D0074226

Monk's tragedies Anelida	1376 Death of Black Prince. Chaucer on mission to Calais. 1377 *February 17, April 30:* Chaucer on missions in France concerning peace treaty and marriage of Richard. *June 22:* death of Edward III and accession of his grandson, Richard II, age 10. Government controlled by Gaunt.
House of Fame Boece Boethian balades Palamon and Arcite	1378 *January 16–March 9:* Chaucer in France concerning marriage of Richard to French king's daughter Marie. *April 18:* daily pitcher of wine replaced by annuity of 20 marks. *May 28–September 19:* Chaucer in Lombardy to treat with Barnabo Visconti (Gower given Chaucer's power of attorney). 1380 *May 1:* Chaucer released from suit for "raptus" of Cecily Champain. (?) Birth of Lewis Chaucer. 1381 Peasants' Revolt. *June 19:* deed of Geoffrey Chaucer, son of John Chaucer, vintner of London, quitclaiming his father's house.
Troylus and Criseyde Legend of Good Women	1382 Richard II marries Anne of Bohemia. 1383 Chaucer obtains first loan against his annuity. 1385 *October 12:* Chaucer appointed justice of the peace in Kent. Political struggle between Gaunt and his brother, Thomas of Woodstock. *September:* death of Joan of Kent. 1386 Justice of peace reaffirmed. *February 19:* Philippa admitted to fraternity of Lincoln Cathedral. *August:* Chaucer elected member of Parliament from Kent. *October 5:* Aldgate house rented to Richard Forester. *October 15:* Scrope-Grosvenor trial. *December 4:* Adam Yardley appointed controller of customs.
Canterbury Prologue early Tales (Knight, Part VII)	1387 *June 18:* last payment of annuity of Philippa Chaucer.
Fabliaux (Miller, Reeve)	1388 *May 1:* Chaucer surrenders his royal annuities to John Scalby of Lincolnshire. 1389 King Richard assumes power. Chaucer appointed clerk of the King's works (more than £30 a year).
Marriage group (Wife of Bath, Friar, Summoner, Merchant, Clerk, Franklin) Astrolabe Equatorie	1390 Commissions to repair St. George's Chapel, Windsor; to oversee repairs on the lower Thames sewers and conduits; to build bleachers for jousts at Smithfield, etc. The three robberies. Chaucer appointed subforester of North Petherton, Somerset. 1391 *June 17:* another clerk of the works appointed. 1393 Chaucer granted a gift of £10 from Richard for services rendered "in this year now present." 1394 Death of Queen Anne. Chaucer granted a new annuity of £20.
	1395 Richard marries Isabella of France. Thomas Chaucer marries heiress Maud Burghersh.
Balades to Scogan, Bukton	1396 John of Gaunt marries Katherine Swynford. 1398 Chaucer borrows against his annuity; action for debt against Chaucer; letters of protection from the King. 1399 Deposition of Richard II. Election of Henry IV. Death of John of Gaunt. *October 13:* on his coronation day, Henry doubles Chaucer's annuity. *December 24:* Chaucer signs 53-year lease for tenement in the garden of the Lady Chapel, Westminster Abbey.
	1400 *September 29:* last record of Chaucer: quittance given by him for a tun of wine received. *October 25:* date of Chaucer's death on tombstone in Westminster Abbey (erected in 1556).

The Complete Canterbury Tales of Geoffrey Chaucer

Edited by

John H. Fisher

John C. Hodges Professor, Emeritus
University of Tennessee

Mark Allen

The University of Texas
at San Antonio

THOMSON
™
WADSWORTH

Australia • Brazil • Canada • Mexico • Singapore
Spain • United Kingdom • United States

The Complete Canterbury Tales of Geoffrey Chaucer
Fisher/Allen

Publisher: *Michael Rosenberg*
Development Editor: *Camille Adkins*
Technology Project Manager: *Joe Gallagher*
Managing Marketing Manager: *Mandee Eckersley*
Marketing Assistant: *Dawn Giovanniello*
Associate MarCom Manager: *Patrick Rooney*
Associate Project Manager, Production: *Karen Stocz*
Print Buyer: *Betsy Donaghey*
Permissions Editor: *Bob Kauser*
Production Service: *G&S Book Services*
Photo Manager: *Sheri Blaney*
Art Director: *Bruce Bond*
Cover Designer: *Dutton & Sherman Design*
Compositor: *G&S Book Services*
Printer: *Courier Westford*
Cover photos: *Background image:* © *Huntington Library/
SuperStock:* Canterbury Tales: Prioress Tale *ca. 1400.
Inset painting: Tate Gallery, London/Art Resource, NY:*
Thomas Stothard, The Pilgrimage to Canterbury.
1806–07.

List of Plates:

Plate A. *Portrait of Chaucer in Hoccleve's* Regement of
Princes. *Anonymous, 15th century, Geoffrey Chaucer.
From the manuscript of Thomas Hoccleve's poem* De
Regimine Principium. *Location: British Library,
London. Photo: HIP/Art Resource, NY.*

Plate B. *Illuminated manuscript of the General Prologue.
Ellesmere MS, The Huntington Library, San
Marino, CA.*

Plate C. *Illuminated manuscript of the opening page of the
Knight's Tale. Ellesmere MS, The Huntington Library,
San Marino, CA.*

Plate D. *Illuminated manuscript of the opening page of the Wife
of Bath's Tale. Ellesmere MS, The Huntington Library,
San Marino, CA.*

© 2006 Thomson Wadsworth, a part of The Thomson
Corporation. Thomson, the Star logo, and Wadsworth
are trademarks used herein under license.

ALL RIGHTS RESERVED. No part of this work covered by
the copyright hereon may be reproduced or used in any form
or by any means—graphic, electronic, or mechanical, including photocopying, recording, taping, web distribution, information storage and retrieval systems, or in any other manner—without the written permission of the publisher.

Printed in the United States of America
1 2 3 4 5 6 7 09 08 07 06 05

Library of Congress Control Number: 2005930215

Thomson Higher Education
25 Thomson Place
Boston, MA 02210-1202
USA

ISBN 0-8384-5708-8

For more information about our products, contact us at:
Thomson Learning Academic Resource Center
1-800-423-0563

For permission to use material from this text or product,
submit a request online at **http://www.thomsonrights.com**
Any additional questions about permissions can be submitted
by e-mail to **thomsonrights@thomson.com**

FOR JUDY

In memory of Jane

Contents

Preface

This edition presents the text of *The Canterbury Tales* as it appeared in John H. Fisher's *The Complete Poetry and Prose of Geoffrey Chaucer,* first published in 1977. For the few changes to Fisher's text, see The Text of This Edition at the back of this volume. The glosses to the text have been thoroughly revised, designed to enable students to understand Chaucer's work without recourse to glossaries or dictionaries, although advanced students will seek available dictionaries and commentaries for the nuances they can provide. Since readers of the *Canterbury Tales* do not always progress from start to finish through the work, glosses are repeated from tale to tale, often within tales, included on the same page as the text and separated from explanatory notes for ease of reference.

The notes, also thoroughly revised from Fisher's original, provide basic information, identify allusions, clarify unfamiliar concepts, and indicate where Chaucer has adapted his sources. No effort has been made to specify the origins of this information as it has passed or is passing from scholarly research to familiar knowledge. The introductions to the parts of *The Canterbury Tales* are also new, but they follow Fisher's model of surveying scholarship and identifying illuminating studies. Earlier editions, especially those of Skeat, Robinson, Benson, Fisher, and the Chaucer Variorum project, have been regular guides in the process of revision, and a number of handbooks, dictionaries, and reference works have been constant companions as well. It is hoped that the notes and introductions combine the succinct utility of Fisher's originals with the perspectives gained through more than twenty-five years of subsequent Chaucer study and commentary.

The vast and growing tradition of Chaucer scholarship and criticism has made increasingly unlikely the synthesis attempted by Skeat, Robinson, and the contributors to Benson's *Riverside Chaucer.* As a result, following Fisher, I have included an extensive bibliography, intended to enable students and scholars to explore issues of interest and contemporary concern. The classification of the bibliography, the cross listing of many works, and the index of authors indicate the topics and directions of Chaucer scholarship and identify the scholars who have made important contributions to study of *The Canterbury Tales.* Citation numbers included in the introductions refer to this bibliography.

Readers who have helped make this volume possible—and who have certainly made it better—include, first and foremost, my wife, Judith Law Fisher, and several friends and colleagues among Chaucer students and scholars: Kenneth Bleeth, Mary Flowers Braswell, James M. Dean, Matthew Giancarlo, Terri Pantuso, Daniel J. Ransom, Mark Womack, Susan Yager, and one reader who preferred to remain anonymous. My thanks to them, one and all. I also wish to thank the staffs of the following libraries that provided assistance and space to work during various phrases of the process of research and revision: Trinity University Library (San Antonio, Texas), the Huntington Library, the British Library, the Bodleian Library, and the National Library of Scotland. Special thanks to the staff of the John Peace Library at the University of Texas at San Antonio, especially Sue McCray of the Interlibrary Loan service. Above all, my thanks go to John Hurt Fisher for the opportunity to undertake this task, and for his patience and confidence.

Mark Allen
The University of Texas at San Antonio

INTRODUCTION: CANTERBURY TALES

The Canterbury Tales is a collection of stories framed as a tale-telling contest. The contest begins as a means to pass time while a group of pilgrims journey to Canterbury, the holiest site in England. As a literary journey, the pilgrimage is metaphoric, a spiritual movement through life to death, passage beyond sin to salvation. As a form of competition, the contest is realistic, a record of the diversity of humanity and an enactment of the tensions that result from such variety and competition. Told by the various pilgrims, the tales themselves vary widely so that while Chaucer gives us an allegory of human life and a drama of social competition, he also gives us a tour-de-force exploration of the range and limits of literature at the time.

Eclectic in its various genres, verse forms, tones, and themes, *The Canterbury Tales* tests the potential of the English language against literary standards of its day. English was a provincial language at the time—hardly the international patois that it is today—and Chaucer adapts Latin, French, and Italian models to experiment, it seems, with how well such models might succeed in English. Of the twenty-four Canterbury tales, more or less complete, only one follows an English model, and that is a parody (the *Tale of Sir Thopas*). Other kinds of imitation, adaptation, and exploration characterize the tales, and in this respect, *The Canterbury Tales* is an *ars poetica* that teaches by example rather than by precept. The metafictional elements of the work—it is, after all, a story *about* storytelling—make it evident that Chaucer was self-conscious about the exploratory nature of his work and that he was deeply engaged with issues of how author, audience, and text collaborate to make meaning.

When Chaucer died in 1400, he left ten parts of the unfinished *Canterbury Tales,* some parts well polished and others less thoroughly integrated into the pilgrimage / contest frame. The outlines of his plan are clear enough, although many details are not. At one point, he envisioned thirty storytellers, each telling two tales on the trip to Canterbury and two tales on the return trip (see 1.792–94)—a total of 120. At some time, perhaps more than once, he altered his plan (see 5.698, 10.25), either expanding it to the ambitious 120 or scaling down from this initial idea. Several tales lack prologues or epilogues, and a few are fragmentary or interrupted. Some details indicate that Chaucer rearranged the sequence of his tales and reassigned some of the plots to different tellers (see, e.g., 7.19n). Parts 1 and 10 are clearly the opening and closing of the sequence, but the order of the parts within these twin peaks differs in some of the surviving manuscripts, with parts 4 and 5 being particularly variable, perhaps indicating that Chaucer was rearranging or reconsidering them.

The order of the tales in this book is generally accepted as the best one, although it is in no way certain that it was Chaucer's. The order follows the lavish Ellesmere manuscript (Ellesmere 26.C.9 in the Huntington Library, San Marino, CA). Copied soon after Chaucer's death, the Ellesmere is one of the earliest and most authoritative of extant manuscripts, produced by the same scribe as the Hengwrt manuscript (National Library of Wales, MS Peniarth 392D). Slightly earlier than the Ellesmere, the Hengwrt has a much less acceptable ordering of the parts, although individual words and spellings are often more authoritative than those in the Ellesmere.

At the 2004 meeting of the New Chaucer Society, Linne R. Mooney stunned and delighted the world of Chaucer scholarship by identifying the copyist of the two manuscripts as Adam Pinkhurst, someone who had been, Mooney shows, Chaucer's copyist for many years and, by extension, someone familiar with the poet's habits, perhaps his intentions. It is probable that Pinkhurst copied the workmanlike Hengwrt piecemeal, following Chaucer's linguistic habits as he gained access to the parts, perhaps late in Chaucer's lifetime or, more likely, soon after the poet's death. In the Ellesmere, Pinkhurst (or someone who guided him) imposed order on the relative chaos that Chaucer left behind in his working papers—making of them a work that is reflected in this volume, complete in design though lacking several portions.

The Ellesmere and the Hengwrt are two among more than fifty manuscripts of *The Canterbury Tales* that survive from the time before William Caxton first printed the work in 1476–77. Almost thirty more surviving manuscripts include selections from the work, often a single tale. None of the versions is exactly the same, so that the version you have in this book is an attempt to reconstruct the most probable readings. Because Chaucer himself was obviously not done with his work, this version (like all edited versions) is a reconstruction of a draft of an incomplete work—challenging in all its indeterminacies and rewarding for the ways that it engages us in the process of making meaning. The most complete information about the manuscripts and their variations is still the daunting eight-volume edition, *The Text of the Canterbury Tales* (1940, no. 37), edited by John M. Manly and Edith Rickert. Two more recent projects, however, are of value for textual questions: the Variorum edition, at present under the general editorship of Daniel J. Ransom (nos. 38–45), and the electronic *Canterbury Tales* Project, spearheaded by Peter W. Robinson (no. 3). On the editorial tradition that has kept *The Canterbury Tales* steadily in print since Caxton, see Paul Ruggiers, *Editing Chaucer* (1984, no. 33).

The frame or organizing plot of a fictional pilgrimage was not new in Chaucer's time, nor was the idea of a literary contest. However, the incorporation of tale-tellers from a variety of occupations and social ranks was unique in its time, and, despite the enormous influence of Chaucer's work, the superb fusion of journey, contest, and tellers from various social stations has not been duplicated in English literature. Early Chaucer scholars spent considerable effort identifying the sources and models for the frame and individual tales, and clarifying the literary debt of Chaucer's allusions to other works. Much of this work was published first by the Chaucer Society (1868–1925), usefully developed in *Sources and Analogues of Chaucer's Canterbury Tales* (1941, no. 186), edited by W. F. Bryan and Germaine Dempster, and brought up to date by the contributors to *Sources and Analogues of the Canterbury Tales* (2002, no. 187), edited by Robert M. Correale and Mary Hamel. Knowledge of Chaucer's sources continues to inform almost all critical approaches because it helps us understand how Chaucer shaped his materials.

Responding to Chaucer's realism, early critics identified real-life models for his pilgrims and mapped the day-by-day progress of the journey. Others examined the allegorical or symbolic import of the astrological references mentioned in the pilgrimage / contest frame or assessed Chaucer's imagery and characters for the ways they echo the Bible, the classics, and the vast medieval commentary on both. Still others treated the pilgrims as complex characters whose tales exist primarily to reflect the motives and desires of their tellers. This so-called dramatic school of criticism was inspired by George Lyman Kittredge's essay "Chaucer's Discussion of Marriage" (1912, no. 444), and it dominated twentieth-century Chaucer studies, continuing to be influential today despite awareness that Chaucer's "drama" is more a matter of rhetoric than character. See C. David Benson, *Chaucer's Drama of Style* (1986, no. 568a). Chaucer's long-lived reputation as the "father" of English poetry also encouraged scholars to assess his contributions to English vocabulary, prosody, and narrative traditions. More recently, the patriarchal assumptions in the term "father" have led critics to challenge the attitudes and biases that are embedded in various critical approaches themselves, as well as to direct attention to questions of gender and class that underlie almost all of Chaucer's tales.

One of the most striking features of recent criticism of *The Canterbury Tales* is the extent to which it is concerned with sociopolitical issues: class, gender, the Hundred Years' War, plague, Lollardy, the uprising of 1381 (Peasants' Revolt), acts of parliament, and the like. This would be no surprise at all if traditional Chaucer criticism had not been so adamant in its conviction that Chaucer—despite his lifelong personal involvement with international trade and the affairs of court—remained aloof to such concerns in his fiction. Another recent critical trend has been to examine individual tales for the ways that they represent the late-medieval cultural forces at work in shaping nascent English nationalism and English notions of other peoples, places, and ideologies rather than the imagination or psychology of the teller. Many such analyses concentrate on particular tales rather than the work in general, but efforts to find unity in *The Canterbury Tales* as a whole continues to strain against the incomplete state of the work. Donald R. Howard's *The Idea of the Canterbury Tales* (1976, no. 575) is perhaps still the most successful reading of the work as a structured, unified whole.

A number of valuable guides to Chaucer and his criticism ease the challenges of coming to grips with the complexities of *The Canterbury Tales* and the capacious scholarship and criticism that have accumulated over six hundred years. The best of the guides is Helen Cooper's Oxford Guide, entitled simply *The Canterbury Tales* (2d ed. 1996, no. 82). The *Cambridge Companion to Chaucer,* edited by Piero Boitani and Jill Mann (2d ed. 2003, no. 78), covers more territory, including discussion of Chaucer's cultural context and his other works as well as *The Canterbury Tales.* Among the others most worthy of mention is Helen Phillips's *An Introduction to the Canterbury Tales: Reading, Fiction, Context* (2000, no. 88). The best one-volume encyclopedia of Chaucer is *The Oxford Companion to Chaucer* (2003, no. 84), by Douglas Gray, and the handiest glossaries are Norman Davis's *A Chaucer Glossary* (1979, no. 67) and the one included in *The Riverside Chaucer* (1987, no. 31), edited by Larry D. Benson. Neither of these glossaries, however, compares with the full lexical description of *The Middle English Dictionary,* which we recommend to all readers of Chaucer.

CANTERBURY TALES PART 1

INTRODUCTION

THE *GENERAL PROLOGUE* establishes the basic plot of *The Canterbury Tales*—the pilgrimage and the tale-telling contest. It introduces the pilgrim-tellers, the Host who conducts the contest, and the narrator who recounts the journey. Its springtime setting connotes renewal, and the opening of the poem aligns the pilgrims' journey with the revitalization of the created universe. The stars, the earth, animals, and plants—the entire "cheyne of love" as it is called in the *Knight's Tale* (2988)—participate in the annual cosmic cycle of rejuvenation. As part of this chain, human beings undertake the spiritual renewal of pilgrimage, a symbolic journey that mirrors the journey from life to death and from this world to the next.

Often called "sketches" or "portraits," the descriptions of the individual pilgrims are deeply influenced by traditional literary satires of the social and moral failings of various professions or occupations—the so-called estates satire of medieval society, not unlike modern complaints against doctors and lawyers. Chaucer enlivens and particularizes his descriptions by recording the successes of his characters as well as the failings that usually make up such satires. Friars were widely condemned for associating with the rich rather than the poor, a habit Chaucer's Friar shares; yet he is also the "beste beggere" in his house (252). The Miller overcharges his clients, a typical complaint against millers, but he is also a superb wrestler. Specific details counteract the stereotypical aspects of the descriptions, personalizing them and reminding the reader that generality and specificity are interdependent. The Friar is a generic friar, but he also has the unusual name Huberd. The Miller is a stereotype of millers, but his hairy wart, black nostrils, and bagpipes help to individuate him. Laura C. Lambdin and Robert T. Lambdin, editors of *Chaucer's Pilgrims* (1996, no. 771), provide

background to each of the individual descriptions; Jill Mann discusses the tradition of estates satire in *Chaucer and Medieval Estates Satire* (1972, no. 772). For full scholarly discussion of the descriptions, see Malcolm Andrew's Variorum notes to *The General Prologue* (1993, no. 38).

The interplay between particular and universal within individual descriptions is magnified by connections among them that help to convey the distinct sense of a society. Some descriptions are clearly paired. The Knight and Squire are father and son, and they embody two aspects of chivalry. The Parson and Plowman are brothers and ideals of clerical and secular Christian labor. The pairing of the Sergeant at Law and the Franklin suggests financial collusion, and homosocial bonding is evident in the harmonious singing of the Summoner and Pardoner. On the other hand, the contrast in attitudes toward money in the descriptions of the Merchant and the Clerk (note the echoic verb *sownynge,* "suggesting," in 275 and 307) remind us that not all people pursue the same goals. Refusing to resolve themselves into a simple social formula, these and many more echoes among the descriptions communicate a rich variety of social relations.

The organization of the descriptions moves from the aristocratic Knight and his retinue to the socially pretentious Prioress and Monk down the social scale through the middle ranks to the churls and scalawags at the end. Yet this apparent hierarchy is disturbed or complicated by the recurrent presence of one character or another who seems out of order—the Physician or the Manciple, for example, or perhaps the Wife of Bath. The upshot is that even though the society depicted seems to have a shape or pattern, it is not a simple or placid one.

Through such techniques, Chaucer's society brings to literary life the affiliations and struggles of late-medieval English society. Much of the sense of vibrancy has to do with aspects of rank and finance—wealthy or impoverished attire, varying table manners, the relative excellence of the horses ridden by the pilgrims (horses were status symbols much as cars are today). Yet subtler reverberations are at work too. It is startling, for example, to observe the varieties of meaning in words such as *worthy, good,* or *gentle* in the *General Prologue*. The Knight is resoundingly worthy, but when the word is applied to the Friar and the Franklin (269, 360) and to the townswomen with whom the Friar flirts (217), it has quite different nuances and compels consideration of what it really means to be "worthy." One learns quickly that the Wife of Bath is a "good" woman in a sense different from the Parson being a "good" man (445, 477), that the meaning of "gentle" must have had a wide semantic field to be applied to the Manciple and the Pardoner (567, 669). These linguistic reverberations between the descriptions lure the reader, almost unaware, to feel the cohesion of the society, while they remind us that neither language nor society is altogether stable.

In *Chaucer and the Politics of Discourse* (1996, no. 304), Michaela Paasche Grudin tallies the variety of ways in which the pilgrims themselves speak—the professional bragging implicit in the Physician's description (429ff.), the laughing and joking of the Wife of Bath (474), the Summoner's rote Latin (646), the boldness of the Host (755), and so on—making clear how the society of the pilgrims is constituted in large part in, through, and by language. After all, the narrator describes the pilgrims only after he has spoken with each of them, "everichon" (31). This concern with language anticipates the variety of forms and genres in the Canterbury collection, although this plurality is here represented in indirect rather than direct speech. We seem to overhear snatches of the narrator's many conversations, and when the Host does propose the contest in direct discourse—the agreement or "foreward" (829) that brings this society into speaking life—the scene indicates that human society is fundamentally verbal and competitive, that language makes community.

Overarching all this is a narrator who reports from memory what he has seen and heard. He tells us that his own "wit is short" (746) and thereby raises questions about his reliability and about the reliability of literature. Critics have argued whether this narrator is better seen as a projection of Chaucer himself (a shrewd but disarming critic of others) or as a naïve persona (whose generosity of spirit enables us to take what he says ironically). He is perhaps both and more, a shifting perspective that compels us to make our own judgments and everywhere reminds us not to take things at face value. The classic discussion of the persona is E. Talbot Donaldson's "Chaucer the Pilgrim" (1954, no. 351), but see also H. Marshall Leicester's "The Art of Impersonation: A General Prologue to *The Canterbury Tales*" (1980, no. 357), and Barbara Nolan's "A Poet Ther Was: Chaucer's Voices in the *General Prologue*" (1986, no. 360).

There is evidence that, like *The Canterbury Tales* itself, the *General Prologue* is unfinished, that Chaucer was still adjusting it or intending to adjust it when he died in 1400. Thus, efforts to date it are futile, but it is likely that he had a notion of a prologue as he began to develop the collection of various tales sometime in the late 1380s. Quite possibly Chaucer intended to develop the description of the Second Nun with a description of the Nun's Priest to follow (see 164n). Certainly the plan for a two-way journey and four tales told by each pilgrim (792–94) was left in need of revision.

Coming first as it does in the Canterbury sequence, the *Knight's Tale* is the secular yardstick against which the tales to follow can be measured. Its epic setting and lofty tone, its concern with hierarchy and order, and its profound message have encouraged critics to regard the tale as the philosophical backbone of *The Canterbury Tales*, at least with regard to the major themes of love, order, and divine Providence. It can be described as a "philosophical romance" because it so successfully fuses weighty themes with the subjects of chivalry and aristocratic love.

The story of Palamon and Arcite's noble but destructive love for Emelye derives from Giovanni Boccaccio's *Il Teseida*. Chaucer compressed the plot and deepened it by increasing its concern for astrological determinism (represented in classical planetary gods) and by lending it a strong sense of organization and balance (see, e.g., 2051n, 2156n). Living under threat of violence, humans seek to restrain social chaos through law and reasoned pity. Hedged in by what appears to be unknowable fate or chance, humans must restrain their passions to avoid the emotional chaos of sorrow and despair. Similarly hedged in by history and literary tradition, storytelling must restrain digression through orderly narration. Thematically and stylistically the tale counsels restraint, suggesting that we not allow impulses to overwhelm order.

Expressed in Duke Theseus's speech at the end of the tale, this theme of orderly restraint derives from Boethius's *Consolation of Philosophy,* which Chaucer translated as his *Boece* and which deeply influenced many of his works. Theseus explains the influence of the planets as manifestations of omniscient Providence and counsels that humans make a "vertu of necessitee" (3042) by accepting what we cannot avoid. Set against love, battle, and death, this counsel leaves little space for human freedom beyond embracing the inevitable. It is freedom tinged with regret, but—to the extent that we assume a Boethian outlook—this freedom is made grand by the opportunity to participate willingly in providential order.

This rarefied idealism has been scrutinized from alternative points of view, often class or gender based. Feminist critics, for example, challenge the hierarchical assumptions taken for granted in Emelye's passivity and Theseus's defeat of "Femenye" (866). In "Chaucerian Ritual and Patriarchal Discourse" (1992, no. 801), John Ganim attributes this masculinist outlook to the Knight rather than to Chaucer; in *Gender and Romance in Chaucer's Canterbury Tales* (1994, no. 695), Susan Crane explores the unresolved "gendered oppositions" of the tale as an aspect of its romance genre. In *Feminizing Chaucer,* Jill Mann (2002, no. 636a) argues that feminine pity is more strongly present in the tale than a masculinist warrior ethos.

In a manner of speaking, the Miller is the first critic of the *Knight's Tale,* although he challenges not its depiction of women but its high-mindedness and the limitations it sets on human self-determination. Chaucer composed his story of Palamon and Arcite before he conceived of the Canterbury pilgrimage, and by incorporating it into the frame (see 889–91n), he exposed it to competing points of view. The *Miller's Tale,* the *Reeve's Tale,* and the unfinished *Cook's Tale* are all "fabliaux"—humorous tales, usually indecent, about middle- or low-class characters and situations. One of the principal comic devices of the genre is burlesque of pretentious values and behaviors, and Chaucer's stacking of three sequential fabliaux enables him to explore and expose a range of outlooks.

The *Miller's Tale* pokes fun at the theological speculations and astrological learning of the *Knight's Tale* as well as its courtly attitudes, and it does so with unrestrained vitality, even rebellion. Its comic outcome has a distinct air of inevitability about it, but it is the inevitability of poetic justice— if it is justice at all—rather than the astrological determinism of the opening tale. As Charles Muscatine discusses in *Chaucer and the French Tradition* (1957, no. 137), the interrelation of style and substance in the *Miller's Tale* is particularly successful, effectively communicating that character is fate. Arguably, each of the male characters gets his "just deserts," even though the question of justice for Alisoun goes unasked. In this respect, the Miller's Alisoun parallels the Knight's Emelye; despite the striking differences in the tales, their similarities are evocative as well.

The *Reeve's Tale* is set in rural Trumpington (near Cambridge) instead of the court of Athens (*Knight's Tale*) or civic Oxford (*Miller's Tale*), and there is little cosmic inevitability or poetic justice in the plot. Chance, animal passion, and vengeance dominate. The two clerks, John and Aleyn (paralleling Palamon and Arcite and the Miller's Nicholas and Absolon), stumble into blunt sexual escapades and win their competition with Symkyn the miller by an accidental stroke in the dark. They are country bumblers whose lack of sophistication is marked by their northern dialect—the first time in English literature that dialect is used for characterization (see the glosses to 4022ff.). The Reeve tells the tale, he informs us, to punish the Miller for a perceived offense, an intensification of the Miller's claim that he will "quite" (repay, 3127) the *Knight's Tale* and an invitation that we consider the role of intention in storytelling. This concern with intention recurs throughout *The Canterbury Tales,* as do issues of competition among classes, professions, and individuals.

In these first three tales, Chaucer explores the social and stylistic implications of competing attitudes in what appears to be a descending sequence, but he seems unwilling to investigate a thoroughly debauched outlook. Breaking off just as it is getting under way, the *Cook's Tale* is set in the London underworld and populated by downright scoundrels, particularly the apprentice Perkyn, who steals, plays at dice, abuses the contract of his apprenticeship, and takes up residence with a prostitute. The major motifs of the tales of the Miller and the

Reeve are found elsewhere in fabliau tradition, but the Cook's fragment seems to be based in contemporary reality. No single source, however, is universally accepted for any of the three. Dating them is similarly uncertain, although they are usually ascribed to the late 1380s or early 1390s. Although much or all of the *Knight's Tale* had been written previously, the formulation of part 1 as a whole almost certainly dates from this time.

We do not know whether Chaucer had more of a plot in mind, but the *Cook's Tale* is effective as it stands. In his first four tales, he establishes a range of values, classes, and styles. The vitality of the *Miller's Tale* successfully challenges the stoicism of the *Knight's Tale,* but it may be a step on a slippery slope to the relative rudeness of the *Reeve's Tale* and the debauchery of the *Cook's Tale.* In *Chaucer and the Subject of History* (1991, no. 619), Lee Patterson shows how conflicting assumptions about social control and human agency underlie various class-based outlooks and how Chaucer's depiction of these outlooks lays the assumptions bare. In "The Three Styles of Fragment I of the *Canterbury Tales*" (1973, no. 755), John H. Fisher argues that the *Knight's Tale* illustrates *high style;* the *Miller's Tale, middle style;* and the *Reeve's Tale, low style.* Thematically, ideologically, and stylistically, the variety of the *Canterbury Tales* begins to emerge, and each tale gains dimension through juxtaposition.

CANTERBURY TALES PART 1

GENERAL PROLOGUE

Here bigynneth the Book of the Tales of Caunterbury.

Whan that Aprill with his shoures soote°
The droghte° of March hath perced° to the
    roote,
And bathed every veyne° in swich licour°
Of which vertu° engendred° is the flour°;
Whan Zephirus eek° with his sweete breeth° 5
Inspired hath° in every holt and heeth°
The tendre croppes°, and the yonge sonne°
Hath in the Ram his halfe cours yronne°,
And smale foweles° maken melodye,
That slepen° al the nyght with open eye— 10
So priketh hem nature° in hir corages°—
Thanne longen folk to goon° on pilgrimages,
And palmeres for to seken straunge
    strondes°
To ferne halwes°, kowthe° in sondry londes°;
And specially from every shires° ende 15
Of Engelond to Caunterbury they wende°

---

1 **his shoures soote,** *its sweet showers* 2 **droghte,** *dryness,* **hath perced,** *has pierced* 3 **veyne,** *vein* (of the plants), **swich licour,** *such liquid* 4 **Of which vertu,** *by which potency,* **engendred,** *born,* **flour,** *flower* 5 **eek,** *also,* **breeth,** *breath* 6 **Inspired hath,** *has breathed into,* **holt and heeth,** *woodland and plain* 7 **tendre croppes,** *new foliage,* **yonge sonne,** *young sun* 8 **his halfe cours yronne,** *run his half-course* 9 **smale foweles,** *small fowls* 10 **slepen,** *sleep* 11 **priketh hem nature,** *nature incites them,* **hir corages,** *their hearts* 12 **Thanne longen folk to goon,** *then people yearn to go* 13 **seken straunge strondes,** *seek foreign shores* 14 **ferne halwes,** *faraway saints,* **kowthe,** *known,* **sondry londes,** *various lands* 15 **shires,** *district's* 16 **wende,** *travel*

---

1 **Aprill,** accented on the first syllable. The first two feet of the poem begin with accented beats. 2 **droghte of March,** early spring is a relatively dry season in southern England. 5 **Zephirus,** the west wind, associated with spring and renewal; in classical mythology husband of Flora, goddess of flowers, and father of Carpus, god of fruit. 7 **yonge sonne,** the sun is young because the poem is set soon after the springtime equinox, when the days begin to lengthen toward summer. 8 **in the Ram,** Aries, the zodiacal sign of the Ram. **halfe cours,** in April the sun passes through the last half of Aries and first half of Taurus, so the sun has already passed Aries and entered Taurus. In Chaucer's time, the sun entered Taurus on April 12. At *MLP* 2.5–6 (perhaps the second day of the pilgrimage), April 18 is indicated, so the beginning of the pilgrimage may be set on April 17. 13 **palmeres,** professional pilgrims whose emblem was a frond from a palm tree, a sign they had been to the Holy Land.

The hooly blisful martir for to seke°
That hem hath holpen° whan that they were
    seeke°. ⚔

    Bifil° that in that seson° on a day
In Southwerk at the Tabard as I lay   20
Redy to wenden° on my pilgrymage
To Caunterbury with ful devout corage°,
At nyght was come into that hostelrye°
Wel nyne and twenty in a compaignye
Of sondry folk°, by aventure yfalle°   25
In felaweship°, and pilgrimes were they alle,
That toward Caunterbury wolden ryde°.
The chambres° and the stables weren wyde°,
And wel we weren esed atte beste°.
And shortly, whan the sonne was to reste,   30
So hadde I spoken with hem everichon°
That I was of hir felaweship anon°,
And made forward° erly° for to ryse,
To take oure wey ther as I yow devyse°.
    But nathelees°, whil I have tyme and
    space,   35
Er° that I ferther in this tale pace°,
Me thynketh it° acordaunt to° resoun
To telle yow al the condicioun°
Of ech of hem°, so as it semed me,
And whiche° they weren, and of what
    degree°,   40
And eek° in what array° that they were inne,
And at a knyght than wol° I first bigynne.

    A KNYGHT ther was, and that a worthy man,
That fro the tyme° that he first bigan
To riden out, he loved chivalrie,   45
Trouthe and honour, fredom and curteisie.
Ful worthy was he in his lordes werre°,
And therto hadde he riden, no man ferre°,
As wel in cristendom° as in hethenesse°,
And evere honoured for his worthynesse.   50
    At Alisaundre he was whan it was wonne.
Ful ofte tyme° he hadde the bord bigonne°
Aboven alle nacions° in Pruce.
In Lettow hadde he reysed° and in Ruce,
No Cristen man so ofte° of his degree°.   55
In Gernade at the seege° eek hadde he be°
Of Algezir, and riden in Belmarye.
At Lyeys was he and at Satalye,
Whan they were wonne, and in the Grete See
At many a noble armee° hadde he be.   60
At mortal batailles hadde he been fiftene°,
And foughten for oure feith at Tramyssene
In lystes thries°, and ay slayn his foo°.
This ilke° worthy knyght hadde been also
Somtyme with the lord of Palatye   65
Agayn° another hethen in Turkye,
And everemoore he hadde a sovereyn prys°.
And though that he were worthy, he was wys,
And of his port° as meeke as is a mayde.
He nevere yet no vileynye ne sayde°   70
In al his lyf unto no maner wight°.

---

17 seke, *seek* **18 hem hath holpen,** *has helped them,* **seeke,** *sick* **19 Bifil,** *it happened,* **seson,** *season* **21 Redy to wenden,** *ready to travel* **22 ful devout corage,** *very devout spirit* **23 hostelrye,** *inn* **25 sondry folk,** *various people,* **by aventure yfalle,** *by chance fallen* **26 In felaweship,** *into fellowship* **27 wolden ryde,** *intended to ride* **28 chambres,** *bedrooms,* **weren wyde,** *were roomy* **29 esed atte beste,** *accommodated in the best manner* **31 hem everichon,** *every one of them* **32 anon,** *immediately* **33 made forward,** *(we) made agreement,* **erly,** *early* **34 I yow devyse,** *I (will) tell you* **35 nathelees,** *nonetheless* **36 Er,** *before,* **pace,** *go* **37 Me thynketh it,** *I think it,* **acordaunt to,** *in accord with* **38 condicioun,** *circumstances* **39 ech of hem,** *each of them* **40 whiche,** *what* **degree,** *social*

rank **41 eek,** *also,* **array,** *clothing,* **42 wol,** *will* **44 fro the tyme,** *from the time* **47 lordes werre,** *lord's war* **48 ferre,** *further* **49 cristendom,** *Christian lands,* **hethenesse,** *heathen lands* **52 Ful ofte tyme,** *very often,* **bord bigonne,** *sat at the head of the table* (board) **53 nacions,** *nationalities* **54 reysed,** *campaigned* **55 so ofte,** *as often,* **degree,** *social rank* **56 seege,** *siege,* **eek hadde he be,** *also had he been* **60 armee,** *expedition* **61 mortal batailles . . . fiftene,** *fifteen mortal battles* **63 In lystes thries,** *thrice in duels,* **ay slayn his foo,** *always killed his foe* **64 ilke,** *same* **66 Agayn,** *against* **67 sovereyn prys,** *supreme reputation* **69 of his port,** *in his behavior* **70 no vileynye ne sayde,** *said nothing villainous* **71 no maner wight,** *any kind of person*

17 blisful martir, blessed martyr, St. Thomas Becket, martyred in Canterbury Cathedral in 1170, making it among the most popular pilgrimage sites in England. **20 In Southwerk at the Tabard,** in the area south of London Bridge at the Tabard Inn, identified by its sign shaped like a smock or sleeveless surcoat. The site of the inn is still identified on Borough High Street in modern Southwark. **24 nyne and twenty,** Chaucer evidently intended thirty pilgrims here (including the narrator), but the number does not fit the text (see 164n); the Host and later the Canon's Yeoman join this group. **43 KNYGHT . . . ,** the Knight is emphatically worthy and his virtues include a wide range—from integrity or fidelity (**Trouthe**) to generosity and good manners (**fredom and curteisie**). The wide-flung campaigns attributed to him—all against pagans at war with Christians—were fought over some forty years, unlikely for any real person. **51 Alisaundre,** Alexandria (in Egypt), won in 1365. **53–54 in Pruce,** fighting in Prussia (on the Baltic Sea), the Knights of the Teutonic Order were organized by nationality. The Teutonic Knights fought also in Lithuania (**Lettow**) and Russia (**Ruce**). **56–57 Gernade at . . . Algezir,** Algeciras, a port in Granada of southern Spain, taken in 1344. **57 Belmarye,** a fourteenth-century Moorish kingdom in modern Morocco, attacked by Christians in the 1360s. **58 Lyeys,** Ayash, a seaport in Turkey, captured in 1367. **Satalye,** Antalya, also in Turkey, was attacked in 1361. **59 Grete See,** Mediterranean Sea. **62 Tramyssene,** Tlemcen, in Algeria, is not known to have been attacked by Christians in the fourteenth century. **63 lystes,** lists were enclosures for battle in which single champions fought to decide the outcome of a larger battle; also used in tournaments. **65 lord of Palatye,** a title used by rulers of the Turkish city Balat (Byzantine Palation; Greek Miletus); it is uncertain who the other Turkish leader may be (line 66). **68 worthy . . . wys,** strength and wisdom were the most valued qualities of the hero from classical times onward.

He was a verray, parfit, gentil° knyght.
But for to tellen yow of his array°,
His hors° weren goode, but he was nat gay°.
Of fustian° he wered° a gypoun°　　75
Al bismotered with° his habergeoun°,
For he was late ycome° from his viage°,
And wente for to doon° his pilgrymage.

　　With hym ther was his sone, a yong SQUIER,
A lovyere° and a lusty bacheler°,　　80
With lokkes crulle° as they were leyd in presse°.
Of twenty yeer° of age he was, I gesse.
Of his stature he was of evene lengthe°,
And wonderly delyvere°, and of greet strengthe.
And he hadde been somtyme in chyvachie°　　85
In Flaundres, in Artoys, and Pycardie,
And born hym weel°, as of so litel space°,
In hope to stonden in his lady grace°.
Embrouded was he, as it were a meede°
Al ful of fresshe floures, whyte and reede°.　　90
Syngynge he was or floytynge° al the day.
He was as fressh as is the monthe of May.
Short was his gowne, with sleves longe and wyde.
Wel koude° he sitte on hors and faire ryde.
He koude songes make and wel endite°,　　95
Juste° and eek° daunce, and weel purtreye° and
　　write.

So hoote° he lovede that by nyghtertale°
He slepte namoore° than dooth a nyghtyngale.
Curteis° he was, lowely°, and servysable°,
And carf biforn° his fader at the table.　　100

　　A YEMAN° hadde he and servantz namo°
At that tyme, for hym liste° ride so,
And he was clad in cote° and hood of grene°.
A sheef of pecok arwes°, bright and kene°,
Under his belt he bar ful thriftily°—　　105
Wel koude he dresse his takel yemanly°;
His arwes drouped noght° with fetheres
　　lowe—
And in his hand he baar° a myghty bowe.
A not-heed° hadde he, with a broun visage°.
Of wodecraft wel koude° he al the usage°.　　110
Upon his arm he baar a gay bracer°,
And by his syde a swerd and a bokeler°,
And on that oother syde a gay daggere
Harneised° wel and sharp as point of spere;
A Cristophre on his brest° of silver sheene.　　115
An horn he bar°, the bawdryk° was of grene;
A forster° was he, soothly°, as I gesse.

　　Ther was also a Nonne°, a PRIORESSE,
That of hir smylyng° was ful symple and coy°;
Hire gretteste ooth° was but by Seint Loy.　　120

72 verray, parfit, gentle, *true, perfect, noble* **73 array,** *equipment* **74 hors,** *horses,* **gay,** *extravagant* **75 fustian,** *coarse cloth,* **wered,** *wore,* **gypoun,** *tunic* **76 bismotered with,** *stained by,* **habergeoun,** *coat of mail* **77 late ycome,** *lately come,* **viage,** *journey* **78 to doon,** *to do* **80 lovyere,** *lover,* **lusty bacheler** *lively young man or aspirant to knighthood* **81 lokkes crulle,** *hair curled,* **leyd in presse,** *laid in a press* **82 yeer,** *years* **83 evene lengthe,** *average height* **84 wonderly delyvere,** *wondrously agile* **85 chyvachie,** *cavalry action* **87 born hym weel,** *conducted himself well,* **litel space,** *short time* **88 stonden in his lady grace,** *stand in his lady's favor* **89 Embrouded . . . meede,** *embroidered . . . as if a meadow* **90 floures, whyte and reede,** *flowers, white and red* **91 floytynge,** *playing a flute or pipes* **94 koude,** *could* **95 songes make and wel endite,** *compose music and lyrics,* **96 Juste,** *joust,* **eek,** *also,* **weel purtreye,** *draw well* **97 hoote,** *hotly,* **by nyghtertale,** *at nighttime* **98 namoore,** *no more* **99 Curteis,** *courteous,* **lowely,** *humble,* **servysable,** *willing to serve* **100 carf biforn,** *carved in front of* **101 YEMAN,** *Yeoman (servant),* **namo,** *no more* **102 hym liste,** *(it) pleased him (to)* **103 cote,** *coat,* **grene,** *green* **104 sheef of pecok arwes,** *bundle of arrows with peacock feathers,* **kene,** *sharp* **105 bar ful thriftily,** *bore very appropriately* **106 Wel koude he dresse his takel yemanly,** *he knew how to care for his equipment as a yeoman should* **107 drouped noght,** *drooped not* **108 baar,** *carried* **109 not-heed,** *closely cropped head,* **broun visage,** *tanned face* **110 koude,** *knew,* **usage,** *practice* **111 gay bracer,** *fancy arm guard* **112 swerd and a bokeler,** *sword and a small shield* **114 Harneised,** *decorated* **115 brest,** *breast* **116 bar,** *bore,* **bawdryk,** *chest strap* **117 forster,** *forest keeper,* **soothly,** *truly* **118 Nonne,** *Nun,* **119 hir smylyng,** *her smiling,* **coy,** *reserved (Lat. quietus) or affecting reserve (see* LGW *1548)* **120 Hire gretteste ooth,** *her greatest oath*

79 SQUIER, the rank of Squire is just below that of his father, the Knight, whom he serves humbly and properly. Yet the contrast of the two portraits is clear: the Knight battles for Christendom in faraway lands; the Squire for his lady's favor in familiar Flanders and France. Their clothes and their activities also contrast. **80 bacheler,** the term has a range of meaning from "young unmarried man" to "aspirant to knighthood" to "a rank of knighthood not qualified to carry his own banner." **86 Flaundres, in Artoys, and Pycardie,** apparently an allusion to the 1383 English "crusade" against Flanders and adjoining districts in northeastern France in support of Urban IV of Rome and against the French supporters of Clement VII of Avignon, two claimants to the papacy. The campaign was part of the Hundred Years' War. **93ff. gowne . . . sleves . . . ,** the short gown and long sleeves are very fashionable, and the Squire's skills in the following lines indicate his aristocratic accomplishments. **98 nyghtyngale,** it was thought that the nightingale sang all night long in the mating season. **100 carf . . . at the table,** a characteristic activity of squires. **101 YEMAN,** a freeborn servant, the well-equipped yeoman serves the Knight (the referent of **he** in this line), apparently as a huntsman and the keeper of his forests. Like the Squire and several other pilgrims, he is decked out in his finery. **108 myghty bowe,** the English longbow was the most effective weapon in the Hundred Years' War. **115 Cristophre,** a badge or metal of St. Christopher, who was the patron of travelers. **118 PRIORESSE,** a high-ranking nun, in this case probably the superior of an independent Benedictine convent. The Prioress's courtly demeanor is emphasized over her Christian piety, although she is in some ways also rather provincial. **120 ooth . . . Seint Loy,** strictly speaking, the Prioress should swear no oaths whatsoever, even one by the genteel French St. Eligius (Fr. *Eloi*).

And she was cleped° madame Eglentyne.
Ful weel° she soong the service dyvyne°,
Entuned° in hir nose ful semely°,
And Frenssh she spak ful faire and fetisly°,
After the scole° of Stratford atte Bowe, 125
For Frenssh of Parys was to hire unknowe°.
At mete° wel ytaught was she with-alle°:
She leet° no morsel from hir lippes falle,
Ne wette° hir fyngres in hir sauce depe°.
Wel koude she° carie a morsel and wel kepe° 130
That no drope ne fille° upon hire brest.
In curteisie was set ful muchel hir lest°.
Hir over-lippe° wyped° she so clene
That in hir coppe° ther was no ferthyng sene°
Of grece°, whan she dronken hadde hir
      draughte°. 135
Ful semely° after hir mete° she raughte°.
And sikerly° she was of greet desport°,
And ful plesaunt, and amyable of port°,
And peyned hire° to countrefete cheere°
Of court, and to been estatlich of manere°, 140
And to ben holden digne° of reverence.
But, for to speken of hire conscience,
She was so charitable and so pitous°

She wolde wepe°, if that she saugh° a mous
Kaught in a trappe, if it were deed or
      bledde°. 145
Of smale houndes° hadde she that she fedde°
With rosted flessh°, or milk and wastel-breed°.
But soore wepte she° if oon° of hem were deed,
Or if men smoot° it with a yerde smerte°—
And al was conscience and tendre herte. 150
Ful semyly° hir wympul pynched was°,
Hir nose tretys°, hir eyen° greye as glas,
Hir mouth ful smal, and therto softe and reed.
But sikerly° she hadde a fair forheed;
It was almoost a spanne brood°, I trowe°, 155
For, hardily°, she was nat undergrowe.
Ful fetys° was hir cloke°, as I was war°.
Of smal coral aboute hire arm she bar°
A peire of bedes°, gauded° al with grene,
And theron heng° a brooch of gold ful
      sheene° 160
On which ther was first write° a crowned A,
And after *Amor vincit omnia.*

    Another NONNE with hir hadde she,
That was hir chapeleyne°, and preestes thre.

---

121 **cleped,** *named* 122 **Ful weel,** *very well,* **service dyvyne,** *liturgy (a cycle of prayers)* 123 **Entuned,** *intoned,* **ful semely,** *very attractively* 124 **fetisly,** *elegantly* 125 **After the scole,** *in accord with the school* 126 **unknowe,** *unknown* 127 **mete,** *dining,* **with-alle,** *in addition* 128 **leet,** *let* 129 **Ne wette,** *nor wet,* **depe,** *deeply* 130 **Wel koude she,** *she was well able to,* **kepe,** *take care* 131 **fille,** *fell* 132 **ful muchel hir lest,** *her greatest pleasure* 133 **over-lippe,** *upper lip,* **wyped,** *wiped* 134 **coppe,** *cup,* **no ferthyng sene,** *no spot seen (farthing = small coin)* 135 **grece,** *grease* **draughte,** *drink* 136 **Ful semely,** *very attractively,* **after hir mete,** *for her food,* **raughte,** *reached* 137 **sikerly,** *certainly* **greet desport,** *excellent conduct* 138 **amyable of port,** *agreeable in demeanor* 139 **peyned hire,** *took pains,* **countrefete cheere,** *imitate the behavior* 140 **to been**

estatlich of manere, *to be stately in manner* 141 **to ben holden digne,** *to be considered worthy* 143 **pitous,** *tenderhearted* 144 **wolde wepe,** *would weep,* **saugh,** *saw* 145 **deed or bledde,** *dead or bleeding* 146 **smale houndes,** *small dogs,* **fedde,** *fed* 147 **rosted flessh,** *cooked meat,* **wastel-breed,** *high-quality bread* 148 **soore wepte she,** *she wept sorely,* **oon,** *one* 149 **smoot,** *hit,* **yerde smerte,** *stick smartly* 151 **Ful semyly,** *very attractively,* **wympul pynched was,** *headdress was pleated* 152 **tretys,** *well shaped,* **eyen,** *eyes* 154 **sikerly,** *certainly* 155 **spanne brood,** *hand-span broad,* **I trowe,** *I believe* 156 **hardily,** *assuredly* 157 **Ful fetys,** *very elegant,* **cloke,** *cloak,* **war,** *aware* 158 **bar,** *bore* 159 **peire of bedes,** *string of beads (a rosary),* **gauded,** *ornamented* 160 **heng,** *hung,* **ful sheene,** *very shiny* 161 **write,** *written* 164 **chapeleyne,** *assistant*

---

121 **Eglentyne,** a typical romance heroine's name, meaning "briar rose," although there was a Madam Argentyn in St. Leonard's convent near Stratford-at-Bow (two miles from London; see *HF* 117), which Chaucer visited as a youth. She was not prioress. 123 **Entuned in hir nose,** the appropriate way to sing or chant the long services. 125 **scole of Stratford atte Bowe,** a convent school, located near London. 126 **Frenssh of Parys,** the Parisian dialect was more prestigious than provincial Anglo-Norman. 127 **At mete . . . ,** the Prioress's table manners follow proper etiquette, but they are modeled on the advice of La Vieille (Old Woman) of *RR* 13,374ff. on how to attract men. 146–47 **small houndes . . . fedde . . . ,** nuns were ordinarily forbidden lapdogs, popular among fashionable ladies. The food that the Prioress feeds to her dogs is also extraordinary, as meat was generally reserved for the ill in Benedictine convents and **wastel-breed** was vastly superior to the dark breads eaten by peasants. 151 **wympul,** the nun's wimple, or headdress, normally covered much of her face (including the forehead) and neck as well as the rest of her head. The pleating (**pynched was**) is a fashionable touch. 152 **greye,** the precise color is uncertain (blue? gray?), although it is typical of the eyes of romance heroines. 155 **spanne brood,** the breadth of a hand span, about seven to nine inches. A broad forehead was thought to be beautiful. 159–62 **peire of bedes . . . ,** a rosary, i.e., a string of beads used to organize the recitation of prayers, although the rosary did not develop a standard form until the fifteenth century. Like much church equipment, the Prioress's rosary is splendid, the coral beads articulated (**gauded**) by green beads and hung with a pendant ornament (**brooch**) which is inscribed with a crowned letter *A* and the Latin phrase *Amor vincit omnia,* "Love conquers all." 163 **NONNE,** the most salient feature of the so-called Second Nun is the lack of description. As chaplain (**chapeleyne**), she was assistant secretary to the Prioress. 164 **preestes thre,** the three priests bring the number of pilgrims in the *Prologue* to thirty-two (compare line 24), and only one priest appears later (at *CT* 7.2809). Chaucer may have left the line incomplete, intending to develop the portraits of the Second Nun and the Nun's Priest, providing opportunity for an early scribe to complete the rhyme, which is in all manuscripts.

A MONK ther was, a fair for the maistrie°, 165
An outridere, that lovede venerie,
A manly man, to been an abbot able°.
Ful many a deyntee° hors hadde he in stable.
And whan he rood, men myghte his brydel° heere
Gynglen in a whistlynge wynd als cleere° 170
And eek as loude as dooth the chapel belle
Ther as this lord° was kepere of the celle°.
The reule° of Seint Maure or of Seint Beneit,
By cause° that it was old and somdel streit°,
This ilke° Monk leet olde thynges pace°, 175
And heeld after the newe world the space°.
He yaf nat of that text a pulled hen°
That seith° that hunters been nat hooly men,
Ne that a monk, whan he is recchelees°,
Is likned til° a fissh that is waterlees°— 180
This is to seyn°, a monk out of his cloystre°.
But thilke° text heeld he nat worth an oystre°.
And I seyde° his opinioun was good.
What, sholde he studie and make hymselven wood°,
Upon a book in cloystre alwey to poure°, 185
Or swynken° with his handes, and laboure,

As Austyn bit?° How shal the world be served?
Lat° Austyn have his swynk to hym reserved!
Therfore he was a prikasour aright°.
Grehoundes° he hadde as swift as fowel° in flight. 190
Of prikyng° and of huntyng for the hare
Was al his lust°; for no cost wolde° he spare.
I seigh° his sleves ypurfiled° at the hond
With grys°, and that the fyneste° of a lond.
And, for to festne° his hood under his chyn, 195
He hadde of gold ywroght° a ful curious pyn°,
A love-knotte in the gretter° ende ther was.
His heed was balled°, that shoon as any glas,
And eek° his face, as° he hadde been enoynt°.
He was a lord ful fat and in good poynt°; 200
His eyen stepe° and rollynge in his heed,
That stemed as a forneys of a leed°;
His bootes souple°; his hors in greet estaat°.
Now certeinly he was a fair prelaat°.
He nas nat° pale as a forpyned goost°. 205
A fat swan loved he best of any roost.
His palfrey° was as broun as is a berye°.

---

165 **a fair for the maistrie,** *an extremely fine* (one) 167 **to been an abbot able,** *able to be an abbot* (monastic superior) 168 **deyntee,** *excellent* 169 **brydel,** *bridle* 170 **als cleere,** *as clearly* 172 **Ther as this lord,** *where this lord* (i.e., the Monk), **celle,** *dependent monastery* 173 **reule,** *rule* 174 **By cause,** *because,* **somdel streit,** *somewhat strict* 175 **ilke,** *same,* **leet . . . pace,** *let pass* 176 **heeld after the newe world the space,** *held with the custom of the modern world* 177 **yaf nat of that text a pulled hen,** *gave not a plucked chicken for that* (written) *text* 178 **seith,** *says* 179 **recchelees,** *disobedient* 180 **likned til,** *likened to,* **waterlees,** *waterless* 181 **seyn,** *say,* **cloystre,** *monastery* (cloister) 182 **thilke,** *this,* **oystre,** *oyster* 183 **seyde,** *said* 184 **wood,** *crazy* 185 **poure,** *pore* over 186 **swynken,** *work* 187 **Austyn bit,** *St. Augustine commands* 188 **Lat,** *let* 189 **prikasour aright,** *hunter on horseback truly* 190 **Grehoundes,** *greyhounds,* **fowel,** *bird* 191 **prikyng,** *riding* 192 **lust,** *pleasure,* **wolde,** *would* 193 **seigh,** *saw,* **ypurfiled,** *trimmed* 194 **grys,** *gray fur,* **fyneste,** *finest* 195 **festne,** *fasten* 196 **of gold ywroght,** *made of gold,* **curious pyn,** *intricate pin* 197 **gretter,** *larger* 198 **balled,** *bald* 199 **eek,** *also* **as,** *as if,* **enoynt,** *oiled* 200 **in good poynt,** *stout* (French *en bon poynt*) 201 **eyen stepe,** *eyes prominent* 202 **stemed as a forneys of a leed,** *glowed like a furnace under a pot* 203 **souple,** *supple,* **greet estaat,** *fine condition* 204 **prelaat,** *churchman* 205 **nas nat,** *was not,* **forpyned goost,** *tortured spirit* 207 **palfrey,** *riding horse,* **berye,** *berry*

165 **MONK,** by definition, is a man who dedicates his life to work and prayer, generally expected to remain within the walls of his monastery ("cloistered") and obey its rules. Chaucer's Monk is commissioned to leave the monastery, and, rejecting regulations, he pursues his genteel interests in horses and hunting. 166 **outridere,** an "agent of a monastery who rides out to administer to its affairs" (*MED*), overseeing its farms and manors (see *CT* 7.65–66). **venerie,** the primary meaning is "hunting," but there may be connotations of "sexual pursuit." This line clearly contrasts with *CT* 1.45. 170 **Gynglen,** jingling; small bells were fashionable decorations for bridles; the flowers "Canterbury bells" later took their name from the clusters of bells adorning pilgrims' horses. 172 **celle,** a monk's cell could be his own small enclosure, but here and elsewhere the term means a subordinate monastery. 173 **reule of Seint Maure or of Seint Beneit,** a "rule" is a set of regulations for the goals and activities of a monastery—its hierarchy, schedule of prayers, organization of labor, etc. St. Benedict (480–ca. 550) wrote the influential *Benedictine Rule,* which according to legend was brought to France by his pupil St. Maurus. 178 **hunters been nat hooly men,** hunters are criticized as unholy in a number of medieval texts, rooted perhaps in the biblical story of Nimrod, Genesis 109. 179–80 **monk . . . recche-lees, / . . . fissh . . . waterlees,** a common comparison in medieval comments on monks who break the rules of their monasteries. 184–86 **studie . . . laboure,** book learning and manual labor are, with prayer, the major monastic activities. 187 **Austyn,** St. Augustine (354–430), one of the four Latin "fathers" of the Catholic Church, thought to have written a rule for monks, *De Opere Monachorum* ("Concerning the Work of Monks"). **world be served,** ideally, monks served the world by praying for the salvation of souls. 191–92 **prikyng . . . hare . . . lust,** the language and imagery here may associate hunting with sexual pursuit (compare *CT* 1.4231 and Gower, *Mirour de l'omme* 21,053), although the hare was highly regarded as the object of sport hunting. 197 **love-knotte,** an interlace design, but the term suggests amorousness. 201 **eyen stepe,** bright, prominent eyes, often attributed to heroes in medieval romances.

A FRERE° ther was, a wantowne and a merye°,
A lymytour°, a ful solempne° man.
In alle the ordres foure° is noon that kan°   210
So muchel of daliaunce° and fair langage°.
He hadde maad° ful many a mariage
Of yonge wommen at his owene cost°.
Unto his ordre he was a noble post°.
Ful wel biloved and famulier° was he   215
With frankeleyns° over al in his contree,
And eek° with worthy wommen of the toun,
For he hadde power of confessioun,
As seyde° hymself, moore than a curat°,
For of his ordre he was licenciat°. *excessive*   220
                                      labido ↑
Ful swetely herde he confessioun,
And plesaunt was his absolucioun°—
He was an esy° man to yeve penaunce°
Ther as he wiste° to have a good pitaunce°.
For unto a poure ordre for to yive°   225
Is signe° that a man is wel yshryve°,
For if he yaf°, he dorste make avaunt°,
He wiste° that a man was repentaunt;
For many a man so hard is of his herte,
He may nat wepe, althogh hym soore smerte°.   230
Therfore in stede of wepynge and preyeres
Men moote yeve° silver to the poure freres°.
His typet° was ay farsed° ful of knyves
And pynnes° for to yeven faire wyves.

And certeinly he hadde a murye note°:   235
Wel koude° he synge and pleyen on a rote°;
Of yeddynges he baar outrely the pris°.
His nekke whit was° as the flour delys°;
Therto he strong was as a champioun.
He knew the tavernes wel in every toun,   240
And everich hostiler° and tappestere°
Bet° than a lazar° or a beggestere°,
For unto swich° a worthy man as he
Acorded nat°, as by his facultee°,
To have with sike° lazars aqueyntaunce.   245
It is nat honeste°, it may nat avaunce°,
For to deelen° with no swich poraille°,
But al with riche and selleres of vitaille°.
And over al ther as° profit sholde arise
Curteis° he was and lowely° of servyse.   250
Ther nas no man nowher so vertuous.
He was the beste beggere in his hous,
And yaf° a certeyn ferme° for the graunt°—   252ᵇ
Noon of his bretheren cam ther in his
      haunt°—   252ᶜ
For thogh a wydwe° hadde noght a sho°,
So plesaunt was his "In principio,"
Yet wolde he have a ferthyng° er he wente°.   255
His purchas° was wel bettre than his rente.
And rage he koude°, as it were right a
      whelpe°.

---

208 FRERE, *Friar,* **a wantowne and a merye,** *a flirtatious and merry* (one) **209 lymytour,** *limiter* (see note) **ful solempne,** *very solemn* **210 ordres foure** *four orders of friars,* **kan,** *knows* **211 daliaunce,** *light talk,* **langage,** *language* **212 maad,** *arranged* **213 owene cost,** *own expense* **214 post,** *support* **215 famulier,** *familiar* **216 frankeleyns,** *independent landowners* **217 eek,** *also* **219 seyde,** *said* **curat,** *parish priest* **220 licenciat,** *licensed* **222 absolucioun,** *forgiving of sin* **223 esy,** *lenient,* **yeve penaunce,** *give penance* **224 Ther as he wiste,** *when he expected,* **good pitaunce,** *large donation* **225 yive,** *give* **226 signe,** *sign* **yshryve,** *forgiven* **227 he yaf,** *the penitent gave* **he dorst make avaunt,** *the Friar dared to boast* **228 He wiste,** *the Friar knew* **230 soore smerte,** *hurts sorely* **232 moote yeve,** *may give,* **freres,** *friars* **233 typet,** *end of his hood,* **ay farsed,** *always crammed* **234 pynnes,** *pins* **235 murye note,** *merry voice* **236 koude,** *could,* **rote,** *stringed instrument* **237 Of yeddynges he baar outrely the pris,** *for ballads he absolutely took the prize* **238 nekke whit was,** *neck was white* **flour delys,** *lily* **241 everich hostiler,** *every innkeeper,* **tappestere,** *barmaid* **242 Bet,** *better,* **lazar,** *leper,* **beggestere,** *beggarmaid* **243 swich,** *such* **244 Acorded nat,** *it was not suitable,* **facultee,** *ability* **245 sike,** *sick* **246 honeste,** *respectable* **avaunce,** *advance* **247 deelen** *deal,* **swich poraille,** *such poor folks* **248 vitaille,** *food* **249 over al ther as,** *everywhere where* **250 Curteis,** *courteous,* **lowely,** *humble* **252b yaf** *gave,* **ferme,** *fee,* **graunt,** *license* **252c haunt,** *locale* **253 wydwe,** *widow,* **sho,** *shoe* **255 ferthyng,** *farthing* (small coin), **er he wente,** *before he departed* **256 purchas,** *profits* **257 rage he koude,** *he could flirt,* **whelpe,** *puppy*

208 FRERE, friars were members of clerical orders but they differed from monks insofar as they were not cloistered in monasteries but made their way in the world by begging, preaching, hearing confessions, administering to the poor, etc. Chaucer's Friar embodies many of the abuses satirized by critics of the friars. **209 lymytour,** "a friar whose begging, preaching, and hearing of confessions was limited" to a particular territory (*MED*). **210 ordres foure,** Franciscans (Gray Friars), Dominicans (Black Friars), Carmelites (White Friars), Augustinians (Austin Friars). Other orders were suppressed in 1274. The depiction of Chaucer's Friar does not specify a particular order. **212–13 maad . . . mariage . . . at his owene cost,** the friar paid for many marriages, perhaps generously, but perhaps to marry off his mistresses. **218–20** A principal tension of the late-medieval church was the conflicting authority of friars and parish priests to hear confession and grant absolution of sins, especially since friars sometimes assumed special authority. The fact that pardoners could also absolve the guilt due to sins further complicated the situation; see lines 669–714 below. **licenciat,** licensed specifically to hear confessions, in contrast to parish priests who had additional spiritual responsibilities. **223–24 to yeve penaunce . . . pitaunce,** the sacrament of penance normally required that the penitent pray or do other acts of contrition (including giving alms—donations for the poor or support of the church) assigned by the confessor. This Friar assigns light punishments when he expects a sizable donation. **238 nekke whit,** a white neck was a sign of sensuality. **241–42 tappestere . . . beggestere,** *–stere* is the OE feminine suffix. **252b–c** This couplet is omitted in a large number of manuscripts, including El; Chaucer may have marked it for deletion. **254 "In principio,"** "In the beginning," the opening words of St. John's gospel (and of Genesis), the first fourteen lines of which were used by friars as a greeting, and perhaps as kind of incantation.

In love-dayes ther koude he muchel helpe°,
For ther he was nat lyk° a cloysterer°
With a thredbare cope°, as is a poure scoler°,   260
But he was lyk a maister or a pope.
Of double worstede° was his semycope°,
That rounded° as a belle out of the presse°.
Somwhat he lipsed° for his wantownesse°
To make his Englissh sweete upon his tonge.   265
And in his harpyng, whan that he hadde songe,
His eyen twynkled in his heed aryght°,
As doon the sterres in the frosty nyght.
This worthy lymytour was cleped° Huberd.

A MARCHANT was ther with a forked berd,   270
In mottelee°, and hye on horse° he sat,
Upon his heed a Flaundryssh bevere hat°,
His bootes clasped faire and fetisly°.
His resons° he spak ful solempnely°,
Sownynge alwey° th'encrees° of his wynnyng°.   275
He wolde the see were kept for any thyng°
Bitwixe Middelburgh and Orewelle.
Wel koude° he in eschaunge sheeldes selle.
This worthy man ful wel his wit bisette°—
Ther wiste no wight° that he was in dette,   280

So estatly° was he of his governaunce°
With his bargaynes° and with his chevyssaunce°.
For sothe° he was a worthy man withalle°,
But, sooth to seyn°, I noot° how men hym calle.

A CLERK ther was of Oxenford also   285
That unto logyk hadde longe ygo°.
As leene° was his hors as is a rake,
And he nas nat° right fat, I undertake°,
But looked holwe°, and therto sobrely°.
Ful thredbare was his overeste courtepy°,   290
For he hadde geten hym yet no benefice°,
Ne was so worldly for to have office°.
For hym was levere° have at his beddes heed°
Twenty bookes, clad in blak or reed,
Of Aristotle and his philosophie,   295
Than robes riche, or fithele°, or gay sautrie°.
But al be that he was a philosophre,
Yet hadde he but litel gold in cofre.
But al that he myghte of his freendes hente°,
On bookes and on lernynge he it spente,   300
And bisily gan for the soules preye°
Of hem° that yaf hym wherwith to scoleye°.
Of studie took he moost cure° and moost heede°.

---

258 **koude he muchel helpe,** *he could do much good* 259 **nat lyk,** *not like,* **cloysterer,** *monastic* 260 **thredbare cope,** *worn-out cloak,* **poure scoler,** *poor scholar* 262 **double worstede,** *high-quality wool,* **semycope,** *short cloak* 263 **rounded,** *was round,* **presse,** *bell mold* 264 **lipsed,** *lisped,* **wantownesse,** *affectation* 267 **aryght,** *exactly* 269 **cleped,** *named* 271 **mottelee,** *cloth of mixed color,* **hye on horse,** *in a high saddle* 272 **Flaundryssh bevere hat,** *beaverskin hat made in Flanders* 273 **fetisly,** *elegantly* 274 **resons,** *opinions,* **solempnely,** *solemnly* 275 **Sownynge alwey,** *indicating always,* **th'encrees,** *the increase,* **wynnyng,** *profit* 276 **wolde the see were kept for any thyng,** *wanted the sea protected at any cost* 278 **koude,** *could* 279 **bisette,** *used* 280 **Ther wiste no wight,** *no person knew* 281 **estatly,** *dignified* **governaunce,** *management* 282

bargaynes, *transactions,* **chevyssaunce,** *investments* 283 **For sothe,** *in truth,* **withalle,** *indeed* 284 **sooth to seyn,** *to tell the truth,* **noot,** *don't know* 286 **unto logyk hadde longe ygo,** *had long studied logic* 287 **leene,** *skinny* 288 **nas nat,** *wasn't,* **undertake,** *declare* 289 **holwe,** *emaciated,* **therto sobrely,** *therefore serious* 290 **overeste courtepy,** *outermost jacket* 291 **benefice,** *ecclesiastical or academic job* 292 **office,** *secular job* 293 **hym was levere,** *he would rather,* **beddes heed,** *bed's head* 296 **fithele,** *fiddle,* **gay sautrie,** *fine psaltery* (harp) 299 **hente,** *acquire* 301 **bisily gan . . . preye,** *busily did pray* 302 **hem,** *those,* **yaf hym wherwith to scoleye,** *gave him support to attend school* 303 **cure,** *care,* **heede,** *attention*

---

258 **love-dayes,** days set apart for settlement of social or domestic disputes; church officials often acted as arbiters. 267 **eyen twynkled,** contrast the flashing eyes of the Monk, line 201 above. 269 **Huberd,** not a common name in the fourteenth century, but in *Roman de Renart,* the name of the kite, a bird of prey. 270 **MARCHANT,** fourteenth-century merchants were traders in commodities, not small businessmen, and of considerable economic importance. The brief description of Chaucer's Merchant emphasizes the expense of his clothing, his commercial dealings, and little else. **forked berd,** high fashion for the time. 277 **Middelburgh and Orewelle,** the Dutch port Middelburgh was licensed to import English wool 1384–88 and the center thereafter for the Merchant Adventurers, a commercial organization of growing influence. Middelburgh lies across the English Channel from the Orwell River, where the English wool-exporting port of Ipswich is located. 278 **eschaunge sheeldes selle,** make money by trafficking in currencies; "shields" were French coins or Flemish money on account. 282 **bargaynes . . . chevyssaunce,** may suggest shrewd or perhaps shady dealings. 284 **noot how men hym calle,** contrast with the narrator's knowledge of the Friar's name, line 269. 285 **CLERK,** student, although the term was coming to mean a man who was skilled in reading and writing or keeping accounts. It is related to "clergy" because medieval university curricula had as their goal the study of theology. In his disregard for money, the Clerk clearly contrasts several of the other pilgrims, most pointedly the Merchant. **Oxenford,** Oxford is home to the oldest university in England. 286 **logyk,** logic, or dialectic, was the top of the undergraduate curriculum, the so-called trivium (grammar, rhetoric, logic). The quadrivium (arithmetic, geometry, astronomy, music) were studied by students seeking master of arts degrees before going on to study theology. Together, the trivium and quadrivium were the seven liberal arts. The Clerk's long study of logic may be humorous. 290 **thredbare,** unlike the Friar's (line 260), the Clerk's clothing was well worn. 294 **Twenty bookes,** a large library for a poor student, especially since books were very expensive. 295 **Aristotle,** preeminent authority on logic in the Middle Ages when he was known as "the Philosopher." 297 **philosophre,** applied to alchemists as well as those who studied philosophy, because the goal of alchemy was to turn base metals to gold with the help of the "philosopher's stone." The wordplay underscores the Clerk's failure to make money. 301–2 **soules . . . Of hem that yaf hym,** patrons often supported students who in turn were expected to pray for the souls of their benefactors.

Explication ⁊ (handwritten in left margin)

Noght o° word spak he moore than was neede,
And that was seyd° in forme and reverence°,   305
And short and quyk and ful of hy sentence°.
Sownynge in° moral vertu was his speche,
And gladly wolde he lerne° and gladly teche°.

  A SERGEANT OF THE LAWE, war° and wys°,
That often hadde been at the Parvys,   310
Ther was also, ful riche of° excellence.
Discreet° he was and of greet reverence°—
He semed swich°, his wordes weren so wise.
Justice he was ful often in assise,
By patente° and by pleyn commissioun°.   315
For his science° and for his heigh renoun°,
Of fees and robes hadde he many oon°.
So greet a purchasour° was nowher noon°:
Al was fee symple° to hym in effect,
His purchasyng myghte nat been infect°.   320
Nowher so bisy a man as he ther nas°,
And yet he semed bisier than he was.
In termes° hadde he caas° and doomes° alle
That from the tyme of Kyng William° were
       yfalle°.
Therto he koude endite and make a thyng°,   325

Ther koude no wight pynche° at his writyng;
And every statut koude he pleyn by rote°.
He rood but hoomly° in a medlee cote°,
Girt° with a ceint° of silk, with barres° smale—
Of his array telle I no lenger tale.   330

  A FRANKELEYN was in his compaignye.
Whit was his berd° as is the dayesye°;
Of his complexioun he was sangwyn°.
Wel loved he by the morwe° a sop in wyn°.
To lyven in delit was evere his wone°,   335
For he was Epicurus owene sone,
That heeld opinioun that pleyn delit°
Was verray felicitee parfit°.
An housholdere, and that a greet, was he;
Seint Julian he was in his contree.   340
His breed, his ale, was always after oon°.
A bettre envyned° man was nowher noon.
Withoute bake mete° was nevere his hous,
Of fissh and flessh°, and that so plenteuous,
It snewed° in his hous of mete and drynke,   345
Of alle deyntees° that men koude thynke.
After the sondry sesons° of the yeer,
So chaunged he his mete and his soper.

---

304 Noght o, *not one* **305 seyd**, *said*, **in forme and reverence**, *formally and respectfully* **306 hy sentence**, *lofty meaning* **307 Sownynge in**, *reflecting* **308 lerne**, *learn*, **teche**, *teach* **309 war**, *careful*, **wys**, *wise* **311 ful riche of**, *well endowed with* **312 Discreet**, *prudent* **of greet reverence**, *highly dignified* **313 semed swich**, *seemed such* **315 patente**, *royal letter*, **pleyn commissioun**, *full commission* **316 science**, *knowledge*, **heigh renoun**, *high reputation* **317 many oon**, *many* (a one) **318 purchasour**, *land buyer*, **nowher noon**, *nowhere none* **319 fee symple**, *owned without restriction* **320 infect**, *invalidated* **321 nas**, *wasn't* **323 termes**, *legal language*, **caas**, *cases*, **doomes**, *decisions* **324 William**, *William the Conqueror*, **were yfalle**, *had happened* **325 Therto he**

koude endite and make a thyng, *also he was able to compose and draw up a legal document* **326 Ther koude no wight pynche**, *where no one could find fault* **327 every statut koude he pleyn by rote**, *knew every statute fully by heart* **328 hoomly**, *informally* **medlee cote**, *multicolored coat* **329 Girt**, *belted* **ceint**, *sash*, **barres**, *stripes* **332 berd**, *beard* **dayesye**, *daisy* **333 sangwyn**, *reddish* **334 by the morwe**, *in the morning*, **sop in wyn**, *bread soaked in wine* **335 wone**, *habit* **337 pleyn delit**, *complete pleasure* **338 verray felicitee parfit**, *true perfect happiness* **341 after oon**, *uniformly good* **342 envyned**, *stocked with wine* **343 bake mete**, *dinner pies* **344 flessh**, *meat* **345 snewed**, *snowed* **346 deyntees**, *delicacies* **347 sondry sesons**, *various seasons*

---

307 Sownynge . . ., contrast line 275 above. **309 SERGEANT OF THE LAWE,** a small faction of high-ranking lawyers from whom all judges were chosen. Chaucer's Sergeant (later, "Man of Law") has the wealth and deep knowledge of the law required for the position, although he also seems concerned with appearances. **310 Parvys,** the porch before St. Paul's Cathedral in London, a traditional place for lawyers and clients to conduct legal business. **314 Justice . . . in assise,** sergeants of the law had exclusive rights to act as judge in courts of the assize, district courts originally concerned with questions of land rights. **315 patente . . . pleyn commissioun,** kings issued open or "patent" letters to appoint judges, and full commission enabled a judge to hear all cases. **317 robes,** fee payment was frequently in the form of clothing or jewelry, often an annual gift for life or a specified term. **318–19 purchasour . . . fee symple,** in the late fourteenth century, people began to be able to purchase real estate (etymologically, *royal estate*, because under William the Conqueror, all land belonged to the King); until that time, the only way to acquire land had been to inherit or receive by gift. The most desirable kind of purchase was "fee simple," without any restrictions on future sale or transfer. **326 pynche,** a possible play on the name of a sergeant of the law, Thomas Pynchbeck, whom Chaucer probably knew. **331 FRANKELEYN,** a country landowner, who traditionally served as justice of the peace and knight of the shire (representative to Parliament) for his locale. The Franklin rides with the Sergeant at Law, his social superior, with whom he shares interest in land ownership and district courts. This association and the Franklin's obsession with fine dining may indicate social climbing. **333 complexioun . . . sangwyn,** the physiological combination or "complexion" of four humors, or bodily fluids, was thought to influence or determine an individual's health and personality. The sanguine or hopeful person was dominated by blood; the phlegmatic or dull, by phlegm; the choleric or excitable, by yellow bile; the melancholic, by black bile. See 420–21n below. **336 Epicurus owene sone,** Epicurus's own son, an Epicurean, a pursuer of pleasure; Epicurus (341–270 BC) was a Greek philosopher whose name was attached (with little real justification) to a philosophy of pleasure. **340 Seint Julian,** the legendary patron saint of hospitality, here used metaphorically to indicate the Franklin's hospitality. **347–48 sondry sesons . . . chaunged,** changed his menu according to the climatic (summer, winter) and / or liturgical seasons (e.g., Lent, Christmas, etc.).

Ful many a fat partrich hadde he in muwe°,
And many a breem° and many a luce° in
   stuwe°.   350
Wo° was his cook but if° his sauce were
Poynaunt° and sharp, and redy al his geere°.
His table dormant° in his halle alway
Stood redy covered al the longe day.
At sessiouns ther was he lord and sire.   355
Ful ofte tyme he was knyght of the shire.
An anlaas° and a gipser° al of silk
Heeng at his girdel, whit as morne° milk.
A shirreve° hadde he been, and a contour°.
Was nowher swich° a worthy vavasour°.   360

    An HABERDASSHERE° and a CARPENTER,
A WEBBE°, a DYERE°, and a TAPYCER°,
And they were clothed alle in o lyveree°
Of a solempne° and a greet fraternitee.
Ful fressh and newe hir geere apiked was°:   365
Hir knyves were chaped noght° with bras
But al with silver; wroght° ful clene and weel
Hire girdles° and hir pouches everydeel°.
Wel semed ech of hem° a fair burgeys°
To sitten in a yeldehalle° on a deys°.   370

Everich°, for the wisdowm that he kan°,
Was shaply° for to been an alderman°.
For catel° hadde they ynogh° and rente,
And eek hir° wyves wolde it wel assente°;
And elles° certeyn were they to blame.   375
It is ful fair to been ycleped° "madame,"
And goon to vigilies al bifore°,
And have a mantel roialliche ybore°.

    A COOK they hadde with hem for the nones°
To boille the chiknes° with the marybones°,   380
And poudre-marchant tart° and galyngale°.
Wel koude he knowe° a draughte° of Londoun ale.
He koude° rooste and sethe° and broille and
   frye,
Maken mortreux°, and wel bake a pye.
But greet harm was it, as it thoughte me°,   385
That on his shyne a mormal° hadde he.
For blankmanger°, that made he with the beste.

    A SHIPMAN was ther, wonynge fer by weste°.
For aught I woot°, he was of Dertemouthe.
He rood upon a rouncy°, as he kouthe°,   390
In a gowne of faldyng° to the knee.

---

349 **muwe,** *coop* 350 **breem,** *bream* (a fish), **luce,** *pike* (a fish), **stuwe,** *pond* 351 **Wo,** *woeful* **but if,** *unless* 352 **Poynaunt,** *spicy,* **geere,** *equipment* 353 **table dormant** *removable table* 357 **anlaas,** *dagger,* **gipser,** *purse* 358 **morne,** *morning* 359 **shirreve,** *sheriff,* **contour,** *tax collector* 360 **swich,** *such,* **vavasour,** *feudal landowner* 361 **HABERDASSHERE,** *dealer in men's clothing* 362 **WEBBE,** *weaver,* **DYERE,** *one who dyes cloth,* **TAPYCER,** *tapestry maker* 363 **o lyveree,** *one uniform* 364 **solempne,** *solemn* 365 **geere apiked was,** *equipment was adorned* 366 **chaped noght,** *mounted not* 367 **wroght,** *made* 368 **Hire girdles,** *their belts* **everydeel,** *every part* 369 **ech of hem,** *each of them,* **fair burgeys,** *impressive citizen* 370 **yeldehalle,** *guildhall,* **deys,** *platform* 371 **Everich,** *each one,* **kan,** *knew* 372 **shaply,** *suitable,* **alderman,** *city or guild official* 373 **catel,** *property,* **ynogh,** *enough* 374 **eek hir,** *also their,* **wolde it wel assente,** *would well agree to it* 375 **And elles,** *or else* 376 **ycleped,** *called* 377 **goon to vigilies al bifore,** *go to services in front of all* 378 **mantel roialliche ybore,** *robe carried royally* 379 **nones,** *occasion* 380 **chiknes,** *chickens* **marybones,** *marrowbones* 381 **poudre-marchant tart,** *pungent spice,* **galyngale,** *aromatic spice* 382 **knowe,** *recognize,* **draughte,** *drink* 383 **he koude,** *he knew how to,* **sethe,** *boil* 383 **mortreux,** *stews* 385 **as it thoughte me,** *as it seemed to me* 386 **shyne,** *shin,* **mormal,** *scabby sore* 387 **blankmanger,** *a spiced mousse* 388 **wonynge fer by west,** *living far in the west* 389 **For aught I woot,** *for all I know* 390 **rouncy,** *workhorse,* **as he kouthe,** *as well as he could* 391 **faldyng,** *coarse wool*

349–50 **muwe . . . stuwe,** bird coops and fish ponds were kept on manors to supply the household. 353 **table dormant,** tables were normally removed from the hall after meals, although the Franklin keeps his set up. 355 **sessiouns,** district courts at which the lord of the manor presided. 356 **knyght of the shire,** member of Parliament for his district. 359 **shirreve,** sheriff (from *shire-reeve*), the legal and administrative representative of the Crown in a given district. 361–62 **HABERDASSHERE . . . CARPENTER . . . WEBBE . . . DYERE . . . TAPYCER,** generally referred to as the "Guildsmen" because their common livery (a kind of uniform) indicates that they were members of a parish guild, a social and charitable organization influential because of its collective membership. None is assigned an extant tale. 363 **lyveree,** as in modern fraternities and organizations, members of medieval guilds identified themselves by wearing distinctive dress, often a robe or hood. 364 **fraternitee,** perhaps the fraternity or brotherhood of St. Fabian and St. Sebastian of St. Botolph's Church in Aldersgate Ward, a center of cloth trade. 367 **silver,** silver ornamentation on knives was allowed by law only to citizens and others who had property worth five hundred pounds or more, a considerable amount. 370 **sitten in yeldehalle on a deys,** sitting on the dais, or raised platform, in a guildhall was a sign of importance. 377 **goon to vigilies al bifore,** to lead the congregation in a procession as part of a church service. 378 **mantel,** a ceremonial robe, perhaps a reference to some particular ritual, though none has been identified. 379 **COOK,** a servant of the Guildsmen, who apparently preferred their food prepared specially for them. The Cook later names himself Roger, and it is suggested that he operates a shop or booth in London (*CT* 1.4325, 4336, 4346–47). Here the praise of his culinary skill is punctuated abruptly by mention of a disgusting sore. **for the nones,** a phrase often used as a line filler, it seems here to mean "for the occasion," i.e., for the pilgrimage. 386–87 **mormal . . . blankmanger,** this juxtaposition of a sore and a soft gelatinous mousse or pudding is revolting. The "For" that links the two lines underscores the juxtaposition, especially in the manuscripts, which are largely unpunctuated; its primary meaning is "As for." 388 **SHIPMAN,** a sailor, although this one owns his own vessel. His nautical skill is emphasized, along with indications of piracy. 389 **Dertemouthe,** Dartmouth is a port in the west of England, notorious for smugglers and pirates. 390 **as he kouthe,** implies that the Shipman does not ride well.

A daggere hangynge on a laas° hadde he
Aboute his nekke, under his arm adoun°.
The hoote somer hadde maad his hewe° al broun.
And certeinly he was a good felawe.   395
Ful many a draughte of wyn° had he ydrawe°
Fro Burdeux-ward, whil that the chapman sleepe°.
Of nyce° conscience took he no keepe°.
If that he faught, and hadde the hyer° hond,
By water he sente hem hoom° to every lond.   400
But of his craft to rekene° wel his tydes°,
His stremes, and his daungers hym bisides°,
His herberwe°, and his moone, his lodemenage°,
Ther nas noon swich° from Hulle to Cartage.
Hardy he was and wys to undertake°.   405
With many a tempest hadde his berd been shake°.
He knew alle the havenes°, as they were,
Fro Gootlond to the cape of Fynystere,
And every cryke° in Britaigne and in Spayne.
His barge ycleped was° the Maudelayne.   410

    With us ther was a DOCTOUR OF PHISIK°;
In al this world ne was ther noon hym lik,
To speke of phisik and of surgerye,
For he was grounded in astronomye°. *astrology*

He kepte° his pacient a ful greet deel   415
In houres° by his magyk natureel.
Wel koude he fortunen° the ascendent
Of his ymages for his pacient.
He knew the cause of everich° maladye,
Were it of hoot, or coold, or moyste, or drye,   420
And where engendred°, and of what humour°.
He was a verray, parfit praktisour°.
The cause yknowe°, and of his° harm the roote,
Anon he yaf° the sike man his boote°. *like his daughter*
Ful redy hadde he his apothecaries°   425
To sende hym drogges° and his letuaries°,
For ech of hem° made oother for to wynne°—
Hir° frendshipe nas nat newe° to bigynne.
Wel knew he the olde Esculapius,
And Deyscorides, and eek Rufus,   430
Olde Ypocras, Haly, and Galyen,
Serapion, Razis, and Avycen,
Averrois, Damascien, and Constantyn,
Bernard, and Gatesden, and Gilbertyn.
Of his diete mesurable° was he,   435
For it was of no superfluitee°,
But of greet norissyng° and digestible.
His studie was but litel on the Bible.

---

392 laas, *cord* **393 under his arm adoun,** *below his arm* **394 hewe,** *color* **396 draughte of wyn,** *drink of wine,* **ydrawe,** *taken* **397 chapman sleepe,** *merchant slept* **398 nyce,** *scrupulous,* **keepe,** *notice* **399 hyer,** *upper* **400 sente hem hoom,** *sent them home* **401 craft to rekene,** *skill to calculate* **tydes,** *tides* **402 daungers hym bisides,** *dangers nearby* **403 herberwe,** *harbors,* **lodemenage,** *navigating* **404 nas noon swich,** *wasn't another such* **405 wys to undertake,** *wise in his management* **406 shake,** *shaken* **407 havenes,** *safe spots* **409 cryke,** *creek* **410 barge ycleped was,** *ship was called* **411 DOCTOUR OF PHISIK,** *Doctor of Medicine* **414**

grounded in astronomy, *learned in astrology* **415 kepte,** *took care of* **416 In houres,** *according to astrological times* **417 fortunen,** *determine* **419 everich,** *every* **421 engendred,** *generated,* **humour,** *bodily liquid* **422 verray, parfit praktisour,** *true perfect practitioner* **423 yknowe,** *known,* **his,** *its* **424 Anon he yaf,** *immediately he gave,* **boote,** *remedy* **425 apothecaries,** *pharmacists* **426 drogges,** *drugs,* **letuaries,** *mixtures* **427 hem,** *them,* **wynne,** *profit* **428 Hir,** *their,* **nas nat newe,** *wasn't new* **435 mesurable,** *moderate* **436 superfluitee,** *excess* **437 of greet norissyng,** *very nourishing*

397 Fro Burdeux-ward . . . , transporting from Bordeaux, renowned for its wine; the Shipman stole from the wine merchants. **399–400 faught . . . ,** those that the Shipman fought and defeated he threw overboard. **404 Hulle to Cartage,** port cities, Hull in northern England; Carthage in North Africa, or Cartagena in southeastern Spain. **408 Gootlond,** Gotland, an island off Sweden. **cape of Fynystere,** Cape Finistere ("end of the earth") in western Spain. **409 Britaigne,** Brittany, in western France. **410 Maudelayne,** Peter Risshenden was in 1391 recorded as the master of a ship named the *Maudeleyne* out of Dartmouth. **411 DOCTOUR OF PHISIK,** doctors of medicine were learned in astrology, since it was believed that the configuration of the stars and planets interacted with the physiology of the human body. Like the stereotype of modern doctors, Chaucer's Physician (as he is generally called) is wealthy and concerned only with physical things. **413 phisik and surgerye,** physic (or medicine) and surgery were related though separate fields, the first concerned with treatment through diet, hygiene, and pharmaceuticals; the latter, with operations. **416 magyk natureel,** natural magic had no occult connotations; it meant the understanding of natural forces. **417 ascendent,** an astrological configuration at an important moment, such as the time of birth or illness. An ascendant is the point on the zodiacal circle (or path of a planet) that ascends above the horizon at the particular moment. **418 ymages,** doctors constructed images—graphic representations—of patients or their astrological configurations by which health could be studied and treated. The images were either drawn or molded of specific materials at specific times. **420 hoot, or coold, or moyste, or drye,** these four qualities, or contraries, were thought to define the four fluids (or humors; see 333n above) of the human body as well as the four elements of the physical cosmos. Combining hot and moist qualities, blood parallels air; cold and moist, phlegm parallels water; hot and dry, yellow bile is like fire; and cold and moist, black bile is like earth. Understanding these parallels and their appropriate hours and seasons enabled physicians to treat their patients according to ancient science, seeking to keep things in proper balance by administering medicines, heating or cooling the patient, letting blood, etc. **422** This line echoes line 72. **425–28** The friendship and mutual profit making of the Physician and his **apothecaries** (pharmacists) reflect a traditional complaint that the two professions collaborated to take advantage of the ill. **429–34** Aescalapius, Dioscorides, Rufus, Hippocrates, and Galen were famous Greek medical authorities. Ali ibn Abbas or Ali ibn Ridwan (**Haly**), Serapion, Rhazes, Avicenna (**Avycen**), and Averroes, were Persian, Egyptian, and Arabic medical authorities. Pseudo-John of Damascus (**Damascien**) and Constantinus Africanus translated medical works into Latin. Bernard of Gordon lectured at the medical school at Montpelier. John Gaddesden (**Gatesden**) and Gilbertus Anglicanus were famous English physicians.

In sangwyn° and in pers° he clad° was al,
Lyned° with taffata and with sendal°,   440
And yet he was but esy of dispence°.
He kepte that he wan in pestilence°,
For gold in phisik is a cordial°; *? alchemy*
Therefore he lovede gold in special°.

A good WIF° was ther OF biside° BATHE,   445
But she was somdel deef°, and that was scathe°.
Of clooth makyng she hadde swich an haunt°,
She passed hem° of Ypres and of Gaunt.
In al the parisshe° wif ne was ther noon°
That to the offrynge° bifore hire sholde goon°;   450
And if ther dide, certeyn so wrooth° was she
That she was out of alle° charitee.
Hir coverchiefs° ful fyne weren of ground°.
I dorste swere° they weyeden° ten pound
That on a Sonday weren upon hir heed.   455
Hir hosen° weren of fyn scarlet reed,
Ful streite yteyd°, and shoes ful moyste° and newe.
Boold was hir face, and fair, and reed of hewe°.
She was a worthy womman al hir lyve.
Housbondes at chirche dore she hadde fyve,   460
Withouten° oother compaignye in youthe—
But therof nedeth nat to speke as nowthe°.
And thries° hadde she been at Jerusalem.

She hadde passed many a straunge strem°.
At Rome she hadde been, and at Boloigne,   465
In Galice at Seint-Jame, and at Coloigne.
She koude muchel° of wandrynge by the weye.
Gat-tothed° was she, soothly for to seye°.
Upon an amblere° esily she sat,
Ywympled wel°, and on hir heed an hat   470
As brood as is a bokeler or a targe°,
A foot-mantel° aboute hir hipes large,
And on hir feet a paire of spores° sharpe.
In felaweshipe wel koude she laughe and carpe°.
Of remedies of love she knew per chaunce°,   475
For she koude° of that art the olde daunce.

A good man was ther of religioun,
And was a poure PERSOUN of a toun,
But riche he was of hooly thoght and werk.
He was also a lerned man, a clerk,   480
That Cristes gospel trewely wolde preche.
His parisshens° devoutly wolde he teche.
Benygne° he was, and wonder° diligent,
And in adversitee ful pacient°,
And swich° he was preved° ofte sithes°.   485
Ful looth were hym° to cursen for his tithes,
But rather wolde he yeven°, out of doute°,
Unto his poure parisshens aboute

---

439 sangwyn, *red,* **pers,** *blue,* **clad,** *dressed* **440 Lyned,** **lined,** **taffata . . . sendal,** *taffeta . . . sendal (kinds of rich cloth)* **441 esy of dispence,** *moderate in spending* **442 that he wan in pestilence,** *what he acquired during plague* **443 cordial,** *heart medicine* **444 in special,** *especially* **445 WIF,** *wife or woman,* **biside,** *near* **446 somdel deef,** *somewhat deaf,* **scathe,** *unfortunate* **447 haunt,** *skill* **448 passed hem,** *surpassed them (clothmakers)* **449 parisshe,** *locale of a church,* **wif ne was ther noon,** *there was no woman* **450 offrynge,** *offering* **sholde goon,** *should go* **451 wrooth,** *angry* **452 out of alle,** *without any* **453 coverchiefs,** *headcloths or kerchiefs,* **ful fyne weren of ground,** *were very fine of texture* **454 dorste swere,** *dare say* **weyeden,** *weighed* **456 hosen,** *leggings* **457 streite yteyd,** *closely tied,* **moyste,** *supple* **458 reed of hewe,** *rosy in color* **461**

Withouten, *without counting* **462 as nowthe,** *now* **463 thries,** *three times* **464 straunge strem,** *foreign river* **467 koude muchel,** *knew much* **468 Gat-tothed,** *gap-toothed,* **soothly for to seye,** *to speak truly* **469 amblere,** *easy-gaited saddle horse* **470 Ywympled wel,** *wearing a large head-dress that covered much of her face* **471 bokeler . . . targe,** *buckler . . . targe (kinds of shields)* **472 foot-mantel,** *protective outer skirt* **473 spores,** *spurs* **474 carpe,** *talk* **475 per chaunce,** *it so happened* **476 koude,** *knew* **482 His parisshens,** *members of his church* **483 Benygne,** *kind,* **wonder,** *wondrously* **484 ful pacient,** *completely patient* **485 swich,** *such,* **preved,** *proved,* **ofte sithes,** *oftentimes* **486 Ful looth were hym,** *very reluctant was he* **487 yeven,** *give,* **out of doute,** *no doubt*

---

443 gold . . . cordial, a play on words: gold was used in heart medicines and it was also dear to the Physician's heart. **445 WIF . . . OF . . . BATHE,** the association of the Wife with the city of Bath is appropriate because it was a center for cloth weaving, a skill traditionally associated with women. In the autobiographical prologue to the *Wife of Bath's Tale*, the Wife of Bath is depicted as profiting from her many marriages, putting to use her knowledge of love and sex, introduced here. **448 Ypres . . . Gaunt,** Ypres and Ghent, cities in Flanders, modern Belgium, famous for their cloth making. English cloth was widely regarded as inferior, so the praise of the Wife's weaving may be comic exaggeration. **450 offrynge,** the Offertory, part of the liturgy of the Mass, a procession in which bread, wine, and other offerings were brought to the priest by the faithful, among whom social precedence was evidently important. See line 377 above and *CT, ParsT* 10.407, where the desire to lead the procession indicates pride. **452 out of alle charitee,** ironic because Offertory gifts symbolize charity. **454 weyeden ten pound,** probably an exaggeration, although multiple coverchiefs were sometimes worn over wire frames. **460 chirche dore,** the marriage ceremony took place at the door, after which the couple entered the church for Mass. **463ff. Jerusalem . . . ,** on pilgrimages to Jerusalem, Rome, Boulogne (France), St. James de Compostela in Galicia (Spain), and Cologna (Germany), an impressive array. See *WBP* 3.555ff. **468 Gat-tothed,** gap-toothed, thought to indicate a bold, envious, and suspicious nature. The Wife later claims (*WBP* 3.603–5) that her spaced teeth help explain her sensuous nature. **475–76 remedies of love . . . that art,** remedies are cures for love, although the phrase translates the title of Ovid's *Remedia amoris,* and "art of love" translates the title of his *Ars Amatoria,* both books of erotic verse. **olde daunce,** all the techniques, perhaps a euphemism for copulation. **478 PERSOUN,** parish priest, responsible for the spiritual welfare of his congregation. The Parson's description echoes scriptural and social ideals of a priest, and contradicts criticism leveled by contemporary satirists. **486 cursen for his tithes,** tithes equaled 10 percent of a person's income, due for support of the church. Failure to pay tithes could lead to being cursed or excommunicated, i.e., excluded from participation in the church.

Of his offryng° and eek of his substaunce°.
He koude° in litel thyng have suffisaunce°.   490
Wyd° was his parisshe° and houses fer
    asonder°,
But he ne lefte nat°, for reyn ne thonder,
In siknesse nor in meschief° to visite
The ferreste° in his parisshe, muche and
    lite°,
Upon his feet, and in his hand a staf°.   495
This noble ensample° to his sheep he yaf°,
That first he wroghte°, and afterward he
    taughte.
Out of the gospel he tho wordes caughte°,
And this figure° he added eek° therto,
That if gold ruste, what shal iren° do?   500
For if a preest be foul, on whom we truste,
No wonder is a lewed° man to ruste.
And shame it is, if a preest take keep°,
A shiten° shepherde and a clene° sheep.
Wel oghte° a preest ensample for to yive,   505
By his clennesse°, how that his sheep sholde
    lyve.
He sette nat his benefice to hyre
And leet° his sheep encombred in the myre°
And ran to Londoun unto Seinte Poules
To seken hym° a chaunterie° for soules,   510
Or with a bretherhed° to been withholde°,
But dwelte at hoom, and kepte wel his folde°
So that the wolf ne made it nat myscarie°.
He was a shepherde and noght a mercenarie°.

And though he hooly were and vertuous,   515
He was nat to synful men despitous°,
Ne of his speche daungerous ne digne°,
But in his techyng discreet and benygne.
To drawen folk to hevene by fairnesse,
By good ensample, this was his bisynesse.   520
But it were any persone° obstinat,
What so° he were, of heigh or lough estat°,
Hym wolde he snybben° sharply for the nonys°.
A bettre preest I trowe° that nowher noon ys.
He waited after° no pompe and reverence   525
Ne maked hym a spiced° conscience,
But Cristes loore° and his apostles twelve
He taughte, but first he folwed it hymselve.

  With hym ther was a PLOWMAN, was his
    brother,
That hadde ylad° of dong° ful many a
    fother°.   530
A trewe swynkere° and a good was he,
Lyvynge in pees° and parfit° charitee.
God loved he best with al his hoole herte
At alle tymes, thogh him gamed or smerte°,
And thanne° his neighebore right as°
    hymselve.   535
He wolde thresshe°, and therto° dyke° and
    delve°,
For Cristes sake, for every poure wight°,
Withouten hire°, if it lay in his myght.
His tithes payde° he ful faire and wel,

---

489 **Of his offryng,** *from his donations,* **substaunce,** *income* 490 **koude,** *could,* **suffisaunce,** *sufficiency* 491 **Wyd,** *large,* **parisshe,** *parish,* **fer asonder,** *far apart* 492 **ne lefte nat,** *refrained not* 493 **meschief,** *trouble* 494 **ferreste,** *farthest,* **muche and lite,** *great and small* 495 **staf,** *walking staff* 496 **ensample,** *example* **yaf,** *gave* 497 **wroghte,** *performed* 498 **tho wordes caughte,** *those words took* 499 **figure,** *metaphor,* **eek,** *also* 500 **iren,** *iron* 502 **lewed,** *unlearned* 503 **keep,** *heed* 504 **shiten,** *filthy,* **clene,** *clean* 505 **oghte,** *ought* 506 **clennesse,** *purity* 508 **leet,** (*did not*) *leave,* **encombred in the myre,** *stuck in the mud* 510 **seken hym,** *seek for himself,* **chaunterie,** *endowed chapel* 511 **bretherhed,** *guild* **withholde,** *supported* 512 **folde,** *flock* 513 **ne made it nat myscarie,** *did not make it go wrong* 514 **mercenarie,** *hired priest* 516 **despitous,** *contemptuous* 517

daungerous ne digne, *disdainful nor haughty* 521 **But it were any persone,** *but if it happened that any person was* 522 **What so,** *whatever,* **heigh or lough estat,** *high or low class* 523 **snybben,** *scold,* **for the nonys,** *because of it* 524 **trowe,** *believe* 525 **waited after,** *expected* 526 **Ne maked hym a spiced,** *nor made (of or for) himself a fussy* 527 **loore,** *teachings* 530 **ylad,** *hauled* **dong,** *dung* **fother,** *load* 531 **trewe swynkere,** *true worker* 532 **pees,** *peace,* **parfit,** *perfect* 534 **thogh him gamed or smerte,** *whether it pleased or hurt him* 535 **thanne,** *then,* **right as,** *just as* 536 **thresshe,** *separate grain* **therto,** *also,* **dyke,** *make dikes,* **delve,** *dig* 537 **poure wight,** *poor person* 538 **hire,** *payment* 539 **tithes payde,** *church dues paid*

495ff. **staf . . . sheep . . . shepherde,** the pastoral (from Lat. *pastor,* "shepherd") imagery throughout the description aligns the Parson with Christ as the Good Shepherd, an ancient ideal that in Christian tradition is rooted in John 10.11ff. 497 The Parson practices what he preaches, an echo of Matthew 5.19. 500 **gold . . . iren,** a proverbial notion. 507ff. **benefice to hyre . . . ,** a benefice is a religious appointment that pays the priest an income, in this case his income for tending to his parish. It was a common complaint that parish priests rented their benefices to others (at less than the stipulated income) and, for additional profit, accepted positions as chaplains for guilds or at endowed chapels, known as "chantries." Chantries were endowed so that priests would pray for the souls of the endowers. 509 **Seinte Poules,** St. Paul's Cathedral in London had a notorious number of chantries. 513–14 An echo of John 10.12–13. 523 **for the nonys,** i.e., the Parson would scold obstinate or stubborn sinners (regardless of their class) for their obstinacy. 528 **taughte . . . folwed,** like line 497, an echo of Matthew 5.19, in which those who follow and teach the commandments of God are called great in the kingdom of heaven. 529 **PLOWMAN,** a free laborer, here an idealized Christian worker. No tale is assigned to the Plowman. **brother,** the brotherhood of the Plowman and Parson is spiritual as well as by birth. 533–35 An echo of Matthew 22.27–29, Christ's commandments to love God and neighbor. 539–40 The plowman paid tithes

Bothe of his propre swynk° and his catel°.   540
In a tabard° he rood upon a mere°.

   Ther was also a REVE, and a MILLERE,
A SOMNOUR, and a PARDONER also,
A MAUNCIPLE, and myself—ther were
     namo°.

   The MILLERE was a stout carl° for the
     nones;   545
Ful byg° he was of brawn°, and eek of bones.
That proved wel, for over al ther he cam°,
At wrastlynge he wolde have alwey the ram°.
He was short-sholdred, brood, a thikke
     knarre°;
Ther was no dore° that he nolde heve of
     harre°,   550
Or breke° it at a rennyng° with his heed.
His berd as any sowe or fox was reed°,
And therto brood, as though it were a spade.
Upon the cop right° of his nose he hade
A werte°, and theron stood a toft of herys°   555
Reed as the brustles° of a sowes erys°.
His nosethirles° blake were and wyde.
A swerd and bokeler° bar° he by his syde.
His mouth as greet was as a greet forneys°.
He was a janglere° and a goliardeys°,   560

And that was moost of synne° and harlotries°.
Wel koude he stelen° corn and tollen thries°.
And yet he hadde a thombe° of gold, pardee°.
A whit cote° and a blew° hood wered° he.
A baggepipe wel koude he blowe and sowne°,   565
And therwithal he broghte us out of towne.

   A gentil MAUNCIPLE was ther of a temple°,
Of which achatours° myghte take exemple
For to be wise in byynge of vitaille°.
For wheither that he payde or took by taille°,   570
Algate° he wayted° so in his achaat°
That he was ay biforn° and in good staat°.
Now is nat that of God a ful fair grace°
That swich a lewed mannes wit° shal pace°
The wisdom of an heep° of lerned men?   575
Of maistres hadde he mo than thries ten°
That weren of lawe expert and curious°,
Of which ther were a duszeyne° in that hous
Worthy to been stywardes° of rente and lond
Of any lord that is in Engelond,   580
To maken hym lyve by his propre good°
In honour dettelees°, but if° he were wood°,
Or lyve as scarsly as hym list desire°;
And able for to helpen al a shire°
In any caas° that myghte falle or happe°—   585
And yet this Manciple sette hir aller cappe°.

---

540 propre swynk, *own work* **catel,** *possessions* **541 tabard,** *long sleeveless overshirt,* **mere,** *mare* **544 namo,** *no more* **545 carl,** *fellow* **546 byg, strong,* **brawn,** *muscle* **547 over al ther he cam,** *wherever he went* **548 wolde have alwey the ram,** *would always take the prize* **549 thikke knarre,** *broad fellow* **550 dore,** *door,* **nolde heve of harre,** *couldn't heave off hinges* **551 breke,** *break* **rennyng,** *butting* **552 reed,** *red* **554 Upon the cop right,** *right on the top of* **555 werte,** *wart,* **toft of herys,** *tuft of hair* **556 brustles,** *bristles,* **sowes erys,** *sow's ears* **557 nosethirles,** *nostrils* **558 bokeler,** *shield,* **bar,** *carried* **559 forneys,** *furnace* **560 janglere,** *constant talker,* **goliardeys,** *tale-teller* **561 synne,** *sin,* **harlotries, dirty stories* **562 koude he stelen,** *could he steal,* **tollen thries,** *take three times his due* **563 thombe,** *thumb,* **pardee,** *by God* **564 whit cote,** *white*

coat, **blew,** *blue,* **wered,** *wore* **565 sowne,** *play* **566 therewithal,** *with that* **567 temple,** *law school* **568 achatours,** *purchasers* **569 byynge of vitaille,** *buying of food* **570 by taille,** *on credit* **571 Algate,** *always,* **wayted,** *watched,* **achaat,** *buying* **572 ay biforn,** *always ahead,* **in good staat,** *financially sound* **573 grace,** *favor* **574 swich a lewed mannes wit,** *(the) wit of such an unlearned man,* **pace,** *surpass* **575 heep,** *heap* **576 mo than thries ten,** *more than thirty* **577 curious,** *clever* **578 duszeyne,** *dozen* **579 stywardes,** *managers* **581 lyve by his propre good,** *live within his own means* **582 dettelees,** *debt-free,* **but if,** *unless,* **wood,** *crazy* **583 as scarsly as hym list desire,** *as economically as he wishes* **584 al a shire,** *an entire district* **585 caas,** *case,* **falle or happe,** *occur or happen* **586 sette hir aller cappe,** *deceived them all*

on what he earned and what he owned; see 486n above. **545 MILLERE,** one who owns or operates a mill for grinding grain into flour, a crucial role in medieval rural economy. Chaucer's Miller, named Robin at *MilP* 1.3129, is notable for his physicality, his bawdy tongue, and his thievery. **for the nones,** the phrase could mean "for the occasion" (line 379 above) or "for this reason" (523 above), but here and elsewhere Chaucer used it (as did other writers) as a line filler, meaning something like "indeed" or "surely." **548 wrastlynge . . . the ram,** a ram was a traditional prize for wrestling matches. **550–51** Door heaving and door butting are evidently the Miller's idea of sport, although scholars have tallied a number of people who butted doors. Door heaving takes place in the *MilT* 1.3470. **559 mouth . . . forneys,** recalls medieval representations of the gaping mouth of hell. **560 goliardeys,** a rare word, meaning something like "windbag, teller of tales"; the phrase "goliardeis, a gloton of wordes" (goliard, glutton of words) occurs in *PP,* B. Pro. 139. **563 thombe of gold,** a metaphor (compare modern "green thumb"); it implies he kept his thumb on the scales. There was also a proverb "An honest miller has a golden thumb," meaning there is no such thing as an honest miller. **567 MAUNCIPLE,** a business agent, a buyer of provisions for an institution, in this case one of the Inns of Court, residences for lawyers and their apprentices during court sessions. As a bureaucratic official in London, Chaucer would have known these Inns. He may have known someone like the shrewd and deceptive Manciple. **temple,** two of the four Inns of Court were the Inner Temple and Middle Temple (with Lincoln's Inn and Gray's Inn) because they occupied land and buildings once owned by the Knights Templars. **586 sette hir aller cappe,** this idiom is similar to the modern expression "pulled the wool over their eyes."

The REVE° was a sclendre° colerik man.
His berd was shave as ny as ever he kan°.
His heer was by his erys° ful round yshorn°.
His top was dokked° lyk a preest biforn°. 590
Ful longe were his legges and ful lene°,
Ylyk° a staf: ther was no calf ysene°.
Wel koude he kepe° a gerner° and a bynne°.
Ther was noon auditour koude on him wynne°.
Wel wiste° he by the droghte and by the reyn° 595
The yeldynge of his seed° and of his greyn.
His lordes sheep, his neet°, his dayerye°,
His swyn°, his hors, his stoor°, and his pultrye°
Was hoolly° in this Reves governynge°,
And by his covenant° yaf the rekenynge°, 600
Syn that° his lord was twenty yeer of age.
Ther koude no man brynge hym in arrerage°.
Ther nas baillif°, ne hierde°, nor oother hyne°
That he ne knew his sleighte° and his covyne°;
They were adrad° of hym as of the deeth. 605
His wonyng° was ful faire upon an heeth°;
With grene trees shadwed° was his place.
He koude bettre than his lord purchace°;
Ful riche he was astored pryvely°.
His lord wel koude he plesen subtilly°, 610
To yeve and lene hym of his owene good°,

And have a thank°, and yet a cote and hood.
In youthe he hadde lerned a good myster°,
He was a wel good wrighte°, a carpenter.
This Reve sat upon a ful good stot°, 615
That was al pomely grey° and highte° Scot.
A long surcote of pers° upon he hade,
And by his syde he baar° a rusty blade.
Of Northfolk was this Reve of which I telle,
Biside a toun men clepen° Baldeswelle. 620
Tukked he was as is a frere aboute°,
And evere he rood the hyndreste° of oure route°.

A SOMONOUR was ther with us in that place
That hadde a fyr-reed cherubynnes° face,
For sawcefleem° he was, with eyen narwe°. 625
As hoot he was and lecherous as a sparwe°,
With scalled browes blake° and piled berd°.
Of his visage° children were aferd°.
Ther nas quyksilver°, lytarge°, ne brymstoon°,
Boras°, ceruce°, ne oille of tartre° noon, 630
Ne oynement that wolde clense and byte°,
That hym myghte helpen of his whelkes white°,
Nor of the knobbes sittynge on his chekes.
Wel loved he garleek°, oynons, and eek lekes°,
And for to drynken strong wyn, reed as blood. 635

---

587 REVE, *manager of a farm,* **sclendre,** *skinny* **588 ny as ever he kan,** *as close as he could* **589 erys,** *ears* **round yshorn,** *closely cut* **590 His top was dokked . . . biforn,** *the top of his head was cropped . . . in front* **591 lene,** *lean* **592 Ylyk,** *like,* **ysene,** *seen* **593 koude he kepe,** *could he manage,* **gerner,** *storehouse,* **bynne,** *storage bin* **594 noon auditour koude on him wynne,** *no accountant (who) could get the best of him* **595 wiste,** *knew,* **reyn,** *rain* **596 yeldynge of his seed,** *what his seed would produce* **597 neet,** *cattle,* **dayerye,** *dairy herd* **598 swyn,** *pigs,* **stoor,** *livestock,* **pultrye,** *poultry* **599 hoolly,** *completely,* **governynge,** *control* **600 covenant,** *contract,* **yaf the rekenynge,** *gave the reckoning* **601 Syn that,** *since* **602 Ther koude no man brynge hym in arrerage,** *no man knew how to find him behind in his accounts* **603 nas baillif,** *was no foreman,* **hierde,** *herdsman,* **hyne,** *peasant* **604 sleighte,** *tricks,* **covyne,** *dishonesty* **605 adrad,** *afraid* **605 wonyng,** *home,* **heeth,** *heath* **607 shadwed,** *shadowed* **608 He koude bettre . . . purchace,** *he could better . . . buy land*

609 astored pryvely, *stocked up secretly* **610 His lord wel koude he plesen subtilly,** *he knew well how to please his lord craftily* **611 yeve and lene hym of his owene good,** *give and loan to his lord from his lord's own goods* **612 have a thank,** *have thanks* **613 myster,** *craft* **614 wrighte,** *woodworker* **615 stot,** *farm horse* **616 pomely grey,** *dapple gray,* **highte,** *named* **617 surcote of pers,** *blue overcoat* **618 baar,** *carried* **620 clepen,** *call* **621 Tukked . . . as is a frere aboute,** *tucked up . . . like a friar* **622 hyndreste,** *furthest back,* **route,** *company* **624 fyr-reed cherubynnes,** *fire-red cherub's* **625 sawcefleem,** *inflamed with pustules,* **eyen narwe,** *narrow eyes* **626 sparwe,** *sparrow* **627 scalled browes blake,** *scabby black eyebrows,* **piled berd,** *mangy beard* **628 visage,** *face,* **aferd,** *afraid* **629 quyksilver,** *mercury,* **lytarge,** *lead oxide,* **byrmstoon,** *sulphur* **630 Boras,** *borax,* **ceruce,** *white lead,* **oille of tartre,** *cream of tartar* **631 clense and byte,** *cleanse and sting* **632 whelkes white,** *pus-filled pimples* **634 garleek,** *garlic,* **eek lekes,** *also leeks*

---

587 REVE, the term meant the manager or overseer of a farm or estate, a rural parallel to the Manciple's urban occupation. Chaucer's Reeve is a watchful, calculating man, thin and quick to anger, who uses his skills to his own advantage. Later named Oswald (*RvP* 1.3860), the Reeve is the physical opposite of the Miller, a contrast Chaucer develops in their tales. **colerik,** choleric or irritable, dominated by yellow bile. On the four humors, see 333n. **590 lyk a preest biforn,** a reference to the clerical tonsure, the shaving of the crown of the head; see 675–79n below. **603–5** The Reeve knew the secrets of his underlings and apparently used his knowledge to strike fear in them. **609 astored,** wealth was reckoned in stored food and possessions rather than money in the bank. **612 cote and hood,** payment was frequently in clothing; see line 317 above. **616 Scot,** a common name for a horse. **619–20 Northfolk . . . Baldeswelle,** modern Bawdeswell in Norfolk, eastern England. **622 hyndreste,** last in the group; if line 566 indicates that the Miller led the travelers, this underscores the opposition between Miller and Reeve. **623 SOMONOUR,** a summoner, or *apparitor,* was a subpoena server for an ecclesiastical court that oversaw moral and religious behavior—cases involving clerics, tithes, sexual conduct, etc. Chaucer's Summoner is physically and morally grotesque. **624–28** The Summoner's skin disease gives him a face swollen with pimply sores and knobs, and his facial hair is falling out. The disease is a form of leprosy, or perhaps syphilis, both thought to result from moral debauchery. **624 cherubynnes,** cherubim (sing., *cherub*) were the second of nine orders of angels, burning with divine love. **626 lecherous as a sparwe,** the association of the sparrow with lechery was traditional. **629–31** Unsuccessful remedies for the Summoner's condition. **634–35** Strong food and drink were thought to promote lechery and skin disease. Such food and drink have negative moral connotations in Numbers 11.5 and Psalms 23.31–33.

Thanne° wolde he speke and crie as he were
    wood°,
And whan that he wel dronken hadde the wyn,
Thanne wolde he speke no word but Latyn.
A fewe termes hadde he, two or thre,
That he had lerned out of som decree°—   640
No wonder is, he herde it al the day,
And eek ye° knowen wel how that a jay°
Kan clepen "Watte°" as wel as kan the pope.
But whoso koude° in oother thyng hym
    grope°,
Thanne hadde he spent° al his philosophie.   645
Ay "Questio quid iuris°" wolde he crie.
He was a gentil harlot° and a kynde;
A bettre felawe sholde men noght fynde.
He wolde suffre° for a quart of wyn
A good felawe to have his concubyn°   650
A twelf-monthe°, and excuse hym atte fulle°.
Ful prively° a fynch° eek koude he pulle.
And if he foond owher° a good felawe,
He wolde techen° hym to have noon awe°
In swich caas of° the ercedekenes curs,   655
But if° a mannes soule were in his purs°,
For in his purs he sholde ypunysshed° be.
"Purs is the ercedekenes helle," seyde he.
But wel I woot° he lyed right in dede°.

Of cursyng oghte ech gilty man him drede°,   660
For curs wol slee right as assoillyng savith°,
And also war hym° of a *Significavit*°.
In daunger° hadde he at his owene gise°
The yonge girles° of the diocise°,
And knew hir conseil, and was al hir reed°.   665
A gerland° hadde he set upon his heed
As greet as it were for an alestake°.
A bokeleer° hadde he maad° hym of a cake°.

    With hym ther rood a gentil PARDONER
Of Rouncivale, his freend and his compeer°,   670
That streight was comen fro the court of
    Rome.
Ful loude° he soong "Com hider°, love, to me!"
This Somonour bar to hym a stif burdoun°.
Was nevere trompe° of half so greet a soun.
This Pardoner hadde heer° as yelow as wex°,   675
But smothe it heeng° as dooth a strike of flex°.
By ounces henge his lokkes° that he hadde,
And therwith he his shuldres overspradde°,
But thynne° it lay, by colpons oon and oon°.
But hood, for jolitee°, wered he noon°,   680
For it was trussed° up in his walet°.
Hym thoughte° he rood al of the newe jet°;
Dischevelee°, save his cappe, he rood al bare°.

---

636 **Thanne,** *then,* **wood,** *crazed* 640 **lerned out of som decree,** *learned out of some legal decree* 642 **eek ye,** *also you,* **jay,** *talking bird* 643 **Kan clepen "Watte,"** *can say "Walter"* 644 **whoso koude . . . hym grope,** *whoever could . . . test him* 645 **spent,** *used up* 646 **Ay "Questio quid iuris,"** *always "What point of law is the question"* 647 **harlot,** *rascal* 649 **suffre,** *allow* 650 **have his concubyn,** *keep his whore* 651 **A twelf-monthe,** *for a year,* **atte ful,** *completely* 652 **Ful prively,** *very secretively,* **fynch,** *finch (see note)* 653 **owher,** *anywhere* 654 **techen,** *teach,* **noon awe,** *no respect* 655 **swich caas of,** *such cases as* 656 **But if,** *unless,* **purs,** *purse* 657 **ypunysshed,** *punished* 659 **woot,** *know,* **lyed right in dede,** *lied indeed* 660 **oghte,** *ought,* **him drede,** *be afraid (for himself)* 661 **curs wol slee right as assoillyng savith,** *excommunication will slay just as absolution saves* 662 **war hym,** *(let) him beware,* **Significavit,** *"Be it*

known . . ." 663 **daunger,** *power,* **owene gise,** *own pleasure* 664 **girles,** *males and females,* **diocise,** *church territory* 665 **hir reed,** *their counselor* 666 **gerland,** *wreath* 667 **alestake,** *tavern sign* 668 **bokeleer,** *shield,* **maad,** *made,* **cake,** *round loaf* 670 **compeer,** *companion* 672 **Ful loude,** *very loudly,* **hider,** *hither* 673 **bar to hym a stif burdoun,** *accompanied him in a strong bass* (voice) 674 **trompe,** *trumpet* 675 **heer,** *hair,* **wex,** *wax* 676 **heeng,** *hung,* **strike of flex,** *length of flax* 677 **By ounces henge his lokkes,** *in strings hung the hair* 678 **shuldres overspradde,** *spread over his shoulders* 679 **thynne,** *thin,* **colpons oon and oon,** *strands one by one* 680 **jolitee,** *playfulness,* **wered he noon,** *he wore none* 681 **trussed,** *tied,* **walet,** *pouch* 682 **Hym thoughte,** *he thought (that),* **newe jet,** *new fashion* 683 **Dischevelee,** *with loose hair,* **bare,** *bare-headed*

637–38 These lines are not in Hg. **639ff.** The Summoner understands the few words of Latin he speaks no better than a trained bird understands what it says. **646 "Questio quid iuris,"** the equivalent of senselessly repeating "Point of order!" **650–51** Though it was the Summoner's responsibility to bring fornicators to ecclesiastical court, he accepts bribes instead. **652 a fynch . . . pulle,** to "pull a finch" or "pluck a bird" meant to trick or deceive, but it seems also to have had sexual overtones. **655 ercedekenes curs,** the archdeacon's curse, or excommunication, could exclude the sinner from all church activities, and hence from hope of salvation. The archdeacon, a bishop's representative, presided over church courts. **657 in his purs . . . ypunysshed,** to be punished in one's purse meant to pay fines. **658 "Purs is the ercedekenes helle,"** i.e., "the purse is the archdeacon's hell"; it's the only place he will (can?) punish you. **662 Significavit,** "Be it known," the opening phrase of the written order that authorized civil arrest if the excommunicated person did not fulfill the demands of the church court. **664 diocise,** diocese, the territory in which a bishop and his officials (including archdeacon and summoners) had jurisdiction. **669 PARDONER,** sins were forgiven by priests in the sacrament of confession, or penance, but the sinner's punishment (also commonly known as his penance) due for sinning could be alleviated or eliminated through pardons or indulgences, available from pardoners, or *questors*. The sale of pardons was a source of revenue for the church, intended to support worthy causes. Chaucer's Pardoner traffics in relics as well as pardons for personal gain. His association with the Summoner implies financial and perhaps sexual collusion. **670 Rouncivale,** the Pardoner was a fund-raiser for the chapel and hospital of St. Mary of Roncevalles, at Charing Cross just west of medieval London. **672 "Com hider . . . ,"** line from a popular song, now lost. **673 burdoun,** critics read homosexual connotations here, since the word could mean either "staff" or the bass part of a melody. **675–79 heer . . . ,** the Pardoner's hair suggests extravagance; clerics cut their hair in a specified way (the "tonsure") as a sign of their dedication to God.

Swiche glarynge eyen° hadde he as an hare.
A vernycle° hadde he sowed upon his cappe. 685
His walet lay biforn hym in his lappe,
Bretful of° pardoun, comen from Rome al hoot°.
A voys° he hadde as smal° as hath a goot°.
No berd hadde he, ne nevere sholde have.
As smothe it was as it were late shave. 690
I trowe° he were a geldyng or a mare.
But of his craft, fro Berwyk into Ware,
Ne was ther swich another° pardoner.
For in his male° he hadde a pilwe-beer°,
Which that he seyde° was Oure Lady veyl°. 695
He seyde he hadde a gobet° of the seyl°
That Seint Peter hadde, whan that he wente
Upon the see°, til Jhesu Crist hym hente°.
He hadde a croys of latoun° ful of stones,
And in a glas° he hadde pigges bones. 700
But with thise relikes°, whan that he fond°
A poure person dwellynge upon lond°,
Upon a day he gat hym° moore moneye
Than that the person gat in monthes tweye°.
And thus, with feyned flaterye° and japes°, 705
He made the person° and the peple his apes°.
But trewely° to tellen atte laste°,
He was in chirche a noble ecclesiaste°.
Wel koude he rede a lessoun° or a storie,
But alderbest° he song an offertorie, 710
For wel he wiste°, whan that song was songe,

He moste preche° and wel affile° his tonge
To wynne silver, as he ful wel koude;
Therefore he song the murierly° and loude.

Now have I toold you shortly, in a clause°, 715
Th'estaat°, th'array°, the nombre, and eek the
  cause°
Why that assembled was this compaignye
In Southwerk at this gentil hostelrye°
That highte° the Tabard, faste° by the Belle.
But now is tyme to yow for to telle 720
How that we baren° us that ilke° nyght,
Whan we were in that hostelrie alyght°.
And after wol I telle of oure viage°
And al the remenaunt of oure pilgrimage.
But first I pray yow°, of youre curteisye, 725
That ye n'arette it nat° my vileynye°
Thogh that I pleynly° speke in this mateere,
To telle yow hir wordes and hir cheere°,
Ne thogh I speke hir wordes proprely°.
For this ye knowen al so° wel as I, 730
Whoso shal telle a tale after a man,
He moot reherce as ny° as evere he kan
Everich a° word, if it be in his charge°,
Al° speke he never so rudeliche° and large°,
Or ellis° he moot° telle his tale untrewe, 735
Or feyne thyng°, or fynde wordes newe.
He may nat spare°, althogh he were his brother;

---

684 eyen, *eyes* **685 vernycle,** *veronica* (see note) **687 Bretful of,** *crammed with,* **al hoot,** *all hot* **688 voys,** *voice,* **smal,** *high-pitched,* **goot,** *goat* **691 trowe,** *believe* **693 Ne was ther swich another,** *there was no comparable* **694 male,** *sack,* **pilwe-beer,** *pillowcase* **695 seyde,** *said,* **Oure Lady veyl,** *our Lady's veil* **696 gobet,** *piece,* **seyl,** *sail* **698 see,** *sea,* **hente,** *grabbed* **699 croys of latoun,** *cross of copper alloy* **700 glas,** *jar* **701 relikes,** *relics,* **fond,** *found* **702 person dwellynge upon lond,** *peasant laborer* **703 gat hym,** *got himself* **704 monthes tweye,** *two months* **705 feyned flaterye,** *fake flattery,* **japes,** *tricks* **706 person,** *parson,* **apes,** *dupes* **707 trewely,** *truly,* **atte laste,** *finally* **708 ecclesiaste,** *churchman* **709 Wel koude he rede a lessoun,** *he knew well how to read a scripture* **710 alderbest,** *best of all* **711 wiste,** *knew* **712 preche,** *preach,* **affile,** *polish* **713 koude,** *was able to* **714 murierly,** *more merrily* **715 in a clause,** *briefly* **716 Th'estaat,** *the rank,* **th'array,** *the clothing,* **eek the cause,** *also the reason* **718 hostelrye,** *inn* **719 highte,** *is called,* **faste,** *near* **721 baren,** *conducted,* **ilke,** *same* **722 alyght,** *stopped* **723 viage,** *journey* **725 pray yow,** *ask you* **726 ye n'arette it nat,** *you blame not,* **vileynye,** *vulgarity* **727 pleynly,** *directly* **728 hir cheere,** *their attitudes* **729 proprely,** *exactly* **730 al so,** *as* **732 moot reherce as ny,** *must repeat as closely* **733 Everich a,** *every single,* **charge,** *responsibility* **734 Al,** *although,* **rudeliche,** *discourteously,* **large,** *freely* **735 ellis,** *else* **moot,** *may* **736 feyne thyng,** *invent something* **737 spare,** *refrain*

---

684 glarynge eyen . . . as an hare, glaring eyes were thought to be indications of folly and excess; the hare, to have characteristics of both sexes. **685 vernycle,** a badge or token named after St. Veronica, whose cloth was thought to have the miraculous imprint of Christ's face. Copies of the "vera icon" (true likeness) were sold to pilgrims who visited Rome. **688–91** The Pardoner's high voice and beardlessness apparently lead the narrator to conclude that he is effeminate, or perhaps a eunuch or homosexual, notions reflected in metaphoric comparison with a **geldyng,** a castrated horse, and a mare. The suggestion of infertility or infertile behavior is underscored by the fact that he keeps his pardons and (if the **walet** [line 686] and **male** [line 694] are the same) his false relics in the sack on his lap. **692 fro Berwyk into Ware,** from Berwick-upon-Tweed in northernmost England to Ware in southern England, i.e., from one end of England to the other. **694–701** Relics are material remains of saints and other holy people, objects of veneration that were thought capable of producing miracles. Trafficking in false relics was criticized by satirists and condemned by the church. **696–98** Matthew 14.24–31 describes how Jesus grasped St. Peter on the water. **710 song an offertorie,** sang the prayers of the Offertory (see 450n above), followed soon after by the preaching of the sermon. **719 the Tabard . . . Belle,** no inn named the Bell has been identified near the Tabard (see 20n above), although the Bell was a licensed house of prostitution in Southwark in the sixteenth century. **725–42** This explanation or "apology" raises several literary and linguistic issues: Is it possible to retell a tale exactly in a new context? In what sense(s) can fiction be unfeigned or true? What is the relation between scripture and other literature? What is the relation between word and deed? **737 He . . . althogh he were his brother,** even if the original teller or speaker (i.e., the "man" of line 731) is his brother, the reteller must not refrain from his retelling. The pronouns reflect the complexities of literary responsibility.

He moot as wel seye o° word as another.
Crist spak hymself ful brode° in hooly writ,
And wel ye woot° no vileynye° is it. 740
Eek° Plato seith°, whoso kan hym rede°,
The wordes moote be cosyn° to the dede.
Also I prey yow to foryeve° it me,
Al have I nat° set folk in hir degree°
Heere in this tale, as that they sholde
      stonde. 745
My wit is short, ye may wel understonde.
   Greet chiere made oure Hoost us everichon°,
And to the soper° sette he us anon.
He served us with vitaille at the beste°.
Strong was the wyn, and wel to drynke us
      leste°. 750
A semely° man oure HOOSTE was withalle°
For to been a marchal in an halle°.
A large man he was with eyen stepe°—
A fairer burgeys° was ther noon in Chepe—
Boold of his speche, and wys, and wel ytaught, 755
And of manhod hym lakked right naught°.
Eek therto° he was right a myrie° man,
And after soper pleyen he bigan°,
And spak of myrthe° amonges othere thynges,
Whan that we hadde maad our rekenynges°, 760
And seyde thus: "Now, lordynges, trewely,
Ye been to me right welcome, hertely°;
For by my trouthe, if that I shal nat lye,
I saugh° nat this yeer so myrie a compaignye
Atones° in this herberwe° as is now. 765

Fayn wolde I doon yow myrthe°, wiste I° how.
And of a myrthe° I am right now bythoght°,
To doon yow ese°, and it shal coste noght.
   "Ye goon to Caunterbury—God yow
      speede!
The blisful martir quite° yow youre meede°! 770
And wel I woot°, as ye goon by the weye,
Ye shapen yow° to talen° and to pleye.
For trewely, confort ne myrthe is noon°
To ride by the weye doumb° as a stoon°.
And therfore wol I maken yow disport°, 775
As I seyde erst°, and doon yow som confort.
And if yow liketh alle by oon assent°
For to stonden at my juggement°,
And for to werken° as I shal yow seye°,
To-morwe, whan ye riden by the weye, 780
Now, by my fader° soule that is° deed,
But ye be° myrie, I wol yeve° yow myn heed!
Hoold up youre hondes, withouten moore
      speche."
   Oure conseil° was nat longe for to seche°.
Us thoughte° it was noght worth to make
      it wys°, 785
And graunted hym° withouten moore avys°,
And bad him seye his voirdit° as hym leste°.
   "Lordynges," quod° he, "now herkneth° for
      the beste,
But taak° it nought, I prey yow, in desdeyn°.
This is the poynt, to speken short and pleyn, 790
That ech of yow, to shorte with° oure weye,

---

738 o, *one* **739 brode,** *freely* **740 ye woot,** *you know,* **vileynye,** *vulgarity* **741 Eek,** *also,* **seith,** *says,* **whoso kan hym rede,** *whoever can read him* **742 moote be cosyn,** *must be related* **743 foryeve,** *forgive* **744 Al have I nat,** *although I have not,* **hir degree,** *their social order* **747 us everichon,** *to each one of us* **748 soper,** *supper* **749 vitaille at the beste,** *the best of food* **750 wel to drynke us leste,** *we were well pleased to drink* **751 semely,** *impressive,* **withalle,** *indeed* **752 marchal in an halle,** *master of ceremonies* **753 eyen stepe,** *prominent eyes* **754 burgeys,** *citizen* **756 right naught,** *nothing at all* **757 Eek therto,** *besides that,* **right a myrie,** *a very merry* **758 pleyen he bigan,** *began to entertain* **759 spak of myrthe,** *spoke of enjoyment* **760 maad our rekenynges,** *paid our bills* **762 hertely,** *sincerely* **764 saugh,** *saw* **765 Atones,** *at one time,* **herberwe,** *inn* **766 Fayn wolde I doon yow myrthe,** *I would gladly make you happy,* **wiste I,** *if I knew* **767 a myrthe,** *an entertainment,* **am . . .**

bythoght, *have thought* **768 doon yow ese,** *give you pleasure* **770 quite,** *pay,* **meede,** *reward* **771 woot,** *know* **772 Ye shapen yow,** *you plan,* **talen,** *tell tales* **773 confort ne myrthe is noon,** *there is no comfort nor mirth* **774 doumb,** *silent,* **stoon,** *stone* **775 disport,** *a diversion* **776 seyde erst,** *said before* **777 yow liketh alle by oon assent,** (it) *pleases you all together* **778 stonden at my juggement,** *accept my direction* **779 to werken,** *act,* **seye,** *tell* **781 fader,** *father's,* **that is,** *who is* **782 But ye be,** *unless you are,* **yeve,** *give* **784 conseil,** *discussion,* **for to seche,** *in deliberation* **785 Us thoughte,** *it seemed to us that,* **worth to make it wys,** *worthwhile to make an issue of it* **786 graunted hym,** *agreed with him,* **avys,** *discussion* **787 seye his voirdit,** *give his verdict,* **as hym leste,** *as he wished* **788 quod,** *said,* **herkneth,** *listen* **789 But taak,** *and take,* **desdeyn,** *disdain* **791 shorte with,** *shorten*

741–42 Plato seith . . . wordes moote be cosyn to the dede, the notion that words must relate ("be a cousin") to actuality is found in Plato's *Timaeus* 29, but Chaucer took it from Boethius; see his translation, *Bo* 3pr12.207. Like his contemporaries, Chaucer could not read Greek. The *MED* records *cosyn* as "fraud, trickery" as early as 1453. **743 foryeve,** the narrator, perhaps Chaucer himself, asks for a different forgiveness at the end of the Canterbury fiction; see *Ret* 10.1084. **751 HOOSTE,** the Host is an innkeeper, later named Harry Bailly (*CkP* 1.4358). A "Henri Bayliff" is recorded as an innkeeper in Southwark in 1380–81, perhaps Chaucer's inspiration and no doubt an inside joke for some of Chaucer's original audience. The Host is an impressive man, concerned with his accounts and with keeping his guests well entertained. His literary judgment (or lack of) is a theme that recurs throughout the work. **752 marchal in an halle,** an officer responsible for managing the arrangements and service in a royal or noble dining hall. **753 eyen stepe,** see 201n above. **754 Chepe,** Cheapside was an important commercial district in medieval London.

In this viage° shal telle tales tweye°
To Caunterbury-ward, I mene it so,
And homward he shal tellen othere° two,
Of aventures that whilom han bifalle°.   795
And which of yow that bereth hym° best of alle,
That is to seyn, that telleth in this caas°
Tales of best sentence° and moost solaas°,
Shal have a soper at oure aller cost°
Heere in this place, sittynge by this post,   800
Whan that we come agayn fro Caunterbury.
And for to make yow the moore mury°,
I wol myselven goodly° with yow ryde,
Right at myn owene cost, and be youre gyde°.
And whoso° wole my juggement withseye°   805
Shal paye al that we spenden by the weye.
And if ye vouchesauf° that it be so,
Tel me anon° withouten wordes mo,
And I wol erly shape me° therfore."
      This thyng was graunted, and oure othes°
          swore   810
With ful glad herte, and preyden° hym also
That he wolde vouchesauf for to do so,
And that he wolde been oure governour,
And of our tales juge and reportour°,
And sette a soper at a certeyn pris°,   815
And we wol reuled been° at his devys°
In heigh and lough°. And thus by oon assent°
We been acorded to his juggement.
And therupon the wyn was fet anon°.
We dronken, and to reste wente echon°   820
Withouten any lenger taryynge°.
Amorwe°, whan that day gan for to sprynge°,
Up roos oure Hoost, and was oure aller cok°,
And gadrede° us togidre alle in a flok,
And forth we riden a litel moore than paas°   825

Unto the wateryng of Seint Thomas.
      And there oure Hoost bigan his hors areste°
And seyde, "Lordynges, herkneth°, if yow leste°.
Ye woot° youre foreward°, and it yow recorde°.
If even-song and morwe-song accorde,   830
Lat se now who shal telle the firste tale.
As evere mote° I drynke wyn or ale,
Whoso be rebel to my juggement
Shal paye for al that by the wey is spent.
Now draweth cut°, er° that we ferrer twynne°;   835
He which that hath the shorteste shal bigynne.
Sire Knyght," quod° he, "my mayster and my lord,
Now draweth cut, for that is myn accord.
Cometh neer," quod he, "my lady Prioresse.
And ye, sire Clerk, lat be youre
          shamefastnesse°,   840
Ne studieth noght; ley hond to°, every man!"
      Anon to drawen every wight° bigan,
And shortly for to tellen as it was,
Were it by aventure, or sort, or cas°,
The sothe° is this, the cut fil to° the Knyght,   845
Of which ful blithe° and glad was every wyght,
And telle he moste° his tale, as was resoun,
By foreward° and by composicioun°,
As ye han herd. What nedeth wordes mo?
And whan this goode man saugh° that it
          was so,   850
As he that wys was and obedient
To kepe his foreward by his free assent,
He seyde, "Syn° I shal bigynne the game,
What, welcome be the cut, a Goddes name°!
Now lat us ryde, and herkneth what I seye."   855
And with that word we ryden forth oure weye,
And he bigan with right a myrie cheere°
His tale anon, and seyde in this manere.

---

792 viage, *journey,* **tweye,** *two* **794 othere,** *another* **795 whilom han bi-f_alle,** *once upon a time have happened* **796 bereth hym,** *conducts himself* **797 caas,** *case* **798 best sentence,** *highest wisdom,* **solaas,** *delight* **799 soper at oure aller cost,** *supper at the expense of all of us* **802 mury,** *merry* **803 goodly,** *gladly* **804 gyde,** *guide* **805 whoso,** *whoever,* **wole . . . withseye,** *contradicts* **807 vouchesauf,** *agree* **808 anon,** *immediately* **809 wol erly shape me,** *will prepare myself early* **810 othes,** *oaths* **811 preyden,** *(we) asked* **814 reportour,** *scorekeeper* **815 pris,** *price* **816 wol reuled been,** *will be ruled,* **at his devys,** *by his will* **817 In heigh and lough,** *in all ways,* **oon assent,** *common agreement* **819 fet anon,** *fetched quickly* **820 echon,** *each one* **821 taryynge,** *delay* **822 Amorwe,** *in the* morning, **gan . . . sprynge,** *did break* **823 oure aller cok,** *rooster for us all* **824 gadrede,** *gathered* **825 litel moore than paas,** *at a slow pace* **827 areste,** *stop* **828 herkneth,** *listen,* **leste,** *please* **829 woot,** *know,* **foreward,** *agreement,* **recorde,** *remember* **832 mote,** *may* **835 draweth cut,** *draw straws,* **er,** *before,* **ferrer twynne,** *depart further* **837 quod,** *said* **840 lat be youre shamefastnesse,** *give up your modesty* **841 ley hond to,** *pick one* **842 wight,** *person* **844 Were it by aventure, or sort, or cas,** *whether by chance, fate, or destiny* **845 sothe,** *truth,* **fil to,** *fell to* **846 blithe,** *happy* **847 moste,** *must* **848 foreward,** *promise,* **composicioun,** *agreement* **850 saugh,** *saw* **853 Syn,** *since* **854 a Goddes name,** *in God's name* **857 right a myrie cheere,** *a most happy expression*

792–94 This plan of four tales per pilgrim (two going and two returning) evidently changed as Chaucer developed his work; see *CT* 5.698 and 10.16. **798 sentence . . . solaas,** a balance between meaning (sentence) and pleasure (solaas) is an aesthetic ideal rooted in Cicero's assertion that the goal of oratory is to teach, delight, and move (*De optimo genere oratorum* 16); both Horace (*Ars Poetica* 343) and Philip Sidney (*Defence of Poesy*) say that the dual aim of writing is to teach and to delight. **826 wateryng of Seint Thomas,** a brook convenient for watering horses about a mile and a half from the Tabard Inn. **835 draweth cut,** drawing straws or sticks, one of which is "cut" or shortened, was (and is) a familiar way of making a random selection in a competition; compare the "cut" of a deck of cards. Some critics have suggested that it is no luck or coincidence at all that when the Host offers first draw to the Knight, he is the one to whom the cut falls.

KNIGHT'S TALE

Heere bigynneth the Knyghtes Tale.

Iamque domos patrias Scithice post aspera gentis Prelia laurigero &c.

Whilom°, as olde stories° tellen us,
Ther was a duc° that highte° Theseus. 860
Of Atthenes he was lord and governour,
And in his tyme swich° a conquerour,
That gretter was ther noon under the sonne.
Ful many a riche contree hadde he wonne,
What with° his wysdom and his chivalrie; 865
He conquered al the regne° of Femenye°,
That whilom was ycleped° Scithia,
And wedded the queene Ypolita,
And broghte hire hoom with hym in his
    contree
With muchel° glorie and greet solempnytee°, 870
And eek° hir yonge suster° Emelye.
And thus with victorie and with melodye
Lete I° this noble duc to Atthenes ryde,

And al his hoost° in armes hym bisyde.
    And certes°, if it nere° to long to heere, 875
I wolde yow have toold fully the manere
How wonnen° was the regne of Femenye
By Theseus and by his chivalrye°,
And of the grete bataille° for the nones°
Bitwixen Atthenes and Amazones, 880
And how asseged° was Ypolita,
The faire, hardy queene of Scithia,
And of the feste° that was at hir° weddynge,
And of the tempest at hir hoom-
    comynge—
But al that thyng I moot as now forbere°. 885
I have, God woot°, a large feeld to ere°,
And wayke° been the oxen in my plough°.
The remenant° of the tale is long ynough.

---

859 **Whilom,** *once,* **stories,** *histories* 860 **duc,** *duke,* **highte,** *was called* 862 **swich,** *such* 865 **What with,** *as a result of* 866 **regne,** *realm,* **Femenye,** *land of women* 867 **ycleped,** *called* 870 **muchel,** *much,* **solempnytee,** *ceremony* 871 **eek,** *also,* **suster,** *sister* 873 **Lete I,** *I let* 874 **hoost,** *army* 875 **certes,** *certainly,* **nere,** *weren't* 877 **wonnen,** *won* 878 **chivalrye,** *knights*

879 **grete bataille,** *great battle,* **for the nones,** *on that occasion* 881 **asseged,** *besieged* 883 **feste,** *festivities,* **hir,** *their* 885 **moot as now forbere,** *must now forsake* 886 **woot,** *knows,* **ere,** *plow* 887 **wayke,** *weak,* **plough,** *plow* 888 **remenant,** *rest*

Iamque domos . . . , "And now to his native land in a decorated chariot after fierce struggles with the Scithians, etc." This line and a half is from Statius, *Thebaid* 12.519–20, the ultimate source of the *KnT,* although Chaucer modeled his version on Boccaccio's *Teseida,* influenced by a glossed version of the *Thebaid* and twelfth-century French *Roman de Thèbes.* An expanded form of the motto is in Chaucer's short poem *Anelida and Arcite* (line 22), which appears to have been a trial run for some of the *KnT* material. **861 Atthenes,** Athens was regarded by medieval people as a social and political ideal. **866 Femenye,** derived from Lat. *femina,* "woman," Chaucer's name for the land of the Amazons. **867 Scithia,** Scythia, on the shores of the Black Sea. **867 Ypolita,** Hippolyta, queen of the Amazons. **884 tempest,** Chaucer invents the detail of the tempest, possibly an allusion to the storm that occurred just as Anne of Bohemia arrived in 1382 in England for her wedding to Richard II.

I wol nat letten eek° noon of this route°.
Lat every felawe telle his tale aboute°,   890
And lat se now who shal the soper wynne°;
And ther° I lefte, I wol ayeyn° bigynne.

   This duc, of whom I make mencioun,
Whan he was come almoost unto the toun,
In al his wele° and in his mooste° pride,   895
He was war°, as he caste his eye aside°,
Where that ther kneled° in the heighe weye°
A compaignye of ladyes, tweye° and tweye,
Ech after oother, clad in clothes blake.
But swich° a cry and swich a wo they make   900
That in this world nys° creature lyvynge
That herde swich another waymentynge°,
And of this cry they nolde nevere stenten°
Til they the reynes° of his brydel henten°.

   "What folk been ye, that at myn hom-
        comynge   905
Perturben° so my feste° with criynge?"
Quod Theseus. "Have ye so greet envye
Of myn honour, that thus compleyne and crye?
Or who hath yow mysboden° or offended?
And telleth me if it may been amended,   910
And why that ye been clothed thus in blak."

   The eldeste lady of hem° alle spak,
Whan she hadde swowned° with a deedly cheere°,
That it was routhe° for to seen and heere,
And seyde: "Lord, to whom Fortune hath
        yeven°   915
Victorie, and as a conqueror to lyven°,
Nat greveth us youre glorie° and youre honour,
But we biseken° mercy and socour°.
Have mercy on oure wo and oure distresse!
Som drope of pitee, thurgh thy gentillesse°,   920

Upon us wrecched wommen lat° thou falle.
For, certes, lord, ther is noon of us alle,
That she ne hath been a duchesse or a queene.
Now be we caytyves°, as it is wel seene,
Thanked be Fortune and hire false wheel,   925
That noon estaat assureth° to be weel°.
And certes, lord, to abyden° youre presence,
Heere in this temple of the goddesse Clemence°
We han ben waitynge al this fourtenyght°.
Now help us, lord, sith° it is in thy myght.   930

   "I, wrecche, which that wepe and wayle thus,
Was whilom° wyf to Kyng Cappaneus,
That starf° at Thebes—cursed be that day!
And alle we that been in this array
And maken al this lamentacioun,   935
We losten alle oure housbondes at that toun,
Whil that the seege° theraboute lay.
And yet now the olde Creon, weylaway°,
That lord is now of Thebes the citee,
Fulfild of ire° and of iniquitee°,   940
He, for despit° and for his tirannye,
To do the dede° bodyes vileynye°
Of alle oure lordes whiche that been yslawe°,
He hath alle the bodyes on an heep ydrawe°,
And wol nat suffren hem°, by noon assent,   945
Neither to been yburyed° nor ybrent°,
But maketh houndes ete hem° in despit°."

   And with that word, withouten moore respit°,
They fillen gruf° and criden pitously,
"Have on us wrecched wommen som mercy,   950
And lat oure sorwe synken in thyn herte."

   This gentil duc doun from his courser sterte°
With herte pitous°, whan he herde hem° speke.
Hym thoughte that his herte wolde breke

---

889 wol nat letten eek, *also will not hinder,* **route,** *company* **890 aboute,** *in turn* **891 the soper wynne,** *win the supper* **892 ther,** *where,* **wol ayeyn,** *will again* **895 wele,** *prosperity,* **mooste,** *greatest* **896 war,** *aware,* **caste . . . aside,** *looked around* **897 kneled,** *kneeled,* **heighe weye,** *main road* **898 tweye,** *two* **900 swich,** *such* **901 nys,** *(there) isn't* **902 waymentynge,** *lamenting* **903 nolde nevere stenten,** *would never stop* **904 reynes,** *reins,* **henten,** *grasped* **906 Perturben,** *disturb,* **feste,** *festivities* **909 mysboden,** *injured* **912 hem,** *them* **913 swowned,** *fainted,* **deedly cheere,** *deathly expression* **914 routhe,** *pity* **915 yeven,** *given* **916 lyven,** *live* **917 Nat greveth us youre glorie,** *your glory doesn't distress us* **918 biseken,** *request,* **socour,** *aid* **920 thurgh thy gentillesse,** *through*

your nobility **921 lat,** *let* **924 caytyves,** *wretches* **926 noon estaat assureth,** *assures no class,* **weel,** *prosperous* **927 abyden,** *await* **928 Clemence,** *Pity* **929 fourtenyght,** *two weeks* **930 sith,** *since* **932 whilom,** *once* **933 starf,** *died* **937 seege,** *siege* **938 weylaway,** *alas* **940 ire,** *anger,* **iniquitee,** *wickedness* **941 for despit,** *because of spite* **942 dede,** *dead,* **vileynye,** *dishonor* **943 yslawe,** *slain* **944 on an heep ydrawe,** *pulled into a heap* **945 wol nat suffren hem,** *will not allow them* **946 yburyed,** *buried,* **ybrent,** *burned* **947 ete hem,** *eat them,* **despit,** *scorn* **948 respit,** *delay* **949 fillen gruf,** *fell groveling* **952 courser sterte,** *steed leapt* **953 pitous,** *compassionate,* **hem,** *them*

889–91 A reference in *LGW* (F420–21) indicates that Chaucer composed a version of the story of Palamon and Arcite before he had begun the *CT*, but these lines show that he adapted the material to some extent before incorporating it into *CT*. **925 Fortune and hire false wheel,** the wheel of the goddess Fortuna, described in *Bo* 2.pr2, is an image of random fate. The theme of fortune and its relation to destiny and freedom are major concerns in *KnT* and elsewhere in Chaucer's works. **932 Cappaneus,** Capaneus was one of the "seven against Thebes" in Greek legend. In the assault on the city, he was destroyed by Zeus for presuming to be invulnerable. His wife, Evadne, committed suicide. **938 olde Creon,** Creon, who became ruler of Thebes after the conclusion of the war with the seven, was the medieval stereotype of a tyrant. His fixed epithet in *Roman de Thèbes* is "Creon li Vieuz" (Creon the old).

Whan he saugh° hem so pitous° and so maat°,   955
That whilom weren of so greet estaat,
And in his armes he hem alle up hente°,
And hem conforteth in ful good entente°,
And swoor his ooth, as he was trewe knyght,
He wolde doon so ferforthly° his myght   960
Upon the tiraunt Creon hem to wreke°,
That al the peple of Grece sholde speke
How Creon was of Theseus yserved°
As he that hadde his deeth ful wel deserved.
    And right anoon°, withouten moore abood°,   965
His baner° he desplayeth, and forth rood
To Thebes-ward°, and al his hoost° biside.
No neer° Atthenes wolde° he go ne ride,
Ne take his ese fully half a day,
But onward on° his wey that nyght he lay°,   970
And sente anon Ypolita the queene,
And Emelye, hir yonge suster sheene°,
Unto the toun of Atthenes to dwelle,
And forth he rit°; ther is namoore to telle.
    The rede° statue of Mars, with spere and
        targe°, *shield*   975
So shyneth in his white baner large,
That alle the feeldes glyteren° up and doun,
And by° his baner° born is his penoun°
Of gold ful riche, in which ther was ybete° *beaten gold*
The Mynotaur, which that he slough° in Crete.   980
    Thus rit° this duc, thus rit this conquerour,
And in his hoost of chivalrie the flour°,
Til that he cam to Thebes and alighte°
Faire in a feeld, ther as° he thoughte to fighte.
But shortly for to speken of this thyng,   985
With Creon, which that was of Thebes kyng,
He faught, and slough hym manly as a knyght
In pleyn bataille°, and putte the folk to flyght.
And by assaut he wan° the citee after,

And rente adoun° bothe wall and sparre° and
        rafter.   990
And to the ladyes he restored agayn
The bones of hir housbondes that were slayn,
To doon obsequies°, as was tho the gyse°.
But it were al to longe for to devyse°
The grete clamour and the waymentynge°   995
That the ladyes made at the brennynge°
Of the bodies, and the grete honour
That Theseus, the noble conquerour,
Dooth to the ladyes, whan they from hym wente;
But shortly for to telle is myn entente.   1000
    Whan that this worthy duc, this Theseus,
Hath Creon slayn, and wonne Thebes thus,
Stille in that feeld he took al nyght his reste,
And dide with al the contree as hym leste°.
    To ransake° in the taas° of bodyes dede,   1005
Hem° for to strepe° of harneys° and of wede°,
The pilours° diden bisynesse° and cure°
After the bataille and disconfiture°.
And so bifel° that in the taas they founde,
Thurgh-girt° with many a grevous blody
        wounde,   1010
Two yonge knyghtes liggynge by and by°,
Bothe in oon armes°, wroght° ful richely,
Of whiche two Arcita highte that oon°,
And that oother knyght highte Palamon.
Nat fully quyke°, ne fully dede they were.   1015
But by hir cote-armures° and by hir gere°
The heraudes° knewe hem best in special°
As they that weren of the blood roial°
Of Thebes, and of sustren° two yborn.
Out of the taas the pilours han hem torn°,   1020
And han hem caried softe° unto the tente
Of Theseus, and he ful soone hem sente
To Atthenes, to dwellen in prisoun

---

955 saugh, *saw,* **pitous,** *pitiable,* **maat,** *defeated* **957 hente,** *took* **958 entente,** *intention* **960 wolde doon so ferforthly,** *would impose so thoroughly* **961 hem to wreke,** *to avenge them* **963 of Theseus yserved,** *treated by Theseus* **965 right anoon,** *immediately,* **abood,** *delay* **966 baner,** *banner* **967 To Thebes-ward,** *toward Thebes,* **hoost,** *army* **968 neer,** *nearer,* **wolde,** *would* **970 onward on,** *further on,* **that nyght he lay,** *he spent the night* **972 sheene,** *beautiful* **974 rit,** *rides* **975 rede,** *red,* **targe,** *shield* **977 feeldes glyteren,** *fields glittered* **978 by,** *near,* **born,** *carried,* **penoun,** *pennant* **979 ybete,** *embroidered* **980 slough,** *slew* **981 rit,** *rides* **982 of chivalrie the flour,** *the flower of chivalry* **983 alighte,** *dismounts* **984 ther as,** *where* **988 pleyn bataille,** *open combat* **989 wan,** *conquered* **990 rente adoun,** *tore down,* **sparre,**

beam 993 obsequies, *funeral services,* **tho the gyse,** *then the custom* **994 devyse,** *describe* **995 waymentynge,** *lamenting* **996 brennynge,** *burning* **1004 hym leste,** (it) *pleased him* **1005 ransake,** *search,* **taas,** *heap* **1006 Hem,** *them,* **strepe,** *strip,* **harneys,** *armor,* **wede,** *clothes* **1007 pilours,** *pillagers,* **diden bisynesse,** *did business,* **cure,** *care* **1008 disconfiture,** *defeat* **1009 bifel,** *it happened* **1010 Thurgh-girt,** *pierced through* **1011 liggynge by and by,** *lying side by side* **1012 oon armes,** *identical armor,* **wroght,** *made* **1013 highte that oon,** *one was named* **1015 quyke,** *alive* **1016 hir cote-armures,** *their coats of arms,* **gere,** *equipment* **1017 heraudes,** *heralds,* **best in special,** *especially well* **1018 roial,** *royal* **1019 sustren,** *sisters* **1020 han hem torn,** *have them pulled* **1021 softe,** *gently*

---

966 baner he desplayeth, displaying or unfurling the flags was a sign of going to battle. Theseus's military insignia included images of **Mars** (line 975), the red or bloody god of war, on his banner; and on his pennant, the **Mynotaur** (Minotaur, line 980), a half-man, half-bull figure of bestiality, defeated by Theseus in the labyrinth on Crete. **1005 To ransake . . . ,** ransacking or pillaging the bodies of the slain was normal medieval practice. **1019 of sustren two yborn,** Palamon and Arcite are first cousins.

Perpetuelly—he nolde no raunsoun°.

And whan this worthy duc hath thus ydon°, 1025
He took his hoost, and hoom he rood anon
With laurer° crowned as a conquerour.
And ther he lyveth in joye and in honour
Terme° of his lyf; what nedeth wordes mo?
And in a tour°, in angwissh and in wo, 1030
This Palamon and his felawe° Arcite
For everemoore; ther may no gold hem quite°.

This passeth yeer by yeer and day by day
Til it fil ones°, in a morwe° of May,
That Emelye, that fairer was to sene° 1035
Than is the lylie upon his stalke grene,
And fressher than the May with floures newe—
For with the rose colour stroof hire hewe°,
I noot° which was the fyner of hem° two—
Er° it were day, as was hir wone° to do, 1040
She was arisen and al redy dight°,
For May wole° have no slogardie a-nyght°.
The sesoun priketh° every gentil herte,
And maketh hym out of his slep to sterte°,
And seith, "Arys, and do thyn observaunce." 1045
This maked Emelye have remembraunce
To doon honour to May, and for to ryse.
Yclothed was she fressh, for to devyse°.
Hir yelow heer was broyded° in a tresse
Bihynde hir bak, a yerde long, I gesse. 1050
And in the gardyn, at the sonne upriste°,
She walketh up and doun, and as hire liste°
She gadereth floures°, party° white and rede,
To make a subtil gerland° for hire hede.
And as an aungel hevenysshly° she soong. 1055

The grete tour that was so thikke and stroong,
Which of the castle was the chief dongeoun°—
Ther as° the knyghtes weren in prisoun

Of whiche I tolde yow and tellen shal—
Was evene joynant° to the gardyn wal 1060
Ther as this Emelye hadde hir pleyynge°.
Bright was the sonne and cleer that morwenynge°,
And Palamoun, this woful prisoner,
As was his wone°, by leve° of his gayler°,
Was risen and romed° in a chambre an
  heigh°, 1065
In which he al the noble citee seigh°,
And eek the gardyn, ful of braunches grene,
Ther as this fresshe Emelye the shene°
Was in hir walk, and romed up and doun.
This sorweful prisoner, this Palamoun, 1070
Goth° in the chambre romynge to and fro,
And to hymself compleynynge of his wo.
That he was born, ful ofte he seyde, "Allas!"

And so bifel, by aventure or cas°,
That thurgh a wyndow, thikke of many a
  barre° 1075
Of iren greet and square as any sparre°,
He cast his eye upon Emelya.
And therwithal he bleynte° and cride, "A!"
As though he stongen° were unto the herte.
And with that cry Arcite anon up sterte°, 1080
And seyde, "Cosyn myn, what eyleth° thee,
That art so pale and deedly on to see°?
Why cridestow°? Who hath thee doon offence?
For Goddes love, taak° al in pacience
Oure prisoun, for it may noon oother be. 1085
Fortune hath yeven° us this adversitee.
Som wikke° aspect or disposicioun
Of Saturne, by sum° constellacioun,
Hath yeven us this, although we hadde it sworn°.
So stood the hevene whan that we were born. 1090
We moste endure; this is the short and playn."

1024 **nolde no raunsoun,** *would accept no ransom* 1025 **ydon,** *done* 1027 **laurer,** *laurel wreath* 1029 **Terme,** (for the) *duration,* 1030 **tour,** *tower* 1031 **felawe,** *companion* 1032 **hem quite,** *pay for them* 1034 **Til it fil ones,** *until it happened once,* **morwe,** *morning* 1035 **to sene,** *to look at* 1038 **stroof hire hewe,** *competed her complexion* 1039 **noot,** *don't know,* **fyner of hem,** *finer of them* 1040 **Er,** *before,* **wone,** *custom* 1041 **dight,** *dressed* 1042 **wole,** *will,* **slogardie a-nyght,** *laziness at night* 1043 **sesoun priketh,** *season prods* 1044 **sterte,** *awaken* 1048 **devyse,** *describe* 1049 **broyded,** *braided* 1051 **upriste,** *rising* 1052 **hire leste,** (it) *pleased her* 1053 **gadereth floures,** *gathered flowers,* **party,** *of mixed colors* 1054 **subtil gerland,** *skillful wreath* 1055 **hevenysshly,** *in a heavenly way* 1057

dongeoun, *fortification* 1058 **Ther as,** *where* 1060 **evene joynant,** *directly adjoining* 1061 **pleyynge,** *entertainment* 1062 **morwenynge,** *morning* 1064 **wone,** *custom,* **leve,** *permission,* **gayler,** *jailer* 1065 **romed,** *roamed,* **an heigh,** *high up* 1066 **seigh,** *saw* 1068 **shene,** *beautiful* 1071 **Goth,** *goes* 1074 **aventure or cas,** *accident or chance* 1075 **thikke of many a barre,** *heavily barred* 1076 **sparre,** *beam* 1078 **bleynte,** *turned pale* 1079 **stongen,** *stung* 1080 **anon up sterte,** *leapt up immediately* 1081 **eyleth,** *ails* 1082 **on to see,** *to look at* 1083 **cridestow,** *did you cry out* 1084 **taak,** *take* 1086 **yeven,** *given* 1087 **Som wikke,** *some wicked* 1088 **sum,** *some* 1089 **hadde it sworn,** *had sworn the opposite*

1024 **raunsoun,** there is no concern with ransom in Chaucer's sources. Theseus seeks no ransom for Palamon and Arcite because, presumably, they have not surrendered and, if released, might seek revenge for the defeat of Thebes. Ransom was a source of income in medieval practice, but Theseus's interests are not financial. 1027 **laurer,** the crown of laurel leaves was traditionally awarded to the hero (or the poet). 1047 **honour to May,** May was celebrated as a time of rejuvenation and fertility. 1077 **eye,** in courtly tradition, love enters through the eye and lodges in the heart. Arcite sees Emily first in Chaucer's source, and Emily, noticing the attention of the knight, sings coyly; *Teseida* 3.11ff. 1087–88 **wikke aspect . . . Of Saturne . . . ,** Arcite equates Fortune with the astrological influence of Saturn, the most malevolent of the planets, blaming it for their imprisonment.

This Palamon answerde and seyde agayn°,
"Cosyn, for sothe°, of this opinioun
Thow hast a veyn ymaginacioun°.
This prison caused me nat for to crye,   1095
But I was hurt right now thurghout myn° eye
Into myn herte, that wol my bane° be.
The fairnesse of that lady that I see
Yond° in the gardyn romen to and fro
Is cause of al my criyng and my wo.   1100
I noot wher° she be womman or goddesse,
But Venus is it soothly°, as I gesse."
And therwithal on knees doun he fil,
And seyde, "Venus, if it be thy wil
Yow in this gardyn thus to transfigure   1105
Bifore me, sorweful, wrecched creature,
Out of this prisoun help that we may scapen°.
And if so be my destynee be shapen°
By eterne° word to dyen in prisoun,
Of oure lynage° have som compassioun,   1110
That is so lowe ybroght by tirannye."
    And with that word Arcite gan espye°
Wher as this lady romed to and fro,
And with that sighte hir beautee hurte hym so
That, if that Palamon was wounded soore,   1115
Arcite is hurt as muche as he, or moore.
And with a sigh he seyde pitously,
"The fresshe beautee sleeth° me sodeynly°
Of hire that rometh in the yonder place,
And but° I have hir mercy and hir grace,   1120
That I may seen° hire atte leeste weye°,
I nam° but deed; ther nis namoore to seye."
    This Palamon, whan he tho° wordes herde,
Dispitously° he looked and answerde,
"Wheither seistow this° in ernest or in pley?"   1125
    "Nay," quod Arcite, "in ernest, by my fey°!
God helpe me so, me list ful yvele pleye°."
    This Palamon gan knytte his browes tweye°.
"It nere°," quod he, "to thee no greet honour

For to be fals, ne for to be traitour   1130
To me, that am thy cosyn and thy brother
Ysworn ful depe°, and ech of us til° oother,
That nevere, for to dyen in the peyne°
Til that deeth departe shal us tweyne°,
Neither of us in love to hyndre° oother,   1135
Ne in noon oother cas°, my leeve° brother,
But that thou sholdest trewely forthren° me
In every cas, as I shal forthren thee:
This was thyn ooth, and myn also, certeyn.
I woot° right wel, thou darst it nat withseyn°.   1140
Thus artow of my conseil°, out of doute,
And now thow woldest falsly been aboute
To love my lady, whom I love and serve,
And evere shal til that myn herte sterve°.
Nay, certes°, false Arcite, thow shalt nat so.   1145
I loved hire first, and tolde thee my wo
As to my conseil° and to my brother sworn
To forthre° me, as I have toold biforn.
For which thou art ybounden as a knyght
To helpen me, if it lay in thy myght,   1150
Or elles artow fals°, I dar wel seyn."
    This Arcite ful proudly spak ageyn°:
"Thow shalt," quod he, "be rather fals than I,
And thou art fals, I telle thee outrely°,
For paramour I loved hire first er thow°.   1155
What wiltow seyen°? Thou wistest° nat
        yet now
Wheither she be a womman or goddesse!
Thyn is affeccioun of hoolynesse°,
And myn is love as to a creature,
For which I tolde thee myn aventure°   1160
As to my cosyn and my brother sworn.
I pose° that thow lovedest hire biforn:
Wostow nat° wel the olde clerkes sawe°,
That 'who shal yeve° a lovere any lawe?'
Love is a gretter lawe, by my pan°,   1165
Than may be yeve to any erthely man.

1092 **agayn,** *in response* 1093 **for sothe,** *truly* 1094 **veyn ymaginacioun,** *foolish notion* 1096 **thurghout myn,** *through my* 1097 **bane,** *death* 1099 **Yond,** *there* 1101 **noot wher,** *don't know whether* 1102 **soothly,** *truly* 1107 **scapen,** *escape* 1108 **shapen,** *predetermined* 1109 **eterne,** *eternal* 1110 **lynage,** *lineage* 1112 **gan espye,** *did see* 1118 **sleeth,** *slays,* **sodeynly,** *suddenly* 1120 **but,** *unless* 1121 **seen,** *see,* **atte leeste weye,** *at least* 1122 **nam,** *am nothing* 1123 **tho,** *those* 1124 **Dispitously,** *scornfully* 1125 **Wheither seistow this,** *do you say this* 1126 **fey,** *faith* 1127 **me list ful yvele pleye,** *play is very unpleasing to me* 1128 **gan knytte his browes tweye,** *knitted his two eyebrows* (frowned) 1129 **nere,** *would not be* 1132 **ful depe,** *very deeply,* **til,** *to* 1133 **for to dyen in the peyne,** *to the extent*

of dying by torture 1134 **departe shal us tweyne,** *shall separate the two of us* 1135 **hyndre,** *hinder* 1136 **cas,** *situation,* **leeve,** *dear* 1137 **forthren,** *further* 1140 **woot,** *know,* **darst it nat withseyn,** *dare not deny it* 1141 **artow of my conseil,** *you are in my confidence* 1144 **sterve,** *dies* 1145 **certes,** *surely* 1147 **conseil,** *confidant* 1148 **forthre,** *further* 1151 **elles artow fals,** *else you are false* 1152 **spak ageyn,** *replied* 1154 **outrely,** *utterly* 1155 **For paramour,** *as a lover,* **er thow,** *before you* 1156 **wiltow seyen,** *will you say,* **wistest,** *knew* 1158 **affeccioun of hoolynesse,** *spiritual love* 1160 **aventure,** *condition* 1162 **pose,** *posit,* **biforn,** *earlier* 1163 **Wostow nat,** *don't you know,* **clerkes sawe,** *scholarly saying* 1164 **yeve,** *give* 1165 **pan,** *head*

1131 **cosyn . . . brother,** Palamon and Arcite are first cousins (line 1019) and sworn brothers, joined by blood and by formal oath. These bonds, familiar in medieval romance, are disrupted by the sight of Emily. 1165 The line is nearly identical to Chaucer's translation in *Bo* 3.m12.55, where passionate love is criticized.

And therfore positif lawe° and swich decree°
Is broken alday° for love in ech degree°.
A man moot nedes° love, maugree his heed°.
He may nat flee it, thogh he sholde be deed,   1170
Al be she° mayde or wydwe° or elles wyf.
And eek° it is nat likly al thy lif
To stonden in hir grace. Namoore shal I.
For wel thou woost° thyselven, verraily°,
That thou and I be dampned° to prisoun   1175
Perpetuelly—us gayneth no raunsoun°.
We stryven° as dide the houndes for the boon°.
They foughte al day, and yet hir part° was noon.
Ther cam a kyte°, whil that they weren so wrothe°,
And baar° awey the boon bitwixe hem° bothe.   1180
And therfore, at the kynges court, my brother,
Ech man for hymself, ther is noon oother°.
Love, if thee list°, for I love and ay° shal.
And soothly°, leeve° brother, this is al.
Heere in this prisoun moote° we endure,   1185
And everich° of us take his aventure°."

   Greet was the strif° and long bitwix hem
      tweye°,
If that I hadde leyser° for to seye,
But to th'effect°. It happed on a day,
To telle it yow as shortly as I may,   1190
A worthy duc that highte° Perotheus,
That felawe° was unto Duc Theseus
Syn thilke day° that they were children lite°,
Was come to Atthenes his felawe to visite,
And for to pleye as he was wont° to do,   1195
For in this world he loved no man so,
And he loved hym als° tendrely agayn°.
So wel they lovede, as olde bookes sayn,
That whan that oon was deed, soothly to telle,

His felawe wente and soughte hym doun in
      helle—   1200
But of that storie list me nat° to write.
Duc Perotheus loved wel Arcite,
And hadde hym knowe° at Thebes yeer by yere°,
And finally at requeste and preyere
Of Perotheus, withouten any raunsoun,   1205
Duc Theseus hym leet out of prisoun
Frely to goon wher that hym liste over al°,
In swich a gyse° as I you tellen shal.

   This was the forward°, pleynly for t'endite°,
Bitwixen Theseus and hym Arcite,   1210
That if so were that Arcite were yfounde
Evere in his lif, by day or nyght or stounde°,
In any contree of this Theseus,
And he were caught, it was acorded° thus,
That with a swerd he sholde lese° his heed.   1215
Ther nas noon° oother remedie ne reed°,
But taketh his leve, and homward he him
      spedde°.
Lat hym be war. His nekke° lith to wedde°.
   How greet a sorwe suffreth now Arcite!
The deeth he feeleth thurgh his herte smyte°.   1220
He wepeth, wayleth, crieth pitously;
To sleen° hymself he waiteth prively°.
He seyde, "Allas that day that I was born!
Now is my prisoun worse than biforn.
Now is me shape° eternally to dwelle   1225
Nat in purgatorie, but in helle.
Allas, that evere knew I Perotheus!
For elles hadde I dwelled with Theseus,
Yfetered° in his prisoun everemo.
Thanne hadde I been in blisse and nat in wo.   1230
Oonly the sighte of hire whom that I serve,

1167 **positif lawe,** *man-made law,* **swich decree,** *similar rules* 1168 **alday,** *always,* **degree,** *social class* 1169 **moot nedes,** *must necessarily,* **maugree his heed,** *in spite of anything* 1171 **Al be she,** *whether she is,* **wydwe,** *widow* 1172 **eek,** *also* 1174 **woost,** *know,* **verraily,** *truly* 1175 **dampned,** *condemned* 1176 **us gayneth no raunsoun,** *no ransom can help us* 1177 **stryven,** *fight,* **boon,** *bone* 1178 **hir part,** *their portion* 1179 **kyte,** *bird of prey,* **wrothe,** *angry* 1180 **baar,** *carried,* **bitwixe,** *from between* 1182 **noon oother,** *no other (way)* 1183 **thee list,** (it) *pleases you,* **ay,** *always* 1184 **soothly,** *truly,* **leeve,** *dear* 1185 **moote,** *must* 1186 **everich,** *each,* **aventure,** *chance* 1187 **strif,** *strife,* **hem tweye,** (the) *two of them* 1188 **leyser,** *time* 1189 **th'effect,**

the point 1191 **highte,** *was called* 1192 **felawe,** *companion* 1193 **Syn thilke day,** *since the time,* **lite,** *little* 1195 **wont,** *accustomed* 1197 **als,** *as,* **agayn,** *in return* 1201 **list me nat,** *I wish not* 1203 **knowe,** *known,* **yeer by yere,** *for years* 1207 **hym liste over al,** *anywhere it pleased him* 1208 **swich a gyse,** *such a manner* 1209 **forward,** *agreement,* **t'endite,** *to write* 1212 **stounde,** *moment* 1214 **acorded,** *agreed* 1215 **lese,** *lose* 1216 **Ther nas noon,** *there was no,* **reed,** *help* 1217 **him spedde,** *hurried himself* 1218 **nekke,** *neck,* **lith to wedde,** *is pledged* 1220 **smyte,** *strike* 1222 **sleen,** *slay,* **waiteth prively,** *awaits* (a time) *secretly* 1225 **is me shape,** *I am destined* 1229 **Yfetered,** *shackled*

1167 positif lawe, Lat. *lex positiva,* or "placed" (rather than unchangeable), man-made law. **1182 Ech man for hymself,** the first recorded instance of this proverb. **1191 Perotheus,** the friendship of Pirithous and Theseus was legendary. Pirithous's suit in favor of Arcite was known to Chaucer from *Teseida* 3.47ff. but the story of Theseus's descent into hell to save Pirithous is from *RR* 8148ff. **1201 list me nat to write,** "it pleases me not to write," a break in literary decorum since the Knight is talking. Such breaks are not unusual in medieval literature, but this may be a vestige of Chaucer's story before he adapted it to the *CT.* **1212 or stounde,** one MS (Dd.4.24) reads *o stounde* ("a moment" rather than "or moment"), and many editors have followed Tyrwhitt's adoption of this reading. **1226 purgatorie,** purgatory, in Roman Catholic tradition, the place where souls suffer extended but not eternal punishment for their sins.

Though that I nevere hir grace may deserve,
Wolde han° suffised right ynough for me.
O deere cosyn Palamon," quod he,
"Thyn is the victorie of this aventure.   1235
Ful blisfully in prison maistow dure°—
In prison? Certes nay°, but in paradys!
Wel hath Fortune yturned thee the dys°,
That hast the sighte of hire, and I th'absence.
For possible is, syn° thou hast hire presence,   1240
And art a knyght, a worthy and an able,
That by som cas°, syn Fortune is chaungeable,
Thow maist to thy desir somtyme atteyne°.
But I that am exiled and bareyne°
Of alle grace, and in so greet dispeir   1245
That ther nys° erthe, water, fir, ne eir,
Ne creature that of hem maked is,
That may me helpe or doon confort in this,
Wel oughte I sterve° in wanhope° and distresse.
Farwel my lif, my lust°, and my gladnesse!   1250
    "Allas, why pleynen° folk so in commune°
On purveiaunce° of God, or of Fortune,
That yeveth° hem ful ofte in many a gyse°
Wel bettre than they kan hemself devyse°?
Som man desireth for to han° richesse,   1255
That cause is of his moerdre° or greet siknesse.
And som man wolde out of his prisoun fayn°,
That in his hous is of his meynee° slayn.
Infinite harmes been in this mateere.
We witen° nat what thing we preyen° heere: 1260
We faren° as he that dronke° is as a mous.
A dronke man woot° wel he hath an hous,
But he noot which the righte wey is thider°,
And to a dronke man the wey is slider°.
And certes, in this world so faren we.   1265
We seken° faste after felicitee,
But we goon wrong ful often, trewely.

Thus may we seyen alle°, and namely I°,
That wende° and hadde a greet opinioun
That if I myghte escapen from prisoun,   1270
Thanne hadde I been in joye and perfit heele°,
Ther° now I am exiled fro my wele°.
Syn that I may nat seen you, Emelye,
I nam° but deed; ther nys no° remedye."
    Upon that oother syde Palamon,   1275
Whan that he wiste° Arcite was agon°,
Swich sorwe he maketh that the grete tour
Resouneth of his youlyng° and clamour.
The pure fettres° on his shynes° grete
Weren of his bittre salte teeres wete.   1280
"Allas," quod he, "Arcita, cosyn myn,
Of al oure strif, God woot°, the fruyt is thyn.
Thow walkest now in Thebes at thy large°,
And of my wo thow yevest litel charge°.
Thou mayst, syn° thou hast wisdom and
        man-hede,   1285
Assemblen alle the folk of oure kynrede°,
And make a werre° so sharp on this citee
That by som aventure or som tretee
Thow mayst have hire to° lady and to wyf
For whom that I moste nedes lese° my lyf.   1290
For, as by wey of possibilitee,
Sith° thou art at thy large, of prisoun free,
And art a lord, greet is thyn avauntage
Moore than is myn, that sterve° here in a cage.
For I moot° wepe and wayle, whil I lyve,   1295
With al the wo that prison may me yeve°,
And eek with peyne that love me yeveth also
That doubleth al my torment and my wo."
Therwith° the fyr of jalousie up sterte
Withinne his brest, and hente° him by the
        herte   1300
So woodly° that he lyk was to biholde°

1233 **Wolde han,** *would have* 1236 **maistow dure,** *can you live* 1237
Certes nay, *certainly no* 1238 **yturned thee the dys,** *tossed the dice for
you* 1240 **syn,** *since* 1242 **som cas,** *some chance* 1243 **atteyne,** *achieve*
1244 **bareyne,** *barren* 1246 **nys,** *isn't* 1249 **sterve,** *die,* **wanhope,** *despair* 1250 **lust,** *desire* 1251 **pleynen,** *complain,* **in commune,** *commonly*
1252 **On purveiaunce,** *about the providence* 1253 **yeveth hem,** *gives
them,* **gyse,** *way* 1254 **devyse,** *imagine* 1255 **han,** *have* 1256 **moerdre,**
murder 1257 **wolde . . . fayn,** *would like* 1258 **of his meynee,** *by his servants* 1260 **witen,** *know,* **preyen,** *pray for* 1261 **faren,** *act,* **dronke,**
drunk 1262 **woot,** *knows* 1263 **noot which the righte wey is thider,**

knows not which is the right way there 1264 **slider,** *slippery* 1266 **seken,**
seek 1268 **seyen alle,** *all say,* **namely I,** *especially me* 1269 **wende,**
thought 1271 **perfit heele,** *perfect well-being* 1272 **Ther,** *whereas,* **wele,**
joy 1274 **nam,** *am nothing,* **nys no,** *isn't any* 1276 **wiste,** *knew,* **agon,** *gone*
1278 **youlyng,** *howling* 1279 **pure fettres,** *very shackles,* **shynes,** *shins*
1282 **woot,** *knows* 1283 **at thy large,** *free* 1284 **yevest litel charge,** *give
little care* 1285 **syn,** *since* 1286 **kynrede,** *relatives* 1287 **werre,** *war* 1289
to, *as* 1290 **moste nedes lese,** *must necessarily lose* 1292 **Sith,** *since* 1294
sterve, *die* 1295 **moot,** *must* 1296 **yeve,** *give* 1299 **Therwith,** *with this*
1300 **hente,** *grabbed* 1301 **woodly,** *madly,* **lyk was to biholde,** *looked like*

1252 **purveiaunce of God, or of Fortune . . .** , in Boethian thought, divine Providence or foresight is omniscient, atemporal awareness of all
events; human beings know only sequentially in time and therefore mistakenly consider events to be the whims of fortune. Chaucer fash-
ioned Arcite's speech from *Bo* 3.pr2. Later in *Bo* the difference between Providence and fortune is made clear, so Arcite's speech reflects incomplete or erroneous understanding. 1260 **We witen nat what thing we preyen,** we don't what it is that we pray for, an echo of Romans 8.26,
which contrasts human desires and divine knowledge. 1262–64 From *Bo* 3.pr2.88, where the drunken man who cannot find his home exemplifies how improper desires confuse humans.

The boxtree or the asshen° dede and colde.
  Thanne seyde he, "O crueel goddes that governe
This world with byndyng of youre word eterne,
And writen in the table of atthamaunt° 1305
Youre parlement° and youre eterne graunt°,
What is mankynde moore unto you holde°
Than is the sheep that rouketh° in the folde°?
For slayn is man right° as another beest,
And dwelleth eek in prison and arreest, 1310
And hath siknesse and greet adversitee,
And ofte tymes giltelees, pardee°.
  "What governance° is in this prescience°,
That giltelees tormenteth innocence?
And yet encresseth this al my penaunce, 1315
That man is bounden to his observaunce°,
For Goddes sake, to letten of° his wille,
Ther as° a beest may al his lust fulfille.
And whan a beest is deed he hath no peyne,
But after his deeth man moot° wepe and pleyne°, 1320
Though in this world he have care and wo.
Withouten doute it may stonden so.
The answere of this lete I° to dyvynys°,
But wel I woot° that in this world greet pyne ys°.
Allas, I se° a serpent or a theef, 1325
That many a trewe man hath doon mescheef°,
Goon at his large°, and where hym list may turne°.
But I moot° been in prisoun thurgh° Saturne,
And eek thurgh Juno, jalous and eek wood°,
That hath destroyed wel ny al° the blood 1330
Of Thebes with his waste° walles wyde.
And Venus sleeth me on that oother syde

For jalousie and fere° of hym Arcite."
  Now wol I stynte of° Palamon a lite,
And lete hym in his prisoun stille dwelle, 1335
And of Arcita forth I wol yow telle.
The somer passeth, and the nyghtes longe
Encressen double wise the peynes stronge
Bothe of the lovere and the prisoner.
I noot° which hath the wofuller mester°. 1340
For, shortly for to seyn, this Palamoun
Perpetuelly is dampned° to prisoun,
In cheynes and in fettres to been deed.
And Arcite is exiled upon his heed°
For, evere mo, as out of that contree, 1345
Ne nevere mo he shal his lady see.
  Yow loveres axe° I now this questioun:
Who hath the worse, Arcite or Palamoun?
That oon may seen his lady day by day,
But in prison he moot° dwelle alway; 1350
That oother wher hym list° may ride or go°,
But seen his lady shal he nevere mo.
Now demeth as yow liste°, ye that kan,
For I wol telle forth as I bigan.

Explicit prima pars. Sequitur pars secunda.

  Whan that Arcite to Thebes comen was, 1355
Ful ofte a day he swelte° and seyde "Allas!"
For seen his lady shal he nevere mo.
And shortly to concluden al his wo,
So muche sorwe hadde nevere creature
That is, or shal, whil that the world may dure°. 1360
His slep, his mete°, his drynke, is hym biraft°,
That lene he wex° and drye as is a shaft°;

1302 asshen, *ashes* **1305 atthamaunt,** *adamant* **1306 parlement,** *decision,* **eterne graunt,** *eternal decree* **1307 holde,** *obliged* **1308 rouketh,** *cowers,* **folde,** *pen* **1309 right,** *just* **1312 pardee,** *by God* **1313 governance,** *caretaking,* **prescience,** *foreknowledge* **1316 observaunce,** *duty* **1317 letten of,** *refrain from* **1318 Ther as,** *whereas* **1320 moot,** *must,* **pleyne,** *complain* **1323 lete I,** *I let,* **dyvynys,** *theologians* **1324 woot,** *know,* **greet pyne ys,** *is great pain* **1325 se,** *see* **1326 doon mescheef,** *done wrong* (to) **1327 Goon at his large,** *go freely,* **where hym list**

may turne, *and go where he likes* **1328 moot,** *must,* **thurgh,** *because of* **1329 wood,** *angry* **1330 wel ny al,** *almost all* **1331 his waste,** *its wasted* **1333 fere,** *fear* **1334 stynte of,** *stop* (talking) *about* **1340 noot,** *don't know,* **mester,** *occupation* **1342 dampned,** *condemned* **1344 upon his heed,** *on threat of death* **1347 axe,** *ask* **1350 moot,** *must* **1351 wher hym list,** *wherever he pleases,* **go,** *walk* **1353 demeth as yow liste,** *judge as you please* **1356 swelte,** *fainted* **1360 dure,** *endure* **1361 mete,** *food,* **is hym biraft,** *he is deprived* (of) **1362 lene he wex,** *he grew lean,* **shaft,** *stick*

1302 boxtree, the boxwood shrub has pale wood. **1303 crueel goddes,** Palamon's complaint against the gods resembles *Bo* 1.m5, another instance where a prisoner mistakenly thinks that the suffering of the innocent evinces a breakdown in divine governance. **1320 man,** the word appears in the MSS in various places in the line, perhaps indicating late insertion or scribal efforts to smooth meter. **1329 Juno,** in the *Thebaid,* the goddess Juno hated Thebes because Zeus, her husband and king of the gods, loved Theban women. **1347 questioun,** a love question (*demande d'amour*), often included in courtly literature as an exercise or demonstration of refined speech and attitude. **1354a Explicit prima pars. Sequitur pars secunda.** "Here ends part one. Here follows part two." These and the other headings help give the *KnT* its formal atmosphere. **1361ff. His slep, his mete . . . ,** Arcite's symptoms are of lovesickness, a malady known as **hereos** (line 1374, from Gk. *eros*). In advanced stages it could produce mania (**manye,** line 1374), a disease of the front (**Biforen,** line 1376) cell of the brain (**celle fantastik,** line 1376). The brain was thought to be divided into three cells: rear (memory), middle (reason), front (image making). Mania could be caused by an influx of the **humour malencolik** (line 1375), i.e., black bile (see *GP* 1.333n), into the front cell, impairing the individual's ability to imagine anything new—a severe form of fixation that could be fatal.

His eyen holwe° and grisly to biholde,
His hewe falow° and pale as asshen colde,
And solitarie he was and evere allone, 1365
And waillynge al the nyght, makynge his mone°.
And if he herde song or instrument,
Thanne wolde he wepe, he myghte nat be stent°.
So feble eek were his spiritz, and so lowe,
And chaunged so, that no man koude knowe° 1370
His speche nor his voys°, though men it herde.
And in his geere° for al the world he ferde°,
Nat oonly lik the loveris maladye
Of hereos°, but rather lyk manye°,
Engendred° of humour malencolik 1375
Biforen, in his celle fantastik°.
And shortly°, turned was al up so doun°
Bothe habit and eek disposicioun
Of hym, this woful lovere daun° Arcite.
  What sholde I al day of his wo endite°? 1380
Whan he endured hadde a yeer or two
This crueel torment and this peyne and wo,
At Thebes, in his contree, as I seyde,
Upon a nyght in sleep as he hym leyde°,
Hym thoughte how that the wynged god
    Mercurie 1385
Biforn hym stood and bad hym to be murie°.
His slepy yerde° in hond he bar° uprighte,
An hat he werede upon his heris° brighte.
Arrayed was this god, as he took keep°,
As he was whan that Argus took his sleep. 1390
And seyde hym thus, "To Atthenes shaltou
    wende°,
Ther is thee shapen of° thy wo an ende."
And with that word Arcite wook and sterte.
"Now trewely, hou soore that me smerte°,"
Quod he, "to Atthenes right now wol I fare, 1395
Ne for the drede of deeth shal I nat spare°

To se my lady that I love and serve.
In hire presence I recche nat to sterve°."
  And with that word he caughte° a greet mirour
And saugh that chaunged was al his colour, 1400
And saugh his visage° al in another kynde°.
And right anon° it ran hym in his mynde°
That, sith° his face was so disfigured
Of maladye the which he hadde endured,
He myghte wel, if that he bar hym lowe°, 1405
Lyve in Atthenes everemoore unknowe
And seen his lady wel ny day by day°.
And right anon he chaunged his array,
And cladde hym° as a poure laborer,
And al allone, save oonly a squier 1410
That knew his privetee° and al his cas°,
Which was disgised pourely° as he was,
To Atthenes is he goon the nexte° way.
And to the court he wente upon a day,
And at the gate he profreth° his servyse 1415
To drugge and drawe°, what so° men wol devyse°.
And shortly of this matere for to seyn°,
He fil in office° with a chamberleyn°
The which that dwellynge was with Emelye,
For he was wys and koude soone espye° 1420
Of every servaunt which that serveth here°.
Wel koude he hewen wode° and water bere,
For he was yong and myghty for the nones°,
And therto he was long° and big° of bones
To doon that° any wight° kan hym devyse. 1425
  A yeer or two he was in this servyse,
Page° of the chambre of Emelye the brighte,
And Philostrate he seyde that he highte°.
But half so wel biloved a man as he
Ne was ther nevere in court of his degree°. 1430
He was so gentil of condicioun°
That thurghout al the court was his renoun°.

1363 **eyen holwe,** *eyes hollow* 1364 **hewe falow,** *complexion yellow* 1366 **mone,** *moan* 1368 **stent,** *stopped* 1370 **koude knowe,** *could recognize* 1371 **voys,** *voice* 1372 **geere,** *manner,* **ferde,** *behaved* 1374 **hereos,** *lovesickness* (see 1361n), **manye,** *mania* 1375 **Engendred,** *born* 1376 **Biforen . . . celle fantastik,** *in the frontal lobe of his imagination* 1377 **shortly,** *in short,* **up so doun,** *upside down* 1379 **daun,** *sir* 1380 **endite,** *write* 1384 **leyde,** *laid* 1386 **murie,** *merry* 1387 **slepy yerde,** *sleep stick,* **bar,** *bore* 1388 **heris,** *hair* 1389 **he took keep,** *he* (Arcite) *was aware* 1391 **shaltou wende,** *you shall go* 1392 **shapen of,** *destined for* 1394 **hou . . . smerte,** *however sorely I suffer* 1396–97 **spare / To se,** *refrain from seeing* 1398 **recche . . . sterve,** *care not if I die* 1399 **caughte,** *took* 1401 **visage,** *face,* **in another kynde,** *of a different nature*

1402 **right anon,** *immediately,* **ran hym in his mynde,** *ran through his mind* 1403 **sith,** *since* 1405 **bar hym lowe,** *acted humbly* 1407 **wel ny day by day,** *nearly every day* 1409 **cladde hym,** *dressed himself* 1411 **privetee,** *secret,* **cas,** *situation* 1412 **pourely,** *as a poor man* 1413 **nexte,** *nearest* 1415 **profreth,** *offers* 1416 **drugge and drawe,** *drudge and pull,* **what so,** *whatever,* **devyse,** *command* 1417 **seyn,** *say* 1418 **fil in office,** *happened to be employed,* **chamberleyn,** *personal attendant* 1420 **espye,** *make assessment* 1421 **here,** *her* 1422 **hewen wode,** *cut wood* 1423 **for the nones,** *in this way* 1424 **long,** *tall,* **big,** *strong* 1425 **that,** *what,* **wight,** *person* 1427 **Page,** *servant* 1428 **highte,** *was named* 1430 **degree,** *status* 1431 **condicioun,** *manners* 1432 **renoun,** *reputation*

1385 **Mercurie,** Mercury, the divine messenger, bears the staff with which he put to sleep the hundred-eyed guardian, **Argus** (line 1390); Ovid, *Metamorphoses* 1.670ff. There is no parallel dream in Chaucer's sources; Chaucer's addition increases the influence of the planets (gods). **1428 Philostrate,** the name means "one vanquished by love." Chaucer borrowed it, not from the *Teseida* (where the assumed name is "Penteo"), but from the title of Boccaccio's *Il Filostrato,* the source of *TC.* In *Teseida,* Emelye recognizes Arcite but lets no one know.

They seyden that it were a charitee°
That Theseus wolde enhauncen his degree,
And putten hym in worshipful° servyse,   1435
Ther as he myghte his vertu exercise.
And thus withinne a while his name is spronge°,
Bothe of his dedes and his goode tonge,
That° Theseus hath taken hym so neer
That of his chambre he made hym a squier,   1440
And gaf° hym gold to mayntene his degree.
And eek men broghte hym out of his contree,
From yeer to yeer, ful pryvely° his rente°.
But honestly° and slyly he it spente,
That no man wondred how that he it hadde.   1445
And thre yeer in this wise° his lif he ladde,
And bar hym so, in pees and eek in werre,
Ther was no man that Theseus hath derre°.
And in this blisse lete I now Arcite,
And speke I wole of Palamon a lite.   1450

In derknesse and horrible and strong prisoun
Thise seven yeer hath seten Palamoun
Forpyned°, what for wo and for distresse.
Who feeleth double soor° and hevynesse
But Palamon, that love destreyneth° so   1455
That wood° out of his wit he goth for wo?
And eek therto° he is a prisoner
Perpetuelly, noght oonly for a yer.

Who koude ryme in Englyssh proprely
His martirdom? For sothe° it am nat I.   1460
Therfore I passe as lightly as I may.

It fel that in the seventhe yer, of May
The thridde° nyght, as olde bookes seyn,
That al this storie tellen moore pleyn,
Were it by aventure° or destynee—   1465
As whan a thyng is shapen it shal be—
That soone after the mydnyght Palamoun,
By helpyng of a freend, brak his prisoun
And fleeth the citee faste as he may go.
For he hadde yeve° his gayler° drynke so   1470
Of a clarree° maad of a certeyn wyn,

With nercotikes and opie° of Thebes fyn°,
That al that nyght, thogh that men wolde him
    shake,
The gayler sleep—he myghte nat awake.
And thus he fleeth as faste as evere he may.   1475
The nyght was short and faste by° the day
That nedes cost° he moot° hymselven hyde,
And til° a grove faste° ther bisyde
With dredeful° foot thanne stalketh Palamoun.
For, shortly, this was his opinioun,   1480
That in that grove he wolde hym hyde al day,
And in the nyght thanne wolde he take his way
To Thebes-ward°, his freendes for to preye°
On Theseus to helpe hym to werreye°.
And shortly, outher° he wolde lese his lif,   1485
Or wynnen Emelye unto his wyf.
This is th'effect° and his entente pleyn.

Now wol I turne to Arcite ageyn,
That litel wiste° how ny° that was his care
Til that Fortune had broght him in the snare.   1490

The bisy larke, messager of day,
Salueth° in hir song the morwe° gray,
And firy Phebus° riseth up so brighte
That al the orient laugheth of the lighte,
And with his stremes° dryeth in the greves°   1495
The silver dropes hangynge on the leves.
And Arcita, that in the court roial
With Theseus is squier principal,
Is risen and looketh on the myrie° day.
And for to doon his observaunce to May,   1500
Remembrynge on the poynt° of his desir,
He on a courser°, startlynge° as the fir,
Is riden into the feeldes hym to pleye,
Out of the court were it a myle or tweye.
And to the grove of which that I yow tolde   1505
By aventure his wey he gan to holde°,
To maken hym a gerland of the greves°
Were it of wodebynde° or hawethorn leves.
And loude he song ayeyn the sonne shene°,

1433 **charitee,** *kindness* 1435 **worshipful,** *honorable* 1437 **name is spronge,** *reputation spreads* 1439 **That,** *so that* 1441 **gaf,** *gave* 1443 **pryvely,** *secretly,* **rente,** *income* 1444 **honestly,** *fittingly* 1446 **wise,** *manner* 1448 **derre,** *more dear* 1453 **Forpyned,** *agonized* 1454 **soor,** *pain* 1455 **destreyneth,** *afflicts* 1456 **wood,** *crazed* 1457 **eek therto,** *also* 1460 **For sothe,** *in truth* 1463 **thridde,** *third* 1465 **aventure,** *chance* 1470 **yeve,** *give,* **gayler,** *jailer* 1471 **clarree,** *wine punch* 1472 **opie,** *opium,* **fyn,** *special* 1476 **faste by,** *so close* 1477 **nedes cost,** *at any cost,* **moot,** *must* 1478 **til,** *to,* **faste,** *near* 1479 **dredeful,** *fearful*

1483 **To Thebes-ward,** *toward Thebes,* **preye,** *beseech* 1484 **werreye,** *make war* 1485 **outher,** *either* 1487 **th'effect,** *the point* 1489 **wiste,** *knew,* **ny,** *near* 1492 **Salueth,** *greets,* **morwe,** *morning* 1493 **firy Phebus,** *the sun* 1495 **stremes,** *beams,* **greves,** *branches* 1499 **myrie,** *merry* 1501 **Remembrynge on the poynt,** *thinking about the focus* 1502 **courser,** *steed,* **startlynge,** *active* 1506 **gan to holde,** *followed* 1507 **greves,** *branches* 1508 **wodebynde,** *woodbine* 1509 **ayeyn the sonne shene,** *facing the bright sun*

1463 **thridde,** May 3 is apparently an auspicious and perhaps an unlucky or unfortunate day, the date when the fox seizes Chanticleer (*NPT* 7.3190) and the night before Pandarus first approaches Criseyde on Troilus's behalf (*TC* 2.56). **1472 of Thebes,** the Egyptian city of Thebes was reputed for its exotic drugs.

"May, with alle thy floures and thy grene,   1510
Welcome be thou, faire, fresshe May,
In hope that I som grene gete may."
And from his courser, with a lusty herte,
Into the grove ful hastily he sterte,
And in a path he rometh up and doun   1515
Theras by aventure this Palamoun
Was in a bussh, that no man myghte hym se,
For soore afered° of his deeth was he.
Nothyng ne knew he that it was Arcite,
God woot° he wolde have trowed° it ful lite°.   1520
But sooth is seyd, gon sithen many yeres°,
That "feeld hath eyen and the wode hath eres."
It is ful fair° a man to bere hym evene°
For alday° meeteth men at unset stevene°.
Ful litel woot° Arcite of his felawe   1525
That was so ny° to herknen al his sawe°,
For in the bussh he sitteth now ful stille.

    Whan that Arcite hadde romed al his fille°,
And songen al the roundel lustily°,
Into a studie° he fil sodeynly°,   1530
As doon thise loveres in hir queynte geres°,
Now in the crope°, now doun in the breres°,
Now up, now doun, as boket° in a welle.
Right as° the Friday, soothly for to telle,
Now it shyneth°, now it reyneth° faste,   1535
Right so kan geery° Venus overcaste
The hertes of hir folk. Right as hir day
Is gereful°, right so chaungeth she array.
Selde° is the Friday al the wowke° ylike.

    Whan that Arcite had songe, he gan
        to sike°,   1540
And sette hym doun withouten any moore.
"Allas," quod he, "that day that I was bore!
How longe, Juno, thurgh thy crueltee,

Woltow werreyen° Thebes the citee?
Allas, ybroght is to confusioun   1545
The blood roial of Cadme and Amphioun—
Of Cadmus, which that was the firste man
That Thebes bulte°, or first° the toun bigan,
And of the citee first was crouned kyng.
Of his lynage° am I and his ofspryng   1550
By verray ligne°, as of the stok roial°,
And now I am so caytyf° and so thral°
That he that is my mortal enemy,
I serve hym as his squier pourely°.
And yet dooth Juno me wel moore shame,   1555
For I dar noght biknowe° myn owene name,
But ther as I was wont to highte° Arcite
Now highte I Philostrate, noght worth a myte°.
Allas, thou felle° Mars! Allas, Juno!
Thus hath youre ire° oure lynage al fordo°,   1560
Save oonly me and wrecched Palamoun,
That Theseus martireth° in prisoun.
And over al this, to sleen me outrely°,
Love hath his firy dart so brennyngly
Ystiked° thurgh my trewe°, careful° herte,   1565
That shapen° was my deeth erst° than my sherte°.
Ye sleen me with youre eyen, Emelye!
Ye been the cause wherfore that° I dye.
Of al the remenant of myn oother care
Ne sette I nat the montance° of a tare°,   1570
So that° I koude doon aught° to youre
        plesaunce°."
And with that word he fil doun in a traunce
A longe tyme, and after he up sterte°.

    This Palamoun, that thoughte that thurgh his
        herte
He felte a coold swerd sodeynliche° glyde,   1575
For ire he quook°, no lenger wolde he byde°.

1518 soore afered, *sorely afraid* **1520 woot,** *knows,* **trowed,** *believed,* **ful lite,** *very little* **1521 sooth is seyd, gon sithen many yeres,** *truly it is said for many years gone* **1523 ful fair,** *very good* (for), **evene,** *evenly* **1524 alday,** *always,* **unset stevene,** *unplanned appointments* **1525 woot,** *knows* **1526 ny,** *near,* **sawe,** *saying* **1528 romed al his fille,** *roamed as he wished* **1529 roundel lustily,** *song energetically* **1530 a studie,** *deep thought,* **sodeynly,** *suddenly* **1531 queynte geres,** *curious ways* **1532 crope,** *leaves,* **breres,** *briars* **1533 boket,** *bucket* **1534 Right as,** *just as* **1535 shyneth,** *shines,* **reyneth,** *rains* **1536 geery,** *variable* **1538 gereful,** *changeable* **1539 Selde,** *seldom,* **wowke,** *week* **1540 sike,** *sigh* **1544 Woltow werreyen,** *will you make war on* **1548 bulte,** *established,* **or first,** *before* **1550 lynage,** *lineage* **1551 verray ligne,** *true line,* **stok roial,** *royal stock* **1552 caytyf,** *wretched,* **thral,** *enslaved* **1554 pourely,** *humbly* **1556 biknowe,** *reveal* **1557 wont to highte,** *accustomed to being called* **1558 myte,** *tiny Flemish coin* **1559 felle,** *cruel* **1560 ire,** *anger,* **fordo,** *destroyed* **1562 martireth,** *torments* **1563 sleen me outrely,** *slay me utterly* **1564 brennyngly,** *burningly* **1565 Ystiked,** *stuck,* **trewe,** *sincere,* **careful,** *sorrowful* **1566 shapen,** *destined,* **erst,** *earlier,* **sherte,** *shirt* (see note) **1568 wherfore that,** *why* **1570 montance,** *value,* **tare,** *weed* **1571 So that,** *if only,* **aught,** *anything,* **plesaunce,** *pleasure* **1573 up sterte,** *leapt up* **1575 sodeynliche,** *suddenly* **1576 quook,** *quaked,* **byde,** *wait*

1512 I som grene gete may, "I may get some green," apparently an allusion to some sort of May custom. **1516–20 by aventure . . . ,** Chaucer emphasizes the accidental nature (compare line 1506) of the meeting of Arcite and Palamon; in *Teseida,* Palamon plans the meeting and comes ready for battle. **1522** A common proverb, "Fields have eyes and woods have ears." **1524** Also proverbial. **1529 roundel,** a kind of French song sung as a round with a refrain; one example concludes *PF.* **1536–39 Venus . . . Friday,** Friday, legendary for its changeable weather, was Venus's day, named for Frigg, the Scandinavian goddess of fertility and love. **1546ff. Cadme and Amphioun,** Cadmus and Amphion were the legendary founders of Thebes. For Juno's animosity toward Thebes, see 1329n above. **1566** His fate was woven before his first shirt.

And whan that he had herd Arcites tale,
As° he were wood°, with face deed and pale,
He stirte hym up out of the buskes° thikke,
And seide, "Arcite, false traytour wikke,   1580
Now artow hent°, that lovest my lady so,
For whom that I have al this peyne and wo,
And art my blood, and to my conseil sworn,
As I ful ofte have told thee heerbiforn°,
And hast byjaped° heere Duc Theseus,   1585
And falsly chaunged hast thy name thus!
I wol be deed, or elles thou shalt dye.
Thou shalt nat love my lady Emelye,
But I wol love hire oonly and namo°,
For I am Palamon, thy mortal foo.   1590
And though that I no wepene° have in this place,
But out of prison am astert° by grace,
I drede° noght that outher° thow shalt dye,
Or thow ne shalt nat loven Emelye.
Chees° which thou wolt, or thou shalt nat
     asterte!"   1595
    This Arcite, with ful despitous° herte,
Whan he hym knew and hadde his tale herd,
As fiers° as leon pulled out his swerd,
And seyde thus, "By God that sit above,
Nere it° that thou art sik° and wood for love,   1600
And eek that thow no wepne° hast in this place,
Thou sholdest nevere out of this grove pace°,
That thou ne sholdest dyen of myn hond.
For I defye° the seurete° and the bond
Which that thou seist° that I have maad°
     to thee.   1605
What, verray° fool, thynk wel that love is free,
And I wol love hire mawgree° al thy myght!
But for as muche thou art a worthy knyght,
And wilnest to darreyne° hire by bataille,
Have heer my trouthe°, tomorwe I wol nat
     faille,   1610
Withoute wityng° of any oother wight°,
That heere I wol be founden as a knyght,

And bryngen harneys° right ynough for thee,
And ches° the beste, and leve the worste for me.
And mete and drynke this nyght wol I brynge   1615
Ynough for thee, and clothes for thy beddynge.
And if so be that thou my lady wynne,
And sle° me in this wode ther° I am inne,
Thow mayst wel have thy lady as for me°."
    This Palamon answerde, "I graunte it
     thee."   1620
And thus they been departed til amorwe°,
Whan ech of hem had leyd his feith to borwe°.
    O Cupide, out of alle° charitee!
O regne°, that wolt no felawe have with thee!
Ful sooth is seyd° that love ne lordshipe   1625
Wol noght, his thankes°, have no felaweshipe.
Wel fynden that Arcite and Palamoun.
Arcite is riden anon unto the toun,
And on the morwe, er it were dayes light,
Ful prively two harneys° hath he dight°,   1630
Bothe suffisaunt and mete to darreyne°
The bataille in the feeld bitwix hem tweyne°,
And on his hors, allone as he was born,
He carieth al the harneys hym biforn.
And in the grove, at tyme and place yset,   1635
This Arcite and this Palamon ben met.
To chaungen gan° the colour in hir° face,
Right as the hunters in the regne of Trace,
That stondeth at the gappe° with a spere,
Whan hunted is the leon or the bere,   1640
And hereth hym° come russhyng in the greves°,
And breketh bothe bowes and the leves,
And thynketh, "Heere cometh my mortal enemy!
Withoute faile, he moot° be deed, or I,
For outher° I moot sleen hym at the gappe,   1645
Or he moot sleen me, if that me myshappe°."
So ferden° they in chaungyng of hir hewe,
As fer as everich° of hem oother knewe°.
    Ther nas no good day, ne no saluyng°,
But streight, withouten word or rehersyng,   1650

1578 As, *as if,* **wood,** *crazed* **1579 buskes,** *bushes* **1581 artow hent,** *are you caught* **1584 heerbiforn,** *before this* **1585 byjaped,** *tricked* **1589 namo,** *no others* **1591 wepene,** *weapon* **1592 astert,** *escaped* **1593 drede,** *doubt,* **outher,** *either* **1595 Chees,** *choose* **1596 despitous,** *spiteful* **1598 fiers,** *fierce* **1600 Nere it,** *were it not,* **sik,** *sick* **1601 wepne,** *weapon* **1602 pace,** *pass* **1604 defye,** *renounce,* **seurete,** *pledge* **1605 seist,** *say,* **maad,** *made* **1606 verray,** *absolute* **1607 mawgree,** *despite* **1609 wilnest to darreyne,** *wish to decide the right to* **1610 trouthe,** *pledge* **1611 wityng,** *knowledge,* **wight,** *person* **1613 harneys,** *armor* **1614 ches,** *(you can) choose* **1618 sle,** *slay,* **ther,** *which* **1619 as for me,** *as far as I am concerned* **1621 til amorwe,** *until the next day* **1622 to borwe,** *as a pledge* **1623 out of alle,** *without any* **1624 regne,** *ruler* **1625 Ful sooth is seyd,** *very truly it is said* **1626 Wol nought, his thankes,** *will not, willingly* **1630 harneys,** *suits of armor,* **dight,** *prepared* **1631 mete to darreyne,** *fit to decide* **1632 tweyne,** *both* **1637 gan, began,** **hir face,** *their faces* **1639 gappe,** *gap* **1641 hereth hym,** *hears it,* **greves,** *brush* **1644 moot,** *must* **1645 outher,** *either* **1646 me myshappe,** *misfortune comes to me* **1647 ferden,** *seemed* **1648 As fer as everich,** *to the extent that each,* **knewe,** *understood* **1649 saluyng,** *greeting*

1600–3 The syntax is strained, but the meaning clear: Arcite threatens Palamon, saying that if Palamon were not love crazed and unarmed, Arcite would never let him leave the grove without killing him. **1638 regne of Trace,** realm of Thrace, an area north of ancient Greece. **1639 gappe,** the space or opening to which the hunted animal is driven.

Everich of hem heelp for to armen oother
As freendly as he were his owene brother,
And after that, with sharpe speres stronge
They foynen° ech at oother wonder longe.
Thou myghtest wene° that this Palamoun   1655
In his fightyng were as a wood leoun°,
And as a crueel tigre was Arcite.
As wilde bores° gonne they to smyte°,
That frothen° whit as foom° for ire wood.
Up to the ancle° foghte they in hir blood.   1660
And in this wise I lete hem fightyng dwelle,
And forth I wole of Theseus yow telle.

    The destinee, ministre general,
That executeth° in the world over al
The purveiaunce° that God hath seyn biforn°,   1665
So strong it is that, though the world had sworn
The contrarie of a thyng by ye or nay,
Yet somtyme it shal fallen on a day
That falleth nat eft° withinne a thousand yeere.
For certeinly, oure appetites° heere,   1670
Be it of werre, or pees, or hate, or love,
Al is this reuled° by the sighte above.

    This mene° I now by myghty Theseus,
That for to hunten is so desirus°,
And namely at° the grete hert° in May,   1675
That in his bed ther daweth° hym no day
That he nys clad°, and redy for to ryde
With hunte° and horn and houndes hym bisyde.
For in his huntyng hath he swich delit
That it is al his joye and appetit   1680
To been hymself the grete hertes bane°,
For after Mars he serveth now Dyane.

    Cleer was the day, as I have toold er this,
And Theseus with alle joye and blis,
With his Ypolita, the faire queene,   1685
And Emelye, clothed al in grene,
On huntyng be they riden roially.
And to the grove that stood ful faste° by,
In which ther was an hert, as men hym tolde,

Duc Theseus the streighte wey hath holde.   1690
And to the launde° he rideth hym ful right,
For thider° was the hert wont° have his flight,
And over a brook, and so forth on his weye.
This duc wol han° a cours° at hym or tweye
With houndes swiche as that hym list
          comaunde°.   1695
    And whan this duc was come unto the launde,
Under° the sonne he looketh, and anon
He was war° of Arcite and Palamon,
That foughten breme° as it were bores two.
The brighte swerdes wenten to and fro   1700
So hidously that with the leeste strook
It semed as it wolde felle an ook.
But what° they were, nothyng he ne woot°.
This duc his courser with his spores° smoot,
And at a stert° he was bitwix hem two,   1705
And pulled out a swerd and cride, "Hoo!
Namoore, up peyne° of lesynge of youre heed!
By myghty Mars, he shal anon be deed
That smyteth any strook that I may seen.
But telleth me what myster° men ye been   1710
That been so hardy for to fighten heere
Withouten juge or oother officere,
As it were in a lystes roially°?"

    This Palamon answerde hastily,
And seyde, "Sire, what nedeth wordes mo?   1715
We have the deeth disserved bothe two.
Two woful wrecches been we, two caytyves°,
That been encombred of° oure owene lyves.
And as thou art a rightful lord and juge,
Ne yeve° us neither mercy ne refuge.   1720
But sle me first, for seinte° charitee!
But sle my felawe eek as wel as me,
Or sle hym first, for though thow knowest it lite°,
This is thy mortal foo, this is Arcite,
That fro thy lond is banysshed on his heed,   1725
For which he hath deserved to be deed.
For this is he that cam unto thy gate

1654 **foynen,** *thrust* 1655 **Thou myghtest wene,** *you might believe* 1656
wood leoun, *mad lion* 1658 **bores,** *boars,* **gonne . . . smyte,** *did they
strike* 1659 **frothen,** *slather,* **foom,** *foam* 1660 **ancle,** *ankle* 1664 **exe-
cuteth,** *brings about* 1665 **purveiaunce,** *providence,* **seyn biforn,** *foreseen* 1669 **eft,** *again* 1670 **appetites,** *desires* 1672 **reuled,** *ruled* 1673
mene, *mean* 1674 **so desirus,** *full of desire* 1675 **namely at,** *especially
for,* **grete hert,** *stag* 1676 **daweth,** *dawns* 1677 **nys clad,** *isn't dressed*
1678 **hunte,** *huntsman,* 1681 **bane,** *slayer* 1688 **faste,** *near* 1691

launde, *clearing* 1692 **thider,** *there,* **wont,** *accustomed to* 1694 **wol han,**
would have, **cours,** *chase* 1695 **houndes . . . comaunde,** *hounds he selected for each chase* 1697 **Under,** *toward* 1698 **war,** *aware* 1699 **breme,**
fiercely 1703 **what,** *what (kind of men),* **woot,** *knew* 1704 **spores,** *spurs*
1705 **at a stert,** *in a leap* 1707 **up peyne,** *upon threat* 1710 **myster,** *kind
of* 1713 **lystes roially,** *royal tournament* 1717 **caytyves,** *wretches* 1718
encombred of, *burdened with* 1720 **Ne yeve,** *do not give* 1721 **seinte,**
holy 1723 **lite,** *little*

1652 **owene brother,** it is ironic that the two are indeed sworn brothers. 1663 **destinee, ministre general . . . ,** destiny, the general minister
of Providence (**purveiaunce,** line 1665) or divine foresight (**seyn biforn,** line 1665), is the enactment in time of what Providence perceives
from its supratemporal, omniscient vantage; from *Bo* 4.pr6.108ff. 1673 **This mene I now by myghty Theseus . . . ,** the statement associates
Theseus with divine foresight. Also, his desire to hunt is equated with the human "appetites" of line 1670. 1682 **Mars . . . Dyane,** god of war,
goddess of hunting. 1698 **He was war,** in the *Teseida* 5.80, it is Emily who finds the knights fighting.

And seyde that he highte° Philostrate.
Thus hath he japed° thee ful many a yer,
And thou hast maked hym thy chief squier.   1730
And this is he that loveth Emelye.
For sith° the day is come that I shal dye,
I make pleynly my confessioun
That I am thilke° woful Palamoun
That hath thy prisoun broken wikkedly.   1735
I am thy mortal foo, and it am I
That loveth so hoote° Emelye the brighte
That I wol dye present in hir sighte.
Wherfore I axe° deeth and my juwise°;
But sle my felawe in the same wise°,   1740
For bothe han° we deserved to be slayn."
    This worthy duc answerde anon agayn,
And seyde, "This is a short conclusioun.
Youre owene mouth, by youre confessioun,
Hath dampned° yow, and I wol it recorde°.   1745
It nedeth noght to pyne° yow with the corde°.
Ye shal be deed, by myghty Mars the rede!"
    The queene anon, for verray wommanhede°,
Gan for to wepe, and so dide Emelye,
And alle the ladyes in the compaignye.   1750
Greet pitee was it, as it thoughte hem alle°,
That evere swich a chaunce sholde falle°,
For gentil men they were of greet estaat,
And no thyng but for love was this debaat°;
And saugh hir blody woundes wyde and
        soore,   1755
And alle crieden, bothe lasse and moore°,
"Have mercy, Lord, upon us wommen alle!"
And on hir bare knees adoun they falle,
And wolde have kist his feet ther as he stood,
Til at the laste aslaked° was his mood,   1760
For pitee renneth soone in gentil herte.
And though he first for ire quook° and sterte°,
He hath considered shortly, in a clause°,
The trespas of hem bothe, and eek the cause,

And although that his ire hir gilt° accused,   1765
Yet in his resoun he hem bothe excused,
As thus: he thoghte wel that every man
Wol helpe hymself in love, if that he kan,
And eek delivere hymself out of prisoun.
And eek his herte hadde compassioun   1770
Of wommen, for they wepen evere in oon°,
And in his gentil herte he thoughte anon,
And softe unto hymself he seyde, "Fy°
Upon a lord that wol have no mercy,
But been a leon, bothe in word and dede,   1775
To hem that been in repentaunce and drede,
As well as to a proud, despitous° man
That wol mayntene that° he first bigan.
That lord hath litel of discrecioun,
That in swich cas° kan no divisioun°,   1780
But weyeth° pride and humblesse after oon°."
And shortly, whan his ire is thus agoon°,
He gan to looken up with eyen lighte,
And spak thise same wordes al on highte°:
    "The god of love, a, benedicite°!   1785
How myghty and how greet a lord is he!
Ayeyns° his myght ther gayneth none obstacles°.
He may be cleped° a god for his myracles,
For he kan maken, at his owene gyse°,
Of everich° herte as that hym list divyse°.   1790
Lo heere this Arcite and this Palamoun,
That quitly° weren out of my prisoun,
And myghte han lyved in Thebes roially,
And witen° I am hir mortal enemy,
And that hir deth lith in my myght also,   1795
And yet hath love, maugree hir eyen° two,
Broght hem hyder bothe for to dye.
Now looketh, is nat that an heigh folye?
    "Who may been a fool but if° he love?
Bihoold, for Goddes sake that sit° above,   1800
Se how they blede! Be they noght wel arrayed°?
Thus hath hir lord, the god of love, ypayed°

1728 **highte,** *is named* 1729 **japed,** *fooled* 1732 **sith,** *since* 1734 **thilke,** *that* 1737 **hoote,** *passionately* 1739 **axe,** *ask,* **juwise,** *sentence* 1740 **wise,** *way* 1741 **han,** *have* 1745 **dampned,** *condemned,* **recorde,** *confirm* 1746 **pyne,** *torture,* **corde,** *rope* 1748 **verray wommanhede,** *true womanhood* 1751 **it thoughte hem alle,** *it seemed to them all* 1752 **falle,** *occur* 1754 **debaat,** *battle* 1756 **lasse and moore,** *lesser and greater* (in rank) 1760 **aslaked,** *diminished* 1762 **for ire quook,** *quaked in anger,* **sterte,** *trembled* 1763 **clause,** *moment* 1765 **hir gilt,** *their guilt* 1771 **evere in oon,** *continuously* 1773 **Fy,** *shame* 1777 **despitous,** *scornful* 1778

mayntene that, *persist in what* 1780 **swich cas,** *such situations,* **kan no divisioun,** *recognizes no distinctions* 1781 **weyeth,** *weighs,* **after oon,** *the same* 1782 **agoon,** *gone* 1784 **on highte,** *aloud* 1785 **a, benedicite,** *ah, bless us* 1787 **Ayeyns,** *against,* **ther gayneth none obstacles,** *no barriers are effective* 1788 **cleped,** *called* 1789 **gyse,** *inclination* 1790 **everich,** *each,* **as that hym list divyse,** *whatever it pleases him to create* 1792 **quitly,** *freely* 1794 **witen,** *know* 1796 **maugree hir eyen,** *despite their eyes* 1799 **but if,** *unless* 1800 **sit,** *sits* 1801 **arrayed,** *adorned* 1802 **ypayed,** *paid*

1745 Hath dampned yon, the knights are not condemned in the *Teseida,* so the queen and her ladies have no cause to intercede. Scholars have suggested that actual intercessions by either Queen Philippa or Queen Anne inspired Chaucer's scene, although he may have invented it to parallel the weeping of the Theban women, lines 900ff. above. **1761** The statement recurs in *MLT* 2.660, *MerT* 4.1986, *SqT* 5.479, *TC* 3.5, and *LGW* F503, with parallels in a number of classical and medieval sources. **1785ff.** A familiar medieval sentiment, although not in the *Teseida* at this point; compare *RR* 4221ff. **1796 maugree hir eyen two,** an idiom meaning despite their wishes or actions.

Hir° wages and hir fees for hir servyse!
And yet they wenen° for to been ful wyse
That serven love, for aught that may bifalle°. 1805
But this is yet the beste game of alle,
That she for whom they han this jolitee°
Kan hem therfore° as muche thank° as me.
She woot° namoore of al this hoote fare°,
By God, than woot a cokkow° or an hare! 1810
But all moot ben assayed°, hoot and coold.
A man moot ben a fool, or° yong or oold—
I woot it by myself ful yore agon°,
For in my tyme a servant was I oon°.
And therfore, syn I knowe of loves peyne, 1815
And woot hou soore it kan a man distreyne°,
As he that hath ben caught ofte in his laas°,
I yow foryeve al hoolly this trespaas,
At requeste of the queene, that kneleth heere,
And eek of Emelye, my suster deere. 1820
And ye shul bothe anon unto me swere
That nevere mo ye shal my contree dere°,
Ne make werre upon me nyght ne day,
But been my freendes in al that ye may.
I yow foryeve this trespas every deel°." 1825
And they hym sworen his axyng° faire and weel,
And hym of lordshipe and of mercy preyde,
And he hem graunteth grace°, and thus he seyde,
    "To speke of roial lynage° and richesse,
Though that she were a queene or a
        princesse, 1830
Ech of you bothe is worthy, doutelees,
To wedden whan tyme is, but nathelees°—
I speke as for my suster Emelye,
For whom ye have this strif and jalousye—
Ye woot yourself she may nat wedden two 1835
Atones°, though ye fighten everemo.
That oon of you, al be hym looth or lief°,
He moot go pipen° in an yvy leef.
This is to seyn, she may nat now han bothe,
Al be ye never° so jalouse ne so wrothe°. 1840

And forthy° I yow putte in this degree°,
That ech of yow shal have his destynee
As hym is shape°, and herkneth° in what wyse°:
Lo heere youre ende of that° I shal devyse.
    "My wyl is this, for plat° conclusioun, 1845
Withouten any repplicacioun°—
If that you liketh, take it for the beste:
That everich° of you shal goon where hym leste°
Frely, withouten raunson or daunger,
And this day fifty wykes fer ne ner°, 1850
Everich of you shal brynge an hundred knyghtes
Armed for lystes° up at alle rightes°,
Al redy to darreyne hire° by bataille.
And this bihote° I yow withouten faille,
Upon my trouthe, and as I am a knyght, 1855
That wheither° of yow bothe that hath myght—
This is to seyn, that wheither he or thow
May with his hundred, as I spak of now,
Sleen his contrarie, or out of lystes dryve,
Thanne shal I yeve Emelya to wyve° 1860
To whom that Fortune yeveth° so fair a grace.
The lystes shal I maken in this place.
And God so wisly on my soule rewe°,
As I shal evene° juge been and trewe,
Ye shul noon oother ende° with me maken 1865
That oon of yow ne shal be deed or taken.
And if yow thynketh this is weel ysayd°,
Seyeth youre avys° and holdeth you apayd°.
This is youre ende and youre conclusioun."
    Who looketh lightly° now but Palamoun? 1870
Who spryngeth up for joye but Arcite?
Who kouthe° telle, or who kouthe endite°
The joye that is maked in the place
Whan Theseus hath doon so fair a grace?
But doun on knees wente every maner
        wight°, 1875
And thonken hym with al hir herte and myght,
And namely the Thebans often sithe°.
And thus with good hope and with herte blithe

1803 **Hir,** *their* 1804 **wenen,** *think* (themselves) 1805 **for aught that may bifalle,** *whatever happens* 1807 **jolitee,** *passion* 1808 **Kan hem therfore,** *gives them for it,* **thank,** *thanks* 1809 **woot,** *knows,* **hoote fare,** *hot business* 1810 **cokkow,** *cuckoo* 1811 **moot ben assayed,** *must be tested* 1812 **or . . . or,** *either . . . or* 1813 **yore agon,** *long ago* 1814 **oon,** *one* (a servant of love) 1816 **distreyne,** *afflict* 1817 **laas,** *net* 1822 **dere,** *harm* 1825 **deel,** *part* 1826 **axyng,** *request* 1828 **grace,** *favor* 1829 **lynage,** *lineage* 1832 **nathelees,** *nonetheless* 1836 **Atones,** *at the same time* 1837 **al be hym looth or lief,** *whether he likes it or not* 1838 **moot go pipen,** *may go whistle* 1840 **Al be ye never,** *even if you weren't,* **wrothe,** *angry* 1841 **forthy,** *therefore,* **degree,** *position* 1843 **shape,** *foreordained,* **herkneth,** *listen,* **wyse,** *way* 1844 **ende of that,** *outcome from what* 1845 **plat,** *plain* 1846 **Withouten any repplicacioun,** *allowing no argument* 1848 **everich,** *each,* **hym leste,** *he wishes* 1850 **wykes fer ne ner,** *weeks more or less* 1852 **lystes,** *battle,* **up at alle rightes,** *in all respects* 1853 **darreyne hire,** *lay claim to her* 1854 **bihote,** *promise* 1856 **wheither,** *whichever* 1860 **to wyve,** *as wife* 1861 **yeveth,** *gives* 1863 **rewe,** *have pity* 1864 **evene,** *impartial* 1865 **ende,** *conclusion* 1867 **weel ysayd,** *well said* 1868 **avys,** *agreement,* **holdeth you apayd,** *consider yourself satisfied* 1870 **lightly,** *delighted* 1872 **kouthe,** *is able to,* **endite,** *write* 1875 **maner wight,** *kind of person* 1877 **sithe,** *times*

1850 **fifty wykes fer ne ner,** apparently a poetic expression for a full year.

They taken hir leve, and homward gonne they
    ride
To Thebes, with his olde walles wyde.   1880

Explicit secunda pars. Sequitur pars tercia.

    I trowe° men wolde deme° it necligence
If I foryete° to tellen the dispence°
Of Theseus, that gooth so bisily
To maken up the lystes roially,
That swich° a noble theatre as it was,   1885
I dar wel seyn in this world ther nas.
The circuit a myle was aboute,
Walled of stoon, and dyched al withoute°.
Round was the shape, in manere of
    compas°,
Ful of degrees°, the heighte of sixty pas°,   1890
That whan a man was set on o degree,
He lette nat° his felawe for to see.
    Estward ther stood a gate of marbul whit,
Westward right swich another in the opposit.
And shortly to concluden, swich a place   1895
Was noon in erthe, as in so litel space.
For in the lond ther was no crafty° man
That geometrie or ars-metrik kan°,
Ne portreitour°, ne kervere° of ymages,
That Theseus ne yaf mete° and wages,   1900
The theatre for to maken and devyse°.
And for to doon his ryte° and sacrifise,
He estward hath, upon the gate above,
In worshipe of Venus, goddesse of love,
Doon make an auter° and an oratorie°.   1905
And on the gate westward, in memorie
Of Mars, he maked hath right swich another,
That coste largely° of gold a fother°.

And northward, in a touret° on the wal,
Of alabastre whit and reed coral,   1910
An oratorie, riche for to see,
In worshipe of Dyane of chastitee°,
Hath Theseus doon wroght° in noble wyse°.
    But yet hadde I foryeten to devyse
The noble kervyng and the portreitures,   1915
The shape, the contenaunce°, and the
    figures,
That weren in thise oratories thre.
    First in the temple of Venus maystow se°
Wroght on the wal, ful pitous to biholde,
The broken slepes and the sikes° colde,   1920
The sacred teeris and the waymentynge°,
The firy strokes of the desirynge
That loves servantz in this lyf enduren,
The othes° that hir covenantz° assuren;
Plesaunce° and Hope, Desir, Foolhardynesse,   1925
Beautee and Youthe, Bauderie°, Richesse,
Charmes and Force, Lesynges°, Flaterye,
Despense°, Bisynesse°, and Jalousye
That wered° of yelewe gooldes° a gerland
And a cokkow° sittynge on hir hand;   1930
Festes°, instrumentz, caroles, daunces,
Lust° and array°, and alle the circumstaunces
Of love, whiche that I rekned° and rekne shal
By ordre, weren peynted on the wal,
And mo than I kan make of mencioun.   1935
For soothly° al the mount of Citheroun,
Ther° Venus hath hir principal dwellynge,
Was shewed on the wal in portreyynge,
With al the gardyn and the lustynesse.
Nat was foryeten° the porter, Ydelnesse,   1940
Ne Narcisus the faire of yore agon°,

1881 trowe, *believe,* **deme,** *judge* **1882 foryete,** *forget,* **dispence,** *expenditure* **1885 That swich,** *so that such* **1888 dyched al withoute,** *ditched all around* **1889 in manere of compas,** *circular* **1890 degrees,** *steps,* **pas,** *paces* **1892 lette nat,** *didn't hinder* **1897 crafty,** *skilled* **1898 ars-metrik kan,** *arithmetic knows* **1899 portreitour,** *painter,* **kervere,** *sculptor* **1900 yaf mete,** *gave food* **1901 devyse,** *design* **1902 ryte,** *rites* **1905 Doon make an auter,** *had an altar made,* **oratorie,** *place for praying* **1908 largely,** *nearly,* **fother,** *load* **1909 touret,** *small tower* **1912 of chastitee,** *the chaste* **1913 doon wroght,** *had made,* **wyse,** *fashion* **1916 contenaunce,** *appearance* **1918 maystow se,** *you can see* **1920 sikes,** *sighs* **1921 waymentynge,** *lamenting* **1924 othes,** *oaths,* **hir covenantz,** *their promises* **1925 Plesaunce,** *Pleasure* **1926 Bauderie,** *Pimping* **1927 Lesynges,** *Lies* **1928 Despence,** *Expenditure,* **Bisynesse,** *Preoccupation* **1929 wered,** *wore,* **yelewe gooldes,** *yellow marigolds* **1930 cokkow,** *cuckoo* **1931 Festes,** *festivities* **1932 Lust,** *desire,* **array,** *clothing* **1933 rekned,** *counted* **1936 soothly,** *truly* **1937 Ther,** *where* **1940 foryeten,** *forgotten* **1941 of yore agon,** *from long ago*

1880a Explicit secunda pars. Sequitur pars tercia. "Here ends part two. Here follows part three." **1885 noble theatre,** Chaucer's description of the arena differs somewhat from Boccaccio's in *Teseida.* Most important, it is built especially for the battle, and in attaching the temples to the arena and equalizing the descriptions, Chaucer communicates a greater sense of unity and symmetry. Venus, Mars, and Diana are the deities of love, war, and chastity and hunting, respectively. **1918 temple of Venus,** the description is modeled on *Teseida* 7.53ff., although in this description and those of the temples of Mars and Diana below, Chaucer creates a sense of immediacy by direct address to the reader and by depicting the first-person narrator as present in the temples, a break in literary decorum. Chaucer also describes the temple of Venus in *HF* 119–39 and *PF* 211–94 (a close translation). **1928–29 Jalousye . . . ,** yellow is the traditional color of jealousy, and the cuckoo symbolizes adultery. **1936 mount of Citheroun,** the mountain of Cithaeron was often conflated with the island Cythera, where Venus rose from the sea. **1941 Narcisus,** the mythical Narcissus fell in love with his own reflection.

Ne yet the folye° of Kyng Salamon,
Ne yet the grete strengthe of Ercules,
Th'enchauntementz of Medea and Circes,
Ne of Turnus, with the hardy fiers corage, 1945
The riche Cresus, kaytyf in servage°.
Thus may ye seen that wysdom ne richesse,
Beautee ne sleighte°, strengthe ne hardynesse,
Ne may with Venus holde champartie°,
For as hir list° the world than° may she gye°. 1950
Lo, alle thise folk so caught were in hir las°,
Til they for wo ful ofte seyde allas.
Suffiseth heere ensamples oon or two,
And though I koude rekene° a thousand mo.

The statue of Venus, glorious for to se, 1955
Was naked, fletynge° in the large see,
And fro the navele doun al covered was
With wawes° grene, and brighte as any glas.
A citole° in hir right hand hadde she,
And on hir heed, ful semely for to se, 1960
A rose gerland, fressh and wel smellynge;
Above hir heed hir dowves flikerynge°.
Biforn hire stood hir sone Cupido;
Upon his shuldres wynges hadde he two,
And blynd he was, as it is often seene; 1965
A bowe he bar and arwes brighte and kene.

Why sholde I noght as wel eek telle yow al
The portreiture that was upon the wal
Withinne the temple of myghty Mars the rede?
Al peynted was the wal, in lengthe and brede°, 1970
Lyk to the estres° of the grisly place
That highte° the grete temple of Mars in Trace,
In thilke° colde, frosty regioun
Ther as Mars hath his sovereyn mansioun°.

First on the wal was peynted a forest, 1975

In which ther dwelleth neither man ne best,
With knotty, knarry°, bareyne° trees olde,
Of stubbes° sharpe and hidouse to biholde,
In which ther ran a rumbel and a swough°,
As though a storm sholde bresten° every
  bough. 1980
And dounward from an hille, under a bente°,
Ther stood the temple of Mars armypotente°,
Wroght al of burned° steel, of which the entree°
Was long and streit° and gastly for to see.
And therout cam a rage° and swich a veze° 1985
That it made al the gate for to rese°.
The northren lyght in at the dores shoon,
For wyndowe on the wal ne was ther noon,
Thurgh which men myghten any light discerne.
The dore was al of adamant° eterne, 1990
Yclenched° overthwart and endelong°
With iren tough; and for to make it strong,
Every pyler°, the temple to sustene°,
Was tonne-greet°, of iren bright and shene.

Ther saugh° I first the dirke ymaginyng° 1995
Of Felonye, and al the compassyng°,
The crueel Ire°, reed as any gleede°;
The pykepurs°, and eek the pale Drede;
The smylere° with the knyfe under the cloke;
The shepne brennynge° with the blake
  smoke; 2000
The tresoun of the mordrynge in the bedde;
The open werre°, with woundes al bibledde°;
Contek°, with blody knyf and sharp manace°.
Al ful of chirkyng° was that sory place.

The sleere° of hymself yet saugh I ther— 2005
His herte-blood hath bathed al his heer°;
The nayl ydryven in the shode a-nyght°;

1942 **folye,** *folly* 1946 **kaytyf in servage,** *wretched in captivity* 1948 **sleighte,** *trickery* 1949 **holde champartie,** *compete successfully* 1950 **hir list,** *she desires,* **than,** *so,* **gye,** *rule* 1951 **las,** *snare* 1954 **rekene,** *tally* 1956 **fletynge,** *floating* 1958 **wawes,** *waves* 1959 **citole,** *stringed instrument* 1962 **dowves flikerynge,** *doves fluttering* 1970 **brede,** *breadth* 1971 **estres,** *interior* 1972 **highte,** *is called,* **Trace,** *Thrace* 1973 **thilke,** *that same* 1974 **sovereyn mansioun,** *highest dwelling* 1977 **knarry,** *gnarled,* **bareyne,** *barren* 1978 **stubbes,** *stumps* 1979 **swough,** *sound of wind* 1980 **bresten** *break* 1981 **under a bente,** *near an open field* 1982 **armypotente,** *potent in arms* 1983 **burned,** *polished,* **entree,** *entrance*

1984 **streit,** *narrow* 1985 **rage,** *roar,* **veze,** *blast* 1986 **rese,** *shake* 1990 **adamant,** *indestructible stone* 1991 **Yclenched,** *bound,* **overthwart and endelong,** *horizontally and vertically* 1993 **pyler,** *pillar,* **sustene,** *support* 1994 **tonne-greet,** *big around as a barrel* 1995 **saugh,** *saw,* **dirke imaginyng,** *dark plans* 1996 **compassyng,** *plotting* 1997 **Ire,** *Anger,* **gleede,** *glowing coal* 1998 **pykepurs,** *pickpocket* 1999 **smylere,** *smiler* 2000 **shepne brennynge,** *barn burning* 2002 **werre,** *war,* **bibledde,** *bloodied* 2003 **Contek,** *strife,* **manace,** *menace* 2004 **chirkyng,** *creaking* 2005 **sleere,** *slayer* 2006 **heer,** *hair* 2007 **shode a-nyght,** *head at night*

1942 **Salamon,** King Solomon had many wives, loves, and concubines who turned his heart from God; 1 Kings 11. 1943 **Ercules,** despite his great strength, Hercules was killed through the love and jealousy of his wife, Deianira; see *MkT* 7.2119ff. 1944 **Medea and Circes,** classical sorceresses who used magic on their lovers. 1945 **Turnus,** killed by Aeneas, his opponent in love; *Aeneid* 12. 1946 **Cresus,** Croesus, king of Lydia, was not known as a lover but was imprisoned after being defeated by Cyrus; see *MkT* 7.2727ff. 1956 **fletynge,** the traditional figure of Venus rising from the sea; doves and the citole are also familiar icons of Venus. 1963 **Cupido,** son of Venus, Cupid was the blind (or blindfold) winged god whose arrows strike lovers. 1969 **temple . . . of Mars,** modeled on *Teseida* 7.30ff., preceding the temple of Venus. 1987 **northren lyght,** light coming in from the north indicates that the temple is oriented toward the north, away from the sun, whereas most temples point east. 2007 Scholars note similarities with Jael's killing of Sisera in Judges 4.21; see *WBP* 3.769.

The colde deeth, with mouth gapyng upright.
Amyddes° of the temple sat Meschaunce°,
With disconfort and sory contenaunce.   2010
 Yet saugh I Woodnesse°, laughynge in his rage,
Armed Compleint, Outhees°, and fiers° Outrage;
The careyne° in the busk°, with throte ycorve°;
A thousand slayn, and nat of qualm ystorve°;
The tiraunt, with the pray° by force yraft°;   2015
The toun destroyed, ther was nothyng laft.
 Yet saugh I brent° the shippes hoppesteres°;
The hunte° strangled with° the wilde beres;
The sowe freten° the child right in the cradel;
The cook yscalded, for al° his longe ladel°.   2020
 Noght° was foryeten° by the infortune° of Marte
The cartere overryden with° his carte—
Under the wheel ful lowe he lay adoun.
 Ther were also, of Martes divisioun°,
The barbour, and the bocher°, and the smyth,   2025
That forgeth sharpe swerdes on his styth°.
 And al above, depeynted° in a tour°,
Saugh I Conquest, sittynge in greet honour,
With the sharpe swerd over his heed
Hangynge by a soutil twynes threed°.   2030
 Depeynted was the slaughtre of Julius,
Of grete Nero, and of Antonius—
Al be° that thilke° tyme they were unborn,
Yet was hir deth depeynted ther-biforn°
By manasynge° of Mars, right by figure°.   2035
So was it shewed° in that portreiture
As is depeynted in the sterres above
Who shal be slayn or elles deed for love.
Suffiseth oon ensample° in stories olde;
I may nat rekene hem alle though I wolde.   2040
 The statue of Mars upon a carte° stood

Armed, and looked grym as he were wood°,
And over his heed ther shynen° two figures
Of sterres°, that been cleped° in scriptures°
That oon Puella, that oother Rubeus.   2045
This god of armes was arrayed thus.
A wolf ther stood biforn hym at his feet
With eyen rede, and of a man he eet°.
With soutil° pencel was depeynt this storie
In redoutynge° of Mars and of his glorie.   2050
 Now to the temple of Dyane the chaste
As shortly as I kan I wol me haste,
To telle yow al the descripsioun.
Depeynted been the walles up and doun
Of huntyng and of shamefast° chastitee.   2055
 Ther saugh I how woful Calistopee,
Whan that Diane agreved was° with here,
Was turned from a womman til a bere°,
And after was she maad the loode-sterre°,
Thus was it peynted, I kan sey yow no ferre°.   2060
Hir sone is eek° a sterre, as men may see.
 Ther saugh I Dane, yturned til a tree—
I mene nat the goddesse Diane,
But Penneus doghter, which that highte° Dane.
 Ther saugh I Attheon an hert° ymaked,   2065
For vengeaunce that he saugh Diane al naked.
I saugh how that his houndes have hym caught
And freeten° hym, for that they knewe hym
    naught.
 Yet peynted was a litel forther moor°
How Atthalante hunted the wilde boor,   2070
And Meleagre, and many another mo,
For which Dyane wroghte hym care and wo.
Ther saugh I many another wonder storie,
The whiche me list nat° drawen to memorie.

2009 Amyddes, *in the middle,* **Meschaunce,** *Mischance* **2011 Wood-nesse,** *Madness* **2012 Outhees,** *Outcry,* **fiers,** *fierce* **2013 careyne,** *corpse,* **busk,** *bush,* **throte ycorve,** *throat cut* **2014 of qualm ystorve,** *by plague killed* **2015 pray,** *prey,* **yraft,** *taken* **2017 brent,** *burned,* **hoppesteres,** *dancing* **2018 hunte,** *hunter,* **strangled with,** *killed by* **2019 freten,** *eat* **2020 for al,** *despite,* **ladel,** *ladle* **2021 Noght,** *nor,* **foryeten,** *neglected,* **infortune,** *evil influence* **2022 overryden with,** *run over by* **2024 Martes divisioun,** *Mars's numbers* **2025 bocher,** *butcher* **2026 styth,** *anvil* **2027 depeynted,** *depicted,* **tour,** *tower* **2030 soutil twynes threed,** *thin thread*

of twine **2033 Al be,** *although,* **thilke,** *at that time* **2034 ther-biforn,** *before then* **2035 manasynge,** *menacing,* **right by figure,** *precisely in figures* **2036 shewed,** *shown* **2039 ensample,** *example* **2041 carte,** *chariot* **2042 wood,** *insane* **2043 shynen,** *shine* **2044 sterres,** *stars,* **cleped,** *called,* **scriptures,** *writings* **2048 eet,** *ate* **2049 soutil,** *subtle* **2050 redoutynge,** *honor* **2055 shamefast,** *modest* **2057 agreved was,** *was upset* **2058 til a bere,** *to a bear* **2059 loode-sterre,** *lodestar* (see note) **2060 ferre,** *further* **2061 eek,** *also* **2064 highte,** *is called* **2065 hert,** *stag* **2068 freeten,** *eaten* **2069 forther moor,** *further on* **2074 me list nat,** *I prefer not* (to)

2017 shippes hoppesteres, apparently a misunderstanding of "navi ballatrici" (dancing ships) for *Teseida* 7.37 "navi bellatrici" (fighting ships). **2031–32** Chaucer recounts the violent deaths of **Julius** (Caesar) in *MkT* 7.2695ff., **Nero** in *MkT* 7.2519ff, and Marc Antony (**Antonius**) in *LGW* 624ff. **2045 oon Puella . . . other Rubeus,** names for figures in geomancy, a form of divination that predicts the future by interpreting dots and lines thought to indicate astrological patterns. **2051 temple of Dyane,** there is no similar description in *Teseida;* Chaucer adds it for balance. **2056ff. Calistopee . . . ,** Callisto was transformed by Diana into the constellation of the Great Bear (Ursa Major) for surrendering her virginity to Jupiter; her son, Arcas, became the Lesser Bear (Ursa Minor). **2059 loode-sterre,** also known as the polestar or North Star, the lodestar is a single star in Ursa Minor, so there is some confusion in Chaucer's account. **2062 Dane,** Daphne was transformed by her father, Peneus (**Penneus,** line 2064), into a laurel tree to save her from Apollo. **2065 Attheon,** because he saw Diana naked, Acteon was transformed into a stag and killed by his own hounds. **2070–71 Atthalante . . . Meleagre,** Meleager killed the Caledonian boar, first wounded by Atalanta; the beast was sent by Diana.

This goddesse on an hert ful hye seet°,   2075
With smale houndes al aboute hir feet,
And undernethe hir feet she hadde a moone,
Wexynge° it was and sholde wanye° soone.
In gaude° grene hir statue clothed was,
With bowe in honde and arwes in a cas.   2080
Hir eyen caste she ful lowe adoun,
Ther° Pluto hath his derke regioun.

A womman travaillynge° was hire biforn;
But for° hir child so longe was unborn,
Ful pitously Lucyna gan she calle,   2085
And seyde, "Help, for thou mayst best of alle!"
Wel koude he peynten lifly° that it wroghte°;
With many a floryn° he the hewes° boghte.

Now been thise lystes maad°, and Theseus,
That at his grete cost arrayed thus   2090
The temples and the theatre every deel°,
Whan it was doon, hym lyked wonder weel.
But stynte° I wole of Theseus a lite,
And speke of Palamon and of Arcite.

The day approcheth of hir retournynge,   2095
That everich sholde an hundred knyghtes brynge
The bataille to darreyne°, as I yow tolde.
And til Atthenes, hir covenantz° for to holde,
Hath everich of hem broght an hundred
        knyghtes,
Wel armed for the werre at alle rightes°.   2100
And sikerly° ther trowed° many a man
That nevere sithen° that the world bigan,
As for to speke of knyghthod of hir hond°,
As fer° as God hath maked see or lond,
Nas° of so fewe so noble a compaignye.   2105
For every wight that lovede chivalrye,
And wolde, his thankes°, han° a passant° name,
Hath preyed that he myghte been of that game°;
And wel° was hym that therto chosen was.
For if ther fille° tomorwe swich a cas°,   2110
Ye knowen wel that every lusty knyght
That loveth paramours° and hath his myght,

Were it in Engelond or elleswhere,
They wolde, hir thankes, wilnen° to be there—
To fighte for a lady, benedicitee°!   2115
It were a lusty° sighte for to see.

And right so ferden° they with Palamon.
With hym ther wenten knyghtes many on°;
Som wol ben armed in an haubergeoun°,
And in a bristplate and a light gypoun°,   2120
And somme woln° have a paire plates° large;
And somme woln have a Pruce° sheeld or a targe°;
Somme woln ben armed on hir legges weel,
And have an ax, and somme a mace° of steel—
Ther is no newe gyse° that it nas old.   2125
Armed were they, as I have yow told,
Everych after his opinioun.

Ther maistow° seen comynge with Palamoun
Lygurge hymself, the grete kyng of Trace.
Blak was his berd and manly was his face;   2130
The cercles of his eyen in his heed,
They gloweden bitwixen yelow and reed,
And lik a grifphon° looked he aboute,
With kempe heeris° on his browes stoute°,
His lymes grete°, his brawnes° harde and
        stronge,   2135
His shuldres brode, his armes rounde and longe.
And as the gyse was in his contree,
Ful hye upon a chaar° of gold stood he,
With foure white boles° in the trays°.
Instede of cote-armure° over his harnays°,   2140
With nayles yelewe° and brighte as any gold,
He hadde a beres skyn°, col-blak for old°.
His longe heer was kembd° bihynde his bak—
As any ravenes fethere it shoon for blak;
A wrethe of gold, arm-greet°, of huge
        wighte°,   2145
Upon his heed, set ful of stones brighte,
Of fyne rubyes and of dyamauntz.
Aboute his chaar ther wenten white alauntz°,
Twenty and mo, as grete as any steer,

2075 **ful hye seet,** *sat very high* 2078 **Wexynge,** *waxing,* **wanye,** *wane* 2079 **gaude,** *yellowish* 2082 **Ther,** *where* 2083 **travaillynge,** *in labor* 2084 **for,** *because* 2087 **lifly,** *lifelike,* **wroghte,** *created* 2088 **floryn,** *coin,* **hewes, paints** 2089 **maad,** *made* 2091 **deel,** *part* 2093 **stynte,** *cease* 2097 **darreyne,** *decide* 2098 **covenantz,** *pledges* 2100 **at alle rightes,** *in all ways* 2101 **sikerly,** *surely,* **trowed,** *thought* 2102 **sithen,** *since* 2103 **knyghthod of hir hond,** *their knightly ability* 2104 **fer,** *far* 2105 **Nas** (there) *wasn't* 2107 **his thankes,** *willingly,* **han,** *have,* **passant,** *outstanding* 2108 **game, contest** 2109 **wel,** *happy* 2110 **fille,** *happened,* **cas,** *event* 2112 **paramours,** *passionately* 2114 **wilnen,** *crave* 2115 **benedicitee,** *bless us* 2116

lusty, *pleasurable* 2117 **ferden,** *did* 2118 **many on,** *many* 2119 **haubergeoun,** *mail armor* 2120 **gypoun,** *tunic* 2121 **woln,** *will,* **paire plates, plate armor** 2122 **Pruce,** *Prussian,* **targe,** *light shield* 2124 **mace,** *war club* 2125 **gyse,** *fashion* 2128 **maistow,** *you may* 2133 **grifphon,** *griffin* 2134 **kempe heeris,** *shaggy hair,* **stoute,** *strong* 2135 **lymes grete,** *large limbs,* **brawnes,** *muscles* 2138 **chaar,** *chariot* 2139 **boles,** *bulls,* **trays,** *harness* 2140 **cote-armure,** *coat of arms,* **harnays,** *armor* 2141 **nayles yelewe, claws yellow** 2142 **beres skyn,** *bearskin,* **for old,** *from age* 2143 **kembd, combed** 2145 **arm-greet,** *thick as an arm,* **wighte,** *weight* 2148 **alauntz, wolfhounds**

2075–77 **goddesse on an hert . . . moone,** the stag and the moon are typical icons of Diana. 2082 **Pluto,** classical god of the underworld. 2085 **Lucyna,** Lucina is another name for Diana in her manifestation as goddess of childbirth. 2129 **Lygurge,** Lycurgus of Nemea is mentioned in *Teseida* 6.14, although Chaucer conflates him with Lycurgus of Thrace and associates him with Saturn.

To hunten at the leoun or the deer,   2150
And folwed hym with mosel° faste ybounde,
Colered of° gold, and tourettes fyled rounde°.
An hundred lordes hadde he in his route°,
Armed ful wel, with hertes stierne° and stoute.

    With Arcite, in stories as men fynde,   2155
The grete Emetreus, the kyng of Inde,
Upon a steede bay° trapped in° steel,
Covered in clooth of gold, dyapred weel°,
Cam ridynge lyk the god of armes, Mars.
His cote-armure was of clooth of Tars   2160
Couched° with perles white and rounde and grete;
His sadel was of brend° gold newe ybete°;
A mantel° upon his shulder hangynge,
Bratful° of rubyes rede as fyr sparklynge;
His crispe heer° lyk rynges was yronne°,   2165
And that was yelow, and glytered as the sonne.
His nose was heigh°, his eyen bright citryn°,
His lippes rounde, his colour was sangwyn°;
A fewe frakenes° in his face yspreynd°,
Bitwixen yelow and somdel° blak ymeynd°;   2170
And as a leoun he his lookyng caste°.
Of fyve and twenty yeer his age I caste°.
His berd was wel bigonne for to sprynge;
His voys was as a trompe° thonderynge.
Upon his heed he wered° of laurer° grene   2175
A gerland, fressh and lusty° for to sene.
Upon his hand he bar for his deduyt°
An egle tame, as any lilye whyt.
An hundred lordes hadde he with hym there,
Al armed, save hir heddes, in al hir gere,   2180
Ful richely in alle maner thynges.
For trusteth wel that dukes, erles, kynges
Were gadered° in this noble compaignye,
For love and for encrees° of chivalrye.

Aboute this kyng ther ran on every part°   2185
Ful many a tame leoun and leopart.
And in this wise thise lordes, alle and some,
Been on the Sonday to the citee come
Aboute pryme°, and in the toun alight°.

    This Theseus, this duc, this worthy knyght,   2190
Whan he had broght hem into his citee,
And inned hem°, everich at his degree°,
He festeth° hem, and dooth so greet labour
To esen hem° and doon hem al honour,
That yet men wenen° that no mannes wit   2195
Of noon estaat ne koude amenden° it.

    The mynstralcye°, the service at the feeste,
The grete yiftes to the meeste° and leeste°,
The riche array of Theseus paleys°,
Ne who sat first ne last upon the deys°,   2200
What ladyes fairest been or best daunsynge,
Or which of hem kan carole best and synge,
Ne who moost felyngly° speketh of love,
What haukes° sitten on the perche above,
What houndes liggen° on the floor adoun—   2205
Of al this make I now no mencioun,
But al th'effect°, that thynketh me the beste.
Now cometh the point, and herkneth if yow leste.

    The Sonday nyght, er° day bigan to sprynge,
Whan Palamon the larke herde synge,   2210
Although it nere nat° day by houres two,
Yet song the larke; and Palamon right tho°
With hooly herte and with an heigh corage°,
He roos to wenden on his pilgrymage
Unto the blisful Citherea benigne°,   2215
I mene Venus, honurable and digne°.
And in hir houre he walketh forth a pas°
Unto the lystes ther hire° temple was,
And doun he kneleth, and with humble cheere

2151 **mosel,** *muzzle* 2152 **Colered of,** *collared with,* **tourettes fyled rounde,** *leash rings filed smooth* 2153 **route,** *company* 2154 **stierne,** *stern* 2157 **steede bay,** *red brown horse,* **trapped in,** *ornamented with* 2158 **dyapred weel,** *well adorned with crisscross quilting* 2161 **Couched,** *decorated* 2162 **brend,** *refined,* **ybete,** *adorned* 2163 **mantel,** *short robe* 2164 **Bratful,** *brimful* 2165 **crispe heer,** *curly hair,* **yronne,** *arranged* 2167 **heigh,** *prominent,* **citryn,** *amber* 2168 **sangwyn,** *reddish* 2169 **frakenes,** *freckles,* **yspreyned,** *sprinkled* 2170 **somdel,** *somewhat,* **ymeynd,** *mingled* 2171 **his lookyng caste,** *set his gaze* 2172 **caste,** *estimate* 2174 **trompe,** *trumpet* 2175 **wered,** *wore,* **laurer,** *laurel* 2176

lusty, *attractive* 2177 **deduyt,** *delight* 2183 **gadered,** *gathered* 2184 **encrees,** *increase* 2185 **part,** *side* 2189 **pryme,** *9 a.m.,* **alight,** *dismount* 2192 **inned hem,** *housed them,* **degree,** *rank* 2193 **festeth,** *feasts* 2194 **esen hem,** *make them comfortable* 2195 **wenen,** *suppose* 2196 **estaat,** *rank,* **koude amenden,** *could improve* 2197 **mynstralcye,** *music* 2198 **meeste,** *greatest,* **leeste,** *least* 2199 **paleys,** *palace* 2200 **deys,** *platform* 2203 **felyngly,** *feelingly* 2204 **haukes,** *hawks* 2205 **liggen,** *lie* 2207 **al th'effect,** *the total effect* 2209 **er,** *before* 2211 **nere nat,** *weren't* 2212 **right tho,** *precisely then* 2213 **heigh corage,** *high spirit* 2215 **benigne,** *gracious* 2216 **digne,** *worthy* 2217 **a pas,** *quickly* 2218 **ther hire,** *where her*

2156 Emetreus, king of India, not mentioned in *Teseida;* Chaucer makes him a martial figure, introducing him to balance Lycurgus. **2160 cote-armure was of clooth of Tars,** cloth vest bearing heraldic insignia, of silk from Tarsia in the Middle East. **2188 Sonday,** Chaucer is precise about day and time in *KnT.* Palamon breaks prison on May 3 "after the mydnyght" (line 1467). Hence it is Friday, May 4, when Arcite comes to the grove (line 1534), and they fight on Saturday, May 5 (line 1629). Theseus sets the tournament for one year later (line 1850), and the knights now assemble on Sunday. **2200 sat . . . upon the deys,** sat on the dais, a raised platform in a position of prominence. **2215 Citherea,** another name for Venus; see 1936n. **2211 nere nat day by houres two,** two hours before sunrise on Monday, the twenty-third hour of Sunday, which belongs to Venus **(2217 hir houre);** Chaucer describes the assignment of hours to planets in *Astr* 2.12.

And herte soor, he seyde as ye shal heere: 2220
   "Faireste of faire, O lady myn, Venus,
Doughter to Jove, and spouse of Vulcanus,
Thow gladere of° the mount of Citheron,
For thilke° love thow haddest to Adoon,
Have pitee of my bittre teeris smerte°,   2225
And taak myn humble preyere at thyn herte.
Allas! I ne have no langage to telle
Th'effectes ne the tormentz of myn helle.
Myn herte may myne harmes° nat biwreye°.
I am so confus that I kan noght seye   2230
But, 'Mercy, lady bright, that knowest weele
My thought, and seest what harmes that I feele!'
Considere al this and rewe° upon my soore°
As wisly° as I shal for everemoore,
Emforth° my myght, thy trewe servant be,   2235
And holden werre° alwey with chastitee.
That make I myn avow°, so° ye me helpe.
I kepe° noght of armes for to yelpe°,
Ne I ne axe° nat tomorwe to have victorie,
Ne renoun in this cas, ne veyne glorie   2240
Of pris of° armes blowen° up and doun.
But I wolde have fully possessioun
Of Emelye, and dye in thy servyse.
Fynd thow the manere hou°, and in what wyse.
I recche° nat, but° it may bettre be,   2245
To have victorie of hem, or they of me,
So that° I have my lady in myne armes.
For though so be that Mars is god of armes,
Youre vertu° is so greet in hevene above
That if yow list°, I shal wel have my love.   2250
   "Thy temple wol I worshipe everemo,
And on thyn auter°, where° I ride or go,
I wol doon sacrifice and fires beete°.
And if ye wol nat so, my lady sweete,
Thanne preye I thee, tomorwe with a spere   2255
That Arcita me thurgh the herte bere°.
Thanne rekke° I noght, whan I have lost my lyf,

Though that Arcita wynne hire to his wyf.
This is th'effect and ende of my preyere:
Yif° me my love, thow blisful lady deere."   2260
   Whan the orison° was doon of Palamon,
His sacrifice he dide and that anon,
Ful pitously° with alle circumstaunce°,
Al° telle I noght as now his observaunce.
But atte laste the statue of Venus shook,   2265
And made a signe°, wherby that he took
That his preyere accepted was that day.
For thogh the signe shewed a delay,
Yet wiste he wel that graunted was his boone°;
And with glad herte he wente hym hoom ful
   soone.   2270
   The thridde houre inequal that° Palamon
Bigan to Venus temple for to gon,
Up roos the sonne and up roos Emelye,
And to the temple of Dyane gan hye°.
Hir maydens, that she thider with hir ladde,   2275
Ful redily° with hem the fyr they hadde,
Th'encens°, the clothes°, and the remenant al
That to the sacrifice longen shal°,
The hornes° fulle of meeth°, as was the gyse°—
Ther lakked noght to doon hir sacrifise.   2280
   Smokynge° the temple, ful of clothes faire,
This Emelye, with herte debonaire°,
Hir body wessh with water of a welle.
But hou° she dide hir ryte° I dar nat telle,
But it be anything in general,   2285
And yet it were a game° to heeren al.
To hym that meneth wel it were no charge°,
But it is good a man been at his large°.
   Hir brighte heer was kembd, untressed° al;
A coroune° of a grene ook cerial°   2290
Upon hir heed was set ful fair and meete°.
Two fyres on the auter gan she beete°,
And dide hir thynges, as men may biholde
In Stace of Thebes and thise bookes olde.

2223 gladere of, *one who brings joy to* **2224 thilke**, *that* **2225 smerte**, *painful* **2229 harmes**, *pains*, **biwreye**, *reveal* **2233 rewe**, *have pity*, **soore**, *pain* **2234 wisly**, *surely* **2235 Emforth**, *to the extent of* **2236 holden werre**, *wage war* **2237 That make I myn avow**, *I make that my vow*, **so**, *if* **2238 kepe**, *care*, **yelpe**, *boast* **2239 axe**, *ask* **2241 pris of**, *praise of*, **blowen**, *announced* **2244 hou**, *how* **2245 recche**, *care*, **but**, *unless* **2247 So that**, *as long as* **2249 vertu**, *power* **2250 list**, *wish* **2252 auter**, *altar*, **where**, *wherever* **2253 beete**, *kindle* **2256 bere**, *pierce* **2257 rekke**, *care* **2260 Yif**, *give* **2261 orison**, *prayer* **2263 pitously**, *pitifully*,

alle circumstaunce, *full ceremony* **2264 Al**, *although* **2266 signe**, *sign* **2268 boone**, *request* **2271 that**, *after* **2274 gan hye**, *did hurry* **2276 Ful redily**, *very properly* **2277 Th'encens**, *the incense*, **clothes**, *cloths* **2278 longen shal**, *were appropriate* **2279 hornes**, *drinking horns*, **meeth**, *mead*, **gyse**, *custom* **2281 Smokynge**, *incensing* **2282 debonaire**, *gentle* **2284 hou**, *how*, **ryte**, *rite* **2286 game**, *pleasure* **2287 charge**, *burden* **2288 at his large**, *at liberty* (to be selective) **2289 untressed**, *unbraided* **2290 coroune**, *crown*, **ook cerial**, *evergreen oak* **2291 meete**, *appropriate* **2292 beete**, *kindle*

2224 Adoon, Adonis, beloved of Venus. **2271 thridde houre inequal that**, the calculation is in planetary hours (not clock hours), which are not equal because they are based upon the duration of daylight. Only at the equinoxes (when there are twelve hours of daylight and of darkness) are planetary hours and clock hours the same. This is the first hour of Monday (three hours after Palamon began), which was assigned to the moon, the planet of Diana. **2294 In Stace of Thebes**, in Statius, concerning Thebes, i.e., the *Thebaid*, which does not include this scene. Chaucer obscures his debt to Boccaccio's *Teseida* here, as he obscures his debt to *Filostrato* in *TC* (1.394).

Whan kyndled was the fyr, with pitous
    cheere   2295
Unto Dyane she spak as ye may heere:
  "O chaste goddesse of the wodes grene,
To whom bothe hevene and erthe and see is
    sene°,
Queene of the regne° of Pluto derk and lowe,
Goddesse of maydens, that myn herte hast
    knowe   2300
Ful many a yeer, and woost° what I desire,
As keep° me fro thy vengeaunce and thyn ire,
That Attheon aboughte° cruelly.
Chaste goddesse, wel wostow° that I
Desire to ben a mayden al my lyf,   2305
Ne nevere wol I be no love ne wyf.
I am, thow woost, yet of thy compaignye,
A mayde, and love huntynge and venerye°,
And for to walken in the wodes wilde,
And noght to ben a wyf and be with childe.   2310
Noght wol I knowe the compaignye of man.
Now help me, lady, sith° ye may and kan,
For tho thre° formes that thou hast in thee.
And Palamon, that hath swich love to me,
And eek Arcite, that loveth me so soore—   2315
This grace I preye thee withoute moore,
As sende love and pees bitwixe hem two,
And fro me turne awey hir hertes so
That al hire hoote love and hir desir,
And al hir bisy° torment and hir fir   2320
Be queynt°, or turned in another place.
And if so be thou wolt do me no grace,
Or if my destynee be shapen so
That I shal nedes° have oon of hem two,
As sende° me hym that moost desireth me.   2325
Bihoold, goddesse of clene chastitee,
The bittre teeris that on my chekes falle.
Syn° thou art mayde and kepere of us alle,
My maydenhede thou kepe and wel conserve,
And whil I lyve, a mayde I wol thee serve."   2330
    The fires brenne upon the auter cleere°,
Whil Emelye was thus in hir preyere.
But sodeynly she saugh a sighte queynte°,

For right anon oon of the fyres queynte°,
And quyked° agayn, and after that anon   2335
That oother fyr was queynt and al agon°,
And as it queynte it made a whistelynge
As doon thise wete brondes° in hir brennynge°,
And at the brondes ende out ran anon
As it were blody dropes many oon.   2340
For which so soore agast° was Emelye
That she was wel ny° mad, and gan to crye,
For she ne wiste° what is signyfied,
But oonly for the feere thus hath she cried,
And weep that it was pitee for to heere.   2345
And therwithal° Dyane gan appeere,
With bowe in honde, right as an hunteresse,
And seyde, "Doghter, stynt° thyn hevynesse°.
Among the goddes hye it is affermed,
And by eterne word writen and conformed,   2350
Thou shalt ben wedded unto oon of tho°
That han for thee so muchel care and wo,
But unto which of hem I may nat telle.
Farwel, for I ne may no lenger dwelle.
The fires whiche that on myn auter
    brenne   2355
Shulle thee declaren, er that thou go henne°,
Thyn aventure of love, as in this cas."
And with that word, the arwes in the caas°
Of the goddesse clateren faste and rynge,
And forth she wente and made a
    vanysshynge   2360
For which this Emelye astoned° was,
And seyde, "What amounteth° this, allas?
I putte me in thy proteccioun,
Dyane, and in thy disposicioun."
And hoom she goth anon the nexte° weye.   2365
This is th'effect; ther is namoore to seye.
    The nexte houre of Mars folwynge this,
Arcite unto the temple walked is
Of fierse Mars, to doon his sacrifise
With alle the rytes of his payen wyse°.   2370
With pitous herte and heigh devocioun,
Right thus to Mars he seyde his orisoun°.
    "O stronge god, that in the regnes° colde

2298 see is sene, *sea is seen* **2299 regne,** *realm* **2301 woost,** *know* **2302 As keep,** *keep* **2303 aboughte,** *paid for* **2304 wostow,** *you know* **2308 venerye,** *hunting* **2312 sith,** *since* **2313 tho thre,** *those three* (see note) **2320 bisy,** *intense* **2321 queynt,** *quenched* **2324 nedes,** *necessarily* **2325 As sende,** *send* **2328 Syn,** *since* **2331 cleere,** *brightly* **2333 queynte,** *strange* **2334 queynte,** *died out* **2335 quyked,** *came alive* **2336 agon,** *gone* **2338 wete brondes,** *damp logs,* **hir brennynge,** *their burning* **2341 agast,** *frightened* **2342 wel ny** *nearly* **2343 wiste,** *knew* **2346 therwithal,** *with that,* **gan appeere,** *did appear* **2348 stynt,** *stop,* **hevynesse,** *sorrow* **2351 tho,** *those* **2356 henne,** *hence* **2358 caas,** *quiver* **2361 astoned,** *astonished* **2362 amounteth,** *means* **2365 nexte,** *nearest* **2370 payen wyse,** *pagan ways* **2372 orisoun,** *prayer* **2373 regnes,** *regions*

2299 regne of Pluto derk and lowe, Pluto was god of the underworld. Diana, goddess of the moon, was sometimes identified with Greek Hecate and thus regarded also as goddess of the underworld. **2303 Attheon,** Acteon; see 2065n above. **2313 tho thre formes,** those three manifestations of the goddess: Luna in the heavens, Diana on earth, Hecate or Proserpina in the underworld. **2367 nexte houre,** i.e., the fourth hour, belonging to Mars; see 2271n.

Of Trace honoured art° and lord yholde°,
And hast in every regne and every lond   2375
Of armes al the brydel in thyn hond,
And hem fortunest° as thee lyst devyse°,
Accepte of me my pitous sacrifise.
If so be that my youthe may deserve,
And that my myght be worthy for to serve   2380
Thy godhede, that I may been oon of thyne,
Thanne preye I thee to rewe° upon my pyne°.
For thilke° peyne and thilke hoote fir
In which thow whilom brendest° for desir,
Whan that thow usedest° the beautee   2385
Of faire, yonge, fresshe Venus free°,
And haddest hire in armes at thy wille—
Although thee ones on a tyme mysfille°,
Whan Vulcanus hadde caught thee in his las°,
And foond thee liggynge° by his wyf, allas—   2390
For thilke° sorwe that was in thyn herte,
Have routhe° as wel upon my peynes smerte.
I am yong and unkonnynge°, as thow woost°,
And, as I trowe°, with love offended moost°
That evere was any lyves° creature.   2395
For she that dooth° me al this wo endure
Ne reccheth nevere wher° I synke or fleete°.
And wel I woot°, er she me mercy heete°,
I moot° with strengthe wynne hire in the place.
And wel I woot, withouten help or grace   2400
Of thee, ne may my strengthe noght availle°.
Thanne help me, lord, tomorwe in my bataille
For thilke° fyr that whilom° brente thee
As wel as thilke fyr now brenneth me,
And do° that I tomorwe have victorie.   2405
Myn be the travaille°, and thyn be the glorie!
Thy sovereyn temple wol I moost honouren
Of any place, and alwey moost labouren
In thy plesaunce° and in thy craftes stronge,
And in thy temple I wol my baner honge°   2410

And alle the armes of my compaignye,
And everemo, unto that day I dye,
Eterne fir I wol biforn thee fynde°.
And eek to this avow° I wol me bynde:
My beerd, myn heer, that hongeth long
   adoun,   2415
That nevere yet ne felte offensioun°
Of rasour° nor of shere°, I wol thee yeve,
And ben thy trewe servant whil I lyve.
Now, lord, have routhe upon my sorwes soore.
Yif me the victorie, I aske thee namoore."   2420
   The preyere stynt° of Arcita the stronge,
The rynges on the temple dore that honge,
And eek the dores, clatereden ful faste,
Of which Arcita somwhat hym agaste°.
The fyres brenden upon the auter brighte,   2425
That it gan al the temple for to lighte.
A sweete smel the ground anon up yaf°,
And Arcita anon his hand up haf°,
And moore encens° into the fyr he caste,
With othere rytes mo; and atte laste   2430
The statue of Mars bigan his hauberk° rynge,
And with that soun he herde a murmurynge
Ful lowe and dym, and seyde thus, "Victorie!"
For which he yaf to Mars honour and glorie.
And thus with joye and hope wel to fare   2435
Arcite anon unto his in° is fare°,
As fayn as fowel° is of the brighte sonne.
   And right anon swich strif ther is bigonne,
For thilke grauntyng°, in the hevene above,
Bitwixe Venus, the goddesse of love,   2440
And Mars, the stierne° god armypotente°,
That Juppiter was bisy it to stente°,
Til that the pale Saturnus the colde,
That knew so manye of aventures olde,
Foond in his olde experience an art°   2445
That he ful soone hath plesed every part.

2374 **art,** *are,* **lord yholde,** *treated as lord* 2377 **hem fortunest,** *determines the fortune of them,* **thee lyst devyse,** *you choose to arrange* 2382 **rewe,** *have pity,* **pyne,** *pain* 2383 **thilke,** *that* 2384 **whilom brendest,** *once burned* 2385 **usedest,** *enjoyed* 2386 **free,** *generous* 2388 **thee . . . mysfille,** *for you at one time* (things) *went wrong* 2389 **las,** *snare* 2390 **liggynge,** *lying* 2391 **thilke,** *that* 2392 **routhe,** *pity* 2393 **unkonnynge,** *inexperienced,* **woost,** *know* 2394 **trowe,** *believe,* **with love offended moost,** *by love hurt most* 2395 **lyves,** *living* 2396 **dooth,** *makes* 2397 **Ne reccheth nevere wher,** *cares not whether,* **fleete,** *float* 2398 **woot,** *know,* **heete,** *promises* 2399 **moot,** *must* 2401 **availle,**

succeed 2403 **thilke,** *that,* **whilom,** *once* 2405 **do,** *cause* 2406 **travaille,** *suffering* 2409 **In thy plesaunce,** *for your pleasure* 2410 **my baner honge,** *hang my banner* 2413 **fynde,** *provide for* 2414 **avow,** *vow* 2416 **offensioun,** *damage* 2417 **rasour,** *razor,* **shere,** *scissors* 2421 **stynt,** *stopped* 2424 **hym agaste,** *was frightened* 2427 **yaf,** *gave* 2428 **haf,** *lifted* 2429 **encens,** *incense* 2431 **his hauberk,** *its mail armor* 2436 **in,** *dwelling,* **is fare,** *goes* 2437 **fayn as fowel,** *happy as a bird* 2439 **thilke grauntyng,** *that promise* 2441 **stierne,** *stern,* **armypotente,** *potent in arms* 2442 **stente,** *stop* 2445 **art,** *strategy*

2389 **Vulcanus,** Vulcan, husband of Venus, trapped Mars and Venus in bed together. **2415–17 My beerd, myn heer . . . thee yeve,** dedication of beards and hair was an ancient custom among the Greeks and the Nazarites. **2442–43 Juppiter . . . Saturnus,** throughout *KnT,* Chaucer blends notions of divine powers with notions of planetary influence. Jupiter (Jove) was the king of the gods, but Saturn was older. Jupiter was thought to be the largest of the planets (except the sun), although the orbit of Saturn (**cours . . . wyde,** line 2454) was the largest known in the Middle Ages. Because of age and distance from earth, Saturn was thought to have malevolent influence on humankind. It is Chaucer's invention to include him in the plot.

As sooth is seyd, elde° hath greet avantage;
In elde is bothe wysdom and usage°;
Men may the olde atrenne°, and noght atrede°.
Saturne anon, to stynten° strif and drede,   2450
Al be it that° it is agayn his kynde°,
Of al this strif he gan remedie fynde.
  "My deere doghter Venus," quod Saturne,
"My cours°, that hath so wyde for to turne,
Hath moore power than woot° any man.   2455
Myn is the drenchyng° in the see so wan°;
Myn is the prison in the derke cote°;
Myn is the stranglyng and hangyng by the throte;
The murmure and the cherles rebellyng;
The groynynge°, and the pryvee°
    empoysonyng.   2460
I do vengeance and pleyn correccioun°,
Whil I dwelle in the signe of the leoun.
Myn is the ruyne° of the hye° halles;
The fallynge of the toures° and of the walles
Upon the mynour° or the carpenter.   2465
I slow° Sampsoun, shakynge the piler;
And myne be the maladyes colde,
The derke tresons, and the castes° olde;
My lookyng is the fader° of pestilence.
Now weep namoore, I shal doon diligence°   2470
That Palamon, that is thyn owene knyght,
Shal have his lady, as thou hast him hight°.
Though Mars shal helpe his knyght, yet nathelees°
Bitwixe yow ther moot° be som tyme pees,
Al be ye° noght of o compleccioun°,   2475
That causeth al day swich divisioun.
I am thyn aiel°, redy at thy wille;
Weep now namoore, I wol thy lust° fulfille."
  Now wol I stynten of the goddes above,
Of Mars and of Venus, goddesse of love,   2480
And telle yow as pleynly as I kan
The grete effect for which that I bygan.

Explicit tercia pars. Sequitur pars quarta.

  Greet was the feeste in Atthenes that day,
And eek the lusty seson of that May
Made every wight to been in swich plesaunce   2485
That al that Monday justen° they and daunce,
And spenden it in Venus heigh servyse.
But by the cause° that they sholde ryse
Eerly, for to seen the grete fight,
Unto hir reste wenten they at nyght.   2490
And on the morwe, whan that day gan sprynge,
Of hors and harneys noyse and claterynge
Ther was in hostelryes° al aboute,
And to the paleys° rood ther many a route°
Of lordes upon steedes and palfreys°.   2495
Ther maystow° seen devisynge° of harneys
So unkouth° and so riche, and wroght so weel
Of goldsmythrye, of browdynge°, and of steel,
The sheeldes brighte, testeres, and trappures°,
Gold-hewen helmes°, hauberkes°,
    cote-armures°,   2500
Lordes in paramentz° on hir courseres°,
Knyghtes of retenue°, and eek squieres
Nailynge° the speres, and helmes bokelynge°,
Giggynge° of sheeldes, with layneres lacynge°—
There as nede is they° weren nothyng ydel.   2505
The fomy° steedes on the golden brydel
Gnawynge, and faste the armurers also
With fyle and hamer prikynge to and fro,
Yemen° on foote, and communes° many oon
With shorte staves°, thikke as they may goon;   2510
Pypes, trompes°, nakers°, clariounes°,
That in the bataille blowen blody sounes;
The paleys ful of peple up and doun,
Heere thre, ther ten, holdynge hir questioun,
Dyvynynge of° thise Thebane knyghtes two.   2515
Somme seyden thus, somme seyde, "It shal be so."

2447 elde, *age* **2448 usage,** *experience* **2449 atrenne,** *outrun,* **atrede,** *outwit* **2450 stynten,** *stop* **2451 Al be it that,** *although,* **agayn his kynde,** *against his nature* **2454 cours,** *orbit* **2455 woot,** *knows* **2456 drenchyng,** *drowning,* **wan,** *dark* **2457 cote,** *hut* **2460 groynynge,** *grumbling,* **pryvee,** *secret* **2461 pleyn correccioun,** *full punishment* **2463 ruyne,** *ruin,* **hye,** *high* **2464 toures,** *towers* **2465 mynour,** *miner* **2466 slow,** *slew* **2468 castes,** *plots* **2469 My lookyng is the fader,** *my influence is the cause* **2470 doon diligence,** *make sure* **2472 hight,** *promised* **2473 nathelees,** *nonetheless* **2474 moot,** *must* **2475 Al be ye,** *although you are,* **o compleccioun,** *the same temperament* **2477 aiel,** *grandfather* **2478 lust,** *desire* **2486 justen,** *joust* **2488 by the cause,** *because* **2493 hostel-** ryes, *lodgings* **2494 paleys,** *palace,* **route,** *company* **2495 palfreys,** *riding horses* **2496 maystow,** *you may,* **devisynge,** *preparation* **2497 unkouth,** *unfamiliar* **2498 browdynge,** *embroidering* **2499 testeres and trappures,** *horse armor* **2500 Gold-hewen helmes,** *gold-colored helmets,* **hauberkes,** *coats of mail,* **cote-armures,** *coats of arms* **2501 paramentz,** *rich robes,* **hir courseres,** *their war horses* **2502 retenue,** *service* **2503 Nailynge,** *fastening* (heads on to), **bokelynge,** *buckling* **2504 Giggynge,** *fitting out,* **layneres lacynge,** *lacing with straps* **2505 they,** i.e., *everyone* **2506 fomy,** *foamy* **2509 Yemen,** *yeomen,* **communes,** *commoners* **2510 staves,** *staffs* **2511 trompes,** *trumpets,* **nakers,** *kettledrums,* **clariounes,** *bugles* **2515 Dyvynynge of,** *speculating about*

2453 doghter, granddaughter; Venus is daughter of Jupiter, who is son of Saturn. **2459 cherles rebellyng,** peasants' rebelling, perhaps one of Chaucer's few allusions to the Peasants' Revolt of 1381. **2462 signe of the leoun,** the influence of Saturn was most malevolent when the planet was aligned with the astrological sign of Leo, the lion. **2466 Sampsoun,** Samson died when he pulled the pillars and roof down on the heads of the Philistines; Judges 16.25ff., retold in *MkT* 7.2079ff. **2482a Explicit tercia pars. Sequitur pars quarta.** "Here ends part three. Here follows part four." **2491 the morwe,** Tuesday, a day belonging to Mars, named after Tiw, a Scandinavian god of war.

Somme helden with hym with the blake berd,
Somme with the balled°, somme with the thikke
    herd°;
Somme seyde he° looked grymme, and he wolde
    fighte:
"He hath a sparth° of twenty pound of
    wighte." 2520
Thus was the halle ful of divynynge°,
Longe after that the sonne gan to sprynge.
    The grete Theseus, that of his sleep awaked
With mynstralcie and noyse that was maked,
Heeld yet° the chambre of his paleys riche 2525
Til that the Thebane knyghtes, bothe yliche°
Honured, were into the paleys fet°.
Duc Theseus was at a wyndow set,
Arrayed right as he were a god in trone°.
The peple preesseth thiderward° ful soone 2530
Hym for to seen, and doon heigh reverence,
And eek to herkne his heste° and his sentence°.
    An heraud° on a scaffold made an "Oo!"
Til al the noyse of peple was ydo°,
And whan he saugh the peple of noyse
    al stille, 2535
Tho shewed° he the myghty dukes wille.
    "The lord hath of his heigh discrecioun
Considered that it were destruccioun
To gentil blood to fighten in the gyse°
Of mortal bataille now in this emprise°. 2540
Wherfore, to shapen° that they shal nat dye,
He wol his firste purpos modifye.
No man therfore, up° peyne of los of lyf,
No maner shot°, ne polax°, ne short knyf
Into the lystes sende, or thider brynge, 2545
Ne short swerd, for to stoke° with poynt bitynge,
No man ne drawe, ne bere it by his syde.
Ne no man shal unto° his felawe° ryde
But o cours°, with a sharpe ygrounde spere,
Foyne°, if hym list, on foote, hymself to were°. 2550
And he that is at meschief° shal be take
And noght slayn, but be broght unto the stake

That shal ben ordeyned° on either syde;
But thider° he shal by force, and there abyde.
And if so falle° the chieftayn be take 2555
On outher° syde, or elles sleen° his make°,
No lenger shal the turneiynge° laste.
God spede° you! Gooth forth, and ley on faste!
With long swerd and with maces° fighteth youre
    fille.
Gooth now youre wey, this is the lordes wille." 2560
    The voys of peple touchede the hevene,
So loude cride they with murie stevene°,
"God save swich a lord, that is so good!
He wilneth no destruccion of blood."
Up goon the trompes° and the melodye, 2565
And to the lystes rit° the compaignye,
By ordinance°, thurghout the citee large,
Hanged with clooth of gold, and nat with sarge°.
    Ful lik a lord this noble duc gan ryde,
Thise two Thebans upon either syde, 2570
And after rood the queene, and Emelye,
And after that another compaignye
Of oon and oother, after hir degree°.
And thus they passen thurghout the citee,
And to the lystes come they by° tyme. 2575
It nas nat of the day yet fully pryme°
Whan set was Theseus ful riche° and hye,
Ypolita the queene, and Emelye,
And othere ladys in degrees aboute.
Unto the seetes preesseth° al the route°. 2580
And westward, thurgh the gates under Marte°,
Arcite and eek the hondred of his parte°
With baner reed° is entred right anon.
And in that selve° moment Palamon
Is under Venus, estward in the place, 2585
With baner whyt and hardy chiere° and face.
In al the world, to seken up and doun,
So evene°, withouten variacioun,
Ther nere swiche° compaignyes tweye,
For ther was noon so wys that koude seye 2590
That any hadde of oother avauntage

2518 **balled,** *bald,* **thikke herd,** *thick haired* 2519 **he,** *that one* 2520 **sparth,** *battle-ax* 2521 **divynynge,** *speculation* 2525 **Heeld yet,** *stayed in* 2526 **yliche,** *alike* 2527 **fet,** *fetched* 2529 **trone,** *throne* 2530 **thiderward,** *toward this* 2532 **herkne his heste,** *hear his command,* **sentence,** *judgment* 2533 **heraud,** *herald* 2534 **ydo,** *done* 2536 **shewed,** *made clear* 2539 **gyse,** *manner* 2540 **emprise,** *undertaking* 2541 **shapen,** *make sure* 2543 **up,** *upon* 2544 **maner shot,** *kind of arrow,* **polax,** *long battle-ax* 2546 **stoke,** *stab* 2548 **unto,** *against,* **felawe,** *opponent* 2549 **But o cours,** *more than one charge* 2550 **Foyne,** *(let him) thrust,* **were,** *defend* 2551 **at meschief,** *in danger* 2553 **ordeyned,** *established* 2554 **thider**

(brought) there 2555 **if so falle,** *if it happens that* 2556 **outher,** *either,* **sleen,** *slain,* **make,** *match (the other leader)* 2557 **turneiynge,** *tournament* 2558 **spede,** *assist* 2559 **maces,** *war clubs* 2562 **murie stevene,** *merry sound* 2565 **trompes,** *trumpets* 2566 **rit,** *rides* 2567 **ordinance,** *proper order* 2568 **sarge,** *wool* 2573 **after hir degree,** *in order of their rank* 2575 **by,** *in* 2576 **fully pryme,** *9 a.m.* 2577 **ful riche,** *very richly* 2580 **preesseth,** *crowded,* **route,** *company* 2581 **Marte,** *Mars* 2582 **parte,** *group* 2583 **baner reed,** *red banner* 2584 **selve,** *same* 2586 **chiere,** *expression* 2588 **evene,** *equal* 2589 **Ther nere swiche,** *there weren't such*

2541 **that they shal nat dye,** most of these humane restrictions on the use of deadly force were added to the story by Chaucer. 2552 **broght unto the stake,** yielding at the stake (a post or marker) was medieval tournament practice; such technicalities are not in *Teseida.*

Of worthynesse, ne of estaat, ne age,
So evene were they chosen, for to gesse°.
And in two renges° faire they hem dresse°.
Whan that hir names rad° were everichon,   2595
That in hir nombre gyle° were ther noon,
Tho were the gates shet, and cried was loude,
"Do now youre devoir°, yonge knyghtes proude!"

   The heraudes lefte hir prikyng° up and doun;
Now ryngen trompes loude and clarioun°.   2600
Ther is namoore to seyn, but west and est
In goon the speres ful sadly in arrest°,
In gooth the sharpe spore° into the syde.
Ther seen° men who kan juste and who kan ryde.
Ther shyveren° shaftes upon sheeldes thikke;   2605
He° feeleth thurgh the herte-spoon° the prikke;
Up spryngen speres twenty foot on highte;
Out goon the swerdes as the silver brighte;
The helmes they tohewen° and toshrede°;
Out brest° the blood with stierne° stremes
    rede;   2610
With myghty maces the bones they tobreste°;
He thurgh the thikkeste of the throng gan
    threste°;
Ther stomblen steedes stronge, and doun
    gooth al;
He rolleth under foot as dooth a bal;
He foyneth° on his feet with his tronchoun°;   2615
And he hym hurtleth with his hors adoun;
He thurgh the body is hurt and sithen ytake°,
Maugree his heed°, and broght unto the stake.
As forward° was, right ther he moste abyde°.
Another lad is° on that oother syde.   2620

   And somtyme dooth hem° Theseus to reste,
Hem to fresshen and drynken, if hem leste.
Ful ofte a day° han thise Thebanes two
Togydre ymet and wroght his felawe wo;
Unhorsed hath ech oother of hem tweye°.   2625
Ther nas no tygre in the vale of Galgopheye,

Whan that hir whelp° is stole° whan it is lite°,
So crueel on the hunte° as is Arcite
For jelous herte upon this Palamoun.
Ne in Belmarye ther nys so fel° leoun   2630
That hunted is, or for his hunger wood°,
Ne of his praye° desireth so the blood,
As Palamon to sleen his foo Arcite.
The jelous strokes on hir helmes byte;
Out renneth blood on bothe hir sydes rede.   2635

   Somtyme° an ende ther is of every dede.
For er the sonne unto the reste wente,
The stronge kyng Emetreus gan hente°
This Palamon, as he faught with Arcite,
And made his swerd depe in his flessh
    to byte,   2640
And by the force of twenty is he take°,
Unyolden°, and ydrawe unto the stake.
And in the rescus° of this Palamoun
The stronge kyng Lygurge is born adoun°,
And Kyng Emetreus, for al his strengthe,   2645
Is born out of his sadel a swerdes lengthe,
So hitte him Palamoun er he were take.
But al for noght—he was broght to the stake.
His hardy herte myghte hym helpe naught:
He most abyde°, whan that he was caught,   2650
By force and eek by composicioun°.

   Who sorweth now but woful Palamoun,
That moot° namoore goon agayn to fighte?
And whan that Theseus hadde seyn this sighte,
Unto the folk that foghten thus echon°   2655
He cryde, "Hoo! namoore, for it is doon!
I wol be trewe juge, and no partie°.
Arcite of Thebes shal have Emelie,
That by his fortune hath hire faire° ywonne."
Anon ther is a noyse of peple bigonne°   2660
For joye of this, so loude and heighe withalle,
It semed that the lystes sholde falle.

   What kan now faire Venus doon above?

2593 for to gesse, *at an estimate* **2594 renges,** *lines,* **hem dresse,** *arrange themselves* **2595 rad,** *read* **2596 gyle,** *deceits* **2598 devoir,** *best* **2599 lefte hir prikyng,** *stopped their spurring* **2600 clarioun,** *clearly* **2602 ful sadly in arrest,** *very firmly against the breastplates* **2603 spore,** *spur* **2604 seen** (are) *seen,* **2605 shyveren,** *shatter* **2606 He,** *one,* **herte-spoon,** *breastbone* **2609 tohewen,** *chop thoroughly,* **toshrede,** *shred thoroughly* **2610 brest,** *bursts,* **stierne,** *cruel* **2611 tobreste,** *break completely* **2612 threste,** *thrust* **2615 foyneth,** *stabs,* **tronchoun,** *spear shaft* **2617 sithen ytake,** *after taken* **2618 Maugree his heed,** *despite his wishes*

2619 forward, *agreement,* **moste abyde,** *must remain* **2620 lad is,** *is led* **2621 dooth hem,** *compels them* **2623 a day,** *during the day* **2625 tweye,** *twice* **2627 whelp,** *cub,* **stole,** *stolen,* **lite,** *little* **2628 hunte,** *hunter* **2630 fel,** *cruel* **2631 wood,** *insane* **2632 praye,** *prey* **2636 Somtyme,** *eventually* **2638 gan hente,** *did seize* **2641 take,** *taken* **2642 Unyolden,** *unyielding* **2643 rescus,** *attempted rescue* **2644 born adoun,** *brought down* **2650 abyde,** *remain* **2651 composicioun,** *agreement* **2653 moot,** *might* **2655 echon,** *each one* **2557 partie,** *partisan* **2659 faire,** *fairly* **2660 bigonne,** *begun*

2605ff. shyveren shaftes upon sheeldes . . . , alliteration, present tense, and syntactic manipulation lend power to this battle scene; *LGW* 635ff. achieves the same effect, as does the alliteration in *TC* 4.38–42. **2626 vale of Galgopheye,** the valley of Gargaphie, where Acteon, seeing Diana naked, was punished by being torn apart by his dogs; Ovid, *Metamorphoses* 3.155ff. **2630 Belmarye,** Benmarin, once a district in north-western Africa; also cited in *GP* 1.57. **2655** This line is omitted in many MSS and a new line 2657 supplied: "Ne non lenger unto his felawe gon."

What seith she now? What dooth this queene of
    love,
But wepeth so, for wantynge° of hir wille,   2665
Til that hir teeres in the lystes fille?
She seyde, "I am ashamed, doutelees°."

    Saturnus seyde, "Doghter, hoold thy pees!
Mars hath his wille, his knyght hath al his boone°,
And, by myn heed, thow shalt been esed°
    soone."   2670

    The trompours° with the loude mynstralcie,
The heraudes that ful loude yolle° and crie,
Been in hire wele° for joye of daun° Arcite.
But herkneth me, and stynteth° noyse a lite°,
Which a° myracle ther bifel anon.   2675

    This fierse Arcite hath of his helm ydon°,
And on a courser, for to shewe his face,
He priketh endelong° the large place,
Lokynge upward upon this Emelye,
And she agayn° hym caste a freendlich° eye—   2680
For wommen, as to speken in comune,
Thei folwen alle the favour of Fortune—
And was al his chiere° as in his herte.

    Out of the ground a furie infernal sterte°,
From Pluto sent at requeste of Saturne,   2685
For which his hors for fere gan to turne,
And leep aside, and foundred° as he leep;
And er that Arcite may taken keep°,
He pighte° hym on the pomel° of his heed,
That° in the place he lay as he were deed,   2690
His brest tobrosten° with his sadel-bowe°.
As blak he lay as any cole° or crowe,
So was the blood yronnen in his face.
Anon° he was yborn° out of the place,
With herte soor, to Theseus paleys.   2695
Tho was he korven° out of his harneys°,
And in a bed ybrought ful faire and blyve°,
For he was yet in memorie° and alyve,

And alwey criynge after Emelye.
    Duc Theseus, with al his compaignye,   2700
Is comen hoom to Atthenes his citee,
With alle blisse° and greet solempnitee.
Al be it that this aventure was falle°,
He nolde noght disconforten° hem alle.
Men seyde eek that Arcite shal nat dye,   2705
He shal been heeled of his maladye.
And of another thyng they weren as fayn°,
That of hem alle was ther noon yslayn,
Al° were they soore yhurt, and namely oon°
That with a spere was thirled° his brest-boon.   2710
To othere woundes and to broken armes
Somme hadden salves, and somme hadden
    charmes.
Fermacies° of herbes and eek save°
They dronken, for they wolde hir lymes have°.
For which this noble duc, as he wel kan,   2715
Conforteth and honoureth every man,
And made revel al the longe nyght
Unto the straunge° lordes, as was right.
Ne ther was holden no disconfitynge°,
But as a justes° or a tourneiynge,   2720
For soothly° ther was no disconfiture°.
For fallyng nys nat but an aventure°,
Ne to be lad by force unto the stake
Unyolden°, and with° twenty knyghtes take,
O° persone allone, withouten mo°,   2725
And haryed° forth by arme, foot, and too°,
And eke his steede dryven forth with staves°
With footmen, bothe yemen and eek knaves—
It nas arretted hym° no vileynye°,
Ther may no man clepen° it cowardye.   2730
    For which anon Duc Theseus leet crye°,
To stynten° alle rancour° and envye°,
The gree° as wel of o syde as of oother,
And eyther syde ylik° as ootheres brother;

2665 wantynge, *lacking* **2667 doutelees,** *doubtless* **2669 boone,** *request* **2670 esed,** *satisfied* **2671 trompours** *trumpeters* **2672 yolle,** *yell* **2673 Been in hire wele,** *are in their happiness,* **daun,** *sir* **2674 stynteth,** *stop,* **lite,** *little* **2675 Which a,** *what a* **2676 of his helm ydon,** *taken off his helmet* **2678 endelong,** *the length of* **2680 agayn,** *upon,* **freendlich,** *friendly* **2683 chiere,** *appearance* **2684 furie infernal sterte,** *hellish spirit of anger leapt* **2687 foundred,** *stumbled* **2688 keep,** *care* **2689 pighte,** *threw,* **pomel,** *top* **2690 That,** *so that* **2691 tobrosten,** *shattered,* **sadel-bowe,** *rigid front piece of the saddle* **2692 cole,** *coal* **2694 Anon,** *at once,* **yborn,** *carried* **2696 korven,** *cut,* **harneys,** *armor* **2697 blyve,** *quickly* **2698 in memorie,** *conscious* **2702 blisse,** *celebration*

2703 aventure was falle, *accident had happened* **2704 disconforten,** *upset* **2707 fayn,** *glad* **2709 Al,** *although,* **namely oon,** *especially one* **2710 thirled,** *pierced* **2713 Fermacies,** *medicines,* **eek save,** *also sage* **2714 wolde hir lymes have,** *wished to save their limbs* **2718 straunge,** *foreign* **2719 holden no disconfitynge,** *thought to be no defeat* **2720 justes,** *joust* **2721 soothly,** *truly,* **disconfiture,** *defeat* **2722 aventure,** *accident* **2724 Unyolden,** *unyielded,* **with,** *by* **2725 O,** *one,* **mo,** *more* **2726 haryed,** *dragged,* **too,** *toe* **2727 staves,** *staffs* **2729 nas arretted hym,** *was not attributed to him,* **vileynye,** *shame* **2730 clepen,** *call* **2731 leet crye,** *had announced* **2732 stynten,** *stop,* **rancour,** *ill will,* **envye,** *hostility* **2733 gree,** *esteem* **2734 ylik,** *alike*

2668 Saturnus, Saturn's intervention is Chaucer's addition; in *Teseida,* Venus calls the fury (line 2685) herself. **2681–82** These lines do not appear in some of the best MSS, perhaps indicating that Chaucer canceled them or that they are a later addition. **2683** The line has various readings in the MSS, suggesting scribal uncertainty about the idiom **al his chiere as;** the line can be paraphrased "And his expression mirrored the joy in his heart."

And yaf hem yiftes after hir degree,　　　　　　2735
And fully heeld a feeste dayes three,
And convoyed° the kynges worthily
Out of his toun a journee largely°.
And hoom wente every man the righte way.
Ther was namoore but "Farewel, have good
　　　day!"　　　　　　　　　　　　　　　　　　　2740
Of this bataille I wol namoore endite°,
But speke of Palamon and of Arcite.
　　Swelleth the brest of Arcite, and the soore°
Encreesseth at his herte moore and moore.
The clothered° blood, for any lechecraft°,　　2745
Corrupteth° and is in his bouk° ylaft°,
That neither veyne-blood°, ne ventusynge°,
Ne drynke of herbes may ben his helpynge.
The vertu expulsif, or animal°,
Fro thilke vertu cleped° natural　　　　　　　　2750
Ne may the venym voyden° ne expelle.
The pipes of his longes° gonne to swelle,
And every lacerte° in his brest adoun
Is shent° with venym and corrupcioun°.
Hym gayneth° neither, for to gete° his lif,　　2755
Vomyt upward, ne dounward laxatif°.
Al is tobrosten° thilke regioun°,
Nature hath now no dominacioun.
And certeinly, ther° Nature wol nat wirche°,
Farewel phisik°—go ber° the man to chirche!　2760
This al and som°, that Arcita moot° dye;
For which he sendeth after Emelye,
And Palamon, that was his cosyn deere.
Thanne seyde he thus, as ye shal after heere:
　　"Naught may the woful spirit in myn herte　2765
Declare o point° of alle my sorwes smerte°
To yow, my lady, that I love moost,
But I biquethe the servyce of my goost°
To yow aboven every creature,

Syn° that my lyf may no lenger dure°.　　　　　2770
Allas, the wo, allas, the peynes stronge
That I for yow have suffred, and so longe;
Allas, the deeth, allas, myn Emelye,
Allas, departynge° of oure compaignye;
Allas, myn hertes queene, allas, my wyf,　　　2775
Myn hertes lady, endere of my lyf!
What is this world? What asketh men° to have?
Now with his love, now in his colde grave,
Allone, withouten any compaignye.
Farewel, my swete foo°, myn Emelye.　　　　　2780
And softe° taak me in youre armes tweye°,
For love of God, and herkneth what I seye.
　　"I have heer with my cosyn Palamon
Had strif and rancour many a day agon
For love of yow, and for my jalousye.　　　　　2785
And Juppiter so wys° my soule gye°
To speken of a servaunt proprely,
With alle circumstances° trewely—
That is to seyn, trouthe, honour, knyghthede,
Wysdom, humblesse, estaat°, and heigh
　　　kynrede°,　　　　　　　　　　　　　　　　　　2790
Fredom°, and al that longeth to that art°—
So° Juppiter have of my soule part°,
As in this world right now ne knowe I non
So worthy to ben loved as Palamon,
That serveth yow, and wol doon al his lyf.　　2795
And if that evere ye shul ben a wyf,
Foryet nat Palamon, the gentil man."
And with that word his speche faille gan°,
For from his feet up to his brest was come
The coold of deeth, that hadde hym
　　　overcome,　　　　　　　　　　　　　　　　　　2800
And yet moore over, for in his armes two
The vital strengthe is lost and al ago°.
Oonly the intellect withouten moore,

2737 **convoyed,** *accompanied* 2738 **journee largely,** *a full day's journey* 2741 **endite,** *write* 2743 **soore,** *pain* 2745 **clothered,** *clotted,* **for
any lechecraft,** *despite any medical skill* 2746 **Corrupteth,** *becomes
infected,* **bouk,** *body,* **ylaft,** *left* 2747 **That,** *so that,* **veyne-blood,** *bleeding,* **ventusynge,** *cupping* 2749 **vertu expulsif, or animal,** *power to
expel, also known as the animal power* 2750 **Fro thilke vertu cleped,**
from that power called 2751 **voyden,** *remove* 2752 **longes,** *lungs* 2753
lacerte, *muscle* 2754 **shent,** *destroyed,* **corrupcioun,** *infection* 2755
Hym gayneth, *it helps him,* **gete,** *save* 2756 **laxatif,** *to defecate* 2757
tobrosten, *shattered,* **thilke regioun,** *(in) this area (of his body)*

2759 **ther,** *where,* **wirche,** *work* 2760 **phisik,** *medicine,* **ber,** *carry* 2761
This al and som, *this is the extent of it,* **moot,** *must* 2766 **o point,** *one
bit,* **sorwes smerte,** *painful sorrows* 2768 **goost,** *spirit* 2770 **Syn,** *since,*
dure, *last* 2774 **departynge,** *the parting* 2777 **asketh men,** *do men ask*
2780 **swete foo,** *sweet enemy* 2781 **softe,** *softly,* **tweye,** *two* 2786 **wys,**
wise, **gye,** *guide* 2788 **circumstances,** *features* 2790 **estaat,** *rank,* **heigh
kynrede,** *high lineage* 2791 **Fredom,** *generosity,* **art,** *i.e., art of love* 2792
So, *so that,* **have of my soule part,** *(may) have my spiritual portion*
2798 **faille gan,** *did fail* 2802 **ago,** *gone*

2743ff. This follows medical theory of the time. Because his internal organs have been severely damaged (**tobrosten,** line 2757) Arcite's thick-
ened (**clothered,** line 2745) blood becomes infected (**Corrupteth,** line 2746) and produces poison (**venym,** line 2751). Bloodletting (**veyne-
blood,** line 2747, release of "excess" blood), cupping (**ventusynge,** line 2747, extraction or suction by heating a glass cup applied to the skin),
and medicines cannot remove the poison; Arcite's own **animal** (line 2749) and **natural** (line 2750) power of purgation is also ineffective. **2776
endere of my lyf,** "one who ends my life"; like "swete foo" (line 2780), the phrase is courtly oxymoron. **2775 wyf,** in *Teseida* 9.83, Arcite marries Emelye soon after the tournament; here the term is an acknowledgment of their betrothal or a term of endearment. **2787 speken of a
servaunt,** the syntax is difficult, but the use of **serveth** below (line 2795) makes it clear that Arcite thinks of Palamon as a servant of love.

That dwelled in his herte syk and soore,
Gan faillen whan the herte felte deeth. 2805
Dusked° his eyen two, and failled breeth,
But on his lady yet caste he his eye;
His laste word was, "Mercy, Emelye!"
His spirit chaunged hous° and wente ther
As I cam nevere, I kan nat tellen wher. 2810
Therfore I stynte°, I nam no divinistre°;
Of° soules fynde I nat in this registre°,
Ne me ne list thilke° opinions to telle
Of hem, though that they writen wher they
    dwelle.
Arcite is coold, ther° Mars his soule gye°. 2815
Now wol I speken forth of Emelye.

    Shrighte° Emelye, and howleth Palamon,
And Theseus his suster took anon
Swownynge°, and baar hire fro the corps away.
What helpeth it to tarien forth the day° 2820
To tellen how she weep bothe eve and morwe?
For in swich cas° wommen have swich sorwe,
Whan that hir housbondes ben from hem ago°,
That for the moore part they sorwen so,
Or ellis fallen in swich maladye 2825
That at the laste certeinly they dye.

    Infinite been the sorwes and the teeres
Of olde folk and folk of tendre yeeres
In al the toun for deeth of this Theban.
For hym ther wepeth bothe child and man. 2830
So greet wepyng was ther noon, certayn,
Whan Ector was ybroght, al fressh yslayn,
To Troye. Allas, the pitee that was ther,
Cracchynge° of chekes, rentynge° eek of heer.
"Why woldestow° be deed," thise wommen
    crye, 2835
"And haddest gold ynough, and Emelye?"
    No man myghte gladen Theseus,
Savynge° his olde fader Egeus,
That knew this worldes transmutacioun,
As he hadde seyn it chaunge bothe up
    and doun, 2840

Joye after wo, and wo after gladnesse,
And shewed hem ensamples° and liknesse°.
    "Right as ther dyed nevere man," quod he,
"That he ne lyvede in erthe in som degree,
Right so ther lyvede never man," he seyde, 2845
"In al this world, that som tyme he ne deyde.
This world nys° but a thurghfare° ful of wo,
And we been pilgrymes, passynge to and fro.
Deeth is an ende of every worldly soore°."
And over al this yet seyde he muchel moore 2850
To this effect, ful wisely to enhorte°
The peple that they sholde hem reconforte°.

    Duc Theseus, with al his bisy cure°,
Caste° now wher that the sepulture°
Of goode Arcite may best ymaked be, 2855
And eek moost honurable in his degree.
And at the laste he took conclusioun°
That ther as first Arcite and Palamoun
Hadden for love the bataille hem bitwene,
That in that selve° grove, swoote° and grene, 2860
Ther as he hadde his amorouse desires,
His compleynte°, and for love his hoote fires,
He wolde make a fyr in which the office
Funeral° he myghte al accomplice°.
And leet comande° anon to hakke and hewe 2865
The okes° olde, and leye hem on a rewe°
In colpons° wel arrayed° for to brenne°.
His officers with swifte feet they renne
And ryden anon at his comandement.
And after this, Theseus hath ysent 2870
After a beere°, and it al overspradde
With clooth of gold, the richeste that he
    hadde.
And of the same suyte° he cladde Arcite.
Upon his hondes hadde he gloves white,
Eek on his heed a coroune° of laurer° grene, 2875
And in his hond a swerd ful bright and kene.
He leyde hym, bare the visage°, on the beere;
Therwith he weep that pitee was to heere.
And for the peple sholde seen hym alle,

[handwritten marginalia, illegible]

2806 Dusked, *darkened* **2809 hous,** *houses* **2811 stynte,** *stop,* **divinistre,** *theologian* **2812 Of,** *concerning,* **registre,** *book* **2813 Ne me ne list thilke,** *nor does it please me those* **2815 ther,** *where,* **gye,** *guides* **2817 Shrighte,** *shrieked* **2819 Swownynge,** *swooning* **2820 tarien forth the day,** *waste time* **2822 swich cas,** *such circumstances* **2823 ago,** *gone* **2834 Cracchynge,** *scratching,* **rentynge,** *tearing* **2835 woldestow,** *would you* **2838 Savynge,** *except* **2842 ensamples,** *examples,* **liknesse,** *analogies* **2847 nys,** *is nothing,* **thurghfare,** *road* **2849 soore,** *pain* **2851 enhorte,**

urge **2852 hem reconforte,** *comfort themselves* **2853 cure,** *care* **2854 Caste,** *considered,* **sepulture,** *tomb* **2857 took conclusioun,** *concluded* **2860 selve,** *same,* **swoote,** *sweet* **2862 compleynte,** *lament* **2863–64 office / Funeral,** *funeral ceremony,* **accomplice,** *fulfill* **2865 leet comande,** *commanded* **2866 okes,** *oaks,* **on a rewe,** *in a row* **2867 colpons,** *piles,* **arrayed,** *arranged,* **brenne,** *burn* **2871 beere,** *bier* **2873 suyte,** *material* **2875 coroune,** *crown,* **laurer,** *laurel* **2877 bare the visage,** *with face uncovered*

2812 in this registre, Chaucer's source, *Teseida,* recounts that Arcite's spirit rose through the spheres, but Chaucer uses the scene elsewhere—as a model for the ascent of Troilus's soul in *TC* 5.1807ff. **2832 Ector,** Hector, hero of Troy, lamented by all after his defeat by Achilles; ultimate source, *Iliad* 22.405ff. **2841 Joye after wo,** similar sentiments are expressed by the Knight when he interrupts the Monk in *NPP* 7.2767ff. **2874 gloves white,** funeral emblem for an unmarried person.

Whan it was day, he broghte hym to the
    halle,   2880
That roreth of the criyng and the soun.
   Tho came this woful Theban Palamoun,
With flotery° berd and ruggy°, asshy heeres°,
In clothes blake, ydropped al with teeres;
And, passynge othere of° wepynge, Emelye,   2885
The rewefulleste° of al the compaignye.
In as muche as the servyce sholde be
The moore noble and riche in his degree,
Duc Theseus leet forth thre steedes brynge°,
That trapped° were in steel al gliterynge,   2890
And covered with the armes of daun° Arcite.
Upon thise steedes grete and white
Ther sitten folk, of whiche oon baar° his sheeld,
Another his spere up on his hondes heeld,
The thridde baar with hym his bowe
    Turkeys°—   2895
Of brend gold was the caas° and eek the
    harneys°—
And riden forth a paas° with sorweful cheere°
Toward the grove, as ye shul after heere.
The nobleste of the Grekes that ther were
Upon his shuldres caryeden the beere   2900
With slak paas°, and eyen° rede and wete,
Thurghout the citee by the maister strete°,
That sprad was al° with blak, and wonder hye
Right of the same is the strete ywrye°.
Upon the right hond wente olde Egeus,   2905
And on that oother syde Duc Theseus,
With vessels in hir hand of gold ful fyn,
Al ful of hony, milk, and blood, and wyn;
Eek Palamon, with ful greet compaignye;
And after that cam woful Emelye,   2910
With fyr° in honde, as was that tyme the gyse°,
To do the office of funeral servyse.
   Heigh° labour and ful greet apparaillynge°
Was at the service and the fyr-makynge,

That with his° grene top the heven raughte°;   2915
And twenty fadme of brede° the armes
    straughte°—
This is to seyn, the bowes weren so brode.
Of stree° first ther was leyd ful many a lode°.
But how the fyr was maked upon highte°,
Ne eek the names that the trees highte°,   2920
As ook, firre, birch, asp°, alder, holm°, popler,
Wylugh°, elm, plane, assh, box, chasteyn°, lynde°,
    laurer,
Mapul, thorn, bech°, hasel, ew°, whippeltree°,
How they weren fild°, shal nat be toold
    for me;
Ne hou the goddes ronnen° up and doun,   2925
Disherited° of hire habitacioun,
In which they woneden° in reste and pees,
Nymphus, fawnes, and amadrides;
Ne hou the beestes and the briddes alle
Fledden for fere, whan the wode was falle;   2930
Ne how the ground agast° was of the light,
That was nat wont° to seen the sonne bright;
Ne how the fyr was couched° first with stree°,
And thanne with drye stikkes cloven a thre°,
And thanne with grene wode and spicerye°,   2935
And thanne with clooth of gold and with
    perrye°,
And gerlandes, hangynge with ful many a flour;
The mirre°, th'encens, with al so greet odour;
Ne how Arcite lay among al this,
Ne what richesse aboute his body is;   2940
Ne how that Emelye, as was the gyse°,
Putte in° the fyr of funeral servyse;
Ne how she swowned whan men made the fyr,
Ne what she spak, ne what was hir desir;
Ne what jeweles men in the fyre caste,   2945
Whan that the fyr was greet and brente° faste;
Ne how somme caste hir sheeld, and somme hir
    spere,

2883 flotery, *fluttering,* **ruggy,** *shaggy,* **asshy heeres,** *ash-covered hair* **2885 passynge othere of,** *surpassing others in* **2886 rewefulleste,** *most sorrowful* **2889 leet forth . . . brynge,** *had brought forth* **2890 trapped,** *equipped* **2891 daun,** *sir* **2893 oon baar,** *one carried* **2895 bowe Turkeys,** *Turkish bow* **2896 caas,** *quiver,* **harneys,** *fittings* **2897 a paas,** *slowly,* **cheere,** *expression* **2901 slak paas,** *slow pace,* **eyen,** *eyes* **2902 maister strete,** *main street* **2903 That sprad was,** *the bier was covered* **2904 ywrye,** *draped* **2911 fyr,** *fire,* **gyse,** *custom* **2913 Heigh,** *great,* **apparaillynge,** *preparation* **2915 his,** *the woodpile's,* **raughte,** *reached to*

2916 twenty fadme of brede, *120 feet across,* **armes straughte,** *cross pieces stretched* **2918 stree,** *straw,* **lode,** *load* **2919 highte,** *height* **2920 highte,** *were called* **2921 asp,** *aspen,* **holm,** *holly* **2922 Wylugh,** *willow,* **chasteyn,** *chestnut,* **lynde,** *linden* **2923 bech,** *beech,* **ew,** *yew,* **whippeltree,** *dogwood* **2924 fild,** *felled* **2925 ronnen,** *ran* **2926 Disherited,** *deprived* **2927 woneden,** *lived* **2931 agast,** *afraid* **2932 wont,** *accustomed* **2933 couched,** *laid,* **stree,** *straw* **2934 cloven a thre,** *split into three* **2935 spicerye,** *spices* **2936 perrye,** *gems* **2938 mirre,** *myrrh* **2941 gyse,** *custom* **2942 Putte in,** *lit* **2946 brente,** *burned*

2911 fyr in honde, Emelye is prepared to light Arcite's funeral fire. **2924 shal nat be toold for me,** this description of what will *not* be described (what rhetoricians call *occupatio*) is the longest and clearest example of several in *KnT;* compare 875ff., 994ff., and 2197ff. **2925 the goddes,** in classical mythology minor deities inhabited forests and trees—nymphs (**nymphus,** line 2928) were nature spirits; fauns (**fawnes,** line 2928) were half-man and half-goat; hamadryads (**amadrides,** line 2928), spirits that lived in trees.

And of hire vestimentz°, whiche that they were°,
And coppes° fulle of wyn, and milk, and blood,
Into the fyr, that brente as it were wood°;　2950
Ne how the Grekes, with an huge route°,
Thries° riden al the fyr aboute
Upon the left hand, with a loud shoutynge,
And thries with hir speres claterynge;
And thries how the ladyes gonne crye;　2955
Ne how that lad° was homward Emelye;
Ne how Arcite is brent to asshen colde;
Ne how that lyche-wake° was yholde
Al thilke nyght; ne how the Grekes pleye
The wake-pleyes°, ne kepe° I nat to seye;　2960
Who wrastleth best naked with oille enoynt°,
Ne who that baar hym best, in no disjoynt°.
I wol nat tellen eek how that they goon
Hoom til Atthenes, whan the pley is doon;
But shortly to the point thanne wol I wende°,　2965
And maken of my longe tale an ende.
　By processe° and by lengthe of certeyn yeres,
Al stynted° is the moornynge and the teres
Of Grekes, by oon general assent.
Thanne semed me ther was a parlement°　2970
At Atthenes, upon certein pointz and caas°,
Among the whiche pointz yspoken° was
To have with certein contrees alliaunce,
And have fully of Thebans obeisaunce°.
For which this noble Theseus anon　2975
Leet senden after° gentil Palamon,
Unwist of° hym what was the cause and why,
But in his blake clothes sorwefully
He cam at his comandement in hye°.
Tho° sente Theseus for Emelye.　2980
Whan they were set, and hust° was al the place,

And Theseus abiden° hadde a space
Er any word cam fram his wise brest,
His eyen sette he ther as was his lest°.
And with a sad visage° he siked stille°,　2985
And after that right thus he seyde his wille°:
　"The Firste Moevere of the cause above°,
Whan he first made the faire cheyne of love,
Greet was th'effect and heigh was his entente.
Wel wiste° he why and what therof he mente,　2990
For with that faire cheyne of love he bond°
The fyr, the eyr, the water, and the lond
In certeyn° boundes, that they may nat flee.
That same Prince and that same Moevere," quod he,
"Hath stabilissed° in this wrecched world adoun°　2995
Certeyn dayes and duracioun
To al that is engendred° in this place,
Over the whiche day they may nat pace°,
Al mowe they° yet tho dayes wel abregge°.
Ther nedeth noght noon auctoritee allegge°,　3000
For it is preeved° by experience,
But that° me list declaren my sentence°.
Thanne may men by this ordre wel discerne
That thilke° Moevere stable is and eterne.
Wel may men knowe, but° it be a fool,　3005
That every part dirryveth° from his hool°,
For nature hath nat taken his° bigynnyng
Of no partie° or cantel° of a thyng,
But of a thyng that parfit° is and stable,
Descendynge so til it be corrumpable°.　3010
And therfore, of his wise purveiaunce°,
He hath so wel biset his ordinaunce°,
That speces° of thynges and progressiouns°

2948 hire vestimentz, *their clothing,* were, *wear* 2949 coppes, *cups* 2950 wood, *crazed* 2951 route, *company* 2952 Thries, *three times* 2956 lad, *led* 2958 lyche-wake, *body watch* 2960 wake-pleyes, *funeral games,* kepe, *care* 2961 enoynt, *anointed* 2962 in no disjoynt, *without difficulty* 2965 wende, *pass* 2967 processe, *course of events* 2968 stynted, *ceased* 2970 parlement, *formal discussion* 2971 pointz and caas, *issues and cases* 2972 yspoken, *decided* 2974 obeisaunce, *submission* 2976 Leet senden after, *sent for* 2977 Unwist of, *unknown to* 2979 in hye, *in haste* 2980 Tho, *then,* 2981 hust, *hushed* 2982 abiden, *waited* 2984 ther as was his lest, *where it pleased him* 2985 sad visage, *steady expression,* siked stille, *sighed quietly* 2986 seyde his wille,

announced his decision 2987 cause above, *ultimate cause* 2990 wiste, *knew* 2991 bond, *bound* 2993 certeyn, *fixed* 2995 stabilissed, *established,* adoun, *down here* 2997 engendred, *born* 2998 pace, *pass* 2999 Al mowe they, *although they may,* abregge, *shorten* 3000 allegge, *to call on* 3001 preeved, *proved* 3002 But that, *except,* me list declaren, *it pleases me to clarify,* sentence, *meaning* 3004 thilke, *the same* 3005 but, *unless* 3006 dirryveth, *derives,* hool, *whole* 3007 his, *its* 3008 partie, part, *cantel, portion* 3009 parfit, *perfect* 3010 corrumpable, *able to decay* 3011 purveiaunce, *providence* 3012 ordinaunce, *hierarchy* 3013 speces, *species,* progressiouns, *processes*

2967 certeyn yeres, the passing of years is Chaucer's adjustment; in *Teseida,* the wedding takes place only days after the funeral. 2973–74 alliaunce . . . Thebans, the political motivation for the marriage of Palamon and Emelye is not found in the *Teseida.* 2987 Firste Moevere, the *primum mobile* (first mover; God) of *Bo* 1.m5, 3.pr12, etc., who sets all things in motion. 2988 faire cheyne of love, the Platonic concept of a great ontological hierarchy descending from God through humans to other forms of animate and inanimate life, all held together by love, appears in *Bo* 2.m8 and elsewhere. 2992 fyr . . . eyr . . . water . . . lond, according to classical and medieval cosmology, all physical creation is composed of these four elements. 3006 dirryveth . . . hool, the Platonic notion that partiality derives from wholeness, as imperfection descends from perfection; *Bo* 3 pr.10. 3011 purveiaunce, Chaucer's usual form for "providence," i.e., foresight.

Shullen enduren by sucessiouns°,
And nat eterne°, withouten any lye°.   3015
This maystow understonde and seen at eye°.
    "Loo° the ook°, that hath so long a norisshynge
From tyme that it first bigynneth sprynge,
And hath so long a lif, as we may see,
Yet at the laste wasted is the tree.   3020
    "Considereth eek how that the harde stoon
Under oure feet, on which we trede and goon°,
Yet wasteth it as it lyth by the weye.
The brode ryver somtyme wexeth° dreye.
The grete tounes se we wane and wende°.   3025
Thanne may ye se that al this thyng° hath ende.
    "Of man and womman seen we wel also
That nedeth°, in oon of thise termes two°,
This is to seyn in youthe or elles age,
He moot be deed, the kyng as shal a page,   3030
Som in his bed, som in the depe see,
Som in the large feeld, as men may see—
Ther helpeth noght, al goth that ilke° weye.
Thanne may I seyn that al this thyng moot deye°.
    "What maketh this but Juppiter, the kyng,   3035
That is prince and cause of alle thyng,
Convertynge° al unto his propre welle°
From which it is dirryved°, sooth° to telle?
And heer-agayns° no creature on lyve°,
Of no degree, availleth° for to stryve.   3040
    "Thanne is it wysdom, as it thynketh me,
To maken vertu of necessitee,
And take it weel° that we may nat eschue°,
And namely that° to us alle is due.
And whoso gruccheth ought°, he dooth
        folye,   3045
And rebel is to hym that al may gye°.
And certeinly a man hath moost honour
To dyen in his excellence and flour°,
Whan he is siker° of his goode name;
Thanne hath he doon his freend, ne hym, no
        shame.   3050
And gladder oghte his freend been of his deeth,

Whan with honour up yolden° is his breeth,
Than whan his name apalled° is for age,
For° al forgeten is his vassellage°.
Thanne is it best, as for a worthy fame,   3055
To dyen whan that he is best of name.
    "The contrarie of al this is wilfulnesse.
Why grucchen° we, why have we hevynesse,
That goode Arcite, of chivalrie flour°,
Departed is with duetee° and honour   3060
Out of this foule prisoun of this lyf?
Why grucchen heere his cosyn and his wyf
Of his welfare, that loved hem° so weel?
Kan he hem° thank—nay, God woot°, never a
        deel°—
That bothe his soule and eek hemself
        offende°?   3065
And yet they mowe hir lustes nat amende°.
    What may I concluden of this longe serye°?
But after wo I rede° us to be merye,
And thanken Juppiter of al his grace.
And er that we departen from this place   3070
I rede we make of sorwes two
O parfit joye, lastynge everemo.
And looketh now wher moost sorwe is herinne,
Ther wol we first amenden° and bigynne.
    "Suster," quod he, "this is my fulle assent°,   3075
With al th'avys° heere of my parlement,
That gentil Palamon, youre owene knyght,
That serveth yow with wille, herte, and myght,
And ever hath doon syn° ye first hym knewe,
That ye shul of youre grace upon hym rewe°,   3080
And taken hym for housbonde and for lord.
Lene° me youre hond, for this is oure accord.
Lat se° now of youre wommanly pitee.
He is a kynges brother sone, pardee,
And though he were a poure bacheler°,   3085
Syn he hath served yow so many a yeer,
And had for yow so greet adversitee,
It moste been considered, leeveth° me,
For gentil mercy oghte to passen right°."

3014 **by sucessiouns,** *in succession* 3015 **eterne,** *eternally,* **lye,** *lie* 3016 **at eye,** *plainly* 3017 **Loo,** *behold,* **ook,** *oak* 3022 **trede and goon,** *tread and walk* 3024 **wexeth,** *becomes* 3025 **wende,** *pass away* 3026 **al this thyng,** *everything* 3028 **nedeth,** *necessarily,* **termes two,** *two periods of life* 3033 **ilke,** *same* 3034 **moot deye,** *must die* 3037 **Convertynge,** *returning,* **his propre welle,** *its own source* 3038 **dirryved,** *derived,* **sooth,** *truth* 3039 **heer-agayns,** *against this,* **on lyve,** *alive* 3040 **availleth,** *benefits* 3043 **weel,** *well,* **eschue,** *avoid* 3044 **namely that,** *especially that which* 3045 **whoso gruccheth ought,** *whoever grumbles at all* 3046 **may gye,** *guides* 3048 **flour,** *flower* 3049 **siker,** *certain* 3052 **up yolden,** *yielded up* 3053 **apalled,** *grown pale* 3054 **For,** *because,* **vassellage,** *service* 3058 **grucchen,** *complain* 3059 **of chivalrie flour,** *flower of chivalry* 3060 **duetee,** *respect* 3063 **hem,** *him* 3064 **hem,** *them,* **woot,** *knows,* **never a deel,** *not a bit* 3065 **offende,** *injure* 3066 **mowe hir lustes nat amende,** *cannot resolve their desires* 3067 **serye,** *series of points* 3068 **rede,** *advise* 3074 **amenden,** *make better* 3075 **fulle assent,** *sincere desire* 3076 **th'avys,** *the advice* 3079 **syn,** *since* 3080 **rewe,** *take pity* 3082 **Lene,** *give* 3083 **Lat se,** *show* 3085 **bacheler,** *young knight* 3088 **leeveth,** *believe* 3089 **passen right,** *surpass prerogative*

3042 **maken vertu of necessitee,** the same proverbial phrase occurs in *SqT* 5.593 and *TC* 4.1586.

Thanne seyde he thus to Palamon the
    knight,   3090
"I trowe° ther nedeth litel sermonyng°
To make yow assente to this thyng.
Com neer, and taak youre lady by the hond."
    Bitwixen hem was maad anon the bond
That highte° matrimoigne or mariage,   3095
By al the conseil and the baronage.
And thus with alle blisse and melodye
Hath Palamon ywedded Emelye.
And God, that al this wyde world hath wroght,

Sende hym his love that hath it deere
    aboght°,   3100
For now is Palamon in alle wele°,
Lyvynge in blisse, in richesse, and in heele°,
And Emelye hym loveth so tendrely,
And he hire serveth also gentilly°,
That nevere was ther no word hem bitwene   3105
Of jalousie or any oother teene°.
Thus endeth Palamon and Emelye,
And God save al this faire compaignye. Amen.

Heere is ended the Knyghtes Tale.

3091 trowe, *believe,* **sermonyng,** *preaching* **3095 highte,** *is called* **3100
deere aboght,** *dearly bought* **3101 alle wele,** *complete joy* **3102 heele,**
health **3104 gentilly,** *nobly* **3106 teene,** *pain*

MILLER'S TALE

PROLOGUE

Heere folwen the wordes bitwene the Hoost and the Millere.

Whan that the Knyght had thus his tale
    ytoold,
In al the route° ne was ther yong ne oold   3110
That he ne seyde it was a noble storie
And worthy for to drawen to memorie°,
And namely the gentils everichon°.
Oure Hooste lough and swoor, "So moot° I gon°,
This gooth aright; unbokeled° is the male°.   3115
Lat se° now who shal telle another tale.
For trewely the game is wel bigonne.
Now telleth ye, sire Monk, if that ye konne
Somwhat to quite with° the Knyghtes tale."
    The Millere, that fordronken° was al pale   3120
So that unnethe° upon his hors he sat,
He nolde avalen° neither hood ne hat,
Ne abyde° no man for his curteisie,
But in Pilates voys he gan to crie,
And swoor, "By armes and by blood and
    bones,   3125

I kan° a noble tale for the nones°,
With which I wol now quite° the Knyghtes
    tale."
Oure Hooste saugh that he was dronke of ale,
And seyde, "Abyd°, Robyn, my leeve° brother,
Som bettre man shal telle us first another.   3130
Abyd, and lat us werken thriftily°."
    "By Goddes soule," quod he, "that wol nat I,
For I wol speke or elles go my wey."
Oure Hoost answerde, "Tel on, a devele wey°!
Thou art a fool; thy wit is overcome."   3135
    "Now herkneth°," quod the Millere, "alle and
    some°.
But first I make a protestacioun:
That I am dronke, I knowe it by my soun°.
And therfore if that I mysspeke or seye,
Wyte° it the ale of Southwerk, I you preye.   3140
For I wol telle a legende and a lyf
Bothe of a carpenter and of his wyf,

3110 route, *company* **3112 drawen to memorie,** *remember* **3113 gentils
everichon,** *each upper-class person* **3114 moot,** *might,* **gon,** *go* **3115 un-
bokeled,** *unbuckled,* **male,** *purse* **3116 Lat se,** *let's see* **3119 quite with,**
repay **3120 fordronken,** *very drunk* **3121 unnethe,** *barely* **3122 nolde**

avalen, *would not remove* **3123 abyde,** *wait for* **3126 kan,** *know,* **nones,**
occasion **3127 quite,** *pay back* **3129 Abyd,** *wait,* **leeve,** *dear* **3131 thriftily,**
properly **3134 a devele wey,** *by the devil's path* **3136 herkneth,** *listen,* **alle
and some,** *everybody* **3138 soun,** *sound* **3140 Wyte,** *recognize*

3114 So moot I gon, an exclamation meaning something like "As I may walk" or "(I swear) by the fact that I am walking." **3124 Pilates
voys,** in popular religious plays, Pontius Pilate was a roaring loudmouth. **3125 By armes . . . ,** by God's arms and blood and bones, an
extravagant oath.

How that a clerk hath set the wrightes° cappe."
   The Reve answerde and seyde, "Stynt thy clappe°!
Lat be thy lewed° dronken harlotrye°.   3145
It is a synne and eek a greet folye
To apeyren° any man, or hym defame,
And eek to bryngen wyves in swich fame°.
Thou mayst ynogh° of othere thynges seyn°."
   This dronke Millere spak ful soone ageyn   3150
And seyde, "Leve brother Osewold,
Who° hath no wyf, he is no cokewold°.
But I sey nat therfore that thou art oon°.
Ther been ful goode wyves many oon,
And evere a thousand goode ayeyns° oon badde.   3155
That knowestow wel thyself, but° if thou madde°.
Why artow° angry with my tale now?
I have a wyf, pardee°, as wel as thow,
Yet nolde I°, for the oxen in my plogh,
Take upon me moore than ynogh,   3160
As demen° of myself that I were oon.
I wol bileve wel that I am noon.
An housbonde shal nat been inquisityf

Of Goddes pryvetee°, nor of his wyf.
So° he may fynde Goddes foyson° there,   3165
Of the remenant nedeth nat° enquere."
   What sholde I moore seyn, but this Millere
He nolde° his wordes for no man forbere°,
But tolde his cherles° tale in his manere.
M'athynketh° that I shal reherce it heere.   3170
And therfore every gentil wight° I preye,
For Goddes love, demeth° nat that I seye
Of yvel entente, but that I moot° reherce
Hir° tales alle, be they bettre or werse,
Or elles falsen° som of my mateere.   3175
And therfore, whoso list° it nat yheere,
Turne over the leef° and chese° another tale;
For he shal fynde ynowe°, grete and smale,
Of storial° thyng that toucheth gentillesse°,
And eek moralitee and hoolynesse.   3180
Blameth nat me if that ye chese amys°.
The Millere is a cherl°, ye knowe wel this,
So was the Reve and other manye mo,
And harlotrie° they tolden bothe two°.
Avyseth yow°, and put me out of blame;   3185
And eek men shal nat maken ernest of game°.

Heere bigynneth the Millere his tale.

   Whilom° ther was dwellynge at Oxenford°
A riche gnof° that gestes heeld to bord°,
And of his craft he was a carpenter.
With hym ther was dwellynge a poure scoler,   3190
Hadde lerned art°, but al his fantasye°
Was turned for to lerne astrologye,
And koude° a certeyn° of conclusiouns°,
To demen° by interrogaciouns°,

If that men asked hym in certein houres   3195
Whan that men sholde have droghte° or elles shoures°,
Or if men asked hym what sholde bifalle°
Of every thyng—I may nat rekene° hem alle.
   This clerk was cleped hende° Nicholas.
Of deerne° love he koude° and of solas°,   3200
And therto he was sleigh° and ful privee°,

3143 wrightes, *carpenter's* **3144 Stynt thy clappe,** *stop your chatter* **3145 lewed,** *ignorant,* **harlotrye,** *vulgarity* **3147 apeyren,** *injure* **3148 swich fame,** *such reputation* **3149 ynogh,** *enough,* **seyn,** *say* **3152 Who,** *whoever,* **cokewold,** *cuckold* **3153 oon,** *one* **3155 ayeyns,** *compared with* **3156 but if,** *unless,* **madde** *(are) crazy* **3157 artow,** *are you* **3158 pardee,** *by God* **3159 nolde I,** *I wouldn't* **3161 demen,** *to consider* **3164 Goddes pryvetee,** *God's secrets* **3165 So,** *if,* **foyson,** *plenty* **3166 nedeth nat,** *(he) need not* **3168 nolde,** *wouldn't* **forbere,** *hold back* **3169 cherles,** *peasant's* **3170 M'athynketh,** *I regret* **3171 gentil wight,** *gentleperson* **3172 demeth,** *judge* **3173 moot,** *must* **3174 Hir,** *their* **3175 falsen,** *falsify* **3176 whoso list,** *whoever wants* **3177 leef,** *page,* **chese,** *choose* **3178**

ynowe, *enough* **3179 storial,** *narrative,* **gentillesse,** *gentility* **3181 amys,** *improperly* **3182 cherl,** *low-born fellow* **3184 harlotrie,** *vulgarity,* **bothe two,** *both of them* **3185 Avyseth yow,** *be advised* **3186 ernest of game,** *seriousness from play* **3187 Whilom,** *once,* **Oxenford,** *Oxford* **3188 gnof,** *oaf,* **gestes heeld to bord,** *took in guests as boarders* **3191 art,** *the liberal arts,* **fantasye,** *desire* **3193 koude,** *(he) knew,* **certeyn,** *number,* **conclusiouns,** *formulas* **3194 demen,** *assess,* **interrogaciouns,** *questions* **3196 droghte,** *drought,* **shoures,** *showers* **3197 sholde bifalle,** *might happen* **3198 rekene,** *tally* **3199 cleped hende,** *called handy (see note)* **3200 deerne,** *secret,* **koude,** *knew,* **solas,** *pleasure* **3201 sleigh,** *sly,* **ful privee,** *very secretive*

3143 set the . . . cappe, "set the cap," an idiom meaning make a fool of him. The Reeve is a carpenter; see *RvP* 1.3861 **3155–56** This couplet, perhaps added late, appears only in some manuscripts. **3159 oxen in my plogh,** euphemism for genitalia, as plowing is a traditional sexual metaphor. This also seems to echo *KnT* 1.887. **3160–61 Take upon me . . . ,** assume more than is necessary and consider myself to be a cuckold. **3170–86** The epilogue to Boccaccio's *Decameron* includes an apology that is in some ways similar to Chaucer's. **3195 certein houres,** astrological predictions depend on the positions of the stars at certain hours. **3199 hende,** consistently applied to Nicholas, the adjective means "handy" and "nearby" as well as "courteous." **3200 deerne love,** secret love, in the courtly tradition thought to intensify desire.

And lyk a mayden meke° for to see.
A chambre hadde he in that hostelrye
Allone, withouten any compaignye,
Ful fetisly ydight° with herbes swoote°,   3205
And he hymself as sweete as is the roote
Of lycorys° or any cetewale°.
His Almageste° and bookes grete and smale,
His astrelabie° longynge for° his art,
His augrym° stones layen faire apart,   3210
On shelves couched° at his beddes heed;
His presse° ycovered with a faldyng reed°;
And al above ther lay a gay sautrie°,
On which he made a-nyghtes melodie
So swetely that al the chambre rong,   3215
And *Angelus ad virginem* he song,
And after that he song the Kynges Noote.
Ful often blessed was his myrie throte.
And thus this sweete clerk his tyme spente
After° his freendes fyndyng° and his rente°.   3220
    This carpenter hadde wedded newe° a wyf,
Which that he lovede moore than his lyf.
Of eighteeene yeer she was of age.
Jalous he was, and heeld hire narwe° in cage,
For she was yong and wylde, and he was old,   3225
And demed° hymself been lik a cokewold.
He knew nat Catoun, for his wit was rude°,
That bad° man sholde wedde his simylitude°.
Men sholde wedden after hire estaat°,
For youthe and elde is often at debaat.   3230
But sith° that he was fallen in the snare,
He moste° endure, as oother folk, his care.
    Fair was this yonge wyf, and therwithal°
As any wezele° hir body gent° and smal°.

A ceynt° she werede°, ybarred° al of silk,   3235
A barmclooth° eek as whit as morne° milk
Upon hir lendes°, ful of many a goore°;
Whit was hir smok°, and broyden° al bifoore
And eek bihynde, on hir coler° aboute,
Of col-blak silk, withinne and eek withoute;   3240
The tapes° of hir white voluper°
Were of the same suyte of° hir coler;
Hir filet° brood of silk, and set ful hye.
And sikerly° she hadde a likerous° eye.
Ful smale ypulled° were hire browes° two,   3245
And tho° were bent and blake as any sloo°.
She was ful moore blisful° on to see°
Than is the newe pere-jonette° tree,
And softer than the wolle is of a wether°.
And by hir girdel heeng° a purs of lether,   3250
Tasseled with silk and perled° with latoun°.
In al this world, to seken up and doun,
Ther nys° no man so wys that koude thenche°
So gay a popelote° or swich° a wenche.
Ful brighter was the shynyng of hir hewe°   3255
Than in the Tour the noble° yforged newe.
    But of hir song, it was as loude and yerne°
As any swalwe° sittynge on a berne°.
Therto° she koude skippe and make game
As any kyde° or calf folwynge his dame°.   3260
Hir mouth was sweete as bragot° or the meeth°,
Or hoord of apples leyd in hey° or heeth°.
Wynsynge° she was as is a joly colt,
Long as a mast, and upright° as a bolt°.
A brooch she baar° upon hir lowe coler   3265
As brood as is the boos° of a bokeler°.
Hir shoes were laced on hir legges hye.

3202 meke, *meek* **3205 Ful fetisly ydight,** *very elegantly furnished,* **swoote,** *sweet* **3207 lycorys,** *licorice,* **cetewale,** *zedoary* (*a spice*) **3208 Almageste,** *astrology book* **3209 astrelabie,** *astrolabe,* **longynge for,** *belonging to* **3210 augrym,** *arithmetic* **3211 couched,** *arranged* **3212 presse,** *cupboard,* **faldyng reed,** *red coarse cloth* **3213 sautrie,** *harp* **3220 After,** *according to,* **freendes fyndyng,** *support from friends,* **rente,** *income* **3221 newe,** *recently* **3224 narwe,** *closely* **3226 demed,** *thought* **3227 rude,** *ignorant* **3228 That bad,** *who asserted,* **simylitude,** *equal* **3229 after hire estaat,** *according to their condition* **3231 sith,** *since* **3232 moste,** *must* **3233 therwithal,** *moreover* **3234 wezele,** *weasel,* **gent,** *delicate,* **smal,** *slender* **3235 ceynt,** *belt,* **werede,** *wore,* **ybarred,** *striped* **3236 barmclooth,** *apron,* **morne,** *morning* **3237 lendes,** *loins,* **goore,** *attached pleat* **3238 smok,** *dress,* **broyden,** *embroidered* **3239 coler,** *collar* **3241 tapes,** *ties,* **voluper,** *bonnet* **3242 suyte of,** *pattern as* **3243 filet,** *headband* **3244 sikerly,** *certainly,* **likerous,** *inviting* **3245 ypulled,** *plucked,* **browes,** *eyebrows* **3246 tho,** *those,* **sloo,** *blackthorn berry* **3247 blisful,** *splendid,* **on to see,** *to look at* **3248 pere-jonette,** *blossoming pear* **3249 wether,** *sheep* **3250 heeng,** *hung* **3251 perled,** *decorated,* **latoun,** *brass* **3253 nys,** *isn't,* **koude thenche,** *could imagine* **3254 popelote,** *doll,* **swich,** *such* **3255 hewe,** *complexion* **3256 noble,** *gold coin* **3257 yerne,** *lively* **3258 swalwe,** *swallow,* **berne,** *barn* **3259 Therto,** *also* **3260 kyde,** *kid,* **dame,** *mother* **3261 bragot,** *honey ale,* **meeth,** *mead* **3262 hey,** *hay,* **heeth,** *heather* **3263 Wynsynge,** *skittish* **3264 upright,** *straight,* **bolt,** *arrow* **3265 baar,** *wore* **3266 boos,** *central disk,* **bokeler,** *small shield***

3204 The line echoes *KnT* 1.2779. **3209 astrelabie,** astrolabe, a device for determining the position of the stars. **3210 augrym stones,** cubes marked with Arabic numerals for computation. **3216 *Angelus ad virginem,*** "The Angel to the Virgin," a hymn commemorating the angel Gabriel's Annunciation of the coming birth of Jesus to Mary (whose husband was a carpenter, as is Alisoun's). **3217 Kynges Noote,** an unidentified song, "The King's Tune." **3220 freendes fyndyng,** compare *GP* 1.299–302 and 301–2n. **3224 narwe in cage,** a metaphor for restricting her closely. **3227 Catoun,** Dionysius Cato, supposed author of *Disticha Catonis* (Cato's Couplets), a collection of maxims used as a medieval schoolbook. **3248 pere-jonette tree,** pear trees were symbols of sexuality. **3254 wenche,** the connotations ranged from "lass" to "prostitute." **3256 Tour,** Tower of London, site of the mint. **3258 swalwe,** the swallow was thought to be lascivious.

She was a prymerole°, a piggesnye°,
For any lord to leggen° in his bedde,
Or yet for any good yeman° to wedde.   3270
　　Now sire, and eft° sire, so bifel the cas°
That on a day this hende Nicholas
Fil° with this yonge wyf to rage° and pleye,
Whil that hir housbonde was at Oseneye—
As clerkes ben ful subtile and ful queynte°—   3275
And prively he caughte hire by the queynte°,
And seyde, "Ywis°, but if ich° have my wille,
For deerne° love of thee, lemman°, I spille°,"
And heeld hire harde by the haunche-bones°,
And seyde, "Lemman, love me al atones,   3280
Or I wol dyen, also God me save!"
And she sproong as a colt dooth in the trave°,
And with hir heed she wryed° faste awey,
And seyde, "I wol nat kisse thee, by my fey°.
Why, lat be," quod she, "lat be, Nicholas,   3285
Or I wol crie, 'out, harrow°' and 'allas'!
Do wey youre handes, for youre curteisye."
　　This Nicholas gan mercy for to crye,
And spak so faire, and profred him° so faste°,
That she hir love hym graunted atte laste,   3290
And swoor hir ooth by Seint Thomas of Kent
That she wol been at his comandement,
Whan that she may hir leyser° wel espie°.
"Myn housbonde is so ful of jalousie
That but ye wayte wel and been privee°,   3295
I woot° right wel I nam° but deed," quod she.
"Ye moste been ful deerne°, as in this cas."
　　"Nay, therof care° thee noght," quod Nicholas.
"A clerk hadde litherly biset° his whyle°,
But if he koude° a carpenter bigyle°."   3300
And thus they been accorded and ysworn

To wayte a tyme, as I have told biforn.
　　Whan Nicholas had doon thus everideel°,
And thakked° hire aboute the lendes° weel,
He kist hire sweete and taketh his sawtrie°,   3305
And pleyeth faste, and maketh melodie.
　　Thanne fil it thus, that to the paryssh chirche°,
Cristes owene werkes for to wirche°,
This goode wyf wente on an haliday°.
Hir forheed shoon as bright as any day,   3310
So was it wasshen whan she leet° hir werk.
　　Now was ther of that chirche a parissh clerk°,
The which that° was ycleped° Absolon.
Crul° was his heer, and as the gold it shoon,
And strouted° as a fanne° large and brode—   3315
Ful streight and evene lay his joly shode°.
His rode° was reed°, his eyen greye as goos°.
With Poules° wyndow corven° on his shoos,
In hoses rede° he wente fetisly°.
Yclad° he was ful smal° and proprely   3320
Al in a kirtel° of a lyght waget°—
Ful faire and thikke been the poyntes° set—
And therupon he hadde a gay surplys°
As whit as is the blosme° upon the rys°.
A myrie child° he was, so God me save.   3325
Wel koude he laten° blood, and clippe,
　　and shave,
And maken a chartre of lond or acquitaunce°.
In twenty manere° koude he trippe° and daunce
After the scole° of Oxenforde tho°,
And with his legges casten° to and fro,   3330
And pleyen songes on a smal rubible°,
Therto he song somtyme a loud quynyble°,
And as wel koude he pleye on a giterne°.
In al the toun nas° brewhous ne taverne

3268 **prymerole**, *primrose*, **piggesnye**, *pig's eye* 3269 **leggen**, *lay* 3270 **yeman**, *yeoman* 3271 **eft**, *again*, **bifel the cas**, *happened the chance* 3273 **Fil**, *happened*, **rage**, *romp* 3275 **queynte**, *clever* 3276 **queynte**, *crotch* 3277 **Ywis**, *surely*, **but if ich**, *unless I* 3278 **deerne**, *secret*, **lemman**, *beloved*, **spille**, *die* (with play on *ejaculate?*) 3279 **haunchebones**, *thighs* 3280 **atones**, *at once* 3282 **trave**, *pen for shoeing unruly horses* 3283 **wryed**, *twisted* 3284 **fey**, *faith* 3286 **harrow**, *help* 3289 **profred him**, *urged himself* (on her), **faste**, *eagerly* 3293 **leyser**, *opportunity*, **espie**, *spy* 3295 **privee**, *cautious* 3296 **woot**, *know*, **nam**, *am not* 3297 **deerne**, *secretive* 3298 **care**, *concern* 3299 **litherly biset**, *badly used*, **whyle**, *time* 3300 **But if he koude**, *unless he could*, **bigyle**, *trick* 3303 **everideel**, *every bit* 3304 **thakked**, *patted*, **lendes**, *loins* 3305

sawtrie, *harp* 3307 **paryssh chirche**, *parish church* 3308 **wirche**, *perform* 3309 **haliday**, *holy day* 3311 **leet**, *left* 3312 **parissh clerk**, *assistant to the priest* 3313 **The which that**, *who*, **ycleped**, *named* 3314 **Crul**, *curled* 3315 **strouted**, *spread out*, **fanne**, *fan* 3316 **joly shode**, *pretty part in his hair* 3317 **rode**, *complexion*, **reed**, *rosy*, **goos**, *goose* 3318 **Poules**, *Paul's*, **corven**, *cut* 3319 **hoses rede**, *red stockings*, **fetisly**, *elegantly* 3320 **Yclad**, *dressed*, **smal**, *daintily* 3321 **kirtel**, *tunic*, **lyght waget**, *pale blue* 3322 **poyntes**, *laces* 3323 **surplys**, *outer gown* 3324 **blosme**, *blossom*, **rys**, *branch* 3325 **child**, *young man* 3326 **laten**, *let* 3327 **acquitaunce**, *legal release* 3328 **manere**, *ways*, **trippe**, *cavort* 3329 **scole**, *fashion*, **tho**, *then* 3330 **casten**, *fling* 3331 **rubible**, *fiddle* 3332 **quynyble**, *high treble* 3333 **giterne**, *guitar* 3334 **nas**, *(there) was no*

3268 prymerole . . . piggesnye, flower names, and perhaps terms of endearment. **3274 Oseneye**, Osney, less than a mile from central Oxford and site of an abbey of Augustinian canons at whose church carpenter John works; see lines 3659ff. below. **3291 Seint Thomas of Kent**, Thomas Becket. **3313 Absolon**, recalls the biblical Absolom, a beautiful man who was killed after his long hair tangled him in a tree; 2 Samuel 14.25,18.9ff. **3318 Poules wyndow**, the design of a window at St. Paul's Cathedral was cut into his shoes; very fashionable. **3326 laten blood, and clippe, and shave**, the clerk Absolon was also a bloodletter (minor surgeon) and a barber, skilled with cutting instruments; see 3766n. On bloodletting, see *KnT* 1.2743n.

That he ne visited with his solas°,   3335
Ther° any gaylard tappestere° was.
But sooth° to seyn, he was somdeel
    squaymous°
Of fartyng, and of speche daungerous°.
    This Absolon, that jolif° was and gay,
Gooth with a sencer° on the haliday,   3340
Sensynge° the wyves of the parisshe faste.
And many a lovely° look on hem he caste,
And namely on this carpenteris wyf.
To looke on hire hym thoughte a myrie lyf,
She was so propre and sweete and likerous°.   3345
I dar wel seyn, if she hadde been a mous,
And he a cat, he wolde hire hente anon°.
This parissh clerk, this joly Absolon,
Hath in his herte swich a love-longynge
That of no wyf took he noon offrynge—   3350
For curteisie, he seyde, he wolde noon.
    The moone, whan it was nyght, ful brighte
    shoon,
And Absolon his gyterne° hath ytake,
For paramours° he thoghte for to wake°.
And forth he gooth, jolif and amorous,   3355
Til he cam to the carpenteres hous
A litel after cokkes hadde ycrowe°,
And dressed hym up° by a shot-wyndowe°
That was upon the carpenteris wal.
He syngeth in his voys gentil and smal,   3360
"Now, deere lady, if thy wille be,
I praye yow that ye wole rewe° on me,"
Ful wel acordaunt° to his gyternynge.
This carpenter awook and herde him synge,
And spak unto his wyf and seyde anon,   3365
"What, Alison, herestow nat° Absolon,
That chaunteth thus under oure boures° wal?"
And she answerde hir housbonde therwithal,
"Yis, God woot°, John, I heere it every deel°."

This passeth forth; what wol ye bet° than
    weel°?   3370
Fro day to day this joly Absolon
So woweth° hire that hym is wobigon°.
He waketh al the nyght and al the day;
He kembeth° his lokkes brode, and made hym
    gay;
He woweth hire by meenes° and brocage°,   3375
And swoor he wolde been hir owene page;
He syngeth, brokkynge° as a nyghtyngale;
He sente hire pyment°, meeth°, and spiced ale,
And wafres°, pipyng hoot out of the gleede°;
And, for° she was of towne, he profreth
    meede°—   3380
For som folk wol ben wonnen for richesse,
And somme for strokes°, and somme for
    gentillesse.
    Somtyme, to shewe° his lightnesse° and
    maistrye°,
He pleyeth Herodes upon a scaffold hye°.
But what availleth° hym as in this cas?   3385
She loveth so this hende Nicholas
That Absolon may blowe the bukkes horn°;
He ne hadde for his labour but a scorn.
And thus she maketh Absolon hire ape,
And al his ernest turneth til a jape°.   3390
Ful sooth° is this proverbe, it is no lye,
Men seyn right thus, "Alwey the nye slye°
Maketh the ferre leeve° to be looth°."
For though that Absolon be wood or wrooth°
By cause that he fer° was from hire sighte,   3395
This nye° Nicholas stood in his lighte.
    Now bere thee wel, thou hende Nicholas,
For Absolon may waille and synge, "Allas!"
And so bifel it on a Saterday
This carpenter was goon til Osenay,   3400
And hende Nicholas and Alisoun

3335 **solas,** *entertainment* 3336 **Ther,** *where,* **gaylard tappestere,** *lively barmaid* 3337 **sooth,** *true,* **somdeel squaymous,** *somewhat squeamish* 3338 **daungerous,** *standoffish* 3339 **jolif,** *merry* 3340 **sencer,** *censer* 3341 **Sensynge,** *incensing* 3342 **lovely,** *amorous* 3345 **likerous,** *desirable* 3347 **hente anon,** *seize at once* 3353 **gyterne,** *guitar* 3354 **paramours,** *love, wake, stay up* 3357 **ycrowe,** *crowed* 3358 **dressed hym up,** *situated himself,* **shot-wyndowe,** *hinged window* 3362 **rewe,** *have pity* 3363 **acordaunt,** *harmonious* 3366 **herestow nat,** *don't you hear* 3367 **boures,** *bedroom's* 3368 **therwithal,** *in that regard* 3369 **woot,** *knows,* **deel,** *bit* 3370 **bet,** *better,* **weel,** *well* 3372 **woweth,** *woos,* **wobigon,**

woeful 3374 **kembeth,** *combs* 3375 **meenes,** *go-betweens,* **brocage,** *use of agents* 3377 **brokkynge,** *trilling* 3378 **pyment,** *wine punch,* **meeth,** *mead* 3379 **wafres,** *cakes,* **gleede,** *coals* 3380 **for,** *because,* **profreth meede,** *offered money* 3382 **for strokes,** *by force* 3383 **shewe,** *show off,* **lightnesse,** *agility,* **maistrye,** *skill* 3384 **scaffold hye,** *raised platform (a stage)* 3385 **availleth,** *benefits* 3387 **blowe the bukkes horn,** *go whistle* 3390 **jape,** *joke* 3391 **sooth,** *true* 3392 **nye slye,** *sly one nearby* 3393 **ferre leeve,** *distant lover,* **looth,** *loathed* 3394 **wood or wrooth,** *crazy or angry* 3395 **fer,** *far* 3396 **nye,** *nearby*

3339 jolif, frequently applied to Absolon, the term meant "merry," even "frisky" or "amorous." **3340 sencer,** a portable incense burner used in church rituals. The aromatic smoke symbolized Christian zeal and the act of censing conveyed honor, although Absolon uses it otherwise. **3350 offrynge,** priests and their clerks usually accepted offerings to support themselves and the local church. **3370 what wol ye bet than weel,** an idiom meaning "what more do you expect?" **3384 pleyeth Herodes,** played Herod, a raging bully in religious dramas. **3396 stood in his lighte,** i.e., got in his way.

Acorded been to this conclusioun,
That Nicholas shal shapen° hym a wyle°
This sely° jalous housbonde to bigyle°,
And if so be the game wente aright,   3405
She sholde slepen in his arm al nyght,
For this was his desir and hire also.
And right anon, withouten wordes mo,
This Nicholas no lenger wolde tarie°,
But dooth ful softe° unto his chambre carie   3410
Bothe mete and drynke for a day or tweye°,
And to hire housbonde bad hire for to seye,
If that he axed° after Nicholas,
She sholde seye she nyste° where he was,
Of al that day she saugh hym nat with eye;   3415
She trowed° that he was in maladye,
For for no cry hir mayde koude hym calle,
He nolde answere for thyng° that myghte falle°.

This passeth forth al thilke° Saterday,
That Nicholas stille in his chambre lay,   3420
And eet° and sleep, or dide what hym leste°,
Til Sonday, that the sonne gooth to reste.

This sely carpenter hath greet merveyle°
Of Nicholas, or what thyng myghte hym eyle°,
And seyde, "I am adrad°, by Seint Thomas,   3425
It stondeth nat aright with Nicholas.
God shilde° that he deyde° sodeynly!
This world is now ful tikel°, sikerly°.
I saugh° today a cors° yborn to chirche
That now°, on Monday last, I saugh hym
        wirche.   3430

"Go up," quod he unto his knave° anoon,
"Clepe° at his dore, or knokke with a stoon.
Looke how it is, and tel me boldely."

This knave gooth hym up ful sturdily°,
And at the chambre dore whil that he stood   3435
He cride and knokked as that he were wood°,
"What? How? What do ye, maister Nicholay?
How may ye slepen al the longe day?"

But al for noght; he herde nat a word.
An hole he foond, ful lowe upon a bord,   3440
Ther as the cat was wont° in for to crepe,
And at that hole he looked in ful depe,
And at the laste he hadde of hym a sighte.
This Nicholas sat capyng° evere uprighte,
As he had kiked° on the newe moone.   3445
Adoun he gooth and tolde his maister soone
In what array° he saugh this ilke° man.

This carpenter to blessen hym bigan,
And seyde, "Help us, Seinte Frydeswyde!
A man woot° litel what hym shal bityde°.   3450
This man is falle, with his astromye,
In som woodnesse° or in som agonye.
I thoghte ay° wel how that it sholde be—
Men sholde nat knowe of Goddes pryvetee°.
Ye°, blessed be alwey a lewed° man   3455
That noght but oonly his bileve kan°!
So ferde° another clerk with astromye;
He walked in the feeldes for to prye°
Upon the sterres, what ther sholde bifalle°,
Til he was in a marle-put yfalle°—   3460
He saugh nat that. But yet, by Seint
        Thomas,
Me reweth soore of° hende Nicholas.
He shal be rated of° his studiyng,
If that I may, by Jhesus, hevene kyng!
Get me a staf, that I may underspore°,   3465
Whil that thou, Robyn, hevest up the dore.
He shal out° of his studiyng, as I gesse."
And to the chambre dore he gan hym dresse°.
His knave was a strong carl° for the nones°,
And by the haspe° he haaf it of° atones;   3470
Into the floor the dore fil anon.
This Nicholas sat ay° as stille as stoon,
And evere caped° upward into the eir.
This carpenter wende° he were in despeir,
And hente° hym by the sholdres myghtily,   3475

3403 **shapen,** *plan,* **wyle,** *scheme* 3404 **sely,** *foolish* (see note), **bigyle,** *deceive* 3409 **tarie,** *delay* 3410 **softe,** *quietly* 3411 **tweye,** *two* 3413 **axed,** *asked* 3414 **nyste,** *didn't know* 3416 **trowed,** *believed* 3418 **thyng,** *anything,* **falle,** *happen* 3419 **passeth forth al thilke,** *goes on all that* 3421 **eet,** *ate,* **hym leste,** *pleased him* 3423 **merveyle,** *wonder* 3424 **eyle,** *ail* 3425 **adrad,** *afraid* 3427 **shilde,** *forbid,* **deyde,** *should die* 3428 **ful tikel,** *very uncertain,* **sikerly,** *certainly* 3429 **saugh,** *saw,* **cors,** *corpse* 3430 **now,** *now* (come to think of it) 3431 **knave,** *servant* 3432 **Clepe,** *call* 3434 **sturdily,** *confidently* 3436 **wood,** *crazed* 3441 **was wont,** *was accustomed* 3444 **capyng,** *gaping,* **uprighte,** *straight up* 3445 **kiked,** *stared* 3447 **array,** *condition,* **ilke,** *same* 3450 **woot,** *knows,* **hym shal bityde,** *will happen to him* 3452 **woodnesse,** *madness* 3453 **ay,** *always* 3454 **pryvetee,** *secrets* 3455 **Ye,** *yes,* **lewed,** *ignorant* 3456 **bileve kan,** *faith knows* 3457 **ferde,** *fared* 3458 **prye,** *study* 3459 **what ther sholde bifalle,** *to predict the future* 3460 **marle-put yfalle,** *clay pit fallen* 3462 **Me reweth soore of,** *I have much pity for* 3463 **rated of,** *scolded for* 3465 **underspore,** *pry up* 3467 **shal out,** *shall come out* 3468 **gan hym dresse,** *turned his attention* 3469 **carl,** *fellow,* **for the nones,** *for the task* 3470 **haspe,** *latch,* **haaf it of,** *heaved it off* 3472 **ay,** *all this time* 3473 **caped,** *gaped* 3474 **wende,** *thought* 3475 **hente,** *seized*

3404 sely, recurrently applied to John, the term is the ancestor of "silly," ranging in meaning from "innocent" or "simple" to "not shrewd, doltish." **3449 Seinte Frydeswyde,** St. Frideswide was the patron saint of Oxford, known for her ability to heal the sick. **3451 astromye,** perhaps a malapropism for astronomy; compare line 3818 below. **3465 underspore,** John pries the door up because medieval doors were hung on upright hinge pins.

And shook hym harde and cride spitously°,
"What, Nicholay, what? How? What, looke adoun!
Awake and thenk on Cristes passioun!
I crouche° thee from elves and fro wightes°."
Therwith the nyght-spel° seyde he
      anon-rightes°   3480
On foure halves° of the hous aboute,
And on the threshfold° of the dore withoute:
"Jhesu Crist and Seint Benedight,
Blesse this hous from every wikked wight,
For nyghtes verye°, the White Pater Noster.   3485
Where wentestow°, Seint Petres soster?"
    And atte laste this hende Nicholas
Gan for to sike° soore, and seyde, "Allas,
Shal al the world be lost eftsoones° now?"
    This carpenter answerde, "What seystow°?   3490
What! Thynk on God, as we doon, men that
      swynke°."
    This Nicholas answerde, "Fecche me drynke,
And after wol I speke in pryvetee
Of certeyn thyng that toucheth me and thee.
I wol telle it noon oother man, certeyn."   3495
    This carpenter goth doun and comth ageyn,
And broghte of myghty° ale a large quart.
And whan that ech of hem had dronke his part,
This Nicholas his dore faste shette°,
And doun the carpenter by hym he sette.   3500
    He seyde, "John, myn hooste, lief° and deere,
Thou shalt upon thy trouthe swere me heere
That to no wight° thou shalt this conseil wreye°,
For it is Cristes conseil that I seye.
And if thou telle it man, thou art forlore°,   3505
For this vengeaunce thou shalt han therfore°,
That if thou wreye me, thou shalt be wood°."
    "Nay, Crist forbede it, for his hooly blood,"

Quod tho° this sely man. "I nam no labbe°,
Ne, though I seye°, I nam nat lief to gabbe°.   3510
Sey what thou wolt, I shal it nevere telle
To child ne wyf, by hym that harwed° helle!"
    "Now, John," quod Nicholas, "I wol nat lye.
I have yfounde in myn astrologye,
As I have looked in the moone bright,   3515
That now a Monday next, at quarter nyght°,
Shal falle a reyn°, and that so wilde and wood°
That half so greet was nevere Noees flood.
This world," he seyde, "in lasse° than an hour
Shal al be dreynt°, so hidous is the shour.   3520
Thus shal mankynde drenche°, and lese hir lyf°."
    This carpenter answerde, "Allas, my wyf!
And shal she drenche? Allas, myn Alisoun!"
For sorwe of this he fil almoost adoun,
And seyde, "Is ther no remedie in this cas?"   3525
    "Why, yis, for Gode," quod hende Nicholas,
"If thou wolt werken after loore and reed°.
Thou mayst nat werken after thyn owene heed°,
For thus seith Salomon, that was ful trewe,
'Werk al by conseil, and thou shalt nat rewe°.'   3530
And if thou werken wolt by good conseil,
I undertake°, withouten mast and seyl°,
Yet shal I saven hire and thee and me.
Hastow nat herd hou saved was Noe,
Whan that oure Lord hadde warned hym
      biforn   3535
That al the world with water sholde be lorn°?"
    "Yis," quod this Carpenter, "ful yoore° ago."
    "Hastou nat herd," quod Nicholas, "also
The sorwe° of Noe with his felaweshipe,
Er° that he myghte gete his wyf to shipe?   3540
Hym hadde be levere°, I dar wel undertake,
At thilke° tyme, than alle his wetheres blake°

3476 spitously, *roughly* **3479 crouche,** *bless,* **wightes,** *creatures* **3480 nyght-spel,** *nighttime charm,* **anon-rightes,** *immediately* **3481 halves,** *sides* **3482 threshfold,** *threshold* **3485 For nyghtes verye,** *from night spirits* (?) **3486 wentestow,** *did you go* **3488 sike,** *sigh* **3489 eftsoones,** *again soon* **3490 seystow,** *say you* **3491 swynke,** *work* **3497 myghty,** *strong* **3499 shette,** *shut* **3501 lief,** *beloved* **3503 wight,** *person,* **wreye,** *reveal* **3505 forlore,** *lost* **3406 han therfore,** *have for this* **3407 be wood,** *go crazy* **3409 tho,** *then,* **labbe,** *blabbermouth* **3510 seye,** *speak,*

nam nat lief to gabbe, *don't like to gab* **3512 harwed,** *broke open* **3516 quarter nyght,** *about 9 p.m.* **3517 reyn,** *rain,* **wood,** *violent* **3519 lasse,** *less* **3520 dreynt,** *drowned* **3521 drenche,** *drown,* **lese hir lyf,** *lose their lives* **3527 werken after loore and reed,** *follow learning and advice* **3528 heed,** *notions* **3530 rewe,** *regret* **3532 undertake,** *declare,* **seyl,** *sail* **3536 lorn,** *lost* **3537 yoore,** *long* **3539 sorwe,** *sorrow* **3540 Er,** *before* **3541 Hym hadde be levere,** *he would have rather* **3542 thilke,** *that,* **wetheres blake,** *black rams*

3478 Cristes passioun, the sufferings of Jesus that culminated in his crucifixion. **3483–86** MSS variants indicate that the scribes were as confused as we are by aspects of this superstitious incantation. **3483 Seint Benedight,** St. Benedict, a convenient rhyme. **3485 White Pater Noster,** white Our Father, a charm. **3486 Seint Petres soster,** otherwise unknown, St. Peter's sister is cited in at least one English charm. **3512 hym that harwed helle,** Jesus' breaking down the gates of hell is described in the popular though apocryphal Gospel of Nicodemus, 16–17. **3518 Noees flood,** recounted in Genesis 7.11ff., Noah's Flood was understood to separate the righteous from the sinful. The Flood began April 17 (Genesis 7.11), perhaps the first day of the Canterbury pilgrimage (see *GP* 1.8n). **3529–30 Salomon . . . ,** the quotation is Ecclesiasticus 32.24, a book in the Catholic Bible often attributed to Solomon by confusion with Ecclesiastes. See *MerT* 4.1485–86 and *Mel* 7.1003. **3539 sorwe of Noe,** in popular religious dramas, the shrewish reluctance of Noah's wife to board the ark is a comic scene; the Bible has no parallel scene.

That she hadde had a ship hirself allone.
And therfore, woostou° what is best to doone?
This asketh° haste, and of an hastif° thyng 3545
Men may nat preche or maken tariyng°.

"Anon go gete us faste into this in°
A knedyng trogh°, or ellis° a kymelyn°,
For ech of us, but looke that they be large,
In which we mowe swymme° as in a barge, 3550
And han° therinne vitaille° suffisant
But for a day—fy on° the remenant°!
The water shal aslake° and goon away
Aboute pryme° upon the nexte day.
But Robyn may nat wite° of this, thy knave, 3555
Ne eek thy mayde Gille I may nat save.
Axe° nat why, for though thou aske me,
I wol nat tellen Goddes pryvetee.
Suffiseth thee, but if thy wittes madde°,
To han as greet a grace° as Noe hadde. 3560
Thy wyf shal I wel saven, out of doute.
Go now thy wey, and speed thee heer-aboute°.

"But whan thou hast for hire and thee
          and me
Ygeten° us thise knedyng tubbes thre,
Thanne shaltow hange hem in the roof
          ful hye°, 3565
That no man of oure purveiaunce° spye.
And whan thou thus hast doon as I have seyd,
And hast oure vitaille faire° in hem yleyd°,
And eek° an ax to smyte° the corde atwo°,
Whan that the water comth that we may go, 3570
And breke an hole an heigh upon° the gable
Unto the gardyn-ward°, over the stable,
That we may frely passen forth oure way,
Whan that the grete shour is goon away,
Thanne shaltou swymme as myrie, I
          undertake, 3575
As dooth the white doke after hire drake.
Thanne wol I clepe°, 'How, Alison! How, John!
Be myrie, for the flood wol passe anon.'
And thou wolt seyn, 'Hayl, maister Nicholay!
Good morwe, I se thee wel, for it is day.' 3580
And thanne shul we be lordes al oure lyf

Of al the world, as Noe and his wyf.
"But of o thyng I warne thee ful right:
Be wel avysed on that ilke° nyght
That we ben entred into shippes bord°, 3585
That noon of us ne speke nat a word,
Ne clepe°, ne crie, but been in his preyere,
For it is Goddes owene heeste° deere.

"Thy wyf and thou moote° hange fer atwynne°,
For° that bitwixe yow shal be no synne, 3590
Namoore in lookyng than ther shal in deede.
This ordinance° is seyd. Go, God thee speede.
Tomorwe at nyght, whan folk ben alle aslepe,
Into oure knedyng tubbes wol we crepe,
And sitten there, abidyng° Goddes grace. 3595
Go now thy wey, I have no lenger space°
To make of this no lenger sermonyng°.
Men seyn thus, 'sende the wise, and sey nothyng.'
Thou art so wys it needeth thee nat teche°.
Go, save oure lyf, and that I the biseche°." 3600

This sely carpenter goth forth his wey.
Ful ofte he seith "allas" and "weylawey,"
And to his wyf he tolde his pryveetee,
And she was war° and knew it bet° than he,
What al this queynte cast was for to seye°. 3605
But nathelees she ferde° as she wolde deye,
And seyde, "Allas! go forth thy wey anon,
Help us to scape°, or we been dede echon!
I am thy trewe, verray° wedded wyf—
Go, deere spouse, and help to save oure lyf." 3610

Lo, which° a greet thyng is affeccioun°!
Men may dyen of ymaginacioun,
So depe may impressioun be take.
This sely carpenter bigynneth quake°.
Hym thynketh verraily that he may see 3615
Noees flood come walwynge° as the see
To drenchen° Alisoun, his hony deere.
He wepeth, weyleth, maketh sory cheere°;
He siketh° with ful many a sory swogh°;
He gooth and geteth hym a knedyng trogh, 3620
And after that a tubbe and a kymelyn,
And pryvely he sente hem° to his in°,
And heng hem in the roof in pryvetee.

3544 **woostou,** *do you know* 3545 **asketh,** *requires,* **hastif** *hasty* 3546 **maken tariyng,** *delay* 3547 **in,** *house* 3548 **knedyng trogh,** *kneading trough,* **ellis,** *else,* **kymelyn,** *brewing vat* 3550 **mowe swymme,** *may float* 3551 **han,** *have,* **vitaille,** *food* 3552 **fy on,** *damn,* **remenant,** *rest* 3553 **aslake,** *subside* 3554 **pryme,** *9 a.m.* 3555 **wite,** *know* 3557 **Axe,** *ask* 3559 **but if thy wittes madde,** *unless you are crazy* 3560 **grace,** *favor* 3562 **speed thee heer-aboute,** *hasten yourself in doing this* 3564 **Ygeten,** *gotten* 3565 **hye,** *high* 3566 **purveiaunce,** *foresight or prepara-tion* 3568 **faire,** *duly,* **yleyd,** *laid* 3569 **eek,** *also,* **smyte,** *cut,* **atwo,** *in two* 3571 **an heigh upon,** *high up in* 3572 **Unto the gardyn-ward,** *toward the garden* 3577 **clepe,** *call* 3584 **ilke,** *same* 3585 **into shippes bord,** *aboard ship* 3587 **clepe,** *call* 3588 **heeste,** *command* 3589 **moote,** *must,* **fer atwynne,** *far apart* 3590 **For,** *so* 3592 **ordinance,** *decree* 3595 **abidyng,** *waiting for* 3596 **space,** *time* 3597 **sermonyng,** *preaching* 3599 **teche,** *teach* 3600 **the biseche,** *beg you* 3604 **war,** *aware,* **bet,** *bet-ter* 3605 **queynte cast was for to seye,** *clever plan meant* 3606 **ferde,** *acted* 3608 **scape,** *escape* 3609 **verray,** *faithful* 3611 **which,** *what,* **af-feccioun,** *emotion* 3614 **quake,** *to tremble* 3616 **walwynge,** *billowing* 3617 **drenchen,** *drown* 3618 **sory cheere,** *sad faces* 3619 **siketh,** *sighs,* **swogh,** *groan* 3622 **hem,** *them,* **in,** *dwelling*

His° owene hand he made laddres thre
To clymben by the ronges° and the stalkes°   3625
Into the tubbes hangynge in the balkes°,
And hem vitailleth°, bothe trogh and tubbe,
With breed and chese and good ale in a jubbe°,
Suffisynge right ynogh as for a day.
But er that he hadde maad al this array,   3630
He sente his knave and eek his wenche also
Upon his nede° to London for to go.
And on the Monday, whan it drow° to nyght,
He shette his dore withoute candel lyght,
And dresseth° alle thyng as it shal be.   3635
And shortly, up they clomben° alle thre;
They seten° stille wel a furlong way.
    "Now, Pater Noster°, clom°!" seyde Nicolay,
And "Clom," quod John, and "Clom," seyde
    Alisoun.
This carpenter seyde his devocioun°,   3640
And stille he sit and biddeth° his preyere,
Awaitynge on the reyn, if he it heere.
    The dede sleep, for wery bisynesse,
Fil on this carpenter right as I gesse
Aboute corfew-tyme°, or litel moore.   3645
For travaille° of his goost° he groneth soore,
And eft° he routeth°, for his heed myslay°.
Doun of the laddre stalketh Nicholay,
And Alisoun ful softe° adoun she spedde.
Withouten wordes mo they goon to bedde,   3650
Ther as the carpenter is wont° to lye.
Ther was the revel and the melodye,
And thus lith° Alison and Nicholas,
In bisynesse of myrthe and of solas°,
Til that the belle of laudes° gan to rynge,   3655
And freres° in the chauncel° gonne synge.
    This parissh clerk, this amorous Absolon,
That is for love alwey so wobigon,
Upon the Monday was at Oseneye

With compaignye, hym to disporte°
    and pleye,   3660
And axed° upon cas° a cloisterer°
Ful prively after John the carpenter.
And he drough° hym apart out of the chirche
And seyde, "I noot°, I saugh hym heere nat
    wirche°
Syn° Saterday. I trowe° that he be went°   3665
For tymber, ther° our abbot hath hym sent.
For he is wont° for tymber for to go
And dwellen at the grange° a day or two.
Or elles he is at his hous, certeyn.
Where that he be, I kan nat soothly seyn."   3670
    This Absolon ful joly was and light°,
And thoghte, "Now is tyme to wake al nyght,
For sikirly° I saugh hym nat stirynge
Aboute his dore syn day bigan to sprynge.
    "So moot I thryve°, I shal at cokkes crowe   3675
Ful pryvely knokke at his wyndowe
That stant° ful lowe upon his boures° wal.
To Alison now wol I tellen al
My love-longynge, for yet I shal nat mysse
That at the leeste wey° I shal hire kisse.   3680
Som maner confort shal I have, parfay°.
My mouth hath icched° al this longe day—
That is a signe of kissyng atte leeste.
Al nyght me mette eek° I was at a feeste.
Therfore I wol go slepe an houre or tweye,   3685
And al the nyght thanne wol I wake and pleye."
    Whan that the firste cok hath crowe, anon
Up rist° this joly lovere Absolon,
And hym arraieth gay° at poynt devys°.
But first he cheweth greyn of lycorys°,   3690
To smellen sweete, er he hadde kembd his heer.
Under his tonge a trewe-love° he beer,
For therby wende° he to ben gracious°.
He rometh° to the carpenteres hous,

3624 **His**, *by his* 3625 **ronges**, *rungs*, **stalkes**, *poles* 3626 **balkes**, *beams* 3527 **hem vitailleth**, *supplies them with food* 3628 **jubbe**, *jug* 3632 **nede**, *errand* 3533 **drow**, *drew* 3635 **dresseth**, *organized* 3636 **clomben**, *climbed* 3637 **seten**, *sat* 3638 **Pater Noster**, *(by) Our Father*, **clom**, *hush* 3640 **devocioun**, *prayers* 3641 **biddeth**, *prays* 3645 **corfew-tyme**, *curfew (see note)* 3646 **travaille**, *suffering*, **goost**, *spirit* 3647 **eft**, *after*, **routeth**, *snores*, **myslay**, *lay wrong* 3649 **softe**, *quietly* 3651 **wont**, *accustomed* 3653 **lith**, *lie* 3654 **solas**, *enjoyment* 3655 **of laudes**, *before dawn* 3656 **freres**, *friars*, **chauncel**, *choir stalls* 3660 **disporte**, *entertain* 3661 **axed**, *asked*, **upon cas**, *by chance*, **cloisterer**,

member of the abbey 3663 **drough**, *drew* 3664 **noot**, *don't know*, **wirche**, *work* 3665 **Syn**, *since*, **trowe**, *believe*, **be went**, *has gone* 3666 **ther**, *where* 3667 **wont**, *accustomed* 3668 **grange**, *farm* 3671 **light**, *delighted* 3673 **sikirly**, *certainly* 3675 **moot I thryve**, *I might succeed* 3677 **stant**, *stands*, **boures**, *bedroom's* 3680 **at the leeste wey**, *at least* 3681 **parfay**, *by faith* 3682 **icched**, *itched* 3684 **me mette eek**, *I dreamed also* 3688 **rist**, *rises* 3689 **hym arraieth gay**, *dresses himself gaily*, **at poynt devys**, *in every way* 3690 **greyn of lycorys**, *cardamom seed* 3692 **trewe-love**, *herb* 3693 **wende**, *thought*, **gracious**, *favorable* 3694 **rometh**, *walks*

3637 a furlong way, "a short while," an idiom derived from the time it takes to walk a furlong (220 yards). **3645 corfew-tyme**, about 9 p.m., when fires were to be covered. **3655 bell of laudes**, the bell rung to indicate that it is time for the morning prayers called lauds. Lauds follows matins (or are recited in conjunction with matins), followed later in the day by prime, terce, sext, none, vespers, and compline, known collectively as the canonical hours or the Divine Office, a cycle of prayer required of priests and other clerics. **3659 Oseneye**, see 3274n. **3692 trewe-love**, an herbal breath sweetener and love charm. **3694 rometh**, the same verb is used to describe romantic walking in *KnT* 1.1065, 1069, 1071, etc.

And stille he stant° under the
      shot-wyndowe°—   3695
Unto his brest it raughte°, it was so lowe—
And softe he cougheth with a semy soun°:
"What do ye, honycomb, sweete Alisoun,
My faire bryd°, my sweete cynamome°?
Awaketh, lemman° myn, and speketh to me!   3700
Wel litel thynken ye upon my wo,
That for youre love I swete ther° I go.
No wonder is thogh that I swelte° and swete;
I moorne° as dooth a lamb after the tete°.
Ywis°, lemman, I have swich love-longynge   3705
That lik a turtel° trewe is my moornynge.
I may nat ete° na moore than a mayde."
   "Go fro the wyndow, Jakke° fool," she sayde.
"As help me God, it wol nat be 'com pa me°.'
I love another—and elles I were to blame—   3710
Wel bet° than thee, by Jhesu, Absolon.
Go forth thy wey or I wol caste a ston,
And lat me slepe, a twenty devel wey°!"
   "Allas," quod Absolon, "and weylawey,
That trewe love was evere so yvel biset°!   3715
Thanne kysse me, syn° it may be no bet°,
For Jhesus love and for the love of me."
   "Wiltow thanne go thy wey therwith°?"
      quod she.
   "Ye, certes, lemman," quod this Absolon.
   "Thanne make thee redy," quod she, "I come
      anon."   3720
And unto Nicholas she seyde stille°,
"Now hust°, and thou shalt laughen al thy fille."
   This Absolon doun sette hym on his knees
And seyde, "I am a lord at alle degrees°,
For after this I hope ther cometh moore.   3725
Lemman°, thy grace, and sweete bryd°, thyn
      oore°!"
   The wyndow she undoth° and that in haste.

"Have do°," quod she, "com of°, and speed the
      faste,
Lest that oure neighebores thee espie."
   This Absolon gan wype his mouth ful drie.   3730
Dirk was the nyght as pich°, or as the cole°,
And at the wyndow out she putte hir hole,
And Absolon, hym fil° no bet ne wers°,
But with his mouth he kiste hir naked ers°
Ful savourly°, er he were war° of this.   3735
   Abak he stirte, and thoughte it was amys,
For wel he wiste° a womman hath no berd°.
He felte a thyng al rough and long yherd°,
And seyde, "Fy! allas! what have I do°?"
   "Tehee," quod she and clapte the
      wyndow to.   3740
And Absolon gooth forth a sory pas°.
   "A berd°, a berd!" quod hende Nicholas.
"By Goddes corpus°, this goth faire and weel."
   This sely Absolon herde every deel°,
And on his lippe he gan for anger byte,   3745
And to hymself he seyde, "I shal thee quyte°."
   Who rubbeth now, who froteth° now his lippes
With dust, with sond, with straw, with clooth, with
      chippes,
But Absolon, that seith ful ofte, "Allas."
"My soule bitake° I unto Sathanas°,   3750
But me were levere than al this toun," quod he,
"Of this despit awroken for to be.
Allas," quod he, "allas, I ne hadde ybleynt°!"
His hoote love was coold and al yqueynt°,
For fro that tyme that he hadde kist hir ers   3755
Of paramours° he sette nat a kers°,
For he was heeled of his maladie.
Ful ofte paramours he gan deffie°,
And weep as dooth a child that is ybete°.
A softe paas° he wente over the strete   3760
Until° a smyth men cleped daun° Gerveys,

3695 stant, *stands,* **shot-wyndowe,** *hinged window* **3696 raughte,**
reached **3697 a semy soun,** *half a sound* (cf. Lat. *semisonus*) **3699 bryd,**
bird or bride, **cynamome,** *cinnamon* **3700 lemman,** *beloved* **3702 swete*
*ther,** *sweat where* **3703 swelte,** *melt* **3704 moorne,** *yearn,* **tete,** *udder*
3705 Ywis, *surely* **3706 turtel,** *turtledove* **3707 ete,** *eat* **3708 Jakke,** *Jack*
3709 'com pa me, *"come kiss me"* **3711 Wel bet,** *much better* **3713 a*
*twenty devel wey,** *by twenty devils' ways* **3715 yvel biset,** *poorly treated*
3716 syn, *since,* **bet,** *better* **3718 therwith,** *with that* **3721 stille,** *quietly*
3722 hust, *hush* **3724 degrees,** *respects* **3726 Lemman,** *beloved,* **bryd,**
bird or bride, **oore,** *mercy* **3727 undoth,** *opens* **3728 Have do,** *get fin-*

ished, **com of,** *hurry* **3731 pich,** *pitch,* **cole,** *coal* **3733 hym fil,** *to him*
happened, **wers,** *worse* **3734 ers,** *rump* **3735 Ful savoury,** *with great*
delight, **war,** *aware* **3737 wiste,** *knew,* **berd,** *beard* **3738 yherd,** *haired*
3739 do, *done* **3741 a sory pas,** *at sad pace* **3742 berd,** *trick* (with
pun *on beard*) **3743 corpus,** *body* **3744 deel,** *bit* **3746 quyte,** *repay*
3747 froteth, *scrubs* **3750 bitake,** *pledge,* **Sathanas,** *Satan* (see note)
3753 ybleynt, *turned away* **3754 yqueynt,** *quenched* **3756 Of para-*
*mours,** *for amorousness,* **kers,** *watercress* (see note) **3758 gan deffie,** *did*
defy **3759 ybete,** *beaten* **3760 softe paas,** *subdued pace* **3761 Until,** *unto,*
cleped daun, *called master*

3698–3707 The language is comically reminiscent of Songs of Songs (esp. 4.11–14) and perhaps Psalms 19.10, and an imitation (or parody)
of courtly wooing. **3706 turtel,** the turtledove was thought to be the most loyal of lovebirds. **3721** In early analogues of this scene, the successful male lover (not the woman) plans and enacts the trick. **3750–52** "Curse me, but I would rather be revenged for this insult than have
the whole town." **3756 sette nat a kers,** "set not (the value of) at a (water)cress," i.e., didn't value at all.

That in his forge smythed plough harneys°;
He sharpeth shaar° and kultour° bisily.
This Absolon knokketh al esily,
And seyde, "Undo°, Gerveys, and that anon."   3765
    "What, who artow?" "It am I, Absolon."
"What, Absolon, for Cristes sweete tree°,
Why rise ye so rathe°? Ey, benedicitee°,
What eyleth° yow? Som gay gerl°, God it woot°,
Hath broght yow thus upon the viritoot°.   3770
By Seinte Note, ye woot wel what I mene."
    This Absolon ne roghte° nat a bene°
Of° al his pley; no word agayn he yaf°.
He hadde moore tow° on his distaf
Than Gerveys knew, and seyde, "Freend so
     deere,   3775
That hoote kultour in the chymenee° heere,
As lene° it me, I have therwith to doone,
And I wol brynge it thee agayn ful soone."
Gerveys answerde, "Certes, were it gold
Or in a poke° nobles alle untold°,   3780
Thou sholdest have, as I am trewe smyth.
Ey, Cristes foo°, what wol ye do therwith?"
    "Therof," quod Absolon, "be as be may°.
I shal wel telle it thee tomorwe day"—
And caughte the kultour by the colde stele°.   3785
Ful softe out at the dore he gan to stele°,
And wente unto the carpenteris wal.
He cogheth first and knokketh therwithal
Upon the wyndowe, right as he dide er.
    This Alison answerde, "Who is ther   3790
That knokketh so? I warante° it a theef."
    "Why, nay," quod he, "God woot°, my sweete
     leef°,

I am thyn Absolon, my deerelyng°.
Of gold," quod he, "I have thee broght a ryng.
My mooder yaf° it me, so God me save.   3795
Ful fyn° it is and therto° wel ygrave°.
This wol I yeve thee, if thou me kisse."
    This Nicholas was risen for to pisse,
And thoughte he wolde amenden al° the jape°;
He sholde kisse his ers er that he scape°.   3800
And up the wyndowe dide he hastily,
And out his ers he putteth pryvely°
Over the buttok, to the haunche-bon°.
And therwith spak this clerk, this Absolon,
"Spek, sweete bryd, I noot nat° where
     thou art."   3805
    This Nicholas anon leet fle° a fart
As greet as it had been a thonder-dent°
That with the strook° he was almoost yblent°,
And he was redy with his iren hoot,
And Nicholas amydde° the ers he smoot°.   3810
    Of gooth° the skyn an hande-brede° aboute,
The hoote kultour brende° so his toute°,
And for the smert° he wende for to dye°.
As° he were wood°, for wo he gan to crye,
"Help! Water! Water! Help, for Goddes
     herte°!"   3815
    This carpenter out of his slomber sterte°,
And herde oon° crien° "water" as he were wood,
And thoughte, "Allas, now comth Nowelis flood!"
He sit hym up withouten wordes mo,
And with his ax he smoot the corde atwo,   3820
And doun gooth al; he foond neither to selle°
Ne breed ne° ale til he cam to the celle°,
Upon the floor, and ther aswowne° he lay.

3762 **smythed plough harneys,** *made plowing equipment* 3763 **sharpeth shaar,** *sharpened plow blades,* **kultour,** *turf cutters* 3765 **Undo,** *open up* 3767 **tree,** *cross* 3768 **rathe,** *early,* **benedicitee,** *bless you* 3769 **eyleth,** *ails,* **gerl,** *girl,* **woot,** *knows* 3770 **viritoot,** *prowl* (?) 3772 **roghte,** *cared,* **bene,** *bean* 3773 **Of,** *for,* **agayn he yaf,** *gave he in response* 3774 **tow,** *flax* (see note) 3777 **chymenee,** *fireplace* 3776 **As lene,** *lend* 3780 **poke,** *sack,* **nobles alle untold,** *coins uncounted* 3782 **Cristes foo,** (by) *Christ's foe* 3783 **be as be may,** (it will) *be as it may be* (i.e., never mind) 3785 **stele,** *handle* 3786 **stele,** *sneak* 3791 **warante,** *swear* 3792 **woot,** *knows,* **leef,** *beloved* 3793 **deerelyng,** *darling* 3795 **yaf,** *gave* 3796 **Ful fyn,** *excellent,* **therto,** *also,* **ygrave,** *engraved* 3799 **amenden**

al, *improve considerably,* **jape,** *joke* 3800 **scape,** *escapes* 3802 **pryvely,** *secretly* 3803 **haunche-bon,** *thigh* 3805 **noot nat,** *don't know* 3806 **leet fle,** *let fly* 3807 **thonder-dent,** *thunderclap* 3808 **strook,** *blast,* **yblent,** *blinded* 3810 **amydde,** *in the middle of,* **smoot,** *struck* 3811 **Of gooth,** *off goes,* **hande-brede,** *hand's breadth* 3812 **brende,** *burned,* **toute,** *rump* 3813 **smert,** *pain,* **wende for to dye,** *thought he would die* 3814 **As,** *as if,* **wood,** *crazed* 3815 **herte,** *heart* 3816 **sterte,** *jerked* 3817 **oon,** *someone,* **crien,** *crying* 3821 **foond neither to selle,** *didn't find for selling* 3822 **Ne . . . ne,** *neither . . . nor,* **celle,** *floor* 3823 **aswowne,** *unconscious*

3766 **"It am I, Absolon,"** their familiarity is understandable since Absolon, a bloodletter and barber (line 3326 above), would have known Gerveys the smith, who made and sharpened metal tools. Contemporary records show that smiths did work at night. 3770 **viritoot,** the word is not found elsewhere; meaning uncertain. 3771 **Seinte Note,** in legend St. Neot urged King Alfred to establish Oxford University. Musical notes are associated with the sound of anvils in Boethius *De Musica* 1.10. 3774 **tow on his distaf,** flax on his distaf, i.e., raw material on the staff used to spin thread by hand. An idiom meaning "more on his mind." 3806 **fart,** compare lines 3337–38 above. 3810 **amydde,** several MSS read "in" or "into." All MSS except two have "in" or "into" at line 3853 below. 3811 **hande-brede,** recalls "hende," the adjective used of Nicholas throughout; see line 3199 above. 3818 **Nowelis,** John's ignorant confusion of "Noel's" for "Noah's." It is repeated or mocked at line 3834 below. 3820 Compare line 3569 above. 3821–22 A French saying, meaning "he wasted no time": "Ainc tant come il mist à descendre, / Ne trouva pas point de pain a vendre" (When he began to fall, he found no bread to sell at all).

Up stirte hire° Alison and Nicholay,
And criden "out°" and "harrow°" in the
    strete.   3825
The neighebores, bothe smale and grete°,
In ronnen° for to gauren° on this man,
That aswowne lay bothe pale and wan,
For with the fal he brosten° hadde his arm.
But stonde he moste unto his owene harm°,   3830
For whan he spak, he was anon bore doun°
With° hende Nicholas and Alisoun.
They tolden every man that he was wood,
He was agast° so of Nowelis flood
Thurgh fantasie°, that of his vanytee°   3835
He hadde yboght° hym knedyng tubbes thre,
And hadde hem hanged in the roof above;
And that he preyed hem°, for Goddes love,
To sitten in the roof, *par compaignye°*.

The folk gan laughen at his fantasye.   3840
Into the roof they kiken° and they cape°,
And turned al his harm° unto a jape°.
For what so° that this carpenter answerde,
It was for noght, no man his reson herde.
With othes° grete he was so sworn adoun°   3845
That he was holde wood° in al the toun,
For every clerk anonright° heeld with other°.
They seyde, "The man is wood, my leeve
    brother,"
And every wight gan laughen° at this stryf°.
Thus swyved° was this carpenteris wyf,   3850
For al his kepyng° and his jalousye,
And Absolon hath kist hir nether eye°,
And Nicholas is scalded° in the towte°.
This tale is doon, and God save al the
    rowte°!

Heere endeth the Millere his Tale.

3824 **hire,** *herself* 3825 **out,** *come out,* **harrow,** *help* 3826 **smale and grete,** *unimportant and important* 3827 **In ronnen,** *ran in,* **gauren,** *stare* 3829 **brosten,** *broken* 3830 **unto his owene harm,** *to his own disadvantage* 3831 **bore doun,** *brought down* 3832 **With,** *by* 3834 **agast,** *afraid* 3835 **fantasie,** *delusion,* **vanytee,** *folly* 3836 **yboght,** *bought* 3838 **preyed hem,** *begged them* 3839 ***par compaignye,*** *for companionship* 3841 **kiken,** *gaze,* **cape,** *gape* 3842 **harm,** *injury,* **jape,** *joke* 3843 **what so,** *whatever* 3845 **othes,** *oaths,* **sworn adoun,** *talked down* 3846 **holde wood,** *thought crazy* 3847 **anonright,** *immediately,* **heeld with other,** *sided with each other* 3849 **wight gan laughen,** *person did laugh,* **stryf,** *disagreement* 3850 **swyved,** *screwed* 3851 **kepyng,** *guarding* 3852 **nether eye,** *lower eye* 3853 **scalded,** *burned,* **towte,** *rump* 3854 **rowte,** *company*

REEVE'S TALE

PROLOGUE

The Prologe of the Reves Tale.

Whan folk hadde laughen at this nyce cas° 3855
Of Absolon and hende Nicholas,
Diverse folk diversely they seyde,
But for the moore part they loughe and pleyde.
Ne at this tale I saugh no man hym greve°,
But it were° oonly Osewold the Reve. 3860
By cause he was of carpenteris craft°,
A litel ire° is in his herte ylaft°.
He gan to grucche°, and blamed it a lite.
    "So theek," quod he, "ful wel koude I yow
        quite°
With bleryng° of a proud milleres eye, 3865
If that me liste° speke of ribaudye°.
But ik° am oold, me list no pley for age—

Gras tyme° is doon, my fodder° is now forage°;
This white top writeth° myne olde yeris;
Myn herte is mowled° also as myne heris°— 3870
But if I fare° as dooth an open-ers°.
That ilke° fruyt is ever lenger the wers°,
Til it be roten in mullok° or in stree°.
We olde men, I drede°, so fare we:
Til we be roten, kan we nat be rype; 3875
We hoppen ay whil° that the world wol pype°.
For in oure wyl° ther stiketh evere a nayl,
To have an hoor° heed and a grene tayl°,
As hath a leek; for thogh oure myght° be
        goon,
Oure wyl desireth folie evere in oon°. 3880

3855 **nyce cas,** *silly incident* 3859 **hym greve,** *trouble himself* 3860 **But it were,** *unless it was* 3861 **carpenteris craft,** *carpenter's training* 3862 **ire,** *anger,* **is . . . ylaft,** *remains* 3863 **grucche,** *complain* 3864 **quite,** *repay* 3865 **bleryng of . . . eye,** *tricking* 3866 **me liste,** (it) *pleased me,* **ribaudye,** *vulgar things* 3867 **ik,** *I* 3868 **Gras tyme,** *fruitful time* (see note), **fodder,** *food,* **forage,** *grazing* 3869 **white top writeth,** *white hair indicates* 3870 **mowled,** *moldy,* **heris,** *hair* 3871 **But if I fare,** *unless I do,* **open-ers,** *open arse* (see note) 3872 **ilke,** *same,* **wers,** *worse* 3873 **mullok,** *compost,* **stree,** *straw* 3874 **drede,** *fear* 3876 **hoppen ay whil,** *dance as long as,* **wol pype,** *plays a tune* 3877 **wyl,** *will* 3878 **hoor,** *white,* **tayl,** *tail* 3879 **myght,** *potency* 3880 **evere in oon,** *continually*

3860 **Osewold,** the name Oswald is common in the north of England. 3864 **theek,** a dialect form from the north and east of England, a contraction of *thee ik* (might I prosper). East Anglian forms recur in the Reeve's speech, and northern forms characterize the speech of the two students in the *RvT.* Both dialects are provincial, perhaps satiric, the first sustained, self-conscious use of dialect in English literature. 3868 **Gras tyme . . . ,** a livestock metaphor: "Good times are done; my food now is only what I can find in the fields after they have been harvested." 3871 **open-ers,** slang for medlar, an applelike fruit that must be stored a long time before it ripens. The slang term derives from its shape. 3876 **hoppen ay . . . ,** recalls Luke 7.32. 3877 **stiketh evere a nayl,** recalls the "thorn of the flesh" of sexual desire; see 2 Corinthians 12.7. 3878–79 The same (phallic?) comparison between old men and leeks is made by the old man in the introduction to book 4 of Boccaccio's *Decameron.*

For whan we may nat doon, than wol we speke;
Yet in oure asshen° olde is fyr yreke°.
　"Foure gleedes han° we, whiche I shal devyse°,
Avauntyng°, liyng, anger, coveitise°.
Thise foure sparkles longen unto eelde°.　3885
Oure olde lemes° mowe° wel been unweelde°,
But wyl ne shal nat faillen, that is sooth.
And yet ik have alwey a coltes tooth,
As many a yeer as it is passed henne°
Syn° that my tappe of lif bigan to renne°.　3890
For sikerly°, whan I was bore°, anon
Deeth drough° the tappe of lyf and leet it gon,
And ever sithe° hath so the tappe yronne°
Til that almoost al empty is the tonne°.
The streem of lyf now droppeth° on the
　　chymbe°.　3895
The sely tonge° may wel rynge and chymbe°
Of wrecchednesse° that passed is ful yoore°;
With olde folk, save dotage°, is namoore!"
　Whan that our Hoost hadde herd this
　　sermonyng°,

He gan to speke as lordly as a kyng.　3900
He seide, "What amounteth° al this wit?
What° shul we speke alday° of hooly writ°?
The devel made a reve for to preche,
Or of a soutere° a shipman or a leche°.
Sey forth thy tale, and tarie° nat the tyme.　3905
Lo Depeford, and it is half-wey pryme°.
Lo Grenewych, ther° many a shrewe° is inne.
It were al tyme thy tale to bigynne."
　"Now, sires," quod this Osewold the Reve,
"I pray yow alle that ye nat yow greve　3910
Thogh I answere and somdeel sette his howve°,
For leveful° is with force force of-showve°.
　"This dronke Millere hath ytoold us heer
How that bigyled° was a carpenteer—
Peraventure° in scorn, for I am oon.　3915
And, by youre leve, I shal hym quite° anoon.
Right in his cherles termes° wol I speke.
I pray to God his nekke mote tobreke°.
He kan wel in myn eye seen a stalke°,
But in his owene he kan nat seen a balke°."　3920

Heere bigynneth the Reves Tale.

　At Trumpyngtoun, nat fer fro Cantebrigge,
Ther gooth a brook, and over that a brigge°,
Upon the whiche brook ther stant° a melle°;
And this is verray sooth° that I yow telle.
A millere was ther dwellynge many a day;　3925
As eny pecok° he was proud and gay.
Pipen° he koude, and fisshe, and nettes beete°,
And turne coppes°, and wel wrastle and sheete°.
Ay° by his belt he baar a long panade°,

And of° a swerd ful trenchant° was the blade.　3930
A joly poppere° baar he in his pouche—
Ther was no man, for peril, dorste° hym touche.
A Sheffeld thwitel° baar he in his hose.
Round was his face, and camuse° was his nose;
As piled° as an ape was his skulle.　3935
He was a market-betere° atte fulle°—
Ther dorste no wight° hand upon hym legge°
That he ne swoor he sholde anon abegge°.

3882 **asshen,** *ashes,* **yreke,** *raked up* 3883 **gleedes han,** *live coals have,* **devyse,** *describe* 3884 **Avauntyng,** *boasting,* **coveitise,** *greed* 3885 **sparkles longen unto eelde,** *sparks belong to old age* 3886 **lemes,** *limbs,* **mowe,** *might,* **unweelde,** *weak* 3889 **henne,** *by* 3890 **Syn,** *since,* **tappe,** *spigot,* **renne,** *run* 3891 **sikerly,** *certainly,* **bore,** *born* 3892 **Deeth drough,** *death opened* 3893 **sithe,** *since,* **yronne,** *run* 3894 **tonne,** *barrel* 3895 **droppeth,** *drips,* **chymbe,** *barrel rim* 3896 **sely tonge,** *foolish tongue,* **chymbe,** *chime* 3897 **Of wrecchednesse,** *about wickedness,* **ful yoore,** *long ago* 3898 **save dotage,** *except senility* 3899 **sermonyng,** *preaching* 3901 **amounteth,** *value has* 3902 **What,** *why,* **alday,** *always,* **hooly writ,** *scripture* 3904 **soutere,** *shoemaker,* **leche,** *physician* 3905 **tarie,** *delay* 3906 **half-wey pryme,** *about 7:30 a.m.* 3907 **ther,**

where, **shrewe,** *rascal* 3911 **howve,** *hood* 3912 **leveful,** *permissible,* **of-showve,** *to overthrow* 3914 **bigyled,** *tricked* 3915 **Peraventure,** *perhaps* 3916 **quite,** *repay* 3917 **cherles termes,** *low-life language* 3918 **mote tobreke,** *might shatter* 3919 **stalke,** *stem* 3920 **balke,** *beam* 3922 **brigge,** *bridge* 3923 **stant,** *stands,* **melle,** *mill* 3924 **verray sooth,** *absolute truth* 3926 **eny pecok,** *any peacock* 3927 **Pipen,** *play the pipes,* **beete,** *mend* 3928 **coppes,** *cups,* **sheete,** *shoot a bow* 3929 **Ay,** *always,* **panade,** *cutlass* 3930 **of,** *as,* **trenchant,** *sharp* 3931 **joly poppere,** *bright dagger* 3932 **dorste,** *dared* 3932 **thwitel,** *knife* 3934 **camuse,** *snub* 3935 **piled,** *bald* 3936 **market-betere,** *market-beater, bully* (?), **atte fulle,** *complete* 3937 **wight,** *person,* **legge,** *lay* 3938 **abegge,** *pay for it*

3888 **coltes tooth,** an idiom meaning "youthful desire"; see *WBP* 3.602. 3906–7 **Depeford . . . Grenewych,** Deptford and Greenwich, villages on the Canterbury way, four to five miles from Southwark. Chaucer may have been living in Greenwich when he wrote this. 3911 **sette his howve,** set his hood; an idiom meaning to "get the best of"; see *GP* 1.586 and *MilP* 1.3143. 3919–20 Recalls Matthew 7.3. 3921 **Trumpyngtoun,** Trumpington, about two miles south of central Cambridge (**Cantebrigge**), where the site of an old mill can still be located. 3928 **turne coppes,** produce wooden cups on a lathe? play a drinking game? 3933 **Sheffeld,** Sheffield, a city still famous for its knives.

A theef he was forsothe° of corn° and mele°,
And that a sly, and usaunt° for to stele.   3940
His name was hoote deynous° Symkyn.
A wyf he hadde, ycomen of noble kyn—
The person° of the toun hir fader was.
With hire he yaf ful many a panne° of bras,
For° that Symkyn sholde in his blood allye°.   3945
She was yfostred° in a nonnerye;
For Symkyn wolde no wyf, as he sayde,
But she were wel ynorissed° and a mayde°,
To saven his estaat of yomanrye°.
And she was proud, and peert° as is a pye°.   3950
A ful fair sighte was it upon hem° two:
On halydayes biforn hire wolde he go
With his typet° bounde aboute his heed,
And she cam after in a gyte of reed°;
And Symkyn hadde hosen of the same.   3955
Ther dorste° no wight clepen hire but°
     "dame";
Was noon so hardy that wente by the weye
That with hire dorste rage° or ones° pleye,
But if he wolde be slayn of Symkyn
With panade°, or with knyf, or boidekyn°.   3960
For jalous folk ben perilous everemo—
Algate° they wolde hire wyves wenden° so.
And eek, for she was somdel smoterlich°,
She was as digne° as water in a dich°,
And ful of hoker° and of bisemare°.   3965
Hir thoughte that a lady sholde hire spare°,
What for hire kynrede° and hir nortelrie°
That she hadde lerned in the nonnerie.

    A doghter hadde they bitwixe hem two
Of twenty yeer, withouten any mo,   3970
Savynge a child that was of half yeer age;

In cradel it lay and was a propre page°.
This wenche thikke and wel ygrowen was,
With kamuse° nose and eyen greye as glas,
Buttokes brode and brestes rounde and hye,   3975
But right fair was hire heer, I wol nat lye.

    This person° of the toun, for she was feir,
In purpos was° to maken hire his heir,
Bothe of his catel° and his mesuage°,
And straunge° he made it of hir mariage°.   3980
His purpos was for to bistowe hire hye°
Into som worthy blood of auncetrye°,
For hooly chirches good° moot been despended°
On hooly chirches blood, that is descended.
Therfore he wolde his hooly blood honoure,   3985
Though that he hooly chirche sholde devoure.

    Greet sokene° hath this millere, out of doute,
With whete and malt of al the land aboute;
And nameliche° ther was a greet collegge,
Men clepen° the Soler Halle at Cantebregge,   3990
Ther was hir° whete and eek hir malt ygrounde.
And on a day it happed, in a stounde°,
Sik lay the maunciple° on a maladye.
Men wenden wisly° that he sholde dye,
For which this millere stal° bothe mele
     and corn   3995
And hundred tyme moore than biforn;
For therbiforn° he stal but curteisly,
But now he was a theef outrageously,
For which the wardeyn° chidde and made fare°.
But therof sette the millere nat a tare°;   4000
He craketh boost°, and swoor it was nat so.

    Thanne were ther yonge poure° clerkes two,
That dwelten in this halle, of which I seye.
Testif° they were, and lusty° for to pleye,

3939 forsothe, *truly,* **corn,** *whole grain,* **mele,** *ground grain* **3940 usaunt,** *accustomed* **3941 hoote deynous,** *called proud* **3943 person,** *parson* **3944 panne,** *pan (see note)* **3945 For,** *so,* **in his blood allye,** *make
an alliance into the family* **3946 yfostred,** *brought up* **3948 ynorissed,
raised,* **mayde,** *virgin* **3949 saven his estaat of yomanrye,** *keep up his
status as a freeholder* **3950 peert,** *saucy,* **pye,** *magpie* **3951 upon hem,**
(to look) at them **3953 typet,** *long end of his hood* **3954 gyte of reed,*
red garment* **3956 dorste,** *dared,* **clepen hire but,** *call her (anything)
but* **3958 rage,** *flirt,* **ones,** *once* **3960 panade,** *cutlass,* **boidekyn,** *dagger* **3962 Algate,** *at least,* **wenden,** *believed* **3963 somdel smoterlich,*
somewhat stained* (by illegitimacy) **3964 digne,** *proud,* **dich,** *ditch* **3965
hoker,** *scorn,* **bisemare,** *contempt* **3966 hire spare,** *be aloof* **3967**

kynrede, *kindred,* **nortelrie,** *nurture* **3972 page,** *boy* **3974 kamuse,*
snub* **3977 person,** *parson* **3978 In purpos was,** *intended* **3979 catel,*
possessions,* **mesuage,** *house* **3980 straunge,** *difficult,* **of hir mariage,*
for her to marry* **3981 hye,** *high* **3982 auncetrye,** *ancestry* **3983 good,*
goodness or goods,* **moot been despended,** *must be spent* **3987 Greet
sokene,** *large monopoly* **3989 nameliche,** *especially* **3990 clepen,** *call*
3991 hir, *their* **3992 in a stounde,** *at one time* **3993 maunciple,** *purchaser* **3994 wenden wisly,** *thought certainly* **3995 stal,** *stole* **3997
therbiforn,** *previously* **3999 wardeyn,** *head of the college,* **chidde
and made fare,** *complained and fussed* **4000 tare,** *weed* **4001 craketh
boost,** *exclaimed loudly* **4002 poure,** *poor* **4004 Testif,** *willful,* **lusty,*
eager*

3941 Symkyn, familiar form of Symond or Simon. **3944 he yaf ful many a panne of bras,** the parson gave a dowry (to marry off his illegitimate daughter). **3949 estaat of yomanrye,** there were serfs, who were legally bound to the land they worked, and free peasants (the yeo-
manry), whose limited rights enabled them to work for their own profits as well as those they owed to lords of the manor. Symkyn has an ex-
aggerated sense of his social class. **3973 wenche,** the connotations ranged from "lass" to "prostitute"; the following description is a comic
mixture of stereotypic plebeian and aristocratic features. **3987–88 Greet sokene . . . ,** Symkyn has exclusive legal rights to grind raw grain
(for bread) and sprouted grain (**malt,** for beer) in the region. **3990 Soler Halle,** Solar Hall (having many windows to admit sunlight), also
known as King's Hall, now part of Trinity College, Cambridge.

And, oonly for hire myrthe and reverye°, 4005
Upon the wardeyn bisily they crye
To yeve° hem leve but a litel stounde°
To goon to mille and seen hir corn ygrounde;
And hardily° they dorste leye° hir nekke
The millere sholde nat stele hem° half
    a pekke 4010
Of corn by sleighte, ne by force hem reve°;
And at the laste the wardeyn yaf hem leve.
John highte° that oon, and Aleyn highte that
    oother;
Of o° toun were they born, that highte
    Strother,
Fer in the north, I kan nat telle where. 4015
  This Aleyn maketh redy al his gerc,
And on an hors the sak he caste anon.
Forth goth Aleyn the clerk and also John
With good swerd and bokeler° by hir side.
John knew the wey—hem nedede no gyde— 4020
And at the mille the sak adoun he layth.
Aleyn spak first, "Al hayl, Symond, y-fayth°!
Hou fares thy faire doghter and thy wyf?"
  "Aleyn, welcome," quod Symkyn, "by my lyf.
And John also, how now, what do ye heer°?" 4025
  "Symond," quod John, "by God, nede has na°
    peer°.
Hym boes° serve hymselve that has na swayn°,
Or elles he is a fool, as clerkes sayn.
Oure manciple, I hope° he wil be deed,
Swa werkes° ay the wanges° in his heed; 4030
And forthy is I° come, and eek Alayn,
To grynde oure corn and carie it ham° agayn.
I pray yow spede us heythen° that ye° may."
  "It shal be doon," quod Symkyn, "by
    my fay°!
What wol ye doon whil that it is in hande?" 4035
  "By God, right by the hopur° wil I stande,"
Quod John, "and se how that the corn gas° in.

Yet saugh I nevere, by my fader kyn,
How that the hopur wagges° til and fra°."
  Aleyn answerde, "John, and wiltow swa°? 4040
Thanne wil I be bynethe°, by my croun°,
And se how that the mele° falles doun
Into the trough; that sal° be my disport°.
For John, yfaith, I may been of youre sort;
I is° as ille° a millere as ar° ye." 4045
  This millere smyled of hir nycetee°,
And thoghte, "Al this nys doon but for a wyle°.
They wene° that no man may hem bigyle°,
But by my thrift°, yet shal I blere hir eye°,
For al the sleighte° in hir philosophye°. 4050
The moore queynte crekes° that they make,
The moore wol I stele whan I take.
Instide of flour yet wol I yeve hem bren°.
The gretteste clerkes been noght wisest men,
As whilom° to the wolf thus spak the mare. 4055
Of al hir art° ne counte I noght a tare°."
  Out at the dore he gooth ful pryvely°,
Whan that he saugh his tyme, softely.
He looketh up and doun til he hath founde
The clerkes hors, ther as it stood ybounde 4060
Bihynde the mille, under a lefesel°,
And to the hors he goth hym faire and wel;
He strepeth of° the brydel right anon.
And whan the hors was laus°, he gynneth gon°
Toward the fen ther° wilde mares renne°, 4065
And forth with "wehee," thurgh thikke and
    thurgh thenne.
  This millere gooth agayn, no word he seyde,
But dooth his note° and with the clerkes pleyde
Til that hir corn was faire and weel ygrounde.
And whan the mele is sakked and ybounde°, 4070
This John goth out and fynt° his hors away,
And gan to crie "Harrow°!" and "Weylaway!
Oure hors is lorn°, Alayn, for Goddes banes°,
Step on thy feet! Com of°, man, al at anes°!"

4005 reverye, *wildness* 4007 yeve, *give,* stounde, *time* 4009 hardily, *confidently,* dorste leye, *dare bet* 4010 hem, *from them* 4011 reve, *rob* 4013 highte, *was called* 4014 o, *one* 4019 bokeler, *small shield* 4022 *y-fayth, *in faith* 4025 heer, *here* 4026 *na, *no,* peer, *equal* 4027 Hym *boes, *it benefits him* (to), swayn, *servant* 4029 hope, *expect* 4030 *Swa werkes, *so aches,* *wanges, *teeth* 4031 forthy *is I, *therefore am I* 4032 *ham, *home* 4033 *heythen, *hence,* that ye, *as fast as you* 4034 fay, *faith* 4036 hopur, *hopper* (intake bin) 4037 *gas, *goes* 4039 wagges, *shakes,* *til and *fra, *to and fro* 4040 wiltow *swa, *will you so* 4041 bynethe, *beneath,* croun, *head* 4042 mele, *ground grain* 4043 *sal, *shall,* disport,

entertainment 4045 *is, *am,* ille, *incompetent,* *ar, *are* 4046 of hir nycetee, *at their simplemindedness* 4047 for a wyle, *as a strategy* 4048 wene, *think,* hem bigyle, *trick them* 4049 thrift, *profit,* blere hir eye, *blur their eyes* 4050 sleighte, *cleverness,* philosophye, *learning* 4051 queynte crekes, *clever zigzags* 4053 bren, *husks* (bran) 4055 whilom, *once* 4056 hir art, *their strategy,* tare, *weed* 4057 pryvely, *secretly* 4061 under a lefesel, *in the shade* 4063 strepeth of, *strips off* 4064 laus, *loose,* gynneth gon, *did go* 4065 fen ther, *marsh where,* renne, *run* 4068 note, *task* 4070 sakked and ybounde, *put in a sack and tied* 4071 fynt, *finds* 4072 Harrow, *help* 4073 lorn, *lost,* *banes, *bones* 4074 Com of, *hurry,* *anes, *once*

4010 pekke, peck; a unit of measure, about one-quarter bushel. 4014 Strother, the town has not been identified. 4022ff. Glosses marked with an asterisk (*) are northern words, forms, or constructions; they characterize the dialect of the students as provincial. 4049 blere hir eye, an idiom meaning "trick them." 4055 to the wolf . . . spak the mare, in various traditional tales, a mare tells the wolf (or fox) who wants to buy her colt that the price is written on her back hoof. When the wolf goes to read it, she kicks him and, in the Reynard the fox story, comments on how clerks are not always wise.

Allas, oure wardeyn has his palfrey° lorn."   4075
This Aleyn al forgat bothe mele and corn;
Al was out of his mynde his housbondrie°.
"What, whilk° way is he gane°?" he gan to crie.

    The wyf cam lepynge inward with a ren.
She seyde, "Allas! youre hors goth to the fen   4080
With wilde mares, as faste as he may go.
Unthank° come on his hand that boond hym so,
And he that bettre sholde han knyt° the reyne!"

    "Allas," quod John, "Aleyn, for Cristes peyne,
Lay doun thy swerd, and I wil myn alswa°.   4085
I is ful wight°, God waat°, as is a raa°;
By Goddes herte, he sal° nat scape us bathe°.
Why nadstow pit° the capul° in the lathe°?
Il-hayl°, by God, Alayn, thou is a fonne°!"

    This sely° clerkes han ful faste yronne   4090
Toward the fen, bothe Aleyn and eek John.

    And whan the millere saugh that they were
      gon,
He half a busshel of hir flour hath take
And bad his wyf go knede it in a cake°.
He seyde, "I trowe° the clerkes were aferd°.   4095
Yet kan a millere make a clerkes berd°
For al his art; now lat hem goon hir weye.
Lo, wher they goon! Ye, lat the children pleye.
They gete° hym nat so lightly°, by my croun."

    Thise sely clerkes rennen up and doun   4100
With "Keep°! Keep! Stand! Stand! Jossa°!
    Warderere°!
Ga° whistle thou, and I sal kepe hym heere!"
But shortly°, til that it was verray° nyght,
They koude nat°, though they dide al hir myght,
Hir capul cacche°, he ran alwey so faste,   4105
Til in a dych they caughte hym atte laste.

    Wery and weet, as beest° is in the reyn°,
Comth sely John, and with him comth Aleyn.
"Allas," quod John, "the day that I was born!
Now are we dryve til hethyng° and til scorn.   4110

Oure corn is stoln, men wil us fooles calle,
Bathe° the wardeyn and oure felawes alle,
And namely the millere, weylaway!"

    Thus pleyneth John as he gooth by the way
Toward the mille, and Bayard in his hond.   4115
The millere sittynge by the fyr he fond,
For it was nyght, and forther° myghte they noght.
But for the love of God they hym bisoght°
Of herberwe° and of ese°, as for hir peny°.

    The millere seyde agayn°, "If ther be eny,   4120
Swich° as it is, yet shal ye have youre part.
Myn hous is streit°, but ye han lerned art.
Ye konne° by argumentes make a place
A myle brood of° twenty foot of space.
Lat se now if this place may suffise,   4125
Or make it rowm° with speche as is your gise°."

    "Now, Symond," seyde John, "by Seint
      Cutberd,
Ay is° thou myrie, and this is faire answered.
I have herd seyd, man sal taa° of twa thynges—
Slyk° as he fyndes, or taa slyk as he brynges.   4130
But specially I pray thee, hooste deere,
Get us som mete° and drynke and make us
    cheere°,
And we wil payen trewely atte fulle.
With empty hand men may none haukes tulle°.
Loo, heere° oure silver, redy for to spende."   4135

    This millere into toun his doghter sende
For ale and breed, and rosted hem a goos,
And boond hire hors, it sholde namoore go loos,
And in his owene chambre hem made a bed
With sheetes and with chalons° faire yspred,   4140
Noght from his owene bed ten foot or twelve.
His doghter hadde a bed al by hirselve
Right in the same chambre by and by°.
It myghte be no bet°, and cause why°?
Ther was no roumer herberwe° in the place.   4145
They soupen° and they speke, hem to solace°,

4075 **palfrey,** *riding horse* 4077 **housbondrie,** *responsible management* 4078 ***whilk,** *which,* ***gane,** *gone* 4082 **Unthank,** *bad luck* 4083 **han knyt,** *have tied* 4085 ***alswa,** *also* 4086 **wight,** *swift,* ***waat,** *knows,* ***raa,** *deer* 4087 ***sal,** *shall,* ***bathe,** *both* 4088 **nadstow *pit,** *didn't you put,* **capul,** *horse,* ***lathe,** *barn* 4089 ***Il-hayl,** *ill health,* **fonne,** *fool* 4090 **This sely,** *these foolish* 4094 **cake,** *loaf* 4095 **trowe,** *believe,* **aferd,** *cautious* 4096 **make a . . . berd,** *deceive* 4099 **gete,** *(will) get,* **so lightly,** *very easily* 4101 **Keep,** *stay,* **Jossa,** *whoa,* **Warderere,** *look out behind* 4102 ***Ga,** *go* 4103 **shortly,** *in short,* **verray,** *truly* 4104 **koude nat,** *were not able to* 4105 **Hir capul cacche,** *catch their horse* 4107 **as beest,** *as an*

animal, **reyn,** *rain* 4110 **dryve *til *hethyng,** *driven to derision* 4112 ***Bathe,** *both* 4117 **forther,** *(go) further* 4118 **bisoght,** *asked* 4119 **Of herberwe,** *for lodging,* **ese,** *food,* **peny,** *money* 4120 **agayn,** *in reply* 4121 **Swich,** *such* 4122 **streit,** *small* 4123 **konne,** *are able to* 4124 **of,** *from* 4126 **rowm,** *roomy,* **gise,** *habit* 4128 **Ay *is,** *always are* 4129 ***sal *taa,** *shall take* 4130 ***Slyk,** *such* 4132 **mete,** *food,* **make us cheere,** *be friendly* 4134 **tulle,** *lure* 4135 **heere,** *here* (is) 4140 **chalons,** *blankets* 4143 **by and by,** *alongside* 4144 **bet,** *better,* **cause why,** *why's that* 4145 **roumer herberwe,** *roomier lodging* 4146 **soupen,** *ate,* **hem to solace,** *to satisfy themselves*

4115 **Bayard,** a conventional name for a horse. 4123 **konne by argumentes,** Symkyn's satire of learned arguments was not uncommon. 4127 **Seint Cutberd,** Cuthbert was a famous monk and bishop of northern England. The pronunciation may play upon the meaning of "berd" in line 4096. 4129–30 The proverb means "one must put up with what is available." Later, the students do take both what they find in Symkyn's house and what they brought to it, at the expense of his pride in his lineage and in his cleverness.

And drynken evere strong ale atte beste.
Aboute mydnyght wente they to reste.
　Wel hath this millere vernysshed° his heed;
Ful pale he was fordronken and nat reed°.　4150
He yexeth° and he speketh thurgh the nose
As° he were on the quakke° or on the pose°.
To bedde he goth, and with hym goth his wyf.
As any jay° she light was and jolyf,
So was hir joly whistle wel ywet°.　4155
The cradel at hir beddes feet° is set,
To rokken, and to yeve the child to sowke°.
And whan that dronken al was in the crowke°,
To bedde wente the doghter right anon.
To bedde gooth Aleyn and also John—　4160
Ther nas na° moore; hem nedede no dwale°.
This millere hath so wisly bibbed° ale
That as an hors he fnorteth° in his sleep,
Ne of his tayl bihynde he took no keep°.
His wyf bar hym a burdon°, a ful strong;　4165
Men myghte hir rowtyng° heere two furlong°;
The wenche rowteth eek, par° compaignye.
　Aleyn the clerk, that herde this melodye,
He poked John, and seyde, "Slepestow?
Herdestow evere slyk a sang° er now?　4170
Lo, whilk° a complyn° is ymel° hem alle.
A wilde fyr upon thair bodyes falle!
Wha° herkned evere slyk a ferly° thyng?
Ye, they sal have the flour of il endyng°.
This lange° nyght ther tydes° me na reste;　4175
But yet, na fors°, al sal° be for the beste.
For, John," seyde he, "als evere moot I thryve°,
If that I may, yon wenche wil I swyve°.
Som esement° has lawe yshapen° us,
For, John, ther is a lawe that says thus,　4180
That gif° a man in a point be ygreved°,
That in another he sal be releved.

Oure corn is stoln, sothly, it is na nay°,
And we han had an il fit° al this day,
And syn° I sal have neen° amendement　4185
Agayn my los, I wil have esement.
By Goddes saule°, it sal neen other bee°!"
　This John answerde, "Alayn, avyse thee°.
The millere is a perilous man," he seyde,
"And gif that he out of his sleep abreyde°,　4190
He myghte doon us bathe a vileynye°."
　Aleyn answerde, "I counte hym nat a flye."
And up he rist, and by the wenche he crepte.
This wenche lay uprighte° and faste slepte,
Til he so ny° was er she myghte espie　4195
That it had been to late for to crie,
And shortly for to seyn, they were aton°.
Now pley, Aleyn, for I wol speke of John.
　This John lith° stille a furlong wey or two°,
And to hymself he maketh routhe° and wo.　4200
"Allas," quod he, "this is a wikked jape°.
Now may I seyn° that I is but an ape°.
Yet has my felawe somwhat for his harm;
He has the milleris doghter in his arm.
He auntred hym°, and has his nedes sped°,　4205
And I lye as a draf-sek° in my bed.
And when this jape is tald another day,
I sal been halde a daf°, a cokenay°.
I wil arise and auntre° it, by my fayth.
Unhardy° is unseely°, thus men sayth."　4210
And up he roos, and softely he wente
Unto the cradel, and in his hand it hente°,
And baar° it softe° unto his beddes feet.
　Soone after this the wyf hir rowtyng leet°,
And gan awake, and wente hire out to pisse,　4215
And cam agayn, and gan hir cradel mysse,
And groped heer and ther, but she foond noon.
"Allas," quod she, "I hadde almoost mysgoon°."

4149 vernysshed, *polished* (see note) **4150 reed,** *red* **4151 yexeth,**
belches **4152 As,** *as if,* **on the quakke,** *hoarse,* **on the pose,** *had a cold*
4154 jay, *noisy bird* **4155 ywet,** *wet* (see note) **4156 hir beddes feet,**
foot of her bed **4157 yeve . . . to sowke,** *breast-feed* **4158 crowke,** *crock*
4161 nas *na, *wasn't any,* **dwale,** *sleeping potion* **4162 wisly bibbed,**
surely imbibed **4163 fnorteth,** *snorts* **4164 keep,** *care* **4165 bar hym a*
burdon, *accompanied him* **4166 rowtyng,** *snoring,* **furlong,** *220 yards*
4167 par, *for* **4170 *slyk a *sang,** *such a song* **4171 *whilk,** *such,* **com-**
plyn, *prayer* (see note), ***ymel,** *among* **4173 *Wha,** *who,* **ferly,** *strange*
4174 *sal, *shall,* **flour of il endyng,** *result of bad outcome* **4175 *lange,**
long, **tydes,** *comes to* **4176 *na fors,** *no matter* **4177 als evere moot I**
thryve, *so may I ever succeed* **4178 swyve,** *screw* **4179 esement,** *compen-*

sation, **yshapen,** *provided* **4181 gif,** *if,* **ygreved,** *injured* **4183 it is *na**
nay, *there is no denying* **4184 il fit,** *bad time* **4185 syn,** *since,* ***neen,** *no*
4187 *saule, *soul,* ***sal *neen other bee,** *shall not be otherwise* **4188**
avyse thee, *be careful* **4190 abreyde,** *awakes* **4191 *bathe a vileynye,**
both harm **4194 uprighte,** *on her back* **4195 ny,** *close* **4197 aton,** *joined*
4199 lith, *lies,* **furlong wey or two,** *about five minutes* **4200 routhe,** *pity*
4201 wikked jape, *nasty trick* **4202 seyn,** *say,* **ape,** *monkey* **4205 aun-**
tred hym, *chanced it,* **nedes sped,** *needs met* **4206 draf-sek,** *sack of chaff*
4208 halde a daf, *thought a fool,* **cokenay,** *idiot* **4209 auntre,** *venture*
4210 Unhardy, *unbrave,* **unseely,** *unlucky* **4212 hente,** *took* **4213 baar,*
carried, **softe,** *quietly* **4214 hir rowtyng leet,** *stopped her snoring* **4218**
mysgoon, *gone wrong*

4149 vernysshed his heed, "polished his head," i.e., had a lot to drink. **4155 whistle wel ywet,** i.e., had a lot to drink. **4171 complyn,** compline, the last in the daily cycle of prayers; see *MilT* 1.3655n. **4172 wilde fyr,** common name for erysipelas, a painful skin disease. **4178 The**
form "if" is southern, a (scribal?) lapse in the representation of northern dialect that should have "gif," as in lines 4181 and 4190. **4192**
counte hym nat a flye, "consider him not (worth) a fly," i.e., don't consider him at all.

I hadde almoost goon to the clerkes bed.
Ey, benedicite°, thanne hadde I foule ysped°." 4220
And forth she gooth til she the cradel fond.
She gropeth alwey forther with hir hond,
And foond the bed, and thoghte noght but good,
By cause that the cradel by it stood,
And nyste° wher she was, for it was derk, 4225
But faire and wel she creep° in to the clerk,
And lith° ful stille, and wolde han caught a sleep°.
Withinne a while this John the clerk up leep°,
And on this goode wyf he leith on soore°.
So myrie a fit° ne hadde she nat ful yoore°; 4230
He priketh° harde and depe as he were mad.
This joly lyf han thise two clerkes lad°
Til that the thridde cok° bigan to synge.
    Aleyn wax wery° in the dawenynge,
For he had swonken° al the longe nyght, 4235
And seyde, "Fareweel, Malyne, sweete wight°.
The day is come, I may no lenger byde°;
But everemo, wherso I go or ryde,
I is thyn awen° clerk, swa have I seel°!"
    "Now, deere lemman°," quod she, "go,
        fareweel. 4240
But er thow go, o thyng I wol thee telle:
Whan that thou wendest° homward by the melle°,
Right at the entree of the dore bihynde°
Thou shalt a cake of half a busshel fynde
That was ymaked of thyn owene mele°, 4245
Which that I heelp° my fader for to stele.
And, goode lemman, God thee save and kepe."
And with that word almoost she gan to wepe.
    Aleyn up rist, and thoughte, "Er that it dawe°,
I wol go crepen in by my felawe," 4250
And fond the cradel with his hand anon.
"By God," thoughte he, "al wrang° I have mysgon°.
Myn heed is toty° of my swynk° tonyght;

That maketh me that I go nat aright.
I woot° wel by the cradel I have mysgo°; 4255
Heere lith the millere and his wyf also."
And forth he goth, a twenty devel way°,
Unto the bed ther as the millere lay.
He wende° have cropen° by his felawe John,
And by the millere in he creep anon, 4260
And caughte hym by the nekke, and softe he
        spak.
He seyde, "Thou John, thou swynes-heed°, awak°,
For Cristes saule, and heer a noble game°.
For by that lord that called is Seint Jame,
As I have thries° in this shorte nyght 4265
Swyved° the milleres doghter bolt upright°,
Whil thow hast°, as a coward, been agast°."
    "Ye, false harlot°," quod the millere, "hast?
A, false traitour, false clerk," quod he,
"Thow shalt be deed°, by Goddes dignitee! 4270
Who dorste° be so boold to disparage°
My doghter, that is come of swich lynage°?"
And by the throte-bolle° he caughte Alayn,
And he hente° hym despitously agayn°,
And on the nose he smoot hym with his fest; 4275
Doun ran the blody streem upon his brest.
And in the floor, with nose and mouth tobroke°,
They walwe° as doon two pigges in a poke°,
And up they goon, and doun agayn anon,
Til that the millere sporned at° a stoon, 4280
And doun he fil bakward upon his wyf
That wiste° nothyng of this nyce stryf°—
For she was falle° aslepe a lite wight°
With John the clerk, that waked hadde al nyght—
And with the fal out of hir sleep she breyde°. 4285
"Help, hooly croys° of Bromeholm!" she seyde,
"*In manus tuas!* Lord, to thee I calle!
Awak, Symond, the feend is on us falle.

4220 Ey, benedicite, *whew, bless me,* **foule ysped,** *gone wrong* **4225 nyste,** *did not know* **4226 creep,** *crept* **4227 lith,** *lies,* **wolde han caught a sleep,** *would have fallen asleep* **4228 leep,** *leapt* **4229 leith on soore,** *attacks aggressively* **4230 So myrie a fit,** *such a good time,* **ful yoore,** *for a long time* **4231 priketh,** *pokes* **4232 lad,** *led* **4233 thridde cok,** *third rooster* **4234 wex wery,** *grew tired* **4235 swonken,** *worked* **4236 wight,** *creature* **4237 lenger byde,** *longer remain* **4239 I *is thyn *awen,** *I am your own,* ***swa have I seel,** *so I swear* **4240 lemman,** *beloved* **4242 wendest,** *go,* **melle,** *mill* **4243 of the dore bihynde,** *behind the door* **4245 mele,** *ground grain* **4246 heelp,** *helped* **4249 dawe,** *dawns* **4252 *wrang,** *wrong,* **mysgon,** *misgone* **4253 toty,** *dizzy,* **swynk,** *labor* **4255**

woot, *know,* **mysgo,** *gone wrong* **4257 a twenty devel wey,** *by twenty devils' ways* **4259 wende,** *thought,* **cropen,** *crept* **4262 swynes-heed,** *pig's head,* **awak,** *awake* **4263 game,** *joke* **4265 thries,** *three times* **4266 Swyved,** *screwed,* **bolt upright,** *lying flat* **4267 hast,** *have,* **agast,** *afraid* **4268 harlot,** *scoundrel* **4270 deed,** *dead* **4271 dorste,** *dares,* **disparage,** *dishonor* **4272 swich lynage,** *such lineage* **4273 throte-bolle,** *Adam's apple* **4274 hente,** *grabbed,* **despitously agayn,** *fiercely in return* **4277 tobroke,** *smashed* **4278 walwe,** *wallow,* **poke,** *sack* **4280 sporned at,** *tripped on* **4282 wiste,** *knew,* **nyce stryf,** *ridiculous struggle* **4283 was falle,** *had fallen,* **lite wight,** *little while* **4285 breyde,** *jerked* **4286 croys,** *cross*

4222–33 Changes in verb tense here help to create narrative pace. **4236 Fareweel, Malyne . . . ,** the following exchange is a burlesque of the courtly *alba* or *aube* ("dawn song") in which lovers lament their parting. **4255–56** The *o*-forms here (**mysgo, also**) and elsewhere are southern forms, lapses (scribal?) in the representation of a northern dialect that should have *a*-forms. **4262 swynes-heed,** i.e., you are drunk as a pig. **4264 Seint Jame,** St. James, a convenient rhyme. **4286 croys of Bromeholm,** a reputed piece of Christ's cross was kept at a religious institution at Bromhom, in Norfolk. **4287 *In manus tuas,*** "Into your hands"; from Luke 23.46; a prayer for protection.

Myn herte is broken; help, I nam but deed°!
Ther lyth oon upon my wombe° and on myn
    heed.   4290
Help, Symkyn, for the false clerkes fighte!"
   This John stirte up as soone as ever he myghte,
And graspeth by° the walles to and fro
To fynde a staf; and she stirte up also,
And knew the estres bet° than dide this John,   4295
And by the wal a staf she foond anon,
And saugh° a litel shymeryng of a light,
For at an hole in shoon the moone bright,
And by that light she saugh hem bothe two,
But sikerly° she nyste° who was who,   4300
But as she saugh a whit thyng in° hir eye.
And whan she gan the white thyng espye,
She wende° the clerk hadde wered a volupeer°,
And with the staf she drow ay neer° and neer°,
And wende han hit this Aleyn at the fulle°,   4305
And smoot the millere on the pyled° skulle

That doun he gooth, and cride, "Harrow°! I
    dye!"
Thise clerkes beete° hym weel and lete hym lye,
And greythen hem°, and tooke hir hors anon,
And eek hire mele°, and on hir wey they gon,   4310
And at the mille yet they tooke hir cake°
Of half a busshel flour ful wel ybake.
   Thus is the proude millere wel ybete°,
And hath ylost° the gryndynge of the whete,
And payed for the soper everideel°   4315
Of Aleyn and of John, that bette° hym weel.
His wyf is swyved°, and his doghter als°.
Lo, swich° it is a millere to be fals!
And therfore this proverbe is seyd ful sooth°:
Hym thar nat wene wel that yvele dooth°.   4320
A gylour° shal hymself bigyled be.
And God, that sitteth heighe in magestee,
Save al this compaignye, grete and smale.
Thus have I quyt° the Millere in my tale.

Heere is ended the Reves Tale.

4289 I nam but deed, *I'm all but dead* **4290 wombe,** *stomach* **4293 graspeth by,** *gropes around* **4295 estres bet,** *interior better* **4297 saugh,** *saw* **4300 sikerly,** *surely,* **nyste,** *knew not* **4301 in,** *with* **4303 wende,** *thought,* **volupeer,** *nightcap* **4304 drow ay neer,** *went always nearer* **4305 wende han . . . at the fulle,** *fully intended to have* **4306 pyled,** *bald* **4307 Harrow,** *help* **4308 beete,** *beat* **4309 greythen hem,** *dressed themselves* **4310 mele,** *ground grain* **4311 cake,** *loaf* **4313 ybete,** *beaten* **4314 hath ylost,** *has not been paid for* **4315 the soper everideel,** *every bit of the supper* **4316 bette,** *beat* **4317 swyved,** *screwed,* **als,** *also* **4318 swich,** *such* **4319 seyd ful sooth,** *said quite truly* **4320 Hym thar nat wene wel that yvele dooth,** *he should not expect good who does evil* **4321 gylour,** *deceiver* **4324 quyt,** *repaid*

COOK'S TALE

PROLOGUE

The Prologe of the Cokes Tale.

The Cook of Londoun, whil the Reve spak,
For joye him thoughte he clawed° him on
   the bak.
"Haha," quod he, "for Cristes passioun°,
This millere hadde a sharp° conclusioun
Upon° his argument of herbergage°!
Wel seyde Salomon in his langage,   4330
"Ne brynge nat every man into thyn hous";
For herberwynge° by nyghte is perilous.
Wel oghte a man avysed for to be°
Whom that he broghte into his pryvetee.
I pray to God so yeve me sorwe and care   4335
If evere, sitthe I highte° Hogge of Ware,
Herde I a millere bettre yset a werk°.
He hadde a jape of malice° in the derk.
But God forbede that we stynte° heere;
And therfore, if ye vouchesauf° to heere   4340

A tale of me, that am a poure man,
I wol yow telle as wel as evere I kan
A litel jape that fil° in oure citee."
   Oure Hoost answerde and seide, "I graunte
   it thee.
Now telle on, Roger, looke that it be good,   4345
For many a pastee° hastow laten blood°,
And many a Jakke of Dovere hastow soold
That hath been twies hoot and twies coold.
Of many a pilgrym hastow Cristes curs
For of° thy percely° yet° they fare the
   wors,   4350
That° they han eten with thy stubbel goos°,
For in thy shoppe is many a flye loos°.
Now telle on, gentil Roger by thy name.
But yet I pray thee, be nat wroth for game°:
A man may seye ful sooth in game and pley."   4355

4326 clawed, *scratched* **4327 for Cristes passioun,** *by the suffering of Christ* **4328 sharp,** *painful* **4329 Upon,** *to,* **herbergage,** *lodging* **4332 herberwynge,** *giving shelter* **4333 avysed for to be,** *be careful* **4336 sitthe I highte,** *since I was named* **4337 yset a werk,** *put to work* **4338 jape of malice,** *spiteful joke* **4339 stynte,** *stop* **4340 vouchesauf,** *consent* **4343 fil,** *happened* **4346 pastee,** *meat pie,* **hastow laten blood,** *have you bled (removed the filling)* **4350 For of,** *because from,* **percely,** *parsley (stuffing?),* **yet,** *still* **4351 That,** *which,* **stubbel goos,** *stubble-fed goose* **4352 loos,** *loose* **4354 wroth for game,** *angry because of play*

4326 For joye . . . , the Cook enjoyed the tale so much that it felt as if the Reeve scratched his back. **4328–29 conclusioun . . . ,** this recalls Symkyn's badgering of the clerks, *RvT* 1.4120–26. **4331** The saying is from Ecclesiasticus 11.29, traditionally ascribed to Solomon. **4336 Hogge of Ware,** Hodge is short for Roger; Ware is a small town near London. A "Roger Ware, Cook" has been found in London records, as has "Roger Knight de Ware of London, Cook." **4337 yset a werk,** an idiom meaning "had a job done on him." **4347 Jakke of Dovere,** unidentified, but perhaps a fish or meat pie.

"Thou seist ful sooth," quod Roger, "by my fey°.
But sooth pley, quaad pley°, as the Flemyng°
    seith.
And therfore, Herry Bailly, by thy feith,
Be thou nat wrooth°, er we departen° heer,

Though that my tale be of an hostileer°.   4360
But nathelees I wol nat telle it yit,
But er we parte, ywis°, thou shalt be quit°."
And therwithal he lough° and made cheere°,
And seyde his tale as ye shul after heere.

Heere bigynneth the Cookes Tale.

A prentys whilom° dwelled in our citee,   4365
And of a craft of vitailliers° was hee.
Gaillard° he was as goldfynch in the shawe°,
Broun as a berye, a propre° short felawe,
With lokkes blake, ykembd° ful fetisly°;
Dauncen he koude so wel and jolily   4370
That he was cleped° Perkyn Revelour.
He was as ful of love and paramour°
As is the hyve ful of hony sweete—
Wel° was the wenche with hym myghte meete°.
At every bridale° wolde he synge and hoppe°.   4375
He loved bet° the taverne than the shoppe,
For whan ther any ridyng° was in Chepe
Out of the shoppe thider° wolde he lepe—
Til that he hadde al the sighte yseyn,
And daunced wel, he wolde nat come
    ayeyn°—   4380
And gadered hym° a meynee° of his sort
To hoppe and synge and maken swich disport°.
And ther they setten stevene° for to meete
To pleyen at the dys° in swich a streete.
For in the toun nas ther no prentys   4385
That fairer koude caste a paire of dys

Than Perkyn koude, and therto° he was free°
Of his dispense° in place of pryvetee°.
That fond° his maister° wel in his chaffare°,
For often tyme he foond his box ful bare.   4390
For sikerly° a prentys revelour°
That haunteth dys°, riot°, or paramour,
His maister shal it in his shoppe abye°,
Al have he° no part of the mynstralcye.
For thefte and riot, they been convertible°,   4395
Al konne he° pleye on gyterne° or ribible°.
Revel and trouthe, as in a lowe degree°,
They been ful wrothe al day°, as men may see.
    This joly prentys with his maister bood°
Til he were ny° out of his prentishood°,   4400
Al were he snybbed° bothe erly and late,
And somtyme lad° with revel to Newegate.
But atte laste his maister hym bithoghte°,
Upon a day, whan he his papir soghte°,
Of a proverbe that seith this same word: 4405
Wel bet is° roten appul° out of hoord°
Than that it rotie° al the remenaunt.
So fareth it by° a riotous servaunt;
It is wel lasse° harm to lete hym pace°

4356 **fey**, *faith* 4357 **sooth pley, quaad play**, *true play is no play*, **Flemyng**, *native of Flanders* (Belgium) 4359 **wrooth**, *angry*, **departen**, *separate* 4360 **hostileer**, *innkeeper* 4362 **ywis**, *surely*, **quit**, *repaid* 4363 **lough**, *laughed*, **made cheere**, *acted friendly* 4365 **prentys whilom**, *apprentice once* 4366 **vitailliers**, *food suppliers* 4367 **Gaillard**, *lively*, **shawe**, *woods* 4368 **propre**, *handsome* 4369 **lokkes**, *hair*, **ykembd**, *combed*, **fetisly**, *elegantly* 4371 **cleped**, *called* 4372 **paramour**, *sexual desire* 4374 **Wel**, *happy*, **hym myghte meete**, *(that) might meet him* 4375 **bridale**, *wedding celebration*, **hoppe**, *dance* 4376 **bet**, *better* 4377 **ridyng**, *parade* 4378 **thider**, *there* 4380 **come ayeyn**, *return* (to the shop) 4381 **gadered hym**, *he gathered*, **meynee**, *group* 4382 **swich disport**, *such fun* 4383 **setten stevene**, *made appointments* 4384 **dys**, *dice* 4387 **therto**, *also*, **free**, *generous* 4388 **dispense**, *spending*, **place of**

pryvetee, *a private place* 4389 **fond**, *found*, **maister**, *master*, **chaffare**, *business* 4391 **sikerly**, *surely*, **prentys revelour**, *party-going apprentice* 4392 **haunteth dys**, *frequents dice*, **riot**, *debauchery* 4393 **abye**, *pay for* 4394 **Al have he**, *although he has* 4395 **convertible**, *interchangeable* 4396 **Al konne he**, *even though he can*, **gyterne**, *guitar*, **ribible**, *fiddle* 4397 **as in a lowe degree**, *in a low-life person* 4398 **been ful wrothe al day**, *are always in conflict* 4399 **bood**, *lived* 4400 **Til he were ny**, *until he was nearly*, **prentishood**, *apprenticeship* 4401 **Al were he snybbed**, *even though he was scolded* 4402 **lad**, *led* 4403 **hym bithoghte**, *thought to himself* 4404 **he his papir soghte**, *Perkyn sought his release from apprenticeship* 4406 **Wel bet**, *much better*, **appul**, *apple*, **hoord**, *the pile* 4407 **rotie**, *rots* 4408 **So fareth it by**, *so it goes with* 4409 **wel lasse**, *much less*, **pace**, *leave*

4358 Herry Bailly, the Host's name, here given for the first time. A "Henricus Bayliff, Ostyler" is listed in Southwark records of the 1380s. That the Cook apparently knows the Host (an innkeeper) may suggest professional rivalry, also reflected in their verbal sparring. **4365 prentys,** apprentices were legally contracted to work for their masters for a period of time in exchange for training in a particular skill or business. **4366 craft of vitailliers,** food suppliers' guild. In the 1380s, there were inflammatory struggles for political and economic power between the London guilds of food suppliers and those that supplied other commodities. **4371 Perkyn Revelour,** "Pete the Partier." **4377 Chepe,** Cheapside was an important commercial area in London. **4402 Newegate,** London's Newgate prison. When unruly persons were taken to prison, they were preceded by musicians to call attention to their disgrace.

Than he shende° alle the servantz in
    the place.   4410
Therfore his maister yaf hym acquitance°,
And bad° hym go with sorwe and with
    meschance°.
And thus this joly prentys hadde his leve.
Now lat hym riote° al the nyght or leve°.
And for° ther is no theef withoute a lowke°   4415

That helpeth hym to wasten and to sowke°
Of that he brybe° kan or borwe° may,
Anon he sente his bed and his array°
Unto a compier° of his owene sort,
That lovede dys and revel and disport,   4420
And hadde a wyf that heeld for contenance°
A shoppe, and swyved° for hir sustenance° . . .

4410 **shende,** *ruin* 4411 **yaf hym acquitance,** *released him from his contract of apprenticeship* 4412 **bad,** *told,* **meschance,** *bad luck* 4414 **riote,** *dissipate,* **leve,** *stop* (leave off) 4415 **for,** *because,* **lowke,** *accomplice*

4416 **sowke,** *suck* 4417 **brybe,** *bribe,* **borwe,** *borrow* 4418 **array,** *clothing* 4419 **compier,** *companion* 4421 **heeld for contenance,** *kept for appearance's sake* 4422 **swyved,** *had sex,* **sustenance,** *living*

CANTERBURY TALES PART 2

INTRODUCTION

THE MAN OF LAW MATERIALS follow part 1 in nearly all manuscripts. The *Man of Law's Prologue* sets the date of the pilgrimage as April 18, and in it—emulating or mocking lawyerly language—the Host restates the conditions of the storytelling contest (33ff.). The Man of Law's statement that he will tell a tale in "prose" (see 96n) and the references to law and philosophy in the *Epilogue* (see 1189n) suggest that the *Tale of Melibee* (now in part 7) may have been originally assigned to the Man of Law. Chaucer apparently canceled the *Epilogue* when he rearranged the tales to follow it (see 1163–90n, 1179n), as it is omitted in twenty-two manuscripts, including the most reliable ones. It may be that in an earlier stage in the evolution of *The Canterbury Tales*, the Man of Law told the *Tale of Melibee*, which was then followed by the present *Shipman's Tale*, told by the Wife of Bath.

The source of the tale of Constance—Custance in Chaucer—is an episode in Nicholas Trivet's *Chronicle* (ca. 1335), an Anglo-Norman account of the history of the Western world. Trivet's episode has its roots in folklore, examined by Margaret Schlauch in *Constance and the Accused Queens* (1927, no. 935) and Nancy B. Black, *Medieval Narratives of Accused Queens* (2003, no. 903). Chaucer's friend John Gower also adapted Trivet's tale about the same time that Chaucer did (ca. 1390), but there is no convincing evidence that Chaucer relied upon Gower, or vice versa, although the former is more likely. Gower's version is closer to Trivet's and a straightforward exemplum of the wickedness of jealousy.

In contrast, Chaucer's tale is concerned with Christian Providence, and it achieves a high (some say too high) degree of pathos by incorporating a number of rhetorical apostrophes and exclamations not found in Trivet or Gower, heightened by the rhyme royal stanza form. The relation between Providence and pathos raises questions for many modern readers because it is difficult for us to see why a world governed by Providence should inspire such lamentation. The events of the plot are guided by the "wyl of Crist" (e.g., 511, 721, 825, etc.), and they are subject to the direct intervention of God and Mary (669, 920). Yet the narrator bewails the influence of the stars, the devil, and wicked mothers-in-law, and his references to divine assistance are cast as rhetorical questions (e.g., 473ff.) rather than confident assertions of faith. Divine aid seems not to respond directly to Custance's prayers, nor does it save her from floating at sea for years in a rudderless boat. Such aid arrives only sporadically, not easily explained by human reason.

This is consistent with late-medieval notions of the world as a place of misery. Several portions of the *Man of Law's Prologue* and *Tale* derive from the early thirteenth-century Latin treatise by Pope Innocent III, *On the Misery of the Human Condition*, which Chaucer says he translated (*LGWP* G414; see note to *MLT* 99–121), although no translation by him survives. The treatise epitomized for the Middle Ages the attitude of *contemptus mundi* (disdain for the world), which encouraged detachment from the world and its affairs on the logic that they cause only sorrow. In *Chaucer's Narrators* (1985, no. 356), David Lawton claims that the rhetoric of the *Man of Law's Tale* echoes Innocent's own rhetoric. The contributors to *Chaucer's Religious Tales*, edited by C. David Benson and Elizabeth Robertson (1990, no. 396), argue that the tale reflects late-medieval spirituality. Morton W. Bloomfield, "The *Man of Law's Tale:* A Tragedy of Victimization and Christian Comedy" (1972, no. 905), describes how the tale distances the audience while provoking deep pathos.

Not everyone agrees, of course. Some critics who regard the rhetoric of the tale as excessive rather than genuine rationalize it as characteristic of legal pleading—the Man of Law's attempt to convince the jury, as it were. In these readings, rhetorical excess and uncertain faith in Providence are blamed on the Man of Law, absolving Chaucer of responsibility for either. In his contribution to Benson and Robertson's collection of essays, A. S. G. Edwards (1990, no. 917) surveys such approaches, although he has little sympathy with them.

Custance's lack of agency in directing the events of her life has encouraged critics to read her as an emblem of women subordinated by patriarchy (God, her father, and her husbands) and the demands of lineage (her mothers-in-law). As such, her story can be seen as a transition between part 1, where men are central and active in and out of marriage, to part 3, where the Wife of Bath takes center stage as one who controls her own marital affairs. In "Worlds Apart: Orientalism, Antifeminism, and Heresy in Chaucer's *Man of Law's Tale*" (1996, no. 934), Susan Schibanoff argues that the Man of Law dehumanizes women and non-Christians alike to affirm male Christian control. In "New Approaches to Chaucer" (2003, no. 915), Carolyn Dinshaw surveys feminist, queer, and postcolonial studies of the *Man of Law's Tale*.

In *Chaucerian Polity* (1997, no. 251), David Wallace examines the shadowy presence of mercantilism in the tale as it correlates with the role of merchants in late-medieval English politics, and he explores similarities between the medieval legal profession and fiction making as a way of explaining Chaucer's references to his own poetry in the *Man of Law's Prologue* (47ff.). In his contribution to a collection of essays edited by Leonard Michael Koff and Brenda Deen Schildgen, *The Decameron and the Canterbury Tales* (2000, no. 918a), Robert W. Hanning discusses mercantile exchange as one of the several forms of distorted mediation in the tale, a means to reveal the Man of Law's own distortion of the message intrinsic to the narrative. Joseph Hornsby, *Chaucer and the Law* (1988, no. 610), and Mary Flowers Braswell, *Chaucer's "Legal Fiction"* (2001, no. 603), explore law and legal notions in Chaucer's life and works.

CANTERBURY TALES PART 2

MAN OF LAW'S TALE

PROLOGUE

The wordes of the Hoost to the compaignye.

Oure Hooste saugh° wel that the brighte sonne
The ark of his artificial day hath ronne°
The ferthe part, and half an houre and moore,
And though he were nat depe ystert in loore°,
He wiste° it was the eightetethe day   5
Of Aprill, that is messager to May;
And saugh wel that the shadwe° of every tree
Was as in lengthe the same quantitee
That was the body erect that caused it.
And therfore by the shadwe he took his wit°   10
That Phebus°, which that shoon so clere and
      brighte,

Degrees was fyve and fourty clombe° on highte,
And for that day, as in that latitude,
It was ten at the clokke°, he gan conclude°;
And sodeynly he plighte° his hors aboute.   15
    "Lordynges," quod he, "I warne yow, al this
      route°,
The fourthe party° of this day is gon.
Now, for the love of God and of Seint John,
Leseth° no tyme as ferforth° as ye may.
Lordynges, the tyme wasteth nyght and day,   20
And steleth° from us, what pryvely° slepynge,
And what thurgh necligence in oure wakynge,

[handwritten marginalia: April 18]
[handwritten marginalia: Showing off knowledge of Astrology.]

---

1 **saugh,** *saw* 2 **ronne,** *run* 4 **depe ystert in loore,** *deeply advanced in learning* 5 **wiste,** *knew* 7 **shadwe,** *shadow* 10 **took his wit,** *decided* 11 **Phebus,** *the sun* 12 **was . . . clombe,** *had climbed* 14 **at the clokke,** o'clock, **gan conclude,** *did deduce* 15 **plighte,** *pulled* 16 **route,** *company* 17 **party,** *part* 19 **Leseth,** *lose,* **ferforth,** *far* 21 **steleth,** *slips away,* **what pryvely,** *what with secretly*

2 **ark of his artificial day,** the arc of the sun moving across the sky. The artificial day is the time from sunrise to sunset, distinguished from the natural day of twenty-four hours. 3 **ferthe part,** a quarter of the way through the sun's artificial day plus an hour and a half is somewhat earlier than 10 o'clock on this date. 5–6 **eightetethe day / Of Aprill,** the date and the following details of the tree's shadow, the angle of the sun, and the time align closely. They are documented in Nicholas of Lynn's *Kalendarium* as occurring April 18, 1386, discussed in Sigmund Eisner's edition of the *Kalendarium,* pp. 30–31.

As dooth° the streem that turneth nevere agayn,
Descendynge fro° the montaigne into° playn.
Wel kan Senec and many a philosophre   25
Biwaillen° tyme moore than gold in cofre°,
For "los of catel° may recovered be,
But los of tyme shendeth° us," quod he.
It wol° nat come agayn, withouten drede°,
Namoore than wole° Malkynes maydenhede,   30
Whan she hath lost it in hir wantownesse.
Lat us nat mowlen° thus in ydelnesse.

   "Sire Man of Lawe," quod he, "so have ye blis°,
Telle us a tale anon, as forward° is.
Ye been submytted, thurgh youre free assent,   35
To stonden° in this cas at my juggement.
Acquiteth yow° now of youre biheeste°;
Thanne have ye do° youre devoir° atte leeste°."

   "Hooste," quod he, "depardieux°, ich assente°;
To breke forward is nat myn entente.   40
Biheste is dette°, and I wole holde fayn°
Al my biheste; I kan no bettre sayn.
For swich° lawe as a man yeveth° another wight°,
He sholde hymselven usen it, by right;
Thus wole° oure text. But nathelees, certeyn,   45
I kan right now no thrifty° tale seyn°
That Chaucer, thogh he kan but lewedly°
On° metres and on rymyng craftily°,
Hath seyd hem° in swich° Englissh as he kan

Of olde tyme°, as knoweth many a man.   50
And if he have noght seyd hem, leve brother,
In o book°, he hath seyd hem in another.
For he hath toold of loveris up and doun°
Mo° than Ovide made of mencioun
In his *Episteles* that been ful olde.   55
What sholde I tellen hem, syn° they ben
      tolde?

   "In youthe he made of° Ceys and Alcione,
And sitthen° hath he spoken of everichone°
Thise noble wyves and thise loveris eke°.
Whoso° that wole his large volume seke°   60
Cleped° the Seintes Legende of Cupide,
Ther may he seen° the large woundes wyde°
Of Lucresse, and of Babilan Tesbee;
The swerd° of Dido for the false Enee;
The tree of Phillis for hire Demophon;   65
The pleinte° of Dianire and of Hermyon,
Of Adriane, and of Isiphilee—
The bareyne yle° stondynge in the see—
The dreynte° Leandre for his Erro;
The teeris° of Eleyne, and eek the wo   70
Of Brixseyde, and the°, Ladomya;
The crueltee of the°, queene Medea,
Thy litel children hangynge by the hals°,
For thy Jason, that was in love so fals!
O Ypermystra, Penelopee, Alceste,   75

---

23 dooth, *does* **24 fro,** *from,* **montaigne into,** *mountain to* **26 Biwaillen,** *lament,* **cofre,** *chest* **27 catel,** *possessions* **28 shendeth,** *ruins* **29 wol,** *will,* **drede,** *doubt* **30 wole,** *will* **32 mowlen,** *get moldy* **33 so have ye blis,** *may you have happiness* **34 forward,** *promise* **36 stonden,** *stand* **37 Acquiteth yow,** *fulfill,* **biheeste,** *promise* **38 do,** *done,* **devoir,** *obligation,* **atte leeste,** *at the least* **39 depardieux,** *by God,* **ich assente,** *I agree* **41 Biheste is dette,** *promise is duty,* **wole holde fayn,** *will maintain gladly* **43 swich,** *such,* **yeveth,** *gives,* **wight,** *person* **45 wole,** *asserts* **46 thrifty,** *fitting,* **seyn,** tell **47 kan but lewedly,** *knows little* **48 On,** *about,* **rymyng craftily,** *skillful rhyming* **49 seyd hem,** *told them,* **swich,** *such* **50 Of olde tyme,** *in the past* **52 o book,** *one book* **53 loveris up and doun,** *lovers here and there* **54 Mo,** *more* **56 syn,** *since* **57 made of,** *wrote about* **58 sitthen,** *since then,* **everichone,** *every one* (of) **59 eke,** *also* **60 Whoso,** *whoever,* **wole . . . seke,** *will . . . seek* **61 Cleped,** *called* **62 seen,** *see,* **wyde,** *wide* **64 swerd,** *sword* **66 pleinte,** *lament* **68 bareyne yle,** *barren isle* **69 dreynte,** *drowned* **70 teeris,** *tears* **71 the,** *thee* **72 the,** *thee* **73 hals,** *neck*

25 Senec, Seneca the younger, a Roman philosopher in whose *Epistle* 1.3 a proverbial sentiment like that in lines 27–28 can be found. **30 Malkynes maydenhede,** Malkin's virginity; Malkin is a name for a rustic female. **35 Ye been submytted,** i.e., you have submitted yourself, the first in a series of legal phrases exchanged by the Host and Man of Law. **45 oure text,** the preceding statement is proverbial, but derives from a legal textbook, the *Digests* of Justinian, 2.2. **47 Chaucer,** this reference and the following metafictive references to some of Chaucer's actual poems simultaneously create and challenge the illusion that the fictional pilgrimage really happened. **55 Episteles,** Ovid's *Heroides,* presented as a series of letters, contains many of the stories listed below. **57 Ceys and Alcione,** Chaucer writes of the lovers Ceyx and Alcione at the beginning of *BD,* 62–220. **61 Seintes Legende of Cupide,** Lives of Cupid's Saints, a reference to *LGW,* which Chaucer calls the *Book of the XXV Ladies* in the *CT* 10.1086. The following list does not match the nineteen tales of the incomplete *LGW*; eight in the list are not found in *LGW,* and the list lacks two that are (Cleopatra, Philomela). Asterisks below indicate those found in *LGW.* **63 *Lucresse,** the rape and suicide of Lucrece; Ovid's *Fasti* 2.685–852.*Babilan Tesbee,** Thisbe, a Babylonian, and her beloved Pyramus committed suicide; Ovid, *Metamorphoses* 4.55–166. **64 *Dido . . . Enee,** Dido killed herself with a sword because Aeneas abandoned her; Virgil, *Aeneid* 4, and Ovid, *Heroides* 7. **65 *Phillis,** in *LGW* 2484 and *HF* 394, Phyllis hangs herself because she was deserted by Demophon; the account in Ovid *Heroides* 2 does not include this detail. **66 Dianire,** Dianeira laments that she caused the death of Hercules, her husband, in *Heroides* 9. **Hermyon,** Hermione laments that Orestes is banished in *Heroides* 8. **67 *Adriane,** Ariadne laments that Theseus abandons her in *Heroides* 10. *Isiphilee,** Hypsipile laments the falseness of Jason in *Heroides* 6; he left her on the isle of Naxos. **69 Leandre . . . Erro,** Leander drowned swimming across the Hellespont to visit Hero; *Heroides* 18. **70 Eleyne,** Helen's love of Paris caused the Trojan war; *Heroides* 16 and elsewhere. **71 Brixseyde,** the original name of the lover of Troilus, changed by Boccaccio to Criseyde; *Heroides* 3. **Ladomya,** Laodamia lamented the death of her husband, Protesilaus, the first man killed in the Trojan War; *Heroides* 13. **72 *Medea,** who killed their children when deserted by Jason; *Heroides* 6. **75 *Ypermystra,** Hypermnestra was killed by her father because she would not kill her husband; *Heroides* 14. **Penelopee,** Penelope long awaited the return of her husband, Ulysses; *Heroides* 14. **Alceste,** who was faithful to her husband, Admetus, and in his place; *LGW* F511ff.

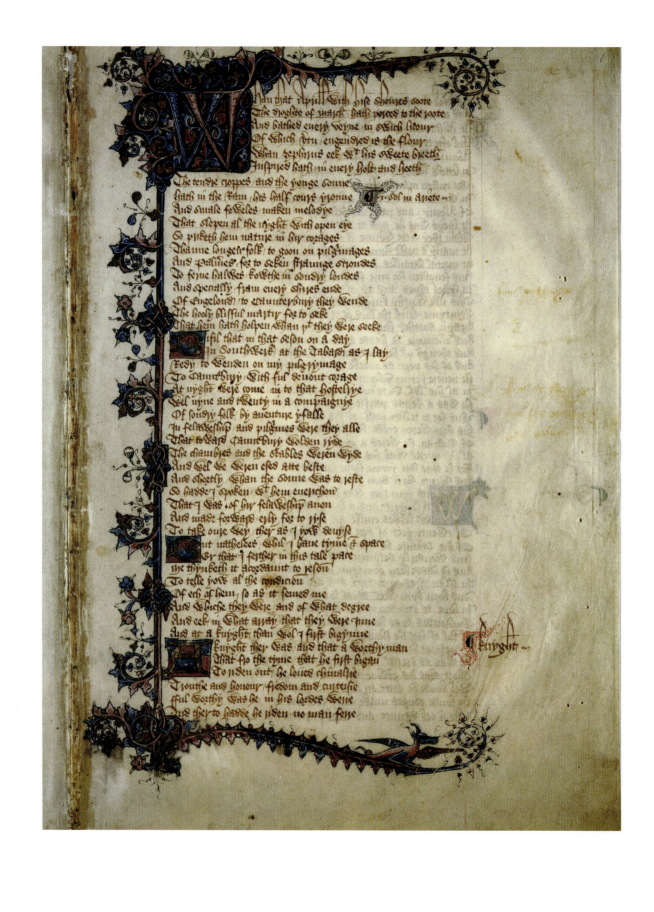

Whan that Aprill with his shoures soote
The droghte of March hath perced to the roote
And bathed every veyne in swich licour
Of which vertu engendred is the flour
Whan zephirus eek with his sweete breeth
Inspired hath in every holt and heeth
The tendre croppes and the yonge sonne
Hath in the Ram his half cours yronne ~ Sol in ariete
And smale foweles maken melodye
That slepen al the nyght with open eye
So priketh hem nature in hir corages
Thanne longen folk to goon on pilgrimages
And palmeres for to seken straunge strondes
To ferne halwes kowthe in sondry londes
And specially from every shires ende
Of Engelond to Caunterbury they wende
The hooly blisful martir for to seke
That hem hath holpen whan þat they were seeke
Bifil that in that seson on a day
In Southwerk at the Tabard as I lay
Redy to wenden on my pilgrymage
To Caunterbury with ful devout corage
At nyght was come in to that hostelrye
Wel nyne and twenty in a compaignye
Of sondry folk by aventure yfalle
In felaweshipe and pilgrimes were they alle
That toward Caunterbury wolden ryde
The chambres and the stables weren wyde
And wel we weren esed atte beste
And shortly whan the sonne was to reste
So hadde I spoken with hem everichon
That I was of hir felaweshipe anon
And made forward erly for to ryse
To take oure wey ther as I yow devyse
But nathelees whil I have tyme and space
Er that I ferther in this tale pace
Me thynketh it acordaunt to resoun
To telle yow al the condicioun
Of ech of hem so as it semed me
And whiche they were and of what degree
And eek in what array that they were inne
And at a knyght than wol I first bigynne ~ Knyght
A knyght ther was and that a worthy man
That fro the tyme that he first bigan
To riden out he loved chivalrie
Trouthe and honour fredom and curteisie
Ful worthy was he in his lordes werre
And therto hadde he riden no man ferre

Iamque domos patrias Scithice post aspera gentis
prelia laurigero &c

Heere bigynneth the knyghtes tale

Whilom as olde stories tellen us
Ther was a duc þt highte Theseus
Of Atthenes he was lord and governour
And in his tyme swich a conquerour
That gretter was ther noon under the sonne
Ful many a riche contree hadde he wonne
What with his wysdom and his chivalrie
He conquered al the regne of ffemenye
That whilom was ycleped Scithia
And weddede the queene Ypolita
And broghte hir hoom with hym in his contree
With muchel glorie and greet solempnytee
And eek hir fayre suster Emelye
And thus with victorie and with melodye
Lete I this noble duc to Atthenes ryde
And al his hoost in armes hym bisyde
And certes if it nere to long to heere
I wolde yow have toold fully the manere
How wonnen was the regne of ffemenye
By Theseus and by his chivalrye
And of the grete bataille for the nones
Bitwixen Atthenes and Amazones
And how asseged was Ypolita
The fayre hardy queene of Scithia
And of the feste þt was at hir weddynge
And of the tempest at hir hoom comynge
But al that thyng I moot as now forbere
I haue god woot a large feeld to ere
And wayke been the oxen in my plough
The remenant of the tale is long ynough
I wol nat letten eek noon of this route
Lat euery felawe tolde his tale aboute
And lat se now who shal the soper wynne
And ther I lefte I wol ayeyn bigynne

This duc of whom I make mencioun
Whan he was come almoost vn to the toun
In al his wele and in his mooste pride
He was war as he caste his eye aside
Where that ther kneled in the weye
A compaignye of ladyes tweye and tweye

Quod this Somonour and a bisshe me
But if I telle tales two or thre
Of freres er I come to Sydyngborne
That I shal make thyn herte for to morne
For wel I woot thy pacience is gon
Oure hooste cride pees and that anon
And seyde lat the womman telle hir tale
Ye fare as folk that dronken been of ale
Do dame telle forth youre tale and that is best
Al redy sir quod she right as yow lest
If I have licence of this worthy frere
Yis dame quod he tel forth and I wol heere

Heere endeth the wyf of Bathe hir prologe and
bigynneth hir tale

In tholde dayes of kyng Arthour
Of which that Britons speken greet honour
Al was this land fulfild of fairye
The elf queene with hir Ioly compaignye
Daunced ful ofte in many a grene mede
This was the olde opinion as I rede
I speke of manye hundred yeres ago
But now kan no man se none elves mo
For now the grete charitee and prayeres
Of lymytours and othere hooly freres
That serchen every lond and every streem
As thikke as motes in the sonne beem
Blessynge halles chambres kichenes boures
Citees burghes castels hye toures
Thropes bernes shipnes dayeryes
This maketh that ther been no fairyes
For ther as wont to walken was an elf
Ther walketh now the lymytour hym self
In undermeles and in morwenynges
And seyth his matyns and his hooly thynges
As he gooth in his lymytacioun
Wommen may go saufly up and doun
In every bussh or under every tree
Ther is noon oother incubus but he
And he ne wol doon hem but dishonour
And so bifel that this kyng Arthour
Hadde in his hous a lusty bacheler
That on a day cam ridynge fro ryver
And happed that allone as he was born
He saugh a mayde walkynge hym biforn

Youre wifhede he comendeth° with the beste.
  "But certeinly no word ne writeth he
Of thilke° wikke ensample° of Canacee,
That loved hir owene brother synfully—
Of swiche° cursed stories I sey fy°!   80
Or ellis° of Tyro Appollonius,
How that the cursed kyng Antiochus
Birafte° his doghter of hir maydenhede.
That is so horrible a tale for to rede—
Whan he hir threw upon the pavement.   85
And therfore he°, of ful avysement°,
Nolde nevere° write in none of his sermons°

Of swiche unkynde° abhomynacions,
Ne I wol noon reherce°, if that I may.
  "But of my tale how shal I doon° this
       day?   90
Me were looth be likned, doutelees°,
To muses that men clepe° Pierides—
Methamorphosios woot° what I mene°;
But nathelees, I recche noght a bene°
Though I come after hym with hawebake.   95
I speke in prose, and lat him rymes make."
And with that word he, with a sobre cheere°,
Bigan his tale, as ye shal after heere.

The Prologe of the Mannes Tale of Lawe.

O hateful harm°, condicion of poverte,
With thurst, with coold, with hunger so
       confounded°!   100
To asken help thee shameth in thyn herte;
If thou noon aske°, so soore artow° ywounded
That verray nede unwrappeth° al thy wounde hid°.
Maugree thyn heed°, thou most° for indigence
Or stele°, or begge, or borwe thy despence°.   105

Thow blamest Crist and seist° ful bitterly
He mysdeparteth richesse temporal°;
Thy neighebore thou wytest° synfully
And seist° thou hast to lite° and he hath al.
"Parfay°," seistow, "somtyme he rekene° shal,   110
Whan that his tayl° shal brennen° in the gleede°,
For he noght helpeth needfulle° in hir° neede."

Herke° what is the ~~message~~ sentence° of the wise:
Bet is° to dyen than have indigence;
Thy selve° neighebor wol° thee despise.   115
If thou be poure, farwel thy reverence°.
Yet of the wise man take this sentence:
Alle the dayes of poure men been wikke°.
Bewar, therfore, er° thou come to that prikke°!

If thou be poure, thy brother hateth thee,   120
And alle thy freendes fleen° from thee, allas.
O riche marchauntz°, ful of wele been yee°;
O noble, O prudent folk, as in this cas°,
Youre bagges been nat fild° with ambes as
But with sys cynk that renneth° for youre
       chaunce°.   125
At Cristemasse myrie° may ye daunce!

---

76 comendeth, *praises* **78 thilke,** *that,* **ensample,** *example* **80 swiche,** *such,* **sey fy,** *say shame* **81 ellis,** *else* **83 Birafte,** *deprived* **86 he,** i.e., "Chaucer," **of ful avysement,** *in wise consideration* **87 Nolde nevere,** *would never,* **sermons,** *discourses* **88 swiche unkynde,** *such unnatural* **89 noon reherce,** *none repeat* **90 doon,** *do* **91 Me were looth be likned, doutelees,** *I would hate to be compared, doubtless* **92 clepe,** *call* **93 woot,** *knows,* **mene,** *mean* **94 recche noght a bene,** *care not a bean* **97 cheere,** *expression* **99 harm,** *injury* **100 confounded,** *mixed* **102 noon aske,** *ask for none,* **soore artow,** *sorely are you* **103 verray nede unwrappeth,** *sheer need discloses,* **hid,** *hidden* **104 Maugree thyn heed,**

despite your head (i.e., yourself), **most,** *must* **105 Or stele,** *either steal,* **despence,** *expenses* **106 seist,** *say* **107 mysdeparteth richesse temporal,** *unfairly divides worldly wealth* **108 wytest,** *blame* **109 seist,** *say,* **to lite,** *too little* **110 Parfay,** *by my faith,* **seistow,** *you say,* **rekene,** *account* (for it) **111 tayl,** *tail,* **brennen,** *burn,* **gleede,** *coals* **112 needfulle,** *(the) needy,* **hir,** *their* **113 Herke,** *hear,* **sentence,** *message* **114 Bet is,** *it is better* **115 Thy selve,** *your own,* **wol,** *will* **116 reverence,** *dignity* **118 wikke,** *wicked* **119 er,** *before,* **prikke,** *point* **121 fleen,** *flee* **122 marchauntz,** *merchants,* **wele been yee,** *prosperity are you* **123 cas,** *situation* **124 fild,** *filled* **125 renneth,** *runs,* **chaunce,** *luck* **126 myrie,** *merry*

---

78 Canacee, Canace; *Heroides* 11. Since Tyrwhitt, critics have taken the criticism of incest here and in the reference to Apollonius of Tyre (line 81) as Chaucer's jibes at his friend John Gower, who told both tales in *Confessio Amantis,* 3.143ff., 8.271ff. **81 Tyro Appollonius,** Apollonius of Tyre, hero of a medieval narrative of the same name, solved the riddle by which King **Antiochus** (line 82) sought to keep his daughter for his own pleasure. **92 muses . . . Pierides,** the nine daughters of Pierus who were changed into magpies for presuming to compete with the muses, goddesses of inspiration; Ovid's *Metamorphoses* 5.300ff. The Man of Law does not want to be compared with Chaucer. **95 come after hym with hawebake,** i.e., follow him with a hawthorn berry pie (inedible). **96 prose,** since *MLPT* are in poetry (seven-line rhyme royal stanzas), this is either a joke or indication that Chaucer once intended to have a prose tale follow, perhaps the present *Melibee.* The first stanza below is also found in the *Melibee* (7.1568–70), encouraging the connection. Yet it is hard to see how the "poverty prologue" below (lines 99–121) is an appropriate introduction to either *MLT* or *Melibee.* **99–121** A paraphrase from *De Miseria Conditionis Humane* (On the Misery of the Human Condition) 1.14 of Pope Innocent III, which in *LGW* G414 Chaucer says he translated, although no complete Chaucerian translation has been found. Other echoes of the work are at lines 421–27, 771–77, 925–31, 1132–38 below, and elsewhere in *CT;* see *PardT* 6.484n. **124–25 ambes as . . . sys cynk,** two aces (snake eyes) . . . six and five (eleven), i.e., a losing throw versus a winning throw in dice.

Ye seken° lond and see for yowre wynnynges;
As wise folk ye known° al th'estaat°
Of regnes°; ye been fadres° of tidynges
And tales bothe of pees° and of debaat°.   130

I were° right now of tales desolaat°
Nere° that a marchant, goon is many a yeere°,
Me taughte° a tale which that ye shal heere.

Heere bigynneth the Man of Lawe his Tale.

In Surrye whilom° dwelte a compaignye
Of chapmen° riche, and therto sadde° and
          trewe,   135
That wyde-where° senten hir spicerye°,
Clothes of gold, and satyns riche of hewe°.
Hir chaffare° was so thrifty° and so newe
That every wight° hath deyntee to chaffare°
With hem°, and eek to sellen hem hire ware°.   140

Now fil it° that the maistres of that sort°
Han shapen hem° to Rome for to wende°,
Were it° for chapmanhode° or for disport°.
Noon oother message° wolde they thider° sende,
But comen hemself° to Rome, this is
          the ende°,   145
And in swich° place as thoughte hem avantage°
For hire entente, they take hir herbergage°.

Sojourned han° thise marchantz in that toun
A certein tyme, as fil° to hire plesance°.
And so bifel that th'excellent renoun   150
Of the Emperoures doghter, dame Custance,
Reported was with every circumstance°
Unto thise Surryen marchantz in swich wyse°,
Fro day to day, as I shal yow devyse°.

This was the commune voys° of every man: 155
"Oure Emperour of Rome—God hym see°—
A doghter hath that syn° the world bigan,
To rekene° as wel hir goodnesse as beautee,
Nas nevere swich° another as is shee.

I prey to God in honour hire susteene,   160
And wolde° she were of al Europe the queene.

"In hire is heigh° beautee withoute pride,
Yowthe withoute grenehede° or folye°;
To alle hire werkes vertu is hir gyde°;
Humblesse hath slayn in hire al tirannye;   165
She is mirour of alle curteisye;
Hir herte is verray° chambre of hoolynesse;
Hir hand, ministre of fredam for almesse°."

And al this voys° was sooth°, as God is trewe.
But now to purpos lat us turne agayn.   170
Thise marchantz han doon fraught hir shippes
          newe°,
And whan they han this blisful mayden sayn°,
Hoom° to Surrye been they went ful fayn°,
And doon hir nedes° as they han doon yoore°,
And lyven in wele°; I kan sey yow namoore.   175

Now fil it that thise marchantz stode° in grace°
Of hym that was the Sowdan° of Surrye,
For whan they cam from any strange° place
He wolde, of his benigne° curteisye,
Make hem good chiere°, and bisily espye°   180
Tidynges° of sondry regnes° for to leere°
The wondres that they myghte° seen or heere.

Amonges othere thynges, specially,
Thise marchantz han° hym toold of dame
          Custance

---

127 **seken,** *search* 128 **known,** *know,* **th'estaat,** *the condition* 129 **regnes,** *kingdoms,* **been fadres,** *are fathers* 130 **pees,** *peace,* **debaat,** *conflict* 131 **were,** *would be,* **of tales desolaat,** *without tales* 132 **Nere,** *were it not,* **goon is many a yeere,** *a long time ago* 133 **Me taughte,** *taught me* 134 **Surrye whilom,** *Syria once* 135 **chapmen,** *merchants,* **therto sadde,** *also steady* 136 **wyde-where,** *far and wide,* **hir spicerye,** *their spices* 137 **hewe,** *color* 138 **chaffare,** *merchandise,* **thrifty,** *profitable* 139 **wight,** *person,* **hath deyntee to chaffare,** *is pleased to trade* 140 **hem,** *them,* **hire ware,** *their goods* 141 **fil it,** *it happened,* **sort,** *company* 142 **Han shapen hem,** *arranged* (for) *themselves,* **wende,** *travel* 143 **Were it,** *either,* **chapmanhode,** *business,* **disport,** *pleasure* 144 **message,** *messenger,* **thider,** *there* 145 **hemself,** *themselves,* **ende,** *goal* 146 **swich,** *such,* **avantage,** *advantageous* 147 **hir herbergage,** *their lodging* 148 **Sojourned han,** *stayed* have 149 **fil,** *happened,* **plesance,** *pleasure* 152 **circumstance,** *detail* 153 **swich wyse,** *such a manner* 154 **devyse,** *describe* 155 **voys,** *voice* 156 **see,** *watch over* 157 **syn,** *since* 158 **rekene,** *take into account* 159 **Nas nevere swich,** *there was never such* 161 **wolde,** *wish* 162 **heigh,** *high* 163 **grenehede,** *immaturity,* **folye,** *folly* 164 **hir gyde,** *their guide* 167 **verray,** *true* 168 **fredam for almesse,** *generosity in giving alms* 169 **voys,** *report,* **sooth,** *true* 171 **han doon fraught hir shippes newe,** *have had their ships loaded again* 172 **sayn,** *seen* 173 **Hoom,** *home,* **fayn,** *pleased* 174 **nedes,** *business,* **han doon yoore,** *had done before* 175 **wele,** *prosperity* 176 **stode,** *stood,* **grace,** *favor* 177 **Sowdan,** *Sultan* 178 **strange,** *foreign* 179 **benigne,** *gentle* 180 **Make hem good chiere,** *make them welcome,* **bisily espye,** *eagerly seek* 181 **Tidyngs,** *news,* **sondry regnes,** *various kingdoms,* **leere,** *learn* 182 **myghte,** *might have* 184 **han,** *have*

---

152 Reported was, in Trivet and Gower, the Syrian merchants are converted to Christianity when they meet and hear Custance.

So° greet noblesse, in ernest, ceriously°,   185
That this Sowdan hath caught so greet plesance°
To han hir figure in his remembrance
That al his lust° and al his bisy cure°
Was for to love hire whil his lyf may dure°.

Paraventure° in thilke° large book   190
Which that men clipe° the hevene ywriten was
With sterres°, whan that° he his birthe took°,
That he for love sholde han° his deeth, allas!
For in the sterres, clerer° than is glas,
Is writen, God woot°, whoso koude° it rede,   195
The deeth of every man, withouten drede°.

In sterres many a wynter therbiforn°
Was writen the deeth of Ector, Achilles,
Of Pompei, Julius, er° they were born;
The strif° of Thebes; and of Ercules,   200
Of Sampson, Turnus, and of Socrates
The deeth; but mennes wittes ben° so dulle
That no wight kan wel rede it atte fulle°.

   This Sowdan for his privee conseil° sente,
And, shortly of this matiere° for to pace°,   205
He hath to hem declared his entente,
And seyde hem°, certein, but° he myghte have
      grace°
To han° Custance withinne a litel space°,
He nas but deed°; and charged hem in hye°
To shapen° for his lyf som remedye.   210

   Diverse men diverse thynges seyden°.
They argumenten, casten° up and doun.
Many a subtil resoun forth they leyden°.
They speken° of magyk and abusioun°.
But finally, as in conclusioun,   215
They kan nat seen in that noon avantage°,
Ne in noon oother wey, save° mariage.

Thanne sawe they therinne swich° difficultee
By wey of reson, for to speke al playn,
By cause° that ther was swich diversitee   220
Bitwene hir bothe lawes°, that they sayn°
They trowe°, "that no Cristen prince wolde fayn°
Wedden his child under oure lawes sweete
That us° were taught by Mahoun, oure
      prophete."

   And he answerde, "Rather than I lese°   225
Custance, I wol be cristned°, doutelees.
I moot been hires°, I may noon oother chese°.
I prey yow hoold youre argumentz in pees.
Saveth° my lyf, and beth noght recchelees°
To geten hire that° hath my lyf in cure°;   230
For in this wo I may nat longe endure."

   What nedeth gretter dilatacioun°?
I seye°, by tretys° and embassadrie°,
And by the popes mediacioun,
And al the chirche, and al the chivalrie°,   235
That in destruccioun of maumettrie°,
And in encrees° of Cristes lawe deere,
They been acorded°, so as ye shal heere:

How that the Sowdan and his baronage°
And alle his liges° sholde ycristned° be,   240
And he shal han Custance in mariage,
And certein gold, I noot° what quantitee;
And heer-to founden° sufficient suretee°.
This same accord was sworn on eyther syde.
Now, faire Custance, almyghty God thee gyde!   245

   Now wolde som men waiten°, as I gesse,
That I sholde tellen al the purveiance°
That th'Emperour, of his grete noblesse,
Hath shapen° for his doghter, dame Custance.

---

185 So, *such,* **ceriously,** *in detail* **186 plesance,** *desire* **188 lust,** *pleasure,* **cure,** *care* **189 dure,** *last* **190 Paraventure,** *perhaps,* **thilke,** *that* **191 clipe,** *call* **192 sterres,** *stars,* **whan that,** *when,* **his birthe took,** *was born* **193 sholde han,** *should have* **194 clerer,** *clearer* **195 woot,** *knows,* **whoso koude,** *whoever could* **196 drede,** *doubt* **197 therbiforn,** *before that time* **199 er,** *before* **200 strif,** *strife* **202 ben,** *are* **203 wel rede it atte fulle,** *interpret it completely* **204 privee conseil,** *private advisers* **205 matiere,** *matter,* **pace,** *pass* **207 seyde hem,** *told them,* **but,** *unless,* **grace,** *(the) good fortune* **208 han,** *have,* **litel space,** *short time* **209 nas but deed,** *was nothing but dead,* **charged hem in hye,** *ordered them in haste* **210 shapen,** *arrange* **211 seyden,** *said* **212 casten,** *deliberated* **213 leyden,** *laid* **214 speken,** *speak,* **abusioun,** *deception* **216 noon avan-**

tage, *no advantage* **217 save,** *except* **218 swich,** *such* **220 By cause,** *because* **221 hir bothe lawes,** *both their religions,* **sayn,** *said* **222 trowe,** *believe,* **wolde fayn,** *would willingly* **225 That us,** *which (to) us* **225 lese,** *lose* **226 cristned,** *baptized* **227 moot been hires,** *must be hers,* **chese,** *choose* **229 Saveth,** *preserve,* **beth noght recchelees,** *be not negligent* **230 geten hire that,** *win her who,* **cure,** *keeping* **232 gretter dilatacioun,** *more amplification* **233 seye,** *say,* **tretys,** *treaty,* **embassadrie,** *diplomacy* **235 chivalrie,** *knights* **236 destruccioun of maumettrie,** *defeat of idolatry* **237 encrees,** *increase* **238 been acorded,** *came to agreement* **239 baronage,** *barons* **240 liges,** *subjects,* **ycristned,** *baptized* **242 noot,** *know not* **243 heer-to founden,** *for this established,* **suretee,** *guaranty* **246 waiten,** *expect* **247 purveiance,** *preparation* **249 Hath shapen,** *has made*

---

198 Ector, Trojan hero of the Trojan War. **Achilles,** Greek hero of the Trojan War. **199 Pompei, Julius,** Pompey and Julius Caesar were rival Roman generals **200 Thebes,** city of turmoil in Greek legend and history. **Ercules,** Hercules, Greek hero and demigod. **201 Sampson,** biblical hero; Judges 13–16. **Turnus,** Aeneus's rival in Italy. **Socrates,** Greek philosopher. **224 Mahoun,** Mohammed, the prophet of Islam.

Wel may men knowen that so greet ordinance° 250
May no man tellen in a litel clause°
As was arrayed° for so heigh° a cause.

Bisshopes been shapen° with hire for to wende°,
Lordes, ladies, knyghtes of renoun,
And oother folk ynogh°, this is th'ende; 255
And notified is thurghout the toun
That every wight°, with greet devocioun,
Sholde preyen° Crist that he this mariage
Receyve in gree°, and spede this viage°.

The day is comen of hir° departynge— 260
I seye°, the woful day fatal is come,
That ther may be no lenger tariynge°,
But forthward they hem dressen°, alle and some°.
Custance, that was with sorwe al overcome,
Ful pale arist°, and dresseth hire to wende°; 265
For wel she seeth° ther is noon oother ende.

Allas, what wonder is it thogh she wepte,
That shal be sent to strange nacioun°
Fro freendes that so tendrely hire kepte°,
And to be bounden under subjeccioun 270
Of oon° she knoweth nat his condicioun°?
Housbondes been° alle goode, and han ben
yoore°.
That knowen wyves—I dar sey yow na moore.

"Fader," she seyde, "thy wrecched child
Custance,
Thy yonge doghter fostred° up so softe°, 275
And ye, my mooder, my soverayn plesance°

Over alle thyng, out-taken° Crist on-lofte°,
Custance youre child hire recomandeth ofte°
Unto youre grace°, for I shal to Surrye,
Ne shal I nevere seen° yow moore with eye. 280

"Allas, unto the Barbre nacioun°
I moste goon°, syn° that it is youre wille;
But Crist, that starf° for our savacioun
So yeve° me grace his heestes° to fulfille!
I, wrecche° womman, no fors° though I spille°! 285
Wommen are born to thraldom° and penance,
And to been under mannes° governance."

I trowe° at Troye, whan Pirrus brak° the wal,
Or° Ilion brende°, at Thebes the citee,
N'at° Rome, for the harm thurgh° Hanybal 290
That Romayns hath venquysshed tymes thre,
Nas herd swich° tendre wepyng for pitee
As in the chambre was for hire departynge;
But forth she moot°, wher so° she wepe or synge.

O firste moevyng°, crueel firmament°, 295
With thy diurnal sweigh° that crowdest ay°
And hurlest° al from est til occident°
That naturelly wolde holde° another way,
Thy crowdyng° set the hevene in swich array°
At the bigynnyng of this fiers viage° 300
That crueel Mars hath slayn° this mariage.

Infortunat ascendent tortuous,
Of° which the lord° is helplees falle°, allas,
Out of his angle° into the derkeste hous°!
O Mars, o atazir°, as in this cas! 305

---

250 **ordinance,** *arrangements* 251 **litel clause,** *short account* 252 **arrayed,** *arranged,* **heigh,** *high* 253 **been shapen,** *were prepared,* **wende,** *travel* 255 **ynogh,** *enough* 257 **wight,** *person* 258 **preyen,** *beseech* **gree,** *favor,* **spede this viage,** *bring success to this journey* 260 **hir,** *their* 261 **seye,** *say* 262 **tariynge,** *delaying* 263 **hem dressen,** *prepare themselves,* **alle and some,** *everybody* 265 **Ful,** *very,* **arist,** *arises,* **dresseth hire to wende,** *prepares herself to travel* 266 **seeth,** *sees* 268 **strange nacioun,** *foreign country* 269 **hire kepte,** *cared for her* 271 **oon,** *someone,* **condicioun,** *nature* 272 **been,** *are,* **ben yoore,** *been for a long time* 275 **fostred,** *raised,* **softe,** *gently* 276 **soverayn plesance,** *supreme pleasure* 277 **out-taken,** *excepting,* **on-lofte,** *above* 278 **hire recomandeth ofte,** *commends herself often* 279 **grace,** *favor* 280 **seen,** *see* 281 **Barbre nacioun,** *barbarous* (pagan) *country* 282 **moste goon,** *must go,* **syn,** *since*

283 **starf,** *died* 284 **yeve,** *give,* **heestes,** *commands* 285 **wrecche,** *wretched,* **no fors,** *no matter,* **spille,** *die* 286 **thraldom,** *servitude* 287 **mannes,** *man's* 288 **trowe,** *believe,* **brak,** *broke* 289 **Or,** *before,* **brende,** *burned* 290 **N'at,** *nor at,* **for the harm thurgh,** *for the damage accomplished by* 291 **venquysshed tymes thre,** *overcome three times* 292 **Nas herd swich,** *was not heard such* 294 **moot,** *must,* **wher so,** *whether* 295 **moevyng,** *moving,* **firmament,** *sky* 296 **diurnal sweigh,** *daily motion,* **crowdest ay,** *pushes always* 297 **hurlest,** *forces,* **est til occident,** *east to west* 298 **wolde holde,** *would hold* (to) 299 **crowdyng,** *pushing,* **swich array,** *such* (an) *arrangement* 300 **fiers viage,** *dangerous voyage* 301 **slayn,** *destroyed* 303 **Of,** *by,* **lord,** *i.e., the planet Mars,* **falle,** *fallen* 304 **angle,** *beneficial position,* **derkeste hous,** *most malevolent position* 305 **atazir,** *dominant influence*

274–87 Lines not in Chaucer's source. **288 Pirrus,** Pyrrhus, son of Achilles, breached the walls of Troy. **289 Ilion,** citadel at Troy or Troy itself. **Thebes,** Greek city that was defeated by siege. **290 Hanybal,** Hannibal, general of Carthage, invaded Italy and threatened Rome in the Second Punic War. **291 tymes thre,** an allusion to the three Punic Wars. **295–315,** lines not in Chaucer's source; they contribute a sense of astrological determinism. **295 firste moevyng,** *primum mobile,* first mover, the outermost sphere of the Ptolemaic universe that conveys east-to-west motion to the planets, despite the fact that their movement through the zodiac indicates a "natural" motion from west to east. The first mover was usually thought to be beneficial; see, e.g., *KnT* 1.2987ff. **302 Infortunat ascendent tortuous,** unfortunate, inauspicious astrological arrangement. This stanza includes technical astrological terms, indicating a configuration that dooms Custance's marriage at the outset of her voyage.

O fieble° moone, unhappy been thy paas°.
Thou knyttest thee ther° thou art nat receyved°;
Ther° thou were weel°, fro thennes artow weyved°.

Inprudent Emperour of Rome, allas,
Was ther no philosophre in al thy toun?   310
Is no tyme bet° than oother in swich cas°?
Of viage° is ther noon eleccioun°,
Namely° to folk of heigh condicioun°?
Noght whan a roote is of a burthe yknowe?
Allas, we been to lewed° or to slowe!   315

To ship is brought this woful faire mayde
Solempnely, with every circumstance°.
"Now Jhesu Crist be with yow alle!" she sayde.
Ther nys namoore° but "Farewel, faire Custance!"
She peyneth hire° to make good contenance°;   320
And forth I lete° hire saille in this manere,
And turne I wole° agayn to my matere.

The mooder° of the Sowdan, welle° of vices,
Espied° hath hir sones pleyn entente,
How he wol lete° his olde sacrifices;   325
And right anon° she for hir conseil sente,
And they been come° to knowe what she mente°.
And whan assembled was this folk in-feere°,
She sette hire° doun, and seyde as ye shal heere.

"Lordes," she said, "ye knowen everichon°,   330
How that my sone in point is for to lete°
The hooly lawes of oure Alkaron,
Yeven° by Goddes message Makomete°.
But oon avow° to grete God I heete°:
The lyf shall rather out of my body sterte°   335
Than Makometes lawe out of myn herte.

"What sholde us tyden of° this newe lawe
But thraldom° to oure bodies and penance,
And afterward in helle to be drawe°
For we reneyed Mahoun° oure creance°?   340
But, lordes, wol ye maken assurance°,
As I shal seyn, assentynge to my loore°,
And I shal make us sauf° for everemoore?"

They sworen and assenten, every man,
To lyve with hire and dye, and by hire stonde,   345
And everich°, in the beste wise° he kan,
To strengthen hire shal alle his frendes fonde°.
And she hath this emprise ytake on honde°
Which ye shal heren° that I shal devyse,
And to hem alle she spak° right in this wyse: 350

"We shul first feyne° us Cristendom to take—
Coold water shal nat greve° us but a lite°!
And I shal swich° a feeste° and revel make
That, as I trowe°, I shal the Sowdan quite°.
For thogh his wyf be cristned never so° white,   355
She shal have nede to wasshe awey the rede°,
Thogh she a font-ful° water with hire lede°."

O Sowdanesse°, roote of iniquitee!
Virago°, thou Semyrame the secounde!
O serpent under femynynytee,   360
Lik to the serpent depe in helle ybounde!
O feyned° womman, al that may confounde°
Vertu and innocence, thurgh thy malice,
Is bred in thee, as nest of every vice.

O Sathan°, envious syn thilke° day   365
That thou were chaced° from oure heritage°,

---

306 fieble, *weak,* **unhappy been thy paas,** *unfortunate was your passing* **307 knyttest thee ther,** *conjoined yourself where,* **receyved,** *welcome* **308 Ther,** *where,* **weel,** *well-positioned,* **fro thennes artow weyved,** *from there are you moved* **311 bet,** *better,* **swich cas,** *such a case* **312 Of viage,** *concerning the voyage,* **noon eleccioun,** *no selection of a beneficial time* **313 Namely,** *especially,* **heigh condicioun,** *high class* **315 lewed,** *ignorant* **317 circumstance,** *ceremony* **319 nys namoore,** *is no more* **320 peyneth hire,** *takes pains,* **make good contenance,** *appear happy* **321 lete,** *let* **322 wole,** *will* **323 mooder,** *mother,* **welle,** *source* **324 Espied,** *recognized* **325 wol lete,** *will abandon* **326 right anon,** *immediately* **327 been come,** *came,* **mente,** *intended* **328 in-feere,** *together* **329 hire,** *herself* **330 everichon,** *everyone* **331 in point is for to lete,** *is on the point of abandoning* **333 Yeven,** *given,* **Goddes message Makomete,** *God's* messenger Mohammed **334 oon avow,** *one vow,* **heete,** *promise* **335 sterte,** *leap* **337 us tyden of,** (for) *us result from* **338 thraldom,** *slavery* **339 drawe,** *pulled* **340 reneyed Mahoun,** *renounced Mohammed,* **creance,** *faith* **341 wol ye maken assurance,** *will you promise* **342 loore,** *advice* **343 sauf,** *safe* **346 everich,** *each one,* **wise,** *way* **347 fonde,** *test* **348 emprise ytake on honde,** *enterprise taken in hand* **349 heren,** *hear* **350 spak,** *spoke* **351 feyne,** *pretend* **352 greve,** *hurt,* **lite,** *little* **353 swich,** *such* **feeste,** *feast* **354 trowe,** *believe,* **Sowdan quite,** *Sultan repay* **355 cristned never so,** *baptized no matter how* **356 rede,** *red* (blood) **357 font-ful,** *baptismal font full of,* **lede,** *bring* **358 Sowdanesse,** *Sultaness* **359 Virago,** *mannish woman* **362 feyned,** *counterfeit,* **confounde,** *undermine* **365 Sathan,** *Satan,* **syn thilke,** *since that* **366 chaced,** *chased,* **heritage,** *salvation*

314 Noght whan a roote is of a burthe yknowe, not (even) when the basis for calculating the horoscope is known? **332 Alkaron,** the Koran, the sacred book of Islam. **352 Coold water,** disparaging reference to baptism, the sacrament whereby people become Christian, typically involving water administered from a receptacle known as a font (see lines 357 and 723) **359 Semyrame,** Semiramis, an Assyrian queen who usurped the throne from her son. **360 serpent under femynynytee,** in medieval art the serpent in Eden had the face of a woman. **361 depe in helle ybounde,** bound deep in hell; Satan is depicted so in much medieval art, following the apocryphal Gospel of Nicodemus.

Wel knowestow° to wommen the olde way.
Thou madest Eva brynge us in servage°;
Thou wolt fordoon° this Cristen mariage.
Thyn instrument so—weylawey the while°—   370
Makestow° of wommen, whan thou wolt bigile°.

   This Sowdanesse, whom I thus blame and
      warye°,
Leet prively° hire conseil goon hire way°.
What sholde I in this tale lenger tarye?
She rydeth to the Sowdan on a day   375
And seyde° hym that she wolde reneye hir lay°,
And Cristendom of° preestes handes fonge°,
Repentynge hire she hethen was so longe;

Bisechynge hym° to doon hire that honour
That she moste han° the Cristen folk
     to feeste—   380
"To plesen hem I wol do my labour."
The Sowdan seith, "I wol doon at youre heeste°,"
And knelynge thanketh hire of° that requeste.
So glad he was he nyste° what to seye.
She kiste hir sone, and hoom she gooth hir
     weye.   385

Explicit prima pars. Sequitur pars secunda.

   Arryved been° this Cristen folk to londe
In Surrye, with a greet solempne route°,
And hastifliche° this Sowdan sente his sonde°
First to his mooder, and al the regne° aboute,
And seyde his wyf was comen, out of doute°,   390
And preyde hire° for to ryde agayn° the queene,
The honour of his regne to susteene.

Greet was the prees° and riche was th'array
Of Surryens and Romayns met yfeere°.
The mooder of the Sowdan, riche and gay,   395
Receyveth hire with also° glad a cheere°

As any mooder myghte hir doghter deere,
And to the nexte° citee ther bisyde
A softe paas solempnely° they ryde.

   Noght trowe I° the triumphe of Julius,   400
Of which that Lucan maketh swich a boost,
Was roialler° or moore curius°
Than was th'assemblee of this blisful hoost.
But this scorpioun, this wikked goost°,
The Sowdanesse, for al hire flaterynge   405
Caste under this° ful mortally to stynge.

   The Sowdan comth° hymself soone after this
So roially that wonder is to telle,
And welcometh hire with alle joye and blis.
And thus in murthe and joye I lete hem
     dwelle;   410
The fruyt° of this matiere is that° I telle.
Whan tyme cam, men thoughte it for the beste;
The revel stynte° and men goon to hir reste.

   The tyme cam° this olde Sowdanesse
Ordeyned° hath this feeste of which I tolde,   415
And to the feeste Cristen folk hem dresse°
In general, ye°, bothe yonge and olde.
Heere may men feeste and roialtee° biholde,
And deyntees mo° than I kan yow devyse°;
But al to deere° they boghte it er° they ryse.   420

   O sodeyn° wo, that evere art successour
To worldly blisse, spreynd° with bitternesse,
The ende of the joye of oure worldly labour!
Wo occupieth the fyn° of oure gladnesse.
Herke° this conseil for thy sikernesse°:   425
Upon thy glade day have in thy mynde
The unwar° wo or harm that comth bihynde°.

For shortly for to tellen, at o° word,
The Sowdan and the Cristen everichone°

---

367 knowestow, *do you know* **368 in servage,** *into slavery* **369 wolt fordoon,** *will destroy* **370 weylawey the while,** *alas the time* **371 Makestow,** *do you make,* **wolt bigile,** *will mislead* **372 warye,** *curse* **373 Leet prively,** *let secretly,* **hire way,** *their way* **376 seyde,** *told,* **wolde reneye hir lay,** *would renounce her religion* **377 of,** *from,* **fonge,** *receive* **379 Bisechynge hym,** *requesting* (of) *him* **380 moste han,** *might have* **382 wol doon at youre heeste,** *will act as you request* **383 of,** *for* **384 nyste,** *knew not* **386 Arryved been,** *arrived have* **387 solempne route,** *impressive company* **388 hastifliche,** *hastily,* **sonde,** *message* **389 regne,** *kingdom* **390 doute,** *doubt* **391 preyde hire,** *asked her,* **ryde agayn,** *meet* **393 prees,** *crowd* **394 yfeere,** *together* **396 also,** *as,* **cheere,** *expression*

398 nexte, *nearest* **399 softe paas solempnely,** *slow solemn pace* **400 Noght trowe I,** *I do not believe* **402 roialler,** *more royal,* **curius,** *elaborate* **404 goost,** *spirit* **406 Caste under this,** *planned under this* (deception) **407 comth,** *comes* **411 fruyt,** *outcome,* **that,** *what* **413 stynte,** *stopped* **414 cam,** *came* (when) **415 Ordeyned,** *ordered* **416 hem dresse,** *prepare themselves* **417 ye,** *yes* **418 roialtee,** *royalty* **419 deyntees mo,** *more delicacies,* **yow devyse,** *describe for you* **420 to deere,** *too dearly,* **er,** *before* **421 sodeyn,** *sudden* **422 spreyned,** *sprinkled* **424 fyn,** *end* **425 Herke,** *listen to,* **sikernesse,** *security* **427 unwar,** *unexpected,* **comth bihynde,** *comes afterward* **428 at o,** *in one* **429 everichone,** *every one*

385a *Explicit prima pars. Sequitur pars secunda.* "Here ends part one. Here follows part two." **400 triumphe of Julius,** a great triumph, or victory procession, of Julius Caesar is mentioned in Lucan's *Pharsalia* 3.73–39 as something that may have occurred; it never takes place in the classical account, but French versions add them. **404 scorpioun,** the scorpion was a familiar symbol of treachery. **421–27** Not in Trivet or Gower; from Innocent, *De Miseria* 1.23; see 99–121n above.

Been al tohewe° and stiked° at the bord°, 430
But it were° oonly dame Custance allone.
This olde Sowdanesse, cursed krone,
Hath with hir freendes doon this cursed dede,
For she hirself wolde° al the contree lede°.

Ne was ther Surryen noon that° was
    converted, 435
That of the conseil of the Sowdan woot°,
That he nas al tohewe er he asterted°.
And Custance han they take anon°, foot-hoot°,
And in a ship al steerelees°, God woot°,
They han hir° set, and bidde hire lerne saille° 440
Out of Surrye agaynward to Ytaille°.

A certein tresor° that she with hire ladde°,
And, sooth to seyn°, vitaille° greet plentee
They han hire yeven°, and clothes eek she hadde,
And forth she sailleth in the salte see. 445
O my Custance, ful of benignytee°,
O Emperoures yonge doghter deere,
He that is Lord of Fortune be thy steere°!

She blesseth hire°, and with ful pitous voys
Unto the croys° of Crist thus seyde she, 450
"O cleere°, o welful auter°, hooly croys,
Reed of° the Lambes blood ful of pitee,
That wessh° the world fro the olde iniquitee°,
Me fro the feend and fro his clawes kepe,
That day° that I shal drenchen° in the depe. 455

Victorious tree, proteccioun of trewe°,
That oonly worthy were° for to bere
The Kyng of Hevene with his woundes newe,
The white Lamb, that hurt was with a spere°,
Flemere of feendes out° of hym° and here° 460

On which° thy lymes° feithfully extenden°,
Me helpe, and yif° me mycht my lyf t'amenden°."

    Yeres and dayes fleet° this creature
Thurghout the See of Grece unto the Strayte
Of Marrok, as it was hire aventure°; 465
On many a sory meel° now may she bayte°;
After° hir deeth ful often may she wayte°,
Er° that the wilde wawes° wol hire dryve
Unto the place ther° she shal arryve.

    Men myghten asken why she was nat slayn 470
Eek° at the feeste? Who myghte hir body save?
And I answere to that demande agayn°,
Who saved Danyel in the horrible cave
Ther° every wight° save he, maister and knave,
Was with° the leon frete er° he asterte°? 475
No wight but God, that he bar° in his herte.

God liste to shewe° his wonderful myracle
In hire, for we sholde seen his myghty werkis°.
Crist, which that is to every harm triacle°,
By certeine meenes ofte°, as knowen clerkis, 480
Dooth thyng° for certein ende° that ful derk° is
To mannes wit, that for° oure ignorance
Ne konne noght knowe° his prudent purveiance°.

    Now sith° she was nat at the feeste yslawe°,
Who kepte hire fro° the drenchyng°
    in the see? 485
Who kepte Jonas in the fisshes mawe°
Til he was spouted up at Nynyvee°?
Wel may men knowe it was no wight° but he
That kepte the peple Ebrayk from hir
    drenchynge°,
With drye feet thurghout the see passynge. 490

---

430 tohewe, *cut to pieces*, **stiked**, *stabbed*, **bord**, *table* **431 But it were**, *except* **434 wolde**, *wanted to*, **lede**, *rule* **435 Ne was ther Surryen noon that**, *nor was there any Syrian who* **436 woot**, *knew* **437 tohewe er he asterted**, *slaughtered before he escaped* **438 take anon**, *taken quickly*, **foot-hoot**, *immediately* **439 steerelees**, *rudderless*, **woot**, *knows* **440 han hir**, *have her*, **lerne saille**, *learn to sail* **441 agaynward to Ytaille**, *back to Italy* **442 tresor**, *treasure*, **ladde**, *brought* **443 sooth to seyn**, *truth to tell*, **vitaille**, *food* **444 han hire yeven**, *have given to her* **446 benignytee**, *goodness* **448 steere**, *rudder* **449 hire**, *herself* **450 croys**, *cross* **451 cleere**, *shining*, **welful auter**, *beneficial altar* **452 Reed of**, *red from* **453 wessh**, *washed*, **iniquitee**, *wickedness* **455 That day**, *on the day*, **drenchen**, *drown* **456 trewe**, *true* (ones) **457 That oonly worthy were**, *the only one that was worthy* **459 spere**, *spear* **460 Flemere of feendes**

out, *one who drives fiends out*, **hym**, *him*, **here**, *her* **461 which**, *whom*, **lymes**, *arms*, **extenden**, *stretch* **462 yif**, *give*, **t'amenden**, *to correct* **463 fleet**, *floated* **465 aventure**, *fortune* **466 sory meel**, *miserable meal*, **bayte**, *eat* **467 After**, *for*, **wayte**, *wait* **468 Er**, *before*, **wawes**, *waves* **469 ther**, *where* **471 Eek**, *also* **472 agayn**, *in response* **474 Ther**, *where*, **wight**, *person* **475 with**, *by*, **frete er**, *eaten before*, **asterte**, *escaped* **476 bar**, *carried* **477 liste to shewe**, *was pleased to demonstrate* **478 werkis**, *works* **479 triacle**, *medicine* **480 meenes ofte**, *means often* **481 Dooth thyng**, *does something*, **ende**, *purpose*, **derk**, *mysterious* **482 for**, *because of* **483 Ne konne noght knowe**, *can not know*, **purveiance**, *providence* **484 sith**, *since*, **yslawe**, *slain* **485 fro**, *from*, **drenchyng**, *drowning* **486 fisshes mawe**, *fish's mouth* **487 Nynyvee**, *Nineveh* **488 wight**, *person* **489 hir drenchynge**, *their drowning*

449–62 Not in Trivet or Gower. Addresses to Christ's cross occur in medieval lyrics and liturgy. **452 Lambes**, Jesus'; John 1.29. **464–65 See of Grece**, eastern Mediterranean Sea. **Strayte / Of Marrok**, Strait of Morocco (of Gibraltar). **470–504** Not in Trivet or Gower. **473 Danyel**, Daniel, through the power of God, survived being locked in a lion's den, where his accusers perished; Daniel 6.16–24. **486 Jonas**, Jonah, preserved by God, survived in a whale's belly for three days before being spewed up near Nineveh; Jonah 1.17–2.10. **489 peple Ebrayk**, the Hebrew people were protected by God when they passed through the Red Sea; Exodus 14.21–22.

Who bad° the foure spirites of tempest
That power han t'anoyen° lond and see,
Bothe north and south and also west and est,
"Anoyeth, neither see, ne land, ne tree"?
Soothly°, the comandour of that was he   495
That fro the tempest ay° this womman kepte
As wel whan she wook as whan she slepte.

Where myghte this womman mete and drynke have
Thre yeer and moore? How lasteth hire vitaille°?
Who fedde the Egipcien Marie in the cave,   500
Or in desert? No wight but Crist, sanz faille°.
Fyve thousand folk it was as greet mervaille°
With loves fyve and fisshes two to feede.
God sente his foyson° at hir grete neede.

She dryveth forth° into oure occian°   505
Thurghout oure wilde see, til atte laste
Under an hoold° that nempnen° I ne kan
Fer° in Northhumberlond the wawe° hire caste,
And in the sond° hir ship stiked° so faste
That thennes wolde it noght of al a tyde°;   510
The wyl of Crist was that she sholde abyde°.

The constable of the castel doun is fare°
To seen this wrak, and al the ship° he soghte,
And foond this wery womman ful of care;
He foond also the tresor° that she broghte.   515
In hir langage mercy she bisoghte°,
The lyf out of hire body for to twynne°,
Hire to delivere of° wo that she was inne.

A maner Latyn corrupt was hir speche,
But algates° therby was she understonde.   520
The constable, whan hym lyst° no lenger seche°,

This woful womman broghte he to the londe.
She kneleth doun and thanketh Goddes sonde°;
But what she was she wolde no man seye°,
For foul ne fair, thogh that° she sholde deye°.   525

She seyde she was so mazed° in the see
That she forgat hir mynde, by hir trouthe°.
The constable hath of hire so greet pitee,
And eek his wyf, that they wepen for routhe°.
She was so diligent, withouten slouthe°,   530
To serve and plesen everich° in that place
That alle hir loven that looken in hir face.

This constable and dame Hermengyld, his wyf,
Were payens°, and that contree everywhere;
But Hermengyld loved hire right° as hir lyf,   535
And Custance hath so longe sojourned° there,
In orisons°, with many a bitter teere,
Til Jhesu hath converted thurgh his grace
Dame Hermengyld, constablesse of that place.

In al that lond no Cristen dorste route°;   540
Alle Cristen folk been fled fro that contree
Thurgh payens that conquereden al aboute
The plages° of the north by land and see.
To Walys° fledde the Cristyanytee°
Of olde Britons dwellynge in this ile°;   545
Ther was hir refut° for the meene while.

But yet nere° Cristene Britons so exiled
That ther nere somme that in hir privetee°
Honoured Crist and hethen folk bigiled°,
And ny° the castel swiche° ther dwelten three.   550
That oon° of hem was blynd and myghte nat see,
But° it were with thilke eyen° of his mynde

---

491 **bad,** *ordered* 492 **han t'anoyen,** *have to damage* 495 **Soothly,** *truly* 496 **ay,** *always* 499 **vitaille,** *food* 501 **sanz faille,** *without doubt* 502 **mervaille,** *marvel* 504 **foyson,** *plenty* 505 **dryveth forth,** *continues on,* **occian,** *ocean* 507 **hoold,** *castle,* **nempnen,** *name* 508 **Fer,** *far,* **wawe,** *waves* 509 **sond,** *sand,* **stiked,** *stuck* 510 **thennes wolde it noght of al a tyde,** *from there it would not move even at high tide* 511 **abyde,** *remain* 512 **doun is fare,** *goes down* 513 **al the ship,** *the entire ship* 515 **tresor,** *treasure* 516 **bisoghte,** *requested* 517 **twynne,** *separate* 518 **of,** *from* 520 **algates,** *nevertheless* 521 **hym lyst,** *it pleased him,* **lenger seche,** *longer*

(to) *search* 523 **Goddes sonde,** *God's sending* 524 **seye,** *tell* 525 **thogh that,** *even if,* **deye,** *die* 526 **mazed,** *dazed* 527 **by hir trouthe,** *upon her word* 529 **routhe,** *pity* 530 **slouthe,** *laziness* 531 **everich,** *everyone* 534 **payens,** *pagans* 535 **right,** *just* 536 **sojourned,** *remained* 537 **orisons,** *prayers* 540 **dorste route,** *dared to assemble* 543 **plages,** *coastal regions* 544 **Walys,** *Wales,* **Christyanytee,** *Christian community* 545 **ile,** *island* 546 **refut,** *refuge* 547 **nere,** *were not* 548 **in hir privetee,** *in secrecy* 549 **bigiled,** *deceived* 550 **ny,** *near,* **swiche,** *such* 551 **oon,** *one* 552 **But,** *unless,* **eyen,** *eyes*

---

491 **foure spirites of tempest,** four angels, commanded by God, hold back the winds of destruction in Revelation 7.1–3. 500 **Egipcien Marie,** St. Mary the Egyptian, a legendary hermit who survived forty-seven years in the desert. 503 **loves . . . and fisshes,** Christ miraculously fed a crowd of five thousand with only five loaves and two fish; Matthew 14.16–21. 508 **Northhumberlond,** an area in northern England that eventually became a part of Northumbria. 512 **constable,** the chief officer of the king's household or court. 519 **maner Latyn corrupt,** a kind of mixed or popular Latin, a historically accurate dialect for a sixth-century Roman princess. Trivet says she spoke to the constable in Saxon; Gower does not specify. 525 **For foul ne fair,** an idiom meaning "under no circumstances." 534 **that contree everywhere,** i.e., the entire country was pagan.

With whiche men seen, whan that they ben
  blynde.

Bright was the sonne as in that someres° day,
For° which the constable and his wyf also   555
And Custance han ytake° the righte° way
Toward the see a furlong wey° or two,
To pleyen and to romen° to and fro.
And in hir walk this blynde man they mette,
Croked° and oold, with eyen faste yshette°.   560

"In name of Crist," cride this blinde Britoun,
"Dame Hermengyld, yif° me my sighte agayn!"
This lady weex affrayed° of the soun,
Lest° that hir housbonde, shortly for to sayn,
Wolde hire for Jhesu Cristes love han slayn°,   565
Til Custance made hire boold, and bad hire
  wirche°
The wyl of Crist, as doghter of his chirche.

The constable weex abasshed° of that sight,
And seyde, "What amounteth° al this fare°?"
Custance answerde, "Sire, it is Cristes myght,   570
That helpeth folk out of the feendes° snare."
And so ferforth° she gan oure lay° declare
That she the constable, er that° it was eve,
Converteth, and on Crist maketh hym bileve.

This constable was nothyng° lord of this place   575
Of which I speke, ther° he Custance fond,
But kepte° it strongly many wyntres space°
Under Alla, kyng of al Northhumbrelond,
That was ful wys and worthy of his hond
Agayn the Scottes, as men may wel heere.   580
But turne I wole° agayn to my mateere.

Sathan°, that evere us waiteth to bigile°,
Saugh of° Custance al hire perfeccioun,
And caste anon° how he myghte quite hir while°,

And made a yong knyght that dwelte in that
  toun   585
Love hire so hoote of° foul affeccioun
That verraily hym thoughte° he sholde spille°
But° he of hire myghte ones° have his wille.

He woweth° hire, but it availleth noght°;
She wolde do no synne, by no weye.   590
And for despit° he compassed° in his thoght
To maken hire on shameful deeth to deye.
He wayteth° whan the constable was aweye,
And pryvely° upon a nyght he crepte
In Hermengyldes chambre, whil she slepte.   595

Wery, forwaked in hire orisouns°,
Slepeth Custance and Hermengyld also.
This knyght, thurgh Sathanas temptaciouns,
Al softely is to the bed ygo°,
And kitte the throte of Hermengyld atwo°,   600
And leyde° the blody knyf by dame Custance,
And wente his wey, ther God yeve hym
  meschance°!

Soone after cometh this constable hoom
  agayn,
And eek Alla, that kyng was of that lond,
And saugh his wyf despitously yslayn°,   605
For which ful ofte he weep and wroong his hond°.
And in the bed the blody knyf he fond
By dame Custance. Allas, what myghte she seye?
For verray wo hir wit was° al aweye.

To Kyng Alla was toold al this meschance°,   610
And eek the tyme, and where, and in what wise
That in a ship was founden dame Custance,
As heerbiforn° that ye han herd devyse°.
The kynges herte of pitee gan agryse°
Whan he saugh° so benigne° a creature   615
Falle in disese° and in mysaventure.

---

554 **someres,** *summer's* **555** **For,** *on account of* **556** **han ytake,** *have taken,* **righte,** *direct* **557** **furlong wey,** *220 yards* **558** **romen,** *roam* **560** **Croked,** *bent,* **yshette,** *shut* **562** **yif,** *give* **563** **weex affrayed,** *grew frightened* **564** **Lest,** *for fear* **565** **han slayn,** *have slain* **566** **bad hire wirche,** *urged her to work* **568** **weex abasshed,** *grew amazed* **569** **amounteth,** *means,* **fare,** *business* **571** **feendes,** *devil's* **572** **so ferforth,** *in such a manner,* **lay,** *law* **573** **er that,** *before* **575** **nothyng,** *not at all,* **576** **ther,** *where* **577** **kepte,** *defended,* **wyntres space,** *years* **581** **wole,** *will* **582** **Sathan,** *Satan,* **bigile,** *deceive* **583** **Saugh of,** *saw in* **584** **caste anon,** *soon plotted,* **quite hir while,** *repay her* **586** **hoote of,** *hotly with* **587** **verraily hym thoughte,**

truly he thought, **spille,** *die* **588** **But,** *unless,* **ones,** *once* **589** **woweth,** *woos,* **availleth noght,** *has no effect* **591** **for despit,** *out of spite,* **compassed,** *planned* **593** **wayteth,** *sought a time* **594** **pryvely,** *secretly* **596** **forwaked in hire orisouns,** *from being awake in their prayers* **599** **ygo,** *gone* **600** **kitte . . . atwo,** *cut in two* **601** **leyde,** *laid* **602** **ther God yeve hym meschance,** *may God give him bad fortune* **605** **despitously yslayn,** *cruelly slain* **606** **wroong his hond,** *wrung his hands* **609** **verry wo hir wit was,** *true sorrow her wits were* **610** **meschance,** *disaster* **613** **heerbiforn,** *before,* **herd devyse,** *heard described* **614** **gan agryse,** *did shudder* **615** **saugh,** *saw,* **benigne,** *good* **616** **disese,** *distress*

---

578 **Alla,** Aella, historical sixth-century king of Anglian Deira, an Old English kingdom. **579** **worthy of his hond,** i.e., strong in battle. For the formula "wise and worthy," see *GP* 1.68. **580** **Agayn the Scottes,** against the Scots, who threatened the northern kingdoms of England.

For as the lomb° toward his deeth is broght,
So stant° this innocent bifore the kyng.
This false knyght, that hath this tresoun wroght°,
Berth hire on hond° that she hath doon thys
    thyng.   620
But nathelees, ther was greet moornyng
Among the peple, and seyn° they kan nat gesse°
That she had doon so greet a wikkednesse,

For they han seyn° hire evere so vertuous,
And lovynge Hermengyld right as° hir lyf.   625
Of this baar° witnesse everich° in that hous,
Save° he that Hermengyld slow° with his knyf.
This gentil kyng hath caught a greet motyf°
Of° this witnesse°, and thoghte he wolde enquere
Depper° in this, a trouthe for to lere°.   630

    Allas, Custance, thou hast no champioun,
Ne fighte kanstow noght°, so weylaway°!
But he that starf° for oure redempcioun,
And boond° Sathan—and yet lith ther° he lay—
So be thy stronge champion this day.   635
For, but if° Crist open myracle kithe°,
Withouten gilt° thou shalt be slayn as swithe°.

She sette hire doun on knees, and thus she sayde,
"Immortal God, that savedest Susanne
Fro° false blame, and thou, merciful mayde,   640
Marie I meene, doghter of Seint Anne,
Bifore whos child angeles synge Osanne°,
If I be giltlees of this felonye,
My socour° be, for ellis° shal I dye!"

    Have ye nat seyn° somtyme a pale face   645
Among a prees°, of hym that hath be lad°
Toward his deeth, wher as hym gat no grace,

And swich° a colour in his face hath had,
Men myghte knowe his face that was bistad°
Amonges alle the faces in that route°?   650
So stant° Custance, and looketh hire aboute.

    O queenes, lyvynge in prosperitee,
Duchesses, and ye ladyes everichone°,
Haveth som routhe° on hire adversitee!
An Emperoures doghter stant allone;   655
She hath no wight° to whom to make hire mone°.
O blood roial, that stondest in this drede,
Fer been° thy freendes at thy grete nede!

    This Alla kyng hath swich compassioun,
As gentil herte is fulfild° of pitee,   660
That from his eyen ran the water doun.
"Now hastily do fecche° a book," quod he,
"And if this knyght wol sweren° how that she
This womman slow°, yet wol we us avyse°
Whom that we wole° that shal been oure
    justise°."   665

A Britoun book written with Evaungiles
Was fet°, and on this book he swoor anoon
She gilty was. And in the meene whiles°,
An hand hym smoot° upon the nekke-boon,
That° doun he fil atones° as a stoon,   670
And bothe his eyen broste° out of his face
In sighte of everybody in that place.

    A voys was herd in general audience°,
And seyde, "Thou hast desclaundred°, giltelees,
The doghter of hooly chirche in heigh
    presence°;   675
Thus hastou° doon, and yet holde I my pees°?"
Of this mervaille agast° was al the prees°;

---

617 lomb, *lamb* **618 stant,** *stands* **619 tresoun wroght,** *betrayal contrived* **620 Berth hire on hond,** *accuses her* **622 seyn,** (they) *say,* **gesse,** *imagine* **624 han seyn,** *have seen* **625 right as,** *as much as* **626 baar,** *bore,* **everich,** *everyone* **627 Save,** *except,* **slow,** *slew* **628 hath caught a greet motyf,** *was greatly moved* **629 Of,** *by,* **witnesse,** *witnessing* **630 Depper,** *deeper,* **lere,** *learn* **632 kanstow noght,** *can you not at all,* **weylaway,** *alas* **633 starf,** *died* **634 boond,** *bound,* **lith ther he,** *lies he* (Satan) *where* **636 but if,** *unless,* **kithe,** *shows* **637 Withouten gilt,** *guiltless,* **as swithe,** *quickly* **640 Fro,** *from* **642 angeles synge Osanne,** *angels sing Hosanna* **644 socour,** *help,* **ellis,** *else* **645 seyn,** *seen* **646 prees,** *crowd,* **be lad,** *been led* **648 swich,** *such* **649 bistad,** *under threat* **650 route,** *crowd*

651 stant, *stands* **653 everichone,** *every one* **654 som routhe,** *some pity* **656 wight,** *person,* **mone,** *appeal* **658 Fer been,** *far* (away) *are* **660 fulfild,** *filled* **662 do fecche,** *bring* **663 wol sweren,** *will swear* **664 slow,** *slew,* **wol we us avyse,** *we will consider* **665 wole,** *choose,* **justise,** *judge* **667 fet,** *fetched* **668 in the meene whiles,** i.e., *while he was doing this* **669 hym smoot,** *struck him* **670 That,** (so) *that,* **atones,** *at once* **671 broste,** *burst* **673 general audience,** *the hearing of all* **674 desclaundred,** *slandered* **675 in heigh presence,** *before God* **676 hastou,** *have you,* **yet holde I my pees,** *yet* (should) *I hold my peace* **677 mervaille agast,** *marvel frightened,* **prees,** *crowd*

631–58 Lines not in Trivet or Gower. **639 Susanne,** Susanna, who in the apocryphal version of the book of Daniel (ch. 13) is falsely accused of adultery by two lecherous elders and saved by the inspired wisdom of Daniel; the topic was popular in medieval and Renaissance art. **641 Marie,** Mary, mother of Jesus and daughter of St. Anne. **647 wher as hym gat no grace,** "it being the case that he got no reprieve"; seeing a condemned person conducted to public execution was not uncommon in the Middle Ages. **660** A familiar chivalric sentiment; see *KnT* 1.1761n. **666 Britoun book written with Evaungiles,** i.e., a gospel book written in Briton; the specification is Chaucer's addition. Also, this formal judicial scene has been thought appropriate to the Man of Law.

As mazed° folk they stoden everichone°
For drede of wreche°, save Custance allone.

Greet was the drede and eek the
    repentance   680
Of hem that hadden wrong suspecioun
Upon this sely° innocent, Custance.
And for this miracle, in conclusioun°,
And by Custances mediacioun,
The kyng, and many another in that place,   685
Converted was, thanked be Cristes grace!

This false kynght was slayn for his untrouthe
By juggement of Alla hastifly°;
And yet Custance hadde of his deeth greet
    routhe°.
And after this Jhesus, of his mercy,   690
Made Alla wedden ful solempnely°
This hooly mayden, that is so bright and sheene°;
And thus hath Crist ymaad° Custance a queene.

But who was woful, if I shal nat lye,
Of this weddyng but Donegild, and namo°,   695
The kynges mooder, ful of tirannye?
Hir thoughte° hir cursed herte brast atwo°.
She wolde noght° hir sone had do° so;
Hir thoughte a despit° that he sholde take
So strange° a creature unto his make°.   700

Me list nat° of the chaf°, ne of the stree°,
Maken so long a tale as of the corn°.
What° sholde I tellen of the roialtee°
At mariage; or which cours goth biforn°;
Who bloweth in a trumpe° or in an horn?   705
The fruyt° of every tale is for to seye°:
They ete, and drynke, and daunce, and synge,
    and pleye.

They goon to bedde, as it was skile° and right;
For thogh that wyves be ful hooly thynges,
They moste° take in pacience at nyght   710
Swiche manere necessaries° as been plesynges°
To folk that han ywedded hem with rynges,
And leye a lite° hir hoolynesse aside,
As for the tyme—it may no bet bitide°.

On hire he gat° a knave child anon°,   715
And to a bisshop and his constable eke°
He took his wyf to kepe°, whan he is gon
To Scotland-ward°, his foomen° for to seke.
Now faire Custance, that is so humble and
    meke,
So longe is goon with childe til that stille°   720
She halt° hire chambre, abidyng° Cristes wille.

The tyme is come a knave child she beer°;
Mauricius at the font-stoon they hym calle.
This constable dooth forth come° a messageer,
And wroot° unto his kyng, that cleped°
    was Alle,   725
How that this blisful tidyng is bifalle°,
And othere tidynges spedeful° for to seye.
He taketh the lettre, and forth he gooth his
    weye.

This messager, to doon his avantage°,
Unto the kynges mooder rideth swithe°,   730
And salueth° hire ful faire in his langage.
"Madame," quod he, "ye may be glad and blithe°,"
And thanketh God an hundred thousand sithe°.
My lady queene hath child, withouten doute°,
To joye and blisse to al this regne° aboute.   735

"Lo°, heere the lettres seled° of this thyng,
That I moot bere° with al the haste I may.

---

678 **mazed,** *stunned,* **stoden everichone,** *all stood* 679 **drede of wreche,** *fear of vengeance* 682 **sely,** *blessed* 683 **in conclusioun,** *as a result* 688 **hastifly,** *immediately* 689 **routhe,** *pity* 691 **ful solempnely,** *with all ceremony* 692 **sheene,** *shining* 693 **ymaad,** *made* 695 **namo,** *no more* 697 **Hir thoughte,** *she thought,* **brast atwo,** *burst in two* 698 **wolde noght,** *did not at all wish,* **do,** *done* 699 **Hir thoughte a despit,** *she thought* (it) *a disgrace* 700 **strange,** *foreign,* **unto his make,** *as his mate* 701 **Me list nat,** *I do not wish* (to), **chaf,** *chaff,* **stree,** *straw* 702 **corn,** *grain* 703 **What,** *why,* **roialtee,** *royalty* 704 **cours goth biforn,** *course* (of the marriage feast) *goes first* 705 **trumpe,** *trumpet* 706 **fruyt,** *essence,* **for to seye,** *to be told* 708 **skile,** *proper* 710 **moste,** *must*

711 **Swiche manere necessaries,** *such kinds of necessities,* **plesynges,** *pleasures* 713 **leye a lite,** *lay a little* 714 **no bet bitide,** *happen no better* 715 **gat,** *begot,* **knave child anon,** *boy soon* 716 **eke,** *also* 717 **kepe,** *care for* 718 **To Scotland-ward,** *toward Scotland,* **foomen,** *enemies* 720 **stille,** *constantly* 721 **halt,** *stays* (in), **abidyng,** *awaiting* 722 **beer,** *bears* 724 **dooth forth come,** *summoned* 725 **wroot,** *wrote,* **cleped,** *called* 726 **blisful tidyng is bifalle,** *happy news has occurred* 727 **spedeful,** *useful* 729 **doon his avantage,** *gain himself an advantage* 730 **swithe,** *quickly* 731 **salueth,** *greets* 732 **blithe,** *happy* 733 **sithe,** *times* 734 **doute,** *doubt* 735 **regne,** *kingdom* 736 **Lo,** *behold,* **seled,** *sealed* 737 **moot bere,** *must bear*

701–2 chaf . . . corn, the image of chaff (husk) and grain (or shell and nut or rind and fruit) is traditional, conveying the contrast between vehicle and tenor or plot and meaning, although here it seems to contrast only details and major action; compare *NPT* 7.3443. **715 knave,** in the El manuscript, erased and changed to *man* here and at 722; some later manuscripts also have *man*. Compare *CIT* 4.444n. **723 font-stoon they hym calle,** i.e., they call him at the baptismal font. The sacrament of baptism involves the giving of a name as well as blessing with water; see 352n above. **736 lettres seled,** letters were kept shut with wax seals of their senders in order to indicate authenticity.

If ye wol aught° unto youre sone the kyng,
I am youre servant, bothe nyght and day."
Donegild answerde, "As now at this tyme, nay; 740
But heere al nyght I wol° thou take thy reste.
Tomorwe wol° I seye° thee what me leste°."

This messager drank sadly° ale and wyn,
And stolen were his lettres pryvely°
Out of his box, whil he sleep as a swyn°; 745
And countrefeted was ful subtilly
Another lettre, wroght° ful synfully,
Unto the kyng direct, of° this mateere,
Fro his constable, as ye shal after heere.

The lettre spak° the queene delivered was 750
Of so horrible a feendly° creature
That in the castel noon° so hardy was
That any while dorste ther° endure.
The mooder° was an elf°, by aventure°
Ycomen°—by charmes or by sorcerie— 755
And everich wight° hateth hir compaignye.

Wo° was this kyng whan he this lettre had sayn°,
But to no wight° he tolde his sorwes soore°,
But of° his owene hand he wroot agayn°,
"Welcome the sonde° of Crist for everemoore 760
To me that am now lerned in his loore°.
Lord, welcome be thy lust° and thy plesaunce°;
My lust I putte al in thyn ordinaunce°.

"Kepeth° this child, al be it foul or feir,
And eek° my wyf, unto myn hoom-comynge°. 765
Crist, whan hym list°, may sende me an heir
Moore agreable than this to my likynge."
This lettre he seleth, pryvely wepynge,
Which to the messager was take° soone,
And forth he gooth; ther is na moore
   to doone. 770

O messager, fulfild° of dronkenesse,
Strong is thy breeth, thy lymes faltren ay°,
And thou biwreyest° alle secreenesse°.
Thy mynde is lorn°, thou janglest as° a jay°,
Thy face is turned in a newe array°. 775
Ther° dronkenesse regneth° in any route°,
Ther is no conseil hyd°, withouten doute.

O Donegild, I ne have noon Englissh digne°
Unto thy malice and thy tirannye!
And therfore to the feend I thee resigne°; 780
Lat hym enditen° of thy traitorie!
Fy, mannysh°, fy!—O nay, by God, I lye°—
Fy, feendlych° spirit, for I dar wel telle
Thogh thou heere walke thy spirit is in helle.

This messager comth fro° the kyng agayn, 785
And at the kynges moodres court he lighte°,
And she was of this messager ful fayn°,
And plesed hym in al that ever she myghte.
He drank and wel his girdel underpighte°;
He slepeth and he fnorteth° in his gyse° 790
Al nyght, til the sonne gan aryse°.

Eft° were his lettres stolen everychon°,
And countrefeted lettres in this wyse:
"The king comandeth his constable anon,
Up peyne° of hangyng, and on heigh juyse°, 795
That he ne sholde suffren° in no wyse
Custance in-with his reawme° for t'abyde
Thre dayes and o quarter of a tyde.

"But in the same ship as he hire fond°,
Hire, and hir yonge sone, and al hir geere, 800
He sholde putte, and croude° hire fro the lond,
And chargen hire that she never eft° coome
   theere."
O my Custance, wel may thy goost° have feere,

---

738 ye wol aught, *you wish* (to send) *anything* **741 wol,** *wish* **742 seye, tell, me leste,** *pleases me* **743 sadly,** *constantly* **744 pryvely,** *secretly* **745 as a swyn,** *like a pig* **747 wroght,** *made* **748 of,** *concerning* **750 spak,** *said* **751 feendly,** *fiendlike* **752 noon,** *no one* **753 dorste ther,** *dared there* **754 mooder,** *mother,* **elf,** *wicked creature,* **aventure,** *misfortune* **755 Ycomen,** *come* **756 everich wight,** *every person* **757 Wo,** *woeful,* **sayn,** *seen* **758 wight,** *person,* **sorwes soore,** *painful sorrows* **759 of,** *by,* **wroot agayn,** *wrote in response* **760 sonde,** *sending* **761 loore,** *teachings* **762 lust,** *wishes,* **plesaunce,** *pleasure* **762 thyn ordinaunce,** *your control* **764 Kepeth,** *protect* **765 eek,** *also,* **unto myn hoom-comynge,** *until I return home* **766 whan hym list,** *when it pleases him* **769 take,** *taken* **771**

fulfild, *full* **772 lymes faltren ay,** *limbs always falter* **773 biwreyest,** *betrays,* **secreenesse,** *secrecy* **774 lorn,** *lost,* **janglest as,** *chatter like,* **jay,** *bird* **775 array,** *appearance* **776 Ther,** *where,* **regneth,** *rules,* **route,** *company* **777 hyd,** *hidden* **778 digne,** *suitable* **780 resigne,** *renounce* **781 enditen,** *write* **782 Fy, mannysh,** *shame, manlike,* **lye,** *lie* **783 feendlych,** *fiendlike* **785 comth fro,** *comes from* **786 lighte,** *arrives* **787 fayn,** *pleased* **789 his girdel underpighte,** *stuffed his belt* **790 fnorteth,** *snores,* **gyse,** *way* **791 gan aryse,** *did arise* **792 Eft,** *again,* **everychon,** *each one* **795 Up peyne,** *under pain,* **heigh juyse,** *high judgment* **796 ne sholde suffren,** *should not allow* **797 in-with his reawme,** *within his realm* **799 fond,** *found* **801 croude,** *push* **802 eft,** *again* **803 thy goost,** *your spirit*

771–77 From Innocent, *De Miseria* 2.19; see 99–121n above. **798 o quarter of a tyde,** either one-quarter of a tide (a maritime calculation; see line 510 above) or, more loosely, a quarter of an hour.

And slepynge, in thy dreem, been in penance°,
Whan Donegild cast° al this ordinance°.   805

This messager on morwe whan he wook
Unto the castel halt° the nexte° way,
And to the constable he the lettre took.
And whan that he this pitous lettre say°,
Ful ofte he seyde "allas" and "weylaway."   810
"Lord Crist," quod he, "how may this world
          endure,
So ful of synne is many a creature?

"O myghty God, if that it be thy wille,
Sith° thou art rightful juge, how may it be
That thou wolt suffren innocentz to spille°,   815
And wikked folk regnen° in prosperitee?
O goode Custance, allas, so wo is me
That I moot° be thy tormentour or deye
On shames deeth°; ther is noon oother weye."

Wepen° bothe yonge and olde in al that
          place   820
Whan that the kyng this cursed lettre sente,
And Custance, with a deedly pale face,
The ferthe° day toward hir ship she wente.
But nathelees she taketh in good entente
The wyl of Crist, and knelynge on the stronde°   825
She seyde, "Lord, ay° welcome be thy sonde°!

"He that me kepte fro the false blame
While I was on the lond amonges yow,
He kan me kepe from harm and eek fro shame
In salte see, althogh I se noght how.   830
As strong as evere he was, he is yet now.
In hym triste° I, and in his mooder deere°,
That is to me my seyl° and eek my steere°."

Hir litel child lay wepyng in hir arm,
And knelynge, pitously to hym she seyde,   835

"Pees°, litel sone, I wol do thee noon harm."
With that hir coverchief of° hir heed she breyde°,
And over his litel eyen° she it leyde,
And in hir arm she lulleth it° ful faste,
And into hevene hire eyen up she caste.   840

"Mooder," quod she, "and mayde bright°,
          Marie,
Sooth° is that thurgh wommanes eggement°
Mankynde was lorn°, and dampned ay° to dye,
For which thy child was on a croys yrent°.
Thy blisful eyen sawe al his torment.   845
Thanne is ther no comparison bitwene
Thy wo and any wo man may sustene°.

"Thow sawe thy child yslayn° bifore thyne eyen,
And yet now lyveth my litel child, parfay°.
Now, lady bright, to whom alle woful° cryen,   850
Thow glorie of wommanhede°, thow faire may°,
Thow haven of refut°, brighte sterre° of day,
Rewe° on my child, that° of thy gentillesse
Rewest on every reweful° in distresse.

"O litel child, allas, what is thy gilt,   855
That nevere wroghtest synne° as yet, pardee°?
Why wil thyn harde fader han thee spilt°?
O mercy, deere constable," quod she,
"As lat my litel child dwelle° heer with thee;
And if thou darst° nat saven hym, for blame°,   860
Yet kys° hym ones in his fadres° name."

Therwith° she looked bakward to the londe,
And seyde, "Farewel, housbonde routhelees°!"
And up she rist°, and walketh doun the stronde°
Toward the ship—hir folweth al the prees°.   865
And evere she preyeth° hire child to holde his
          pees;
And taketh hir leve, and with an hooly entente
She blissed hire°, and into ship she wente.

---

804 penance, *suffering* **805 cast,** *planned,* **ordinance,** *arrangement* **807 halt,** *took,* **nexte,** *nearest* **809 say,** *saw* **814 Sith,** *since* **815 spille,** *die* **816 regnen,** *rule* **818 moot,** *must* **819 On shames deeth,** *in a death of shame* **820 Wepen,** *weep* **823 ferthe,** *fourth* **825 stronde,** *shore* **826 ay,** *always,* **sonde,** *sending* **832 triste,** *trust,* **mooder deere,** *dear mother* **833 seyl,** *sail,* **steere,** *rudder* **836 Pees,** *peace* **837 coverchief of,** *kerchief from,* **breyde,** *removed* **838 eyen,** *eyes* **839 lulleth it,** *quieted him* **841 mayde bright,** *beautiful maiden* **842 Sooth,** *truth,* **eggement,** *encouragement* **843 lorn,** *lost,* **dampned ay,** *condemned always* **844 croys rent,** *cross torn* **847 sustene,** *endure* **848 yslayn,** *slain* **849 parfay,** *by my faith* **850 alle woful,** *all who suffer* **851 wommanhede,** *womanhood,* **may,** *maiden* **852 haven of refut,** *shelter for refuge,* **sterre,** *star* **853 Rewe,** *have pity,* **that,** *you who* **854 every reweful,** *everyone pitiable* **856 wroghtest synne,** *sinned,* **pardee,** *by God* (Fr.) **857 thyn hard fader han thee,** *your cruel father have you killed* **859 As lat . . . dwelle,** *and let . . . live* **860 darst,** *dare,* **blame,** *fear of blame* **861 kys,** *kiss,* **fadres,** *father's* **862 Therwith,** *with this* **863 routhelees,** *pitiless* **864 rist,** *rises,* **stronde,** *shore* **865 hir folweth al the prees,** *the whole crowd follows her* **866 preyeth,** *asks* **868 blissed hire,** *blessed herself***

813–26 Lines not in Trivet or Gower. The question raised in these lines is a common one in the face of trials; compare *Bo* 1.m5.34ff. **843 wommanes eggement,** the misogynist commonplace that a woman (Eve) was the cause of the fall of humankind is rooted in Genesis 3.6. It is often paired with the notion that salvation was achieved through Mary and her suffering.

Vitailled° was the ship, it is no drede°,
Habundantly for hire ful longe space°,   870
And othere necessaries that sholde nede°
She hadde ynogh°, heryed° be Goddes grace.
For° wynd and weder°, almyghty God purchace°,
And brynge hire hoom! I kan no bettre seye,
But in the see she dryveth° forth hir weye.   875

Explicit secunda pars. Sequitur pars tercia.

Alla the kyng comth hoom° soone after this
Unto his castle, of the which I tolde,
And asketh where his wyf and his child is°.
The constable gan aboute his herte colde°,
And pleynly° al the manere° he hym tolde   880
As ye han herd—I kan telle it no bettre—
And sheweth° the kyng his seel and eek his lettre,

And seyde, "Lord, as ye comanded me
Up peyne° of deeth, so have I doon, certein."
This messager tormented° was til he   885
Moste biknowe° and tellen, plat° and pleyn,
Fro nyght to nyght, in what place he had leyn°.
And thus, by wit and sotil° enquerynge,
Ymagined° was by° whom this harm gan sprynge°.

The hand was knowe° that the lettre wroot,   890
And al the venym° of this cursed dede,
But in what wise°, certeinly, I noot°.
Th'effect is this, that Alla, out of drede°,
His mooder slow°—that may men pleynly rede—
For that she traitoure was to hire ligeance°.   895
Thus endeth olde Donegild, with meschance°.

The sorwe that this Alla nyght and day
Maketh for his wyf, and for his child also,
Ther is no tonge that it telle may.
But now wol I unto Custance go,   900

That fleteth° in the see, in peyne and wo,
Fyve yeer and moore, as liked Cristes sonde,
Er that° hir ship approched unto the londe.

Under° an hethen castel, atte laste,
Of which the name in my text noght I fynde°,   905
Custance, and eek hir child, the see up caste.
Almyghty God, that saved al mankynde,
Have on Custance and on hir child som mynde°,
That fallen is in hethen hand eftsoone°,
In point to spille°, as I shal telle yow soone.   910

Doun fro the castle comth ther many a wight°
To gauren° on this ship and on Custance.
But shortly, from the castle, on a nyght,
The lordes styward—God yeve° hym
        meschance°—
A theef that hadde reneyed oure creance°,   915
Cam into the ship allone, and seyde he sholde
Hir lemman be°, wher so she wolde or nolde°.

Wo was this wrecched womman tho bigon°;
Hir child cride, and she cride pitously.
But blisful Marie heelp° hire right anon°,   920
For with hir struglyng wel and myghtily
The theef fil overbord al sodeynly°,
And in the see he dreynte for vengeance°.
And thus hath Crist unwemmed° kept Custance.

O foule lust of luxurie°, lo, thyn ende°!   925
Nat oonly that thou feyntest° mannes mynde,
But verraily thou wolt his body shende°.
Th'ende of thy werk, or of thy lustes blynde°,
Is compleynyng°. Hou many oon° may men fynde
That noght for werk somtyme°, but for
        th'entente   930
To doon this synne, been outher slayn or
        shente°!

---

869 **Vitailled,** *stocked with food,* **drede,** *doubt* 870 **space,** *time* 871 **sholde nede,** *(she) would need* 872 **ynogh,** *enough,* **heryed,** *praised* 873 **For,** *(as) for,* **weder,** *weather,* **purchace,** *provide* 875 **dryveth,** *goes* 876 **comth hoom,** *comes home* 878 **is,** *are* 879 **gan . . . colde,** *did* (grow) *cold* 880 **pleynly,** *clearly,* **al the manere,** *the whole proceeding* 882 **sheweth,** *shows* 884 **Up peyne,** *under pain* 885 **tormented,** *tortured* 886 **Moste biknowe,** *must reveal,* **plat,** *clear* 887 **leyn,** *slept* 888 **sotil,** *subtle* 889 **Ymagined,** *deduced,* **by,** *from,* **gan sprynge,** *did originate* 890 **knowe,** *ascertained* 891 **venym,** *poison* 892 **wise,** *way,* **noot,** *know not* 893 **out of drede,** *without doubt* 894 **slow,** *slew* 895 **ligeance,** *allegiance* 896 **meschance,** *bad fortune* 901 **fleteth,** *floats* 903 **Er that,** *before* 904 **Under,** *near* 905 **noght I fynde,** *I do not find* 908 **som mynde,** *some attention* 909 **eftsoone,** *again* 910 **point to spille,** *danger of death* 911 **comth,** *comes,* **many a wight,** *many people* 912 **gauren,** *stare* 914 **yeve,** *give,* **meschance,** *bad fortune* 915 **reneyed oure creance,** *renounced our faith* 917 **Hir lemman be,** *be her lover,* **wher so she wolde or nolde,** *whether she wished it or not* 918 **Wo . . . tho bigon,** *miserable then* 920 **heelp,** *helped,* **right anon,** *right away* 922 **sodeynly,** *suddenly* 923 **dreynte for vengeance,** *drowned as punishment* 924 **unwemmed,** *untainted* 925 **lust of luxurie,** *desire of lechery,* **ende,** *outcome* 926 **feyntest,** *dims* 927 **shende,** *destroy* 928 **lustes blynde,** *blind desires* 929 **compleynyng,** *lamenting,* **Hou many oon,** *how many* 930 **werk somtyme,** *(the) deed sometimes* 931 **been outher slayn or shente,** *are either killed or destroyed*

Explicit secunda pars. Sequitur pars tercia. "Here ends part two. Here follows part three." 882 **seel,** wax seal; see 736n above. 902 **as liked Cristes sonde,** so it pleased the sending of Christ, an idiom that means something like "as it accorded with the dispensation of Christ." 914 **lordes styward,** the steward or manager of the castle who represented his lord. 922 **theef fil,** villain fell; in Trivet, she pushes him. 925–31 From Innocent, *De Miseria* 2.21; see 99–121n above.

How may this wayke° womman han this
    strengthe
Hire to defende agayn° this renegat°?
O Golias, unmesurable of lengthe,
Hou myghte David make thee so maat°,   935
So yong and of armure so desolaat°?
Hou dorste° he looke upon thy dredful face?
Wel may men seen, it nas° but Goddes grace.

Who yaf° Judith corage or hardynesse°
To sleen° hym Oloferne in his tente,   940
And to deliveren out of wrecchednesse
The peple of God? I seye, for this entente°,
That right° as God spirit of vigour sente
To hem°, and saved hem out of meschance,
So sente he myght and vigour to Custance.   945

    Forth gooth hir ship thurghout the narwe°
    mouth
Of Jubaltare and Septe, dryvynge ay°
Somtyme west and somtyme north and south
And somtyme est, ful many a wery day,
Til Cristes mooder—blessed be she ay—   950
Hath shapen°, thurgh hir endelees goodnesse,
To make an ende of al hir hevynesse°.

    Now lat us stynte° of Custance but a throwe°,
And speke we of the Romayn Emperour,
That out of Surrye° hath by lettres knowe°   955
The slaughtre of Cristen folk, and dishonour
Doon to his doghter by a fals traytour,
I mene the cursed wikked Sowdanesse°
That at the feeste leet sleen° both moore and
    lesse°.

For which this Emperour hath sent anon   960
His senatour, with roial ordinance°,
And othere lordes, God woot°, many oon,
On Surryens to taken heigh° vengeance.

They brennen°, sleen°, and brynge hem to
    meschance°
Ful many a day; but shortly, this is th'ende,   965
Homward to Rome they shapen hem to wende°.

    This senatour repaireth° with victorie
To Rome-ward°, saillynge ful roially°,
And mette° the ship dryvynge°, as seith the storie,
In which Custance sit ful pitously.   970
Nothyng° knew he what she was, ne why
She was in swich array°, ne she nyl seye°
Of hire estaat°, although° she sholde deye.

He bryngeth hire to Rome, and to his wyf
He yaf° hire and hir yonge sone also;   975
And with the senatour she ladde° hir lyf.
Thus kan Oure Lady bryngen out of wo
Woful Custance, and many another mo°.
And longe tyme dwelled she in that place,
In hooly werkes evere, as was hir grace°.   980

The senatoures wyf hir aunte was,
But for al that° she knew hire never the moore.
I wol no lenger tarien° in this cas,
But to Kyng Alla, which I spak of yoore°,
That wepeth for his wyf and siketh soore°,   985
I wol retourne°, and lete° I wol Custance
Under the senatoures governance.

    Kyng Alla, which that hadde his mooder slayn,
Upon a day fil in swich repentance°
That, if I shortly tellen shal and playn,   990
To Rome he comth to receyven his penance,
And putte hym in° the Popes ordinance°
In heigh and logh°, and Jhesu Crist bisoghte°
Foryeve his wikked werkes° that he wroghte°.

    The fame anon° thurghout the toun
    is born°,   995
How Alla kyng shal comen in pilgrymage,

---

932 wayke, *weak* **933 agayn,** *against,* **renegat,** *turncoat* (see line 915) **935 maat,** (check)*mated* **936 of armure so desolaat,** *without armor* **937 Hou dorste,** *how dares* **938 nas,** *is nothing* **939 yaf,** *gave,* **hardynesse,** *boldness* **940 sleen,** *slay* **942 entente,** *opinion* **943 right,** *just* **944 hem,** *them* **946 narwe,** *narrow* **947 dryvynge ay,** *moving always* **951 Hath shapen,** *has arranged* **952 hevynesse,** *sorrow* **953 stynte,** *pause,* **but a throwe,** *briefly* **955 Surrye,** *Syria,* **knowe,** *known* **958 Sowdanesse,** *Sultaness* **959 leet sleen,** *caused to be killed,* **moore and lesse,** *upper and lower* (classes) **961 roial ordinance,** *royal command* **962 woot,** *knows* **963 heigh,** *extreme* **964 brennen,** *burn,* **sleen,** *slay,* **meschance,** *ill fate* **966 shapen hem to wende,** *prepare themselves to*

travel **967 repaireth,** *returns* **968 To Rome-ward,** *toward Rome,* **roially,** *royally* **969 mette,** *met,* **dryvynge,** *moving* **971 Nothyng,** *not at all* **972 swich array,** *such a condition,* **ne she nyl seye,** *nor will she speak* **973 estaat,** *social rank,* **althogh,** *even if* **975 yaf,** *gave* **976 ladde,** *led* **978 another mo,** *others more* **980 grace,** *good fortune* **982 for al that,** *even so* **983 tarien,** *delay* **984 yoore,** *earlier* **985 siketh soore,** *sighs sorely* **986 wol retourne,** *will return,* **lete,** *leave* **989 fil in swich repentance,** *fell into such remorse* **992 in,** *under,* **ordinance,** *orders* **993 In heigh and logh,** *in high and low* (i.e., in all respects), **bisoghte,** *asked* **994 werkes,** *deeds,* **wroghte,** *worked* (i.e., had done) **995 fame anon,** *news quickly,* **born,** *carried*

---

934 Golias, Goliath, the gigantic warrior slain by David in 1 Samuel 17.4ff. **939–40 Judith . . . hym Oloferne,** Judith saves the Israelites by killing Holofernes in the apocryphal book of Judith; compare *MkT* 7.2251ff. Redundant pronouns such as *hym* recur in Middle English. **947 Jubaltare and Septe,** Gibraltar and Ceuta, separated by the Strait of Gibraltar at the western end of the Mediterranean Sea.

By herbergeours° that wenten hym biforn;
For which the senatour, as was usage°,
Rood hym agayns°, and many of his lynage°,
As wel to shewen his heighe magnificence   1000
As to doon any kyng a reverence°.

Greet cheere dooth° this noble senatour
To Kyng Alla, and he to hym also;
Everich of hem° dooth oother greet honour.
And so bifel that inwith° a day or two   1005
This senatour is to Kyng Alla go°
To feste°, and shortly, if I shal nat lye,
Custances sone° wente in his compaignye.

Som men wolde seyn° at requeste of Custance
This senatour hath lad this child to feeste;   1010
I may nat tellen every circumstance:
Be as be may°, ther was he at the leeste°.
But sooth° is this, that at his moodres heeste°
Biforn° Alla, durynge the metes space°,
The child stood, lookyng in the kynges face.   1015

This Alla kyng hath of this child greet wonder,
And to the senatour he seyde anon,
"Whos is that faire child that stondeth yonder?"
"I noot°," quod he, "by God, and by Seint John.
A mooder he hath, but fader hath he noon   1020
That I of woot°"; but and shortly, in a stounde°,
He tolde Alla how that this child was founde.

"But God woot°," quod this senatour also,
"So vertuous a lyvere° in my lyf
Ne saugh I nevere° as she, ne herde of mo°,   1025
Of worldly wommen, mayde, ne of wyf.
I dar wel seyn° hir hadde levere° a knyf
Thurghout hir brest than ben° a womman wikke;

There is no man koude° brynge hire to that
    prikke°."

Now was this child as lyk unto Custance   1030
As possible is a creature to be.
This Alla hath the face in remembrance
Of dame Custance, and ther on mused° he
If that the childes mooder were aught° she
That is his wyf, and pryvely° he sighte°,   1035
And spedde hym fro° the table that° he myghte.

"Parfay°," thoghte he, "fantome° is in myn heed.
I oghte deme°, of skilful° juggement,
That in the salte see my wyf is deed."
And afterward he made his argument: 1040
"What woot I if that° Crist have hyder ysent°
My wyf by see, as wel as he hire sente
To my contree fro thennes that° she wente°?"

And after noon, hoom° with the senatour
Goth Alla, for to seen this wonder chaunce°.   1045
This senatour dooth Alla greet honour,
And hastifly° he sente after Custaunce.
But trusteth weel, hire liste nat to daunce°
Whan that she wiste wherfore was that sonde°;
Unnethe° upon hir feet she myghte stonde.   1050

Whan Alla saugh his wyf, faire° he hire grette°,
And weep that it was routhe° for to see;
For at the firste look he on hire sette,
He knew wel verraily° that it was she.
And she, for sorwe, as doumb stant° as a tree,   1055
So was hir herte shet° in hir distresse,
Whan she remembred his unkyndenesse.

Twyes° she swowned° in his owene sighte.
He weep°, and hym excuseth° pitously.

---

997 herbergeours, *servants who arrange for lodgings* **998 usage,** *custom* **999 Rood hym agayns,** *rode to meet him,* **lynage,** *kindred* **1001 doon . . . a reverence,** *revere* **1002 Greet cheere dooth,** *great attention gives* **1004 Everich of hem,** *each of them* **1005 inwith,** *within* **1006 is . . . go,** *goes* **1007 To feste,** *for a feast* **1008 sone,** *son* **1009 wolde seyn,** *would say* **1012 Be as be may,** *whatever the case,* **leeste,** *least* **1013 sooth,** *(the) truth,* **moodres heeste,** *mother's request* **1014 Biforn,** *before,* **metes space,** *mealtime* **1019 noot,** *know not* **1021 woot,** *know,* **stounde,** *moment* **1023 woot,** *knows* **1024 lyvere,** *living person* **1025 Ne saugh I nevere,** *I never saw,* **herde of mo,** *heard of any* **1027 dar wel seyn,** *dare say,* **hir hadde levere,** *she would rather have* **1028 ben,** *be* **1029 koude,** *(who) could,* **prikke,** *point* **1033 ther on mused,** *considered* **1034**

aught, *none other than* **1035 pryvely,** *quietly,* **sighte,** *sighed* **1036 spedde hym fro,** *hurried himself from,* **that,** *as soon as* **1037 Parfay,** *by my faith,* **fantome,** *fantasy* **1038 deme,** *to accept,* **of skilful,** *by reasonable* **1041 woot I if that,** *do I know whether,* **have hyder ysent,** *has sent here* **1043 fro thennes that,** *from where,* **wente,** *traveled* **1044 hoom,** *home* **1045 wonder chaunce,** *wondrous possibility* **1047 hastifly,** *quickly* **1048 hire liste nat to daunce,** *she did not want to dance* (with joy) **1049 wiste wherfore was that sonde,** *knew the reason for the summons* **1050 Unnethe,** *scarcely* **1051 faire,** *fairly,* **grette,** *greeted* **1052 routhe,** *pity* **1054 verraily,** *truly* **1055 doumb stant,** *silent stands* **1056 shet,** *enclosed* **1058 Twyes,** *twice,* **swowned,** *fainted* **1059 weep,** *weeps,* **hym excuseth,** *excuses himself*

1000 As wel to shewen his, "Both to show his own"; the Roman senator meets King Aella as something of an equal, to show his own high station as well as to acknowledge the king's. **1009 Som men,** Tyrwhitt and later editors have taken this and the reference at line 1086 below as disparaging allusions to Gower's version of the story and indications that Chaucer thought it less decorous than his own. In Gower and Trivet, Custance instructs Maurice how to act at the meal.

"Now God," quod he, "and alle his halwes°
    brighte   1060
So wisly° on my soule as have mercy,
That of youre harm as giltelees am I
As is Maurice my sone, so lyk youre face;
Elles° the feend me fecche out of this place!"

Long was the sobbyng and the bitter
    peyne,   1065
Er that hir° woful hertes myghte cesse°;
Greet was the pitee for to heere hem pleyne°,
Thurgh whiche pleintes° gan hir° wo encresse.
I pray yow alle my labour to relesse°;
I may nat telle hir wo until tomorwe,   1070
I am so wery for to speke° of sorwe.

But finally, whan that the sothe is wist°
That Alla giltelees was of hir wo,
I trowe° an hundred tymes been they kist°,
And swich° a blisse is ther bitwix hem° two   1075
That, save° the joye that lasteth everemo°,
Ther is noon lyk that any creature
Hath seyn° or shal, whil that the world may dure°.

Tho preyde she° hir housbonde mekely,
In relief of hir longe, pitous pyne°,   1080
That he wolde preye° hir fader specially
That of his magestee he wolde enclyne°
To vouchesauf° som day with hym to dyne°.
She preyde hym eek he sholde by no weye
Unto hir fader no word of hire seye°.   1085

Som men wolde seyn° how that the child
    Maurice
Dooth° this message unto this Emperour;
But, as I guesse, Alla was nat so nyce°
To hym that was of so sovereyn° honour
As he that is of Cristen folk the flour,   1090
Sente° any child, but it is bet to deeme°
He wente hymself, and so it may wel seeme.

This Emperour hath graunted° gentilly
To come to dyner, as he hym bisoughte°;
And wel rede I° he looked bisily°   1095
Upon this child, and on his doghter thoghte.
Alla goth to his in°, and as hym oghte°,
Arrayed for this feste in every wise
As ferforth° as his konnyng° may suffise.

The morwe° cam, and Alla gan hym
    dresse°,   1100
And eek his wyf, this Emperour to meete.
And forth they ryde in joye and in gladnesse.
And whan she saugh° hir fader in the strete,
She lighte doun and falleth hym to feete°.
"Fader," quod she, "youre yonge child
    Custance   1105
Is now ful clene° out of youre remembrance.

"I am youre doghter Custance," quod she,
"That whilom° ye han sent unto Surrye.
It am I, fader, that in the salte see
Was put allone and dampned° for to dye.   1110
Now, goode fader, mercy I yow crye!
Sende me namoore unto noon hethenesse°,
But thonketh my lord heere of his kyndenesse."

Who kan the pitous joye tellen al
Bitwixe hem thre°, syn° they been thus
    ymette°?   1115
But of my tale make an ende I shal;
The day goth faste, I wol no lenger lette°.
This glade folk to dyner they hem sette°;
In joye and blisse at mete° I lete hem dwelle
A thousand foold° wel moore than I kan telle.   1120

This child Maurice was sithen° Emperour
Maad° by the Pope, and lyved cristenly.
To Cristes chirche he dide greet honour.
But I lete al his storie passen by;
Of Custance is my tale specially.   1125

1060 halwes, *saints* 1061 wisly, *truly* 1064 Elles, *or else* (may) 1066 Er that hir, *before their,* cesse, *cease* 1067 hem pleyne, *them lament* 1068 pleintes, *lamentation,* gan hir, *did their* 1069 relesse, *release* (me from) 1071 for to speke, *of speaking* 1072 sothe is wist, *truth is known* 1074 trowe, *believe,* been they kist, *they kissed* 1075 swich, *such,* bitwix hem, *between them* 1076 save, *except for,* everemo, *eternally* 1078 seyn, *seen,* dure, *last* 1079 Tho preyde she, *then she asked* 1080 pyne, *pain* 1081 preye, *ask* 1082 enclyne, *consent* 1083 vouchesauf, *agree,* dyne, *dine* 1085 seye, *speak* 1086 wolde seyn, *would say* 1087 Dooth, *conveys* 1088 nyce, *insensitive* 1089 so sovereyn, *such supreme* 1091 Sente,

(to) *send,* bet to deeme, *better to think* 1093 graunted, *agreed* 1094 bisoughte, *requested* 1095 wel rede I, *I well read,* bisily, *intently* 1097 in, *lodging* (inn), hym oghte, *he ought to* 1099 ferforth, *far,* konnyng, *ability* 1100 morwe, *morning,* gan hym dresse, *prepared himself* 1103 saugh, *saw* 1104 hym to feete, *at his feet* 1106 ful clene, *completely* 1108 whilom, *once* 1110 dampned, *condemned* 1112 hethenesse, *heathen land* 1115 Bitwixe hem thre, *among the three of them,* syn, *since,* ymette, *met* 1117 lette, *delay* 1118 hem sette, *set themselves* 1119 mete, (the) *meal* 1120 foold, *times* 1121 sithen, *afterward* 1122 Maad, *made*

1086 See 1009n above. In Trivet and Gower, Maurice conveys the invitation. 1090 flour, flower, i.e., the emperor is the apex of Christianity.

In the olde Romayn geestes may men fynde
Maurices lyf; I bere it noght in mynde.

    This Kyng Alla, whan he his tyme say°,
With his Custance, his hooly wyf so sweete,
To Engelond been they come the righte° way, 1130
Wher as they lyve in joye and in quiete.
But litel while it lasteth, I yow heete°,
Joye of this world, for tyme wol nat abyde.
Fro day to nyght it changeth as the tyde.

Who lyved evere in swich delit o° day 1135
That hym ne moeved outher° conscience,
Or ire°, or talent, or somkynnes affray°,
Envye, or pride, or passion, or offence?
I ne seye but for this ende this sentence°.
That litel while in joye or in plesance 1140
Lasteth the blisse of Alla with Custance.

For deeth, that taketh of heigh and logh° his
    rente°,
Whan passed was a yeer, evene as I gesse,
Out of this world this Kyng Alla he hente°,
For whom Custance hath ful greet hevynesse°. 1145

Now lat° us praye to God his soule blesse.
And dame Custance, finally to seye,
Toward the toun of Rome goth hire weye°.

    To Rome is come this hooly creature,
And fyndeth hire freendes hoole° and
    sounde°. 1150
Now is she scaped° al hire aventure.
And whan that she hir fader hath yfounde°,
Doun on hir knees falleth she to grounde;
Wepynge for tendrenesse in herte blithe°,
She heryeth° God an hundred thousand
    sithe°. 1155

    In vertu and in hooly almus-dede°
They lyven alle, and nevere asonder wende°;
Til deeth departed hem°, this lyf they lede.
And fareth now weel, my tale is at an ende.
Now Jhesu Crist, that of his myght may
    sende 1160
Joy after wo, governe us in his grace,
And kepe° us alle that been in this place!

                         Amen.

Heere endeth the Tale of the Man of Lawe.

[EPILOGUE]

Owre Hoost upon his stiropes° stood anon°,
And seyde, "Goode men, herkeneth everych on°!
This was a thrifty° tale for the nones°! 1165
Sir Parisshe Prest," quod he, "for Goddes bones,
Telle us a tale, as was thi forward yore°.
I se wel that ye lerned men in lore
Can moche° good, by Goddes dignite!"

The Parson him answerde, "Benedicite°! 1170
What eyleth° the man, so synfully to swere°?"
Oure Host answerde, "O Jankin, be ye there?
I smelle a Lollere in the wynd," quod he.
"Now, goode men," quod oure Host,
    "herkeneth° me;
Abydeth°, for Goddes digne passioun°, 1175

1128 **say,** *saw* 1130 **righte,** *direct* 1132 **yow heete,** *assure you*
1135 **swich delit o,** *such delight one* 1136 **hym ne moeved outher,** *disturbed him not either* 1137 **ire,** *anger,* **somkynnes affray,** *some kind of fear* 1139 **ne seye but for this ende this sentence,** *make this observation only for this purpose* 1142 **heigh and logh,** *high and low,* **rente,** *payment* 1144 **hente,** *snatched* 1145 **hevynesse,** *sorrow* 1146 **lat,** *let* 1148 **goth hire weye,** *takes her way* 1150 **hoole,** *undamaged,* **sounde,** *healthy* 1151 **is . . . scaped,** *has escaped* 1152 **hir fader hath yfounde,** *has*

found her father 1154 **blithe,** *happy* 1155 **heryeth,** *praises,* **sithe,** *times* 1156 **almus-dede,** *charitable deeds* 1157 **asonder wende,** *traveled separately* 1158 **departed hem,** *separated them* 1162 **kepe,** *protect* 1163 **stiropes,** *stirrups,* **anon,** *quickly* 1164 **herkeneth everych on,** *listen everyone* 1165 **thrifty,** *successful,* **nones,** *occasion* 1167 **thi forward yore,** *your promise earlier* 1169 **Can moche,** *know much* 1170 **Benedicite,** *bless us* 1171 **eyleth,** *ails,* **swere,** *utter oaths* 1174 **herkeneth,** *listen to* 1175 **Abydeth,** *wait,* **digne passioun,** *worthy suffering*

1126 **olde Romayn geestes,** old Roman stories or histories. The life of Maurice is found in Trivet's *Chronicle* along with that of Constance in the section entitled "Les gestes des apostles, emperours, et rois" (Accounts of Apostle, Emperors, and Kings). 1132–38 Ecclesiasticus 18.26 and Job 21.12, both from Innocent, *De Miseria* 1.20; see 99–121n above. 1163–90 These lines are included in thirty-five MSS but omitted in El, Hg, and twenty-two others, probably canceled from Chaucer's original. The text here is based on MS. Corpus Christi 198. 1172 **Jankin,** familiar form of John (like Johnny), a traditional name for a priest. 1173 **smelle a Lollere in the wynd,** i.e., think I detect a Lollard. The Lollards were followers of John Wycliffe, fourteenth-century church reformer, who objected to swearing (and to pilgrimages). *Lollard* derives from Dutch for "mumbler" and was applied to many kinds of religious zealot.

For we schal han a predicacioun°;
This Lollere heer wil prechen° us somwhat."
  "Nay, by my fader soule, that schal he nat!"
Seyde the Wif of Bath; "he schal nat preche;
He schal no gospel glosen° here ne teche°.   1180
We leven alle° in the grete God," quod she;
"He wolde sowen° som difficulte,
Or springen cokkel° in our clene corn.

And therfore, Hoost, I warne thee biforn°,
My joly body schal a tale telle,   1185
And I schal clynken° you so mery a belle,
That I schal waken al this compaignie.
But it schal not ben of philosophie,
Ne phislyas, ne termes queinte° of lawe.
Ther is but litel Latyn in my mawe°!"   1190

1176 schal han a predicacioun, *shall have a sermon* **1177 prechen,**
preach **1180 glosen,** *gloss* (comment on), **teche,** *teach* **1181 leven alle,**
all believe **1182 wolde sowen,** *will plant* **1183 springen cokkel,** *raise*
weeds **1184 biforn,** *in advance* **1186 clynken,** *jingle* **1189 termes
queinte,** *curious words* **1190 mawe,** *mouth*

1179 Wif of Bath This reading is found in no MS; all read "Squyer," "Sumnour," or "Shipman," two-syllable words beginning with S. "Wife of Bath" is assumed to have been in Chaucer's original when this epilogue linked the present *ShT* (originally assigned to the Wife of Bath) to *MLT*. When Chaucer changed his plans and substituted another pilgrim name for "Wif of Bath," he had to supply a syllable; in the MSS "heer" is found in various positions, indicating that it may have been written with a caret in the margin of the original. **1185 joly body,** merry self; the same phrase occurs in *ShT* 7.423, referring to a woman. In both instances, Chaucer may have had the Wife of Bath in mind. **1189 phisylas,** uncertain meaning, but it may be a malapropism for "filace" (file of documents), some form of "physick" (medicine), or even the *Physics* of Aristotle. The original word confused the scribes, who provided a number of variants. This and the other terms of learning in lines 1188–89 may be seen as an appropriate response to *Mel,* which may once have stood in the place of *MLT;* see 96n above.

CANTERBURY TALES PART 3

INTRODUCTION

IN 1908, Eleanor Prescott Hammond (1933, no. 57) heralded much modern Chaucer criticism when she labeled parts 3, 4, and 5 of *The Canterbury Tales* the "marriage group," arguing that the sequence is the product of Chaucer's most mature art (after 1390?) and identifying a major source of the group: St. Jerome's *Epistola adversus Jovinianum* (Letter against Jovinian)—Jerome's tendentious argument that virginity is morally superior to marriage. Almost everyone agrees that among Chaucer's most remarkable achievements is the creation of the proto-feminist Wife of Bath out of Jerome's antimatrimonial, antifeminist material. Insofar as her strategies of argument can be seen to be similar to Jerome's own—interpreting authorities for one's own purposes—the Wife may be seen to "read like a man," to adapt Carolyn Dinshaw's felicitous phrase in *Chaucer's Sexual Poetics* (1989, no. 629).

Dinshaw focuses on how Jankyn (husband number five) treats (and beats!) the Wife and identifies several correlations between the manipulation of texts and the treatment of women in Western tradition. In this line of thinking, Alisoun's uses and abuses of scripture and other written authorities parallel her manipulations of her husbands, an inversion of the traditional control of books and women by men, and an inversion of the traditional hierarchy of husband and wife in marriage.

In the Middle Ages, male control in marriage was a figure for the well-ordered hierarchical society, thought to parallel Christ's marriage to the church, the king to the commonwealth, and reason to the senses. When the Wife of Bath asserts that her own experiences are equal or superior to the authority of Jerome and others, she verges on heresy; yet she does so with such gusto that it is difficult not to side with her. When we recognize that Chaucer constructs her experiences from the very authorities the Wife imitates and simultaneously rejects, we find ourselves in an interpretive circle from which escape is difficult: the Wife of Bath is a product of the very system she challenges.

The character of the Wife of Bath overshadows part 3 and much of the marriage group. The acrimonious exchange of tales between the Friar and Summoner begins as an altercation that interrupts her prologue (829–56), following an earlier interruption by the Pardoner (163–92). Interruption occurs elsewhere in the Canterbury fiction, but only the Wife succeeds in quelling her interrupters. References to the Wife by the Clerk (4.1170) and in the *Merchant's Tale* (4.1685) contribute to her looming presence, but our sense of a real person speaking results largely from the confessional mode of her prologue, the tensions and contradictions in her claims, and the stylistic virtuosity through which Chaucer brings her to life.

Though Jerome is the major source for topics and arguments in the *Wife of Bath's Prologue*, La Vieille (Old Woman) of Jean de Meun's portion of the *Roman de la Rose* is the immediate model for her character, derived ultimately from the experienced old bawd found in Ovid. Works by Walter Map, Jehan LeFévre, Eustace Deschamps, and others contributed to the large antifeminist tradition from which the Wife of Bath arose, and they provide many echoes of details and diction. None of them achieves, however, as strong a sense of a living person speaking. In *The Disenchanted Self* (1990, no. 668), H. Marshall Leicester offers a feminist-psychoanalytical-deconstructive reading of the speaking voice in the *Wife of Bath's Prologue*. In *Chaucer and the Subject of History* (1991, no. 619), Lee Patterson examines the subjectivity of the Wife in light of the genre of *sermons joyeux* (parodic literary sermons), and he assesses her relation to La Vieille. Ralph Hanna III and Traugott Lawler collect materials for studying the tradition from which the *Wife of Bath's Prologue* arose—Jerome, Walter

Map's *Dissuasio Valerii* (Dissuasion of Valerius), and Theophrastus's *Liber de Nuptiis* (Book of Marriage)—in *Jankyn's Book of Wikked Wyves* (1997, no. 972).

The *Wife of Bath's Tale* is a version of the "loathly lady" story that is also found in John Gower's "Tale of Florent" and in two fifteenth-century Arthurian tales, *The Weddynge of Sir Gawen and Dame Ragnell* (a romance) and *The Marriage of Sir Gawaine* (a ballad). Chaucer's version stands out for the ways it emphasizes female wisdom and female sovereignty, even though it ends in marital compromise (as does the *Wife of Bath's Prologue*). Among the changes Chaucer makes to the traditional tale (see, e.g., 889n, 1220n), the most apparent is the addition of the loathly lady's lecture on "gentillesse" (1109ff.), which converts the knight from rapist to compliant husband, a parallel to the lady's own transformation to youthful beauty. The lecture overturns traditional notions of class by suggesting that gentle deeds are more important than gentle birth, and, rooted in Dante's *Convivio*, it marks a stage in the slow growth of the ideal of human equality in Western thought. The topics of sovereignty in marriage and gentility are paired elsewhere in the marriage group, aligning issues of gender and class and cementing the cohesion of parts 3, 4, and 5.

As much as the Wife's materials are about marital sovereignty and gentility, they are also concerned with texts and their meanings, orality in opposition to literacy, and, arguably, the *truth* of marriage be*troth*als. The *Friar's Tale* focuses more narrowly on what language *does* and under what conditions speech has real effects. It depicts a pledge of brotherhood between a demon and a summoner (a slap at the pilgrim Summoner) and a pair of curses. The carter's curse produces no effect because he does not really intend to send his cart and horses to the devil, but the old lady's curse of the summoner is powerful and effective because she does intend it, because the summoner does not intend to repent, and because (as his questions to the demon show) he genuinely wants to know about hell. The speech acts of pledging, cursing, and questioning are brought together in this seemingly simple tale to explore the efficacy of language and its relation to the intentions of a speaker. See Daniel T. Kline, "'Myne By Right': Oath Making and Intent in *The Friar's Tale*" (1998, no. 1011).

No central pledge occurs in analogous accounts, and Penn R. Szittya, in "The Green Man as Loathly Lady" (1975, no. 946), shows how the pledge in the *Friar's Tale* links it with the pledge of marriage between knight and loathly lady in the *Wife of Bath's Tale* and how the pairing of the two tales recalls the echoic relation of the Knight's and Miller's tales in part 1 of *The Canterbury Tales*.

As the Reeve sought to outdo the Miller, his working-class rival, the Summoner goes after the Friar, his ecclesiastical rival—and (it is suggested) his equal in anger and avarice. Commissioned by the papacy, friars were outside the jurisdiction of the diocesan hierarchy of archbishops, bishops, and parish priests. Summoners were the subpoena servers of the judicial branch of this structure, notorious for using the office to bilk the poor, just as friars were notorious for currying favor with the rich. The vicious antagonism of Chaucer's Summoner and Friar embodies the social and spiritual upheavals latent in their greed and abuse of their respective offices. The *Summoner's Tale* is dominated by antifraternal satire through which the Summoner ridicules the claims of friars to be the new apostles (see, e.g., 1737n, 2185–88n), and he undercuts these claims through scatology, recurrent puns (1707n), and a blasphemous parody of the Pentecost. The great wind of the Holy Spirit that brought the gift of speaking in tongues to Christ's apostles (Acts 2.1–6) is equated with the fart of an ailing man. Human speech, like all sound, is reduced to reverberating air (2234). We have no clear source for the plot of either the *Friar's Tale* or the *Summoner's Tale*, although parallels to many details can be found in sermon handbooks, anecdotes, and other popular materials. It is striking that Chaucer adapts medieval popular culture to create the tales of these two ecclesiastical officers when he uses more learned material to create the Wife of Bath.

On the treatment of antifraternalism and Pentecost in the tale, see Glending Olson, "The End of *The Summoner's Tale* and the Uses of Pentecost" (1999, no. 1034); on the role of puns, D. Thomas Hanks Jr., "Chaucer's *Summoner's Tale* and 'the first smel of fartes thre'" (1997, no. 1027). In the introduction to his Variorum edition of *The Summoner's Tale* (1995, no. 40), John F. Plummer III surveys the thematic and structural unity of part 3 and its parallels with part 1.

CANTERBURY TALES
PART 3

WIFE OF BATH'S TALE

PROLOGUE

The Prologue of the Wyves Tale of Bathe.

Experience though noon auctoritee	But me was toold, certeyn, nat longe agoon is°,
Were in this world is right ynogh for me	That sith that Crist ne wente nevere but onis° 10
To speke of wo that is in mariage.	To weddyng in the Cane of Galilee,
For, lordynges, sith° I twelve yeer was of age,	That by the same ensample° taughte he me
Thonked be God that is eterne° on lyve, 5	That I ne sholde wedded be but ones°.
Housbondes at chirche dore I have had fyve—	Herkne eek°, which a sharp word for the
If I so ofte myghte have ywedded bee°—	nones°:
And alle were worthy men in hir degree°.	Biside a welle, Jhesus, God and man, 15

---

4 sith, *since* **5 eterne,** *eternal* **7 ywedded bee,** *been married* **8 hir degree,** *their social standing* **9 nat longe agoon is,** (it) *is not long ago* **10 onis,** *once* **12 ensample,** *example* **13 ne . . . but ones,** *only once* **14 Herkne eek, which,** *listen also* (to this), **which** (is), **for the nones,** *indeed*

1 auctoritee, especially *written* authority, as the battle over Jankyn's book dramatizes in lines 788ff. below. The theme of experience and authority recurs throughout *CT.* **3 wo . . . in mariage,** the unhappiness of marriage was a standard argument in medieval antimatrimonial—often antifeminist—literature written to convince priests and nuns to remain celibate. These writings are the sources of the *WBP,* especially St. Jerome's *Epistola adversus Jovinianum* (Letter against Jovinian), although *WBP* confronts its antifeminist assumptions and arguments. **4 twelve yeer was of age,** twelve years old, the age at which a girl could marry under church law. **6 chirche dore,** the marriage ceremony was performed at the church door, after which the couple went inside for the nuptial mass; the line echoes *GP* 1.460. **11 Cane of Galilee,** John 2.1–11 tells of Christ's going to a wedding in the town of Cana in Galilee. Jerome 1.40 asserts that Christ went to only one wedding in order to teach Christians to marry only once.

Spak° in repreeve° of the Samaritan,
"Thou hast yhad° fyve housbondes," quod he,
"And that man the which that hath now thee
Is noght thyn housbonde." Thus seyde he
    certeyn.
What that he mente therby, I kan nat seyn°,   20
But that I axe° why that the fifthe man
Was noon° housbonde to the Samaritan?
How manye myghte she have in mariage?
Yet herde I nevere tellen in myn age
Upon this nombre diffinicioun.   25
Men may devyne° and glosen° up and doun,
But wel I woot°, expres°, withoute lye,
God bad° us for to wexe and multiplye;
That gentil text kan I wel understonde.
Eek wel I woot, he seyde° myn housbonde   30
Sholde lete° fader and mooder and take to me.
But of no nombre mencioun made he,
Of bigamye or of octogamye.
Why sholde men speke of it vileynye?
   Lo, heere the wise kyng, daun Salomon,   35
I trowe° he hadde wyves mo than oon°.
As wolde God° it were leveful unto° me
To be refreshed half so ofte as he.
Which yifte° of God hadde he for alle his wyvys°!
No man hath swich° that in this world alyve° is.   40
God woot°, this noble kyng, as to my wit°,
The firste nyght had many a myrie fit
With ech of hem°, so wel was hym on lyve°.
Yblessed° be God that I have wedded fyve,
Of whiche I have pyked° out the beste,
Bothe of here nether purs° and of here cheste°.
Diverse scoles° maken parfyt clerkes°,

And diverse practyk° in many sondry° werkes
Maketh the werkman parfit sekirly°;
Of fyve husbondes scoleiyng° am I.
Welcome the sixte, whan that evere he shal.   45
For sothe, I wol° nat kepe° me chaast° in al.
Whan myn housbonde is fro the world ygon°,
Som Cristen man shal wedde me anon°,
For thanne° th'apostle seith that I am free
To wedde, a Goddes half°, where it liketh me°.   50
He seith that to be wedded is no synne;
Bet° is to be wedded than to brynne°.
What rekketh me°, thogh folk seye vileynye°
Of shrewed° Lameth and his bigamye?
I woot° wel Abraham was an hooly man,   55
And Jacob eek, as ferforth° as I kan°,
And ech of hem hadde wyves mo° than two,
And many another holy man also.
Wher can ye seye, in any manere age°,
That hye° God defended° mariage   60
By expres° word? I pray yow, telleth me.
Or where comanded he virginitee?
I woot as wel as ye, it is no drede°,
Th'apostel, whan he speketh of maydenhede°,
He seyde that precept therof° hadde he noon.   65
Men may conseille° a womman to been oon°,
But conseillyng is nat comandement.
He putte it in oure owene juggement;
For hadde God comanded maydenhede,
Thanne hadde he dampned° weddyng with the
    dede.   70
And certain, if ther were no seed ysowe°,
Virginitee wherof thanne° sholde it growe?
Poul dorste° nat comanden, atte leeste°,

---

16 Spak, *spoke,* **repreeve,** *criticism* **17 hast yhad,** *have had* **20 seyn,** *say* **21 axe,** *ask* **22 noon,** *no* **26 devyne,** *speculate,* **glosen,** *interpret* **27 woot,** *know,* **expres,** *clearly* **28 bad,** *commanded* **30 seyde,** *said* **31 lete,** *leave* **36 trowe,** *believe,* **mo than oon,** *more than one* **37 As wolde God,** *I wish to God,* **leveful unto,** *permitted for* **39 Which yifte,** *what a gift,* **wyvys,** *wives* **40 swich,** *such,* **alyve,** *alive* **41 woot,** *knows,* **wit,** *understanding* **43 ech of hem,** *each of them,* **wel was hym on lyve,** *lively was he* **44 Yblessed,** *blessed* **44a pyked,** *picked* **44b here nether purs,** *their lower purs,* **cheste,** *money box* **44c scoles,** *schools,* **parfyt clerkes,** *perfect students* **44d practyk,** *practice,* **sondry,** *various* **44e parfit sekirly,** *perfect certainly* **44f scoleiyng,** *schooling* **46 wol,** *will,* **kepe,** *keep,* **chaast,** *chaste* **47 ygon,** *gone* **48 anon,** *quickly* **49 thanne,** *then* **50 a Goddes half,** *by God's flank,* **where it liketh me,** *whoever I want* **52 Bet,** *better,* **brynne,** *burn* **53 What rekketh me,** *what do I care,* **seye vileynye,** *speak ill* **54 shrewed,** *wicked* **55 woot,** *know* **56 ferforth,** *far,* **kan,** *know* **57 mo,** *more* **59 any manere age,** *any time period* **60 hye,** *high,* **defended,** *forbade* **61 expres,** *specific* **63 drede,** *doubt* **64 maydenhede,** *virginity* **65 precept therof,** *command concerning this* **66 conseille,** *counsel,* **been oon,** *be one* (a virgin) **70 dampned,** *condemned* **71 ysowe,** *planted* **72 wherof thanne,** *from where then* **73 Poul dorste,** *Paul dared,* **atte leeste,** *to say the least*

16 Samaritan, Jesus' discussion with the Samaritan woman at the well is in John 4.5ff., interpreted by Jerome 1.14 as discouragement of remarriage after the death of a spouse. **25 diffinicioun,** clear limit, echoing Jerome's Latin *definitum* (1.15). **28 wexe and multiplye,** increase and procreate; from Genesis 1.28, etc., quoted in Jerome 1.24. **31 lete fader and mooder,** from Matthew 19.5; Jerome 1.5. **33 bigamye or octogamye,** twice married or eight times married; Jerome 1.15 and other medieval thinkers used the terms for successive marriages. **35 Lo, heere,** an idiom meaning "think for example of." **daun Salomon,** master Solomon, the biblical king who had seven hundred wives and three hundred concubines; 1 Kings 11.3; Jerome 1.24. **44a–f** Lines not found in several important manuscripts, perhaps canceled by Chaucer or added late. **46 For sothe,** means "truly," but several manuscripts have "For sith" (For since . . .), a different reading that demands different punctuation. **49–52 th'apostle seith . . . ,** the apostle (St. Paul) says . . . ; from 1 Corinthians 7.9 and 39; Jerome 1.10. **54 Lameth,** Lamech. In Genesis 4.19, he takes two wives; Jerome 1.14. **55–56** Abraham and Jacob each had multiple wives (Genesis 25.1, 35:22–26); Jerome 1.5. **64–67** Paul in 1 Corinthians 7.25; Jerome 1.12, whose argument is echoed through line 76.

A thyng of which his maister yaf noon heeste°.
The dart° is set up for virginitee: 75
Cacche whoso° may; who renneth best lat° see.
　But this word° is nat taken of° every wight°,
But ther as God lust gyve it of his myght°.
I woot wel that th'apostel was a mayde°,
But nathelees, thogh that he wroot and sayde   80
He wolde° that every wight were swich° as he,
Al nys but° conseil° to virginitee.
And for to been a wyf he yaf me leve°
Of indulgence; so it is no repreve°
To wedde me if that my make° dye,   85
Withoute excepcioun of° bigamye.
Al were it° good no womman for to touche—
He mente as in his bed or in his couche—
For peril is bothe fyr and tow t'assemble°—
Ye knowe what this ensample may resemble.   90
This is al and som°: he heeld virginitee
Moore parfit° than weddyng in freletee°.
Freletee clepe I°, but if that° he and she
Wolde leden° al hir° lyf in chastitee.
　I graunte it wel, I have noon envie,   95
Thogh maydenhede preferre bigamye°.
Hem liketh° to be clene, body and goost°.
Of myn estaat° I nyl nat° make no boost,
For wel ye knowe, a lord in his houshold
He nath nat° every vessel al of gold;   100
Somme been of tree°, and doon hir° lord servyse.
God clepeth° folk to hym in sondry wyse°,
And everich° hath of God a propre yifte,
Som this, som that, as hym liketh shifte°.
　Virginitee is greet perfeccioun,   105
And continence° eek with devocioun,

But Crist, that of perfeccioun is welle°,
Bad nat° every wight° he sholde go selle
Al that he hadde and gyve it to the poore,
And in swich wise° folwe hym and his foore°.   110
He spak to hem that wolde lyve parfitly;
And lordynges, by youre leve°, that am nat I.
I wol bistowe° the flour° of al myn age°
In the actes and in fruyt of mariage.
　Telle me also, to what conclusioun°   115
Were membres ymaad° of generacioun°,
And of so parfit wys a wight ywroght?
Trusteth right wel, they were nat maad for noght.
Glose whoso wole° and seye bothe up and doun°
That they were maked for purgacioun   120
Of uryne, and oure bothe thynges smale°
Were eek to knowe a femele from a male,
And for noon oother cause—say ye no?
The experience woot° wel it is noght so.
So that the clerkes be nat with me wrothe°,   125
I sey this, that they beth maked° for bothe,
This is to seye, for office° and for ese
Of engendrure°, ther° we nat God displese.
Why sholde men elles° in hir bookes sette
That a man shal yelde° to his wyf hire dette?   130
Now wherwith° sholde he make his paiement°,
If he ne used° his sely instrument?
Thanne were they maad upon a creature
To purge uryne, and eek for engendrure.
　But I seye noght that every wight is holde°,   135
That° hath swich harneys° as I to yow tolde,
To goon and usen hem in engendrure.
Thanne sholde men take of chastitee no cure°.
Crist was a mayde° and shapen as a man,

---

74 **maister yaf noon heeste,** *master gave no commandment* 75 **dart,** *prize* 76 **Cacche whoso,** *catch* (it) *whoever,* **lat,** *let* (us) 77 **word,** *advice,* **taken of,** *intended for,* **wight,** *person* 78 **ther as God lust gyve it of his myght,** *only where God wants to give it through his strength* 79 **mayde,** *virgin* 81 **wolde,** *wants,* **swich,** *such* 82 **Al nys but,** *it is nothing except,* **conseil,** *counsel* 83 **yaf me leve,** *gave me permission* 84 **repreve,** *disgrace* 85 **make,** *mate* 86 **excepcioun of,** *criticism for* 87 **Al were it,** *although it is* 89 **bothe fyr and tow t'assemble,** *bring together fire and tinder* 91 **al and som,** *the sum total* 92 **parfit,** *perfect,* **freletee,** *weakness* 93 **clepe I,** *I call it,* **but if that,** *unless* 94 **Wolde leden,** *would lead,* **hir,** *their* 96 **preferre bigamye,** *be considered better than remarrying* 97 **Hem liketh,** (it) *pleases them* (virgins), **goost,** *spirit* 98 **estaat,** *status,* **nyl nat,** *will not* 100 **nath nat,** *has not* 101 **tree,** *wood,* **doon hir,** *do their* 102 **clepeth,** *calls,* **sondry**

wyse, *many ways* 103 **everich,** *each one* 104 **hym liketh shifte,** (it) *pleases God to ordain* 106 **continence,** *self-restraint* 107 **welle,** *the source* 108 **Bad nat,** *did not command,* **wight,** *person* 110 **swich wise,** *such a way,* **foore,** *footsteps* 112 **by youre leve,** *with your permission* 113 **wol bistowe,** *will give,* **flour,** *best part,* **age,** *life* 115 **conclusioun,** *purpose* 116 **membres ymaad of generacioun,** *sexual organs made* 119 **Glose whoso wole,** *interpret whoever wants* (to), **bothe up and doun,** *in every way* 121 **bothe thynges smale,** *the small things of both* (genders) 124 **woot,** *knows* 125 **wrothe,** *angry* 126 **beth maked,** *were made* 127 **office,** *service* (excretion) 128 **engendrure,** *procreation,* **ther,** *where* 129 **elles,** *otherwise* 130 **yelde,** *yield* 131 **wherwith,** *with what,* **paiement,** *payment* 132 **ne used,** *did not use* 135 **holde,** *obligated* 136 **That,** *who,* **swich harneys,** *such equipment* 138 **cure,** *care* 139 **mayde,** *virgin*

84 **Of indulgence,** by concession; from 1 Corinthians 7.6 (*indulgentium*); Jerome 1.8. 87 **womman . . . touche,** from 1 Corinthians 7.1; Jerome 1.7. 100 **every vessel . . . ,** Paul distinguishes between vessels of gold and wood in 2 Timothy 2.20; Jerome 1.40. 103 **propre yifte,** special gift; from 1 Corinthians 7.7; Jerome 1.8. 107–11 From Matthew 19.21; Jerome 1.34. 113–14 Echoes *RR* 11453–56. 117 "And by so wise a Being created," although the MSS have various readings. Jerome asks the same question but argues that the existence of sexual organs does not mean that we must use them for sex. 127–28 Critics point out that we have no evidence whether or not the Wife has borne children. 130 **hire dette,** the marital obligation (or debt) of intercourse. From Lat. *debitum,* 1 Corinthians 7.3; Jerome 1.7. 132 **sely,** triple meaning: silly, innocent, blessed.

And many a seint° sith that the world bigan, 140
Yet lyved they evere in parfit chastitee.
I nyl nat° envye no virginitee.
Lat hem be breed° of pured whete seed°,
And lat us wyves hoten° barly-breed;
And yet with barly-breed, Mark telle kan, 145
Oure Lord Jhesu refresshed many a man.
In swich estaat° as God hath cleped° us
I wol persevere; I nam nat precius°.
In wyfhode I wol use myn instrument
As frely as my Makere hath it sent. 150
If I be daungerous°, God yeve° me sorwe.
Myn housbonde shal it have bothe eve and morwe°,
Whan that hym list° com forth and paye his dette°.
An housbonde I wol have, I nyl nat lette°,
Which° shal be bothe my dettour° and
      my thral°, 155
And have his tribulacioun withal°
Upon his flessh whil that I am his wyf.
I have the power durynge al my lyf
Upon his propre body, and noght he.
Right thus the Apostel° tolde it unto me, 160
And bad° oure housbondes for to love us weel°.
Al this sentence me liketh° every deel°—

      Up stirte° the PARDONER, and that anon°:
"Now, dame," quod he, "by God and by Seint John,
Ye been° a noble prechour° in this cas. 165
I was aboute to wedde a wyf. Allas,
What° sholde I bye° it on my flessh so deere°?
Yet hadde I levere° wedde no wyf to-yeere°."
      "Abyde," quod she, "my tale is nat bigonne.
Nay, thou shalt drynken of another tonne 170
Er° that I go, shal savoure wors° than ale.
And whan that I have toold thee forth my tale

Of tribulacioun in mariage,
Of which I am expert in al myn age—
This is to seyn, myself have been the
      whippe— 175
Than maystow chese° wheither thou wolt sippe
Of thilke tonne° that I shal abroche°.
Be war of it, er thou to ny° approche,
For I shal telle ensamples mo° than ten.
'Whoso that nyl be war by° othere men, 180
By hym shul othere men corrected be.'
The same wordes writeth Ptholomee;
Rede in his Almageste and take it there."
      "Dame, I wolde praye yow, if youre wyl it were,"
Seyde this Pardoner, "as ye bigan, 185
Telle forth youre tale; spareth° for no man,
And teche us yonge men of youre praktike°."
      "Gladly," quod she, "sith it may yow like°.
But yet I praye to al this compaignye
If that I speke after my fantasye° 190
As taketh not agrief of that° I seye,
For myn entente nys° but for to pleye."

      Now, sire, now wol I telle forth my tale:
As evere moote I° drynken wyn or ale,
I shal seye sooth°, of tho° housbondes that I
      hadde, 195
As thre of hem were goode, and two were badde.
The thre men were goode, and riche, and olde.
Unnethe° myghte they the statut holde
In which that they were bounden unto me.
Ye woot° wel what I meene of this, pardee°. 200
As help me God, I laughe whan I thynke
How pitously a-nyght° I made hem swynke°!
And, by my fey°, I tolde of it no stoor°;
They had me yeven hir° lond and hir tresoor.

---

140 seint, *saint* **142 nyl nat,** *will not* **143 breed,** *bread,* **pured whete seed,** *refined wheat grain* **144 hoten,** *be called* **147 swich estaat,** *such condition,* **cleped,** *called* **148 precius,** *valuable* or *fussy* **151 daungerous,** *standoffish,* **yeve,** *give* **152 morwe,** *morning* **153 hym list,** *it pleases him,* **dette,** *debt* **154 nyl nat lette,** *will not stop* **155 Which,** *who,* **dettour,** *debtor,* **thral,** *servant* **156 withal,** *as well* **160 the Apostel,** *St. Paul* **161 bad,** *ordered,* **weel,** *well* **162 sentence me liketh,** *message pleases me,* **deel,** *bit* **163 stirte,** *started,* **anon,** *quickly* **165 Ye been,** *you are,* **prechour,** *preacher* **167 What,** *why,* **bye,** *pay for,* **deere,** *dearly* **168 Yet hadde I levere,** *I would rather,* **to-yeere,** *this year* **171 Er,** *before,*

savoure wors, *taste worse* **176 maystow chese,** *may you choose* **177 thilke tonne,** *that cask,* **abroche,** *tap* **178 to ny,** *too near* **179 mo,** *more* **180 Whoso that nyl be war by,** *whoever will not be made wary by* (the examples of) **186 spareth,** *stop* **187 praktike,** *practice* **188 sith it may yow like,** *since it may please you* **190 after my fantasye,** *in accord with my whims* **191 As taketh not agrief of that,** *don't be grieved by what* **192 nys,** *is not* **194 As evere moote I,** *as I might ever* **195 seye sooth,** *tell the truth,* **tho,** *those* **198 Unnethe,** *barely* **200 Ye woot,** *you know,* **pardee,** *by God* **202 a-nyght,** *at night,* **hem swynke,** *them work* **203 fey,** *faith,* **tolde . . . no stoor,** *took no account* **204 yeven hir,** *given their*

---

144 barly-breed, bread made from coarse rather than fine grain. The reference to **Mark** (line 145) is incorrect, since only John's gospel records how Jesus used barley loaves (and fishes) to feed the multitude. Comparison of wheat and barley as degrees of perfection echoes Jerome 1.7. **156 tribulacioun,** tribulation; the word comes from 1 Corinthians 7.28; Jerome 1.13. **158–59** From 1 Corinthians 7.4; Jerome 1.7. **161 bad oure housbondes,** from Ephesians 5.25; Jerome 1.16. **170 drynken of another tonne,** drink from another wine cask; metaphor for "get worse treatment from me." The image is used of fortune in *RR* 6762ff. and elsewhere. **182–83 Ptholomee . . . Almageste,** although not in the Greek original, this proverb and the one at line 326 are in the preface of the 1515 Venice edition of the *Almagest,* a treatise by the classical astrologer Ptolemy. **198 statut,** obligation; see marital debt at lines 130 and 153 above.

Me neded nat do lenger diligence° 205
To wynne hir love, or doon hem° reverence.
They loved me so wel, by God above,
That I ne tolde no deyntee of° hir love.
A wys womman wol sette hire evere in oon°
To gete hire love, ye, ther as° she hath noon. 210
But sith° I hadde hem hoolly° in myn hond,
And sith they hadde me yeven al hir lond,
What° sholde I taken heede hem° for to plese
But° it were for my profit and myn ese?
I sette hem so a-werke°, by my fey, 215
That many a nyght they songen° "weilawey."
The bacon was nat fet for hem, I trowe°,
That som men han° in Essex at Dunmowe.
I governed hem so wel, after my lawe,
That ech of hem ful blisful was and fawe° 220
To brynge me gaye thynges fro the fayre°.
They were ful glad whan I spak to hem faire,
For, God it woot°, I chidde hem spitously°.
   Now herkneth hou° I baar me° proprely,
Ye wise wyves, that kan understonde. 225
Thus shul ye speke and bere hem wrong on
    honde,
For half so boldely kan ther no man
Swere and lyen as a womman kan.
I sey nat this by° wyves that been wyse,
But° if it be whan they hem mysavyse°. 230
A wys wyf, if that she kan hir good°,
Shal beren hym on hond the cow is wood,
And take witnesse of hir owene mayde
Of hir assent°. But herkneth how I sayde:
   Sire olde kaynard°, is this thyn array? 235
Why is my neighebores wyf so gay°?
She is honoured over al ther° she gooth;
I sitte at hoom; I have no thrifty clooth°.
What dostow° at my neighebores hous?

Is she so fair? Artow° so amorous? 240
What rowne° ye with oure mayde, benedicite°?
Sire olde lecchour, lat thy japes° be.
And if I have a gossib° or a freend
Withouten gilt, thou chidest as a feend
If that I walke or pleye unto his hous. 245
Thou comest hoom as dronken as a mous
And prechest on thy bench with yvel preef°.
Thou seist° to me it is a greet meschief
To wedde a poure womman for costage°;
And if that she be riche, of heigh parage°, 250
Thanne seistow that it is a tormentrie°
To suffren hire pride and hire malencolie°.
And if that she be fair, thou verray knave°,
Thou seyst° that every holour° wol hire have;
She may no while in chastitee abyde° 255
That is assailled upon ech a° syde.
   Thou seyst som folk desire us for richesse,
Somme for oure shap, and somme for oure
    fairnesse,
And som for she kan synge and daunce,
And som for gentillesse° and daliaunce°, 260
Som for hir handes and hir armes smale°—
Thus goth al to the devel, by thy tale°.
Thou seyst men may nat kepe° a castel wal
It may so longe assailed been over al°.
   And if that she be foul°, thou seist that
    she 265
Coveiteth° every man that she may se,
For as a spaynel° she wol on hym lepe
Til that she fynde som man hire to chepe°.
Ne noon so grey goos gooth° ther in the lake
As, seistow, wol been withoute make°. 270
And seyst it is an hard thyng for to welde°
A thyng that no man wole, his thankes, helde°.
Thus seistow, lorel°, whan thow goost to bedde,

---

205 **do lenger diligence,** *make more effort* 206 **doon hem,** *show them* 208 **tolde no deyntee of,** *placed no value on* 209 **evere in oon,** *constantly* 210 **ther as,** *where* 211 **sith,** *since,* **hem hoolly,** *them completely* 213 **What,** *why,* **taken heede hem,** *pay attention them* 214 **But,** *unless* 215 **a-werke,** *to working* 216 **songen,** *sang* 217 **trowe,** *trust* 218 **han,** *have* 220 **fawe,** *eager* 221 **fro the fayre,** *from the fair* 223 **woot,** *knows,* **chidde hem spitously,** *scolded them spitefully* 224 **hou,** *how,* **baar me,** *bore myself* 229 **by,** *about* 230 **But,** *except,* **hem mysavyse,** *mistake themselves* 231 **kan hir good,** *knows what's good for her* 234 **hir assent,** *(the maid's) agreement* 235 **kaynard,** *sluggard* 236 **gay,** *gaily dressed* 237 **over al ther,** *wherever* 238 **thrifty clooth,** *appropriate clothes* 239

dostow, *do you do* 240 **Artow,** *are you* 241 **rowne,** *whisper,* **benedicite,** *bless us* 242 **japes,** *jokes* 243 **gossib,** *confidant* 247 **yvel preef,** *inaccurate evidence* 248 **seist,** *say* 249 **costage,** *expense* 250 **heigh parage,** *high lineage* 251 **tormentrie,** *torment* 252 **malencolie,** *sullenness* 253 **verray knave,** *absolute villain* 254 **seyst,** *say,* **holour,** *lecher* 255 **abyde,** *remain* 256 **ech a,** *every* 260 **gentillesse,** *courtesy,* **daliaunce,** *small talk* 261 **smale,** *slender* 262 **tale,** *account* 263 **kepe,** *defend* 264 **over al,** *in every way* 265 **foul,** *ugly* 266 **Coveiteth,** *lusts for* 267 **spaynel,** *spaniel* 268 **hire to chepe,** *to buy her* 269 **Ne noon so grey goos gooth,** *nor is there any gray goose (that) goes* 270 **make,** *mate* 271 **welde,** *control* 272 **wole, his thankes, helde** *wishes, willingly, to hold* 273 **lorel,** *wretch*

---

217 **bacon was nat fet,** bacon was not fetched; at Dunmow in Essex (southeastern England) and other places, a married couple who had not quarreled for a year could claim a side of bacon as reward. 226 **bere hem wrong on honde,** an idiom meaning "accuse them wrongfully." 232 **beren hym . . . cow is wood,** make him think the chough (a talking bird) is crazy, an allusion to a folk tale in which a bird tattles on his mistress—the plot of the *ManT*. 235–378 Most of the details here derive from well-known antifeminist material, based on Theophrastus, preserved in Jerome 1.47, and popularized by Matheolus, LeFèvre, *RR*, and Deschamps.

And that no wys man nedeth for to wedde,
Ne no° man that entendeth unto° hevene—   275
With wilde thonder-dynt° and firy levene°
Moote° thy welked nekke° be tobroke°!
　　Thow seyst that droppyng° houses and eek
　　　smoke
And chidyng wyves maken men to flee
Out of hir owene° hous—a, benedicitee°!   280
What eyleth swich° an old man for to chide?
　　Thow seyst we wyves wol oure vices hide
Til we be fast°, and thanne we wol hem shewe°—
Wel may that be a proverbe of a shrewe°!
　　Thou seist that oxen, asses, hors°, and
　　　houndes,   285
They been assayed° at diverse stoundes°;
Bacyns°, lavours°, er° that men hem bye,
Spoones and stooles, and al swich housbondrye°,
And so been pottes, clothes, and array°;
But folk of wyves maken noon assay,   290
Til they be wedded—olde dotard shrewe°!
Thanne, seistow, we wol oure vices shewe.
　　Thou seist also that it displeseth me
But if that thou wolt preyse my beautee,
And but thou poure° alwey upon my face   295
And clepe° me "faire dame" in every place,
And but thou make a feeste° on thilke day
That I was born, and make me fressh and gay,
And but thou do to my norice° honour,
And to my chamberere° withinne my bour°,   300
And to my fadres° folk and his allyes°—
Thus seistow, olde barelful of lyes°!
　　And yet of oure apprentice Janekyn,
For° his crisp° heer, shynynge as gold so fyn,
And for he squiereth° me bothe up and doun,   305
Yet hastow° caught a fals suspecioun.
I wol° hym noght, thogh thou were deed
　　tomorwe.

But tel me, why hydestow with sorwe°
The keyes of thy cheste awey fro me?
It is my good as wel as thyn, pardee°.   310
What, wenestow° to make an ydiot of oure dame?
Now by that lord that called is Seint Jame,
Thou shalt nat bothe, thogh that thou were
　　wood°,
Be maister of my body and of my good°;
That oon° thou shalt forgo, maugree thyne
　　eyen.   315
What needeth thee of me to enquere or spyen?
I trowe thou woldest loke° me in thy chiste°.
Thou sholdest seye, "Wyf, go where thee liste°;
Taak° youre disport°, I wol nat leve no talys°.
I knowe yow for a trewe wyf, dame Alys°."   320
We love no man that taketh kepe° or charge°
Wher that we goon; we wol ben at oure large°.
　　Of alle men yblessed moot° he be,
The wise astrologien°, daun Ptholome,
That seith this proverbe in his Almageste,   325
"Of alle men his wysdom is the hyeste°
That rekketh° nevere who hath the world in
　　honde°."
By this proverbe thou shalt understonde,
Have thou ynogh°, what thar thee recche°
　　or care
How myrily° that othere folkes fare?   330
For certeyn, olde dotard°, by youre leve,
Ye shul have queynte° right ynogh at eve.
He is to greet° a nygard° that wolde werne°
A man to lighte a candle at his lanterne;
He shal have never the lasse° light, pardee°.   335
Have thou ynogh, thee thar nat pleyne thee°.
Thou seyst also that if we make us gay
With clothyng and with precious array
That it is peril of° oure chastitee;
And yet with sorwe°, thou most enforce thee°,   340

275 **Ne no,** *nor* (does any), **entendeth unto,** *intends to go to* 276 **thonder-dynt,** *thunderclap,* **levene,** *lightning* 277 **Moote,** *may,* **welked nekke,** *withered neck,* **tobroke,** *completely broken* 278 **droppyng,** *leaking* 280 **hir owene,** *their own,* **a, benedicitee,** *ah, bless us* 281 **eyleth swich,** *ails such* 283 **fast,** *secure* (married), **wol hem shewe,** *will reveal them* 284 **shrewe,** *villain* 285 **hors,** *horses* 286 **assayed,** *tested,* **diverse stoundes,** *various times* 287 **Bacyns,** *basins,* **lavours,** *washbowls,* **er,** *before* 288 **swich housbondrye,** *such household items* 289 **array,** *equipment* 291 **dotard shrewe,** *senile villain* 295 **poure,** *gaze* 296 **clepe,** *call* 297 **feeste,** *celebration,* **thilke,** *that* 299 **norice,** *nurse* 300 **chamberere,** *chambermaid,* **bour,** *bedroom* 301 **fadres,** *father's,* **allyes,** *relatives* 302 **lyes,** *dregs or lies* 304 **For,** *because of,* **crisp,** *curled* 305 **squiereth,** *accompanies* 306 **hastow,** *have you* 307 **wol,** *want* 308 **hydestow with**

sorwe, *do you hide with such great care* 310 **pardee,** *by God* 311 **wenestow,** *do you think* 313 **wood,** *enraged* 314 **good,** *possessions* 315 **oon,** *one* 317 **loke,** *lock,* **chiste,** *strongbox* 318 **thee liste,** *you wish* 319 **Taak,** *take,* **disport,** *pleasure,* **nat leve no talys,** *not believe any reports* 320 **Alys,** *Alice* 321 **kepe,** *care,* **charge,** *responsibility* 322 **wol ben at oure large,** *will be free* 323 **yblessed moot,** *blessed may* 324 **astrologien,** *astronomer* 326 **hyeste,** *highest* 327 **rekketh,** *cares,* **honde,** *control* 329 **Have thou ynogh,** (if) *you have enough,* **what thar thee recche,** *why concern yourself* 330 **myrily,** *happily* 331 **dotard,** *fool* 332 **queynte,** *vagina* 333 **to greet,** *too great,* **nygard,** *miser,* **werne,** *refuse* 335 **lasse,** *less,* **pardee,** *by God* 336 **thee thar nat pleyne thee,** *you shouldn't complain* 339 **peril of,** *a threat to* 340 **sorwe,** *trouble,* **enforce thee,** *belabor yourself*

278–80 The often repeated comparison of wives and leaky houses derives from Proverbs 27.15; see *Mel* 7.1086 and *ParsT* 10.631. **311 oure dame,** the Wife is referring to herself as the lady of the house. **312 Seint Jame,** St. James; two apostles were named James. **315 maugree thyne eyen,** despite your eyes; an idiom meaning something like "regardless of what you think." **324–25 Ptholome . . . Almageste,** see 182–83n above.

And seye this wordes in the Apostles name,
"In habit maad° with chastitee and shame
Ye wommen shul apparaille yow°," quod he,
"And noght in tressed° heer and gay perree°,
As° perles, ne with gold, ne clothes riche."   345
After thy text, ne after thy rubriche,
I wol nat wirche° as muchel° as a gnat.

   Thou seydest this, that I was lyk a cat;
For whoso° wolde senge° a cattes skyn
Thanne wolde the cat wel dwellen in his in°,   350
And if the cattes skyn be slyk° and gay
She wol nat dwelle in house half a day,
But forth she wole°, er° any day be dawed°,
To shewe hir skyn and goon a-caterwawed°.
This is to seye, if I be gay, sire shrewe°,   355
I wol renne° out my borel° for to shewe.

   Sire olde fool, what helpeth thee° to spyen?
Thogh thou preye° Argus with his hundred eyen
To be my warde-cors°, as he kan best,
In feith, he shal nat kepe° me but me lest°;   360
Yet koude I make his berd°, so moot I thee°!

   Thou seydest eek that ther been thynges thre
The whiche thynges troublen al this erthe,
And that no wight° may endure the ferthe°—
O leeve sire shrewe°, Jhesu shorte° thy lyf!   365
Yet prechestow° and seyst an hateful wyf
Yrekened is for oon° of thise meschances.
Been° ther none othere maner resemblances
That ye may likne° youre parables to,
But if° a sely° wyf be oon of tho°?   370

   Thou liknest° eek wommenes love to helle,
To bareyne lond°, ther° water may nat dwelle.

   Thou liknest it also to wilde fyr,
The moore it brenneth°, the moore it hath
   desir
To consume every thyng that brent wole be°.   375

Thou seyest, right as° wormes shende° a tree,
Right so a wyf destroyeth hire housbonde;
This knowe they that been to wyves bonde.

   Lordynges, right thus, as ye have understonde,
Baar I stifly myne olde housbondes on
   honde°   380
That thus they seyden in hir dronknesse—
And al was fals, but° that I took witnesse
On Janekyn and on my nece° also.
O Lord, the peyne I dide hem and the wo,
Ful giltelees, by Goddes° sweete pyne°!   385
For as an hors I koude byte° and whyne°.
I koude pleyne°, thogh I were in the gilt,
Or elles° often tyme hadde I been spilt°.
Whoso comth first to mille, first grynt°;
I pleyned first, so was oure werre ystynt°.   390
They were ful glad to excuse hem blyve°
Of thyng of which they nevere agilte hir lyve°.

   Of wenches wolde I beren hym on honde°,
Whan that for syk° unnethes° myghte he stonde.
Yet tikled it° his herte, for that he   395
Wende° that I hadde of hym so greet chiertee°.
I swoor that al my walkynge out by nyghte
Was for t'espye wenches that he dighte°.
Under that colour° hadde I many a myrthe°.
For al swich° wit is yeven us° in oure byrthe: 400
Deceite, wepyng, spynnyng God hath yeve
To wommen kyndely° whil that they may lyve.
And thus of o° thyng I avaunte me°,
Atte° ende I hadde the bettre in ech degree°,
By sleighte° or force, or by som maner thyng,   405
As by continueel murmur or grucchyng°.
Namely abedde° hadden they meschaunce°.
Ther wolde I chide° and do hem no plesaunce;
I wolde no lenger in the bed abyde°
If that I felte his arm over my syde   410

---

342 habit maad, *clothes made* **343 apparaille yow,** *dress yourselves* **344 tressed,** *arranged,* **perree,** *jewels* **345 As,** *(such) as* **347 wirche,** *work,* **muchel,** *much* **349 whoso,** *whoever,* **senge,** *singe* **350 in his in,** *in his house* **351 slyk,** *sleek* **353 wole,** *will (go),* **er,** *before,* **dawed,** *dawned* **354 goon a-caterwawed,** *gone caterwauling* **355 sire shrewe,** *sir villain* **356 renne,** *run,* **borel,** *cloth* **357 helpeth thee,** *good does it do you* **358 preye,** *ask* **359 warde-cors,** *bodyguard* **360 kepe,** *guard,* **but me lest,** *unless I wish* **361 make his berd,** *deceive him,* **moot I thee,** *might I prosper* **364 wight,** *person,* **ferthe,** *fourth* **365 leeve sire shrewe,** *dear sir villain,* **shorte,** *shorten* **366 prechestow,** *you preach* **367 Yrekened is for oon,** *is considered one* **368 Been,** *are* **369 likne,** *compare* **370 But if,** *unless,* **sely,** *innocent,* **oon of those,** *one of them* **371 liknest,** *compare* **372 bareyne lond,** *barren land,* **ther,** *where* **374 brenneth,** *burns* **375 brent**

wole be, *can be burned* **376 right as,** *just as,* **shende,** *destroys* **380 Baar I stifly . . . on honde,** *I strongly accused* **382 but,** *except* **383 nece,** *female relative* **385 Goddes,** *God's,* **pyne,** *pain* **386 koude byte,** *could bite,* **whyne,** *whinny* **387 pleyne,** *complain* **388 elles,** *else,* **spilt,** *ruined* **389 grynt,** *grinds* **390 werre ystynt,** *war stopped* **391 blyve,** *quickly* **392 agilte hir lyve,** *(were) guilty in their lives* **393 beren hym on honde,** *accuse him* **394 syk,** *sickness,* **unnethes,** *barely* **395 tikled it,** *it pleased* **396 Wende,** *thought,* **chiertee,** *love* **398 dighte,** *had sex with* **399 colour,** *pretense,* **myrthe,** *happy time* **400 swich,** *such,* **yeven us,** *given us (women)* **402 kyndely,** *by nature* **403 o,** *one,* **avaunte me,** *boast* **404 Atte,** *at the,* **ech degree,** *each respect* **405 sleighte,** *trickery* **406 grucchyng,** *complaining* **407 abedde,** *in bed,* **meschaunce,** *bad luck* **408 chide,** *scold* **409 abyde,** *remain*

---

341 the Apostles name, St. Paul's name; the quotation that follows is from 1 Timothy 2.9; Jerome 1.27. **346 After thy text . . . rubriche,** to follow neither your text nor your rubrics (words written in red for emphasis). **349–54 cattes skyn . . . ,** cat's skin; a proverbial figure. **358 Argus,** mythic watchman who is deceived by Io despite his one hundred eyes; Ovid, *Metamorphoses* 1.625. **362–64 thynges thre . . . ,** from Proverbs 30.21–23; Jerome 1.28. **371–78 wommenes love . . . ,** from Proverbs 30.16 and a version of Proverbs 25.20; Jerome 1.28.

Til he had maad his raunsoun unto me°;
Thanne wolde I suffre hym do° his nycetee°.
And therfore every man this tale I telle,
Wynne whoso° may, for al is for to selle;
With empty hand men may none haukes° lure. 415
For wynnyng wolde I° al his lust endure
And make me a feyned° appetit—
And yet in bacon° hadde I nevere delit.
That made me that evere I wolde hem chide;
For thogh the pope hadde seten hem biside°, 420
I wolde nat spare hem at hir owene bord°,
For, by my trouthe, I quitte° hem word for word.
As helpe me verray° God omnipotent,
Though I right now sholde make my testament°,
I ne owe hem nat a word that it nys quit°. 425
I broghte it so aboute by my wit
That they moste yeve° it up as for the beste,
Or elles hadde we nevere been in reste.
For thogh he looked as a wood leoun°,
Yet sholde he faille of his conclusioun°. 430

  Thanne wolde I seye, "Goode lief°, taak keep°,
How mekely° looketh Wilkyn°, oure sheep!
Com neer°, my spouse, lat me ba° thy cheke!
Ye sholde been al pacient and meke,
And han° a sweete spiced conscience, 435
Sith° ye so preche of Jobes pacience.
Suffreth alwey, syn° ye so wel kan preche;
And but° ye do, certein we shal yow teche
That it is fair° to have a wyf in pees°.
Oon of us two moste bowen°, douteless, 440
And sith a man is moore resonable
Than womman is, ye moste been suffrable°.
What eyleth° yow to grucche° thus and grone?
Is it for ye wolde have my queynte° allone?
Wy°, taak it al—lo, have it every deel°. 445
Peter, I shrewe° yow, but° ye love it weel.

For if I wolde selle my bele chose,
I koude walke as fressh as is a rose,
But I wol kepe it for youre owene tooth°.
Ye be to blame, by God, I sey yow sooth°." 450
  Swiche manere° wordes hadde we on honde.
Now wol I speken of my fourthe housbonde.
  My fourthe housbonde was a revelour°—
This is to seyn, he hadde a paramour°,
And I was yong and ful of ragerye°, 455
Stibourne° and strong, and joly as a pye°.
Wel koude I daunce to an harpe smale,
And synge, ywis°, as any nyghtyngale,
Whan I had dronke a draughte of sweete wyn.
Metellius, the foule cherl°, the swyn°, 460
That with a staf birafte° his wyf hir lyf
For she drank wyn, thogh I hadde been his wyf,
He sholde nat han daunted° me fro drynke!
And after wyn on Venus moste° I thynke,
For al so siker° as cold engendreth hayl°, 465
A likerous mouth moste han a likerous tayl.
In wommen vinolent° is no defence—
This knowen lecchours by experience.
  But, Lord Crist, whan that it remembreth me°
Upon my yowthe and on my jolitee, 470
It tikleth° me about myn herte roote°.
Unto this day it dooth myn herte boote°
That I have had my world as in my tyme.
But age, allas, that al wole envenyme°,
Hath me biraft° my beautee and my pith°. 475
Lat go, farewel, the devel go therwith!
The flour is goon, ther is namoore to telle;
The bren°, as I best kan, now moste I selle;
But yet to be right myrie wol I fonde°.
Now wol I tellen of my fourthe housbonde. 480
  I seye, I hadde in herte greet despit°
That he of any oother had delit.

---

411 **maad his raunsoun unto me,** *paid me* 412 **suffre hym do,** *allow him to do,* **nycetee,** *foolishness* 414 **whoso,** *whoever* 415 **none haukes,** *no hawks* 416 **For wynnyng wolde I,** *in order to profit I would* 417 **feyned,** *pretended* 418 **bacon,** *preserved meat* 420 **seten hem biside,** *sat beside them* 421 **hir owene bord,** *their own table* 422 **quitte,** *repaid* 423 **verray,** *true* 424 **testament,** *will* 425 **nys quit,** *isn't repaid* 427 **yeve,** *give* 429 **wood leoun,** *enraged lion* 430 **faille of his conclusioun,** *fail to get his goal* 431 **Goode lief,** *dearest,* **taak keep,** *take heed* 432 **mekely,** *meekly,* **Wilkyn,** *Willie* 433 **neer,** *nearer,* **ba,** *kiss* 435 **han,** *have* 436 **Sith,** *since* 437 **syn,** *since* 438 **but,** *unless* 439 **fair,** *well,* **pees,** *peace* 440 **moste bowen,** *must bend* 442 **suffrable,** *accepting* 443 **eyleth,** *ails,* **grucche,** *complain* 444 **queynte,** *vagina* 445 **Wy,** *why,* **every deel,** *completely* 446 **Peter,** *by St. Peter,* **shrewe,** *curse,* **but,** *unless* 449 **owene tooth,** *own taste* 450 **sey yow sooth,** *tell you truly* 451 **Swiche manere,** *such kinds of* 453 **revelour,** *pleasure seeker* 454 **paramour,** *mistress* 455 **ragerye,** *high spirits* 456 **Stibourne,** *stubborn,* **pye,** *magpie* 458 **ywis,** *surely* 460 **cherl,** *lowlifer,* **swyn,** *pig* 461 **birafte,** *deprived* 463 **han daunted,** *have scared* 464 **moste,** *must* 465 **al so siker,** *as certainly,* **engendreth hayl,** *produces hail* 467 **vinolent,** *drunken* 469 **it remembreth me,** *I remember* 471 **tikleth,** *pleases,* **about myn herte roote,** *to the bottom of my heart* 472 **boote,** *good* 474 **al wole envenyme,** *will poison all* 475 **me biraft,** *deprived me* (of), **pith,** *strength* 478 **bren,** *bran* 479 **fonde,** *strive* 481 **despit,** *resentment*

---

435 sweete spiced conscience, a difficult phrase that seems to mean "tender adaptable sensibility." **436 Jobes pacience,** Job's patience is proverbial, deriving from the biblical book of Job. **447 bele chose,** French for "pretty thing," a sexual euphemism to match the English euphemism at line 444 and the Latin one at line 608. **460 Metellius,** killed his wife with his staff because she had been drinking; recorded in a medieval schoolbook, the *Memorabilium Exempla* of Valerius Maximus. Chaucer cites materials from the same chapter (6.3) at lines 643 and 647 below. **466 likerous mouth . . . likerous tayl,** gluttony produces lechery, with play on *liquorous* and *lecherous*.

But he was quit°, by God and by Seint Joce.
I made hym of the same wode a croce°—
Nat of my body, in no foul manere, 485
But certeinly, I made folk swich cheere°
That in his owene grece° I made hym frye
For angre, and for verray jalousye.
By God, in erthe I was his purgatorie,
For which I hope his soule be in glorie. 490
For, God it woot°, he sat ful ofte and song°
Whan that his shoo ful bitterly hym wrong.
There was no wight save° God and he that wiste°,
In many wise°, how soore° I hym twiste°.
He deyde° whan I cam fro Jerusalem, 495
And lith ygrave° under the roode beem,
Al is his tombe° noght so curyus°
As was the sepulcre° of hym Daryus,
Which that Appelles wroghte subtilly;
It nys but wast° to burye hym preciously°. 500
Lat hym fare wel; God yeve° his soule reste.
He is now in his grave and in his cheste°.

    Now of my fifthe housbonde wol I telle.
God lete his soule nevere come in helle—
And yet was he to me the mooste shrewe°; 505
That feele I on my ribbes al by rewe°,
And evere shal unto myn endyng day.
But in oure bed he was so fresshe and gay,
And therwithal° so wel koude he me glose°,
Whan that he wolde han my bele chose°, 510
That thogh he hadde me bet° on every bon,
He koude wynne agayn my love anon°.
I trowe° I loved hym best for that he
Was of his love daungerous° to me.
We wommen han°, if that I shal nat lye, 515
In this matere a queynte fantasye°:
Wayte what° thyng we may nat lightly° have,

Therafter wol we crie al day and crave.
Forbede us thyng°, and that desiren we;
Preesse on° us faste, and thanne wol we fle°. 520
With daunger oute we° al oure chaffare°;
Greet prees° at market maketh deere ware°,
And to greet cheep° is holde at litel prys°.
This knoweth every womman that is wys.

    My fifthe housbonde—God his soule
      blesse— 525
Which that I took for love and no richesse,
He somtyme° was a clerk of Oxenford,
And hadde left scole°, and wente at hom to bord°
With my gossib°, dwellynge in oure toun—
God have hir soule—hir name was Alisoun; 530
She knew myn herte and eek my privetee°
Bet° than oure parisshe preest, so moot I thee°!
To hire biwreyed° I my conseil° al.
For hadde myn housbonde pissed on a wal,
Or doon a thyng that sholde han cost his lyf, 535
To hire, and to another worthy wyf,
And to my nece°, which that I loved weel,
I wolde han toold his conseil every deel°.
And so I dide ful often, God it woot°,
That made his face ful often reed and hoot 540
For verray shame, and blamed hymself for he
Had toold to me so greet a pryvetee.

    And so bifel that ones in a Lente—
So often tymes I to my gossyb wente,
For evere yet I loved to be gay, 545
And for to walke in March, Averill, and May,
Fro hous to hous, to heere sondry talys°—
That Jankyn clerk and my gossyb dame Alys
And I myself into the feeldes wente.
Myn housbonde was at Londoun al the Lente; 550
I hadde the bettre leyser° for to pleye,

---

483 quit, *repaid* **484 croce,** *stick or cross* **486 folk swich cheere,** (to) *people such a welcoming disposition* **487 owene grece,** *own grease* **491 woot,** *knows,* **song,** *sang* **493 wight save,** *person except,* **wiste,** *knew* **494 wise,** *ways,* **soore,** *sorely,* **twiste,** *tormented* **495 deyde,** *died* **496 lith ygrave,** *lies buried* **497 Al is his tombe,** *although his tomb is,* **curyus,** *ornate* **498 sepulcre,** *sepulcher* **500 nys but wast,** *is nothing but waste,* **preciously,** *expensively* **501 yeve,** *give* **502 cheste,** *coffin* **505 mooste shrewe,** *greatest villain* **506 by rewe,** *in a row* **509 therwithal,** *with that,* **glose,** *coax or interpret* **510 bele chose,** *pretty thing* (vagina) **511 bet,** *beat* **512 anon,** *quickly* **513 trowe,** *believe* **514 daungerous,** *standoffish*

515 han, *have* **516 queynte fantasye,** *strange desire* **517 Wayte what,** *observe whatever,* **lightly,** *easily* **519 Forbede us thyng,** *forbid us something* **520 Preesse on,** *pursue,* **fle,** *run* **521 daunger oute we,** *aloofness we put out,* **chaffare,** *merchandise* **522 prees,** *crowd,* **deere ware,** *expensive goods* **523 to greet cheep,** *too good a bargain,* **prys,** *value* **527 somtyme,** *for a while* **528 scole,** *school,* **bord,** *board* **529 gossib,** *friend* **531 privetee,** *secrets* **532 Bet,** *better,* **moot I thee,** *might I prosper* **532 biwreyed,** *revealed,* **conseil,** *confidences* **537 nece,** *female relative* **538 conseil every deel,** *secrets completely* **539 woot,** *knows* **547 heere sondry talys,** *hear various stories* **551 leyser,** *opportunity*

---

483 Seint Joce, St. Judocus, a Breton saint, whose emblem was a pilgrim's staff. **489 purgatorie,** place of punishment for sin, but purgatory was a common image for the pains of marriage. **492 shoo . . . hym wrong,** shoe wrung (or pinched) him, another common image for the pains of marriage. **495 fro Jerusalem,** in *GP* 1.463, it is said that the Wife went to Jerusalem on pilgrimage three times. **496 roode beem,** crossbeam; a special place to be buried in a church, under the beam upon which the crucifix is hung. **498–99 Daryus . . . Appelles,** an account of the splendid tomb of Darius, built by Appelles, is in Gautier de Chatillon's *Alexandreis.* **530 Alisoun,** a diminutive of Alice. The Wife (line 320) and her gossip have the same name, suggesting deep intimacy. **543 Lente,** the liturgical season of repentance that precedes Easter.

[handwritten margin note: "Its like shes on the prowl for husband #6?"]

And for to se, and eek for to be seye°
Of lusty° folk. What wiste I° wher my grace°
Was shapen° for to be, or in what place?
Therfore I made my visitaciouns   555
To vigilies and to processiouns,
To prechyng eek, and to thise pilgrimages,
To pleyes of myracles, and to mariages,
And wered upon° my gaye scarlet gytes°—
Thise wormes, ne thise motthes°, ne thise
   mytes°,   560
Upon my peril, frete° hem never a deel°;
And wostow° why? For they were used weel.
  Now wol I tellen forth what happed me.
I seye° that in the feeldes walked we,
Til trewely we hadde swich daliance°,   565
This clerk and I, that of my purveiance°
I spak to hym and seyde hym how that he,
If I were wydwe°, sholde wedde me.
For certeinly, I sey for no bobance°,
Yet was I nevere withouten purveiance   570
Of mariage, n'of° othere thynges eek.
I holde a mouses herte nat worth a leek
That hath but oon hole for to sterte° to,
And if that faille°, thanne is al ydo°.
  I bar hym on honde° he hadde enchanted
   me—   575
My dame° taughte me that soutiltee°.
And eek I seyde I mette° of hym al nyght:
He wolde han slayn me as I lay upright°,
And al my bed was ful of verray° blood,
But yet I hope that he shal do me good,   580
For blood bitokeneth° gold, as me was taught—
And al was fals; I dremed of it right naught°,
But I folwed ay my dames loore°,
As wel of this as of othere thynges moore.

But now, sire, lat me se, what I shal seyn°?   585
Aha, by God, I have my tale ageyn°!
  Whan that my fourthe housbonde was on
   beere°,
I weep algate° and made sory cheere°,
As wyves mooten° for it is usage°,
And with my coverchief covered my visage°;   590
But for that° I was purveyed of° a make°,
I wepte but smal°, and that I undertake°.
  To chirche was myn housbonde born a-morwe°
With neighebores that for hym maden sorwe,
And Jankyn oure clerk was oon of tho°.   595
As help me God, whan that I saugh° hym go
After the beere°, me thoughte he hadde a paire
Of legges and of feet so clene° and faire
That al myn herte I yaf° unto his hoold°.
He was, I trowe°, a twenty wynter° oold,   600
And I was fourty, if I shal seye sooth;
But yet I hadde alwey a coltes tooth.
Gat-tothed I was, and that bicam° me weel;
I hadde the prente of Seinte Venus seel.
As help me God, I was a lusty oon,   605
And faire and riche and yong and wel bigon°,
And trewely, as myne housbondes tolde me,
I hadde the beste quonyam myghte be.
For certes, I am al Venerien
In feelynge, and myn herte is Marcien.   610
Venus me yaf° my lust, my likerousnesse°,
And Mars yaf me my sturdy hardynesse°.
Myn ascendent was Taur, and Mars therinne—
Allas, allas, that evere love was synne!
I folwed ay° myn inclinacioun   615
By vertu of my constellacioun,
That made me I koude noght withdrawe°
My chambre of Venus° from a goode felawe.

---

552 be seye, *be seen* **553 Of lusty**, *by pleasant*, **What wiste I**, *how did I know what*, **grace**, *fortune* **554 shapen**, *destined* **559 wered upon**, *wore*, **gytes**, *gowns* **560 motthes**, *moths*, **mytes**, *insects* **561 frete**, *ate*, **never a deel**, *not a bit* **562 wostow**, *do you know* **564 seye**, *say* **565 daliance**, *flirting* **566 purveiance**, *foresight* **568 wydwe**, *widow* **569 bobance**, *boast* **571 n'of**, *nor of* **573 sterte**, *escape* **574 faille**, *fail*, **ydo**, *done* **575 bar hym on honde**, *convinced him* **576 dame**, *mother*, **soutiltee**, *subtlety* **577 mette**, *dreamed* **578 upright**, *on my back* **579 verray**, *actual* **581 bitokeneth**, *signifies* **582 right naught**, *not at all* **583 dames loore**, *mother's advice* **585 seyn**, *say* **586 ageyn**, *again*

587 beere, *bier* **588 algate**, *continuously*, **made sory cheere**, *acted sad* **589 mooten**, *must*, **usage**, *customary* **590 visage**, *face* **591 But for that**, *except because*, **purveyed of**, *provided with*, **make**, *mate* **592 smal**, *little*, **undertake**, *declare* **593 a-morwe**, *in the morning* **595 oon of tho**, *one of them* **596 saugh**, *saw* **597 After the beere**, *behind the bier* **598 clene**, *trim* **599 yaf**, *gave*, **hoold**, *possession* **600 trowe**, *think*, **wynter**, *years* **603 bicam**, *suited* **606 wel bigon**, *well situated* **611 me yaf**, *gave me*, **likerousnesse**, *sexuality* **612 hardynesse**, *boldness* **615 ay**, *always* **617 withdrawe**, *withhold* **618 chambre of Venus**, *vagina*

556 vigilies, vigils, services held before religious holidays. **558 pleyes of myracles,** popular religious dramas. **602 coltes tooth,** an idiom meaning "youthful desire"; see *RvP* 1.3888. **603 Gat-tothed,** gap-toothed, thought to indicate a bold, envious, suspicious, and perhaps sensuous nature; see *GP* 1.468. **604 prente of Seinte Venus seel,** a birthmark associated with Venus and sensuality. **608 quonyam,** Latin, meaning "because" or "whereas," a euphemism for vagina; see 447n above. **609–12** Lines not found in several important manuscripts, perhaps canceled by Chaucer or added late. **609–10 Venerien . . . Marcien,** under the influence of Venus (planet of love) and Mars (planet of war). **613 ascendent . . . therinne,** the constellation of Taurus (the Bull) was rising with Mars within when the Wife was born. **616 vertu of my constellacioun,** the power of my constellation; i.e., the Wife blames her inclinations on her horoscope.

Yet have I Martes mark upon my face,
And also in another privee° place.   620
For God so wys be my savacioun°,
I ne loved nevere by no discrecioun°,
But evere folwede myn appetit,
Al were he° short, or long, or blak, or whit;
I took no kepe°, so that° he liked° me,   625
How poore he was, ne eek° of what degree°.
    What sholde I seye but at the monthes
        ende
This joly clerk Jankyn that was so hende°
Hath wedded me with greet solempnytee,
And to hym yaf° I al the lond and fee°   630
That evere was me yeven° therbifoore—
But afterward repented me ful soore.
He nolde suffre° nothyng of my list°;
By God, he smoot° me ones° on the lyst°,
For that° I rente° out of his book a leef°,   635
That of the strook myn ere wax al deef°.
Stibourne° I was as is a leonesse,
And of my tonge a verray jangleresse°,
And walke I wolde, as I had doon biforn°,
From hous to hous, although he had it
        sworn°;   640
For which he often tymes wolde preche°,
And me of olde Romayn geestes° teche:
How he Symplicius Gallus lefte his wyf,
And hire forsook for terme of al his lyf°,
Noght but for open-heveded° he hir say°   645
Lokynge out at° his dore upon a day.
    Another Romayn tolde he me by name
That for° his wyf was at a someres game°
Withouten his wityng°, he forsook hire eke.

And thanne wolde he upon his Bible seke°   650
That ilke° proverbe of Ecclesiaste
Where he comandeth and forbedeth faste°
Man shal nat suffre° his wyf go roule° aboute.
Thanne wolde he seye right thus, withouten
        doute:
"Whoso that buyldeth his hous al of salwes°,   655
And priketh his blynde hors over the
        falwes°,
And suffreth° his wyf to go seken halwes°,
Is worthy to been hanged on the galwes°."
But al for noght; I sette° noght an hawe°
Of his proverbes n'of° his olde sawe°,   660
Ne I wolde nat of hym corrected be.
I hate hym that my vices telleth me,
And so doo mo°, God woot°, of us than I.
This made hym with me wood al outrely°.
I nolde noght forbere° hym in no cas.   665
    Now wol I seye yow sooth, by Seint
        Thomas,
Why that I rente° out of his book a leef°,
For which he smoot° me so that I was deef.
    He hadde a book that gladly, nyght and
        day,
For his desport° he wolde rede alway.   670
He cleped° it Valerie and Theofraste,
At which book he lough alwey ful faste°.
And eek ther was somtyme a clerk° at Rome,
A cardinal, that highte° Seint Jerome,
That made a book agayn Jovinian;   675
In which book eek ther was Tertulan,
Crisippus, Trotula, and Helowys,
That was abbesse nat fer fro Parys°;

---

620 privee, *private* **621 so wys be my savacioun,** *so certainly be my salvation* **622 discrecioun,** *thoughtful decision* **624 Al were he,** *although he was* **625 kepe,** *notice,* **so that,** *as long as,* **liked,** *pleased* **626 ne eek,** *nor also,* **degree,** *class* **628 hende,** *courteous* or *handy* **630 yaf,** *gave,* **fee,** *wealth* **631 yeven,** *given* **633 nolde suffre,** *wouldn't allow,* **list,** *desire* **634 smoot,** *hit,* **ones,** *once,* **lyst,** *ear* **635 For that,** *because,* **rente,** *tore,* **leef,** *page* **636 ere wax al deef,** *ear became deaf* **637 Stibourne,** *stubborn* **638 verray jangleresse,** *true loudmouth* **639 biforn,** *before* **640 sworn,** *forbidden* **641 preche,** *lecture* **642 geestes,** *stories* **644 terme of al his lyf,** *his entire life* **645 open-heveded,** *bareheaded,* **hir say,** *saw her* **646 at,**

of **648 for,** *because,* **someres game,** *summer celebration* **649 wityng,** *knowledge* **650 upon his Bible seke,** *look up in his Bible* **651 ilke,** *same* **652 faste,** *firmly* **653 suffre,** *allow,* **roule,** *roam* **655 salwes,** *willow sticks* **656 falwes,** *unused plowed fields* **657 suffreth,** *allows,* **seken halwes,** *seek shrines* **658 galwes,** *gallows* **659 sette,** *valued* (at), **hawe,** *hawthorn berry* **660 n'of,** *nor of,* **sawe,** *saying* **663 mo,** *more,* **woot,** *knows* **664 wood al outrely,** *utterly furious* **665 nolde noght forbere,** *would not put up with* **667 rente,** *tore,* **leef,** *page* **668 smoot,** *hit* **670 desport,** *enjoyment* **671 cleped,** *called* **672 ful faste,** *very loudly* **673 clerk,** *scholar* **674 highte,** *was called* **678 fer fro Parys,** *far from Paris*

619–26 Lines not found in several important manuscripts, perhaps canceled by Chaucer or added late. **619 Martes mark,** a birthmark associated with Mars or boldness. **636 deef,** see *GP* 1.446. **643 Symplicius Gallus,** Sulpicius Gallus divorced his wife for appearing without her kerchief on; see 460n above. **647 Another Romayn,** Sempronius Sophus divorced his wife because she went to games; see 460n above. **651 Ecclesiaste,** Ecclesiasticus, a book in the Catholic Bible; see Ecclesiasticus 25.34–35. **655–58** A familiar saying. **671 Valerie and Theofraste,** Walter Map's *Dissuasio Valerii ad Rufinum* (Valerius's Dissuasion of Rufinus) and Theophrastus's *Liber de Nuptiis* (Book of Marriage), the latter surviving in Jerome. More than sixty extant medieval manuscripts contain combinations of or selections from the antimatrimonial and antifeminist materials listed in lines 671–80. **674 cardinal,** an important church official; historically, Jerome was not a cardinal but was often represented as such. **675 book agayn Jovinian,** Jerome's *Epistola adversus Jovinianum* (Letter against Jovinian). **676 Tertulan,** Tertullian, a classical writer mentioned in Jerome, although not quoted in *WBP*. **677 Crisippus,** mentioned by Jerome but otherwise obscure. **Trotula,** a female physician and writer on gynecology. **Helowys,** Heloise, whose *Letters* record why she chose not to marry Peter Abelard.

And eek the Parables of Salomon,
Ovides Art, and bookes many on°.   680
And alle thise were bounden in o° volume,
And every nyght and day was his custume,
Whan he hadde leyser and vacacioun°
From oother worldly occupacioun,
To reden on this book of wikked wyves.   685
He knew of hem mo° legendes and lyves
Than been° of goode wyves in the Bible.
For trusteth wel, it is an inpossible°
That any clerk° wol speke good of wyves,
But if° it be of hooly seintes lyves,   690
Ne of noon oother womman never the mo.
Who peyntede the leon, tel me who?
By God, if wommen hadde writen stories,
As clerkes han withinne hire oratories°,
They wolde han writen of men moore
    wikkednesse   695
Than al the mark of Adam° may redresse°.
The children of Mercurie and of Venus
Been in hir wirkyng° ful contrarius°:
Mercurie loveth wysdam and science°,
And Venus loveth ryot° and dispence°,   700
And for hire° diverse disposicioun
Ech falleth in otheres exaltacioun.
And thus, God woot°, Mercurie is desolat
In Pisces wher Venus is exaltat,
And Venus falleth ther° Mercurie is reysed°.   705
Therfore no womman of° no clerk is preysed.
The clerk, whan he is oold and may noght do
Of Venus werkes worth his olde sho°,
Thanne sit he doun and writ in his dotage°

That wommen kan nat kepe hir mariage.   710
    But now to purpos°, why I tolde thee
That I was beten for a book, pardee°!
Upon a nyght Jankyn, that was oure sire°,
Redde on his book, as he sat by the fire,
Of Eva first, that for hir wikkednesse   715
Was al mankynde broght to wrecchednesse,
For which that° Jhesu Crist hymself was slayn
That boghte° us with his herte blood agayn—
Lo, heere expres° of womman may ye fynde
That womman was the los° of al mankynde.   720
Tho redde he me how Sampson loste his
    heres°.
Slepynge, his lemman kitte° it with hir sheres°,
Thurgh which treson loste he bothe his eyen.
    Tho redde he me, if that I shal nat lyen,
Of Hercules and of his Dianyre,   725
That caused hym to sette hymself afyre.
    Nothyng forgat he the sorwe and the wo
That Socrates hadde with his wyves two,
How Xantippa caste pisse upon his heed.
This sely° man sat stille as° he were deed;   730
He wiped his heed, namoore dorste° he seyn°
But "Er° that thonder stynte°, comth a reyn!"
    Of Phasifpha, that was the queene of Crete,
For shrewednesse° hym thoughte the tale swete.
Fy! Spek namoore—it is a grisly° thyng—   735
Of hire horrible lust and hir likyng.
    Of Clitermystra, for hire lecherye,
That falsly made hire housbonde for to dye,
He redde it with ful good devocioun.
    He tolde me eek for what occasioun   740

---

680 **bookes many on,** *many a book* 681 **o,** *one* 683 **leyser and vaca-cioun,** *leisure and spare time* 686 **of hem mo,** *about them more* 687 **been,** *are* 688 **inpossible,** *impossibility* 689 **clerk,** *scholar, member of the clergy* 690 **But if,** *unless* 694 **oratories,** *places for prayer* 696 **mark of Adam,** i.e., *all men,* **redresse,** *amend* 698 **hir wirkyng,** *their activities,* **ful con-trarius,** *completely opposite* 699 **science,** *knowledge* 700 **ryot,** *partying,* **dispence,** *extravagance* 701 **for hire,** *because of their* 703 **woot,** *knows* 705 **ther,** *when,* **reysed,** *raised* 706 **of,** *by* 708 **sho,** *shoe* 709 **dotage,**

senility 711 **to purpos,** *to the point* 712 **pardee,** *by God* 713 **oure sire,** *master of the household* 717 **For which that,** *on account of which* 718 **That boghte,** *who redeemed* 719 **expres,** *specifically* 720 **los,** *loss* 721 **heres,** *hair* 722 **lemman kitte,** *lover cut,* **hir sheres,** *her scissors* 730 **sely,** *silly or innocent,* **as,** *as if* 731 **namoore dorste,** *no more dared,* **seyn,** *say* 732 **Er,** *before,* **stynte,** *stops* 734 **shrewednesse,** *cursedness* 735 **grisly,** *terrible*

---

679 Parables of Salomon, a medieval name for the Book of Proverbs. **680 Ovides Art,** Ovid's *Ars Amatoria* (Art of Love). **692 peyntede the leon,** an allusion to a fable in which a lion sees a picture of a man killing a lion and remarks that the picture would be different if a lion had painted it. **697 children of Mercurie and of Venus,** people associated with the planets Mercury (scholars) and Venus (lovers) **701–2 diverse disposicioun . . . exaltacioun,** semitechnical astronomical language, meaning that Mercury and Venus are so situated that when one exerts its strongest influence on the affairs of humans, the other exerts its least influence. A planet is at its exaltation when it is in the constellation of the zodiac thought to empower it; it is at its dejection (or desolation or declination) when in the constellation where it is weakest. **704 Pisces,** constellation of the Fish; the exaltation of Venus and dejection of Mars. **715 Eva,** Eve, blamed for causing the fall of humanity in Genesis. **717–20** Lines not found in several important manuscripts, perhaps canceled by Chaucer or added late. **721 Sampson,** on Samson's hair-cut, loss of strength, and blindness, see Judges 16.15–21 and *MkT* 7.2015–94. This and most of the following antifeminist commonplaces are mentioned in Jerome, although some details come from elsewhere. **725 Hercules . . . Dianyre,** accidentally betrayed by his wife, Deianira, Hercules leapt into a burning fire; see *MkT* 7.2095–2142. **728–29 Socrates . . . Xantippa,** the account comes from Jerome 1.48. **733 Phasif-pha,** Pasiphae's passion for a bull led to the birth of the Minotaur; Jerome 1.48. **737 Clitermystra,** Clytemnestra, committed adultery and helped kill her husband, Agamemnon; Jerome 1.48.

Amphiorax at Thebes loste his lyf.
Myn housbonde hadde a legende of his wyf
Eriphilem, that for an ouche° of gold
Hath prively° unto the Grekes told
Wher that hir housbonde hidde hym in
    a place   745
For which he hadde at Thebes sory grace°.
    Of Lyvia tolde he me, and of Lucye:
They bothe made hir housbondes for to dye,
That oon for love, that oother was for hate.
Lyvia hir housbonde, upon an even late°,   750
Empoysoned° hath for that she was his fo;
Lucia, likerous°, loved hire housbonde so
That for° he sholde alwey upon hire thynke,
She yaf° hym swich a manere love-drynke
That he was deed er it were by the morwe°—   755
And thus algates° housbondes han sorwe.
    Thanne tolde he me how that oon Latumyus
Compleyned unto his felawe Arrius
That in his gardyn growed° swich a tree
On which he seyde how that his wyves thre   760
Hanged hemself° for herte despitus°.
"O leeve° brother," quod this Arrius,
"Yif° me a plante of thilke° blissed tree,
And in my gardyn planted it shal bee."
    Of latter date°, of wyves hath he red°   765
That somme han slayn hir housbondes in hir bed
And lete hir lecchour° dighte hire° al the nyght,
Whan that the corps° lay in° the floor upright°.
And somme han dryve nayles° in hir brayn
Whil that they slepte, and thus they han hem
    slayn.   770
Somme han hem yeve° poysoun in hire drynke.
    He spak moore harm than herte may bithynke°,
And therwithal° he knew of mo° proverbes
Than in this world ther growen gras or herbes.
"Bet is°," quod he, "thyn habitacioun°   775

Be with a leoun or a foul dragoun
Than with a womman usynge for to chyde°."
"Bet is," quod he, "hye° in the roof abyde°
Than with an angry wyf doun in the hous;
They been so wikked and contrarious°,   780
They haten that° hir housbondes loveth ay°."
He seyde, "A womman cast hir shame away
Whan she cast of hir smok°," and forthermo,
"A fair womman, but° she be chaast also,
Is lyk a gold ryng in a sowes° nose."   785
Who wolde leeve° or who wolde suppose
The wo that in myn herte was, and pyne°?
    And whan I saugh he wolde nevere fyne°
To reden on this cursed book al nyght,
Al sodeynly thre leves° have I plyght°   790
Out of his book right as he radde°, and eke
I with my fest° so took° hym on the cheke
That in oure fyr he fil bakward adoun.
And he up stirte° as dooth a wood° leoun,
And with his fest he smoot° me on the heed   795
That in° the floor I lay as I were deed.
And whan he saugh° how stille that I lay,
He was agast and wolde han° fled his way,
Til atte lasted out of my swogh° I breyde°.
"O, hastow° slayn me, false theef?" I seyde,   800
"And for my land thus hastow mordred me?
Er° I be deed yet wol I kisse thee."
    And neer he cam and kneled faire° adoun,
And seyde, "Deere suster° Alisoun,
As help me God, I shal thee nevere smyte°.   805
That° I have doon, it is thyself to wyte°.
Foryeve it me, and that I thee biseke°."
And yet eftsoones° I hitte hym on the cheke,
And seyde, "Theef, thus muchel° am I wreke°.
Now wol I dye; I may no lenger speke."   810
But atte laste with muchel care and wo
We fille acorded° by us selven° two.

---

743 **ouche,** *jeweled ornament* 744 **prively,** *secretly* 746 **sory grace,** *bad fortune* 750 **upon an even late,** *late one evening* 751 **Empoysoned,** *poisoned* 752 **likerous,** *lecherous* 753 **for,** *so* 754 **yaf,** *gave* 755 **morwe,** *morning* 756 **algates,** *always* 759 **growed,** *grew* 761 **hemself,** *themselves,* **for herte despitus,** *because of spiteful hearts* 762 **leeve,** *dear* 763 **Yif,** *give,* **thilke,** *that* 765 **Of latter date,** *later on,* **red,** *read* 767 **lecchour,** *lecher,* **dighte hire,** *have sex with her* 768 **corps,** *dead body,* **in,** *on,* **upright,** *flat* 769 **dryve nayles,** *driven nails* 771 **han hem yeve,** *have given them* 772 **bithynke,** *think of* 773 **therwithal,** *further,* **mo,** *more* 775 **Bet it,** *it is better,* **thyne habitacioun,** *your dwelling* 777 **usynge for to chyde,** *accustomed to scold* 778 **hye,** *high,* **abyde,**

(to) *stay* 780 **contrarious,** *quarrelsome* 781 **that,** *what,* **ay,** *always* 783 **smok,** *dress* 784 **but,** *unless* 785 **sowes,** *pig's* 786 **leeve,** *believe* 787 **pyne,** *pain* 788 **fyne,** *cease* 790 **leves,** *pages,* **plyght,** *snatched* 791 **radde,** *read* 792 **fest,** *fist,* **took,** *hit* 794 **stirte,** *leaped,* **wood,** *enraged* 795 **smoot,** *struck* 796 **in,** *on* 797 **saugh,** *saw* 798 **wolde han,** *wished to have* 799 **swogh,** *faint,* **breyde,** *awoke* 800 **hastow,** *have you* 802 **Er,** *before* 803 **faire,** *gently* 804 **suster,** *sweetheart* 805 **smyte,** *hit* 806 **That,** (for) *what,* **wyte** *blame* 807 **thee biseke,** *plead of you* 808 **eftsoones,** *again* 809 **muchel,** *much,* **wreke,** *avenged* 812 **fille acorded,** *came to agreement,* **us selven,** *ourselves*

---

741 **Amphiorax,** Amphiaraus died at Thebes after Eriphyle, his wife, disclosed his hiding place in exchange for a necklace; Jerome 1.48. 747–55 **Lyvia . . . ,** the accounts come from Walter Map (see 671n); not in Jerome. 757–64 **Latumyus . . . Arrius . . . ,** the story is found, with different names, in Walter Map. 765–71 Similar stories are found together in John of Salisbury's *Policraticus* 8. 773 **proverbes,** Jerome 1.28 and 48 quote most of the following proverbs from scriptural sources.

He yaf° me al the bridel° in myn hond,
To han the governance of hous and lond,
And of his tonge, and of his hond also; 815
And made hym brenne° his book anon° right tho°.
And whan that I hadde geten° unto me
By maistrie° al the soveraynetee°,
And that he seyde, "Myn owene trewe wyf,
Do as thee lust° the terme° of al thy lyf; 820

Keep° thyn honour, and keep eek myn estaat°."
After that day we hadden never debaat.
God helpe me so, I was to hym as kynde
As any wyf from Denmark unto Ynde,
And also trewe, and so was he to me. 825
I prey to God that sit in magestee°
So blesse his soule for his mercy deere.
Now wol I seye my tale if ye wol heere.

Biholde the wordes bitwene the Somonour and the Frere.

The Frere lough° whan he hadde herd al this.
"Now dame," quod he, "so have I joye or blis, 830
This is a long preamble of a tale."
And whan the Somonour herde the Frere
        gale°,
"Lo," quod the Somonour, "Goddes armes two,
A frere wol entremette hym° everemo.
Lo, goode men, a flye and eek a frere 835
Wol falle in every dyssh and eek mateere.
What spekestow of preambulacioun?
What, amble° or trotte or pees° or go sit doun!
Thou lettest° oure disport° in this manere."
    "Ye, woltow so, sire Somonour?" quod the
        Frere. 840
"Now, by my feith, I shal er° that I go
Telle of a somonour swich° a tale or two

That alle the folk shal laughen in this place."
    "Now elles, Frere, I bishrewe° thy face,"
Quod this Somonour, "and I bishrewe me 845
But if° I telle tales two or thre
Of freres er I come to Sidyngborne,
That I shal make thyn herte for to morne,
For wel I woot° thy pacience is gon."
    Oure Hoost cride, "Pees°, and that anon°!" 850
And seyde, "Lat the womman telle hire tale.
Ye fare as° folk that dronken ben° of ale.
Do, dame, telle forth youre tale, and that is
        best."
    "Al redy, sire," quod she, "right as yow lest°,
If I have licence° of this worthy Frere." 855
    "Yis, dame," quod he, "tel forth and I wol
        heere."

Heere endeth the Wyf of Bathe hir Prologe and bigynneth hir Tale.

In th'olde dayes of the Kyng Arthour,
Of which that Britons° speken greet honour,
Al was this land fulfild of fairye°.
The elf-queene with hir joly compaignye 860
Daunced ful ofte in many a grene mede°.
This was the olde opinion, as I rede—
I speke of manye hundred yeres ago.

But now kan no man se none elves mo°,
For now the grete charitee and prayeres 865
Of lymytours° and othere hooly freres,
That serchen° every lond and every streem
As thikke as motes° in the sonne-beem°,
Blessynge halles, chambres, kichenes, boures°,
Citees, burghes°, castels, hye toures°, 870

---

813 yaf, *gave*, bridel, *bridle* 816 brenne, *burn*, anon, *immediately*, tho, *then* 817 geten, *gotten* 818 maistrie, *mastery*, soveraynetee, *dominance* 820 lust, *desire*, terme, *time* 821 Keep, *protect*, estaat, *rank* 826 sit in magestee, *sits in majesty* 829 Frere lough, *Friar laughed* 832 gale, *exclaim* 834 entremette hym, *intrude himself* 838 amble, *walk leisurely*, pees, *peace* (shut up!) 839 lettest, *hinder*, disport, *fun* 841 er, *before* 842 swich, *such* 844 bishrewe, *curse* 846 But if, *unless* 849 woot, *know*

850 Pees, *peace*, anon, *immediately* 852 fare as, *act like*, ben, *are* 854 lest, *wish*, 855 licence, *permission* 858 Britons, *people from Celtic Britain* 859 fulfild of fairye, *filled with fairy folk* 861 grene mede, *green meadow* 864 se none elves mo, *see any more elves* 866 lymytours, *friars licensed to beg in a certain area* (limit) 867 serchen, *seek out* 868 motes, *dust specks*, sonne-beam, *sunbeam* 869 boures, *bedrooms* 870 burghes, *towns*, hye toures, *high towers*

824 **Denmark unto Ynde,** Denmark to India, i.e., in the whole world. 833 **Goddes armes two,** by God's arms, a mild oath. 837 **What spekestow of preambulacioun?** Why do you speak about making preambles? (line 831)—with a play on *perambulation*, which means "walking or traveling," echoed by *amble* in the next line. The Summoner and the Friar are professional antagonists because their religious offices (and abuses of these offices) led to conflicts or competition between them. 840 **woltow so,** will you do so? i.e., are you trying to start something? 847 **Sidyngborne,** Sittingbourne, about forty miles from London.

Thropes°, bernes°, shipnes°, dayeryes°—
This maketh that ther been no fairyes.
For ther as wont to walken was an elf°
Ther walketh now the lymytour hymself,
In undermeles° and in morwenynges°,   875
And seyth his matyns° and his hooly thynges
As he gooth in his lymytacioun°.
Wommen may go now saufly° up and doun;
In every bussh or under every tree
Ther is noon oother incubus but he,   880
And he ne wol doon hem but° dishonour.
   And so bifel that this Kyng Arthour
Hadde in his hous a lusty bacheler *[handwritten: squire described exactly the same way]*
That on a day cam ridynge fro ryver,
And happed° that, allone as he was born,   885
He saugh° a mayde walkynge hym biforn°,
Of whiche mayde anon°, maugree hir heed°,
By verray° force he rafte hire maydenhed°; *[handwritten: raped her]*
For which oppressioun was swich clamour°
And swich pursute° unto the Kyng Arthour,   890
That dampned° was this knyght for to be deed,
By cours of lawe, and sholde han lost his heed—
Paraventure swich° was the statut tho°—
But° that the queene and othere ladyes mo
So longe preyeden° the kyng of° grace   895
Til he his lyf hym graunted in the place,
And yaf° hym to the queene, al at hir wille,
To chese° wheither she wolde hym save or spille°.
   The queene thanketh the kyng with al hir
     myght,
And after this thus spak she to the knyght,   900
Whan that she saugh hir tyme upon a day,
"Thou standest yet," quod she, "in swich array°
That of thy lyf yet hastow no suretee°.
I grante thee lyf if thou kanst tellen me
What thyng is it that wommen moost desiren.   905
Bewar and keep thy nekke-boon from iren°.

And if thou kanst nat tellen it anon°,
Yet shal I yeve° thee leve° for to gon
A twelf-month and a day to seche and leere°
An answere suffisant in this mateere;   910
And suretee wol I han° er that thou pace,
Thy body for to yelden° in this place."
   Wo° was this knyght and sorwefully he siketh°.
But what, he may nat do al as hym liketh;
And at the laste he chees hym for to wende°   915
And come agayn right at the yeres ende
With swich answere as God wolde hym purveye°,
And taketh his leve and wendeth° forth his weye.
   He seketh every hous and every place
Where as he hopeth for to fynde grace°   920
To lerne what thyng wommen loven moost,
But he ne koude arryven° in no coost°
Wher as he myghte fynde in this mateere
Two creatures accordynge in-feere°.
   Somme seyde wommen loven best richesse,   925
Somme seyde honour, somme seyde jolynesse,
Somme riche array, somme seyden lust
    a-bedde°,
And oftetyme to be wydwe° and wedde.
Somme seyde that oure hertes been moost esed°
Whan that we been yflatered and yplesed—   930
He gooth ful ny the sothe°, I wol nat lye.
A man shal wynne us best with flaterye,
And with attendance° and with bisynesse°
Been we ylymed°, bothe moore and lesse.
   And somme seyn that we loven best   935
For to be free and do right° as us lest°,
And that no man repreve° us of oure vice,
But seye that we be wise and nothyng nyce°.
For trewely ther is noon of us alle,
If any wight wol clawe us on the galle°,   940
That we nel kike for° he seith us sooth°;
Assay°, and he shal fynde it that so dooth°,

---

871 **Thropes,** *villages,* **bernes,** *barns,* **shipnes,** *animal pens,* **dayeryes,* dairies* 873 **ther as wont to walken was an elf,** *where an elf was accustomed to walk* 875 **undermeles,** *afternoons,* **morwenynges,** *mornings* 876 **seyth his matyns,** *says his morning prayers* 877 **lymytacioun,** *licensed district* 878 **saufly,** *safely* 881 **ne wol doon hem but,** *will not do (to)* them *(anything)* but 883 **bacheler,** *young knight* 885 **happed,** *(it) happened* 886 **saugh,** *saw,* **hym biforn,** *before him* 887 **anon,** *soon,* **maugree hir heed,** *despite anything she could do* 888 **verray,** *sheer,* **rafte hire maydenhed,** *stole her virginity* 889 **swich clamour,** *such outcry* 890 **swich pursute,** *such pleading* 891 **dampned,** *condemned* 893 **Paraventure swich,** *it happens (that) such,* **statut tho,** *law then* 894 **But,** *except* 895 **preyeden,** *pleaded with,* **of,** *for* 897 **yaf,** *gave* 898 **chese,** *choose,* **spille,** *kill* 902 **swich array,** *such a condition* 903 **hastow no suretee,**

you have no certainty 906 **iren,** *ax (iron)* 907 **anon,** *immediately* 908 **yeve,** *give,* **leve,** *permission* 909 **seche and leere,** *seek and learn* 911 **suretee wol I han,** *I will have a pledge* 912 **yelden,** *yield* 913 **Wo,** *woeful,* **siketh,** *sighs* 915 **chees hym for to wende,** *chose to travel* 917 **purveye,** *provide* 918 **wendeth,** *goes* 920 **grace,** *the good fortune* 922 **ne koude arryven,** *could not arrive,* **coost,** *coast (region)* 924 **accordynge in-feere,** *agreeing together* 927 **lust a-bedde,** *pleasure in bed* 928 **wydwe,** *widowed* 929 **esed,** *comforted* 931 **gooth ful ny the sothe,** *comes very near the truth* 933 **attendance,** *service,* **bisynesse,** *attention* 934 **ylymed,** *captured (with birdlime)* 936 **right,** *just,* **us lest,** *we please* 937 **repreve,** *accuse* 938 **nothyng nyce,** *not at all foolish* 940 **wight wol clawe us on the galle,** *person will hit us on a sore spot* 941 **nel kike for,** *will not kick because,* **seith us sooth,** *tells us truth* 942 **Assay,** *try it,* **so dooth,** *does so*

880 **incubus,** an evil spirit who had sex with humans. 889 **oppressioun,** rape; there is no rape in other versions of the story. 909 **twelf-month and a day,** a year and a day, a legal formula that occurs in other romances, e.g., *Sir Gawain and the Green Knight* 297.

For be we° never so vicious withinne,
We wol been holden° wise and clene of synne.
   And somme seyn that greet delit han° we   945
For to been holden stable°, and eek secree°,
And in o purpos stedefastly to dwelle°,
And nat biwreye thyng° that men° us telle.
But that tale is nat worth a rake-stele°.
Pardee°, we wommen konne° nothyng hele°:   950
Witnesse on Myda—wol ye heere the tale?
   Ovyde, amonges othere thynges smale,
Seyde Myda hadde under his longe heres°
Growynge upon his heed two asses eres°,
The which vice° he hydde as he best myghte   955
Ful subtilly from every mannes sighte,
That save° his wyf ther wiste° of it namo°.
He loved hire moost and trusted hire also.
He preyde hire that to no creature
She sholde tellen of his disfigure°.   960
   She swoor him nay for al this world to wynne,
She nolde° do that vileynye or synne
To make hir housbonde han so foul a name;
She nolde nat telle it for hir owene shame.
But nathelees, hir thoughte° that she dyde°   965
That she so longe sholde a conseil° hyde;
Hir thoughte it swal° so soore° aboute hir herte
That nedely° som word hire moste asterte°.
And sith° she dorste° telle it to no man,
Doun to a mareys° faste° by she ran—   970
Til she cam there hir herte was afyre—
And as a bitore bombleth in the myre,
She leyde hir mouth unto the water doun:
"Biwreye° me nat, thou water, with thy soun°,"
Quod she; "to thee I telle it and namo°;   975
Myn housbonde hath longe asses erys two.
Now is myn herte al hool, now is it oute.
I myghte no lenger kepe° it, out of doute°."
Heere may ye se°, thogh we a tyme abyde°,

Yet out it moot°; we kan no conseil hyde.   980
The remenant° of the tale if ye wol heere,
Redeth Ovyde and ther ye may it leere°.
   This knyght of which my tale is specially,
Whan that he saugh° he myghte nat come
    therby—
This is to seye, what wommen love moost—   985
Withinne his brest ful sorweful was the goost°.
But hoom he gooth, he myghte nat sojourne°;
The day was come that homward moste he
    tourne.
And in his wey it happed hym° to ryde
In al this care under° a forest syde,   990
Wher as° he saugh upon a daunce go°
Of ladyes foure and twenty° and yet mo;
Toward the whiche daunce he drow ful yerne°,
In hope that som wysdom sholde he lerne.
But certeinly, er° he cam fully there,   995
Vanysshed was this daunce, he nyste° where.
Ne creature saugh he that bar lyf°
Save° on the grene° he saugh sittynge a wyf—
A fouler wight° ther may no man devyse°.
Agayn the knyght this olde wyf gan ryse°,   1000
And seyde, "Sire knyght, heer forth ne lith° no
    wey.
Tel me what that ye seken, by youre fey°.
Paraventure° it may the bettre be;
Thise olde folk kan muchel° thyng," quod she.
   "My leeve mooder°," quod this knyght,
    "certeyn   1005
I nam° but deed but if° that I kan seyn
What thyng it is that wommen moost desire.
Koude ye me wisse°, I wolde wel quite youre
    hire°."
   "Plight me thy trouthe° heere in myn hand,"
    quod she,
"The nexte thyng that I requere° thee   1010

---

943 be we, *we are* **944 wol been holden**, *would like to be considered* **945 han**, *have* **946 For to been holden stable**, *to be considered dependable*, **eek secree**, *also able to keep a secret* **947 in o purpos stedefastly to dwelle**, *able to keep to one goal steadily* **948 biwreye thyng**, *betray things*, **men**, *people* **949 rake-stele**, *rake handle* **950 Pardee**, *by God*, **konne**, *can*, **hele**, *hide* **953 heres**, *hair* **954 eres**, *ears* **955 vice**, *flaw* **957 save**, *except for*, **wiste**, *knew*, **namo**, *none more* **960 disfigure**, *deformity* **962 nolde**, *would not* **965 hir thoughte**, *she thought*, **dyde**, *would die* **966 conseil**, *secret* **967 swal**, *swelled*, **soore**, *sorely* **968 nedely**, *necessarily*, **hire moste asterte**, *from her must escape* **969 sith**, *since*, **dorste**, *dared* **970 mareys**, *marsh*, **faste**, *near* **974 Biwreye**, *betray*, **soun**, *sound* **975 namo**, *no more* **978 kepe**, *contain*, **out of doute**, *without doubt* **979 se**, *see*, **tyme abyde**, *wait awhile* **980 moot**, *must* **981 remenant**, *remainder*

982 leere, *learn* **984 saugh**, *saw* **986 goost**, *spirit* **987 sojourne**, *stay* **989 it happed hym**, *he happened* **990 under**, *near* **991 Wher as**, *where*, **saugh upon a daunce go**, *saw dancing* **992 Of ladyes foure and twenty**, *twenty-four ladies* **993 drow ful yerne**, *approached very eagerly* **995 er**, *before* **996 nyste**, *knew not* **997 bar lyf**, *was alive* **998 Save**, *except*, **grene**, *grassy place*, **wyf**, *woman* **999 fouler wight**, *uglier creature*, **devyse**, *describe* **1000 Agayn . . . gan ryse**, *before . . . arose* **1001 heer forth ne lith**, *in this direction lies* **1002 fey**, *faith* **1003 Paraventure**, *perhaps* **1004 kan muchel**, *know many* **1005 leeve mooder**, *dear old lady* **1006 nam**, *am nothing*, **but if**, *unless* **1008 Koude ye me wisse**, *if you can instruct me*, **quite youre hire**, *repay your efforts* **1009 Plight me thy trouthe**, *pledge me your solemn promise* **1010 requere**, *demand of*

---

951 Myda, Midas; from Ovid, *Metamorphoses* 11, where his secret is betrayed by his barber, not his wife. **972 as a bitore bombleth in the myre**, as a bittern (a wading bird) burbles in the mud.

Thou shalt it do, if it lye in thy myght,
And I wol telle it yow er it be nyght."
   "Have heer my trouthe," quod the knyght. "I
     grante°."
   "Thanne," quod she, "I dar me wel avante°
Thy lyf is sauf°, for I wol stonde therby.   1015
Upon my lyf, the queene wol seye as I°.
Lat se which is the proudeste of hem alle
That wereth on° a coverchief or a calle°
That dar seye nat of that° I shal thee teche.
Lat us go forth withouten lenger speche."   1020
Tho rowned° she a pistel° in his ere
And bad hym to be glad and have no fere.
   Whan they be comen° to the court, this knyght
Seyde he had holde his day° as he hadde hight°,
And redy was his answere, as he sayde.   1025
Ful many a noble wyf, and many a mayde,
And many a wydwe°—for that they been wise—
The queene hirself sittynge as justise,
Assembled been, his answere for to heere;
And afterward this knyght was bode appeere°.   1030
   To every wight° comanded was silence,
And that the knyght sholde telle in audience°
What thyng that worldly wommen loven best.
This knyght ne stood nat stille° as doth a best°,
But to his questioun anon° answerde   1035
With manly voys that al the court it herde.
   "My lige lady, generally," quod he,
"Wommen desiren to have sovereynetee
As wel over hir housbond as hir love,
And for to been in maistrie hym above.   1040
This is youre mooste° desir thogh ye me kille.
Dooth as yow list°; I am heer at youre wille."
   In al the court ne was ther wyf ne mayde
Ne wydwe that contraried° that he sayde,
But seyden he was worthy han his lyf.   1045
   And with that word up stirte° the olde wyf
Which that° the knyght saugh° sittynge on the
     grene°:

"Mercy," quod she, "my sovereyn lady queene!
Er that° youre court departe, do me right.
I taughte this answere unto the knyght,   1050
For which he plighte me his trouthe° there
The firste thyng I wolde hym requere°
He wolde it do, if it lay in his myght.
Bifore the court thanne preye I thee, sir
     knyght,"
Quod she, "that thou me take unto thy wyf°,   1055
For wel thou woost° that I have kept° thy lyf.
If I seye° fals, sey nat, upon thy fey°."
   This knyght answerde, "Allas and weylawey!
I woot° right wel that swich° was my biheste°.
For Goddes love, as chees° a newe requeste;   1060
Taak al my good° and lat my body go."
   "Nay thanne," quod she, "I shrewe° us bothe
     two!
For thogh that I be foul and oold and poore,
I nolde° for all the metal ne for oore°
That under erthe is grave° or lith° above,   1065
But if° thy wyf I were, and eek thy love."
   "My love?" quod he, "nay, my dampnacioun!
Allas, that any of my nacioun°
Sholde evere so foule disparaged° be."
But al for noght; th'ende is this, that he   1070
Constreyned was, he nedes moste° hire wedde;
And taketh his olde wyf and gooth to bedde.
   Now wolden som men seye, paraventure°,
That for my necligence I do no cure°
To tellen yow the joye and al th'array°   1075
That at the feeste° was that ilke° day.
To which thyng shortly answere I shal:
I seye ther nas no° joye ne feeste at al.
Ther nas° but hevynesse and muche sorwe.
For prively he wedded hire on morwe°,   1080
And al day after hidde hym as an owle,
So wo was hym, his wyf looked so foule.
   Greet was the wo the knyght hadde in his
     thoght.

1013 **grante,** *agree* 1014 **dar me wel avante,** *I dare well boast* 1015 **sauf,** *safe* 1016 **seye as I,** *say as I say* 1018 **wereth on,** *wears,* **calle,** *headdress* 1019 **dar seye nat of that,** *dare deny what* 1021 **rowned,** *whispered,* **pistel,** *message* 1023 **be comen,** *are come* 1024 **holde his day,** *returned on time,* **hight,** *promised* 1027 **wydwe,** *widow* 1030 **bode appeere,** *bidden to appear* 1031 **wight,** *person* 1032 **in audience,** *publicly* 1034 **stille,** *quiet,* **best,** *beast* 1035 **anon,** *immediately* 1041 **mooste,** *greatest* 1042 **list,** *please* 1044 **contraried,** *contradicted* 1046 **stirte,** *leapt* 1047 **Which that,** *the one who,* **saugh,** *saw,* **grene,** *grassy place* 1049 **Er that,** *before* 1051 **plighte me his trouthe,** *pledged me his solemn promise* 1052

requere, *demand* 1055 **unto thy wyf,** *as your wife* 1056 **woost,** *know,* **kept,** *saved* 1057 **seye,** *speak,* **fey,** *faith* 1059 **woot,** *know,* **swich,** *such,* **biheste,** *promise* 1060 **as chees,** *choose* 1061 **good,** *possessions* 1062 **shrewe,** *curse* 1064 **nolde,** *don't want,* **oore,** *ore* 1065 **grave,** *buried,* **lith,** *lies* 1066 **But if,** *unless* 1068 **nacioun,** *kindred* 1069 **disparaged,** *degraded* 1071 **nedes moste,** *necessarily must* 1073 **paraventure,** *perhaps* 1074 **do no cure,** *take no care* 1075 **th'array,** *the arrangements* 1076 **feeste,** *celebration,* **ilke,** *same* 1078 **nas no,** *was no* 1079 **nas,** *was nothing* 1080 **on morwe,** *in the morning*

1028 **queene . . . as justise,** the queen presides as judge, recalling the "courts of love" associated with Eleanor of Aquitaine and Marie de Champagne, and written about by Andreas Capellanus, *De Amore.* **1038–40 sovereynetee . . . maistrie,** see line 818.

Whan he was with his wyf abedde ybroght°
He walweth° and he turneth to and fro. 1085
His olde wyf lay smylynge everemo,
And seyde, "O deere housbonde, benedicitee°,
Fareth° every knyght thus with his wyf as ye?
Is this the lawe of Kyng Arthures hous?
Is every knyght of his so dangerous°? 1090
I am youre owene love and eek youre wyf;
I am she which that saved hath youre lyf,
And certes° yet ne dide I yow nevere unright°;
Why fare° ye thus with me this firste nyght?
Ye faren lyk a man had lost his wit°. 1095
What is my gilt? For Goddes love, tel it,
And it shal been amended°, if I may."
  "Amended?" quod this knyght, "allas, nay, nay,
It wol nat been amended nevere mo.
Thou art so loothly°, and so oold also, 1100
And therto comen of so lough a kynde°,
That litel wonder is thogh I walwe and wynde°.
So wolde God myn herte wolde breste°!"
  "Is this," quod she, "the cause of youre
    unreste?"
  "Ye, certeinly," quod he, "no wonder is." 1105
  "Now sire," quod she, "I koude° amende al this,
If that me liste°, er° it were dayes thre,
So° wel ye myghte bere° yow unto me.
  "But, for ye speken of swich gentillesse
As is descended out of old richesse, 1110
That therfore sholden ye be gentil men,
Swich arrogance is nat worth an hen.
Looke who that° is moost vertuous alway,
Pryvee and apert°, and moost entendeth ay°
To do the gentil dedes that he kan, 1115
Taak hym for the grettest gentil man.
Crist wole° we clayme of hym oure gentillesse,
Nat of oure eldres for hire old richesse.

For thogh they yeve° us al hir heritage,
For which we clayme to been of heigh
    parage°, 1120
Yet may they nat biquethe° for no thyng
To noon of us hir vertuous lyvyng°,
That made hem gentil men ycalled be°,
And bad us folwen° hem in swich degree°.
  "Wel kan the wise poete of Florence 1125
That highte° Dant speken in this sentence.
Lo, in swich maner rym° is Dantes tale:
'Ful selde up riseth° by his branches smale
Prowesse° of man, for God of his goodnesse
Wole° that of hym we clayme oure
    gentillesse.' 1130
For of oure eldres may we no thyng clayme
But temporel thyng that man may hurte and
    mayme°.
  "Eek every wight woot° this as wel as I,
If gentillesse were planted natureelly
Unto a certeyn lynage doun the lyne, 1135
Pryvee and apert, thanne wolde they nevere fyne°
To doon of gentillesse the faire office°—
They myghte do no vileynye or vice.
  "Taak fyr° and ber° it in the derkeste hous
Bitwix this and the mount of Kaukasous, 1140
And lat men shette° the dores and go thenne°,
Yet wole the fyr as faire lye° and brenne°
As twenty thousand men myghte it biholde;
His office° natureel ay° wol it holde,
Up peril of my lyf, til that it dye. 1145
  "Heere may ye se wel how that genterye°
Is nat annexed° to possessioun,
Sith° folk ne doon hir operacioun°
Alwey, as dooth the fyr, lo, in his kynde°.
For God it woot° men may wel often fynde 1150
A lordes sone° do shame and vileynye;

1084 abedde ybroght, *brought to bed* **1085 walweth,** *tosses* **1087 benedicitee,** *bless you* **1088 Fareth,** *acts* **1090 dangerous,** *standoffish* **1093 certes,** *certainly,* **unright,** *wrong* **1094 fare,** *act* **1095 had lost his wit,** *(who) has gone mad* **1097 been amended,** *be put right* **1100 loothly,** *hideous* **1101 therto comen of so lough a kynde,** *also come from so low a lineage* **1102 walwe and wynde,** *toss and turn* **1103 wolde brest,** *would burst* **1106 koude,** *could* **1107 me liste,** *it pleased me,* **er,** *before* **1108 So,** *so that,* **bere,** *behave* **1113 Looke who that,** *observe who* **1114 Pryvee and apert,** *in private and public,* **entendeth ay,** *tries always* **1117 Crist wole,** *Christ wishes that* **1119 yeve,** *give* **1120 heigh parage,** *upper-class birth* **1121 biquethe,** *hand down* **1122 hir vertuous lyvyng,**

their virtuous living **1123 ycalled be,** *be called* **1124 bad us folwen,** *ordered us to follow,* **swich degree,** *same manner* **1126 highte,** *is named* **1127 swich maner rym,** *rhyme like this* **1128 Ful selde up riseth,** *very seldom rises up,* **branches smale,** *descendants (branches of the family tree)* **1129 Prowesse,** *worth* **1130 Wole,** *wishes* **1132 mayme,** *injure* **1133 wight woot,** *person knows* **1136 fyne,** *cease* **1137 faire office,** *good actions* **1139 Taak fyr,** *take fire,* **ber,** *carry* **1140 Bitwix this,** *between here* **1141 shette,** *shut,* **thenne,** *from there* **1142 lye,** *blaze,* **brenne,** *burn* **1144 His office,** *its function,* **ay,** *always* **1146 genterye,** *gentility* **1147 annexed,** *attached* **1148 Sith,** *since,* **ne doon hir operacioun,** *do not operate* **1149 his kynde,** *its nature* **1150 woot,** *knows* **1151 sone,** *son*

1103 So wolde God, an idiom meaning something like "I wish to God." **1109 swich gentillesse,** such nobility. The idea that nobility depends on virtuous deeds rather than on lineage is commonplace, but the fourth tractate and the commentary on the third canzone of Dante's *Convivio* have the closest parallels; compare also *RR* 6579–92, 18,607–946; *Bo* 3.pr6 m6; Gower, *Mirour de l'omme* 17,329–64, 17,394–400. **1110 old richesse,** traditional wealth; Dante uses *antica ricchezza.* **1126 Dant,** Dante is the poet of Florence. **1128–30** From Dante's *Purgatorio* 7.121–23. **1140 Kaukasous,** Caucasus, in Russia. **1145 Up peril of my lyf,** an idiom meaning "I assure you on my life."

And he that wole han pris° of his gentrye—
For he was born of a gentil hous
And hadde his eldres noble and vertuous—
And nel° hymselven do no gentil dedis   1155
Ne folwen his gentil auncestre that deed° is,
He nys nat° gentil, be he duc or erl,
For vileyns° synful dedes make a cherl.
For gentillesse nys° but renomee°
Of thyne auncestres for hire heigh bountee°,   1160
Which is a strange thyng° to thy persone.
Thy gentillesse cometh fro God allone. ←
Thanne comth oure verray° gentillesse of grace;
It was no thyng° biquethe° us with oure place°.

 "Thenketh hou° noble, as seith Valerius,   1165
Was thilke° Tullius Hostillius
That out of poverte roos to heigh noblesse.
Reed° Senek, and redeth eek Boece;
Ther shul ye seen expres° that it no drede is°
That he is gentil that dooth gentil dedis.   1170
And therfore, leeve° housbonde, I thus conclude:
Al were it that° myne auncestres were rude°,
Yet may the hye° God—and so hope I—
Grante me grace to lyven vertuously.
Thanne am I gentil whan that I bigynne   1175
To lyven vertuously and weyve° synne.

 "And there as ye of poverte me repreeve°,
The hye God, on whom that we bileeve,
In wilful° poverte chees° to lyve his lyf.
And certes every man, mayden, or wyf,   1180
May understonde that Jhesus, hevene kyng,
Ne wolde nat chese a vicious lyvyng.
Glad poverte is an honeste° thyng, certeyn;
This wole Senec and othere clerkes seyn°.
Whoso that halt hym payd of° his poverte,   1185
I holde hym riche al° hadde he nat a sherte.
He that coveiteth° is a poure wight°,

For he wolde han° that is nat in his myght;
But he that noght hath°, ne coveiteth have°,
Is riche, although ye holde hym but a knave°.   1190
 "Verray° poverte it syngeth proprely°.
Juvenal seith° of poverte myrily°,
'The poure man, whan he goth by the weye°,
Bifore the theves° he may synge and pleye.'
Poverte is hateful good and, as I gesse,   1195
A ful greet bryngere out of bisynesse°;
A greet amendere eek° of sapience°
To hym that taketh it in pacience.
Poverte is this, although it seme alenge°,
Possessioun that no wight wol chalenge.   1200
Poverte ful ofte, whan a man is lowe,
Maketh his God and eek hymself to knowe.
Poverte a spectacle° is, as thynketh me,
Thurgh which he may his verray° freendes see.
And therfore, sire, syn° that I noght yow
       greve°,   1205
Of my poverte namoore ye me repreve°.

 "Now, sire, of elde° ye repreve me;
And certes°, sire, thogh noon auctoritee°
Were in no book, ye gentils of honour
Seyn° that men sholde an oold wight doon
       favour°   1210
And clepe° hym fader for youre gentillesse—
And auctours° shal I fynden, as I gesse.
 "Now ther° ye seye that I am foul and old,
Than drede° you noght to been a cokewold°,
For filthe° and eelde°, also moot I thee°,   1215
Been grete wardeyns° upon chastitee.
But nathelees, syn I knowe youre delit,
I shal fulfille youre worldly appetit.
 "Chese now," quod she, "oon of thise thynges
       tweye:
To han° me foul and old til that I deye°   1220

1152 wol han pris, *will have praise* **1155 nel,** *will not* **1156 deed,** *dead*
1157 nys nat, *is not* **1158 vileyns,** *wicked* **1159 nys,** *is nothing,* **renomee,**
fame **1160 hire heigh bountee,** *their high goodness* **1161 strange thyng,**
something alien **1163 verray,** *true* **1164 no thyng,** *nothing,* **biquethe,**
passed on to, **place,** *social rank* **1165 Thenketh hou,** *think how* **1166**
thilke, *that* **1168 Reed,** *read* **1169 expres,** *specifically,* **it no drede is,**
there is no doubt **1171 leeve,** *dear* **1172 Al were it that,** *although,* **rude,** *of*
low class **1173 hye,** *high* **1176 weyve,** *abandon* **1177 repreeve,** *accuse*
1179 wilful, *voluntary,* **chees,** *chose* **1183 honeste,** *honorable* **1184 seyn,**
say **1185 Whoso that halt hym payd of,** *whoever is content with* **1186 al,**
although **1187 coveiteth,** *yearns for* (covets), **wight,** *person* **1188 wolde**
han, *would have* **1189 noght hath,** *has nothing,* **ne coveiteth have,**

nor yearns to have **1190 knave,** *servant* **1191 Verray,** *true,* **syngeth pro-**
prely, *sings appropriately* **1192 seith,** *says,* **myrily,** *merrily* **1193 by the**
weye, *on the road* **1194 theves,** *thieves* **1196 bryngere out of bisynesse,**
encourager of productive action **1197 amendere eek,** *improver also,* **sapi-**
ence, *wisdom* **1199 seme alenge,** *seems wearisome* **1203 spectacle,** *lens*
1204 verray, *true* **1205 syn,** *since,* **noght yow greve,** *don't injure you* **1206**
repreve, *accuse,* **1207 elde,** *old age* **1208 certes,** *certainly,* **auctoritee,**
authority **1210 Seyn,** *say,* **an oold wight doon favour,** *respect an old per-*
son **1211 clepe,** *call* **1212 auctours,** *authors* (who agree) **1213 ther,**
since **1214 drede,** *fear,* **cokewold,** *cuckold* **1215 filthe,** *foulness,* **eelde,**
age, **also moot I thee,** *so I may prosper* **1216 Been grete wardeyns,** *are*
great guardians **1220 han,** *have,* **deye,** *die*

1165–67 Valerius . . . , Valerius Maximus 3.4 tells the legend of Tullius Hostilius, who rose from the peasantry to become third king of Rome.
1168 Senek, Seneca, *Epistle* 44. **Boece,** Boethius, *Bo* 3.pr6. **1184 Senec,** Seneca, *Epistle* 17. **1191 proprely,** appropriately or by its own nature;
scribes had trouble with the word, offering many variants. **1192 Juvenal,** *Satire* 10.21. **1219 Chese now . . . ,** in other versions of the tale, the
loathly lady offers a different choice (fair by day and foul by night, or vice versa) and shows her beauty to the knight before he must choose.

And be to yow a trewe humble wyf,
And nevere yow displese in al my lyf,
Or elles° ye wol han° me yong and fair,
And take youre aventure° of the repair°
That shal be to youre hous by cause° of me,　　1225
Or in som oother place, may wel be.
Now chese yourselven, wheither° that yow liketh."
　　This knyght avyseth hym° and sore siketh°,
But atte laste he seyde in this manere,
"My lady and my love, and wyf so deere,　　1230
I put me in youre wise governance;
Cheseth youreself which may be moost plesance°
And moost honour to yow and me also.
I do no fors the wheither° of the two,
For as yow liketh it suffiseth° me."　　1235
　　"Thanne have I gete° of yow maistrie," quod
　　　she,
"Syn° I may chese and governe as me lest°?"
　　"Ye, certes°, wyf," quod he. "I holde it best."
　　"Kys me," quod she. "We be no lenger wrothe°,
For, by my trouthe, I wol be to yow bothe—　　1240
This is to seyn, ye°, bothe fair and good.
I prey to God that I moote sterven wood°

But° I to yow be also° good and trewe
As evere was wyf syn that the world was newe.
And but I be tomorn° as fair to seene°　　1245
As any lady, emperice, or queene,
That is bitwixe the est and eke the west,
Dooth with my lyf and deth right as yow lest°.
Cast up the curtyn, looke how that it is."
　　And whan the knyght saugh verraily°
　　　al this,　　1250
That she so fair was, and so yong therto°,
For joye he hente° hire in his armes two.
His herte bathed in a bath of blisse,
A thousand tyme a-rewe° he gan hire kisse°,
And she obeyed hym in every thyng　　1255
That myghte doon hym plesance or likyng.
　　And thus they lyve unto hir lyves ende
In parfit joye. And Jhesu Crist us sende
Housbondes meeke, yonge, and fressh abedde,
And grace t'overbyde hem° that we wedde.　　1260
And eek I pray Jhesu shorte hir° lyves
That wol nat be governed by hir wyves.
And olde and angry nygardes of dispence°,
God sende hem soone verray pestilence°!

Heere endeth the Wyves Tale of Bathe.

1223 **elles**, *else,* **wol han**, *will have* 1224 **aventure**, *chances,* **repair**, *visitors* 1225 **by cause**, *because* 1227 **wheither**, *whichever* 1228 **avyseth hym**, *ponders,* **sore siketh**, *sighs painfully* 1232 **plesance**, *happiness* 1234 **do no fors the wheither**, *I don't care which* 1235 **suffiseth**, *satisfies* 1236 **gete**, *gotten* 1237 **Syn**, *since,* **me lest**, *I please* 1238 **Ye, certes**, *yes, certainly* 1239 **lenger wrothe**, *longer at odds* 1241 **seyn, ye**, *say, yes* 1242 **moote sterven wood**, *might die insane* 1243 **But**, *unless,* **also**, *as* 1245 **tomorn**, *tomorrow,* **seene**, *see* 1248 **yow lest**, *you wish* 1250 **saugh verraily**, *saw truly* 1251 **therto**, *also* 1252 **hente**, *grasped* 1254 **a-rewe**, *in a row,* **gan hire kisse**, *kissed her* 1260 **t'overbyde hem**, *to outlive them* 1261 **shorte hir**, *shorten their* 1263 **nygardes of dispence**, *misers of money* 1264 **verray pestilence**, *true plague*

1249 **Cast up the curtyn**, the drapes of the canopy bed had been drawn for privacy.

somonour - always looking for fornication. Is beaten @ every town.

FRIAR'S TALE

PROLOGUE

The Prologe of the Freres Tale.

This worthy lymytour, this noble Frere,　1265
He made alwey a maner louryng chiere°
Upon the Somonour, but for honestee°
No vileyns° word as yet to hym spak he.
But atte laste he seyde unto the wyf,
"Dame," quod he, "God yeve° yow right good
　　lyf.　1270
Ye han heer° touched, also moot I thee,
In scole-matere greet difficultee.
Ye han seyd° muche thyng right wel,
　I seye.
But dame, heere as we ryde by the weye
Us nedeth nat to speken but of game°,　1275
And lete auctoritees°, on° Goddes name,
To prechyng and to scole° of clergye.
But if it lyke° to this compaignye,
I wol yow of a somonour telle a game.
Pardee°, ye may wel knowe by the name°　1280

That of a somonour may no good be sayd;
I praye that noon of you be yvele apayd°.
A somonour is a rennere° up and doun
With mandementz° for fornicacioun,
And is ybet° at every townes ende."　1285
　　Oure Hoost tho° spak, "A, sire, ye sholde
　　be hende°
And curteys, as a man of youre estaat°;
In compaignye we wol have no debaat°.
Telleth youre tale and lat the Somonour be."
　　"Nay," quod the Somonour, "lat hym seye
　　to me　1290
Whatso hym list°. Whan it comth to
　my lot°,
By God, I shal hym quiten° every grot°.
I shal hym tellen which° a greet honour
It is to be a flaterynge lymytour,
And of many another manere° cryme　1295

1266 **maner louryng chiere,** *kind of angry expression* 1267 **for honestee,** *to keep his dignity* 1268 **vileyns,** *rude* 1270 **yeve,** *give* 1271 **han heer,** *have here* 1273 **han seyd,** *have said* 1275 **of game,** *for entertainment* 1276 **lete auctoritees,** *leave learned texts,* **on,** *in* 1277 **scole,** *studies* 1278 **lyke,** *is pleasing* 1280 **Pardee,** *by God,* **the name,** *reputation* 1282 **yvele apayd,** *displeased* 1283 **rennere,** *runner* 1284 **mandementz,** *summonses* 1285 **ybet,** *beaten* 1286 **tho,** *then,* **hende,** *gracious* 1287 **estaat,** *status* 1288 **debaat,** *quarreling* 1291 **Whatso hym list,** *whatever he wishes,* **lot,** *turn* 1292 **quiten,** *repay,* **grot,** *bit* (coin) 1293 **hym tellen which,** *tell him what* 1295 **another manere,** *more kinds of*

1265 **lymytour,** "a friar whose begging, preaching, and hearing of confessions was limited" to a particular territory (*MED*); see *GP* 1.208n and 209n. 1271 **also moot I thee,** "as I may prosper," an idiom meaning something like "if I do say so myself." 1272 **scole-matere,** school matter, i.e., intellectual things. 1283 **somonour,** summoner, a subpoena server for an ecclesiastical court.

Which nedeth° nat rehercen for° this tyme.
And his office° I shal hym telle, ywis°."
　　Oure Hoost answerde, "Pees, namoore of this."

And after this he seyde unto the Frere,
"Tel forth youre tale, leeve° maister deere."　　1300

Heere bigynneth the Freres Tale.

Whilom° ther was dwellynge in my contree
An erchedekene, a man of heigh degree,
That boldely dide execucioun°
In punysshynge of fornicacioun,
Of wicchecraft, and eek of bawderye°,　　1305
Of diffamacioun°, and avowtrye°,
Of chirche reves°, and of testamentz°,
Of contractes°, and of lakke of° sacramentz,
Of usure°, and of symonye° also.
But certes, lecchours dide he grettest wo°—　　1310
They sholde syngen° if that they were hent°—
And smale tytheres° weren foule yshent°
If any persone° wolde upon hem pleyne°.
Ther myghte asterte hym no pecunyal peyne°.
For smale tithes and for smal offrynge°　　1315
He made the peple pitously to synge,
For er° the bisshop caughte hem° with his hook°,
They were in the erchedeknes° book.
And thanne hadde he, thurgh his jurisdiccioun,
Power to doon on hem correccioun.　　1320
He hadde a somonour redy to his hond—
A slyer boye nas noon° in Engelond,
For subtilly he hadde his espiaille°
That taughte hym wher that hym myghte availle°.
He koude spare of lecchours oon or two　　1325
To techen° hym to foure and twenty mo.
For thogh this somonour wood was as an hare,

To telle his harlotrye° I wol nat spare,
For we been out of his correccioun.
They han of us no jurisdiccioun,　　1330
Ne nevere shullen, terme° of alle hir lyves.
　　"Peter°, so been° wommen of the styves°,"
Quod the Somonour, "yput out of my cure°!"
　　"Pees, with myschance and with mysaventure,"
Thus seyde oure Hoost, "and lat hym telle his
　　tale.　　1335
Now telleth forth, thogh that the Somonour gale°,
Ne spareth nat, myn owene maister deere."
　　This false theef, this somonour, quod the
　　Frere,
Hadde alwey bawdes° redy to his hond,
As any hauk to lure in Engelond,　　1340
That tolde hym al the secree° that they knewe,
For hire acqueyntance was nat come of newe.
They weren his approwours prively°.
He took hymself a greet profit therby;
His maister knew nat alwey what he wan°.　　1345
Withouten mandement° a lewed° man
He koude somne°, on peyne° of Cristes curs,
And they were glade for to fille his purs
And make hym grete feestes atte nale°.
And right as Judas hadde purses smale,　　1350
And was a theef, right swich a theef was he;
His maister hadde but half his duetee°.

1296 nedeth, (I) *need,* **for,** *at* **1297 office,** *function,* **ywis,** *surely* **1300 leeve,** *beloved* **1301 Whilom,** *once* **1303 dide execucioun,** *executed the laws* **1305 eek of bawderye,** *also of pimping* **1306 diffamacioun,** *slander,* **avowtrye,** *adultery* **1307 reves,** *robberies,* **of testamentz,** *pertaining to wills* **1308 contractes,** *(marriage) contracts,* **lakke of,** *failure to perform* **1309 usure,** *lending money for interest,* **symonye,** *buying or selling church offices* **1310 dide he grettest wo,** *he hurt most* **1311 syngen,** *wail,* **hent,** *caught* **1312 foule yshent,** *harshly punished* **1313 persone,** *parson (parish priest),* **upon hem pleyne,** *complain about them* **1314 Ther myghte asterte hym no pecunyal peyne,** *he would not escape financial*

suffering **1315 offrynge,** *voluntary contribution* **1317 er,** *before,* **hem, them, hook,** *curved staff* **1318 erchedeknes,** *archdeacon's* **1322 A slyer boye nas noon,** *there was no slyer rascal* **1323 espiaille,** *spy network* **1324 availle,** *profit* **1326 techen,** *lead* **1328 harlotrye,** *(sexual?) wickedness* **1331 terme,** *(for the) time* **1332 Peter,** *by St. Peter,* **been,** *are,* **styves, brothels** **1333 cure,** *responsibility* **1336 gale,** *makes noise* **1339 bawdes, pimps** **1341 secree,** *secrets* **1343 approwours prively,** *undercover agents* **1345 wan,** *acquired* **1346 mandement,** *summons,* **lewed,** *ignorant* **1347 koude somne,** *could summon,* **on peyne,** *under threat* **1349 atte nale, at the alehouse* **1352 his duetee,** *amount due to him*

1302 erchedekene, archdeacon; in medieval church hierarchy, the officer just below the bishop, responsible for a subdivision of the diocese and the overseeing of its ecclesiastical court. **1308 sacramentz,** church rites, including baptism, confirmation, Eucharist or communion, penance or confession, marriage, last rites, and ordination of priests. **1312 smale tytheres,** small tithers, those who fail to pay complete tithes, a 10 percent income tax due the church. **1327 wood was an hare,** proverbial: crazy as a (marsh or March) hare, i.e., out of control. **1329 we . . . correccioun,** we (friars) . . . authority. Friars were under the authority of their own orders rather than the diocesan courts. **1334 with myschance and with mysaventure,** an idiom meaning "bad luck to you." **1340 hauk to lure,** a hawk was trained to return to its handler when a "lure" (false bird on a rope) was swung. **1350 Judas . . . purses,** Judas Iscariot, who betrayed Jesus, was a thief and keeper of the disciples' money; John 12.4–6.

He was, if I shal yeven° hym his laude°,
A theef and eek a somnour and a baude°.
He hadde eek wenches at his retenue°   1355
That wheither that Sir Robert or Sir Huwe,
Or Jakke, or Rauf, or whoso that it were
That lay by hem°, they tolde it in his ere.
Thus was the wenche and he of oon assent°;
And he wolde fecche a feyned mandement°   1360
And somne hem° to chapitre° bothe two,
And pile° the man and lete the wenche go.
   Thanne wolde he seye, "Freend, I shal for thy
     sake
Do striken hire out of° oure lettres blake.
Thee thar namoore, as in this cas, travaille°;   1365
I am thy freend ther° I thee may availle°."
Certeyn he knew of briberyes mo
Than possible is to telle in yeres two.
For in this world nys dogge for the bowe°
That kan an hurt deer from an hool° knowe   1370
Bet° than this somnour knew a sly lecchour
Or an avowtier° or a paramour°.
And for° that was the fruyt° of al his rente°,
Therfore on it he sette al his entente. — *intution*
   And so bifel that ones° on a day   1375
This somnour evere waityng on his pray°
Rood for to somne an old wydwe°, a ribibe,
Feynynge a cause, for he wolde brybe°.
And happed° that he saugh bifore hym ryde
A gay yeman° under a forest syde°.   1380
A bowe he bar° and arwes° brighte and kene°;
He hadde upon a courtepy° of grene;
An hat upon his heed with frenges blake°.
   "Sire," quod this somnour, "hayl, and wel
     atake."
   "Welcome," quod he, "and every good
     felawe.   1385

Wher rydestow°, under this grenewode shawe°?"
Seyde this yeman, "Wiltow fer° to day?"
   This somnour hym answerde and seyde, "Nay.
Heere faste° by," quod he, "is myn entente
To ryden for to reysen up° a rente   1390
That longeth to my lordes duetee°."
   "Artow° thanne a bailly°?" "Ye," quod he.
He dorste° nat, for verray° filthe and shame
Seye that he was a somonour, for the name°.
   "Depardieux°," quod this yeman, "deere
     broother,   1395
Thou art a bailly, and I am another.
I am unknowen as in this contree;
Of thyn aqueyntance I wolde praye thee°
And eek of bretherhede, if that yow leste°.
I have gold and silver in my cheste;   1400
If that thee happe° to comen in oure shire°,
Al shal be thyn, right° as thou wolt desire."
   "Grantmercy°," quod this somnour, "by my
     feith!"
Everych° in ootheres hand his trouthe leith°,
For to be sworne bretheren til they deye.   1405
In daliance° they ryden forth hir weye.
   This somonour, that was as ful of jangles°
As ful of venym been thise waryangles
And evere enqueryng upon everythyng,
"Brother," quod he, "where is now youre
     dwellyng   1410
Another day if that I sholde yow seche°?"
This yeman hym answerde in softe speche,
   "Brother," quod he, "fer° in the north contree,
Where as° I hope som tyme I shal thee see.
Er° we departe I shal thee so wel wisse°   1415
That of myn hous ne shaltow nevere° mysse."
   "Now, brother," quod this somonour, "I yow
     preye,

1353 yeven, *give,* **laude**, *proper praise* **1354 baude**, *pimp* **1355 at his retenue**, *in his service* **1358 hem**, *them* **1359 of oon assent**, *in agreement* **1360 feyned mandement**, *false document* **1361 somne hem**, *summon them*, **chapitre**, *court session* **1362 pile**, *rob* **1364 Do striken hire out of**, *erase her from* **1365 Thee thar . . . travaille**, *about this . . . trouble yourself* **1366 ther**, *where*, **thee may availle**, *may help you* **1369 nys dogge for the bowe**, *there is no hunting* (archery) *dog* **1370 hool**, *whole* (unwounded) *one* **1371 Bet**, *better* **1372 avowtier**, *adulterer*, **paramour**, *lover* **1373 for**, *because*, **fruyt**, *best part*, **rente**, *income* **1375 ones**, *once* **1376 pray**, *prey* **1377 wydwe**, *widow* **1378 brybe**, *blackmail* **1379 happed**, (it) *happened* **1380 gay yeman**, *well-dressed yeoman*, **under a forest syde**, *at the forest's edge* **1381 bar**, *carried*, **arwes**, *arrows,*

kene, *sharp* **1382 courtepy**, *jacket* **1383 frenges blake**, *black fringe* **1386 rydestow**, *do you ride*, **shawe**, *grove* **1387 Wiltow fer**, *will you go far* **1389 faste**, *near* **1390 reysen up**, *collect* **1391 longeth to my lordes duetee**, *belongs to my lord* **1392 Artow**, *are you*, **bailly**, *bailiff* (agent or representative) **1393 dorste**, *dared*, **verray**, *true* **1394 for the name**, *because of the reputation* **1395 Depardieux**, *by God* **1398 wolde praye thee**, *would like to ask you* **1399 yow leste**, (it) *pleases you* **1401 happe**, *happen*, **shire**, *county* **1402 right**, *just* **1403 Grantmercy**, *thank you* **1404 Everych**, *each*, **his trouthe leith**, *laid his pledge* (i.e., they shook on it) **1405 deye**, *die* **1406 daliance**, *small talk* **1407 ful of jangles**, *talkative* **1411 seche**, *seek* **1413 fer**, *far* **1414 Where as**, *where* **1415 Er**, *before*, **wisse**, *teach* **1416 ne shaltow nevere**, *you shall never*

1374 entente, intention, a word that recurs throughout the tale. **1377 ribibe**, fiddle, slang term for an old woman, perhaps from a confusion of Lat. *vetula* (old woman) and *vitula* (viol). **1384 hayl, and wel atake**, greetings, and I am happy I met (have overtaken) you. **1408 As ful of venym been thise waryangles**, as full of poison (as) are these butcher birds, or shrikes, who impaled their prey on thorns that were thought to be poisonous as a result. **1413 north contree**, hell was often located in the north; e.g., Isaiah 14.14 and Jeremiah 6.1.

Teche me whil that we ryden by the weye—
Syn that ye been a baillif as am I—
Som subtiltee, and tel me feithfully   1420
In myn office how that I may moost wynne;
And spareth nat° for conscience ne synne,
But as my brother tel me how do ye°."
      "Now by my trouthe, brother deere," seyde he,
"As I shal tellen thee a feithful tale: 1425
My wages been ful streite° and ful smale.
My lord is hard to me and daungerous°,
And myn office is ful laborous,
And therfore by extorcions I lyve.
For sothe°, I take al that men wol me yeve°.   1430
Algate°, by sleyghte° or by violence
Fro yeer to yeer I wynne° al my dispence°.
I kan no bettre telle°, feithfully."
      "Now certes," quod this somonour, "so fare° I.
I spare nat° to taken, God it woot°,   1435
But if° it be to hevy or to hoot.
What I may gete in conseil prively°,
No maner conscience of° that have I.
Nere myn° extorcioun, I myghte nat lyven,
Nor of swiche japes° wol I nat be shryven°.   1440
Stomak ne conscience ne knowe I noon;
I shrewe° thise shrifte-fadres° everychoon°.
Wel be we met, by God and by Seint Jame!
But, leeve° brother, tel me thanne thy name,"
Quod this somonour. In this meene while   1445
This yeman gan a litel for to smyle.
      "Brother," quod he, "wiltow° that I thee telle?
I am a feend; my dwellyng is in helle.
And heere I ryde about my purchasyng°
To wite where° men wold me yeven°
          anythyng.   1450
My purchas° is th'effect° of al my rente°.
Looke how thou rydest for the same entente—
To wynne good°, thou rekkest° nevere how.
Right so fare° I, for ryde I wold right now

Unto the worldes ende for a preye°."   1455
      "A," quod this somonour, "benedicite°, what
          sey ye?
I wende° ye were a yeman trewely.
Ye han° a mannes shap° as wel as I.
Han ye a figure thanne determinat
In helle, ther ye been in youre estat°?"   1460
      "Nay, certeinly," quod he, "ther have
          we noon;
But whan us liketh° we kan take us oon°,
Or elles make yow seme° we been shape°.
Somtyme lyk a man, or lyk an ape,
Or lyk an angel kan I ryde or go.   1465
It is no wonder thyng thogh it be so;
A lowsy jogelour° kan deceyve thee,
And pardee°, yet kan° I moore craft than he."
      "Why," quod this somonour, "ryde ye thanne
          or goon
In sondry shap° and nat alwey in oon?"   1470
      "For° we," quod he, "wol° us swiche° formes
          make
As moost able° is oure preyes° for to take."
      "What maketh yow to han° al this labour?"
      "Ful many a cause, leeve° sire somonour,"
Seyde this feend, "but alle thyng hath tyme.   1475
The day is short and it is passed pryme,
And yet ne wan I nothyng in this day.
I wol entende to wynnen, if I may,
And nat entende oure wittes to declare°.
For, brother myn, thy wit is al to bare°   1480
To understonde althogh I tolde hem thee°.
But, for thou axest° why labouren we,
For somtyme we been Goddes instrumentz
And meenes to doon his comandementz,
Whan that hym list°, upon his creatures,   1485
In divers art° and in diverse figures°.
Withouten hym we have no myght, certayn,
If that hym list to stonden ther-agayn°."

1422 spareth nat, *don't refrain* **1423 do ye,** *you operate* **1426 ful streite,** *very limited* **1427 daungerous,** *demanding* **1430 sothe,** *truth,* **yeve,** *give* **1431 Algate,** *always,* **sleyghte,** *trickery* **1432 wynne,** *acquire,* **dispence,** *money* **1433 telle,** *tally* **1434 fare,** *act* **1435 spare nat,** *don't refrain,* **woot,** *knows* **1436 But if,** *unless* **1437 conseil prively,** *secret counsel* **1438 No maner conscience of,** *no kind of moral concern about* **1439 Nere myn,** *if it were not for my* **1440 swiche japes,** *such tricks,* **shryven,** *confessed* **1442 shrewe,** *curse,* **shrifte-fadres,** *confessors,* **everychoon,** *every one* **1444 leeve,** *beloved* **1447 wiltow,** *do you wish* **1449 purchasyng,** *acquiring* **1450 wite where,** *know whether,* **yeven,** *give* **1451 purchas,** *acquisition,* **th'effect,** *the sum total,* **rente,** *income* **1453 wynne good,** *gain wealth,*

rekkest, *care* **1454 fare,** *act* **1455 preye,** *victim* **1456 benedicite,** *bless you* **1457 wende,** *thought* **1458 han,** *have,* **shap,** *shape* **1462 us liketh,** *it pleases us,* **oon,** *one* (a shape) **1463 make yow seme,** *make it seem to you,* **been shape,** *are shaped* **1467 jogelour,** *conjurer* **1468 pardee,** *by God,* **kan,** *know* **1470 sondry shap,** *various shapes* **1471 For,** *because,* **wol,** *will,* **swiche,** *such* **1472 able,** *effective,* **preyes,** *victims* **1473 han,** *have* **1474 leeve,** *beloved* **1479 oure wittes to declare,** *to show off our* (demonic) *intellects* **1480 al to bare,** *altogether incapable* **1481 tolde hem thee,** *explained them to you* **1482 for thou axest,** *because you ask* **1485 hym list,** (it) *pleases him* **1486 divers art,** *various methods,* **figures,** *shapes* **1488 hym list to stonden ther-agayn,** (it) *pleases him to oppose* (what we do)

1459–60 Han ye . . . estat, "Do you have, then, a definite or particular form when you are in hell, where you are in your (proper) condition?"—a debated metaphysical question. **1475 alle thyng hath tyme,** the demon quotes Ecclesiastes 3.1. **1476 pryme,** one of medieval times of the day, about 9:00 a.m.; see *MilT* 1.3655n.

And somtyme, at oure prayere°, han we leve°
Oonly the body and nat the soule greve°: 1490
Witnesse on° Job, whom that we diden wo.
And somtyme han we myght of° bothe two,
This is to seyn, of soule and body eke.
And somtyme be we suffred for to seke
Upon° a man and doon his soule unreste, 1495
And nat his body, and al is for the beste.
Whan he withstandeth oure temptacioun,
It is a cause of his savacioun,
Al be it that it was nat oure entente
He sholde be sauf but° that we wolde hym
    hente°. 1500
And somtyme be we servant unto man,
As to the erchebisshop Seint Dunstan,
And to the apostles servant eek was I.”
    “Yet tel me,” quod the somonour, “feithfully,
Make ye yow newe bodies thus alway 1505
Of elementz?” The feend answerde, “Nay.
Somtyme we feyne°, and somtyme we aryse
With dede° bodyes in ful sondry wyse°,
And speke as renably° and faire and wel
As to the Phitonissa dide Samuel— 1510
And yet wol som men seye it was nat he;
I do no fors of° youre dyvynytee°.
But o thyng warne I thee, I wol nat jape°:
Thou wolt algates wite° how we been shape;
Thou shalt herafterwardes°, my brother
    deere, 1515
Come there° thee nedeth nat of me to leere°,
For thou shalt by thyn owene experience
Konne in a chayer rede° of this sentence°
Bet° than Virgile while he was on lyve,
Or Dant also. Now lat us ryde blyve°, 1520
For I wole holde compaignye with thee
Til it be so that thou forsake me.”

“Nay,” quod this somonour, “that shal nat
    bityde°.
I am a yeman knowen is ful wyde°;
My trouthe° wol I holde, as in this cas. 1525
For though thou were the devel Sathanas,
My trouthe wol I holde to thee my brother,
As I am sworn—and ech of us til° oother—
For to be trewe brother in this cas.
And bothe we goon abouten oure purchas°. 1530
Taak thou thy part, what that° men wol thee yeve°,
And I shal myn; thus may we bothe lyve.
And if that any of us have moore than oother,
Lat hym be trewe and parte° it with his
    brother.”
    “I graunte,” quod the devel, “by my fey°.” 1535
And with that word they ryden forth hir wey.
And right at the entryng of the townes ende°,
To which this somonour shoop hym for to wende°,
They saugh° a cart that charged° was with hey,
Which that a cartere° droof forth in his wey. 1540
Deep° was the wey, for which the carte stood.
The cartere smoot° and cryde as he were wood°,
“Hayt°, Brok! Hayt, Scot! What, spare ye for° the
    stones?
The feend,” quod he, “yow fecche°, body and
    bones,
As ferforthly° as evere were ye foled°, 1545
So muche wo as I have with yow tholed°!
The devel have al, bothe hors and cart and hey.”
    This somonour seyde, “Heere shal we have a
    pley°.”
And neer the feend he drough°, as noght ne
    were°,
Ful prively°, and rowned° in his ere, 1550
“Herkne°, my brother, herkne, by thy feith!
Herestow nat how that° the cartere seith?

1489 prayere, *request,* leve, *permission* 1490 greve, *afflict* 1491 Witnesse on, *take as evidence* 1492 myght of, *power over* 1494–95 suffred for to seke / Upon, *allowed to attack* 1500 sauf but that, *saved unless,* hente, *grab* 1507 feyne, *create illusion* 1508 dede, *dead,* ful sondry wyse, *very many ways* 1509 renably, *reasonably* 1512 do no fors of, *care not at all about,* dyvynytee, *theological dispute* 1513 jape, *joke* 1514 wolt algates wite, *will nevertheless know* 1515 herafterwardes, *soon after this* 1516 there, *where,* leere, *learn* 1518 Konne in a chayer rede, *be able in a* (professor's) *chair to lecture,* sentence, *topic* 1519 Bet, *better* 1520 blyve, *quickly* 1523 bityde, *happen* 1524 knowen is ful wyde, (as) is

very widely known 1525 trouthe, *pledge* 1528 til, *to* 1530 purchas, *acquisition* 1531 what that, *whatever,* yeve, *give* 1534 parte, *divide* 1535 fey, *faith* 1537 ende, *edge* 1538 shoop . . . to wende, *planned to go* 1539 saugh, *saw,* charged, *loaded* 1540 cartere, *cart driver* 1541 Deep, *rutted,* stood, *was stuck* 1542 smoot, *struck,* wood, *crazed* 1543 Hayt, *giddy up,* spare ye for, *do you hold back because* (of) 1544 yow fecche, *fetch you* 1545 ferforthly, *surely,* foled, *foaled* (born) 1546 tholed, *suffered* 1548 a pley, *some fun* 1549 drough, *approached,* as noght ne were, *as* (if it) *were nothing* 1550 Ful prively, *very secretly,* rowned, *whispered* 1551 Herkne, *listen* 1552 Herestow nat how that, *don't you hear what*

1491 Job, God allowed Satan to afflict Job; Job 1.12, 2.6. 1502 erchebisshop Seint Dunstan, St. Dunstan, Archbishop of Canterbury (960–88), was reputed to have controlled demons. 1503 apostles servant, in scripture (Acts 19.11–12) and saints' legends, the apostles had power over demons. 1506 elementz, the four elements: fire, air, water, earth. 1510–11 Phitonissa . . . , in the Vulgate version of the biblical Chronicles (1 Paralipomenon 10.13), the Witch of Endor is called "pythonissam." In the Vulgate 1 Samuel 28.11 (1 Kings), she conjures the spirit of Samuel, who predicts to Saul the downfall of the Israelites. The spirit was later thought to be a demon, not Samuel's spirit. 1519–20, Virgile . . . Dant, Virgil's *Aeneid* and Dante's *Inferno* include visits to hell or the underworld. 1543 Brok . . . Scot, horse names.

Hent it anon°, for he hath yeve° it thee,
Bothe hey and cart, and eek his caples° thre."
    "Nay," quod the devel, "God woot°, never a
      deel°.   1555
It is nat his entente, trust thou me weel.
Axe° hym thyself, if thou nat trowest me°;
Or elles stynt° a while, and thou shalt see."
    This cartere thakketh° his hors upon the
      croupe°,
And they bigonne drawen and to stoupe°.   1560
"Heyt° now," quod he, "ther° Jhesu Crist yow
      blesse,
And al his handwerk°, bothe moore and lesse!
That was wel twight°, myn owene lyard° boy.
I pray God save thee, and Seinte Loy!
Now is my cart out of the slow°, pardee°."   1565
    "Lo, brother," quod the feend, "what tolde I
      thee?
Heere may ye se, myn owene deere brother,
The carl° spak oon°, but he thoghte another.
Lat us go forth abouten oure viage°;
Heere wynne I nothyng upon cariage."   1570
    Whan that they coomen somwhat out of towne,
This somonour to his brother gan to rowne°:
"Brother," quod he, "heere woneth° an old
      rebekke
That hadde almoost as lief to lese° hire nekke
As for to yeve a peny° of hir good°.   1575
I wole han twelf pens°, though that she be wood°,
Or I wol sompne° hire unto oure office°;
And yet, God woot°, of hire knowe I no vice.
But for° thou kanst nat, as in this contree,
Wynne° thy cost°, taak heer ensample°
      of me."   1580
    This somonour clappeth° at the wydwes° gate.
"Com out," quod he, "thou olde virytrate°!
I trowe° thou hast som frere° or preest with thee."
    "Who clappeth?" seyde this wyf, "Benedicitee°,

God save you, sire; what is youre sweete
      wille?"   1585
    "I have," quod he, "of somonce here a bille°.
Upon peyne of cursyng, looke that thou be
Tomorn° bifore the erchedeknes knee
T'answere to the court of certeyn thynges."
    "Now, Lord," quod she, "Crist Jhesu, kyng
      of kynges,   1590
So wisly° helpe me, as I ne may°.
I have been syk, and that ful many a day.
I may nat go so fer," quod she, "ne ryde,
But I be deed°, so priketh it in my syde.
May I nat axe a libel°, sire somonour,   1595
And answere there by my procuratour°
To swich thyng as men wole opposen° me?"
    "Yis," quod this somonour, "pay anon°—
      lat se—
Twelf pens to me, and I wol thee acquite.
I shal no profit han therby but lite;   1600
My maister hath the profit and nat I.
Com of°, and lat me ryden hastily;
Yif° me twelf pens; I may no lenger tarye°."
    "Twelf pens!" quod she, "Now, lady Seinte
      Marie
So wisly° help me out of care and synne,   1605
This wyde world thogh that I sholde wynne,
Ne have I nat twelf pens withinne myn hoold°.
Ye knowen wel that I am poure and oold;
Kithe° youre almesse° on me, poure wrecche."
    "Nay thanne," quod he, "the foule feend me
      fecche   1610
If I th'excuse°, though° thou shul be spilt°!"
    "Allas!" quod she, "God woot°, I have
      no gilt."
    "Pay me," quod he, "or by the sweete Seinte
      Anne,
As I wol° bere awey thy newe panne
For dette° which that thou owest me of old.   1615

1553 Hent it anon, *seize it now,* **yeve,** *given* **1554 caples,** *cart horses* **1555 woot,** *knows,* **never a deel,** *not at all* **1557 Axe,** *ask,* **nat trowest,** *don't believe* **1558 elles stynt,** *else wait* **1559 thakketh,** *pats,* **hors,** *horses,* **croupe,** *rump* **1560 stoupe,** *lean forward* **1561 Heyt,** *giddy up,* **ther,** *so that* **1562 handwerk,** *handiwork* **1563 twight,** *pulled,* **lyard,** *dappled* **1565 slow,** *mud,* **pardee,** *by God* **1568 carl,** *worker,* **oon,** *one* (thing) **1569 viage,** *journey* **1572 rowne,** *whisper* **1573 woneth,** *dwells* **1574 That hadde almoost as lief to lese,** *who would almost as willingly lose* **1575 yeve,** *give,* **good,** *property* **1576 wole han twelf pens,** *will have twelve pennies,* **wood,** *mad* **1577 sompne,** *summon,* **office,** *court* **1578 woot,** *knows* **1579 for,** *because* **1580 Wynne,** *earn,* **cost,** *expenses,* **taak**

heer ensample, *take an example here* **1581 clappeth,** *knocks,* **wydwes,** *widow's* **1582 virytrate,** *hag* **1583 trowe,** *think,* **frere,** *friar* **1584 Benedicitee,** *bless you* **1586 of somonce . . . bille,** *a document of summons* **1588 Tomorn,** *in the morning* **1591 wisly,** *surely,* **ne may,** *cannot* **1594 But I be deed,** *or it will kill me* **1595 axe a libel,** *ask for a written copy* **1596 procuratour,** *representative* **1597 wole opposen,** *will bring against* **1598 anon,** *now* **1602 Com of,** *hurry* **1603 Yif,** *give,* **tarye,** *delay* **1605 wisly,** *surely,* **1607 hoold,** *possession* **1609 Kithe,** *show,* **almesse,** *charity* **1611 th'excuse,** *excuse you,* **though,** *even if,* **spilt,** *ruined* **1612 woot,** *knows* **1614 As I wol,** *I will* **1615 dette,** *debt*

1564 Seinte Loy, St. Eligius, patron saint of carters; see *GP* 1.120. **1570 cariage,** a fee paid to a feudal lord in lieu of the lord's right to use his tenant's cart and horses; i.e., the devil knows he will profit nothing here. **1573 rebekke,** another term for fiddle, slang for old woman; see 1377n. **1613 Seinte Anne,** mother of Mary, grandmother of Jesus.

Whan that thou madest thyn housbonde
    cokewold°,
I payde at hoom for thy correccioun°."
    "Thou lixt°," quod she, "by my savacioun,
Ne was I nevere er° now, wydwe ne wyf,
Somoned unto youre court in al my lyf;   1620
Ne nevere I nas but° of my body trewe°.
Unto the devel, blak and rough of hewe°,
Yeve° I thy body and my panne also!"
    And whan the devel herde hire cursen so
Upon hir knees, he seyde in this manere,   1625
"Now Mabely, myn owene moder deere,
Is this youre wyl in ernest that ye seye°?"
    "The devel," quod she, "so fecche hym er he
    deye°,
And panne and al, but he wol hym° repente!"
    "Nay, olde stot°, that is nat myn entente,"   1630
Quod this somonour, "for to repente me
For any thyng that I have had of thee.
I wolde° I hadde thy smok and every clooth."
    "Now brother," quod the devel, "be nat wrooth°;
Thy body and this panne been myne°
    by right.   1635
Thou shalt° with me to helle yet tonyght,
Where thou shalt knowen of oure privetee°
Moore than a maister of dyvynytee°."
And with that word this foule feend hym hente°;
Body and soule he with the devel wente   1640

Where as that somonours han hir° heritage.
And God, that maked after his ymage
Mankynde, save and gyde us alle and some,
And leve° thise somonours goode men bicome!

    Lordynges, I koude han° toold yow, quod this
    Frere,   1645
Hadde I had leyser° for this Somnour heere,
After the text of Crist, Poul, and John,
And of oure othere doctours many oon°,
Swiche peynes° that youre hertes myghte agryse°,
Al be it° so no tonge may it devyse°,   1650
Thogh that I myghte a thousand wynter° telle,
The peynes of thilke cursed hous of helle.
But for to kepe us fro that cursed place,
Waketh and preyeth Jhesu for his grace
So kepe us fro the temptour Sathanas.   1655
Herketh this word, beth war° as in this cas:
The leoun sit in his awayt alway
To sle° the innocent, if that he may.
Disposeth ay° youre hertes to withstonde
The feend that yow wolde make thral° and
    bonde°.   1660
He may nat tempte yow over youre myght,
For Crist wol be youre champion and knyght.
And prayeth that thise somonours hem repente
Of hir mysdedes er° that the feend hem hente°!

Heere endeth the Freres Tale.

1616 madest . . . cokewold, *made your husband a victim of your adultery* **1617 correccioun,** *fine* **1618 Thou lixt,** *you lie* **1619 er,** *before* **1621 Ne nevere I nas but,** *nor was I ever* (anything) *but,* **trewe,** *faithful* (to my husband) **1622 hewe,** *appearance* **1623 Yeve,** *give* **1627 that ye seye,** *what you say* **1628 er he deye,** *before he dies* **1629 but he wol hym,** *unless he will* **1630 stot,** *cow* **1633 wolde,** *wish* **1634 wrooth,** *angry* **1635 been myne,** *are mine* **1636 shalt,** *shall* (go) **1637 privetee,** *secrets* **1638 dyvynytee,** *theology* **1639 hente,** *grabbed* **1641 han hir,** *have their* **1644 leve,** *let* **1645 koude han,** *could have* **1646 leyser,** *time* **1648 othere doctours many oon,** *many other theologians* **1649 Swiche peynes,** *such pains,* **agryse,** *terrify* **1650 Al be it so,** *even though,* **devyse,** *describe* **1651 wynter,** *years* **1656 beth war,** *be aware* **1658 sle,** *slay* **1659 Disposeth ay,** *prepare always* **1660 thral,** *slave,* **bonde,** *bound* **1664 mysdedes er,** *misdeeds before,* **hente,** *seizes*

1636 A parody of Christ's words to the thief who repents; Luke 23.43. **1647 After the text . . . ,** following scripture—the Gospels, Paul's letters, and John's Revelation. **1657 leoun . . . awayt,** lion sits waiting; Psalms 10.8–9. **1661** 1 Corinthians 10.13. **1663–64 thise somonours . . . ,** some manuscripts have "this somonour," with singular pronouns following.

SUMMONER'S TALE

PROLOGUE

The Prologe of the Somonours Tale.

This Somonour in his styropes hye° stood;   1665
Upon this Frere his herte was so wood°
That lyk an aspen leef he quook° for ire°.
   "Lordynges," quod he, "but o° thyng I desire:
I yow biseke° that, of youre curteisye,
Syn° ye han herd this false Frere lye,   1670
As suffreth me° I may my tale telle.
This Frere bosteth° that he knoweth helle,
And God it woot° that it is litel wonder—
Freres and feendes been but lyte asonder°.
For, pardee°, ye han ofte tyme herd telle   1675
How that a frere ravysshed° was to helle
In spirit ones° by a visioun,
And as an angel ladde° hym up and doun
To shewen hym the peynes that ther were
In al the place saugh° he nat a frere;   1680
Of oother folk he saugh ynowe° in wo.
Unto this angel spak the frere tho°,
   'Now, sire,' quod he, 'han freres swich° a grace°
That noon of hem shal come to this place?'

'Yis,' quod this angel, 'many a millioun.'   1685
And unto Sathanas° he ladde hym doun.
'And now hath Sathanas,' seith he, 'a tayl
Brodder than of a carryk° is the sayl.
Hold up thy tayl, thou Sathanas,' quod he.
'Shewe forth thyn ers°, and lat the frere se   1690
Where is the nest of freres in this place!'
And er that half a furlong wey of space,
Right so° as bees out swarmen from an hyve,
Out of the develes ers ther gonne dryve
Twenty thousand freres in a route°,   1695
And thurghout helle swarmeden aboute,
And comen agayn as faste as they may gon,
And in his ers they crepten everychon°.
He clapte° his tayl agayn and lay ful stille.
This frere, whan he hadde looke al his fille   1700
Upon the tormentz of this sory place,
His spirit God restored, of his grace,
Unto his body agayn, and he awook.
But natheles for fere° yet he quook°,

1665 styropes hye, *stirrups high* **1666 wood,** *angry* **1667 quook,** *trembled,* **ire,** *anger* **1668 but o,** *only one* **1669 biseke,** *request* **1670 Syn,** *since* **1671 As suffreth me,** *so allow me* **1672 bosteth,** *boasts* **1673 woot,** *knows* **1674 been but lyte asonder,** *are only a little different* **1675 pardee,** *by God* **1676 ravysshed,** *abducted* **1677 ones,** *once* **1678 ladde,** *led* **1680 saugh,** *saw* **1681 ynowe,** *enough* **1682 tho,** *then* **1683 swich, such,** **grace,** *favor* **1686 Sathanas,** *Satan* **1688 carryk,** *large ship* **1690 thyn ers,** *your arse* **1693 Right so,** *just* **1695 route,** *company* **1698 everychon,** *every one* **1699 clapte,** *closed* **1704 fere,** *fear,* **quook,** *trembled*

1692 er that half a furlong wey of space, before a minute or two (had passed). See *MilT* 1.3637n.

So was the develes ers ay in his mynde— 1705
That is his heritage of verray kynde°.

God save yow alle, save this cursed Frere!
My prologe wol I ende in this manere."

Heere bigynneth the Somonour his Tale.

Lordynges, ther is in Yorkshire, as I gesse,
A mersshy° contree called Holdernesse 1710
In which ther wente a lymytour aboute
To preche and eek to begge, it is no doute.
And so bifel that on a day this frere
Hadde preched at a chirche in his manere,
And specially, aboven every thyng, 1715
Excited he the peple in his prechyng
To trentals, and to yeve° for Goddes sake
Wherwith men myghte hooly houses make°
Ther as divine servyce is honoured,
Nat ther as it is wasted and devoured, 1720
Ne ther it nedeth nat for to be yeve°,
As to possessioners that mowen lyve°,
Thanked be God, in wele° and habundaunce.
"Trentals," seyde he, "deliveren fro penaunce
Hir° freendes soules, as wel olde as° yonge, 1725
Ye°, whan that they been hastily ysonge,
Nat for to holde° a preest joly and gay—
He syngeth nat but o masse in a day.
Delivereth out," quod he, "anon° the soules.
Ful hard it is with flesshhook° or with oules° 1730
To been yclawed°, or to brenne° or bake.
Now spede yow hastily, for Cristes sake!"
And whan this frere had seyd al his entente,
With *qui cum patre* forth his wey he wente.

Whan folk in chirche had yeve° him what
hem leste°, 1735
He wente his wey—no lenger wolde he reste—
With scrippe° and tipped staf°, ytukked hye°.
In every hous he gan to poure° and prye°,
And beggeth mele° and chese, or elles corn°.
His felawe hadde a staf tipped with horn, 1740
A peyre of tables al of yvory,
And a poyntel° polysshed fetisly°,
And wroot the names alwey, as he stood,
Of alle folk that yaf° hym any good,
Ascaunces° that he wolde for hem preye. 1745
"Yif° us a busshel whete, malt, or reye°,
A Goddes kechyl°, or a tryp° of chese,
Or elles what yow lyst°—we may nat cheese°—
A Goddes halfpeny, or a masse peny,
Or yif us of youre brawn°, if ye have eny, 1750
A dagon° of youre blanket—leeve° dame,
Oure suster deere—lo, heere I write youre
name—
Bacon or boef°, or swich thyng° as ye fynde."
A sturdy harlot° wente ay hem bihynde°,
That was hir hostes man°, and bar a sak°, 1755
And what men yaf hem°, leyde it on his bak.
And whan that he was out at dore, anon
He planed° awey the names everichon°

1706 **verray kynde,** *true nature* 1710 **mersshy,** *marshy* 1717 **yeve,** *give* 1718 **make,** *build* 1721 **yeve,** *given* 1722 **mowen lyve,** *are able to live* 1723 **wele,** *prosperity,* 1725 **Hir,** *their,* **as wel . . . as,** *both . . . and* 1726 **Ye,** *indeed* 1727 **holde,** *keep* (support) 1729 **anon,** *immediately* 1730 **Ful hard,** *very painful,* **flesshhook,** *meat hook,* **oules,** *awls* 1731 **been yclawed,** *be torn,* **brenne,** *burn* 1735 **yeve,** *given,* **hem leste,** *pleased them* 1737 **scrippe,** *bag,* **tipped staf,** *metal- or horn-tipped staff,* **ytukked hye,** (and cloak) *tucked up high* 1738 **poure,** *examine,* **prye,**

peek (into) 1739 **mele,** *ground grain,* **elles corn,** *else whole grain* 1742 **poyntel,** *stylus,* **fetisly,** *elegantly* 1744 **yaf,** *gave* 1745 **Ascaunces,** *as if to indicate* 1746 **Yif,** *give,* **reye,** *rye* 1747 **Goddes kechyl,** *small charity cake,* **tryp,** *bit* 1748 **yow lyst,** *pleases you,* **cheese,** *choose* 1750 **brawn,** *meat* 1751 **dagon,** *piece,* **leeve,** *beloved* 1753 **boef,** *beef,* **swich thyng,** *whatever* 1754 **harlot,** *servant,* **wente ay hem bihynde,** *always traveled behind them* 1755 **hir hostes man,** *their innkeeper's servant,* **bar,** *carried* 1756 **yaf hem,** *gave them* 1758 **planed,** *smoothed,* **everichon,** *every one*

1706 **heritage,** compare *FrT* 3.1641. 1707 **save . . . save,** a powerful pun that initiates a series of word plays in *SumT*; see notes to lines 1793, 1877–78, 1916–17, 1934, 1967, 2148, 2185–87, and 2222. 1710 **Holdernesse,** a district in Yorkshire, in northern England. Chaucer does not reproduce a northern accent here as he does in *RvT*. 1711 **lymytour,** "a friar whose begging, preaching, and hearing of confessions was limited" to a particular territory (*MED*). See *GP* 1.209 and *FrT* 3.1265. 1717 **trentals,** (the money paid for) thirty masses for the dead, conducted to release a soul from purgatory. 1722 **possessioners,** clergy (other than friars) who live on revenue from property or other endowments. 1726 **hastily ysonge,** the friar recommends that the thirty masses be conducted (sung) simultaneously (by a group of friars rather than a single priest), presumably a quicker route to salvation than conducting one per day. 1734 **qui cum patre,** "who with the father," a formula beginning for the closing of a prayer or sermon. 1737 **scrippe and tipped staf,** satirizes friars' claims to be the new apostles, because Christ commanded his disciples to travel with neither sack nor staff (Luke 9.3). For other satiric details, see notes to lines 1740, 1770, 1820, and 2186–87. 1740 **felawe,** friars were supposed to travel in pairs, in imitation of Christ's command to his disciples in Luke 10.1, but the "sturdy harlot" (line 1754) makes three. 1741 **peyre of tables,** folding tablets, covered with wax for taking notes. 1749 **Goddes halfpeny . . . masse peny,** money given as charity or as payment for a mass.

That he biforn had writen in his tables;
He served hem with nyfles° and with fables.   1760
  "Nay, ther thou lixt°, thou Somonour!" quod
      the Frere.
  "Pees," quod oure Hoost, "for Cristes mooder
      deere.
Tel forth thy tale, and spare it nat at al°."
  "So thryve I°," quod this Somonour, "so I shal."
  So longe he wente, hous by hous, til he   1765
Cam til° an hous ther he was wont° to be
Refresshed moore than in an hundred placis.
Syk° lay the goode man whos that the place is;
Bedrede° upon a couche lowe he lay.
"*Deus hic!*" quod he, "O Thomas, freend, good
      day,"   1770
Seyde this frere, curteisly and softe.
"Thomas," quod he, "God yelde° yow. Ful ofte
Have I upon this bench faren ful weel°;
Heere have I eten many a myrie° meel."
And fro the bench he droof° awey the cat   1775
And leyde adoun his potente° and his hat,
And eek his scrippe°, and sette hym softe adoun.
His felawe was go walked° into toun
Forth with his knave into that hostelrye
Where as he shoop° hym thilke° nyght to lye.   1780
  "O deere maister," quod this sike man,
"How han ye fare sith° that March bigan?
I saugh° yow noght this fourtenyght° or moore."
  "God woot°," quod he, "laboured I have ful
      soore°,
And specially for thy savacioun   1785
Have I seyd many a precious orisoun°,
And for oure othere freendes, God hem blesse!
I have to day been at youre chirche at messe,°
And seyd a sermon after my symple wit,
Nat al after the text of hooly writ;   1790
For it is hard to° yow, as I suppose,

And therfore wol I teche° yow al the glose°.
Glosynge is a glorious thyng, certeyn,
For lettre sleeth, so as we clerkes seyn.
There° have I taught hem to be charitable,   1795
And spende hir good ther° it is resonable;
And there I saugh oure dame—a, where is she?"
  "Yond° in the yerd I trowe° that she be,"
Seyde this man, "and she wol come anon."
  "Ey, maister, welcome be ye, by Seint
      John!"   1800
Seyde this wyf, "How fare ye, hertely°?"
  The frere ariseth up ful curteisly°
And hire embraceth in his armes narwe°,
And kiste hire sweete, and chirketh° as a sparwe
With his lyppes. "Dame," quod he, "right weel,   1805
As he that is youre servant every deel°,
Thanked be God that yow yaf° soule and lyf.
Yet saugh I nat this day so fair a wyf
In al the chirche, God so save me!"
  "Ye, God amende defautes°, sire," quod she.   1810
"Algates°, welcome be ye, by my fey°!"
  "Graunt mercy, dame, this have I founde alwey.
But of youre grete goodnesse, by youre leve,
I wolde prey yow that ye nat yow greve°,
I wole with Thomas speke a litel throwe°.   1815
Thise curatz° been ful necligent and slowe
To grope° tendrely a conscience
In shrift; in prechyng is my diligence°,
And studie in Petres wordes and in Poules.
I walke and fisshe Cristen mennes soules   1820
To yelden° Jhesu Crist his propre rente°;
To sprede his word is set al myn entente."
  "Now, by your leve, O deere sire," quod she,
"Chideth° him weel, for seinte° Trinitee.
He is as angry as a pissemyre°   1825
Though that he have al that he kan desire.
Though I hym wrye a-nyght° and make hym warm,

1760 nyfles, *trifles* **1761 lixt,** *lie* **1763 spare it nat at al,** *don't hold back* **1764 So thryve I,** *as I may prosper* **1766 til,** *to,* **wont,** *accustomed* **1768 Syk,** *sick* **Bedrede,** *bedridden* **1772 yelde,** *reward* **1773 faren ful weel,** *done very well* **1774 myrie,** *merry* **1775 droof,** *drove* **1776 potente,** *staff* **1777 scrippe,** *bag* **1778 go walked,** *gone walking* **1780 shoop,** *planned,* **thilke,** *that* **1782 han ye fare sith,** *have you done since* **1783 saugh,** *saw,* **fourtenyght,** *fortnight* (two weeks) **1784 woot,** *knows,* **ful soore,** *very sorely* **1786 orisoun,** *prayer* **1788 messe,** *mass* **1791 hard to,** *difficult for* **1792 teche,** *teach,* **glose,** *interpretation* **1795 There,** i.e., "in

church" **1796 hir good ther,** *their money where* **1798 Yond,** *over there,* **trowe,** *believe* **1801 hertely,** *with all my heart* **1802 curteisly,** *courteously* **1803 narwe,** *closely* **1804 chirketh,** *chirps* **1806 every deel,** *in every way* **1807 yow yaf,** *gave to you* **1810 amende defautes,** *repair* (my) *faults* **1811 Algates,** *always,* **fey,** *faith* **1814 yow greve,** *be upset* **1815 throwe,** *while* **1816 curatz,** *resident priests* **1817 grope,** *examine* **1818 diligence,** *concern* **1821 yelden,** *pay,* **propre rente,** *due income* **1824 Chideth,** *scold,* **seinte,** (the) *holy* **1825 pissemyre,** *ant* **1827 wrye a-nyght,** *cover at night*

1770 "*Deus hic,*" "God be here"; see Matthew 10.12. **1781 maister,** address of respect, accepted by the friar here and at lines 1800 and 1836, but see lines 2185–87 below. **1793 Glosynge . . . ,** "glossing" or interpreting (but also distorting or deceiving, a potent double entendre; see *MED gloze*). The friar defends his practice of interpreting scripture by alluding to St. Paul's assertion that the "letter slays" and the "spirit gives life" (2 Corinthians 3.6). The distinction recurs in lines 1919–20 below. **1804 sparwe,** sparrow, thought to be lecherous. **1818 shrift,** confession, the sacrament of the forgiveness of sins that involves a preparatory examination of conscience. **1820 fisshe . . . mennes soules,** the friar here claims to be a disciple of Christ; see Matthew 4.19.

And on hym leye my leg outher° myn arm;
He groneth lyk oure boor lith° in oure sty.
Oother desport° right noon of hym have I; 1830
I may nat plese hym in no maner cas."
    "O Thomas, *je vous dy,* Thomas! Thomas!
This maketh the feend; this moste ben amended.
Ire° is a thyng that hye° God defended°,
And therof wol I speke a word or two." 1835
    "Now, maister," quod the wyf, "er that I go,
What wol ye dyne°? I wol go theraboute."
    "Now, dame," quod he, "now *je vous dy sanz
        doute,*
Have I nat of a capon° but the lyvere°,
And of youre softe breed nat but a shyvere°, 1840
And after that a rosted pigges heed—
But° that I nolde no° beest for me were deed—
Thanne hadde I with yow hoomly suffisaunce°.
I am a man of litel sustenaunce°;
My spirit hath his fostryng° in the Bible. 1845
The body is ay° so redy and penyble°
To wake° that my stomak° is destroyed.
I prey yow, dame, ye be nat anoyed,
Though I so freendly yow my conseil shewe°.
By God, I wolde nat telle it but a fewe." 1850
    "Now, sire," quod she, "but o word er I go.
My child is deed withinne thise wykes two,
Soone after that ye wente out of this toun."
    "His deeth saugh° I by revelacioun,"
Seith this frere, "at hoom in oure dortour°. 1855
I dar wel seyn that er that half an hour
After his deeth I saugh hym born° to blisse
In myn avisioun, so God me wisse°.
So dide oure sexteyn and oure fermerer,
That han been trewe freres fifty yeer; 1860

They may now—God be thanked of his loone°—
Maken hir° jubilee and walke allone.
And up I roos, and al oure covent eke°,
With many a teere trillyng° on my cheke,
Withouten noyse or claterynge of belles; 1865
Te Deum was oure song, and nothyng elles,
Save that to Crist I seyde an orisoun°,
Thankynge hym of° his revelacioun.
For, sire and dame, trusteth me right weel,
Oure orisons been moore effectueel°, 1870
And moore we seen of Cristes secree° thynges,
Than burel° folk, although they weren kynges.
We lyve in poverte and in abstinence,
And burell folk in richesse and despence°
Of mete and drynke, and in hir foul delit. 1875
We han this worldes lust al in despit°.
Lazar and Dives lyveden° diversly,
And diverse gerdon° hadden they therby.
Whoso wol preye, he moot° faste and be clene°,
And fatte° his soule, and make his body lene. 1880
We fare as seith th'apostle; clooth° and foode
Suffisen us, though they be nat ful° goode.
The clennesse° and the fastynge of us freres
Maketh that Crist accepteth oure preyeres.
    "Lo, Moyses fourty dayes and fourty nyght 1885
Fasted er° that the heighe God of myght
Spak with hym in the Mount of Synay.
With empty wombe°, fastynge many a day,
Receyved he the lawe that was writen
With Goddes fynger; and Elye, wel ye witen°, 1890
In Mount Oreb, er he hadde any speche
With hye God that is oure lyves leche°,
He fasted longe and was in contemplaunce°.
    "Aaron, that hadde the temple in governaunce,

1828 outher, *or* **1829 lyk oure boor lith,** *like our* (male) *pig* (that) *lies* **1830 desport,** *entertainment* **1832 je vous dy,** *I say to you* **1834 Ire,** *anger,* **hye,** *high,* **defended,** *forbade* **1837 dyne,** *eat* **1839 capon,** *chicken,* **lyvere,** *liver* **1840 shyvere,** *sliver* **1842 But,** *except,* **nolde no,** *wish no* **1843 hoomly suffisaunce,** *family fare* **1844 of litel sustenaunce,** *who eats little* **1845 his fostryng,** *its nourishment* **1846 ay,** *always,* **penyble,** *painstaking* **1847 To wake,** *to stay awake,* **stomak,** *appetite* **1849 conseil shewe,** *secrets reveal* **1854 saugh,** *saw* **1855 dortour,**

dormitory 1857 born, *carried* **1858 wisse,** *instruct* **1861 loone,** *gift* **1862 hir,** *their* **1863 covent eke,** *assembly also* **1864 trillyng,** *trickling* **1867 orisoun,** *prayer* **1868 of,** *for* **1870 effectueel,** *effective* **1871 secree,** *secret* **1872 burel,** *nonreligious* **1874 despence,** *consumption* **1876 despit,** *scorn* **1877 lyveden,** *lived* **1878 gerdon,** *reward* **1879 moot,** *must,* **clene,** *pure* **1880 fatte,** *fatten* **1881 clooth,** *clothing* **1882 ful,** *very* **1883 clennesse,** *purity* **1886 er,** *before* **1888 wombe,** *stomach* **1890 witen,** *know* **1892 leche,** *physician* **1893 contemplaunce,** *contemplation*

1838 je vous dy sanz doute, "I say to you without doubt." The use of French and the repetition from line 1832 suggest affectation. **1859 sexteyn . . . fermerer,** two officers in the friar's convent, the first responsible for the sacred vessels and vestments, the second for the infirmary. **1862 jubilee . . . walke allone,** privileges such as walking without a companion (see 1740n above) were granted to friars at jubilee (fiftieth) anniversaries. **1866 Te Deum,** "To You O God," a hymn of praise, regularly sung to conclude matins (see *MilT* 1.3655n) but also sung to celebrate outstanding events or occasions. **1877 Lazar and Dives,** the biblical poor man and rich man; Luke 16.19–31. This and the other biblical allusions from here to line 1917 derive from St. Jerome's *Epistola adversus Jovinianum* (Letter against Jovinian), book 2, here 2.17. Also, note the play with *Dives, diversly,* and *diverse,* lines 1877–78. **1881 th'apostle,** Paul, in 1 Timothy 6.8; Jerome 2.11. **1885–90 Moyses . . . ,** on Mt. Sinai, Moses fasted (Exodus 34.28) before he received for the second time the Ten Commandments written by God (see Exodus 31.18); Jerome 2.15. **1890–93 Elye . . . ,** Elijah fasted and spoke with God on Mount Horeb (1 Kings 19.8; Vulgate 3 Kings); Jerome 2.15. **1894–1901 Aaron . . . ,** Leviticus 10.8–9; Jerome 2.15.

And eek the othere preestes everichon° 1895
Into the temple whan they sholde gon
To preye for the peple and do servyse,
They nolden° drynken in no maner wyse
No drynke which that myghte hem dronke
    make,
But there in abstinence preye and wake 1900
Lest that they deyden°. Taak heede what I seye.
But° they be sobre that for the peple preye,
War° that I seye—namoore, for it suffiseth.
    "Oure Lord Jhesu, as hooly writ devyseth°,
Yaf° us ensample of fastynge and preyeres. 1905
Therfore we mendynantz°, we sely° freres,
Been wedded to poverte and continence°,
To charite, humblesse, and abstinence,
To persecucioun for rightwisnesse°,
To wepynge, misericorde°, and clennesse°. 1910
And therfore may ye se that oure preyeres—
I speke of us, we mendynantz, we freres—
Been to the hye God moore acceptable
Than youres, with youre feestes at the table.
Fro Paradys first, if I shal nat lye, 1915
Was man out chaced for his glotonye—
And chaast was man in Paradys, certeyn.
    "But herkne° now, Thomas, what I shal seyn°.
I ne have no text of° it, as I suppose,
But I shal fynde it in a maner glose° 1920
That specially oure sweete Lord Jhesus
Spak this by° freres whan he seyde thus,
'Blessed be they that povere° in spirit been.'
And so forth al the gospel may ye seen
Wher it be likker° oure professioun 1925
Or hirs° that swymmen in possessioun.
Fy° on hire° pompe and on hire glotonye,

And for hir lewednesse I hem diffye°.
    "Me thynketh they been lyk Jovinyan,
Fat as a whale and walkynge as a swan, 1930
Al vinolent° as botel in the spence°.
Hir° preyere is of ful greet reverence
Whan they for soules seye the psalm of Davit:
Lo, 'buf°!' they seye, '*cor meum eructavit!*'
Who folweth Cristes gospel and his foore° 1935
But we that humble been, and chaast, and poore,
Werkeris° of Goddes word, nat auditours°?
Therfore, right° as an hauk up at a sours°
Up springeth into th'eir, right so prayeres
Of charitable and chaste bisy freres 1940
Maken hir sours° to Goddes eres two.
Thomas, Thomas, so moote I° ryde or go,
And by that lord that clepid° is Seint Yve,
Nere thou° oure brother, sholdestou° nat thryve.
In oure chapitre° praye we day and nyght 1945
To Crist that he thee sende heele° and myght
Thy body for to weelden hastily°."
    "God woot°," quod he, "nothyng therof feele I!
As help me Crist, as° I in a fewe yeres
Have spended upon diverse manere freres° 1950
Ful many a pound, yet fare I never the bet°.
Certeyn, my good° I have almoost biset°.
Farwel, my gold, for it is al ago°."
    The frere answerde, "O Thomas, dostow° so?
What nedeth yow diverse freres seche°? 1955
What nedeth hym that hath a parfit leche°
To sechen othere leches in the toun?
Youre inconstance° is youre confusioun.
Holde ye thanne° me, or elles oure covent°,
To praye for yow been insufficient? 1960
Thomas, that jape° nys nat worth a myte°.

1895 everichon, *each one* 1898 nolden, *would not* 1901 Lest . . . deyden, *in order that they would not die* 1902 But, *unless* 1903 War, *beware* 1904 devyseth, *describes* 1905 Yaf, *gave* 1906 mendynantz, *begging friars* (mendicants), sely, *blessed* 1907 continence, *restraint* 1909 for rightwisnesse, *for the sake of righteousness* 1910 misericorde, *mercy*, clennesse, *purity* 1918 herkne, *listen*, seyn, *say* 1919 ne have no text of, *have no biblical quotation for* 1920 maner glose, *kind of interpretation* 1922 by, *about* 1923 povere, *poor* 1925 Wher it be likker, *whether the gospel be closer to* 1926 hirs, *theirs* 1927 Fy, *fie*, hire, *their* 1928 diffye, *defy* 1931 vinolent, *full of wine*, spence, *storeroom* 1932 Hir, *their* 1934 buf, *burp* 1935 foore, *footsteps* 1937 Werkeris, *doers*, auditours, *listen-* ers 1938 right, *just*, up at a sours, *soaring* 1941 hir sours, *their soarings* 1942 so moote I, *as I might* 1943 clepid, *named* 1944 Nere thou, *(if) you were not*, sholdestou, *you should* 1945 chapitre, *assembly* 1946 heele, *health* 1947 weelden hastily, *use soon* 1948 woot, *knows* 1949 as, *though* 1950 diverse maner freres, *various kinds of friars* 1951 bet, *better* 1952 good, *wealth*, biset, *spent* 1953 ago, *gone* 1954 dostow, *do you* 1955 What nedeth yow . . . seche, *why do you need to seek* 1956 parfit leche, *perfect physician* 1958 inconstance, *inconsistency* 1959 Holde ye thanne, *do you consider then*, covent, *assembly* 1961 jape, *joke*, myte, *worthless coin*

1916–17 chaced . . . chaast, chased . . . chaste; the play links gluttony in Paradise (Adam's eating of the apple) and lechery (desire for Eve). Genesis 3.6–7; Jerome 2.15. 1919–20 text . . . glose, see 1793n above. 1923 Matthew 5.3. The claim is ironic since friars in the fourteenth century were notorious for self-indulgence. 1929 Jovinyan, the target of St. Jerome's ascetic defense of celibacy and fasting, *Letter against Jovinian;* Jovinian is described in similar terms in the treatise, 1.40. See 1877n above. 1933 Davit, King David, thought to be the composer of the biblical book of Psalms. 1934 *cor meum eructavit,* "my heart has uttered," the opening words of Psalm 45 (Vulgate 44), but a pun because *eructavit* also means "belched." 1935 Echoes Matthew 19.21, but also Jerome 2.6. 1937 James 1.22, but also Jerome 2.3. 1943 Seint Yve, there were several saints named Ives, none clearly appropriate here. 1944 oure brother, a lay member of the friar's convent.

Youre maladye is for° we han to lyte°.
A, yif° that covent half a quarter otes°!
A, yif that covent foure and twenty grotes°!
A, yif that frere a peny and lat hym go! 1965
Nay, nay, Thomas, it may no thyng be so!
What is a ferthyng° worth parted in twelve?
Lo, ech thyng that is oned° in itselve
Is moore strong than whan it is toscatered°.
Thomas, of me thou shalt nat been yflatered; 1970
Thou woldest han° oure labour al for noght.
The hye God, that al this world hath wroght,
Seith that the werkman worthy is his hyre°.
Thomas, noght of youre tresor I desire
As for myself, but that al oure covent 1975
To preye for yow is ay° so diligent,
And for to buylden Cristes owene chirche.
Thomas, if ye wol lernen for to wirche°,
Of buyldynge up of chirches may ye fynde
If it be good in Thomas lyf of Inde. 1980
Ye lye heere ful of anger and of ire,
With which the devel set youre herte afyre,
And chiden° heere the sely° innocent,
Youre wyf, that is so meke and pacient.
And therfore, Thomas, trowe° me if thee
     leste°, 1985
Ne stryve nat with thy wyf, as for thy beste°.
And ber° this word awey now, by thy feith,
Touchynge this thyng, lo, what the wise seith:
'Withinne thyn hous ne be° thou no leoun;
To thy subgitz° do noon oppressioun; 1990
Ne make thyne aqueyntance nat for to flee.'
And, Thomas, yet eftsoones° I charge° thee,
Bewar from° ire that in thy bosom slepeth,
Bewar fro the serpent that so slily crepeth
Under the gras and styngeth subtilly°. 1995
Bewar, my sone, and herkne° paciently

That twenty thousand men han° lost hir lyves
For stryvyng with hir lemmans° and hir wyves.
Now sith° ye han so hooly meke° a wyf,
What nedeth yow, Thomas, to maken stryf? 2000
Ther nys, ywys°, no serpent so cruel
Whan man tret° on his tayl, ne half so fel°
As womman is, whan she hath caught an ire;
Vengeance is thanne al that they desire.
Ire is a synne, oon of the grete of sevene, 2005
Abhomynable unto the God of hevene;
And to hymself it is destruccioun.
This every lewed viker° or persoun°
Kan seye, how ire engendreth° homycide.
Ire is, in sooth°, executour of pryde°. 2010
I koude° of ire seye so muche sorwe
My tale sholde laste til tomorwe.
And therfore preye I God bothe day and nyght
An irous° man, God sende hym litel myght!
It is greet harm and certes° greet pitee 2015
To sette an irous man in heigh degree°.
     "Whilom° ther was an irous potestat°,
As seith Senek, that durynge his estaat°
Upon a day out ryden knyghtes two,
And as Fortune wolde that it were so 2020
That oon of hem° cam hoom that oother noght.
Anon the knyght bifore the juge is broght,
That seyde thus, 'Thou hast thy felawe slayn
For which I deme° thee to the deeth, certayn.'
And to another knyght comanded he, 2025
'Go lede hym to the deeth, I charge° thee.'
And happed as they wente by the weye
Toward the place ther° he sholde deye,
The knyght cam which° men wenden° had be
     deed.
Thanne thoughte they it were the beste reed° 2030
To lede hem bothe to the juge agayn.

1962 for, *because,* **to lyte,** *too little* **1963 yif,** *give,* **quarter otes,** *quarter (measure of) oats* **1964 grotes,** *silver coins (worth four pennies)* **1967 ferthyng,** *farthing (coin worth a quarter penny)* **1968 oned,** *united* **1969 toscatered,** *scattered around* **1971 woldest han,** *wish to have* **1973 hyre,** *pay* **1976 ay,** *always* **1978 for to wirche,** *to do good works* **1983 chiden,** *scold,* **sely,** *blessed* **1985 trowe,** *believe,* **leste,** *will* **1986 beste,** *benefit* **1987 ber,** *carry* **1989 ne be,** *do not be* **1990 subgitz,** *subjects* **1992 eftsoones,** *again,* **charge,** *order* **1993 Bewar from,** *beware of,* **1995 subtilly,** *stealthily* **1996 herkne,** *listen* **1997 han,** *have*

1998 lemmans, *lovers* **1999 sith,** *since,* **hooly meke,** *wholly meek* **2001 ywys,** *certainly* **2002 tret,** *steps,* **fel,** *dangerous* **2008 lewed viker,** *unlearned vicar (priest's representative),* **persoun,** *parson* **2009 engendreth,** *produces* **2010 sooth,** *truth,* **executour of pryde,** *pride's representative* **2011 koude,** *could* **2014 irous,** *angry* **2015 certes,** *certainly* **2016 degree,** *rank* **2017 Whilom,** *once,* **potestat,** *ruler* **2018 estaat,** *time of rule* **2021 oon of hem,** *one of them* **2024 deme,** *judge* **2026 charge,** *order* **2028 ther,** *where* **2029 which,** *who,* **wenden,** *believed* **2030 reed,** *counsel*

1967 ferthyng . . . parted in twelve, this punningly anticipates lines 2253ff. below. **1968–69** Proverbial, but its application to "thyng" is unusual, emphasized here by repetition, lines 1966–68. **1973** Translates Luke 10.7, which continues, "Go not from house to house." **1980 Thomas lyf of Inde,** the life of Thomas of India; Thomas the Apostle was reputed to have traveled to India as a preacher and carpenter. **1989–91** Ecclesiasticus 4.35. **2005 grete of sevene,** greatest of seven; Ire (Anger or Wrath) is one of the seven deadly sins, along with Pride, Envy, Sloth, Avarice, Gluttony, and Lechery. **2018 Senek . . . ,** the following illustrations derive from Seneca's *De Ira* (first century CE), although Chaucer probably got them from a preachers' manual such as John of Wales's *Communiloquium* (Common Sayings) 1.4.4, 1.3.11, and 2.8.2–3. Such illustrations were common in sermons against Ire.

They seiden, 'Lord, the knyght ne hath nat slayn
His felawe; heere he standeth hool° alyve.'
'Ye shul be deed,' quod he, 'so moot I thryve°,
That is to seyn, bothe oon, and two, and
    thre.'   2035
And to the firste knyght right thus spak he,
'I dampned° thee; thou most algate° be deed.
And thou also most nedes lese° thyn heed
For thou art cause why thy felawe deyth°.'
And to the thridde knyght right thus he
    seith,   2040
'Thou hast nat doon that° I comanded thee.'
And thus he dide doon sleen hem° alle thre.

   "Irous Cambises was eek dronkelewe°
And ay° delited hym to been a shrewe°.
And so bifel°, a lord of his meynee°   2045
That loved vertuous moralitee
Seyde on a day bitwene hem two right thus,
'A lord is lost if he be vicius,
And dronkenesse is eek a foul record
Of any man, and namely° in a lord.   2050
Ther is ful many an eye and many an ere
Awaityng on° a lord and he noot° where.
For Goddes love, drynk moore attemprely°!
Wyn maketh° man to lesen° wrecchedly
His mynde and eek his lymes° everichon.'   2055
   'The revers° shaltou se,' quod he, 'anon°,
And preve it by thyn owene experience,
That wyn ne dooth to folk no swich° offence.
Ther is no wyn bireveth me° my myght
Of hand ne foot, ne of myne eyen sight.'   2060
And for despit° he drank ful muchel moore
An hondred part° than he hadde bifoore;
And right anon this irous, cursed wrecche
Leet this knyghtes sone bifore hym fecche°,
Comandynge hym he sholde bifore hym
    stonde.   2065
And sodeynly he took his bowe in honde,

And up the streng he pulled to his ere,
And with an arwe he slow° the child right there.
'Now wheither° have I a siker° hand or noon?'
Quod he. 'Is al my myght and mynde agon? 2070
Hath wyn byreved me° myn eyen sight?'
   "What sholde I telle th'answere of the knyght?
His sone was slayn, ther is namoore to seye.
Beth war, therfore, with lordes how ye pleye.
Syngeth *Placebo* and 'I shal if I kan,'   2075
But if° it be unto a poure man.
To a poure man men sholde his vices telle,
But nat to a lord thogh he sholde go to helle.
   "Lo° irous Cirus, thilke Percien,
How he destroyed the ryver of Gysen   2080
For that° an hors of his was dreynt° therinne
Whan that he wente Babiloigne to wynne°.
He made that the ryver was so smal
That wommen myghte wade it over al.
Lo, what seyde he that so wel teche kan: 2085
Ne be no° felawe to an irous man,
Ne with no wood° man walke by the weye,
Lest thee repente—I wol no ferther seye.
   "Now, Thomas, leeve° brother, lef thyn° ire;
Thou shalt me fynde as just as is a squyre°. 2090
Hoold nat the develes knyf ay° at thyn herte—
Thyn angre dooth thee al to soore smerte°—
But shewe to me al thy confessioun."
   "Nay," quod the sike man, "by Seint Symoun,
I have be shryven° this day at° my curat°. 2095
I have hym toold hoolly al myn estat°.
Nedeth° namoore to speken of it," seith he,
"But if me list°, of myn humylitee."
   "Yif° me thanne of thy gold, to make oure
    cloystre,"
Quod he, "for many a muscle° and many an
    oystre,   2100
Whan othere men han° ben ful wel at eyse°,
Hath been oure foode, oure cloystre for to reyse°.

2033 **hool**, *wholly* 2034 **so moot I thryve**, *as I may thrive* 2037 **damp-ned**, *condemned*, **algate**, *surely* 2038 **nedes lese**, *necessarily lose* 2039 **deyth**, *dies* 2041 **that**, *what* 2042 **dide doon sleen hem**, *did have them slain* 2043 **eek dronkelewe**, *also a drunkard* 2044 **ay**, *always*, **shrewe**, *wicked person* 2045 **bifel**, *it happened*, **meynee**, *household* 2050 **namely**, *especially* 2052 **Awaityng on**, *watching*, **noot**, *knows not* 2053 **attem-prely**, *temperately* 2054 **Wyn maketh**, *wine causes*, **lesen**, *lose* 2055 **lymes**, *limbs* 2056 **revers**, *opposite*, **anon**, *immediately* 2058 **swich**, *such* 2059 **bireveth me**, *(that) deprives me of* 2061 **despit**, *spite* 2062 **part**, *times*

2064 **Leet . . . fecche**, *had . . . brought* 2068 **slow**, *slew* 2069 **wheither**, *(tell me) whether*, **siker**, *steady* 2071 **byreved me**, *deprived me of* 2076 **But if**, *unless* 2079 **Lo**, *consider* 2081 **For that**, *because*, **dreynt**, *drowned* 2082 **Babiloigne to wynne**, *to conquer Babylon* 2086 **Ne be no**, *do not be a* 2087 **wood**, *angry* 2089 **leeve**, *dear*, **lef thyn**, *abandon your* 2090 **squyre**, *carpenter's square* 2091 **ay**, *always* 2092 **to soore smerte**, *too much pain* 2095 **be shryven**, *been absolved*, **at**, *by*, **curat**, *local priest* 2096 **estat**, *(spiritual) condition* 2097 **Nedeth**, *I need* 2098 **list**, *wish* 2099 **Yif**, *give* 2100 **muscle**, *mussel* 2101 **han**, *have*, **eyse**, *ease* 2102 **reyse**, *build*

2043 **Cambises**, king of Persia. In Seneca's *De Ira*, but see 2018n above. 2075 *Placebo*, "I will please"; Vulgate Psalm 114.9. The word came to imply subservient flattery; see *MerT* 4.1476ff. 2079 **Cirus, thilke Percien**, Cyrus (the Great), the Persian. In Seneca's *De Ira*, but see 2018n above. 2080 **ryver of Gysen**, Gyndes River, a tributary of the Tigris in southwestern Asia. 2085 **he**, Solomon, author of Proverbs. 2086–87 Proverbs 22.24–25; John of Wales 2.8.2. See 2018n above. 2094 **Symoun**, St. Simon the disciple (Mark 3.18) or possibly Simon Magus, a sorcerer who competed with the apostles and sought to purchase their spiritual power (Acts 8.9ff.). 2099 **cloystre**, cloister, the friars' place of residence.

And yet, God woot°, unnethe° the fundement°
Parfourned° is, ne° of oure pavement°
Nys nat° a tyle° yet withinne oure wones°.　　2105
By God, we owen fourty pound for stones.
　"Now help, Thomas, for hym that harwed
　　helle!
For elles moste° we oure bookes selle.
And if yow lakke oure predicacioun°,
Thanne goth the world al to destruccioun.　　2110
For whoso wolde us fro this world bireve°,
So God me save, Thomas, by youre leve,
He wolde bireve out of this world the sonne°.
For who kan teche and werchen as we konne°?
And that is nat of litel tyme°," quod he,　　2115
"But syn° Elye was, or Elise,
Han° freres been, that fynde I of record,
In charitee, ythanked be oure Lord.
Now Thomas, help, for seinte° charitee!"
And doun anon he sette hym on his knee°.　　2120
　This sike man wax wel ny wood° for ire;
He wolde that the frere had been on fire,
With his false dissymulacioun.
"Swich° thyng as is in my possessioun,"
Quod he, "that may I yeven°, and noon
　oother.　　2125
Ye sey° me thus, that I am youre brother?"
　"Ye, certes," quod the frere, "trusteth weel.
I took oure dame oure lettre and oure seel."
　"Now wel," quod he, "and somwhat shal I yeve
Unto youre hooly covent whil I lyve;　　2130
And in thyn hand thou shalt it have anon°
On this condicion and oother noon,
That thou departe° it so, my leeve brother,
That every frere have also muche as oother.
This shaltou° swere on thy professioun°,　　2135

Withouten fraude or cavillacioun°."
　"I swere it," quod this frere, "by my feith!"
And therwithal his hand in his he leith°,
"Lo, heer° my feith°; in me shal be no lak."
　"Now thanne, put in thyn hand doun by
　　my bak,"　　2140
Seyde this man, "and grope wel bihynde.
Bynethe° my buttok ther shaltow° fynde
A thyng that I have hyd in pryvetee."
　"A," thoghte this frere, "this shal go with me!"
And doun his hand he launcheth° to the
　clifte°　　2145
In hope for to fynde there a yifte.
And whan this sike man felte this frere
Aboute his tuwel° grope there and heere,
Amydde his hand he leet the frere a fart—
Ther nys no capul drawynge in° a cart　　2150
That myghte have lete a fart of swich° a soun.
　The frere up stirte as dooth a wood leoun°,
"A, false cherl°," quod he, "for Goddes bones!
This hastow° for despit° doon for the nones°.
Thou shalt abye° this fart, if that I may."　　2155
　His meynee°, whiche that herden this affray°,
Cam lepynge in and chaced out the frere.
And forth he gooth with a ful angry cheere°
And fette° his felawe, ther° as lay his stoor°.
He looked as it° were a wilde boor;　　2160
He grynte with his teeth, so was he wrooth°.
A sturdy paas° doun to the court he gooth
Wher as ther woned° a man of greet honour
To whom that he was alwey confessour.
This worthy man was lord of that village.　　2165
This frere cam as he were in a rage
Where as this lord sat etyng at his bord°.
Unnethes° myghte the frere speke a word,

2103 woot, *knows,* **unnethe,** *scarcely,* **fundement,** *foundation* **2104 Parfourned,** *completed,* **ne,** *nor,* **pavement,** *flooring* **2105 Nys nat,** (there) *is not,* **tyle,** *tile,* **wones,** *dwelling* **2108 moste,** *must* **2109 predicacioun,** *preaching* **2111 us fro this world bireve,** *deprive the world of us* **2113 sonne,** *sun* **2114 konne,** *can* **2115 is nat of litel tyme,** *has not* (been true) *for only a short time* **2116 syn,** *since* **2117 Han,** *have* **2119 seinte,** *holy* **2120 sette hym on his knee,** *knelt* **2121 wax wel ny wood,** *grew nearly insane* **2124 Swich,** *such* **2125 yeven,** *give* **2126 sey,** *tell* **2131 anon,** *soon* **2133 departe,** *divide,* **leeve,** *beloved* **2135 shaltou,** *shall you,* **professioun,** *sacred vows* **2136 cavillacioun,**

quibbling **2138 leith,** *lays* **2139 heer,** *here is,* **feith,** *pledge* **2142 Bynethe,** *beneath,* **shaltow,** *shall you* **2145 launcheth,** *thrusts,* **clifte,** *crack* (of the butt) **2148 tuwel,** *chimney* (anus) **2150 nys no capul drawynge in,** *is no horse pulling* **2151 swich,** *such* **2152 wood leoun,** *enraged lion* **2153 cherl,** *rascal* **2154 hastow,** *have you,* **despit,** *spite,* **for the nones,** *at this time* **2155 abye,** *pay for* **2156 meynee,** *household,* **affray,** *disruption* **2158 cheere,** *expression* **2159 fette,** *fetched,* **ther,** *where,* **stoor,** *loot* **2160 as it,** *as* (if) *he* **2161 wrooth,** *angered* **2162 sturdy paas,** *quick pace* **2163 woned,** *dwelled* **2167 bord,** *table* **2168 Unnethes,** *scarcely*

2107 hym that harwed helle, Christ, whose breaking down of the gates of hell to release meritorious souls ("harrowing of hell") is recounted in the apocryphal Gospel of Nicodemus. **2111–13** Cicero, *De Amicitia* (On Friendship) 13.47; John of Wales 2.8.3. See 2018n above. **2116 Elye . . . Elise,** Elijah . . . Elisha, who gathered the Israelites on Mt. Carmel; 1 Kings 18. Carmelite friars claimed that their order was founded by Elijah, but no orders of friars were created before the thirteenth century. **2128 oure dame oure lettre and oure seel,** the friar has given to Thomas's wife a letter embossed with the convent's seal that confirms that Thomas and his wife are lay members of the convent; see 1944n above. **2148 grope,** at line 1817, the friar says he has "groped" Thomas's conscience. **2158** In seven MSS the tale ends here with the following conclusion: "He had noght elles for his longe sermoun / To parte amonge his bredern when he come home / And thus is this tale of the Frere ydo, / For we were almost at the toune."

Til atte laste he seyde, "God yow see°!"
  This lord gan looke°, and seide,
    "Benedicitee°,   2170
What, Frere John, what maner world is this°?
I se wel that some thyng ther is amys°;
Ye looken as° the wode were ful of thevys°.
Sit doun anon and tel me what youre grief is,
And it shal been amended, if I may."   2175
  "I have," quod he, "had a despit° this day,
God yelde° yow, adoun in youre village,
That in this world is noon so poure a page°
That he nolde° have abhomynacioun
Of that° I have receyved in youre toun.   2180
And yet ne greveth me nothyng° so soore
As that this olde cherl with lokkes hoore°
Blasphemed hath oure hooly covent eke."
  "Now, maister," quod this lord, "I yow
    biseke°—"
  "No maister, sire," quod he, "but
    servitour°,   2185
Thogh I have had in scole that honour.
God liketh nat that 'Raby' men us calle
Neither in market ne in youre large halle."
  "No fors°," quod he, "but tel me al youre grief."
  "Sire," quod this frere, "an odious
    meschief   2190
This day bityd is° to myn ordre and me,
And so, *per consequens*°, to ech degree°
Of hooly chirche, God amende it soone."
  "Sire," quod the lord, "ye woot° what is to
    doone.
Distempre yow noght°; ye be my confessour; 2195
Ye been the salt of the erthe and the savour°.
For Goddes love, youre pacience ye holde!
Tel me youre grief." And he anon hym tolde
As ye han herd biforn, ye woot wel what.
  The lady of the hous ay° stille sat   2200

Til she had herd what the frere sayde.
  "Ey, Goddes mooder," quod she, "blisful mayde!
Is ther oght elles°? Telle me feithfully."
  "Madame," quod he, "how thynke ye herby°?"
  "How that me thynketh?" quod she. "So God
    me speede°,   2205
I seye, a cherl° hath doon a cherles dede.
What shold I seye? God lat° hym nevere thee°.
His sike heed is ful of vanytee;
I holde hym in a manere frenesye°."
  "Madame," quod he, "by God, I shal
    nat lye,   2210
But° I on hym oother weyes be wreke°,
I shal disclaundre° hym over al ther° I speke,
This false blasphemour that charged me
To parte° that wol nat departed be
To every man yliche°, with meschaunce°!"   2215
  The lord sat stille as he were in a traunce,
And in his herte he rolled up and doun°:
How hadde the cherl this ymaginacioun
To shewe swich° a probleme to the frere?
Nevere erst er° now herde I of swich mateere. 2220
I trowe° the devel putte it in his mynde.
In ars-metrik shal ther no man fynde
Biforn this day of swich a questioun°.
Who sholde make a demonstracioun°
That every man sholde have yliche his part   2225
As of the soun or savour of a fart?
O nyce°, proude cherl, I shrewe° his face!
  "Lo, sires," quod the lord, "with harde grace°,
Who herde evere of swich a thyng er now?
To every man ylike, tel me how?   2230
It is an inpossible, it may nat be.
Ey, nyce cherl, God lete him nevere thee°!
The rumblynge of a fart, and every soun,
Nis° but of eir reverberacioun,
And evere it wasteth litel and litel awey.   2235

2169 God yow see, (may) *God watch over you* **2170 gan looke,** *looked,* **Benedicitee,** *bless you* **2171 what maner world is this,** *what in the world is wrong* **2172 amys,** *wrong* **2173 as,** *as if,* **thevys,** *thieves* **2176 despit,** *insult* **2177 yelde,** *reward* **2178 is noon so poure a page,** (there) *is no serving boy so lowly* **2179 nolde,** *would not* **2180 that,** *what* **2181 ne greveth me nothyng,** *nothing grieves me* **2182 lokkes hoore,** *white hair* **2184 biseke,** *request* **2185 servitour,** *servant* **2189 fors,** *matter* **2191 bityd is,** *has happened* **2192 per consequens,** *as a result,* **degree,** *rank* **2194 woot,** *know* **2195 Distempre yow noght,** *don't be angry* **2196**

savour, *flavoring* **2200 ay,** *completely* **2203 oght elles,** *nothing else* **2204 herby,** *by this* **2205 speede,** *help* **2206 cherl,** *rascal* **2207 lat,** *let,* **thee,** *prosper* **2209 manere frenesye,** *kind of madness* **2211 But,** *unless,* **be wreke,** *am avenged* **2212 disclaundre,** *slander,* **over al ther,** *everywhere* **2214 parte,** *divide* **2215 yliche,** *equally,* **meschaunce,** *bad fortune* **2217 rolled up and doun,** *contemplated* **2219 shewe swich,** *set such* **2220 erst er,** *before* **2221 trowe,** *believe* **2223 questioun,** *problem* **2224 demonstracioun,** *proof* **2227 nyce,** *foolish,* **shrewe,** *curse* **2228 with harde grace,** *curse it all* **2232 thee,** *prosper* **2234 Nis,** *is nothing*

2185–88 maister . . . Raby, the friar here refuses the religious title "rabbi" (Hebrew "my master"), purporting to follow Christ's commands that his disciples not accept the title (Matthew 23.7–8), even though he accepts the academic title "master of arts." See 1781n above. **2196 salt of the erthe,** Christ addresses his disciples in this way in Matthew 5.13 **2222 ars-metrik,** arithmetic, but also a pun on "arse-measurement." **2226 savour,** fragrance, but at line 2196 the word means "flavoring" when applied to the friar. **2231 an inpossible,** a textbook exercise in mathematics or logic. **2234 of eir reverberacioun,** vibration of air. In *HF* 765, Chaucer refers to speech as broken air.

Ther is no man kan deemen°, by my fey°,
If that it were departed° equally.
What, lo, my cherl, lo, yet how shrewedly°
Unto my confessour today he spak.
I holde hym certeyn a demonyak°! 2240
Now ete youre mete and lat the cherl go pleye;
Lat hym go honge° hymself a devel weye°."

*The wordes of the lordes squier and his kervere for
departynge of the fart on twelve.*

Now stood the lordes squier at the bord,
That karf° his mete, and herde word by word
Of alle thynges whiche I have yow sayd. 2245
"My lord," quod he, "beth nat yvele apayd°,
I koude° telle, for a gowne-clooth°,
To yow, sire frere, so ye be nat wrooth°,
How that this fart sholde evene ydeled° be
Among youre covent, if it lyked me." 2250
    "Tel," quod the lord, "and thou shalt have
        anon
A gowne-clooth, by God and by Seint John!"
    "My lord," quod he, "whan that the weder° is
        fair,
Withouten wynd or perturbynge° of air,
Lat brynge a cartwheel heere into this
        halle— 2255
But look that it have his° spokes alle;
Twelve spokes hath a cartwheel comunly°—
And bryng me thanne twelve freres, woot° ye why?
For thrittene is a covent, as I gesse.
Youre confessour heere, for his worthynesse, 2260
Shal parfourne up° the nombre of his covent.
Thanne shal they knele doun by oon assent°

And to every spokes ende, in this manere,
Ful sadly leye° his nose shal a frere.
Youre noble confessour—there God hym
        save— 2265
Shal holde his nose upright under the nave°.
Thanne shal this cherl, with bely stif and toght°
As any tabour°, been hyder ybroght°;
And sette hym on the wheel right of this cart,
Upon the nave, and make hym lete a fart. 2270
And ye shul seen, up peril of my lyf°,
By preeve° which that is demonstratif°,
That equally the soun of it wol wende°,
And eke° the stynk, unto the spokes ende,
Save° that this worthy man, youre confessour, 2275
By cause he is a man of greet honour,
Shal have the first fruyt, as resoun is.
As yet the noble usage° of freres is
The worthy men of hem shul first be served,
And certeinly he hath it weel disserved. 2280
He hath today taught us so muche good
With prechyng in the pulpit ther° he stood
That I may vouchesauf°, I sey for me,
He hadde the firste smel of fartes thre;
And so wolde al his covent hardily, 2285
He bereth hym so faire and hoolily."
    The lord, the lady, and ech man save the frere
Seyde that Jankyn spak in this matere
As wel as Euclide or Protholomee.
Touchynge° this cherl°, they seyde, subtiltee 2290
And heigh° wit made hym speke as he spak;
He nys no° fool, ne no demonyak°.
And Jankyn hath ywonne° a newe gowne—
My tale is doon; we been almoost at towne.

Heere endeth the Somonours Tale.

agreement **2264 Ful sadly leye,** *very steadily place* **2266 nave,** *hub* **2267**
2236 deemen, *judge,* **fey,** *faith* **2237 departed,** *divided* **2238 shrewedly,**
toght, *tight* **2268 tabour,** *drum,* **been hyder ybroght,** *be brought here*
evilly **2240 a demonyak,** *one possessed by a demon* **2242 honge,** *hang,* **a**
2271 up peril of my lyf, *I bet my life* **2272 preeve,** *proof,* **demonstratif,**
devel weye, *in the devil's name* **2244 karf,** *carved* **2246 yvele apayd,** *up-*
demonstrable **2273 wende,** *travel* **2274 eke,** *also* **2275 Save,** *except* **2278**
set **2247 koude,** *could,* **gowne-clooth,** *robe* (a reward) **2248 wrooth,**
usage, *custom* **2282 ther,** *where* **2283 vouchesauf,** *grant* **2290 Touch-**
angry **2249 evene ydeled,** *evenly divided* **2253 weder,** *weather* **2254**
ynge, *concerning,* **cherl,** *rascal* **2291 heigh,** *high* **2292 nys no,** *is no,*
perturbynge, *disturbance* **2256 his,** *its* **2257 comunly,** *commonly* **2258**
demonyak, *one possessed by a demon* **2293 ywonne,** *won*
woot, *know* **2261 parfourne up,** *complete* **2262 oon assent,** *unanimous*

2242a kervere, carver; the squire cuts the lord's food; see *GP* 1.100. **2259 thrittene is a covent,** in their aspirations to imitate the apostles
and Christ, friars convened themselves in groups of twelve, plus a leader, to make thirteen. The scene of the friars around a cart wheel
parodies visual representations of the first Pentecost (Acts 2), when the Holy Spirit visited the apostles in a great wind and tongues of
fire, enabling the apostles to speak many languages and spread the Christian message. **2289 Euclide or Protholomee,** Euclid or Ptolemy, classical mathematicians.

CANTERBURY TALES PART 4

INTRODUCTION

THE CENTER OF THE MARRIAGE GROUP, part 4 is striking for its contrasts and for the ways it develops the connected concerns of gender and class initiated by the Wife of Bath: marital sovereignty and the nature of true gentility. The celibate Clerk tells an exemplum in which a well-loved aristocrat (Walter) who initially wishes not to marry chooses a peasant woman (Griselda) and then tests her cruelly. The recently married Merchant tells a fabliau in which a doddering tyrant (January) selects with lascivious deliberation an attractive young wife (May) and then is cuckolded when she has sex in a pear tree with a squire (Damian). Christian allusions echo in the *Clerk's Tale* (see, e.g., 207n) and are brought to the foreground when the Clerk explains that his tale encourages not wifely submissiveness but human acceptance of God's will (1149–62). By contrast, fairy deities with classical names (Pluto and Proserpine, replacing Christ and St. Peter in some of the analogues) intervene directly in the action of the *Merchant's Tale;* in doing so, they show that the battle of the sexes extends beyond human affairs. In the *Clerk's Tale* Walter's aristocratic lineage (gentility of blood) is counterpointed by Griselda's extraordinary patience (gentility of action). The *Merchant's Tale* satirizes gentility of all sorts (1986) and exposes its delusions through January's blindness (both psychological and physical), May's outhouse disposal of Damian's love letter, and the absurdity of sex in a tree. Funny, though mordant in its criticism of human self-delusion, the *Merchant's Tale* is generalized through its use of allegorical names. Few have found humor in the tale of Griselda and Walter, and the tale both offers and resists allegorical interpretation.

Griselda's passivity and Walter's tyranny challenge modern sensibility, making it difficult for us to understand why the plot was so popular in the late Middle Ages and beyond. Of the many fourteenth- and early fifteenth-century versions, three were by the most famous authors of the age: Boccaccio, Petrarch, and Chaucer. Boccaccio first included it in the *Decameron* (1352); Petrarch translated it into Latin (1373), giving it wider currency; and Sercambi did another Italian version (after 1399). There is an anonymous Latin translation, at least four translations of Petrarch into French, and a dramatic adaptation of the tale. Chaucer worked from Petrarch (as he tells us through the Clerk) and an anonymous, updated French version, *Le Livre Griseldis;* he may also have been influenced by Philippe de Mézière's rendering (ca. 1385). In *Chaucerian Polity* (1997, no. 251), David Wallace argues that Chaucer's version critiques Petrarchan humanism for its collusion with tyranny. In *Faith, Ethics, and the Church* (2000, no. 594), David Aers thinks that it posits a Stoic alternative to dominant Catholic orthodoxy. Judith Bronfman documents the popularity of the tale into the twentieth century in *Chaucer's Clerk's Tale* (1994, no. 1043).

Chaucer's version is unique for the ways that it creates pathos through allusion and narrative perspective. The tale allows us to share Griselda's thoughts and increases the potential for regarding her as a figure of holy suffering (see, e.g., 281–94, 554–67). At times, the narrator laments her suffering (e.g., 460–62, 621–23); at others, he discloses the opinions of others (990–91, 995–1008). Yet Griselda's willingness to accept the cruelty of her husband and to give up her children opens her up to proto-feminist charges of collusion with her patriarchal tormentor, charges that Chaucer may well have had in mind since he has the Clerk address the Wife of Bath and "al hire secte" at the end of the tale (1163ff).

The reference sharply recalls the Wife's claim that it is an "inpossible" (an impossibility) that any clerk "wol speke good of wyves" unless she be a saint

(3.688–90), and the rapid shift from the Clerk's allegorical reading of the tale to his reference to the Wife makes it seem as if the tale can be read as personal rejoinder as well as a secular saint's life or a macabre fairy tale. If Chaucer composed his tale of Griselda with the Canterbury frame in mind, he must have shaped the material to produce the neck-whip reversals of the conclusion and the envoy. More likely, he assigned a previously written tale to the Clerk and sat back to watch the fun, if fun it is. Critical responses to the tale are intense in their castigations of Walter (and sometimes Griselda), and they often ignore the fact that gentility of deed overwhelms gentility of blood in both the *Clerk's Tale* and the *Wife of Bath's Tale,* even though the sexual politics of the two tales vary so widely. For a survey of criticism, see Charlotte C. Morse, "Critical Approaches to the *Clerk's Tale*" (1990, no. 1066).

Tone and pace are crucial to understanding the *Merchant's Tale.* The opening praise of marriage (1267–1392) makes most sense in context if read as sarcastic, and the sexual efficiency of May and Damian in the tree (2353, "in he throng") is set provocatively against pages of January's rationalization about his choice of a wife; his (non)debate with his counselors, Placebo and Justinus; and his sexual fantasies and delusions. The revolting description of January's lovemaking and the blunt irony of being told that we know not what May thinks of him (1851) clash with the idealized language of January's praise of May, drawn from the biblical Song of Songs (2138–48). The sardonic tone of the tale is palpable, though critics divide over whether we should attribute it to the bitterness of the narrator or to the traditional plot—the fabliau of the *senex amans* (old man) cuckolded by a young wife. Chaucer's use of a similar plot in the *Miller's Tale* is much less acerbic, but he treats aging sexuality with bitterness in the *Reeve's Prologue* and

with a kind of nostalgia in the Wife of Bath's recollections (3.469–79).

No specific source of the pear-tree episode has been identified, although it is embellished here by some of the same sources found in the Wife of Bath's materials, particularly Jerome's *Epistola adversus Jovinianum* (Letter against Jovinian) and the *Roman de la Rose.* The intervention of the fairy gods recalls the planetary influences of the *Knight's Tale.* The *Merchant's Tale* also shares materials with the *Tale of Melibee:* much of the mock encomium of marriage (1311–88) derives ultimately from Albertano of Brescia, *Liber Consolationis et Consilii* (translated by Chaucer in *Melibee*) and *De Amore Dei.* The successful combination of such eclectic materials indicates that Chaucer shaped the Merchant about the same time as he did the Wife of Bath, probably late in his development of *The Canterbury Tales.*

A. S. G. Edwards, "The Merchant's Tale and Moral Chaucer" (1990, no. 1088), assesses the thematic implications of perspective and tone in the tale, documenting how readers, from the earliest scribes to modern critics, have reacted to such shifts. In an illuminating essay that focuses on the *Clerk's Tale* and the Middle English *Pearl,* "Satisfaction and Payment in Middle English Literature" (1983, no. 1064), Jill Mann explores the theme of sufficiency or "enoughness" in these works. The idea is reflected in the "suffisant answere" that the fairy goddess gives to May in order to sustain the deception of January in the *Merchant's Tale* (2266), an echo of the "answere suffisant" to the life question that the court demands of the rapist knight in the *Wife of Bath's Tale* (3.910). These and many more echoes among the tales of parts 3 and 4—as well as part 5—create a unity that is simultaneously thematic, dramatic, and rhetorical, encouraging us to read them as a single sequence, even though the manuscripts arrange them in different ways.

Canterbury Tales
Part 4

CLERK'S TALE

PROLOGUE

Heere folweth the Prologe of the Clerkes Tale of Oxenford.

"Sire Clerk of Oxenford°," oure Hooste sayde,
"Ye ryde as coy° and stille as dooth° a mayde
Were newe spoused°, sittynge at the bord°;
This day ne herde I of youre tonge a word.
I trowe° ye studie aboute som sophyme°,   5
But Salomon seith, everythyng hath tyme.
For Goddes sake, as beth° of bettre cheere°!
It is no tyme for to studien heere.
Telle us som myrie° tale, by youre fey°,
For what man that is entred in a pley°,   10
He nedes moot° unto the pley assente.
But precheth nat, as freres doon in Lente,
To make us for oure olde synnes wepe,

Ne that thy tale make us nat to slepe.
"Telle us som murie° thyng of aventures.   15
Youre termes, youre colours, and youre figures,
Keepe hem° in stoor° til so be that° ye endite°
Heigh style, as whan that men to kynges write.
Speketh so pleyn at this tyme, we yow preye,
That we may understonde what ye seye."   20
This worthy clerk benignely° answerde,
"Hooste," quod he, "I am under youre yerde°.
Ye han° of us as now the governance,
And therfore wol I do yow obeisance°
As fer as resoun axeth°, hardily°.   25
I wol yow telle a tale which that I

---

1 **Oxenford,** *Oxford* 2 **coy,** *quiet,* **dooth,** *does* 3 **Were newe spoused,** *who is newly married,* **bord,** *table* 5 **trowe,** *believe,* **sophyme,** *logical argument* 7 **as beth,** *be,* **cheere,** *mood* 9 **myrie,** *merry,* **fey,** *faith* 10 **pley,** *game* 11 **nedes moot,** *must necessarily* 15 **murie,** *merry* 17 **hem,** *them,*

stoor, *reserve,* **til so be that,** *until,* **endite,** *compose* 21 **benignely,** *graciously* 22 **yerde,** *yardstick* (authority) 23 **han,** *have* 24 **do yow obeisance,** *obey you* 25 **axeth,** *asks,* **hardily,** *with all my heart*

---

6 **Ecclesiastes** 3.1, attributed to Solomon. 10–11 Proverbial. 12 **Lente,** a church season of repentance and fasting. 16 **termes . . . colours . . . figures,** technical terms, rhetorical flourishes, figures of speech—all part of academic training. 18 **Heigh style,** elaborate rhetorical style suited to high purpose, as described in the medieval art of letter writing (*ars dictaminis*).

149

Lerned at Padwe of° a worthy clerk,
As preved° by his wordes and his werk.
He is now deed and nayled in his cheste°—
I prey to God so yeve his soule reste.   30
    "Fraunceys Petrak, the lauriat poete,
Highte° this clerk, whos rethorike sweete
Enlumyned al Ytaille of° poetrie,
As Lynyan dide of philosophie,
Or lawe, or oother art particuler;   35
But deeth, that wol° nat suffre us dwellen° heer,
But as it were a twynklyng of an eye,
Hem bothe hath slayn, and alle shul we dye.
    "But forth to tellen of this worthy man
That taughte me this tale, as I bigan   40
I seye that first with heigh stile he enditeth°,

Er° he the body of his tale writeth,
A prohemye, in the which discryveth° he
Pemond and of Saluces the contree,
And speketh of Apennyn, the hilles hye°,   45
That been the boundes of West Lumbardye,
And of Mount Vesulus in special
Where as the Poo out of a welle smal
Taketh his firste spryngyng and his sours°,
That estward ay° encresseth in his cours   50
To Emele-ward, to Ferrare, and Venyse,
The which a long thyng were to devyse°.
And trewely, as to my juggement,
Me thynketh it a thyng impertinent°,
Save that he wole convoyen° his mateere.   55
But this his tale, which that ye may heere."

Heere bigynneth the Tale of the Clerk of Oxenford.

    Ther is at the west syde of Ytaille,
Doun at the roote of Vesulus the colde,
A lusty playne, habundant of vitaille°,
Where many a tour° and toun thou mayst
    biholde   60
That founded were in tyme of fadres olde°,
And many another delitable° sighte,
And Saluces this noble contree highte°.

A markys° whilom° lord was of that lond,
As were his worthy eldres° hym bifore;   65
And obeisant°, ay redy to his hond°,
Were alle his liges°, bothe lasse and moore.
Thus in delit he lyveth and hath doon yoore°,
Biloved and drad° thurgh favour of Fortune
Bothe of° his lordes and of his commune°.   70

Therwith he was, to speke as of lynage°,
The gentilleste yborn of Lumbardye:
A fair persone, and strong, and yong of age,
And ful of honour and of curteisye,
Discreet° ynogh his contree for to gye°—   75
Save in somme thynges that he was to blame.
And Walter was this yonge lordes name.

    I blame hym thus, that he considered noght°
In tyme comynge what hym myghte bityde°,
But on his lust° present was al his thoght,   80
As for to hauke and hunte on every syde.
Wel ny° alle othere cures° leet he slyde°.
And eek° he nolde°—and that was worst of
    alle—
Wedde no wyf for noght that may bifalle°.

27 of, *from* **28 preved,** *proved* **29 cheste,** *coffin* **32 Highte,** *was named* **33 Enlumyned al Ytaille of,** *made famous all of Italy for* **36 wol,** *will,* **suffre us dwellen,** *allow us to remain* **41 enditeth,** *composed* **42 Er,** *before* **43 discryveth,** *describes* **45 hye,** *high* **49 sours,** *source* **50 ay,** *always* **52 devyse,** *describe* **54 impertinent,** *irrelevant* **55 wole convoyen,** *will introduce* **59 habundant of vitaille,** *rich in produce* **60 tour,** *tower* **61 fadres olde,** *ancient fathers* **62 delitable,** *delightful* **63 highte,** *was named* **64 markys,** *marquis (a noble rank)*, **whilom,** *once* **65 eldres,**

ancestors **66 obeisant,** *obedient,* **ay redy to his hond,** *always attentive to his rule* **67 liges,** *subjects* **68 hath doon yoore,** *has long done* **69 drad,** *respected* **70 of,** *by,* **commune,** *common people* **71 lynage,** *lineage* **75 Discreet,** *wise,* **gye,** *lead* **78 noght,** *not* **79 bityde,** *happen* (to) **80 lust,** *pleasure* **82 Wel ny,** *nearly,* **cures,** *cares,* **leet he slyde,** *he ignored* **83 eek,** *also,* **nolde,** *would not* **84 for noght that may bifalle,** *whatever might happen*

27 Padwe, Padua, city in northeastern Italy. **31 Fraunceys Petrak, the lauriat,** Francis Petrarch (d. 1374) was awarded the poet's crown of laurel leaves by the Roman Senate in 1341; Chaucer may have met him on his first visit to Italy, 1372–73. Petrarch translated into Latin Boccaccio's original Italian version of this story. Chaucer knew of both versions, as well as a French one, but he depends primarily on Petrarch's. **34 Lynyan,** Giovanni di Lignano (d. 1383), professor of canon law at Padua, visited England as papal legate. **43 prohemye,** prologue; Petrarch added a prologue to Boccaccio's tale. **44 Pemond . . . Saluces,** Piedmont, Saluzzo. **45 Apennyn,** the Apennine hills. **46 Lumbardye,** Lombardy, a region of Italy. **47 Vesulus,** Monte Viso. **48 Poo,** River Po. **51 To Emele-ward . . . Ferrare . . . Venyse,** toward Emilia (region), Ferrara, Venice (cities). **58 the colde,** Chaucer adds this adjective, line 61, and lines 64–70, emphasizing time and lineage in the tale. **72 Lumbardye,** Lombardy, a region of Italy associated with tyranny. Chaucer added this detail here. **81 hauke,** hunt with a hawk, a noble pastime.

Oonly that point his peple bar so soore°   85
That flokmeele° on a day they to hym wente,
And oon° of hem, that wisest was of loore,
Or elles° that the lord best wolde assente°
That he sholde telle hym what his peple mente,
Or elles koude° he shewe wel swich° mateere,   90
He to the markys seyde as ye shul heere:

      "O noble markys, youre humanitee
Asseureth° us to yeve° us hardinesse°
As ofte as tyme is of necessitee°
That we to yow mowe° telle oure hevynesse°.   95
Accepteth, lord, now for youre gentillesse,
That we with pitous herte unto yow pleyne°,
And lat youre eres nat my voys° desdeyne°.

"Al have I noght to doone in this mateere
Moore than another man hath in this place,   100
Yet for as muche as° ye, my lord so deere,
Han° alwey shewed me favour and grace,
I dar the bettre aske of yow a space°
Of audience to shewen oure requeste,
And ye, my lord, to doon right as yow leste°.   105

"For certes°, lord, so wel us liketh yow
And al youre werk, and evere han doon°, that we
Ne koude nat us self devysen how°
We myghte lyven in moore felicitee,
Save o thyng, lord, if it youre wille be,   110
That for to been a wedded man yow leste°—
Thanne were youre peple in sovereyn hertes
      reste°.

"Boweth youre nekke under that blisful yok°
Of soveraynetee, noght of servyse,
Which that men clepe° spousaille or wedlok.   115
And thenketh, lord, among youre thoghtes wyse
How that oure dayes passe in sondry wyse°,
For thogh we slepe, or wake, or rome°, or ryde,
Ay fleeth° the tyme; it nyl no man abyde°.

"And thogh youre grene youthe floure° as yit,   120
In crepeth age alwey as stille° as stoon,
And deeth manaceth° every age, and smyt°
In ech estaat°, for ther escapeth noon.
And also° certein as we knowe echoon°
That we shul deye, as uncerteyn we alle   125
Been of that day whan deeth shal on us falle.

"Accepteth thanne of us the trewe entente,   A
That nevere yet refuseden youre heeste°,   B
And we wol°, lord, if that ye wole assente,   A
Chese° yow a wyf in short tyme atte leeste,   B   130
Born of the gentilleste° and of the meeste°   B
Of al this land, so that it oghte seme   C
Honour to God and yow, as we kan deeme°.   C

Rhyme Royal

"Delivere us out of al this bisy drede°
And taak a wyf, for hye Goddes° sake!   135
For if it so bifelle, as God forbede,
That thurgh youre deeth youre lyne sholde slake°,
And that a straunge° successour sholde take
Youre heritage, O wo were us alyve.
Wherfore we pray you hastily to wyve°."   140

      Hir° meeke preyere and hir pitous cheere°
Made the markys herte° han pitee.
"Ye wol°," quod he, "myn owene peple deere,
To that° I nevere erst° thoughte streyne me°.
I me rejoysed of my liberte,   145
That seelde° tyme is founde in mariage.
Ther° I was free I moot° been in servage.

"But nathelees I se youre trewe entente,
And truste upon youre wit°, and have doon ay°;
Wherfore of my free wyl I wole assente   150
To wedde me as soone as evere I may.
But ther° as ye han profred° me today
To chese° me a wyf, I yow relesse°
That choys, and prey yow of that profre cesse°.

---

85 **bar so soore**, *took so badly* 86 **flokmeele**, *in a group* 87 **oon**, *one* 88 **elles**, *else*, **best wolde assente**, *would most willingly agree* 90 **koude**, *could*, **swich**, *such* 93 **Asseureth**, *assures*, **yeve**, *give*, **hardinesse**, *courage* 94 **As ofte as tyme is of necessitee**, *whenever it is necessary* 95 **mowe**, *may*, **hevynesse**, *worry* 97 **pleyne**, *lament* 98 **voys**, *voice*, **desdeyne**, *disdain* 101 **for as muche as**, *because* 102 **Han**, *have* 103 **space**, *moment* 105 **leste**, *please* 106 **certes**, *certainly*, **so wel us liketh yow**, *we like you so well* 107 **han doon**, *have done (so)* 108 **us self devysen**, *ourselves imagine* 111 **leste**, *chose* 112 **in sovereyn hertes reste**, *most perfectly content* 113 **yok**, *yoke* 115 **clepe**, *call* 117 **sondry wyse**, *various ways* 118 **rome**, *walk* 119 **Ay fleeth**, *always flies*, **nyl no man abyde**, *will*

await no man 120 **floure**, *flourishes* 121 **stille**, *quietly* 122 **manaceth**, *menaces*, **smyt**, *strikes* 123 **ech estaat**, *each social class* 124 **also**, *as*, **echoon**, *each one* 128 **heeste**, *command* 129 **wol**, *will* 130 **Chese**, *choose* 131 **gentilleste**, *most noble*, **meeste**, *greatest* 133 **deeme**, *judge* 134 **bisy drede**, *constant fear* 135 **hye Goddes**, *high God's* 137 **lyne sholde slake**, *lineage should diminish* 138 **straunge**, *foreign* 140 **wyve**, *marry* 141 **Hir**, *their*, **cheere**, *expression* 142 **herte**, *heart* 143 **wol**, *wish* 144 **To that**, *for what*, **erst**, *before*, **streyne me**, *(to) constrain myself* 146 **seelde**, *seldom* 147 **Ther**, *there*, **moot**, *may* 149 **wit**, *wisdom*, **doon ay**, *done always* 152 **ther**, *where*, **profred**, *offered* 153 **chese**, *choose*, **relesse**, *release (from)* 154 **cesse**, *cease*

114 **soveraynetee**, supremacy; see *WBP* 3.818. 119 Proverbial after Chaucer.

"For God it woot° that children ofte been   155
Unlyk hir worthy eldres hem bifore;
Bountee° comth al of God, nat of the streen°
Of which they been engendred and ybore°.
I truste in Goddes bountee, and therfore
My mariage and myn estaat and reste   160
I hym bitake°; he may doon as hym leste°.

"Lat me allone in chesynge of my wyf.
That charge° upon my bak I wole endure.
But I yow preye, and charge° upon youre lyf,
What wyf that I take, ye me assure   165
To worshipe hire whil that hir lyf may dure°,
In word and werk, bothe heere and everywheere,
As° she an emperoures doghter weere.

"And forthermoore, this shal ye swere, that ye
Agayn my choys shul neither grucche ne
     stryve°.   170
For sith° I shal forgoon° my libertee
At youre requeste, as evere moot° I thryve,
Ther° as myn herte is set, ther wol I wyve°.
And but° ye wole assente in swich manere,
I prey yow speketh namoore of this matere."   175

With hertely wyl° they sworen and assenten
To al this thyng—ther seyde no wight° nay—
Bisekynge° hym of grace, er that they wenten,
That he wolde graunten hem a certein day°
Of his spousaille°, as soone as evere he may,   180
For yet alwey the peple somwhat dredde°,
Lest that° the markys no wyf wolde wedde.

He graunted hem a day swich° as hym leste°
On which he wolde be wedded sikerly°,
And seyde he dide al this at hir requeste.   185
And they with humble entente buxomly°,
Knelynge upon hir knees ful reverently,
Hym thonken alle°, and thus they han an ende°
Of hire entente and hoom agayn they wende°.

And heerupon° he to his officeres   190
Comaundeth for the feste to purveye°,
And to his privee° knyghtes and squieres
Swich charge yaf° as hym liste on hem leye;
And they to his comandement obeye,
And ech of hem dooth al his diligence   195
To doon unto the feeste reverence°.

Explicit prima pars. Incipit secunda pars.

Noght fer fro thilke paleys° honurable
Ther as° this markys shoop° his mariage
There stood a throop° of site delitable°,
In which that poure folk of that village   200
Hadden hir beestes and hir herbergage°,
And of hire labour tooke hir sustenance,
After° that the erthe yaf hem° habundance.

Amonges thise poure folk ther dwelte a man
Which that° was holden° pourest of hem
     alle,   205
But hye° God somtyme senden kan°
His grace into a litel oxes stalle.
Janicula men of that throop hym calle.
A doghter hadde he, fair ynogh to sighte,
And Grisildis this yonge mayden highte°.   210

But for to speke of vertuous beautee,
Thanne was she oon the faireste° under sonne.
For poureliche yfostred up° was she,
No likerous lust° was thurgh hire herte yronne°.
Wel ofter° of the welle than of the tonne°   215
She drank, and for° she wolde vertu plese
She knew wel labour but noon ydel ese.

But thogh this mayde tendre were of age,
Yet in the brest of hire virginitee
Ther was enclosed rype and sad corage°;   220
And in greet reverence and charitee
Hir olde poure fader fostred shee°.

---

155 woot, *knows* **157 Bountee,** *goodness,* **streen,** *family* **158 engendred and ybore,** *produced and born* **161 hym bitake,** *entrust (to) him,* **leste,** *pleases* **163 charge,** *burden* **164 charge,** *order* **166 dure,** *last* **168 As,** *as if* **170 grucche ne stryve,** *complain nor struggle* **171 sith,** *since,* **forgoon,** *give up* **172 moot,** *may* **173 Ther,** *where,* **wyve,** *marry* **174 but,** *unless* **176 hertely wyl,** *heartfelt will* **177 wight,** *person* **178 Bisekynge hym of grace,** *asking him by favor* **179 graunten hem a certein day,** *name for them the day* **180 spousaille,** *wedding* **181 dredde,** *feared* **182 Lest that,** *that* **183 swich,** *such,* **hym leste,** *it pleased him* **184 sikerly,** *certainly* **186 buxomly,** *humbly* **188 Hym thonken alle,** *all thanked him,* **han an ende,** *have a fulfillment* **189 wende,** *go*

190 heerupon, *after this* **191 for the feste to purveye,** *to prepare for the feast* **192 privee,** *personal* **193 Swich charge yaf,** *such orders gave* **196 doon unto . . . reverence,** *make worthy* **197 Noght fer fro thilke paleys,** *not far from this palace* **198 Ther as,** *where,* **shoop,** *arranged* **199 throop,** *village,* **delitable,** *delightful* **201 herbergage,** *dwelling* **203 After,** *to the extent,* **yaf hem,** *gave them* **205 Which that,** *who,* **holden** *considered* **206 hye,** *high,* **senden kan,** *can send* **210 highte,** *was called* **212 oon the faireste,** *fairest of all* **213 poureliche yfostred up,** *raised in poverty* **214 likerous lust,** *sensual desire,* **was . . . yronne,** *ran* **215 Wel ofter,** *more often,* **tonne,** *wine cask* **216 for,** *because* **220 rype and sad corage,** *mature and steady spirit* **222 fostred shee,** *she took care of*

196a *Explicit prima pars. Incipit secunda pars.* "Here ends part one. Here begins part two." **207 oxes stalle,** Chaucer added this image that recalls the humble birth of Christ; see 281–94n. **208 Janicula,** Latin word meaning "little gate." The name is in Boccaccio and Petrarch and may have suggested to Chaucer the themes of the Annunciation and Nativity. **215–17** Chaucer's addition.

A fewe sheep, spynnynge°, on feeld she kepte;
She wolde noght been ydel til she slepte.

And whan she homward cam, she wolde
    brynge   225
Wortes° or othere herbes tymes ofte,
The whiche she shredde and seeth° for hir
    lyvynge,
And made hir bed ful harde and nothyng softe;
And ay° she kepte hir fadres lyf on-lofte°
With everich° obeisaunce and diligence   230
That child may doon to fadres reverence.

    Upon Grisilde, this poure creature,
Ful ofte sithe° this markys caste his eye
As he on huntyng rood, paraventure°;
And whan it fil° that he myghte hire espye,   235
He noght with wantowne lookyng of folye
His eyen caste on hire, but in sad wyse°
Upon hir chiere° he wolde hym ofte avyse°,

Commendynge in his herte hir wommanhede,
And eek hir vertu, passynge any wight°   240
Of so yong age, as wel in chiere as dede.
For thogh the peple° have no greet insight
In vertu, he considered ful right
Hir bountee, and disposed° that he wolde
Wedde hire oonly, if evere he wedde sholde.   245

    The day of weddyng cam, but no wight° kan
Telle what womman that it sholde be.
For which merveille° wondred many a man,
And seyden whan they were in privetee,
"Wol nat oure lord yet leve his vanytee°?   250
Wol he nat wedde? Allas, allas, the while!
Why wole he thus hymself and us bigile?"

    But natheless this markys hath doon make°,
Of gemmes set in gold and in asure°,

Brooches and rynges for Grisildis sake;   255
And of hir clothyng took he the mesure
By a mayde lyk to hire stature,
And eek of othere aornementes° alle
That unto swich a weddyng sholde falle°.

The time of undren of the same day   260
Approcheth that this weddyng sholde be,
And al the paleys° put was in array,
Bothe halle and chambres, ech in his° degree—
Houses of office° stuffed with plentee
Ther maystow seen°, of deynteuous vitaille°   265
That may be founde as fer as last Ytaille°.

This roial° markys richely arrayed,
Lordes and ladyes in his compaignye,
The whiche that to the feeste weren yprayed°,
And of his retenue° the bachelrye°,   270
With many a soun of sondry° melodye,
Unto the village of the which I tolde
In this array the righte° wey han holde°.

    Grisilde of this, God woot°, ful innocent
That for hire shapen° was al this array,   275
To fecchen water at a welle is went°,
And comth hoom as soone as ever she may;
For wel she hadde herd seyd that thilke° day
The markys sholde wedde, and if she myghte
She wolde fayn han seyn° som of that sighte.   280

She thoghte, "I wole with othere maydens stonde,
That been my felawes, in oure dore and se
The markysesse°; and therfore wol I fonde°
To doon at hoom as soone as it may be
The labour which that longeth° unto me,   285
And thanne I may at leyser hire biholde
If she this wey unto the castel holde°."

And as she wolde over hir thresshfold° gon,
The markys cam and gan hire for to calle°,

---

223 **spynnynge,** *while spinning* 226 **Wortes,** *plants* 227 **shredde and seeth,** *chopped and cooked* 229 **ay,** *always,* **kepte . . . on-lofte,** *maintained* 230 **everich,** *every* 233 **sithe,** *times* 234 **paraventure,** *by chance* 235 **fil,** *happened* 237 **sad wyse,** *serious manner* 238 **chiere,** *demeanor,* **avyse,** *consider* 240 **passynge any wight,** *surpassing anyone* 242 **peple,** *populace* 244 **disposed,** *decided* 246 **wight,** *person* 248 **merveille,** *marvel* 250 **leve his vanytee,** *abandon his foolishness* 253 **hath doon make,** *has had made* 254 **asure,** *lapis lazuli* 258 **aornements,** *ornaments* 259 **sholde falle,** *are appropriate* 262 **paleys,** *palace* 263 **his,** *its* 264 **Houses of office,** *utility buildings* 265 **maystow seen,** *may you see,* **deynteuous vitaille,** *delicious food* 266 **last Ytaille,** *the ends of Italy* 267 **roial,** *royal* 269 **yprayed,** *invited* 270 **retenue,** *service,* **bachelrye,** *young knights* 271 **sondry,** *various* 273 **righte,** *nearest,* **han holde,** *have taken* 274 **woot,** *knows* 275 **shapen,** *prepared* 276 **is went,** *has gone* 278 **thilke,** *this* 280 **fayn han seyn,** *like to see* 283 **markysesse,** *marquise* (wife of a marquis), **fonde,** *try* 285 **longeth,** *belongs* 287 **holde,** *takes* 288 **thresshfold,** *threshold* 289 **gan hire for to calle,** *called her*

249–52 Chaucer adds the subjects' questions. **260 undren,** midmorning, but also a time for auspicious encounters in romance tradition; Petrarch does not specify the hour, nor does he elaborate upon the household preparations. **281–94** Largely Chaucer's addition, including the description of Griselda's thoughts. The threshold and the mention of the Lord's will suggest the Annunciation, i.e., Mary's acceptance of God's will that she give birth to Jesus. The oxen's stall (also in line 207) recalls the scene of Jesus' birth, the Nativity. The water pot from the well (line 276) recalls the divine selection of Rebecca as wife for Isaac; Genesis 24.

And she set doun hir water pot anon°,   290
Biside the thresshfold, in an oxes stalle,
And doun upon hir knes she gan to falle,
And with sad contenance° kneleth stille°
Til she had herd what was the lordes wille.

This thoghtful markys spak unto this
    mayde   295
Ful sobrely, and seyde in this manere,
"Where is youre fader, O Grisildis?" he sayde.
And she with reverence, in humble cheere,
Answerde, "Lord, he is al redy heere."
And in she gooth withouten lenger lette°,   300
And to the markys she hir fader fette°.

He by the hand thanne took this olde man
And seyde thus whan he hym hadde asyde°,
"Janicula, I neither may ne kan
Lenger the plesance° of myn herte hyde.   305
If that thou vouchesauf°, what so bityde°,
Thy doghter wol I take er that I wende°
As for my wyf, unto hir lyves ende.

"Thou lovest me, I woot° it wel certeyn,
And art my feithful lige man ybore°,   310
And al that liketh° me, I dar wel seyn
It liketh thee, and specially therfore
Tel me that poynt° that I have seyd bifore,
If that thou wolt unto that purpos drawe°
To take me as for thy sone-in-lawe."   315

The sodeyn cas° this man astonyed° so
That reed he wax°; abayst° and al quakynge
He stood. Unnethes° seyde he wordes mo
But oonly thus, "Lord," quod he, "my willynge
Is as ye wole°, ne ayeyns° youre likynge   320
I wol no thyng. Ye be my lord so deere,
Right° as yow lust°, governeth this mateere."

"Yet wol I," quod this markys softely,
"That in thy chambre I and thou and she

Have a collacioun°. And wostow° why?   325
For I wol axe° if it hire wille be
To be my wyf and reule hire after° me.
And al this shal be doon in thy presence;
I wol noght speke out of thyn audience°."

And in the chambre whil they were aboute   330
Hir tretys° which as ye shal after heere,
The peple cam unto the hous withoute°,
And wondred hem in how honeste° manere
And tentifly° she kepte hir fader deere.
But outrely° Grisildis wondre myghte,   335
For nevere erst° ne saugh she swich° a sighte.

No wonder is thogh she were astoned
To seen so greet a gest come in that place;
She nevere was to swiche gestes woned°,
For which she looked with ful pale face.   340
But shortly forth this matere for to chace°,
Thise arn° the wordes that the markys sayde
To this benigne°, verray°, feithful mayde.

"Grisilde," he seyde, "ye shal wel understonde
It liketh to° youre fader and to me   345
That I yow wedde, and eek° it may so stonde,
As I suppose, ye wol° that it so be.
But thise demandes axe° I first," quod he,
"That, sith° it shal be doon in hastif wyse°,
Wol ye assente, or elles yow avyse°?   350

"I seye this, be ye redy with good herte
To al my lust°, and that I frely may
As me best thynketh do yow° laughe or smerte°,
And nevere ye to grucche° it, nyght ne day?
And eek whan I sey 'ye' ne sey nat 'nay,'   355
Neither by word ne frownyng contenance?
Swere this, and heere I swere oure alliance."

Wondrynge upon this word, quakynge for
    drede,
She seyde, "Lord, undigne° and unworthy

---

290 anon, *immediately* **293 sad contenance,** *sober looks,* **stille,** *quietly*
300 lette, *delay* **301 fette,** *fetched* **303 hadde asyde,** *had* (taken) *aside*
305 plesance, *desire* **306 vouchesauf,** *agree,* **what so bityde,** *whatever*
happens **307 wende,** *leave* **309 woot,** *know* **310 lige man ybore,** *subject*
born **311 liketh,** *pleases* **313 Tel me that poynt,** *respond to the issue*
314 unto that purpos drawe, *accept that plan* **316 sodeyn cas,** *sudden*
situation, **astonyed,** *astonished* **317 reed he wax,** *he turned red,* **abayst,**
abashed **318 Unnethes,** *scarcely* **320 wole,** *wish,* **ne ayeyns,** *nor against*
322 Right, *just,* **lust,** *desire* **325 collacioun,** *discussion,* **wostow,** *do you*
know **326 axe,** *ask* **327 reule hire after,** *obey* **329 audience,** *hearing*

331 Hir tretys, *their negotiation* **332 cam unto . . . withoute,** *approached*
the outside (of) **333 wondred hem in how honeste,** *they wondered at*
what an honorable **334 tentifly,** *attentively* **335 outrely,** *utterly* **336 erst,**
before, **swich,** *such* **339 to swiche gestes woned,** *accustomed to such*
guests **341 chace,** *pursue* **342 arn,** *are* **343 benigne,** *good,* **verray,** *true*
345 It liketh to, *it pleases* **346 eek,** *also* **347 wol,** *wish* **348 demandes*
*axe,** *questions ask* **349 sith,** *since,* **hastif wyse,** *hurried manner* **350 elles*
*yow avyse,** *else think about it* **352 lust,** *desire* **353 do yow,** *make you,*
smerte, *hurt* **354 grucche,** *complain about* **359 undigne,** *undeserving*

Am I to thilke° honour that ye me beede°, 360
But as ye wole° yourself, right so wol I.
And heere I swere that nevere willyngly
In werk ne thoght I nyl° yow disobeye,
For to be deed°, though me were looth to deye."

"This is ynogh, Grisilde myn," quod he. 365
And forth he gooth with a ful sobre cheere°
Out at the dore, and after that cam she,
And to the peple he seyde in this manere,
"This is my wyf," quod he, "that standeth heere.
Honoureth hire and loveth hire, I preye, 370
Whoso me loveth; ther is namoore to seye."

And for° that nothyng of hir olde geere°
She sholde brynge into his hous, he bad°
That wommen sholde dispoillen° hire right
   theere;
Of which thise ladyes were nat right glad 375
To handle hir clothes wherinne she was clad.
But nathelees this mayde bright of hewe
Fro foot to heed they clothed han al newe.

Hir heris han they kembd°, that lay untressed°
Ful rudely°, and with hir° fyngres smale 380
A corone° on hire heed they han ydressed°,
And sette hire ful of nowches° grete and smale.
Of hire array what sholde I make a tale?
Unnethe° the peple hir knew for hire fairnesse
Whan she translated was in swich richesse. 385

This markys hath hire spoused with a ryng
Broght for the same cause°, and thanne hire
   sette
Upon an hors snow-whit and wel amblyng°,
And to his paleys er he lenger lette°
With joyful peple that hire ladde and mette 390
Convoyed hire, and thus the day they spende
In revel til the sonne gan descende°.

And shortly forth this tale for to chace°,
I seye that to this newe markysesse°
God hath swich favour sent hire of his grace 395
That it ne semed nat by liklynesse°
That she was born and fed in rudenesse°,
As in a cote° or in an oxe-stalle,
But norissed° in an emperoures halle.

To every wight° she woxen° is so deere 400
And worshipful that folk ther° she was bore°,
And from hire birthe knew hire yeer by yeere,
Unnethe trowed° they—but dorste han° swore—
That to Janicle, of which I spak bifore,
She doghter were, for as by conjecture 405
Hem thoughte she was another creature.

For though that evere vertuous was she,
She was encressed in swich excellence
Of thewes° goode, yset in heigh bountee°,
And so discreet and fair of eloquence, 410
So benigne° and so digne° of reverence,
And koude so the peples herte embrace,
That ech hire lovede that looked on hir face.

Noght oonly of Saluces in the toun
Publiced° was the bountee° of hir name, 415
But eek biside° in many a regioun,
If oon seide° wel, another seyde the same;
So spradde of hire heighe bountee the fame
That men and wommen, as wel yonge as olde,
Goon° to Saluce upon hire to biholde. 420

Thus Walter lowely—nay, but roially—
Wedded with fortunat honestetee°,
In Goddes pees lyveth ful esily
At hoom, and outward grace ynogh had he;
And for° he saugh that under low degree 425
Was ofte vertu hid, the peple hym heelde
A prudent man, and that is seyn° ful seelde°.

---

360 thilke, *this,* **beede,** *offer* **361 wole,** *wish* **363 nyl,** *will not* **364 For to be deed,** *upon pain of death* **366 cheere,** *expression* **372 for,** *so,* **geere,** *clothing* **373 bad,** *ordered* **374 dispoillen,** *undress* **379 han . . . kembd,** *have combed,* **untressed,** *unbraided* **380 Ful rudely,** *very disorderly,* **hir,** *their* **381 corone,** *nuptial garland,* **han ydressed,** *have placed* **382 nowches,** *brooches* **384 Unnethe,** *hardly* **387 cause,** *purpose* **388 wel amblyng,** *a gentle walker* **389 er he lenger lette,** *with no delay* **392 sonne gan descende,** *sun went down* **393 chace,** *follow* **394 markysesse,**

marquise 396 nat by liklynesse, *unlikely* **397 rudenesse,** *humbleness* **398 cote,** *pen* **399 norissed,** *raised* **400 wight,** *person,* **woxen,** *grown* **401 ther,** *where,* **bore,** *born* **403 Unnethe trowed,** *hardly believed,* **dorste han,** *necessarily* **409 thewes,** *qualities,* **heigh bountee,** *great generosity* **411 benigne,** *good,* **digne,** *worthy* **415 Publiced,** *made known,* **bountee,** *goodness* **416 eek biside,** *also nearby* **417 oon seide,** *one said* **420 Goon,** *went* **422 honestetee,** *virtue* **425 for,** *because* **427 seyn,** *seen,* **seelde,** *seldom*

---

365 Repeated at line 1051, framing the narrative and highlighting the theme of sufficiency. **375–76** Chaucer follows the French version rather than Petrarch here and develops its concern with clothing in greater detail elsewhere. **385 translated,** transformed; the term was used for various changes of state, including sanctification and deification.

Nat oonly this Grisildis thurgh hir wit
Koude° al the feet° of wyfly hoomlinesse°,
But eek, whan that the cas° required it,   430
The commune profit koude she redresse°.
Ther nas° discord, rancour, ne hevynesse°
In al that land that she ne koude apese°,
And wisely brynge hem alle in reste and ese.

Though that° hire housbonde absent were,
        anon   435
If gentil men or othere° of hire contree
Were wrothe°, she wolde bryngen hem aton°;
So wise and rype wordes hadde she,
And juggementz of so greet equitee°,
That she from hevene sent was, as men
        wende°,   440
Peple to save and every wrong t'amende.

    Nat longe tyme after that this Grisild
Was wedded, she a doghter hath ybore,
Al had hire levere° have born a knave° child.
Glad was this markys and the folk therfore,   445
For though a mayde child coome al bifore,
She may unto a knave child atteyne°
By liklihede, syn° she nys nat bareyne°.

Explicit secunda pars. Incipit tercia pars.

    Ther fil°, as it bifalleth tymes mo°,
Whan that this child had souked° but a
        throwe°,   450
This markys in his herte longeth so
To tempte his wyf, hir sadnesse° for to knowe,
That he ne myghte out of his herte throwe
This merveillous desir his wyf t'assaye—
Nedelees, God woot°, he thoghte hire for
        t'affraye°.   455

He hadde assayed hire ynogh bifore
And foond hire evere good. What neded it
Hire for to tempte, and alwey moore and moore,
Though som men preise it for a subtil wit°?
But as for me, I seye that yvele it sit°   460
To assaye a wyf whan that it is no nede,
And putten hire in angwyssh and in drede.

For which this markys wroghte° in this manere:
He cam allone a-nyght ther as she lay,
With stierne° face and with ful trouble
        cheere°,   465
And seyde thus, "Grisilde," quod he, "that day
That I yow took out of youre pouere° array
And putte yow in estaat of heigh noblesse—
Ye have nat that forgeten, as I gesse?

"I seye, Grisilde, this present dignitee°   470
In which that I have put yow, as I trowe°,
Maketh° yow nat foryetful for to be°
That I yow took in poure estaat ful lowe,
For any wele° ye moot yourselven knowe°.
Taak heede of every word that Y° yow seye;   475
Ther is no wight that hereth it but we tweye°.

"Ye woot° youreself wel how that ye cam heere
Into this hous, it is nat longe ago;
And though to me that ye be lief° and deere,
Unto my gentils° ye be no thyng so.   480
They seyn to hem° it is greet shame and wo
For to be subgetz° and been in servage°
To thee, that born art of a low lynage.

"And namely sith° thy doghter was ybore
Thise wordes han they spoken, doutelees.   485
But I desire, as I have doon bifore,

---

429 **Koude,** *knew,* **feet,** *feats,* **hoomlinesse,** *domesticity* 430 **cas,** *situation* 431 **koude she redresse,** *she was able to restore* 432 **nas,** *was no,* **hevynesse,** *unhappiness* 433 **apese,** *quell* 435 **Though that,** *even if* 436 **othere,** *others* 437 **wrothe,** *angry,* **hem aton,** *them to accord* 439 **equitee,** *fairness* 440 **wende,** *believed* 444 **Al had hire levere,** *though she would rather,* **knave,** *male* 447 **unto . . . atteyne,** *achieve* 448 **syn,** *since,* **bareyne,** *barren* 449 **Ther fil,** *it happened,* **tymes mo,** *often* 450 **souked,** *breast-fed,* **throwe,** *short time* 452 **sadnesse,** *steadfastness* 455 **woot,** *knows,* **t'affraye,** *to frighten* 459 **subtil wit,** *clever idea* 460 **yvele it sit,** *it is evil* 463 **wroghte,** *worked* 465 **stierne,** *stern,* **trouble cheere,** *troubled expression* 467 **pouere,** *poor* 470 **dignitee,** *high rank* 471 **trowe,** *trust* 472 **Maketh,** *causes,* **foryetful for to be,** *to forget* 474 **For any wele,** *despite any prosperity,* **knowe,** *experience (now)* 475 **Y,** *I,* 476 **tweye,** *two* 477 **woot,** *know* 479 **lief,** *beloved* 480 **gentils,** *noble people* 481 **to hem,** *among themselves* 482 **subgetz,** *subject,* **servage,** *servitude* 484 **sith,** *since*

429 **hoomlinesse,** the best manuscripts read "humblenesse," but the words in Petrarch and the French version suggest the household here. 431 **commune profit,** public good; the medieval social ideal in which each class performed its proper function and individuals put the social good ahead of personal advantage. 444 **knave,** in the El manuscript, erased and changed to "man" here and at lines 447 and 612. Some later manuscripts also have "man." Compare *MLT* 2.715n. 448a *Explicit secunda pars. Incipit tercia pars.* "Here ends the second part. Here begins the third part." 452–54 **To tempte . . . t'assaye,** both mean "to test," but *tempte* has more potential for negative connotations; *assaye* means "to gauge the perfection of." 456–70 Expanded by Chaucer. 483 **thee,** the uses of "thee" and "thy" here and in the next stanza are disrespectful, in contrast with Walter's respectful address in, for example, lines 491–97. Compare the more complex uses of second-person pronouns in, for example, lines 890–91 and 963–73.

To lyve my lyf with hem in reste and pees.
I may nat in this caas° be recchelees°;
I moot doon° with thy doghter for the beste—
Nat as I wolde, but as my peple leste°.   490

"And yet, God woot°, this is ful looth° to me.
But nathelees withoute youre wityng°
I wol° nat doon. But this wol I," quod he,
"That ye to me assente as in this thyng.
Shewe now youre pacience in youre werkyng°   495
That° ye me highte° and swore in youre village
That day that maked was oure mariage." ⚓

Whan she had herd al this she noght ameved°,
Neither in word or chiere or contenaunce°,
For, as it semed, she was nat agreved°.   500
She seyde, "Lord, al lyth° in your plesaunce°.
My child and I, with hertely obeisaunce°,
Been youres al, and ye mowe° save or spille°
Youre owene thyng; werketh after youre wille.

"Ther may nothyng, God so my soule save,   505
Liken to° yow that may displese me;
Ne I desire nothyng for to have,
Ne drede for to leese, save oonly yee.
This wyl is in myn herte and ay° shal be;
No lengthe of tyme or deeth may this deface°, 510
Ne chaunge my corage° to another place."

Glad was this markys of hire answeryng,
But yet he feyned° as he were nat so;
Al drery was his cheere° and his lookyng
Whan that he sholde out of the chambre go.   515
Soone after this, a furlong wey or two,
He prively hath toold al his entente
Unto a man, and to his wyf hym sente.

A maner sergeant° was this privee° man,
The which that feithful ofte he founden
        hadde   520
In thynges grete, and eek swich folk° wel kan

Doon execucioun in thynges badde—
The lord knew wel that he hym loved and dradde°.
And whan this sergeant wiste° his lordes wille,
Into the chambre he stalked° hym ful stille°.   525

"Madame," he seyde, "ye moote foryeve it° me
Though I do thyng to which I am constreyned.
Ye been so wys° that ful wel knowe ye
That lordes heestes mowe° nat been yfeyned°;
They mowe° wel been biwailled and
        compleyned,   530
But men moote nede° unto hire lust° obeye,
And so wol I; ther is namoore to seye.

"This child I am comanded for to take—"
And spak namoore, but out the child he hente°
Despitously°, and gan a cheere make°   535
As though he wolde han slayn it er he wente.
Grisildis moot° al suffren and consente,
And as a lamb she sitteth meke and stille
And leet this crueel sergeant doon his wille.

Suspecious was the diffame° of this man,   540
Suspect his face, suspect his word also,
Suspect the tyme in which he this bigan.
Allas, hir doghter that she loved so,
She wende° he wolde han slawen° it right tho°.
But nathelees she neither weep ne syked°,   545
Conformynge hire to that° the markys lyked.

But atte laste to speken she bigan,
And mekely she to the sergeant preyde
So as he was a worthy gentilman
That she moste° kisse hire child er that° it
        deyde.   550
And in hir barm° this litel child she leyde°
With ful sad° face, and gan the child to blisse°,
And lulled it, and after gan it kisse.

And thus she seyde in hire benigne voys°,
"Fareweel, my child! I shal thee nevere see.   555

---

488 **caas**, *situation*, **be recchelees**, *pay no attention* 489 **moot doon**, *must do* 490 **leste**, *desire* 491 **woot**, *knows*, **looth**, *hateful* 492 **wityng**, *knowledge* 493 **wol**, *will* 495 **werkyng**, *actions* 496 **That**, *what*, **highte**, *promised* 498 **ameved**, *moved* 499 **chiere or contenaunce**, *disposition or looks* 500 **agreved**, *upset* 501 **lyth**, *lies*, **plesaunce**, *pleasure* 502 **hertely obeisaunce**, *sincere obedience* 503 **mowe**, *may*, **spille**, *kill* 506 **Liken to**, *be pleasing to* 509 **ay**, *always* 510 **deface**, *erase* 511 **corage**, *heart* 513 **feyned**, *pretended* 514 **cheere**, *disposition* 519 **A maner sergeant**, *a kind of agent*, **privee**, *confidential* 521 **eek swich folk**, *also*

such persons 523 **dradde**, *revered* 524 **wiste**, *knew* 525 **stalked**, *crept*, **stille**, *quietly* 526 **moote foryeve it**, *must forgive* 528 **wys**, *wise* 529 **lordes heestes mowe**, *lords' commands may*, **yfeyned**, *evaded* 530 **mowe**, *may* 531 **moote nede**, *necessarily*, **lust**, *desire* 534 **hente**, *seized* 535 **Despitously**, *pitilessly*, **gan a cheere make**, *made actions* 537 **moot**, *must* 540 **diffame**, *bad reputation* 544 **wende**, *thought*, **han slawen**, *have killed*, **tho**, *then* 545 **syked**, *sighed* 546 **that**, *what* 550 **moste**, *might*, **er that**, *before* 551 **in hir barm**, *to her breast*, **leyde**, *laid* 552 **sad**, *steady*, **blisse**, *bless* 554 **benigne voys**, *kind voice*

516 **furlong wey or two**, an idiom meaning the "time it takes to travel about 220 yards" (furlong), i.e., a short while. 554–67 Chaucer's addition.

But sith° I thee have marked° with the croys°
Of thilke° Fader—blessed moote° he be—
That for us deyde upon a croys of tree°,
Thy soule, litel child, I hym bitake°,
For this nyght shaltow° dyen for my sake."   560

   I trowe° that to a norice° in this cas°
It had been hard this reuthe° for to se°;
Wel myghte a mooder thanne han cryd "allas."
But nathelees so sad stidefast° was she
That she endured al adversitee,   565
And to the sergeant mekely she sayde,
"Have heer agayn youre litel yonge mayde.

"Gooth now," quod she, "and dooth my lordes
   heeste°.
But o thyng wol I prey yow of youre grace,
That, but° my lord forbad yow, atte leeste   570
Burieth this litel body in som place
That beestes ne no briddes° it torace°."
But he no word wol to that purpos° seye,
But took the child and wente upon his weye.

   This sergeant cam unto his lord ageyn,   575
And of Grisildis wordes and hire cheere
He tolde hym point for point, in short and pleyn,
And hym presenteth with his doghter deere.
Somwhat this lord hath routhe° in his manere,
But nathelees his purpos heeld he stille,   580
As lordes doon whan they wol han hir° wille.

And bad° his sergeant that he pryvely°
Sholde this child softe wynde and wrappe°,
With alle circumstances° tendrely,
And carie it in a cofre° or in a lappe°;   585
But upon peyne his heed of° for to swappe°
That no man sholde knowe of his entente,
Ne whenne° he cam, ne whider° that he wente;

But at Boloigne to his suster deere,
That thilke° tyme of Panik was countesse,   590

He sholde it take and shewe hire° this mateere,
Bisekynge° hire to doon hire bisynesse°
This child to fostre in alle gentillesse;
And whos child that it was he bad° hire hyde
From every wight°, for oght that may bityde°.   595

   The sergeant gooth and hath fulfild this
   thyng.
But to this markys now retourne we.
For now gooth he ful faste ymaginyng°
If by his wyves cheere° he myghte se,
Or by hire word aperceyve, that she   600
Were chaunged. But he nevere hire koude
   fynde
But evere in oon ylike sad° and kynde.

As glad, as humble, as bisy in servyse
And eek in love as she was wont° to be,
Was she to hym in every maner wyse,   605
Ne of hir doghter noght a word spak she.
Noon accident° for noon adversitee
Was seyn° in hire, ne nevere hir doghter name
Ne nempned° she, in ernest nor in game.

Explicit tercia pars. Sequitur pars quarta.

   In this estaat° ther passed been foure yeer   610
Er° she with childe was, but as God wolde°
A knave° child she bar by this Walter,
Ful gracious and fair for to biholde.
And whan that folk it to his fader tolde,
Nat oonly he but al his contree merye°   615
Was for this child, and God they thanke and
   herye°.

   Whan it was two yeer old, and fro the brest
Departed of° his norice°, on a day
This markys caughte yet another lest°
To tempte his wyf yet ofter° if he may.   620
O nedelees was she tempted in assay!
But wedded men ne knowe no mesure°
Whan that they fynde a pacient creature.

---

556 **sith**, *since*, **marked**, *signed*, **croys**, *cross* 557 **thilke**, *that*, **moote**, *must* 558 **tree**, *wood* 559 **hym bitake**, *to him entrust* 560 **shaltow**, *shall you* 561 **trowe**, *believe*, **norice**, *nurse*, **cas**, *situation* 562 **reuthe**, *pity*, **se**, *see* 564 **sad stidefast**, *firmly steadfast* 568 **lordes heeste**, *lord's command* 570 **but**, *unless* 572 **briddes**, *birds*, **torace**, *tear to pieces* 573 **purpos**, *proposal* 579 **routhe**, *pity* 581 **wol han hir**, *will have their* 582 **bad**, *ordered*, **pryvely**, *secretly* 583 **softe wynde and wrappe**, *carefully clothe* 584 **With alle circumstances**, *in all ways* 585 **cofre**, *cradle*, **lappe**, *sling* 586 **of**, *off*, **swappe**, *cut* 588 **whenne**, *where from*, **whider**, *where to* 590

thilke, *at this* 591 **shewe hire**, *explain to her* 592 **Bisekynge**, *requesting*, **doon hire bisynesse**, *undertake* 594 **bad**, *ordered* 595 **wight**, *person*, **for oght that may bityde**, *whatever might happen* 598 **ful faste imaginyng**, *pondering very intensely* 599 **wyves cheere**, *wife's behavior* 602 **in oon ylike sad**, *constantly steadfast* 604 **wont**, *accustomed* 607 **Noon accident**, *no change* 608 **seyn**, *seen* 609 **nempned**, *named* 610 **estaat**, *condition* 611 **Er**, *before*, **wolde**, *wished* 612 **knave**, *male* 615 **merye**, *merry* 616 **herye**, *praise* 618 **Departed of**, *separated from*, **norice**, *(wet) nurse* 619 **lest**, *desire* 620 **ofter**, *again* 622 **mesure**, *moderation*

589–90 Boloigne . . . of Panik, perhaps the castle Panico, which is near the city of Bologna. **609a** *Explicit tercia pars. Sequitur pars quarta.* "Here ends part three. Here follows part four." **621–23** Chaucer's addition; see 452–54n above.

"Wyf," quod this markys, "ye han herd er this
My peple sikly berth° oure mariage,   625
And namely sith° my sone yboren is,
Now is it worse than evere in al oure age°.
The murmur sleeth° myn herte and my corage°,
For to myne eres° comth the voys so smerte°
That it wel ny° destroyed hath myn herte.   630

"Now sey they thus, 'Whan Walter is agon,
Thanne shal the blood of Janicle succede
And been oure lord, for oother have we noon.'
Swiche° wordes seith my peple, out of drede°.
Wel oughte I of swich murmur taken heede,   635
For certeinly I drede° swich sentence°,
Though they nat pleyn° speke in myn audience°.

"I wolde lyve in pees, if that I myghte;
Wherfore I am disposed outrely°,
As I his suster servede° by nyghte   640
Right so thenke° I to serve hym pryvely.
This warne I yow that ye nat sodeynly
Out of youreself for no wo sholde outreye°;
Beth pacient, and therof I yow preye."

"I have," quod she, "seyd thus, and evere
      shal: 645
I wol no thyng, ne nyl no° thyng, certayn,
But as yow list°. Naught greveth me° at al
Though that my doughter and my sone be
      slayn—
At youre comandement, this is to sayn°.
I have noght had no part of children tweyne°   650
But first siknesse and after wo and peyne.

"Ye been oure lord—dooth with youre owene
      thyng
Right as yow list; axeth no reed at° me.
For as I lefte at hoom al my clothyng,
Whan I first cam to yow, right° so," quod she,   655
"Lefte I my wyl and al my libertee,

And took youre clothyng; wherfore° I yow preye,
Dooth youre plesaunce°; I wol youre lust° obeye.

"And certes°, if I hadde prescience°
Youre wyl to knowe er ye youre lust me tolde,   660
I wolde it doon withouten necligence.
But now I woot° youre lust and what ye wolde,
Al youre plesance ferme and stable° I holde.
For wiste I° that my deeth wolde do yow ese°,
Right gladly wolde I dyen yow to plese.   665

"Deth may noght make no comparisoun
Unto youre love." And whan this markys say°
The constance of his wyf, he caste adoun
His eyen two, and wondreth that she may
In pacience suffre al this array°.   670
And forth he goth with drery contenance,
But to his herte it was ful greet plesance.

   This ugly sergeant in the same wyse
That he hire doghter caughte, right so he—
Or worse, if men worse kan devyse—   675
Hath hent° hire sone that ful was of beautee.
And evere in oon° so pacient was she
That she no chiere° maade of hevynesse°,
But kiste hir sone and after gan it blesse.

Save° this, she preyde° hym that if he myghte   680
Hir litel sone he wolde in erthe grave°,
His tendre lymes, delicaat to sighte°,
Fro foweles° and fro beestes for to save.
But she noon answere of hym myghte have.
He wente his wey as hym no thyng ne roghte°,   685
But to Boloigne he tendrely it broghte.

   This markys wondred evere lenger the moore
Upon hir pacience, and if that he
Ne hadde soothly° knowen therbifoore
That parfitly° hir children loved she,   690
He wolde have wend° that of som subtiltee°,

---

625 sikly berth, *poorly accept* **626 namely sith**, *especially since* **627 age,** *time* **628 murmur sleeth**, *murmuring slays*, **corage**, *feelings* **629 myne eres**, *my ears*, **smerte**, *painful* **630 wel ny**, *nearly* **634 Swiche**, *such*, **out of drede**, *doubtless* **636 drede**, *fear*, **sentence**, *opinion* **637 pleyn**, *openly*, **audience**, *hearing* **639 disposed outrely**, *firmly decided* **640 servede**, *was treated* **641 thenke**, *think* **643 outreye**, *burst out* **646 wol . . . ne nyl no**, *desire . . . nor will not* (*desire*) *any* **647 list**, *wish*, **Naught greveth me**, *it grieves me not* **649 sayn**, *say* **650 tweyne**, *two* **653 axeth no reed at**, *ask no advice from* **655 right**, *just* **657 wherfore**, *therefore* **658 Dooth youre plesaunce**, *do as you please*, **lust, de-*

sire **659 certes**, *surely*, **prescience**, *foreknowledge* **662 woot**, *know* **663 ferme and stable**, *firmly and solidly* **664 wiste I**, (*if*) *I knew*, **ese**, *ease* **667 say**, *saw* **670 array**, *condition* **676 Hath hent**, *has seized* **677 in oon**, *constantly* **678 chiere**, *expression*, **hevynesse**, *sorrow* **680 Save**, *except*, **preyde**, *pleaded with* **681 grave**, *bury* **682 delicaat to sighte**, *beautiful to see* **683 Fro foweles**, *from birds* **685 as hym no thyng ne roghte**, *as if he cared nothing* **689 Ne hadde soothly**, *had not truly* **690 parfitly**, *perfectly* **691 wend**, *thought*, **of som subtiltee**, *out of some treachery*

647–49 Chaucer's addition.

And of malice, or for crueel corage°,
That she hadde suffred° this with sad visage°.

But wel he knew that next hymself, certayn,
She loved hir children best in every wyse.   695
But now of wommen wolde I axen fayn°
If thise assayes° myghte nat suffise?
What koude a sturdy° housbonde moore devyse
To preeve° hir wyfhod and hir stedefastnesse,
And he continuynge evere in sturdinesse°?   700

But ther been° folk of swich° condicioun
That whan they have a certein purpos take°,
They kan nat stynte of° hire entencioun,
But right as° they were bounded° to that stake
They wol nat of that firste purpos slake°.   705
Right so this markys fulliche° hath purposed
To tempte his wyf as he was first disposed.

He waiteth if by word or contenance
That she to hym was changed of corage°,
But nevere koude he fynde variance.   710
She was ay oon° in herte and in visage,
And ay the forther° that she was in age,
The moore trewe—if that it were possible—
She was to hym in love, and moore penyble°.

For which it semed thus, that of hem two   715
Ther nas° but o wyl, for as Walter leste°
The same lust° was hire plesance° also.
And, God be thanked, al fil° for the beste.
She shewed wel° for no worldly unreste°
A wyf, as of hirself°, nothing ne sholde   720
Wille in effect, but as hir housbonde wolde.

The sclaundre° of Walter ofte and wyde
spradde°
That of a crueel herte he wikkedly,
For he a poure womman wedded hadde,
Hath mordred bothe his children prively.   725
Swich murmur was among hem comunly°;

No wonder is, for to the peples ere
Ther cam no word but that they mordred were.

For which, where as his peple therbifore
Hadde loved hym wel, the sclaundre of his
diffame°   730
Made hem that they hym hatede therfore—
To been a mordrere is an hateful name.
But nathelees, for ernest ne for game,
He of his crueel purpos nolde stente°;
To tempte his wyf was set al his entente.   735

Whan that his doghter twelve yeer was of age,
He to the court of Rome, in subtil wyse
Enformed of his wyl, sente his message°,
Comaundynge hem swiche bulles to devyse°
As to his crueel purpos may suffyse—   740
How that the pope, as for his peples reste°,
Bad hym to wedde another if hym leste°.

I seye, he bad they sholde countrefete
The popes bulles, makynge mencioun
That he hath leve° his firste wyf to lete°   745
As by the popes dispensacioun°,
To stynte° rancour and dissencioun
Bitwixe his peple and hym; thus seyde the bulle,
The which they han publiced atte fulle°.

The rude° peple, as it no wonder is,   750
Wenden° ful wel that it hadde be right so;
But whan thise tidynges cam to Grisildis,
I deeme that hire herte was ful wo.
But she, ylike sad° for everemo,
Disposed was, this humble creature,   755
The adversitee of Fortune al t'endure,

Abidynge evere his lust and his plesance
To whom that she was yeven° herte and al
As to° hire verray° worldly suffisance°.
But shortly if this storie I tellen shal,   760
This markys writen hath in special

---

692 **corage,** *feelings* 693 **suffred,** *allowed,* **sad visage,** *sober expression*
696 **axen fayn,** *would like to ask* 697 **assayes,** *tests* 698 **sturdy,** *cruel* 699
preeve, *test* 700 **sturdinesse,** *cruelty* 701 **been,** *are,* **swich,** *such* 702
take, *taken* 703 **stynte of,** *refrain from* 704 **right as,** *just as* (if),
bounded, *bound* 705 **slake,** *stop* 706 **fulliche,** *fully* 709 **corage,** *heart*
711 **ay oon,** *always one* 712 **forther,** *more advanced* 714 **penyble,**
painstaking 716 **nas,** *was not,* **leste,** *wanted* 717 **lust,** *desire,* **plesance,**
wish 718 **fil,** *happened* 719 **shewed wel,** *demonstrated well* (that), **for
no worldly unreste,** *on account of no earthly distress* 720 **as of hirself,**

in and of herself 722 **sclaundre,** *bad reputation,* **spradde,** *spread* 726
hem comunly, *them* (the people) *generally* 730 **diffame,** *ill repute* 734
nolde stente, *would not stop* 738 **message,** *messenger,* **devyse,** *compose*
741 **peples reste,** *people's contentment* 742 **leste,** *wished* 745 **hath leve,**
has permission, **lete,** *leave* 746 **dispensacioun,** *allowance* 747 **stynte,**
stop 749 **publiced atte fulle,** *made fully known* 750 **rude,** *ignorant* 751
Wenden, *believed* 754 **ylike sad,** *constantly steadfast* 758 **yeven,** *given*
759 **As to,** *concerning,* **verray,** *complete,* **suffisance,** *satisfaction*

---

736 **twelve yeer,** the legal age for a girl to marry. 739 **bulles,** documents from the pope, so called because of their lead (Lat. *bulla*) seals.

A lettre in which he sheweth his entente,
And secreely he to Boloigne it sente.

To the Erl of Panyk, which that hadde tho°
Wedded his suster, preyde he specially   765
To bryngen hoom agayn his children two
In honourable estaat° al openly.
But o thyng he hym preyede outrely°,
That he to no wight°, though men wolde
          enquere,
Sholde nat telle whos children that they were,   770

But seye the mayden sholde ywedded be
Unto the Markys of Saluce anon.
And as this erl was preyed° so dide he;
For at day set° he on his wey is goon
Toward Saluce, and lordes many oon°   775
In riche array, this mayden for to gyde,
Hir yonge brother ridynge hire bisyde.

   Arrayed was toward° hir mariage
This fresshe mayde, ful of gemmes cleere°;
Hir brother, which that seven yeer was of age,   780
Arrayed eek ful fressh in his manere.
And thus in greet noblesse and with glad cheere,
Toward Saluces shapynge hir° journey,
Fro day to day they ryden in hir wey.

Explicit quarta pars. Sequitur pars quinta.

   Among al this after his wikke usage°,   785
This markys yet his wyf to tempte moore
To the outtreste preeve° of hir corage°,
Fully to han experience and loore°
If that she were as stidefast as bifoore,
He on a day in open audience°   790
Ful boistously° hath seyd hire this sentence:

   "Certes°, Grisilde, I hadde ynogh plesance°
To han yow to° my wyf for youre goodnesse,
As for youre trouthe and for youre obeisance°,

Noght for youre lynage ne for youre richesse;   795
But now knowe I in verray soothfastnesse°
That in greet lordshipe, if I wel avyse°,
Ther is greet servitude in sondry wyse°.

"I may nat doon as every plowman may.
My peple me constreyneth for to take   800
Another wyf, and crien day by day;
And eek the pope, rancour for to slake°,
Consenteth it, that dar I undertake°.
And treweliche° thus muche I wol yow seye,
My newe wyf is comynge by the weye.   805

"Be strong of herte and voyde anon° hir place,
And thilke dowere that ye broghten me,
Taak it agayn°; I graunte it of my grace.
Retourneth to youre fadres hous," quod he.
"No man° may alwey han prosperitee.   810
With evene° herte I rede° yow t'endure
The strook of Fortune or of aventure°."

   And she answerde agayn in pacience,
"My lord," quod she, "I woot°, and wiste° alway,
How that bitwixen youre magnificence   815
And my poverte no wight° kan ne may
Maken comparisoun; it is no nay°.
I ne heeld me nevere digne° in no manere
To be youre wyf, no, ne youre chamberere°.

"And in this hous, ther° ye me lady maade,   820
The heighe God take I for my witnesse,
And also wysly° he my soule glaade°,
I nevere heeld me° lady ne maistresse
But humble servant to youre worthynesse,
And evere shal whil that my lyf may dure°,   825
Aboven every worldly creature.

"That ye so longe of youre benignitee°
Han holden° me in honour and nobleye,
Where as I was noght worthy for to bee,
That thonke I God and yow, to whom I preye   830

---

764 tho, *then* **767 estaat,** *fashion* **768 outrely,** *utterly* **769 wight,** *person*
773 preyed, *asked* **774 day set,** (the) *established day* **775 many oon,*
many **778 toward,** *on the way to* **779 cleere,** *bright* **783 shapynge hir,*
taking their **785 wikke usage,** *evil habit* **787 outtreste preeve,** *utmost
test,* **corage,** *heart* **788 loore,** *knowledge* **790 audience,** *hearing* **791
boistously,** *roughly* **792 Certes,** *surely,* **plesance,** *pleasure* **793 han yow
to,** *have you for* **794 obeisance,** *obedience* **796 verray soothfastnesse,*
full truth **797 avyse,** *consider* **798 sondry wyse,** *many ways* **802 slake,*

quell 803 dar I undertake, *I dare claim* **804 treweliche,** *truly* **806 voyde
anon,** *vacate immediately* **808 agayn,** *back* **810 man,** *person* **811 evene,*
steady, **rede,** *advise* **812 aventure,** *chance* **814 woot,** *know,* **wiste,** *knew*
816 wight, *person* **817 no nay,** *undeniable* **818 digne,** *worthy* **819 chamberere,** *chambermaid* **820 ther,** *where* **823 also wysly,** *as surely* (as),
glaade, *may gladden* **823 me,** *myself* **825 dure,** *last* **827 benignitee,*
goodness **828 Han holden,** *have held*

784a Explicit quarta pars. Sequitur pars quinta. "Here ends part four. Here follows part five." **807 thilke dowere,** that dowry, i.e., the property
or money brought by a bride to her husband when they marry.

Foryelde° it yow; ther is namoore to seye.
Unto my fader gladly wol I wende°,
And with hym dwelle unto my lyves ende.

"Ther° I was fostred of° a child ful smal,
Til I be deed my lyf ther wol I lede,   835
A wydwe° clene in body, herte, and al.
For sith I yaf° to yow my maydenhede,
And am youre trewe wyf, it is no drede°,
God shilde swich° a lordes wyf to take
Another man to housbonde or to make°.   840

"And of youre newe wyf God of his grace
So graunte yow wele° and prosperitee.
For I wol gladly yelden hire my place,
In which that I was blisful wont° to bee.
For sith it liketh° yow, my lord," quod shee,   845
"That whilom° weren al myn hertes reste,
That I shal goon, I wol goon whan yow leste°.

"But ther as ye me profre swich dowaire°
As I first broghte, it is wel in my mynde
It were my wrecched clothes nothyng faire°,   850
The whiche to me were hard now for to fynde—
O goode God, how gentil and how kynde
Ye semed by youre speche and youre visage
The day that maked was oure mariage!

"But sooth is seyd°—algate° I fynde it trewe,   855
For in effect it preeved is on me—
Love is noght oold° as whan that it is newe.
But certes°, lord, for noon adversitee,
To dyen in the cas°, it shal nat bee
That evere in word or werk I shal repente   860
That I yow yaf myn herte in hool entente°.

"My lord, ye woot° that in my fadres place
Ye dide me streepe° out of my poure weede°,
And richely me cladden of youre grace.
To yow broghte I noght elles, out of drede°,   865

But feith, and nakednesse, and maydenhede.
And heere agayn your clothyng I restoore,
And eek my weddyng ryng, for everemore.

"The remenant of youre jueles° redy be
Inwith° youre chambre, dar I saufly sayn°.   870
Naked out of my fadres hous," quod she,
"I cam, and naked moot I turne° agayn.
Al youre plesance° wol I folwen fayn°.
But yet I hope it be nat youre entente
That I smoklees° out of youre paleys wente°.   875

"Ye koude nat doon so dishonest° a thyng
That thilke° wombe in which youre children
        leye
Sholde biforn the peple in my walkyng
Be seyn al bare; wherfore I yow preye,
Lat me nat lyk a worm go by the weye.   880
Remembre yow, myn owene lord so deere,
I was youre wyf, though I unworthy weere.

"Wherfore, in gerdon of° my maydenhede,
Which that I broghte and noght agayn I bere,
As voucheth sauf to yeve me°, to my meede°,   885
But swich° a smok as I was wont° to were,
That I therwith may wrye° the wombe of here°
That was youre wyf. And heer take I my leeve
Of yow, myn owene lord, lest I yow greve."

   "The smok," quod he, "that thou hast on
        thy bak,   890
Lat it be stille and bere it forth with thee."
But wel unnethes thilke° word he spak,
But wente his wey, for routhe° and for pitee.
Biforn the folk hirselven strepeth° she,
And in hir smok, with heed and foot al bare,   895
Toward hir fader hous forth is she fare°.

   The folk hire folwe, wepynge in hir weye,
And Fortune ay° they cursen as they goon.

---

831 Foryelde, *repay* **832 wende,** *go* **834 Ther,** *where,* **fostred of,** *raised as* **836 wydwe,** *widow* **837 sith I yaf,** *since I gave* **838 drede,** *doubt* **839 shilde swich,** *forbid such* **840 make,** *mate* **842 wele,** *happiness* **844 wont,** *accustomed* **845 sith it liketh,** *since it pleases* **846 whilom,** *once* **847 leste,** *wish* **848 profre swich dowaire,** *offer such dowry* **850 nothyng faire,** *not at all attractive* **855 sooth is seyd,** *truth is said,* **algate,** *always* **857 Love is noght oold,** *love is not* (the same when) *old* **858 certes,** *surely* **859 To dyen in the cas,** *upon my life* **861 in hool entente,** *in complete conviction* **862 woot,** *know* **863 dide me streepe,** *had me stripped,* **weede,** *clothing*

865 drede, *doubt* **869 jueles,** *jewels* **870 Inwith,** *within,* **dar I saufly sayn,** *I safely dare say* **872 moot I turne,** *must I return* **873 plesance,** *pleasure,* **fayn,** *happily* **875 smoklees,** *without undergarments,* **paleys wente,** *palace go* **876 dishonest,** *dishonorable* **877 That thilke,** *that this* **883 gerdon of,** *return for* **885 As voucheth sauf to yeve me,** *so grant me,* **meede,** *reward* **886 But swich,** *only such,* **wont,** *accustomed* **887 wrye,** *cover,* **here,** *her* **892 wel unnethes thilke,** *barely this* **893 routhe,** *sympathy* **894 strepeth,** *strips* **896 is . . . fare,** *goes* **898 ay,** *always*

834–61 Expanded by Chaucer. **871–72** Similar to Job 1.21; see 932n. **880 lyk a worm,** Chaucer adds the proverbial comparison and lines 881–82. **890–91 thy . . . thee,** see 483n.

But she fro wepyng kepte hire eyen dreye,
Ne in this tyme word ne spak she noon.　　　900
Hir fader, that this tidynge herde anoon,
Curseth the day and tyme that Nature
Shoop° hym to been a lyves° creature.

For out of doute this olde poure man
Was evere in suspect° of hir mariage;　　　905
For evere he demed sith° that it bigan
That whan the lord fulfild hadde his corage°,
Hym wolde thynke it were a disparage°
To his estaat so lowe for t'alighte°,
And voyden° hire as soone as ever he myghte.　　　910

Agayns° his doghter hastiliche° goth he,
For he by noyse of folk knew hire comynge,
And with hire olde coote as it myghte be°
He covered hire, ful sorwefully wepynge.
But on° hire body myghte he it nat brynge,　　　915
For rude° was the clooth, and she moore of age°
By dayes fele° than at hire mariage.

Thus with hire fader for a certeyn space°
Dwelleth this flour° of wyfly pacience,
That neither by hire wordes ne hire face,　　　920
Biforn the folk, ne eek in hire° absence,
Ne shewed she that hire° was doon offence,
Ne of hire heighe estaat no remembraunce
Ne hadde she, as by hire contenaunce°.

No wonder is, for in hire grete estaat°　　　925
Hire goost° was evere in pleyn° humylitee;
No tendre mouth, noon herte delicaat°,
No pompe, no semblant° of roialtee,
But ful of pacient benyngnytee°,
Discreet and pridelees°, ay° honurable,　　　930
And to hire housbonde evere meke and
　　　stable°.

Men speke of Job, and moost° for his
　　　humblesse,
As clerkes whan hem list konne wel endite°,
Namely° of men, but as in soothfastnesse°,
Though clerkes preise wommen but a lite,　　　935
Ther kan no man in humblesse hym acquite°
As womman kan, ne kan been half so trewe
As wommen been, but it be falle of newe°.

[*Pars sexta.*]

Fro Boloigne is this Erl of Panyk come,
Of which the fame up sprang to moore and
　　　lesse°,　　　940
And in the peples eres° alle and some
Was kouth eek° that a newe markysesse
He with hym broghte, in swich pompe and
　　　richesse
That nevere was ther seyn with mannes eye
So noble array in al West Lumbardye.　　　945

The markys, which that shoop° and knew al this,
Er° that this erl was come sente his message
For thilke sely° poure Grisildis,
And she with humble herte and glad visage°,
Nat with no swollen thoght in hire corage°,　　　950
Cam at his heste° and on hire knees hire sette,
And reverently and wisely she hym grette°.

"Grisilde," quod he, "my wyl is outrely°
This mayden, that shal wedded been to me,
Received be tomorwe as roially　　　955
As it possible is in myn hous to be,
And eek that every wight° in his degree°
Have his estaat° in sittyng and servyse
And heigh plesaunce°, as I kan best devyse.

"I have no wommen suffisaunt°, certayn,　　　960
The chambres for t'arraye in ordinaunce°

---

903 Shoop, *created,* **lyves,** *living* **905 suspect,** *suspicion* **906 demed sith,** *judged since* **907 corage,** *feelings* **908 disparage,** *disgrace* **909 t'alighte,** *to descend* **910 voyden,** *dispense with* **911 Agayns,** *toward,* **hastiliche,** *hastily* **913 as it myghte be,** *as well as possible* **915 on,** *around* **916 rude,** *ragged,* **moore of age,** *older* **917 fele,** *many* **918 space,** *time* **919 flour,** *ideal* (flower) **921 ne eek in hire,** *nor also in their* **922 hire,** *to her* **924 contenaunce,** *behavior* **925 grete estaat,** *exalted status* **926 goost,** *spirit,* **pleyn,** *complete* **927 delicaat,** *fussy* **928 semblant,** *display* **929 benyngnytee,** *kindness* **930 pridelees,** *without pride,* **ay,** *always* **931 stable,** *faithful* **932 moost,** *mostly* **933 hem list konne wel endite,** *they*

wish can well write **934 Namely,** *especially,* **soothfastnesse,** *truth* **936 hym acquite,** *behave themselves* **938 but it be falle of newe,** *unless it happened recently* **940 moore and lesse,** (people of) *greater and lesser* (class) **941 eres,** *ears* **942 kouth eek,** *known also* **946 which that shoop,** *who created* **947 Er,** *before* **948 thilke sely,** *this innocent* **949 visage,** *looks* **950 corage,** *heart* **951 heste,** *command* **952 grette,** *greeted* **953 outrely,** *utterly* (that) **957 wight,** *person,* **degree,** *rank* **958 estaat,** *proper due* **959 heigh plesaunce,** *lofty pleasures* **960 suffisaunt,** *satisfactory* **961 t'arraye in ordinaunce,** *to prepare in proper fashion*

---

913 olde coote, old coat; Petrarch and the French versions explain that her father kept the coat in anticipation of her disgrace. **916** Some manuscripts omit "she," which makes it the cloth that is older, as in Petrarch. **901–02** Chaucer's addition, an echo of Job's curse of the day he was born; Job 3.1–3. **932 Job,** known for his patient suffering and the protagonist of the biblical book of Job. **935** See *WBP* 3.688–91. **938a [*Pars sexte.*],** "Part six." This indication of a division occurs in only a limited number of MSS.

After my lust°, and therfore wolde I fayn°
That thyn were al swich manere governaunce.
Thou knowest eek of old al my plesaunce.
Thogh thyn array° be badde and yvel biseye°,   965
Do thou thy devoir° at the leeste weye°."

     "Nat oonly, lord, that I am glad," quod she,
"To doon youre lust, but I desire also
Yow for to serve and plese in my degree°
Withouten feyntyng°, and shal everemo;   970
Ne nevere, for no wele° ne no wo,
Ne shal the goost° withinne myn herte stente°
To love yow best with al my trewe entente."

And with that word she gan the hous to
     dighte°,
And tables for to sette, and beddes make,   975
And peyned hire° to doon al that she myghte,
Preyynge° the chambereres°, for Goddes sake,
To hasten hem and faste swepe and shake,
And she, the mooste servysable° of alle,
Hath every chambre arrayed and his halle.   980

     Abouten undren° gan this erl alighte°,
That with hym broghte thise noble children
     tweye,
For which the peple ran to seen the sighte
Of hire° array so richely biseye°;
And thanne at erst° amonges hem they seye   985
That Walter was no fool, thogh that hym leste°
To chaunge his wyf, for it was for the beste.

For she is fairer, as they deemen° alle,
Than is Grisilde, and moore tendre of age,
And fairer fruyt° bitwene hem sholde falle°,   990
And moore plesant, for hire heigh lynage°.
Hir brother eek so fair was of visage°
That hem to seen the peple hath caught
     plesaunce°,
Commendynge now the markys governaunce.

"O stormy peple, unsad° and evere
     untrewe!   995
Ay undiscreet° and chaungynge as a vane°,
Delitynge evere in rumbul° that is newe,
For lyk the moone ay wexe ye° and wane!
Ay ful of clappyng°, deere ynogh a jane,
Youre doom° is fals, youre constance yvele
     preeveth°,   1000
A ful greet fool is he that on yow leeveth°."

Thus seyden sadde° folk in that citee,
Whan that the peple gazed up and doun
For they were glad right for the noveltee
To han a newe lady of hir toun.   1005
Namoore of this make I now mencioun,
But to Grisilde agayn wol I me dresse°,
And telle hir constance and hir bisynesse.

     Ful bisy was Grisilde in everythyng
That to the feeste was apertinent°.   1010
Right noght was she abayst° of hire clothyng,
Thogh it were rude° and somdeel eek torent°,
But with glad cheere to the yate is went°
With oother folk, to greete the markysesse,
And after that dooth forth° hire bisynesse°.   1015

With so glad chiere his gestes she receyveth,
And konnyngly°, everich in his degree,
That no defaute° no man aperceyveth°,
But ay they wondren what she myghte bee
That in so poure array was for to see   1020
And koude° swich honour and reverence,
And worthily they preisen° hire prudence.

In al this meenewhile she ne stente°
This mayde and eek hir brother to commende
With al hir herte, in ful benyngne entente°,   1025
So wel that no man koude hir pris amende°.
But atte laste, whan that thise lordes wende°
To sitten doun to mete°, he gan to calle
Grisilde as she was bisy in his halle.

---

962 **lust**, *wishes*, **fayn**, *wish* 965 **array**, *clothing*, **yvel biseye**, *wretched to see* 966 **devoir**, *duty*, **at the leeste weye**, *at least* 969 **degree**, *place* 970 **feyntyng**, *diminishing* 971 **wele**, *prosperity* 972 **goost**, *spirit*, **stente**, *cease* 974 **dighte**, *prepare* 976 **peyned hire**, *took pains* 977 **Preyynge**, *asking*, **chambereres**, *chambermaids* 979 **servysable**, *dedicated* 981 **undren**, *midmorning*, **gan . . . alighte**, *arrived* 984 **hire**, *their*, **richely biseye**, *rich to see* 985 **at erst**, *for the first time* 986 **leste**, *wished* 988 **deemen**, *judge* 990 **fruyt**, *offspring*, **falle**, *be born* 991 **heigh lynage**, *high lineage* 992 **visage**, *face* 993 **hath caught plesaunce**, *were pleased* 995 **unsad**, *inconstant* 996 **Ay undiscreet**, *always thoughtless*, **vane**, *weather vane* 997 **rumbul**, *rumor* 998 **ay wexe ye**, *you always wax* 999 **clappyng**, *chattering* 1000 **doom**, *judgment*, **constance yvele preeveth**, *constancy tests poorly* 1001 **leeveth**, *believes* 1002 **sadde**, *steadfast* 1007 **dresse**, *address* 1010 **was apertinent**, *pertained* 1011 **abayst**, *ashamed* 1012 **rude**, *rough*, **somdeel eek torent**, *somewhat tattered too* 1013 **yate is went**, *street goes* 1015 **dooth forth**, *does more* (of), **bisynesse**, *tasks* 1017 **konnyngly**, *skillfully* 1018 **defaute**, *flaw*, **aperceyveth**, *perceives* 1021 **koude**, *understood* 1022 **preisen**, *praise* 1023 **ne stente**, *never ceased* 1025 **benyngne entente**, *kind intention* 1026 **hir pris amende**, *correct her praise* 1027 **wende**, *went* 1028 **mete**, *dinner*

963–73 See 483n. **990–91** Chaucer's addition. **995–1008** Chaucer's addition. **999 deere ynogh a jane**, costly enough at a halfpenny, i.e., worth nothing. **1009–15** In Chaucer's sources, Griselda greets the new bride personally. **1028 gan to calle**, called; see line 289 above.

"Grisilde," quod he, as it were in his pley, 1030
"How liketh thee my wyf, and hire beautee?"
"Right wel," quod she, "my lord, for in good fey°
A fairer saugh I nevere noon than she.
I prey to God yeve° hire prosperitee,
And so hope I that he wol to yow sende 1035
Plesance ynogh unto youre lyves ende.

"O thyng biseke° I yow, and warne also,
That ye ne prikke with no tormentynge
This tendre mayden as ye han doon mo°,
For she is fostred in hire norissynge 1040
Moore tendrely, and to my supposynge
She koude nat adversitee endure
As koude a poure fostred creature."

And whan this Walter saugh hire pacience,
Hir glade chiere, and no malice at al, 1045
And he so ofte had doon to hire offence,
And she ay sad° and constant as a wal,
Continuynge evere hire innocence overal,
This sturdy° markys gan his herte dresse°
To rewen° upon hire wyfly stedfastnesse. 1050

"This is ynogh, Grisilde myn," quod he.
"Be now namoore agast° ne yvele apayed°.
I have thy feith and thy benyngnytee°
As wel as evere womman was assayed°,
In greet estaat and poureliche arrayed. 1055
Now knowe I, dere wyf, thy stedfastnesse"—
And hire in armes took and gan hire kesse°.

And she for wonder took of it no keep°;
She herde nat what thyng he to hire seyde;
She ferde as° she had stert° out of a sleep, 1060
Til she out of hir mazednesse abreyde°.
"Grisilde," quod he, "by God that for us deyde°,
Thou art my wyf, ne noon oother I have,
Ne nevere hadde, as God my soule save.

"This is thy doghter, which thou hast
    supposed 1065

To be my wyf; that oother feithfully°
Shal be myn heir, as I have ay disposed°—
Thou bare hym in thy body trewely.
At Boloigne have I kept hem prively°.
Taak hem agayn, for now maystow nat seye° 1070
That thou hast lorn° noon of thy children tweye.

"And folk that ootherweys° han seyd of me,
I warne hem wel that I have doon this deede
For no malice ne for no crueltee,
But for t'assaye in thee thy wommanheede, 1075
And nat to sleen my children—God forbeede°—
But for to kepe hem pryvely and stille°,
Til I thy purpos° knewe and al thy wille."

Whan she this herde, aswowne° doun she
    falleth
For pitous joye, and after hire swownynge 1080
She bothe hire yonge children to° hire calleth,
And in hire armes, pitously wepynge,
Embraceth hem, and tendrely kissynge
Ful lyk a mooder, with hire salte teeres
She bathed bothe hire visage° and hire
    heeres°. 1085

O which° a pitous thyng it was to se
Hir swownyng, and hire humble voys to heere!
"Grauntmercy, lord°, God thanke it yow,"
    quod she,
"That ye han saved me my children deere.
Now rekke I nevere to been° deed right
    heere, 1090
Sith° I stonde in youre love and in youre grace,
No fors of deeth ne° whan my spirit pace°.

"O tendre, O deere, O yonge children myne!
Youre woful mooder wende stedfastly°
That cruel houndes or som foul vermyne 1095
Hadde eten yow; but God of his mercy,
And youre benyngne fader tendrely
Hath doon yow kept°"—and in that same stounde°
Al sodeynly she swapte° adoun to grounde.

1032 **fey**, *faith* 1034 **yeve**, *give* 1037 **biseke**, *beg* 1039 **mo**, (to) *others* 1047 **ay sad**, *always steady* 1049 **sturdy**, *cruel*, **gan . . . dresse**, *arranged* 1050 **rewen**, *take pity* 1052 **agast**, *afraid*, **yvele apayed**, *treated evilly* 1053 **benyngnytee**, *goodness* 1054 **assayed**, *tested* 1057 **gan hire kesse**, *kissed her* 1058 **took . . . no keep**, *paid no attention* 1060 **ferde as**, *acted as if*, **stert**, *started* 1061 **mazednesse abreyde**, *dazedness awoke* 1062 **deyde**, *died* 1066 **feithfully**, *truly* 1067 **ay disposed**, *always planned* 1069 **prively**, *secretly* 1070 **maystow nat seye**, *may you not say* 1071

lorn, *lost* 1072 **ootherweys**, *otherwise* 1076 **sleen**, *slay*, **forbeede**, *forbid* 1077 **pryvely and stille**, *secretly and quietly* 1078 **purpos**, *intention* 1079 **aswowne**, *fainting* 1085 **hire visage**, *their faces*, **heeres**, *hair* 1086 **which**, *what* 1090 **rekke I nevere to been**, *don't care* (if I were to) *be* 1091 **Sith**, *since* 1092 **No fors of deeth ne**, *death does not matter*, **pace**, *passes* 1094 **wende stedfastly**, *believed firmly* 1098 **doon yow kept**, *protected you*, **stounde**, *moment* 1099 **swapte**, *collapsed*

1051 See 365n. **1075 wommanheede**, see line 239 above. **1079–1113** Chaucer's longest addition.

And in hire swough° so sadly° holdeth she   1100
Hire children two whan she gan hem t'embrace
That with greet sleighte° and greet difficultee
The children from hire arm they gonne arace°.
O many a teere on many a pitous face
Doun ran of hem that stooden hire bisyde;   1105
Unnethe abouten° hire myghte they abyde°.

    Walter hire gladeth and hire sorwe slaketh°.
She riseth up abaysed° from hire traunce,
And every wight° hire joye and feeste maketh°
Til she hath caught agayn hire contenaunce°.   1110
Walter hire dooth so feithfully plesaunce°
That it was deyntee° for to seen the cheere°
Bitwixe hem two, now they been met yfeere°.

    Thise ladyes, whan that they hir tyme say°,
Han taken hire and into chambre gon,   1115
And strepen hire out of hire rude array,
And in a clooth of gold that brighte shoon,
With a coroune of many a riche stoon
Upon hire heed, they into halle hire broghte,
And ther she was honured as hire oghte.   1120

Thus hath this pitous day a blisful ende,
For every man and womman dooth his myght°
This day in murthe° and revel to dispende°
Til on the welkne° shoon the sterres lyght.
For moore solempne in every mannes syght   1125
This feste° was, and gretter of costage°,
Than was the revel of hire mariage.

    Ful many a yeer in heigh prosperitee
Lyven this two in concord and in reste,
And richely his doghter maryed° he   1130
Unto a lord, oon of the worthieste
Of al Ytaille; and thanne in pees and reste
His wyves fader in his court he kepeth
Til that the soule out of his body crepeth.

His sone succedeth in his heritage   1135
In reste and pees after his fader° day,
And fortunat was eek in mariage,
Al° putte he nat his wyf in greet assay.
This world is nat so strong, it is no nay°,
As it hath been in olde tymes yoore°,   1140
And herkneth° what this auctour° seith therfoore°.

    This storie is seyd, nat for that wyves sholde
Folwen Grisilde as in humylitee,
For it were inportable° though they wolde°,
But for° that every wight° in his degree°   1145
Sholde be constant in adversitee
As was Grisilde. Therfore Petrak writeth
This storie, which with heigh stile he enditeth°.

For sith° a womman was so pacient
Unto a mortal man, wel moore us oghte   1150
Receyven al in gree° that God us sent°.
For greet skile is° he preeve° that he wroghte°.
But he ne tempteth no man that he boghte°
As seith Seint Jame, if ye his pistel° rede;
He preeveth folk al day°, it is no drede°,   1155

And suffreth° us, as for oure exercise,
With sharpe scourges of adversitee
Ful ofte to be bete° in sondry wise°,
Nat for to knowe oure wyl, for certes° he
Er° we were born knew al oure freletee°,   1160
And for oure beste is al his governaunce.
Lat us thanne lyve in vertuous suffraunce.

    But o° word, lordynges, herkneth er I go:
It were ful hard to fynde now-a-dayes
In al a toun Grisildis thre or two,   1165
For if that they were put to swiche assayes°,
The gold of hem hath now so badde alayes°
With bras°, that thogh the coyne be fair at eye,
It wolde rather breste a-two than plye.

1100 swough, *swoon,* **sadly,** *firmly* **1102 sleighte,** *skill* **1103 gonne arace,** *did separate* **1106 Unnethe abouten hire,** *scarcely nearby her,* **abyde,** *remain* **1107 slaketh,** *decreased* **1108 abaysed,** *disoriented* **1109 wight,** *person,* **hire joye and feeste maketh,** *celebrates and attends to her* **1110 caught agayn hire contenaunce,** *regained her composure* **1111 hire dooth . . . plesaunce,** *does her wishes* **1112 deyntee,** *a delight,* **cheere,** *joy* **1113 met yfeere,** *together* **1114 hir tyme say,** *saw their time* **1116 rude,** *rough* **1122 dooth his myght,** *does his best* **1123 murthe,** *mirth,* **dispende,** *spend* **1124 welkne,** *sky* **1126 feste,** *celebration,* **costage,** *expense* **1130 maryed,** *married* **1136 fader,** *father's* **1138 Al,**

although **1139 no nay,** *undeniable* **1140 yoore,** *long ago* **1141 herkneth,** *listen,* **auctour,** *author,* **seith therfoore,** *says concerning this* **1144 inportable,** *unsustainable* or *intolerable,* **wolde,** *wished to* **1145 for,** *so,* **wight,** *person,* **degree,** *social position* **1148 enditeth,** *composed* **1149 sith,** *since* **1151 in gree that,** *happily what,* **sent,** *sends* **1152 greet skile is,** *it is very reasonable that,* **preeve,** *test,* **wroghte,** *made* **1153 boghte,** *redeemed* **1154 pistel,** *epistle* **1155 al day,** *always,* **drede,** *doubt* **1156 suffreth,** *allows* **1158 bete,** *beaten,* **sondry wise,** *various ways* **1159 certes,** *surely* **1160 Er,** *before,* **freletee,** *frailty* **1163 o,** *one* **1166 swiche assayes,** *such tests* **1167 alayes,** *alloys* **1168 bras,** *brass*

1137–41 Added by Chaucer. **1148 heigh stile,** high style; see 18n above. **1154 Jame,** James 1.13. **1155 preeveth,** tests, but the connotations include "prove the quality of." See 452–54n. **1162** Petrarch's and the French version end here. **1168–69 coyne . . . breste-a-two than plye,** the coin . . . would break in two rather than bend; pliability is one test for the purity of gold.

For which, heere for the Wyves love of
    Bathe—   1170
Whos lyf and al hire secte God mayntene
In heigh maistrie, and elles° were it scathe°—
I wol with lusty herte, fressh and grene,
Seyn yow a song to glade° yow, I wene°.
And lat us stynte of ernestful° matere.   1175
Herkneth my song that seith in this manere:

Lenvoy de Chaucer.   *—is it really or Chaucer or the clerk?*

  Grisilde is deed, and eek hire pacience,
And bothe atones° buryed in Ytaille,
For which I crie in open audience°
No wedded man so hardy be t'assaille°   1180
His wyves pacience in hope to fynde
Grisildis, for in certein he shal faille.

O noble wyves, ful of heigh prudence,
Lat noon humylitee youre tonge naille°,
Ne lat no clerk have cause or diligence°   1185
To write of yow a storie of swich mervaille
As of Grisildis, pacient and kynde,
Lest Chichevache yow swelwe in hire entraille.

Folweth Ekko°, that holdeth no silence,
But evere answereth at the countretaille°.   1190
Beth° nat bidaffed for° youre innocence,
But sharply taak on yow the governaille°.
Emprenteth wel this lessoun in youre mynde
For commune profit°, sith° it may availle°.

Ye archewyves, stondeth at defense,   1195
Syn° ye be strong as is a greet camaille°;
Ne suffreth° nat that men yow doon offense.
And sklendre° wyves, fieble as in bataille,
Beth egre° as is a tygre yond in Ynde°;
Ay clappeth° as a mille, I yow consaille°.   1200

Ne dreed hem nat; doth hem no reverence.
For though thyn housbonde armed be in maille°,
The arwes° of thy crabbed° eloquence
Shal perce his brest and eek his aventaille°.
In jalousie I rede eek° thou hym bynde,   1205
And thou shalt make hym couche° as doth a
    quaille.

If thou be fair, ther° folk been in presence°,
Shewe thou thy visage and thyn apparaille;
If thou be foul, be fre° of thy dispence°;
To gete thee freendes ay° do thy travaille°;   1210
Be ay of chiere as light as leef on lynde°,
And lat hym care and wepe and wrynge° and
    waille.

Bihoolde the murye wordes of the Hoost.

  This worthy Clerk whan ended was his tale,   1212ª
Oure Hoost seyde and swoor by Goddes bones,
"Me were levere than a barel ale°
My wyf at hoom had herd this legende ones°.
This is a gentil tale for the nones°
As to my purpos°, wiste° ye my wille.
But thyng that wol nat be, lat it be stille°."   1212ᵍ

Heere endeth the Tale of the Clerk of Oxenford.

1172 and elles, *or else,* **scathe,** *too bad* **1174 glade,** *gladden,* **wene,** *hope* **1175 stynte of ernestful,** *stop with serious* **1178 atones,** *together* **1179 open audience,** *public* **1180 t'assaille,** *to test* **1184 naille,** *nail* (stop) **1185 diligence,** *eagerness* **1189 Ekko,** *Echo* **1190 at the countretaille,** *in reply* **1191 Beth,** *be,* **bidaffed for,** *tricked because of* **1192 taak . . . governaille,** *take control* **1194 commune profit,** *general welfare,* **sith,** *since,* **availle,** *be useful* **1196 Syn,** *since,* **camaille,** *camel* **1197 suffreth,** *allow* **1198 sklendre,** *slender* **1999 Beth egre,** *be eager,* **tygre yond in Ynde,** *tiger yonder in India* **1200 Ay clappeth,** *always make noise,*

consaille, *counsel* **1202 maille,** *chain mail* **1203 arwes,** *arrows,* **crabbed,** *angry* **1204 aventaille,** *neck protector* **1205 rede eek,** *advise also* **1206 couche,** *cower* **1207 ther,** *where,* **been in presence,** *are present* **1209 fre,** *generous,* **dispence,** *spending* **1210 ay,** *always,* **travaille,** *effort* **1211 leef on lynde,** *leaf on linden tree* **1212 wrynge,** *wring* (his hands) **1212ᶜ Me were levere than a barel ale,** *I would prefer to a barrel of ale* (that) **1212ᵈ legende ones,** *story once* **1212ᵉ nones,** *occasion* **1212ᶠ purpos,** *thinking,* **wiste,** (if you) *knew* **1212ᵍ stille,** *quiet*

1170 Wyves love of Bathe, love of the Wife of Bath, clear indication that the tale can be read as a response to *WBPT*. Yet this stanza is lacking in one group of sixteen MSS, where lines 1195–1200 also occur at the end of the envoy, both suggesting that Chaucer's version of the tale existed earlier than the Canterbury collection. The *Bathe-scathe* rhyme occurs also at *GP* 1.446. **1171 secte,** pun on sect (group of people) and sex. **1176a Lenvoy de Chaucer,** the envoy by Chaucer, probably composed independently by Chaucer but appropriate to the Clerk as well. An envoy is a set of stanzas, often metrically ornate, and usually concludes a longer poem with a summary, directive, or message. **1188 Lest Chichevache . . . swelwe,** so that Chichevache will not swallow you into her guts. A reference to a French fable of a very lean cow whose only food is patient wives; Bicorne, very fat, eats only patient husbands. **1195 archewyves,** leaders of the female sex (or sect); see 1171n above. Chaucer's coinage. **1200 as a mille,** like the waterwheel at a mill, which produces a repetitive noise. **1212ª⁻ᵍ** Perhaps a canceled link, found in twenty-two MSS; note that the rhyme scheme matches that of *ClT* rather than that of the envoy.

MERCHANT'S TALE

PROLOGUE

The Prologe of the Marchantes Tale.

"Wepyng and waylyng, care and oother sorwe
I knowe ynogh, on even and a-morwe°,"
Quod the Marchant, "and so doon
    othere mo° 1215
That wedded been. I trowe° that it be so,
For wel I woot° it fareth° so with me.
I have a wyf, the worste that may be;
For thogh the feend to hire ycoupled were,
She wolde hym overmacche, I dar wel swere. 1220
What sholde I yow reherce in special
Hir hye° malice? She is a shrewe at al°.
Ther is a long and large difference
Bitwix Grisildis grete pacience
And of my wyf the passyng° crueltee. 1225
Were I unbounden°, also moot I thee°,
I wolde nevere eft° comen in the snare.
We wedded men lyve in sorwe and care.
Assaye whoso wole° and he shal fynde

I seye sooth°, by Seint Thomas of Ynde, 1230
As for the moore part°—I sey nat alle.
God shilde° that it sholde so bifalle°!
    "A, goode sire Hoost, I have ywedded bee°
Thise monthes two, and moore nat, pardee°,
And yet, I trowe°, he that al his lyve° 1235
Wyflees° hath been, though that men wolde him
    ryve°
Unto the herte, ne koude in no manere
Tellen so muchel sorwe as I now heere
Koude tellen of my wyves cursednesse."
    "Now," quod oure Hoost, "Marchaunt, so God
    yow blesse, 1240
Syn° ye so muchel knowen of that art,
Ful hertely° I pray yow telle us part."
    "Gladly," quod he, "but of myn owene
    soore°
For soory herte I telle may namoore."

1214 on even and a-morwe, *in evenings and mornings* **1215 othere mo,** *others* **1216 trowe,** *believe* **1217 woot,** *know,* **fareth,** *goes* **1222 hye,** *high,* **at al,** *in every way* **1225 passyng,** *surpassing* **1226 unbounden,** *not bound,* **also moot I thee,** *as I may prosper* **1227 eft,** *again* **1229 Assaye whoso wole,** *test it whoever will* **1230 seye sooth,** *speak truth* **1231**

moore part, *greater number* **1232 shilde,** *forbid,* **bifalle,** *happen* **1233 bee,** *been* **1234 pardee,** *by God* **1235 trowe,** *believe,* **lyve,** *life* **1236 Wyflees,** *wifeless,* **ryve,** *pierce* **1241 Syn,** *since* **1242 hertely,** *heartily* **1243 soore,** *suffering*

1213 Wepyng and waylyng . . . , echoes line 1212 above. **1219–20 feend . . . overmacche,** recalls the folk theme of the shrewish wife who defeats the devil after he carries her off. **1230 Thomas of Ynde,** cf. *SumT* 3.1980n. Perhaps merely a convenient rhyme. **1241 that art,** the art of marriage.

Heere bigynneth the Marchantes Tale.

Whilom° ther was dwellynge in Lumbardye 1245
A worthy knyght that born was of Pavye,
In which he lyved in greet prosperitee;
And sixty yeer a wyflees° man was hee,
And folwed ay° his bodily delyt
On wommen ther as was his appetyt, 1250
As doon thise fooles that been seculeer.
And whan that he was passed sixty yeer,
Were it for hoolynesse or for dotage°
I kan nat seye, but swich a greet corage°
Hadde this knyght to been a wedded man 1255
That day and nyght he dooth al that he kan
T'espien where° he myghte wedded be,
Preyinge oure Lord to graunten him that he
Mighte ones knowe of thilke° blisful lyf
That is bitwixe an housbonde and his wyf, 1260
And for to lyve under that hooly boond°
With which that first God man and womman
    bond°.
"Noon oother lyf," seyde he, "is worth a bene°,
For wedlok is so esy and so clene
That in this world it is a paradys." 1265
Thus seyde this olde knyght, that was so wys.

And certeinly, as sooth° as God is kyng,
To take a wyf it is a glorious thyng,
And namely° whan a man is oold and hoor°;
Thanne is a wyf the fruyt° of his tresor. 1270
Thanne sholde he take a yong wyf and a feir,
On which he myghte engendren hym an heir,
And lede his lyf in joye and in solas°,
Where as thise bacheleris synge allas,
Whan that they fynden any adversitee 1275
In love, which nys° but childyssh vanytee.
And trewely it sit wel to be so°

That bacheleris have often peyne and wo.
On brotel° ground they buylde, and
    brotelnesse
They fynde whan they wene sikernesse°. 1280
They lyve but as a bryd° or as a beest,
In libertee and under noon arreest°,
Ther as a wedded man in his estaat°
Lyveth a lyf blisful and ordinaat°
Under this yok of mariage ybounde. 1285
Wel may his herte in joye and blisse habounde°.
For who kan be so buxom° as a wyf?
Who is so trewe and eek so ententyf°
To kepe° hym, syk and hool°, as is his make°?
For wele° or wo she wole hym nat forsake. 1290
She nys nat wery° hym to love and serve
Thogh that he lye bedrede° til he sterve°.
And yet somme clerkes seyn it nys nat so,
Of whiche he Theofraste is oon of tho°.
What force° though Theofraste liste lye°? 1295
    "Ne take no wyf," quod he, "for housbondrye°,
As for to spare° in houshold thy dispence°.
A trewe servant dooth moore diligence
Thy good° to kepe than thyn owene wyf,
For she wol clayme half part al hir lyf. 1300
And if that thou be syk°, so God me save,
Thy verray° freendes or a trewe knave°
Wol kepe thee bet° than she that waiteth ay
After° thy good and hath doon many a day.
And if thou take a wyf unto thyn hoold°, 1305
Ful lightly maystow been a cokewold°."
This sentence° and an hundred thynges worse
Writeth this man, ther° God his bones corse°!
But take no kepe of al swich vanytee;
Deffie° Theofraste and herke° me. 1310

1245 **Whilom,** *once* 1248 **wyflees,** *wifeless* 1249 **folwed ay,** *followed always* 1253 **dotage,** *senility* 1254 **corage,** *feeling* 1257 **where,** *how* 1259 **ones knowe of thilke,** *once experience that* 1261 **boond,** *bond* 1262 **bond,** *bonded* 1263 **bene,** *bean* 1267 **sooth,** *truly* 1269 **namely,** *especially,* **hoor,** *gray* 1270 **fruyt,** *fruit* 1273 **solas,** *pleasure* 1276 **nys,** *is nothing* 1277 **sit wel to be so,** *is well fitting* 1279 **brotel,** *insecure* 1280 **wene sikernesse,** *expect security* 1281 **bryd,** *bird* 1282 **arreest,** *constraint* 1283 **estaat,** *condition* 1284 **ordinaat,** *regulated* 1286 **habounde,** *abound* 1287 **buxom,** *obedient* 1288 **ententyf,** *attentive* 1289 **kepe,** *care for,* **hool,** *healthy,* **make,** *mate* 1290 **wele,** (in) *prosperity* 1291 **nys nat wery,** *is not weary* 1292 **lye bedrede,** *lie bedridden,* **sterve,** *dies* 1294 **oon of tho,** *one of those* 1295 **force,** (does it) *matter,* **liste lye,** *chooses to lie* 1296 **housbondrye,** *domestic management* 1297 **spare,** *reduce,* **dispence,** *spending* 1299 **good,** *possessions* 1301 **syk,** *ill* 1302 **verray,** *true,* **knave,** *serving man* 1303 **bet,** *better* 1303–4 **waiteth ay / After,** *waits always for* 1305 **hoold,** *keeping* 1306 **Ful lightly maystow been a cokewold,** *very easily may you be a victim of adultery* 1307 **sentence,** *message* 1308 **ther,** *where,* **corse,** *curse* 1310 **Deffie,** *defy,* **herke,** *listen to*

1245 **Lumbardye,** Lombardy; see *ClT* 4.72n. 1246 **Pavye,** Pavia, near Milan. 1251 **seculeer,** lay persons, or perhaps, worldly people; see lines 1322 and 1390. Chaucer may have originally intended the tale for a member of the clergy. 1266 **so wys,** so wise; blunt sarcasm, as much of what follows may be. 1286–92 Echoes (mocks?) contemporary wedding vows. 1294 **Theofraste,** Theophrastus, author of the lost antimatrimonial *Liber Aureolus de Nuptiis* (Golden Book of Marriage), part of which is preserved in Jerome's *Epistola adversus Jovinianum* (Letter against Jovinian) 1.47; see *WBP* 3.3n and 3.235–378n above. 1305–6 This reading is found in only two MSS; the many variants suggest Chaucer may not have completed the couplet.

A wyf is Goddes yifte verraily°;
Alle othere manere yiftes hardily°,
As londes, rentes, pasture, or commune,
Or moebles°, alle been yiftes° of Fortune,
That passen as a shadwe upon a wal.   1315
But drede° nat, if pleynly speke I shal,
A wyf wol laste and in thyn hous endure
Wel lenger than thee list°, paraventure°.

   Mariage is a ful greet sacrement.
He which that hath no wyf, I holde hym
    shent°.   1320
He lyveth helplees and al desolat—
I speke of folk in seculer estaat°.
And herke° why, I sey nat this for noght,
That womman is for mannes help ywroght°.
The hye God, whan he hadde Adam maked,   1325
And saugh him al allone, bely-naked,
God of his grete goodnesse seyde than,
"Lat us now make an help unto this man
Lyk to hymself," and thanne he made him Eve.
Heere may ye se, and heerby may ye preve°,   1330
That wyf is mannes help and his confort,
His paradys terrestre° and his disport°.
So buxom° and so vertuous is she
They moste nedes° lyve in unitee.
O flessh they been, and o flessh, as I gesse,   1335
Hath but oon herte in wele° and in distresse.

   A wyf, a Seinte Marie°, benedicite°,
How myghte a man han any adversitee
That hath a wyf? Certes, I kan nat seye.
The blisse which that is bitwixe hem tweye°   1340
Ther may no tonge telle or herte thynke.
If he be poure, she helpeth hym to swynke°;
She kepeth his good°, and wasteth never a deel°;
Al that hire housbonde lust°, hire liketh° weel;
She seith nat ones nay, whan he seith ye.   1345

"Do this," seith he. "Al redy, sire," seith she.
O, blisful ordre of wedlok precious,
Thou art so murye° and eek so vertuous,
And so commended and appreved eek°
That every man that halt hym° worth a leek   1350
Upon his bare knees oughte al his lyf
Thanken his God that hym hath sent a wyf,
Or elles preye to God hym for to sende
A wyf to laste unto his lyves ende,
For thanne his lyf is set in sikernesse°.   1355
He may nat be deceyved, as I gesse,
So that° he werke after° his wyves reed°.
Thanne may he boldely beren up his heed—
They been so trewe and therwithal° so wyse.
For which, if thou wolt werken as the wyse,   1360
Do alwey so as wommen wol thee rede°.

   Lo how that Jacob, as thise clerkes rede°,
By good conseil of his mooder Rebekke
Boond° the kydes° skyn aboute his nekke,
Thurgh which his fadres benysoun° he wan.   1365

   Lo Judith, as the storie eek telle kan,
By wys conseil she Goddes peple kepte°,
And slow° hym Olofernus whil he slepte.

   Lo Abigayl, by good conseil how she
Saved hir housbonde Nabal whan that he   1370
Sholde han be slayn. And looke° Ester also
By good conseil delyvered out of wo
The peple of God, and made hym Mardochee
Of Assuere enhaunced° for to be.

   Ther nys nothyng in gree superlatyf°,   1375
As seith Senek, above an humble wyf.

   Suffre° thy wyves tonge, as Catoun bit°;
She shal comande, and thou shalt suffren it,
And yet she wole obeye of curteisye°.
A wyf is kepere of thyn housbondrye°.   1380
Wel may the sike man biwaille and wepe

1311 **verraily,** *truly* 1312 **hardily,** *certainly* 1314 **moebles,** *movable possessions,* **been yiftes,** *are gifts* 1316 **drede,** *doubt* 1318 **list,** *wish,* **paraventure,** *perhaps* 1320 **shent,** *lost* 1322 **folk in seculer estaat,** *lay people* 1323 **herke,** *listen* 1324 **is . . . ywroght,** *is created* 1330 **preve,** *prove* 1332 **paradys terreste,** *worldly paradise,* **disport,** *entertainment* 1333 **buxom,** *obedient* 1334 **moste nedes,** *must necessarily* 1336 **wele,** *happiness* 1337 **Seinte Marie,** *Holy Mary,* **benedicite,** *bless us* 1340 **tweye,** *two* 1342 **swynke,** *work* 1343 **good,** *goods,* **deel,** *bit* 1344 **lust,** desires, **hire liketh,** (it) pleases her 1348 **murye,** merry 1349 **appreved eek,** approved of too 1350 **halt hym,** thinks himself 1355 **sikernesse,** security 1357 **So that,** as long as, **werke after,** follows, **reed,** advice 1359 **therwithal,** also 1362 **rede,** advise, teach 1364 **Boond,** tied, **kydes,** goat's 1365 **benysoun,** blessing 1367 **kepte,** protected 1368 **slow,** slew 1371 **looke,** consider 1374 **enhaunced,** advanced 1375 **in gree superlatyf,** in highest degree 1377 **Suffre,** endure, **bit,** ordered 1379 **of curteisye,** for proper manners 1380 **housbondrye,** domestic arrangements

1311–14 From Albertano of Brescia, *Liber de Amore Dei* (Book of the Love of God). 1313 **commune,** rights to use common lands for grazing, woodcutting, etc. 1325–35 **Adam . . . O flessh,** one flesh; Genesis 2.18, 24; from Albertano of Brescia, *De Amore.* 1362–88 These examples and sayings are all found in Albertano's *De Amore* or his *Liber Consolationis et Consilii* (Book of Consolation and Counsel). Chaucer uses the same biblical examples in *Mel* 7.1098–1101. 1362–63 **Jacob . . . Rebekke,** Jacob is told by his mother, Rebecca, how to deceive his father, Isaac, with a goat's skin and gain Isaac's blessing; Genesis 27. 1366–68 **Judith . . . Olofernus,** in the apocryphal book of Judith 12–13, Judith kills the intoxicated warrior Holofernes to protect the Israelites. 1369–70 **Abigayl . . . Nabal,** Abigail convinces David not to seek revenge for the offense of her husband, Nabal; David later marries Abigail; 1 Samuel 25.10–42. 1371–74 **Ester . . . Mardochee . . . Assuere,** outfoxing the enemy of Mordecai, Esther convinces her husband, King Ahasuerus, to promote Mordecai and save the Jews; Esther 7–8. 1376 **Senek,** not actually in Seneca; from Albertano *De Consolationis.* 1377 **Catoun,** Cato, *Distiches,* but from Albertano, *De Amore.*

Ther as ther nys no° wyf the hous to kepe.
I warne thee, if wisely thou wolt wirche°,
Love wel thy wyf as Crist loved his chirche.
If thou lovest thyself, thou lovest thy wyf. 1385
No man hateth his flessh, but in his lyf
He fostreth it, and therfore bidde I thee
Cherisse° thy wyf or thou shalt nevere thee°.
Housbonde and wyf, whatso° men jape° or pleye,
Of worldly° folk holden the siker° weye. 1390
They been so knyt° ther may noon harm bityde°,
And namely° upon the wyves syde.
For which this Januarie, of whom I tolde,
Considered hath, in with his dayes olde,
The lusty lyf, the vertuous quyete°, 1395
That is in mariage hony-sweete,
And for his freendes on a day he sente
To tellen hem th'effect° of his entente.
    With face sad° his tale he hath hem toold.
He seyde, "Freendes, I am hoor° and oold, 1400
And almoost, God woot°, on my pittes brynke°;
Upon my soule somwhat moste I thynke.
I have my body folily despended°.
Blessed be God that it shal been amended,
For I wol be, certeyn, a wedded man, 1405
And that anoon° in al the haste I kan,
Unto som mayde fair and tendre of age.
I prey yow, shapeth° for my mariage
Al sodeynly°, for I wol nat abyde°;
And I wol fonde t'espien°, on my syde°, 1410
To whom I may be wedded hastily.
But forasmuche as° ye been mo than I°,
Ye shullen rather swich° a thyng espyen
Than I, and where me best were to allyen°.
    "But o thyng warne I yow, my freendes
        deere, 1415
I wol noon oold wyf han° in no manere.
She shal nat passe twenty yeer, certayn.

Oold fissh and yong flessh wolde I have fayn°.
Bet° is," quod he, "a pyk than a pykerel°,
And bet than old boef° is the tendre veel. 1420
I wol no womman thritty yeer of age;
It is but bene-straw° and greet forage°.
And eek thise olde wydwes°, God it woot°,
They konne so muchel craft on Wades boot,
So muchel broken harm° whan that hem
        leste°, 1425
That with hem sholde I nevere lyve in reste.
For sondry scoles maken sotile° clerkis:
Womman of manye scoles half a clerk is.
But certeynly, a yong thyng may men gye°
Right as men may warm wex with handes
        plye°. 1430
Wherfore I sey yow pleynly, in a clause,
I wol noon oold wyf han right for this cause.
For if so were° I hadde swich myschaunce
That I in hire ne koude han no plesaunce°,
Thanne sholde I lede my lyf in avoutrye°, 1435
And streight° unto the devel whan I dye.
Ne children sholde I none upon hire geten°,
Yet were me levere° houndes had me eten
Than that myn heritage sholde falle
In straunge hand°. And this I telle yow alle: 1440
I dote nat°, I woot° the cause why
Men sholde wedde, and forthermoore woot I
Ther speketh many a man of mariage
That woot namoore of it than woot my page°
For whiche causes man sholde take a wyf. 1445
Siththe° he may nat lyven chaast° his lyf,
Take hym a wyf with greet devocioun
By cause of leveful° procreacioun
Of children, to th'onour of God above,
And nat oonly for paramour° or love; 1450
And for° they sholde leccherye eschue°
And yelde hir dette when that it is due;

1382 **Ther as ther nys no,** *where there is no* 1383 **wirche,** *do* 1388
Cherisse, *cherish,* **thee,** *prosper* 1389 **whatso,** *however,* **jape,** *joke* 1390
Of worldly, *among lay,* **siker,** *certain* 1391 **knyt,** *tied,* **bityde,** *happen*
1392 **namely,** *especially* 1395 **quyete,** *quiet* 1398 **hem th'effect,** *them
the purpose* 1399 **sad,** *sober* 1400 **hoor,** *gray* 1401 **woot,** *knows,* **pittes
brynke,** *grave's edge* 1403 **folily despended,** *foolishly spent* 1406
anoon, *soon* 1408 **shapeth,** *prepare* 1409 **sodeynly,** *suddenly,* **abyde,**
wait 1410 **fonde t'espien,** *try to discover,* **syde,** *part* 1412 **forasmuche
as,** *because,* **been mo than I,** *outnumber me* 1413 **rather swich,** *more
readily such* 1414 **allyen,** *ally (myself)* 1416 **wol noon . . . han,** *will
have no* 1418 **wolde I have fayn,** *I prefer* 1419 **Bet,** *better,* **pykerel,**

pickerel (young pike) 1420 **boef,** *beef* 1422 **bene-straw,** *dried bean
stalks,* **greet forage,** *coarse feed* 1423 **wydwes,** *widows,* **woot,** *knows*
1425 **So muchel broken harm,** *so much to cause damage,* **hem leste,** *it
pleases them* 1427 **sotile,** *subtle* 1429 **gye,** *guide* 1430 **plye,** *shape* 1433
if so were, *if it happened* 1434 **han no plesaunce,** *have no pleasure* 1435
avoutrye, *adultery* 1436 **streight,** *(go) straight* 1437 **geten,** *beget* 1438
were me levere, *I would rather that* 1440 **In straunge hand,** *into the
hands of someone unrelated to me* 1441 **dote nat,** *am not senile,* **woot,**
know 1444 **page,** *servant* 1446 **Siththe,** *since,* **chaast,** *chastely* 1448 **By
cause of leveful,** *for the purpose of lawful* 1450 **paramour,** *passion* 1451
for, *because,* **eschue,** *avoid*

1384–88 Ephesians 5.25, 28–29, 33, but from Albertano, *De Amore.* **1393 Januarie,** the suggestive name of the old knight contrasts
with the youthful name of his future wife, May; see line 1693 below. **1424 konne so muchel craft on Wades boot,** know or can do so much
cunning in Wade's boat, an obscure allusion to a mythical hero. The following lines suggest it means to cause sexual or domestic
sorrow. **1427 sondry scoles,** many schools; a clear echo of the Wife of Bath, *WBP* 3.44[c–d]. **1452 yelde hir dette,** pay their marital debt;
WBP 3.130n.

Or for that ech of hem sholde helpen oother
In meschief°, as a suster shal the brother,
And lyve in chastitee ful holily—   1455
But sires, by youre leve, that am nat I.
For, God be thanked, I dar make avaunt°,
I feele my lymes stark° and suffisaunt
To do al that a man bilongeth to;
I woot myselven best what I may do.   1460
Though I be hoor°, I fare° as dooth a tree
That blosmeth er that° fruyt ywoxen bee°,
And blosmy tree nys neither° drye ne deed.
I feele me nowhere hoor but on myn heed;
Myn herte and alle my lymes been as grene   1465
As laurer° thurgh the yeer is for to sene°.
And syn that° ye han herd al myn entente,
I prey yow to my wyl ye wole assente."

    Diverse men diversely hym tolde
Of mariage manye ensamples olde.   1470
Somme blamed it, somme preysed it, certeyn,
But atte laste, shortly for to seyn,
As alday falleth° altercacioun
Bitwixen freendes in disputisoun,
Ther fil° a stryf bitwixe his bretheren two,   1475
Of whiche that oon was cleped° Placebo.
Justinus soothly° called was that oother.

    Placebo seyde, "O Januarie, brother,
Ful litel nede hadde ye, my lord so deere,
Conseil to axe° of any that is heere,   1480
But° that ye been so ful of sapience°
That yow ne liketh°, for youre heighe prudence,
To weyven fro° the word of Salomon.
This word seyde he unto us everychon:
'Wirk alle thyng by conseil,' thus seyde he,   1485
'And thanne shaltow° nat repente thee.'
But though that Salomon spak swich° a word°,
Myn owene deere brother and my lord,
So wysly° God my soule brynge at reste,
I holde youre owene conseil is the beste.   1490

For, brother myn, of me taak this motyf°,
I have now been a court-man al my lyf,
And God it woot°, though I unworthy be,
I have stonden° in ful greet degree°
Abouten lordes of ful heigh estaat;   1495
Yet hadde I nevere with noon of hem debaat°.
I nevere hem contraried, trewely;
I woot wel that my lord kan° moore than I.
What that° he seith, I holde it ferme° and stable;
I seye the same or elles thyng semblable°.   1500
A ful greet fool is any conseillour
That serveth any lord of heigh honour
That dar presume, or elles thenken it,
That his conseil sholde passe his lordes wit.
Nay, lordes been no fooles, by my fay°.   1505
Ye han° youreselven shewed heer today
So heigh sentence°, so holily° and weel,
That I consente and conferme everydeel°
Youre wordes alle and youre opinioun.
By God, ther nys no° man in al this toun,   1510
N'yn Ytaille°, that koude bet han sayd°!
Crist halt hym° of this conseil ful wel apayd°.
And trewely, it is an heigh corage°
Of any man that stapen° is in age
To take a yong wyf. By my fader kyn°,   1515
Youre herte hangeth on a joly pyn!
Dooth now in this matiere right as yow leste°,
For finally I holde it for the beste."

    Justinus that ay stille° sat and herde
Right in this wise° he to Placebo answerde: 1520
"Now, brother myn, be pacient I preye,
Syn° ye han seyd°, and herkneth what I seye.
Senek among his othere wordes wyse
Seith° that a man oghte hym right wel avyse°
To whom he yeveth° his lond or his catel°.   1525
And syn I oghte avyse me right wel
To whom I yeve my good awey fro me,
Wel muchel moore I oghte avysed be

1454 **meschief,** *misfortune* 1457 **avaunt,** *boast* 1458 **lymes stark,** *limbs strong* 1461 **hoor,** *gray,* **fare,** *act* 1462 **blosmeth er that,** *blossoms before,* **ywoxen bee,** *is grown* 1463 **nys neither,** *is neither* 1466 **laurer,** *laurel (evergreen),* **is for to sene,** *can be seen* 1467 **syn that,** *since* 1473 **alday falleth,** *always happens in* 1475 **fil,** *occurred* 1476 **cleped,** *called* 1477 **soothly,** *truly* 1480 **axe,** *ask* 1481 **But,** *except,* **sapience,** *wisdom* 1482 **ne liketh,** *don't like* 1483 **weyven fro,** *deviate from* 1486 **shaltow,** *you shall* 1487 **swich,** *such,* **word,** *saying* 1489 **wysly,** *surely* 1491 **motyf,** *sentiment* 1493 **woot,** *knows* 1494 **stonden,** *stood,* **greet degree,** *high rank* 1496 **debaat,** *disagreement* 1498 **kan,** *knows* 1499 **What that,**

whatever, **holde it ferme,** *consider it solid* 1500 **elles thyng semblable,** *else something similar* 1505 **fay,** *faith* 1506 **han,** *have* 1507 **So heigh sentence,** *such noble judgment,* **holily,** *wholly* 1508 **everydeel,** *completely* 1510 **nys no,** *is no* 1511 **N'yn Ytaille,** *nor in Italy,* **bet han sayd,** *have said better* 1512 **halt hym,** *considers himself,* **ful wel apayd,** *very well satisfied* 1513 **an heigh corage,** *grand impulse* 1514 **stapen,** *advanced* 1515 **fader kyn,** *father's relatives* 1517 **leste,** *please* 1519 **ay stille,** *completely still* 1520 **wise,** *way* 1522 **Syn,** *since,* **han seyd,** *have spoken* 1524 **Seith,** *says,* **hym . . . avyse,** *consider* 1525 **yeveth,** *gives,* **catel,** *possessions*

1456 Another echo of the Wife of Bath, *WBP* 3.112. **1476 Placebo,** "I will please." See *SumT* 3.2075n. **1477 Justinus,** "the just one." **1485–86** Ecclesiasticus 32.24, attributed to Solomon. **1516 hangeth on a joly pyn,** hangs on a jolly hinge, i.e., is merry. **1523 Senek,** Seneca, but the maxim recurs in antifeminist tradition.

To whom I yeve my body for alwey.
I warne yow wel, it is no childes pley 1530
To take a wyf withouten avysement°.
Men moste enquere°, this is myn assent°,
Wher she be wys, or sobre, or dronkelewe°,
Or proud, or elles ootherweys a shrewe,
A chidestere°, or wastour of thy good°, 1535
Or riche, or poore, or elles mannyssh wood°.
Al be it so that° no man fynden shal
Noon in this world that trotteth hool in al,
Ne man, ne beest, swich as men koude devyse°.
But nathelees it oghte ynough suffise 1540
With any wyf, if so were° that she hadde
Mo° goode thewes° than hire vices badde.
And al this axeth leyser for t'enquere°.
For, God it woot°, I have wept many a teere
Ful pryvely syn° I have had a wyf. 1545
Preyse whoso wole° a wedded mannes lyf,
Certein I fynde in it but° cost and care,
And observances° of alle blisses bare°.
And yet, God woot, my neighebores aboute,
And namely° of wommen many a route°, 1550
Seyn° that I have the mooste stedefast wyf,
And eek the mekeste oon that bereth lyf°—
But I woot° best where wryngeth me my sho.
Ye mowe°, for me°, right as yow liketh do.
Avyseth yow—ye been a man of age— 1555
How that ye entren into mariage,
And namely with a yong wyf and a fair.
By hym that made water, erthe, and air,
The yongeste man that is in al this route°
Is bisy ynough° to bryngen it aboute 1560
To han his wyf allone°. Trusteth me,
Ye shul nat plesen hire fully yeres thre°—
This is to seyn, to doon hire ful plesaunce°.
A wyf axeth° ful many an observaunce°.

I prey yow that ye be nat yvele apayd°." 1565
  "Wel," quod this Januarie, "and hastow ysayd°?
Straw for thy Senek, and for thy proverbes.
I counte nat a panyer ful of herbes
Of scole-termes. Wyser men than thow,
As thou hast herd, assenteden right now 1570
To my purpos. Placebo, what sey ye?"
  "I seye it is a cursed man," quod he,
"That letteth° matrimoigne, sikerly°."
And with that word they rysen sodeynly
And been assented fully that he sholde 1575
Be wedded whanne hym liste° and where he
    wolde°.
  Heigh fantasye° and curious bisynesse°
Fro day to day gan in the soule impresse°
Of Januarie aboute his mariage.
Many fair shap and many a fair visage 1580
Ther passeth thurgh his herte nyght by nyght.
As whoso° tooke a mirour, polisshed bryght,
And sette it in a commune market-place,
Thanne sholde he se ful many a figure pace
By his mirour, and in the same wyse 1585
Gan Januarie inwith his thoght devyse°
Of maydens whiche that dwelten hym bisyde.
He wiste° nat wher that he myghte abyde°.
For if that oon have° beaute in hir face,
Another stant° so in the peples grace° 1590
For hire sadnesse° and hire benyngnytee°
That of the peple grettest voys° hath she;
And somme were riche and hadden badde name.
But nathelees, bitwixe ernest and game°,
He atte laste apoynted hym° on oon, 1595
And leet alle othere from his herte goon,
And chees° hire of his owene auctoritee—
For love is blynd alday° and may nat see.
And whan that he was in his bed ybroght,

1531 avysement, *consideration* **1532 moste enquere,** *must inquire,* **assent,** *opinion* **1533 dronkelewe,** *inclined to drink* **1535 chidestere,** *scolder,* **good,** *goods* **1536 mannyssh wood,** *crazy as a man* or *man crazy* **1537 Al be it so that,** *even though* **1539 devyse,** *imagine* **1541 if so were,** *if* (it) *were so* **1542 Mo,** *more,* **thewes,** *qualities* **1543 axeth leyser for t'enquere,** *takes time to investigate* **1544 woot,** *knows* **1545 Ful pryvely syn,** *in complete secrecy since* **1546 Preyse whoso wol,** (regardless of) *who will praise* **1547 but,** (nothing) *except* **1548 observances,** *duties,* **of alle blisses bare,** *without any joys* **1550 namely,** *especially,* **route,** *group* **1551 Seyn,** *say* **1552 bereth lyf,** *is alive* **1553 woot,** *know* **1554 mowe,** *may,* **for me,** *as far as I am concerned* **1559 route,** *company* **1560 bisy ynough,** *sufficiently occupied* **1561 allone,** *alone* (i.e., to

himself) **1562 yeres thre,** (for) *three years* **1563 doon . . . plesaunce,** *give . . . pleasure* **1564 axeth,** *requires,* **observaunce,** *attention* **1565 yvele apayd,** *displeased* **1566 hastow ysayd,** *have you spoken* (i.e., are you done?) **1573 letteth,** *opposes,* **sikerly,** *surely* **1576 hym liste,** (it) *pleased him,* **wolde,** *wished* **1577 Heigh fantasye,** *intense imagining,* **curious bisynesse,** *complicated activity* **1578 gan in the soule impresse,** *impressed in the soul* **1582 As whoso,** *like someone who* **1586 Gan . . . devyse,** *did . . . fantasize* **1588 wiste,** *knew,* **abyde,** *stop* **1589 oon have,** *one has* **1590 stant,** *stands,* **grace,** *favor* **1591 sadnesse,** *seriousness,* **benyngnytee,** *goodness* **1592 voys,** *praise* **1594 game,** *play* **1595 apoynted hym,** *fixed himself* **1597 chees,** *chose* **1598 alday,** *always*

1530–36 Compare *WBP* 3.285–92. **1538 trotteth hool in al,** an idiom that means "goes perfect in every respect." **1553 where wryngeth me my sho,** where my shoe pinches me; see *WBP* 3.492n. **1567 Straw for,** an idiom meaning "I care nothing for." **1568–69 I counte . . . / Of scole termes,** I value school terms (i.e., educated talk) no more than a wicker basket full of herbs. **1582–83 mirour . . . market-place,** the image of the mirror of the mind is also used in *TC* 1.365 and *Bo* 5.m4.27, but the mercantile comparison here makes January's fixation obnoxious.

He purtreyed° in his herte and in his thoght   1600
Hir fresshe beautee and hir age tendre,
Hir myddel smal, hire armes longe and sklendre°,
Hir wise governaunce°, hir gentillesse,
Hir wommanly berynge, and hire sadnesse°.
And whan that he on hire was
    condescended°,   1605
Hym thoughte his choys myghte nat ben
    amended.
For whan that he hymself concluded hadde,
Hym thoughte ech oother mannes wit so badde
That inpossible it were to repplye°
Agayn° his choys—this was his fantasye.   1610
His freendes sente he to at his instaunce°,
And preyed hem° to doon hym that plesaunce
That hastily they wolden to hym come;
He wolde abregge hir° labour alle and some.
Nedeth namoore for hym to go ne ryde°;   1615
He was apoynted ther° he wolde abyde°.

    Placebo cam and eek his freendes soone
And alderfirst° he bad hem° alle a boone°,
That noon of hem none argumentes make
Agayn° the purpos which that he hath take,   1620
Which purpos was plesant to God, seyde he,
And verray ground° of his prosperitee.

    He seyde ther was a mayden in the toun,
Which that of beautee hadde greet renoun.
Al were it so° she were of smal degree°,   1625
Suffiseth hym hir yowthe and hir beautee.
Which mayde, he seyde, he wolde han to his wyf,
To lede in ese and hoolynesse his lyf;
And thanked God that he myghte han hire al°,
That no wight° his blisse parten shal°.   1630
And preyde hem to laboure in this nede°
And shapen° that he faille nat to spede°;
For thanne, he seyde, his spirit was at ese.
"Thanne is," quod he, "nothyng may me displese,
Save o thyng priketh in my conscience   1635
The which° I wol reherce° in youre presence.

"I have," quod he, "herd seyd ful yoore° ago,
Ther may no man han parfite° blisses two—
This is to seye, in erthe and eek in hevene.
For though he kepe hym fro the synnes
    sevene   1640
And eek from every branche of thilke° tree,
Yet is ther so parfit felicitee
And so greet ese and lust° in mariage,
That evere I am agast° now in myn age
That I shal lede now so myrie a lyf,   1645
So delicat°, withouten wo and stryf,
That I shal have myn hevene in erthe heere.
For sith that verray° hevene is boght so deere°
With tribulacioun and greet penaunce,
How sholde I thanne, that lyve° in swich
    plesaunce°,   1650
As alle wedded men doon with hire wyvys,
Come to the blisse ther° Crist eterne on lyve ys°?
This is my drede, and ye, my bretheren tweye°,
Assoilleth° me this questioun, I preye."

    Justinus, which that° hated his folye,   1655
Answerde anon right in his japerye°;
And for° he wolde his longe tale abregge°,
He wolde noon auctoritee allegge°,
But seyde, "Sire, so ther be° noon obstacle
Oother than this, God of his hygh myracle°   1660
And of his mercy may so for yow wirche°
That er° ye have youre right of hooly chirche
Ye may repente of wedded mannes lyf,
In which ye seyn° ther is no wo ne stryf.
And elles°, God forbede but he sente°   1665
A wedded man hym grace to repente
Wel ofte rather° than a sengle° man.
And therfore, sire, the beste reed I kan°:
Dispeire yow noght, but have in youre memorie
Paraunter° she may be youre purgatorie.   1670
She may be Goddes meene° and Goddes whippe.
Thanne shal youre soule up to hevene skippe
Swifter than dooth an arwe out of the bowe.

1600 purtreyed, *portrayed* **1602 sklendre,** *slender* **1603 governaunce,** *behavior* **1604 sadnesse,** *seriousness* **1605 condescended,** *settled* **1609 repplye,** *argue* **1610 Agayn,** *against* **1611 instaunce,** *insistence* **1612 preyed hem,** *prayed them* **1614 abregge hir,** *shorten their* **1615 to go ne ryde,** *to walk nor ride* (i.e., to search) **1616 apoynted ther,** *fixed where* (i.e., with whom), **abyde,** *stay* **1618 alderfirst,** *first of all,* **bad hem,** *asked them,* **boone,** *request* **1620 Agayn,** *against* **1622 verray ground,** *true basis* **1625 Al were it so,** *even though,* **smal degree,** *humble class* **1629 han hire al,** *have her completely* **1630 wight,** *man,* **parten shal,** *shall share* **1631 nede,** *desire* **1632 shapen,** *arrange,* **spede,** *succeed* **1636 The which,** *which,* **reherce,** *describe* **1637 yoore,** *long* **1638**

parfite, *perfect* **1641 thilke,** *that* **1643 lust,** *pleasure* **1644 agast,** *terrified* **1646 delicat,** *delightful* **1648 sith that verray,** *since true,* **deere,** *dearly* **1650 that lyve,** *who lives,* **swich plesaunce,** *such pleasure* **1652 ther,** *where,* **on lyve ys,** *is alive* **1653 tweye,** *two* **1654 Assoilleth,** *solve* **1655 which that,** *who* **1656 japerye,** *mockery* **1657 for,** *because,* **abregge,** *shorten* **1658 allegge,** *appeal to* **1659 so ther be,** *as there is* **1660 myracle,** *power* **1661 wirche,** *bring about* **1662 er,** *before* **1664 seyn,** *say* **1665 And elles,** *or else,* **but he sente,** *unless he sends* **1667 Wel ofte rather,** *more often,* **sengle,** *single* **1668 the beste reed I kan,** (here is) *the best advice I know* **1670 Paraunter,** (that) *perhaps* **1671 Goddes meene,** *God's means*

1640–41 synnes sevene . . . tree, the Seven Deadly Sins were represented as a tree with branches and twigs; see *ParsT* 10.388–90 and elsewhere. **1662 right of hooly chirche,** extreme unction, or the anointing of the sick, one of the seven sacraments. **1666 hym grace,** grace; "hym" is a redundant reference to "wedded man." **1670–71 purgatorie . . . whippe,** these images of marital suffering echo *WBP* 3.175 and 489.

I hope to God herafter shul ye knowe
That ther nys no so° greet felicitee   1675
In mariage, ne nevere mo shal bee,
That yow shal lette of° youre savacioun,
So that ye° use, as skile° is and resoun°,
The lustes° of youre wyf attemprely°,
And that ye plese hire nat to° amorously,   1680
And that ye kepe yow eek from oother synne.
My tale is doon for my wit is thynne.
Beth nat agast herof°, my brother deere,
But lat us waden° out of this mateere.
The Wyf of Bathe, if ye han understonde°,   1685
Of mariage, which ye have on honde,
Declared hath ful wel in litel space.
Fareth now wel. God have yow in his grace."
    And with that word this Justyn and his brother
Han take hir leve°, and ech of hem of
        oother.   1690
For whan they saugh that it moste nedes° be,
They wroghten° so, by sly° and wys tretee°,
That she, this mayden, which that Mayus highte°,
As hastily as evere that she myghte
Shal wedded be unto this Januarie.   1695
I trowe° it were to longe yow to tarie°
If I yow tolde of every scrit° and bond
By which that she was feffed in° his lond,
Or for to herknen° of hir riche array°.
But finally ycomen° is the day   1700
That to the chirche bothe be they went
For to receyve the hooly sacrement.
Forth comth° the preest, with stole aboute his
        nekke,
And bad hire be lyk Sarra and Rebekke
In wysdom and in trouthe of mariage,   1705

And seyde his orisons°, as is usage°,
And croucheth hem°, and bad° God sholde hem
        blesse,
And made al siker° ynogh with hoolynesse.
    Thus been they wedded with solempnitee,
And at the feeste sitteth he and she   1710
With othere worthy folk upon the deys°.
Al ful of joye and blisse is the paleys°,
And ful of instrumentz and of vitaille°,
The mooste deynteuous° of al Ytaille.
Biforn° hem stoode instrumentz of swich
        soun°   1715
That Orpheus ne of Thebes Amphioun
Ne maden nevere swich a melodye.
At every cours thanne cam loud mynstralcye
That nevere tromped° Joab for to heere,
Nor he Theodomas yet half so cleere   1720
At Thebes whan the citee was in doute.
Bacus the wyn hem skynketh° al aboute,
And Venus laugheth upon every wight°,
For Januarie was bicome hir knyght
And wolde bothe assayen° his corage°   1725
In libertee and eek in mariage;
And with hire fyrbrond° in hire hand aboute
Daunceth biforn the bryde and al the route°.
And certeinly, I dar right wel seyn this,
Ymeneus that god of weddyng is   1730
Saugh nevere his° lyf so myrie a wedded man.
Hoold thou thy pees°, thou poete Marcian,
That writest us that ilke° weddyng murie°
Of hire Philologie and hym Mercurie,
And of the songes that the Muses songe!   1735
To° smal is bothe thy penne, and eek thy tonge
For to descryven of° this mariage

1675 nys no so, *is no such* **1677 yow shal lette of,** *shall keep you from* **1678 So that ye,** *as long as you,* **skile,** *proper,* **resoun,** *reasonable* **1679 lustes,** *pleasures,* **attemprely,** *moderately* **1680 to,** *too* **1683 Beth nat agast herof,** *be not frightened of this* **1684 waden,** *move* **1685 han understonde,** *have understood* **1690 Han take hir leve,** *take their leave* **1691 moste nedes,** *must necessarily* **1692 wroghten,** *worked* (it), **sly,** *skillful,* **tretee,** *negotiation* **1693 highte,** *was called* **1696 trowe,** *think,* **yow to tarie,** *to delay you* **1697 scrit,** *document* **1698 feffed in,** *endowed with* **1699 herknen,** *hear,* **array,** *clothing* **1700 ycomen,** *arrived* **1703**

comth, *comes* **1706 orisons,** *prayers,* **usage** *customary* **1707 croucheth hem,** *made the sign of the cross over them,* **bad,** *asked* **1708 siker,** *certain* **1711 deys,** *dais* (platform) **1712 paleys,** *palace* **1713 vitaille,** *food* **1714 deynteuous,** *extravagant* **1715 Biforn,** *before,* **swich soun,** *such sound* **1719 tromped,** *trumpeted* **1722 hem skynketh,** *pours for them* **1723 wight,** *person* **1725 assayen,** *test,* **corage,** *desire* **1727 hire fyrbrond,** *her torch* (Venus's) **1728 route,** *company* **1731 Saugh nevere his,** *saw never* (in) *his* **1732 pees,** *peace* **1733 us that ilke,** *for us that same,* **murie,** *merry* **1736 To,** *too* **1737 descryven of,** *describe*

1685–87 Wyf of Bathe . . . , this break in literary decorum has been thought Chaucer's mistake or the Merchant's, but it neatly compels the reader (or listener) to compare the sentiments of *MerT* with *WBPT*. **1693 Mayus,** May; see 1393n above. **1703 stole,** an ecclesiastical vestment like a long scarf, worn by priest or bishop when performing the sacraments, including marriage. **1704 Sarra and Rebekke,** Sara and Rebecca, biblical figures of wise and faithful wives, referred to in the traditional marriage ceremony. This brisk summary of the ceremony is bitterly ironic, as is the following rhetorical excess. **1716 Orpheus,** mythic musician who freed his wife from Hades by music. **Amphioun,** mythic musician who built Thebes by charming stones to move. **1719 Joab,** King David's trumpeter; 2 Samuel 2.28. **1720 Theodomas,** seer in *Thebaid* (8.343) whose predictions of war came true when the trumpets of the armies sounded. **1722 Bacus,** Bacchus, god of wine. **1723 Venus,** goddess of love, whose laughter, phallic torch, and dance in the following lines are metaphoric and, given the unseemliness of January's desire, parodic. **1730 Ymeneus,** Hymen. **1732 Marcian,** Marcianus Capella, fifth-century author of *De Nuptiis Philologiae et Mercurii* (Concerning the Marriage of Philology and Mercury), an allegorical poem about the liberal arts that is antithetical to the libidinous marriage described here.

Whan tendre youthe hath wedded stoupyng age.
Ther is swich myrthe that it may nat be writen.
Assayeth° it youreself, thanne may ye witen°   1740
If that I lye or noon° in this matiere.

Mayus, that sit° with so benyngne a chiere°,
Hire to biholde it semed fairye°.
Queene Ester looked nevere with swich an eye
On Assuer, so meke a look hath she.   1745
I may yow nat devyse° al hir beautee,
But thus muche of hire beautee telle I may,
That she was lyk the brighte morwe° of May,
Fulfild of alle beautee and plesaunce.

This Januarie is ravysshed in a traunce   1750
At every tyme he looked on hir face;
But in his herte he gan hire to manace° *threaten*
That he that nyght in armes wolde hire streyne°
Harder than evere Parys dide Eleyne.
But nathelees yet hadde he greet pitee   1755
That thilke° nyght offenden° hire moste° he,
And thoughte, "Allas, O tendre creature,
Now wolde God° ye myghte wel endure
Al my corage°, it is so sharp and keene!
I am agast° ye shul it nat susteene°—   1760
But God forbede that I dide al my myght!
Now wolde God that it were woxen nyght°,
And that the nyght wolde lasten everemo.
I wolde that al this peple were ago°."
And finally he dooth al his labour°,   1765
As he best myghte, savynge° his honour,
To haste hem fro the mete° in subtil wyse.

The tyme cam that resoun was° to ryse,
And after that men° daunce and drynken faste,
And spices al aboute the hous they caste,   1770
And ful of joye and blisse is every man—
Al but a squyer highte° Damyan,
Which carf biforn the knyght ful many a day.

He was so ravysshed on his lady May
That for the verray peyne° he was ny wood°.   1775
Almoost he swelte° and swowned ther° he stood,
So soore hath Venus hurt hym with hire brond°,
As that° she bar it daunsynge in hire hond,
And to his bed he wente hym hastily.
Namoore of hym as at this tyme speke I,   1780
But there I lete hym wepe ynogh and pleyne°,
Til fresshe May wol rewen° on his peyne.

O perilous fyr that in the bedstraw bredeth°!
O famulier foo° that his servyce bedeth°!
O servant traytour, false hoomly hewe°,   1785
Lyk to the naddre° in bosom sly untrewe°!
God shilde° us alle from youre aqueyntaunce.
O Januarie, dronken in plesaunce
In mariage, se how thy Damyan,
Thyn owene squier and thy boren man°,   1790
Entendeth for to do thee vileynye.
God graunte thee thy hoomly fo t'espye°!
For in this world nys° worse pestilence
Than hoomly foo al day° in thy presence.

Parfourned° hath the sonne his ark
      diurne;   1795
No lenger may the body of hym sojurne°
On th'orisonte as in that latitude.
Night with his mantel° that is derk and rude°
Gan oversprede the hemysperie aboute,
For which departed is this lusty route°   1800
Fro Januarie with thank° on every syde.
Hoom to hir houses lustily they ryde,
Where as they doon hir thynges as hem leste°,
And whan they sye° hir tyme goon to reste.
Soone after that, this hastif° Januarie   1805
Wolde go to bedde, he wolde no lenger tarye.
He drynketh ypocras, clarree, and vernage
Of spices hoote t'encreessen his corage,

1740 **Assayeth**, *test,* **witen**, *know* 1741 **noon**, *not* 1742 **sit**, *sits,* **benyn-gne a chiere**, *serene an expression* 1743 **fairye**, *enchanting* 1746 **devyse**, *describe* 1748 **morwe**, *morning* 1752 **manace**, *threaten* 1753 **streyne**, *bind* 1756 **thilke**, *that,* **offenden**, *attack,* **moste**, *must* 1758 **wolde God**, *(I) wish (to) God* 1759 **corage**, *desire* 1760 **I am agast**, *I fear,* **sus-teene**, *survive* 1762 **it were woxen nyght**, *it would become night* 1764 **ago**, *gone* 1765 **dooth al his labour**, *does all he can* 1766 **savynge**, *with-out compromising* 1767 **mete**, *meal* 1768 **resoun was**, (*it*) *was reason-able* 1769 **men**, *people* 1772 **highte**, *named* 1775 **verray peyne**, *sheer pain,* **ny wood**, *nearly crazed* 1776 **swelte**, *fainted,* **swowned ther**, *swooned where* 1777 **brond**, *torch* 1778 **As that**, *the one that* 1781 **pleyne**, *lament* 1782 **rewen**, *have pity* 1783 **bedstraw bredeth**, *mattress begins* 1784 **foo**, *foe,* **bedeth**, *offers* 1785 **hoomly hewe**, *domestic pre-tense* 1786 **naddre**, *snake,* **sly untrewe**, *secretly false* 1787 **shilde**, *protect* 1790 **boren man**, *servant since birth* 1792 **hoomly fo t'espye**, *to see the enemy at home* 1793 **nys**, *there is no* 1794 **al day**, *always* 1795 **Par-fourned**, *performed* 1796 **sojurne**, *remain* 1798 **mantel**, *cloak,* **rude**, *rough* 1800 **route**, *company* 1801 **thank**, *thanks* 1803 **as hem leste**, *as pleases them* 1804 **sye**, *saw* 1805 **hastif**, *eager*

1744–45 **Ester . . . Assuer**, Esther married King Ahasuerus to manipulate him and used her looks effectively; see Esther 2.15ff. and (in the Vulgate) 15.4–19. 1754 **Parys . . . Eleyne**, Paris's abduction of Helen caused the Trojan War. 1773 **Which carf biforn**, who carved before, i.e., Damian carved January's meat as his personal retainer; see *GP* 1.100. 1786 In *Gesta Romanorum*, Tale 174, and elsewhere is found the story of the man who put the frozen serpent in his bosom to warm it only to have it bite him when it thawed. 1795–97 **sonne his ark diurne . . . th'orisonte**, the diurnal or daily arc of the sun across the sky and its descent below the horizon, an elaborate way of saying that day is end-ing. 1799 **hemysperie**, hemisphere, the half of the heavens seen from Earth. 1807 **ypocras, clarree, and vernage**, three kinds of strong wine, sweetened and spiced, all thought to increase the lustiness and fertility of the drinker.

And many a letuarie° hath he ful fyn°,
Swiche° as the cursed monk daun°
    Constantyn   1810
Hath writen in his book *De Coitu;*
To eten hem alle he nas no thyng eschu°.
And to his privee° freendes thus seyde he,
"For Goddes love, as soone as it may be,
Lat voyden° al this hous in curteys wyse°."   1815
And they han doon right as he wol devyse°.
Men drynken and the travers drawe anon.
The bryde was broght abedde as stille as stoon;
And whan the bed was with° the preest yblessed,
Out of the chambre hath every wight hym
    dressed°.   1820
And Januarie hath faste in armes take
His fresshe May, his paradys, his make°.
He lulleth hire, he kisseth hire ful ofte.
With thikke brustles of his berd unsofte— *don't shave well.*
Lyk to the skyn of houndfyssh, sharp as
    brere°,   1825
For he was shave al newe in his manere—
He rubbeth hire aboute hir tendre face,
And seyde thus, "Allas, I moot trespace°
To yow, my spouse, and yow greetly offende°
Er tyme come° that I wil doun descende.   1830
But nathelees, considereth this," quod he,
"Ther nys no° werkman, whatsoevere he be,
That may bothe werke wel and hastily.
This wol be doon at leyser parfitly°.
It is no fors° how longe that we pleye;   1835
In trewe wedlok coupled be we tweye°,
And blessed be the yok° that we been° inne,
For in oure actes we mowe° do no synne.
A man may do no synne with his wyf,
Ne hurte hymselven with his owene knyf,   1840
For we han leve to pleye us° by the lawe."
Thus laboureth he til that the day gan dawe°,
And thanne he taketh a soppe in fyn clarree°,
And upright in his bed thanne sitteth he,

And after that he sang ful loude and cleere,   1845
And kiste his wyf, and made wantown cheere°.
He was al coltissh°, ful of ragerye°,
And ful of jargon° as a flekked pye°.
The slakke skyn aboute his nekke shaketh
Whil that he sang, so chaunteth he and
    craketh°.   1850
But God woot° what that May thoughte in hir
    herte
Whan she hym saugh up sittynge in his sherte,
In his nyght-cappe, and with his nekke lene.
She preyseth° nat his pleyyng worth a bene°.
Thanne seide he thus, "My reste wol I take.   1855
Now day is come I may no lenger wake."
And doun he leyde his heed and sleep til pryme°.
And afterward whan that he saugh his tyme
Up ryseth Januarie. But fresshe May
Heeld hire chambre unto the fourthe day,   1860
As usage° is of wyves for the beste,
For every labour° somtyme moot° han reste
Or elles longe may he nat endure,
This is to seyn, no lyves° creature
Be it of fyssh or bryd or beest or man.   1865
    Now wol I speke of woful Damyan,
That langwissheth for love, as ye shul heere.
Therfore I speke to hym in this manere,
I seye, "O sely° Damyan, allas,
Andswere to my demaunde°, as in this cas°.   1870
How shaltow° to thy lady, fresshe May,
Telle thy wo? She wole alwey seye nay.
Eek° if thou speke, she wol thy wo biwreye°.
God be thyn help! I kan no bettre seye."
    This sike° Damyan in Venus fyr   1875
So brenneth° that he dyeth for desyr,
For which he putte his lyf in aventure°.
No lenger myghte he in this wise° endure,
But prively a penner° gan he borwe°,
And in a lettre wroot he al his sorwe,   1880
In manere of a compleynt or a lay,

It wasn't good in bed.

1809 letuarie, *medicine,* **ful fyn,** *very fine* **1810 Swiche,** *such,* **daun,** *master* **1812 nas no thyng eschu,** *was not at all averse* **1813 privee,** *intimate* **1815 Lat voyden,** *empty out,* **curteys wyse,** *a courteous way* **1816 wol devyse,** *wished* **1819 with,** *by* **1820 wight hym dressed,** *man taken himself* **1822 make,** *mate* **1825 brere,** *a briar* **1828 moot trespace,** *must do wrong* **1829 offende,** *displease or injure* **1830 Er tyme come,** *before the time comes* **1832 nys no,** *is no* **1834 parfitly,** *perfectly* **1835 It is no fors, it doesn't matter** **1836 tweye,** *two* **1837 yok,** *yoke,* **been,** *are* **1838 mowe, are able to** **1841 pleye us,** *entertain ourselves* **1842 gan dawe,** *dawned*

1843 soppe in fyn clarree, *bread soaked in wine* **1846 made wantown cheere,** *behaved lecherously* **1847 coltissh,** *frisky,* **ragerye,** *frolics* **1848 ful of jargon,** *talkative,* **flekked pye,** *spotted magpie* **1850 craketh,** *croaks* **1851 woot,** *knows* **1854 preyseth,** *praised,* **bene,** *bean* **1857 pryme,** *about 9 a.m.* **1861 usage,** *custom* **1862 labour,** *laborer,* **moot,** *must* **1864 lyves,** *living* **1869 sely,** *foolish* **1870 demaunde,** *question,* **cas,** *situation* **1871 shaltow,** *will you* **1873 Eek,** *and,* **biwreye,** *betray* **1875 sike,** *sick* **1876 brenneth,** *burns* **1877 aventure,** *jeopardy* **1878 wise,** *manner* **1879 penner,** *a case for pen and ink,* **gan he borwe,** *he borrowed*

1810 Constantyn, Constantinus Africanus, eleventh-century author of *De Coitu* (On Intercourse), which includes suggestions for virility and remedies for impotence. **1817 travers drawe anon,** the curtain is soon drawn, separating the bedchamber from the hall. **1825 houndfyssh,** dogfish, a small shark with rough skin. **1826 shave al newe,** recently shaven, even though older men usually wore beards in Chaucer's time. **1839–40 wyf . . . owene knyf,** *ParsT* 10.859 gives the opposite, orthodox view. **1881 compleynt or a lay,** complaint or song, both lyric forms.

It really does love her.

Unto his faire, fresshe lady May;
And in a purs of sylk heng° on his sherte
He hath it put, and leyde it at his herte.

    The moone, that at noon was thilke° day   1885
That Januarie hath wedded fresshe May
In two of Tawr, was into Cancre glyden.
So longe hath Mayus in hir chambre byden°
As custume is unto thise nobles alle.
A bryde shal nat eten in the halle   1890
Til dayes foure, or thre dayes atte leeste,
Ypassed been; thanne lat hire go to feeste.
The fourthe day compleet fro noon to noon,
Whan that the heighe masse was ydoon°,
In halle sit this Januarie and May   1895
As fressh as is the brighte someres day.
And so bifel how that° this goode man
Remembred hym upon this Damyan,
And seyde, "Seynte° Marie, how may this be
That Damyan entendeth° nat to me?   1900
Is he ay syk°, or how may this bityde°?"
His squieres whiche that stooden ther bisyde
Excused hym by cause of his siknesse,
Which letted hym to doon° his bisynesse;
Noon oother cause myghte make hym tarye.   1905
    "That me forthynketh°," quod this Januarie.
"He is a gentil squier, by my trouthe.
If that he deyde°, it were harm and routhe°.
He is as wys, discreet, and as secree°
As any man I woot° of his degree°,   1910
And therto manly° and eek servysable°,
And for to been a thrifty° man right able.
But after mete° as soone as evere I may,
I wol myself visite hym, and eek May,
To doon hym al the confort that I kan."   1915
And for that word hym blessed every man
That of his bountee° and his gentillesse
He wolde so conforten in siknesse
His squier, for it was a gentil dede.
"Dame," quod this Januarie, "taak good hede,   1920

At after-mete ye° with youre wommen alle,
Whan ye han been in chambre out of this halle,
That alle ye go se this Damyan.
Dooth hym disport°—he is a gentil man;
And telleth hym that I wol hym visite,   1925
Have I no thyng but° rested me a lite.
And spede yow faste, for I wole abyde°
Til that ye slepe faste° by my syde."
And with that worde he gan to hym to calle°
A squier that was marchal° of his halle   1930
And tolde hym certeyn thynges what he wolde°.
    This fresshe May hath streight hir wey yholde°
With alle hir wommen unto Damyan.
Doun by his beddes syde sit she than°,
Confortynge hym as goodly as she may.   1935
This Damyan, whan that his tyme he say°,
In secree wise his purs and eek his bille°,
In which that he ywriten hadde his wille,
Hath put into hire hand withouten moore,
Save that he siketh° wonder depe and soore,   1940
And softely to hire right thus seyde he,
"Mercy, and that° ye nat discovere° me,
For I am deed if that this thyng be kyd°."
This purs hath she in with hir bosom hyd
And wente hire wey—ye gete namoore of me.   1945
But unto Januarie ycomen is she
That on his beddes syde sit ful softe.
He taketh hire and kisseth hire ful ofte,
And leyde hym doun to slepe, and that anon.
She feyned hire as° that she moste gon°   1950
Ther as ye woot° that every wight° moot neede°,
And whan she of this bille hath taken heede,
She rente° it al to cloutes° atte laste,
And in the pryvee° softely° it caste.
    Who studieth° now but faire fresshe May?   1955
Adoun by olde Januarie she lay,
That sleep° til that the coughe hath hym awaked.
Anon he preyde hire strepen hire° al naked;
He wolde of hire, he seyde, han som plesaunce°,

1883 heng, *which hung* **1885 thilke,** *that same* **1888 byden,** *remained* **1894 ydoon,** *done* **1897 bifel how that,** *it happened that* **1899 Seynte,** *holy* **1900 entendeth,** *attends* **1901 ay syk,** *very sick,* **bityde,** *happen* **1904 letted hym to doon,** *prevented him from doing* **1906 That me forthynketh,** *I am sorry about that* **1908 deyde,** *died,* **routhe,** *pity* **1909 secree,** *confidential* **1910 woot,** *know,* **degree,** *rank* **1911 manly,** *reliable,* **eek servysable,** *also willing to serve* **1912 thrifty,** *accomplished* **1913 mete,** *dinner* **1917 bountee,** *goodness* **1921 At after-mete ye,** *after dinner you* **1924 Dooth hym disport,** *entertain him* **1926 Have I no thyng**

but, *only after I have* **1927 abyde,** *wait* **1928 faste,** *close* **1929 gan . . . to calle,** *called* **1930 marchal,** *chief officer* **1931 wolde,** *wished* **1932 hath streight hir wey yholde,** *goes straight* **1934 than,** *then* **1936 say,** *saw* **1937 bille,** *plea* **1940 siketh,** *sighed* **1942 and that,** *and (I ask) that,* **discovere,** *betray* **1943 kyd,** *known* **1950 feyned hire as,** *pretended,* **moste gon,** *must go* **1951 woot,** *know,* **wight,** *person,* **moot neede,** *necessarily must (go)* **1953 rente,** *tears,* **cloutes,** *shreds* **1954 pryvee,** *toilet,* **softely,** *quietly* **1955 studieth,** *thinks* **1957 That sleep,** *who sleeps* **1958 preyde hire strepen hire,** *asked her to strip herself* **1959 plesaunce,** *pleasure*

1885–87 moone . . . / In two of Tawr . . . into Cancre glyden, the moon was in the second degree of Taurus, the zodiacal sign of the Bull, moving into Cancer, the sign of the Crab. This takes four days. **1894 heigh masse,** High Mass; an elaborate form of the daily liturgy. **1909–12** Given Damian's passion for May, the sexual connotations of several of the adjectives here are ironic.

He seyde hir clothes dide hym encombraunce°,   1960
And she obeyeth, be hire lief or looth°.
But lest that precious folk be° with me wrooth°,
How that he wroghte° I dar nat to yow telle,
Or wheither hire thoughte it° paradys or helle.
But heere I lete hem werken in hir wyse   1965
Til evensong rong and that they moste aryse.

    Were it by destynee or by aventure°,
Were it by influence° or by nature,
Or constellacioun°, that in swich estaat°
The hevene stood, that tyme fortunaat   1970
Was for to putte a bille° of Venus werkes—
For alle thyng hath tyme, as seyn° thise clerkes—
To any womman for to gete hire love,
I kan nat seye, but grete God above
That knoweth that noon act is causelees,   1975
He deme° of al, for I wole holde my pees°.
But sooth° is this, how that this fresshe May
Hath take swich impressioun that day
For pitee of this sike Damyan
That from hire herte she ne dryve kan°   1980
The remembrance for to doon hym ese°.
"Certeyn," thoghte she, "whom that this thyng displese,
I rekke° noght, for heere I hym assure°
To love hym best of any creature,
Though he namoore hadde than his sherte."   1985
Lo, pitee renneth° soone in gentil herte!

    Heere may ye se how excellent franchise°
In wommen is whan they hem narwe avyse°.
Som tyrant is°, as ther be many oon,
That hath an herte as hard as any stoon,   1990
Which wolde han let hym sterven° in the place
Wel rather than han graunted hym hire grace,
And hem rejoysen° in hire crueel pryde,
And rekke nat to been° an homycide.

This gentil May, fulfilled of pitee,   1995
Right of° hire hand a lettre made she
In which she graunteth hym hire verray grace°.
Ther lakketh noght oonly but day and place
Wher that she myghte unto his lust suffise°,
For it shal be right as he wole devyse°.   2000
And whan she saugh hir tyme upon a day,
To visite this Damyan gooth May,
And sotilly° this lettre doun she threste°
Under his pilwe: rede it if hym leste°.
She taketh hym by the hand and harde hym twiste   2005
So secrely that no wight° of it wiste°,
And bad hym been al hool°, and forth she wente
To Januarie whan that he for hire sente.

    Up riseth Damyan the nexte morwe.
Al passed was his siknesse and his sorwe.   2010
He kembeth° hym, he preyneth° hym and pyketh°,
He dooth al that his lady lust° and lyketh,
And eek to Januarie he gooth as lowe°
As evere dide a dogge for the bowe°.
He is so plesant unto every man—   2015
For craft is al, whoso that do it kan—
That every wight is fayn° to speke hym good,
And fully in his lady grace° he stood.
Thus lete I Damyan aboute his nede°,
And in my tale forth I wol procede.   2020

    Somme clerkes holden° that felicitee
Stant° in delit, and therfore certeyn he,
This noble Januarie, with al his myght
In honest wyse as longeth° to a kynght,
Shoop hym° to lyve ful deliciously.   2025
His housynge, his array, as honestly
To his degree was maked as a kynges.
Amonges othere of his honeste thynges,
He made a gardyn walled al with stoon.
So fair a gardyn woot° I nowher noon,   2030

1960 dide hym encombraunce, *encumbered him* **1961 be hire lief or looth,** *whether* (it was) *to her pleasing or offensive* **1962 lest that precious folk be,** *for fear that prudish people will be,* **wrooth,** *angry* **1963 wroghte,** *worked* **1964 hire thoughte it,** *it seemed to her* **1967 aventure,** *chance* **1968 influence,** *planetary influence* **1969 constellacioun,** *configuration of the stars,* **swich estaat,** *such arrangement* **1971 putte a bille,** *present a petition* **1972 seyn,** *say* **1976 He deme,** (may) *he judge,* **pees,** *peace* **1977 sooth,** *the truth* **1980 ne dryve kan,** *cannot drive* **1981 remembrance for to doon hym ease,** *thought of making him comfortable* **1983 rekke,** *care,* **assure,** *promise* **1986 renneth,** *runs* **1987 franchise,** *generosity* **1988 hem narwe avyse,** *consider carefully* **1989 Som**

tyrant is, (perhaps) *there is some tyrant* **1991 sterven,** *die* **1993 hem rejoysen,** *take pleasure from him* **1994 rekke nat to been,** *not care about being* **1996 Right of,** *properly by* **1997 verray grace,** *complete favor* **1999 unto his lust suffise,** *satisfy his desire* **2000 wole devyse,** *will wish* **2003 sotilly,** *cleverly,* **threste,** *thrust* **2004 hym leste,** (it) *pleases him* **2006 wight,** *person,* **wiste,** *knew* **2007 hool,** *healthy* **2011 kembeth,** *combs,* **preyneth,** *preens,* **pyketh,** *cleans* **2012 lust,** *wants* **2013 lowe,** *lowly* (humbly) **2014 for the bowe,** *trained for hunting with a bow* **2017 fayn,** *pleased* **2018 lady grace,** *lady's grace* **2019 aboute his nede,** *pursuing his desire* **2021 holden,** *think* **2022 Stant,** *exists* **2024 longeth,** *pertains* **2025 Shoop hym,** *arranged* (for) *himself* **2030 woot,** *know*

1966 evensong rong, bells were rung to signal the beginning of evening religious service. **1986** The familiar chivalric sentiment is mocked here; for other occurrences see *KnT* 1.1761n. **2021 felicitee,** supreme happiness. The pursuit of worldly pleasure is attributed to Epicurus and condemned by Philosophy in *Bo* 3.pr2.77ff. **2024–28 honest . . . honestly . . . honeste,** honorable / honorably, but the repetition three times in five lines mocks the meaning.

For out of doute I verraily° suppose
That he that wroot the *Romance of the Rose*
Ne koude° of it the beautee wel devyse°,
Ne Priapus ne myghte nat suffise°,
Though he be god of gardyns, for to telle   2035
The beautee of the gardyn and the welle°
That stood under a laurer° alwey grene.
Ful ofte tyme he Pluto and his queene
Proserpina and al hire fairye°
Disporten hem° and maken melodye   2040
Aboute that welle, and daunced, as men tolde.
    This noble knyght, this Januarie the olde,
Swich deyntee° hath in it to walke and pleye
That he wol no wight suffren bere° the keye
Save he hymself; for of the smale wyket°   2045
He baar° alwey of silver a clyket°
With which, whan that hym leste°, he it unshette°.
And whan he wolde paye his wyf hir dette
In somer seson, thider wolde he go,
And May his wyf, and no wight but they two,   2050
And thynges whiche that were nat doon abedde,
He in the gardyn parfourned hem° and spedde°.
And in this wyse many a murye day
Lyved this Januarie and fresshe May.
But worldly joye may nat alwey dure°   2055
To Januarie, ne to no creature.
    O sodeyn hap°, O thou Fortune unstable,
Lyk to the scorpion so deceyvable°,
That flaterest with thyn heed whan thou wolt
        stynge!
Thy tayl is deeth, thurgh thyn envenymynge°.   2060
O brotil° joye, O sweete venym queynte°,
O monstre that so subtilly kanst peynte°
Thy yiftes° under hewe° of stidefastnesse,
That° thou deceyvest bothe moore and lesse,
Why hastow Januarie thus deceyved,   2065
That haddest hym for thy fulle freend receyved?

And now thou hast biraft hym° bothe his eyen
For sorwe of which desireth he to dyen.
    Allas, this noble Januarie free
Amydde his lust and his prosperitee   2070
Is woxen° blynd, and that al sodeynly.
He wepeth and he wayleth pitously;
And therwithal the fyr of jalousie
Lest° that his wyf sholde falle in som folye
So brente° his herte that he wolde fayn°   2075
That som man bothe hym and hire had slayn.
For neither after his deeth nor in his lyf
Ne wolde he that she were love° ne wyf,
But evere lyve as wydwe° in clothes blake
Soul° as the turtle that lost hath hire make°.   2080
But atte laste, after a month or tweye,
His sorwe gan aswage°, sooth° to seye.
For whan he wiste° it may noon oother be,
He paciently took his adversitee
Save°, out of doute, he may nat forgoon°   2085
That he nas jalous everemoore in oon°.
Which jalousye it was so outrageous
That neither in halle n'yn° noon oother hous,
N'yn noon oother place neverthemo,
He nolde suffre° hire for to ryde or go   2090
But if that he had hond on hire alway;
For which ful ofte wepeth fresshe May
That loveth Damyan so benyngnely°
That she moot outher° dyen sodeynly
Or elles she moot han hym as hir leste°.   2095
She wayteth whan° hir herte wolde breste°.
    Upon that oother syde Damyan
Bicomen is the sorwefulleste man
That evere was, for neither nyght ne day
Ne myghte he speke a word to fresshe May,   2100
As to his purpos of no swich mateere,
But if that° Januarie moste it heere°,
That hadde an hand upon hire everemo.

2031 verraily, *truly* **2033 Ne koude,** *could not,* **devyse,** *describe* **2034 myghte nat suffise,** *might not be capable* **2036 welle,** *fountain* **2037 laurer,** *laurel tree* **2039 hire fairye,** *their fairies* **2040 Disporten hem,** *entertained themselves* **2043 Swich deyntee,** *such delight* **2044 no wight suffren bere,** *allow no one to carry* **2045 wyket,** *gate* **2046 baar,** *carried,* **clyket,** *key* **2047 hym leste,** *(it) pleased him,* **unshette,** *unlocked* **2052 parfourned hem,** *performed them,* **spedde,** *succeeded* **2055 alwey dure,** *forever sustain* **2057 sodeyn hap,** *sudden happening* **2058 deceyvable,** *able to deceive* **2060 envenymynge,** *poisoning* **2061 brotil,** *unstable,* **queynte,** *strange* **2062 kanst peynte,** *can disguise* **2063 yiftes,** *gifts,*

hewe, *illusion* **2064 That,** *(so) that* **2067 biraft hym,** *deprived him* (of) **2071 woxen,** *become* **2074 Lest,** *for fear* **2075 brente,** *burned,* **wolde fayn,** *would have been happy* **2078 love,** *lover* **2079 wydwe,** *widow* **2080 Soul,** *solitary,* **make,** *mate* **2082 gan aswage,** *lessened,* **sooth,** *true* **2083 wiste,** *knew* **2085 Save,** *except that,* **forgoon,** *cease* **2086 nas jalous everemoore in oon,** *was jealous constantly* **2088 n'yn,** *nor in* **2090 nolde suffre,** *would not allow* **2093 benyngnely,** *graciously* **2094 moot outher,** *must either* **2095 hir leste,** *she desired* **2096 wayteth whan,** *expects the time,* **breste,** *burst* **2102 But if,** *except,* **moste it heere,** *would hear it*

2032 Romance of the Rose, the thirteenth-century allegory, *Roman de la Rose,* by Guillaume de Lorris and Jean de Meun, which opens in a garden of idleness and narcissistic love; translated by Chaucer, at least in part, as *Romaunt of the Rose.* **2034 Priapus,** Roman god of gardens and fertility, represented with an enormous phallus. **2038–39 Pluto . . . Proserpina,** traditionally, god and goddess of the underworld, but here king and queen, associated with fairies and later presented as comic. **2048 paye . . . hir dette,** see 1452n above. **2080 turtle,** turtledove, a bird fabled for its fidelity to its mate.

But nathelees, by writyng to and fro
And privee° signes wiste° he what she mente,　2105
And she knew eek the fyn° of his entente.
　　O Januarie, what myghte it thee availle,
Thogh thou myghtest se as fer as shippes saille?
For as good is blynd deceyved be
As to be deceyved whan a man may se.　2110
　　Lo Argus, which that hadde an hondred
　　　eyen,
For al that evere he koude poure or pryen,
Yet was he blent°, and God woot° so been mo°
That wenen wisly° that it be nat so.
Passe over is an ese, I sey namoore.　2115
　　This fresshe May that I spak of so yoore°,
In warm wex hath emprented the clyket°
That Januarie bar of the smale wyket°,
By which into his gardyn ofte he wente;
And Damyan, that knew al hire entente,　2120
The cliket countrefeted pryvely°.
Ther nys namoore to seye, but hastily°
Som wonder by this clyket shal bityde°,
Which ye shul heeren, if ye wole abyde.
　　O noble Ovyde, ful sooth seystou°,
　　　God woot°,　2125
What sleighte° is it, thogh it be long and hoot°,
That he nyl° fynde it out in som manere?
By Piramus and Tesbee may men leere°,
Thogh they were kept ful longe streite overal°,
They been accorded rownynge° thurgh a wal,　2130
Ther° no wight° koude han founde out swich a
　　　sleighte°.
　　But now to purpos: er that° dayes eighte
Were passed, er the month of Juyl, bifille°

That Januarie hath caught so greet a wille,
Thurgh eggyng° of his wyf, hym for to pleye　2135
In his gardyn, and no wight but they tweye,
That in a morwe° unto his May seith he,
"Rys up, my wyf, my love, my lady free°;
The turtles voys° is herd, my dowve° sweete;
The wynter is goon with alle his reynes weete°.　2140
Com forth now, with thyne eyen columbyn°.
How fairer been thy brestes than is wyn!
The gardyn is enclosed al aboute;
Com forth, my white spouse! Out of doute
Thou hast me wounded in myn herte, O wyf.　2145
No spot of° thee ne knew I al my lyf.
Com forth and lat us taken oure disport°;
I chees° thee for my wyf and my confort."
　　Swiche olde lewed wordes used he.
On° Damyan a signe made she　2150
That he sholde go biforn with his cliket.
This Damyan thanne hath opened the wyket
And in he stirte°, and that in swich manere
That no wight° myghte it se neither yheere,
And stille he sit under a bussh anon.　2155
　　This Januarie, as blynd as is a stoon,
With Mayus in his hand, and no wight mo,
Into his fresshe gardyn is ago°,
And clapte to° the wyket sodeynly.
　　"Now wyf," quod he, "heere nys° but thou
　　　and I,　2160
That art the creature that I best love.
For by that Lord that sit in hevene above
Levere ich hadde to° dyen on a knyf
Than thee offende, trewe deere wyf.
For Goddes° sake, thenk how I thee chees°,　2165

[handwritten margin note: Song on Psalm]

2105 privee, *secret,* **wiste,** *knew* **2106 eek the fyn,** *also the goal* **2113 blent,** *blinded* or *deceived* **woot,** *knows,* **so been mo,** *so (have) more been* **2114 wenen wisly,** *think confidently* **2116 so yoore,** *such a while ago* **2117 clyket,** *key* **2118 wyket,** *gate* **2121 pryvely,** *secretly* **2122 hastily,** *soon* **2123 shal bityde,** *will happen* **2125 sooth seystou,** *truly you speak,* **woot,** *knows* **2126 sleighte,** *deception,* **long and hoot,** *long-lasting and impassioned (?)* **2127 nyl,** *will not* **2128 leere,** *learn* **2129 kept ful longe streite overal,** *separated for a long time strictly in every way* **2130 been accorded rownynge,** *came to an agreement whispering* **2131 Ther,**

2132 er that, *before* **2133 bifille,** *it happened* **2135 eggyng,** *urging* **2137 morwe,** *morning* **2138 free,** *gracious* **2139 turtles voys,** *turtledove's song,* **dowve,** *dove* **2140 reynes weete,** *wet rains* **2141 eyen columbyn,** *dovelike eyes* **2146 spot of,** *blemish on* **2147 disport,** *pleasure* **2148 chees,** *chose* **2150 On,** *to* **2153 stirte,** *leapt* **2154 wight,** *person* **2158 ago,** *gone* **2159 clapte to,** *slammed* **2160 nys,** *no one is* **2163 Levere ich hadde to,** *I would rather* **2165 Goddes,** *God's,* **chees,** *chose*

where, **wight,** *person,* **sleighte,** *deception*

2109–10 i.e., it is no better to be deceived when you are blind as when you can see. **2111 Argus,** one-hundred-eyed guardian who is blinded and killed; Ovid *Metamorphoses* 1.625ff. **2115 Passe over is an ese,** proverbial, meaning something like "The easy way is to ignore it." **2117 warm wex . . . emprented the clyket,** ironic and suggestive. January had earlier thought to mold his young bride like warm wax (lines 1429–30), and the recurrent rhyme pair "clyket / wyket" (key / gate) suggests genitalia. Impressions and imprintings recur at lines 1578, 1978, and 2178. **2124–31 Ovyde . . . ,** in the story of Pyramus and Thisbe, two tragic lovers who communicate by whispering through a chink in a wall, the question is asked, "Quid non sentit amor?" (What does love not perceive?); Ovid *Metamorphoses* 4.55–166. **2127 he,** refers to personified love; some MSS have "Love." **2133 Juyl,** July; found in all MSS. The reference in line 2222 to Gemini (May 11–June 11) encourages many to take this as an error for June, but "er" (before) can well mean *in the month before the month of July.* **2138–48 Rys up . . . ,** January's speech echoes the biblical Song of Songs, borrowed via Jerome's *Epistola adversus Jovinianum* (see *WBP* 3.3n) and undercut by January's lasciviousness and several double entendres. **2143 enclosed al aboute,** the enclosed garden (*hortus conclusus*) was a figure for Mary, mother of Jesus. **2149 lewed,** multiple meanings in this context—secular, lascivious, and unlearned—all in contrast to the scriptural source of January's words.

Noght for no coveitise°, doutelees,
But oonly for the love I had to thee.
And though that I be oold and may nat see,
Beth to me trewe, and I wol telle yow why:
Thre thynges, certes°, shal ye wynne therby.   2170
First, love of Crist, and to yourself honour,
And al myn heritage, toun and tour—
I yeve° it yow, maketh chartres° as yow leste°;
This shal be doon tomorwe er sonne reste°,
So wisly° God my soule brynge in blisse.   2175
I prey yow first, in covenant° ye me kisse,
And though that I be jalous, wyte° me noght.
Ye been so depe enprented in my thoght
That whan that I considere youre beautee
And therwithal° the unlikly elde° of me,   2180
I may nat, certes°, though I sholde dye,
Forbere° to been out of youre compaignye
For verray° love. This is withouten doute.
Now kys me, wyf, and lat us rome° aboute."
    This fresshe May, whan she thise wordes
        herde,   2185
Benyngnely° to Januarie answerde,
But first and forward° she bigan to wepe.
"I have," quod she, "a soule for to kepe
As wel as ye, and also myn honur,
And of my wyfhod thilke° tendre flour   2190
Which that I have assured° in youre hond,
Whan that the preest to yow my body bond°.
Wherfore I wole answere in this manere,
By the leve° of yow, my lord so deere:
I prey to God that nevere dawe° the day   2195
That I ne sterve°, as foule as womman may,
If evere I do unto my kyn° that shame,
Or elles I empeyre° so my name,
That I be fals; and if I do that lakke°,
Do strepe° me and put me in a sakke,   2200
And in the nexte ryver do me drenche°.

I am a gentil womman and no wenche.
Why speke ye thus? But men been evere untrewe,
And wommen have repreve° of yow ay newe°.
Ye han noon oother contenance°, I leeve°,   2205
But speke to us of untrust and repreeve°."
    And with that word she saugh wher Damyan
Sat in the bussh, and coughen she bigan,
And with hir fynger signes made she
That Damyan sholde clymbe upon a tree   2210
That charged° was with fruyt, and up he wente.
For verraily° he knew al hire entente,
And every signe that she koude make,
Wel bet° than Januarie, hir owene make°,
For in a lettre she hadde toold hym al   2215
Of this matere, how he werchen shal°.
And thus I lete hym sitte upon the pyrie°,
And Januarie and May romynge ful myrie.
    Bright was the day and blew° the firmament°.
Phebus hath of gold his stremes° doun ysent   2220
To gladen every flour with his warmnesse.
He was that tyme in Geminis, as I gesse,
But litel fro his declynacion
Of Cancer, Jovis exaltacion.
And so bifel° that brighte morwe-tyde°   2225
That in that gardyn in that ferther syde
Pluto, that is kyng of Fairye,
And many a lady in his compaignye,
Folwynge his wyf the queene Proserpyne,
Which that he ravysshed out of Ethna   2230
Whil that she gadered floures in the mede°—
In Claudyan ye may the stories rede,
How in his grisely° carte he hire fette°—
This kyng of Fairye thanne adoun hym sette
Upon a bench of turves°, fressh and grene,   2235
And right anon thus seyde he to his queene,
    "My wyf," quod he, "ther may no wight
        seye nay°,

2166 **coveitise**, *greed* 2170 **certes**, *certainly* 2173 **yeve**, *give*, **chartres**, *documents*, **leste**, *please* 2174 **er sonne reste**, *before sunset* 2175 **wisly**, *surely* (may) 2176 **covenant**, *pledge* 2177 **wyte**, *blame* 2180 **therwithal**, *moreover* 2180 **unlikly elde**, *unsuitable age* 2181 **certes**, *surely*, 2182 **Forbere**, *endure* 2183 **verray**, *true* 2184 **rome**, *walk* 2186 **Benyngnely**, *graciously* 2187 **first and forward**, *first of all* 2190 **thilke**, *that* 2191 **assured**, *entrusted* 2192 **bond**, *bonded* 2194 **leve**, *permission* 2195 **dawe**, *dawn* 2196 **sterve**, *die* 2197 **kyn**, *family* 2198 **empeyre**, *damage*

2199 **lakke**, *misdeed* 2200 **strepe**, *strip* 2201 **drenche**, *drown* 2204 **repreve**, *blame*, **ay newe**, *always* 2205 **contenance**, *attitude*, **leeve**, *believe* 2206 **repreeve**, *blame* 2211 **charged**, *heavy* 2212 **verraily**, *truly* 2214 **Wel bet**, *much better*, **make**, *mate* 2216 **werchen shal**, *should act* 2217 **pyrie**, *pear tree* 2219 **blew**, *blue*, **firmament**, *sky* 2220 **of gold his stremes**, *his golden rays* 2225 **bifel**, *it happened*, **morwe-tyde**, *morning time* 2231 **mede**, *meadow* 2233 **grisely**, *horrifying*, **fette**, *fetched* 2235 **of turves**, *made of turf* 2237 **ther may no wight seye nay**, *no one can deny*

2220–24 Phebus . . . in Geminis . . . Jovis exaltacion, i.e., the sun was in the sign of Gemini shortly before ("litel fro") entering into Cancer, over which Jupiter (Jove) exerted most influence. This perhaps indicates a date of June 8; see 2133n. On declination and exaltation, see *WBP* 3.701–02n. **2227–29 Pluto . . . Proserpyne,** see 2038–39n above. Contrast their intervention with that of the gods in *KnT*. **2230** The off-rhyme and a number of manuscript variants indicate that the line may have been garbled or partial in Chaucer's original. Found in only two MSS, "Ethna" (Enna or Mt. Etna) is scribal, supplied from Claudian. **2232 Claudyan,** Claudian, author of fourth-century *De Raptu Proserpinae* (The Abduction of Proserpine).

Th'experience so preveth every day
The tresons whiche that wommen doon to man.
Ten hondred thousand stories tellen I kan   2240
Notable of youre untrouthe and brotilnesse°.
O Salomon, wys and richest of richesse,
Fulfild of sapience° and of worldly glorie,
Ful worthy been thy wordes to memorie
To every wight that wit and reson kan°.   2245
Thus preiseth he yet the bountee° of man:
'Amonges a thousand men yet foond I oon°,
But of wommen alle foond I noon.'
     "Thus seith the kyng that knoweth youre
          wikkednesse.
And Jhesus filius Syrak, as I gesse,   2250
Ne speketh of yow but seelde reverence°.
A wylde fyr° and corrupt° pestilence
So falle upon youre bodyes yet tonyght!
Ne se ye nat° this honurable knyght,
By cause, allas, that he is blynd and old,   2255
His owene man shal make hym cokewold°.
Lo°, where he sit, the lechour in the tree!
Now wol I graunten, of my magestee,
Unto this olde, blynde, worthy knyght
That he shal have ayeyn° his eyen syght   2260
Whan that his wyf wold doon hym vileynye.
Thanne shal he knowen al hire harlotrye,
Bothe in repreve° of hire and othere mo°."
     "Ye shal?" quod Proserpyne, "Wol ye so?
Now by my moodres sires soule I swere   2265
That I shal yeven° hire suffisant answere,
And alle wommen after, for hir sake,
That though they be in any gilt ytake°
With face boold they shulle hemself° excuse,
And bere hem doun° that wolden hem°
          accuse.   2270

For lakke of answere noon of hem shal dyen.
Al° hadde man seyn a thyng with bothe his eyen,
Yit shul we wommen visage it hardily°,
And wepe, and swere, and visage it subtilly,
So that ye men shul been as lewed as gees°.   2275
What rekketh me° of youre auctoritees?
     "I woot° wel that this Jew, this Salomon,
Foond of° us wommen fooles many oon°.
But though that he ne foond no good womman,
Yet hath ther founde many another man   2280
Wommen ful trewe, ful goode, and vertuous.
Witnesse on hem that dwelle in Cristes hous°;
With martirdom they preved hire constance°.
The Romayn geestes eek° maken remembrance
Of many a verray°, trewe wyf also.   2285
But sire, ne be nat wrooth°, al be it so
Though that he seyde he foond no good
          womman;
I prey yow take the sentence° of the man;
He mente thus, that in sovereyn bontee°
Nis noon° but God that sit° in Trinitee.   2290
Ey°, for verray God that nys but oon°.
     "What make ye so muche of Salomon?
What though he made a temple, Goddes° hous?
What though he were riche and glorious?
So made he eek a temple of false goddis;   2295
How myghte he do a thyng that moore
          forbode° is?
Pardee°, as faire as ye his name emplastre°,
He was a lecchour and an ydolastre°,
And in his elde° he verray God forsook;
And if that God ne hadde, as seith the book,   2300
Yspared hym for his fadres sake, he sholde
Have lost his regne rather° than he wolde°.
I sette right noght of al the vileynye

2241 **brotilnesse,** *untrustworthiness* 2242 **Salomon,** *Solomon* 2243 **sapience,** *wisdom* 2245 **kan,** *knows* 2246 **bountee,** *goodness* 2247 **oon,** *one* (good man) 2251 **seelde reverence,** *seldom honor* 2252 **wylde fyr,** *itchy skin disease,* **corrupt,** *incurable* 2254 **Ne se ye nat,** *don't you see* 2256 **cokewold,** *victim of adultery* (cuckold) 2257 **Lo,** *look* 2260 **ayeyn,** *again* 2263 **repreve,** *blame,* **othere mo,** *others more* 2266 **yeven,** *give* 2268 **ytake,** *taken* 2269 **hemself,** *themselves* 2270 **bere hem doun,** *defeat those,* **hem,** *them* 2272 **Al,** *although* 2273 **visage it hardily,** *face it out boldly* 2275 **lewed as gees,** *ignorant as geese* 2276 **rekketh me,** *do I care* 2277 **woot,** *know* 2278 **Foond of,** *found among,* **many oon,** *many*

2282 **Cristes hous,** i.e., *heaven* 2283 **hire constance,** *their constancy* 2284 **The Romayn geestes eek,** *Roman history also* 2285 **verray,** *genuine* 2286 **wrooth,** *angry* 2288 **sentence,** *meaning* 2289 **sovereyn bontee,** *supreme goodness* 2290 **Nis noon,** *there is none,* **sit,** *sits* 2291 **Ey,** *yes,* **nys but oon,** *there is only one* 2293 **Goddes,** *God's* 2296 **forbode,** *forbidden* 2297 **Pardee,** *by God,* **emplastre,** *whitewash* 2298 **ydolastre,** *idolater* 2299 **elde,** *old age* 2302 **rather,** *sooner,* **wolde,** *wanted* 2303–4 **sette right noght . . . boterflye,** *don't care . . . a butterfly* (for)

2240 **stories,** this word is lacking in the best MSS, evidently omitted in the original. Scribes supply near-synonyms: "stories," "samples," "historyes," and "tales." 2247–48 Ecclesiastes 7.28. 2250 **Jhesus filius Syrak,** Jesus, son of Sirach; supposed author of the apocryphal book of Ecclesiasticus, which contributed to antifeminist tradition. 2265 **moodres sires,** Persephone's grandfather is Saturn, father of Ceres; see *KnT* 1.2441–42n. 2266 **suffisant answere,** compare *WBT* 3.910. 2277–90 The antifeminist sentiment from Solomon (i.e., Ecclesiastes 7.29, attributed to him in the Middle Ages) and Proserpina's interpretation of it parallel Prudence's argument in *Mel* 7.1076–79. 2293–95 **temple . . . temple of false goddis,** Solomon built the first temple to Yahweh in Jerusalem (1 Kings 5.3–18) and temples to foreign gods (1 Kings 11.7–8). 2298–2302 1 Kings 11.1–3; God spared Solomon for the sake of his father, David.

That ye of wommen write a boterflye°.
I am a womman, nedes moot I° speke   2305
Or elles swelle til myn herte breke°.
For sithen° he seyde that we been jangleresses°,
As evere hool I moote brouke my tresses,
I shal nat spare for no curteisye
To speke hym harm that wolde° us vileynye."   2310
    "Dame," quod this Pluto, "be no lenger wrooth°.
I yeve it up! But sith° I swoor myn ooth
That I wolde graunten hym his sighte ageyn,
My word shal stonde, I warne yow certeyn.
I am a kyng; it sit° me noght to lye."   2315
    "And I," quod she, "a queene of Fairye.
Hir answere shal she have, I undertake.
Lat us namoore wordes heerof make.
For sothe°, I wol no lenger yow contrarie."
    Now lat us turne agayn to Januarie   2320
That in the gardyn with his faire May
Syngeth ful murier than the papejay°,
"Yow love I best, and shal, and oother noon."
So long aboute the aleyes° is he goon
Til he was come agayns thilke pyrie°   2325
Where as this Damyan sitteth ful myrie
An heigh° among the fresshe leves grene.
    This fresshe May, that is so bright and sheene°,
Gan for to syke° and seyde, "Allas, my syde!
Now sire," quod she, "for aught that may
        bityde°,   2330
I moste han° of the peres that I see,
Or I moot dye°, so soore longeth me°
To eten of the smale peres grene.
Help, for hir love that is of hevene queene.
I telle yow wel, a womman in my plit   2335
May han to° fruyt so greet an appetit
That she may dyen but she of it have."
    "Allas," quod he, "that I ne had heer a knave°
That koude clymbe! Allas, allas," quod he,
"That I am blynd!" "Ye sire, no fors°," quod
        she,   2340
"But wolde ye vouchesauf°, for Goddes sake,
The pyrie inwith youre armes for to take°—

For wel I woot° that ye mystruste me—
Thanne sholde I clymbe wel ynogh," quod she,
"So I my foot myghte sette upon youre bak."   2345
    "Certes," quod he, "theron shal be no lak,
Mighte I yow helpen with myn herte blood."
He stoupeth doun, and on his bak she stood,
And caughte hire by a twiste°, and up she gooth—
Ladyes, I prey yow that ye be nat wrooth°,   2350
I kan nat glose°, I am a rude° man—
And sodeynly anon this Damyan
Gan pullen up the smok° and in he throng°.
    And whan that Pluto saugh this grete wrong,
To Januarie he gaf° agayn his sighte,   2355
And made hym se as wel as evere he myghte.
And whan that he hadde caught his sighte
        agayn
Ne was ther nevere man of thyng so fayn°
But on his wyf his thoght was everemo.
Up to the tree he caste his eyen two   2360
And saugh that Damyan his wyf had dressed°
In swich manere it may nat been expressed,
But if I wolde speke uncurteisly;
And up he yaf° a roryng and a cry,
As dooth the mooder whan the child
        shal dye.   2365
"Out! Help! Allas! Harrow!" he gan to crye,
"O stronge° lady stoore°, what dostow°?"
    And she answerde, "Sire, what eyleth° yow?
Have pacience and resoun in youre mynde.
I have yow holpe on° bothe youre eyen
        blynde.   2370
Up peril of my soule, I shal nat lyen,
As me was taught, to heele with youre eyen,
Was no thyng bet°, to make yow to see,
Than strugle with a man upon a tree.
God woot°, I dide it in ful good entente."   2375
    "Strugle!" quod he, "Ye, algate° in it wente!
God yeve° yow bothe on shames deth to dyen!
He swyved° thee; I saugh it with myne eyen;
And elles be I° hanged by the hals°."
    "Thanne is," quod she, "my medicyne fals.   2380

2305 nedes moot I, *necessarily I must* **2306 breke,** *breaks* **2307 sithen,**
since, **jangleresses,** *chatterboxes* **2310 wolde,** *wishes* **2311 wrooth,** *angry*
2312 sith, *since* **2315 sit,** *suits* **2319 sothe,** *truly* **2322 papejay,** *parrot*
2324 aleyes, *paths* **2325 agayns thilke pyrie,** *up to that pear tree* **2327 An
heigh,** *on high* **2328 sheene,** *radiant* **2329 syke,** *sigh* **2330 for aught that
may bityde,** *whatever happens* **2331 moste han,** *must have* (some) **2332
moot dye,** *may die,* **soore longeth me,** *sorely I desire* **2336 han to,** *have*
for **2338 knave,** *boy servant* **2340 no fors,** *no matter* **2341 vouchesauf,**

agree **2342 The pyrie inwith youre armes for to take,** *to hug the pear tree*
2343 woot, *know* **2349 twiste,** *branch* **2350 wrooth,** *angry* **2351 glose,**
gloss over, **rude,** *uneducated* **2353 smok,** *dress,* **throng,** *thrust* **2355 gaf,**
gave **2358 fayn,** *happy* **2361 dressed,** *treated* **2364 yaf,** *gave* **2367
stronge,** *bold,* **stoore,** *impudent,* **dostow,** *are you doing* **2368 eyleth,** *ails*
2370 holpe on, *helped in* **2373 bet,** *better* **2375 woot,** *knows* **2376 algate,*
entirely **2377 yeve,** *grant* **2378 swyved,** *screwed* **2379 And elles be I,** *and*
(if it were) *otherwise may I be,* **hals,** *neck*

2308 Literally, "As always healthy I may use (or enjoy) my braids," meaning approximately "I swear by my gender." **2335 in my plit,** in my condition, i.e., pregnant. May never declares herself pregnant, but she alleges an intense craving for green pears. **2364–65** Contrast with
Griselda's thoughts of her children, *ClT* 4.543ff. and 677ff.

For certeinly if that ye myghte° se,
Ye wolde nat seyn thise wordes unto me.
Ye han som glymsyng and no parfit sighte."
    "I se," quod he, "as wel as evere I myghte,
Thonked be God, with bothe myne eyen two,   2385
And by my trouthe, me thoughte he dide
        thee so."
    "Ye maze°, maze, goode sire," quod she.
"This thank have I for I have maad yow see.
Allas," quod she, "that evere I was so kynde!"
    "Now, dame," quod he, "lat al passe out of
        mynde.   2390
Com doun, my lief°, and if I have myssayd°,
God helpe me so as I am yvele apayd°.
But by my fader soule, I wende han seyn°
How that this Damyan hadde by thee leyn°,
And that thy smok hadde leyn upon his
        brest."   2395
    "Ye, sire," quod she, "ye may wene° as yow lest°.
But, sire, a man that waketh out of his sleep
He may nat sodeynly wel taken keep°

Upon a thyng, ne seen it parfitly,
Til that he be adawed verraily°.   2400
Right so a man that longe hath blynd ybe°
Ne may nat sodeynly so wel yse°
First whan his sighte is newe come ageyn
As he that hath a day or two yseyn°.
Til that youre sighte ysatled be° a while   2405
Ther may ful many a sighte yow bigile°.
Beth war°, I prey yow, for by hevene kyng,
Ful many a man weneth° to seen a thyng,
And it is al another than it semeth.
He that mysconceyveth°, he mysdemeth°."   2410
And with that word she leep doun fro the tree.
    This Januarie, who is glad but he?
He kisseth hire and clippeth° hire ful ofte,
And on hire wombe he stroketh hire ful softe,
And to his palays° hoom he hath hire lad°.   2415
Now, goode men, I pray yow to be glad.
Thus endeth heere my tale of Januarie.
God blesse us, and his mooder Seinte Marie.

Heere is ended the Marchants Tale of Januarie.

[EPILOGUE]

    "Ey, Goddes mercy," seyde oure Hoost tho°,
"Now swich a wyf I pray God kepe me fro!   2420
Lo whiche sleightes° and subtilitees
In wommen been, for ay° as bisy as bees
Been they us sely° men for to deceyve,
And from a sooth° evere wol they weyve°
By this Marchauntes tale it preveth weel.   2425
But douteles, as trewe as any steel
I have a wyf, though that she poure be,
But of hir tonge a labbyng° shrewe is she,
And yet she hath an heep of vices mo°—

Therof no fors°. Lat alle swiche° thynges go.   2430
But wyte° ye what? In conseil° be it seyd,
Me reweth soore° I am unto hire teyd°.
For and° I sholde rekenen° every vice
Which that she hath, ywis° I were to nyce°.
And cause why? It sholde reported be   2435
And toold to hire of somme° of this meynee°—
Of whom, it nedeth nat for to declare
Syn° wommen konnen outen swich chaffare°.
And eek my wit suffiseth nat therto
To tellen al, wherfore my tale is do°."   2440

2381 **myghte**, *could* 2387 **maze**, *are dazed* 2391 **lief**, *beloved*, **myssayd**, *misspoken* 2392 **yvele apayd**, *poorly rewarded* 2393 **wende han seyn**, *thought to have seen* 2394 **leyn**, *laid* 2396 **wene**, *think*, **lest**, *please* 2398 **keep**, *heed* 2400 **adawed verraily**, *truly awake* 2401 **ybe**, *been* 2402 **yse**, *see* 2404 **yseyn**, *seen* 2405 **ysatled be**, *is settled* 2406 **bigile**, *deceive* 2407 **Beth war**, *be aware* 2408 **weneth**, *thinks* 2410 **mysconceyveth**, *misperceives*, **mysdemeth**, *misjudges* 2413 **clippeth**, *embraces* 2415 **palays**, *palace*, **lad**, *led* 2419 **tho**, *then* 2421 **whiche sleightes**,

what tricks 2422 **ay**, *always* 2423 **sely**, *innocent* 2424 **sooth**, *truth*, **weyve**, *deviate* 2428 **labbyng**, *blabbing* 2429 **mo**, *more* 2430 **no fors**, *no matter*, **swiche**, *such* 2431 **wyte**, *know*, **In conseil**, *confidentially* 2432 **Me reweth soore**, *I sorely regret*, **teyd**, *tied* 2433 **For and**, *and if*, **rekenen**, *tally* 2434 **ywis**, *surely*, **to nyce**, *very foolish* 2436 **somme**, *someone*, **meynee**, *company* 2438 **Syn**, *since*, **konnen outen swich chaffare**, *know how to present such merchandise* 2440 **do**, *done*

2419–40 These lines appear in the great majority of MSS, although sometimes between *MerT* and *FranT*, with adjustments for context.

CANTERBURY TALES PART 5

INTRODUCTION

Part 5 is made up of two of Chaucer's most exotic tales. The first, the *Squire's Tale,* is a story of adventure and betrayed love set in the Tartar Empire; it introduces a brass horse that can transport a rider anywhere in the world, a sword that both cuts and heals, a seeing mirror, and a ring that allows its bearer to converse with birds. The narrative potential latent in these motifs is not realized, and although the ring does enable its wearer, Canacee, to understand the lament of a female falcon who has been abandoned by her lover, this subplot is left hanging. The fantasy of the tale is muted by rationalization of its magical phenomena (see, e.g., 229–30, 253–57) or juxtaposition with scientific explanation (263–74). As Vincent DiMarco shows in his contribution to *Sources and Analogues* (2002, no. 187), the various explanations of the marvels in the *Squire's Tale* are consistent with medieval understanding of optics, chemistry, and automata. Even in his most magical tales, Chaucer shows a basic distrust of unexplained marvels.

The *Squire's Tale* was long criticized and even ignored for its halting self-consciousness about rhetoric and its agglomeration of motifs that refuse to resolve themselves into formal unity (see 667–69n). Critics wondered whether the Franklin's interruption of the Squire comes when it does because Chaucer (or, according to many critics, the narratively challenged Squire) could not control the story. Early critics found parallels for many of the motifs in the *Thousand and One Nights,* a collection of Eastern stories in Arabic, even though the collection was unavailable to Chaucer in the form we know it. No known tale has been identified as the primary source of the *Squire's Tale.*

Postcolonial studies have brought new perspective to these Eastern connections by assessing narrative digressiveness as part of the "orientalism" of the tale. Edward Said coined the term as the title of his landmark study (1978, no. 661a), and it has come to be used generally for the Western attitude toward Eastern culture that stigmatizes it as excessive, bizarre, and sensual—often particularly feminized and in need of restraint or containment. In this kind of reading, the Squire's apologies for his rhetoric (see, e.g., 67, 105–6, 401–5), his rationalizations of the marvelous, and the unfulfilled promise to cover all bases at the end of the tale become, arguably, Chaucer's orientalist send-up of Eastern tales or his disclosure of the Squire's jingoism or self-interest. Other issues informed by orientalist concerns are the relation of the Squire to his (arguably imperialistic) father, the Knight, and the possibility that historical events underlie those of the tale. See the pertinent essays in *Chaucer's Cultural Geography,* edited by Kathryn L. Lynch (2002, no. 660).

Based ultimately in Arabic learning, the astronomical aspects of the *Squire's Tale* have also been closely interpreted. J. D. North, *Chaucer's Universe* (1988, no. 425), reads a complex structure in the tale's astronomical allusions; and Marijane Osborn, *Time and the Astrolabe in The Canterbury Tales* (2002, no. 426), equates the brass horse with a pointer on the astrolabe (a tool for reading the stars) and argues that the identification helps alert us to the allegory of an astronomical day that runs throughout *The Canterbury Tales.* Useful surveys of the critical reception of the tale are available in Donald C. Baker's Variorum edition (1990, no. 43) and David Lawton's *Chaucer's Narrators* (1985, no. 356).

The *Franklin's Tale* is a Breton lay, a brief form of the romance genre, set in Brittany, the land of enchantment in medieval romance. It starts where many romances leave off, with a happy marriage, and many consider this marriage to be Chaucer's idealistic alternative to the battles of the sexes depicted earlier in the marriage group. This view is rooted ultimately in George Lyman Kittredge's landmark study, "Chaucer's Discussion of Marriage" (1912, no. 444). In this view, Arveragus and Dorigen marry as equals, neither claiming sovereignty, and by the end of the tale, gentilesse is shared among social classes. Yet the magic of the tale is largely a matter of tides and astronomical study, creating illusion. The coastal rocks that endanger Arveragus's return home to his wife are not actually removed; they simply appear to be so, rendering them perhaps more dangerous than ever.

The final turns of the plot result from the sequential grand gestures by three men—Arveragus, Aurelius (a squire who loves Dorigen), and a clerk-magician who had promised to remove the rocks—and after everyone goes away happy, the Franklin closes the tale with a *demande d'amour,* a love question: "Who was most generous?" As a result, many critics read the tale as evidence that human generosity, or virtue more generally, is capable of producing human happiness. Others, however, argue that each of the promises made in the tale (including the marriage vows), the gentilesse of the characters, and even the very notion of "trouthe" are in some way dependent on illusion. This reading is usually connected with the epilogue to the *Squire's Tale,* where the Franklin is thought to reveal himself as something of a social climber, invested in the notion that the nouveaux riches are as capable of gentility as the traditional aristocracy. Here, as is often the case in Chaucer, critical disagreement may reveal much about the outlook of the individual critic. See David M. Seaman, "'As Thynketh Yow': Conflicting Evidence and the Interpretation of *The Franklin's Tale*" (1991, no. 1162).

The same issues of promises, love, happiness, and gentilesse appear in the falcon's lament in the *Squire's Tale,* and they echo resoundingly in the earlier tales of the marriage group, including the *Friar's Tale* and the *Summoner's Tale,* where promising and intention are central. Richard Firth Green, *A Crisis of Truth* (1999, no. 609), and Carolyn P. Collette, *Species, Phantasms, and Images* (2001, no. 665), clarify cultural and psychological aspects of intention and will in late-medieval understanding of promises and troth plighting, important to the *Franklin's Tale* and throughout *The Canterbury Tales.*

Apart from the rocks, the basic plot of the *Franklin's Tale* parallels the tale of Menedon in Boccaccio's *Filocolo,* perhaps known to Chaucer in a version that circulated separately in a collection of love-question narratives. He also probably knew the similar story in the *Decameron* (10.5). In both versions by Boccaccio, the magic is a good deal more magical and idealistic: the lover must create a Maylike garden in the month of January, likely the source for Chaucer's use of these months as names in the *Merchant's Tale.* For the names in the *Franklin's Tale* and perhaps for the motif of removing rocks, Chaucer turned to Geoffrey of Monmouth's *History of the Kings of Britain* (ca. 1138). He used Boethius's *Consolation* (4.pr6) for Dorigen's complaint about the rocks, the *Roman de la Rose* for most of the defense of equality in marriage (761–98), and Jerome's *Epistola adversus Jovinianum* for much of Dorigen's contemplation against her fortune (1368–1456)—sources used with equal brilliance elsewhere in the marriage group. Indeed, the successful pastiche here juxtaposed with the potential for sprawl in the *Squire's Tale* may suggest that Chaucer consciously set in opposition two kinds of composite narrative.

CANTERBURY TALES
PART 5

SQUIRE'S TALE

PROLOGUE

"Squier, com neer, if it youre wille be,
And sey somwhat of love, for certes ye
Konnen° theron as muche as any man."
    "Nay, sire," quod he, "but I wol seye as I kan

With hertly° wyl, for I wol nat rebelle   5
Agayn your lust°. A tale wol I telle;
Have me excused° if I speke amys.
My wyl is good, and lo, my tale is this."

Heere bigynneth the Squieres Tale.

At Sarray, in the land of Tartarye,
Ther dwelte a kyng that werreyed° Russye,   10
Thurgh which ther dyde many a doughty° man.
This noble kyng was cleped° Cambyuskan,
Which in his tyme was of so greet renoun
That ther was nowher in no regioun
So excellent a lord in alle thyng.   15

Hym lakked noght that longeth° to a kyng.
And of the secte° of which that he was born
He kepte his lay°, to which that he was sworn.
And therto he was hardy, wys, and riche,
And pitous and just, alwey yliche°;   20
Sooth° of his word, benigne°, and honurable;
Of his corage as any centre stable;

---

3 Konnen, *know* **5 hertly,** *hearty* **6 lust,** *desire* **7 Have me excused,** *excuse me* **10 werreyed,** *waged war on* **11 doughty,** *valiant* **12 cleped,** *named* **16 longeth,** *is appropriate* **17 secte,** *religion* **18 his lay,** *its law* **20 yliche,** *consistently* **21 Sooth,** *true,* **benigne,** *gracious*

1–8 Lines generally found following 4.2419–40 in the MSS, although they do not often introduce *SqT*. When they introduce other tales, "Squier" is replaced and "somwhat of love" reads "us a tale." **9 Sarray . . . Tartarye,** Sarai (modern Tsarev), capital of the Mongol (Tartar) Empire. In the thirteenth century, the Mongols conquered Russia. **12 Cambyuskan,** Genghis Khan, 1162–1227, founder of the Mongol Empire. Historically, his grandson Batu Khan (1198–1255) conquered Russia. **22 as any centre stable,** stable as the center of a circle; proverbial.

Yong, fressh, strong, and in armes desirous°
As any bacheler° of al his hous.
A fair persone he was and fortunat,   25
And kepte alwey so wel roial estat°
That there was nowher swich another man.
 This noble kyng, this Tartre Cambyuskan,
Hadde two sones on Elpheta his wyf,
Of whiche the eldeste highte° Algarsyf,   30
That oother sone was cleped° Cambalo.
A doghter hadde this worthy kyng also
That yongest was, and highte Canacee.
But for to telle yow al hir beautee,
It lyth° nat in my tonge n'yn° my konnyng°.   35
I dar nat undertake so heigh a thyng;
Myn Englissh eek° is insufficient.
It moste been a rethor° excellent
That koude his colours longynge for° that art
If he sholde hire discryven° every part.   40
I am noon swich; I moot speke as I kan.
 And so bifel° that whan this Cambyuskan
Hath twenty wynter born his diademe°,
As he was wont° fro yeer to yeer, I deme°,
He leet the feeste of his nativitee   45
Doon cryen° thurghout Sarray his citee,
The laste Idus of March°, after the yeer°.
Phebus the sonne ful joly was and cleer,
For he was neigh° his exaltacioun
In Martes face, and in his mansioun   50
In Aries, the colerik hoote signe.
Ful lusty° was the weder° and benigne°,
For which the foweles agayn° the sonne sheene°,
What for° the sesoun and the yonge grene,
Ful loude songen hire affecciouns.   55
Hem semed han geten hem° protecciouns°
Agayn the swerd° of wynter, keene° and coold.
 This Cambyuskan, of which I have yow toold,

In roial vestiment sit° on his deys°,
With diademe°, ful heighe in his paleys,   60
And halt° his feeste so solempne° and so ryche
That in this world ne was ther noon it lyche°.
Of which if I shal tellen al th'array,
Thanne wolde it occupie a someres day,
And eek it nedeth nat° for to devyse°   65
At every cours the ordre of hire servyse.
I wol nat tellen of hir strange sewes°,
Ne of hir swannes°, ne of hire heronsewes°.
Eek in that lond, as tellen knyghtes olde,
Ther is som mete° that is ful deynte holde°   70
That in this lond men recche of it but smal°.
Ther nys no man that may reporten al.
 I wol nat taryen° yow for it is pryme°
And for it is no fruyt° but los° of tyme.
Unto my firste I wole have my recours°.   75
 And so bifel° that after the thridde cours,
Whil that this kyng sit thus in his nobleye°,
Herknynge° his mynstrales hir thynges pleye
Biforn hym at the bord deliciously°,
In at the halle dore al sodeynly   80
Ther cam a knyght upon a steede of bras,
And in his hand a brood mirour of glas,
Upon his thombe he hadde of gold a ryng,
And by his syde a naked swerd hangyng.
And up he rideth to the heighe bord°.   85
In al the halle ne was ther spoken a word
For merveille of this knyght; hym to biholde
Ful bisily ther wayten° yonge and olde.
 This strange knyght, that cam thus sodeynly,
Al armed save his heed ful richely,   90
Saleweth° kyng and queene and lordes alle,
By ordre as they seten in the halle,
With so heigh reverence and obeisaunce°,
As wel in speche as in contenaunce°,

---

23 armes desirous, *battle eager* **24 bacheler,** *young knight* **26 roial estat,** *royal status* **30 highte,** *was called* **31 cleped,** *named* **35 lyth,** *resides,* **n'yn,** *nor in,* **konnyng,** *understanding* **37 eek,** *also* **38 rethor,** *rhetorician* **39 koude his colours longynge for,** *knew his figures of speech belonging to* **40 discryven,** *describe* **42 bifel,** *it happened* **43 born his diademe,** *carried his crown* **44 wont,** *accustomed,* **deme,** *believe* **45–46 leet . . . / Doon cryen,** *proclaimed* **47 laste Idus of March,** *March 15, after the yeer,* in accord with the calendar **49 neigh,** *near* **52 Ful lusty,** *very stirring,* **weder,** *weather,* **benigne,** *inviting* **53 foweles agayn,** *birds in response to,* **sheene,** *shine* **54 What for,** *because of* **56 Hem semed han geten hem,** (it) *seemed to them that they had gotten themselves* **57**

swerd, *sword,* **keene,** *sharp* **59 sit,** *sits,* **deys,** *dais* (platform) **60 diademe,** *crown* **61 halt,** *holds,* **solempne,** *grand* **62 lyche,** *like* **65 eek it nedeth nat,** *also there is no need,* **devyse,** *describe* **67 strange sewes,** *exotic soups* **68 hir swannes,** *their swans,* **heronsewes,** *young herons* **70 mete,** *food,* **ful deynte holde,** *considered very delicious* **71 recche of it but smal,** *think little of it* **73 taryen,** *delay,* **pryme,** *9 a.m.* **74 no fruyt,** *not fruitful,* **los,** *loss* **75 wole have my recours,** *will return* **76 bifel,** *it happened* **77 nobleye,** *nobility* **78 Herknynge,** *listening to* **79 bord deliciously,** *table delightfully* **85 heighe bord,** *high table* **88 wayten,** *watched* **91 Saleweth,** *greets* **93 obeisaunce,** *deference* **94 contenaunce,** *demeanor*

48–51 the sonne . . . exaltacioun . . . signe, the sun (**Phebus,** line 48) was at the point of its greatest influence, which is in the **face** (one-third or ten degrees, line 50) of Mars and the **mansioun** (line 50) or house of **Aries** (the Ram, line 51), a constellation associated with the hot (and dry) choleric humor. **67 I wol nat tellen,** the "occupatio" (see *KnT* 1.2924n) in the following lines and elsewhere in the tale clashes with the claim of rhetorical inability at lines 38–42. **81 Ther cam a knyght,** in *Sir Gawain and the Green Knight* and other romances, the interruption of a feast and / or the arrival of an unknown knight on horseback begins the action.

That Gawayn with his olde° curteisye,   95
Though he were comen ayeyn out of Fairye,
Ne koude hym nat amende° with a word.
And after this, biforn the heighe bord,
He with a manly voys seith his message,
After the forme used in his langage,   100
Withouten vice° of silable° or of lettre,
And for° his tale sholde seme the bettre
Accordant to his wordes was his cheere°,
As techeth art of speche hem° that it leere°.
Al be that° I kan nat sowne his stile,   105
Ne kan nat clymben over so heigh a style,
Yet seye I this, as to commune° entente,
Thus muche amounteth° al that evere he mente,
If it so be that I have it in mynde.
    He seyde, "The kyng of Arabe° and of
        Inde°,   110
My lige° lord, on this solempne day
Saleweth yow, as he best kan and may,
And sendeth yow, in honour of youre feeste,
By me that am al redy at youre heeste°,
This steede of bras, that esily and weel   115
Kan in the space of o day natureel—
This is to seyn, in foure and twenty houres—
Wher so yow lyst°, in droghte or elles shoures°,
Beren° youre body into every place
To which youre herte wilneth° for to pace°,   120
Withouten wem of° yow, thurgh foul or fair,
Or if yow lyst° to fleen° as hye in the air
As dooth an egle whan hym list° to soore,
This same steede shal bere yow evere moore,
Withouten harm, til ye be ther yow leste°,   125
Though that ye slepen on his bak or reste,
And turne ayeyn° with writhyng° of a pyn°.

He that it wroghte° koude° ful many a gyn°.
He wayted many a constellacioun
Er° he had doon this operacioun,   130
And knew ful many a seel and many a bond.
    "This mirour eek, that I have in myn hond,
Hath swich a myght° that men may in it see
Whan ther shal fallen any adversitee
Unto youre regne° or to youreself also,   135
And openly who is youre freend or foo.
And over al this, if any lady bright°
Hath set hire herte on any maner wight°,
If he be fals, she shal his tresoun see,
His newe love, and al his subtiltee,   140
So openly that ther shal no thyng hyde.
Wherfore, ageyn° this lusty someres tyde,
This mirour and this ryng that ye may see,
He hath sent unto my lady Canacee,
Youre excellente doghter that is heere.   145
    "The vertu° of the ryng, if ye wol heere,
Is this, that if hire lust° it for to were°
Upon hir thombe, or in hir purs it bere,
Ther is no fowel° that fleeth° under the hevene
That she ne shal wel understonde his stevene°,   150
And knowe his menyng openly and pleyn,
And answere hym in his langage ageyn;
And every gras° that groweth upon roote
She shal eek knowe, and whom it wol do boote°,
Al be his woundes never so depe and wyde.   155
    "This naked swerd that hangeth by my syde
Swich vertu° hath that what° man so ye smyte°
Thurghout his armure it wole kerve° and byte,
Were it° as thikke as is a branched ook.
And what man that is wounded with the
        strook   160

---

95 olde, *venerable* **97 amende,** *improve* **101 vice,** *error,* **silable,** *syllable*
102 for, *so that* **103 cheere,** *expression* **104 hem,** *to them,* **leere,** *learn*
105 Al be that, *although* **107 commune,** *general* **108 Thus muche
amounteth,** *to this much amounts* **110 Arabe,** *Arabia,* **Inde,** *India* **111
lige,** *liege* **114 heeste,** *command* **118 Wher so yow lyst,** *wherever you
wish,* **elles shoures,** *else showers* **119 Beren,** *carry* **120 wilneth,** *wishes,*
pace, *go* **121 wem of,** *harm to* **122 lyst,** *wish,* **fleen,** *fly* **123 hym list,** *he
wishes* **125 ther yow leste,** *where you please* **127 turne ayeyn,** *return*

again, **writhyng,** *the twisting,* **pyn,** *peg* **128 wroghte,** *made,* **koude,**
understands, **gyn,** *clever device* **130 Er,** *before* **133 myght,** *power* **135
regne,** *kingdom* **137 bright,** *beautiful* **138 maner wight,** *sort of man* **142
ageyn,** *in response to* **146 vertu,** *power* **147 hire lust,** *she wishes,* **were,**
wear **149 fowel,** *bird,* **fleeth,** *flies* **150 stevene,** *speech* **153 gras,** *plant*
154 eek, *also,* **wol do boote,** *will benefit* **157 Swich vertu,** *such power,*
what, *whatever,* **smyte,** *strike* **158 kerve,** *carve* **159 Were it,** *(even if)
it were*

95–96 Gawayn . . . Fairye, Sir Gawain was known for his courtesy and thought to reside in the fairyland, although the latter notion is generally found in romance tradition outside that of English. **99–104** The visitor's etiquette and rhetorical propriety are consistent with medieval ideals and rhetorical handbooks. **105–6 sowne his stile . . . clymben . . . a style,** "reproduce his style . . . climb a stile" (to get over so high a fence). This claim of rhetorical incompetence is expressed, paradoxically, in elaborate verbal play. **115 steede of bras,** there are Eastern analogues to this mechanical flying horse, but the notion may be related ultimately to actual automata or to the indicator on the astrolabe (often brass), known as the "horse." **129 wayted many a constellacioun,** i.e., waited for the proper astrological configuration. **131 seel . . . bond,** occult means of security and secrecy, although precisely what is meant is unclear. **132 mirour . . . ,** magic mirrors recur in medieval literature as a means to learn of enemies' movements; mirrors of love are less frequent. **142 lusty someres tyde,** pleasant summer season, but "lusty" may connote amorous; summer in Middle English included spring (as winter included fall). **146 ryng,** no specific precedent has been found for this ring that conveys the ability to converse with birds and know the medicinal properties of plants; see 250n. **156 swerd,** see 238–39n.

Shal never be hool° til that yow list°, of grace°,
To stroke° hym with the plat° in thilke° place
Ther he is hurt; this is as muche to seyn,
Ye moote° with the platte swerd ageyn
Stroke hym in the wounde and it wol close;   165
This is a verray sooth°, withouten glose°.
It failleth nat whils it is in youre hoold."
    And whan this knyght hath thus his tale toold,
He rideth out of halle and doun he lighte°.
His steede, which that shoon as sonne
        brighte,   170
Stant in the court stille as any stoon.
This knyght is to his chambre lad anoon°,
And is unarmed, and unto mete yset°.
    The presentes been ful roially yfet°—
This is to seyn, the swerd and the mirour—   175
And born° anon into the heighe tour°
With certeine officers ordeyned therfore°;
And unto Canacee this ryng was bore
Solempnely°, ther° she sit at the table.
But sikerly°, withouten any fable,   180
The hors of bras that may nat be remewed°,
It stant as it were to the ground yglewed.
Ther may no man out of the place it dryve°
For noon engyn of wyndas° ne polyve°;
And cause why? For they kan° nat the craft°.   185
And therfore in the place they han it laft
Til that the knyght hath taught hem the manere
To voyden° hym, as ye shal after heere.
    Greet was the prees° that swarmeth to and fro
To gauren° on this hors that stondeth so,   190
For it so heigh was, and so brood and long,
So wel proporcioned for to been strong,
Right as° it were a steede of Lumbardye;
Therwith° so horsly and so quyk° of eye,
As° it a gentil Poilleys courser° were.   195
For certes°, fro his tayl unto his ere,

Nature ne art ne koude hym nat amende°
In no degree, as al the peple wende°.
But everemoore hir mooste° wonder was
How that it koude gon°, and was of bras.   200
It was a fairye°, as the peple semed°.
Diverse folk diversely they demed°;
As many heddes as manye wittes° ther been.
They murmureden as dooth a swarm of been°
And maden skiles° after hir fantasies,   205
Rehersynge of° thise olde poetries°,
And seyde that it was lyk the Pegasee,
The hors that hadde wynges for to flee°,
Or elles it was the Grekes hors Synoun
That broghte Troie to destruccioun,   210
As men mowe° in thise olde geestes° rede.
    "Myn herte," quod oon, "is everemoore in
        drede.
I trowe° som men of armes been therinne,
That shapen hem° this citee for to wynne.
It were right good that al swich thyng were
        knowe."   215
    Another rowned° to his felawe lowe
And seyde, "He lyeth; it is rather lyk
An apparence ymaad° by som magyk,
As jogelours° pleyen at thise feestes grete."
Of sondry doutes° thus they jangle° and trete°.   220
As lewed° peple demeth comunly°
Of thynges that been maad moore subtilly
Than they kan in hir lewednesse comprehende,
They demen gladly° to the badder° ende.
    And somme of hem wondred on the mirour   225
That born was up into the maister tour°,
Hou men myghte in it swiche° thynges se.
    Another answerde and seyde it myghte wel be
Naturelly, by composiciouns
Of anglis° and of slye° reflexiouns,   230
And seyden that in Rome was swich oon°.

---

161 **hool,** *healed,* **yow list,** *you choose,* **of grace,** *graciously* 162 **stroke,** *strike,* **plat,** *flat of the sword,* **thilke,** *that* 164 **moote,** *must* 166 **verray sooth,** *absolute truth,* **glose,** *interpretation* 169 **lighte,** *alights* 172 **lad anoon,** *led immediately* 173 **unto mete yset,** *given a meal* 174 **roially yfet,** *royally brought* 176 **born,** *carried,* **tour,** *tower* 177 **ordeyned therfore,** *assigned for this* 179 **Solempnely,** *ceremoniously,* **ther,** *where* 180 **sikerly,** *certainly* 181 **remewed,** *moved* 183 **dryve,** *move* 184 **wyndas,** *winch,* **polyve,** *pulley* 185 **kan,** *understand,* **craft,** *technique* 188 **voyden,** *remove* 189 **prees,** *crowd* 190 **gauren,** *stare* 193 **Right as,** *just as (if)* 194 **Therwith,** *moreover,* **quyk,** *lively* 195 **As,** *as if,* **courser,** *steed* 196 **certes,** *certainly* 197 **amende,** *improve* 198 **wende,** *thought* 199 **hir**

mooste, *their greatest* 200 **koude gon,** *could move* 201 **fairye,** *magical thing,* **semed,** *thought* 202 **demed,** *judged* 203 **wittes,** *opinions* 204 **been,** *bees* 205 **skiles,** *explanations* 206 **Rehersynge of,** *recalling from,* **poetries,** *poems* 208 **flee,** *fly* 211 **mowe,** *might,* **geestes,** *stories* 213 **trowe,** *believe* 214 **shapen hem,** *plan* 216 **rowned,** *whispered* 218 **apparence ymaad,** *apparition made* 219 **jogelours,** *conjurers* 220 **sondry doutes,** *various fears,* **jangle,** *chatter,* **trete,** *argue* 221 **lewed,** *unlearned,* **demeth comunly,** *generally judge* 224 **demen gladly,** *judge willingly,* **badder,** *worse* 226 **maister tour,** *principal tower* 227 **swiche,** *such* 230 **anglis,** *angles,* **slye,** *clever* 231 **swich oon,** *such a one*

193–95 Lumbardye . . . Poilleys, Lombardy in northern Italy and Apulia in the south were both famous for horses. **203** Proverbial after Chaucer. **207 the Pegasee,** Pegasus, mythological winged horse. **209 Grekes hors Synoun,** the horse of Sinon the Greek, i.e., the Trojan horse (brass in several accounts) involved in the fall of Troy. **231 in Rome,** an allusion to the mirror that Virgil (thought to be a magician as well as a poet) was reputed to have erected in Rome to warn of enemy approach.

They speken of Alocen, and Vitulon,
And Aristotle, that writen in hir lyves
Of queynte° mirours and of perspectives°,
As knowen they that han hir bookes herd.   235

 And oother folk han wondred on the swerd
That wolde percen thurghout everythyng,
And fille in speche of Thelophus the kyng,
And of Achilles with his queynte° spere,
For he koude with it bothe heele and dere°   240
Right in swich wise° as men may with the swerd
Of which right now ye han youreselven herd.
They speken of sondry hardyng° of metal,
And speke of medicynes therwithal°,
And how and whanne it sholde yharded be°,   245
Which is unknowe, algates° unto me.

 Tho° speeke they of Canacees ryng,
And seyden alle that swich a wonder thyng
Of craft° of rynges herde they nevere noon,
Save° that he Moyses and Kyng Salomon   250
Hadde a name of konnyng° in swich art.
Thus seyn the peple and drawen hem apart°.

 But natheless somme seiden that it was
Wonder° to maken of fern-asshen glas,
And yet nys glas nat° lyk asshen of fern.   255
But for° they han knowen it so fern°,
Therfore cesseth hir janglyng° and hir wonder.

 As soore° wondren somme on cause of
  thonder,
On ebbe°, on flood, on gossomer°, and on myst,
And on alle thyng, til that the cause is wyst°.   260
Thus jangle they, and demen°, and devyse°,
Til that the kyng gan fro the bord° aryse.

 Phebus hath laft° the angle meridional,

And yet ascendynge was the beest roial,
The gentil Leon, with his Aldrian,   265
Whan that this Tartre kyng, this Cambyuskan,
Roos fro his bord, ther as he sat ful hye°.
Toforn° hym gooth the loude mynstralcye,
Til he cam to his chambre of parementz°,
Ther as they sownen diverse° instrumentz   270
That it is lyk an hevene for to heere.
Now dauncen lusty Venus children deere,
For in the Fyssh hir lady sat ful hye,
And looketh on hem with a freendly eye.

 This noble kyng is set up in his trone°.   275
This strange knyght is fet° to hym ful soone,
And on the daunce he gooth with Canacee.
Heere is the revel and the jolitee
That is nat able a dul man to devyse°.
He most han° knowen love and his servyse,   280
And been a feestlych° man as fressh as May,
That sholde yow devysen swich array.

 Who koude telle yow the forme of daunces
So unkouthe°, and so fresshe contenaunces°,
Swich subtil° lookyng and dissymulynges°   285
For drede of jalouse mennes aperceyvynges°?
No man but Launcelot, and he is deed.
Therfore I passe of° al this lustiheed°;
I sey namoore, but in this jolynesse
I lete hem til men to the soper dresse°.   290

 The styward bit° the spices for to hye°,
And eek the wyn, in al this melodye.
The usshers and the squiers been ygoon,
The spices and the wyn is come anoon.
They ete and drynke, and whan this hadde an
  ende,   295

---

234 queynte, *ingenious,* **perspectives,** *lenses* **239 queynte,** *marvelous*
240 dere, *injure* **241 Right in swich wise,** *just in the way* **243 sondry*
hardyng, *various* (ways of) *hardening* **244 therwithal,** *also* **245 sholde*
yharded be, *might be hardened* **246 algates,** *in all ways* **247 Tho,** *then*
249 craft, *the making* **250 Save,** *except,* **he Moyses,** *that Moses* **251*
name of konnyng, *reputation for knowledge* **252 drawen hem apart,**
withdrew themselves **254 Wonder,** *wondrous* **255 And yet nys glas nat,**
even though glass is not **256 for,** *because,* **fern,** *long ago* **257 janglyng,**
chattering **258 soore,** *intently* **259 ebbe,** *tides,* **gossomer,** *cobwebs* **260**

wyst, *known* **261 demen,** *judge,* **devyse,** *imagine* **262 bord,** *table* **263*
laft, *left* **267 ful hye,** *very high* **268 Toforn,** *before* **269 chambre of*
parementz, *ornamented chamber* **270 sownen diverse,** *play various* **275*
trone, *throne* **276 fet,** *brought* **279 devyse,** *describe* **280 most han,** *must*
have **281 feestlych,** *festive* **284 unkouthe,** *exotic,* **so fresshe conte-**
naunces, *such fresh expressions* **285 subtil,** *secretive,* **dissymulynges,** *pre-*
tendings **286 jalouse mennes aperceyvynges,** *jealous men's perceptions*
288 of, *over,* **lustiheed,** *pleasure* **290 dresse,** *approach* **291 styward bit,**
steward bid, **for to hye,** *to be brought quickly*

232–33 Alocen . . . Vitulon . . . Aristotle, Alhazen, an Arabian author of a treatise on optics, adapted into Latin by Witelo, a Polish physicist.
Aristotle was known as a scientist as well as a philosopher, hardly separable in the Middle Ages. **235 herd,** books were often read aloud in
the past. **238–39 Thelophus . . . Achilles,** Telephus, king of Mysia, was wounded and then healed by the weapon of Achilles, rationalized by
the curative properties of rust in Pliny's *Natural History* 34.45. **250 Moyses . . . Salomon,** the association of wisdom and magic led to the popular belief that Moses and Solomon were magicians; in legend, each possessed a magic ring. **254 fern-asshen,** the ash of burned ferns was
an ingredient in glass-making. **263–65 Phebus . . . Aldrian,** i.e., it is afternoon, because the sun has passed through the tenth of twelve domiciles, called the *angle meridional* (i.e., 10 a.m. to noon), during which the constellation Leo (the Lion, or royal beast) begins to rise above the
horizon; "Aldrian" may refer to Castor and Pollux, stars in Gemini. **272–73 Venus children . . . Fyssh,** Venus's children (i.e., lovers) dance at
this time because their planet exerts its greatest influence on them while it is in the constellation Pisces, the Fish. **287 Launcelot,** epitome
of chivalry and lover of Guenivere in Arthurian romances.

Unto the temple, as reson was, they wende°.
   The service doon, they soupen° al by day°.
What nedeth yow rehercen hire array?
Ech man woot° wel that a kynges feeste
Hath plentee to the mooste and to the leeste,   300
And deyntees mo° than been in my knowyng.
At after-soper gooth this noble kyng
To seen this hors of bras, with al the route°
Of lordes and of ladyes hym aboute.
   Swich wondryng was ther on this hors of
      bras   305
That syn° the grete sege of Troie was,
Theras° men wondreden on an hors also,
Ne was ther swich a wondryng as was tho°.
But fynally the kyng axeth° this knyght
The vertu° of this courser and the myght,   310
And preyde° hym to telle his governaunce°.
   This hors anoon bigan to trippe° and daunce
Whan that this knyght leyde hand upon his
      reyne,
And seyde, "Sire, ther is namoore to seyne°
But whan yow list° to ryden anywhere,   315
Ye mooten trille a pyn stant° in his ere,
Which I shal yow telle bitwix° us two.
Ye moote nempne hym° to what place also,
Or to what contree, that yow list to ryde.
And whan ye come ther as yow list abyde°,   320
Bidde hym descende and trille another pyn—
For therin lith th'effect° of al the gyn°—
And he wol doun descende and doon youre
      wille,
And in that place he wol abyden stille.
Though al the world the contrarie hadde
      yswore,   325
He shal nat thennes° been ydrawe ne ybore°.
Or if yow liste bidde° hym thennes goon,
Trille this pyn and he wol vanysshe anoon
Out of the sighte of every maner wight°,

And come agayn, be it by day or nyght,   330
Whan that yow list to clepen hym ageyn°
In swich a gyse° as I shal to yow seyn
Bitwixe yow and me and that ful soone.
Ride whan yow list, ther is namoore to doone."
   Enformed whan the kyng was of° that
      knyght,   335
And hath conceyved in his wit aright
The manere and the forme of al this thyng,
Ful glad and blithe° this noble doughty° kyng
Repeireth° to his revel as biforn°.
The brydel is unto the tour yborn°   340
And kept among his jueles leeve° and deere.
The hors vanysshed, I noot° in what manere,
Out of hir sighte; ye gete namoore of me.
But thus I lete° in lust° and jolitee
This Cambyuskan his lordes festeiynge°   345
Til wel ny° the day bigan to sprynge.

Explicit pars prima. Sequitur pars secunda.

   The norice° of digestioun, the sleep,
Gan on hem wynke° and bad hem taken keep°
That muchel drynke and labour wolde han reste,
And with a galpyng° mouth hem alle he
      keste°,   350
And seyde it was tyme to lye adoun,
For blood was in his domynacioun.
"Cherisseth° blood, natures freend," quod he.
They thanken hym galpynge, by two, by thre,
And every wight gan drawe hym° to his reste   355
As sleep hem bad°; they tooke it for the beste.
   Hire dremes shul nat been ytoold for° me;
Ful were hire heddes° of fumositee°
That causeth dreem of which ther nys no
      charge°.
They slepen til that it was pryme large°,   360
The mooste part, but it were° Canacee.
She was ful mesurable° as wommen be,

---

296 **wende**, *go* 297 **soupen**, *eat*, **by day**, *in daylight* 299 **woot**, *knows*
301 **deyntees mo**, *more delicacies* 303 **route**, *company* 306 **syn**, *since*
307 **Theras**, *where* 308 **tho**, *then* 309 **axeth**, *asks* 310 **vertu**, *power* 311
preyde, *requested*, **his governaunce**, *how it is controlled* 312 **trippe**, *cavort* 314 **seyne**, *say* 315 **list**, *wish* 316 **mooten trille a pyn stant**, *turn a
peg* (that) *stands* 317 **bitwix**, *between* 318 **moote nempne hym**, *must
tell him* 320 **list abyde**, *wish to remain* 322 **lith th'effect**, *lies the result*,
gyn, *device* 326 **thennes**, *from there*, **ydrawe ne ybore**, *pulled nor carried*
327 **liste bidde**, *wish to order* 329 **maner wight**, *kind of person* 331
clepen hym ageyn, *call him back* 332 **gyse**, *manner* 335 **of**, *by* 338

blithe, *happy*, **doughty**, *valiant* 339 **Repeireth**, *returns*, **biforn**, *before*
340 **tour yborn**, *tower carried* 341 **jueles leeve**, *jewels beloved* 342 **noot**,
know not 344 **lete**, *leave*, **lust**, *pleasure* 345 **his lordes festeiynge**, *en-
tertaining his lords* 346 **Til wel ny**, *until nearly* 347 **norice**, *nurse* 348
Gan . . . wynke, *winked*, **taken keep**, *pay attention* 350 **galpyng**, *yawn-
ing*, **hem alle he keste**, (sleep) *kissed them all* 353 **Cherisseth**, *cherish*
355 **gan drawe hym**, *took himself* 356 **bad**, *ordered* 357 **for**, *by* 358 **hire
heddes**, *their heads*, **fumositee**, *alcoholic fumes* 359 **nys no charge**, *is
no significance* 360 **pryme large**, *9 a.m.* 361 **but it were**, *except for* 362
ful mesurable, *very moderate*

306 **grete sege of Troie**, Trojan War; see 209n. 346a *Explicit pars prima.
Sequitur pars secunda.* "Here ends part one. Here follows part two."
352 **blood was in his domynacioun**, blood was in his dominance; i.e., the humor of blood (see *GP* 1.333), important to good health, became dominant at night. Both Sleep and Blood are personified here.

For of hir fader hadde she take leve°
To goon to reste soone after it was eve.
Hir liste nat appalled for to be°   365
Ne on the morwe unfeestlich° for to se°.
And slepte hire firste sleep and thanne awook,
For swich a joye she in hir herte took
Bothe of hir queynte° ryng and hire mirour
That twenty tyme she changed hir colour°,   370
And in hire sleep right for impressioun°
Of hire mirour, she hadde a visioun°.
Wherfore°, er that the sonne gan up glyde°
She cleped° on hir maistresse° hire bisyde,
And seyde that hire liste° for to ryse.   375
    Thise olde wommen that been gladly wyse°,
As is hire maistresse, answerde hire anon
And seyde, "Madame, whider° wil ye goon
Thus erly, for the folk been alle on reste?"
    "I wol," quod she, "arise, for me leste°   380
No lenger for to slepe, and walke aboute."
    Hire maistresse clepeth° wommen a greet route°,
And up they rysen, wel a° ten or twelve.
Up riseth fresshe Canacee hirselve,
As rody° and bright as dooth the yonge sonne   385
That in the Ram is foure degrees up ronne—
Noon hyer° was he whan she redy was—
And forth she walketh esily a pas°,
Arrayed after° the lusty° seson soote°
Lightly, for to pleye and walke on foote,   390
Nat but with° fyve or sixe of hir meynee°,
And in a trench° forth in the park gooth she.
    The vapour which that fro the erthe glood°
Made the sonne to seme rody° and brood°,
But nathelees it was so fair a sighte   395

That it made alle hire hertes for to lighte°,
What for the seson and the morwenynge,
And for the foweles° that she herde synge.
For right anon° she wiste° what they mente,
Right by hir song, and knew al hire entente.   400
    The knotte° why that every tale is toold,
If it be taried° til that lust be coold°
Of hem that han it after herkned yoore°,
The savour passeth ever lenger the moore°
For fulsomnesse° of his prolixitee°.   405
And by the same resoun, thynketh me,
I sholde to the knotte condescende°,
And maken of hir walkyng soone an ende.
    Amydde° a tree, fordrye° as whit as chalk,
As Canacee was pleyyng in hir walk,   410
Ther sat a faucon° over hire heed ful hye
That with a pitous voys so gan to crye
That all the wode resouned of hire cry.
Ybeten° hath she hirself so pitously
With bothe hir wynges til the rede blood   415
Ran endelong° the tree ther° as she stood.
And evere in oon° she cryde alwey and shrighte,
And with hir beek hirselven so she prighte°,
That ther nys° tygre ne noon so crueel beest
That dwelleth outher° in wode or in forest   420
That nolde han° wept, if that he wepe koude,
For sorwe of hire, she shrighte alwey so loude.
For ther nas nevere° man yet on lyve°—
If that I koude° a faucon wel discryve°—
That herde of swich another of fairnesse°   425
As wel of plumage as of gentillesse
Of shap, and al that myghte yrekened be°.
A faucon peregryn thanne semed she
Of fremde° land, and everemoore as she stood

---

363 take leve, *received permission* **365 Hir liste nat appalled for to be,** *she wished not to become pale* **366 unfeestlich,** *unfestive,* **for to se,** *to look at* **369 queynte,** *marvelous* **370 changed hir colour,** *blushed* **371 right for impression,** *because of the effect* **372 visioun,** *dream* **373 Wherfore,** *as a result,* **gan up glyde,** *rose* **374 cleped,** *called,* **maistresse,** *governess* **375 hire liste,** *she wished* **376 gladly wyse,** *fortunately wise* **378 whider,** *where* **380 me leste,** *I wish* **382 clepeth,** *called,* **greet route,** *large group* **383 wel a,** *about* **385 rody,** *rosy* **387 Noon hyer,** *no higher* **388 esily a pas,** *slowly* **389 Arrayed after,** *dressed in accord with,* **lusty,** *pleasant,* **soote,** *sweet* **391 Nat but with,** *with only,* **meynee,** *group of attendants* **392 trench,** *path* **393 glood,** *glided* **394 to seme rody,** *seem red,* **brood,** *large* **396 made alle hire hertes for to lighte,** *lightened all their hearts*

398 foweles, *birds* **399 right anon,** *immediately,* **wiste,** *knew* **401 knotte,** *crux* **402 taried,** *delayed,* **lust be coold,** *pleasure is cold* **403 han it after herkned yoore,** *have listened to it for a time* **404 savour passeth ever lenger the moore,** *enjoyment disappears increasingly* **405 fulsomnesse,** *abundance,* **prolixitee,** *lengthiness* **407 condescende,** *give way* **409 Amydde,** *in the middle of,* **fordrye,** *dried out* **411 faucon,** *falcon* **414 Ybeten,** *beaten* **416 endelong,** *down the length of,* **ther,** *where* **417 evere in oon,** *continuously,* **shrighte,** *shrieked* **418 prighte,** *pricked* **419 ther nys,** *there is no* **420 outher,** *either* **421 nolde han,** *would not have* **423 ther nas nevere,** *there was never,* **on lyve,** *alive* **424 koude,** *were able to,* **discryve,** *describe* **425 swich another of fairnesse,** *of another so beautiful* **427 yrekened be,** *be considered* **429 fremde,** *foreign*

385–86 as dooth the yonge sonne . . . up ronne, Canace is compared to the early-morning sun, and simultaneously we are told that it is about 6 a.m. The sun is "yonge" in mid-March (see line 47 above) because it is early in the year; it is just rising (**foure degrees up ronne**) above the horizon into the zodiacal sign of Aries, the Ram. **401–5** An elaborate way of saying that a tale told too long loses the appreciation of its audience. **428 peregryn,** a species of falcon, literally "pilgrim" because young peregrines were caught in passage from their breeding grounds rather than taken from the nest.

She swowneth now and now° for lakke of
    blood,   430
Til wel neigh° is she fallen fro the tree.
   This faire kynges doghter, Canacee,
That on hir fynger baar the queynte° ryng
Thurgh which she understood wel everythyng
That any fowel may in his leden seyn°,   435
And koude answeren hym in his ledene ageyn,
Hath understonde what this faucon seyde,
And wel neigh for the routhe° almoost she deyde.
And to the tree she gooth ful hastily,
And on this faukon looketh pitously,   440
And heeld hir lappe abrood°, for wel she wiste°
The faukon moste fallen fro the twiste°,
Whan that it swowned next, for lakke of blood.
A longe while to wayten° hire she stood
Til atte laste she spak in this manere   445
Unto the hauk, as ye shal after heere:
   "What is the cause, if it be for to telle,
That ye be in this furial pyne° of helle?"
Quod Canacee unto the hauk above.
"Is this for sorwe of deeth or los of love?   450
For as I trowe° thise been causes two
That causen moost a gentil herte wo;
Of oother harm it nedeth nat to speke.
For° ye youreself upon yourself yow wreke°,
Which proveth wel that outher ire° or drede°   455
Moot been enchesoun° of youre cruel dede,
Syn that° I see noon oother wight yow chace°.
For love of God, as dooth youreselven grace°,
Or what may been youre help? For west nor est
Ne saugh° I nevere er now no bryd° ne beest   460
That ferde with hymself° so pitously.
Ye sle° me with youre sorwe verraily°,
I have of yow so greet compassioun.
For Goddes love, com fro the tree adoun;
And as I am a kynges doghter trewe,   465

If that I verraily the cause knewe
Of youre disese°, if it lay in my myght,
I wolde amenden it er° that it were nyght,
As wisly° helpe me the grete God of kynde°!
And herbes shal I right ynowe yfynde°   470
To heele with youre hurtes hastily."
   Tho shrighte° this faucon yet moore pitously
Than ever she dide, and fil to grounde anon,
And lith aswowne°, deed and lyk a stoon,
Til Canacee hath in hire lappe hire take   475
Unto the tyme she gan of swough° awake.
   And after that° she of hir swough gan breyde°,
Right in hir haukes ledene° thus she seyde:
"That pitee renneth soone in gentil herte,
Feelynge his similitude in peynes smerte°,   480
Is preved alday°, as men may it see,
As wel by werk° as by auctoritee,
For gentil herte kitheth° gentillesse.
I se wel ye han of my distresse
Compassion, my faire Canacee,   485
Of verray° wommanly benignytee°
That Nature in youre principles° hath yset.
But for noon° hope for to fare the bet°,
But for° to obeye unto youre herte free°,
And for to maken othere° bewar by me,   490
As by the whelp chasted° is the leoun,
Right for that cause° and that conclusioun°,
Whil that I have a leyser and a space°,
Myn harm I wol confessen er I pace°."
   And evere, whil that oon hir sorwe tolde,   495
That oother weep° as she to water wolde°,
Til that the faucon bad hire to be stille,
And with a syk° right thus she seyde hir wille:
   "That I was bred°—allas, that ilke° day—
And fostred in a roche° of marbul gray   500
So tendrely that nothyng eyled° me,
I nyste nat° what was adversitee

---

430 **swowneth now and now,** *swoons recurrently* 431 **wel neigh,** *nearly*
433 **queynte,** *marvelous* 435 **leden seyn,** *language say* 438 **routhe,** *pity*
441 **heeld hir lappe abrood,** *held out the lap of her dress,* **wiste,** *knew*
442 **twiste,** *branch* 444 **wayten,** *watch* 448 **furial pyne,** *furious pain*
451 **trowe,** *believe* 454 **For,** *because,* **wreke,** *avenge* 455 **outher ire,** *either anger,* **drede,** *fear* 456 **Moot been enchesoun,** *must be the reason*
457 **Syn that,** *since,* **wight yow chace,** *creature pursue you* 458 **as dooth youreselven grace,** *have mercy on yourself* 460 **saugh,** *saw,* **bryd,** *bird*
461 **ferde with hymself,** *treated himself* 462 **sle,** *slay,* **verraily,** *truly* 467
disese, *distress* 468 **amenden it er,** *remedy it before* 469 **wisly,** *surely*
(may), **kynde,** *nature* 470 **right ynowe yfynde,** *find sufficient* 472 **Tho**

shrighte, *then shrieked* 474 **lith aswowne,** *lies fainted* 476 **of swough,**
from the faint 477 **after that,** *after,* **gan breyde,** *awakened with a start*
478 **haukes ledene,** *hawk's language* 480 **peynes smerte,** *the sting of
pain* 481 **preved alday,** *proved continually* 482 **werk,** *actions* 483 **kitheth,** *reveals* 486 **verray,** *true,* **benignytee,** *goodness* 487 **principles,**
innate disposition 488 **But for noon,** *not for any,* **fare the bet,** *to do any
better* 489 **But for,** *except,* **free,** *generous* 490 **othere,** *others* 491
chasted, *corrected* 492 **Right for that cause,** *just for that purpose,* **conclusioun,** *outcome* 493 **space,** *time* 494 **pace,** *depart* 496 **weep,** *wept,*
wolde, *would* (turn) 498 **syk,** *sigh* 499 **bred,** *born,* **ilke,** *same* 500
roche, *rock* 501 **eyled,** *troubled* 502 **nyste nat,** *knew not*

---

479 Familiar chivalric sentiment; see *KnT* 1.1761n. **491 whelp . . . leoun,** from the proverbial notion that a lion can be taught a lesson by
beating a dog. In this highly rhetorical sentence, the falcon says she will tells her story, not because she hopes things will improve but because she wishes to obey Canacee's request and because she hopes she can be a model for others to learn from. **499ff.** The falcon's tale has
many verbal and narrative resemblances to Chaucer's poem *Anelida and Arcite*, lines 105ff.

Til I koude flee° ful hye under the sky.
Tho° dwelte a tercelet° me faste° by
That semed welle° of alle gentillesse.   505
Al were he° ful of treson and falsnesse,
It was so wrapped under humble cheere°,
And under hewe° of trouthe in swich manere,
Under plesance and under bisy peyne°,
That no wight° koude han wend° he koude
          feyne°,   510
So depe in greyn he dyed his coloures°.
Right° as a serpent hit hym° under floures
Til he may seen his tyme for to byte,
Right so this god of loves ypocryte°
Dooth so his cerymonyes and obeisaunces°,   515
And kepeth in semblaunt° alle his observaunces
That sownen into° gentillesse of love.
As in a toumbe° is al the faire above°
And under is the corps°, swich° as ye woot°,
Swich was the ypocrite, bothe coold and hoot.   520
And in this wise he served his entente,
That, save° the feend°, noon wiste° what he
          mente,
Til he so longe hadde wopen° and compleyned,
And many a yeer his service to me feyned°,
Til that myn herte, to pitous and to nyce°,   525
Al innocent of his corouned° malice,
For fered° of his deeth, as thoughte me,
Upon° his othes and his seuretee°,
Graunted hym love upon this condicioun,
That everemoore myn honour and renoun°   530
Were saved°, bothe privee and apert°;
This is to seyn, that after his desert
I yaf° hym al myn herte and al my thoght—
God woot° and he, that ootherwise noght°—
And took his herte in chaunge° of myn for ay°.   535

But sooth° is seyd°, goon sithen many a day°,
A trewe wight° and a theef thenken nat oon°.
And whan he saugh the thyng so fer ygoon
That I hadde graunted hym fully my love
In swich a gyse° as I have seyd above,   540
And yeven hym my trewe herte as free°
As he swoor he yaf his herte to me,
Anon this tigre, ful of doublenesse,
Fil on his knees with so devout humblesse,
With so heigh reverence, and as by his
          cheere°   545
So lyk a gentil lovere of manere,
So ravysshed, as it semed, for the joye
That nevere Jason ne Parys of Troye—
Jason? Certes°, ne noon° oother man
Syn° Lameth was, that alderfirst° bigan   550
To loven two, as writen folk biforn°—
Ne nevere, syn° the firste man was born,
Ne koude man° by twenty thousand part°
Countrefete° the sophymes° of his art,
Ne were worthy unbrokelen his galoche°   555
Ther° doublenesse or feynyng sholde approche°,
Ne so koude thonke a wight° as he dide me!
His manere was an hevene for to see
Til° any womman, were she never so wys,
So peynted° he and kembde at point-devys°,   560
As wel his wordes as his contenaunce°.
And I so loved hym for his obeisaunce°,
And for the trouthe I demed° in his herte,
That if so were that any thyng hym smerte°,
Al were it never so lite°, and I it wiste°,   565
Me thoughte I felte deeth myn herte twiste°.
And shortly so ferforth° this thyng is went
That my wyl was his willes instrument;
This is to seyn, my wyl obeyed his wyl

---

503 koude flee, *was able to fly* **504 Tho,** *then,* **tercelet,** *male falcon,* **faste,** *near* **505 welle,** (a) *source* **506 Al were he,** *although he was* **507 cheere,** *demeanor* **508 hewe,** *illusion* **509 bisy peyne,** *busy efforts* **510 wight,** *creature,* **koude han wend,** *could have believed,* **feyne,** *pretend* **511 depe in greyn he dyed his coloures,** *deeply ingrained* (i.e., successfully) *he painted his words* (or used his rhetoric) **512 Right,** *just,* **hit hym,** *hides himself* **514 ypocryte,** *hypocrite* **515 obeisaunces,** *acts of humility* **516 semblaunt,** *outward show* **517 sownen into,** *contribute to* **518 toumbe,** *tomb,* **faire above,** *beauty on the outside* **519 corps,** *corpse,* **swich,** *such,* **woot,** *know* **522 save,** *except,* **feend,** *devil,* **wiste,** *knew* **523 wopen,** *wept* **524 feyned,** *pretended* **525 to nyce,** *too foolish* **526 corouned,** *sovereyn* **527 For fered,** *because of fear* **528 Upon,** *based on,* **seuretee,** *assurance* **530 renoun,** *reputation* **531 saved,** *preserved,* **privee and apert,** *privately and publicly* **533 yaf,** *gave* **534 woot,** *knows,* **ootherwise noght,** *on any other terms I would not have*

535 chaunge, *exchange,* **for ay,** *forever* **536 sooth,** *truth,* **seyd,** *said,* **goon sithen many a day,** *for a long time* **537 trewe wight,** *true person,* **thenken nat oon,** *think not alike* **540 gyse,** *way* **541 free,** *freely* **545 as by his cheere,** *to judge by his expression* **549 Certes,** *surely,* **ne noon,** *nor any* **550 Syn,** *since,* **that alderfirst,** *who first* **551 biforn,** *before* **552 syn,** *since* **553 Ne koude man,** *could* (any) *man,* **twenty thousand part,** *one twenty thousandth* **554 Countrefete,** *imitate,* **sophymes,** *deceptive arguments* **555 unbrokelen his galoche,** *to unbuckle his sandal* **556 Ther,** *where,* **sholde approche,** *is concerned* **557 so koude thonke a wight,** *could so thank* (i.e., *treat*) *a person* **559 Til,** *to* **560 peynted,** *painted* (i.e., *pretended*), **kembde at point-devys,** *combed* (i.e., *arranged*) *perfectly* **561 contenaunce,** *behavior* **562 obeisaunce,** *acts of humility* **563 demed,** *judged to be* **564 hym smerte,** *pained him* **565 Al were it never so lite,** *regardless how insignificant,* **wiste,** *knew* **566 twiste,** *wring* **567 ferforth,** *far*

---

543 tigre, tiger, thought to be a deceptive animal. **548 Jason,** deserted Hypsipyle and Medea; *LGW* 1370ff. **Parys,** deserted Oenome. **550 Lameth,** Lamech had two wives; Genesis 4.19.

In alle thyng as fer as reson fil°,   570
Kepynge the boundes of my worship evere.
Ne nevere hadde I thyng so lief°, ne levere°,
As hym, God woot°, ne nevere shal namo.
     "This lasteth lenger than a yeer or two
That I supposed of hym noght but good.   575
But finally, thus atte laste it stood,
That Fortune wolde that he moste twynne°
Out of that place which that I was inne.
Wher me° was wo, that is no questioun.
I kan nat make of it discripsioun;   580
For o thyng dar I tellen boldely,
I knowe what is the peyne of deeth therby.
Swich harm° I felte for he ne myghte bileve°.
So on a day of me he took his leve
So sorwefully eek that I wende verraily°   585
That he had felt as muche harm as I,
Whan that I herde hym speke, and saugh his
          hewe°.
But nathelees, I thoughte he was so trewe;
And eek that he repaire sholde° ageyn
Withinne a litel while, sooth° to seyn;   590
And resoun wolde° eek that he moste° go
For his honour, as ofte it happeth so;
That I made vertu of necessitee
And took it wel, syn° that it moste be.
As I best myghte, I hidde fro hym my sorwe,   595
And took hym by the hond, Seint John to borwe,
And seyde hym thus, 'Lo, I am youres al.
Beth swich° as I to yow have been and shal.'
What he answerde, it nedeth noght reherce°.
Who kan sey bet° than he, who kan do werse?   600
Whan he hath al wel seyd, thanne hath he doon°.
Therfore bihoveth hire° a ful long spoon
That shal ete with a feend, thus herde I seye.
So atte laste he moste° forth his weye,
And forth he fleeth° til he cam ther hym leste°. 605
     "Whan it cam hym to purpos° for to reste,

I trowe° he hadde thilke° text in mynde,
That alle thyng, repeirynge° to his kynde°;
Gladeth° hymself—thus seyn men, as I gesse.
Men loven of propre kynde° newefangelnesse°,   610
As briddes doon° that men in cages fede°.
For though thou nyght and day take of hem
          hede°,
And strawe° hir cage faire and softe as silk,
And yeve° hem sugre, hony, breed, and milk,
Yet right anon as that° his dore is uppe,   615
He with his feet wol spurne° adoun his cuppe,
And to the wode he wole° and wormes ete.
So newefangel been they of hire mete°,
And loven novelries of propre kynde°;
No gentillesse of blood ne may hem bynde°.   620
     "So ferde° this tercelet°, allas the day!
Though he were gentil born, and fressh and gay,
And goodlich for to seen°, humble and free°,
He saugh upon a tyme a kyte flee°,
And sodeynly he loved this kyte so   625
That al his love is clene fro° me ago,
And hath his trouthe falsed° in this wyse.
Thus hath the kyte my love in hire servyse,
And I am lorn° withouten remedie."
And with that word this faucon gan to crie   630
And swowned eft in Canacees barm°.
     Greet was the sorwe for the haukes harm
That Canacee and alle hir wommen made.
They nyste hou° they myghte the faucon glade°.
But Canacee hom bereth hire in hir lappe,   635
And softely in plastres° gan hire wrappe,
Ther as° she with hire beek hadde hurt hirselve.
Now kan nat° Canacee but herbes delve°
Out of the ground, and make salves newe
Of herbes preciouse and fyne of hewe°,   640
To heelen with this hauk. Fro day to nyght
She dooth hire bisynesse and al hire myght,
And by hire beddes heed she made a mewe°,

---

fede, *feed* 612 hede, *care* 613 strawe, *line with straw* 614 yeve, *give* 615 right anon as that, *just as soon as* 616 spurne, *kick* 617 wole, *will* (go) 618 mete, *diet* 619 of propre kynde, *by natural disposition* 620 hem bynde, *restrain them* 621 ferde, *acted,* tercelet, *male falcon* 623 goodlich for to seen, *attractive,* free, *generous* 624 kyte flee, *kite* (scavenger bird) *fly* 626 clene fro, *completely from* 627 trouthe falsed, *pledge falsified* 629 lorn, *lost* 631 barm, *lap* 634 nyste hou, *knew not how,* glade, *gladden* 636 plastres, *bandages* 637 Ther as, *where* 638 kan nat, *can do nothing,* delve, *dig* 640 fyne of hewe, *of good color* (i.e., fresh) 643 mewe, *birdhouse*

570 fil, *extended* 572 lief, *dear,* levere, *dearer* 573 woot, *knows* 577 twynne, *depart* 579 Wher me, *whether to me* 583 Swich harm, *such pain,* bileve, *remain* 585 wende verraily, *thought truly* 587 hewe, *color* 589 repaire sholde, *should return* 590 sooth, *truth* 591 wolde, *wished,* moste, *must* 594 syn, *since* 598 Beth swich, *be such* 599 it nedeth noght reherce, *I need not retell* 600 say bet, *speak better* 601 doon, *finished* 602 bihoveth hire, *she needs* 604 moste, *must* (go) 605 fleeth, *flies,* ther hym leste, *where* (it) *pleased him* 606 it cam hym to purpos, *he decided* 607 trowe, *think,* thilke, *that* 608 repeirynge, *returning,* kynde, *nature* 609 Gladeth, *pleases* 610 of proper kynde, *by natural disposition,* newefangelnesse, *novelty* 611 briddes doon, *birds do,*

---

593 See *KnT* 1.3042. 596 **Seint John to borwe,** to pledge by St. John, the Apostle of Truth. 602–3 Proverbial after Chaucer. 608–9 *Bo* 3.m2.42. 610–20 *Bo* 3.m2.21–31. This application of a bird analogy to a bird is incongruous.

And covered° it with velvettes blewe
In signe of trouthe that is in wommen sene.   645
And al withoute°, the mewe is peynted grene,
In which were peynted alle thise false fowles
As beth thise tidyves, tercelettes, and owles;
Right for despit° were peynted hem bisyde
Pyes°, on hem for to crie and chyde°.   650
    Thus lete I Canacee hir hauk kepyng;
I wol namoore as now speke of hir ryng
Til it come eft° to purpos for to seyn
How that this faucon gat hire love ageyn
Repentant, as the storie telleth us,   655
By mediacioun of Cambalus,
The kynges sone, of which that I yow tolde.
But hennesforth I wol my proces holde°
To speke of aventures and of batailles

That nevere yet was herd so grete mervailles.   660
    First wol I telle yow of Cambyuskan,
That in his tyme many a citee wan;
And after wol I speke of Algarsif,
How that he wan° Theodera to his wif,
For whom ful ofte in greet peril he was,   665
Ne hadde he° been holpen° by the steede of bras;
And after wol I speke of Cambalo,
That faught in lystes° with the bretheren two
For Canacee er that he myghte hire wynne.
And ther I lefte I wol ayeyn bigynne.   670

Explicit secunda pars. Incipit pars tercia.

    Appollo whirleth up his chaar° so hye,
Til that the god Mercurius hous, the slye°—

Heere folwen the wordes of the Frankeleyn to the Squier, and the wordes of the Hoost to the Frankeleyn.

"In feith, Squier, thow hast thee wel yquit°
And gentilly. I preise wel thy wit,"
Quod the Frankeleyn, "considerynge thy
        yowthe,   675
So feelyngly thou spekest, sire, I allow° the.
As to my doom°, ther is noon that is heere
Of eloquence that shal be thy peere°,
If that thou lyve—God yeve thee good chaunce°,
And in vertu sende thee continuaunce,   680
For of thy speche I have greet deyntee°.
I have a sone, and by the Trinitee,
I hadde levere than twenty pound worth lond°,
Though it right now were fallen in myn hond,
He were a man of swich discrecioun   685
As that ye been. Fy on possessioun,

But if° a man be vertuous withal°!
I have my sone snybbed°, and yet shal,
For he to vertu listeth nat entende°,
But for to pleye at dees°, and to despende°   690
And lese° al that he hath is his usage°.
And he hath levere° talken with a page
Than to comune° with any gentil wight°
There° he myghte lerne gentillesse aright."
    "Straw for youre gentillesse!" quod oure
        Hoost.   695
"What, Frankeleyn, pardee° sire, wel thou woost°
That ech of yow moot° tellen atte leste
A tale or two, or breken his biheste°."
    "That knowe I wel, sire," quod the Frankeleyn.
"I prey yow, haveth me nat in desdeyn°,   700

---

644 **covered,** *lined,* 646 **al withoute,** *on the outside* 649 **Right for despit,** *just for mockery* 650 **Pyes,** *magpies,* **chyde,** *scold* 653 **eft,** *again* 658 **proces holde,** *story continue* 664 **wan,** *won* 666 **Ne hadde he,** (if) *he had not,* **holpen,** *helped* 668 **lystes,** *single combat* 671 **chaar,** *chariot* 672 **slye,** *cunning* 673 **thee wel yquit,** *accounted well for yourself* 676 **allow,** *praise* 677 **doom,** *judgment* 678 **peere,** *equal* 679 **chaunce,** *fortune* 681 **deyntee,** *pleasure* 683 **hadde levere than twenty pound worth lond,**

would rather (have) *land generating twenty pounds* (income) *annually* 687 **But if,** *unless,* **vertuous withal,** *talented also* 688 **snybbed,** *scolded* 689 **to vertu listeth nat entende,** *wishes not to attend to accomplishments* 690 **dees,** *dice,* **despende,** *spend,* 691 **lese,** *lose,* **in his usage,** *habitually* 692 **hath levere,** *would rather* 693 **comune,** *converse,* **gentil wight,** *gentleman* 694 **There,** *where* 696 **pardee,** *by God,* **woost,** *know* 697 **moot,** *must* 698 **beheste,** *promise* 700 **desdeyn,** *scorn*

644–46 **blewe . . . grene,** blue is the color of constancy and green of inconstancy in the refrain of Chaucer's *Against Women Unconstant.* 648 **tidyves,** an unidentified variety of bird, evidently reputed to be inconstant; cf. *LGW* 154. 663–64 **Algarsif . . . Theodera,** nothing is known for certain of Algarsif (Cambyuskan's oldest son, line 30), nor of his wife. 667–68 **Cambalo . . . bretheren two,** it is impossible to know if this is the younger son of Cambyuskan (line 31) or a suitor of Canace who fights her brothers. At this point, the many plots and magical devices seem to suggest that only a loose and very long narrative could bring them all together. 670a *Explicit secunda pars. Incipit pars tercia.* "Here ends part two. Here begins part three." 671–72 A number of MSS omit these lines. They set the time in mid-May when the sun (Apollo) enters Gemini, one of the houses or domiciles of Mercury, who is the clever or trickster god. 697–98 **moot tellen atte lest / A tale or two,** must tell at least a tale or two. This suggests a less ambitious program of tales than the initial requirement of four tales per pilgrim; see *GP* 1.792–94n.

Though to this man I speke a word or two."
 "Telle on thy tale withouten wordes mo."
 "Gladly, sire Hoost," quod he, "I wole obeye
Unto your wyl. Now herkneth° what I seye.

I wol yow nat contrarien° in no wyse   705
As fer as that my wittes wol suffyse.
I prey to God that it may plesen yow;
Thanne woot° I wel that it is good ynow°."

---

704 herkneth, *listen to* **705 contrarien,** *oppose* **708 woot,** *know,* **ynow,**
enough

FRANKLIN'S TALE

PROLOGUE

— House of Commons
— His social aspirations

The Prologe of the Frankeleyns Tale.

Thise olde gentil Britouns in hir dayes
Of diverse aventures maden layes, 710
Rymeyed° in hir firste° Briton tonge,
Whiche layes with hir instrumentz they songe
Or elles redden° hem for hir plesaunce°;
And oon of hem have I in remembraunce,
Which I shal seyn with good wyl as I kan. 715
  But, sires, by cause I am a burel° man,
At my bigynnyng first I yow biseche,
Have me excused of my rude speche.

I lerned nevere rethorik, certeyn.
Thyng that I speke, it moot° be bare and pleyn. 720
I sleep nevere on the Mount of Pernaso,
Ne lerned Marcus Tullius Scithero.
Colours° ne knowe I none, withouten drede,
But swiche colours° as growen in the mede°,
Or elles swich as men dye or peynte. 725
Colours of rethoryk been to queynte°;
My spirit feeleth noght of swich mateere.
But if yow list, my tale shul ye heere.

Heere bigynneth the Frankeleyns Tale.

In Armorik, that called is Britayne,
Ther was a knyght that loved and dide his
  payne 730
To serve a lady in his beste wise;
And many a labour, many a greet emprise°

He for his lady wroghte° er she were wonne,
For she was oon the faireste under sonne,
And eek therto comen of so heigh kynrede° 735
That wel unnethes dorste° this knyght for drede
Telle hire his wo, his peyne, and his distresse.

---

711 Rymeyed, *composed in rhyme,* **hir firste,** *their original* **713 redden,** *read,* **plesaunce,** *pleasure* **716 burel,** *unlearned* **720 moot,** *must* **723 Colours,** *rhetorical devices* **724 colours,** *flowers,* **mede,** *meadow* **726 to*

queynte, too ingenious **732 emprise,** *enterprise* **733 wroghte,** *undertook* **735 kynrede,** *lineage* **736 wel unnethes dorste,** *scarcely dared*

709 Britouns, Bretons, Celtic peoples of Brittany by whom the Arthurian legend and other Celtic stories are thought to have been conveyed to the French and English. **710 layes,** short romances; the tale fits in the subgenre of brief medieval romance, the Breton lay. **721 Pernaso,** Mt. Parnassus, sacred to the Muses. **722 Scithero,** Cicero, exemplary Latin rhetorician. **729 Armorik,** Armorica, ancient name of Brittany, in northwestern France.

But atte laste she for his worthynesse,
And namely° for his meke obeysaunce°,
Hath swich° a pitee caught of his penaunce°   740
That pryvely° she fil of his accord°
To take hym for hir housbonde and hir lord,
Of swich lordshipe as men han° over hir wyves.
And for to lede the moore in blisse hir lyves,
Of his free wyl he swoor hire° as a knyght   745
That nevere in al his lyf he day ne nyght
Ne sholde upon hym take no maistrie°
Agayn hir wyl, ne kithe° hire jalousie,
But hire obeye and folwe hir wyl in al,
As any lovere to his lady shal,   750
Save that the name of soveraynetee°,
That wolde he have for shame of his degree°.

   She thanked hym, and with ful greet humblesse
She seyde, "Sire, sith° of youre gentillesse
Ye profre° me to have so large a reyne°,   755
Ne wolde nevere God bitwixe us tweyne,
As in my gilt°, were outher werre° or stryf.
Sire, I wol be youre humble trewe wyf—
Have heer my trouthe°—til that myn herte breste°."
Thus been they bothe in quiete and in reste.   760

   For o thyng, sires, saufly° dar I seye,
That freendes everych° oother moot° obeye
If they wol longe holden compaignye.
Love wol nat been constreyned by maistrye.
Whan maistrie comth°, the God of Love anon°   765
Beteth his wynges and farewell, he is gon.
Love is a thyng as any spirit free.
Wommen, of kynde°, desiren libertee,
And nat to been constreyned as a thral°—
And so doon men, if I sooth° seyen shal.   770
Looke who that is moost pacient in love,
He is at his avantage° al above.

Pacience is an heigh vertu, certeyn,
For it venquysseth°, as thise clerkes seyn,
Thynges that rigour° sholde nevere atteyne°.   775
For° every word men may nat chide° or pleyne°.
Lerneth to suffer°, or elles so moot I goon,
Ye shul it lerne wher so ye wole or noon°.
For in this world, certain, ther no wight° is
That he ne dooth or seith somtyme amys°.   780
Ire°, siknesse, or constellacioun°,
Wyn°, wo, or chaungynge of complexioun
Causeth ful ofte to doon amys or speken.
On every wrong a man may nat be wreken°.
After° the tyme moste° be temperaunce°   785
To every wight that kan on° governaunce.
And therfore hath this wise, worthy knyght
To lyve in ese suffrance hire bihight°,
And she to hym ful wisly gan to swere
That nevere sholde ther be defaute in here°.   790

   Heere may men seen an humble, wys accord;
Thus hath she take hir servant and hir lord—
Servant in love and lord in mariage.
Thanne was he bothe in lordshipe and servage°.
Servage? Nay, but in lordshipe above°   795
Sith° he hath bothe his lady and his love;
His lady, certes°, and his wyf also,
The which that lawe of love acordeth to.
And whan he was in this prosperitee,
Hoom with his wyf he gooth to his contree,   800
Nat fer fro Pedmark ther his dwellyng was,
Where as he lyveth in blisse and in solas°.

   Who koude telle but° he hadde wedded be°
The joye, the ese, and the prosperitee
That is bitwixe an housbonde and his wyf?   805
A yeer and moore lasted this blisful lyf,
Til that the knyght of which I speke of thus,
That of Kayrrud was cleped° Arveragus,
Shoop hym° to goon and dwelle a yeer or tweyne
In Engelond, that cleped was eek° Briteyne,   810

---

739 namely, *especially,* **obeysaunce,** *submissiveness* **740 swich,** *such,* **penaunce,** *suffering* **741 pryvely,** *secretly,* **fil of his accord,** *agreed* **743 han,** *have* **745 hire,** *to her* **747 maistrie,** *control* **748 kithe,** *show* **751 soveraynetee,** *dominance* **752 for shame of his degree,** *in consideration of his social rank* **754 sith,** *since* **755 profre,** *offer,* **so large a reyne,** *such free rein* **757 As in my gilt,** *through my fault,* **outher werre,** *either war* **759 trouthe,** *pledge,* **breste,** *burst* **761 saufly,** *surely* **762 everych,** *each,* **moot,** *must* **765 comth,** *comes,* **anon,** *at once* **768 of kynde,** *by nature* **769 thral,** *slave* **770 sooth,** *truth* **772 at his avantage,** *i.e., has the advantage* **774 venquysseth,** *overcomes* **775 rigour,** *strictness,* **atteyne,** *achieve* **776 For,** *at,* **chide,** *scold,* **pleyne,** *complain* **777 suffre,** *tolerate* **778 wher so ye wole or noon,** *whether you want to or not* **779 wight,** *person* **780 amys,** *wrongly* **781 Ire,** *anger,* **constellacioun,** *astrological influence* **782 Wyn,** *wine* **784 wreken,** *avenged* **785 After,** *according to,* **moste,** *(there) must,* **temperaunce,** *tolerance* **786 kan on,** *knows about* **788 suffrance hire bihight,** *promised her patience* **790 defaute in here,** *flaws in her* **794 servage,** *servitude* **795 above,** *higher* **796 Sith,** *since* **797 certes,** *surely* **802 solas,** *pleasure* **803 but,** *unless,* **be,** *been* **808 cleped,** *called* **809 Shoop hym,** *prepared himself* **810 cleped was eek,** *also was called*

756–57 Ne wolde nevere God . . . were, i.e., may there never be by God. **764–67** Similar to *RR* 9440–42. **768–69** Similar to *RR* 13959–66. **773–74** Proverbial. **777 so moot I goon,** as I am able to walk; i.e., by my life. **782 complexioun,** balance of humors (see *GP* 1.333n). The list of causes here are commonplaces of medieval psychology and physiology. **793–98** See *RR* 9449–53. **801 Pedmark,** Penmarch, on the coast of Brittany. **808 of Kayrrud,** Kérity, a village near Penmarch.

To seke in armes worship° and honour—
For al his lust° he sette in swich° labour—
And dwelled there two yeer, the book seith thus.

    Now wol I stynten of° this Arveragus,
And speken I wole of Dorigen his wyf   815
That loveth hire housbonde as hire hertes lyf.
For his absence wepeth she and siketh°,
As doon thise noble wyves whan hem liketh°.
She moorneth, waketh°, wayleth, fasteth,
    pleyneth°.
Desir of his presence hire so destreyneth°   820
That al this wyde world she sette at noght.
Hire freendes, whiche that knewe hir hevy
    thoght,
Conforten hire in al that ever they may.
They prechen hire, they telle hire nyght and day
That causelees she sleeth hirself, allas,   825
And every confort possible in this cas°
They doon to hire with al hire bisynesse,
Al for to make hire leve hire hevynesse.

    By proces°, as ye knowen everichoon°,
Men may so longe graven° in a stoon   830
Til som figure therinne emprented be.
So longe han they conforted hire, til she
Receyved hath, by hope and by resoun,
The emprentyng° of hire consolacioun,
Thurgh which hir grete sorwe gan aswage°;   835
She may nat alwey duren° in swich rage°.

    And eek Arveragus in al this care
Hath sent hire lettres hoom of his welfare,
And that he wol come hastily agayn;
Or elles hadde this sorwe hir herte slayn.   840

    Hire freendes sawe hir sorwe gan to slake°,
And preyde hire on knees, for Goddes sake,
To come and romen hire° in compaignye,
Awey to dryve hire derke fantasye.
And finally she graunted that requeste,   845
For wel she saugh° that it was for the beste.

    Now stood hire castel faste° by the see,
And often with hire freendes walketh shee

Hire to disporte° upon the bank an heigh
Where as she many a ship and barge seigh°   850
Seillynge hir cours°, where as hem liste go°.
But thanne was that a parcel° of hire wo,
For to hirself ful ofte, "Allas," seith she,
"Is ther no ship of so manye as I se
Wol bryngen hom my lord? Thanne were myn
    herte   855
Al warisshed° of his° bittre peynes smerte."

    Another tyme ther wolde she sitte and thynke,
And caste hir eyen dounward fro the brynke.
But whan she saugh the grisly rokkes blake
For verray° feere so wolde hir herte quake   860
That on hire feet she myghte hire noght sustene.
Thanne wolde she sitte adoun upon the grene
And pitously into the see biholde,
And seyn right thus with sorweful sikes° colde:

    "Eterne God, that thurgh thy purveiaunce°   865
Ledest the world by certein governaunce,
In ydel°, as men seyn, ye no thyng make.
But, Lord, thise grisly, feendly° rokkes blake,
That semen rather a foul confusioun
Of werk than any fair creacioun   870
Of swich a parfit° wys God and a stable°,
Why han ye wroght° this werk unresonable?
For by this werk, south, north, ne west, ne eest,
Ther nys yfostred man°, ne bryd°, ne beest;
It dooth no good, to my wit, but anoyeth°.   875
Se ye nat, Lord, how mankynde it destroyeth?
An hundred thousand bodyes of mankynde
Han rokkes slayn, al be they nat in mynde°,
Which mankynde is so fair part of thy werk
That thou it madest lyk to thyn owene merk°.   880

    "Thanne semed it ye hadde a greet chiertee°
Toward mankynde; but how thanne may it bee
That ye swiche meenes° make it° to destroyen,
Whiche meenes do no good but evere anoyen°?
I woot° wel clerkes wol seyn as hem leste°,   885
By argumentz, that al is for the beste
Though I ne kan the causes nat yknowe.

---

811 **worship,** *reputation* 812 **lust,** *desire,* **swich,** *such* 814 **stynten of,** *stop about* 817 **siketh,** *sighs* 818 **hem liketh,** (it) *pleases them* 819 **waketh,** *lies awake,* **pleyneth,** *laments* 820 **destreyneth,** *torments* 826 **cas,** *situation* 829 **By proces,** *in time,* **everichoon,** *everyone* 830 **graven,** *engrave* 834 **emprentyng,** *impression* 835 **gan aswage,** *diminished* 836 **duren,** *endure,* **swich rage,** *such passion* 841 **slake,** *subside* 843 **romen hire,** *walk herself* 846 **saugh,** *saw* 847 **faste,** *near* 849 **Hire to disporte,** *to entertain herself* 850 **seigh,** *sees* 851 **hir cours,** *their way,* **hem liste go,** *they*

wish to go 852 **parcel,** *portion* 856 **warisshed,** *cured,* **his,** *its* 860 **verray,** *genuine* 864 **sikes,** *sighs* 865 **purveiaunce,** *providence* 867 **In ydel,** *to no purpose* 868 **feendly,** *fiendish* 871 **parfit,** *perfect,* **stable,** *stable one* 872 **wroght,** *made* 874 **Ther nys yfostred man,** *there is no man who benefits,* **ne bryd,** *nor bird* 875 **anoyeth,** *afflicts* 878 **al be they nat in mynde,** *although they are forgotten* 880 **lyk to thyn owene merk,** *in your own image* 881 **chiertee,** *charity* (love) 883 **swiche meenes,** *such means,* **it,** i.e., *mankind* 884 **anoyen,** *afflict* 885 **woot,** *know,* **hem leste,** *they wish*

811 **worship and honour,** the tension between the pursuit of knightly honor and love of wife is a romance motif from Chrétien de Troyes (fl. 1160–90) onward. 865–93 This appeal to (questioning of?) Providence has its roots in Boethian thought (*Consolation* 4.pr6) and recalls *KnT* 1.2986ff., although Dorigen fails to perceive or accept the wisdom of divine order.

But thilke° God that made wynd to blowe
As kepe° my lord! This my conclusion.
To clerkes lete I al disputison.   890
But wolde° God that alle thise rokkes blake
Were sonken into helle for his sake!
Thise rokkes sleen myn herte for the feere."
Thus wolde she seyn, with many a pitous teere.
 Hire freendes sawe that it was no disport°   895
To romen by the see, but disconfort,
And shopen° for to pleyen somwher elles.
They leden° hire by ryveres and by welles,
And eek in othere places delitables°;
They dauncen and they pleyen at ches and
  tables°.   900
 So on a day, right in the morwetyde°,
Unto a gardyn that was ther bisyde,
In which that they hadde maad hir ordinaunce°
Of vitaille° and of oother purveiaunce°,
They goon and pleye hem al the longe day.   905
And this was on the sixte morwe of May,
Which May hadde peynted with his softe shoures°
This gardyn ful of leves and of floures;
And craft° of mannes hand so curiously°
Arrayed hadde this gardyn, trewely,   910
That nevere was ther gardyn of swich prys°
But if it were the verray° paradys.
The odour of floures and the fresshe sighte
Wolde han° maked any herte lighte
That evere was born but if to° greet siknesse   915
Or to greet sorwe helde it in distresse,
So ful it was of beautee with plesaunce°.
At after-dyner gonne they to daunce,
And synge also, save Dorigen allone,
Which made alwey hir compleint and hir
  moone°,   920
For she ne saugh hym on the daunce go
That was hir housbonde and hir love also.

But nathelees she moste° a tyme abyde°,
And with good hope lete hir sorwe slyde°.
 Upon this daunce, amonges othere men,   925
Daunced a squier biforn Dorigen,
That fressher was and jolyer° of array,
As to my doom°, than is the monthe of May.
He syngeth, dauunceth, passynge° any man
That is or was sith° that the world bigan.   930
Therwith he was, if men sholde hym discryve°,
Oon of the beste farynge° man on lyve:
Yong, strong, right vertuous, and riche, and wys,
And wel biloved, and holden in greet prys°.
And shortly, if the sothe I tellen shal,   935
Unwityng of° this Dorigen at al
This lusty squier, servant to Venus,
Which that ycleped° was Aurelius,
Hadde loved hire best of any creature
Two yeer and moore, as was his aventure°,   940
But nevere dorste° he tellen hire his grevaunce.
Withouten coppe he drank al his penaunce.
He was despeyred°; nothyng dorste he seye,
Save in his songes somwhat wolde he wreye°
His wo, as in a general compleynyng.   945
He seyde he lovede and was biloved no thyng°.
Of swich matere made he manye layes,
Songes, compleintes, roundels, virelayes,
How that he dorste° nat his sorwe telle,
But langwissheth° as a furye dooth in helle,   950
And dye he moste, he seyde, as dide Ekko
For Narcisus, that dorste nat telle hir wo.
In oother manere than ye heere me seye
Ne dorste he nat to hire his wo biwreye°,
Save that paraventure° somtyme at daunces,   955
Ther° yonge folk kepen hir observaunces°,
It may wel be he looked on hir face
In swich a wise° as man that asketh grace°;
But nothyng wiste° she of his entente.

---

888 thilke, *that* **889 As kepe,** *so protect* **891 wolde,** *I wish to* **895 disport,** *pleasure* **897 shopen,** *arranged* **898 leden,** *led* **899 delitables,** *delightful* **900 tables,** *backgammon* **901 morwetyde,** *morning* **903 hir ordinaunce,** *their arrangements* **904 vitaille,** *food,* **purveiaunce,** *provisions* **907 shoures,** *showers* **909 craft,** *skill,* **curiously,** *ingeniously* **911 swich prys,** *such excellence* **912 verray,** *true* **914 Wolde han,** *would have* **915 but if to,** *unless too* **917 plesaunce,** *pleasure* **920 Which,** *who,* **moone,** *moan* **923 moste,** *must,* **abyde,** *await* **924 slyde,** *pass* **927**

jolyer, *more attractive* **928 doom,** *judgment* **929 passynge,** *surpassing* **930 sith,** *since* **931 discryve,** *describe* **932 beste farynge,** *most handsome* **934 prys,** *honor* **936 Unwityng of,** *unknown to* **938 ycleped,** *named* **940 aventure,** *luck* **941 dorste,** *dared* **943 despeyred,** *in despair* **944 wreye,** *reveal* **946 no thyng,** *not at all* **949 dorste,** *dared* **950 langwissheth,** *suffers* **954 biwreye,** *betray (reveal)* **955 paraventure,** *perhaps* **956 Ther,** *where,* **observaunces,** *courtly rituals* **958 wise,** *manner,* **grace,** *favor* **959 wiste,** *knew*

937 Venus, goddess of love. **942 Withouten coppe . . . his penaunce,** he drank all his sorrow without a cup, i.e., he did it the hard way, suffering extraordinarily. **947–48 layes/Songes, compleintes, roundels, virelayes,** lays (brief songs), songs, complaints (laments), roundels, virelayes. Several of Chaucer's short poems are cast as complaints; roundels and virelays are now verse forms but originally were names for dance songs with refrains. **950 furye dooth in hell,** typically, the classical Furies were figures of punishment, but Chaucer presents them as tormented, perhaps influenced by Dante, *Inferno* 9.37–51. **951–52 Ekko/For Narcisus,** refused love by Narcissus, the nymph Echo faded away to a mere voice; Ovid, *Metamorphoses* 3.353–400 and elsewhere.

[Handwritten margin notes: "Lets the clerks decide if the rocks were created for harm."; "The squire tempts her"; "Squire falls in love w/ her"; "He'll look @ her and sign"]

Nathelees it happed°, er they thennes° wente, 960
By cause that he was hire neighebour,
And was a man of worship° and honour,
And hadde° yknowen hym of tyme yoore°,
They fille in speche; and forthe moore° and
    moore
Unto his purpos drough° Aurelius, 965
And whan he saugh his tyme, he seyde thus:
   "Madame," quod he, "by God that this world
    made,
So° that I wiste it myghte youre herte glade°,
I wolde° that day that youre Arveragus
Wente over the see, that I, Aurelius, 970
Hadde went ther° nevere I sholde have come
    agayn.
For wel I woot° my servyce is in vayn;
My gerdon° is but brestyng° of myn herte.
Madame, reweth° upon my peynes smerte°,
For with a word ye may me sleen° or save. 975
Heere at youre feet God wolde° that I were grave°!
I ne have as now no leyser° moore to seye;
Have mercy, sweete, or ye wol do me deye!"
   She gan to looke upon Aurelius:
"Is this youre wyl°," quod she, "and sey ye
    thus? 980
Nevere erst°," quod she, "ne wiste I what ye mente.
But now, Aurelie, I knowe youre entente,
By thilke° God that yaf° me soule and lyf
Ne shal I nevere been untrewe wyf
In word ne werk, as fer as I have wit. 985
I wol been his to whom that I am knyt°.
Taak this for fynal answere as of me."
But after that in pley thus seyde she:
   "Aurelie," quod she, "by heighe God above,
Yet wolde I graunte yow to been youre love, 990
Syn° I yow se° so pitously complayne°.
Looke° what day that endelong° Britayne
Ye remoeve alle the rokkes, stoon by stoon,
That they ne lette° ship ne boot to goon—

I seye, whan ye han maad the coost so clene 995
Of rokkes that ther nys no stoon ysene°,
Thanne wol I love yow best of any man.
Have heer my trouthe° in al that evere I kan°."
   "Is ther noon oother grace° in yow?" quod he.
   "No, by that Lord," quod she, "that maked
    me! 1000
For wel I woot° that it shal never bityde°.
Lat swiche° folies out of youre herte slyde°.
What deyntee° sholde a man han in his lyf
For to go love another mannes wyf,
That hath hir body whan so that hym liketh?" 1005
   Aurelius ful ofte soore siketh°;
Wo was Aurelie whan that he this herde,
And with a sorweful herte he thus answerde:
   "Madame," quod he, "this were an inpossible°.
Thanne moot I dye° of sodeyn deth horrible." 1010
And with that word he turned hym anon°.
Tho° coome hir othere freendes many oon
And in the aleyes° romeden up and doun,
And nothyng wiste° of this conclusioun,
But sodeynly bigonne revel° newe 1015
Til that the brighte sonne loste his hewe,
For th'orisonte hath reft° the sonne his lyght—
This is as muche to seye as it was nyght.
And hoom they goon in joye and in solas°,
Save° oonly wrecche Aurelius, allas! 1020
He to his hous is goon with sorweful herte.
He seeth° he may nat fro his deeth asterte°;
Hym semed that he felte his herte colde°.
Up to the hevene his handes he gan holde,
And on his knowes° bare he sette hym doun, 1025
And in his ravyng seyde his orisoun°.
For verray° wo out of his wit he breyde°.
He nyste° what he spak, but thus he seyde;
With pitous herte his pleynt° hath he bigonne
Unto the goddes, and first unto the sonne: 1030
   He seyde, "Appollo, god and governour
Of every plaunte, herbe, tree, and flour,

---

960 **happed,** *happened,* **thennes,** *from there* 962 **worship,** *reputation* 963 **hadde,** (she) *had,* **of tyme yoore,** *for a long time* 964 **moore,** *closer* 965 **drough,** *drew* 968 **So,** *if,* **glade,** *gladden* 969 **wolde,** *wish* 971 **went ther,** *gone where* 972 **woot,** *know* 973 **gerdon,** *reward,* **brestyng,** *bursting* 974 **reweth,** *have pity,* **smerte,** *sore* 975 **sleen,** *slay* 976 **God wolde,** *I wish to God,* **grave,** *buried* 977 **leyser,** *time* 980 **wyl,** *desire* 981 **erst,** *before* 983 **thilke,** *that,* **yaf,** *gave* 986 **knyt,** *wedded* (knitted) 991 **Syn,** *since,* **se,** *see,* **complayne,** *lament* 992 **Looke,** *consider,* **endelong,** *the entire length of* 994 **lette,** *hinder* 996 **ysene,** *seen* 998 **trouthe,** *pledge,*

kan, *am able* (to do) 999 **grace,** *kindness* 1001 **woot,** *know,* **bityde,** *happen* 1002 **swiche,** *such,* **slyde,** *pass* 1003 **deyntee,** *pleasure* 1006 **soore siketh,** *sighs sorely* 1009 **inpossible,** *impossibility* 1010 **moot I dye,** *must I die* 1011 **turned hym anon,** *turned himself away quickly* 1012 **Tho,** *then* 1013 **aleyes,** *paths* 1014 **wiste,** *knew* 1015 **bigonne revel,** *began revelry* 1017 **orisonte hath reft,** *horizon has stolen* 1019 **solas,** *pleasure* 1020 **Save,** *except* 1022 **seeth,** *sees that,* **asterte,** *escape* 1023 **colde,** *turn cold* 1025 **knowes,** *knees* 1026 **orisoun,** *prayer* 1027 **verray,** *true,* **breyde,** *leapt* 1028 **nyste,** *knew not* 1029 **pleynt,** *lament*

---

988 in pley, the phrase connotes much the same as in modern English, from "amiably" to "playfully" to "teasingly," all of which seem to qualify Dorigen's promise that follows. In romance tradition, rash promises usually come about when the promise maker is tricked or deceived; the impossibility of a task is another folk motif. **1031 Appollo,** Phoebus Apollo, god of the sun.

That yevest after thy declinacioun°
To ech of hem his tyme and his sesoun,
As thyn herberwe° chaungeth lowe or heighe,   1035
Lord Phebus, cast thy merciable eighe°
On wrecche Aurelie which that am but lorn°.
Lo, lord, my lady hath my deeth ysworn
Withoute gilt, but thy benignytee°
Upon my dedly° herte have som pitee.   1040
For wel I woot°, lord Phebus, if yow lest°,
Ye may me helpen, save° my lady, best.
Now voucheth sauf° that I may yow devyse°
How that I may been holpen° and in what wyse.

"Youre blisful suster, Lucina the sheene,   1045
That of the see° is chief goddesse and queene—
Though Neptunus have deitee° in the see,
Yet emperisse° aboven hym is she—
Ye knowen wel, lord, that right° as hir desir
Is to be quyked° and lightned of youre fir,   1050
For which she folweth yow ful bisily°,
Right° so the see desireth naturelly
To folwen hire, as she that is goddesse
Bothe in the see and ryveres moore and lesse°.
Wherfore, lord Phebus, this is my requeste—   1055
Do this miracle, or do myn herte breste°—
That now next at this opposicioun
Which in the signe shal be of the Leoun,
As preieth hire° so greet a flood° to brynge
That fyve fadme° at the leeste it oversprynge°   1060
The hyeste rokke in Armorik Briteyne;
And lat this flood endure yeres tweyne°.
Thanne certes to my lady may I seye,
'Holdeth° youre heste°, the rokkes been aweye.'

"Lord Phebus, dooth this miracle for me.   1065
Preye° hire she go no faster cours than ye;
I seye, preyeth youre suster that she go
No faster cours than ye thise yeres two.
Thanne shal she been evene atte fulle alway,

And spryng flood laste bothe nyght and day.   1070
And but° she vouchesauf° in swich manere
To graunte me my sovereyn lady deere,
Prey hire to synken every rok adoun
Into hir owene dirke regioun
Under the ground ther° Pluto dwelleth inne,   1075
Or nevere mo shal I my lady wynne.
Thy temple in Delphos wol I barefoot seke°.
Lord Phebus, se the teeris on my cheke,
And of my peyne have som compassioun."
And with that word in swowne° he fil adoun,   1080
And longe tyme he lay forth in a traunce.

His brother, which that knew of his penaunce°,
Up caughte hym, and to bedde he hath hym
     broght.
Dispeyred° in this torment and this thoght
Lete I this woful creature lye;   1085
Chese he, for me°, wheither he wol lyve or dye.

Arveragus, with heele° and greet honour,
As he that was of chivalrie the flour°,
Is comen hoom, and othere worthy men.
O blisful artow° now, thou Dorigen,   1090
That hast thy lusty housbonde in thyne armes,
The fresshe knyght, the worthy man of armes,
That loveth thee as his owene hertes lyf.
No thyng list hym to been ymaginatyf°
If any wight hadde spoke, whil he was oute,   1095
To hire of love; he hadde of it no doute.
He noght entendeth° to no swich mateere,
But daunceth, justeth°, maketh hire good cheere.
And thus in joye and blisse I let hem dwelle,
And of the sike Aurelius I wol yow telle.   1100

In langour° and in torment furyus
Two yeer and moore lay wrecche Aurelyus
Er any foot he myghte on erthe gon°;
Ne confort in this tyme hadde he noon
Save of his brother, which that was a clerk°.   1105

1033 yevest after thy declinacioun, *give according to your angle above the equator* **1035 herberwe,** *house* (in the zodiac) **1036 merciable eighe,** *merciful eye* **1037 lorn,** *lost* **1039 thy benignytee,** (may) *your goodness* **1040 dedly,** *deadlike* **1041 woot,** *know,* **lest,** *wish* **1042 save,** *besides* **1043 voucheth sauf,** *grant,* **yow devyse,** *explain to you* **1044 holpen,** *helped* **1046 see,** *sea* **1047 have deitee,** *has rule* **1048 emperisse,** *empress* **1049 right,** *just* **1050 quyked,** *brought to life* **1051 bisily,** *intently* **1052 Right,** *just* **1054 moore and lesse,** *greater and lesser* **1056 breste,** *burst* **1059 As preieth hire,** *so ask her,* **flood,** *tide* **1060**

fadme, *fathoms* (six feet), **oversprynge,** *rise above* **1062 yeres tweyne,** *two years* **1064 Holdeth,** *keep,* **heste,** *promise* **1066 Preye,** *ask* **1071 but, unless,** **vouchesauf,** *agrees* **1075 ther,** *where* **1077 seke,** *seek* **1080 swowne,** *a faint* **1082 penaunce,** *suffering* **1084 Dispeyred,** *hopeless* **1086 Chese he, for me,** *he can choose, as far as I'm concerned* **1087 heele,** *health* **1088 flour,** *flower* **1090 artow,** *are you* **1094 No thyng list hym to been ymaginatyf,** *he was not at all inclined to wonder* **1097 noght entendeth,** *pays no attention* **1098 justeth,** *jousts* **1101 langour, affliction* **1103 gon,** *walk* **1105 clerk,** *scholar*

1045 Lucina the sheene, Luna the beautiful, goddess of the moon and controller of tides. **1047 Neptunus,** Neptune, god of the sea. **1050 The moon reflects the light of the sun. 1057–58 opposicioun . . . Leoun,** opposition of sun and moon, in the sign of Leo. Tides are highest when the gravity of sun and moon pull together (in conjunction) or against each other (opposition). **1066 no faster cours,** the moon appears to travel faster than the sun through the sky; Aurelius asks that they travel at the same speed to maintain their opposition, keep the moon full, and keep the tide high. **1074 hir owene dirke regioun,** her own dark region, the underworld. The moon goddess was recognized in two other manifestations: Diana, goddess of the hunt, and Hecate, goddess of the underworld. **1075 Pluto,** god of the underworld. **1077 Delphos,** Delphi, Apollo's most famous temple.

He knew of al this wo and al this werk°,
For to noon oother creature, certeyn,
Of this matere he dorste° no word seyn.
Under his brest he baar it moore secree
Than evere dide Pamphilus for Galathee. 1110
His brest was hool withoute° for to sene,
But in his herte ay° was the arwe kene°.
And wel ye knowe that of a sursanure°
In surgerye is perilous the cure,
But° men myghte touche the arwe or come
    therby°. 1115
His brother weep and wayled pryvely°
Til atte laste hym fil in remembraunce°
That whiles he was at Orliens in Fraunce,
As yonge clerkes that been lykerous°
To reden° artes that been curious° 1120
Seken° in every halke° and every herne°
Particuler° sciences for to lerne,
He hym remembred that upon a day
At Orliens in studie a book he say°
Of magyk natureel°, which his felawe, 1125
That was that tyme a bacheler of lawe—
Al were he° ther to lerne another craft—
Hadde prively upon his desk ylaft°.
Which book spak muchel° of the operaciouns
Touchynge the eighte and twenty mansiouns 1130
That longen° to the moone, and swich folye°
As in oure dayes is nat worth a flye,
For hooly chirches feith in oure bileve°
Ne suffreth noon° illusioun us to greve°.
And whan this book was in his
    remembraunce, 1135
Anon for joye his herte gan to daunce,
And to hymself he seyde pryvely:
"My brother shal be warisshed° hastily,
For I am siker° that ther be sciences
By whiche men make diverse apparences° 1140
Swiche° as thise subtile tregetoures pleye°.
For ofte at feestes have I wel herd seye

That tregetours withinne an halle large
Have maad come in a water and a barge,
And in the halle rowen up and doun. 1145
Somtyme hath semed come a grym leoun;
And somtyme floures sprynge as in a mede°;
Somtyme a vyne and grapes white and rede;
Somtyme a castel, al of lym° and stoon;
And whan hym lyked°, voyded it anon°. 1150
Thus semed it to every mannes sighte.
    "Now thanne conclude I thus, that if I myghte
At Orliens som oold felawe° yfynde
That hadde thise moones mansions in mynde,
Or oother magyk natureel above, 1155
He sholde wel make my brother han° his love.
For with an apparence° a clerk may make
To mannes sighte that alle the rokkes blake
Of Britaigne weren yvoyded everichon°,
And shippes by the brynke° comen and gon, 1160
And in swich forme° enduren a wowke° or two.
Thanne were my brother warisshed° of his wo;
Thanne moste she nedes holden hire biheste°,
Or elles he shal shame hire atte leeste."
    What sholde I make a lenger tale of this? 1165
Unto his brotheres bed he comen is,
And swich confort he yaf° hym for to gon
To Orliens that he up stirte° anon
And on his wey forthward thanne is he fare°
In hope for to been lissed° of his care. 1170
    Whan they were come almoost to that citee,
But if it were a° two furlong° or thre,
A yong clerk romynge by hymself they mette,
Which that° in Latyn thriftily° hem grette°,
And after that he seyde a wonder thyng: 1175
"I knowe," quod he, "the cause of youre comyng."
And er they ferther any foote wente,
He told hem al that was in hire entente.
    This Briton° clerk hym asked of felawes°
The whiche that he had knowe in olde
    dawes°, 1180

1106 **werk**, *matter* 1108 **dorste**, *dared* 1111 **hool withoute**, *whole on the outside* 1112 **ay**, *always*, **arwe keen**, *sharp arrow* 1113 **sursanure**, *superficially healed wound* 1115 **But**, *unless*, **arwe**, *arrowhead*, **come therby**, *get at it* 1116 **pryvely**, *in secret* 1117 **fil in remembraunce**, *recalled* 1119 **lykerous**, *eager* 1120 **reden**, *study*, **curious**, *arcane* 1121 **Seken**, *seek*, **halke**, *nook*, **herne**, *corner* 1122 **Particuler**, *specialized* 1124 **say**, *saw* 1125 **magyk natureel**, *astrology* 1127 **Al were he**, *although he was* 1128 **ylaft**, *left* 1129 **spak muchel**, *said much* 1131 **longen**, *pertain*, **swich folye**, *such folly* 1133 **bileve**, *creed* 1134 **Ne suffreth noon**, *allows no*, **greve**, *afflict* 1138 **warisshed**, *healed* 1139 **siker**, *certain* 1140 **ap-**

parences, *apparitions* 1141 **Swiche**, *such*, **tregetoures pleye**, *magicians produce* 1147 **mede**, *meadow* 1149 **lym**, *mortar* 1150 **hym lyked**, (it) *pleased* (the magician), **voyded it anon**, (he) *sent it away at once* 1153 **felawe**, *companion* 1156 **han**, *have* 1157 **apparence**, *illusion* 1159 **yvoyded everichon**, *all removed* 1160 **brynke**, *coast* 1161 **swich forme**, *such appearance*, **wowke**, *week* 1162 **warisshed**, *healed* 1163 **biheste**, *promise* 1167 **yaf**, *gave* 1168 **up stirte**, *leapt up* 1169 **fare**, *gone* 1170 **lissed**, *relieved* 1172 **But if it were a**, *except for*, **furlong**, *eighth of a mile* 1174 **Which that**, *who*, **thriftily**, *suitably*, **grette**, *greeted* 1179 **Briton**, *Breton*, **felawes**, *companions* 1180 **dawes**, *days*

1110 **Pamphilus for Galathee,** Pamphilus yearns for and seduces Galatea in the popular thirteenth-century Latin poem *Pamphilus de Amore.* 1118 **Orliens,** Orleans, site of a famous university in the Middle Ages. 1130 **eighte and twenty mansiouns,** the twenty-eight positions in the lunar month. 1174 **Latyn,** Latin, the international language of scholars and universities in medieval Europe.

And he answerde hym that they dede were,
For which he weep ful ofte many a teere.
    Doun of his hors Aurelius lighte anon°,
And with this magicien forth is he gon
Hoom to his hous, and maden hem wel
    at ese. 1185
Hem lakked° no vitaille° that myghte hem plese.
So wel arrayed hous as ther was oon°
Aurelius in his lyf saugh nevere noon.
    He shewed hym, er he wente to sopeer°,
Forestes, parkes ful of wilde deer: 1190
Ther saugh he hertes° with hir hornes hye°,
The gretteste that evere were seyn with eye.
He saugh of hem an hondred slayn with houndes,
And somme with arwes blede of bittre woundes.
    He saugh, whan voyded° were thise wilde
    deer, 1195
Thise fauconers upon° a fair ryver
That with hir haukes han the heron slayn.
    Tho saugh° he knyghtes justyng in° a playn.
And after this he dide hym swich plesaunce°
That he hym shewed his lady on a daunce, 1200
On which hymself he daunced, as hym thoughte.
And whan this maister that this magyk wroughte°
Saugh it was tyme, he clapte his handes two,
And farewel, al oure revel was ago°.
    And yet remoeved they nevere out of the
    hous 1205
Whil they saugh al this sighte merveillous,
But in his studie, ther as his bookes be,
They seten stille, and no wight° but they thre.
    To hym this maister called his squier
And seyde hym thus: "Is redy oure soper? 1210
Almoost an houre it is, I undertake°,
Sith° I yow bad oure soper for to make,
Whan that thise worthy men wenten with me
Into my studie, ther as my bookes be."
    "Sire," quod this squier, "whan it liketh
    yow, 1215
It is al redy, though ye wol right now."

    "Go we thanne soupe°," quod he, "as for the
    beste.
Thise amorous folk somtyme moote han° hir
    reste."
    At after-soper fille they in tretee°
What somme° sholde this maistres gerdon° be 1220
To remoeven alle the rokkes of Britayne,
And eek from Gerounde to the mouth of Sayne.
    He made it straunge°, and swoor, so God hym
    save,
Lasse than a thousand pound he wolde nat have,
Ne gladly for that somme he wolde nat goon°. 1225
    Aurelius, with blisful herte anoon,
Answerde thus: "Fy on a thousand pound!
This wyde world, which that men seye is round,
I wolde it yeve° if I were lord of it.
This bargayn is ful dryve°, for we been knyt°. 1230
Ye shal be payed trewely, by my trouthe.
But looketh° now, for no necligence or slouthe°
Ye tarie° us heere no lenger than to-morwe."
    "Nay," quod this clerk, "have heer my feith to
    borwe°."
    To bedde is goon Aurelius whan hym
    leste°, 1235
And wel ny° al that nyght he hadde his reste.
What for his labour and his hope of blisse,
His woful herte of penaunce° hadde a lisse°.
    Upon the morwe whan that it was day
To Britaigne tooke they the righte° way, 1240
Aurelius and this magicien bisyde,
And been descended ther° they wolde abyde.
And this was, as thise bookes me remembre°,
The colde, frosty seson of Decembre.
    Phebus wax° old and hewed lyk latoun°, 1245
That in his hoote declynacioun°
Shoon as the burned° gold with stremes brighte;
But now in Capricorn adoun he lighte°,
Where as he shoon ful pale, I dar wel seyn.
The bittre frostes, with the sleet and reyn, 1250
Destroyed hath the grene in every yerd.

1183 lighte anon, *alighted soon* **1186 Hem lakked,** *they lacked,* **vitaille,** *food* **1187 as ther was oon,** i.e., *as this one* **1189 sopeer,** *supper* **1191 hertes,** *harts,* **hornes hye,** *tall antlers* **1195 voyded,** *removed* **1196 fauconers upon,** *falconers near* **1198 Tho saugh,** *then saw,* **justyng in,** *jousting on* **1199 swich plesaunce,** *such pleasure* **1202 wroughte,** *worked* **1204 ago,** *gone* **1208 wight,** *creature* **1211 undertake,** *declare* **1212 Sith,** *since* **1217 soupe,** *to dine* **1218 moote han,** *must have* **1219 tretee,** *negotiation* **1220 somme,** *sum,* **maistres gerdon,** *master's payment* **1223 straunge,** *difficult* **1225 goon,** *go (with them)* **1229 yeve,** *give* **1230 ful dryve,** *completed,* **knyt,** *agreed* **1232 looketh,** *make sure,* **slouthe,** *laziness* **1233 tarie,** *delay* **1234 to borwe,** *in pledge* **1235 hym leste,** *he pleases* **1236 wel ny,** *nearly* **1238 of penaunce,** *from sorrow,* **lisse,** *release* **1240 righte,** *most direct* **1242 been descended ther,** *dismounted where* **1243 me remembre,** *remind me* **1245 Phebus wax,** *the sun grew,* **hewed lyk latoun,** *colored like brass* **1246 hoote declynacioun,** *summertime position* **1247 burned,** *burnished* **1248 adoun he lighte,** *he descends*

1204 al oure revel was ago, all or entertainment was gone; compare Shakespeare's *Tempest* 4.1.148. **1222 Gerounde . . . Sayne,** the rivers Gironde and Seine, marking a coastline that includes much of western France. **1224 thousand pound,** a very large sum of money. **1248 in Capricorn,** the sun descends into the zodiacal sign of Capricorn (the Goat) at the beginning of winter.

Janus sit by the fyr with double berd
And drynketh of his bugle horn° the wyn.
Biforn hym stant° brawen of the tusked swyn,
And "Nowel" crieth every lusty° man.   1255
 Aurelius in al that evere he kan
Dooth to this maister chiere and reverence°,
And preyeth° hym to doon his diligence°
To bryngen hym out of his peynes smerte°,
Or with a swerd that he wolde slitte his herte°.   1260
 This subtil clerk swich routhe° had of this man
That nyght and day he spedde hym that he kan°
To wayten° a tyme of his conclusioun°—
This is to seye, to maken illusioun
By swich an apparence of jogelrye°   1265
(I ne kan no° termes of astrologye)
That she and every wight sholde wene° and seye
That of Britaigne the rokkes were aweye,
Or ellis they were sonken under grounde.
So atte laste he hath his tyme yfounde   1270
To maken his japes° and his wrecchednesse
Of swich a supersticious cursednesse.
His tables Tolletanes forth he brought,
Ful wel corrected; ne ther lakked nought,
Neither his collect ne his expans yeeris,   1275
Ne his rootes, ne his othere geeris°,
As been his centris and his argumentz,
And his proporcioneles convenientz
For his equaciouns in everythyng.
And by his eighte speere in his wirkyng°   1280

He knew ful wel how fer Alnath was shove
Fro° the heed of thilke fixe° Aries above,
That in the ninthe speere considered is;
Ful subtilly he kalkuled° al this.
 Whan he hadde founde his firste
  mansioun°,   1285
He knew the remenaunt° by proporcioun,
And knew the arisyng of his moone weel,
And in whos face°, and terme°, and everydeel°;
And knew ful weel the moones mansioun
Acordaunt to his° operacioun,   1290
And knew also his° othere observaunces°
For° swiche illusiouns and swiche meschaunces°
As hethen folk useden° in thilke° dayes.
For which no lenger maked he delayes,
But thurgh his magik, for a wyke° or tweye°,   1295
It semed that alle the rokkes were aweye.   ← *theyre gone*
 Aurelius, which that yet despeired is°
Wher° he shal han his love or fare amys°,
Awaiteth nyght and day on this myracle;
And whan he knew that ther was noon
  obstacle,   1300
That voyded° were thise rokkes everychon,
Doun to his maistres° feet he fil anon
And seyde, "I woful wrecche, Aurelius,
Thanke yow, lord, and lady myn Venus,
That me han holpen° fro my cares colde."   1305
And to the temple his wey forth hath he holde°,
Where as he knew he sholde his lady see.

[Right margin handwritten note: Takes a long time for the rocks' appearance to disappear]

1253 bugle horn, *drinking horn* **1254 stant,** *stands* **1255 lusty,** *cheerful* **1257 Dooth . . . chiere and reverence,** *entertains and honors* **1258 preyeth,** *asks,* **diligence,** *best* **1259 peynes smerte,** *sharp pains* **1260 slitte his herte,** *commit suicide* **1261 swich routhe,** *such pity* **1262 spedde hym that he kan,** *hastened so that he might be able* **1263 wayten,** *determine,* **conclusioun,** *calculations* **1265 apparence of jogelrye,** *apparition of conjuring* **1266 ne kan no,** *know no* **1267 wene,** *believe* **1271 japes,** *tricks* **1276 geeris,** *equipment* **1280 wirkyng,** *studying* **1282 Fro,** *by means of,* **thilke fixe,** *that fixed* **1284 kalkuled,** *calculated* **1285 mansioun,** *location* (of the moon) **1286 remenaunt,** *the other locations*

1288 whos face, *the first third of which constellation,* **terme,** *which of five unequal divisions of the constellations,* **everydeel,** *everything* **1290 Acordaunt to his,** *in relation to its* **1291 his,** *its* (the moon's), **observaunces,** *regular movements* **1292 For,** *for the purpose of,* **swiche meschaunces,** *such misdoings* **1293 useden,** *were accustomed to,* **thilke,** *those* **1295 wyke,** *week,* **tweye,** *two* **1297 despeired is,** *is in despair* **1298 Wher,** *whether,* **fare amys,** *go wrong* **1301 voyded,** *removed* **1302 maistres,** *master's* **1305 han holpen,** *have helped* **1306 hath he holde,** *has he taken*

1252 Janus, god of gateways with two bearded faces, one looking inward and the other outward; source of the name January. **1254–55 brawen of the tusked swyn . . . "Nowel,"** meat of the boar (the traditional Christmas feast features boar's head); noel is a traditional Christmas song. This portrait of the season has little to do with the plot; it may be a remnant of source material, most likely the narrative accompanying Menedon's fourth question in Boccaccio's *Filocolo,* where the magician makes a garden blossom in winter. **1273–74 tables Tolletanes . . . corrected,** astrological tables originally composed to be used in Toledo, Spain, but calibrated ("corrected") to other cities or locations. Chaucer's familiarity with astrology is evident in this passage, even though the Franklin protests that he knows nothing of the subject (line 1266). **1275 collect,** table recording the degrees of planetary motions in twenty-year periods. **expans yeeris,** table recording the degrees of planetary motions in a single year. **1276 rootes,** base dates from which planetary motions are calculated. **1277 centris,** table recording positions of planetary centers by minutes, days, hours, and minutes. **argumentz,** angles and arcs used in calculating planetary positions. **1278 proporcioneles convenientz,** uncertain, but perhaps table recording the degrees of planetary motions by fractional parts of years. **1279 equaciouns,** method of dividing heavenly sphere into equal sections. **1280–83 eighte speere . . . Alnath . . . Aries . . . ninthe speere,** i.e., he knew from its relation to the eighth sphere (fixed stars) how far the star Alnath had been moved in the head of the zodiacal sign of the Ram (Aries) that is thought to be in the ninth sphere (Primum Mobile). This movement marks the gradual westward shift of the equinoxes. **1288 whos face . . . terme . . . everydeel,** i.e., he knew when the moon would rise in the first third of which zodiacal sign, which division of those signs, and everything else.

And whan he saugh his tyme, anon-right° hee
With dredful° herte and with ful humble cheere°
Salewed hath° his sovereyn lady deere: 1310
  "My righte° lady," quod this woful man,
"Whom I moost drede° and love as I best kan,
And lothest were of al this world displese°,
Nere it° that I for yow have swich disese°
That I moste dyen heere at youre foot anon   1315
Noght wolde° I telle how me is wo bigon°.
But certes° outher° moste I dye or pleyne°;
Ye sle me giltelees for verray peyne°.
But of my deeth thogh that ye have no routhe°,
Avyseth yow er that° ye breke youre trouthe.   1320
Repenteth yow, for thilke° God above,
Er ye me sleen by cause that I yow love.
For, madame, wel ye woot° what ye han hight°—
Nat that I chalange° any thyng of right°
Of yow, my sovereyn lady, but youre grace°—   1325
But in a gardyn yond°, at swich a place,
Ye woot° right wel what ye bihighten° me,
And in myn hand youre trouthe plighten ye°
To love me best—God woot, ye seyde so,
Al be that° I unworthy am therto.   1330
Madame, I speke it for the honour of yow
Moore than to save myn hertes lyf right now.
I have do° so as ye comanded me,
And if ye vouchesauf°, ye may go see.
Dooth as yow list; have youre biheste° in
      mynde;   1335
For, quyk° or deed, right there ye shal me fynde.
In yow lith al to do° me lyve or deye—
But wel I woot° the rokkes been aweye."
  He taketh his leve, and she astoned° stood;
In al hir face nas a drope of blood.   1340
She wende° nevere han° come in swich a trappe.
"Allas," quod she, "that evere this sholde happe°!
For wende I nevere by possibilitee

That swich a monstre° or merveille myghte be.
It is agayns the proces of nature."   1345
And hoom she goth a sorweful creature.
For verray feere unnethe° may she go°.
She wepeth, wailleth, al a day or two,
And swowneth that° it routhe° was to see.
But why it was to no wight° tolde shee,   1350
For° out of towne was goon Arveragus.
But to hirself she spak and seyde thus,
With face pale and with ful sorweful cheere°,
In hire compleynt°, as ye shal after heere:
  "Allas," quod she, "on thee, Fortune, I
      pleyne°,   1355
That unwar° wrapped hast me in thy cheyne°,
Fro which t'escape woot° I no socour°
Save oonly deeth or elles dishonour;
Oon of thise two bihoveth° me to chese°.
But nathelees, yet have I levere° to lese   1360
My lif than of my body to have a shame,
Or knowe myselven fals, or lese my name°;
And with my deth I may be quyt°, ywis°.
Hath ther nat many a noble wyf er this,
And many a mayde, yslayn hirself, allas,   1365
Rather than with hir body doon trespas?
  "Yis, certes°, lo, thise stories beren witnesse.
Whan thritty tirauntz° ful of cursednesse
Hadde slayn Phidon in Atthenes atte feste°,
They comanded his doghtres for t'areste°,   1370
And bryngen hem biforn hem in despit°,
Al naked, to fulfille hir foul delit,
And in hir fadres° blood they made hem daunce
Upon the pavement, God yeve° hem
      myschaunce°!
For which thise woful maydens, ful of drede,   1375
Rather than they wolde lese hir maydenhede°,
They prively been stirt° into a welle
And dreynte° hemselven, as the bookes telle.

1308 anon-right, *at once* **1309 dredful,** *fearful,* **cheere,** *manner* **1310 Salewed hath,** *has greeted* **1311 righte,** *true* **1312 moost drede,** *must fear* **1313 lothest . . . displese,** *most reluctant to displease* **1314 Nere it,** *were it not,* **disese,** *pain* **1316 Noght wolde,** *not at all would,* **wo bigon,** *in such woe* **1317 certes,** *surely,* **outher,** *either,* **pleyne,** *lament* **1318 verray peyne,** *true pain* **1319 routhe,** *pity* **1320 Avyseth yow er that,** *consider before* **1321 thilke,** *that* **1323 woot,** *know,* **hight,** *promised* **1324 chalange,** *claim,* **of right,** *as a right* **1325 youre grace,** (by) *your favor* **1326 yond,** *yonder* **1327 woot,** *know,* **bihighten,** *promised* **1328 youre trouthe plighten ye,** *you pledged your truth* **1330 Al be that,** *even though* **1333 do,** *done* **1334 vouchesauf,** *consent* **1335 biheste,** *promise* **1336 quyk,** *alive* **1337 lith al to do,** *lies all to make* **1338 woot,** *know* **1339**

astoned, *astonished* **1341 wende,** *thought,* **han,** *to have* **1342 happe, happen* **1344 monstre,** *wonder* **1347 unnethe,** *hardly, go, walk* **1349 swowneth that,** *faints so that,* **routhe,** *pity* **1350 why . . . tolde shee,** (the reason) *why she told no one was* **1351 For,** *because* **1353 cheere,** *manner* **1354 compleynt,** *lament* **1355 pleyne,** *complain* **1356 unwar,** *unexpectedly,* **cheyne,** *chain* **1357 woot,** *know,* **socour,** *help* **1359 bihoveth,** *is necessary for,* **chese,** *choose* **1360 have I levere,** *I would prefer* **1362 name,** *reputation* **1363 quyt,** *free,* **ywis,** *surely* **1367 certes,** *surely* **1368 thritty tirauntz,** *thirty tyrants* **1369 feste,** *feast* **1370 for t'areste,** *to be arrested* **1371 despit,** *scorn* **1373 hir fadres,** *their father's* **1374 yeve,** *give,* **myschaunce,** *ill fate* **1376 Rather . . . maydenhede,** i.e., *to preserve their virginity* **1377 prively been stirt,** *secretly jumped* **1378 dreynte,** *drowned*

1369–78 Phidon . . . , this account and the twenty-two that follow are all from Jerome, *Epistola adversus Jovinianum* (here 1.41; see *WBP* 3.3n), although Chaucer rearranges the order. Some critics think the reordering and sheer number produce comedy or bathos, whereas others assess them as a reflection of Dorigen's psychology or as a rhetorical set piece.

"They of° Mecene leete enquere and seke°
Of Lacedomye fifty maydens eke°,   1380
On whiche they wolden doon hir lecherye.
But was ther noon of al that compaignye
That she nas slayn°, and with a good entente
Chees° rather for to dye than assente
To been oppressed of hir maydenhede°.   1385
Why sholde I thanne to dye been in drede?
    "Lo, eek the tiraunt Aristoclides,
That loved a mayden heet° Stymphalides,
Whan that hir fader slayn was on a nyght,
Unto Dianes temple goth she right°   1390
And hente the ymage° in hir handes two,
Fro which ymage wolde she nevere go.
No wight° ne myghte hir handes of it arace°
Til she was slayn right in the selve° place.
    "Now sith° that maydens hadden swich
        despit°   1395
To been defouled with mannes foul delit,
Wel oghte a wyf rather hirselven slee
Than be defouled, as it thynketh me.
    "What shal I seyn of Hasdrubales wyf
That at Cartage birafte° hirself hir lyf?   1400
For whan she saugh that Romayns wan the
        toun,
She took hir children alle and skipte° adoun
Into the fyr, and chees rather to dye
Than any Romayn dide° hire vileynye.
    "Hath nat Lucresse yslayn hirself, allas,   1405
At Rome whan that she oppressed° was
Of° Tarquyn, for hire thoughte it was a shame
To lyven whan that she had lost hir name°?
    "The sevene maydens of Melesie also
Han slayn hemself for verrey drede° and wo   1410

Rather than folk of Gawle hem sholde
        oppresse.
Mo° than a thousand stories as I gesse
Koude I now telle as touchynge this mateere.
    "Whan Habradate was slayn, his wyf so
        deere
Hirselven slow° and leet hir blood to glyde   1415
In Habradates woundes depe and wyde,
And seyde, 'My body, at the leeste way,
Ther shal no wight° defoulen, if I may.'
    "What sholde I mo ensamples heerof sayn,
Sith that° so manye han hemselven slayn   1420
Wel rather than they wolde defouled be?
I wol conclude that it is bet° for me
To sleen myself than been defouled thus.
I wol be trewe unto Arveragus,
Or rather sleen myself in som manere,   1425
As dide Demociones doghter deere
By cause that she wolde nat defouled be.
    "O Cedasus, it is ful greet pitee
To reden how thy doghtren° deyde, allas,
That slowe hemself° for swich a manere cas°.   1430
    "As greet a pitee was it, or wel moore,
The Theban mayden that for Nichanore
Hirselven slow right for swich manere wo.
    "Another Theban mayden dide right so°
For oon of Macidonye hadde hire oppressed;   1435
She with hire deeth hir maydenhede
        redressed°.
    "What shal I seye of Nicerates wyf
That for swich cas birafte° hirself hir lyf?
How trewe eek was to Alcebiades
His love, that rather for to dyen chees°   1440
Than for to suffre° his body unburyed be.

1379 They of, *the men of,* **leete enquere and seke,** *did request and select* **1380 eke,** *also* **1383 nas slayn,** *did not die* **1384 Chees,** *chose* **1385 oppressed of hir maydenhede,** *raped* **1388 heet,** *called* **1390 right,** *directly* **1391 hente the ymage,** *clung to the statue* **1393 wight,** *person,* **arace,** *tear away* **1394 selve,** *same* **1395 sith,** *since,* **swich despit,** *such scorn* **1400 birafte,** *deprived* **1402 skipte,** *leapt* **1404 Than . . . dide,** *than* (let) . . . *do* **1406 oppressed,** *raped* **1407 Of,** *by* **1408 name,**

reputation 1410 verrey drede, *true fear* **1412 Mo,** *more* **1415 slow,** *slew* **1418 wight,** *man* **1420 Sith that,** *since* **1422 bet,** *better* **1429 doghtren,** *daughters* **1430 slowe hemself,** *slew themselves,* **swich a manere cas,** *this kind of situation* **1434 right so,** *the same* **1436 redressed,** *amended* **1438 swich cas birafte,** *such a situation deprived* **1440 chees,** *chose* **1441 suffre,** *allow*

1379–80 Mecene . . . Lacedomye, Jerome 1.41 reports that Messene and Sparta (Lacedaemonia) exchanged virgins in connection with religious ritual; one time, when the Spartans attempted rape, the Messenian virgins all committed suicide. **1387–94 Aristoclides . . . ,** follows the account in Jerome 1.41. **1390 Dianes temple,** Diana was goddess of virginity. **1399–1404 Hasdrubales wyf . . . ,** Jerome 1.43 reports that when the Roman Scipio conquered Carthage, the wife of King Hasdrubal burned herself and her children to escape capture; see *NPT* 7.3363–68. **1405–8 Lucresse,** unlike the preceding women, Lucretia killed herself after being raped (by Tarquinus); *LGW* 1680ff.; Jerome 1.46. **1409–11 Melesie . . . ,** Jerome 1.41 mentions the seven virgins of Melitus (Asia Minor) who commit suicide to escape the invading Galatians (**folk of Gawle,** line 1411); unattested elsewhere. **1414–18 Habradate . . . ,** Chaucer expands Jerome's account (1.45) by adding a quotation from Abradatas's wife (named Panthea). **1426 Demociones doghter,** the daughter of Demotion; Jerome 1.41. **1428 Cedasus,** Scedasus; Jerome 1.41. **1432 Theban mayden,** unnamed suicide, lusted after by Nicanor; Jerome 1.41. **1434 Another Theban mayden,** unnamed in Jerome 1.41; killed her Macedonian rapist and herself. **1437 Nicerates wyf,** wife of Niceratus, committed suicide to avoid rape; Jerome 1.44. **1439 Alcebiades,** after Alcibiades was killed, his concubine risked death to bury him; Jerome 1.44.

"Lo, which° a wyf was Alceste," quod she.
"What seith° Omer of goode Penalopee?
Al Grece knoweth of hire chastitee.
Pardee°, of Laodomya is writen thus, 1445
That whan at Troie was slayn Protheselaus,
No lenger wolde she lyve after his day.
"The same of noble Porcia telle I may;
Withoute Brutus koude she nat lyve,
To whom she hadde al hool hir herte yeve°. 1450
"The parfit wyf hod° of Arthemesie
Honured is thurgh al the barbarie°.
O Teuta, queene, thy wyfly chastitee
To alle wyves may a mirour bee.
The same thyng I seye of Bilyea, 1455
Of Rodogone, and eek Valeria."
Thus pleyned° Dorigen a day or tweye,
Purposynge° evere that she wolde deye.
But nathelees, upon the thridde nyght
Hoom cam Arveragus, this worthy knyght, 1460
And asked hire why that she weep so soore°,
And she gan wepen ever lenger the moore.
"Allas," quod she, "that evere I was born!
Thus have I seyd," quod she, "thus have I
sworn—"
And toold hym al as ye han herd bifore°; 1465
It nedeth nat reherce it yow namoore.
This housbonde with glad chiere° in freendly
wyse
Answerde and seyde as I shal yow devyse°,
"Is ther oght elles°, Dorigen, but this?"
"Nay, nay," quod she, "God helpe me so as
wys°! 1470
This is to muche, and it were Goddes° wille."
"Ye, wyf," quod he, "lat slepen that is stille.

It may be wel, paraventure°, yet today.
Ye shul youre trouthe° holden, by my fay°,
For God so wisly° have mercy upon me, 1475
I hadde wel levere ystiked for to be°,
For verray love which that I to yow have,
But if° ye sholde youre trouthe kepe and save.
Trouthe is the hyeste thyng that man may kepe."
But with that word he brast anon° to wepe, 1480
And seyde, "I yow forbede," up° peyne of deeth,
That nevere whil thee° lasteth lyf ne breeth
To no wight° telle thou of this aventure°.
As I may best I wol my wo endure,
Ne make no contenance of hevynesse°, 1485
That folk of yow may demen° harm or gesse."
And forth he cleped° a squier and a mayde:
"Gooth forth anon with Dorigen," he sayde,
"And bryngeth hire to swich a place anon."
They take hir leve and on hir wey they gon, 1490
But they ne wiste° why she thider° wente.
He nolde no wight tellen° his entente.
Paraventure° an heep° of yow, ywis°,
Wol holden hym a lewed° man in this,
That he wol putte his wyf in jupartie°. 1495
Herkneth° the tale er ye upon hire crie°.
She may have bettre fortune than yow semeth°;
And whan that ye han herd the tale, demeth°.
This squier, which that highte° Aurelius,
On Dorigen that was so amorus, 1500
Of aventure happed° hire to meete
Amydde° the toun, right in the quykkest strete°,
As she was bown° to goon the wey forth right
Toward the gardyn ther as she had hight°.
And he was to the gardyn-ward° also, 1505
For wel he spyed° whan she wolde go

1442 **which,** *such* 1443 **seith,** *says* 1445 **Pardee,** *by God* 1450 **yeve,** *given* 1451 **parfit wyf hod,** *perfect fidelity* 1452 **barbarie,** *heathen world* 1457 **pleyned,** *lamented* 1458 **Purposynge,** *intending* 1461 **weep so soore,** *wept so bitterly* 1465 **han herd biforn,** *have heard earlier* 1467 **glad chiere,** *joyful expression* 1468 **devyse,** *describe* 1469 **oght elles,** *nothing else* 1470 **so as wys,** *surely* 1471 **and it were Goddes,** *even if it is God's* 1473 **paraventure,** *perhaps* 1474 **trouthe,** *pledge,* **fay,** *faith* 1475 **God so wisly,** *(may) God surely* 1476 **wel levere ystiked for to be,** *much prefer to be stabbed* 1478 **But if,** *unless* 1480 **brast anon,** *burst at once* 1481 **forbede,** *forbid,* **up,** *upon* 1482 **thee,** *to you* 1483 **wight,** *person,* **aventure,** *incident* 1485 **make no contenance of hevynesse,** *give no appearance of sorrow* 1486 **demen,** *judge* 1487 **cleped,** *called* 1491 **ne wiste,** *did not know,* **thider,** *there* 1492 **nolde no wight tellen,** *did not want to tell anyone* 1493 **Paraventure,** *perhaps,* **an heep,** *many,* **ywis,** *surely* 1494 **lewed,** *ignorant* 1495 **jupartie,** *jeopardy* 1496 **Herkneth,** *listen to,* **er,** *before,* **upon hire crie,** *lament her* 1497 **yow semeth,** *seems to you* 1498 **demeth,** *judge* 1499 **highte,** *was called* 1501 **Of aventure happed,** *by chance happened* 1502 **Amydde,** *in the middle of,* **quykkest strete,** *liveliest street* 1503 **bown,** *preparing* 1504 **hight,** *promised* 1505 **to the gardyn-ward,** *(going) to the garden* 1506 **spyed,** *watched*

1442–45 **Alceste . . . Penalopee . . . Laodomya,** the three are mentioned together in Jerome 1.45: Alcestis offered her life for that of her husband, Admetus (see *LGWP* F510ff.); Penelope, loyal wife of Odysseus in Homer (**Omer,** line 1443); Laodamia wished not to outlive her husband, Protesilaus, when he was killed at Troy. 1448 **Porcia,** Portia could not live without her husband, Brutus; Jerome 1.46. 1451–53 **Arthemesie . . . Teuta,** mentioned together in Jerome 1.44. Artemisia, renowned for chastity, loved her husband even after he died. Teuta, queen of Illyrica, gained power through chastity. 1455–56 Lines found in two MSS only, probably from the margin of Chaucer's original. **Bilyea,** Bilia, famed for chastity and for tolerating her husband's bad breath; Jerome 1.46. **Rodogone,** Rhodogune killed her maid for recommending that she remarry; Jerome 1.45. **Valeria,** refused to remarry; Jerome 1.46. 1493–98 Lines found in the same two MSS as lines 1455–56.

Out of hir hous to any maner place.
But thus they mette, of aventure or grace°,
And he saleweth° hire with glad entente,
And asked of hire whiderward° she wente.   1510

    And she answerde, half as she were mad,
"Unto the gardyn, as myn housbonde bad°,
My trouthe° for to holde°, allas, allas!"

    Aurelius gan wondren on this cas°,
And in his herte hadde greet compassioun   1515
Of hire and of hire lamentacioun,
And of Arveragus, the worthy knyght,
That bad hire holden al that she had hight°,
So looth hym was° his wyf sholde breke hir
        trouthe;
And in his herte he caughte of this greet
        routhe°,   1520
Considerynge the beste on every syde,
That fro his lust° yet were hym levere abyde°
Than doon so heigh a cherlyssh° wrecchednesse
Agayns franchise° and alle gentillesse;
For which in fewe wordes seyde he thus: 1525
    "Madame, seyth to° youre lord Arveragus
That sith° I se his grete gentillesse
To yow, and eek I se wel youre distresse,
That him were levere han shame°—and that were
        routhe—
Than ye to me sholde breke thus youre
        trouthe,   1530
I have wel levere evere° to suffre wo
Than I departe° the love bitwix yow two.
I yow relesse°, madame, into youre hond
Quyt every serement° and every bond
That ye han maad to me as heerbiforn°,   1535
Sith thilke° tyme which that ye were born.
My trouthe° I plighte°, I shal yow never repreve°
Of no biheste°, and heere I take my leve
As of the treweste and the beste wyf
That evere yet I knew in al my lyf.   1540
But every wyf be war of hire biheeste;

On Dorigen remembreth atte leeste.
Thus kan a squier doon a gentil dede
As wel as kan a knyght, withouten drede°."
    She thonketh hym upon hir knees al bare,   1545
And hoom unto hir housbonde is she fare°,
And tolde hym al, as ye han herd me sayd;
And be ye siker°, he was so weel apayd°
That it were inpossible me to wryte.
What sholde I lenger of this cas endyte°?   1550
    Arveragus and Dorigen his wyf
In sovereyn blisse leden forth hir lyf.
Nevere eft° ne was ther angre hem bitwene.
He cherisseth hire as though she were a queene,
And she was to hym trewe for everemoore.   1555
Of thise two folk ye gete of me namoore.
    Aurelius, that his cost° hath al forlorn°,
Curseth the tyme that evere he was born:
"Allas," quod he, "allas that I bihighte°
Of pured° gold a thousand pound of wighte°   1560
Unto this philosophre. How shal I do?
I se namoore but that I am fordo°.
Myn heritage° moot I nedes° selle
And been a beggere. Heere may I nat dwelle
And shamen al my kynrede° in this place,   1565
But° I of hym may gete bettre grace°.
But nathelees, I wole of hym assaye°,
At certeyn dayes, yeer by yeer, to paye,
And thanke hym of his grete curteisye.
My trouthe wol I kepe, I wol nat lye."   1570
    With herte soor he gooth unto his cofre°,
And broghte gold unto this philosophre
The value of fyve hundred pound, I gesse,
And hym bisecheth of his gentillesse
To graunte hym dayes of the remenaunt°,   1575
And seyde, "Maister, I dar° wel make avaunt°,
I failled nevere of my trouthe° as yit.
For sikerly° my dette shal be quyt°
Towardes yow, howevere that I fare
To goon a-begged° in my kirtle° bare.   1580

1508 **of aventure or grace**, *by chance or providence* 1509 **saleweth**, *greets* 1510 **whiderward**, *where* 1512 **bad**, *directed* 1513 **trouthe**, *promise*, **holde**, *keep* 1514 **cas**, *situation* 1518 **hight**, *promised* 1519 **So looth hym was**, *so hateful (to) him (it) was (that)* 1520 **routhe**, *pity* 1522 **lust**, *desire*, **yet were hym levere abyde**, *he would rather refrain* 1523 **cherlyssh**, *churlish* 1524 **franchise**, *liberality* 1526 **seyth to**, *tell* 1527 **sith**, *since* 1529 **him were levere han shame**, *he would rather have shame* 1531 **have wel levere evere**, *much prefer always* 1532 **departe**, *separate* 1533 **relesse**, *release* 1534 **serement**, *oath* 1535 **as heerbiforn**, *before this* 1536 **Sith thilke**, *since that* 1537 **trouthe**, *word*, **plighte**, *pledge*, **repreve**, *accuse* 1538 **biheste**, *promise* 1544 **drede**, *doubt* 1546

is she fare, *she goes* 1548 **siker**, *certain*, **apayd**, *pleased* 1550 **cas endyte**, *situation compose* 1553 **eft**, *after* 1557 **cost**, *payment*, **forlorn**, *forfeited* 1559 **bihighte**, *promised* 1560 **pured**, *refined*, **wighte**, *weight* 1562 **fordo**, *destroyed* 1563 **heritage**, *inheritance*, **moot I nedes**, *I must necessarily* 1565 **kynrede**, *kindred* 1566 **But**, *unless*, **grace**, *favor* 1567 **assaye**, *try* 1570 **trouthe**, *pledge* 1571 **cofre**, *money chest* 1575 **dayes of the remenaunt**, *time to pay the remainder* 1576 **dar**, *dare*, **avaunt**, *boast* 1577 **trouthe**, *pledge* 1578 **sikerly**, *certainly*, **quyt**, *repaid* 1579–80 **howevere . . . a-begged**, *i.e., even if I have to go beg* 1580 **kirtle**, *undergarments*

1541–44 In two late MSS, these lines follow line 1550.

But wolde ye vouchesauf°, upon seuretee°,
Two yeer or thre for to respiten me°,
Thanne were I wel, for elles moot° I selle
Myn heritage; ther is namoore to telle."

   This philosophre sobrely answerde,   1585
And seyde thus, whan he thise wordes herde,
"Have I nat holden covenant° unto thee?"
   "Yes, certes, wel and trewely," quod he.
   "Hastow nat had thy lady as thee liketh?"
   "No, no," quod he, and sorwefully he
      siketh°.   1590
   "What was the cause? Tel me if thou kan."
   Aurelius his tale anon bigan,
And tolde hym al as ye han herd bifoore;
It nedeth nat to yow reherce it moore.
   He seide, "Arveragus, of gentillesse,   1595
Hadde levere° dye in sorwe and in distresse
Than that his wyf were of hir trouthe fals."
The sorwe of Dorigen he tolde hym als°,
How looth hire was to been° a wikked wyf,
And that she levere had° lost that day hir lyf,   1600
And that hir trouthe she swoor thurgh
     innocence,
She nevere erst° hadde herd speke of apparence°.

"That made me han of hire so greet pitee;
And right as frely as he sente hire me,
As frely sente I hire to hym ageyn.   1605
This al and som°; ther is namoore to seyn."
   This philosophre answerde, "Leeve° brother,
Everich° of yow dide gentilly til oother.
Thou art a squier, and he is a knyght;
But God forbede, for his blisful myght,   1610
But if° a clerk koude° doon a gentil dede
As wel as any of yow, it is no drede°.
   "Sire, I releesse thee thy thousand pound
As° thou right now were cropen° out of the
     ground
Ne nevere er now ne haddest knowen me.   1615
For, sire, I wol nat taken a peny of thee
For al my craft°, ne noght for my travaille°.
Thou hast ypayed wel for my vitaille°.
It is ynogh, and farewel, have good day."
And took his hors, and forth he goth his way.   1620
   Lordynges, this question, thanne, wol I aske
     now,
Which was the mooste fre°, as thynketh yow?
Now telleth me, er that ye ferther wende°.
I kan° namoore; my tale is at an ende.

Heere is ended the Frankeleyns Tale.

1581 **wolde ye vouchesauf,** *if you would consent,* **seuretee,** *security* 1582 **respiten me,** *grant me an extension* 1583 **elles moot,** *otherwise must* 1587 **holden covenant,** *kept my promise* 1590 **siketh,** *sighs* 1596 **Hadde levere,** *would rather* 1598 **als,** *also* 1599 **looth hire was to been,** *she would have hated to be* 1600 **levere had,** *would rather have*

1602 **erst,** *before,* **apparence,** *illusions* 1606 **This al and som,** *this is all of it* 1607 **Leeve,** *dear* 1608 **Everich,** *each* 1611 **But if,** *unless,* **koude,** *could* 1612 **drede,** *doubt* 1614 **As,** *as if,* **cropen,** *crept* 1617 **craft,** *skill,* **travaille,** *labor* 1618 **vitaille,** *food* 1622 **fre,** *noble* or *generous* 1623 **wende,** *travel* 1624 **kan,** *know*

1584 **Myn heritage,** presumably Aurelius does not want to sell inherited property that is the source of an annual income.

CANTERBURY TALES
PART 6

INTRODUCTION

ART 6 OF *The Canterbury Tales* focuses on death. The tellers of the paired tales are healers by profession: a physical healer, the Physician, and a spiritual healer, the Pardoner. There is, however, no healing in these tales, but death instead—not the deaths that result from epic battle, or tragic misfortune, or ideological struggle found elsewhere in *The Canterbury Tales,* but deaths that result from relatively naked vices (lechery and greed), with little or no evidence of honor, reward, or salvation. The moral categories of the tales appear to be stark, and death dominates the plots, seeming to invite easy interpretation. The experience of reading the tales, however, belies this ease and raises questions about the relation of virtue to reward, about tale-telling as a form of moral discourse, and about the relationship between the material world and the spiritual realm.

Derived from the *Roman de la Rose,* ultimately from Livy's *History of Rome,* the *Physician's Tale* is more disturbing morally and aesthetically than its predecessors. Livy uses it to exemplify degenerate justice in a straightforward exemplum. In the *Roman de la Rose,* the character Reason uses the plot to demonstrate that love is preferable to justice. In analogous versions by Gower and Boccaccio (of no apparent influence on Chaucer), the exemplum illustrates bad government. Chaucer suppresses the social and political concerns and heightens the contrast between virtue and the mortal power of vice. He adds prefatory material in praise of the protagonist's beauty and virginity, advises parental governance, and intensifies the personal relation of the father-daughter pair in the tale, Virginius and Virginia.

As a result, when Virginius slays Virginia to save her from the lechery of the judge, Appius, the act can be seen as more horrifying than exemplary or pathos ridden. Then, when Appius commits suicide after his lechery is disclosed and his henchman

Claudius is exiled instead of executed, the final message of the tale—forsake sin—seems only loosely applicable to these villains and not at all applicable to Virginius, much less Virginia. The tale is cast as an exemplum drawn from history (155–56), but its digressions threaten to overwhelm its plot, which itself seems unjust and unjustified by its moralization. By setting us such challenges, the tale can be seen to engage us in the process of seeking the purpose and efficacy of exemplary tales; see Anne Middleton, "The *Physician's Tale* and Love's Martyrs: 'Ensamples Mo Than Ten' as a Method in the *Canterbury Tales*" (1973, no. 1187). Various studies address the issues of virginity and violence in the tale, among them R. Howard Bloch's "Chaucer's Maiden's Head: *The Physician's Tale* and the Poetics of Virginity" (1989, no. 1175) and Sandra Pierson Prior's "Virginity and Sacrifice in Chaucer's *Physician's Tale*" (1999, no. 1189). The best available survey of critical approaches is in Helen Storm Corsa's Variorum edition of the tale (1987, no. 44), and see Emerson Brown's "What Is Chaucer Doing with the Physician and His Tale?" (1981, no. 1178).

Impersonal and dislocating, the *Physician's Tale* sets up various aspects of the Pardoner's stunningly personal performance: virginity is juxtaposed with suggestions of sterility, imitation of nature with hypocrisy, governance with unrestrained indulgence, physical with spiritual death. Both tales deal with the self-destructiveness of evil, but where the Physician asserts this as a moral platitude, the Pardoner effectively dramatizes the truism and embodies it himself.

Like the Wife of Bath, the Pardoner reveals his defects through a confessional mode in his *Prologue.* The inspiration is again the *Roman de la Rose,* this time Faus-Semblant (False Seeming or Hypocrisy, lines 11065ff.), who proclaims his own avarice, hypocrisy, and disdain for those who fear God. Chaucer naturalizes these attitudes as actions when the Pardoner tallies his past successes in selling relics and (after his tale) attempts to sell pardons to the pilgrim audience. Underlying such efforts is the Pardoner's willful, cynical disregard for the power of the spiritual gifts that he purveys. In Chaucer's time (and for believers today), relics mediate between the material and the spiritual realms; they embody holiness in material objects. Pardons (also called indulgences) remove the need for temporal punishment due for sin in order to pave the way to heavenly reward. In his knowing abuse of relics and pardons the Pardoner is on a headlong crash course with spiritual death.

Traffic in relics and pardons was a real danger to the church, because it had itself come to depend upon profits derived from them and because the essential connection between the material and the spiritual lay at the very core of its worldly mission. Through the Pardoner, Chaucer condemns the spiritual arrogance of refusing to acknowledge spiritual reality, and he explores how such transgression can threaten to corrupt the entire system. As Alan J. Fletcher has shown in "The Topical Hypocrisy of Chaucer's Pardoner" (1990, no. 1208), Wycliffite concerns with religious hypocrisy lend considerable dimension to the Pardoner's performance, and A. L. Kellogg and L. A. Haselmayer, "Chaucer's Satire on the Pardoner" (1951, no. 1217), long ago documented that the orthodox church was well aware of systemic dangers.

The rioters in the *Pardoner's Tale* believe that they can destroy death, a parody or perversion of Christian salvation by this unholy trinity. Unlike the Pardoner himself, they seem unaware of their blasphemy, and they fall easy and unwitting victims to their own greed. Along the way, they exemplify not only greed but also the so-called tavern vices against which the Pardoner preaches—oath taking, gluttony, and gambling—contributing to the power of the tale, often regarded as Chaucer's greatest success in brief narration.

No clear source has been identified for the tale, but worldwide analogues ranging from the Far East

to Africa and Hollywood (John Huston's *The Treasure of the Sierra Madre*) attest to the ironic power of the plot: we find death, or death finds us, when we least expect it, especially when distracted by vice. The Old Man is especially uncanny in Chaucer's version, elsewhere a more easily defined figure. Critics have read him as, among other suggestions, Death itself, Death's messenger, the Wandering Jew, a demon, and even a projection of the Pardoner's own psyche. The uncanny power of the Old Man to tug at the mind is perhaps best reflected in a pair of essays by Lee Patterson, who first attempts to psychoanalyze the Pardoner and later retracts his own analysis. See "Chaucerian Confession: Penitential Literature and the Pardoner" (1976, no. 1227) and "Chaucer's Pardoner on the Couch: Psyche and Clio in Medieval Literary Studies" (2001, no. 1228).

Perhaps the most vigorously debated crux of the *Pardoner's Prologue* and *Tale* is the Pardoner's offer to sell his wares to the pilgrims after admitting his own avarice and hypocrisy. Some critics read a self-destructive impulse here, whereas others find sheer arrogance, cynicism, and even despair. The offer provokes the Host's brutal response to the Pardoner, which with its threat of castration recalls the narrator's comment in the *General Prologue* that he believes the Pardoner may be a gelding or a mare (1.691)—that he may be sterile, a eunuch, or homosexual. Most critics find at least a touch of queerness in the scene, although Richard Firth Green has argued against this trend in "The Pardoner's Pants (and Why They Matter)" (1993, no. 1211). Monica A. McAlpine surveys the topic of the Pardoner's homosexuality in "The Pardoner's Homosexuality and How It Matters" (1980, no. 1220). For recent, theoretically charged approaches, see Robert S. Sturges's *Chaucer's Pardoner and Gender Theory* (2000, no. 1238) and Glenn Burger's *Chaucer's Queer Nation* (2003, no. 648).

CANTERBURY TALES
PART 6

PHYSICIAN'S TALE

Heere folweth the Phisiciens Tale.

Ther was, as telleth Titus Livius,
A knyght that called was Virginius,
Fulfild of honour and of worthynesse,
And strong of freendes and of greet richesse.

This knyght a doghter hadde by his wyf; 5
No children hadde he mo in al his lyf.
Fair was this mayde in excellent beautee
Aboven every wight° that man may see,
For Nature hath with sovereyn° diligence
Yformed hire in so greet excellence, 10
As though she wolde seyn, "Lo, I, Nature,
Thus kan I forme and peynte a creature
Whan that me list°. Who kan me countrefete°?
Pigmalion noght°, though he ay° forge° and bete°,
Or grave° or peynte, for I dar wel seyn 15

Apelles, Zanzis, sholde werche in veyn°
Outher° to grave or peynte or forge or bete,
If they presumed me to countrefete.
For He that is the formere principal°
Hath maked me his vicaire general, 20
To forme and peynten erthely creaturis
Right as me list°, and ech thyng in my cure° is
Under the moone that may wane and waxe°,
And for my werk right no thyng wol I axe°.
My lord and I been ful of oon accord°. 25
I made hire to the worship° of my lord.
So do I alle myne othere creatures,
What° colour that they han or what figures."
Thus semeth me that Nature wolde seye.

This mayde of age twelve yeer was and tweye°, 30

---

8 wight, *creature* **9 sovereyn,** *ultimate* **13 me list,** (it) *pleases me,* **countrefete,** *imitate* **14 noght,** (could) *not,* **ay,** *always,* **forge,** *shape in metal,* **bete,** *hammer* **15 grave,** *engrave* **16 werche in veyn,** *work in vain* **17 Outher,** *either* **19 formere principal,** *creator* **22 Right as me list,** *just as it pleases me,* **cure,** *care* **23 wane and waxe,** *decrease and increase* **24 axe,** *ask* **25 ful of oon accord,** *fully in agreement* **26 to the worship,** *in honor of* **28 What,** *whatever* **30 and tweye,** *plus two*

---

1 Titus Livius, Livy, Roman historian, the ultimate source of this story, although Chaucer adapted it from *RR* 5589ff. **14–16 Pigmalion . . . Apelles, Zanzis,** famous artists, mentioned together in a discussion of nature vs. art in *RR* 16177ff. **20 vicaire general,** general deputy, a common title for Nature, found, e.g., in *RR* 16782 and 19505 and elsewhere. **23 Under the moone,** below the moon, where all is natural, i.e., in the realm of Nature; above is the realm of the supernatural.

In which that° Nature hadde swich delit°.
For right as° she kan peynte a lilie whit
And reed a rose, right° with swich peynture°
She peynted hath this noble creature
Er she were born, upon hir lymes fre°,   35
Where as by right° swiche colours sholde be.
And Phebus° dyed hath hire tresses grete°
Lyk to the stremes° of his burned heete°.
And if that excellent was hire beautee,
A thousand foold moore vertuous was she.   40
In hire ne lakked no condicioun
That is to preyse, as by discrecioun°.
As wel in goost° as body chast was she,
For which she floured in virginitee
With alle humylitee and abstinence,   45
With alle attemperaunce° and pacience,
With mesure eek° of beryng° and array.
Discreet she was in answeryng alway,
Though° she were wis as Pallas, dar I seyn,
Hir facound° eek ful wommanly and pleyn.   50
No countrefeted° termes hadde she
To seme wys, but after° hir degree°
She spak, and alle hire wordes moore and lesse
Sownynge in° vertu and in gentillesse.
Shamefast° she was in maydens shamefastnesse,   55
Constant in herte, and evere in bisynesse
To dryve hire° out of ydel slogardye°.
Bacus hadde of hir mouth right no maistrie°;
For wyn and youthe dooth Venus° encresse
As° men in fyr wol casten oille or greesse°.   60
And of hir owene vertu, unconstreyned,
She hath ful ofte tyme syk hire feyned°
For that° she wolde fleen° the compaignye
Where likly was to treten of° folye,
As is at feestes, revels, and at daunces,   65
That been occasions of daliaunces°.
Swich thynges maken children for to be
To soone rype and boold, as men may se,

Which is ful perilous and hath been yoore°.
For al to soone may she lerne loore   70
Of booldnesse, whan she woxen is° a wyf.
   And ye maistresses°, in youre olde lyf,
That lordes doghtres han° in governaunce,
Ne taketh of my wordes no displesaunce°.
Thenketh° that ye been set in governynges   75
Of lordes doghtres oonly for two thynges°,
Outher for° ye han kept youre honestee,
Or elles ye han falle in freletee°
And knowen wel ynough the olde daunce°,
And han forsaken fully swich meschaunce°   80
For everemo; therfore for Cristes sake,
To teche hem vertu looke that ye ne slake°.
   A theef of venysoun° that hath forlaft°
His likerousnesse° and al his olde craft
Kan kepe a forest best of any man.   85
Now kepeth wel, for if ye wole°, ye kan.
Looke wel that ye unto no vice assente
Lest ye be dampned° for youre wikke entente,
For whoso dooth°, a traitour is certeyn.
And taketh kepe of° that that I shal seyn: 90
Of alle tresons sovereyn pestilence°
Is whan a wight bitrayseth° innocence.
   Ye fadres and ye moodres eek also,
Though° ye han children, be it oon or mo,
Youre° is the charge of al hire surveiaunce°   95
Whil that they been under youre governaunce.
Beth war if by ensample of youre lyvynge
Or by youre necligence in chastisynge
That they perisse°; for I dar wel seye
If that they doon ye shul it deere abeye°.   100
Under a shepherde softe and necligent
The wolf hath many a sheep and lamb torent°.
Suffiseth oon ensample° now as heere,
For I moot° turne agayn to my matere.
   This mayde, of which I wol this tale expresse, 105
So kepte hirself hir neded° no maistresse,

---

31 which that, *whom,* **swich delit,** *such delight* **32–33 right as . . . right,** *just as . . . so* **33 swich peynture,** *such painting* **35 lymes fre,** *noble limbs* **36 by right,** *appropriately* **37 Phebus,** *the sun,* **tresses grete,** *long hair* **38 stremes,** *rays,* **burned heete,** *burnished heat* **42 discrecioun,** *discrimination* **43 goost,** *spirit* **46 attemperaunce,** *temperance* **47 mesure eek, moderation also,** **beryng,** *manners* **49 Though,** *as though* **50 facound, way of speaking* **51 countrefeted,** *false* **52 after,** *in accord with,* **degree, social rank* **54 Sownynge in,** *resounding* **55 Shamefast,** *modest* **57 hire, herself,* **ydel slogardye,** *idle laziness* **58 right no maistrie,** *no dominance at all* **59 Venus,** *i.e., sexual desire* **60 As,** *as when,* **greesse, grease* **62 syk hire feyned,** *pretended illness* **63 For that,** *because,* **wolde fleen,** *wished to avoid* **64 treten of,** *deal with* **66 daliaunces,** *flirtation* **69 yoore,** *for a* long time **71 woxen is,** *has become* **72 maistresses,** *governesses* **73 han, have* **74 displesaunce,** *displeasure* **75 Thenketh,** *realize* **76 thynges,** *reasons* **77 Outher for,** *either because* **78 han falle in freletee,** *have fallen in frailty* **79 olde daunce,** *i.e., lovemaking* **80 meschaunce,** *misconduct* **82 ne slake,** *do not slacken* **83 theef of venysoun,** *deer poacher,* **forlaft, abandoned* **84 likerousnesse,** *evil hunger* **86 wole,** *wish to* **88 Lest ye be dampned,** *so you will not be damned* **89 whoso dooth,** *whoever does* **90 taketh kepe of,** *pay attention to* **91 sovereyn pestilence,** *the ultimate evil* **92 bitrayseth,** *betrays* **94 Though,** *since* **95 Youre,** *yours,* **surveiaunce, protection* **99 perisse,** *perish* **100 it deere abeye,** *pay for it dearly* **102 torent,** *torn to pieces* **103 Suffiseth oon ensample,** *one example suffices* **104 moot,** *must* **106 hir neded,** *for her (was) needed*

39–71 This idealized portrait of virtuous virginity reflects the tradition of the virgin martyr, here in implicit tension with the fecundity of Nature, as in *RR* 18999ff. **49 Pallas,** Pallas Athena, goddess of wisdom. **58 Bacus,** Bacchus, god of wine. **101–2** Proverbial.

For in hir lyvyng maydens myghten rede
As in a book every good word or dede
That longeth° to a mayden vertuous,
She was so prudent and so bounteuous°.   110
For which the fame out sprong on every syde
Bothe of hir beautee and hir bountee wyde,
That thurgh that land they preised hire echone°
That loved vertu, save Envye allone
That sory is of oother mennes wele°,   115
And glad is of his sorwe and his unheele°—
The doctour maketh this descripcioun.

   This mayde upon a day wente in the toun
Toward a temple, with hire mooder deere,
As is of yonge maydens the manere.   120

   Now was ther thanne a justice° in that toun
That governour was of that regioun.
And so bifel° this juge his eyen caste
Upon this mayde, avysynge hym ful faste°
As she cam forby ther as° this juge stood.   125
Anon his herte chaunged and his mood,
So was he caught with beautee of this mayde,
And so hymself ful pryvely he sayde,
"This mayde shal be myn, for° any man!"

   Anon the feend into his herte ran   130
And taughte hym sodeynly that he by slyghte
The mayden to his purpos wynne myghte.
For certes°, by no force ne by no meede°,
Hym thoughte, he was nat able for to speede°.
For she was strong of freendes° and eek she   135
Confermed was in swich soverayn bountee°
That wel he wiste° he myghte hire nevere wynne
As for to make hire with hir body synne.
For which, by° greet deliberacioun,
He sente after a cherl, was in the toun,   140
Which that he knew for subtil and for boold.
This juge unto this cherl his tale hath toold
In secree wise, and made hym to ensure°
He sholde telle it to no creature,
And if he dide, he sholde lese his heed.   145

[handwritten margin notes, partly illegible:] way in which her beauty is also responsible for destroying her — so who's at fault here? thinking to hi...

Whan that assented was this cursed reed°,
Glad was this juge, and maked him greet cheere°,
And yaf° hym yiftes precīouse and deere°.

   Whan shapen° was al hire° conspiracie
Fro point to point, how that his lecherie   150
Parfourned° sholde been ful subtilly°,
As ye shul heere it after openly,
Hoom gooth the cherl, that highte° Claudius.
This false juge, that highte Apius—
So was his name, for this is no fable°,   155
But knowen for historial° thyng notable;
The sentence° of it sooth° is out of doute—
This false juge gooth now faste aboute°
To hasten his delit al that he may.
And so bifel° soone after on a day   160
This false juge, as telleth us the storie,
As he was wont°, sat in his consistorie°,
And yaf° his doomes° upon sondry cas°.
This false cherl cam forth a ful greet pas°,
And seyde, "Lord, if that it be youre wille,   165
As dooth me right° upon this pitous bille°
In which I pleyne upon° Virginius;
And if that he wol seyn it is nat thus,
I wol it preeve° and fynde good witnesse
That sooth° is that° my bille wol expresse."   170

   The juge answerde, "Of this, in his absence,
I may nat yeve diffynytyve° sentence.
Lat do hym calle°, and I wol gladly heere.
Thou shalt have al right and no wrong heere."

   Virginius cam to wite° the juges wille,   175
And right anon was rad° this cursed bille.
The sentence of it was as ye shul heere:

   "To yow, my lord, sire Apius so deere,
Sheweth youre poure servant Claudius
How that a knyght, called Virginius,   180
Agayns the lawe, agayn al equitee°,
Holdeth, expres agayn° the wyl of me,
My servant, which that is my thral° by right,
Which fro myn hous was stole upon a nyght,

---

109 longeth, *pertains* **110 bounteuous,** *good* **113 echone,** *each one* **115 mennes wele,** *men's prosperity* **116 unheele,** *misfortune* **121 justice,** *judge* **123 bifel,** *it happened that* **124 avysynge hym ful faste,** *considering very intensely* **125 forby ther as,** *past where* **129 for,** *despite* **131 slyghte,** *deception* **133 certes,** *surely,* **meede,** *bribery* **134 speede,** *succeed* **135 strong of freendes,** i.e., *had powerful friends* **136 soverayn bountee,** *supreme goodness* **137 wiste,** *knew* **139 by,** *with* **143 made hym to ensure,** *made him promise* **146 reed,** *plan* **147 maked hym greet cheere,** i.e., *acted pleasantly toward him* **148 yaf,** *gave,* **deere,** *valuable* **149 shapen,** *planned,* **hire,** *their* **151 Parfourned,** *accomplished,* **subtilly,** *secretly* **153

highte, *was named* **155 fable,** *fiction* **156 historial,** *historical* **157 sentence,** *significance,* **sooth,** *true* **158 faste aboute,** *quickly all around* **160 bifel,** *it happened* **162 wont,** *accustomed,* **consistorie,** *court* **163 yaf,** *gave,* **doomes,** *judgments,* **sondry cas,** *various cases* **164 a ful greet pas,** *in a great hurry* **166 As dooth me right,** *do me justice,* **bille,** *formal complaint* **167 pleyne upon,** *accuse* **169 preeve,** *prove* **170 sooth,** *true,* **that,** *what* **172 yeve diffynytyve,** *give definitive* **173 Lat do hym calle,** *let him be summoned* **175 wite,** *know* **176 rad,** *read* **181 equitee,** *justice* **182 expres agayn,** *specifically against* **183 thral,** *slave*

---

117 the doctour, epithet of St. Augustine; the preceding sentiment about Envy is also attributed to Augustine in *ParsT* 10.484. **140 cherl,** low-class fellow or ruffian; some MSS have "clerk," but *RR* 5599 reads "Li ribauz" (the debauched one). **169 witnesse,** either "testimony" or "evidence." In medieval law, witnesses' testimony to the character or statements of the claimants was important; *RR* 5612–14.

Whil that she was ful yong—this wol I preeve° 185
By witnesse, lord, so that it nat yow greeve°.
She nys° his doghter nat, what so° he seye.
Wherfore to yow, my lord the juge, I preye,
Yeld° me my thral, if that it be youre wille."
Lo, this was al the sentence of his bille. 190

    Virginius gan upon the cherl biholde°,
But hastily, er° he his tale° tolde
And wolde have preeved it as sholde a knyght°,
And eek by witnessyng of many a wight°,
That al was fals that seyde his adversarie, 195
This cursed juge wolde nothyng tarie°
Ne heere a word moore of Virginius,
But yaf° his juggement, and seyde thus:
    "I deeme anon° this cherl his servant have;
Thou shalt no lenger in thyn hous hir save°. 200
Go bryng hire forth and put hire in oure warde°.
The cherl shal have his thral. This I awarde."

    And whan this worthy knyght Virginius
Thurgh sentence of this justice Apius
Moste° by force his deere doghter yeven° 205
Unto the juge, in lecherie to lyven,
He gooth hym hoom and sette him in his halle,
And leet anon his deere doghter calle°,
And with a face deed as asshen colde
Upon hir humble face he gan biholde, 210
With fadres pitee stikynge thurgh his herte,
Al° wolde he from his purpos nat converte°.

    "Doghter," quod he, "Virginia, by thy name,
Ther been two weyes, outher° deeth or shame,
That thou most suffre. Allas, that I was bore°! 215
For nevere thou deservedest wherfore°
To dyen with a swerd or with a knyf.
O deere doghter, endere° of my lyf,
Which° I have fostred up with swich plesaunce°
That thou were nevere out of my
      remembraunce! 220
O doghter, which that art my laste wo,

And in my lyf my laste joye also,
O gemme of chastitee, in pacience
Take thou thy deeth, for this is my sentence°.
For love, and nat for hate, thou most be deed°; 225
My pitous hand moot smyten of° thyn heed.
Allas, that evere Apius the say°!
Thus hath he falsly jugged the today."
And tolde hire al the cas, as ye bifore
Han herd; nat nedeth for to telle it moore. 230

    "O mercy, deere fader!" quod this mayde,
And with that word she bothe hir armes layde
Aboute his nekke, as she was wont° to do.
The teeris bruste° out of hir eyen two,
And seyde, "Goode fader, shal I dye? 235
Is ther no grace, is ther no remedye?"

    "No, certes°, deere doghter myn," quod he.

    "Thanne yif me leyser°, fader myn," quod she,
"My deeth for to compleyne° a litel space°;
For, pardee°, Jepte yaf° his doghter grace 240
For to compleyne er he hir slow°, allas!
And God it woot°, nothyng was hir trespas°
But for° she ran hir fader first to see
To welcome hym with greet solempnitee."
And with that word she fil aswowne anon°, 245
And after whan hir swownyng is agon
She riseth up and to hir fader sayde,
"Blissed be God that I shal dye a mayde.
Yif° me my deeth er that I have a shame.
Dooth with youre child youre wyl, a Goddes°
      name!" 250

    And with that word she preyed hym ful ofte
That with his swerd he wolde smyte softe°.
And with that word aswowne doun she fil.
Hir fader, with ful sorweful herte and wil,
Hir heed of smoot°, and by the top it hente°, 255
And to the juge he gan it to presente°
As he sat yet in doom° in consistorie°.
And whan the juge it saugh°, as seith the storie,

---

185 preeve, *prove* **186 greeve,** *displease* **187 nys,** *is not,* **what so,** *whatever* **189 Yeld,** *give* **191 gan . . . biholde,** *stared at* **192 er,** *before,* **tale,** *version* **193 as sholde a knyght,** i.e., *in trial by combat* **194 wight,** *person* **196 wolde nothyng tarie,** *would not delay* **198 yaf,** *gave* **199 deeme anon,** *judge at once* **200 save,** *keep* **201 warde,** *custody* **205 Moste,** *must,* **yeven,** *give* **208 leet anon . . . calle,** *at once summoned* **212 Al,** *although,* **converte,** *turn* **214 outher,** *either* **215 bore,** *born* **216 wherfore,** *for any reason* **218 endere,** *one who ends* **218 Which,** *who,* **swich plesaunce,** *such pleasure* **224 sentence,** *decision* **225 most be deed,** *must be dead*

226 moot smyten of, *must strike off* **227 the say,** *saw you* **233 wont,** *accustomed* **234 teeris bruste,** *tears burst* **237 certes,** *certainly* **238 leyser,** *time* **239 compleyne,** *lament,* **space,** *while* **240 pardee,** *by God,* **yaf,** *gave* **241 slow,** *slew* **242 woot,** *knows,* **trespas,** *wrongdoing* **243 But for,** *except that* **245 fil aswowne anon,** *fainted at once* **249 Yif,** *give* **250 a Goddes,** *in God's* **252 smyte softe,** *strike softly* **255 of smoot,** *struck off,* **hente,** *grasped* **256 gan . . . presente,** *presented* **257 doom,** *judgment,* **consistorie,** *court* **258 saugh,** *saw*

207 his halle, the great hall of his manor. In all other versions, Virginius executes Virginia without deliberation in a public act. From here to line 255, Chaucer reshapes his source. **240 Jepte,** in Judges 11.30ff., Jephthah vows to God, if given victory in battle, to sacrifice whoever comes out of the house first. His daughter is first, and he allows her two months to bewail the fact that she must die a virgin. Virginia, of course, wants to remain virginal. Chaucer's addition.

He bad° to take hym and anhange° hym faste.
But right anon° a thousand peple in thraste°   260
To save the knyght, for routhe° and for pitee,
For knowen was the false iniquitee°.
The peple anon had suspect° in this thyng,
By manere of the cherles chalangyng°,
That it was by the assent of Apius;   265
They wisten° wel that he was lecherus.
For which unto this Apius they gon
And caste hym in a prisoun right anon,
Ther as° he slow° hymself; and Claudius,
That servant was unto this Apius,   270
Was demed° for to hange upon a tree,
But that Virginius of his pitee
So preyde for hym that he was exiled,

And elles°, certes°, he had been bigyled°.
The remenant° were anhanged, moore and
    lesse,   275
That were consentant of° this cursednesse.
  Heere may men seen how synne hath his
    merite°.
Beth war°, for no man woot° whom God wol smyte
In no degree°, ne in which manere wyse
The worm of conscience may agryse   280
Of° wikked lyf, though it so pryvee° be
That no man woot° therof but God and he.
For be he lewed° man or ellis lered   – *regardless of whether*
                                                              he's not learned
                                                              or learned
He noot° how soone that he shal been afered°.
Therfore I rede° yow this conseil take: 285
Forsaketh° synne er synne yow forsake°.

Heere endeth the Phisiciens Tale.

---

259 bad, *ordered,* **anhange,** *hang* **260 right anon,** *immediately,* **in thraste,** *rushed in* **261 routhe,** *compassion* **262 iniquitee,** *wickedness* **263 suspect,** *suspicion* **264 chalangyng,** *accusation* **266 wisten,** *knew* **269 Ther as,** *where,* **slow,** *slew* **271 demed,** *judged* **274 elles,** *otherwise,* **certes,** *certainly,* **bigyled,** *tricked* (i.e., killed) **275 remenant,** *remainder*

276 consentant of, *in support of* **277 his merite,** *its reward* **278 Beth war,** *beware,* **woot,** *knows* **279 In no degree,** *of any social rank* **280–81 agryse / Of,** *be terrified by* **281 pryvee,** *secret* **282 woot,** *knows* **283 lewed,** *uneducated* **284 noot,** *knows not,* **afered,** *frightened* (by death) **285 rede,** *advise* **286 Forsaketh,** *abandon,* **forsake,** *betrays*

286 This common proverb is echoed in *ParsT* 10.83; it here raises questions since it applies to Appius and Claudius rather than Virginia.

PARDONER'S TALE

PROLOGUE

The wordes of the Hoost to the Phisicien and the Pardoner.

Oure Hooste gan to swere as he were wood°,
"Harrow°," quod he, "by nayles and by blood!
This was a fals cherl and a fals justise.
As shameful deeth as herte may devyse   290
Come to thise false juges and hire advocatz°.
Algate° this sely° mayde is slayn, allas!
Allas, to deere° boughte she beautee!
Wherfore I seye al day° as men may see
That yiftes° of Fortune and of Nature   295
Been cause of deeth to many a creature.
Of bothe yiftes that I speke of now
Men han ful ofte moore for harm than prow°.

"But trewely, myn owene maister deere,
This is a pitous tale for to heere.   300
But nathelees, passe over, is no fors°.
I pray to God so save thy gentil cors°,

And eek thyne urynals and thy jurdones,
Thyn ypocras, and eek thy galiones,
And every boyste° ful of thy letuarie°;   305
God blesse hem, and oure lady Seinte Marie.
   "So moot I theen°, thou art a propre man,
And lyk a prelat°, by Seint Ronyan!
Seyde I nat wel? I kan nat speke in terme°;
But wel I woot° thou doost myn herte to erme° 310
That I almoost have caught a cardynacle.
By corpus bones, but° I have triacle°,
Or elles a draughte° of moyste° and corny° ale,
Or but I heere anon° a myrie tale,
Myn herte is lost for pitee of this mayde.   315
Thou beel amy, thou Pardoner," he sayde,
"Telle us som myrthe or japes° right anon."
   "It shal be doon," quod he, "by Seint Ronyon.

---

287 **wood,** *crazed* 288 **Harrow,** *alas* 291 **hire advocatz,** *their lawyers* 292 **Algate,** *at any rate,* **sely,** *innocent* 293 **to deere,** *too dearly* 294 **al day,** *always* 295 **yiftes,** *gifts* 298 **prow,** *profit* 301 **no fors,** *no matter* 302 **cors,** *body* 305 **boyste,** *jar,* **letuarie,** *medicine* 307 **So moote I theen,** *as*

I may thrive 308 **prelat,** *clergyman* 309 **terme,** *in learned terms* 310 **woot,** *know,* **erme,** *grieve* 312 **but,** *unless,* **triacle,** *medicine* 313 **draughte,** *drink,* **moyste,** *fresh,* **corny,** *malty* (?) 314 **heere anon,** *hear soon* 317 **japes,** *jokes*

287–326 Variants in the MSS suggest that Chaucer expanded and revised this link when he decided to place *PardT* after *PhyT.* See MR 2.325–28 and 4.78–81 for discussion and details. **288 by nayles and by blood,** by the nails and blood of Christ's Crucifixion, a strong oath. **303 urynals . . . jurdones,** chamber pots, but also vessels used for urinalysis. **304 ypocras . . . galiones,** concoctions named for the famous physicians Hippocrates and Galen, although the latter seems to have been invented by the Host, who (in this passage and elsewhere) imitates professional jargon. **308 Seint Ronyan,** a Scottish saint, Ronan, but with play upon *runnion,* "kidney, sexual organ." **311 cardynacle,** evidently the Host's error, corrected in many MSS to "cardiacle" (heart attack). **312 By corpus bones,** a distortion of the oath *Corpus Dei* (By the Lord's Body). See 472n below. **316 beel amy,** French feminine *belle amie,* "pretty friend"; here derisive.

But first," quod he, "heere at this ale stake
I wol bothe drynke and eten of a cake°." 320
     And right anon thise gentils° gonne to crye,
"Nay, lat hym telle us of no ribaudye°!
Telle us som moral thyng that we may leere°

Som wit°, and thanne wol we gladly heere."
     "I graunte, ywis°," quod he, "but I moot°
          thynke 325
Upon som honest° thyng while that I drynke."

Heere folweth the Prologe of the Pardoners Tale.

Lordynges, quod he, in chirches whan I preche,
I peyne me° to han an hauteyn° speche
And rynge it out as round° as gooth° a belle,
For I kan° al by rote° that I telle. 330
My theme is alwey oon°, and evere was:
Radix malorum est cupiditas.
     First I pronounce whennes° that I come,
And thanne my bulles° shewe I, alle and some.
Oure lige lordes seel on my patente, 335
That shewe I first my body to warente°,
That no man be so boold, ne preest ne° clerk,
Me to destourbe of° Cristes hooly werk.
And after that thanne telle I forth my tales.
Bulles of popes and of cardynales, 340
Of patriarkes and bisshopes I shewe,
And in Latyn I speke a wordes fewe,
To saffron with° my predicacioun°,
And for to stire° hem to devocioun.
Thanne shewe I forth my longe cristal stones, 345
Ycrammed ful of cloutes° and of bones—
Relikes been they, as wenen they echoon°.
Thanne have I in latoun° a sholder-boon
Which that was of an hooly Jewes° sheep.
"Goode men," I seye, "taak of my wordes
          keep°; 350
If that this boon be wasshe° in any welle,
If cow, or calf, or sheep, or oxe swelle°

That any worm° hath ete° or worm ystonge,
Taak water of that welle and wassh his tonge,
And it is hool anon°; and forthermoor, 355
Of pokkes° and of scabbe° and every soor
Shal every sheep be hool that of this welle
Drynketh a draughte. Taak kepe eek° what I telle:
If that the goode man that the beestes oweth°
Wol° every wyke°, er that the cok hym
          croweth°, 360
Fastynge, drynken of this welle a draughte,
As thilke° hooly Jew oure eldres taughte,
His beestes and his stoor° shal multiplie.
     "And, sires, also it heeleth jalousie;
For though a man be falle in jalous rage, 365
Lat maken with this water his potage°,
And nevere shal he moore his wyf mystriste°,
Though he the soothe of hir defaute wiste°,
Al° had she taken preestes two or thre.
     "Heere is a miteyn eek°, that ye may se. 370
He that his hand wol putte in this mitayn,
He shal have multipliyng of his grayn,
Whan he hath sowen, be it whete or otes—
So that he offre° pens, or elles grotes.
     "Goode men and wommen, o thyng warne
          I yow: 375
If any wight° be in this chirche now
That hath doon synne horrible, that he

---

320 cake, *loaf* **321 gentils,** *gentlefolk* **322 ribaudye,** *coarse humor* **323 leere,** *learn* **324 wit,** *wisdom* **325 ywis,** *certainly,* **moot,** *must* **326 honest,** *moral* **328 peyne me,** *take pains,* **hauteyn,** *loud* **329 round,** *resoundingly,* **gooth,** *goes* **330 kan,** *know,* **rote,** *repetition* **331 alwey oon,** *always the same* **333 pronounce whennes,** *proclaim whence* (i.e., *from* Rome) **334 bulles,** *official documents* **336 warente,** *protect* **337 ne . . . ne,** *neither . . . nor* **338 destourbe of,** *prevent from doing* **343 saffron with,** i.e., *add spice to,* **predicacioun,** *preaching* **344 stire,** *stir* **346 cloutes,** *rags* **347 wenen they echoon,** *they all believe* **348 latoun,** *brass*

349 Jewes, *Jew's* **350 keep,** *heed* **351 wasshe,** *washed* **352 swelle,** *swells up* **353 worm,** *snake,* **ete,** *bitten* **355 hool anon,** *healed at once* **356 pokkes,** *pox,* **scabbe,** *scabs* **358 Taak kepe eek,** *take heed also* **359 oweth,** *owns* **360 Wol,** *will,* **wyke,** *week,* **er that the cok hym croweth,** i.e., *before dawn* **362 thilke,** *that* **363 stoor,** *livestock* **366 Lat maken . . . his potage,** *make his soup* **367 mystriste,** *mistrust* **368 soothe of hir defaute wiste,** *knew the truth of her fault* **369 Al,** *although* **370 miteyn eek,** *mitten also* **374 So that he offre,** *as long as he offers* **376 wight,** *person*

---

319 ale stake, projecting pole hung with a garland or bush; sign of an alehouse. **332 *Radix malorum est cupiditas,*** "the root of all evil is greed"; 1 Timothy 6.10. Cupidity is the opposite of charity. **335 lige lordes seel . . . patente,** the seal of the pope or bishop on the open (or "patent") letter that granted authority to the bearer. **340–41 popes . . . cardynales . . . patriarkes . . . bisshopes,** popes, cardinals, patriarchs, bishops—all high-ranking church officials. **347 Relikes,** relics, objects of religious veneration, often parts of the body of saints or material objects associated with the saints or Christ. The Pardoner traffics in false relics and false pardons, both growing problems in the late Middle Ages; see *GP* 1.669n. **349 hooly Jewes sheep,** reference uncertain, but probably related to line 362. **362 hooly Jew,** Genesis 30.32–43 recounts how Jacob multiplied the number of sheep he could claim from Laban. **374 pens, or elles groats,** pennies or silver coins worth four pennies.

Dar nat for shame of it yshryven° be,
Or any womman, be she yong or old,
That hath ymaked hir housbonde cokewold°,   380
Swich° folk shal have no power ne no grace
To offren to° my relikes in this place.
And whoso fyndeth hym out of swich blame,
They wol come up and offre in Goddes name,
And I assoille hem° by the auctoritee   385
Which that by bulle° ygraunted was to me."
   By this gaude° have I wonne, yeer by yeer,
An hundred mark sith° I was pardoner.
I stonde lyk a clerk in my pulpet,
And whan the lewed° peple is doun yset,   390
I preche so as ye han herd bifoore,
And telle an hundred false japes° moore.
Thanne peyne I me° to strecche forth the nekke,
And est and west upon the peple I bekke°,
As dooth a dowve° sittynge on a berne°.   395
Myne handes and my tonge goon so yerne°
That it is joye to se my bisynesse°.
Of avarice° and of swich cursednesse
Is al my prechyng, for to make hem free°
To yeven hir pens°, and namely unto me,   400
For myn entente is nat but for to wynne°,
And nothyng for correccioun of synne.
I rekke° nevere, whan that they been beryed°,
Though that hir soules goon a-blakeberyed!
For certes°, many a predicacioun°   405
Comth ofte tyme of yvel entencioun;
Som for plesance° of folk and flaterye,
To been avaunced° by ypocrisye,
And som for veyne glorie°, and som for hate.
For whan I dar noon oother weyes debate°,   410
Thanne wol I stynge hym with my tonge smerte°
In prechyng, so that he shal nat asterte°
To been defamed° falsly, if that he
Hath trespased to° my bretheren or to me.

For though I telle noght his propre name,   415
Men shal wel knowe that it is the same
By signes and by othere circumstances.
Thus quyte° I folk that doon us displesances°;
Thus spitte I out my venym under hewe°
Of hoolynesse, to semen hooly and trewe.   420
   But shortly myn entente I wol devyse°:
I preche of nothyng but for coveityse°.
Therfore my theme is yet, and evere was,
Radix malorum est cupiditas.
Thus kan I preche agayn° that same vice   425
Which that I use, and that is avarice°.
But though myself be gilty in that synne,
Yet kan I maken oother folk to twynne°
From avarice, and soore to repente.
But that is nat my principal entente—   430
I preche nothyng but for coveitise.
Of this mateere it oghte ynogh suffise.
   Thanne telle I hem ensamples many oon°
Of olde stories longe tyme agoon.
For lewed° peple loven tales olde;   435
Swiche° thynges kan they wel reporte° and holde°.
What, trowe ye the whiles° I may preche,
And wynne gold and silver for° I teche,
That I wol lyve in poverte wilfully°?
Nay, nay, I thoghte it nevere, trewely,   440
For I wol preche and begge in sondry° landes;
I wol nat do no labour with myne handes,
Ne make baskettes and lyve therby,
By cause I wol nat beggen ydelly°.
I wol noon of the apostles countrefete°;   445
I wol have moneie°, wolle°, chese, and whete,
Al° were it yeven of° the povereste page°,
Or of the povereste wydwe° in a village,
Al° sholde hir children sterve° for famyne.
Nay, I wol drynke licour of the vyne   450
And have a joly wenche in every toun.

---

378 **yshryven,** *forgiven* 380 **cokewold,** *a cuckold* 381 **Swich,** *such* 382 **offren to,** *make an offering for* 385 **assoille hem,** *absolve them* 386 **bulle,** *official document* 387 **gaude,** *trick* 388 **sith,** *since* 390 **lewed,** *ignorant* 392 **japes,** *tricks* 393 **peyne I me,** *I take pains* 394 **bekke,** *nod* 395 **dowve,** *dove,* **on a berne,** *in a barn* 396 **yerne,** *rapidly* 397 **bisynesse,** *intensity* 398 **avarice,** *greed* 399 **free,** *generous* 400 **yeven hir pens,** *give their pennies* 401 **wynne,** *acquire* 403 **rekke,** *care,* **beryed,** *buried* 405 **certes,** *certainly,* **predicacioun,** *sermon* 407 **plesance,** *pleasure* 408 **avaunced,** *advanced* 409 **veyne glorie,** *empty pride* 410 **debate,** *dispute* 411 **smerte,** *painfully* 412 **asterte,** *escape* 413 **defamed,**

slandered 414 **trepased to,** *offended* 418 **quyte,** *repay,* **displesances,** *displeasure* 419 **hewe,** *disguise* 421 **devyse,** *describe* 422 **coveityse,** *greed* 425 **agayn,** *against* 426 **avarice,** *greed* 428 **twynne,** *turn away* 433 **ensamples many oon,** *many examples* 435 **lewed,** *ignorant* 436 **Swiche,** *such,* **reporte,** *repeat,* **holde,** *remember* 437 **trowe ye the whiles,** *do you think that while* 438 **for,** *because* 439 **wilfully,** *voluntarily* 441 **sondry,** *various* 444 **ydelly,** *idly* 445 **countrefete,** *imitate* 446 **moneie,** *money,* **wolle,** *wool* 447 **Al,** *although,* **yeven of,** *given by,* **povereste page,** *poorest servant* 448 **wydwe,** *widow* 449 **Al,** *even if,* **sterve,** *die*

---

383 **out of swich blame,** not guilty of such offenses; the Pardoner's insidious implication is that anyone who does not offer money *is* guilty of such offenses. 388 **mark,** coin worth two-thirds pound; one hundred marks was a healthy income. 404 **goon a-blakeberyed,** pick blackberries; the precise meaning is uncertain, but it is clearly dismissive. 424 See 332n. 439–45 The ideals rejected here—voluntary poverty, manual labor, imitation of the apostles, and begging—underlie clerical vows.

But herkneth°, lordynges, in conclusioun:
Youre likyng is that I shal telle a tale.
Now have I dronke a draughte of corny° ale,
By God, I hope I shal yow telle a thyng   455
That shal by reson been at youre likyng.

For though myself be a ful vicious man,
A moral tale yet I yow telle kan,
Which I am wont° to preche for to wynne°.
Now hoold youre pees; my tale I wol bigynne.   460

Heere bigynneth the Pardoners Tale.

In Flaundres whilom° was a compaignye
Of yonge folk that haunteden folye°,
As riot°, hasard°, stywes°, and tavernes,
Where as with harpes, lutes, and gyternes°
They daunce and pleyen at dees° bothe day and
          nyght,   465
And eten also and drynken over hir myght°,
Thurgh which they doon the devel sacrifise
Withinne that develes temple in cursed wise
By superfluytee° abhomynable.
Hir othes been° so grete and so dampnable   470
That it is grisly for to heere hem swere.
Oure blissed Lordes body they totere—
Hem thoughte° that Jewes rente° hym noght
          ynough—
And ech of hem at otheres synne lough°.
And right anon° thanne comen tombesteres°   475
Fetys° and smale°, and yonge frutesteres°,
Syngeres with harpes, baudes°, wafereres°,
Whiche been the verray° develes officeres
To kyndle and blowe the fyr of lecherye
That is annexed unto glotonye.   480
   The hooly writ° take I to my witnesse
That luxurie° is in wyn and dronkenesse.

Lo, how that dronken Looth, unkyndely°,
Lay by his doghtres two, unwityngly°;
So dronke he was, he nyste° what he wroghte°.   485
Herodes, whoso wel the stories soghte°,
Whan he of wyn was repleet° at his feeste,
Right at his owene table he yaf° his heeste°
To sleen° the Baptist John, ful giltelees.
   Senec seith a good word doutelees;   490
He seith he kan no difference fynde
Bitwix a man that is out of his mynde
And a man which that is dronkelewe°
But that woodnesse°, fallen in a shrewe°,
Persevereth° lenger than dooth dronkenesse.   495
O glotonye, ful of cursednesse!
O cause first of oure confusioun!
O original of oure dampnacioun,
Til Crist hadde boght° us with his blood° agayn!
Lo, how deere°, shortly for to sayn,   500
Aboght° was thilke° cursed vileynye!
Corrupt° was al this world for glotonye.
   Adam oure fader and his wyf also
Fro Paradys to labour and to wo
Were dryven for that vice, it is no drede°.   505
For whil that Adam fasted, as I rede,

---

452 **herkneth**, *listen* 454 **corny**, *malty* (?) 459 **wont**, *accustomed*, **wynne**, *acquire* 461 **whilom**, *once* 462 **haunteden folye**, *lived in folly* 463 **As riot**, *such as partying*, **hasard**, *gambling*, **stywes**, *brothels* 464 **gyternes**, *guitars* 465 **dees**, *dice* 466 **myght**, *capacity* 469 **superfluytee**, *over-indulgence* 470 **Hir othes been**, *their oaths are* 473 **Hem thoughte**, (it was) *thought by them*, **rente**, *tore* 474 **lough**, *laughed* 475 **right anon**, *soon*, **tombesteres**, *female acrobats* 476 **Fetys**, *shapely*, **smale**, *slim*, **frutesteres**, *female fruit sellers* 477 **baudes**, *pimps*, **wafereres**, *cake sellers*

478 **verray**, *actual* 481 **hooly writ**, *Bible* 482 **luxurie**, *lechery* 483 **unkyndely**, *unnaturally* 484 **unwityngly**, *unknowingly* 485 **nyste**, *knew not*, **wroghte**, *did* 486 **whoso . . . soghte**, *whoever . . .* (may) *investigate* 487 **repleet**, *filled* 488 **yaf**, *gave*, **heeste**, *order* 489 **sleen**, *slay* 493 **dronkelewe**, *regularly drunk* 494 **woodnesse**, *madness*, **fallen in a shrewe**, *happening to a wretch* 495 **Persevereth**, *lasts* 499 **boght**, *redeemed*, **blood**, i.e., *death* 500 **deere**, *expensively* 501 **Aboght**, *redeemed*, **thilke**, *that* 502 **Corrupt**, *corrupted* 505 **drede**, *doubt*

461 **Flaundres**, Flanders, in modern Belgium. 468 **develes temple**, devil's temple, i.e., tavern. 472 **totere**, tear apart. Swearing was thought to tear the body of Christ, since many oaths cite parts of Christ's body or aspects of his Crucifixion. See lines 649–62 below and *ParsT* 10.591. 482 Ephesians 5.18, but Chaucer may have taken it from Pope Innocent III, *De Miseria Conditionis Humane* (On the Misery of the Human Condition) 2.19; see *MLT* 2.99–121n. Other materials below that may derive from *De Miseria*—all from sections 2.17–19—are at lines 486–89, 515–18, 519–21, 525–26, 533–34, 535–44, 547–48, 549–50, and 558–59. There is related material from St. Jerome, *Epistola adversus Jovinianum* 2.10–17 (Letter against Jovinian) at lines 506–9, 515–18, 525–26, and 547–48; see *WBP* 3.3n. 483 **Looth**, Lot; Genesis 19.30–35. 486–89 **Herodes . . . Baptist John**, at a meal Herod fulfilled an oath to a dancing girl by ordering the decapitation of John the Baptist; Mark 6.22–28 and Matthew 14.7–11. Drunkenness is not mentioned in the biblical accounts, although the association was common; see *PP* C.11.176–79. Alluded to in Innocent 2.18; see 482n above. 490–95 **Senec . . .**, Seneca, *Letters* 83.18–19. 497 **cause first**, gluttony was commonly condemned as the primary reason why Adam and Eve ate the forbidden fruit and were expelled from Paradise. See *SumT* 3.1915–17; *ParsT* 10.819.

He was in Paradys; and whan that he
Eet° of the fruyt deffended° on the tree,
Anon° he was out cast to wo and peyne.
O glotonye, on thee° wel oghte us pleyne°!   510
O, wiste a man° how manye maladyes
Folwen of excesse and of glotonyes,
He wolde been the moore mesurable°
Of his diete, sittynge at his table.
Allas, the shorte throte, the tendre mouth,   515
Maketh that est and west and north and south,
In erthe, in eir, in water, men to swynke°
To gete a glotoun deyntee mete° and drynke.
Of this matiere, O Paul, wel kanstow trete°:
"Mete unto wombe°, and wombe eek unto
       mete,   520
Shal God destroyen bothe," as Paulus seith.
Allas, a foul thyng is it, by my feith,
To seye this word, and fouler is the dede,
Whan man so drynketh of the white and rede°
That of his throte he maketh his pryvee°   525
Thurgh thilke° cursed superfluitee°.
    The apostel wepyng seith ful pitously,
"Ther walken manye of whiche yow toold
       have I—
I seye it now wepyng, with pitous voys—
They been enemys of Cristes croys°,   530
Of whiche the ende is deeth; wombe is hir god!"
O wombe, O bely, O stynkyng cod°,
Fulfilled of° donge and of corrupcioun!
At either ende of thee foul is the soun°.
How greet labour and cost is thee to fynde°!   535
Thise cookes, how they stampe and streyne and
       grynde
And turnen substaunce into accident

To fulfille al thy likerous talent°.
Out of the harde bones knokke they
The mary°, for they caste noght° awey   540
That may go thurgh the golet° softe and
       swoote°.
Of spicerie° of leef and bark and roote
Shal been his sauce ymaked by delit°,
To make hym yet a newer° appetit.
But certes°, he that haunteth swiche delices°   545
Is deed whil that he lyveth in tho° vices.
    A lecherous thyng is wyn, and dronkenesse
Is ful of stryvyng° and of wrecchednesse.
O dronke man, disfigured is thy face,
Sour is thy breeth, foul artow° to embrace,   550
And thurgh thy dronke nose semeth the soun
As though thou seydest ay° "Sampsoun,
       Sampsoun."
And yet, God woot°, Sampsoun drank nevere
       no wyn.
Thou fallest as it were a styked swyn°;
Thy tonge is lost, and al thyn honeste cure°;   555
For dronkenesse is verray sepulture°
Of mannes wit° and his discrecioun.
In whom that drynke hath dominacioun
He kan no conseil° kepe, it is no drede°.
Now kepe yow fro the white and fro the rede,   560
And namely° fro the white wyn of Lepe,
That is to selle° in Fysshstrete or in Chepe.
This wyn of Spaigne crepeth subtilly
In othere wynes, growynge faste by,
Of which ther ryseth swich fumositee°   565
That whan a man hath dronken draughtes thre,
And weneth° that he be at hoom in Chepe,
He is in Spaigne right at the toune of Lepe—

---

508 **Eet**, *ate,* **deffended**, *forbidden* 509 **Anon**, *soon* 510 **on thee**, *against you,* **pleyne**, *lament* 511 **wiste a man**, *if a person knew* 513 **mesurable**, *moderate* 517 **swynke**, *work* 518 **mete**, *food* 519 **kanstow trete**, *can you explain* 520 **wombe**, *stomach* 524 **the white and rede**, *wine* 525 **pryvee**, *toilet* 526 **thilke**, *this,* **superfluitee**, *overindulgence* 530 **croys**, *cross* 532 **cod**, *sack* 533 **Fulfilled of**, *filled with* 534 **soun**, *sound* 535 **is thee to fynde**, *is it to provide for you* 538 **likerous talent**, *greedy desire* 540 **mary**, *marrow,* **noght**, *nothing* 541 **golet**, *gullet,*

swoote, *sweet* 542 **spicerie**, *aromatic mixture* 543 **by delit**, *for delight* 544 **newer**, *renewed* 545 **certes**, *surely,* **haunteth swiche delices**, *lives in such delicacies* 546 **tho**, *those* 548 **stryvyng**, *quarreling* 550 **artow**, *are you* 552 **ay**, *always* 553 **woot**, *knows* 554 **styked swyn**, *stuck pig* 555 **honeste cure**, *noble concern* 556 **verray sepulture**, *true burial* 557 **wit**, *reason* 559 **conseil**, *confidences,* **drede**, *doubt* 561 **namely**, *especially* 562 **to selle**, *for sale* 564 **faste by**, *nearby* 565 **fumositee**, *potency* 567 **weneth**, *believes*

515–18 Echoes Innocent 2.17 and Jerome 2.8; see 482n. **519–21 Paul . . . ,** 1 Corinthians 6.13, perhaps by way of Innocent 2.17; see 482n above. **525–26** Echoes Jerome 2.17; see 482n. **527 The apostel,** St. Paul. **528–31** Philippians 3.18–19; also *ParsT* 10.820. **533–34** Echoes Innocent 2.18 and 2.17; see 482n. **537 substaunce into accident,** essential nature into outward appearance; a grim philosophical joke that claims culinary preparation to be deeply unnatural, even blasphemous. In Catholic doctrine, in the sacrament of the Eucharist, the substance of the bread and wine becomes the body and blood of Christ, while the outward appearance remains the same. **545–46** 1 Timothy 5.6; Jerome 2.9. **547–48** A version of Proverbs 20.1, in Innocent 2.19 and Jerome 2.10; see 482n. **549–50** Echoes Innocent 2.19; see 482n. **552–53 Sampsoun . . . ,** imitation of loud, nasal breathing. The biblical Samson was conceived by his mother while she abstained, and he lived as a Nazarite, in abstention; Judges 13.4–7. **558–59** The Vulgate version of Proverbs 31.4, in Innocent 2.19; see 482n above. Referred to again in 582n below. **561 Lepe,** in Spain. **562 Fysshstrete . . . Chepe,** commercial areas of medieval London. **563 crepeth subtilly,** sneaks slyly, a reference to the practice of adulterating expensive (usually French) wines with cheaper ones.

Nat at the Rochele, ne at Burdeux toun—
And thanne wol he seye "Sampsoun,
    Sampsoun!"   570

But herkneth, lordynges, o word I yow preye,
That alle the sovereyn° actes, dar I seye,
Of victories in the Olde Testament,
Thurgh verray° God that is omnipotent,
Were doon in abstinence and in preyere.   575
Looketh the Bible and ther ye may it leere°.

Looke° Attilla, the grete conquerour,
Deyde in his sleep with shame and dishonour,
Bledynge ay° at his nose in dronkenesse.
A capitayn sholde lyve in sobrenesse.   580
And over al this, avyseth yow right wel
What was comaunded unto Lamwel—
Nat Samuel, but Lamwel, seye I—
Redeth the Bible, and fynde it expresly°
Of wyn-yevyng° to hem that han justise°.   585
Namoore of this, for it may wel suffise.

And now that I have spoken of glotonye,
Now wol I yow deffenden hasardrye°.
Hasard is verray mooder° of lesynges°,
And of deceite, and cursed forswerynges°,   590
Blaspheme of° Crist, manslaughtre, and wast° also
Of catel° and of tyme; and forthermo,
It is repreeve° and contrarie of honour
For to ben holde° a commune hasardour°.
And ever the hyer° he is of estaat°,   595
The moore is he yholden desolaat°.
If that a prynce useth hasardrye,
In alle governaunce and policye
He is, as by commune opinioun,
Yholde the lasse in reputacioun.   600

Stilboun, that was a wys embassadour,
Was sent to Corynthe in ful greet honour
Fro Lacidomye to make hire alliaunce.

And whan he cam, hym happede par chaunce°
That alle the gretteste that were of that lond   605
Pleyynge atte hasard he hem fond°.
For which as soone as it myghte be
He stal hym hoom° agayn to his contree
And seyde, "Ther wol I nat lese° my name,
Ne I wol nat take on me so greet defame°   610
Yow for to allie° unto none hasardours.
Sendeth othere wise embassadours,
For by my trouthe me were levere dye°
Than I yow sholde to hasardours allye.
For ye that been so glorious in honours   615
Shul nat allyen yow with hasardours
As by my wyl, ne as by my tretee°."
This wise philosophre, thus seyde hee.

Looke eek° that to the kyng Demetrius
The kyng of Parthes, as the book seith us,   620
Sente him a paire of dees° of gold in scorn,
For he hadde used hasard ther-biforn°,
For which he heeld his glorie or his renoun
At no value or reputacioun.
Lordes may fynden oother maner° pley   625
Honeste° ynough to dryve the day awey.

Now wol I speke of othes° false and grete
A word or two, as olde bookes trete.
Gret sweryng is a thyng abhominable,
And fals sweryng is yet moore reprevable.   630
The heighe God forbad sweryng at al,
Witnesse on Mathew, but in special
Of sweryng seith the hooly Jeremye,
"Thou shalt swere sooth° thyne othes and
    nat lye,
And swere in doom° and eek in rightwisnesse°, 635
But ydel sweryng is a cursednesse."
Bihoold and se that in the firste table
Of heighe Goddes heestes° honurable

---

572 sovereyn, *supreme* **574 Thurgh verray,** *through true* **576 leere,**
learn **577 Looke,** *consider* **579 ay,** *steadily* **584 expresly,** *specifically* **585**
Of wyn-yevyng, *about giving wine,* **han justise,** *dispense justice* **588 def-**
fenden hasardye, *speak against gambling* **589 verray mooder,** *true*
mother, **lesynges,** *lies* **590 forswerynges,** *broken oaths* **591 Blaspheme**
of, *blasphemy against,* **wast,** *waste* **592 catel,** *possessions* **593 repreeve,**
shame **594 ben holde,** *be considered,* **hasardour,** *gambler* **595 hyer,**
higher, **estaat,** *class* **596 yholden desolaat,** *considered wretched* **604 hym**

happede par chaunce, *to him it happened by chance* **606 fond,** *found*
608 stal hym hoom, i.e., *slipped home quietly* **609 lese,** *lose* **610 so greet**
defame, *such great dishonor* **611 Yow for to allie,** *to ally you* **613 me**
were levere dye, *I would rather die* **617 tretee,** *negotiation* **619 Looke**
eek, *consider also* **621 dees,** *dice* **622 ther-biforn,** *before that* **625 oother**
maner, *other kinds of* **626 Honeste,** *noble* **627 othes,** *oaths* **634 sooth,**
truly **635 doom,** *judgment,* **rightwisnesse,** *righteousness* **638 Goddes**
heestes, *God's commandments*

---

569 Rochele . . . Burdeux, La Rochelle . . . Bordeaux, regions that produce expensive French wines. **577–79 Attilla . . . ,** the Hun, reported
to have passed out and died from drink. **582 What was comaunded unto Lamwel,** the command is in the Vulgate version of Proverbs 31.4:
"Do not to kings, O Lamuel, do not to kings give wine, for there is no secret where drunkenness reigns." See 558–59n above. **589** From John
of Salisbury *Policraticus* 1.5 [36], although Chaucer probably derived much of lines 589–624 from a preacher's manual such as that of John
of Wales, *Communiloquium* 1.10.7. **601–18 Stilboun . . . Corynthe . . . Lacidomye,** an attempted alliance between Corinth and Sparta (Lacedae-
mon). John of Salisbury, *Policraticus* 1.5 [37] and John of Wales 1.10.7; the ambassador's name is *Chilon* in both. **619 Demetrius,** is sent dice
by the king of Parthia; John of Salisbury *Policraticus* 1.5 [38] and John of Wales 1.10.7. **629 Gret sweryng,** solemn oaths, i.e., those sworn by
something holy or serious. **632 Mathew,** see Matthew 5.34–37, quoted in *ParsT* 10.589–90. **633 Jeremye,** Jeremiah 4.2 is adapted in lines
634–36, quoted in *ParsT* 10.592. **637 firste table,** first tablet; the Ten Commandments were given to Moses on two tablets; *MED* 1c.

Hou that the seconde heeste of hym is this,
"Take nat my name in ydel° or amys°." 640
Lo, rather he forbedeth swich sweryng
Than homycide or many a cursed thyng—
I seye that as by ordre° thus it stondeth,
This knoweth that his heestes understondeth
How that the seconde heeste of God is that. 645
And fortherover I wol thee telle al plat°
That vengeance shal nat parten° from his hous
That of his othes is to outrageous.
"By Goddes precious herte and by his nayles°,"
And "By the blood of Crist that is in Hayles, 650
Sevene is my chaunce and thyn is cynk and
      treye,"
"By Goddes armes, if thou falsly pleye
This daggere shal thurghout thyn herte go,"
This fruyt° cometh of the bicched bones° two—
Forsweryng°, ire°, falsnesse, homycide. 655
Now for the love of Crist, that for us dyde,
Lete° youre othes bothe grete and smale.
But, sires, now wol I telle forth my tale.

   Thise riotoures° thre of whiche I telle,
Longe erst er prime rong° of any belle, 660
Were set hem in a taverne for to drynke,
And as they sat they herde a belle clynke
Biforn a cors° was caried to his grave.
That oon of hem gan callen to his knave°,
"Go bet°," quod he, "and axe redily° 665
What cors is this that passeth heer forby°,
And looke that thou reporte his name weel."

   "Sire," quod this boy, "it nedeth never-a-deel°;
It was me toold er ye cam heer two houres.
He was, pardee°, an old felawe° of youres, 670
And sodeynly he was yslayn° tonyght,
Fordronke° as he sat on his bench upright.
Ther cam a privee° theef men clepeth° Deeth
That in this contree al the peple sleeth°,
And with his spere he smoot his herte atwo° 675

And wente his wey withouten wordes mo.
He hath a thousand slayn this pestilence°.
And, maister, er ye come in his presence,
Me thynketh that it were necessarie
For to be war of swich an adversarie. 680
Beth redy for to meete hym everemoore—
Thus taughte me my dame°. I sey namoore."
   "By Seinte Marie," seyde this taverner,
"The child seith sooth°, for he hath slayn this
      yeer
Henne° over a mile withinne a greet village 685
Bothe man and womman, child, and hyne°, and
      page°.
I trowe° his habitacioun be there.
To been avysed° greet wysdom it were
Er that° he dide a man a dishonour."
   "Ye, Goddes armes," quod this riotour, 690
"Is it swich° peril with hym for to meete?
I shal hym seke by wey° and eek by strete,
I make avow to Goddes digne° bones!
Herkneth, felawes, we thre been al ones°;
Lat ech of us holde up his hand til° oother, 695
And ech of us bicomen otheres brother,
And we wol sleen this false traytour Deeth.
He shal be slayn, he that so manye sleeth,
By Goddes dignitee, er it be nyght."
   Togidres han thise thre hir trouthes plight° 700
To lyve and dyen ech of hem for oother
As though he were his owene ybore° brother.
And up they stirte°, al dronken in this rage,
And forth they goon towardes that village
Of which the taverner hadde spoke biforn. 705
And many a grisly ooth thanne han they sworn,
And Cristes blessed body they torente°—
Deeth shal be deed, if that they may hym hente°!
   Whan they han goon nat fully half a mile,
Right° as they wolde han troden over a stile, 710
An oold man and a poure with hem mette.

---

640 ydel, *vain,* **amys,** *wrongly* **643 by ordre,** *in order of occurrence* **646 al plat,** *plainly* **647 parten,** *depart* **649 nayles,** *nails* **654 fruyt,** *result,* **bicched bones,** *bitched* (i.e., *cursed*) *dice* **655 Forsweryng,** *breaking oaths,* **ire,** *anger* **657 Lete,** *abandon* **659 riotoures,** *villains* **660 Longe erst er prime rong,** *well before 9 a.m. was rung* **663 cors,** *corpse* (that) **664 knave,** *servant boy* **665 Go bet,** *go now,* **axe redily,** *ask quickly* **666 heer forby,** *by here* **668 it nedeth never-a-deel,** *it is not necessary at all* **670 pardee,** *by God,* **felawe,** *companion* **671 yslayn,** *killed* **672**

Fordronke, *completely drunk* **673 privee,** *stealthy,* **clepeth,** *call* **674 sleeth,** *slays* **675 smoot . . . atwo,** *struck in two* **677 this pestilence,** (during) *this outbreak of the plague* **682 dame,** *mother* **684 seith sooth,** *tells the truth* **685 Henne,** *from here* **686 hyne,** *farm worker,* **page,** *court servant* **687 trowe,** *believe* **688 avysed,** *prepared* **689 Er that,** *before* **691 swich,** *such* **692 wey,** *path* **693 digne,** *honored* **694 al ones,** *together* **695 til,** *to* **700 hir trouthes plight,** *pledged their words* **702 ybore,** *born* **703 stirte,** *leapt* **707 torente,** *tore* (see 472n) **708 hente,** *seize* **710 Right,** *just*

639 seconde heeste, second commandment for Catholics; third for many Protestants. **647–48** Echoes Ecclesiasticus 23.11, quoted in *ParsT* 10.593. **650 Hayles,** Hayles Abbey in Gloucestershire had a vial said to contain Christ's blood. **651 Sevene . . . cynk and treye,** seven . . . five and three (eight); combinations in a dice game. **662 belle clynke,** handbell ring, before a funeral procession. **710 wolde han troden over a stile,** would have crossed a fence by means of a stile, a low stone or wooden ladder on each side of the fence. **711 oold man,** this enigmatic figure who desires but cannot find death has been assessed as Old Age, Death, the Wandering Jew, and a projection of the Pardoner himself.

This olde man ful mekely hem grette°,
And seyde thus, "Now, lordes, God yow see!"
    The proudeste of thise riotoures three
Answerde agayn°, "What, carl with sory grace°,   715
Why artow° al forwrapped° save thy face?
Why lyvestow° so longe in so greet age?"
    This olde man gan looke in his visage°,
And seyde thus: "For° I ne kan nat fynde
A man, though that I walked into Ynde,   720
Neither in citee ne in no village,
That wolde chaunge° his youthe for myn age;
And therfore moot° I han myn age stille
As longe tyme as it is Goddes wille.
Ne Deeth, allas, ne wol nat han° my lyf.   725
Thus walke I lyk a restelees kaityf°,
And on the ground, which is my moodres° gate,
I knokke with my staf bothe erly and late,
And seye, 'Leeve° mooder, leet me in!
Lo, how I vanysshe°, flessh and blood
        and skyn.   730
Allas, whan shul my bones been at reste?
Mooder, with yow wolde I chaunge my cheste°
That in my chambre longe tyme hath be,
Ye, for an heyre clowt° to wrappe me.'
But yet to me she wol nat do that grace°,   735
For which ful° pale and welked° is my face.
    "But, sires, to yow it is no curteisye
To speken to an old man vileynye
But he trespasse° in word or elles in dede.
In Hooly Writ ye may yourself wel rede,   740
'Agayns° an oold man, hoor° upon his heed,
Ye sholde arise.' Wherfore I yeve° yow reed°,
Ne dooth unto an oold man noon harm now
Namoore than that ye wolde men did to yow
In age, if that ye so longe abyde°.   745
And God be with yow, where ye go° or ryde.
I moot go thider as° I have to go."
    "Nay, olde cherl°, by God thou shalt nat so,"
Seyde this oother hasardour anon.

"Thou partest nat so lightly, by Seint John!   750
Thou spak right now of thilke° traytour Deeth,
That in this contree alle oure freendes sleeth.
Have heer my trouthe, as thou art his espye°,
Telle where he is or thou shalt it abye°,
By God and by the hooly sacrement!   755
For soothly° thou art oon of his assent°
To sleen us yonge folk, thou false theef!"
    "Now, sires," quod he, "if that ye be so leef°
To fynde Deeth, turne up this croked wey,
For in that grove I lafte hym, by my fey°,   760
Under a tree and there he wole abyde°.
Noght for youre boost he wole him nothyng°
        hyde.
Se ye that ook°? Right there ye shal hym fynde.
God save yow, that boghte agayn° mankynde,
And yow amende°." Thus seyde this olde man.   765
And everich° of thise riotoures ran
Til he cam to that tree, and ther they founde
Of floryns fyne° of gold ycoyned° rounde
Wel ny an° eighte busshels as hem thoughte.
No lenger thanne after Deeth they soughte,   770
But ech of hem so glad was of that sighte,
For that° the floryns been so faire and brighte,
That doun they sette hem by this precious
        hoord.
The worste of hem he spak the firste word.
    "Bretheren," quod he, "taak kepe° what
        I seye;   775
My wit is greet, though that I bourde° and pleye.
This tresor hath Fortune unto us yeven°
In myrthe and jolitee oure lyf to lyven,
And lightly° as it comth so wol we spende.
Ey, Goddes precious dignitee, who wende°   780
Today that we sholde han so fair a grace°?
But myghte this gold be caried fro this place
Hoom to myn hous—or elles unto youres—
For wel ye woot° that al this gold is oures,
Thanne were we in heigh felicitee°.   785

---

712 **grette**, *greeted* 715 **agayn**, *in return,* **carl with sory grace**, *bad luck to you fellow* 716 **artow**, *are you,* **al forwrapped**, *all wrapped up* 717 **lyvestow**, *do you live* 718 **gan looke in his visage**, *gazed into his face* 719 **For**, *because* 722 **chaunge**, *exchange* 723 **moot**, *must* 725 **ne wol nat han**, *will not have* 726 **kaityf**, *wretch* 729 **Leeve**, *dear* 730 **vanysshe**, *waste away* 732 **cheste**, *money chest* 734 **heyre clowt**, *haircloth* (burial shroud) 735 **grace**, *favor* 736 **ful**, *very,* **welked**, *withered* 739 **But he trespasse**, *unless he offends* 741 **Agayns**, *in the presence of,* **hoor**, *white* 742 **yeve**, *give,* **reed**, *advice* 745 **abyde**, *live* 746 **go**, *walk* 747 **thider as,**

where 748 **cherl**, *peasant* 751 **thilke**, *this* 753 **espye**, *spy* 754 **abye**, *pay for* 756 **soothly**, *truly,* **oon of his assent**, *in agreement with him* 758 **leef**, *eager* 760 **fey**, *faith* 761 **wole abyde**, *will remain* 762 **nothyng**, *not at all* 763 **ook**, *oak* 764 **boghte agayn**, *redeemed* 765 **amende**, *correct* 766 **everich**, *each* 768 **floryns fyne**, *coins pure,* **ycoyned**, *coined* 769 **Wel ny an**, *nearly* 772 **For that**, *because* 775 **taak kepe**, *heed* 776 **bourde**, *joke* 777 **yeven**, *given* 779 **lightly**, (as) *easily* 780 **wende**, *thought* 781 **han so fair a grace**, *have such luck* 784 **woot**, *know* 785 **heigh felicitee**, *high happiness*

---

713 God yow see, may God look over you; a blessing. **720 Ynde,** India, i.e., the end of the earth. **727 moodres gate,** mother's (and Mother Earth's) entrance; the image and the Old Man's desire for death, neither found in analogous tales, parallel Maximianus Etruscus *Elegies* 1.227–34. Rebirth and reentry into the womb are associated in John 3.4. **741–42** Leviticus 19.32. **755 hooly sacrement,** Eucharist, another blasphemous oath. **784 this gold is oures,** in English law, found treasure was property of the monarch.

But trewely, by daye it may nat bee.
Men wolde seyn° that we were theves stronge°,
And for oure owene tresor doon us honge°.
This tresor moste ycaried be by nyghte
As wisely and as slyly as it myghte.   790
Wherfore I rede° that cut° among us alle
Be drawe°, and lat se wher the cut wol falle;
And he that hath the cut with herte blithe°
Shal renne° to towne, and that ful swithe°,
And brynge us breed and wyn ful prively°.   795
And two of us shul kepen subtilly°
This tresor wel. And if he wol nat tarie°,
Whan it is nyght we wol this tresor carie
By oon assent° where as us thynketh best."
That oon of hem the cut broghte in his fest   800
And bad hem° drawe and looke° where it wol falle,
And it fil on the yongeste of hem alle,
And forth toward the toun he wente anon.
    And also° soone as that he was gon
That oon of hem spak thus unto that oother,   805
"Thow knowest wel thou art my sworn brother;
Thy profit wol I telle thee anon.
Thou woost° wel that oure felawe is agon.
And heere is gold, and that ful greet plentee,
That shal departed° been among us thre.   810
But nathelees, if I kan shape° it so
That it departed were among us two,
Hadde I nat doon a freendes torn° to thee?"
    That oother answerde, "I noot hou° that
        may be.
He woot° wel that the gold is with us tweye°.   815
What shal we doon? What shal we to hym seye?"
    "Shal it be conseil°?" seyde the firste shrewe°,
"And I shal tellen in a wordes fewe
What we shal doon, and brynge it wel aboute."
    "I graunte," quod that oother, "out of doute,   820
That by my trouthe I shal thee nat biwreye°."
    "Now," quod the firste, "thou woost° wel we be
        tweye,
And two of us shul strenger be than oon.
Looke whan that° he is set that right anoon

Arys° as though thou woldest with hym pleye,   825
And I shal ryve° hym thurgh the sydes tweye
Whil that thou strogelest° with hym as in game,
And with thy daggere looke° thou do the same.
And thanne shal al this gold departed be,
My deere freend, bitwixen me and thee.   830
Thanne may we bothe oure lustes° all fulfille,
And pleye at dees° right° at oure owene wille."
And thus acorded been thise shrewes tweye°
To sleen the thridde, as ye han herd me seye.
    This yongeste, which that wente unto
        the toun,   835
Ful ofte in herte he rolleth up and doun°
The beautee of thise floryns° newe and brighte.
"O Lord," quod he, "if so were that I myghte
Have al this tresor to myself allone
Ther is no man that lyveth under the trone°   840
Of God that sholde lyve so murye° as I."
And atte laste the feend, oure enemy,
Putte in his thought that he sholde poyson beye°
With which he myghte sleen his felawes tweye—
Forwhy° the feend foond hym in swich lyvynge°   845
That he hadde leve° hem to sorwe brynge.
For this was outrely° his fulle entente,
To sleen hem bothe and nevere to repente.
And forth he gooth, no lenger wolde he tarie,
Into the toun unto a pothecarie°,   850
And preyde° hym that he hym wolde selle
Som poyson that he myghte his rattes quelle°,
And eek ther was a polcat° in his hawe°
That, as he seyde, his capouns° hadde yslawe°,
And fayn he wolde wreke hym°, if he myghte,   855
On vermyn that destroyed° hym by nyghte.
    The pothecarie answerde, "And thou shalt have
A thyng that, also° God my soule save,
In al this world ther is no creature
That eten or dronken hath of this confiture°   860
Noght but the montance° of a corn° of whete
That he ne shal his lif anon forlete°—
Ye, sterve° he shal and that in lasse while°
Than thou wold goon a paas nat but° a mile,

787 seyn, *say,* **theves stronge,** *a band of thieves* **788 doon us honge,** *hang us* **791 rede,** *advise,* **cut,** *straws (i.e., drawing for the short straw)* **792 drawe,** *drawn* **793 blithe,** *happy* **794 renne,** *run,* **ful swithe,** *very quickly* **795 prively,** *secretly* **796 kepen subtilly,** *protect carefully* **797 tarie,** *delay* **799 oon assent,** *mutual consent* **801 bad hem,** *told them,* **looke,** *consider* **804 also,** *as* **808 woost,** *know* **810 departed,** *divided* **811 shape,** *arrange* **813 freendes torn,** *friendly favor* **814 noot hou,** *don't know how* **815 woot,** *knows,* **tweye,** *two* **817 conseil,** *confidential,* **shrewe,** *villain* **821 biwreye,** *betray* **822 woost,** *know* **824 Looke whan that,** *see to it that when* **825 Arys,** *get up* **826 ryve,** *stab* **827 strogelest,** *struggle* **828 looke,** *make sure* **831 lustes,** *desires* **832 dees,** *dice,*

right, *completely* **833 shrewes tewye,** *two villains* **836 rolleth up and doun,** *contemplates* **837 floryns,** *coins* **840 trone,** *throne* **841 murye, merrily* **843 beye,** *buy* **845 Forwhy,** *because,* **swich lyvynge,** *such a condition of life* **846 leve,** *permission* **847 outrely,** *utterly* **850 pothecarie, druggist* **851 preyde,** *asked* **852 quelle,** *kill* **853 polcat,** *weasel,* **hawe,** *yard* **854 capouns,** *chickens,* **yslawe,** *slain* **855 fayn he wolde wreke hym,** *he wished to have revenge* **856 destroyed,** *injured* **858 also,** *as (may)* **860 confiture,** *concoction* **861 Noght but the montance,** *nothing more than the size,* **corn,** *grain* **862 anon forlete,** *immediately lose* **863 sterve,** *die,* **lasse while,** *less time* **864 goon a paas nat but,** *go at a pace only*

The poysoun is so strong and violent." 865
    This cursed man hath in his hond yhent°
This poysoun in a box, and sith° he ran
Into the nexte strete unto a man
And borwed of hym large botels° thre,
And in the two his poyson poured he. 870
The thridde he kepte clene for his owene drynke
For al the nyght he shoop° hym for to swynke°
In cariynge of the gold out of that place.
And whan this riotour, with sory grace°,
Hadde filled with wyn his grete botels thre, 875
To his felawes agayn repaireth° he.
    What nedeth it to sermone° of it moore?
For right as they hadde cast° his deeth bifoore,
Right so they han hym slayn, and that anon.
And whan that this was doon, thus spak
        that oon, 880
"Now lat us sitte and drynke and make us merie,
And afterward we wol his body berie°."
And with that word it happed hym par cas°
To take the botel ther° the poyson was,
And drank, and yaf° his felawe drynke also, 885
For which anon they storven° bothe two.
    But certes, I suppose that Avycen
Wroot° nevere in no canon° ne in no fen°
Mo wonder signes° of empoisonyng
Than hadde thise wrecches two er hir°
        endyng. 890
Thus ended been thise homycides two
And eek the false empoysonere also.
    O cursed synne of alle cursednesse!
O traytours homycide, O wikkednesse!
O glotonye, luxurie°, and hasardrye°! 895
Thou blasphemour of Crist with vileynye
And othes° grete of usage° and of pride!
Allas, mankynde, how may it bitide°
That to thy creatour, which that the wroghte°
And with his precious herte-blood thee
        boghte°, 900
Thou art so fals and so unkynde°, allas?

Now goode men, God foryeve yow youre
        trespas,
And ware yow fro° the synne of avarice.
Myn hooly pardoun may yow alle warice°—
So that° ye offre nobles° or sterlynges° 905
Or elles silver broches, spoones, rynges.
Boweth youre heed under this hooly bulle°!
Com up, ye wyves, offreth of youre wolle°!
Youre names I entre heer in my rolle anon°;
Into the blisse of hevene shul ye gon. 910
I yow assoille° by myn heigh power,
Yow that wol offre, as clene and eek as cleer
As ye were born.—And lo, sires, thus I preche.
And Jhesu Crist, that is oure soules leche°,
So graunte yow his pardoun to receyve, 915
For that is best—I wol yow nat deceyve.
    But, sires, o word forgat I in my tale:
I have relikes° and pardoun in my male°
As faire as any man in Engelond,
Whiche were me yeven° by the popes hond. 920
If any of yow wole° of devocioun
Offren, and han myn absolucioun,
Com forth anon and kneleth heere adoun
And mekely receyveth my pardoun,
Or elles taketh pardoun as ye wende° 925
Al newe and fressh at every miles ende—
So that ye offren, alwey newe and newe,
Nobles or pens° whiche that be goode and trewe.
It is an honour to everich° that is heer
That ye mowe° have a suffisant° pardoneer 930
T'assoille° yow in contree as ye ryde
For aventures° whiche that may bityde°.
Paraventure° ther may fallen oon or two
Doun of his hors and breke his nekke atwo.
Looke which a seuretee° is it to yow alle 935
That I am in youre felaweship yfalle°,
That may assoille yow bothe moore and lasse
Whan that the soule shal fro the body passe.
I rede° that oure Hoost heere shal bigynne,
For he is moost envoluped° in synne. 940

---

866 **yhent,** *seized* 867 **sith,** *then* 869 **botels,** *bottles* 872 **shoop,** *planned,* **swynke,** *work* 874 **sory grace,** *ill fate* 876 **repaireth,** *returns* 877 **sermone,** *preach* 878 **cast,** *planned* 882 **berie,** *bury* 883 **it happed hym par cas,** *he happened by chance* 884 **ther,** *where* 885 **yaf,** *gave* 886 **storven,** *died* 888 **Wroot,** *wrote,* **canon,** *chart,* **fen,** *section* 889 **Mo wonder signes,** *more extreme symptoms* 890 **er hir,** *before their* 895 **luxurie,** *lechery,* **hasardrye,** *gambling* 897 **othes,** *oaths,* **usage,** *habit* 898 **bitide,** *happen* 899 **the wroghte,** *made you* 900 **boghte,** *redeemed* 901 **unkynde,** *unnatural* 903 **ware yow fro,** *beware* 904 **warice,** *save* 905 **So**

that, *as long as,* **nobles,** *gold coins,* **sterlynges,** *silver coins* 907 **bulle,** *document* 908 **wolle,** *wool* 909 **rolle anon,** *records immediately* 911 **assoille,** *absolve* 914 **leche,** *physician* 918 **relikes,** *relics,* **male,** *bag* 920 **yeven,** *given* 921 **wole,** *will* 925 **wende,** *travel* 928 **pens,** *pennies* 929 **everich,** *everyone* 930 **mowe,** *are able to,* **suffisant,** *capable* 931 **T'assoille,** *to absolve* 932 **aventures,** *accidents,* **bityde,** *happen* 933 **Paraventure,** *perhaps* 935 **which a seuretee,** *what an assurance* 936 **am in youre felaweship yfalle,** *have happened into your company* 939 **rede,** *advise* 940 **envoluped,** *enveloped*

887–88 **Avycen . . . canon . . . fen,** Avicenna, medieval Islamic physician, whose famous treatise, *Liber Canonis Medicinae* (Book of the Rules of Medicine), is divided into fens (Arabic *fann,* a unit of technical discussion); *Liber* 4.6 discusses poisons. 927–28 Echoes lines 905–6.

Com forth, sire Hoost, and offre first anon,
And thou shalt kisse my relikes everychon°—
Ye, for a grote°: unbokele anon° thy purs."
   "Nay, nay," quod he, "thanne have I Cristes curs.
Lat be," quod he, "it shal nat be, so theech°!   945
Thou woldest make me kisse thyn olde breech°
And swere it were a relyk of a seint,
Though it were with thy fundement depeint°.
But by the croys which that Seint Eleyne fond
I wolde I hadde thy coillons in myn hond   950
Instide of relikes or of seintuarie°.
Lat kutte hem of°, I wol thee helpe hem carie.
They shul be shryned° in an hogges toord°."
   This Pardoner answerde nat a word.

So wrooth° he was, no word ne wolde he seye.   955
   "Now," quod oure Hoost, "I wol no lenger
      pleye
With thee ne with noon oother angry man."
But right anon the worthy Knyght bigan,
Whan that he saugh that al the peple lough°,
"Namoore of this, for it is right ynough.   960
Sire Pardoner, be glad and myrie of cheere°;
And ye, sire Hoost, that been to me so deere,
I prey yow that ye kisse the Pardoner.
And Pardoner, I prey thee drawe thee neer,
And as we diden lat us laughe and pleye."   965
Anon they kiste and ryden° forth hir weye.

Heere is ended the Pardoners Tale.

---

942 everychon, *each one* **943 grote,** *four-penny silver coin,* **unbokele anon,** *unbuckle quickly* **945 theech,** *may I prosper* **946 breech,** *underpants* **948 fundement depeint,** *bottom stained* **951 seintuarie,** *sacred objects* **952 Lat kutte hem of,** *let them be cut off* **953 shryned,** *enshrined,* **hogges toord,** *hog's turd* **955 wrooth,** *enraged* **959 lough,** *laughed* **961 myrie of cheere,** *good humored* **966 ryden,** *rode*

949 croys . . . Seint Eleyne, St. Helen was thought to have found the cross of Christ's Crucifixion. **950 coillons,** testicles, recalling the earlier suggestions of the Pardoner's castration or infertility, *GP* 1.688–91n. The association of relics and coillons was inspired by Reason's theory of names and allegory in *RR* 7081ff., especially 7108–09.

CANTERBURY TALES PART 7

INTRODUCTION

PART 7 IS THE LONGEST and most varied section of *The Canterbury Tales,* with six tales of differing genre, one of them in prose, two in rhymed couplets, and the others in various verse forms. The pilgrim Chaucer tells two of the tales himself, and in the links among the tales, the Host comments recurrently on literature and its effects. Throughout *The Canterbury Tales,* Chaucer explores the commonplace that diverse people speak diversely (see, e.g., *KnT* 1.2516ff., *WBT* 3.925ff., *SqT* 5.202), and in part 7 he experiments with literary form while exploring how and to what extent tales are appropriate to individual tellers and our expectations of them. The briefer sections of *The Canterbury Tales* often juxtapose two different or opposed literary genres or modes, but here the variety is greater and the complexity richer.

The teller's use of first-person female pronouns in the *Shipman's Tale* indicates that the story was once intended by Chaucer to be told by the Wife of Bath (see 11–19). Its reassignment in unrevised form to the Shipman may be due to the mercantile concerns of the tale since the Shipman makes a shady living in the business of nautical transport (*GP* 1.395ff.). The tale commodifies sex rather than celebrates it or moralizes about it, and the fabliau lacks the slapstick humor and bawdiness of Chaucer's other examples of the genre. In their place it offers restrained conversation and double entendre (see 36, 416). The sex-for-money device of the traditional plot—the "lover's gift regained"—does not rebound on the monk who trades in sex with a merchant's wife and in money with the merchant. Nor does adultery negatively affect the married couple. Unlike in the closest analogues to the tale, Boccaccio's *Decameron* 8.1 and 8.2 and Sercambi's *Novelle,* the wife is not compelled to repay the money for which she prostitutes herself, perhaps a vestige of the Wife of Bath as original teller. Sex and money pay dividends in a world where everyone profits, so the class and gender inequalities of the fabliau are muted by urbanity, opportunism, and accommodation. Albert H. Silverman, "Sex and Money in Chaucer's *Shipman's Tale*" (1953, no. 1262) long ago identified the punning equation of sex and money in the tale. In "Thinking about Money in Chaucer's *Shipman's Tale*" (2003, no. 1259), William E. Rogers and Paul Dower survey subsequent criticism and argue that varying attitudes toward money produce varying interpretations of the tale.

The bourgeois urbanity of the *Shipman's Tale* is contrasted sharply by lofty idealism, bloody action, and heightened sentimentality in the *Prioress's Tale.* We leave a gray world for one that is black and white. Medieval miracles of the Virgin (the genre of the tale) promoted piety by depicting the rewards of steadfast devotion in the face of persecution. As are so many stereotyped "bad guys" of popular literature, the Jews in this tale are demonized, here quite literally (558–64), and the ending of the tale reminds us sharply that such demonizing occurs in history as well as literature, with brutal consequences. The devotion of the little choirboy slain by the Jews is emphasized by the fact that he does not understand the Latin words he sings, only that they praise Mary. The Prioress identifies with such innocent or unthinking devotion (481–87), encouraging many to blame her for the goriness and anti-Semitism of the tale. Others blame the genre itself, and still others argue that the anti-Semitism was Chaucer's own, unavoidable in his time. The Prioress's pity for mice and dogs (see *GP* 1.144–50) at a time when human beings were dying from plague and starvation encourages the first view. However we read the brutality of the tale, it confronts us with the powers of speech and narrative to affect human lives and with the dangers that lie in the gaps between intention, understanding, and language use. The essays edited by

Sheila Delany in *Chaucer and the Jews* (2002, no. 656) explore Judaism in Chaucer's works and bring postcolonial perspective to bear on the issues surveyed by Florence Ridley in *The Prioress and the Critics* (1965, no. 1298) and Beverly Boyd in the Variorum edition of the tale (1987, no. 45).

The rhyme royale stanza form of the *Prioress's Tale* heightens its emotional effects, and the verse form is tellingly sustained—and perhaps undercut—in the comic prologue that follows and sets up the *Tale of Sir Thopas*. Told by the pilgrim-narrator Chaucer at the invitation of the Host, the tale is a burlesque of tail-rhyme romances popular in late-medieval England. To appreciate the fun, we must recognize the brilliant clichés by which Chaucer systematically parodies every convention of the genre—verse form, setting, plot, character, diction, imagery, and so on. On the clichés, see Laura Hibbard Loomis's chapter in Bryan and Dempster's *Sources and Analogues* (1941, no. 186) and Alan T. Gaylord's "Chaucer's Dainty 'Dogerel'" (1979, no. 1305). Twenty-first century readers may be forgiven for missing some of the joke, but the Host is not let off so easily. His brusque interruption of Chaucer's parody exposes literary ignorance or insensitivity. As well, the plumpness and naïveté of the narrator-persona in the *Thopas* prologue make Chaucer himself a comic target. Nowhere is his humor more genial or inclusive, yet there is more here than literary fun. The contrast with the seriousness of the *Prioress's Tale* is emphatic, and the parody touches on the aesthetic aspects of many issues from the previous tale: ignorance versus understanding, intention and effect, and the function of conventions and stereotypes.

The *Tale of Melibee* has also been read as something of a joke—a lengthy, sententious treatise that is introduced as a "litel thyng in prose" (937). Little it is not, and at the end the joke seems again to be on the Host, who misses the political and personal allegory of the tale and reveals himself to be intimidated by his wife. The very serious issues of the tale—the value of taking counsel and the desirability of peace—are appropriate to late fourteenth-century England, which was embroiled in the Hundred Years' War and the shifting power struggles of the minority of Richard II and his troubled reign. Chaucer may have written the work before Richard took full control of the kingdom (see 1199n), but the message is apposite under almost any political conditions. As well, the allegory

encourages individual self-reflection, as Prudence eventually convinces her husband, Melibee, to pursue the personal calm that parallels social peace. Female advice is a positive force, and marriage is a figure for moral or psychological balance as well as political stability. The tale translates Renaud de Louens's *Livre de Melibée et de Dame Prudence* (1336), itself a French translation of Albertanus of Brescia's Latin *Liber Consolationis et Consilii* (Book of Consolation and Counsel). On the allegory of the tale, see Paul Strohm, "The Allegory of the *Tale of Melibee*" (1967, no. 1330); and, for political concerns, Lynn Staley Johnson, "Inverse Counsel: Contexts for the *Melibee*" (1990, no. 1322), and Judith Ferster, "Chaucer's *Tale of Melibee:* Contradictions and Context" (2000, no. 1320).

The weightiness of *Melibee* contrasts the fun of *Thopas* as *sentence* contrasts *solaas;* and the message of *Melibee* can be seen as a secular complement to Chaucer's other prose tale, the *Parson's Tale,* and crucial to understanding *The Canterbury Tales* overall. The *Thopas / Melibee* pairing represents the poet's traditional roles of entertainer and adviser, and the Host's responses suggest Chaucer's concerns about audience reception. See Alan T. Gaylord, "*Sentence* and *Solaas* in Fragment VII of the *Canterbury Tales:* Harry Bailly as Horseback Editor" (1967, no. 744), and Lee W. Patterson, "'What Man Artow?': Authorial Self-Definition in *The Tale of Sir Thopas* and *The Tale of Melibee*" (1989, no. 1312).

The *Monk's Tale* continues Chaucer's experimentation with form and genre. Its eight-line stanza is used elsewhere in Chaucer's poetry only in the *ABC,* and the tale is really an anthology of tales that mirrors part 7 and *The Canterbury Tales* overall, though it tellingly lacks their variety. The Monk labels his brief narratives "tragedies" (1971), defining them as stories of men who fall from prosperity, leaving aside concern with the cause(s) of the fall or the merit of the victim. This definition and the persistent lamenting of Fortune's effects in the tale encourage negative judgments of the Monk, who by vocation, the argument goes, ought to be more concerned with spiritual merit than the vagaries of fortune. The definition of *tragedy* has prompted commentary on Chaucer's medieval understanding of the term in contrast with Aristotle's classic definition in his *Poetics,* which better fits later works by Shakespeare and Arthur Miller, for example. For discussion of Chaucer's notion of tragedy and its legacy, see Henry Ansgar Kelly,

Chaucerian Tragedy (1997, no. 701). *Studies in the Age of Chaucer* 22 (2000, no. 1342) includes a cluster of articles that discuss a range of issues that pertain to the *Monk's Tale*.

"De casibus" tragedy, as medieval tragedy is also called, derives from Boccaccio's collection *De Casibus Virorum Illustrium* (On the Falls of Famous Men). Chaucer took little or none of his material from Boccaccio's collection, although the rubric to the *Monk's Tale* (1990a) borrows the Latin title. Chaucer's sources are eclectic, including the Bible, the *Romance of the Rose*, Boethius, Ovid, Dante, and others. Consistent with Chaucer's recurrent disguising of his debt to Boccaccio, the account of Zenobia, the only woman in this list, uses Boccaccio's *De Claris Mulieribus* (On Famous Women) while suggesting that Petrarch is the source (2325). The four accounts about Chaucer's near contemporaries raise textual questions because they appear in two different places in the manuscripts (see 2375–2461n). These "modern instances" align ancient history with events of Chaucer's day, in two cases with the lives of men whom Chaucer met.

The Knight's interruption of the Monk comes as a relief to many readers since he suggests an alternative to a tragic view of life and a different kind of story. The Host agrees, and his responses to the Monk's performance are a comic screen through which Chaucer extends his concern with audience response to tales, setting up the literary tour de force that is the *Nun's Priest's Tale*. We arrive at this tale with barely any expectations because the teller is not introduced in the *General Prologue* and we have come to distrust the Host's evaluations of people and tales. The *Nun's Priest's Tale* returns to the rhymed couplets of the *Shipman's Tale* and fulfills the narrative and ethical potential in that earlier tale for tricking a trickster—in this case a rooster outdoing a fox. Within its beast-fable genre, it balances the mock heroism of *Thopas* and the sententiousness of *Melibee*, combining *solaas* and *sentence* as well as anywhere in the Canterbury fiction. It mentions the murder of a little boy (3110ff.), recalling the *Prioress's Tale*, and it echoes both the Prioress's table manners and at least one of her phrases (2834, 3052). Most emphatically, it counters the Monk's catastrophes with delight, renders absurd the self-seriousness that underlies them,

and shows that though people (and chickens) may fall, they also can rise again.

The themes and digressions of the *Nun's Priest's Tale* are kaleidoscopic, shifting among serious concerns such as free will, dream psychology, gender relations, Adam's fall, the uprising of 1381 (Peasants' Revolt), and the morality of fiction—all rendered comic by reminders that the tale is set in a barnyard. The widow's modest living in the narrative frame casts into relief the rooster's self-centeredness, which in turn occasions a number of exempla and rhetorical set pieces that offer contradictory proverbs and other kinds of wisdom literature. The effect is rather like a set of Chinese boxes or Russian dolls, so the serious concerns of the tale are constantly undercut but never disappear from view. When the rooster offers one moral at the end of the tale, the fox offers another. The narrator hints at a third in language that implies everything written must be taken seriously. These "nested" morals, like the narrative layers of the tale, challenge the reader to make sense of it all without losing awareness of the tale's playfulness.

The basic plot derives from Marie de France's "Del Cok e del Gupil" (The Cock and the Fox), a beast-fable in the tradition of Aesop, and from medieval beast epics that centered on the adventures of Reynard the fox, especially the *Roman de Renart* and perhaps the *Renart le Contrefait* (Reynard the Trickster). Robert A. Pratt (1972, no. 1370; 1977, no. 1369) has shown that Chaucer adapted these and fleshed them out with a variety of materials, particularly Robert Holcott's commentary of the biblical Book of Wisdom attributed to Solomon, *Super Sapientiam Salomonis*. Edward Wheatley summarizes Pratt's arguments in the recent *Sources and Analogues* (2002, no. 187). Derek Pearsall's Variorum edition (1984, no. 41) of the tale is thorough and judicious in its judgments, and his reading of the tale in his *The Canterbury Tales* (1985, no. 87) has not been superseded.

Two versions of the *Nun's Priest's Prologue* survive, and Chaucer evidently canceled the *Epilogue* (see 2767n, 3447–62n). These and other features of part 7 left unrevised or in process indicate that Chaucer's exploration of—perhaps anxiety about—poetics and literary reception was an ongoing concern.

CANTERBURY TALES PART 7

SHIPMAN'S TALE

Heere bigynneth the Shipmannes Tale.

A marchant whilom° dwelled at Seint Denys,
That riche was, for which men helde hym wys.
A wyf he hadde of excellent beautee,
And compaignable and revelous° was she,
Which is a thyng that causeth more dispence°   5
Than worth is al the chiere° and reverence°
That men hem doon° at festes and at daunces.
Swiche salutaciouns° and contenaunces°
Passen as dooth a shadwe upon the wal.
But wo is hym that payen moot° for al!   10
The sely° housbonde algate° he moot paye,
He moot us clothe, and he moot us arraye°,
Al for his owene worship°, richely—
In which array we daunce jolily.
And if that he noght may°, par aventure°,   15

Or ellis list no swich dispence endure°,
But thynketh it is wasted and ylost,
Thanne moot another payen for oure cost,
Or lene° us gold—and that is perilous.
    This noble marchaunt heeld° a worthy hous,   20
For which he hadde alday° so greet repair°
For his largesse°, and for his wyf was fair,
That wonder is. But herkneth° to my tale:
Amonges alle his gestes grete and smale
Ther was a monk, a fair man and a boold—   25
I trowe a thritty wynter° he was oold—
That evere in oon° was drawynge to that place.
This yonge monk that was so fair of face
Aqueynted was so with the goode man
Sith that hir° firste knoweliche° bigan,   30

---

1 whilom, *once* 4 revelous, *inclined to partying* 5 dispence, *expense* 6 chiere, *attention,* reverence, *respect* 7 hem doon, *give them* 8 Swiche salutaciouns, *such greetings,* contenaunces, *courtesies* 10 moot, *must* 11 sely, *innocent* or *foolish,* algate, *always* 12 arraye, *adorn* 13 worship, *esteem* 15 noght may, *is unable to,* par aventure, *by chance* 16 ellis list no swich dispence endure, *else does not wish to endure such expense* 19 lene, *lend* 20 heeld, *maintained* 21 alday, *always,* so greet repair, *so many visitors* 22 largesse, *generosity* 23 herkneth, *listen* 26 trowe a thritty wynter, *believe about thirty years* 27 evere in oon, *constantly* 30 Sith that hir, *since their,* knoweliche, *acquaintance*

1 Seint Denys, town north of Paris, known in the Middle Ages for trade and a major abbey. 11–19 us . . . we . . . , the first-person pronouns in these lines require a female speaker, almost certainly the Wife of Bath before this tale was reassigned and left unrevised. 29 goode man, the usual label for the head of a household.

236

That in his hous as famulier was he
As it is possible any freend to be.
And for as muchel as° this goode man
And eek this monk of which that I bigan
Were bothe two yborn in o° village,　　　35
The monk hym claymeth as for cosynage;
And he agayn°, he seith nat ones nay
But was as glad therof as fowel° of day,
For to his herte it was a greet plesaunce°.
Thus been they knyt with eterne alliaunce,　　　40
And ech of hem gan oother for t'assure°
Of bretherhede whil that hir lyf may dure°.

　　Free° was daun John and namely° of dispence°
As in that hous, and ful of diligence
To doon plesaunce and also greet costage°.　　　45
He noght forgat to yeve° the leeste page°
In al the hous, but after hir degree°
He yaf° the lord and sitthe° al his meynee°,
Whan that he cam, som manere honest° thyng,
For which they were as glad of his comyng　　　50
As fowel° is fayn° whan that the sonne up riseth.
Namoore of this as now, for it suffiseth.

　　But so bifel, this marchant on a day
Shoop hym° to make redy his array
Toward the toun of Brugges for to fare°,　　　55
To byen° there a porcioun of ware°.
For which he hath to Parys° sent anon
A messager, and preyed hath° daun John
That he sholde come to Seint Denys to pleye
With hym and with his wyf a day or tweye,　　　60
Er° he to Brugges wente, in alle wise°.

　　This noble monk of which I yow devyse
Hath of his abbot as hym list licence°,
By cause he was a man of heigh prudence
And eek an officer, out for to ryde　　　65
To seen° hir graunges° and hire bernes° wyde°,
And unto Seinte Denys he comth anon.

Who was so welcome as my lord daun John,
Oure deere cosyn, ful of curteisye?
With hym broghte he a jubbe° of malvesye°,　　　70
And eek another, ful of fyn vernage°,
And volatyl°, as ay° was his usage°.
And thus I lete hem ete and drynke and pleye,
This marchant and this monk, a day or tweye.

　　The thridde day this marchant up ariseth　　　75
And on his nedes sadly hym avyseth°,
And up into his countour-hous° gooth he
To rekene with° hymself, wel may be,
Of thilke° yeer how that it with hym stood,
And how that he despended° hadde his good°,　　　80
And if that he encressed were or noon.
His bookes and his bagges many oon
He leith° biforn hym on his countyng-bord.
Ful riche was his tresor and his hord,
For which ful faste° his countour-dore he
　　shette°;　　　85
And eek he nolde that no man° sholde hym
　　lette°
Of his acountes for the meene tyme;
And thus he sit til it was passed pryme°.

　　Daun John was rysen in the morwe° also
And in the gardyn walketh to and fro　　　90
And hath his thynges° seyd ful curteisly°.

　　This goode wyf cam walkynge pryvely°
Into the gardyn there° he walketh softe°,
And hym saleweth° as she hath doon ofte.
A mayde child cam in hire compaignye　　　95
Which as hir list° she may governe and gye°
For yet under the yerde° was the mayde.
"O deere cosyn myn, daun John," she sayde,
"What eyleth° yow so rathe° for to ryse?"

　　"Nece," quod he, "it oghte ynough suffise　　　100
Fyve houres for to slepe upon a nyght
But° it were for an old appalled wight°,

---

33 for as muchel as, *on account of the fact that* **35 o,** *the same* **37 agayn,** *in return* **38 fowel,** *bird* **39 plesaunce,** *pleasure* **41 gan . . . for t'assure,** *did assure* **42 dure,** *last* **43 Free,** *generous, namely, especially,* **dispence,** *spending* **45 doon . . . costage,** *spend money* **46 yeve,** *give,* **page,** *servant boy* **47 after hir degree,** *in accord with their rank* **48 yaf,** *gave,* **sitthe,** *after,* **meynee,** *household* **49 manere honest,** *kind of appropriate* **51 fowel,** *bird,* **fayn,** *happy* **54 Shoop hym,** *prepared himself* **55 fare,** *go* **56 byen,** *buy,* **porcioun of ware,** *quantity of goods* **57 Parys,** *Paris* **58 preyed hath,** *has asked* **61 Er,** *before,* **wise,** *ways* **62 devyse,** *describe* **63 as hym list licence,** *permission as he wishes* **66 seen,** *oversee,* **graunges,** *farms,* **bernes,** *barns,* **wyde,** *widespread* **70 jubbe,** *jug,* **malvesye,** *sweet*

Greek wine **71 vernage,** *sweet Italian wine* **72 volatyl,** *game fowl,* **ay,** *always,* **usage,** *habit* **76 his nedes sadly hym avyseth,** *thinks seriously about his business* **77 countour-hous,** *counting house* (office) **78 rekene with,** *reckon by* **79 thilke,** *that* **80 despended,** *spent,* **good,** *assets* **83 leith,** *lays* **85 ful faste,** *very tightly,* **shette,** *shut* **86 nolde that no man,** *wished that no one,* **lette,** *hinder* **88 pryme,** *about 9 a.m.* **89 morwe,** *morning* **91 thynges,** *prayers,* **ful curteisly,** *very courteously* **92 pryvely,** *secretly* **93 there,** *where,* **softe,** *softly* **94 saleweth,** *greets* **96 as hir list,** *as it pleases her,* **gye,** *guide* **97 the yerde,** *supervision* **99 eyleth,** *ails,* **rathe,** *early* **102 But,** *unless,* **appalled wight,** *feeble person*

---

36 cosynage, kinship. The kinship terms *cosynage* and *cosyn* recur frequently throughout the tale, arguably punning with forms of *cosin* (trickery or deception), which the *MED* first records some fifty years after Chaucer's death. **43 daun,** master, a formulaic address of respect. **55 Brugges,** Bruges in Flanders (modern Belgium), a mercantile city. **65 out for to ryde,** i.e., he is an "outrider," like the Monk in the *GP* 1.166n. **100 Nece,** kinswoman; a term of address for a female relative.

As been thise wedded men that lye and dare°
As in a fourme° sit a wery hare
Were° al forstraught° with houndes grete and
    smale.   105
But deere nece, why be ye so pale?
I trowe°, certes°, that oure goode man
Hath yow laboured sith° the nyght bigan
That yow were nede to resten hastily°."
And with that word he lough° ful murily,   110
And of his owene thought he wax al reed°.
    This faire wyf gan for to shake hir heed
And seyde thus, "Ye, God woot° al," quod she.
"Nay, nay, cosyn myn, it stant° nat so with me;
For by that God that yaf° me soule and lyf,   115
In al the reawme° of France is ther no wyf
That lasse lust hath to° that sory pley.
For I may synge 'allas and weylawey
That I was born,' but to no wight°," quod she,
"Dar I nat telle how that it stant with me.   120
Wherfore I thynke out of this land to wende°,
Or elles of myself to make an ende,
So ful am I of drede and eek of care."
    This monk bigan upon this wyf to stare,
And seyde, "Allas, my nece, God forbede   125
That ye for any sorwe or any drede
Fordo° youreself. But telleth me youre grief—
Paraventure° I may in youre meschief°
Conseille or helpe; and therfore telleth me
Al youre anoy°, for it shal been secree°.   130
For on my porthors° I make an ooth
That nevere in my lyf, for lief ne looth°,
Ne shal I of no conseil yow biwreye°."
    "The same agayn to yow," quod she, "I seye.
By God and by this porthors I yow swere,   135
Though men me wolde al into pieces tere,
Ne shal I nevere, for to goon to helle,
Biwreye a word of thyng that ye me telle,
Nat for no cosynage° ne alliance
But verraily° for love and affiance°."   140
Thus been they sworn, and heerupon they kiste

And ech of hem tolde oother what hem liste°.
    "Cosyn," quod she, "if that I hadde a space°,
As I have noon, and namely° in this place,
Thanne wolde I telle a legende of my lyf,   145
What I have suffred sith° I was a wyf
With myn housbonde, al be he youre cosyn."
    "Nay," quod this monk, "by God and Seint
        Martyn,
He is na moore cosyn unto me
Than is this leef that hangeth on the tree.   150
I clepe° hym so, by Seint Denys of Fraunce,
To have the moore cause of aqueyntaunce
Of yow, which I have loved specially
Aboven alle wommen, sikerly°.
This swere I yow on my professioun°.   155
Telleth youre grief, lest that° he come adoun,
And hasteth yow, and gooth youre wey anon."
    "My deere love," quod she, "O my daun John,
Ful lief were me° this conseil° for to hyde,
But out it moot°; I may namoore abyde°.   160
Myn housbonde is to me the worste man
That evere was sith° that the world bigan.
But sith I am a wyf, it sit° nat me
To tellen no wight of oure privetee,
Neither abedde ne in noon oother place;   165
God shilde° I sholde it tellen, for his grace!
A wyf ne shal nat seyn of hir housbonde
But al honour, as I kan understonde—
Save° unto yow thus muche I tellen shal:
As helpe me God, he is noght worth at al   170
In no degree° the value of a flye.
But yet me greveth moost his nygardye°.
And wel ye woot° that wommen naturelly
Desiren thynges sixe as wel as I:
They wolde that hir housbondes sholde be   175
Hardy°, and wise, and riche, and therto free°,
And buxom° unto his wyf, and fressh abedde°.
But by that ilke° Lord that for us bledde,
For his honour myself for to arraye,
A° Sonday next I most nedes paye°   180

---

103 **dare,** *cower* 104 **fourme,** *burrow* 105 **Were,** *when it is,* **forstraught,** *distraught* 107 **trowe,** *think,* **certes,** *surely* 108 **sith,** *since* 109 **hastily,** *soon* 110 **lough,** *laughed* 111 **wax al reed,** i.e., *blushed* 113 **woot,** *knows* 114 **stant,** *stands* 115 **yaf,** *gave* 116 **reawme,** *realm* 117 **lasse lust hath to,** *less pleasure has for* 119 **wight,** *person* 121 **wende,** *travel* 127 **Fordo,** *kill* 128 **Paraventure,** *perhaps,* **meschief,** *misfortune* 130 **anoy,** *trouble,* **secree,** *secret* 131 **porthors,** *breviary* (prayer book) 132 **lief ne looth,** *love nor hate* 133 **biwreye,** *betray* 139 **cosynage,** *kinship* (see 36n) 140 **verraily,** *truly,* **affiance,** *trust* 142 **hem liste,** *they pleased* 143 **space,**

while 144 **namely,** *especially* 146 **sith,** *since* 151 **clepe,** *call* 154 **sikerly,** *certainly* 155 **professioun,** *monastic vows* 156 **lest that,** *before* 159 **Ful lief were me,** *very much I would like,* **conseil,** *secret* 160 **out it moot,** *it must come out,* **abyde,** *wait* 162 **sith,** *since* 163 **sit,** *suits* 166 **shilde,** *forbid* 169 **Save,** *except* 171 **In no degree,** *in no way* 172 **nygardye,** *stinginess* 173 **woot,** *know* 175 **wolde,** *wish* 176 **Hardy,** *bold,* **therto free,** *also generous* 177 **buxom,** *obedient,* **fressh abedde,** *lively in bed* 178 **ilke,** *same* 180 **A,** *by,* **most nedes paye,** *need to pay*

148 **Seint Martyn,** St. Martin of Tours, founded the first monastery in France. 151 **Seint Denys,** St. Denis, patron saint of France. 156 **lest that he come adoun,** i.e., quickly before he comes down. As in modern usage, *lest that* is used to express fear or apprehension.

An hundred frankes, or ellis I am lorn°.
Yet were me levere° that I were unborn
Than me were doon a sclaundre or vileynye.
And if myn housbonde eek it myghte espye°,
I nere° but lost. And therfore I yow preye,   185
Lene° me this somme°, or ellis moot° I deye.
Daun John, I seye lene me thise hundred frankes.
Pardee°, I wol nat faille yow my thankes,
If that yow list° to doon that I yow praye.
For at a certeyn day I wol yow paye,   190
And doon to yow what plesance° and service
That I may doon, right° as yow list devise°.
And but° I do, God take on me vengeance
As foul as evere hadde Genylon of France."

This gentil monk answerde in this manere,   195
"Now trewely, myn owene lady deere,
I have," quod he, "on yow so greet a routhe°
That I yow swere and plighte° yow my trouthe°
That whan youre housbonde is to Flaundres fare°,
I wol delyvere yow out of this care,   200
For I wol brynge yow an hundred frankes."
And with that word he caughte hire by the flankes,
And hire embraceth harde, and kiste hire ofte.
"Gooth now youre wey," quod he, "al stille and
      softe°,
And lat us dyne as soone as that ye may,   205
For by my chilyndre° it is pryme of day°.
Gooth now, and beeth as trewe as I shal be."

"Now elles° God forbede, sire," quod she,
And forth she gooth as jolif as a pye,
And bad° the cookes that they sholde
      hem hye°   210
So that men myghte dyne, and that anon.
Up to hir housbonde is this wyf ygon,
And knokketh at his countour° boldely.

"Qui la°?" quod he. "Peter, it am I,"
Quod she; "what sire, how longe wol ye faste?   215
How longe tyme wol ye rekene° and caste°

Youre sommes°, and youre bookes, and youre
      thynges?
The devel have part on° alle swiche rekenynges!
Ye have ynough, pardee, of Goddes sonde°.
Com doun today, and lat youre bagges stonde.   220
Ne be ye nat ashamed that daun John
Shal fasting al this day alenge goon°?
What, lat us heere a messe° and go we dyne."

"Wyf," quod this man, "litel kanstow devyne°
The curious° bisynesse that we have.   225
For of us chapmen°, also° God me save,
And by that lord that clepid° is Seint Yve,
Scarsly amonges twelve tweye° shul thryve
Continuelly, lastynge unto oure age.
We may wel make chiere and good visage°,   230
And dryve forth° the world as it may be,
And kepen oure estaat in pryvetee°
Til we be deed, or elles that° we pleye°
A pilgrymage, or goon out of the weye°.
And therfore have I greet necessitee   235
Upon this queynte° world t'avyse me,
For everemoore we moote° stonde in drede
Of hap° and fortune in oure chapmanhede°.

"To Flaunders wol I go tomorwe at day,
And come agayn as soone as evere I may.   240
For which, my deere wyf, I thee biseke°
As be to every wight° buxom° and meke,
And for to kepe° oure good° be curious°,
And honestly governe wel oure hous.
Thou hast ynough, in every maner wise,   245
That to a thrifty houshold may suffise.
Thee lakketh noon array° ne no vitaille°;
Of silver in thy purs shaltow° nat faille°."
And with that word his countour-dore he shette,
And doun he gooth, no lenger wolde he lette°.   250
But hastily a messe° was ther seyd,
And spedily the tables were yleyd°,
And to the dyner faste they hem spedde,

---

181 lorn, *lost* **182 were me levere,** *I would rather* **184 espye,** *discover* **185 nere,** *would be nothing* **186 Lene,** *loan,* **somme,** *sum,* **moot,** *must* **188 Pardee,** *by God* **189 list,** *choose* **191 plesance,** *pleasure* **192 right,** *just,* **list devise,** *wish to devise* **193 but,** *unless* **197 routhe,** *pity* **198 plighte,** *pledge,* **trouthe,** *word* **199 fare,** *gone* **204 al stille and softe,** i.e., *quietly* **206 chilyndre,** *pocket sundial,* **pryme of day,** *9 a.m.* **208 elles,** *otherwise* **210 bad,** *ordered,* **hem hye,** *hurry themselves* **213 countour,** *counting house* (see line 77) **214 Qui la,** *who's there* (Fr.) **216 rekene,** *reckon,* **caste,** *project* **217 sommes,** *sums* **218 have part on,** *take a portion of* **219 sonde,** *gifts*

222 alenge goon, *go unhappy* **223 messe,** *mass* **224 kanstow devyne,** *can you imagine* **225 curious,** *intricate* **226 chapmen,** *merchants,* **also,** *so (may)* **227 clepid,** *named* **228 tweye,** *two* **230 visage,** *face* **231 dryve forth,** *advance* **232 pryvetee,** *secrecy* **233 elles that,** *otherwise,* **pleye,** *perform* **234 goon out of the weye,** *go into hiding* **236 queynte,** *complicated* **237 moote,** *must* **238 hap,** *chance,* **chapmanhede,** *trading* **241 biseke,** *request* **242 wight,** *person,* **buxom,** *helpful* **243 kepe,** *protect,* **good,** *property,* **curious,** *careful* **247 array,** *clothing,* **vitaille,** *food* **248 shaltow,** *you shall,* **faille,** *lack* **250 lette,** *delay* **251 messe,** *mass* **252 yleyd,** *laid*

---

181 hundred frankes, one hundred gold coins, a sizable sum. **183 Than me were doon a sclaundre or vileynye,** than an embarrassment or dishonor were done to me. The wife fears that her debt (for clothing) will be made known, presumably jeopardizing future borrowing. **194 Genylon,** Ganelon, who betrayed Roland in *Chanson de Roland,* was torn to pieces by horses. **209 jolif as a pye,** jolly as a magpie, i.e., happy as a lark. **214 Peter,** by St. Peter, keeper of the gates of heaven. **227 Seint Yve,** St. Ivo of Chartres? A convenient rhyme?

And richely this monk the chapman fedde.

   At after-dyner daun John sobrely   255
This chapman took apart, and prively
He seyde hym thus, "Cosyn, it standeth so
That wel I se to Brugges wol ye go.
God and Seint Austyn spede yow and gyde°!
I prey yow, cosyn, wisely that ye ryde.   260
Governeth yow also of youre diete
Atemprely°, and namely° in this hete°.
Bitwix us two nedeth no strange fare°.
Farewel, cosyn. God shilde° yow fro care.
And if that any thyng by day or nyght,   265
If it lye in my power and my myght,
That ye me wol comande in any wyse,
It shal be doon right° as ye wol devyse.

   "O thyng, er that ye goon, if it may be:
I wolde prey yow for to lene° me   270
An hundred frankes for a wyke° or tweye,
For certein beestes that I moste beye
To stoore with° a place that is oures.
God helpe me so, I wolde it were youres!
I shal nat faille surely at my day,   275
Nat for a thousand frankes, a mile way.
But lat this thyng be secree°, I yow preye,
For yet tonyght thise beestes moot I beye.
And fare now wel, myn owene cosyn deere;
Graunt mercy of° youre cost and of youre
     cheere°."   280

   This noble marchant gentilly anon
Answerde and seyde, "O cosyn myn, daun John,
Now sikerly° this is a smal requeste.
My gold is youres whan that it yow leste°,
And nat oonly my gold but my chaffare°.   285
Take what yow list°, God shilde° that ye spare°.

   "But o thyng is, ye knowe it wel ynogh,
Of chapmen that hir moneie is hir plogh°.
We may creaunce° whil we have a name°,
But goldlees for to be it is no game.   290
Paye it agayn whan it lith° in youre ese;

After my myght° ful fayn° wolde I yow plese."

   Thise hundred frankes he fette° forth anon,
And prively he took hem to daun John.
No wight° in al this world wiste° of this lone°   295
Savynge this marchant and daun John allone.
They drynke, and speke, and rome° a while and
     pleye,
Til that daun John rideth to his abbeye.

   The morwe cam, and forth this marchant rideth
To Flaundres-ward; his prentys° wel hym
     gydeth°   300
Til he cam into Brugges murily.
Now gooth this marchant faste and bisily
Aboute his nede, and byeth° and creaunceth°.
He neither pleyeth at the dees° ne daunceth,
But as a marchaunt, shortly for to telle,   305
He let° his lyf, and there I lete hym dwelle.

   The Sonday next° this marchant was agon,
To Seint Denys ycomen is daun John,
With crowne° and berd al fressh and newe yshave.
In al the hous ther nas so litel a knave°,   310
Ne no wight elles°, that he nas ful fayn°
That my lord daun John was come agayn.
And shortly to the point right for to gon,
This faire wyf acorded° with daun John
That for thise hundred frankes he sholde al
     nyght   315
Have hire in his armes bolt upright°.
And this acord parfourned° was in dede;
In myrthe al nyght a bisy lyf they lede
Til it was day, that daun John wente his way,
And bad the meynee°, "Farewel, have good
     day,"   320
For noon of hem, ne no wight in the toun,
Hath of daun John right no° suspecioun.
And forth he rydeth hoom to his abbeye,
Or where hym list°; namoore of hym I seye.

   This marchant, whan that ended was the
     faire,   325

---

259 gyde, *guide* **262 Atemprely,** *moderately,* **namely,** *especially,* **hete,** *heat* **263 nedeth no strange fare,** *(there) need be no elaborate parting* **264 shilde,** *protect* **268 right,** *just* **270 lene,** *loan* **271 wyke,** *week* **273 stoore with,** *stock* **277 secree,** *secret* **280 Graunt mercy of,** *many thanks for,* **cheere,** *hospitality* **283 sikerly,** *surely* **284 it yow leste,** *you want it* **285 chaffare,** *merchandise* **286 list,** *desire,* **shilde,** *forbid,* **spare,** *refrain* **288 plogh,** *plow* **289 creaunce,** *obtain credit,* **name,** *reputation* **291 lith,** *lies* **292 myght,** *ability,* **ful fayn,** *very gladly* **293 fette,** *fetched* **295**

wight, *person,* **wiste,** *knew,* **lone,** *loan* **297 rome,** *stroll* **300 prentys,** *apprentice,* **gydeth,** *leads* **303 byeth,** *purchases,* **creaunceth,** *buys on credit* **304 dees,** *dice* **306 let,** *leads* **307 next,** *after* **309 crowne,** *head* **310 knave,** *boy servant* **311 wight elles,** *other person,* **fayn,** *happy* **314 acorded,** *agreed* **316 bolt upright,** *flat on her back* **317 acord parfourned,** *agreement performed* **320 meynee,** *household* **322 right no,** *any* **324 hym list,** *it pleases him*

---

259 Seint Austyn, St. Augustine of Hippo. **272 beestes that I moste beye,** animals that I must buy. The monk is responsible for his monastery's farms; see lines 62–66 above. **276 a mile way,** i.e., I won't be late by even the time it takes to walk a mile, about twenty minutes. **325 faire,** trade fair, where buyers and sellers come together for purchase and exchange. The merchant is evidently there to purchase on credit goods that he later expects to sell at a profit.

To Seint Denys he gan for to repaire°,
And with his wyf he maketh feeste and cheere°,
And telleth hire that chaffare° is so deere°
That nedes moste he make a chevyssaunce°,
For he was bounded in a reconyssaunce° 330
To paye twenty thousand sheeld anon°.
For which this marchant is to Parys gon
To borwe of certeine freendes that he hadde
A certeyn frankes, and somme with him he ladde.
And whan that he was come into the toun, 335
For greet chiertee° and greet affeccioun,
Unto daun John he gooth hym first—to pleye,
Nat for to axe° or borwe of hym moneye,
But for to wite and seen of° his welfare,
And for to tellen hym of his chaffare°, 340
As freendes doon whan they been met yfeere°.
Daun John hym° maketh feeste and murye
    cheere,
And he hym tolde agayn°, ful specially,
How he hadde wel yboght and graciously°,
Thanked be God, al hool° his marchandise, 345
Save° that he moste, in alle maner wise,
Maken a chevyssaunce° as for his beste°,
And thanne he sholde been in joye and reste.
    Daun John answerde, "Certes°, I am fayn°
That ye in heele° ar comen hom agayn. 350
And if that I were riche, as have I blisse,
Of twenty thousand sheeld sholde ye nat mysse°,
For ye so kyndely this oother day
Lente me gold; and as I kan and may,
I thanke yow, by God and by Seint Jame. 355
But nathelees, I took unto oure dame
Youre wyf at hom the same gold ageyn
Upon youre bench; she woot° it wel, certeyn,
By certeyn tokenes° that I kan yow telle.
Now, by youre leve, I may no lenger dwelle. 360
Oure abbot wole out of this toun anon,

And in his compaignye moot° I goon.
Grete° wel oure dame, myn owene nece sweete,
And fare wel, deere cosyn, til we meete."
    This marchant, which that was ful war and
        wys, 365
Creanced° hath, and payd eek in Parys
To certeyn Lumbardes redy in hir hond
The somme of gold, and gat of hem his bond,
And hoom he gooth murie as a papejay°,
For wel he knew he stood in swich array° 370
That nedes moste he wynne° in that viage°
A thousand frankes aboven al his costage°.
    His wyf ful redy mette hym atte gate,
As she was wont of oold usage algate°,
And al that nyght in myrthe they bisette°, 375
For he was riche and cleerly out of dette.
Whan it was day, this marchant gan embrace
His wyf al newe°, and kiste hire on hir face,
And up he gooth° and maketh it ful tough°.
    "Namoore," quod she, "by God, ye have
        ynough!" 380
And wantownely agayn° with hym she pleyde,
Til atte laste thus this marchant seyde,
"By God," quod he, "I am a litel wrooth°
With yow, my wyf, although it be me looth°.
And woote° ye why? By God, as that I gesse 385
That ye han maad a manere straungenesse°
Bitwixen me and my cosyn daun John.
Ye sholde han warned me, er I had gon,
That he yow hadde an hundred frankes payed
By redy tokene°; and heeld hym yvele apayed° 390
For that I to hym spak of chevyssaunce°—
Me semed so° as by his contenaunce.
But nathelees, by God oure hevene kyng,
I thoughte° nat to axen hym° no thyng.
I prey thee, wyf, as do namoore so; 395
Telle me alwey er that I fro thee go

---

326 gan . . . to repaire, *did return* 327 feeste and cheere, *celebration and entertainment* 328 chaffare, *merchandise*, deere, *expensive* 329 nedes moste he make a chevyssaunce, *he must necessarily take a loan* 330 reconyssaunce, *contract* 331 sheeld anon, *units of credit immediately* 336 chiertee, *friendship* 338 axe, *ask* 339 for to wite and seen of, *to know and look after* 340 chaffare, *trading* 341 yfeere, *together* 342 hym, *for him* 343 agayn, *in response* 344 graciously, *favorably* 345 al hool, *completely* 346 Save, *except* 347 Maken a chevyssaunce, *take out a loan*, beste, *advantage* 349 Certes, *surely*, fayn, *happy* 350 in heele, *in prosperity* 352 mysse, *lack* 358 woot, *knows* 359 tokenes, *evidence* 362 moot, *must* 363 Grete, *greet* 366 Creanced, *borrowed* 369 papejay,

parrot (see 209n) 370 swich array, *such an arrangement* 371 wynne, *profit*, viage, *venture* 372 costage, *expenses* 374 wont of oold usage algate, *accustomed to by regular habit always* 375 bisette, *applied* (themselves) 378 al newe, *anew* 379 gooth, *rises*, maketh it ful tough, *acts proud* 381 wantownely agayn, *lasciviously in return* 383 wrooth, *peeved* 384 it be me looth, *I hate to* 385 woote, *know* 386 manere straungenesse, *a kind of distance* 390 By redy tokene, *with clear evidence*, heeld hym yvele apayed, *he thought himself mistreated* 391 chevyssaunce, *borrowing* 392 Me semed so, *it seemed so to me* 394 thoughte, *intended*, axen hym, *ask of him*

333–34 borwe . . . / A certeyn frankes, and somme with him he ladde, borrow . . . some franks (French coins), and he took some with him. 366–68 payd eek in Parys . . . Lumbardes redy in hir hond . . . his bond, repaid in Paris to Lombard bankers the sum of gold (which he borrowed in Bruges, line 330) in return for the original promissory note (bond, line 368). Lombard bankers were well known for their international transactions. Nowhere in the tale is the buying or selling straightforward.

If any dettour hath in myn absence
Ypayed thee, lest thurgh thy necligence
I myghte hym axe a thing that he hath payed."
    This wyf was nat afered° nor affrayed°,   400
But boldely she seyde, and that anon,
"Marie°, I deffie the false monk, daun John!
I kepe° nat of his tokenes° never a deel°.
He took° me certeyn° gold, that woot° I weel.
What, yvel thedam° on his monkes snowte°,   405
For, God it woot°, I wende° withouten doute
That he hadde yeve° it me bycause of yow,
To doon therwith myn honour and my prow°,
For cosynage°, and eek for beele° cheere
That he hath had ful ofte tymes heere.   410
But sith° I se I stonde in this disjoynt°,
I wol answere yow shortly to the poynt:
Ye han mo slakkere° dettours than am I!
For I wol paye yow wel and redily
Fro day to day, and if so be I faille,   415
I am youre wyf; score° it upon my taille

And I shal paye as soone as ever I may.
For by my trouthe, I have on myn array°,
And nat on wast°, bistowed° every deel°,
And for I have bistowed it so weel   420
For youre honour, for Goddes sake, I seye
As° be nat wrooth°, but lat us laughe and pleye.
Ye shal my joly body have to wedde°.
By God, I wol nat paye yow but a-bedde!
Forgyve it me, myn owene spouse deere;   425
Turne hiderward°, and maketh bettre cheere."
    This marchant saugh ther was no remedie,
And for to chide it nere° but greet folie
Sith that° the thyng may nat amended be.
"Now wyf," he seyde, "and I foryeve it thee;   430
But by thy lyf, ne be namoore so large°.
Keep bet° my good, that yeve° I thee in charge."
Thus endeth now my tale, and God us sende
Taillynge ynough unto oure lyves ende.
                               Amen.

Heere endeth the Shipmannes Tale.

Bihoold the murie wordes of the Hoost to the Shipman and to the Lady Prioresse.

    "Wel seyd, by corpus dominus," quod oure
        Hoost,   435
"Now longe moote° thou saille by the cost°,
Sire gentil maister, gentil maryneer!
God yeve° this monk a thousand last quade yeer°.
Aha, felawes, beth war° of swich a jape°!
The monk putte in the mannes hood an ape,   440
And in his wyves eek, by Seint Austyn.
Draweth no monkes moore unto youre in°.
    "But now passe over and lat us seke° aboute:

Who shal now telle first of al this route°
Another tale?" And with that word he sayde,   445
As curteisly as it had been a mayde,
"My lady Prioresse, by youre leve°,
So that I wiste° I sholde yow nat greve°,
I wolde demen° that ye tellen sholde
A tale next, if so were that ye wolde.   450
Now wol ye vouchesauf°, my lady deere?"
    "Gladly," quod she, and seyde as ye shal heere.

Explicit.

---

399 hym axe, *ask him* (for) **400 afered,** *frightened,* **affrayed,** *afraid* **402 Marie,** *by Mary* **403 kepe,** *care,* **tokenes,** *evidence,* **never a deel,** *not at all* **404 took,** *gave,* **certeyn,** *some,* **woot,** *know* **405 yvel thedam,** *evil luck,* **snowte,** *snout* **406 woot,** *knows,* **wende,** *thought* **407 yeve,** *given* **408 prow,** *advantage* **409 cosynage,** *kinship* (see 36n above) **409 beele,** *good* **411 sith,** *since,* **disjoynt,** *difficulty* **413 mo slakkere,** *more unreliable* **416 score,** *record* **418 array,** *clothing* **419 on wast,** *in waste,* **bistowed,** *spent,* **deel,** *bit* **422 As,** *so,* **wrooth,** *angry* **423 to wedde,** *in pledge* **426 hiderward,** *this way* **428 for to chide it nere,** *to scold would be nothing* **429 Sith that,** *since* **430 large,** *unthrifty* **432 bet,** *better,* **yeve,** *give* **436 moote,** *may,* **cost,** *coast* **438 yeve,** *give,* **last quade yeer,** *cartloads of bad years* **439 beth war,** *beware,* **jape,** *trick* **442 in,** *house* (inn) **443 seke,** *look* **444 route,** *company* **447 leve,** *permission* **448 wiste,** *knew,* **greve,** *offend* **449 demen,** *judge* **451 vouchesauf,** *consent*

416 taille, pun on tally (account or tax) and tail (sexual sense). The pun occurs again at line 434. **435 corpus dominus,** the Host's mistake for *corpus domini,* the Lord's body. **440 putte in the mannes hood an ape,** put a monkey in the man's hood, i.e., made a monkey of him. **441 Seint Austyn,** St. Augustine of Hippo.

PRIORESS'S TALE

PROLOGUE

The Prologe of the Prioresses Tale.

Domine dominus noster.

O Lord, oure Lord, thy name how
    merveillous
Is in this large world ysprad°, quod she,
For noght oonly thy laude° precious   455
Parfourned° is by men of dignitee,
But by the mouth of children thy bountee°
Parfourned is, for on the brest soukynge°
Somtyme shewen° they thyn heriynge°.

Wherfore in laude°, as I best kan or may,   460
Of thee and of the white lylye flour
Which that the bar°, and is a mayde alway,
To telle a storie I wol do my labour—
Nat that I may encreessen hir honour,

For she hirself is honour and the roote   465
Of bountee, next hir Sone, and soules boote°.

O mooder mayde, O mayde mooder free°!
O bussh unbrent, brennynge in Moyses sighte,
That ravysedest° doun fro the deitee,
Thurgh thyn humblesse, the goost° that in
    th'alighte°,   470
Of whos vertu° whan he thyn herte lighte°
Conceyved was the Fadres sapience,
Help me to telle it in thy reverence.

Lady, thy bountee, thy magnificence,
Thy vertu, and thy grete humylitee,   475

---

454 **ysprad,** *spread* 455 **laude,** *praise* 456 **Parfourned,** *performed*
457 **bountee,** *goodness* 458 **soukynge,** *sucking* 459 **shewen,** *show,*
heriynge, *praising* 460 **laude,** *praise* 462 **Which that the bar,** *she who*
bore you (i.e., Mary) 466 **boote,** *remedy* 467 **free,** *bountiful* 469 **rav-**
ysedest, *ravished* 470 **goost,** *Holy Spirit,* **th'alighte,** *alighted in you*
471 **vertu,** *power,* **lighte,** *illuminated*

452a Domine dominus noster, Lord, our lord [how excellent is your name]; translated in line 453, a version of Psalms 8.1 (Vulgate 8.2), used in the liturgy of the Blessed Virgin and in the mass of the Holy Innocents (December 23). **454 quod she,** carries on without a break from epilogue of *ShT* (line 452), although the verse form shifts to rhyme royal. **461 white lylye flour,** the white lily is an emblem of Mary's purity. **468 bussh unbrent, brennynge in Moyses sighte,** bush unburned, burning, i.e., the burning bush that Moses saw (Exodus 3.2), a prefiguration of the Virgin Birth. **472 Fadres sapience,** Father's Wisdom, i.e., Christ; 1 Corinthians 1.24. **474–80** Echoes Dante *Paradiso* 3.16–21.

Ther may no tonge expresse in no science°,
For somtyme, Lady, er° men praye to thee,
Thou goost biforn° of thy benyngnytee°,
And getest° us the lyght of thy preyere
To gyden° us unto thy Sone so deere.   480

My konnyng° is so wayk°, O blisful queene,
For to declare thy grete worthynesse

That I ne may the weighte nat susteene,
But as a child of twelf monthe oold or lesse
That kan unnethe° any word expresse,   485
Right so fare° I, and therfore I yow preye,
Gydeth° my song that I shal of yow seye.

Explicit.

Heere bigynneth the Prioresses Tale.

Ther was in Asye° in a greet citee
Amonges Cristene folk a Jewerye°
Sustened by a lord of that contree   490
For foul usure and lucre of vileynye°,
Hateful to Crist and to his compaignye;
And thurgh the strete° men myghte ride or
          wende°,
For it was free and open at eyther ende.

A litel scole° of Cristen folk ther stood   495
Doun at the ferther ende, in which ther were
Children an heep° ycomen of Cristen blood,
That lerned in that scole yeer by yere
Swich manere doctrine° as men used there,
This is to seyn, to syngen and to rede,   500
As smale children doon in hire childhede.

Among thise children was a wydwes° sone,
A litel clergeoun° seven yeer of age,
That day by day to scole was his wone°,
And eek also, where as° he saugh th'ymage   505
Of Cristes mooder, hadde he in usage°,
As hym was taught, to knele adoun and seye
His *Ave Marie* as he goth by the weye.

Thus hath this wydwe hir litel sone ytaught
Oure blisful Lady, Cristes mooder deere,   510
To worshipe ay°, and he forgat it naught,
For sely° child wol alday° soone leere°.
But ay whan I remembre on this mateere,
Seint Nicholas stant° evere in my presence,
For he so yong to Crist dide reverence.   515

This litel child his litel book lernynge,
As he sat in the scole at his prymer,
He *Alma redemptoris* herde synge,
As children lerned hire antiphoner°;
And as he dorste°, he drough° hym ner°
          and ner,   520
And herkned ay° the wordes and the noote,
Til he the firste vers koude al by rote°.

Noght wiste he° what this Latyn was to seye°,
For he so yong and tendre was of age.
But on a day his felawe gan he preye°   525
T'expounden° hym this song in his langage,
Or telle hym why this song was in usage°;
This preyde he hym to construe° and declare
Ful often tyme upon his knowes° bare.

---

476 science, *factual way* **477 er,** *before* **478 goost biforn,** *go before,* **benyngnytee,** *generosity* **479 getest,** *wins* **480 gyden,** *guide* **481 konnyng,** *understanding,* **wayk,** *feeble* **485 unnethe,** *scarcely* **486 Right so fare,** *just so do* **487 Gydeth,** *guide* **488 Asye,** *Asia* **489 Jewerye,** *Jewish ghetto* **491 lucre of vileynye,** *wicked profits* **493 strete,** *area,* **wende,** *walk* **495 scole,** *school* **497 Children an heep,** *a number of children* **499 Swich manere doctrine,** *such kind of teaching* **502 wydwes,** *widow's* **503 clergeoun,** *schoolboy,* **wone,** *custom* **505 where as,** *wherever* **506**

hadde he in usage, *he was accustomed* **511 ay,** *always* **512 sely,** (an) *innocent,* **alday,** *always,* **leere,** *learn* **514 stant,** *stands* **519 antiphoner,** *religious songbook* **520 dorste,** *dared,* **drough,** *drew,* **ner,** *nearer* **521 herkned ay,** *listened constantly to* **522 koude al by rote,** *knew by heart* **523 Noght wiste he,** *he knew not at all,* **was to seye,** i.e., *meant* **525 gan he preye,** *he asked* **526 T'expounden,** *to explain* **527 in usage,** *used* **528 construe,** *interpret* **529 knowes,** *knees*

---

491 usure, usury, i.e., lending money for profit at excessive interest rates. Church law forbade usury, although there was no consistency concerning what rate constituted usury. Royalty often protected Jewish lenders to ensure tax revenue and access to loans. **503 seven yeer,** in analogous tales, he is ten. **508 *Ave Marie,*** "Hail Mary," the most popular prayer to Mary, based on the Annunciation, the greeting of the angel Gabriel to Mary at the time that she conceived Jesus; Luke 1.28, 42. **512** Proverbial. **514 Seint Nicholas,** patron saint of schoolboys, known for his piety when an infant. **517 prymer,** first schoolbook, made up of alphabet, prayers, Ten Commandments, etc. **518 *Alma redemptoris,*** "Mother of the Redeemer," a Latin song used in religious services from four weeks before Christmas until February 2.

His felawe, which that elder was than he,   530
Answerde hym thus, "This song, I have herd seye,
Was maked of oure blisful Lady free°,
Hire to salue°, and eek hire for to preye
To been oure help and socour° whan we deye°.
I kan° namoore expounde in this mateere;   535
I lerne song, I kan° but smal grammeere."

   "And is this song maked in reverence
Of Cristes mooder?" seyde this innocent.
"Now, certes°, I wol do my diligence
To konne° it al er Cristemasse be went°—   540
Though that I for my prymer shal be shent°,
And shal be beten thries° in an houre,
I wol it konne° Oure Lady for to honoure."

His felawe taughte hym homward prively°,
Fro day to day, til he koude it by rote,   545
And thanne he song it wel and boldely.
Fro word to word, acordynge with the note.
Twies a day it passed thurgh his throte,
To scoleward and homward whan he wente,
On Cristes mooder set was his entente.   550

   As I have seyd, thurghout the Juerie°
This litel child, as he cam to and fro,
Ful murily than wolde he synge and crie
O Alma redemptoris everemo.
The swetnesse his herte perced so   555
Of Cristes mooder that to hire to preye
He kan nat stynte° of syngyng by the weye.

   Oure firste foo, the serpent Sathanas°,
That hath in Jues° herte his waspes nest,
Up swal° and seide, "O Hebrayk peple, allas,   560
Is this to yow a thyng that is honest°,
That swich a boy shal walken as hym lest°
In youre despit°, and synge of swich sentence°,
Which is agayn youre lawes reverence°?"

Fro thennes forth the Jues han conspired   565
This innocent out of this world to chace°.
An homycide° therto han they hyred
That in an aleye° hadde a privee° place;
And as the child gan forby for to pace°,
This cursed Jew hym hente° and heeld hym
    faste,   570
And kitte° his throte and in a pit hym caste.

I seye that in a wardrobe° they hym threwe
Where as thise Jewes purgen hire entraille°.
O cursed folk of Herodes al newe,
What may youre yvel entente yow availe°?   575
Mordre wol out, certeyn, it wol nat faille,
And namely ther° th'onour of God shal sprede;
The blood out crieth on youre cursed dede.

   O martir sowded° to virginitee,
Now maystow° syngen, folwynge evere in oon°   580
The white Lamb celestial—quod she—
Of which the grete evaungelist Seint John
In Pathmos wroot, which seith that they that
    goon
Biforn this Lamb and synge a song al newe,
That nevere flesshly° wommen they ne knewe.   585

   This poure wydwe awaiteth al that nyght
After hir litel child, but he cam noght;
For which, as soone as it was dayes lyght,
With face pale of drede and bisy thoght,
She hath at scole and elleswhere hym soght,   590
Til finally she gan so fer espie°
That he last seyn was in the Juerie.

   With moodres pitee in hir brest enclosed,
She gooth, as she were half out of hir mynde,
To every place where she hath supposed   595
By liklihede hir litel child to fynde;
And evere on Cristes mooder meeke and kynde

---

532 **free**, *generous* 533 **salue**, *greet* 534 **socour**, *aid*, **deye**, *die* 535 **kan**, *can* 536 **kan**, *know* 539 **certes**, *surely* 540 **konne**, *know*, **be went**, *is gone* 541 **shent**, *scolded* 542 **beten thries**, *beaten three times* 543 **konne**, *learn* 544 **homward prively**, *on the way home secretly* 551 **Juerie**, *ghetto* 557 **stynte**, *stop* 558 **Sathanas**, *Satan* 559 **Jues**, *Jews'* 560 **swal**, *swelled* 561 **honest**, *honorable* 562 **hym lest**, *he pleases* 563 **despit**, *scorn*, **of swich**

sentence, *with such a meaning* 564 **reverence**, *honor* 566 **chace**, *banish* 567 **homycide**, *murderer* 568 **aleye**, *alley*, **privee**, *secret* 569 **gan forby to pace**, *did walk by* 570 **hente**, *seized* 571 **kitte**, *cut* 572 **wardrobe**, *cesspit* 573 **purgen hire entraille**, *empty their bowels* 575 **availe**, *help* 577 **namely ther**, *especially where* 579 **sowded**, *joined* 580 **maystow**, *may you*, **evere in oon**, *forever* 585 **flesshly**, *sexually* 591 **espie**, *discover*

---

536 I kan but smal grammeere, I know only a little grammar (i.e., Latin). The boy's older friend is not in the analogues, and the fact that neither boy understands the words of the song increases the distance between comprehension and faith. Compare with the Prioress's own lack of understanding, lines 481–85. **545 koude it by rote**, knew it by heart; compare *PardT* 6.332. **574 folk of Herodes al newe**, present-day people of Herod, the ruler of the Jews, who at Christ's birth ordered all newborn children killed; Matthew 2.16. **576** Proverbial. **581–83 white Lamb . . . Pathmos**, the vision of the Heavenly Lamb (Christ) in procession with 144,000 virgins is in Revelation 14.1ff, attributed in the Middle Ages to St. John the evangelist (gospel writer), written on the isle of Patmos. Children who died early were associated with virgins. **581 quod she**, evidently the Prioress (and a convenient rhyme).

She cride, and atte laste thus she wroghte°,
Among the cursed Jues she hym soghte.

She frayneth° and she preyeth pitously   600
To every Jew that dwelte in thilke° place
To telle hire if hir child wente oght forby°.
They seyde "nay"; but Jhesu of his grace
Yaf in hir thoght° in with a litel space°
That in that place after hir sone she cryde   605
Where he was casten in a pit bisyde.

O grete God, that parfournest thy laude°
By mouth of innocentz, lo heere thy myght!
This gemme of chastite, this emeraude°,
And eek of martirdom the ruby bright,   610
Ther° he with throte ykorven° lay upright°,
He *Alma redemptoris* gan to synge
So loude that al the place gan to rynge.

The Cristene folk that thurgh the strete wente
In coomen° for to wondre upon this thyng,   615
And hastily they for the provost° sente.
He cam anon withouten tariyng,
And herieth° Crist that is of hevene kyng,
And eek his mooder, honour of mankynde,
And after that the Jewes leet he bynde°.   620

This child with pitous lamentacioun
Up taken was, syngynge his song alway,
And with honour of greet processioun
They carien hym unto the nexte° abbay.
His mooder swownynge° by his beere° lay;   625
Unnethe° myghte the peple that was theere
This newe Rachel brynge fro his beere.

With torment and with shameful deeth echon°
This provost dooth the Jewes for to sterve°
That of this mordre wiste°, and that anon°.   630
He nolde no swich° cursednesse observe°.
Yvele shal he have that yvele wol deserve;

Therfore with wilde hors he dide hem drawe,
And after that he heng° hem by the lawe.

Upon this beere ay lith° this innocent   635
Biforn the chief auter°, whil the masse laste;
And after that the abbot with his covent°
Han sped hem° for to burien hym ful faste;
And whan they hooly water on hym caste,
Yet spak this child, whan spreynd° was hooly
          water,   640
And song *O Alma redemptoris mater.*

This abbot which that was an hooly man
As monkes been—or elles oghte be—
This yonge child to conjure° he bigan,
And seyde, "O deere child, I halse° thee,   645
In vertu° of the Hooly Trinitee,
Tel me what is thy cause for to synge,
Sith° that thy throte is kut to my semynge°?"

"My throte is kut unto my nekke-boon,"
Seyde this child, "and as by wey of kynde°   650
I sholde have dyed, ye, longe tyme agon.
But Jesu Crist, as ye in bookes fynde,
Wil° that his glorie laste and be in mynde;
And for the worship of his Mooder deere
Yet may I synge *O Alma* loude and cleere.   655

"This welle° of mercy, Cristes mooder sweete,
I loved alwey as after my konnynge°;
And whan that I my lyf sholde forlete°,
To me she cam, and bad me for to synge
This anthem verraily° in my deyynge°,   660
As ye han herd, and whan that I hadde songe,
Me thoughte she leyde a greyn upon my tonge.

"Wherfore I synge and synge I moot°, certeyn,
In honour of that blisful Mayden free°
Til fro my tonge of° taken is the greyn;   665
And afterward thus seyde she to me,

---

598 wroghte, *worked* **600 frayneth,** *asks* **601 thilke,** *that* **602 wente oght forby,** *went by in any way* **604 Yaf in hir thoght,** *put it in her mind,* **in with a litel space,** *in a little while* **607 parfournest thy laude,** *performs your praise* **609 emeraude,** *emerald* **611 Ther,** *where,* **ykorven,** *carved,* **upright,** *on his back* **615 In coomen,** *came in* **616 provost,** *magistrate* **618 herieth,** *praises* **620 leet he bynde,** *he had tied up* **624 nexte,** *nearest* **625 swownynge,** *fainting* **625 beere,** *bier* **626 Unnethe,** *scarcely* **628 echon,** *each one* **629 dooth . . . for to sterve,** *has . . . put to death*

630 wiste, *knew,* **anon,** *immediately* **631 nolde no swich,** *would no such,* **observe,** *overlook* **634 heng,** *hanged* **635 ay lith,** *always lies* **636 auter,** *altar* **637 covent,** *group of monks* **638 Han sped hem,** *hurried themselves* **640 spreynd,** *sprinkled* **644 conjure,** *plead with* **645 halse,** *entreat* **646 In vertu,** *by the power* **648 Sith,** *since,* **to my semynge,** *it seems to me* **650 as by wey of kynde,** *in the course of nature* **653 Wil,** *wishes* **656 welle,** *source* **657 konnynge,** *capability* **658 forlete,** *lose* **660 verraily,** *truly,* **deyynge,** *dying* **663 I moot,** *I must* **664 free,** *generous* **665 of,** *off*

627 newe Rachel, Jewish mother who weeps inconsolably for her lost child; Jeremiah 31.15 and Matthew 2.18. The allusion complicates the anti-Semitism of the tale. **632 Yvele shal he have . . . ,** evil shall he have who evil deserves. Proverbial; compare Exodus 21.23–25 and Matthew 5.38–39. **662 greyn,** seed; in other versions of the story, a lily, a jewel, or a pebble.

'My litel child, now wol I fecche thee
Whan that the greyn is fro thy tonge ytake°.
Be nat agast°, I wol thee nat forsake.'"

This hooly monk, this abbot, hym meene I,   670
His tonge out caughte and took awey the greyn,
And he yaf° up the goost ful softely.
And whan this abbot hadde this wonder seyn,
His salte teeris trikled doun as reyn,
And gruf° he fil al plat° upon the grounde,   675
And stille he lay as he had leyn ybounde.

The covent° eek lay on the pavement
Wepynge, and heryen° Cristes mooder deere,

And after that they ryse and forth been went,
And tooken awey this martir from his beere;   680
And in a tombe of marbul stones cleere°
Enclosen they his litel body sweete.
Ther he is now, God leve° us for to meete!

O yonge Hugh of Lyncoln, slayn also
With° cursed Jewes—as it is notable,   685
For it is but a litel while ago—
Preye eek for us, we synful folk unstable,
That of his mercy, God so merciable
On us his grete mercy multiplie,
For reverence of his mooder Marie. Amen.   690

Heere is ended the Prioresses Tale.

---

668 ytake, *taken* **669 agast,** *frightened* **672 yaf,** *gave* **675 gruf,** *face down,*
plat, *flat*

677 covent, *group of monks* **678 heryen,** *they praise* **681 cleere,** *shining*
683 leve, *grant* **685 With,** *by*

684 Hugh of Lyncoln, a supposed victim of child murder, for which nineteen Jews were executed by Henry III in 1255; accusations of ritual murder against Jews recur throughout European history.

TALE OF SIR THOPAS

PROLOGUE

Bihoold the murye wordes of the Hoost to Chaucer.

Whan seyd was al this miracle, every man
As sobre was that wonder was to se,
Til that oure Hooste japen tho° bigan,
And thanne at erst° he looked upon me,
And seyde thus, "What man artow°?" quod he. 695
"Thou lookest as thou woldest fynde an hare,
For evere upon the ground I se thee stare.

"Approche neer and looke up murily.
Now war yow°, sires, and lat this man have place°—
He in the waast° is shape as wel as I! 700
This were a popet° in an arm t'enbrace

For any womman, smal and fair of face.
He semeth elvyssh° by his contenaunce,
For unto no wight° dooth he daliaunce°.

"Sey now somwhat, syn° oother folk han sayd. 705
Telle us a tale of myrthe, and that anon."
"Hooste," quod I, "ne beth nat yvele apayd°,
For oother tale certes kan° I noon,
But of a rym I lerned longe agoon."
"Ye, that is good," quod he. "Now shul we heere 710
Som deyntee° thyng, me thynketh by his cheere°."

Explicit.

Heere bigynneth Chaucers Tale of Thopas.

Listeth, lordes, in good entent,
And I wol telle verrayment°
    Of myrthe and of solas°;

Al of a knyght was fair and gent° 715
In bataille and in tourneyment—
    His name was Sire Thopas.

---

693 **japen tho,** *to joke then* 694 **at erst,** *for the first time* 695 **artow,** *are you* 699 **war you,** *beware,* **place,** *room* 700 **waast,** *waist* 701 **popet,** *doll* 703 **elvyssh,** *otherworldly* 704 **wight,** *person,* **daliaunce,** *pay attention*

705 **syn,** *since* 707 **yvele apayd,** *displeased* 708 **kan,** *know* 711 **deyntee, delightful,** **cheere,** *expression* 713 **verrayment,** *truly* 714 **solas,** *pleasure* 715 **gent,** *beautiful*

694–704 Chaucer's comic self-portrait here can be compared with that in his short poem, *Lenvoy to Scogan* (lines 27 and 31), and his *HF* 574 and 660 (plumpness) and *HF* 647–59 (bookish isolation). **712 Listeth, lordes,** a formulaic beginning of an oral performance; the tale is a parodic pastiche (in jog-trot verse) of absurdities juxtaposed with clichés and formulas from popular romances. **717 Thopas,** topaz, a yellow semiprecious stone.

Yborn he was in fer° contree,
In Flaundres al biyonde the see,
　At Poperyng in the place°.　720
His fader was a man ful free°,
And lord he was of that contree,
　As it was Goddes grace.

Sire Thopas wax° a doghty swayn°;
Whit was his face as payndemayn,　725
　His lippes rede as rose;
His rode° is lyk scarlet in grayn°,
And I yow telle in good certayn,
　He hadde a semely° nose.

His heer, his berd was lyk saffroun°,　730
That to his girdel raughte° adoun,
　His shoon° of cordewane°.
Of Brugges were his hosen broun°,
His robe was of syklatoun°,
　That coste many a jane°.　735

He koude hunte at wilde deer,
And ride an haukyng for river°
　With grey goshauk° on honde;
Therto he was a good archeer,
Of wrastlyng was ther noon his peer,　740
　Ther° any ram shal stonde°.

Ful many a mayde bright in bour°,
They moorne° for hym paramour°,
　Whan hem were bet° to slepe.
But he was chaast and no lechour,　745
And sweete as is the brembul flour°
　That bereth the rede hepe°.

And so bifel° upon a day,
Forsothe° as I yow telle may,
　Sire Thopas wolde out ride.　750

He worth° upon his steede gray,
And in his hand a launcegay°,
　A long swerd by his side.

He priketh° thurgh a fair forest
Therinne is many a wilde best,　755
　Ye, bothe bukke and hare;
And as he priketh north and est,
I telle it yow, hym hadde almest
　Bitidde° a sory care.

Ther spryngen° herbes grete and smale,　760
The lycorys° and cetewale°,
　And many a clowe-gylofre°,
And notemuge° to putte in ale,
Wheither it be moyste° or stale,
　Or for to leye in cofre°.　765

The briddes synge, it is no nay°,
The sparhauk and the papejay,
　That joye it was to heere;
The thrustelcok made eek hir lay,
The wodedowve upon a spray°　770
　She sang ful loude and cleere.

Sire Thopas fil in love-longynge,
Al whan he herde the thrustel synge,
　And pryked as he were wood°.
His faire steede in his prikynge　775
So swatte° that men myghte him wrynge;
　His sydes were al blood.

Sire Thopas eek so wery was
For prikyng on the softe gras,
　So fiers was his corage,　780
That doun he leyde him in that plas°
To make his steede som solas°,
　And yaf° hym good forage.

718 fer, *distant* 720 place, *plaza* 721 free, *noble* 724 wax, *grew* (up), doghty swayn, *brave squire* 727 rode, *complexion*, in grayn, *deeply dyed* 729 semely, *handsome* 730 saffroun, *yellow orange spice* 731 raughte, *reached* 732 shoon, *shoes*, cordewane, *Spanish leather* 733 hosen broun, *brown stockings* 734 syklatoun, *costly silken fabric* 735 jane, *cheap coin from Genoa* 737 haukyng for river, *hawking for waterfowl* 738 goshauk, *hunting bird* 741 Ther, *where*, stonde, *stand* 742 bright in bour, *beautiful in* (bed) *chamber* 743 moorne, *yearn*, paramour,

sexually 744 bet, *better* 746 brembul flour, *wild rose* 747 rede hepe, *red* (rose) *hip* 748 bifel, *happened* 749 Forsothe, *truly* 751 worth, *climbs* 752 launcegay, *light lance* 754 priketh, *spurs* 759 Bitidde, *happened* 760 spryngen, *grow* 761 lycorys, *licorice*, cetewale, *zedoary* (a spice) 762 clowe-gylofre, *clove* 763 notemuge, *nutmeg* 764 moyste, *fresh* 765 cofre, *a chest* 766 it is no nay, *it can't be denied* 770 spray, *branch* 774 wood, *crazed* 776 swatte, *sweated* 781 plas, *place* 782 solas, *relief* 783 yaf, *gave*

719 Flaundres, bourgeois trade nation, just across the English Channel. 720 Poperyng, a Flemish market town, hardly aristocratic. 725 payndemayn, white bread, with a possible play on "dough" from previous line? 733 Of Brugges, from Bruges, center of Flemish trade. 739–40 archeer . . . wrastlyng, archery and wrestling were distinctly nonaristocratic. A ram was the prize in wrestling contests. 760 herbes, plants, none of which are native to Flanders. 767 sparhauk . . . papejay, the sparrow hawk and parrot are not songbirds. 769 thrustelcok . . . hir lay, male thrush . . . her song; note the gender confusion. 770 wodedowve, wood pigeon, not a songbird. 774 pryked, spurred, but acquires absurd sexual connotations through repetition and context (lines 775, 779, and 798); see *RvT* 1.4231.

"O Seinte Marie, benedicite°,
What eyleth this love at me° 785
    To bynde me so soore?
Me dremed al this nyght, pardee°,
An elf-queene shal my lemman° be
    And slepe under my goore°.

"An elf-queene wol I love, ywis°, 790
For in this world no womman is
    Worthy to be my make°
                In towne;
Alle othere wommen I forsake,
And to an elf-queene I me take 795
    By dale° and eek by downe°."

Into his sadel he clamb° anon,
And priketh over stile and stoon
    An elf-queene for t'espye°,
Til he so longe hadde riden and goon 800
That he foond in a pryve woon°
    The contree of Fairye
                So wilde;
For in that contree was ther noon
That to him durste° ride or goon, 805
    Neither wyf ne childe.

Til that ther cam a greet geaunt°,
His name was Sire Olifaunt°,
    A perilous man of dede.
He seyde, "Child°, by Termagaunt, 810
But if° thou prike out of myn haunt°,
    Anon I sle thy steede
                With mace°.
Heere is the queene of Fairye,
With harpe and pipe and symphonye°, 815
    Dwellynge in this place."

The child seyde, "Also moote I thee°,
Tomorwe wol I meete with thee,
    Whan I have myn armoure;

And yet I hope, *par ma fay*°, 820
That thou shalt with this launcegay
    Abyen° it ful sowre°.
                Thy mawe°
Shal I percen if I may,
Er it be fully pryme of day°, 825
    For heere thow shalt be slawe°."

Sire Thopas drow abak° ful faste;
This geant at hym stones caste
    Out of a fel staf-slynge°;
But faire escapeth Sir Thopas, 830
And al it was thurgh Goddes gras,
    And thurgh his fair berynge°.

[The Second Fit]

Yet listeth, lordes, to my tale,
Murier° than the nightyngale,
    For now I wol yow rowne° 835
How Sir Thopas with sydes smale°,
Prikyng over hill and dale,
    Is comen agayn to towne.

His myrie men comanded he
To make hym bothe game° and glee°, 840
    For nedes moste he fighte°
With a geaunt with hevedes° three,
For paramour° and jolitee°
    Of oon that° shoon ful brighte.

"Do come°," he seyde, "my mynstrales, 845
And geestours° for to tellen tales,
    Anon° in myn armynge,
Of romances that been roiales°,
Of popes and of cardinales,
    And eek of love-likynge." 850

They fette° hym first the sweete wyn,
And mede° eek in a mazelyn°,

---

784 **benedicite,** *bless you* 785 **eyleth this love at me,** *does love have
against me* 787 **pardee,** *by God* 788 **lemman,** *lover* 789 **goore,** *garment*
790 **ywis,** *surely* 792 **make,** *mate* 796 **dale,** *valley,* **downe,** *hill* 797
clamb, *climbed* 799 **t'espye,** *to discover* 801 **pryve woon,** *secret place* 805
durste, *dared* 807 **geaunt,** *giant* 808 **Olifaunt,** *Elephant* 810 **Child,**
knight 811 **But if,** *unless,* **haunt,** *area* 813 **mace,** *a club* 815 **sympho-
nye,** *hurdy-gurdy* 817 **Also moote I thee,** *as I may prosper* 820 *par ma
fay,* *by my faith* (Fr.) 822 **Abyen,** *pay for,* **sowre,** *bitterly* 823 **mawe,**
stomach 825 **pryme of day,** *9 a.m.* 826 **slawe,** *killed* 827 **drow abak,** *re-
treated* 829 **fel staf-slynge,** *deadly slingshot* 832 **fair berynge,** *good conduct* 834 **Murier,** *merrier* 835 **rowne,** *whisper* 836 **sydes smale,** *slender
waist* 840 **game,** *entertainment,* **glee,** *song* 841 **nedes moste he,** *he must
necessarily* 842 **hevedes,** *heads* 843 **paramour,** *love,* **jolitee,** *pleasure*
844 **Of oon that,** *for someone who* 845 **Do come,** *summon* 846 **gees-
tours,** *tale-tellers* 847 **Anon,** *soon* 848 **roiales,** *royal* 851 **fette,** *fetched*
852 **mede,** *mead* (honey liquor), **mazelyn,** *wooden bowl*

---

793 **In towne,** one-foot metrical lines such as this (also at lines 803, 813, etc.) are part of English romance tradition, but here they ring falsely.
805 This line appears in only a few manuscripts. 810 **Termagaunt,** a pagan god in fiction. 832a **Fit,** a section of a poem or song. A number
of scribes indicate a section break here and at line 890a with enlarged capitals. 849 **popes . . . cardinales,** church officials rather than members of royalty, and not usual subjects of romances.

And roial spicerye°
Of gyngebreed that was ful fyn,
And lycorys°, and eek comyn°,   855
  With sugre that is trye°.

He dide next° his white leere°
Of clooth of lake° fyn and cleere°,
  A breech° and eek a sherte,
And next his sherte an aketoun°,   860
And over that an haubergeoun°
  For percynge° of his herte.

And over that a fyn hawberk°,
Was al ywroght° of Jewes werk,
  Ful strong it was of plate;   865
And over that his cote-armour
As whit as is a lilye flour,
  In which he wol debate°.

His sheeld was al of gold so reed,
And therinne was a bores° heed,   870
  A charbocle bisyde.
And there he swoor on ale and breed
How that the geaunt shal be deed,
  Bityde° what bityde!

His jambeux° were of quyrboilly°,   875
His swerdes shethe of yvory,
  His helm of latoun° bright;
His sadel was of rewel-boon°,
His brydel as the sonne shoon,
  Or as the moone light.   880

His spere was of fyn ciprees,
That bodeth werre and nothyng pees,

The heed ful sharpe ygrounde;
His steede was al dappull gray,
It gooth an ambil in the way   885
  Ful softely and rounde°
        In londe.
Loo, lordes myne, heere is a fit!
If ye wol any moore of it,
  To telle it wol I fonde°.   890

[The Third Fit]

Now holde youre mouth, *par charitee,*
Bothe knyght and lady free°,
  And herkneth to my spelle°.
Of bataille and of chivalry
And of ladyes love-drury°   895
  Anon I wol yow telle.

Men speken of romances of prys°,
Of Horn Child and of Ypotys,
  Of Beves and of Sir Gy,
Of Sir Lybeux and Pleyndamour—   900
But Sir Thopas, he bereth the flour
  Of roial chivalry!

His goode steede al he bistrood°,
And forth upon his wey he glood°
  As sparcle° out of the bronde°;   905
Upon his creest° he bar a tour°,
And therinne stiked a lilie flour—
  God shilde° his cors° fro shonde°!

And for° he was a knyght auntrous°,
He nolde° slepen in noon hous,   910

---

853 **roial spicerye,** *royal spice selection* 855 **lycorys,** *licorice,* **comyn,** *cumin* 856 **trye,** *excellent* 857 **dide next,** *put on next to,* **leere,** *flesh* 858 **clooth of lake,** *linen,* **cleere,** *bright* 859 **A breech,** *pants* 860 **aketoun,** *padded jacket* 861 **haubergeoun,** *chain mail shirt* 862 **For percynge,** *to prevent piercing* 863 **hawberk,** *plate mail shirt* 864 **ywroght,** *made* 868 **debate,** *fight* 870 **bores,** *boar's* 874 **Bityde,** *happen* 875 **jambeux,** *leg armor,* **quyrboilly,** *boiled leather* 877 **latoun,** *brasslike alloy* 878 **rewel-**

boon, *whalebone* 886 **rounde,** *confidently* (?) 890 **fonde,** *try* 892 **free,** *generous* 893 **spelle,** *story* 895 **love-drury,** *service in love* 897 **prys,** *excellence* 903 **al he bistrood,** *he completely mounted* 904 **glood,** *glided* 905 **sparcle,** *spark,* **bronde,** *torch* 906 **creest,** *helmet top,* **tour,** *tower* 908 **shilde,** *protect,* **cors,** *body,* **shonde,** *harm* 909 **for,** *because,* **auntrous,** *adventurous* 910 **nolde,** *would not*

---

864 **Jewes werk,** Jews were not known for making armor. 866 **cote-armour,** surcoat (outer shirt) decorated with heraldic insignia, here either blank or not described. 871 **charbocle,** carbuncle, a precious stone or the heraldic device that represents one. 881 **fyn ciprees,** fine cypress. Spears were traditionally made of ash; cypress was known for shipbuilding and fragrance, not weaponry. 884–85 **dappull gray . . . ambil,** dapple gray . . . slow walk; neither the color nor the gait of a warhorse. 888 **here is a fit,** here is a section; a formulaic transition in a number of metrical romances. 891 **holde youre mouth,** *par charitee,* shut your mouth, for charity; a comic combination of rudeness and currying favor. 898–900 **Horn Child,** hero of the ME romance *King Horn.* **Ypotys,** central character in a verse dialogue (not a romance) in which a Christian child converts the pagan emperor of Rome. **Beves,** Bevis of Hampton. **Sir Gy,** Guy of Warwick. **Sir Lybeux,** Libeus Desconus (The Fair Unknown). **Pleyndamour,** "Filled with Love." This romance has not been identified; perhaps facetious. Several of the ME romances cited here are found together in the Auchinleck MS, which suggests Chaucer may have known it or a similar anthology.

But liggen° in his hoode;
His brighte helm was his wonger°,
And by hym baiteth° his dextrer°
    Of herbes fyne and goode.

Hymself drank water of the well,   915
As dide the knyght Sire Percyvell
    So worthy under wede°,
Til on a day . . .

---

911 liggen, *lie* **912 wonger,** *pillow* **913 baiteth,** *grazes,* **dextrer,** *warhorse* **917 wede,** *clothing*

916 Sire Percyvell, Sir Perceval de Galles.

TALE OF MELIBEE

PROLOGUE

Heere the Hoost stynteth° Chaucer of his Tale of Thopas.

"Namoore of this, for Goddes dignitee,"
Quod oure Hooste, "for thou makest me   920
So wery of thy verray lewednesse°
That, also wisly° God my soule blesse,
Myne eres aken of° thy drasty° speche.
Now swich° a rym° the devel I biteche°!
This may wel be rym dogerel," quod he.   925
    "Why so?" quod I, "why wiltow lette° me
Moore of my tale than another man,
Syn that° it is the beste rym I kan?"
    "By God," quod he, "for pleynly, at o word,
Thy drasty rymyng is nat worth a toord°!   930
Thou doost noght elles but despendest tyme°.
Sire, at o word, thou shalt no lenger ryme.
Lat se wher° thou kanst tellen aught in geeste°,
Or telle in prose somwhat at the leeste,
In which ther be som murthe or som
        doctryne."   935

"Gladly," quod I, "by Goddes sweete pyne°,
I wol yow telle a litel thyng in prose
That oghte liken yow, as I suppose,
Or elles certes ye been to daungerous°.
It is a moral tale vertuous,   940
Al be it told somtyme in sondry wyse°
Of sondry folk as I shal yow devyse°.
    "As thus: ye woot° that every Evaungelist°
That telleth us the peyne of Jhesu Crist
Ne seith nat alle thyng as his felawe dooth,   945
But nathelees hir sentence° is al sooth°,
And alle acorden as in hire sentence,
Al be ther in hir tellyng difference.
For somme of hem seyn moore and somme
        seyn lesse
Whan they his pitous passioun expresse—   950
I meene of Mark, Mathew, Luc, and John—
But doutelees hir sentence is al oon°.

918a stynteth, *stops* **921 verray lewednesse,** *genuine ignorance* **922 also wisly,** *as truly as* **923 Myne eres aken of,** *my ears ache from,* **drasty,** *worthless* **924 swich,** *such,* **rym,** *rhyme,* **biteche,** *give* **926 wiltow lette,** *will you hinder* **928 Syn that,** *since* **930 toord,** *turd* **931 despendest tyme,** *waste time* **933 wher,** *whether,* **aught in geeste,** *anything in*

alliterative verse (?) **936 pyne,** *pain* **939 to daungerous,** *too hard to please* **941 sondry wyse,** *various ways* **942 devyse,** *describe* **943 woot,** *know,* **Evaungelist,** *gospel writer* **946 hir sentence,** *their meaning,* **sooth,** *truth* **952 al oon,** *the same*

925 rym dogerel, wretched verse; *doggerel* appears to be Chaucer's coinage. **935 murthe . . . doctryne,** entertainment . . . meaning; these parallel "solaas" and "sentence" in *GP* 1.798. The sheer delight of *Thopas* is matched with the sententiousness of *Melibee*.

"Therfore, lordynges alle, I yow biseche,
If that yow thynke I varie as° in my speche,
As thus, though that I telle somwhat moore   955
Of proverbes than ye han herd bifoore
Comprehended° in this litel tretys heere,
To enforce with° th'effect of my mateere,
And though I nat the same wordes seye

As ye han herd, yet to yow alle I preye   960
Blameth me nat, for as in my sentence
Shul ye nowher fynden difference
Fro the sentence of this tretys lyte°
After the which° this murye tale I write.
And therfore herkneth what that I shal seye   965
And lat me tellen al my tale I preye."

Explicit.

Here biginneth Chaucers Tale of Melibee.

A yong man called Melibeus, mighty and riche, bigat upon his wyf, that called was Prudence, a doghter which that called was Sophie. / Upon a day bifel° that he for his desport° is went into the feeldes hym to pleye. / His wyf and eek his doghter hath he left inwith his hous of which the dores weren fast yshette°. / Thre of his olde foes han it espyed°, and setten laddres to the walles of his hous, and by the wyndowes been entred, / and betten his wyf, and wounded his   970 doghter with fyve mortal woundes in fyve sondry places— / this is to seyn, in hir feet, in hire handes, in hir erys, in hir nose, and in hire mouth— and leften hire for deed, and wenten awey. /

Whan Melibeus retourned was into his hous and saugh al this meschief, he lyk a mad man, rentinge° his clothes, gan to wepe and crye. /

Prudence his wyf, as ferforth° as she dorste°, bisoghte° hym of his wepyng for to stynte°, / but nat forthy° he gan to crie and wepen ever lenger the moore. /   975

This noble wyf Prudence remembered hire upon the sentence of Ovide, in his book that cleped° is *The Remedie of Love,* wher as he seith, / "He is a fool that destourbeth° the mooder to wepen in the deeth of hire child til she have wept hir fille as for a certein tyme, / and thanne shal man doon his diligence with amyable wordes hire to reconforte°, and preyen hire of hir weping for to stynte°." /

For which resoun this noble wyf Prudence suffred hir housbond for to wepe and crie as for a certein space, / and whan she saugh hir tyme she seyde hym in this wise, "Allas, my lord," quod she, "why make ye yourself for to be lyk a fool? / For   980 sothe°, it aperteneth nat° to a wys man to maken swiche a sorwe. / Youre doghter, with the grace of God, shal warisshe° and escape. / And al were it so that° she right now were deed, ye ne oughte nat as for hir deeth yourself to destroye. / Senek seith, 'The wise man shal nat take to greet disconfort for the deeth of his children, / but certes he sholde suffren it in pacience, as wel as he abideth the deeth of his owene propre persone.'" /   985

This Melibeus answerde anon and seyde, "What man," quod he, "sholde of his wepyng stente° that hath so greet a cause for to wepe? / Jesu Crist oure lord hymself wepte for the deeth of Lazarus hys freend." /

Prudence answerde, "Certes, wel I woot attem-

---

954 **varie as,** *deviate* (from expectations) 957 **Comprehended,** *included* 958 **enforce with,** *reinforce,* **th'effect,** *impact* 963 **lyte,** *little* 964 **After the which,** *in imitation of which* 968 **bifel,** *it happened,* **desport,** *recreation* 969 **fast yshette,** *firmly shut* 970 **espyed,** *discovered* 973 **rentinge,** *tearing* 974 **as ferforth,** *as far,* **dorste,** *dared,* **bisoghte,**

asked, **stynte,** *stop* 975 **nat forthy,** *nonetheless* 976 **cleped,** *titled* 977 **destourbeth,** *prevents* 978 **reconforte,** *comfort,* **stynte,** *stop* 981 **For sothe,** *truly,* **aperteneth nat,** *it is not appropriate* 982 **warisshe,** *recover* 983 **al were it so that,** *even if* 986 **stente,** *stop*

967 **Melibeus,** "one who drinks honey"; see line 1410 below. **Prudence,** "the ability to see what is virtuous." **Sophie,** "wisdom"; unnamed in Chaucer's source. The line numbers for this prose tale are conventional, for convenient reference. The numbers indicate the end of the respective lines. **Thre . . . foes,** identified at lines 1420–26 as the world, the flesh, and the devil, the traditional sources of temptation. **hous . . . wyndowes,** in the allegory, temptation enters the mind through the eyes. 972 Signifying the five senses: hand (touch), ears (hearing), nose (smell), mouth (taste), and eyes (seeing). Chaucer follows his French source in mistakenly substituting feet for eyes. 976 **Ovide,** Ovid, *Remedia Amoris* (Remedies for Love) 127–30; note the reversal of gender roles when Prudence remembers the quotation. 984 **Senek,** Seneca, *Letters* 74.30. 987 **Lazarus,** John 11.35.

pree° wepyng is nothing deffended° to hym that sorweful is, amonges folk in sorwe, but it is rather graunted hym to wepe. / The Apostle Paul unto the Romayns writeth, 'Man shal rejoyse with hem that maken joye, and wepen with swich folk as wepen.' / But though attempree wepyng be ygraunted, outrageous wepyng certes is deffended. / Mesure° of wepyng sholde be considered, after the loore that techeth us Senek. / 'Whan that thy frend is deed,' quod he, 'lat nat thyne eyen to moyste been of teeres, ne to muche drye. Although the teeres come to thyne eyen, lat hem nat falle.' / And whan thou hast forgoon° thy freend, do diligence to gete another freend; and this is moore wysdom than for to wepe for thy freend which that thou hast lorn°, for therinne is no boote°. / And therfore if ye governe yow by sapience° put awey sorwe out of your herte. / Remembre yow that Jesus Syrak seith, 'A man that is joyous and glad in herte, it hym conserveth florisshyng in his age°, but soothly sorweful herte maketh his bones drye.' / He seith eek thus, that sorwe in herte sleeth ful many a man. / Salomon seith that right as motthes in the shepes flees° anoyeth to° the clothes, and the smale wormes to the tree, right so anoyeth sorwe to the herte. / Wherfore us oghte as wel in the deeth of oure children as in the losse of oure goodes temporels have pacience. / Remembre yow upon the pacient Job. Whan he hadde lost his children and his temporel substance, and in his body endured and receyved ful many a grevous tribulacioun, yet seyde he thus, / 'Oure Lord hath yeven it me, our Lord hath biraft it me. Right as our Lord hath wold, right so it is doon. Blessed be the name of our Lord.'" / 1000

To this foreseide° thinges answerde Melibeus unto his wyf Prudence, "Alle thy wordes," quod he, "been sothe° and therwith profitable. But trewely myn herte is troubled with this sorwe so grevously that I noot° what to doone." /

"Lat calle," quod Prudence, "thy trewe freendes alle and thy lynage° whiche that been wise. Telleth your cas and herkneth what they seye in conseillyng, and yow governe° after hire sentence°. / Salomon seith, 'Werk alle thy thinges by conseil and thou shalt never repente.'" /

Thanne, by the conseil of his wyf Prudence, this Melibeus leet callen a greet congregacioun of folk, / as surgiens°, phisiciens, olde folk and yonge, and somme of his olde enemys reconsiled as by hir semblaunt° to his love and into his grace. / 1005 And ther with al° ther coomen somme of his neighebores that diden hym reverence more for drede than for love, as it happeth ofte. / Ther coomen also ful many subtille flatereres, and wise advocatz lerned in the lawe. /

And whan this folk togidre assembled weren, this Melibeus in sorweful wise shewed hem his cas, / and by the manere of his speche it semed wel that in herte he baar a crueel ire, redy to doon vengeaunce upon his foes, and sodeynly desired that the werre° sholde bigynne. / But nathelees yet axed° he hire conseil upon this matiere. / 1010 A surgien, by licence and assent of swiche as weren wise, up roos and to Melibeus seyde as ye may heere. /

"Sire," quod he, "as to us surgiens aperteneth° that we do to every wight° the beste that we kan, wher as° we been withholde° and to our pacientz that we do no damage, / wherfore it happeth many tyme and ofte that whan twey° men han everich° wounded oother, oon same surgien heleth hem bothe. / Wherfore unto our art it is nat pertinent° to norice° werre, ne parties to supporte°. / But certes, as to the warisshynge° of youre doghter, al be it so that she perilously be wounded, we shullen do so ententif° bisynesse fro day to nyght that with the grace of God she shal be hool and sound as soone as is possible." / Almoost right 1015 in the same wise the phisiciens answerden,

---

988 woot attempree, *know that temperate,* **nothing deffended,** *not at all forbidden* **991 Mesure,** *moderation* **993 forgoon,** *lost,* **lorn,** *lost,* **boote,** *remedy* **994 sapience,** *wisdom* **995 conserveth florisshyng in his age,** *preserves freshness in his old age* **997 shepes flees,** *wool* (sheep's fleece), **anoyeth to,** *damage* **1001 foreseide,** *previously stated,* **sothe,** *true,* **noot,** *don't know* **1002 lynage,** *relatives,* **yow governe,** *govern your-self,* **sentence,** *advice* **1005 surgiens,** *surgeons,* **as by hir semblaunt,** *apparently* **1006 ther with al,** *also* **1009 werre,** *war* **1010 axed,** *asked* **1012 aperteneth,** *it is appropriate,* **wight,** *person,* **wher as,** *wherever,* **withholde,** *retained* **1013 twey,** *two,* **everich,** *each* **1014 pertinent,** *appropriate,* **norice,** *encourage,* **parties to support,** *to support either party* **1015 warisshynge,** *healing,* **ententif,** *attentive*

989 Paul, Romans 12.15. **991–92 Senek . . . ,** Seneca, *Letters* 63.1. **995 Jesus Syrak,** Jesus, son of Sirach, author of Ecclesiasticus, but the passage is from Proverbs 17.22, an error in Chaucer's source. **996 He seith,** Ecclesiasticus 30.23 (Vulgate). **997 Salomon,** Proverbs 25.20 (Vulgate). **998 goodes temporels,** imitates French grammar, with adjective following noun and agreeing in number. **999–1000** Job 1.21. **1003 Salomon,** Ecclesiasticus 32.24 (Vulgate); see *MilT* 1.3529–30n.

save that they seyden a fewe woordes moore, / that "right as maladies been cured by hir contraries, right so shul men warisshe werre by vengeaunce." / His neighebores ful of envye, his feyned freendes that semeden reconsiled, and his flatereres / maden semblant° of wepyng, and empeireden° and agreggeden° muchel of this matiere in preising greetly Melibee of myght°, of power, of richesse, and of freendes, despisynge the power of his adversaries, / and seiden outrely° that he anon sholde wreken° hym on his foes and bigynne werre. /   1020

Up roos thanne an advocat° that was wys, by leve and by conseil of othere that were wise, and seide, / "Lordynges, the nede for which we been assembled in this place is a ful hevy° thyng and an heigh° matiere, / by cause of the wrong and of the wikkednesse that hath be doon, and eek by resoun of the grete damages that in tyme comynge been possible to fallen° for this same cause, / and eek by resoun of the grete richesse and power of the parties bothe, / for the whiche resouns it were a ful greet peril to erren° in this matiere. / 1025 Wherfore, Melibeus, this is our sentence°: we conseille yow aboven alle thing that right anon thou do thy diligence° in kepynge of° thy propre persone° in swich a wise that thou wante° noon espie° ne wacche° thy body for to save. / And after that we conseille that in thyn hous thou sette sufficeant garnisoun° so that they may as wel thy body as thyn hous defende. / But certes°, for to moeve werre°, or sodeynly for to doon vengeaunce, we may nat demen° in so litel tyme that it were profitable. / Wherfore we axen leyser° and espace° to have deliberacioun in this cas to deme°. / For the commune proverbe seith thus, 'He that sone deemeth, soone shal repente.' / And eek 1030 men seyn that thilke° juge is wys that soone understondeth a matiere and juggeth by leyser°. / For al be it so that° alle tariyng° be anoyful°, algates° it is nat to repreve° in yevynge° of juggement, ne in vengeance-takyng, whan it is sufficeant and resonable. / And that shewed oure lord Jesu Crist by ensample, for whan that the womman that was taken in avowtrie° was broght in his presence, to knowen what sholde be doon with hire persone, al be it so that he wiste° wel hymself what that he wolde answere, yet ne wolde he nat answere sodeynly, but he wolde have deliberacioun, and in the ground he wroot twies°. / And by thise causes° we axen° deliberacioun, and we shal thanne, by the grace of God, conseille thee thyng that shal be profitable." /

Up stirten° thanne the yonge folk at ones, and the mooste partie of that compainye scorned the olde wise men, and bigonnen to make noyse, and seyden that / right so as whil that° iren 1035 is hoot men sholden smyte°, right so men sholde wreken° hir wronges while that they been fresshe and newe. And with loud voys they criden, 'Werre! Werre!' /

Up roos tho° oon of thise olde wise, and with his hand made contenaunce° that men sholde holden hem stille and yeven° hym audience. / "Lordynges," quod he, "ther is ful many a man that crieth 'werre, werre,' that woot° ful litel what werre amounteth°. / Werre at his° bigynnyng hath so greet an entryng° and so large that every wight° may entre whan hym liketh, and lightly° fynde werre. / But certes what ende that shal therof bifalle°, it is nat light° to knowe. / For soothly°, whan 1040 that werre is ones° bigonne, ther is ful many a child unborn of his mooder that shal sterve° yong by cause of that ilke° werre, or elles lyve in sorwe and dye in wrecchednesse. / And therfore, er that° any werre bigynne, men moste have greet conseil and greet deliberacioun." /

1019 semblant, *appearance,* **empeireden,** *made worse,* **agreggedden,** *aggravated,* **Melibee of myght,** *the might of Melibee* **1020 outrely,** *utterly,* **wreken,** *revenge* **1021 advocat,** *lawyer* **1022 hevy,** *serious,* **heigh,** *important* **1023 fallen,** *occur* **1025 to erren,** *to make an error* **1026 sentence,** *advice,* **do thy diligence,** *take care,* **kepynge of,** *protecting,* **thy propre persone,** *yourself,* **wante,** *lack,* **espie,** *spy,* **wacche,** *watchman* **1027 garnisoun,** *guards* **1028 certes,** *certainly,* **moeve werre,** *make war,* **demen,** *decide* **1029 axen leyser,** *ask time,* **espace,** *opportunity,* **deme,** *judge* **1031 thilke,** *that,* **by leyser,** *in time* **1032 al be it so that,** *even though,* **tariyng,** *delaying,* **anoyful,** *disturbing,* **algates,** *nevertheless,*

nat to repreve, *not to be objected to,* **yevynge,** *giving* **1033 avowtrie,** *adultery,* **wiste,** *knew,* **wroot twies,** *wrote twice* **1034 by thise causes,** *for these reasons,* **axen,** *ask* **1035 stirten,** *leapt* **1036 right so as whil that,** *just as when* **smyten,** *strike,* **wreken,** *avenge* **1037 tho,** *then,* **made contenaunce,** *gestured,* **yeven,** *give* **1038 woot,** *knows,* **amounteth,** *amounts to* **1039 his,** *its,* **entryng,** *entry,* **wight,** *person,* **lightly,** *easily* **1040 that shal therof bifalle,** *will result from that,* **light,** *easy* **1041 soothly,** *truly,* **ones,** *once,* **sterve,** *die,* **ilke,** *same* **1042 er that,** *before*

1017 cured by hir contraries, the medieval belief that good health was a matter of balance among the humors; see *GP* 1.333n. Healing war with vengeance, however, is a non sequitur not found in the Latin original but added in Chaucer's French source. **1030 commune proverbe,** Publilius Syrus, first-century BCE dramatist, *Sententiae* 32. **1031–32** Also proverbial. **1033 Jesu Crist,** John 8.3–8. **1036** Proverbial.

And whan this olde man wende to enforcen° his tale by resons°, wel ny° alle at ones bigonne they to rise for to breken° his tale, and beden° hym ful ofte his wordes for to abregge°. / For soothly, he that precheth to hem that listen nat heeren° his wordes, his sermon hem anoieth°. / For Jesus Syrak seith that musik in wepynge is anoyous thing—this is to seyn, as muche availleth° to speken bifore folk to whiche his speche anoyeth, as it is to synge biforn hym that wepeth. / And whan this wyse 1045 man saugh that hym wanted° audience, alshamefast° he sette him doun agayn. / For Salomon seith, "Ther as thou ne mayst have noon audience, enforce thee nat to speke." / "I see wel," quod this wise man, "that the commune proverbe is sooth, that good conseil wanteth° whan it is most nede°." /

Yet hadde this Melibeus in his conseil many folk that prively in his eere conseilled hym certeyn thing and conseilled hym the contrarie in general audience°. /

Whan Melibeus hadde herd that the gretteste partie° of his conseil weren accorded° that he sholde maken werre, anoon he consented to hir conseilling and fully affermed hir sentence°. / Thanne dame Prudence, whan that 1050 she saugh how that hir housbonde shoop hym° for to wreken° hym on his foes and to bigynne werre, she in ful humble wise, when she saugh hir tyme, seide to hym thise wordes, / "My lord," quod she, "I yow biseche as hertely as I dar and kan, ne haste yow nat to faste, and for alle gerdons° as yeveth° me audience. / For Piers Alfonce seith, 'Whoso that dooth to thee oother° good or harm, haste thee nat to quiten° it; for in this wise thy freend wol abyde° and thyn enemy shal the lenger lyve in drede.' / The proverbe seith, 'He hasteth wel that wisely kan abyde,' and in wikked haste is no profit." /

This Melibee answerde unto his wyf Prudence, "I purpose nat," quod he, "to werke by thy conseil for many causes and resouns. For certes°, every wight° wolde holde me thanne a fool— / 1055 this is to seyn, if I for thy conseilling wolde chaungen thynges that been ordeyned and affermed by so manye wyse. / Secoundly, I seye that alle wommen been wikke and noon good of hem alle. For of a thousand men, seith Salomon, I foond o good man, but, certes, of alle wommen, good womman foond I never. / And also certes, if I governed me by thy conseil, it sholde seme that I hadde yeve° to thee over me the maistrie, and God forbede that it so weere. / For Jesus Syrak seith that if the wyf have maistrie, she is contrarious to hir housbonde. / And Salomon seith, 'Never in thy lyf to thy wyf ne to thy child ne to thy freend ne yeve° no power over thyself. For bettre it were that thy children aske of thy persone thynges that hem nedeth than thou be thyself in the handes of thy children.' / And if I wolde werke by thy 1060 conseilling, certes my conseilling moste somtyme° be secree til it were tyme that it moste be knowe, and this ne may noght be. / For it is writen that the janglerie° of wommen kan nat hyden thynges save that° they witen° noght. / Furthermore the philosophre seith, 'In wikked conseil wommen venquisshe° men.' And for thise resouns I ne owe nat usen° thy conseil." /

Whanne dame Prudence ful debonairly° and with greet pacience hadde herd al that hir housbonde lyked for to seye, thanne axed° she of hym licence for to speke, and seyde in this wyse. / "My lord," quod she, "as to your firste resoun, certes it may lightly° been answered. For I seye that it is no folie to chaunge conseil whan the thyng is chaunged, or elles whan the thyng semeth otherweyes than it was biforn. / And moore- 1065 over I seye that though ye han sworn and

himself, **wreken,** *revenge* 1052 **gerdons,** *benefits,* **as yeveth,** *so give* 1053 **oother,** *either,* **quiten,** *repay,* **abyde,** *remain* 1055 **certes,** *sure,* **wight,** *man* 1058 **yeve,** *given* 1060 **yeve,** *give* 1061 **moste somtyme,** *must for a time* 1062 **janglerie,** *blabbing,* **that,** *what,* **witen,** *know* 1063 **venquisshe,** *vanquish,* **ne owe nat usen,** *ought not follow* 1064 **debonairly,** *courteously,* **axed,** *asked* 1065 **lightly,** *easily*

1043 **wende to enforcen,** *thought to convey,* **resons,** *arguments,* **wel ny,** *nearly,* **breken,** *interrupt,* **beden,** *request,* **abregge,** *shorten* (it) 1044 **listen nat heeren,** *don't wish to hear,* **hem anoieth,** *annoys them* 1045 **as muche availleth,** *it accomplishes as much* 1046 **hym wanted,** *he lacked,* **al shamefast,** *ashamed* 1048 **wanteth,** *is lacking,* **nede,** *needed* 1049 **in general audience,** i.e., *publicly* 1050 **partie,** *portion,* **accorded,** *agreed,* **hir sentence,** *their advice* 1051 **shoop hym,** *prepared*

1045 **Jesus Syrak,** Ecclesiasticus 22.6 (Vulgate). 1047 **Salomon,** Ecclesiasticus 32.6 (Vulgate); compare *NPP* 7.2801–2. 1048 **commune proverbe,** Publilius Syrus, *Sententiae* 594. 1053 **Piers Alfonce,** Petrus Alphonsus, author of a popular collection of exempla, *Disciplina Clericalis* (Guide for Scholars) 24.3. 1054 Chaucer's addition; *TC* 1.956 and *ParsT* 10.1003. 1057 **Salomon,** Ecclesiastes 7.28; *MerT* 4.2247–48. 1059 Ecclesiasticus 25.20; compare *WBP* 3.818 and *ParsT* 10.927. 1060 **Salomon,** Ecclesiasticus 33.20–21 (Vulgate). 1062–63 Lines found in no MSS so probably not in Chaucer's immediate source, although in the extant Latin and French versions. Here emended slightly from Skeat's translation of the French. 1063 **the philosophre,** Publilius Syrus, *Sententiae* 324.

bihight° to parfourne° youre emprise°, and nathelees ye weyve° to parfourne thilke same emprise by juste cause, men sholde nat seyn therfore that ye were a lier ne forsworn. / For the book seith that the wise man maketh no lesyng° whan he turneth his corage° to the bettre. / And al be it so that° your emprise be establissed and ordeyned° by greet multitude of folk, yet thar ye nat accomplice thilke ordinaunce but yow lyke°. / For the trouthe of thynges and the profit been rather founden in fewe folk that been wise and ful of resoun than by greet multitude of folk ther° every man crieth and clatereth° what that hym liketh. Soothly swich° multitude is nat honeste°. / As to the seconde resoun, where as ye seyn that alle wommen been wikke, save your grace°, certes ye despisen° alle wommen in this wyse; and he that alle despseth alle displeseth, as seith the book. / And Senec 1070 seith that who so wole° have sapience° shal no man dispreise°, but he shal gladly techen the science° that he kan withouten presumpcioun or pryde. / And swiche thynges as he nought ne kan°, he shal nat been ashamed to lerne hem and enquere of lasse° folk than hymself. / And sire, that ther hath been many a good womman may lightly° be preved°. / For certes, sire, oure lord Jesu Crist wolde nevere have descended to be born of a womman if alle wommen hadden ben wikke. / And after that, for the grete bountee° that is in wommen, our lord Jesu Crist, whan he was risen fro deeth to lyve, appeered rather to a womman than to his apostles. / And though that Salomon seith 1075 that he ne fond never womman good, it folweth nat therfore that alle wommen ben wikke. / For though that he ne fond no good womman, certes, ful many another man hath founden many a womman ful good and trewe. / Or elles peraventure the entente of Salomon was this, that as in

sovereyn bountee° he foond no womman— / this is to seyn, that ther is no wight that hath sovereyn bountee save God allone, as he hymself recordeth in hys Evaungelie. / For ther nys no creature so good that hym ne wanteth° somwhat of the perfeccioun of God that is his maker. / Your 1080 thridde resoun is this: ye seyn if ye governe yow by my conseil, it sholde seme that ye hadde yeve me the maistrie and the lordshipe over your persone. / Sire, save your grace°, it is nat so. For if it were so, that no man sholde be conseilled but oonly of hem that hadden lordshipe and maistrie of his persone, men wolden nat be conseilled so ofte. / For soothly, thilke man that asketh conseil of a purpos°, yet hath he free choys, wheither he wole werke by that conseil or noon°. / And as to youre fourthe resoun, ther ye seyn that the janglerie° of wommen kan nat hyd thynges save that they wiste noght°, as who seith that a womman kan nat hyde that she woot°, / sire, thise wordes been understonde of wommen that been jangleresses and wikked, / of 1085 whiche wommen men seyn that three thinges dryven a man out of his hous, that is to seyn, smoke, dropping of reyn, and wikked wyves. / And of swiche wommen seith Salomon that it were bettre dwelle in desert than with a womman that is riotous°. / And sire, by youre leve, that am nat I. / For ye haan° ful ofte assayed° my grete silence and my gret pacience, and eek how wel that I kan hyde and hele° thynges that men oghte secreely to hyde. / And soothly°, as to youre fifthe resoun, wher as ye seyn that in wikked conseil wommen venquisshe° men, God woot thilke° resoun stant heere in no stede°. / For under- 1090 stoond now, ye asken conseil to do wikkednesse; / and if ye wole werken wikkednesse and your wyf restreyneth thilke° wikked purpos

---

1066 **bihight,** *pledged,* **parfourne,** *perform,* **emprise,** *enterprise,* **natheles ye weyve,** (if) *you nonetheless opt not* 1067 **lesyng,** *lie,* **corage,** *heart* 1068 **al be it so that,** *even if,* **ordeyned,** *planned,* **thar ye nat accomplice thilke ordinaunce but yow lyke,** *you need not fulfill this plan unless you wish* 1069 **ther,** *where,* **clatereth,** *chatters,* **Soothly swich,** *truly such a,* **honeste,** *respectable* 1070 **save your grace,** *i.e., with all due respect,* **despisen,** *insult* 1071 **who so wole,** *whoever will,* **sapience,** *wisdom,* **dispreise,** *slander,* **science,** *knowledge* 1072 **nought ne kan,** *does not know,* **lasse,** *lesser* 1073 **lightly,** *easily,* **preved,** *proved* 1075 **bountee,** *goodness* 1078 **sovereyn bountee,** *supreme goodness* 1080 **ne wanteth,** *lacks not* 1082 **save your grace,** *with all due respect* 1083 **of a purpos,** *about a plan,* **noon,** *not* 1084 **janglerie,** *chatter,* **save that they wiste noght,** *except when they know nothing,* **woot,** *knows* 1087 **riotous,** *contentious* 1088 **haan,** *have,* **assayed,** *tested,* **hele,** *conceal* 1090 **soothly,** *truly,* **venquisshe,** *overwhelm,* **woot thilke,** *knows this,* **stant . . . in no stede,** *is of no value* 1092 **thilke,** *this*

1067 **the book,** Seneca, *De Beneficiis* (On Benefits) 4.38.1. 1071 **Senec,** not in Seneca, but Martinus Dumiensis, *Formula Honestae Vitae* (Formula for a Noble Life), chap. 3. 1075 Matthew 28.9; Mark 16.9. 1076 **Salomon,** Ecclesiastes 7.29, attributed to Solomon in the Middle Ages; see *MerT* 4.2277–79. 1079 **Evaungelie,** gospel; Matthew 19.17; Luke 18.19. 1084 **wommen kan nat hyde,** women's inability to keep a secret is a motif in *WBT* 3.945–80. 1086 Derives from Proverbs 27.15; see *WBP* 3.278–80 and *ParsT* 10.631. 1087 **Salomon,** Proverbs 21.9; compare *WBP* 3.775–80. 1088 **that am nat I,** see *WBP* 3.112 and *MerT* 4.1456. This and other echoes indicate connections between *Melibee* and the marriage group of fragments 3–5.

and overcometh yow by resoun and by good conseil, / certes, youre wyf oghte rather to be preised
than yblamed. / Thus sholde ye understonde the
philosophre that seith, 'In wikked conseil wommen venquisshen hir housbondes.' / And ther as
ye blamen alle wommen and hir resouns°, I shal
shewe yow by manye ensamples that many a womman hath ben ful good, and yet been°, and
hir conseils ful hoolsome and profitable. / 1095
Eek som men han seyd that the conseillinge of
wommen is outher to deere° or elles to litel of
prys°. / But al be it so that ful many a womman is
badde and hir conseil vile and noght worth, yet
han men founde ful many a good womman and ful
discrete and wise in conseillinge. / Loo Jacob by
good conseil of his mooder Rebekka wan the
benysoun° of Ysaak his fader and the lordshipe
over alle his bretheren. / Judith by hire good conseil delivered the citee of Bethulie, in which she
dwelled, out of the handes of Olofernus that
hadde it biseged° and wolde have al destroyed it. /
Abygail delivered Nabal hir housbonde fro David
the kyng that wolde have slayn hym, and apaysed°
the ire of the kyng by hir wit and by hir good
conseillyng. / Hester enhaunced greetly by 1100
hir good conseil the peple of God in the
regne of Assuerus the kyng. / And the same
bountee° in good conseilling of many a good womman may men telle. / And mooreover, whan
our Lord hadde creat Adam our formefader°, he
seyde in this wyse, / 'It is nat good to been a man
alloone. Make we to hym an help semblable° to
hymself.' / Heere may ye se that if that wommen
were nat goode, and hir conseils goode and
profitable, / oure lord God of hevene 1105
wolde neither han wroght hem, ne called hem
help of man, but rather confusioun of man. / And
ther seyde oones a clerk in two vers: 'What
is bettre than gold? Jaspre°. What is bettre than
jaspre? Wisedoom. / And what is bettre than wisedoom? Womman. And what is bettre than a good

womman? Nothyng.' / And sire, by manye of othre
resons may ye seen that manye wommen been
goode and hir conseils goode and profitable. /
And therfore, sire, if ye wol triste to° my conseil,
I shal restoore yow youre doghter hool and
sound. / And eek I wol do to yow so muche 1110
that ye shul have honour in this cause." /

Whan Melibee hadde herd the wordes of his
wyf Prudence he seyde thus, / "I se wel that the
word of Salomon is sooth°. He seith that wordes
that been spoken discreetly by ordinaunce° been
honycombes, for they yeven° swetnesse to the soule
and hoolsomnesse° to the body. / And wyf, by cause
of thy swete wordes and eek for I have assayed and
preved thy grete sapience° and thy grete trouthe, I
wol governe me by thy conseil in alle thing." /

"Now sire," quod dame Prudence, "and syn ye
vouchesauf° to been governed by my conseil, I wol
enforme yow how ye shul governe yourself in
chesynge of° your conseillours. / Ye shul first 1115
in alle youre werkes mekely biseken to° the
heighe God that he wol be your conseillour; / and
shapeth yow° to swich entente that he yeve yow
conseil and confort, as taughte Thobie his sone: /
'At alle tymes thou shalt blesse God, and praye
hym to dresse° thy weyes.' And looke that all thy
conseils been in hym for evermoore. / Seint Jame
eek seith, 'If any of yow have nede of sapience, axe
it of God.' / And afterward thanne shul ye taken
conseil of yourself and examyne wel your thoghtes
of swich thyng as yow thynketh that is best for
your profit. / And thanne shul ye dryve fro 1120
your herte thre thynges that been contrariouse to good conseil, / that is to seyn, ire°, covei-
tise°, and hastifnesse°. /

"First, he that axeth conseil of hymself, certes
he moste been withouten ire, for manye causes. /
The firste is this: he that hath greet ire and
wratthe in hymself, he weneth° alwey that he may
do thyng that he may nat do. / And secoundely,
he that is irous and wrooth, he ne may nat

1095 **hir resouns**, *their arguments*, **yet been**, *still is* 1096 **outher to deere**, *either too costly*, **prys**, *value* 1098 **benysoun**, *blessing* 1099 **biseged**, *besieged* 1100 **apaysed**, *appeased* 1102 **bountee**, *goodness* 1103 **formefader**, *first father* 1104 **semblable**, *similar* 1107 **Jaspre**, *jasper* (semiprecious stone) 1110 **triste to**, *trust* 1113 **sooth**, *true*, **by**

ordinaunce, *in due order*, **yeven**, *give*, **hoolsomnesse**, *health* 1114 **sapience**, *wisdom* 1115 **syn ye vouchesauf**, *since you consent*, **chesynge of**, *choosing* 1116 **biseken to**, *ask* 1117 **shapeth yow**, *bend yourself* 1118 **dresse**, *prepare* 1122 **ire**, *anger*, **coveitise**, *greed*, **hastifnesse**, *hastiness* 1124 **weneth**, *thinks*

1094 See 1063n. 1098–1101 These examples are cited in the same order in *MerT* 4.1362–74. **Jacob . . . Rebekka,** Genesis 27. **Judith . . . Olofernus,** the apocryphal book of Judith 12–13. **Abygail . . . Nabal,** Abigail convinces David not to seek revenge for the offense of her husband, Nabal; 1 Samuel 25.10–42. **Hester . . . Assuerus,** Esther 7–8. **1104 Adam,** Genesis 2.18. **1106 confusioun of man,** see *NPT* 7.3164. **1107 a clerk,** unidentified, but the saying was common. **1113 Salomon,** Proverbs 16.24. **1115** At this point the French text followed by Chaucer omits about ten pages of the Latin original. **1117 Thobie,** Tobias 4.20 (Vulgate). **1119 Seint Jame,** James 1.5.

wel deme°; / and he that may nat wel deme 1125
may nat wel conseille. / The thridde is this,
that he that is irous and wrooth, as seith Senec, ne
may nat speke but blameful thynges; / and with his
viciouse wordes he stireth oother folk to angre
and to ire. / And eek, sire, ye moste° dryve coveitise
out of youre herte. / For the apostle seith
that coveitise is roote of alle harmes. / And 1130
trust wel that a coveitous man ne kan noght
deme° ne thynke, but° oonly to fulfille the ende
of his coveitise. / And certes°, that ne may never
been accompliced, for ever the moore habundaunce that he hath of richesse, the moore he desireth. / And sire, ye moste also dryve out of youre
herte hastifnesse, for certes, / ye may nat deeme°
for the beste by a sodeyn thought that falleth
in youre herte, but ye moste avyse yow° on it ful
ofte. / For as ye herde biforn, the commune
proverbe is this, that he that soone demeth,
soone repenteth. /   1135

  "Sire, ye ne be nat alwey in lyke° disposicioun / for certes somthyng that somtyme semeth
to yow that it is good for to do another tyme it
semeth to yow the contrarie. /

  "Whan ye han taken conseil of yourself, and
han deemed by good deliberacion swich thyng as
you list best°, / thanne rede° I yow that ye kepe it
secree. / Biwrey° nat youre conseil° to no persone
but if so be that ye wenen sikerly° that, thurgh your
biwreying, your condicioun shal be to yow
the moore profitable. / For Jesus Syrak 1140
seith, 'Neither to thy foe ne to thy frend
discovere nat thy secree ne thy folie, / for they wol
yeve° yow audience and looking° and supporta-
cioun° in thy presence and scorne thee in thyn
absence.' / Another clerk seith that scarsly shal-
tou° fynden any persone that may kepe conseil
sikerly°. / The book seith, 'Whil that thou kepest
thy conseil in thyn herte, thou kepest it in thy prisoun, / and whan thou biwreyest° thy conseil
to any wight, he holdeth thee in his snare.' / 1145

And therfore yow is bettre to hyde your
conseil in your herte than praye hem to whom he
han biwreyed youre conseil that he wole kepen it
cloos and stille. / For Seneca seith, 'If so be that
thou ne mayst nat thyn owene conseil hyde, how
darstou prayen any oother wight thy conseil sikerly
to kepe?' / But nathelees, if thou wene sikerly°
that the biwreiyng° of thy conseil to a persone wol
make thy condicioun to stonden in the bettre
plyt°, thanne shaltou tellen hym thy conseil in this
wise. / First, thou shalt make no semblant wheither thee were levere pees° or werre, or this or that,
ne shewe hym nat thy wille and thyn entente. / For
trust wel, that comenli° thise conseillours been
flatereres, / namely° the conseillours of grete 1150
lordes, / for they enforcen hem° alwey rather
to speken plesante wordes, enclynynge to the
lordes lust°, than wordes that been trewe or
profitable. / And therfore men seyn that the riche
man hath seeld° good conseil but if he have it of
hymself. / And after that, thou shalt considere thy
freendes and thyne enemys. / And as touchynge
thy freendes, thou shalt considere wiche of hem
that been moost feithful and moost wise, and
eldest and most approved in conseilling. / 1155
And of hem shalt thou aske thy conseil, as the
caas requireth. /

  "I seye that first ye shul clepe° to youre conseil
your freendes that been trewe. / For Salomon
seith that right as the herte of a man deliteth in
savour° that is soote°, right so the conseil of trewe
freendes yeveth° swetenesse to the soule. / He seith
also, 'Ther may nothing be likned° to the trewe
freend.' / For certes, gold ne silver beth nat so
muche worth as the goode wyl of a trewe
freend. / And eek he seith that a trewe freend 1160
is a strong deffense; whoso that hym fyndeth,
certes he fyndeth a greet tresour. / Thanne shul ye
eek considere if that° your trewe freendes been
discrete and wyse. For the book seith, 'Axe° alwey
thy conseil of hem that been wise.' / And by this

1125 deme, *judge* 1129 moste, *must* 1131 deme, *judge,* but, *except*
1132 certes, *surely* 1134 deeme, *judge,* moste avyse yow, *must deliber-*
ate 1136 lyke, *the same* 1138 you list best, *best pleases you* 1139 rede,
advise 1140 Biwrey, *reveal,* conseil, *decision,* wenen sikerly, *believe*
securely 1142 yeve, *give,* looking, *attention,* supportacioun, *support*
1143 shaltou, *shall you,* sikerly, *securely* 1145 biwreyest, *reveal* 1148

wene sikerly, *think securely,* biwreiyng, *revealing,* plyt, *state* 1149 semblant wheither thee were levere pees, *indication whether you prefer*
peace 1150 comenli, *commonly* 1151 namely, *especially* 1152 enforcen
hem, *compel themselves,* lust, *wishes* 1153 seeld, *seldom* 1157 clepe,
summon 1158 savour, *taste,* soote, *sweet,* yeveth, *gives* 1159 likned,
compared 1162 if that, *whether,* Axe, *ask*

1127 **Senec,** not in Seneca, but Publilius Syrus, *Sententiae* 281. **1130 the apostle,** Paul, 1 Timothy 6.10. See line 1840 below; *PardP* 6.334; and
ParsT 10.739. **1135 commune proverbe,** same as line 1030 above. **1141 Jesus Syrak,** Ecclesiasticus 19.8–9 (Vulgate). **1143 Another clerk,** not
identified. **1144 The book,** not identified. **1147 Seneca,** not in Seneca, but Martinus Dumiensis, *De Moribus* (On Customs) 16. **1158 Salomon,**
Proverbs 27.9. **1159** Ecclesiasticus 6.15 (Vulgate). **1161** Ecclesiasticus 6.14 (Vulgate). **1162 the book,** Tobias 4.19 (Vulgate).

same resoun shul ye clepen° to youre conseil of youre freendes that been of age°, swiche as han seyn° and been expert in manye thynges, and been approved in conseillinges. / For the book seith that in the olde men is the sapience° and in longe tyme the prudence. / And Tullius seith that grete thynges ne been nat ay° accompliced by strengthe, ne by delivernesse° of body, but by good conseil, by auctoritee of persones, and by science°, the whiche thre thynges ne been nat fieble by age, but certes they enforcen° and encreesen day by day. / And thanne shul ye kepe this for a gen- 1165 eral reule. First shul ye clepen° to your conseil a fewe of your freendes that been especiale, / for Salomon seith, 'Manye freendes have thou, but among a thousand chese° thee oon to be thy conseillour.' / For al be it so that thou first ne telle thy conseil but to a fewe, thou mayst afterward telle it to mo° folk if it be nede. / But looke° alwey that thy conseillours have thilke° thre condiciouns that I have seyd bifore, that is to seyn, that they be trewe, wise, and of oold experience. / And werke° nat alwey in every nede by oon counseillour al-lone, for somtyme bihooveth it to been con-seilled by manye. /For Salomon seith, 'Salva- 1170 cioun° of thynges is wher as ther been manye conseillours.' /

"Now sith° I have toold yow of which folk ye sholde been counseilled, now wol I teche yow which conseil ye oghte to eschewe°. / First ye shul escheue the conseillyng of fooles. For Salomon seith, 'Taak no conseil of a fool, for he ne kan noght conseille but after his owene lust° and his affeccioun°.' / The book seith that the propretee° of a fool is this: he troweth lightly° harm of every wight, and lightly troweth alle bountee° in hymself. / Thou shalt eek escheue the conseillyng of flatereres, swiche as enforcen hem° rather to preise your persone by flaterye than for to telle yow the sothfastnesse° of thinges. / 1175

"Wherfore Tullius seith, 'Amonges alle the pestilences° that been in freendshipe, the gretteste is flaterie.' And therfore is it moore nede° that thou escheue and drede flatereres than any oother peple. / The book seith, 'Thou shalt rather drede and flee fro the sweete wordes of flaterynge preis-eres° than fro the egre° wordes of thy freend that seith° thee thy sothes°.' / Salomon seith that the wordes of a flaterere is a snare to cacche with in-nocents. / He seith also that he that speketh to his freend wordes of swetnesse and of plesaunce set-teth a net biforn his feet to cacche hym. / And therfore seith Tullius, 'Enclyne nat thyne eres to flatereres, ne taaketh no conseil of the wordes of flaterye.' / And Caton seith, 1180 'Avyse thee° wel and escheue the wordes of swetnesse and of plesaunce.' / And eek thou shalt escheue the conseillyng of thyne olde ene-mys that been reconsiled. / The book seith that no wight° retourneth saufly° into the grace° of hys olde enemy. / And Isope seith, 'Ne trust nat to hem to whiche thou hast had somtyme werre or enemytee°, ne telle hem nat thy conseil.' / And Seneca telleth the cause why: 'It may nat be,' seith he, 'that where greet fyr hath longe tyme endured that ther ne dwelleth som vapour of warmnesse°.' / And therfore seith Salomon, 1185 'In thyn olde foo trust nevere.' / For sikerly° though thyn enemy be reconsiled and maketh thee chiere° of humylitee and lowteth° to thee with his heed, ne trust him nevere. / For certes°, he maketh thilke feyned° humilitee moore for his profit than for any love of thy persone, by cause° that he deemeth° to have victorie over thy persone by swich feyned contenance°, the which victorie he mighte nat wynne by strif or werre. / And

---

1163 **clepen,** *summon,* **of age,** *mature,* **swiche as han seyn,** *such as have seen* 1164 **sapience,** *wisdom* 1165 **ay,** *always,* **delivernesse,** *agility,* **science,** *knowledge,* **enforcen,** *grow stronger* 1166 **clepen,** *summon* 1167 **chese,** *choose* 1168 **mo,** *more* 1169 **looke,** *be sure,* **thilke,** *those* 1170 **werke,** *act* 1171 **Salvacioun,** *security* 1172 **sith,** *since,* **eschewe,** *avoid* 1173 **lust,** *desire,* **affeccioun,** *gratification* 1174 **propretee,** *quality,* **troweth lightly,** *easily believes,* **bountee,** *goodness* 1175 **enforcen hem,** *strive,* **sothfastnesse,** *truthfulness* 1176 **pestilences,** *plagues,* **nede,** *necessary* 1177 **preiseres,** *praisers,* **egre,** *painful,* **seith,** *tells,* **sothes,** *truths* 1181 **Avyse thee,** *consider* 1183 **wight,** *person,* **saufly,** *securely,* **grace,** *favor* 1184 **enemytee,** *antagonism* 1185 **vapour of warmnesse,** *warm air* 1187 **sikerly,** *certainly,* **chiere,** *expressions,* **lowteth,** *bows* 1188 **certes,** *surely,* **thilke feyned,** *this pretended,* **by cause,** *for the reason,* **deemeth,** *thinks,* **swich feyned contenance,** *such pretended behavior*

1165 **Tullius,** Cicero, *De Senectute* (On Old Age) 6.17. 1167 **Salomon,** Ecclesiasticus 6.6 (Vulgate). 1171 **Salomon,** Proverbs 11.14. 1173 **Salomon,** Ecclesiasticus 8.20 (Vulgate). 1174 **The book,** Cicero, *Disputationes Tusculanae* (Tusculan Disputations) 3.30.73. 1176 **Tullius,** Cicero, *De Amicitia* (On Friendship) 25.91. 1177 **The book,** Martinus Dumiensis, *Formula Honestae Vitae* (Formula for a Noble Life), chap. 3. 1178 **Salomon,** Caecilius Balbus, *De Nugis Philosophorum* (On the Trifles of Philosophers), 27. 1179 Proverbs 29.5. 1180 **Tullius,** Cicero, *De Officiis* (On Duties) 1.91. 1181 **Caton,** Dionysius Cato, supposed author of *Disticha Catonis* (Cato's Couplets) 3.4. 1183 **The book,** Publilius Syrus, *Sententiae* 91. 1184 **Isope,** Aesop's *Fables* and Caecilius Balbus, *De Nugis Philosophorum* (On the Trifles of Philosophers), 25. 1185 **Seneca,** not Seneca, but Publilius Syrus, *Sententiae* 389. 1186 **Salomon,** Ecclesiasticus 12.10 (Vulgate).

Peter Alfonce seith, 'Make no felawshipe with thyne olde enemys, for if thou do hem bountee°, they wol perverten it into wikkednesse.' / And eek thou most escheue° the conseilling of hem that been thy servants and beren thee greet reverence, for peraventure° they doon it moore for drede° than for love. / And therfore seith a 1190 philosophre in this wise, 'Ther is no wight parfitly° trewe to hym that he to soore dredeth°.' / And Tullius seith, 'Ther nys no myght so greet of any emperour that longe may endure but if° he have moore love of the peple than drede.' / Thou shalt also escheue the conseiling of folk that been dronkelewe°, for they kan no conseil hyde. / For Salomon seith, 'Ther is no privetee ther as regneth° dronkenesse.' / Ye shul also han in suspect the conseillyng of swich folk as conseille yow o thyng prively and conseille yow the contrarie openly. / For Cassidorie seith that it is a 1195 manere sleighte to hyndre° whan he sheweth to doon o thyng openly and werketh prively the contrarie. / Thou shalt also have in suspect the conseillyng of wikked folk. For the book seith, 'The conseillyng of wikked folk is alwey full of fraude.' / And David seith, 'Blisful is that man that hath nat folwed the conseilyng of shrewes°.' / Thou shalt also escheue the conseillyng of yong folk, for hir conseil is nat rype. /

"Now sire, sith I have shewed yow of which folk ye shul take your conseil, and of which folk ye shul folwe the conseil, / now wol I teche 1200 yow how ye shal examyne your conseil, after the doctrine of Tullius. / In the examynynge thanne of your conseillour, ye shul considere manye thynges. / Alderfirst° thou shalt considere that in thilke° thyng that thou purposest°, and upon what thyng thou wolt have conseil, that verray°

trouthe be seyd and conserved°, this is to seyn, telle trewely thy tale. / For he that seith fals may nat wel be conseilled in that cas of which° he lieth. / And after this, thou shalt considere the thynges that acorden to that thou purposest° for to do by thy conseillours, if resoun accorde therto, / 1205 and eek if thy myght may atteine therto°, and if the moore part and the bettre part of thy conseillours accorde therto or noon°. / Thanne shaltou° considere what thyng shal folwe after hir conseillyng, as hate, pees, werre, grace°, profit, or damage, and manye othere thynges. / Thanne of alle thise thynges thou shalt chese° the beste and weyve° alle othere thynges. / Thanne shaltow considere of what roote° is engendred° the matiere of thy conseil and what fruyt it may conceyve and engendre. / Thou shalt eek considere alle thise causes fro whennes° they been sprongen°. / 1210 And whan ye han examyned youre conseil as I have seyd, and which partie° is the bettre and moore profitable, and hast approved it by manye wise folk and olde, / thanne shaltou considere if thou mayst parfourne° it and maken of it a good ende. / For certes, resoun wol nat that any man sholde bigynne a thyng but if he myghte parfourne it as hym oghte. / Ne no wight° sholde take upon hym so hevy a charge that he myghte nat bere it. / For the proverbe seith, he that to muche embraceth, distreyneth° litel. / And Catoun 1215 seith, 'Assay° to do swich° thing as thou hast power to doon lest that the charge° oppresse thee so soore° that thee bihoveth to weyve thyng° that thou hast bigonne.' / And if so be that thou be in doute wheither thou mayst parfourne a thyng or noon, chese° rather to suffre° than bigynne. / And Piers Alphonce seith, 'If thou hast myght to doon a thyng of which thou most° repente thee, it is

---

1189 **bountee,** *goodness* 1190 **escheue,** *avoid,* **peraventure,** *perhaps,* **drede,** *fear* 1191 **parfitly,** *perfectly,* **to soore dredeth,** *fears too much* 1192 **but if,** *unless* 1193 **dronkelewe,** *drunkards* 1194 **ther as regneth,** *where reigns* 1196 **a manere sleighte to hyndre,** *a kind of trick intended to do damage* 1198 **shrewes,** *villains* 1203 **Alderfirst,** *first of all,* **thilke,** *that,* **purposest,** *proposes,* **verray,** *genuine,* **conserved,** *preserved* 1204 **cas of which,** *matter about which* 1205 **acorden to that thou purposest,** *suit what you propose* 1206 **atteine therto,** *achieve it,* **accorde**

therto or noon, *agree with it or not* 1207 **shaltou,** *you shall,* **grace,** *kindness* 1208 **chese,** *choose,* **weyve,** *abandon* 1209 **roote,** *source,* **engendred,** *produced* 1210 **whennes,** *where,* **been sprongen,** *have arisen* 1211 **partie,** *choice* 1212 **parfourne,** *fulfill* 1214 **wight,** *person* 1215 **distreyneth,** *keeps* 1216 **Assay,** *attempt,* **swich,** *such,* **lest that the charge,** *so that the weight will not,* **soore,** *painfully,* **thee bihoveth to weyve thyng,** *it requires you to abandon something* 1217 **chese,** *choose,* **suffre,** *be patient* 1218 **most,** *must*

1189 Peter Alfonce, Petrus Alphonsus, *Disciplina Clericalis* (Guide for Scholars) 2.2. **1191 a philosophre,** unidentified. **1192 Tullius,** Cicero, *De Officiis* (On Duties) 2.7.23. **1194 Salomon,** Proverbs 31.4 (Vulgate). **1196 Cassidorie,** Cassiodorus, sixth-century statesman and author who founded two monasteries, *Variae Epistolae* (Various Letters) 10.18. **1197 the book,** Publilius Syrus, *Sententiae* 354. **1198 David,** Psalms 1.1. **1199** Chaucer and his French source omit about two pages of the Latin original here; in addition, Chaucer omits a quotation from Ecclesiastes 10.16 that warns against childhood rulers, leading scholars to think he was translating while Richard II was in his minority. **1200–10 Tullius . . . ,** Cicero, *De Officiis* (On Duties) 2.18; a paraphrase. **1215 proverbe,** see Chaucer's short poem *Proverbe,* lines 7–8. **1216 Catoun,** Dionysius Cato, supposed author of *Disticha Catonis* (Cato's Couplets) 3.14. **1218 Piers Alphonce,** Petrus Alphonsus, *Disciplina Clericalis* (Guide for Scholars) 4.4.

bettre nay than ye.' / This is to seyn that thee is bettre holde thy tonge stille than for to speke. / Thanne may ye understonde by strenger resons that if thou hast power to parfourne a werk of which thou shalt repente, thanne is it bettre that thou suffre than bigynne. / Wel seyn 1220 they° that defenden° every wight to assaye anything of which he is in doute, wheither he may parfourne it or noon. / And after, whan ye han examyned youre conseil as I have seyd biforn and knowen wel that ye may parfourne youre emprise°, conferme° it thanne sadly° til it be at an ende. /

"Now is it resoun and tyme that I shewe yow whannc and whcrforc that yc may chaungc your conseil withouten youre repreve°. / Soothly° a man may chaungen his purpos and his conseil if the cause cesseth° or whan a newe caas bitydeth°. / For the lawe seith that upon thinges that newely bityden bihoveth° newe conseil. / And Senec 1225 seith, 'If thy conseil is comen to the eres of thyn enemy, change thy conseil.' / Thou mayst also chaunge thy conseil if so be that thou mayst fynde that by errour or by oother cause harm or damage may bityde. / Also, if thy conseil be dishonest or ellis cometh of dishoneste cause, chaunge thy conseil. / For the lawes seyn that alle bihestes° that been dishoneste been of no value. / And eek, if so be that it be inpossible or may nat goodly° be parfourned or kept. /   1230

"And take this for a general reule that every conseil that is affermed so strongly that it may nat be chaunged for no condicioun that may bityde°, I seye that thilke° conseil is wikked." /

This Melibeus, whanne he hadde herd the doctrine of his wyf dame Prudence, answerde in this wyse. / "Dame," quod he, "as yet into this tyme ye han wel and convenably° taught me as in general how I shal governe me in the chesynge and in the withholdynge° of my conseillours. / But now wolde

I fayn° that ye wolde condescende in especial° / and telle me how liketh yow°, or what semeth yow°, by° oure conseillours that we han chosen in oure present nede." /   1235

"My lord," quod she, "I biseke° yow in al humblesse that ye wol nat wilfully replie° agayn my resouns, ne distempre° youre herte thogh I speke thyng that yow displese. / For God woot° that, as in myn entente, I speke it for your beste, for youre honour, and for youre profite eke. / And soothly°, I hope that youre benygnytee° wol taken it in pacience. / Trusteth me wel," quod she, "that your conseil as in this caas ne sholde nat, as to speke properly, be called a conseilling, but a mocioun° or a moevyng° of folye°, / in which conseil ye han erred in many a sondry wise°. /   1240

"First and forward°, ye han erred in th'assemblynge of youre conseillours. / For ye sholde first have cleped° a fewe folk to your conseil, and after ye myghte han shewed° it to mo° folk, if it hadde been nede°. / But certes°, ye han sodeynly cleped to your conseil a greet multitude of peple ful chargeant° and ful anoyous° for to heere. / Also ye han erred for there as ye sholden oonly have cleped to youre conseil youre trewe frendes olde and wise, / ye han ycleped straunge° folk and yong folk, false flatereres and enemys reconsiled, and folk that doon yow reverence withouten love. / And eek also ye have erred for 1245 ye han broght with yow to youre conseil ire, coveitise, and hastifnesse, / the whiche thre thynges been contrariouse to every conseil honeste and profitable, / the whiche thre ye han nat anientissed° or destroyed hem, neither in yourself ne in your conseillours as yow oghte. / Ye han erred also for ye han shewed to your conseillours youre talent°, and youre affeccioun° to make werre an on and for to do vengeance. / They han espied by your wordes to what thyng ye been

1221 **Wel seyn they,** *they say well,* **defenden,** *forbid* 1222 **emprise,** *enterprise,* **conferme,** *pursue,* **sadly,** *steadily* 1223 **repreve,** *shame* 1224 **Soothly,** *truly,* **cesseth,** *ceases,* **caas bitydeth,** *situation occurs* 1225 **bihoveth,** *is necessary* 1229 **bihestes,** *promises* 1230 **goodly,** *well* 1231 **may bityde,** *might happen,* **that thilke,** *that that* 1233 **convenably,** *properly,* **withholdynge,** *retaining* 1234 **wolde I fayn,** *I would like,* **condescende in especial,** *proceed to specifics* 1235 **liketh yow,** *you like,* **seemeth yow,** *you think,* **by,** *about* 1236 **biseke,** *ask,* **replie,** *object,*

distempre, *upset* 1237 **woot,** *knows* 1238 **soothly,** *truly,* **benygnytee,** *goodness* 1239 **mocioun,** *motion,* **moevyng,** *movement,* **folye,** *folly* 1240 **sondry wise,** *various way* 1241 **forward,** *foremost* 1242 **cleped,** *summoned,* **shewed,** *revealed,* **mo,** *more,* **nede,** *necessary* 1243 **certes,** *surely,* **ful chargeant,** *very burdensome,* **ful anoyous,** *very bothersome* 1245 **ycleped straunge,** *summoned unfamiliar* 1248 **anientissed,** *eliminated* 1249 **talent,** *inclination,* **affeccioun,** *desire*

1219 Proverbial. **1225 the lawe,** Cicero, *Pro Lege Manilia* (On the Manilian Law) 20.60. **1226 Senec,** not identified in Seneca. **1246 ire, coveitise, and hastifnesse,** see line 1122 above. Such repetitions help organize the work as a scholastic treatise. **1249–51** In *MerT*, Placebo flatters January by echoing January's own opinions (see *MerT* 4.1467–68 and 1478ff.).

enclyned. / And therfore han they rather 1250 conseilled yow to your talent than to your profit. / Ye han erred also for it semeth that it suffiseth to han been conseilled by thise conseillours oonly and with litel avys°, / wher as in so greet and so heigh a nede it hadde been necessarie mo conseillours and moore deliberacioun to parfourne your emprise°. / Ye han erred also for ye ne han nat examyned youre conseil in the forseyde manere, ne in due manere as the caas requireth. / Ye han erred also, for ye han nat maked no divisioun bitwixe your conseillours—this is to seyn bitwixen your trewe freendes and your feyned° conseillours, / ne ye han nat knowe 1255 the wil of youre trewe freendes olde and wise, / but ye han cast alle hire wordes in an hochepot° and enclyned youre herte to the moore partie° and to the gretter nombre, and ther been ye condescended°. / And sith° ye woot° wel that men shal alwey fynde a gretter nombre of fooles than of wise men, / and therfore the conseils that been at° congragaciouns and multitudes of folk ther as men take moore reward° to the nombre than to the sapience° of persones, / ye se wel that in swiche° conseillynges fooles han the maistrie." / 1260

Melibeus answerde agayn, and seyde, "I graunte wel that I have erred; / but ther as° thou hast toold me heerbiforn that he nys nat to blame that chaungeth his conseillours in certein caas and for certeine juste causes, / I am al redy to chaunge my conseillours, right as thow wolt devyse°. / The proverbe seith that for to do synne is mannyssh°, but certes° for to persevere longe in synne is werk of the devel." /

To this sentence° answerde anon dame Prudence and seyde, / "Examineth," quod 1265 she, "your conseil, and lat us see the whiche of hem han spoken most resonably and taught yow best conseil. / And for as muche as that the examynacioun is necessarie, lat us bigynne at the surgiens and at the phisiciens, that first speeken in this matiere. / I sey yow that the surgiens and phisiciens han seyd° yow in your conseil discreetly,

as hem oughte, / and in hir speche seyd ful wisely, that to the office of hem aperteneth°, to doon to every wight honour and profit and no wight for to anoye, / and in hire craft°, to doon greet diligence unto the cure of hem whiche that they han in hire governaunce. / And sire, right as 1270 they han answered wisely and discreetly, / right so rede° I that they been heighly° and sovereynly gerdoned° for hir noble speche, / and eek for° they sholde do the moore ententif° bisynesse in the curacioun of your doghter deere. / For al be it so that° they been your freendes, therfore shal ye nat suffren° that they serve yow for noght, / but ye oghte the rather° gerdone hem° and shewe hem your largesse°. / And 1275 as touchynge the proposicioun which that the phisiciens encreesceden in this caas, this is to seyn, / that in maladies that oon contrarie is warisshed° by another contrarie, / I wolde fayn knowe hou ye understonde this text and what is youre sentence°." /

"Certes," quod Melibeus, "I understonde it in this wise: / that right as they han doon me a contrarie°, right so sholde I doon hem another. / For right as they han venged hem° 1280 on me and doon me wrong, right so shal I venge me upon hem and doon hem wrong, / and thanne have I cured oon contrarie by another." /

"Lo, lo," quod dame Prudence, "how lightly° is every man enclined to his owene desir and to his owene plesaunce! / Certes°," quod she, "the wordes of the phisiciens ne sholde nat han been understonden in thys wise. / For certes, wikkednesse is nat contrarie to wikkednesse, ne vengeaunce to vengeaunce, ne wrong to wrong, but they been semblable°. / And therfore, o 1285 vengeaunce is nat warisshed by another vengeaunce, ne o wrong by another wrong, / but everich° of hem encreesceth and aggreggeth° other. / But certes, the wordes of the phisiciens sholde been understonden in this wise: / for good and wikkednesse been two contraries, and

---

1252 **avys,** *deliberation* 1253 **emprise,** *enterprise* 1255 **feyned,** *pretended* 1257 **hochepot,** *hodgepodge,* **moore partie,** *larger group,* **condescended,** *settled* 1258 **sith,** *since,* **woot,** *know* 1259 **been at,** *are from,* **reward,** *regard,* **sapience,** *wisdom* 1260 **swiche,** *such* 1262 **ther as,** *since* 1263 **devyse,** *advise* 1264 **mannyssh,** *human,* **certes,** *surely* 1265 **sentence,** *truism* 1268 **seyd,** *spoken to* 1269 **aperteneth,** *is appropriate* 1270 **in hire craft,** *in accord with their profession* 1272 **rede,** *advise,*

heighly, *liberally,* **sovereynly gerdoned,** *supremely rewarded* 1273 **eek for,** *also so,* **ententif,** *eager* 1274 **al be it so that,** *even though,* **suffren,** *allow* 1275 **the rather,** *instead,* **gerdone hem,** *reward them,* **largesse,** *generosity* 1277 **warisshed,** *cured* 1278 **sentence,** *interpretation* 1280 **contrarie,** *offense* 1281 **venged hem,** *avenged themselves* 1283 **lightly,** *easily* 1284 **Certes,** *certainly* 1285 **semblable,** *alike* 1287 **everich,** *each,* **aggreggeth,** *aggravates*

1276–77 **proposicioun . . . phisiciens encreesceden in this caas . . . ,** first mentioned in lines 1016–17 above.

pees and werre, vengeaunce and suffraunce°, discord and accord, and manye othere thynges. / But
certes, wikkednesse shal be warisshed by goodnesse, discord by accord, werre by pees, and
so forth of othere thinges. / And heerto 1290
accordeth° Seint Paul the apostle in manye
places. / He seith, 'Ne yeldeth° nat harm for harm,
ne wikked speche for wikked speche, / but do
wel to hym that dooth thee harm, and blesse hym
that seith to thee harm.' / And in manye othere
places he amonesteth pees° and accord. / But now
wol I speke to yow of the conseil which that was
yeven° to yow by the men of lawe and the wise
folk / that seyden alle by oon accord as ye 1295
han herd bifore, / that over alle thynges ye
sholde doon youre diligence to kepen° youre persone and to warnestoore° youre hous. / And seyden also that in this caas yow oghten for to werken
ful avysely° and with greet deliberacioun. / And
sire, as to the firste point that toucheth to the
kepyng° of youre persone, / ye shul understonde
that he that hath werre shal evermore mekely
and devoutly preyen biforn alle thynges / 1300
that Jesus Crist of his grete mercy wol han
hym in his proteccioun and been his sovereyn°
helpyng at his nede. / For certes, in this world
ther is no wight that may be conseilled ne kept
sufficeantly withouten the keping of oure lord Jesu
Crist. / To this sentence accordeth° the prophete
David that seith, / 'If God ne kepe the citee, in
ydel waketh° he that it kepeth°.' / Now sire, thanne
shul ye comitte the kepyng of youre persone to
youre trewe freendes that been approved
and yknowe°, / and of hem shul ye axen° help 1305
youre persone for to kepe. For Catoun seith,
'If thou hast nede of help, axe it of thy freendes, /
for ther nys noon so good a phisicien as thy trewe
freend.' / And after this, thanne shul ye kepe yow
fro alle straunge folk° and fro lyeres°, and have

alwey in suspect hir compaignye. / For Piers Alfonce seith, 'Ne taak no compaignye by the weye
of straunge men but if so be that thou have knowe
hym of a lenger tyme. / And if so be that he be
falle into thy compaignye paraventure° withouten thyn assent, / enquere thanne as sub- 1310
tilly as thou mayst of his conversacioun° and of
his lyf bifore, and feyne° thy wey. Seye that thou
goost thider° as thou wolt nat go. / And if he
bereth° a spere, hoold° thee on the right syde, and
if he bere a swerd, hoold thee on the lift syde.' /
And after this, thanne shul ye kepe yow wisely from
alle swich manere° peple as I have seyd bifore, and
hem and hir conseil escheue°. / And after this,
thanne shul ye kepe yow in swich manere / that
for any presumpcioun of° youre strengthe that ye
ne dispise nat, ne acounte nat the myght of your
adversarie so litel that ye lete° the kepyng of
youre persone for your presumpcioun, / for 1315
every wys man dredeth his enemy. / And
Salomon seith, 'Weleful° is he that of alle hath
drede, / for certes he that thurgh the hardynesse°
of his herte and thurgh the hardynesse of hymself
hath to greet presumpcioun, hym shal yvel
bityde°.' / Thanne shul ye evermoore countre-
wayte° embusshementz° and alle espiaille°. / For
Senec seith that the wyse man that dredeth
harmes escheueth° harmes, / ne he ne falleth° 1320
into perils that perils escheueth. / And al be it
so that it seme that thou art in siker° place, yet
shaltow° alwey do thy diligence in kepynge of thy
persone, / this is to seyn ne be nat necligent to
kepe thy persone nat oonly fro thy gretteste enemys but fro thy leeste enemy. / Senek seith, 'A man
that is wel avysed, he dredeth his leste enemy.' /
Ovyde seith that the litel wesele wol slee the
grete bole° and the wilde hert. / And the 1325
book seith, 'A litel thorn may prikke a greet
kyng ful soore, and an hound wol holde the wilde

1289 suffraunce, *patient endurance* **1291 heerto accordeth,** *with this
agrees* **1292 yeldeth,** *repay* **1294 amonesteth pees,** *encourages peace*
1295 yeven, *given* **1297 kepen,** *protect,* **warnestoore,** *fortify* **1298 ful
avysely,** *very thoughtfully* **1299 kepyng,** *protection* **1301 sovereyn,**
greatest **1303 sentence accordeth,** *advice agrees* **1304 waketh,** *watches,*
it kepeth, *protects it* **1305 yknowe,** *known* **1306 axen,** *ask* **1308
straunge folk,** *strangers,* **lyeres,** *liars* **1310 paraventure,** *perhaps* **1311**

conversacioun, *way of life,* **feyne,** *disguise,* **thider,** *where* **1312 bereth,**
carries, **hoold,** *keep* **1313 swich manere,** *such kind of,* **escheue,** *avoid*
1315 presumpcioun of, *overconfidence about,* **lete,** *neglect* **1317 Wele-
ful,** *fortunate* **1318 hardynesse,** *boldness,* **hym shal yvel bityde,** *to him
shall evil occur* **1319 countrewayte,** *watch for,* **embusshementz,** *am-
bushes,* **espiaille,** *spying* **1320 escheueth,** *avoids* **1321 ne he ne falleth,**
and he falls not **1322 siker,** *a secure,* **shaltow,** *shall you* **1325 bole,** *bull*

1291 Seint Paul . . . manye places, Romans 12.17; 1 Thessalonians 5.15; 1 Corinthians 4.12–13; also 1 Peter 3.9. **1295 men of lawe . . . ,** see
lines 1026ff. above. **1303–4 David,** Psalms 127.1 (Vulgate 126.1). **1306–7 Catoun,** Dionysius Cato, supposed author of *Disticha Catonis* (Cato's
Couplets) 4.13. **1309–12 Piers Alfonce,** Petrus Alphonsus, *Disciplina Clericalis* (Guide for Scholars) 17.2. **1317–18 Salomon,** Proverbs 28.14.
1320 Senec, not in Seneca, but Publilius Syrus, *Sententiae* 607. **1324 Senek,** Publilius Syrus, *Sententiae* 255. **1325 Ovyde,** Ovid, *Remedia Amoris*
(Remedies of Love) 421. **wesele** (weasel) is Chaucer's mistranslation of French *vivre* (viper) as Latin *viverra* (ferret).

boor.' / But nathelees, I sey nat thou shalt be so coward that thou doute° ther wher as is no drede. / The book seith that somme folk han greet lust° to deceyve, but yet they dreden hem to be deceyved. / Yet shaltou drede to been empoisoned and kepe yow from the compaignye of scorneres. / For the book seith, 'With scorneres make no compaignye, but flee hire wordes as venym.' /   1330

"Now as to the seconde point, wher as youre wise conseillours conseilled yow to warnestoore° youre hous with gret diligence, / I wolde fayn° knowe how that ye understonde thilke° wordes and what is your sentence°." /

Melibeus answerde and seyde, "Certes I understande it in this wise, that I shal warnestoore myn hous with toures swiche° as han castelles and othere manere edifices, and armure, and artelries°, / by whiche thinges I may my persone and myn hous so kepen and deffenden that myne enemys shul been in drede myn hous for to approche." /

To this sentence answerde anon Prudence, "Warnestooryng°," quod she, "of heighe toures and of grete edifices apperteneth° somtyme to pryde, / and eek men make heighe toures   1335 and grete edifices with grete costages° and with greet travaille°, and whan that they been accompliced yet be they nat worth a stree° but if they be defended by trewe freendes that been olde and wise. / And understoond wel that the gretteste and the strongeste garnyson° that a riche man may have as wel to kepen his persone as his goodes is / that he be biloved amonges hys subgetz and with his neighebores. / For thus seith Tullius that ther is a manere° garnyson that no man may venquysse° ne disconfite° and that is / a lord to be biloved of his citezeins and of his peple. /   1340

"Now sire, as to the thridde point: wher as your olde and wise conseillours seyden that yow

ne oghte nat sodeynly ne hastily proceden in this nede°, / but that yow oghte purveyen° and apparaillen yow° in this caas with greet diligence and greet deliberacioun, / trewely I trowe° that they seyden right wisely and right sooth°. / For Tullius seith, 'In every nede er thou bigynne it, apparaille thee with greet diligence.' / Thanne seye I that in vengeance takyng, in werre, in bataille, and in warnestooryng, / er thow bigynne, I 1345 rede° that thou apparaille thee ther to, and do it with greet deliberacioun. / For Tullius seith that longe apparaillyng biforn the bataille maketh short victorie. / And Cassidorus seith, 'The garnyson is stronger whan it is longe tyme avysed°.' /

"But now lat us speken of the conseil that was accorded° by your neighebores swiche as doon yow reverence withouten love, / youre olde enemys reconsiled, your flatereres / that con- 1350 seilled yow certeyne thynges prively°, and openly conseilleden yow the contrarie, / the yonge folk also that conseilleden yow to venge yow° and make werre anon. / And certes, sire, as I have seyd biforn, ye han greetly erred to han cleped° swich maner folk to youre conseil, / which conseillours been ynogh repreved by the resouns aforeseyd. / But nathelees lat us now descende to the special°. Ye shuln° first procede after the doctrine of Tullius. / Certes, the trouthe of this 1355 matiere or of this conseil nedeth nat diligently enquere°; / for it is wel wist whiche° they been that han doon to yow this trespas and vileynye, / and how manye trespassours, and in what manere they han to yow doon al this wrong and al this vileynye. / And after this thanne shul ye examyne the seconde condicioun, which that the same Tullius addeth in this matiere. / For Tullius put a thing° which that he clepeth° 'consentynge'; this is to seyn, / who been they, and how manye, 1360 and whiche been they that consenteden

---

1327 doute, *fear* **1328 lust,** *desire* **1331 warnestoore,** *fortify* **1332 fayn,** *like to,* **thilke,** *these,* **sentence,** *interpretation* **1333 toures swiche,** *towers such,* **artelries,** *artillery* **1335 Warnestooryng,** *fortifying,* **apperteneth,** *is related* **1336 costages,** *expense,* **travaille,** *effort,* **stree,** *straw* **1337 garnyson,** *garrison* **1339 manere,** *kind of* **venquysse,** *defeat,* **disconfite,** *overcome* **1341 nede,** *crisis* **1342 purveyen,** *provide for,* **apparaillen**

yow, *prepare yourself* **1343 trowe,** *believe,* **sooth,** *truly* **1346 rede,** *advise* **1348 avysed,** *considered* **1349 accorded,** *agreed to* **1351 prively,** *in private* **1352 venge yow,** *avenge yourself* **1353 cleped,** *summoned* **1355 descende to the special,** *move to the specific,* **shuln,** *shall* **1356 nedeth nat diligently enquere,** *need not be methodically examined* **1357 wist whiche,** *known who* **1360 put a thing,** *added a concern,* **clepeth,** *calls*

1326 Chaucer's addition; note the rhyme. **1328 The book,** Seneca, *Letters* 3.3. **1331 seconde point,** see line 1027 above. **1335–36** Words are missing from these lines in most MSS, a result of scribal eye skip between the two instances of "grete edifices." **1339–40 Tullius,** not in Cicero, but Seneca, *De Clementia* (on Mercy) 1.19.6. **1341 thridde point,** see line 1028 above. **1344 Tullius,** Cicero, *De Officiis* (On Duties) 1.73. **1347 Tullius,** not found in Cicero. **1348 Cassidorus,** *Variae Epistolae* (Various Letters) 1.17. **1349–52** See lines 1035, 1049, and 1182. **1354 repreved by the resouns aforeseyd,** discredited by the arguments above; lines 1243ff. **1355 doctrine of Tullius,** Cicero, *De Officiis* (On Duties) 2.5; paraphrased in lines 1200–10.

to° thy conseil in thy wilfulnesse to doon hastif° vengeance. / And lat us considere also who been they, and how manye been they, and whiche been they that consenteden to your adversaries. / And certes, as to the firste poynt, it is wel knowen whiche folk been they that consenteden to youre hastif wilfulnesse, / for trewely alle tho that conseilleden yow to maken sodeyn werre ne been nat youre freendes. / Lat us now considere whiche been they° that ye holde so greetly youre freendes as to youre persone. / For al be it so that ye be 1365 mighty and riche, certes ye ne been but allone. / For certes, ye ne han no child but a doghter; / ne ye ne han bretheren ne cosyns germayns° ne noon oother neigh kynrede°, / wherfore that° youre enemys for drede sholde stinte° to plede° with yow or to destroye youre persone. / Ye knowen also that youre richesses mooten° been dispended° in diverse parties°; / and 1370 whan that every wight hath his part, they ne wollen taken but litel reward to venge thy deeth. / But thyne enemys been thre, and they han manie children, bretheren, cosyns, and oother ny kynrede. / And though so were° that thou haddest slayn of hem two or thre, yet dwellen ther ynowe° to wreken° hire deeth and to sle thy persone. / And though so be that° youre kynrede be moore siker° and stedefast than the kyn of youre adversarie, / yet nathelees youre kynrede nys° but a fer° kynrede; they been but litel syb° to yow, / and the kyn of your enemys been ny 1375 syb° to hem. And certes, as in that°, hire condicioun is bet than youres. / Thanne lat us considere also if the conseillyng of hem that conseilleden yow to taken sodeyn vengeaunce, wheither it accorde to resoun. / And certes, ye knowe wel nay. / For as by right and resoun, ther may no man taken vengeance on no wight but the juge that hath the jurisdiccioun of it, / whan it is graunted hym to take thilke° vengeance hastily or attemprely°

as the lawe requireth. / And yet mooreover of 1380 thilke word that Tullius clepeth 'consentynge,' / thou shalt considere if thy might and thy power may consenten° and suffise to thy wilfulnesse and to thy conseillours. / And certes, thou mayst wel seyn that nay. / For sikerly°, as for to speke proprely, we may do nothing but oonly swich thyng as we may doon rightfully. / And certes, rightfully ne mowe ye° take no vengeance as of your propre auctoritee. / Thanne mowe° ye seen that 1385 youre power ne consenteth° nat ne accordeth nat with your wilfulnesse. / Lat us now examyne the thridde point that Tullius clepeth 'consequent°.' / Thou shalt understonde that the vengeance that thou purposest for to take is the consequent. / And therof folweth another vengeaunce, peril, and werre, and other damages withoute nombre of whiche we be nat war as at this tyme. / And as touchynge the fourthe point, that Tullius clepeth 'engendrynge°,' thou shalt con- 1390 sidere that this wrong which that is doon to thee is engendred of° the hate of thyne enemys; / and of the vengeance takinge upon that wolde engendre another vengeance and muchel° sorwe and wastinge of richesses, as I seyde. /

"Now sire, as to the point that Tullius clepeth 'causes,' which that is the laste point, / thou shalt understonde that the wrong that thou hast receyved hath certeine causes / whiche that clerkes clepen *oriens* and *efficiens,* and *causa longinqua* and *causa propinqua,* this is to seyn, the fer cause and the ny cause. / The fer cause is Almighty 1395 God, that is cause of alle thinges. / The neer cause is thy thre enemys. / The cause accidental was hate. / The cause material been the fyve woundes of thy doghter. / The cause formal is the manere of hire werkynge that° broghten laddres and cloumben° in at thy wyndowes. / 1400 The cause final was for to sle thy doghter; it letted° nat in as muche as in hem was. / But for to

---

1361 **consenteden to,** *agreed with,* **hastif,** *hasty* 1365 **whiche been they,** *of what kind they are* 1368 **cosyns germayns,** *first cousins,* **neigh kynrede,** *near relatives* 1369 **wherfore that,** *because of whom,* **stinte,** *cease,* **plede,** *dispute* 1370 **mooten,** *must,* **dispended,** *divided* (after death), **diverse parties,** *various parts* 1373 **though so were,** *if it were,* **ynowe,** *enough,* **wreken,** *avenge* 1374 **though so be that,** *even though,* **siker,** *dependable* 1375 **nys,** *is nothing,* **fer,** *distant,* **syb,** *related* 1376 **ny**

syb, *closely related,* **as in that,** *in that respect* 1380 **thilke,** *that,* **hastily or attemprely,** *swiftly or with care* 1382 **consenten,** *accord with* 1384 **sikerly,** *surely* 1385 **ne mowe ye,** *you may not* 1386 **mowe,** *may,* **consenteth,** *matches* 1387 **clepeth 'consequent,'** *calls 'the consequence'* 1390 **clepeth 'engendrynge,'** *calls 'the producing'* 1391 **engendred of,** *produced by* 1392 **muchel,** *much* 1400 **that,** *who,* **cloumben,** *climbed* 1401 **letted,** *lacked* (i.e., they succeeded as far as they were able)

1372 **enemys been thre,** see 970n above. 1395 *oriens,* "rising." *efficiens,* "efficient." *causa longinqua,* "remote cause." *causa propinqua,* "near cause." Chaucer added these Latin words to his French source. 1397–1401 These parallel three of the four Aristotelian categories of cause: *material,* i.e., in matter or material substance; *formal,* i.e., the shape or form; and *final,* i.e., the end or purpose. Aristotle's *efficient* cause is close to the modern notion of cause, and although *accidental* here may mean something similar, it is usually applied to nonessential features.

speken of the fer cause, as to what ende they shul come, or what shal finally bityde of° hem in this caas, ne kan I nat deme° but by conjectynge and by supposinge. / For we shul suppose that they shul come to a wikked ende, / by cause that the Book of Decrees seith, 'Seelden° or with greet peyne been causes ybroght to good ende whanne they been baddely bigonne.' /

"Now sire, if men wolde axe me, why that God suffred men to do yow this vileinye, certes I kan nat wel answere as for no sothfast-nesse°. / For th'apostle seith that the sci- 1405 ences° and the juggementz of oure lord God Almighty been ful depe. / Ther may no man com-prehende ne serchen hem suffisantly. / Nathelees, by certeyne presumpciouns and conjectynges I holde and bileeve / that God which that is ful of justice and of rightwisenesse° hath suffred° this bityde° by juste cause resonable. /

"Thy name is Melibee, this is to seyn, 'a man that drynketh hony.' / Thou hast 1410 ydronke so muchel hony of sweete tem-poreel richesses and delices° and honours of this world / that thou art dronken and hast forgeten Jesu Crist thy creatour. / Thou ne hast nat doon to hym swich honour and reverence as thee oughte. / Ne thou ne hast nat wel ytaken kepe° to the wordes of Ovide that seith, / 'Under the hony of the goodes of the body is hyd the venym that sleeth the soule.' / And Salomon seith, 1415 'If thou hast founden hony, ete of it that suffiseth, / for if thou ete of it out of mesure° thou shalt spewe°,' and be nedy and poure. / And peraventure° Crist hath thee in despit° and hath turned awey fro thee his face and his eereis of mis-ericorde°, / and also he hath suffred° that thou hast been punysshed in the manere that thow has ytres-passed°. / Thou has doon synne agayn our lord Crist, / for certes the thre enemys of 1420 mankynde, that is to seyn, the flessh, the feend, and the world, / thou hast suffred hem en-tre into thyn herte wilfully by the wyndowes of thy body, / and hast nat defended thyself suffisantly agayns hire assautes° and hire temptaciouns, so that they han wounded thy soule in fyve places, / this is to seyn, the deedly synnes that been entred into thyn herte by thy fyve wittes°. / And in the same manere our lord Crist hath woold° and suffred that thy three enemys been entred into thyn hous by the wyndowes / and han 1425 ywounded thy doghter in the forseyde manere." /

"Certes," quod Melibee, "I se wel that ye enforce yow muchel° by wordes to overcome me in swich manere that I shal nat venge me of myne enemys, / shewynge me the perils and the yveles that myghten falle of this vengeance. / But whoso wolde considere in alle vengeances the perils and yveles that myghte sewe of° vengeance takynge, / a man wolde never take vengeance, and that were harm°. / For by the vengeance takinge 1430 been the wikked men dissevered° fro the goode men. / And they that han wyl to do wikked-nesse restreyne hir wikked purpos whan they seen the punyssynge and chastisynge of the trespas-sours." /

And to this answerde dame Prudence, "Certes," seyde she, "I graunte wel that of vengeaunce cometh muchel yvel and muchel good, / but vengeaunce taking aperteneth nat° unto everi-choon° but only unto juges and unto hem that han jurisdiccioun upon the trespassours. / And yet seye I moore, that right as a singuler° persone synneth in takynge vengeance of another man, / right so synneth the juge if he do no 1435 vengeance of hem that it han disserved°. / For Senec seith thus, 'That maister,' he seith, 'is good that proveth shrewes°.' / And as Cassidore seith, 'A man dredeth to do outrages whan he woot° and knoweth that it displeseth to the juges

---

1402 **bityde of,** *happen to,* **deme,** *judge* 1404 **Seelden,** *seldom* 1405 **as for no sothfastnesse,** i.e., *with no certainty* 1406 **sciences,** *wisdom* 1409 **rightwisenesse,** *righteousness,* **suffred,** *allowed,* **bityde,** *to happen* 1411 **delices,** *delights* 1414 **ytaken kepe,** *paid attention* 1417 **out of mesure,** *immoderately,* **spewe,** *vomit* 1418 **peraventure,** *perhaps,* **despit,** *contempt,* **eereis of misericorde,** *ears of mercy* 1419 **suffred,** *allowed,* **ytrespassed,** *sinned* 1423 **hire assautes,** *their assaults* 1424 **wittes,** *senses* 1425 **woold,** *willed* 1427 **enforce yow muchel,** *try hard* 1429 **sewe of,** *result from* 1430 **harm,** *wrong* 1431 **dissevered,** *separated* 1434 **aperteneth nat,** *is not appropriate,* **everichoon,** *everyone* 1435 **singuler,** *individual* 1436 **disserved,** *deserved* 1437 **proveth shrewes,** *tests villains* 1438 **woot,** *understands*

1404 **Book of Decrees,** *Decretum Gratiani* (Gratian's Decrees) 2.1.1.25, a twelfth-century compilation of canon law. 1406 **th'apostle,** Paul, Romans 11.33. 1410 **Melibee . . . ,** the etymology (Lat. *mel bibens,* "honey drinking") helps to make the tale a psychomachia, or internal allegory; see 967n above. 1414–15 **Ovide,** Ovid, *Amores* 1.8.104. 1416–17 **Salomon,** Proverbs 25.16. 1433–34 Lines found in no MSS, although found in the French source; translated by Skeat. 1437 **Senec,** not in Seneca, but Martinus Dumiensis, *De Moribus* (On Customs) 114. 1438 **Cassidore,** Cassiodorus, *Variae Epistolae* (Various Letters) 1.4.

and sovereyns°.' / Another seith, 'The juge that dredeth to do right maketh men shrewes.' / And Seint Paule the apostle seith in his Epistle, whan he wryteth unto the Romayns, that the juges beren nat the spere withouten cause, / but 1440 they beren it to punysse the shrewes and mysdoeres and to defende the goode men. / If ye wol thanne take vengeance of youre enemys, ye shul retourne or have your recours to the juge that hath the jurisdiccion upon hem, / and he shal punysse hem as the lawe axeth and requireth." /

"A," quod Melibee, "this vengeance liketh me nothyng°. / I bithenke me° now and take heede, how fortune hath norissed° me fro my childhede, and hath holpen° me to passe many a stroong paas°. / Now wol I assayen hir°, trowynge° 1445 with Goddes helpe, that she shal helpe me my shame for to venge." /

"Certes," quod Prudence, "if ye wol werke by my conseil, ye shul nat assaye fortune by no wey, / ne ye shul nat lene° or bowe unto hir after the word of Senec / for 'thynges that been folily° doon and that been in hope of fortune shullen never come to good ende.' / And as the same Senec seith, 'The moore cleer and the moore shynyng that fortune is, the moore brotil° and the sonner° broken she is.' / Trusteth nat in hire, for she nys nat 1450 stidefast ne stable, / for whan thow trowest° to be moost seur° and siker° of hire help, she wol faille thee and deceyve thee. / And where as ye seyn that fortune hath norissed yow fro youre childhede, / I seye that in so muchel° shul ye the lasse° truste in hire and in hir wit°. / For Senec seith, 'What man that is norissed by fortune, she maketh hym a greet fool.' / Now thanne, 1455 syn ye desire and axe° vengeance, and the vengeance that is doon after the lawe and bifore the juge ne liketh yow nat, / and the vengeance that is doon in hope of fortune is perilous and

uncertein, / thanne have ye noon oother remedie but for to have youre recours unto the sovereyn juge° that vengeth° alle vileynyes and wronges, / and he shal venge yow after that° hymself witnesseth, where as he seith, / 'Leveth the vengeance to me and I shal do it.'" / 1460

Melibee answerde, "If I ne venge me nat of the vileynye that men han doon to me, / I sompne° or warne° hem that han doon to me that vileynye and alle othere to do me another vileynye. / For it is writen, 'If thou take no vengeance of an oold vileynye, thou sompnest thyne adversaries to do thee a newe vileynye.' / And also, for my suffrance°, men wolden do to me so muchel vileynye that I myghte neither bere it ne susteene, / and so sholde I been put° and holden over lowe°. / For men seyn, 'In muchel suffrynge 1465 shul manye thynges falle unto thee whiche thou shalt nat mowe suffre°.'" /

"Certes," quod Prudence, "I graunte yow that over muchel suffraunce° nys nat good, / but yet ne folweth it nat therof that every persone to whom men doon vileynye take of it vengeance, / for that aperteneth° and longeth° al oonly to the juges, for they shul venge the vileynyes and injuries. / And therfore tho° two auctoritees that ye han seyd above been oonly understonden in the juges, / for whan they suffren° over muchel 1470 the wronges and the vileynyes to be doon withouten punysshynge, / they sompne nat a man al oonly° for to do newe wronges, but they comanden it. / Also a wys man seith that the juge that correcteth nat the synnere comandeth and biddeth hym do synne. / And the juges and sovereyns myghten in hire land so muchel suffre of° the shrewes° and mysdoeres, / that they sholden by swich suffrance°, by proces of tyme°, wexen of swich° power and myght that they sholden putte out the juges and the sovereyns from hire

---

1438 **sovereyns,** *monarchs* 1444 **liketh me nothyng,** *pleases me not at all* 1445 **bithenke me,** *recall,* **norissed,** *nourished,* **holpen,** *helped,* **stroong paas,** *difficult situation* 1446 **assayen hir,** *test her,* **trowynge,** *believing* 1448 **lene,** *bend* 1449 **folily,** *foolishly* 1450 **brotil,** *brittle,* **sonner,** *sooner* 1452 **trowest,** *believe* (yourself), **seur,** *sure,* **siker,** *certain* 1454 **in so muchel,** *for this reason,* **lasse,** *less,* **wit,** *cunning* 1456 **axe,** *ask* 1458 **sovereyn juge,** i.e., *God,* **vengeth,** *avenges* 1459 **after that,** *as* 1462 **sompne,** *summon,* **warne,** *inform* 1464 **suffrance,** *patience* 1465

put, *thrust,* **holden over lowe,** *held overly low* 1466 **shalt nat mowe suffre,** i.e., *cannot endure* 1467 **over muchel suffraunce,** *too much patient endurance* 1469 **aperteneth,** *is appropriate,* **longeth,** *belongs* 1470 **tho,** *those,* **auctoritees,** *writings* 1471 **suffren,** *allow* 1472 **sompne nat a man al oonly,** *not only summon a man* 1474 **so muchel suffre of,** *allow so much from,* **shrewes,** *villains* 1475 **swich suffrance,** *such allowance,* **by proces of tyme,** *eventually,* **wexen of swich,** *grow to such*

1439 **Another seith,** Publilius Syrus, *Sententiae* 528. 1440 **Seint Paule . . . Romayns,** Romans 13.4; "spere" (spear) is an error for sword. 1448–49 **Senec,** not Seneca, but Publilius Syrus, *Sententiae* 320. 1450 **Senec,** Publilius Syrus, 189. 1455 **Senec,** Publilius Syrus, 172. 1460 Romans 12.19. 1463 **it is writen,** Publilius Syrus, 645. 1466 **men seyn,** Publilius Syrus, 487. 1473 **wys man,** Caecilius Balbus, *De Nugis Philosophorum* (On the Trifles of Philosophers) 41.4.

places / and atte laste maken hem lesen° hire 1475
lordshipes. /

"But lat us now putte° that ye have leve° to venge
yow. / I seye ye been nat of myght and power as
now to venge yow. / For if ye wole maken comparisoun unto the myght of youre adversaries, ye shul
fynde in manye thynges that I have shewed yow er
this that hire condicioun is bettre than youres. /
And therfore seye I that it is good as now
that ye suffre and be pacient. /   1480

"Forthermoore, ye knowen wel that, after
the commune sawe°, it is a woodnesse° a man to
stryve with a strenger° or a moore myghty man than
he is hymself, / and for to stryve with a man of
evene strengthe—that is to seyn, with as strong a
man as he—it is peril, / and for to stryve with
a weyker man it is folie. / And therfore sholde a
man flee° stryvynge as muchel as he myghte. / For
Salomon seith, 'It is a greet worship to a man
to kepen him fro noyse and stryf.' / And if it 1485
so bifalle or happe° that a man of gretter
myght and strengthe than thou art do thee grevaunce, / studie and bisye thee rather to stille° the
same grevaunce than for to venge thee. / For
Senec seith that he putteth hym in greet peril that
stryveth with a gretter man than he is hymself. /
And Catoun seith, 'If a man of hyer estaat or degree or moore myghty than thou do thee anoy or
grevaunce°, suffre° hym, / for he that oones° hath
greved thee another tyme may releeve thee
and helpe.' / Yet sette I caas°, ye have bothe 1490
myght and licence for to venge yow. / I seye
that ther be ful manye thynges that shul restreyne
yow of vengeance takinge, / and make yow for to
enclyne to suffre, and for to han pacience in the
thynges that han been doon to yow. / First and
foreward, if ye wole considere the defautes° that
been in youre owene persone, / for whiche defautes God hath suffred yow have this tribu-
lacioun°, as I have seyd yow heer biforn. / For 1495
the poete seith that we oghte paciently taken
the tribulacions that comen to us, whan we
thynken and consideren that we han disserved to
have hem. / And Seint Gregorie seith that whan a
man considereth wel the nombre of his defautes
and of his synnes, / the peynes and the tribulaciouns that he suffreth semen the lesse unto
hym; / and inasmuche as hym thynketh his
synnes moore hevy and grevous, / insomuche
semeth his peyne the lighter and the esier
unto hym. / Also ye owen° for to enclyne and 1500
bowe youre herte to take the pacience of oure
lord Jesu Crist, as seith Seint Peter in his Epistles. /
'Jesu Crist,' he seith, 'hath suffred for us and
yeven° ensample to every man to folwe and sewe°
him, / for he dide never synne, ne nevere cam ther
a vileynous word out of his mouth. / Whan men
cursed hym, he cursed hem noght, and whan men
betten° hym, he manaced° hem noght.' / Also the
grete pacience which the seintes that been in
paradys han had in tribulaciouns that they
han ysuffred withouten hir desert or gilt / 1505
oghte muchel stiren° yow to pacience. /
Forthermoore, ye sholde enforce yow° to have
pacience, / considerynge that the tribulaciouns of
this world but litel while endure and soone passed
been and goone. / And the joye that a man seketh
to have by pacience in tribulaciouns is perdurable°,
after that the apostle seith in his Epistle. / 'The
joye of God,' he seith, 'is perdurable,' that
is to seyn, everlastinge. / Also troweth° and 1510
bileveth stedefastly that he nys nat wel
ynorissed° ne wel ytaught that kan nat have pacience or wol nat receyve pacience. / For Salomon
seith that the doctrine and the wit of a man is
knowen by pacience. / And in another place he
seith that he that is pacient governeth hym by greet
prudence. / And the same Salomon seith, 'The angry and wrathful man maketh noyses, and the pacient man atempreth hym and stilleth°.' / He seith
also, 'It is moore worth° to be pacient than for
to be right strong; / and he that may have the 1515
lordshipe of his owene herte is moore to
preyse than he that by his force or strengthe taketh

1476 **lesen,** *lose* 1477 **putte,** *assume,* **leve,** *permission* 1481 **sawe,** *proverb,* **woodnesse,** *madness* (for); **strenger,** *stronger* 1484 **flee,** *avoid*
1486 **happe,** *happen* 1487 **stille,** *quiet* 1489 **grevaunce,** *injure,* **suffre,**
endure 1490 **oones,** *once* 1491 **sette I cas,** *let me assume* 1494 **defautes,**
faults 1495 **tribulacioun,** *trouble* 1501 **owen,** *ought* 1502 **yeven,** *given,*

sewe, *imitate* 1504 **betten,** *beat,* **manaced,** *threatened* 1506 **stiren,** *encourage* 1507 **enforce yow,** *push yourself* 1509 **perdurable,** *immortal*
1511 **troweth,** *accept,* **nys nat wel ynorissed,** *is not well nourished* 1514
atempreth hym and stilleth, *controls and quiets himself* 1515 **moore
worth,** *worth more*

1485 **Salomon,** Proverbs 20.3. 1488 **Senec,** Publilius Syrus, *Sententiae* 483. 1489–90 **Catoun,** Dionysius Cato, supposed author of *Disticha Catonis* (Cato's Couplets) 4.39. 1496 **the poet,** unidentified. 1497 **Seint Gregorie . . . ,** unidentified passage. 1501–4 **Seint Peter . . . ,** 1 Peter
2.21–23. 1509 **the apostle,** Paul, 2 Corinthians 4.17. 1512 **Salomon,** Proverbs 19.11 (Vulgate). 1513 Proverbs 14.29 (Vulgate). 1514 Proverbs
15.18. 1515–16 Proverbs 16.32.

grete citees.' / And therfore seith Seint Jame in his Epistle that pacience is a greet vertu of perfeccioun." /

"Certes," quod Melibee, "I graunte yow, dame Prudence, that pacience is a greet vertu of perfeccioun. / But every man may nat have the perfeccioun that ye seken; / ne I nam nat° of the nombre of right parfite men, / for myn herte 1520 may never been in pees unto° the tyme it be venged. / And al be it so that it was greet peril to myne enemys to do me a vileynye in takinge vengeance upon me, / yet tooken they noon heede of the peril but fulfilleden hire wikked wyl and hir corage°. / And therfore methynketh° men oghten nat repreve° me though I putte me in a litel peril for to venge me, / and though I do a greet excesse, that is to seyn, that I venge oon outrage by another." / 1525

"A," quod dame Prudence, "ye seyn youre wil and as yow lyketh°; / but in no caas of the world a man sholde nat doon outrage ne excesse for to vengen hym. / For Cassidore seith that as yvel° dooth he that vengeth hym by outrage as he that dooth the outrage. / And therfore ye shul venge yow after the ordre of right, that is to seyn by the lawe, and noght by excesse ne by outrage. / And also, if ye wol venge yow of the outrage of youre adversaries in oother manere than right comandeth, ye synnen. / And therfore seith 1530 Senec that a man shal nevere vengen shrewednesse° by shrewednesse. / And if ye seye that right axeth° a man to defenden violence by violence and fightyng by fightyng, / certes ye seye sooth° whan the defense is doon anon° withouten intervalle or withouten tariyng or delay / for to deffenden hym and nat for to vengen hym. / And it bihoveth° that a man putte swich attemperance° in his deffense, / that men have no 1535 cause ne matiere to repreven° hym that deffendeth hym of° excesse and outrage, for ellis

were it agayn° resoun. / Pardee°, ye knowen wel that ye maken no deffense as now for to deffende yow, but for to venge yow, / and so seweth° it that ye han no wyl to do youre dede attemprely°. / And therfore, methynketh that pacience is good. For Salomon seith that he that is nat pacient shal have greet harm." /

"Certes," quod Melibee, "I graunte yow that whan a man is inpacient and wrooth of° that that toucheth° him noght and that aperteneth° nat unto hym though it harme him, it is no wonder. / For the lawe seith that he is 1540 coupable° that entremetteth° or medleth with swych thyng as aperteneth nat unto hym. / And Salomon seith that he that entremetteth hym of the noyse° or strif of another man is lyk to hym that taketh an hound by the eris. / For right as he that taketh a straunge hound by the eris is outherwhile° biten with° the hound, / right in the same wise is it resoun that he have harm that by his inpacience medleth hym of the noyse of another man wher as it aperteneth nat unto hym. / But ye knowen wel that this dede—that is to seyn, my grief and my disese°—toucheth me right ny°. / And therfore, though I be wrooth and 1545 inpacient, it is no merveille. / And savynge youre grace°, I kan nat seen that it mighte greetly harme me though I tooke vengeaunce, / for I am richer and moore myghty than myne enemys been. / And wel knowen ye that by moneye and by havynge grete possessions been all the thynges of this world governed. / And Salomon seith that alle thynges obeyen to moneye." / 1550

Whan Prudence hadde herd hir housbonde avanten hym° of his richesse and of his moneye, dispreisynge° the power of his adversaries, she spak and seyde in this wise, / "Certes, dere sire, I graunte yow that ye been riche and myghty, / and that the richesses been goode to hem that han wel ygeten° hem and wel konne° usen hem. / For right

---

1520 **ne I nam nat,** *I am not* 1521 **unto,** *until* 1523 **hir corage,** *their desire* 1524 **methynketh,** *it seems to me,* **repreve,** *blame* 1526 **as yow lyketh,** *what pleases you* 1528 **as yvel,** *as much evil* 1531 **shrewednesse,** *wickedness* 1532 **right axeth,** *justice demands* 1533 **sooth,** *truth,* **anon,** *immediately* 1535 **bihoveth,** *is appropriate,* **putte swich attemperance,** *use such moderation* 1536 **repreven,** *blame,* **deffendeth hym of,** *defends himself against,* **agayn,** *against* 1537 **Pardee,** *by God* 1538 **seweth,**

follows, **attemprely,** *temperately* 1540 **wrooth of,** *angered by,* **toucheth,** *involves,* **aperteneth,** *pertains* 1541 **coupable,** *culpable,* **entremetteth,** *interferes* 1542 **noyse,** *uproar* 1543 **outherwhile,** *sometimes,* **with,** *by* 1545 **disese,** *distress,* **right ny,** *very closely* 1547 **savynge youre grace,** *with all due respect* 1551 **avanten hym,** *boast,* **dispreisynge,** *belittling* 1553 **ygeten,** *acquire,* **konne,** *can*

1517 **Seint Jame,** adapted from James 1.4. 1528 **Cassidore,** Cassiodorus; the following is posed as a question in *Variae Epistolae* 1.30. 1531 **Senec,** not in Seneca, but Martinus Dumiensis, *De Moribus* (On Customs) 139. 1539 **Salomon,** Proverbs 19.19. 1541 **entremetteth,** this verb is used in the angry exchange between the Friar and the Summoner in *WBP* 3.834. 1542 **Salomon,** Proverbs 26.17. 1550 **Salomon,** Ecclesiastes 10.19.

as the body of a man may nat lyven withoute the soule, namore may it live withouten temporeel goodes. / And for richesses may a man gete hym grete freendes. / And therfore seith 1555 Pamphilles, 'If a netherdes° doghter,' seith he, 'be riche, she may chesen of a thousand men which she wol take to hir housbonde, / for of a thousand men oon° wol nat forsaken hire ne re-fusen hire.' / And this Pamphilles seith also, 'If thou be right happy (that is to seyn, if thou be right riche) thou shalt fynd a greet nombre of felawes° and freendes. / And if thy fortune change that thou wexe° poure, farewel freendshipe and felaweshipe, / for thou shalt be al alloone withouten any compaignye, but if it be the compaignye of poure folk.' / And yet seith 1560 this Pamphilles moreover that they that been thralle and bonde of lynage° shullen been maad worthy and noble by the richesses. / And right so as by richesses ther comen manye goodes, right so by poverte come ther manye harmes and yveles. / For greet poverte constreyneth a man to do manye yveles. / And therfore clepeth Cassidore poverte 'the moder of ruyne°,' / that is to seyn the mooder of overthrowynge or fallynge doun. / And therfore seith Piers Alfonce, 1565 'Oon of the gretteste adversitees of this world is / whan a free man by kynde or by burthe° is constreyned by poverte to eten° the almesse° of his enemy.' / And the same seith Innocent in oon of his bookes. He seith that sorweful and myshappy is the condicioun of a poure begger, / for if he axe nat his mete° he dyeth for hunger, / and if he axe he dyeth for shame; and algates° necessitee constreyneth hym to axe. / And 1570 therfore seith Salomon that bet it is to dye than for to have swich poverte. / And as the same Salomon seith, 'Bettre it is to dye of bitter deeth than for to lyven in swich wise.' / By thise resons that I have seid unto yow, and by manye

othere resons that I koude seye, / I graunte yow that richesses been goode to hem that geten hem wel, and to hem that wel usen tho° richesses. / And therfore wol I shewe yow hou ye shul have yow°, and how ye shul bere yow in gaderynge° of richesses, and in what manere ye shul usen hem. / 1575

"First, ye shul geten hem withouten greet desir, by good leyser sokyngly°, and nat over hastily. / For a man that is to desirynge to gete richesses abaundoneth hym first to thefte and to alle other yveles. / And therfore seith Salomon, 'He that hasteth hym to bisily to wexe riche shal be noon innocent.' / He seith also that the richesse that hastily cometh to a man soone and lightly gooth and passeth fro a man, / but that richesse that cometh litel and litel° wexeth° alwey and multiplieth. / And sire, ye shul geten 1580 richesses by youre wit and by youre travaille° unto youre profit, / and that withouten wrong or harmdoinge to any oother persone. / For the lawe seith that ther maketh no man himselven riche if he do harm to another wight°, / this is to seyn that nature deffendeth° and forbedeth by right that no man make hymself riche unto the harm of another persone. / And Tullius seith that no sorwe ne no drede of deeth, ne nothing that may falle unto a man / is so muchel agayns nature as a 1585 man to encressen his owene profit to the harm of another man. / And though the grete men and the myghty men geten richesses moore lightly° than thou, / yet shaltou° nat been ydel ne slow to do thy profit°, for thou shalt in alle wise flee ydelnesse. / For Salomon seith that ydelnesse techeth a man to do manye yveles. / And the same Salomon seith that he that travailleth° and bisieth hym to tilien° his land shal eten breed, / but he that is ydel and casteth hym° 1590 to no bisynesse ne occupacioun shal falle into poverte and dye for hunger. / And he that is ydel

---

1556 netherdes, *cowherd's* **1557 oon,** *one* **1558 felawes,** *companions* **1559 wexe,** *become* **1561 thralle and bonde of lynage,** *slaves by birth* **1564 ruyne,** *ruin* **1567 free man by kynde or by burthe,** *a man free by nature or birth,* **eten,** *eat,* **almesse,** *charity* **1569 axe nat his mete,** *doesn't beg for food* **1570 algates,** *always* **1574 tho,** *those* **1575 have yow,** *behave yourself,* **gaderynge,** *gathering* **1576 leyser sokyngly,** *time gradu-ally* **1580 litel and litel,** *little by little,* **wexeth,** *grows* **1581 travaille,** *la-bor* **1583 wight,** *person* **1584 deffendeth,** *prohibits* **1587 lightly,** *easily* **1588 shaltou,** *you should,* **to do thy profit,** *to make profit* **1590 travail-leth,** *labors,* **tilien,** *cultivate* **1591 casteth hym,** *devotes himself*

1556–57 Pamphilles, hero of twelfth-century poetic dialogue *Pamphilus de Amore* (Pamphilius on Love), 53–54. **1558** Not from *Pamphilus,* but Ovid, *Tristia,* 1.9.5–6. **1560** Compare *KnT* 1.2779 and *MilT* 1.3204. **1561 Pamphilles,** not from *Pamphilus;* see Petrus Alphonsus, *Disciplina Clericalis* (Guide for Scholars) ex. 4.2. **1564 Cassidore,** Cassiodorus, *Variae Epistolae* 9.13. **1566–67 Piers Alfonce,** Petrus Alphonsus, *Disciplina Clericalis* (Guide for Scholars) 2.2. **1568–70 Innocent . . . ,** Pope Innocent III, *De Miseria Conditionis Humane* (On the Misery of the Human Condition) 1.16. **1571 Salomon,** Ecclesiasticus 40.29 (Vulgate). **1572 same Salomon,** Ecclesiasticus 30.17 (Vulgate). **1578 Salomon,** Proverbs 28.20. **1579 seith also,** Proverbs 13.11. **1585–86 Tullius . . . ,** Cicero *De Officiis* (On Duties) 3.21. **1589 Salomon,** Ecclesiasticus 33.27 (Vulgate). **1590 Salomon,** Proverbs 28.19.

and slow kan never fynde covenable° tyme for to doon his profit. / For ther is a versifiour° seith that the ydel man excuseth hym in wynter by cause of the grete cold, and in somer by enchesoun° of the heete. / For thise causes seith Caton, 'Waketh° and enclyneth nat yow over muchel for to slepe, for over muchel reste norisseth and causeth manye vices.' / And therfore seith Seint Jerome, 'Dooth somme goode dedes that the devel which is oure enemy ne fynde yow nat unocupied.' / 1595 For the devel ne taketh nat lightly unto his werkynge swiche as he fyndeth occupied in goode werkes.' /

"Thanne thus in getynge richesses ye mosten° flee ydelnesse. / And afterward ye shul use the richesses whiche ye have geten by youre wit and by youre travaille / in swich a manere that men holde nat yow to scars°, ne to sparynge, ne to fool large°, that is to seyn over large a spender. / For right as men blamen an avaricious man by cause of his scarsetee° and chyncherye°, / in the 1600 same wise is he to blame that spendeth over largely. / And therfore seith Caton, 'Use,' he seith, 'thy richesses that thou hast geten / in swich a manere that men have no matiere ne cause to calle thee neither wrecche ne chynche°, / for it is a greet shame to a man to have a pouere° herte and a riche purs.' / He seith also, 'The goodes that thou hast ygeten, use hem by mesure°,' that is to seyn, spende hem mesurably. / For they 1605 that folily wasten and despenden the goodes that they han, / whan they han namore propre° of hire owene, they shapen hem° to take the goodes of another man. / I seye thanne that ye shul fleen avarice° / usynge youre richesses in swich manere that men seye nat that youre richesses been yburyed, / but that ye have hem in youre myght and in youre weeldynge°. / For a wys 1610 man repreveth° the avaricious man and seith thus in two vers: / 'Wherto and why burieth a man

his goodes by his grete avarice, and knoweth wel that nedes moste he dye, / for deeth is the ende of every man as in this present lyf?' / And for what cause or enchesoun° joyneth° he hym or knytteth he hym so faste° unto his goodes, / that alle his wittes mowen nat disseveren° hym or de-parten hym from his goodes, / and knoweth 1615 wel, or oghte knowe, that whan he is deed he shal nothing bere with hym out of this world? / And therfore seith Seint Augustin that the avaricious man is likned° unto helle, / that the moore it swel-weth°, the moore desir it hath to swelwe and de-voure. / And as wel as ye wolde eschewe° to be called an avaricious man or chynche°, / as wel sholde ye kepe yow and governe yow in swich a wise that men calle yow nat fool large°. / 1620 Therfore seith Tullius, 'The goodes,' he seith, 'of thyn hous ne sholde nat been hyd, ne kept so cloos but that they mighte been opened by pitee and debonairetee°' — / that is to seyn, to yeven part to hem that han greet nede — / 'ne thy goodes shullen nat been so opene to been every mannes goodes.' /

"Afterward, in getynge of youre richesses and in usynge hem ye shul alwey have thre thynges in youre herte, / that is to seyn, our lord God, conscience, and good name. / First, ye shul 1625 have God in youre herte, / and for no richesse ye shullen do nothyng which may in any manere displese God that is youre creatour and maker. / For after the word of Salomon, 'It is bettre to have a litel good with the love of God / than to have muchel good and tresour and lese° the love of his lord God.' / And the prophete seith that bettre it is to been a good man and have litel good and tresour / than to been holden° a 1630 shrewe° and have grete richesses. / And yet seye I ferthermoore that ye sholde alwey doon your bisynesse to gete yow richesses, / so that ye gete hem with good conscience. / And th'apostle seith

---

1592 **covenable,** *convenient* 1593 **versifiour,** *poet,* **enchesoun,** *reason* 1594 **Waketh,** *be alert* 1597 **mosten,** *must* 1599 **to scars,** *too stingy,* **to fool large,** *too foolishly generous* 1600 **scarsetee,** *stinginess,* **chyncherye,** *miserliness* 1603 **chynche,** *miser* 1604 **pouere,** *poor* 1605 **by mesure,** *in moderation* 1607 **propre,** *property,* **shapen hem,** *prepare themselves* 1608 **fleen avarice,** *flee from greed* 1610 **weeldynge,** *control* 1611

repreveth, *blames* 1614 **enchesoun,** *reason,* **joyneth,** *attaches,* **faste,** *tightly* 1615 **mowen nat disseveren,** *may not separate* 1617 **likned,** *com-pared* 1618 **swelweth,** *swallows* 1619 **eschewe,** *avoid,* **chynche,** *miser* 1620 **fool large,** *foolishly generous* 1621 **debonairetee,** *graciousness* 1629 **lese,** *lose* 1631 **holden,** *thought,* **shrewe,** *villain*

1593 Not identified, but see Proverbs 20.4. 1594 **Caton,** Dionysius Cato, supposed author of *Disticha Catonis* (Cato's Couplets) 1.2. 1595 **Seint Jerome,** see his *Epistles* 125.11. 1602–3 **Caton . . . ,** *Disticha* 4.16. 1605 *Disticha* 3.21. 1609 **yburyed,** perhaps an allusion to the parable of buried talents; Matthew 25.14–30. 1612–13 Quotation not identified. 1617–18 **Seint Augustin . . . ,** not identified in Augustine; see Proverbs 27.20. 1621–23 **Tullius . . . ,** Cicero, *De Officiis* 2.55. 1628–29 **Salomon,** Proverbs 15.16 has "fear" (Lat. *timore*) rather than "love." 1630–31 **proph-ete . . . ,** Psalms 36.16 (Vulgate). 1634 **th'apostle,** Paul, 2 Corinthians 1.12.

that ther nys thyng in this world of which we sholden have so greet joye as whan oure conscience bereth us good witnesse. / And the wise man seith, 'The substance° of a man is ful good whan synne is nat in mannes conscience.' / After- 1635 ward in getynge of youre richesses and in usynge of hem, / yow moste have greet bisynesse° and greet diligence° that youre goode name be alwey kept° and conserved. / For Salomon seith that bettre it is and moore it availleth a man to have a good name than for to have grete richesses. / And therfore he seith in another place, 'Do greet diligence,' seith Salomon, 'in kepyng of thy freend and of thy goode name, / for it shal lenger abide with thee than any tresour be it never so precious.' / And certes he sholde nat be called a 1640 gentilman that° after God and good conscience, alle thynges left°, ne dooth his diligence and bisynesse to kepen his good name. / And Cassidore seith that it is signe of a gentil herte whan a man loveth and desireth to han a good name. / And therfore seith Seint Augustyn that ther been two thynges that arn necessarie and nedefulle, / and that is good conscience and good loos°— / that is to seyn, good conscience to thyn owene persone inward and good loos for thy neighebore outward. / And he that trusteth 1645 hym so muchel in his goode conscience / that he displeseth and setteth at noght his goode name or loos, and rekketh° noght though° he kepe nat his goode name, nys° but a crueel° cherl. /

"Sire, now have I shewed yow how ye shul do in getynge richesses, and how ye shullen usen hem, / and I se wel that for the trust that ye han in youre richesses ye wole moeve° werre and bataille. / I conseille yow that ye bigynne no werre in trust of youre richesses for they ne suffisen noght werres to mayntene. / And therfore seith a 1650 philosophre, 'That man that desireth and wole algates° han werre shal never have suffisaunce°, / for the richer that he is the gretter despenses° moste he make if he wole have worship and victorie.' / And Salomon seith that the gretter richesses that a man hath the mo despendours° he hath. / And deere sire, al be it so that° for youre richesses ye mowe° have muchel folk, / yet bihoveth it nat°, ne it is nat good, to bigynne werre where as ye mowe in oother manere have pees unto youre worship and profit. / For 1655 the victories of batailles that been in this world lyen nat in greet nombre or multitude of the peple ne in the vertu° of man, / but it lith° in the wyl and in the hand of oure lord God Almyghty. / And therfore Judas Machabeus, which was Goddes knight, / whan he sholde fighte agayn his adversarie that hadde a greet nombre and a gretter multitude of folk and strenger than was this peple of Machabee, / yet he reconforted° his litel compaignye, and seyde right in this wise: / 1660 'Als lightly°,' quod he, 'may oure lord God Almighty yeve° victorie to a fewe folk as to many folk, / for the victorie of bataile comth nat by the grete nombre of peple / but it come from our lord God of Hevene.' / And deere sire, for as muchel as there is no man certein if he be worthy that God yeve hym victorie, namore than he is certein whether he be worthy of the love of God or naught, after that Salomon seith, / therfore every man sholde greetly drede werres to bigynne. / And by cause° that in batailles 1665 fallen° manye perils, / and happeth outher while° that as soone° is the grete man slayn as the litel man, / and as it is writen in the Seconde Book of Kynges, 'The dedes of batailles been aventurouse° and nothing certeyne,' / for as lightly° is oon hurt with a spere as another. / And for ther is gret peril in werre, therfore sholde a man flee° and escheue° werre in as muchel as a man may goodly. / For Salomon seith, 'He that loveth 1670 peril shal falle in peril.'" /

After that dame Prudence hadde spoken in this manere, Melibee answerde and seyde, / "I see wel,

---

1635 **substance**, *property* 1637 **bisynesse**, *attention,* **diligence**, *effort,* **kept**, *protected* 1641 **that**, *who,* **left**, *remaining* 1644 **loos**, *reputation* 1647 **rekketh**, *cares,* **though**, *if,* **nys**, *is nothing,* **crueel**, *crude* 1649 **wole moeve**, *will begin* 1651 **algates**, *always,* **suffisaunce**, *enough* 1652 **despenses moste**, *spending must* 1653 **mo despendours**, *more spenders*

1654 **al be it so that**, *even though,* **mowe**, *may* 1655 **bihoveth it nat**, *it is not appropriate* 1656 **vertu**, *power* 1657 **lith**, *lies* 1660 **reconforted**, *encouraged* 1661 **Als lightly**, *as easily,* **yeve**, *give* 1666 **by cause**, *because,* **fallen**, *occur* 1667 **outher while**, *sometimes,* **soone**, *readily* 1668 **aventurouse**, *variable* 1669 **lightly**, *easily* 1670 **flee**, *shun,* **escheue**, *avoid*

1635 **wise man**, Ecclesiasticus 13.30 (Vulgate). 1638 **Salomon**, Proverbs 22.1. 1639 **another place**, Ecclesiasticus 41.15 (Vulgate); "freend" is Chaucer's adjustment from "fame." 1642 **Cassidore**, Cassiodorus, a version of *Variae Epistolae* (Various Letters) 1.4. 1643 **Seint Augustyn**, Sermon 355.1; this citation not in the Latin. 1644 Chaucer's addition. 1651 **philosophre**, unidentified. 1653 **Salomon**, Ecclesiastes 5.10 (Vulgate); not in the Latin. 1658–63 **Judas Machabeus . . . ,** 1 Maccabees 3.18–19. 1664 **Salomon**, Ecclesiastes 9.1; "namore . . . God" omitted from all MSS; translated from French by Skeat. 1668 **Seconde Book of Kynges,** 2 Samuel 11.25 (Vulgate 2 Kings). 1671 **Salomon**, Ecclesiasticus 3.27 (Vulgate).

dame Prudence, that by youre faire wordes and by youre resons that ye han shewed me, that the werre liketh yow nothing°. / But I have nat yet herd youre conseil, how I shal do in this nede." /

"Certes," quod she, "I conseille yow that ye accorde° with youre adversaries, and that ye have pees with hem. / For Seint Jame seith in 1675 his Epistles that by concord and pees the smale richesses wexen° grete, / and by debaat° and discord the grete richesses fallen doun. / And ye knowen wel that oon of the gretteste and moost sovereyn° thyng that is in this world is unytee° and pees. / And therfore seyde oure lord Jesu Crist to his apostles in this wise, / 'Wel, happy, and blessed been they that loven and purchacen° pees, for they been called children of God.'" / 1680

"A," quod Melibee, "now se I wel that ye loven nat myn honour ne my worshipe. / Ye knowen wel that myne adversaries han bigonnen this debaat and bryge° by hire outrage; / and ye see wel that they ne requeren ne preyen me nat of pees, ne they asken nat to be reconsiled. / Wol ye thanne° that I go and meke me° and obeye me° to hem and crie hem mercy? / Forsothe, that were nat my worship°. / For right° as men 1685 seyn that over greet hoomlynesse engendreth dispreisynge°, so fareth it° by to greet humylitee or mekenesse." /

Thanne bigan dame Prudence to maken semblant° of wratthe° and seyde, / "Certes°, sire, sauf youre grace°, I love youre honour and youre profit as I do myn owene, and ever have doon; / ne ye ne noon oother syen nevere° the contrarie. / And yit, if I hadde seyd that ye sholde han purchaced the pees and the reconsiliacioun, I ne hadde nat muchel mystaken me ne seyd amys°. / For 1690 the wise man seith the dissensioun bygynneth by another man, and the reconsilyng bygynneth by thyself. / And the prophete seith, 'Flee shrewednesse° and do goodnesse; / seke pees and folwe it, as muchel as in thee is.' / Yet seye I nat that ye shul rather° pursue to youre adversaries for pees than they shuln° to yow, / for I knowe wel that ye been so hard herted, that ye wol do nothing for me. / And Salomon seith, 'He 1695 that hath over hard an herte, atte laste° he shal myshappe and mystyde°.'" /

Whanne Melibee hadde herd dame Prudence maken semblant of wratthe, he seyde in this wise, / "Dame, I prey yow that ye be nat displesed of thynges that I seye, / for ye knowe wel that I am angry and wrooth° and that is no wonder, / and they that been wrothe witen° nat wel what they don ne what they seyn°. / Therfore the 1700 prophete seith that troubled eyen han no cleer sighte. / But seyeth and conseileth me as yow liketh for I am redy to do right as ye wol desire, / and if ye repreve° me of my folye I am the moore holden° to love yow and preyse yow. / For Salomon seith that he that repreveth hym that dooth folye, / he shal fynde gretter grace° than he that deceyveth hym by sweete wordes." / 1705

Thanne seide dame Prudence, "I make no semblant° of wratthe ne anger but for youre grete profit°. / For Salomon seith, 'He is moore worth° that repreveth or chideth a fool for his folye shewynge hym semblant of wratthe, / than he that supporteth hym and preyseth hym in his mysdoynge and laugheth at his folye.' / And this same Salomon seith afterward that by the sorweful visage° of a man—that is to seyn, by the sory and hevy countenaunce° of a man— / the fool correcteth and amendeth himself." / 1710

Thanne seyde Melibee, "I shal nat konne° answere to so manye faire resouns as ye putten to me and shewen. / Seyeth shortly youre wyl and youre conseil, and I am al ready to fulfille and parfourne° it." /

Thanne dame Prudence discovered° al hir wyl to hym, and seyde, / "I conseille yow," quod she,

---

1673 **liketh yow nothing,** *pleases you not at all* 1675 **accorde,** *come to agreement* 1676 **wexen,** *grow* 1677 **debaat,** *conflict* 1678 **sovereyn,** *excellent* 1678 **unytee,** *unity* 1680 **purchacen,** *attain* 1682 **bryge,** *trouble* 1684 **Wol ye thanne,** *do you wish then,* **meke me,** *humble myself,* **obeye me,** *subject myself* 1685 **worship,** *honor* 1686 **right,** *just,* **hoomlynesse engendreth dispreisynge,** *familiarity breeds contempt,* **fareth it,** *it results* 1687 **semblant,** *appearance,* **wratthe,** *anger* 1688 **Certes,** *surely,* **sauf youre grace,** *with all due respect* 1689 **ne ye ne noon oother syen nevere,** *and you never saw* 1690 **seyd amys,** *misspoke* 1692 **shrewednesse,** *evil* 1694 **shul rather,** *should more readily,* **shuln,** *should* 1696 **atte laste,** *ultimately,* **myshappe and mystyde,** *be unfortunate and unlucky* 1699 **wrooth,** *wrathful* 1700 **witen,** *know,* **seyn,** *say* 1703 **repreve,** *blame,* **holden,** *compelled* 1705 **grace,** *favor* 1706 **semblant,** *appearance,* **profit,** *benefit* 1707 **moore worth,** *worth more* 1709 **visage,** *face,* **hevy countenaunce,** *serious expression* 1711 **konne,** *be able to* 1712 **parfourne,** *perform* 1713 **discovered,** *revealed*

1676–77 **Seint Jame . . . ,** mistake for *Seneque,* i.e., Seneca, *Letters* 94.46. 1679–80 **Jesu Crist . . . ,** Matthew 5.9. 1691 **wise man,** Martinus Dumiensis, *De Moribus* (On Customs) 49. 1692–93 **prophete . . . ,** Psalms 33.15 (Vulgate). 1696 **Salomon,** Proverbs 28.14. 1701 **prophete,** unidentified. 1704–5 **Salomon . . . ,** Proverbs 28.23. 1707–10 **Salomon . . . ,** see Ecclesiastes 7.4–6.

"aboven alle thynges, that ye make pees bitwene God and yow, / and beth reconsiled unto hym and to his grace. / For as I have seyd 1715 yow heerbiforn°, God hath suffred° yow to have this tribulacioun° and disese° for youre synnes. / And if ye do as I sey yow, God wol sende youre adversaries unto yow, / and maken hem fallen at youre feet, redy to do youre wyl and youre comandementz. / For Salomon seith, 'Whan the condicioun of man is plesaunt° and likynge° to God, / he chaungeth the hertes of the mannes adversaries, and constreyneth hem to biseken hym of° pees and of grace.' / And I 1720 prey yow, lat me speke with youre adversaries in privee° place, / for they shul nat knowe that it be of youre wyl or of youre assent. / And thanne, whan I knowe hire wil and hire entente, I may con- seille yow the moore seurely°." /

"Dame," quod Melibee, "dooth youre wil and youre likynge, / for I putte me hoolly in youre disposicioun° and ordinaunce°." / 1725

Thanne dame Prudence, whan she saugh the goode wil of hire housbonde, delibered° and took avys° in hirself, / thinkynge how she myghte brynge this nede unto a good conclusioun and to a good ende. / And whan she saugh hire tyme, she sente for thise adversaries to come unto hire into a pryvee place, / and shewed wisely unto hem the grete goodes° that comen of pees, / and the grete harmes and perils that been in werre; / 1730 and seyde to hem in a goodly° manere, hou that hem oughten have greet repentaunce / of the injurie and wrong that they hadden doon to Melibee hire lord, and to hire, and to hire doghter. /

And whan they herden the goodliche° wordes of dame Prudence, / they weren so surpprised° and ravysshed°, and hadden so greet joye of hire, that wonder was to telle. / "A, lady," quod they, "ye han shewed unto us the blessynge of swetnesse,

after the sawe° of David the prophete; / for 1735 the reconsilynge which we been nat worthy to have in no manere, / but we oghte requeren° it with greet contricioun and humylitee, / ye of youre grete goodnesse have presented unto us. / Now se we wel that the science° and the konnynge° of Salomon is ful trewe. / For he seith that sweete wordes multiplien and encreesen freendes, and maken shrewes° to be debonaire° and meeke. / 1740

"Certes," quod they, "we putten oure dede° and al oure matere and cause al hoolly° in youre goode wyl, / and been redy to obeye to the speche and comandement of my lord Melibee. / And therfore, deere and benygne° lady, we preien° yow and biseke° yow as mekely as we konne° and mowen° / that it lyke unto° youre grete goodnesse to fulfillen in dede youre goodliche wordes, / for we consideren and knowlichen that we han offended and greved my lord Melibee out of mesure° / so ferforth° that we be nat of 1745 power to maken his amendes°. / And therfore we oblige° and bynden us and oure freendes to doon all his wyl and his comandementz. / But peraventure° he hath swich hevynesse° and swich wratthe° to us-ward° by cause of oure offense / that he wole enjoyne us° swich a peyne° as we mowe° nat bere ne susteene°. / And therfore, noble lady, we biseke° to youre wommanly pitee / to 1750 taken swich avysement in this nede° that we ne oure freendes be nat desherited° ne destroyed thurgh our folye." /

"Certes," quod Prudence, "it is an hard thyng and right perilous / that a man putte hym al out- rely° in the arbitracioun and juggement and in the myght and power of his enemys. / For Salomon seith, 'Leeveth° me, and yeveth credence° to that I shal seyn. I seye,' quod he, 'ye peple, folk and governours of hooly chirche, / to thy sone, to thy wyf, to thy freend, ne to thy broother / 1755

1716 heerbiforn, *before this,* **suffred,** *allowed,* **tribulacioun,** *trouble,* **disese,** *distress* **1719 plesaunt,** *pleasing,* **likynge,** *agreeable* **1720 biseken hym of,** *ask him for* **1721 privee,** *private* **1723 seurely,** *cer- tainly* **1725 disposicioun,** *disposal,* **ordinaunce,** *command* **1726 de- libered,** *deliberated,* **took avys,** *considered* **1729 goodes,** *benefits* **1731 goodly,** *pleasing* **1733 goodliche,** *excellent* **1734 surpprised,** *taken,* **ravysshed,** *overcome* **1735 sawe,** *saying* **1737 requeren,** *to request* **1739 science,** *wisdom,* **konnynge,** *understanding* **1740 shrewes,** *enemies,* **debonaire,** *compliant* **1741 dede,** *action,* **al hoolly,** *completely* **1743**

benygne, *gracious,* **preien,** *ask,* **biseke,** *beseech,* **konne,** *can,* **mowen,** *may* **1744 lyke unto,** *be pleasing to* **1745 out of mesure,** *immoderately* **1746 forforth,** *far,* **maken his amendes,** *make it up to him* **1747 oblige,** *obligate* **1748 peraventure,** *perhaps,* **swiche hevynesse,** *such sternness,* **wratthe,** *anger,* **to us-ward,** *toward us* **1749 enjoyne,** *impose on,* **peyne,** *punishment,* **mowe,** *can,* **susteene,** *endure* **1750 biseke,** *plead* **1751 taken swich avysement in this nede,** *consider in this situation,* **desher- ited,** *impoverished* **1753 outrely,** *utterly* **1754 Leeveth,** *believe,* **yeveth credence,** *accept*

1719 Salomon, Proverbs 16.7. **1735 David,** Psalms 20.4 (Vulgate). **1739–40 Salomon . . . ,** Ecclesiasticus 6.5 (Vulgate). **1754–56 Salomon . . . ,** Ecclesiasticus 33.19–20 (Vulgate).

ne yeve thou nevere myght ne maistrie° of thy body whil thou lyvest.' / Now sithen° he deffend-eth° that man shal nat yeven to his broother ne to his freend the might of his body, / by strenger° re-soun he deffendeth and forbedeth a man to yeven hymself to his enemy. / And nathelees I conseille you that ye mystruste nat my lord. / For I woot° wel and knowe verraily° that he is debonaire° and meeke, large°, curteys, / and nothing desy- 1760 rous ne coveitous° of good ne richesse. / For ther nys nothing in this world that he desireth save° oonly worship° and honour. / Forthermoore I knowe wel and am right seur° that he shal nothyng doon in this nede withouten my con-seil. / And I shal so werken in this cause that by grace of oure lord God ye shul been reconsiled unto us." /

Thanne seyden they with o voys, "Worshipful lady, we putten us and our goodes al fully in youre wil and disposicioun / and been redy 1765 to comen, what day that it lyke unto° youre noblesse to lymyte° us or assigne us, / for to maken oure obligacioun and boond as strong as it liketh unto youre goodnesse / that we mowe° fulfille the wille of yow and of my lord Melibee." /

Whan dame Prudence hadde herd the answeres of thise men, she bad hem goon agayn prively°, / and she retourned to hire lord Melibee and tolde hym how she foond his adversaries ful repentant, / knowlechynge° ful lowely hire 1770 synnes and trespas, and how they were redy to suffren all peyne, / requirynge° and preiynge hym of mercy and pitee. /

Thanne seyde Melibee, "He is wel worthy to have pardoun and foryifnesse of his synne that excuseth nat his synne / but knowlecheth it and repenteth hym, axinge indulgence°. / For Senec seith, 'Ther is the remissioun and foryif-nesse where as confessioun is.' / For confes- 1775 sioun is neighebore to innocence. / And he seith in another place, 'He that hath shame for his synne and knowlecheth it is worthy

remissioun.' And therfore I assente and con-ferme me° to have pees. / But it is good that we do it nat withouten the assent and wyl of oure freendes." /

Thanne was Prudence right glad and joyeful, and seyde, / "Certes, sire," quod she, "ye han wel and goodly answered. / For right as by 1780 the conseil, assent, and help of youre freendes ye han been stired° to venge yow and maken werre, / right so withouten hire conseil shul ye nat accorden yow, ne have pees with youre adver-saries. / For the lawe seith, 'Ther nys nothing so good by wey of kynde° as a thyng to been un-bounde° by hym that° it was ybounde.'" /

And thanne dame Prudence, withouten delay or tariynge, sente anon hire messages° for hire kyn°, and for hyr olde freendes whiche that were trewe and wyse, / and tolde hem by ordre°, in the presence of Melibee, al this mateere as it is aboven expressed and declared, / and prey- 1785 den that they wolde yeven hire avys° and con-seil what best were to doon in this nede. / And whan Melibees freendes hadde taken hire avys and deliberacioun of the forseide mateere, / and had-den examyned it by greet bisynesse° and greet diligence, / they yave ful conseil for to have pees and reste, / and that Melibee sholde receyve with good herte his adversaries to foryifnesse and mercy. /   1790

And whan dame Prudence hadde herd the assent of hir lord Melibee and the conseil of his freendes / accorde with hire wille and hire enten-cioun, / she was wonderly° glad in hire herte, and seyde, / "Ther is an old proverbe," quod she, "seith that the goodnesse that thou mayst do this day, do it, / and abide° nat ne delaye it nat til tomorwe. / And therfore I conseille that 1795 ye sende youre messages, swiche as been dis-crete° and wise, / unto youre adversaries tellynge hem on youre bihalve / that if they wole trete of° pees and of accord, / that they shape° hem with-outen delay or tariyng to comen unto us." /

1756 maistrie, *control* **1757 sithen,** *since,* **deffendeth,** *forbids* **1758 strenger,** *stronger* **1760 woot,** *know,* **verraily,** *truly,* **debonaire,** *willing,* **large,** *generous* **1761 coveitous,** *greedy* **1762 save,** *except,* **worship,** *dignity* **1763 seur,** *certain* **1766 lyke unto,** *is pleasing to,* **lymyte,** *appoint* **1768 mowe,** *may* **1769 prively,** *privately* **1771 knowlechynge,** *acknowledging* **1772 requirynge,** *requesting* **1774 axinge indulgence,** *asking leniency* **1777 conferme me,** *resolve* **1781 stired,** *encouraged* **1783 by wey of kynde,** *in the course of nature,* **unbounde,** *released,* **that,** *by whom* **1784 messages,** *messengers,* **kin,** *relatives* **1785 by ordre,** *in or-der* **1786 yeven hire avys,** *given their advice* **1788 bisynesse,** *attention* **1793 wonderly,** *wonderfully* **1795 abide,** *wait* **1796 discrete,** *thought-ful* **1798 trete of,** *negotiate about* **1799 shape,** *prepare***

1775 Senec, not in Seneca, but Martinus Dumiensis, *De Moribus* (On Customs) 94. **1777** The Latin original follows Publilius Syrus, *Sententiae* 489, but the French differs somewhat. Omitted in several MSS, with a number of variants; see MR 4.506–7. **1783 lawe seith,** Justinian, *Di-gesta* 1.17.35. **1794 old proverbe,** see *LGW* 452.

Which thyng parfourned° was in dede. / 1800 And whanne thise trespassours and repentynge folk of hire folies—that is to seyn, the adversaries of Melibee— / hadden herd what thise messagers seyden unto hem / they weren right glad and joyeful, and answereden ful mekely and benignely°, / yeldynge graces° and thankynges to hire lord Melibee and to al his compaignye, / and shopen hem° withouten delay to go with the messagers and obeye to the comandement of hire lord Melibee. / 1805

And right anon they tooken hire wey to the court of Melibee, / and tooken with hem somme of hire trewe freendes to maken feith° for hem and for to been hire borwes°. / And whan they were comen to the presence of Melibee, he seyde hem thise wordes, / "It standeth thus," quod Melibee, "and sooth° it is, that ye / causelees and withouten skile° and resoun / han doon 1810 grete injuries and wronges to me and to my wyf Prudence and to my doghter also. / For ye han entred into myn hous by violence, / and have doon swich outrage, that alle men knowen wel that ye have disserved the deeth. / And therfore wol I knowe and wite° of yow / wheither ye wol putte the punyssement and the chastisynge and the vengeance of this outrage in the wyl of me and of my wyf Prudence, or ye wol nat?" / 1815

Thanne the wiseste of hem thre answerde for hem alle, and seyde, / "Sire," quod he, "we knowen wel that we been unworthy to comen unto the court of so greet a lord and so worthy as ye been. / For we han so greetly mystaken us and han offended and agilt in swich a wise agayn° youre heigh lordshipe / that trewely we han disserved the deeth. / But yet for the grete goodnesse and debonairetee° that al the world witnesseth in youre persone, / we submytten us to the 1820 excellence and benignitee° of youre gracious lordshipe, / and been redy to obeie to alle youre comandementz, / bisekynge yow that of youre merciable pitee ye wol considere oure grete

repentaunce and lough° submyssioun, / and graunten us foryevenesse of oure outrageous trespas and offense. / For wel we knowe that youre liberal grace and mercy strecchen hem ferther into goodnesse than doon oure outrageouse giltes and trespas into wikkednesse, / al be 1825 it that cursedly and dampnably we han agilt agayn° your heigh lordshipe." /

Thanne Melibee took hem up fro the ground ful benignely, / and receyved hire obligaciouns° and hir boondes° by hire othes upon hire plegges° and borwes°, / and assigned hem a certeyn day to retourne unto his court / for to accepte and receyve the sentence and jugement that Melibee wolde comande to be doon on hem by the causes° aforeseyd; / whiche thynges or- 1830 deyned°, every man retourned to his hous. /

And whan that dame Prudence saugh hire tyme, she freyned° and axed hir lord Melibee / what vengeance he thoughte to taken of his adversaries. /

To which Melibee answerde and seyde, "Certes," quod he, "I thynke and purpose me fully / to desherite° hem of al that ever they han, and for to putte hem in exil forever." / 1835

"Certes," quod dame Prudence, "this were a crueel sentence, and muchel agayn resoun. / For ye been riche ynough, and han no nede of oother mennes good°. / And ye mighte lightly° in this wise gete yow a coveitous name°, / which is a vicious thyng and oghte been escheued of° every good man. / For after the sawe° of the word of the apostle, 'Coveitise is roote of alle harmes.' / 1840 And therfore it were bettre for yow to lese° so muchel good of youre owene than for to taken of hire good in this manere. / For bettre it is to lesen good° with worshipe° than it is to wynne good with vileynye and shame. / And everi man oghte to doon his diligence and his bisynesse to geten hym a good name. / And yet shal he nat oonly bisie hym in kepynge of his good name, / but he shal also enforcen hym° alwey to do somthing by which he may renovelle° his good name. / For 1845

1800 parfourned, *performed* **1803 benignely,** *graciously* **1804 yeldynge graces,** *offering gratitude* **1805 shopen hem,** *prepared themselves* **1807 maken feith,** *bear witness,* **borwes,** *sureties* **1809 sooth,** *true* **1810 skile,** *justification* **1814 wite,** *learn* **1818 agilt in swiche a wise agayn,** *been guilty in such a way against* **1820 debonairetee,** *agreeableness* **1821 benignitee,** *goodness* **1823 lough,** *low* **1826 agilt agayn,** *been guilty against* **1828 obligaciouns,** *promises,* **boondes,** *guarantees,* **pledges,**

pledges, **borwes,** *sureties* **1830 by the causes,** *for the reasons* **1831 ordeyned,** *established* **1832 freyned,** *inquired* **1835 desherite,** *deprive* **1837 good,** *possessions* **1838 lightly,** *easily,* **coveitous name,** *reputation for greed* **1839 escheued of,** *avoided by* **1840 sawe,** *saying* **1841 lese,** *lose* **1842 lesen good,** *lose possessions,* **worshipe,** *honor* **1845 enforcen hym,** *try,* **renovelle,** *renew*

1807 borwes, sureties, i.e., people who pledge to assume the responsibilities of others, especially in case of default on debts or obligations. **1840 the apostle,** Paul, 1 Timothy 6.10; see *PardT* 6.334. **1842** Publilius Syrus, *Sententiae* 479.

it is writen that the olde° good loos° and good name of a man is soone goon and passed whan it is nat newed ne renovelled. / And as touchynge° that ye seyn ye wole exile youre adversaries, / that thynketh me muchel agayn resoun and out of mesure°, / considered the power that they han yeve yow upon hemself. / And it is writen that he is worthy to lesen° his privilege that mysuseth the myght and the power that is yeven hym. / And I sette cas° ye myghte enjoyne° hem that peyne° by right and by lawe, / which I trowe° ye mowe° nat do; / I seye ye mighte nat putten it to execucioun peraventure°, / and thanne were it likly to retourne to the werre as it was biforn. / And therfore, if ye wole° that men do yow obeisance°, ye moste deemen° moore curteisly— / this is to seyn, ye moste yeven° moore esy sentences and juggementz. / For it is writen that he that moost curteisly comandeth, to hym men moost obeyen. / And therfore, I prey yow that in this necessitee and in this nede, ye caste yow° to overcome youre herte. / For Senec seith that he that overcometh his herte, overcometh twies°. / And Tullius seith, 'Ther is nothyng so comendable in a greet lord / as whan he is debonaire° and meeke, and appeseth hym lightly°.' / And I prey yow that ye wole forbere° now to do vengeance / in swich a manere that youre goode name may be kept and conserved; / and that men mowe° have cause and mateere° to preyse yow of° pitee and of mercy; / and that ye have no cause to repente yow of thyng that ye doon. / For Senec seith, 'He overcometh in an yvel manere that repenteth hym of his victorie.' / Wherfore I pray yow, lat mercy been in youre mynde and in your herte / to th'effect and

entente that God Almyghty have mercy on yow in his laste juggement. / For Seint Jame seith in his Epistle, 'Juggement withouten mercy shall be doon to hym that hath no mercy of° another wight°.'" /

Whanne Melibee hadde herd the grete skiles° and resouns of dame Prudence, and hir wise informaciouns and techynges, / his herte gan enclyne to the wil of his wif, considerynge hire trewe entente, / and conformed hym anon, and assented fully to werken after hire conseil, / and thonked God of whom procedeth al vertu and alle goodnesse that hym sente a wif of so greet discrecioun. / And whan the day cam that his adversaries sholde appieren° in his presence, / he spak unto hem ful goodly°, and seyde in this wyse, "Al be it so that° of youre pride and presumpcioun and folie and of youre necligence and unkonnynge°, / ye have mysborn yow° and trespassed unto me, / yet for as much as I see and biholde your grete humylitee, / and that ye been sory and repentant of youre giltes, / it constreyneth° me to doon yow grace and mercy. / Therfore I receyve yow to my grace / and foryeve yow outrely° alle the offenses, injuries, and wronges, that ye have doon agayn me and myne / to this effect and to this ende that God of his endelees mercy / wole at the tyme of oure dyinge foryeven us oure giltes that we han trespassed to hym in this wrecched world. / For doutelees, if we be sory and repentant of the synnes and giltes whiche we han trespassed in the sighte of oure lord God, / he is so free° and so merciable / that he wole foryeven us our giltes / and bryngen us to his blisse that never hath ende. Amen." /

Heere is ended Chaucers Tale of Melibee and of Dame Prudence.

1846 olde, *established,* **loos,** *reputation* **1847 touchynge,** *concerning* **1848 out of mesure,** *immoderate* **1850 lesen,** *lose* **1851 I sette cas,** *let me suppose,* **enjoyne,** *assign,* **peyne,** *punishment* **1852 trowe,** *believe,* **mowe,** *may* **1853 putten it to execucioun peraventure,** *enforce it perhaps* **1855 wole,** *want,* **do yow obeisance,** *respect you,* **deemen,** *judge* **1856 yeven,** *give* **1858 caste yow,** *try* **1859 twies,** *twice* **1861**

debonaire, *agreeable,* **appeseth hym lightly,** *soothes himself easily* **1862 forbere,** *refrain* **1864 mowe,** *may,* **mateere,** *reason,* **of,** *for* **1869 of,** *for,* **wight,** *person* **1870 skiles,** *arguments* **1874 appieren,** *appear* **1875 goodly,** *pleasantly* **1876 Al be it so that,** *even though,* **unkonnynge,** *ignorance* **1877 mysborn yow,** *acted wrongly* **1880 constreyneth,** *compels* **1881 outrely,** *completely* **1885 free,** *generous*

1846 it is writen, Publilius Syrus, *Sententiae* 293. **1850 it is writen,** Gregory, *Decretals* 3.31.18. **1857 it is writen,** Seneca, *De Clementia* (On Mercy) 1.24.1. **1859 Senec,** not in Seneca, but Publilius Syrus, *Sententiae* 64. **1860–61 Tullius . . . ,** Cicero, *De Officiis* (On Duties) 1.88. **1866 Senec,** not in Seneca, but Publilius Syrus, *Sententiae* 366. **1869 Seint Jame,** James 2.13. **1871–72** Chaucer's addition. **1884–88** Chaucer's addition; see 1 John 1.9.

MONK'S TALE

PROLOGUE

The murye wordes of the Hoost to the Monk.

Whan ended was my tale of Melibee
And of Prudence and hire benignytee°,　　1890
Oure Hooste seyde, "As I am feithful man,
And by that precious corpus Madrian,
I hadde levere than a barel ale°
That Goodelief, my wyf, hadde herd this tale.
She nys nothyng° of swich pacience　　1895
As was this Melibeus wyf Prudence.
By Goddes bones, whan I bete my knaves°,
She bryngeth me forth the grete clobbed
　　staves°,
And crieth, 'Slee° the dogges everichoon°,
And brek hem bothe bak and every boon!'　　1900
And if that any neighebore of myne
Wol nat in chirche to my wyf enclyne°,
Or be so hardy° to hire to trespace°,
Whan she comth hoom she rampeth° in my face,
And crieth, 'False coward, wrek° thy wyf!　　1905

By corpus bones, I wol have thy knyf,
And thou shalt have my distaf and go spynne!'
Fro day to nyght right thus she wol bigynne.
'Allas,' she seith, 'that evere I was shape°
To wedden a milksop, or a coward ape,　　1910
That wol been overlad with every wight°.
Thou darst° nat stonden by thy wyves right.'
　　"This is my lif but if that I wol fighte;
And out at dore anon° I moot me dighte°,
Or elles I am but lost but if that° I　　1915
Be lik a wilde leoun, fool-hardy.
I woot° wel she wol do° me slee somday
Som neighebore, and thanne go my way,
For I am perilous with knyf in honde
Al be it that° I dar hire nat withstonde,　　1920
For she is byg° in armes, by my feith—
That shal he fynde that hire mysdooth or seith°.
But lat us passe awey fro this mateere.

1890 benignytee, graciousness 1893 hadde levere than a barel ale, would rather than (have) a barrel of ale 1895 nys nothyng, is nothing 1897 knaves, boy servants 1898 clobbed staves, knobby sticks 1899 Slee, slay, everichoon, each one 1902 enclyne, bow in respect 1903 hardy, bold, trespace, do offense 1904 rampeth, rages 1905 wrek, avenge 1909 shape, destined 1911 overlad with every wight, pushed around by everybody 1912 darst, dare 1914 anon, immediately, moot me dighte, must take myself 1915 but if that, unless 1917 woot, know, do, make 1920 Al be it that, even though 1921 byg, strong 1922 mysdooth or seith, mistreats or misspeaks

1892 corpus Madrian, body of Madrian. Since no St. Madrian is known, apparently the Host's malapropism. 1894 Goodelief, a proper name; found in Kentish records, although some editors treat it as an epithet. The wife of the real Harry Bailly (see GP 1.751n) was named "Christian." 1906 corpus bones, a confusion of corpus Dei (God's body) and God's bones. 1907 distaf, staff used in spinning thread and traditional symbol of female work.

"My lord, the Monk," quod he, "be myrie of
   cheere,
For ye shul telle a tale trewely.   1925
Loo, Rouchestre stant heer faste° by.
Ryde forth, myn owene lord, brek nat oure game.
But by my trouthe, I knowe nat youre name.
Wher° shal I calle yow my lord daun John,
Or daun Thomas, or elles daun Albon?   1930
Of what hous be ye, by youre fader kyn?
I vowe to God, thou hast a ful fair skyn;
It is a gentil pasture ther° thow goost°.
Thou art nat lyk a penant° or a goost°.
Upon my feith, thou art som officer,   1935
Som worthy sexteyn, or som celerer,
For by my fader soule, as to my doom°,
Thou art a maister whan thou art at hoom,
No poure cloysterer° ne no novys,
But a governour, wily and wys,   1940
And therwithal° of brawnes° and of bones,
A wel farynge° persone for the nones°. occasion
I pray to God, yeve hym confusioun°
That first thee broghte unto religioun°!
Thou woldest han been a tredefowel
   aright°.   1945
Haddestow° as greet a leeve° as thou hast myght
To parfourne° al thy lust in engendrure°,
Thou haddest bigeten ful many a creature.
Allas, why werestow° so wyd a cope°?
God yeve° me sorwe but°, and° I were a pope, 1950
Nat oonly thou, but every myghty man,
Though he were shorn ful hye upon his pan,
Sholde have a wyf, for al the world is lorn°—
Religioun hath take up al the corn°

Of tredyng°, and we borel men° been
   shrympes.   1955
Of fieble trees ther comen wrecched ympes°.
This maketh that oure heires been so sklendre°
And feble that they may nat wel engendre°.
This maketh that oure wyves wole assaye°
Religious folk, for ye mowe° bettre paye   1960
Of Venus paiementz° than mowe we.
God woot°, no lussheburgh° payen ye!
But be nat wrooth°, my lord, though that I pleye.
Ful ofte in game a sooth° I have herd seye."
   This worthy Monk took al in pacience,   1965
And seyde, "I wol doon al my diligence°—
As fer as sowneth into honestee°—
To telle yow a tale, or two, or three,
And if yow list° to herkne hyderward°,
I wol yow seyn° the lyf of Seint Edward—   1970
Or ellis, first, tragedies wol I telle
Of whiche I have an hundred in my celle°.
   "Tragedie is to seyn a certeyn storie,
As olde bookes maken us memorie°,
Of hym that stood in greet prosperitee   1975
And is yfallen out of heigh degree
Into myserie, and endeth wrecchedly.
And they ben versified communely
Of six feet which men clepen° exametron.
In prose eek been endited° many oon,   1980
And eek in meetre, in many a sondry wyse°.
Lo, this declaryng° oghte ynogh suffise.
   "Now herkneth, if yow liketh for to heere.
But first I yow biseeke° in this mateere,
Though I by ordre telle nat thise thynges,   1985
Be it of popes, emperours, or kynges,

1926 faste, *near* **1929 Wher,** *whether* **1933 a gentil pasture ther,** *high-class grazing where,* **goost,** *go* **1934 penant,** *penitent,* **goost,** *spirit* **1937 as to my doom,** *by my judgment* **1939 cloysterer,** *typical monk,* **novys,** *novice* **1941 therwithal,** *moreover,* **brawnes,** *muscles* **1942 wel farynge,** *good looking,* **nones,** *occasion* **1943 yeve hym confusioun,** *damn him* **1944 unto religioun,** *into the clergy* **1945 tredefowel aright,** *superb rooster* **1946 Haddestow,** *if you had,* **leeve,** *permission* **1947 parfourne,** *perform,* **engendrure,** *procreation* **1949 werestow,** *do you wear,* **cope,** *cape* **1950 yeve,** *give,* **but,** *unless,* **and,** *if* **1953 lorn,** *lost* **1954 corn,** *seed,* **1955 tredyng,** *copulating,* **borel men,** *laymen* **1956 wrecched ympes,** *weak branches* **1957 sklendre,** *skinny* **1958 engendre,** *procreate* **1959 assaye,** *try out* **1960 mowe,** *can* **1961 Venus paiementz,** *Venus's payments* (i.e., sexual performance) **1962 woot,** *knows,* **lussheburgh,** *counterfeit coins* (from Luxembourg) **1963 wrooth,** *angry* **1964 sooth,** *truth* **1966 diligence,** *effort* **1967 sowneth into honestee,** *contributes to decency* **1969 yow list,** *it pleases you,* **hyderward,** *in this direction* **1970 seyn,** *tell* **1972 celle,** *room* **1974 maken us memorie,** *remind us* **1979 clepen,** *call* **1980 eek been endited,** *also are composed* **1981 sondry wyse,** *various ways* **1982 declaryng,** *explanation* **1984 biseeke,** *request***

1926 Rouchestre, Rochester, thirty miles from London and a little over halfway to Canterbury; ten miles beyond Sittingbourne (mentioned in *WBP* 3.847), prompting some editors to move part 7 to precede part 3, the so-called Bradshaw shift, after Henry Bradshaw who first proposed this order. **1929 daun John,** master John; the Host knows the Monk's name is "daun Piers" (master Peter) in *NPP* 7.2792. **1931 hous,** monastery, although in light of *fader kyn,* it may here mean "noble family," of aristocratic blood. **1936 sexteyn . . . celerer,** monastic officials in charge of sacred vessels and garments (sexton) and of food and wine (cellarer). **1952 shorn ful hye upon his pan,** with hair trimmed full high upon his head (i.e., tonsured) as a sign of monastic vocation. **1970 Seint Edward,** Edward I ("the Confessor"), king of England from 1043 to 1066. Richard II had a special regard for both Edward the Confessor and Edward II. **1973 Tragedie,** similar definitions of tragedy are found at lines 1991–94 and 2761–66 below, all echoing *Bo* 2.pr2.69–74. Thus, the Boethian conception of tragedy frames *MkT,* but see also 2375–2462n. Chaucer was the first to treat tragedy as a narrative genre in English. **1979 exametron,** hexameters, six-foot meters used in Latin heroic poetry.

After hir ages°, as men writen fynde,
But tellen hem som before and som bihynde,

As it now comth unto my remembraunce,
Have me excused of myn ignoraunce."   1990

Heere bigynneth the Monkes Tale De Casibus Virorum Illustrium.

I wol biwaille in manere of tragedie
The harm° of hem that stoode in heigh degree°,
And fillen° so that ther nas no remedie
To brynge hem out of hire adversitee.
For certein, whan that Fortune list° to flee,   1995
Ther may no man the cours of hire withholde.
Lat no man truste on blynd prosperitee;
Be war by thise ensamples trewe and olde.

LUCIFER

At Lucifer, though he an angel were
And nat a man, at hym wol I bigynne.   2000
For though Fortune may noon angel dere°,
From heigh degree yet fel he for his synne
Doun into helle where he yet is inne.
O Lucifer, brightest of angels alle,
Now artow Sathanas°, that mayst nat twynne°   2005
Out of miserie, in which that thou art falle.

ADAM

Loo Adam, in the feeld of Damyssene
With Goddes owene fynger wroght was he,
And nat bigeten° of mannes sperme unclene,
And welte° al paradys savynge o° tree.   2010
Hadde nevere worldly man so heigh degree
As Adam, til he for mysgovernaunce°
Was dryven out of hys hye prosperitee
To labour, and to helle, and to meschaunce°.

SAMPSON

Loo Sampsoun, which that was annunciat°   2015
By the angel longe er° his nativitee,
And was to God Almyghty consecrat°,

And stood in noblesse whil° he myghte see.
Was nevere swich another as was hee,
To speke of strengthe and therwith
        hardynesse°;   2020
But to his wyves toolde he his secree,
Thurgh which he slow° hymself for
        wrecchednesse.

Sampsoun, this noble almyghty champioun,
Withouten wepen save his handes tweye,
He slow and al torente° the leoun,   2025
Toward his weddyng walkynge by the weye.
His false wyf koude° hym so plese and preye°
Til she his conseil knew; and she untrewe
Unto his foos° his conseil gan biwreye°,
And hym forsook and took another newe.   2030

Thre hundred foxes took Sampson for ire°,
And alle hir tayles he togydre bond,
And sette the foxes tayles alle on fire,
For he on every tayl had knyt a brond°.
And they brende° alle the cornes° in that
        lond,   2035
And alle hire olyveres°, and vynes eke°.
A thousand men he slow eek with his hond,
And hadde no wepen but an asses cheke°.

Whan they were slayn, so thursted hym that he
Was wel ny lorn°, for which he gan to preye   2040
That God wolde on his peyne° han som pitee
And sende hym drynke or elles moste he deye,
And of this asses cheke that was dreye,
Out of a wang-tooth° sprang anon a welle°,
Of which he drank anon shortly to seye,   2045
Thus heelp hym God, as Judicum can telle.

1987 After hir ages, *chronologically* **1992 harm,** *sufferings,* **heigh degree,** *high rank* **1993 fillen,** *fell* **1995 list,** *chooses* **2001 dere,** *harm* **2005 artow Sathanas,** *are you Satan,* **twynne,** *escape* **2009 bigeten,** *begotten* **2010 welte,** *ruled,* **savynge o,** *except one* **2012 mysgovernaunce,** *lack of control* **2014 meschaunce,** *ill fate* **2015 which that was annunciat,** *who was foretold* **2016 er,** *before* **2017 consecrat,** *consecrated* **2018 whil,** *as* *long as* **2020 hardynesse,** *courage* **2022 slow,** *slew* **2025 al torente,** *completely tore apart* **2027 koude,** *could,* **preye,** *plead with* **2029 foos,** *foes,* **biwreye,** *betray* **2031 ire,** *anger* **2034 knyt a brond,** *attached a torch* **2035 brende,** *burned,* **cornes,** *grain crops* **2036 olyveres,** *olive trees,* **vynes eke,** *grapevines also* **2038 cheke,** *jawbone* **2040 wel ny lorn,** *nearly lost* **2041 peyne,** *pain* **2044 wang-tooth,** *molar,* **welle,** *spring*

1990a De Casibus Virorum Illustrium, Concerning the Fall of Illustrious Men; the same title as that of Boccaccio's famous collection, although Chaucer does not use it as a source. **1999 Lucifer,** a name for Satan that derives from Isaiah 14.12 and Luke 10.18; the account of the fall of Satan is Revelation 12.7–9. **2007 Adam,** the account of the creation of Adam and the prohibition of eating from one tree are in Genesis 1.27–2.17. **Damyssene,** Damascus, city reputed to have been built on the site where Adam was created. **2015 Sampsoun,** the account of Samson follows mainly Judges 13ff. **2046 Judicum,** biblical book of Judges (*Liber Judicum*).

By verray° force at Gazan° on a nyght,
Maugree° Philistiens of that citee,
The gates of the toun he hath up plyght°
And on his bak ycaryed° hem hath hee   2050
Hye° on an hill wher as men myghte hem see.
O noble, almyghty Sampsoun, lief° and deere,
Had thou nat toold to wommen thy secree,
In al this world ne hadde been thy peere°!

This Sampson nevere ciser° drank ne wyn,   2055
Ne on his heed cam rasour° noon ne sheere°,
By precept° of the messager divyn°,
For alle his strengthes in his heeres weere.
And fully twenty wynter°, yeer by yeere,
He hadde of Israel the governaunce.   2060
But soone shal he wepe many a teere,
For wommen shal hym bryngen to meschaunce°.

Unto his lemman° Dalida he tolde
That in his heeris al his strengthe lay,
And falsely to his foomen° she hym solde.   2065
And slepynge in hir barm° upon a day,
She made to clippe or shere his heres away,
And made his foomen al this craft espyen°,
And whan that they hym foond in this array°,
They bounde hym faste and putten out his
          eyen.   2070

But er his heer were clipped or yshave,
Ther was no boond with which men myghte
          him bynde.
But now is he in prison in a cave,
Where as they made hym at the queerne
          grynde°.
O noble Sampsoun, strongest of mankynde,   2075
O whilom° juge, in glorie and in richesse,
Now maystow° wepen with thyne eyen blynde,

Sith° thou fro wele° art falle in wrecchednesse.

The ende of this caytyf° was as I shal seye.
His foomen made a feeste upon a day,   2080
And made hym as hire fool biforn hem pleye,
And this was in a temple of greet array°.
But atte laste he made a foul affray°,
For he two pilers° shook and made hem falle,
And doun fil temple and al, and ther it lay, 2085
And slow° hymself, and eek his foomen alle.

This is to seyn, the prynces everichoon°
And eek thre thousand bodyes were ther slayn
With fallynge of the grete temple of stoon.
Of Sampson now wol I namoore sayn.   2090
Beth war° by this ensample oold and playn
That no men telle hir conseil til° hir wyves
Of swich thyng as they wolde han secree fayn°,
If that it touche° hir lymes° or hir lyves.

HERCULES

Of Hercules, the sovereyn conquerour,   2095
Syngen his werkes laude° and heigh renoun,
For in his tyme of strengthe he was the flour°.
He slow and rafte° the skyn fro the leoun;
He of centauros leyde the boost adoun°;
He arpies slow, the crueel bryddes felle°;   2100
He golden apples rafte of° the dragoun;
He drow° out Cerberus, the hound of helle;

He slow the crueel tyrant Busirus,
And made his hors to frete° hym, flessh and
          boon;
He slow the firy serpent venymus°;   2105
Of Acheloys hornes two he brak oon°;
And he slow Cacus in a cave of stoon;

2047 **verray,** *sheer,* **Gazan,** *Gaza* 2048 **Maugree,** *despite* 2049 **up plyght,** *torn up* 2050 **ycaryed,** *carried* 2051 **Hye,** *high* 2052 **lief,** *beloved* 2054 **peere,** *equal* 2055 **ciser,** *strong drink* 2056 **rasour,** *razor,* **sheere,** *shears* 2057 **precept,** *command,* **divyn,** *divine* 2059 **wynter,** *years* 2062 **meschaunce,** *ill fate* 2063 **lemman,** *mistress* 2065 **foomen,** *enemies* 2066 **barm,** *lap* 2068 **al this craft espyen,** *understand this secret* 2069 **array,** *fashion* 2074 **queerne grynde,** *mill grind* 2076 **whilom,** *once* 2077 **maystow,** *may you* 2078 **Sith,** *since,* **wele,** *prosperity* 2079 **caytyf,**

wretch 2082 **of greet array,** *ornately decorated* 2083 **foul affray,** *horrible attack* 2084 **pilers,** *pillars* 2086 **slow,** *killed* 2087 **everichoon,** *each one* 2091 **Beth war,** *be warned,* **playn,** *clear* 2092 **conseil til,** *secrets to* 2093 **wolde han secree fayn,** *would want to have secret* 2094 **touche,** *concerns,* **lymes,** *limbs* 2096 **laude,** *praise* 2097 **flour,** *apex* (flower) 2098 **rafte,** *took away* 2099 **leyde the boost adoun,** *laid to rest the boast* 2100 **bryddes felle,** *fearsome birds* 2101 **rafte of,** *took away from* 2102 **drow,** *drew* 2104 **frete,** *eat* 2105 **venymus,** *poisonous* 2106 **brak oon,** *broke one*

2063 Delida, Delilah. **2095 Hercules,** the account follows mainly *Bo* 4.m7, mentioning only some of the twelve traditional labors of Hercules. **2098 leoun,** the first labor of Hercules was to slay the Nemean lion. **2099 centauros,** Hercules killed two centaurs (half-horse, half-man), but the reference is unclear. **2100 arpies,** Hercules destroyed the harpies (man-eating birds) as his sixth labor. **2101 apples,** a dragon guarded the golden apples of the Hesperides, Hercules' eleventh labor. **2102 Cerberus,** the three-headed guard dog of hell that Hercules brought up to earth as his twelfth labor. **2103 Busirus,** Chaucer conflates two stories from *Bo* 2.pr6.68–70 and 4.m7.40–41. **2105 firy serpent,** apparently the many-headed Hydra, even though it was not fiery. **2106 Acheloys,** a river god in the form of a horned bull who fought Hercules. **2107 Cacus,** gigantic, fire-breathing son of Vulcan who lived in a cave and beset the people of Evander.

He slow the geant Antheus the stronge;
He slow the grisly boor, and that anon;
And bar° the hevene on his nekke longe.   2110

Was nevere wight° sith that° this world bigan
That slow so manye monstres as dide he.
Thurghout this wyde world his name ran°,
What for his strengthe and for his heigh bountee°,
And every reawme° wente he for to see.   2115
He was so stroong that no man myghte hym lette°.
At bothe the worldes endes, seith Trophee,
In stide° of boundes° he a pileer° sette.

A lemman° hadde this noble champioun,
That highte° Dianira, fressh as May,   2120
And as thise clerkes maken mencioun,
She hath hym sent a sherte, fressh and gay.
Allas, this sherte, allas and weylaway,
Envenymed° was so subtilly withalle°
That er that he had wered it half a day   2125
It made his flessh al from his bones falle.

But nathelees somme clerkes hire excusen
By oon that highte° Nessus that it maked.
Be as be may, I wol hire noght accusen—
But on his bak this sherte he wered al naked   2130
Til that his flessh was for the venym blaked°.
And whan he saugh° noon oother remedye,
In hoote coles he hath hymselven raked°,
For with no venym deigned hym to dye°.

Thus starf° this worthy, myghty Hercules.   2135
Lo, who may truste on Fortune any throwe°?
For hym that folweth al this world of prees°

Er he be war is ofte yleyd° ful lowe.
Ful wys is he that kan hymselven knowe!
Beth war°, for whan that Fortune list to glose°,   2140
Thanne wayteth° she her man to overthrowe
By swich a wey as he wolde leest suppose.

NABUGODONOSOR

The myghty trone°, the precious tresor,
The glorious ceptre, and roial magestee
That hadde the Kyng Nabugodonosor   2145
With tonge unnethe° may discryved bee°.
He twyes wan° Jerusalem the citee;
The vessel° of the temple he with hym ladde°.
At Babiloigne° was his sovereyn see°,
In which his glorie and his delit he hadde.   2150

The faireste children° of the blood roial
Of Israel he leet do gelde° anoon,
And maked ech of hem to been his thral°.
Amonges othere Daniel was oon
That was the wiseste child of everychon°,   2155
For he the dremes of the kyng expowned°,
Where as in Chaldeye clerk ne was ther noon
That wiste° to what fyn° his dremes sowned°.

This proude kyng leet maken° a statue of gold,
Sixty cubites long and sevene in brede°,   2160
To which ymage bothe yong and oold
Comanded he to loute° and have in drede,
Or in a fourneys° ful of flambes rede
He shal be brent° that wolde noght obeye.
But nevere wolde assente to that dede   2165
Daniel ne his yonge felawes tweye°.

2110 **bar,** *carried* 2111 **wight,** *man,* **sith that,** *since* 2113 **name ran,** *reputation spread* 2114 **bountee,** *goodness* 2115 **reawme,** *realm* 2116 **lette,** *hinder* 2118 **stide,** *stead,* **boundes,** *boundaries,* **pileer,** *pillar* 2119 **lemman,** *lover* 2120 **highte,** *was named* 2124 **Envenymed,** *poisoned,* **withalle,** *as well* 2128 **highte,** *was named* 2131 **blaked,** *burned black* 2132 **saugh,** *saw* 2133 **hymselven raked,** *raked over himself* 2134 **with no venym deigned hym to dye,** *he would not accept death by poison* 2135 **starf,** *died* 2136 **throwe,** *length of time* 2137 **world of prees,** *crowded world* 2138 **yleyd,** *laid* 2140 **Beth war,** *be warned,* **list to glose,** *chooses to deceive* 2141 **wayteth,** *watches* 2143 **trone,** *throne* 2146 **unnethe,** *hardly,* **discryved bee,** *be described* 2147 **twyes wan,** *twice conquered* 2148 **vessel,** *treasure,* **ladde,** *carried off* 2149 **Babiloigne,** *Babylon,* **sovereyn see,** *imperial seat* 2151 **children,** *young men* 2152 **leet do gelde,** *had castrated* 2153 **thral,** *slave* 2155 **everychon,** *everyone* 2156 **expowned,** *explained* 2158 **wiste,** *knew,* **fyn,** *end,* **sowned,** *indicated* 2159 **leet maken,** *had made* 2160 **brede,** *breadth* 2162 **loute,** *bow* 2163 **fourneys,** *furnace* 2164 **brent,** *burned* 2166 **tweye,** *two*

2108 **Antheus,** Antaeus, giant wrestler whose strength increased each time he touched the earth; throttled by Hercules as he held Antaeus off the ground. 2109 **boor,** the Erymanthian boar, which Hercules captured (but did not slay) as his fourth labor. 2110 **hevene,** heavens; in his eleventh labor, Hercules held up the heavens on his shoulders while Atlas took the golden apples from his daughters, the Hesperides. 2117 **bothe the worldes endes,** it was commonplace that Hercules set pillars at the Strait of Gibraltar and the edge of the Far East. **Trophee,** unidentified. 2120 **Dianira,** Deianira, second wife of Hercules, gave him a shirt poisoned with the blood of Nessus, a centaur slain by Hercules. Before dying, Nessus had convinced Deianira that the shirt would restore Hercules' love for her even though he had turned his attention to Iole. 2145 **Nabugodonosor,** Nebuchadnezzar; the account is mostly from Daniel 1–4, although there is no mention of castration (as in line 2152 below) in the Bible nor is Daniel one of the three who refuse to worship the idol (as in lines 2165–66). 2157 **Chaldeye,** Chaldea, often identified with Babylon and associated with occult learning. 2160 **cubites,** measure of the length of a forearm, seventeen to twenty-two inches. 2166 In Daniel 3.20, the three are Shadrach, Meshach, and Abednego, not Daniel.

This kyng of kynges proud was and elaat°.
He wende° that God that sit° in magestee
Ne myghte hym nat bireve° of his estaat.
But sodeynly he loste his dignytee,   2170
And lyk a beest hym semed for to bee,
And eet hey° as an oxe, and lay theroute°
In reyn; with wilde beestes walked hee
Til certein tyme was ycome aboute.

And lik an egles fetheres wax° his heres;   2175
His nayles lyk a briddes° clawes weere;
Til God relessed hym a certeyn yeres°,
And yaf hym wit°, and thanne with many a teere
He thanked God; and evere° his lyf in feere
Was he to doon amys° or moore trespace°;   2180
And til that tyme he leyd was on his beere°,
He knew that God was ful of myght and grace.

BALTHASAR

His sone, which that highte° Balthasar,
That heeld the regne° after his fader° day,
He by his fader koude noght be war°,   2185
For proud he was of herte and of array,
And eek an ydolastre° he was ay°.
His hye estaat assured hym in pryde°;
But Fortune caste hym doun, and ther he lay,
And sodeynly his regne gan divide°.   2190

A feeste he made unto his lordes alle
Upon a tyme, and bad° hem blithe bee,
And thanne his officeres gan he calle.
"Gooth, bryngeth forth the vesseles," quod he,
"Whiche that my fader in his prosperitee   2195
Out of the temple of Jerusalem birafte°;
And to oure hye goddes thanke we
Of° honour that oure eldres with us lafte."

Hys wyf, his lordes, and his concubynes
Ay° dronken whil hire appetites laste   2200

Out of thise noble vessels sondry° wynes.
And on a wal this kyng his eyen caste,
And saugh an hand, armlees, that wroot ful
    faste,
For feere of which he quook° and siked soore°.
This hand that Balthasar so soore agaste°   2205
Wroot *Mane, techel, phares* and namoore.

In al that land magicien was noon
That koude expoune° what this lettre° mente,
But Daniel expowned it anoon,
And seyde, "Kyng, God to thy fader lente   2210
Glorie and honour, regne°, tresour, rente°,
And he was proud, and nothyng God ne dradde°,
And therfore God greet wreche° upon hym
    sente,
And hym birafte° the regne that he hadde.

"He was out cast of mannes compaignye—   2215
With asses was his habitacioun,
And eet hey as a beest in weet and drye,
Til that he knew, by grace and by resoun,
That God of hevene hath domynacioun
Over every regne° and every creature.   2220
And thanne hadde God of hym compassioun,
And hym restored his regne and his figure°.

"Eek° thou that art his sone art proud also,
And knowest alle thise thynges verraily°,
And art rebel to God, and art his foo.   2225
Thou drank eek of his vessels boldely;
Thy wyf eek, and thy wenches, synfully
Dronke of the same vessels sondry wynys°;
And heryest° false goddes cursedly.
Therfore to thee yshapen° ful greet pyne° ys.   2230

"This hand was sent from God that on the wal
Wroot *Mane, techel, phares,* truste me.
Thy regne is doon, thou weyest noght° at al.

2167 **elaat,** *arrogant* 2168 **wende,** *thought,* **sit,** *sits* 2169 **bireve,** *deprive*
2172 **hey,** *hay,* **theroute,** *outside* 2175 **wax,** *grew* 2176 **briddes,** *bird's*
2177 **a certeyn yeres,** *in a period of time* 2178 **yaf hym wit,** *gave him*
reason 2179 **evere,** *i.e., for the rest of* 2180 **doon amys,** *do wrong,* **tre-**
space, *sin* 2181 **beere,** *funeral platform* 2183 **highte,** *was named* 2184
heeld the regne, *ruled,* **fader,** *father's* 2185 **koude noght be war,** *could*
not be warned 2187 **ydolastre,** *idolater,* **ay,** *always* 2188 **assured hym in**
pryde, *confirmed his pride* 2190 **regne gan divide,** *kingdom broke up*
2192 **bad,** *commanded* 2196 **birafte,** *carried off* 2198 **Of,** *for the* 2200

Ay, *continuously* 2201 **sondry,** *various* 2204 **quook,** *trembled,* **siked**
soore, *sighed sorely* 2205 **agaste,** *frightened* 2208 **expoune,** *explain,* **let-**
tre, *writing* 2211 **regne,** *kingdom,* **rente,** *profit* 2212 **nothyng . . . ne**
dradde, *dreaded not at all* 2213 **wreche,** *misery* 2214 **hym birafte,**
deprived him (of) 2220 **regne,** *kingdom* 2222 **figure,** (human) *form*
2223 **Eek,** *moreover* 2224 **verraily,** *truly* 2228 **sondry wynys,** *various*
wines 2229 **heryest,** *worship* 2230 **to thee yshapen,** *to you destined,*
pyne, *pain* 2233 **regne,** *reign,* **weyest noght,** *weigh nothing*

2183 **Balthasar,** Belshazzar, son of Nebuchadnezzar; his story follows that of his father in Daniel 5. 2206 ***Mane, techel, phares,*** the handwrit-
ing on the wall of Daniel 5.25–28, there interpreted to mean "to number," "to weigh," and "to divide."

Dyvyded is thy regne°, and it shal be
To Medes and to Perses yeven°," quod he.   2235
And thilke° same nyght this kyng was slawe°,
And Darius occupieth his degree°,
Thogh he therto hadde neither right ne lawe.

Lordynges, ensample heerby may ye take
How that in lordshipe is no sikernesse°,   2240
For whan Fortune wole a man forsake,
She bereth awey his regne and his richesse,
And eek his freendes, bothe moore and lesse.
For what man that hath freendes thurgh Fortune,
Mishap wol maken hem° enemys as I gesse;   2245
This proverbe is ful sooth° and ful commune°.

CENOBIA

Cenobia, of Palymerie queene,
As writen Persiens of hir noblesse,
So worthy was in armes and so keene°
That no wight° passed hire in hardynesse°,   2250
Ne in lynage°, nor in oother gentilesse.
Of kynges blood of Perce is she descended—
I seye nat that she hadde moost fairnesse,
But of hir shape she myghte nat been amended°.

From hire childhede I fynde that she fledde   2255
Office° of wommen, and to wode° she wente,
And many a wilde hertes° blood she shedde
With arwes brode that she to hem sente.
She was so swift that she anon° hem hente°.
And whan that she was elder, she wolde kille   2260
Leouns, leopardes, and beres al torente°,
And in hir armes weelde° hem at hir wille.

She dorste° wilde beestes dennes seke°,
And rennen in the montaignes al the nyght,

And slepen under a bussh, and she koude
    eke°   2265
Wrastlen by verray° force and verray myght
With any yong man, were he never so wight°.
Ther myghte no thyng in hir armes stonde.
She kepte hir maydenhod from every wight°;
To no man deigned hire for to be bonde°.   2270

But atte laste hir freendes han hire maried°
To Odenake, a prynce of that contree,
Al were it so that° she hem longe taried°.
And ye shul understonde how that he
Hadde swiche fantasies° as hadde she.   2275
But natheless, whan they were knyt in feere°,
They lyved in joye and in felicitee,
For ech of hem hadde oother lief° and deere.

Save o° thyng, that she wolde nevere assente
By no wey that he sholde by hire lye   2280
But ones°, for it was hir pleyn° entente
To have a child the world to multiplye.
And also° soone as that she myghte espye
That she was nat with childe with that dede,
Thanne wolde she suffre° hym doon his
    fantasye°   2285
Eftsoone° and nat but oones, out of drede°.

And if she were with childe at thilke cast°,
Namoore sholde he pleyen thilke game
Til fully fourty wikes weren past.
Thanne wolde she ones suffre hym do the
    same.   2290
Al were this Odenake wilde or tame,
He gat namoore of hire, for thus she seyde,
It was to wyves lecherie and shame,
In oother caas° if that men with hem pleyde.

2234 **regne,** *kingdom* 2235 **yeven,** *given* 2236 **thilke,** *this,* **slawe,** *slain* 2237 **degree,** *rank* 2240 **sikernesse,** *certainty* 2245 **hem,** *them* 2246 **sooth,** *true,* **commune,** *widespread* 2249 **keene,** *courageous* 2250 **wight,** *person,* **hardynesse,** *boldness* 2251 **lynage,** *lineage* 2254 **amended,** *improved* 2256 **Office,** *duties,* **wode,** *the forest* 2257 **hertes,** *deer's* 2259 **anon,** *soon,* **hente,** *caught* 2261 **torente,** *torn to pieces* 2262 **weelde,** *control* 2263 **dorste,** *dared,* **seke,** *to seek* 2265 **eke,** *also* 2266 **verray,** *sheer* 2267 **wight,** *strong* 2269 **wight,** *man* 2270 **deigned hire for to be**

bonde, *did she condescend to be married* 2271 **han hire maried,** *have married her* 2273 **Al were it so that,** *even though,* **hem longe taried,** *long delayed them* 2275 **swiche fantasies,** *such wishes* 2276 **knyt in feere,** *joined together* 2278 **lief,** *beloved* 2279 **Save o,** *except one* 2281 **ones,** *once,* **pleyn,** *simple* 2283 **also,** *as* 2285 **suffre,** *allow,* **fantasye,** *desire* 2286 **Eftsoone,** *again,* **out of drede,** *without doubt* 2287 **at thilke cast,** *in that attempt* 2294 **caas,** *circumstances*

2235 **Medes . . . Perses,** the Medes were a historical people absorbed by the Persians (**Perses**) before the fall of Babylon. 2237 **Darius,** no historical person has been identified, although he is mentioned in Daniel 5.31. Historically Cyrus the Great of Persia defeated Babylonia. 2246 **This proverbe,** see *Bo* 3.pr5.68–70. 2247 **Cenobia . . . Palymerie,** Zenobia, queen of Palmyra, city-state in central Syria. Chaucer follows the account in Boccaccio's *De Claris Mulieribus* (On Famous Women) 98, which is odd, since he borrowed the title but no material from Boccaccio's *De Casibus;* see the note to 1990a above. 2252 **Perce,** Persia, although Boccaccio says Egypt. 2272 **Odenake,** Odenatus, prince of Palmyra. 2289 **fourty wikes,** forty weeks or about nine months. All except two MSS read "days," but Boccaccio's "post partus purgationes" indicates the period of gestation.

Two sones by this Odenake hadde she 2295
The whiche she kepte in vertu and lettrure°.
But now unto oure tale turne we:
I seye, so worshipful° a creature,
And wys therwith, and large with mesure°,
So penyble° in the werre, and curteis° eke, 2300
Ne moore labour° myghte in werre° endure,
Was noon, though al this world men wolde seke.

Hir riche array° ne myghte nat be told,
As wel in vessel° as in hire clothyng.
She was al clad in perree° and in gold, 2305
And eek she lafte° noght, for noon huntyng,
To have of sondry tonges° ful knowyng,
Whan that she leyser° hadde; and for to entende°
To lerne bookes was al hire likyng°,
How she in vertu myghte hir lyf dispende°. 2310

And shortly of this proces° for to trete,
So doghty° was hir housbonde and eek she
That they conquered manye regnes° grete
In the orient, with many a fair citee
Apertenaunt° unto the magestee 2315
Of Rome, and with strong hond held hem ful
       faste°,
Ne nevere myghte hir foomen° doon hem° flee
Ay whil° that Odenakes dayes laste.

Hir batailles, whoso list° hem for to rede,
Agayn Sapor the kyng and othere mo°, 2320
And how that al this proces fil° in dede,
Why she conquered, and what title had therto°,
And after, of hir meschief° and hire wo,
How that she was biseged° and ytake;
Lat hym unto my maister Petrak go, 2325
That writ ynough of this, I undertake°.

Whan Odenake was deed, she myghtily
The regnes° heeld, and with hire propre° hond

Agayn hir foos she faught so cruelly°
That ther nas kyng ne prynce in al that lond 2330
That he nas glad, if he that grace fond,
That she ne wolde upon his lond werreye°.
With hire they maden alliance by bond
To been in pees, and lete hire ride and pleye.

The Emperour of Rome Claudius, 2335
Ne hym bifore the Romayn Galien,
Ne dorste nevere been° so corageus,
Ne noon Ermyn°, ne noon Egipcien°,
Ne Surrien°, ne noon Arabyen,
Withinne the feeldes that dorste with hire
       fighte, 2340
Lest° that she wolde hem with hir handes slen°,
Or with hir meignee° putten hem to flighte.

In kynges habit° wente hir sones two,
As heires of hir fadres regnes° alle,
And Hermanno and Thymalao 2345
Hir names were, as Persiens hem calle.
But ay° Fortune hath in hire hony galle°:
This myghty queene may no while endure.
Fortune out of hir regne made hire falle
To wrecchednesse and to mysaventure. 2350

Aurelian, whan that the governaunce
Of Rome cam into his handes tweye°,
He shoop° upon this queene to doon vengeaunce.
And with his legions he took his weye
Toward Cenobie, and shortly for to seye, 2355
He made hire flee, and atte laste hire hente°,
And fettred° hire, and eek hire children tweye,
And wan the land, and hoom to Rome he wente.

Amonges othere thynges that he wan°,
Hir chaar° that was with gold wroght° and
       perree° 2360
This grete Romayn, this Aurelian,

2296 **lettrure,** *learning* 2298 **worshipful,** *noble* 2299 **large with mesure,** *appropriately generous* 2300 **penyble,** *hardworking,* **curteis,** *courteous* 2301 **labour,** *toil,* **werre,** *war* 2303 **array,** *splendor* 2304 **vessel,** *treasure* 2305 **perree,** *jewels* 2306 **lafte,** *neglected* 2307 **sondry tonges,** *various languages* 2308 **leyser,** *time,* **entende,** *strive* 2309 **likyng,** *desire* 2310 **dispende,** *spend* 2311 **this proces,** *these events* 2312 **doghty,** *brave* 2313 **regnes,** *kingdoms* 2315 **Apertenaunt,** *belonging* 2316 **ful faste,** *very firmly* 2317 **foomen,** *enemies,* **doon hem,** *make them* 2318 **Ay whil,** *for the time* 2319 **list,** *chooses* 2320 **othere mo,** *many others* 2321 **this proces fil,** *these events occurred* 2322 **therto,** *as a result* 2323 **meschief,** *misfortune* 2324 **biseged,** *besieged* 2326 **undertake,** *assert* 2328 **regnes,** *kingdoms,* **propre,** *own* 2329 **cruelly,** *fiercely* 2332 **werreye,** *make war* 2337 **Ne dorste nevere been,** *never dared to be* 2338 **Ermyn,** *Armenian,* **Egipcien,** *Egyptian* 2339 **Surrien,** *Syrian* 2341 **Lest,** *for fear,* **slen,** *slay* 2342 **meignee,** *army* 2343 **habit,** *clothing* 2344 **hir fadres regnes,** *their father's kingdoms* 2347 **ay,** *always,* **galle,** *bitterness* 2352 **tweye,** *two* 2353 **shoop,** *prepared* 2356 **hente,** *captured* 2357 **fettred,** *chained* 2359 **wan,** *won* 2360 **chaar,** *chariot,* **wroght,** *made,* **perree,** *jewels*

2320 **Agayn Sapor,** against Shapur, king of Persia, third century BCE. 2325 **Petrak,** Petrarch, though Chaucer's source was Boccaccio, whom he never acknowledges. **2335–36 Claudius . . . Galien,** Roman emperors, Claudius (268–70 CE) and Gallienus (253–68 CE). **2351 Aurelian,** Roman emperor Aurelianus (270–75 CE).

Hath with hym lad, for that men sholde it see.
Biforen° his triumphe° walketh shee,
With gilte° cheynes on hire nekke hangynge.
Coroned° was she, as after° hir degree°,   2365
And ful of perree charged° hire clothynge.

Allas, Fortune! She that whilom° was
Dredeful to kynges and to emperoures
Now gaureth° al the peple on hire, allas.
And she that helmed° was in starke stoures°,   2370
And wan by force townes stronge and toures°,
Shal on hir heed now were° a vitremyte;
And she that bar the ceptre° ful of floures
Shal bere a distaf° hire costes for to quyte°.

DE PETRO REGE ISPANNIE°

O noble, O worthy Petro, glorie of Spayne,   2375
Whom Fortune heeld so hye in magestee,
Wel oghten men thy pitous deeth complayne°.
Out of thy land thy brother made thee flee,
And after at a seege, by subtiltee°,
Thou were bitraysed° and lad unto his tente,   2380
Where as he with his owene hand slow° thee,
Succedynge in thy regne and in thy rente°.

The feeld of snow, with th'egle of blak therinne,
Caught with the lymerod° coloured as the gleede°,
He brew° this cursednesse and al this synne.   2385
The wikked nest was werkere of this nede°.

Noght Charles Olyver, that took ay heede°
Of trouthe and honour, but of Armorike
Genylon Olyver, corrupt for meede°,
Broghte this worthy kyng in swich a brike°.   2390

DE PETRO REGE DE CIPRO

O worthy Petro, kyng of Cipre, also,
That Alisandre wan by heigh maistrie°,
Ful many an hethen wroghtestow ful wo°,
Of which thyne owene liges° hadde envie,
And for no thyng but for thy chivalrie   2395
They in thy bed han slayn thee by the morwe.
Thus kan Fortune hir wheel governe and gye°,
And out of joye brynge men to sorwe.

DE BARNABO DE LUMBARDIA

Off° Melan grete Barnabo Viscounte,
God of delit and scourge of Lumbardye,   2400
Why sholde I nat thyn infortune acounte°,
Sith° in estaat thow cloumbe° were so hye?
Thy brother sone, that was thy double allye,
For he thy nevew was and sone-in-lawe,
Withinne his prisoun made thee to dye—   2405
But why ne how noot° I that thou were slawe°.

DE HUGELINO COMITE° DE PIZE

Off the Erl Hugelyn of Pyze the langour°
Ther may no tonge telle for pitee.

2363 **Biforen,** *in front of,* **triumphe,** *victory procession* 2364 **gilte,** *gilded* 2365 **Coroned,** *crowned,* **as after,** *in accord with,* **degree,** *rank* 2366 **charged,** *weighted* 2367 **whilom,** *once* 2369 **gaureth,** *stare* 2370 **helmed,** *helmeted,* **starke stoures,** *violent battles* 2371 **toures,** *towers* 2372 **were,** *wear,* **vitremyte,** *headdress* 2373 **ceptre,** *scepter* 2374 **distaf,** *stick for spinning,* **hire costes for to quyte,** *to pay for her upkeep* 2374a **Rege Ispannie,** *king of Spain* 2377 **complayne,** *lament* 2379 **subtiltee,** *deception* 2380 **bitraysed,** *betrayed* 2381 **slow,** *slew* 2382 **rente,** *income*

2384 **lymerod,** *rod smeared with birdlime for trapping birds,* **gleede,** *glowing coal* (red) 2385 **brew,** *brewed* 2386 **nede,** *crisis* 2387 **took ay heede,** *always paid attention* (to) 2389 **corrupt for meede,** *corrupted by payment* 2390 **brike,** *trap* 2392 **heigh maistrie,** *grand victory* 2393 **wroghtestow ful wo,** *you made very sorrowful* 2394 **liges,** *followers* 2397 **gye,** *guide* 2399 **Off,** *of* 2401 **thyn infortune acounte,** *tell your misfortune* 2402 **Sith,** *since,* **cloumbe,** *climbed* 2406 **noot,** *know not,* **slawe,** *slain* 2406a **Comite,** *count* 2407 **langour,** *suffering*

2375–2462 These "modern instances" come at the end of *MkT* in the best MSS, although most MSS and modern editions keep them here, with the result that attention is focused on tragedy at the beginning and end of *MkT;* see 1973n. As RI 1132 suggests, the modern instances may have been on loose sheets, able to be inserted in various places. More generally, the errors tallied in MR 2.403 indicate a flawed exemplar. 2375 **Petro,** Pedro, king of Castile and León, was assassinated in 1369. His daughter married John of Gaunt in 1371. Chaucer's 1366 trip to Spain may have been an embassy to Pedro's court. 2378 **thy brother,** Don Enrique of Trastamare, illegitimate half brother of Pedro who conspired in his defeat and death. In MR 4.511, it is suggested that Chaucer, politically motivated, emended "thy bastard brother," the reading in some MSS. 2383–84 Describes the coat of arms of Bertrand du Guesclin, conspirator in Pedro's overthrow. 2386 **wikked nest,** Skeat 5.238–39 identifies as a play on the name of Olivier de Mauni (Fr. *mau ni,* i.e., *mal nid,* "bad nest"), another conspirator against Pedro. 2387 **Charles Olyver,** Charlemagne's Oliver, loyal retainer and comrade of Roland in the *Chanson de Roland* (Song of Roland). 2388 **Armorike,** Armorica, or Brittany, home of Oliver Mauny. 2389 **Genylon Olyver,** i.e., traitor Oliver. Ganelon betrayed Roland in *Chanson de Roland.* 2391 **Petro . . . Cipre,** Pierre de Lusignan, king of Cyprus, assassinated in 1369; he visited the English court in 1363. Chaucer's account follows Machaut's *La Prise d'Alexandrie* (The Conquest of Alexandria) rather than history. 2399 **Barnabo Viscounte,** Bernabò Visconti, lord of Milan, with whom Chaucer did business on his 1378 trip to Italy. Visconti was arrested, imprisoned, and died under suspicious circumstances in 1385, evidently orchestrated by Gian Galeazzo Visconti, his nephew and son-in-law. 2407 **Erl Hugelyn of Pyze,** Count Ugolino of Pisa. Chaucer cites Dante (line 2461), i.e., *Inferno* 33.1–90, but the accounts vary. Dante has Ugolino in the bottom of hell, among the treasonous, not worthy of pity.

But litel out of° Pize stant a tour°
In which tour in prisoun put was he,   2410
And with hym been his litel children thre—
The eldeste scarsly fyf yeer was of age.
Allas, Fortune, it was greet crueltee
Swiche briddes° for to putte in swich a cage!

Dampned° was he to dyen in that prisoun,   2415
For Roger, which that bisshop was of Pize,
Hadde on hym maad a fals suggestioun°
Thurgh which the peple gan upon hym rise,
And putten hym to prisoun in swich wise°
As ye han herd, and mete° and drynke he
        hadde   2420
So smal that wel unnethe° it may suffise,
And therwithal° it was ful poure and badde.

And on a day bifil° that in that hour
Whan that his mete wont° was to be broght,
The gayler° shette the dores of the tour.   2425
He herde it wel, but he spak° right noght,
And in his herte anon° ther fil° a thoght
That they for hunger wolde doon° hym dyen.
"Allas," quod he, "allas, that I was wroght°!"
Therwith the teeres fillen from his eyen.   2430

His yonge sone that thre yeer was of age
Unto hym seyde, "Fader, why do ye wepe?
Whanne wol the gayler bryngen oure potage°?
Is ther no morsel breed that ye do kepe?
I am so hungry that I may nat slepe.   2435
Now wolde God that I myghte slepen evere!
Thanne sholde nat hunger in my wombe° crepe.
Ther is nothyng but breed that me were levere°."

Thus day by day this child bigan to crye,
Til in his fadres barm° adoun it lay   2440
And seyde, "Farewel, fader, I moot° dye."
And kiste his fader, and dyde the same day.
And whan the woful fader deed it say°,
For wo his armes two he gan to byte.

And seyde, "Allas, Fortune, and weylaway!   2445
Thy false wheel my wo al may I wyte°."

His children wende° that it for hunger was
That he his armes gnow°, and nat for wo,
And seyde, "Fader, do nat so, allas,
But rather ete the flessh upon us two.   2450
Oure flessh thou yaf° us, take oure flessh
        us fro,
And ete ynogh°." Right thus they to hym seyde,
And after that, withinne a day or two,
They leyde hem in his lappe adoun and deyde.

Hymself, despeired, eek for hunger starf°.   2455
Thus ended is this myghty Erl of Pize.
From heigh estaat Fortune awey hym carf°.
Of this tragedie it oghte ynough suffise;
Whoso wol here° it in a lenger wise,
Redeth the grete poete of Ytaille   2460
That highte° Dant, for he kan al devyse°
Fro point to point, nat o word wol he faille.

NERO

        Although that Nero were as vicius°
As any feend that lith in helle adoun,
Yet he, as telleth us Swetonius,   2465
This wyde world hadde in subjeccioun,
Bothe est and west, south, and septemtrioun°.
Of rubies, saphires, and of peerles° white
Were alle his clothes brouded° up and doun,
For he in gemmes greetly gan delite.   2470

Moore delicaat°, moore pompous of array,
Moore proud was nevere emperour than he.
That ilke clooth° that he hadde wered o day
After that tyme he nolde° it nevere see.
Nettes of gold threed hadde he greet plentee   2475
To fisshe in Tybre whan hym liste° pleye.
His lustes° were al lawe in his decree
For Fortune as his freend hym wolde obeye.

2409 **litel out of,** *a little way from,* **tour,** *tower* 2414 **Swiche briddes,** *such birds* 2415 **Dampned,** *condemned* 2417 **suggestioun,** *accusation* 2419 **wise,** *manner* 2420 **mete,** *food* 2421 **unnethe,** *scarcely* 2422 **therwithal,** *also* 2423 **bifil,** *it happened* 2424 **wont,** *usually* 2425 **gayler,** *jailer* 2426 **spak,** *spoke* 2427 **anon,** *immediately,* **fil,** *came* 2428 **doon,** *make* 2429 **wroght,** *made* 2433 **potage,** *soup* 2437 **wombe,** *stomach* 2438 **me were levere,** *to me is more desirable* 2440 **fadres barm,** *father's*

lap 2441 **moot,** *must* 2443 **deed it say,** *saw him dead* 2445 **wyte,** *blame* 2447 **wende,** *thought* 2448 **gnow,** *gnawed* 2451 **yaf,** *gave* 2452 **ynogh,** *sufficiently* 2455 **starf,** *died* 2457 **carf,** *carved* 2459 **here,** *hear* 2461 **highte,** *is named,* **devyse,** *describe* 2463 **vicius,** *wicked* 2467 **septemtrioun,** *north* 2468 **peerles,** *pearls* 2469 **brouded,** *embroidered* 2471 **delicaat,** *fond of luxury* 2473 **ilke clooth,** *same clothing* 2474 **nolde,** *wished not* 2476 **liste,** *wished to* 2477 **lustes,** *desires*

2416 **Roger,** Ruggiero, archbishop of Pisa, Ugolino's enemy, then collaborator; Dante does not mention that he accused Ugolino. 2461 **Dant,** Dante; see 2407n above. 2463–65 **Nero . . . Swetonius,** the Roman historian Suetonius records the life of Nero in *De vita Caesarum* (Lives of the Caesars), Book 1, but Chaucer's details come from *RR* 6183ff., a section on Fortune, which influenced various parts of *MkT;* see, e.g., 2727n, 2758n, and also *NPT* 7.3370n. 2476 **Tybre,** Tiber, river in Rome.

He Rome brende° for his delicasie°;
The senatours he slow° upon a day   2480
To heere how men wolde wepe and crie;
And slow his brother, and by his suster lay.
His mooder made° he in pitous array°,
For he hire wombe slitte to biholde
Where he conceyved was—so weilaway°,   2485
That he so litel of his mooder tolde°!

No teere out of his eyen for that sighte
Ne cam, but seyde, "A fair womman was she."
Greet wonder is how that he koude or myghte
Be domesman° of hire dede beautee.   2490
The wyn to bryngen hym comanded he,
And drank anon—noon oother wo he made.
Whan myght is joyned unto crueltee,
Allas, to depe° wol the venym wade°.

In yowthe a maister° hadde this emperour   2495
To teche hym letterure° and curteisye,
For of moralitee he was the flour°,
As in his tyme, but if° bookes lye,
And whil this maister hadde of hym maistrye°,
He maked hym so konnyng° and so sowple°   2500
That longe tyme it was er tirannye
Or any vice dorste° on hym uncowple°.

This Seneca, of which that I devyse°,
By cause Nero hadde of hym swich drede,
For he fro vices wolde hym ay chastise°   2505
Discreetly, as by word and nat by dede:
"Sire," wolde he seyn, "an emperour moot nede°
Be vertuous and hate tirannye";
For which he in a bath made hym to blede
On bothe his armes, til he moste° dye.   2510

This Nero hadde eek of acustumaunce°
In youthe agayns° his maister for to ryse°,
Which afterward hym thoughte greet grevaunce;

Therfore he made hym dyen in this wise.
But natheless this Seneca the wise   2515
Chees° in a bath to dye in this manere
Rather than han any oother tormentise°.
And thus hath Nero slayn his maister deere.

Now fil° it so that Fortune liste° no lenger
The hye pryde of Nero to cherice°,   2520
For though that he was strong, yet was she
      strenger.
She thoughte thus, "By God, I am to nyce°
To sette a man that is fulfild of vice
In heigh degree, and emperour hym calle.
By God, out of his sete° I wol hym trice°.   2525
Whan he leest weneth°, sonnest shal he falle."

The peple roos upon° hym on a nyght
For his defaute°, and whan he it espied
Out of his dores anon° he hath hym dight°
Allone, and ther° he wende° han been allied°   2530
He knokked faste, and ay the moore he cried
The fastere shette° they the dores alle.
Tho wiste° he wel he hadde himself mysgyed°,
And wente his wey; no lenger dorste° he calle.

The peple cride and rombled° up and doun,   2535
That with his erys° herde he how they seyde,
"Where is this false tiraunt, this Neroun?"
For fere almoost out of his wit he breyde°,
And to his goddes pitously he preyde
For socour°, but it myghte nat bityde°.   2540
For drede of this, hym thoughte that he deyde,
And ran into a gardyn hym to hyde.

And in this gardyn foond he cherles tweye°
That seten by a fyr ful greet and reed.
And to thise cherles two he gan to preye   2545
To sleen hym and to girden of° his heed,
That° to his body whan that he were deed

2479 **brende**, *burned*, **delicasie**, *pleasure* 2480 **slow**, *killed* 2483 **made**, *put*, **array**, *condition* 2485 **weilaway**, *alas* 2486 **tolde**, *thought* 2490 **domesman**, *judge* 2494 **to depe**, *too deep*, **wade**, *go* 2495 **maister**, *teacher* 2496 **letterure**, *literature* 2497 **flour**, *apex* (flower) 2498 **but if**, *unless* 2499 **maistrye**, *control* 2500 **konnyng**, *wise*, **sowple**, *compliant* 2502 **dorste**, *dared*, **uncowple**, *attack* 2503 **devyse**, *describe* 2505 **ay chastise**, *always criticize* 2507 **moot nede**, *must necessarily* 2510 **moste**, *must* 2511 **of acustumaunce**, *by custom* 2512 **agayns**, i.e., *in deference to*, **ryse**, *stand up* 2516 **Chees**, *chose* 2517 **tormentise**, *torment* 2519 **fil**, *happened*, **liste**, *wished* 2520 **cherice**, *protect* 2522 **to nyce**, *too foolish* 2525 **sete**, *position*, **trice**, *snatch* 2526 **weneth**, *expects* 2527 **roos upon**, *rebelled against* 2528 **defaute**, *wickedness* 2529 **anon**, *soon*, **dight**, *gone* 2530 **ther**, *where*, **wende**, *thought*, **han been allied**, *to have allies* 2532 **fastere shette**, *more tightly shut* 2533 **Tho wiste**, *then knew*, **mysgyed**, *misguided* 2534 **dorste**, *dared* 2535 **rombled**, *murmured* 2536 **erys**, *ears* 2538 **breyde**, *went* 2540 **socour**, *help*, **bityde**, *happen* 2543 **cherles tweye**, *two commoners* 2546 **girden of**, *cut off* 2547 **That**, *so that*

2503 **Seneca**, Stoic moral philosopher, dramatist, and tutor of Nero, who caused him to be bled to death (65 CE); Seneca was accused of conspiring against Nero; he selected his own manner of execution. 2533 In El, Hg, and related MSS, line 2541 is here as well as in its proper place.

Were no despit° ydoon for his defame°.
Hymself he slow°, he koude° no bettre reed°,
Of which Fortune lough° and hadde a game. 2550

DE OLOFERNO

Was nevere capitayn under a kyng
That regnes mo° putte in subjeccioun,
Ne strenger was in feeld of alle thyng°,
As in his tyme, ne gretter of renoun,
Ne moore pompous in heigh presumpcioun 2555
Than Oloferne, which Fortune ay kiste°
So likerously°, and ladde hym up and doun
Til that his heed was of er° that he wiste°.

Nat oonly that this world hadde hym in awe
For lesynge of° richesse or libertee, 2560
But he made every man reneyen his lawe°.
"Nabugodonosor was god," seyde hee.
"Noon oother god sholde adoured bee."
Agayns his heeste° no wight dorste° trespace
Save° in Bethulia, a strong citee, 2565
Where Eliachim a preest was of that place.

But taak kepe of° the deeth of Oloferne:
Amydde° his hoost° he dronke lay a-nyght,
Withinne his tente, large as is a berne°,
And yet, for al his pompe and al his myght, 2570
Judith, a womman, as he lay upright°
Slepynge, his heed of smoot° and from his tente
Ful pryvely° she stal° from every wight°,
And with his heed unto hir toun she wente.

DE REGE ANTHIOCHO ILLUSTRI

What nedeth it of Kyng Anthiochus 2575
To telle his hye roial magestee,
His hye pride, his werkes venymus°?

For swich another was ther noon as he.
Rede which that° he was in Machabee,
And rede the proude wordes that he seyde, 2580
And why he fil fro heigh prosperitee,
And in° an hill how wrecchedly he deyde.

Fortune hym hadde enhaunced so in pride
That verraily° he wende° he myghte attayne
Unto the sterres upon every syde, 2585
And in balance weyen° ech montayne,
And alle the floodes of the see restrayne.
And Goddes peple hadde he moost in hate;
Hem wolde he sleen° in torment and in payne
Wenynge° that God ne myghte his pride
abate°. 2590

And for° that Nichanore and Thymothee
Of° Jewes weren venquysshed myghtily,
Unto the Jewes swich an hate hadde he
That he bad° greithen° his chaar° ful hastily,
And swoor and seyde ful despitously° 2595
Unto Jerusalem he wolde eftsoone°
To wreken° his ire° on it ful cruelly,
But of his purpos he was let° ful soone.

God for his manace° hym so soore smoot°
With invisible wounde, ay° incurable, 2600
That in his guttes carf° it so and boot°
That his peynes weren importable°.
And certeinly the wreche° was resonable
For many a mannes guttes dide he peyne.
But from his purpos cursed and dampnable, 2605
For° al his smert°, he wolde hym nat restreyne,

But bad anon apparaillen° his hoost°;
And sodeynly, er he was of it war,
God daunted° al his pride and al his boost.
For he so soore fil° out of his char° 2610

2548 despit, *insult*, defame, *bad reputation* 2549 slow, *killed*, koude, *knew*, reed, *plan* 2550 lough, *laughed* 2552 regnes mo, *more kingdoms* 2553 feeld of alle thyng, *battlefield in any way* 2556 ay kiste, *always kissed* 2557 likerously, *wantonly* 2558 of er, *off before*, wiste, *knew* 2560 lesynge of, *(fear of) losing* 2561 reneyen his lawe, *renounce his religion* 2564 heeste, *command*, wight dorste, *person dared* 2565 Save, *except* 2567 taak kepe of, *pay attention to* 2568 Amydde, *in the middle*, hoost, *army* 2569 berne, *barn* 2571 upright, *on his back* 2572 of smoot, *cut off* 2573 Ful pryvely, *very secretly*, stal, *slipped away*, wight, *person* 2577 venymus, *poisonous* 2579 Rede which that, *read what kind*

2582 in, *on* 2584 verraily, *truly*, wende, *thought* 2586 weyen, *weigh* 2589 Hem wolde he sleen, *he wished to slay them* 2590 Wenynge, *believing*, abate, *lessen* 2591 for, *because* 2592 Of, *by* 2594 bad, *commanded*, greithen, *(to) prepare*, chaar, *chariot* 2595 despitously, *scornfully* 2596 eftsoone, *(go) immediately* 2597 wreken, *inflict*, ire, *anger* 2598 let, *prevented* 2599 manace, *threats*, soore smoot, *painfully struck* 2600 ay, *forever* 2601 carf, *cut*, boot, *bit* 2602 importable, *intolerable* 2603 wreche, *punishment* 2606 For, *despite*, smert, *pain* 2607 bad anon apparaillen, *ordered immediately to prepare*, hoost, *army* 2609 daunted, *defeated* 2610 fil, *fell*, char, *chariot*

2556 **Oloferne,** Holofernes served Nebuchadnazzar, king of Assyria, and was killed by Judith to protect the Jewish people. Chaucer's account is from the apocryphal book of Judith, although he adds the concern with Fortune. 2565 **Bethulia,** unidentified biblical city. 2566 **Eliachim,** encourages resistance to Holofernes in Judith 4; sometimes thought to be author of the book of Judith. 2575 **Anthiochus,** Antiochus, king of Syria (175–63 BCE). 2579 **Machabee,** Chaucer's account is from 2 Maccabees 9, where God punishes Antiochus for attacking the Jews. 2591 **Nichanore and Thymothee,** Nicanor and Timothy, whose defeats by the Jews anger Antiochus; 2 Maccabees 9.3.

That it his limes° and his skyn to-tar°,
So that he neyther myghte go ne ryde,
But in a chayer° men aboute hym bar°
Al forbrused° bothe bak and syde.

The wreche° of God hym smoot° so cruelly   2615
That thurgh his body wikked wormes crepte,
And therwithal° he stank so horribly
That noon of al his meynee° that hym kepte,
Wheither so he wook, or ellis slepte,
Ne myghte noght the stynk of hym endure.   2620
In this meschief° he wayled and eek wepte,
And knew God lord of every creature.

To al his hoost and to hymself also
Ful wlatsom° was the stynk of his careyne°.
No man ne myghte hym bere° to ne fro.   2625
And in this stynk and this horrible peyne
He starf° ful wrecchedly in° a monteyne.
Thus hath this robbour and this homycide°,
That many a man made to wepe and pleyne°,
Swich gerdoun° as bilongeth unto° pryde.   2630

DE ALEXANDRO

   The storie of Alisaundre is so commune°
That every wight° that hath discrecioun
Hath herd somwhat or al of his fortune.
This wyde world, as in conclusioun°,
He wan by strengthe, or for his hye renoun°   2635
They weren glad for pees unto hym sende°.
The pride of man and beest he leyde adoun°
Wher so he cam unto the worldes ende.

Comparisoun myghte nevere yet been maked
Bitwixe hym and another conquerour   2640
For al this world for drede of hym hath quaked°.
He was of knyghthod and of fredom° flour°.

Fortune hym made the heir of hire° honour.
Save° wyn and wommen, no thing myghte aswage°
His hye entente in armes and labour,   2645
So was he ful of leonyn° corage.

What pris° were it to hym, though I yow tolde
Of Darius and an hundred thousand mo
Of kynges, princes, erles, dukes bolde
Whiche he conquered, and broghte hem
        into wo?   2650
I seye, as fer as man may ryde or go
The world was his—what sholde I moore devyse°?
For though I write or tolde yow everemo
Of his knyghthode, it myghte nat suffise.

Twelf yeer he regned, as seith Machabee.   2655
Philippes sone of Macidoyne he was,
That first was kyng in Grece the contree.
O worthy, gentil Alisandre, allas,
That evere sholde fallen swich a cas°!
Empoysoned of thyn owene folk thou weere;   2660
Thy *sys* Fortune hath turned into *aas*,
And for thee ne weep she never a teere.

Who shal me yeven° teeris to compleyne°
The deeth of gentillesse° and of franchise°,
That al the world weelded° in his demeyne°,   2665
And yet hym thoughte it myghte nat suffise?
So ful was his corage of heigh emprise°.
Allas, who shal me helpe to endite°
False Fortune, and poyson to despise,
The whiche two of al this wo I wyte°?   2670

DE JULIO CESARE

   By wisedom, manhede, and by greet labour,
From humble bed to roial magestee
Up roos he Julius, the conquerour,

2611 **limes,** *limbs,* **to-tar,** *tore to shreds* 2613 **chayer,** *chair,* **bar,** *bore*
2614 **Al forbrused,** *completely bruised* 2615 **wreche,** *vengeance,* **smoot,**
struck 2617 **therwithal,** *with that* 2618 **meynee,** *household* 2621
meschief, *bad fortune* 2624 **wlatsom,** *loathsome,* **careyne,** *body* 2625
bere, *carry* 2627 **starf,** *died,* **in,** *on* 2628 **homycide,** *murderer* 2629
pleyne, *lament* 2630 **Swich gerdoun,** *such reward,* **bilongeth unto,** *is
appropriate to* 2631 **commune,** *well known* 2632 **wight,** *person* 2634
as in conclusioun, *in sum* 2635 **hye renoun,** *exalted fame* 2636 **for**

pees unto hym sende, *to send* (messages of) *peace to him* 2637 **leyde
adoun,** *put down* 2641 **quaked,** *trembled* 2642 **fredom,** *generosity,*
flour, *the apex* (flower) 2643 **hire,** *their* 2644 **Save,** *except,* **aswage,** *reduce* 2646 **leonyn,** *lionlike* 2647 **pris,** *praise* 2652 **devyse,** *describe* 2659
swich a cas, *such a situation* 2663 **yeven,** *give,* **compleyne,** *lament* 2664
gentillesse, *nobility,* **franchise,** *magnanimity* 2665 **weelded,** *controlled,*
demeyne, *dominion* 2667 **emprise,** *enterprise* 2668 **endite,** *accuse* 2670
wyte, *blame*

2631 **Alisaundre,** Alexander the Great (356–23 BCE), king of Macedon. No specific source for Chaucer's account has been identified. 2648
Darius, Darius III of Persia, routed by Alexander in 333 and 331 BCE. 2655 **Machabee,** 1 Maccabees 1.1–7. 2656 **Philippes sone,** Philip II of
Macedon, Alexander's father, consolidated the Greek states through conquest. 2660 **Empoysoned,** Alexander died of a fever, although poi-
son is blamed in a number of literary accounts. 2661 *sys . . . aas,* six . . . ace, highest and lowest dice throws. 2673 **Julius,** Julius Caesar (102?–44
BCE), Roman statesman and general. Chaucer's account is too general to indicate a specific source, and many of its inaccuracies were medieval commonplaces, e.g., Caesar was not humbly born (line 2672) and never became emperor (line 2677).

That wan° al th'occident° by land and see,
By strengthe of hand, or elles by tretee°,   2675
And unto Rome made hem tributarie.
And sitthe° of Rome the emperour was he
Til that Fortune weex° his adversarie.

O myghty Cesar, that in Thessalie
Agayn° Pompeus, fader thyn in lawe,   2680
That of the orient hadde al the chivalrie°
As fer as that the day bigynneth dawe,
Thou thurgh thy knyghthod hast hem take and
          slawe°,
Save° fewe folk that with Pompeus fledde,
Thurgh which thou puttest al th'orient°
          in awe.   2685
Thanke Fortune, that so wel thee spedde°.

But now a litel while I wol biwaille
This Pompeus, this noble governour
Of Rome, which that fleigh at° this bataille.
I seye, oon of his men, a fals traitour,   2690
His heed of smoot, to wynnen hym favour
Of Julius, and hym the heed he broghte.
Allas, Pompeye, of th'orient conquerour,
That Fortune unto swich a fyn° thee broghte.

    To Rome agayn repaireth° Julius   2695
With his triumphe, lauriat ful hye;
But on a tyme Brutus Cassius,
That evere hadde of his hye estaat° envye,
Ful prively hath maad conspiracye
Agayns this Julius in subtil wise,   2700
And caste° the place in which he sholde dye
With boydekyns°, as I shal yow devyse°.

This Julius to the Capitolie wente
Upon a day, as he was wont° to goon,

And in the Capitolie anon hym hente°   2705
This false Brutus and his othere foon°,
And stiked hym with boydekyns anoon
With many a wounde, and thus they lete
          hym lye;
But nevere gronte° he at no strook but oon,
Or elles at two, but if his storie lye.   2710

So manly was this Julius of herte,
And so wel lovede estaatly honestee°,
That though his deedly woundes soore smerte°,
His mantel° over his hypes° castyth he
For no man sholde seen his privetee°,   2715
And as he lay of diyng° in a traunce,
And wiste verraily° that deed was hee,
Of honestee° yet hadde he remembraunce.

Lucan, to thee this storie I recomende°,
And to Swetoun, and to Valerius also,   2720
That of this storie writen word and ende°,
How that to thise grete conqueroures two
Fortune was first freend and sitthe° foo.
No man ne truste upon hire favour longe,
But have hire in awayt° for everemoo.   2725
Witnesse on alle thise conqueroures stronge.

CRESUS

    This riche Cresus, whilom° kyng of Lyde,
Of which Cresus Cirus soore hym dradde°,
Yet was he caught amyddes° al his pryde,
And to be brent° men to the fyr hym ladde°.   2730
But swich a reyn doun fro the welkne shadde°
That slow° the fyr and made hym to escape;
But to be war° no grace° yet he hadde,
Til Fortune on the galwes° made hym gape°.

2674 **wan**, *conquered*, **occident**, *Western world* 2675 **tretee**, *treaty* 2677 **sitthe**, *afterward* 2678 **weex**, *became* 2680 **Agayn**, *against* 2681 **chivalrie**, *knights* 2683 **take and slawe**, *taken and killed* 2684 **Save**, *except* 2685 **th'orient**, *the Eastern world* 2686 **spedde**, *helped* 2689 **fleigh at**, *fled from* 2694 **fyn**, *end* 2695 **repaireth**, *returns* 2698 **estaat**, *rank* 2701 **caste**, *planned* 2702 **boydekyns**, *daggers*, **devyse**, *describe* 2704 **wont**, *accustomed* 2705 **anon hym hente**, *immediately seized him* 2706 **foon**, *foes* 2709 **gronte**, *groaned* 2712 **estaatly honestee**, *honorable decency*

2713 **soore smerte**, *hurt grievously* 2714 **mantel**, *cloak*, **hypes**, *hips* 2715 **privetee**, *private parts* 2716 **of diyng**, *dying* 2717 **wiste verraily**, *knew truly* 2718 **honestee**, *decency* 2719 **recomende**, *submit* 2721 **word and ende**, *beginning and end* 2723 **sitthe**, *afterward* 2725 **have hire in awayt**, *keep watch on her* 2727 **whilom**, *once* 2728 **dradde**, *feared* 2729 **amyddes**, *in the middle of* 2730 **brent**, *burned*, **ladde**, *led* 2731 **welkne shadde**, *sky poured* 2732 **slow**, *killed* 2733 **war**, *warned*, **grace**, *favor* 2734 **galwes**, *gallows*, **gape**, *stare*

2679–80 **Thessalie . . . Pompeus**, in 48 BCE, near the city of Pharsala in Thessaly, a region in Greece, Caesar defeated his longtime competitor, Pompey the Great, famous for his conquests in the East. He was Caesar's son-in-law, not father-in-law; this confusion predates Chaucer. 2682 **bigynneth dawe**, begins to dawn, i.e., from where the sun rises. 2691 **of smoot**, cut off; actually Pompey was stabbed in Egypt after fleeing Thessaly. 2696 **lauriat**, crowned with laurel leaves, ancient symbol of victory. 2697 **Brutus Cassius**, Brutus and Cassius were two of the conspirators that killed Caesar; here (and in other medieval accounts) they are conflated into one person. 2705 **Capitolie**, Caesar was killed in the Curia, not the Capitoline Hill; another common medieval error. 2719–20 **Lucan . . . Swetoun . . . Valerius**, three who wrote about Caesar: Lucan, *Pharsalia* (The Story of Pharsala); Suetonius, *De Vita Caesarum* (Lives of the Caesars); Valerius Maximus, *Factorum ac Dictorum Memorabilium* (Memorable Deeds and Sayings). 2727 **Cresus**, Croesus, king of Lydia. Chaucer's account comes from *Bo* 2.pr2.60–65 and *RR* 6489ff. 2728 **Cirus**, Cyrus the Great, king of Persia, was threatened by Croesus but defeated him in 546 BCE.

Whanne he escaped was, he kan nat stente°   2735
For to bigynne a newe werre agayn.
He wende° wel, for that° Fortune hym sente
Swich hap° that he escaped thurgh the rayn,
That of° his foos he myghte nat be slayn,
And eek a swevene° upon a nyght he mette°,   2740
Of which he was so proud and eek so fayn°
That in vengeance he al his herte sette.

Upon a tree he was, as that hym thoughte,
Ther° Juppiter hym wessh°, bothe bak and syde,
And Phebus eek a fair towaille° hym broughte   2745
To dryen hym with. And therfore wax° his pryde,
And to his doghter that stood hym bisyde,
Which that he knew in heigh sentence
     habounde°,
He bad hire telle hym what it signyfyde,
And she his dreem bigan right thus
     expounde: 2750

"The tree," quod she, "the galwes° is to meene°,
And Juppiter bitokneth° snow and reyn,
And Phebus with his towaille so clene,
Tho been the sonne stremes for to seyn°.
Thou shalt anhanged° be, fader, certeyn;   2755
Reyn shal thee wasshe, and sonne shal thee drye."
Thus warned hym ful plat° and eek ful pleyn
His doghter, which that called was Phanye.

Anhanged was Cresus, the proude kyng;
His roial trone° myghte hym nat availle°.   2760
Tragedies noon oother maner° thyng
Ne kan° in syngyng crie ne biwaille
But that Fortune alwey wole assaille°
With unwar strook° the regnes° that been
     proude;
For whan men trusteth hire, thanne wol she
     faille,   2765
And covere hire brighte face with a clowde.

Explicit Tragedia.

Heere stynteth the Knyght the Monk of his tale.

2735 stente, *stop* **2737 wende,** *believed,* **for that,** *because* **2738 Swich hap,** *such chance* **2739 of,** *by* **2740 swevene,** *dream,* **mette,** *dreamed* **2741 fayn,** *pleased* **2744 Ther,** *where,* **wessh,** *washed* **2745 towaille,** *towel* **2746 wax,** *grew* **2748 in heigh sentence habounde,** *abounded in high wisdom* **2751 galwes,** *gallows,* **is to meene,** *signifies* **2752**

bitokneth, *symbolizes* **2754 Tho** *then,* **been the sonne stremes for to seyn,** *stand for the sun rays* **2755 anhanged,** *hanged* **2757 plat,** *clearly* **2760 trone,** *throne,* **availle,** *help* **2761 maner,** *kind of* **2762 Ne kan,** *do not* **2763 assaille,** *attack* **2764 unwar strook,** *unexpected stroke,* **regnes,** *kingdoms*

2744 Juppiter, Jupiter was god of sky and rains. **2745 Phebus,** Phoebus Apollo, god of the sun. **2758 Phanye,** Phania, Croesus's daughter in *RR* 6514. **2761–64** Tragedies cannot lament or bewail in singing any kind of thing except that Fortune will attack with unexpected stroke the reigns that are proud. Repeats the medieval definition of tragedy, introduced at lines 1973ff. and 1991–94 above, helping to frame *MkT*. **2766 clowde,** echoed at *NPT* 7.2782 below; the image may derive from *Bo* 1.pr2.26, 3.m11.10, etc.

NUN'S PRIEST'S TALE

PROLOGUE

The Prologe of the Nonnes Preestes Tale.

"Hoo," quod the Knyght, "good sire, namoore
  of this!
That° ye han seyd is right ynough°, ywis°,
And muchel moore, for litel hevynesse°
Is right ynough to muche° folk, I gesse.   2770
I seye for me, it is a greet disese°,
Where as men han been in greet welthe and
  ese,
To heeren of hire sodeyn° fal, allas.
And the contrarie is joye and greet solas°,
As whan a man hath been in poure estaat°   2775
And clymbeth up and wexeth° fortunat,
And there abideth° in prosperitee.
Swich° thyng is gladsom°, as it thynketh me,
And of swich thyng were goodly for to telle."
    "Ye," quod oure Hooste, "by Seint Poules
  belle,   2780

Ye seye right sooth°. This Monk he clappeth
  lowde°.
He spak how Fortune covered with a clowde
I noot° nevere what; and also of a tragedie
Right now ye herde; and pardee°, no remedie
It is for to biwaille ne compleyne°   2785
That that° is doon, and als° it is a peyne,
As ye han seyd, to heere of hevynesse.
    "Sire Monk, namoore of this, so God yow
  blesse!
Youre tale anoyeth al this compaignye.
Swich talkyng is nat worth a boterflye°,   2790
For therinne is ther no desport° ne game.
Wherfore, sire Monk, daun Piers by youre
  name,
I pray° yow hertely° telle us somwhat elles;
For sikerly°, nere° clynkyng of youre belles

2768 **That,** *what,* **right ynough,** *plenty,* **ywis,** *indeed* 2769 **hevynesse,**
sadness 2770 **muche,** *many* 2771 **disese,** *discomfort* 2773 **hire sodeyn,**
their sudden 2774 **solas,** *pleasure* 2775 **poure estaat,** *miserable condition*
2776 **wexeth,** *grows* 2777 **abideth,** *stays* 2778 **Swich,** *such,* **gladsom,**
pleasing 2781 **right sooth,** *very truly,* **clappeth lowde,** *chatters loudly*

2783 **noot,** *know not* 2784 **pardee,** *by God* 2785 **compleyne,** *lament*
2786 **That that,** *that which,* **als,** *also* 2790 **boterflye,** *butterfly* 2791
desport, *entertainment* 2793 **pray,** *ask,* **hertely,** *earnestly* 2794 **sikerly,**
certainly, **nere,** *(if it)* *were not for*

2767 **Knyght,** a shorter, probably earlier version of the *NPP* (lacking lines 2771–90) exists in fourteen MSS; in some of these the Host
interrupts the Monk. Chaucer's expansion emphasizes the one-sidedness of the Monk's tragedies. 2780 **Seint Poules belle,** the bell of St.
Paul's Cathedral, London. 2782 **covered with a clowde,** this echoes *MkT* 7.2766. 2792 **daun Piers,** master Peter; why the Host did not know
or did not use the Monk's name at *MkT* 7.1929–30 has never been satisfactorily explained. 2794 **belles,** the jingling of the Monk's bridle
bells is referred to in *GP* 1.169–70.

That on youre bridel hange on every syde,   2795
By Hevene Kyng that for us alle dyde°,
I sholde er° this han fallen doun for sleep,
Althogh the slough° had never been so deep.
Thanne hadde youre tale al be toold in
        veyn,
For certeinly, as that thise clerkes seyn,   2800
Where as a man may have noon audience,
Noght helpeth it° to tellen his sentence°.
And wel I woot° the substance° is in me,
If any thyng shal wel reported be.
Sire, sey somwhat of huntyng, I yow preye.”   2805
    “Nay,” quod this Monk, “I have no lust° to
        pleye.
Now lat another telle, as I have toold.”

Thanne spak oure Hoost with rude speche and
        boold,
And seyde unto the Nonnes Preest anon°,
“Com neer, thou preest, com hyder°, thou sir
        John!   2810
Telle us swich thyng as may oure hertes glade°.
Be blithe°, though thou ryde upon a jade°.
What thogh° thyn hors be bothe foul and lene?
If he wol serve thee, rekke° nat a bene°.
Looke that thyn herte be murie° everemo.”   2815
    “Yis, sire,” quod he, “yis, Hoost, so moot I go°.
But I be° myrie, ywis° I wol be blamed.”
And right anon his tale he hath attamed°,
And thus he seyde unto us everichon°,
This sweete preest, this goodly man sir John.   2820

Explicit.

Heere bigynneth the Nonnes Preestes Tale of the Cok and Hen, Chauntecleer and Pertelote.

    A poure wydwe° somdeel stape° in age
Was whilom° dwellyng in a narwe° cotage,
Biside a grove, stondynge in a dale°.
This wydwe, of which I telle yow my tale,
Syn thilke° day that she was last a wyf,   2825
In pacience ladde° a ful symple lyf.
For litel was hir catel° and hir rente°,
By housbondrie° of swich° as God hire sente
She foond° hirself and eek hir doghtren° two.
Thre large sowes hadde she and namo°,   2830
Three keen°, and eek a sheep that highte° Malle.
Ful° sooty was hir bour and eek hir halle,
In which she eet° ful many a sklendre° meel.
Of poynaunt° sauce hir neded never a deel°—
No deyntee morsel passed thurgh hir throte.   2835
Hir diete was accordant to hir cote°.

Repleccioun° ne made hire nevere sik;
Attempree° diete was al hir phisik°,
And exercise, and hertes suffisaunce°.
The goute lette hire nothyng for to daunce°,   2840
N'apoplexie° shente° nat hir heed.
No wyn ne drank she, neither whit ne reed.
Hir bord° was served moost with whit and blak—
Milk and broun breed, in which she foond no
        lak°,
Seynd° bacoun, and somtyme an ey° or tweye°,   2845
For she was, as it were, a maner deye°.
    A yeerd° she hadde enclosed al aboute
With stikkes, and a drye dych withoute,
In which she hadde a cok hight° Chauntecleer.
In al the land of crowyng nas° his peer.   2850
His voys was murier than the murie orgon°

2796 **dyde,** died 2797 **er,** before 2798 **slough,** mud 2802 **Noght helpeth it,** it accomplishes nothing, **sentence,** meaning 2803 **woot,** know, **substance,** essential meaning 2806 **lust,** desire 2809 **anon,** immediately 2810 **hyder,** here 2811 **glade,** gladden 2812 **blithe,** happy, **jade,** nag 2813 **What thogh,** so what if 2814 **rekke,** care, **bene,** bean 2815 **murie,** merry 2816 **so moot I go,** as I may prosper 2817 **But I be,** unless I am, **ywis,** surely 2818 **attamed,** begun 2819 **everichon,** every one 2821 **wydwe,** widow, **somdeel stape,** somewhat advanced 2822 **whilom,** once, **narwe,** small 2823 **dale,** valley 2825 **Syn thilke,** since that 2826 **ladde,** led 2827 **catel,** possessions, **rente,** income 2828 **housbondrie,** careful treatment,

swich, such 2829 **foond,** provided for, **doghtren,** daughters 2830 **namo,** no more 2831 **keen,** cows, **highte,** was named 2832 **Ful,** very 2833 **eet,** ate, **sklendre,** sparse 2834 **poynaunt,** tangy, **deel,** bit 2836 **cote,** cottage 2837 **Repleccioun,** overeating 2838 **Attempree,** moderate, **al hir phisik,** her only medical treatment 2839 **hertes suffisaunce,** heart's content 2840 **lette hire nothyng for to daunce,** hindered her not at all from dancing 2841 **N'apoplexie,** nor apoplexy (a stroke), **shente,** injured 2843 **bord,** table 2844 **lak,** fault 2845 **Seynd,** smoked, **ey,** egg, **tweye,** two 2846 **maner deye,** kind of dairywoman 2847 **yeerd,** yard 2849 **hight,** called 2850 **nas,** none was 2851 **murie orgon,** merry organ

---

2832 **bour . . . halle,** bedroom . . . main room; dignified terms for a humble dwelling, perhaps implying that such extravagances are unnecessary. 2834–35 **sauce . . . morsel,** the widow's diet contrasts directly with the description of the Prioress at table, GP 1.128–29. 2840 **goute,** gout is a disease characterized by inflammation of the joints (often the feet), once thought to result from dietary excess.

On messe-dayes that in the chirche gon.
Wel sikerer° was his crowyng in his logge°,
Than is a clokke or an abbey orlogge°.
By nature° he knew ech ascencioun   2855
Of the equynoxial in thilke toun°;
For whan degrees fiftene weren ascended,
Thanne crew° he that it myghte nat been
    amended°.
His coomb was redder than the fyn° coral,
And batailled° as it were a castel wal;   2860
His byle° was blak, and as the jeet° it shoon°;
Lyk asure° were his legges and his toon°;
His nayles whitter than the lylye flour;
And lyk the burned° gold was his colour.
This gentil cok hadde in his governaunce   2865
Sevene hennes for to doon al his plesaunce°,
Whiche were his sustres° and his paramours°,
And wonder lyk° to hym as of colours;
Of whiche the faireste hewed° on hir throte
Was cleped° faire damoysele Pertelote.   2870
Curteys° she was, discreet, and debonaire°,
And compaignable, and bar° hyrself so faire,
Syn thilke° day that she was seven nyght oold,
That trewely she hath the herte in hoold
Of Chauntecleer, loken° in every lith°.   2875
He loved hire so that wel was hym therwith°.
But swich a joye was it to here hem synge,
Whan that the brighte sonne bigan to
    sprynge,
In sweete accord°, "My lief is faren in londe"—
For thilke° tyme, as I have understonde,   2880
Beestes and briddes° koude speke and synge.
    And so bifel° that in a dawenynge,
As Chauntecleer among his wyves alle
Sat on his perche that was in the halle—
And next hym sat this faire Pertelote—   2885

This Chauntecleer gan gronen° in his throte,
As man that in his dreem is drecched soore°.
And whan that Pertelote thus herde hym roore°,
She was agast° and seyde, "O herte deere,
What eyleth yow to grone in this manere?   2890
Ye been a verray° sleper; fy, for shame!"
    And he answerde and seyde thus, "Madame,
I pray yow that ye take it nat agrief°.
By God, me mette° I was in swich meschief°
Right now that yet myn herte is soore
    afright.   2895
Now God," quod he, "my swevene recche aright°,
And kepe my body out of foul prisoun!
Me mette how that I romed up and doun
Withinne our yeerd, wheer as I saugh a beest
Was lyk an hound, and wolde han° maad
    areest   2900
Upon my body, and wolde han had me deed.
His colour was bitwixe yelow and reed,
And tipped was his tayl and bothe his eeris°
With blak, unlyk the remenant° of his heeris;
His snowte smal, with glowynge eyen tweye°.   2905
Yet of his look for feere almoost I deye°;
This caused me my gronyng, doutelees."
    "Avoy°," quod she, "fy on yow, hertelees°!
Allas," quod she, "for by that God above,
Now han ye lost myn herte and al my love.   2910
I kan nat love a coward, by my feith!
For certes°, what so° any womman seith,
We alle desiren, if it myghte bee,
To han housbondes hardy°, wise, and free°,
And secree°, and no nygard°, ne no fool,   2915
Ne hym that is agast° of every tool°,
Ne noon avauntour°. By that God above,
How dorste ye seyn°, for shame, unto youre love
That any thyng myghte make yow aferd?

2853 sikerer, *more reliable*, logge, *lodging* 2854 orlogge, *chiming clock* 2855 By nature, *instinctively* 2856 thilke toun, *that town* 2858 crew, *crowed*, amended, *improved upon* 2859 fyn, *fine* 2860 batailled, *notched like a battlement* 2861 byle, *beak*, jeet, *dark black gem*, shoon, *shined* 2862 asure, *blue gem*, toon, *toes* 2864 burned, *polished* 2866 plesaunce, *pleasure* 2867 sustres, *sisters*, paramours, *mistresses* 2868 wonder lyk, *wondrously like* 2869 hewed, *colored* 2870 cleped, *called* 2871 Curteys, *courtly*, debonaire, *gracious* 2872 bar, *carried* 2873 Syn thilke, *since that* 2875 loken, *locked*, lith, *limb* 2876 therwith, *with that* 2879 accord, *harmony* 2880 thilke, *at that* 2881 briddes, *birds* 2882

bifel, *it happened* 2886 gan gronen, *began to groan* 2887 drecched soore, *deeply troubled* 2888 roore, *cry out* 2889 agast, *upset* 2891 verray, *sound* 2893 take it nat agrief, *be not upset* 2894 me mette, *I dreamed*, swich mischief, *such misfortune* 2896 my swevene recche aright, *interpret my dream correctly* 2900 wolde han, *would have* 2903 eeris, *ears* 2904 remenant, *rest* 2905 glowynge eyen tweye, *two glowing eyes* 2906 deye, *die* 2908 Avoy, *for shame*, hertelees, *coward* 2912 certes, *certainly*, what so, *whatever* 2914 hardy, *bold*, free, *generous* 2915 secree, *discreet*, nygard, *miser* 2916 agast, *afraid*, tool, *weapon* 2917 noon avauntour, *no boaster* 2918 dorste ye seyn, *dare you say*

2855–57 ech ascensioun / Of the equynoxial . . . degrees fiftene . . . , each time the sun ascended 15 degrees above the horizon in its imaginary circle around the Earth, Chauntecleer crowed the new hour; a 360-degree orbit divides into twenty-four equal units (hours) of 15 degrees. 2879 My lief is faren in londe, "My love is gone away," a popular song. 2882 in a dawenynge, one morning; according to medieval dreamlore, the best time for premonition. 2900 maad areest, a formal term for "seized"; like *prisoun* (line 2897), the physical description of Chantecleer (lines 2859–64), and the courtly description of Pertelote (lines 2870–75), this is the inflated language of the mock heroic. 2913–17 Compare *WBT* 3.925–48 and *ShT* 7.172–77.

Have ye no mannes herte, and han a berd°? 2920
  "Allas, and konne° ye been agast of swevenys°?
Nothyng, God woot°, but vanitee° in swevene is.
Swevenes engendren° of replecciouns°,
And ofte of fume° and of complecciouns,
Whan humours been to habundant° in a
    wight°. 2925
Certes° this dreem which ye han met° tonyght
Cometh of the greet superfluytee
Of youre rede colera°, pardee°,
Which causeth folk to dreden° in hir dremes
Of arwes°, and of fyr with rede lemes°, 2930
Of rede beestes, that they wol hem byte,
Of contek°, and of whelpes° grete and lyte°;
Right° as the humour of malencolie°
Causeth ful many a man in sleep to crie
For feere of blake beres, or boles° blake, 2935
Or elles blake develes wole hem take.
Of othere humours koude° I telle also
That werken many a man in sleep ful wo;
But I wol passe as lightly as I kan.
Lo° Catoun, which that was so wys a man, 2940
Seyde he nat thus, 'Ne do no fors° of dremes'?
  "Now, sire," quod she, "whan ye flee° fro the
    bemes°,
For Goddes love, as taak° som laxatyf.
Up° peril of my soule and of my lyf,
I conseille yow the beste, I wol nat lye, 2945
That bothe of colere and of malencolye
Ye purge yow; and for° ye shal nat tarie,
Though in this toun is noon apothecarie,
I shal myself to herbes techen° yow
That shul been for youre heele and for youre
    prow°; 2950
And in oure yeerd tho° herbes shal I fynde

The whiche han of hire propretee by kynde°
To purge yow bynethe° and eek above.
Foryet nat this, for Goddes owene love,
Ye been ful coleryk of compleccioun. 2955
Ware° the sonne in his ascencioun°
Ne fynde yow nat repleet° of humours hoote°.
And if it do, I dar wel leye° a grote°
That ye shul have a fevere terciane,
Or an agu° that may be youre bane°. 2960
A day or two ye shul have digestyves°
Of wormes, er° ye take youre laxatyves
Of lawriol, centaure, and fumetere,
Or elles of ellebor, that groweth there,
Of katapuece, or of gaitrys beryis, 2965
Of herbe yve, growyng in oure yeerd ther
    mery is°—
Pekke hem up right as they growe and ete
    hem yn.
Be myrie, housbonde, for youre fader kyn°!
Dredeth no dreem; I kan sey yow namoore."
  "Madame," quod he, "graunt mercy of°
    youre loore. 2970
But nathelees, as touchyng daun° Catoun,
That hath of wysdom swich° a greet renoun,
Though that he bad° no dremes for to drede,
By God, men may in olde bookes rede
Of many a man moore of auctorite 2975
Than evere Caton was, so moot I thee°,
That al the revers seyn° of this sentence°,
And han wel founden by experience
That dremes been significaciouns
As wel of joye as of tribulaciouns 2980
That folk enduren in this lif present.
Ther nedeth° make of this noon argument;
The verray preeve° sheweth it in dede.

2920 **berd,** *beard* 2921 **konne,** *can,* **swevenys,** *dreams* 2922 **woot,** *knows,* **vanitee,** *foolishness* 2923 **engendren,** *are bred,* **replecciouns,** *overeating* 2924 **fume,** *gas* 2925 **to habundant,** *too abundant,* **wight,** *person* 2926 **Certes,** *surely,* **met,** *dreamed* 2928 **rede colera,** *reddish bile,* **pardee,** *by God* 2929 **dreden,** *fear* 2930 **arwes,** *arrows,* **lemes,** *flames* 2932 **contek,** *conflict,* **whelpes,** *dogs,* **lyte,** *little* 2933 **Right,** *just,* **malencolie,** *black bile* 2935 **boles,** *bulls* 2937 **koude,** *could* 2940 **Lo,** *consider* 2941 **Ne do no fors of,** *make no matter of* 2942 **flee,** *fly,* **bemes,** *rafters* 2943 **as taak,** *take* 2944 **Up,** *upon* 2947 **for,** *so that* 2949 **techen,** *show* 2950 **prow,** *advantage* 2951 **tho,** *those* 2952 **propretee by kynde,**

natural properties 2953 **bynethe,** *below* 2956 **Ware,** *beware that,* **in his ascencioun,** *when it rises high* 2957 **repleet,** *full,* **hoote,** *hot* 2958 **leye,** *bet,* **grote,** *silver coin* 2960 **agu,** *sharp fever,* **bane,** *death* 2961 **digestyves,** *digestive aids* 2962 **er,** *before* 2966 **ther mery is,** *where it is pleasant* 2968 **fader kyn,** *father's kin* 2970 **graunt mercy of,** *many thanks for* 2971 **touchyng daun,** *regarding master* 2972 **swich,** *such* 2973 **bad,** *told (us)* 2976 **so moot I thee,** *as I may prosper* 2977 **revers seyn,** *opposite say,* **sentence,** *advice* 2982 **Ther nedeth,** *there is no need to* 2983 **verray preeve,** *actual experience*

2924 **complecciouns,** (im)balances among the humors (blood, phlegm, yellow or reddish bile [choler], black bile [melancholy]); see *GP* 1.333n. and 2984n. below. 2940 **Caton,** Dionysius Cato, supposed author of *Disticha Catonis* (Cato's Couplets), a collection of maxims used as a medieval school textbook; see *Disticha* 2.3. 2959 **fevere terciane,** fever that recurs every other day, attributed to an excess of reddish bile, especially when combined with black bile. 2963–66 **lawriol, centaure, and fumetere . . . ellebor . . . katapuece . . . gaitrys beryis** (berries) **. . . herbe yve** (ivy), all herbs used in medieval medicine, although the combination here is overwhelming and perhaps deadly.

"Oon of the gretteste auctour that men rede
Seith thus, that whilom° two felawes° wente   2985
On pilgrimage in a ful good entente,
And happed so° they coomen in a toun
Wher as ther was swich congregacioun
Of peple, and eek so streit of herbergage°,
That they ne founde as muche as o cotage°   2990
In which they bothe myghte logged° bee.
Wherfore they mosten° of necessitee,
As for that nyght, departen° compaignye.
And ech of hem gooth to his hostelrye°,
And took his loggyng as it wolde falle°.   2995
That oon of hem was logged in a stalle,
Fer° in a yeerd, with oxen of the plough;
That oother man was logged wel ynough,
As was his aventure° or his fortune
That us governeth alle as in commune.   3000

"And so bifel that longe er it were° day,
This man mette° in his bed, ther as he lay,
How that his felawe gan° upon hym calle,
And seyde, 'Allas, for in an oxes stalle
This nyght I shal be mordred ther° I lye.   3005
Now help me, deere brother, or I dye!
In alle haste com to me!" he sayde.

"This man out of his sleep for feere abrayde°;
But whan that he was wakened of his sleep,
He turned hym°, and took of it no keep°.   3010
Hym thoughte his dreem nas° but a vanitee°.
Thus twies in his slepyng dremed hee,
And atte thridde tyme yet his felawe
Cam, as hym thoughte, and seide, 'I am now
     slawe°.
Bihold my bloody woundes depe and wyde.   3015
Arys up erly in the morwe tyde,
And at the west gate of the toun,' quod he,
'A carte ful of donge° ther shaltow° se,
In which my body is hid ful prively°.
Do thilke carte arresten° boldely.   3020

My gold caused my mordre, sooth° to sayn.'
And tolde hym every point how he was slayn,
With a ful pitous face, pale of hewe.
And truste wel, his dreem he foond ful trewe,
For on the morwe as soone as it was day   3025
To his felawes in° he took the way,
And whan that he cam to this oxes stalle,
After his felawe he bigan to calle.

"The hostiler° answerede hym anon,
And seyde, 'Sire, youre felawe is agon.   3030
As soone as day he wente out of the toun.'

"This man gan fallen in suspecioun,
Remembrynge on his dremes that he mette°,
And forth he gooth—no lenger wolde he lette°—
Unto the west gate of the town, and fond   3035
A dong-carte, wente° as it were to donge° lond,
That was arrayed° in that same wise
As ye han herd the dede man devyse°.
And with an hardy° herte he gan to crye
Vengeance and justice of this felonye.   3040
'My felawe mordred is this same nyght,
And in this carte heere he lith gapyng upright°.
I crye out on the ministres,' quod he,
'That sholden kepe° and reulen° this citee.
Harrow°, allas, heere lith my felawe slayn!'   3045
What sholde I moore unto this tale sayn?
The peple out sterte° and caste the carte to
     grounde,
And in the myddel of the dong they founde
The dede man that mordred was al newe°.

"O blisful God, that art so just and trewe,   3050
Lo°, how that thou biwreyest° mordre alway!
Mordre wol out, that se we day by day.
Mordre is so wlatsom° and abhomynable
To God, that is so just and resonable,
That he ne wol nat suffre it heled be°,   3055
Though it abyde° a yeer, or two, or thre.
Mordre wol out, this my conclusioun.

2985 **whilom**, *once*, **felawes**, *friends* 2987 **happed so**, (it) *happened that* 2989 **eek so streit of herbergage**, *also shortage of lodging* 2990 **o cotage**, *one cottage* 2991 **logged**, *lodged* 2992 **mosten**, *must* 2993 **departen**, *separate* 2994 **hostelrye**, *lodging* 2995 **wolde falle**, *so happened* 2997 **Fer**, *far* (*away*) 2999 **aventure**, *chance* 3001 **er it were**, *before it was* 3002 **mette**, *dreamed* 3003 **gan**, *did* 3005 **ther**, *where* 3008 **abrayde**, *started up* 3010 **turned hym**, *turned over*, **keep**, *heed* 3011 **nas**, *was nothing*, **vanitee**, *folly* 3014 **slawe**, *slain* 3018 **donge**, *manure*,

shaltow, *you will* 3019 **prively**, *secretly* 3020 **Do thilke carte arresten**, *have this cart seized* 3021 **sooth**, *truth* 3026 **felawes in**, *friend's inn* 3029 **hostiler**, *innkeeper* 3033 **mette**, *dreamed* 3034 **lette**, *hesitate* 3036 **wente**, *going*, **donge**, *fertilize* 3037 **arrayed**, *arranged* 3038 **devyse**, *describe* 3039 **hardy**, *bold* 3042 **gapyng upright**, *face upward* 3044 **kepe**, *protect*, **reulen**, *rule* 3045 **Harrow**, *alack* 3047 **sterte**, *leapt* 3049 **al newe**, *just recently* 3051 **Lo**, *behold*, **biwreyest**, *reveals* 3053 **wlatsom**, *repulsive* 3055 **suffre it heled be**, *allow it to be hidden* 3056 **abyde**, *waits*

2984 **Oon of the gretteste auctour,** *one of the greatest authors*. The stories that follow are adjacent but reversed in Cicero, *De Divinatione* (On Prophecy) 1.27, and reversed and separated in Valerius Maximus, *Facta et Dicta Memorabilia* (Memorable Deeds and Sayings) 1.7; neither has them in sequential chapters as asserted by "next chapitre" (line 3065). Chaucer probably knew these and other versions, especially those in Robert Holcot's fourteenth-century *Super Sapientiam Salomonis* (Commentary on Solomon's Book of Wisdom), which also influenced Chaucer's discussion of dreams and the humors in lines 2923–41, 2974–81, and 3130–35. **3052 Mordre wol out,** echoes *PrT* 7.576.

And right anon, ministres of that toun
Han hent° the cartere and so soore° hym pyned°,
And eek the hostiler so soore engyned°,   3060
That they biknewe° hire wikkednesse anon°,
And were anhanged by the nekke-bon.
Heere may men seen that dremes been to drede°.

"And certes in the same book I rede,
Right in the nexte chapitre after this—   3065
I gabbe° nat, so have I joye or blis—
Two men that wolde han passed over see
For certeyn cause, into a fer contree,
If that the wynd ne hadde been contrarie
That made hem in a citee for to tarie   3070
That stood ful myrie upon an haven-syde°.
But on a day, agayn° the eventyde,
The wynd gan chaunge and blew right as hem
     leste°.
Jolif° and glad they wente unto hir reste,
And casten hem° ful erly for to saille.   3075
But, herkneth, to that o° man fil a greet mervaille:
That oon of hem, in slepyng as he lay,
Hym mette° a wonder dreem agayn° the day.
Hym thoughte a man stood by his beddes syde,
And hym comanded that he sholde abyde°,   3080
And seyde hym thus, 'If thou tomorwe wende°,
Thow shalt be dreynt°; my tale is at an ende.'

"He wook and tolde his felawe what he mette,
And preyde° hym his viage° to lette°;
As for that day, he preyde hym to byde°.   3085
His felawe that lay by his beddes syde
Gan for to laughe°, and scorned him ful faste°.
'No dreem,' quod he, 'may so myn herte agaste°
That I wol lette for to do my thynges.
I sette nat a straw by° thy dremynges,   3090
For swevenes been but° vanytees° and japes°.

Men dreme alday° of owles and of apes,
And eek° of many a maze therwithal°;
Men dreme of thyng that nevere was ne shal.
But sith° I see that thou wolt heere abyde°,   3095
And thus forslewthen wilfully° thy tyde°,
God woot°, it reweth° me; and have good day!'
And thus he took his leve and wente his way.
But er that he hadde half his cours yseyled°,
Noot I nat° why, ne what myschaunce it
     eyled°,   3100
But casuelly° the shippes botme rente°,
And ship and man under the water wente
In sighte of othere shippes it bisyde,
That with hem seyled at the same tyde.

"And therfore, faire Pertelote so deere,   3105
By swiche° ensamples olde yet maistow leere°
That no man sholde been to recchelees°
Of dremes; for I seye° thee, doutelees,
That many a dreem ful soore is for to drede°.
Lo°, in the lyf of Seint Kenelm I rede°,   3110
That was Kenulphus sone, the noble kyng
Of Mercenrike, how Kenelm mette° a thyng
A lite er° he was mordred. On a day
His mordre in his avysioun° he say°.
His norice hym expowned every deel°   3115
His swevene°, and bad° hym for to kepe hym°
     weel
For° traisoun; but he nas but° seven yeer oold,
And therfore litel tale hath he toold°
Of any dreem, so hooly was his herte.
By God, I hadde levere than my sherte   3120
That ye hadde rad° his legende, as have I.
Dame Pertelote, I sey yow trewely,
Macrobeus, that writ° the avisioun
In Affrike° of the worthy Cipioun,

3059 Han hent, *have seized,* **soore,** *painfully,* **pyned,** *tortured* **3060 engyned,** *tortured* **3061 biknewe,** *admitted,* **anon,** *immediately* **3063 been to drede,** *are to be feared* **3066 gabbe,** *lie* **3071 ful myrie upon an haven-syde,** *very pleasantly on a harbor* **3072 agayn,** *before* **3073 right as hem leste,** *just as they wished* **3074 Jolif,** *cheerful* **3075 casten hem,** *planned* **3076 o,** *one* **3078 Hym mette,** *he dreamed,* **agayn,** *before* **3080 abyde,** *wait* **3081 wende,** *travel* **3082 dreynt,** *drowned* **3084 preyde,** *asked,* **viage,** *journey,* **lette,** *delay* **3085 byde,** *wait* **3087 Gan for to laughe,** *laughed,* **ful faste,** *very much* **3088 agaste,** *frighten* **3090 sette nat a straw by,** *don't give a darn about* **3091 swevenes been but,** *dreams are only,* **vanytees,** *empty things,* **japes,** *jokes* **3092 alday,** *always* **3093 eek,** *also,* **a maze therwithal,** *amazements as well* **3095 sith,** *since,* **wolt** **heere abyde,** *will stay here* **3096 forslewthen wilfully,** *deliberately waste by idleness,* **tyde,** *time* **3097 woot,** *knows,* **reweth,** *saddens* **3099 yseyled,** *sailed* **3100 Noot I nat,** *I know not,* **myschaunce it eyled,** *misfortune afflicted it* **3101 casuelly,** *accidentally,* **botme rente,** *bottom split* **3106 swiche,** *such,* **maistow leere,** *may you learn* **3107 to recchelees,** *too dismissive* **3108 seye,** *tell* **3109 soore is for to drede,** *deeply to be feared* **3110 Lo,** *consider,* **rede,** *read* **3112 mette,** *dreamed* **3113 lite er,** *little before* **3114 avysioun,** *prophetic dream,* **say,** *saw* **3115 norice hym expowned every deel,** *nurse explained to him completely* **3116 swevene,** *dream,* **bad,** *told,* **kepe hym,** *protect himself* **3117 For,** *against,* **nas but,** *was only* **3118 litel tale hath he toold,** *little attention did he pay* **3121 rad,** *read* **3123 writ,** *wrote* **3124 Affrike,** *Africa*

3076 herkneth, listen! This hypermetrical word is omitted in a number of MSS, but it produces a dramatic or a colloquial effect. **3092 of owles and of apes,** i.e., of fanciful or ominous things. **3110–17 Seint Kenelm . . . ,** according to legend, Cenhelm, the son of Cenwulf (**Kenulphus,** line 3111), succeeded his father to the throne of Mercia (**Mercenrike,** line 3112) at the age of seven in 821. Though forewarned in a dream, he was betrayed by his aunt, murdered, and concealed under a thorn tree; a miraculous ray of light revealed his body. The "litel clergeoun" is also age seven in *PrT* 7.503. **3120–21 hadde levere than my sherte / That ye hadde rad his legende,** idiomatic expression meaning roughly, "I'd give up my shirt to have you read his story." **3123 Macrobeus,** Macrobius, late-classical author of a commentary on Cicero's *Somnium Scipionis* (The Dream of Scipio) and medieval authority on dreams. Chaucer summarizes Macrobius's commentary in *PF* 31ff.

Affermeth° dremes, and seith that they been   3125
Warnynge of thynges that men after seen°.

    "And forthermoore, I pray yow, looketh wel
In the Olde Testament of Daniel,
If he heeld° dremes any vanitee°.
Reed eek° of Joseph and ther shul ye see   3130
Wher° dremes be somtyme—I sey nat alle—
Warnynge of thynges that shul after falle°.
Looke° of Egipte the kyng, daun° Pharao,
His bakere and his butiller° also,
Wher° they ne felte noon effect in° dremes.   3135
Whoso wol seken actes° of sondry remes°
May rede of dremes many a wonder thyng.

    "Lo° Cresus, which that was of Lyde kyng,
Mette° he nat that he sat upon a tree,
Which signified he sholde anhanged bee°?   3140
Lo heere° Andromacha, Ectores wyf,
That day that Ector sholde lese° his lyf,
She dremed on the same nyght biforn
How that the lyf of Ector sholde be lorn°
If thilke° day he wente into bataille.   3145
She warned hym but it myghte nat availle°.
He wente for to fighte natheles°,
But he was slayn anon of Achilles.
But thilke tale is al to longe to telle,
And eek it is ny° day, I may nat dwelle°.   3150
Shortly I seye, as for conclusioun,
That I shal han of this avisioun
Adversitee—and I seye forthermoor
That I ne telle of laxatyves no stoor°,
For they been venymes°, I woot° it weel;   3155
I hem diffye°, I love hem never a deel°!

    "Now lat us speke of myrthe and stynte° al this.
Madame Pertelote, so have I blis°,

Of o thyng God hath sent me large grace°,
For whan I se the beautee of youre face—   3160
Ye been so scarlet reed aboute youre eyen—
It maketh al my drede for to dyen.
For al so siker° as *In principio,*
Mulier est hominis confusio—
Madame, the sentence° of this Latyn is   3165
'Womman is mannes joye and al his blis.'
For whan I feele a-nyght° youre softe syde—
Al be it that° I may nat on yow ryde
For that oure perche is maad so narwe°, allas—
I am so ful of joye and of solas°   3170
That I diffye bothe swevene° and dreem."

    And with that word he fley° doun fro the beem°,
For it was day, and eek his hennes alle,
And with a chuk° he gan hem for to calle,
For he hadde founde a corn lay° in the yerd.   3175
Real° he was, he was namoore aferd.
He fethered° Pertelote twenty tyme,
And trad° hire eke as ofte, er it was pryme°.
He looketh as it were a grym leoun°,
And on his toos he rometh up and doun;   3180
Hym deigned nat° to sette his foot to grounde.
He chukketh° whan he hath a corn yfounde,
And to hym rennen thanne his wyves alle.
Thus roial, as a prince is in an halle,
Leve I this Chauntecleer in his pasture°,   3185
And after wol I telle his aventure.

    Whan that the monthe in which the world
        bigan,
That highte° March, whan God first maked man,
Was compleet, and passed were also
Syn° March bigan thritty dayes and two,   3190
Bifel° that Chauntecleer in al his pryde,

3125 Affermeth, *confirms* **3126 after seen,** *see afterward* **3129 heeld,** *considered,* **vanitee,** *folly* **3130 Reed eek,** *read also* **3131 Wher,** *whether* **3132 falle,** *happen* **3133 Looke,** *read about,* **daun,** *master* **3134 butiller,** *steward* **3135 Wher,** *whether,* **in,** *from* **3136 seken actes,** *look up histories,* **sondry remes,** *various kingdoms* **3138 Lo,** *consider* **3139 Mette,** *dreamed* **3140 anhanged bee,** *be hanged* **3141 Lo heere,** *consider now* **3142 lese,** *lose* **3144 lorn,** *lost* **3145 thilke,** *that* **3146 myghte nat availle,** *did no good* **3147 natheles,** *nonetheless* **3150 ny,** *nearly,* **dwelle,** *delay* **3154 ne telle of laxatyves no stoor,** *don't consider laxatives to have value* **3155 venymes,** *poisons,* **woot,** *know* **3156 hem**

diffye, *reject them,* **deel,** *bit* **3157 stynte,** *stop* **3158 so have I blis,** i.e., *I swear by heaven* **3159 large grace,** *generous favor* **3163 so siker,** *as certainly* **3165 sentence,** *meaning* **3167 a-nyght,** *at night* **3168 Al be it that,** *even though* **3169 narwe,** *narrow* **3170 solas,** *pleasure* **3171 swevene,** *vision* **3172 fley,** *flew,* **beem,** *rafters* **3174 chuk,** *cluck* **3175 lay,** *lying* **3176 Real,** *royal* **3177 fethered,** *embraced* **3178 trad,** *copulated with,* **pryme,** *9 a.m.* **3179 grym leoun,** *fierce lion* **3181 Hym deigned nat,** *he did not condescend* **3182 chukketh,** *clucks* **3185 pasture,** *enclosure* **3188 highte,** *called* **3190 Syn,** *since* **3191 Bifel,** *it happened***

3128 Daniel, Daniel 7–12 records his prophetic dreams. **3130–35 Joseph . . . ,** Joseph has prophetic dreams and interprets the dreams of Egypt's pharaoh and the pharaoh's baker and steward in Genesis 37, 40, 41; see 2984n above. **3138 Cresus . . . Lyde,** Croesus . . . Lydia; see *MkT* 7.2727–60 and notes. **3141 Andromacha,** Andromache, Hector's wife, who dreamed prophetically of his death. The story first appears in Dares Phrygius's sixth-century *De Excidio Troiae Historica* (The History of the Destruction of Troy) 25. **3163 *In principio,*** "in the beginning"; the opening words of Genesis and of John's gospel. **3164 *Mulier est hominis confusio,*** "woman is man's destruction"; an echo of *Mel* 7.1106 and a medieval commonplace rooted in the story of Adam and Eve. Chantecleer's mistranslation is genuine ignorance, or it is intended to impress and seduce Pertelote—or both. **3188 first maked man,** in medieval tradition, God created the earth and Adam and Eve in March (the spring equinox). **3190 thritty dayes and two,** thirty-two days after the end of March is May 3, the same day that Palamon escapes from prison in *KnT* 1.1462–63 and that Pandarus dreams in *TC* 2.56. When simplified, the elaborate syntax of the sentence means "When the entire month of March and thirty-two more days more have passed, it happened that . . ."

His sevene wyves walkynge by his syde,
Caste up his eyen to the brighte sonne
That in the signe of Taurus hadde yronne°
Twenty degrees and oon° and somwhat
    moore,   3195
And knew by kynde° and by noon oother loore
That it was pryme°, and crew° with blisful stevene°.
"The sonne," he seyde, "is clomben° up on hevene
Fourty degrees and oon, and moore ywis°.
Madame Pertelote, my worldes blis,   3200
Herkneth° thise blisful briddes° how they synge,
And se the fresshe floures how they sprynge!
Ful is myn herte of revel° and solas°."
But sodeynly hym fil° a sorweful cas°,
For evere the latter ende° of joye is wo.   3205
God woot° that worldly joye is soone ago°,
And if a rethor koude faire endite°
He in a cronycle saufly° myghte it write
As for a sovereyn notabilitee°.
Now every wys man, lat him herkne° me: 3210
This storie is also° trewe, I undertake°,
As is the book of Launcelot de Lake,
That wommen holde in ful greet reverence.
Now wol I torne° agayn to my sentence°.
    A colfox ful of sly iniquitee°,   3215
That in the grove hadde woned° yeres three,
By heigh ymaginacioun forncast°,
The same nyght thurghout° the hegges brast°
Into the yerd ther° Chauntecleer the faire
Was wont°, and eek his wyves, to repaire°,   3220

And in a bed of wortes° stille he lay
Til it was passed undren° of the day,
Waitynge his tyme on Chauntecleer to falle,
As gladly doon° thise homycides alle
That in await liggen° to mordre men.   3225
O false mordrour, lurkynge in thy den!
O newe Scariot, newe Genylon,
False dissymulour°, O Greek Synon,
That broghtest Troye al outrely° to sorwe!
O Chauntecleer, acursed be that morwe°   3230
That thou into that yerd flaugh° fro the bemes!
Thou were ful wel ywarned by thy dremes
That thilke° day was perilous to thee;
But what that God forwoot° moot nedes bee°,
After the opinioun of certein clerkis.   3235
Witnesse on° hym that any parfit clerk° is
That in scole° is greet altercacioun
In this mateere, and greet disputisoun,
And hath been of an hundred thousand men.
But I ne kan nat bulte it to the bren°,   3240
As kan the hooly doctour Augustyn,
Or Boece, or the bisshop Bradwardyn,
Wheither that Goddes worthy forwityng°
Streyneth° me nedely° for to doon a thyng—
"Nedely" clepe° I symple necessitee—   3245
Or elles if free choys be graunted me
To do that same thyng or do it noght
Though° God forwoot° it er° that it was wroght°;
Or if his wityng° streyneth never a deel°
But° by necessitee condicioneel.   3250

3194 yronne, *progressed* **3195 oon,** *one* **3196 by kynde,** *instinctively* **3197 pryme,** *9 a.m.,* **crew,** *crowed,* **stevene,** *voice* **3198 clomben,** *ascended* **3199 ywis,** *certainly* **3201 Herkneth,** *listen to,* **briddes,** *birds* **3203 revel,** *joy,* **solas,** *pleasure* **3204 hym fil,** *to him happened,* **cas,** *event* **3205 latter ende,** *eventual outcome* **3206 woot,** *knows,* **ago,** *gone* **3207 koude faire endite,** *could well compose* **3208 saufly,** *confidently* **3209 sovereyn notabilitee,** *notable fact* **3210 herkne,** *listen to* **3211 also,** *as,* **undertake,** *declare* **3214 torne,** *return,* **sentence,** *subject matter* **3215 iniquitee,** *wickedness* **3216 woned,** *lived* **3217 By heigh ymaginacioun forncast,** *planned* or *foreseen by exalted imagination* **3218 thurghout,** *through,* **hegges brast,** *hedges burst* **3219 ther,** *where,* **3220 wont,** *accustomed,* **repaire,** *go* **3221 wortes,** *vegetables* **3222 undren,** *midmorning* (see *CIT* 4.260n) **3224 gladly doon,** *usually do* **3225 liggen,** *lie* **3228 dissymulour,** *deceiver* **3229 al outrely,** *utterly* **3230 morwe,** *morning* **3231 flaugh,** *flew* **3233 thilke,** *that* **3234 forwoot,** *foreknows,* **moot nedes bee,** *must necessarily be* **3236 Witnesse on,** *take the evidence of,* **parfit clerk,** *graduated student* **3237 scole,** *school* **3240 bulte it to the bren,** *sift out the bran* (i.e., *find the answer*) **3243 worthy forwityng,** *exalted foreknowledge* **3244 Streyneth,** *constrains,* **nedely,** *necessarily* **3245 clepe,** *call* **3248 Though,** *even though,* **forwoot,** *foreknows,* **er,** *before,* **wroght,** *enacted* **3249 wityng,** *knowing,* **never a deel,** *not at all* **3250 But,** *except*

3194 signe of Taurus, the zodiacal sign of the Bull; on Friday, May 3, 1392, the sun was 21°6min into Taurus, and at the latitude of central England, 41°5min above the horizon, as precisely indicated in lines 3194–99. **3207 rethor,** rhetorician; the depressing sentiment in the preceding two lines is developed at length in the *Poetria Nova* of rhetorician Geoffrey of Vinsauf and, of course, belied by the outcome of Chaucer's tale. **3211–12 trewe . . . /As is the book of Launcelot,** this seems to be a humorous critique of romances, such as tales of Lancelot and Guenivere. **3215 colfox,** fox with ears, tail, and feet tipped black; see lines 2903–4 above. **3227 Scariot,** Judas Iscariot betrayed Jesus; Matthew 26.48–50. **Genylon,** Ganelon betrayed Roland in *Song of Roland.* **3228 Synon,** betrayed the city of Troy by means of the Trojan horse. **3241–42 Augustyn . . . Boece . . . Bradwardyn,** St. Augustine of Hippo (fourth century), Boethius (sixth century), and Thomas of Bradwardine (Chaucer's near contemporary) were all authorities on the complex and controversial issue of the relation between divine knowledge of all things and human free will. Put briefly: Augustine emphasized God's gifts of grace and choice to humans; Bradwardine emphasized predestination. Boethius sought to explain free will and divine (fore)knowledge by distinguishing between divine and human knowledge and between simple and conditional necessity. **3245–50 symple necessitee . . . necessitee condicioneel,** Boethius's distinction; see *Bo* 5.pr6.183ff. It is simple necessity that all humans are mortal. It is conditional necessity that if we know someone is sitting, then the person

I wol nat han to do of° swich mateere.
My tale is of a cok, as ye may heere,
That took his conseil of his wyf, with sorwe,
To walken in the yerd upon that morwe
That he hadde met° that dreem that I yow
　　tolde.　　　　　　　　　　　　　　　　3255
Wommennes conseils been ful ofte colde°;
Wommannes conseil broghte us first to wo
And made Adam fro Paradys to go
Ther as° he was ful myrie and wel at ese.
But for I noot° to whom it myght displese　3260
If I conseil of wommen wolde blame,
Passe over, for I seyde it in my game.
Rede auctours°, where they trete of swich mateere,
And what they seyn of wommen ye may heere.
Thise been the cokkes wordes and nat
　　myne;　　　　　　　　　　　　　　　　3265
I kan noon harm of no womman divyne°.
　　Faire in the soond° to bathe hire myrily
Lith° Pertelote, and alle hire sustres by,
Agayn° the sonne, and Chauntecleer so free°
Soong murier than the mermayde in the
　　see—　　　　　　　　　　　　　　　　3270
For Phisiologus seith sikerly°
How that they syngen wel and myrily.
And so bifel that as he caste his eye
Among the wortes° on a boterflye,
He was war of this fox that lay ful lowe.　3275
Nothyng ne liste hym° thanne for to crowe,
But cride anon, "Cok, cok!" and up he sterte
As man that was affrayed in his herte.
For natureelly a beest desireth flee
Fro his contrarie° if he may it see,　　　3280
Though he never erst° hadde seyn it with his eye.
　　This Chauntecleer whan he gan hym espye

He wolde han fled, but that the fox anon°
Seyde, "Gentil sire, allas, wher wol ye gon?
Be ye affrayed of me that am youre freend?　3285
Now, certes, I were worse than a feend
If I to yow wolde harm or vileynye.
I am nat come youre conseil for t'espye°,
But trewely the cause of my comynge
Was oonly for to herkne° how that ye synge.　3290
For trewely, ye have as myrie a stevene°
As any aungel hath that is in hevene.
Therwith° ye han in musyk moore feelynge
Than hadde Boece, or any that kan synge.
My lord youre fader—God his soule
　　blesse—　　　　　　　　　　　　　　3295
And eek youre mooder, of hire gentillesse,
Han in myn hous ybeen° to my greet ese.
And certes, sire, ful fayn° wolde I yow plese.
　　"But for men speke of syngyng, I wol seye,
So moote I brouke° wel myne eyen tweye°,　3300
Save yow°, herde I nevere man so synge
As dide youre fader in the morwenynge.
Certes, it was of° herte al that he song.
And for to make his voys the moore strong,
He wolde so peyne hym° that with bothe his
　　eyen　　　　　　　　　　　　　　　　3305
He moste wynke°, so loude he wolde cryen,
And stonden on his tiptoon therwithal°,
And strecche forth his nekke long and smal.
And eek he was of swich discrecioun
That ther nas no man in no regioun　　　3310
That hym in song or wisedom myghte passe°.
I have wel rad° in *Daun Burnel the Asse*,
Among his vers, how that ther was a cok
For that° a preestes sone yaf° hym a knok
Upon his leg whil he was yong and nyce°,　3315

3251 han to do of, *pay attention to* **3255 met,** *dreamed* **3256 colde,** *fatal* **3259 Ther as,** *where* **3260 noot,** *know not* **3263 auctours,** *authors* **3266 divyne,** *suppose* **3267 soond,** *sand* **3268 Lith,** *lies* **3269 Agayn,** *facing,* **free,** *noble* **3271 seith sikerly,** *says certainly* **3274 wortes,** *vegetables* **3276 Nothyng ne liste hym,** *not at all did he wish* **3280 contrarie,** *opposite* **3281 erst,** *before* **3283 anon,** *quickly* **3288 conseil for t'espye,** *to seek*

your secrets **3290 herkne,** *listen* **3291 stevene,** *voice* **3293 Therwith,** *also* **3297 Han . . . ybeen,** *have been* **3298 ful fayn,** *very eagerly* **3300 So moote I brouke,** *as I may enjoy,* **eyen tweye,** *two eyes* **3301 Save yow,** *except for you* **3303 of,** *from the* **3305 peyne hym,** *exert himself* **3306 moste wynke,** *must close* **3307 therwithal,** *also* **3311 passe,** *surpass* **3312 rad,** *read* **3314 For that,** *because,* **yaf,** *gave* **3315 nyce,** *foolish*

must be sitting: the condition is that we know it, although this condition does not affect the person's freedom to sit. God knows all things in one eternal moment, and they must come about by the (conditional) necessity of his knowing them; his knowledge does not affect the free will of the people who are involved. From our perspective in time, what he (fore)knows must necessarily happen, but the necessity may be on the condition of human free choice. **3252 tale is of a cok,** the juxtaposition of philosophical issues with chickens has comic parallels with Boethius's contrast between divine and human knowledge. As God does, we foreknow Chauntecleer's fate without causing it. **3270 mermayde,** the mermaid (or siren) was thought to lure sailors to destruction by singing. **3271 Phisiologus,** the title (sometimes the author) of the bestiary, an ancient collection of animal descriptions (sometimes including the mermaid), moralized to reflect Christian truisms and principles. **3294 Boece,** Boethius's *De Musica* was the standard medieval textbook on music as a mathematical science. **3312 *Daun Burnel the Asse*,** a title (though usually called the *Speculum Stultorum* [Mirror of Fools]) of a twelfth-century beast fable by Nigel Wirecker that satirizes a donkey (Burnel) who was dissatisfied with the length of his tail. It includes an account of a boy who broke the leg of a rooster. Years later, when the boy was scheduled to be ordained a priest, the rooster failed to awaken him.

He made hym for to lese° his benefice°.
But certeyn, ther nys no comparisoun
Bitwixe the wisedom and discrecioun
Of youre fader and of his subtiltee.
Now syngeth, sire, for seinte charitee°;   3320
Lat se, konne° ye youre fader countrefete°?"

    This Chauntecleer his wynges gan to bete,
As man that koude his traysoun° nat espie,
So was he ravysshed° with his flaterie.
Allas, ye lordes, many a fals flatour°   3325
Is in youre courtes, and many a losengeour°,
That plesen yow wel moore, by my feith,
Than he that soothfastnesse° unto yow seith.
Redeth Ecclesiaste of flaterye;
Beth war, ye lordes, of hir trecherye.   3330

    This Chauntecleer stood hye upon his toos,
Strecchynge his nekke, and heeld his eyen
    cloos,
And gan to crowe loude for the nones°.
And daun Russell the fox stirte up atones°,
And by the gargat hente° Chauntecleer,   3335
And on his bak toward the wode hym beer°,
For yet ne was ther no man that hym sewed°.

    O destinee that mayst nat been eschewed°!
Allas that Chauntecleer fleigh° fro the bemes!
Allas his wyf ne roghte° nat of dremes!   3340
And on a Friday fil al this meschaunce°.

    O Venus, that art goddesse of plesaunce°,
Syn° that thy servant was this Chauntecleer,
And in thy servyce dide al his poweer,
Moore for delit than world to multiplye,   3345
Why woldestow suffre° hym on thy day to dye?

    O Gaufred, deere maister soverayn°,
That whan thy worthy Kyng Richard was slayn
With shot°, compleynedest° his deeth so soore,

Why ne hadde I now thy sentence° and thy
    loore°,   3350
The Friday for to chide°, as diden ye?
For on a Friday, soothly°, slayn was he.
Thanne wolde I shewe yow how that I koude
    pleyne°
For Chauntecleres drede and for his peyne.

    Certes°, swich cry ne lamentacioun   3355
Was nevere of ladyes maad° whan Ylioun
Was wonne, and Pirrus with his streite° swerd
Whan he hadde hent° Kyng Priam by the berd
And slayn hym, as seith° us *Eneydos*,
As maden alle the hennes in the clos°,   3360
Whan they had seyn of Chauntecleer the
    sighte.
But sovereynly° dame Pertelote shrighte°
Ful louder than dide Hasdrubales wyf
Whan that hir housbonde hadde lost his lyf,
And that the Romayns hadde brend° Cartage.   3365
She was so ful of torment and of rage
That wilfully° into the fyr she sterte°
And brende hirselven with a stedefast herte.

    O woful hennes°, right so criden ye
As whan that Nero brende the citee   3370
Of Rome cryden senatoures wyves
For that hir husbondes losten alle hir lyves—
Withouten gilt this Nero hath hem slayn.
Now turne I wole to my tale agayn.

    This sely wydwe° and eek hir doghtres two   3375
Herden thise hennes crie and maken wo,
And out at dores stirten they anon
And syen° the fox toward the grove gon,
And bar upon his bak the cok away,
And cryden, "Out, harrow, and weylaway!   3380
Haha, the fox!" and after hym they ran,

3316 **lese**, *lose,* **benefice**, *church appointment* 3320 **seinte charitee**, *holy charity* 3321 **konne**, *can,* **countrefete**, *imitate* 3323 **traysoun**, *betrayal* 3324 **ravysshed**, *carried away* 3325 **flatour**, *flatterer* 3326 **losengeour**, *one who praises falsely* 3328 **soothfastnesse**, *truth* 3333 **for the nones**, *on this occasion* 3334 **stirte up atones**, *leapt up immediately* 3335 **gargat hente**, *throat seized* 3336 **beer**, *carried* 3337 **sewed**, *pursued* 3338 **eschewed**, *avoided* 3339 **fleigh**, *flew* 3340 **roghte**, *cared* 3341 **meschaunce**, *misfortune* 3342 **plesaunce**, *pleasure* 3343 **Syn**, *since* 3346

woldestow suffre, *would you allow* 3347 **maister soverayn**, *master most excellent* 3349 **shot**, *an arrow,* **compleynedest**, *lamented* 3350 **sentence**, *meaningfulness,* **loore**, *learning* 3351 **chide**, *accuse* 3352 **soothly**, *truly* 3353 **koude pleyne**, *could lament* 3355 **Certes**, *surely* 3356 **of ladyes maad**, *made by ladies* 3357 **streite**, *drawn* 3358 **hent**, *seized* 3359 **seith**, *tells* 3360 **clos**, *enclosure* 3362 **sovereynly**, *supremely,* **shrighte**, *shrieked* 3365 **brend**, *burned* 3367 **wilfully**, *deliberately,* **sterte**, *leapt* 3369 **hennes**, *hens* 3375 **sely wydwe**, *innocent widow* 3378 **syen**, *saw*

3329 **Ecclesiaste**, probably Ecclesiasticus 12.10–19. **3341–42 Friday . . . Venus**, Friday was the day of Venus, goddess of love, and the day was associated traditionally with bad luck and disaster—including the expulsion of Adam, the beginning of the flood, Christ's Crucifixion, and the death of Richard I (Lion-Heart) of England. **3347–48 Gaufred . . . Richard**, Geoffrey (or Galfrid) of Vinsauf was the author of the *Poetria Nova,* a textbook on rhetoric. Chaucer burlesques his exemplary lamentation on the death of Richard I (the Lion-Heart) in lines 3347–73. **3356 Ylioun**, Ilium, the citadel of Troy. **3357–59 Pirrus . . . King Priam . . . *Eneydos***, Pyrrhus, son of Achilles, seizes Priam, king of Troy, by the hair (not the beard) and slays him in Virgil's *Aeneid* 2.550–54, although the Trojan women lament before Priam is slain, 2.486–90. **3363 Hasdrubales wyf**, mentioned also in *FranT* 5.1399–1404; see the note there. Chaucer here adds the emphasis on the wife's lament. **3370 Nero brende . . .**, a short version of *MkT* 7.2463–2550; both derive from *RR* 6183ff., although Chaucer adds the emphasis on sorrowing women here.

And eek with staves° many another man.
Ran Colle oure dogge, and Talbot and Gerland,
And Malkyn with a dystaf° in hir hand;
Ran cow and calf, and eek the verray° hogges,   3385
So fered for° the berkyng of the dogges
And shoutyng of the men and wommen eke;
They ronne so hem thoughte hir herte breke.
They yolleden° as feendes doon in helle;
The dokes° cryden as men wolde hem
    quelle°;   3390
The gees for feere flowen° over the trees;
Out of the hyve cam the swarm of bees.
So hydous was the noyse, a benedicitee°,
Certes°, he° Jakke Straw and his meynee°
Ne made nevere shoutes half so shrille   3395
Whan that they wolden any Flemyng kille
As thilke° day was maad upon the fox.
Of bras they broghten bemes°, and of box°,
Of horn, of boon°, in whiche they blewe and
    powped°,
And therwithal° they skriked° and they
    howped°.   3400
It seemed as that hevene sholde falle.
Now, goode men, I prey yow herkneth° alle.
  Lo, how Fortune turneth° sodeynly
The hope and pryde eek of hir enemy.
This cok that lay upon the foxes bak   3405
In al his drede unto the fox he spak,
And seyde, "Sire, if that I were as ye,
Yet wolde I seyn, as wys God helpe me,
'Turneth agayn°, ye proude cherles° alle!
A verray° pestilence upon yow falle!   3410
Now I am come unto the wodes syde.
Maugree youre heed, the cok shal heere abyde°.
I wol hym ete, in feith, and that anon!'"

The fox answerde, "In feith, it shal be don."
And as he spak that word, al sodeynly   3415
This cok brak from his mouth delyverly°,
And heighe upon a tree he fleigh° anon.
And whan the fox saugh that the cok was gon,
"Allas," quod he, "O Chauntecleer, allas!
I have to yow," quod he, "ydoon trespas°,   3420
In as muche as I maked yow aferd
Whan I yow hente° and broghte out of the yerd.
But, sire, I dide it of no wikke entente.
Com doun, and I shal telle yow what I mente.
I shal seye sooth° to yow, God help me so."   3425
  "Nay thanne," quod he, "I shrewe° us bothe two.
And first I shrewe myself bothe blood and bones
If thou bigyle° me any ofter° than ones°.
Thou shalt namoore thurgh thy flaterye
Do° me to synge and wynke° with myn eye;   3430
For he that wynketh whan he sholde see,
Al wilfully°, God lat him nevere thee°!"
  "Nay," quod the fox, "but God yeve° hym
    meschaunce°,
That is so undiscreet of governaunce°
That jangleth° whan he sholde holde his
    pees."   3435
  Lo, swich it is for to be recchelees°
And necligent, and truste on flaterye.
But ye that holden this tale a folye,
As of a fox, or of a cok and hen,
Taketh the moralite, goode men.   3440
For Seint Paul seith that al that writen is,
To° oure doctrine it is ywrite°, ywis.°
Taketh the fruyt and lat the chaf be stille.
Now, goode God, if that it be thy wille,
As seith my Lord, so make us alle goode men,   3445
And brynge us to his heighe bliss. Amen.

Heere is ended the Nonnes Preestes Tale.

3382 staves, *staffs* **3384 dystaf,** *stick for spinning thread* **3385 verray,** *actual* **3386 fered for,** *frightened by* **3389 yolleden,** *yelled* **3390 dokes,** *ducks,* **quelle,** *kill* **3391 flowen,** *flew* **3393 a benedicitee,** *ah bless us* **3394 Certes,** *surely,* **he,** i.e., *the famous,* **meynee,** *company* **3397 thilke,** *that* **3398 bemes,** *trumpets,* **box,** *boxwood* **3399 boon,** *bone,* **powped,** *puffed* **3400 therwithal,** *also,* **skriked,** *shrieked,* **howped,** *whooped* **3402 herkneth,** *hear* **3403 turneth,** *reverses* **3409 Turneth agayn,** *go back,*

cherles, *peasants* **3410 verray,** *genuine* **3412 abyde,** *remain* **3416 delyverly,** *cleverly* **3417 fleigh,** *flew* **3420 ydoon trespas,** *done offense* **3422 hente,** *seized* **3425 sooth,** *truth* **3426 shrewe,** *curse* **3428 bigyle,** *trick,* **ofter,** *more often,* **ones,** *once* **3430 Do,** *make,* **wynke,** *blink* **3432 wilfully,** *intentionally,* **thee,** *prosper* **3433 yeve,** *give,* **meschaunce,** *misfortune* **3434 governaunce,** *control* **3435 jangleth,** *chatters* **3436 recchelees,** *careless* **3442 To,** *for,* **ywrite,** *written,* **ywis,** *surely*

3383 Colle . . . Talbot . . . Gerland, dog names. **3384 Malkyn,** a name for a rustic female. **3394–96 Jakke Straw . . . Flemyng,** Jack Straw is named as a leader of the uprising of 1381 (Peasants' Revolt) in historical records, but it may be a pseudonym or a representative name; many Flemish (Belgian) workers were murdered in the uprising because of their economic success in the wool trade. This is Chaucer's only direct reference to this momentous event. **3412 Maugree youre head,** in spite of your head, i.e., despite anything you do. **3441 Seint Paul seith,** Romans 15.4. Compare *Ret* 10.1083. **3443 fruyt . . . chaf,** wheat and chaff. Like grain and husk or nut and shell, this is a traditional way of distinguishing between the saved and the damned and (clearly applicable here) between the spiritual meaning and the literal meaning of literature. The imagery derives from Matthew 3.12; it is developed in Paul's letters (e.g., 2 Corinthians 3.6) and Augustine's *De Doctrina Christiana* (On Christian Teaching) and is used widely in medieval literature. Compare *MLT* 2.701–2; *ParsP* 10.35–36. **3445 my Lord,** perhaps a reference to Jesus, St. Paul, or the Nun's Priest's bishop or archbishop.

[Epilogue]

"Sire Nonnes Preest," oure Hooste seide anoon,
"Iblessed° be thy breche°, and every stoon°!
This was a murie tale of Chauntecleer.
But by my trouthe, if thou were seculer°,   3450
Thou woldest ben a trede-foul° aright°.
For if thou have corage° as thou hast myght,
Thee were nede of° hennes, as I wene°,
Ya, moo than seven tymes seventene.
See, which braunes° hath this gentil preest,   3455
So gret a nekke, and swich a large breest!
He loketh as a sperhauk with his eyen;
Him nedeth nat his colour° for to dyen
With brasile°, ne with greyn of Portyngale°.
Now, sire, faire falle yow° for youre tale!"   3460
    And after that he, with ful merie chere,
Seide unto another, as ye shuln° heere.

3448 Iblessed, *blessed,* **breche,** *buttocks,* **stoon,** *testicle* **3450 seculer,** *a layman* **3451 trede-foul,** *breeding bird* (rooster), **aright,** *true* **3452 corage,** *heart* **3453 Thee were need of,** *you need,* **wene,** *believe* **3455 braunes,** *muscles* **3458 colour,** *complexion* **3459 brasile,** *red dye,* **greyn of Portyngale,** *red dye* **3460 faire falle yow,** *good luck to you* **3462 shuln,** *shall*

3447–62 Lines found in ten MSS only (not Hg or El), perhaps canceled by Chaucer when he developed the description of the Monk in *MkP*: note the general similarities with *MkP* 7.1943–64, and especially the clear echoes between 7.1945–46 and 3451–52. **3457 as a sperhauk,** like a sparrow hawk, a bird of prey.

CANTERBURY TALES PART 8

INTRODUCTION

IN HER CONTRIBUTION TO *Sources and Analogues* (2002, no. 187), Sherry L. Reames makes clear the likelihood that Chaucer translated the *Second Nun's Tale* from two different sources and combined them with materials from Dante's *Paradiso* 33 and Marian liturgy. It is evident that he translated it before he began *The Canterbury Tales* because he mentions a "lyf" of Saint Cecilia in his *Legend of Good Women* (Prologue F426), dated before the Canterbury fiction. The tale is indeed a saint's life, perhaps the most intellectually charged example of this popular genre in Middle English. Chaucer adapts the saint's-life genre elsewhere (*Legend of Good Women, Man of Law's Tale, Clerk's Tale*), but only here does he give us an example in all of its awe and austerity. When granted its assumptions about Christianity and about language (see the note to line 84a), the tale is powerful in its endorsement of virginity as a spiritual ideal and its belief that spiritual truth is knowable, even palpable, in this world. Presented as history rather than fiction, the tale conveys such intense religious conviction that it reflects either profound spirituality or nostalgia for bygone certainty, perhaps both. In "Chaucer's Tale of the Second Nun and the Strategies of Dissent" (1992, no. 1392), Lynn Staley Johnson argues that Wycliffite concerns with political authority lie close to the surface of the tale as well.

In the context of *The Canterbury Tales*, the tale gains additional dimensions. The Second Nun is not described in the *General Prologue*, though, like the Nun's Priest, she is apparently a member of the retinue of the Prioress (1.163–64). Similarities between the tales of the Second Nun and her superior invite comparison—rhyme royal stanzas, martyrdom, gaping neck or throat wounds—and their differences produce striking contrasts. Unlike the Prioress's unlearned little choirboy, the Second Nun's St. Cecilia comprehends divine mysteries deeply, and her martyrdom is depicted as heroic rather than pathetic. She experiences spiritual reality directly and uses her knowledge to convert others to Christianity and defend herself against charges of false faith. Taken together, the two tales and their prologues pose two different kinds of faith, one rooted in knowledge and the other in devotion. Carolyn P. Collette considers these issues and surveys the criticism in "Critical Approaches to the 'Prioress's Tale' and the 'Second Nun's Tale'" (1990, no. 1272).

Linguistic realism, epistemological certainty, and sequential conversions characterize the *Second Nun's Prologue* and *Tale,* whereas jargon, confusion, and failure to achieve alchemical transmutation recur in the *Canon's Yeoman's Tale* that follows—arguably a juxtaposition of the idealized Christian past with a dystopic view of contemporary society. The church had long condemned alchemy as chicanery, but Chaucer's tale is apparently the earliest fictional account of the science and its potential to frustrate its practitioners and mislead the unwary. The Canon's Yeoman's description of his experiences in the laboratory (part 1 of the tale) emphasizes the frustration that results from thwarted expectations and the limits of human knowledge. The narrative of the priest and the canon (part 2 of the tale) satirizes gullibility and condemns trickery, as do most exposés of con games.

It is clear that Chaucer knew something about the literature of alchemy, if not its practice. The tale reflects rudimentary knowledge of metals (relative melting temperatures, for example) and considerable familiarity with alchemical terminology, which Chaucer may have derived directly from any number of Latin treatises on the subject—those he actually mentions or quotes (1428–28, 1450) or perhaps the standard textbook in the field, Geber's (or Jabir's) thirteenth-century *Summa Perfectionis* (Sum of Perfection). Edgar H. Duncan, "The Literature of Alchemy and Chaucer's Canon's Yeoman's Tale" (1968, no. 1402), discusses sources and Chaucer's knowledge of the practice. The many and provocative echoes between the tales of the Second Nun and the Canon's Yeoman are identified by Joseph E. Grennen, "Saint Cecilia's 'Chemical Wedding'" (1966, no. 1379), and Bruce A. Rosenberg, "The Contrary Tales of the Second Nun and the Canon's Yeoman" (1968, no. 1383). In *Darke Hieroglyphicks* (1996, no. 1408), Stanton J. Linden traces depictions of alchemy in English literature from Chaucer forward, and Peggy A. Knapp, "The Work of Alchemy" (2000, no. 1406a), observes connections between the practice and nascent capitalism.

Because the Canon's Yeoman has not heard the *Second Nun's Tale*—he rides up after she finishes—the echoes between the two tales of part 8 are evidence that Chaucer is communicating to his audience above the heads of his characters. This fact,

the reference to Boughton in the link between the paired tales (556), and the concern in the two tales with the theme of transformation have encouraged critics to regard the tales as preparation for closure in the Canterbury fiction. Boughton-under-Blean is about five miles from Canterbury, and the decision by the Canon's Yeoman to leave his past life and join the pilgrimage at the eleventh hour indicates his own willingness to change. The abrupt departure of his former boss, the Canon, has not been explained satisfactorily, although in "The Canon's Yeoman as Imperfect Paradigm" (1982, no. 1401), Jackson J. Campbell argues that the entire scene anticipates the penitential message of the *Parson's Tale*. Lee Patterson, "Perpetual Motion: Alchemy and the Technology of the Self" (1993, no. 1410), argues that in the *Canon's Yeoman's Prologue and Tale* Chaucer exemplifies how individual subjectivities are shaped by language and society.

Canterbury Tales Part 8

SECOND NUN'S TALE

PROLOGUE

The Prologe of the Seconde Nonnes Tale.

The ministre° and the norice° unto vices,
Which that men clepe° in Englissh ydelnesse,
That porter of the gate is of delices°,
To eschue° and by hire contrarie° hire oppresse°—
That is to seyn, by leveful bisynesse°—   5
Wel oughten we to doon al oure entente
Lest° that the feend thurgh ydelnesse us hente°.

For he that with his thousand cordes slye°
Continuelly us waiteth to biclappe°,
Whan he may man in ydelnesse espye°,   10
He kan so lightly cacche° hym in his trappe—
Til that a man be hent° right by the lappe°

He nys nat war° the feend hath hym in honde.
Wel oghte us werche° and ydelnesse withstonde.

And though men dradden nevere for° to dye,   15
Yet seen men wel by resoun, doutelees,
That ydelnesse is roten slogardye°
Of which ther nevere comth no good n'encrees°;
And seen that slouthe hire holdeth° in a lees°
Oonly to slepe, and for to ete and drynke,   20
And to devouren al that othere swynke°.

And for to putte us fro swich° ydelnesse,
That cause is of so greet confusioun°,

---

1 ministre, *servant,* **norice,** *nurse* **2 clepe,** *call* **3 delices,** *delights* **4 eschue,** *avoid,* **contrarie,** *opposite,* **hire oppresse,** *overcome her* **5 leveful bisynesse,** *permitted activities* **7 Lest,** *for fear,* **hente,** *seize* **8 cordes slye,** *subtle traps* **9 biclappe,** *ensnare* **10 espye,** *see* **11 lightly cacche,** *easily catch* **12 hent,** *seized,* **lappe,** *hem* **13 nys nat war,** *is not aware*

14 werche, *work* **15 dradden nevere for,** *never dread* **17 roten slogardye,** *rotten laziness* **18 n'encrees** *nor profit* **19 slouthe hire holdeth,** *sloth holds her* (idleness), **lees,** *leash* **21 othere swynke,** *others work for* **22 swich,** *such* **23 confusioun,** *destruction*

2–3 ydelnesse . . . porter of the gate, Lady Idleness is gatekeeper to the garden of pleasure in the allegorical *Roman de la Rose.* Cautions against idleness are commonplace in monastic literature, where the activities of copying and translating, as well as manual labor, are presented as alternatives to the spiritual dangers of idleness.

I have heer doon my feithful bisynesse
After the legende in translacioun 25
Right of° thy glorious lif and passioun°—
Thou with thy gerland wroght° of rose and lilie,
Thee meene I°, mayde and martyr Seint Cecilie.

Invocacio ad Mariam.

And thow that flour of virgines art alle°,
Of whom that Bernard list° so wel to write, 30
To thee at my bigynnyng first I calle;
Thou confort of us wrecches, do me endite°
Thy maydens deeth, that wan° thurgh hire merite
The eterneel lyf, and of the feend° victorie,
As man may after reden° in hire storie. 35

Thow mayde and mooder, doghter of thy sone,
Thow welle of mercy, synful soules cure,
In whom that God for bountee° chees° to wone°,
Thow humble and heigh over every creature,
Thow nobledest° so ferforth° oure nature 40
That no desdeyn° the Makere hadde of kynde°
His sone in blood and flessh to clothe and wynde°.

Withinne the cloistre° blisful of thy sydis°
Took mannes shap the eterneel love and pees
That° of the tryne compas lord and gyde is, 45
Whom erthe and see and hevene out of relees°
Ay heryen°; and thou, virgine wemmelees°,
Baar° of thy body—and dweltest mayden pure—
The creatour of every creature.

Assembled is in thee magnificence 50
With mercy, goodnesse, and with swich pitee

That thou that art the sonne° of excellence
Nat oonly helpeth hem that preyen thee,
But often tyme of thy benygnytee°
Ful frely, er that° men thyn help biseche°, 55
Thou goost° biforn and art hir lyves leche°.

Now help, thow meeke and blisful faire mayde,
Me, flemed wrecche°, in this desert of galle°;
Thynk on the womman Cananee that sayde
That whelpes° eten somme of the crommes° alle 60
That from hir lordes table been yfalle;
And though that I, unworthy sone of Eve,
Be synful, yet accepte my bileve°.

And for that° feith is deed withouten werkis,
So for to werken yif° me wit and space°, 65
That I be quit fro thennes° that most derk is.
O thou that art so fair and ful of grace,
Be myn advocat in that heighe place
Theras° withouten ende is songe° Osanne,
Thow Cristes mooder, doghter deere of Anne. 70

And of thy light my soule in prison lighte,
That troubled is by the contagioun
Of my body, and also by the wighte°
Of erthely lust and fals affeccioun;
O havene of refut°, O salvacioun 75
Of hem that been in sorwe and in distresse,
Now help, for to my werk I wol me dresse°.

Yet preye I yow that reden that I write,
Foryeve me that I do no diligence°
This ilke° storie subtilly to endite°, 80

---

flawless **48 Baar,** *bore* **52 sonne,** *sun* **54 benygnytee,** *graciousness* **55 er that,** *before,* **biseche,** *beg for* **56 goost,** *go,* **leche,** *physician* **58 flemed wrecche,** *banished exile,* **galle,** *bitterness* **60 whelpes,** *young dogs,* **crommes,** *crumbs* **63 bileve,** *faith* **64 for that,** *because* **65 yif,** *grant,* **space,** *time* **66 quit fro thennes,** *saved from the place* **69 Theras,** *where,* **songe,** *sung* **73 wighte,** *weight* **75 refut,** *refuge* **77 me dresse,** *address myself* **79 do no diligence,** *take no pains* **80 ilke,** *same,* **endite,** *write*

26 Right of, *true to,* **passioun,** *suffering* **27 wroght,** *made* **28 Thee meene I,** *I mean you* **29 that flour of virgines art alle,** *who are the apex (flower) of all virgins* **30 list,** *chose* **32 do me endite,** *cause me to write* **33 wan,** *won* **34 feend,** *fiend* **35 after reden,** *read below* **38 bountee,** *graciousness,* **chees,** *chose,* **wone,** *dwell* **40 nobledest,** *ennobled,* **ferforth,** *thoroughly* **41 desdeyn,** *disdain,* **kynde,** *(human) nature* **42 wynde,** *wrap* **43 cloistre,** *holy enclosure,* **sydis,** *sides* **45 That,** *he who* **46 out of relees,** *without cease* **47 Ay heryen,** *always praise,* **wemmelees,**

25 legende, biography, usually a saint's life. **28a Invocacio ad Mariam,** Invocation to Mary. Compare with *PrT* 7.467–80; both echo St. Bernard's praise of Mary in Dante's *Paradiso* 33, the liturgy dedicated to Mary, and other poems in her praise. **30 Bernard,** St. Bernard of Clairvaux (ca. 1090–1153), a major advocate of veneration of the Virgin. **45 tryne compas,** threefold universe—the earth, sea, and heavens of the next line. **59 womman Cananee,** Canaanite woman; Matthew 15.21–28. **62 sone of Eve,** son of Eve; indication that Chaucer may have composed this prologue for a male pilgrim or before he conceived of the Canterbury fiction. However, the phrase is used as self-reference in the *Salve Regina* (Hail Queen), sung by medieval nuns every day. **64** Echoes James 2.17 and parallels concern with spiritual labor and production elsewhere in *SNPT.* **69 Osanne,** Hosanna; an exclamation of spiritual triumph and praise. **70 Anne,** St. Anne, by tradition the mother of Mary, first mentioned in the apocryphal Gospel of the Birth of Mary. **72 contagioun,** diseased influence; the notion that the body infects the spirit. **78 reden that,** read what; like the reference to reading (rather than telling the tale orally) in line 35, evidence that Chaucer may have written this before conceiving of the Canterbury fiction.

For bothe have I the wordes and sentence°
Of hym that at the seintes reverence°
The storie wroot, and folwen hire legende,
And I pray yow that ye wole my werk amende°.

Interpretacio nominis Cecilie quam ponit Frater Jacobus Januensis in Legenda

First wolde I yow the name of Seinte Cecilie   85
Expowne°, as men may in hir storie see.
It is to seye in Englissh "hevenes lilie,"
For pure chaastnesse of virginitee;
Or for she whitnesse hadde of honestee°,
And grene of conscience, and of good fame   90
The soote savour°, "lilie" was hir name.

Or Cecilie is to seye "the wey to blynde,"
For she ensample was by good techynge.
Or elles Cecile, as I writen fynde,
Is joyned by a manere° conjoynynge   95
Of "hevene" and "Lia"; and heere in figurynge°
The "hevene" is set for thoght of hoolynesse,
And "Lia" for hire lastynge bisynesse.

Cecile may eek be seyd° in this manere,
"Wantynge of blyndnesse," for hir grete light   100
Of sapience°, and for hire thewes cleere°;
Or elles, loo, this maydens name bright
Of "hevene" and "leos" comth, for which by right
Men myghte hire wel "the hevene of peple" calle,
Ensample of goode and wise werkes alle.   105

For "leos" "peple" in Englissh is to seye,
And right° as men may in the hevene see
The sonne and moone and sterres every weye,
Right so men goostly° in this mayden free
Seyen° of feith the magnanymytee°,   110
And eek the cleernesse hool° of sapience°,
And sondry° werkes brighte of excellence.

And right so as° thise philosophres write
That hevene is swift and round and eek
   brennynge,
Right so was faire Cecilie the white   115
Ful swift and bisy evere in good werkynge,
And round and hool in good perseverynge°,
And brennynge° evere in charite ful brighte.
Now have I yow declared what she highte°.

Explicit

Here bigynneth the Seconde Nonnes Tale of the Lyf of Seinte Cecile.

This mayden bright Cecilie, as hir life
   seith,   120
Was comen of Romayns and of noble kynde,
And from hir cradel up fostred in the feith
Of Crist, and bar° his gospel in hir mynde.
She nevere cessed°, as I writen fynde,

Of hir preyere, and God to love and
   drede,   125
Bisekynge° hym to kepe° hir maydenhede.

And whan this mayden sholde unto a man
Ywedded be, that was ful yong of age,

---

81 **sentence,** *meaning* 82 **at the seintes reverence,** *out of reverence for the saint* 84 **amende,** *correct* 86 **Expowne,** *explain* 89 **honestee,** *virtue* 91 **soote savour,** *sweet scent* 95 **manere,** *kind of* 96 **in figurynge,** *symbolically* 99 **eek be seyd,** *also mean* 101 **sapience,** *wisdom,* **thewes cleere,** *shining virtues* 107 **right,** *just* 109 **goostly,** *spiritually* 110

Seyen, *saw,* **magnanymytee,** *generosity* 111 **cleernesse hool,** *complete brightness,* **sapience,** *wisdom* 112 **sondry,** *various* 113 **right so as,** *just as* 117 **perseverynge,** *constancy* 118 **brennynge,** *burning* 119 **highte,** *is called* 123 **bar,** *kept* 124 **cessed,** *ceased* 126 **Bisekynge,** *asking,* **kepe,** *protect*

84a **Interpretacio . . . Legenda,** Interpretation of the name Cecilia that brother Jacob of Genoa included in the *Legend.* Jacobus of Voragine (ca. 1230–1298), archbishop of Genoa, wrote the most famous collection of saints' lives in the Middle Ages, *Legenda Aurea* (The Golden Legend). More than half of Jacobus's two hundred saints' lives begin with Latin name etymologies, now known to be inaccurate, that reflect the faith in language typical of much medieval thought. Chaucer draws on Jacobus for the Interpretation and the beginning of his tale to line 357; specific sources for the rest of his tale have not been established with certainty. 87 **hevenes lilie,** heaven's lily; Lat. *celi lilia.* 92 **wey to blynde,** pathway for the blind; Lat. *cecis via.* 96 **"hevene" and "Lia,"** Lat. *celo et Lia;* Leah symbolizes the active religious life in scriptural commentary. 100 **Wantynge of blyndnesse,** lacking blindness; Lat. *cecitate carens.* 103 **hevene and leos,** heaven and people; Lat. *celo;* Gk. λαοσ (**leos**). 114 **hevene is swift and round and eek brennynge,** in the medieval cosmos, the uppermost heavenly sphere of the fixed stars moved most swiftly and the Empyrean was the realm of pure fire.

Which that ycleped was° Valerian,
And day was comen of hir° marriage, 130
She ful devout and humble in hir corage°,
Under hir robe of gold that sat ful faire,
Hadde next° hire flessh yclad hire in an haire°.

And whil the orgnes maden melodie,
To God allone in herte thus sang she, 135
"O Lord, my soule and eek my body gye°
Unwemmed°, lest° that it confounded° be."
And for his love that dyde upon a tree,
Every seconde and thridde day she faste°,
Ay biddynge° in hire orisons° ful faste°. 140

The nyght cam and to bedde moste she gon
With hire housbonde, as ofte is the manere,
And pryvely° to hym she seyde anon,
"O sweete and wel biloved spouse deere,
Ther is a conseil°, and ye wolde it heere, 145
Which that right fayn° I wolde unto yow seye,
So that° ye swere ye shul it nat biwreye°."

Valerian gan faste° unto hire swere
That for no cas°, ne thyng that myghte be,
He sholde nevere mo biwreyen here°. 150
And thanne at erst° to hym thus seyde she,
"I have an aungel which that loveth me,
That with greet love, wherso I wake or sleepe,
Is redy ay° my body for to keepe°.

"And if that he may feelen, out of drede°, 155
That ye me touche, or love in vileynye°,
He right anon wol sle yow with the dede,
And in youre yowthe thus ye shullen dye°,
And if that ye in clene° love me gye°,
He wol yow loven as me, for youre
    clennesse, 160
And shewen yow his joye and his brightnesse."

Valerian, corrected as God wolde°,
Answerde agayn°, "If I shal trusten thee,

Lat me that aungel se and hym biholde,
And if that it a verray° angel bee, 165
Thanne wol I doon as thou hast prayed me;
And if thou love another man, for sothe°,
Right with this swerd thanne wol I sle yow
    bothe."

Cecile answerde anon-right° in this wise,
"If that yow list° the angel shul ye see 170
So that ye trowe° in Crist and yow baptize.
Gooth forth to Via Apia," quod shee,
"That fro this toun ne stant but° miles three,
And to the poure folkes that ther dwelle
Sey hem° right thus as that I shal yow telle. 175

"Telle hem that I, Cecile, yow to hem sente
To shewen yow the goode Urban the olde
For secree nedes° and for good entente.
And whan that ye Seint Urban han biholde°,
Telle hym the wordes whiche that I to yow
    tolde. 180
And whan that he hath purged yow fro
    synne,
Thanne shul ye se that angel er° ye twynne°."

Valerian is to the place ygon°,
And right as hym was taught by his lernynge
He foond this hooly olde Urban anon 185
Among the seintes buryeles lotynge°.
And he anon withouten tariynge
Dide his message, and whan that he it tolde
Urban for joye his handes gan up holde.

The teeris from his eyen leet he falle. 190
"Almyghty Lord, O Jhesu Crist," quod he,
"Sowere of chaast conseil°, hierde° of us alle,
The fruyt of thilke° seed of chastitee
That thou hast sowe in Cecile, taak to thee!
Lo, lyk a bisy bee, withouten gile, 195
Thee serveth ay thyn owene thral° Cecile.

---

129 Which that ycleped was, *who was called* **130 hir,** *their* **131 corage,** *spirit* **133 next,** *next to,* **yclad hire in an haire,** *dressed herself in a hair shirt* **136 gye,** *direct* **137 Unwemmed,** *spotless,* **lest,** *for fear,* **confounded,** *condemned* **139 faste,** *fasted* **140 Ay biddynge,** *always praying,* **orisons,** *prayers,* **ful faste,** *very eagerly* **143 pryvely** *privately* **145 conseil,** *secret* **146 right fayn,** *very happily* **147 So that,** *if,* **biwreye,** *betray* **148 gan faste,** *did eagerly* **149 for no cas,** *under no circumstances* **150, here,** *her* **151 at erst,** *for the first time* **154 ay,** *always,* **keepe,** *protect* **155**

out of drede, *without doubt* **156 in vileynye,** *shamefully* **158 shullen dye,** *shall die* **159 clene,** *pure,* **gye,** *keep* **162 wolde,** *wished* **163 agayn,** *in return* **165 verray,** *true* **167 for sothe,** *in truth* **169 anon-right,** *immediately* **170 list,** *wish* **171 trowe,** *believe* **173 ne stant but,** *stands only* **175 Sey hem,** *say to them* **178 secree nedes,** *secret purpose* **179 han biholde,** *do see* **182 er,** *before,* **twynne,** *depart* **183 ygon,** *gone* **186 seintes buryeles lotynge,** *hiding among the saint's burial places* **192 chaast conseil,** *chaste counsel,* **hierde,** *shepherd* **193 thilke,** *that* **196 thral,** *servant*

134 orgnes, organs; Cecilia's associations with organ music evidently led to her becoming patron saint of music in the Renaissance. **171 baptize,** receive baptism, the sacrament whereby someone becomes a Christian. **172 Via Apia,** the Appian Way leads south from Rome past the catacombs (subterranean burial galleries) where Christians may have buried their dead and hid from Roman persecution. **177 Urban,** Pope Urban I, beheaded in 230 CE.

"For thilke spouse that she took riht now,
Ful lyk a fiers leoun, she sendeth heere,
As meke as evere was any lomb, to yow."
And with that word anon ther gan appeere   200
An oold man clad in white clothes cleere°
That hadde a book with lettre of gold in honde,
And gan bifore Valerian to stonde.

Valerian as deed fil doun for drede
Whan he hym saugh, and he up hente° hym
    tho°,   205
And on his book right thus he gan to rede,
"O° Lord, O feith, O God, withouten mo,
O Cristendom, and Fader of alle also,
Aboven alle and over alle everywhere."
Thise wordes al with gold ywriten were.   210

Whan this was rad°, thanne seyde this olde man,
"Leevestow° this thyng or no? Sey ye or nay."
"I leeve° al this thyng," quod Valerian,
"For sother° thyng than this, I dar wel say,
Under the hevene no wight° thynke may."   215
Tho vanysshed this olde man, he nyste° where,
And Pope Urban hym cristened° right there.

Valerian gooth hoom and fynt° Cecilie
Withinne his chambre with an angel stonde°.
This angel hadde of roses and of lilie   220
Corones° two, the whiche he bar in honde,
And first to Cecile, as I understonde,
He yaf° that oon, and after gan he take
That oother to Valerian hir make°.

"With body clene and with unwemmed°
    thoght
Kepeth ay° wel thise corones," quod he.   225
"Fro Paradys to yow have I hem broght,
Ne nevere mo ne shal they roten bee,
Ne lese° hir soote savour°, trusteth me;
Ne nevere wight° shal seen hem with his eye   230
But° he be chaast and hate vileynye.

"And thow, Valerian, for° thow so soone
Assentedest to good conseil also,

Sey what thee list°, and thou shalt han thy boone°.
"I have a brother," quod Valerian tho°,   235
"That in this world I love no man so.
I pray yow that my brother may han grace
To knowe the trouthe, as I do, in this place."

The angel seyde, "God liketh thy requeste,
And bothe with the palm° of martirdom   240
Ye shullen come unto his blisful feste°."
And with that word Tiburce his brother coom°.
And whan that he the savour undernoom°,
Which that the roses and the lilies caste,
Withinne his herte he gan to wondre faste,   245

And seyde, "I wondre, this tyme of the yeer,
Whennes° that soote° savour cometh so
Of rose and lilies that I smelle heer?
For though I hadde hem in myne handes two,
The savour myghte in me no depper° go.   250
The sweete smel that in myn herte I fynde
Hath chaunged me al in° another kynde."

Valerian seyde, "Two corones° han we,
Snow white and rose reed that shynen cleere,
Whiche that thyne eyen° han no myght to
    see;   255
And as thou smellest hem thurgh my preyere,
So shaltow seen° hem, leeve° brother deere,
If it so be thou wolt, withouten slouthe°,
Bileve aright and knowen verray° trouthe."

Tiburce answerde, "Seistow° this to me   260
In soothnesse°, or in dreem I herkne° this?"
"In dremes," quod Valerian, "han we be
Unto this tyme, brother myn, ywis°.
And now at erst° in trouthe oure dwellyng is."
"How woostow° this," quod Tiburce, "and in
    what wyse?"   265
Quod Valerian, "That shal I thee devyse°.

"The aungel of God hath me the trouthe ytaught
Which thou shalt seen if that thou wolt reneye°

---

201 **cleere**, *bright* 205 **hente**, *lifted*, **tho**, *then* 207 **O**, *one* 211 **rad**, *read* 212 **Leevestow**, *do you believe* 213 **leeve**, *believe* 214 **sother**, *truer* 215 **wight**, *person* 216 **nyste**, *knew not* 217 **cristened**, *baptized* 218 **fynt**, *finds* 219 **stonde**, *standing* 221 **Corones**, *crowns* 223 **yaf**, *gave* 224 **make**, *spouse* 225 **unwemmed**, *spotless* 226 **Kepeth ay**, *protect always* 229 **lese**, *lose*, **soote savour**, *sweet scent* 230 **wight**, *person* 231 **But**, *unless* 232 **for**, *because* 234 **thee list**, *you desire*, **boone**, *wish* 235 **tho**, *then* 240 **palm**, *reward* 241 **feste**, *feast* 242 **coom**, *came* 243 **savour under-**

noom, *odor perceived* 247 **Whennes**, *from where*, **soote**, *sweet* 250 **depper**, *deeper* 252 **al in**, *completely into* 253 **corones**, *crowns* 255 **thyne eyen**, *your eyes* 257 **shaltow seen**, *shall you see*, **leeve**, *beloved* 258 **slouthe**, *delay through spiritual laziness* 259 **verray**, *genuine* 260 **Seistow**, *do you say* 261 **soothnesse**, *reality*, **herkne**, *(do I) hear* 263 **ywis**, *certainly* 264 **at erst**, *for the first time* 265 **woostow**, *do you know* 266 **devyse**, *explain* 268 **reneye**, *renounce*

201 **oold man**, probably St. Paul, since lines 207–9 quote his letter to the Ephesians 4.5–6. 220 **roses . . . lilie**, the crowns of roses and lilies symbolize martyrdom and purity.

The ydoles and be clene°, and elles naught."
And of the myracle of thise corones tweye   270
Seint Ambrose in his preface list to seye°;
Solempnely this noble doctour° deere
Commendeth it, and seith in this manere:

  "The palm° of martirdom for to receyve,
Seinte Cecile, fulfild of Goddes yifte,   275
The world and eek hire chambre° gan she
      weyve°—
Witnesse Tyburces and Valerians shrifte°,
To whiche God of his bountee wolde shifte°
Corones two of floures wel smellynge,
And made his angel hem the corones brynge.   280

"The mayde hath broght thise men to blisse
      above;
The world hath wist° what it is worth, certeyn,
Devocioun of chastitee to love."
Tho shewed hym Cecile al open° and pleyn
That alle ydoles nys° but a thyng in veyn,   285
For they been dombe and therto they been
      deve°,
And charged hym his ydoles for to leve.

"Whoso that troweth nat° this, a beest he is,"
Quod tho Tiburce, "if that I shal nat lye."
And she gan kisse his brest, that herde this,   290
And was ful glad he koude° trouthe espye°.
"This day I take thee for myn allye°,"
Seyde this blisful faire mayde deere,
And after that she seyde as ye may heere:

  "Lo, right so as the love of Crist," quod she, 295
"Made me thy brotheres wyf, right in that wise°
Anon for myn allye heer take I thee,
Syn that° thou wolt thyne ydoles despise.
Go with thy brother now and thee baptise,
And make thee clene so that thou mowe°
      biholde   300
The angeles face of which thy brother tolde."

Tiburce answerde and seyde, "Brother deere,
First tel me whider I shal° and to what man?"
"To whom?" quod he, "Com forth with right
      good cheere.
I wol thee lede unto the Pope Urban."   305
"Til Urban? Brother myn Valerian,"
Quod tho Tiburce, "woltow° me thider° lede?
Me thynketh that it were a wonder dede.

"Ne menestow nat° Urban," quod he tho,
"That is so ofte dampned° to be deed,   310
And woneth in halkes° alwey to and fro,
And dar nat ones putte forth his heed?
Men sholde hym brennen° in a fyr so reed
If he were founde, or that men myghte hym
      spye,
And we also, to bere° hym compaignye.   315

"And whil we seken thilke° divinitee
That is yhid in hevene pryvely°,
Algate ybrend° in this world shul we be!"
To whom Cecile answerde boldely,
"Men myghten dreden wel and skilfully°   320
This lyf to lese°, myn owene deere brother,
If this were lyvynge oonly° and noon oother.

"But ther is bettre lif in oother place
That nevere shal be lost, ne drede thee noght,
Which Goddes Sone us tolde thurgh his grace.   325
That Fadres Sone hath alle thyng ywroght°,
And al that wroght is with a skilful° thoght,
The Goost° that fro the Fader gan procede°
Hath sowled° hem, withouten any drede.

By word and by myracle Goddes Sone,   330
Whan he was in this world, declared heere
That ther was oother lyf ther° men may wone°."
To whom answerde Tiburce, "O suster deere,
Ne seydestow° right now in this manere,
Ther nys but o° God, lord in soothfastnesse°?   335
And now of three how maystow bere witnesse?"

---

269 **clene,** *pure* 271 **list to seye,** *chose to tell* 272 **doctour,** *teacher* 274 **palm,** *reward* 276 **chambre,** *bedchamber,* **weyve,** *give up* 277 **shrifte,** *conversion* 278 **shifte,** *assign* 282 **wist,** *learned* 284 **open,** *openly* 285 **nys,** *is nothing* 286 **deve,** *deaf* 288 **Whoso that troweth nat,** *whoever does not believe* 291 **koude,** *could,* **espye,** *see* 292 **allye,** *relative* 296 **wise,** *way* 298 **Syn that,** *because* 300 **mowe,** *might* 303 **whider I shal,** *where I shall (go)* 307 **woltow,** *will you,* **thider,** *there* 309 **Ne menestow nat,** *you can't mean*

310 **dampned,** *condemned* 311 **woneth in halkes,** *lives in hidden places* 313 **brennen,** *burn* 315 **bere,** *keep* 316 **thilke,** *that* 317 **pryvely,** *secretly* 318 **Algate ybrend,** *nevertheless burned* 320 **skilfully,** *reasonably* 321 **lese,** *lose* 322 **lyvynge oonly,** *the only (kind of) life* 326 **ywroght,** *created* 327 **skilful,** *reasoned* 328 **Goost,** *(Holy) Spirit,* **gan procede,** *did come forth* 329 **sowled,** *given them souls* 332 **ther,** *where,* **wone,** *dwell* 334 **Ne seydestow,** *didn't you say* 335 **nys but o,** *is only one,* **soothfastnesse,** *truth*

271 **Ambrose in his preface,** St. Ambrose (ca. 340–397); lines 274–83 derive from the preface to the Mass for St. Cecilia, attributed to Ambrose. 277 **Valerians,** a number of early MSS read "Cecilies," a mistake, probably in Chaucer's original.

"That shal I telle," quod she, "er I go.
Right as a man hath sapiences° three,
Memorie, engyn°, and intellect also,
So in o beynge° of divinitee   340
Thre persones may ther right wel bee."
Tho gan she hym ful bisily to preche
Of Cristes come°, and of his peynes teche°,

And manye pointes of his passioun°:
How Goddes Sone in this world was withholde° 345
To doon mankynde pleyn° remissioun,
That was ybounde in synne and cares colde.
Al this thyng she unto Tiburce tolde.
And after this, Tiburce in good entente
With Valerian to Pope Urban he wente,   350

That thanked God, and with glad herte and
          light
He cristned hym and made hym in that place,
Parfit° in his lernynge, Goddes kynght.
And after this Tiburce gat swich° grace
That every day he saugh in tyme and space   355
The aungel of God; and every maner boone°
That he God axed°, it was sped° ful soone.

It were ful hard by ordre° for to seyn
How manye wondres Jhesus for hem wroghte,
But atte laste, to tellen short and pleyn,   360
The sergeantz° of the toun of Rome hem soghte,
And hem biforn Almache the prefect° broghte,
Which hem apposed°, and knew al hire
          entente,
And to the ymage° of Juppiter hem sente,

And seyde, "Whoso wol nat sacrifise,   365
Swap of° his heed; this° my sentence heer."
Anon thise martirs that I yow devyse°,
Oon Maximus, that was an officer
Of the prefectes and his corniculer°,

Hem hente°, and whan he forth the seintes
          ladde   370
Hymself he weep° for pitee that he hadde.

Whan Maximus had herd the seintes loore°,
He gat hym of the tormentoures leve°,
And ladde hem to his hous withoute moore;
And with hir prechyng er that it were eve   375
They gonnen fro the tormentours to reve°,
And fro Maxime, and fro his folk echone°,
The false feith, to trowe° in God allone.

Cecile cam, whan it was woxen° nyght,
With preestes that hem cristned alle yfeere°;   380
And afterward, whan day was woxen light,
Cecile hem seyde with a ful stedefast cheere°,
"Now, Cristes owene knyghtes leeve° and deere,
Cast alle awey the werkes of derknesse,
And armeth yow in armure of brightnesse.   385

"Ye han forsothe° ydoon a greet bataille,
Youre cours° is doon, youre feith han ye
          conserved.
Gooth to the corone° of lif that may nat faille;
The rightful Juge, which that ye han served,
Shal yeve° it yow as ye han it deserved."   390
And whan this thyng was seyd as I devyse°,
Men ledde hem forth to doon the sacrefise.

But whan they weren to the place broght,
To tellen shortly the conclusioun,
They nolde° encense ne sacrifise right noght,   395
But on hir knees they setten hem adoun
With humble herte and sad° devocioun,
And losten bothe hir hevedes° in the place.
Hir soules wenten to the Kyng of Grace.

This Maximus, that saugh° this thyng bityde°,   400
With pitous teeris tolde it anon-right°,

---

338 sapiences, *mental faculties* **339 engyn,** *imagination* **340 o beynge,** *one being* **343 come,** *coming,* **teche,** *teach* **344 passioun,** *suffering* **345 withholde,** *retained* **346 pleyn,** *complete* **353 Parfit,** *perfect* **354 swich,** *such* **356 boone,** *request* **357 axed,** *asked,* **sped,** *accomplished* **358 by ordre,** *in proper order* **361 sergeantz,** *officers* **362 prefect,** *chief officer* **363 apposed,** *questioned* **364 ymage,** *statue* **366 Swap of,** *strike off,* **this,** *this is* **367 devyse,** *describe* **369 corniculer,** *assistant* **370 Hem hente,** *seized*

them **371 weep,** *wept* **372 loore,** *teaching* **373 gat hym . . . leve,** *obtained permission* **376 gonnen . . . to reve,** *did . . . remove* **377 echone,** *each one* **378 trowe,** *believe* **379 was woxen,** *had become* **380 yfeere,** *together* **382 ful stedefast cheere,** *very resolute expression* **383 leeve,** *beloved* **386 forsothe,** *truly* **387 cours,** *path* **388 corone,** *crown* **390 yeve,** *give* **391 devyse,** *describe* **395 nolde,** *would not* **397 sad,** *steadfast* **398 hevedes,** *heads* **400 that saugh,** *who saw,* **bityde,** *happen* **401 anon-right,** *immediately*

---

341 Thre persones, the Trinity, three persons in one God, one of the central mysteries of Christianity, explained with apparent ease by Cecilia. **342–48** Chaucer here summarizes a portion of the account in the *Legenda Aurea* and begins to follow a liturgical version of Cecilia's life at line 349; see the note to 84a and the introduction to part 8 above. **385 armeth yow,** arm yourselves; see Romans 13.12 and Ephesians 6.11–13. **386–90** See 2 Timothy 4.7–8. **395 encense,** worship by burning aromatic materials (incense). **398 losten bothe hir hevedes,** both Valerian and Tiburce lost their heads.

That he hir soules saugh° to hevene glyde
With aungels ful of cleernesse° and of light,
And with this word converted many a wight°;
For which Almachius dide hym so tobete°   405
With whippe of leed til he his lif gan lete°.

Cecile hym took and buryed hym anon
By Tiburce and Valerian softely°
Withinne hire° buriyng place under the stoon;
And after this Almachius hastily   410
Bad° his ministres fecchen° openly
Cecile, so that she myghte in his presence
Doon sacrifice and Juppiter encense.

But they, converted at° hir wise loore,
Wepten ful soore°, and yaven ful credence°   415
Unto hire word, and cryden moore and moore,
"Crist, Goddes sone, withouten difference,
Is verray° God—this is al oure sentence°—
That hath so good a servant hym to serve.
This with o voys° we trowen°, thogh we sterve°."   420

Almachius, that herde of this doynge,
Bad fecchen° Cecile that he myghte hire see;
And alderfirst°, lo, this was his axynge,
"What maner womman artow°?" tho quod he.
"I am a gentil womman born," quod she.   425
"I axe° thee," quod he, "though it thee greeve,
Of thy religioun and of thy bileeve."

"Ye han bigonne youre questioun folily°,"
Quod she, "that wolden two answeres conclude°
In o demande; ye axed lewedly°."   430
Almache answerde unto that similitude°,
"Of whennes° comth thyn answeryng so rude?"
"Of whennes?" quod she whan that she was
    freyned°,
"Of conscience and of good feith unfeyned°."

Almachius seyde, "Ne takestow noon heede°   435
Of my power?" And she answerde hym this:
"Youre myght," quod she, "ful litel is to dreede,
For every mortal mannes power nys°
But lyk a bladdre ful of wynd, ywys°.
For with a nedles poynt, whan it is blowe°,   440
May al the boost° of it be leyd ful lowe."

"Ful wrongfully bigonne thow," quod he,
"And yet in wrong is thy perseveraunce.
Wostow nat° how oure myghty princes free°
Han thus comanded and maad ordinaunce   445
That every Cristen wight° shal han penaunce°
But if that° he his Cristendom withseye°,
And goon al quit° if he wole it reneye°?"

"Yowre princes erren°, as youre nobleye°
    dooth,"
Quod tho Cecile, "and with a wood sentence°   450
Ye make us gilty, and it is nat sooth°.
For ye, that knowen wel oure innocence,
For as muche as we doon a reverence
To Crist, and for we bere a Cristen name,
Ye putte on us a cryme and eek a blame.   455

But we that knowen thilke° name so
For vertuous, we may it nat withseye°."
Almache answerde, "Chees° oon of thise two:
Do sacrifice, or Cristendom reneye°,
That thou mowe° now escapen by that weye."   460
At which the hooly blisful faire mayde
Gan for to laughe, and to the juge sayde:

"O juge, confus in thy nycetee°,
Woltow° that I reneye° innocence
To make me a wikked wight°?" quod shee.   465
"Lo°, he dissymuleth° heere in audience°;
He stareth and woodeth° in his advertence°."

402 hir soules saugh, *saw their souls* **403 cleernesse,** *brightness* **404 wight,** *person* **405 dide hym so tobete,** *had him so thoroughly beaten* **406 gan lete,** *did lose* **408 softely,** *secretly* **409 hire,** *their* **411 Bad,** *ordered,* **fecchen,** *to seize* **414 at,** *by* **415 ful soore,** *very intensely,* **yaven ful credence,** *gave complete belief* **418 verray,** *true,* **sentence,** *meaning* **420 o voys,** *a single voice,* **trowen,** *affirm,* **sterve,** *die* **422 Bad fecchen,** *ordered seized* **423 alderfirst,** *first of all* **424 artow,** *are you* **426 axe,** *ask* **428 folily,** *foolishly* **429 conclude,** *include* **430 axed lewedly,** *asked ignorantly* **431 similitude,** *comparison* **432 Of whennes,** *from where* **433 freyned,** *asked* **434 unfeyned,** *sincere* **435 Ne takestow noon heede,** *aren't you*

concerned **438 nys,** *is nothing* **439 ywys,** *to be sure* **440 blowe,** *inflated* **441 boost,** *boast* **444 Wostow nat,** *don't you know,* **free,** *generous* **446 wight,** *person,* **penaunce,** *punishment* **447 But if that,** *unless,* **withseye,** *deny* **448 al quit,** *completely free,* **reneye,** *renounce* **449 erren,** *make mistakes,* **nobleye,** *nobility* **450 wood sentence,** *insane mandate* **451 sooth,** *true* **456 thilke,** *that,* **457 withseye,** *deny* **458 Chees,** *choose* **459 reneye,** *renounce* **460 mowe,** *might* **463 nycetee,** *folly* **464 Woltow,** *do you wish,* **reneye,** *renounce* **465 wight,** *creature* **466 Lo,** *behold,* **dissymuleth,** *pretends,* **in audience,** *in public* **467 woodeth,** *raves,* **advertence,** *attention*

406 whippe of leed, a flail with pieces of metal (lead) attached. **429–30 two answeres . . . o demande,** Cecilia gives Almachius a blunt lesson in argumentation.

To whom Almachius, "Unsely° wrecche,
Ne woostow nat° how fer my myght may
    strecche?

"Han noght° oure myghty princes to me
    yiven°,   470
Ye, bothe power and auctoritee
To maken folk to dyen or to lyven?
Why spekestow° so proudly thanne to me?"
"I speke noght but stedfastly," quod she,
"Nat proudly, for I seye, as for my syde,   475
We haten deedly thilke° vice of pryde.

"And if thou drede nat a sooth° to heere,
Thanne wol I shewe al openly, by right,
That thou hast maad a ful gret lesyng° heere.
Thou seyst thy princes han thee yeven° myght   480
Bothe for to sleen and for to quyken° a wight,
Thou that ne mayst but oonly lyf bireve°;
Thou hast noon oother power ne no leve°.

"But thou mayst seyn thy princes han thee
    maked
Ministre of deeth, for if thou speke of mo°,   485
Thou lyest, for thy power is ful naked°."
"Do wey thy booldnesse," seyde Almachius tho,
"And sacrifice to oure goddes er thou go.
I recche° nat what wrong that thou me profre°,
For I kan suffre it as a philosophre,   490

"But thilke° wronges may I nat endure
That thou spekest of oure goddes heere,"
    quod he.
Cecile answerde, "O nyce° creature!
Thou seydest no word syn° thou spak to me
That I ne knew therwith thy nycetee;   495
And that thou were, in every maner wise,
A lewed° officer and a veyn° justise.

"Ther lakketh no thyng to thyne outer eyen
That thou n'art blynd, for thyng that we seen alle
That it is stoon—that men may wel espyen°—   500
That ilke° stoon a god thow wolt it calle.
I rede° thee, lat thyn hand upon it falle
And taste it wel and stoon thou shalt it fynde,
Syn° that thou seest nat with thyne eyen blynde.

"It is a shame that the peple shal   505
So scorne thee and laughe at thy folye,
For communly men woot° it wel overal
That myghty God is in his hevenes hye°.
And thise ymages, wel thou mayst espye
To thee ne to hemself° ne mowen noght
    profite°,   510
For in effect they been nat worth a myte°."

Thise wordes and swiche° othere seyde she,
And he weex wrooth° and bad° men sholde hir
    lede
Hom til hir hous, and "In hire hous," quod he,
"Brenne° hire right in a bath of flambes rede."   515
And as he bad, right so was doon in dede;
For in a bath they gonne hire faste shetten°,
And nyght and day greet fyr they under betten°.

The longe nyght and eek a day also
For al the fyr and eek the bathes heete   520
She sat al coold and feelede no wo;
It made hire nat a drope for to sweete°.
But in that bath hir lyf she moste lete°,
For he Almachius, with ful wikke entente,
To sleen hire in the bath his sonde° sente.   525

Thre strokes in the nekke he smoot° hire tho°,
The tormentour, but for no maner chaunce
He myghte noght smyte al hir nekke atwo°.
And for ther was that tyme an ordinaunce

---

468 **Unsely,** *unfortunate* 469 **Ne woostow nat,** *don't you know* 470 **Han noght,** *have not,* **yiven,** *given* 473 **spekestow,** *do you speak* 476 **deedly thilke,** *that deadly* 477 **sooth,** *truth* 479 **lesyng,** *lying* 480 **yeven,** *given* 481 **quyken,** *bring to life* 482 **bireve,** *deprive* 483 **leve,** *permission* 485 **mo,** *more* 486 **ful naked,** *wholly deficient* 489 **recche,** *care,* **profre,** *offer* 491 **thilke,** *those* 493 **nyce,** *foolish* 494 **syn,** *since* 497 **lewed,** *ignorant,* **veyn,** *ineffective* 500 **espyen,** *perceive* 501 **ilke,** *same* 502 **rede,**

advise 504 **Syn,** *since* 507 **woot,** *know* 508 **hye,** *high* 510 **hemself,** *themselves,* **ne mowen noght profite,** *might they not profit* 511 **myte,** *tiny coin* 512 **swiche,** *such* 513 **weex wrooth,** *grew angry,* **bad,** *ordered* (that) 515 **Brenne,** *burn* 517 **gonne hire faste shetten,** *shut her up tightly* 518 **betten,** *fed* 522 **sweete,** *sweat* 523 **moste lete,** *must give up* 525 **sonde,** *emissary* 526 **smoot,** *struck,* **tho,** *then* 528 **atwo,** *in two*

490 **philosophre,** i.e., Almachius claims he can bear it philosophically, although the word was also used of alchemists, a link to *CYT,* which follows. **498–99 Ther lakketh . . . blynd,** i.e., you are blind despite the fact that your physical eyes lack nothing. **515 bath of flambes rede,** bath of red flames; the flame bath was either a room heated from below in the Roman manner (a hypocaust) or a large pot. The manner of attempting to kill Cecilia is analogous to alchemists' attempts to refine or purify substances by sweating or distillation. Cecilia's lack of sweat (line 522) demonstrates her purity and contrasts the sweat of *CYP* 8.560ff.

That no man sholde doon man swich
    penaunce°   530
The ferthe strook to smyten, softe or soore,
This tormentour ne dorste° do namoore,

But half deed, with hir nekke ycorven there,
He lefte hir lye, and on his wey he went.
The Cristen folk which that aboute hire were   535
With sheetes han the blood ful faire yhent°.
Thre dayes lyved she in this torment,
And nevere cessed hem° the feith to teche
That she hadde fostred°. Hem she gan to preche,

And hem she yaf° hir moebles° and hir
    thyng°,   540

And to the Pope Urban bitook° hem tho,
And seyde, "I axed° this at Hevene Kyng,
To han respit° thre dayes and namo°,
To recomende to yow er that I go
Thise soules, lo, and that I myghte do werche°   545
Heere of myn hous perpetuelly a cherche."

    Seint Urban with his deknes° prively°
The body fette° and buryed it by nyghte
Among his othere seintes honestly°.
Hir hous the chirche of Seinte Cecilie highte°.   550
Seint Urban halwed° it as he wel myghte,
In which into this day in noble wyse
Men doon to Crist and to his seinte servyse.

Heere is ended the Seconde Nonnes Tale.

---

530 swich penaunce, *such punishment* **532 ne dorste,** *dared not* **536 yhent,** *soaked up* **538 hem,** *to them* **539 fostred,** *instructed* **540 yaf,** *gave,* **moebles,** *portable possessions,* **thyng,** *things* **541 bitook,** *entrusted* **542 axed,** *asked* **543 han respit,** *have delay,* **namo,** *no more* **545 do** werche, *have made* **547 deknes,** *deacons,* **prively,** *secretly* **548 fette,** *brought* **549 honestly,** *honorably* **550 highte,** *is called* **551 halwed,** *blessed*

533 nekke ycorven, compare *PrT* 7.611, and contrast the little boy's continued singing with Cecilia's preaching.

CANON'S YEOMAN'S TALE

PROLOGUE

The Prologe of the Chanouns Yemannes Tale.

Whan ended was the lyf of Seinte Cecile,
Er° we hadde riden fully fyve mile, 555
At Boghtoun-under-Blee us gan atake°
A man that clothed was in clothes blake,
And undernethe he hadde a whyt surplys.
His hakeney°, that was al pomely grys°,
So swatte° that it wonder was to see; 560
It semed as he had priked° miles three.
The hors eek that his yeman° rood upon
So swatte that unnethe° myghte it gon.
Aboute the peytrel° stood the foom° ful hye;
He was of foom al flekked as a pye°. 565
A male tweyfoold° upon his croper° lay.
It semed that he caried lite° array.
Al light for somer° rood this worthy man.
And in myn herte to wondren I bigan
What that he was til that I understood 570

How that his cloke was sowed° to his hood,
For which, whan I hadde longe avysed me°,
I demed° hym som chanoun for to be.
His hat heeng at his bak doun by a laas°,
For he hadde riden moore than trot or paas°; 575
He hadde ay priked° lik as he were wood°.
A clote-leef° he hadde under his hood
For swoot°, and for to kepe his heed from
  heete—
But it was joye for to seen hym swete!
His forheed dropped as° a stillatorie 580
Were ful of plantayne° and of paritorie°.
And whan that he was come he gan to crye,
"God save," quod he, "this joly compaignye!
Faste have I priked," quod he, "for youre sake,
By cause that I wolde yow atake°, 585
To riden in som myrie° compaignye."

---

555 **Er,** *before* 556 **gan atake,** *overtook* 559 **hakeney,** *riding horse,*
pomely grys, *dappled gray* 560 **swatte,** *sweated* 561 **priked,** *spurred* 562
yeman, *servant* 563 **unnethe,** *scarcely* 564 **peytrel,** *breast harness,*
foom, *foam* 565 **pye,** *magpie* 566 **male tweyfoold,** *double bag,* **croper,**
harness behind the saddle 567 **lite,** *little* 568 **Al light for somer,** *equipped*

lightly for summer 571 **sowed,** *sewn* 572 **avysed me,** *reflected* 573
demed, *judged* 574 **laas,** *cord* 575 **paas,** *(walking) pace* 576 **ay priked,**
the whole way spurred, **wood,** *crazed* 577 **clote-leef,** *leaf of a large weed*
578 **swoot,** *sweat* 580 **dropped as,** *dripped as if* 581 **plantayne,** *an herb,*
paritorie, *an herb* 585 **atake,** *overtake* 586 **myrie,** *merry*

---

556 **Boghtoun-under-Blee,** Boughton, a town about five miles from Canterbury, in the Blean Forest. 558 **surplys,** surplice; an ecclesiastical garment, usually worn as an outer garment. 573 **chanoun,** canon; a clergyman who lives a communal life and helps administer a cathedral, college, or other ecclesiastical institution. This is probably a secular canon, one who lives under a lax rule (as opposed to a regular canon who lives under strict regulations), or perhaps he has abandoned his office. 580 **stillatorie,** still, distiller; a heating vessel used in medicine, chemistry, and alchemy to extract or purify by distillation. See *SNT* 8.515n.

His yeman eek was ful of curteisye
And seyde, "Sires, now in the morwe-tyde°
Out of youre hostelrie° I saugh yow ryde,
And warned° heer my lord and my soverayn, 590
Which that° to ryden with yow is ful fayn°
For his desport°; he loveth daliaunce°."
 "Freend, for thy warnyng God yeve° thee
  good chaunce,"
Thanne seyde oure Hoost, "for certein it wolde
  seme
Thy lord were wys, and so I may wel deme°. 595
He is ful jocunde° also, dar I leye°!
Can he oght° telle a myrie tale or tweye,
With which he glade° may this compaignye?"
 "Who, sire? My lord? Ye, ye withouten lye.
He kan° of murthe and eek of jolitee 600
Nat but ynough°; also, sire, trusteth me,
And ye hym knewe as wel as do I,
Ye wolde wondre how wel and craftily
He koude werke, and that in sondry wise°.
He hath take on hym many a greet
  emprise°, 605
Which were ful hard for any that is heere
To brynge aboute, but° they of hym it leere°.
As hoomly° as he rit° amonges yow,
If ye hym knewe, it wolde be for youre prow°.
Ye wolde nat forgoon° his aqueyntaunce 610
For muchel good, I dar leye in balaunce°
Al that I have in my possessioun.
He is a man of heigh discrecioun;
I warne° yow wel, he is a passyng° man."
 "Wel," quod oure Hoost, "I pray thee, tel me
  than, 615
Is he a clerk or noon? Telle what he is."
 "Nay, he is gretter than a clerk, ywis°,"
Seyde this Yeman, "and in wordes fewe,
Hoost, of his craft somwhat I wol yow shewe.
 "I seye, my lord kan swich° subtilitee— 620
But al his craft ye may nat wite at° me,
And somwhat helpe I yet to his wirkyng—

That al this ground on which we been ridyng
Til that we come to Caunterbury toun,
He koude al clene° turnen up so doun°, 625
And pave it al of silver and of gold!"
 And whan this Yeman hadde this tale ytold
Unto oure Hoost, he seyde, "Benedicitee°,
This thyng is wonder° merveillous to me,
Syn that° thy lord is of so heigh prudence, 630
By cause of which men sholde hym reverence,
That of his worshipe° rekketh he° so lite.
His oversloppe° nys nat° worth a myte°,
As in effect°, to hym, so moot I go°.
It is al baudy° and totore° also. 635
Why is thy lord so sluttissh°, I the preye,
And is of power° bettre clooth to beye°,
If that his dede° accorde with they speche?
Telle me that, and that I thee biseche°."
 "Why?" quod this Yeman, "Wherto axe ye
  me? 640
God help me so, for he shal nevere thee°—
But I wol nat avowe that° I seye,
And therfore keep it secree, I yow preye—
He is to wys°, in feith, as I bileeve.
That that° is overdoon, it wol nat preeve° 645
Aright, as clerkes seyn; it is a vice.
Wherfore in that I holde hym lewed° and
  nyce°.
For whan a man hath over-greet° a wit,
Ful oft hym happeth to mysusen it.
So dooth my lord, and that me greveth
  soore. 650
God it amende°! I kan sey yow namoore."
 "Therof no fors°, good Yeman," quod oure
  Hoost;
"Syn° of the konnyng° of thy lord thow woost°,
Telle how he dooth, I pray thee hertely,
Syn that he is so crafty and so sly°. 655
Where dwelle ye, if it to telle be°?"
 "In the suburbes of a toun," quod he,
"Lurkynge in hernes° and in lanes blynde°,

---

588 morwe-tyde, *morning* 589 hostelrie, *inn* 590 warned, *advised* 591 Which that, *who,* ful fayn, *very eager* 592 desport, *entertainment,* daliaunce, *conversation* 593 yeve, *give* 595 deme, *judge* 596 jocunde, *cheerful,* dar I leye, *I dare bet* 597 oght, *at all* 598 glade, *please* 600 kan, *knows* 601 Nat but ynough, *more than enough* 604 sondry wise, *many ways* 605 emprise, *enterprise* 607 but, *unless,* leere, *learn* 608 hoomly, *familiarly,* rit, *rides* 609 prow, *profit* 610 forgoon, *give up* 611 leye in balaunce, *bet* 614 warne, *advise,* passyng, *excellent* 617 ywis, *certainly* 620 kan swich, *knows such* 621 wite at, *know from* 625 koude al clene, *could completely,* up so doun, *upside down* 628 Benedicitee, *bless you*

629 wonder, *wonderfully* 630 Syn that, *since* 632 worshipe, *honor,* rekketh he, *he cares* 633 oversloppe, *overshirt,* nys nat, *is not,* myte, *tiny coin* 634 As in effect, *in fact,* so moot I go, *as far as I can tell* 635 baudy, *dirty,* totore, *torn* 636 sluttissh, *sloppy* 637 of power, *able,* beye, *buy* 638 dede, *actions* 639 biseche, *ask* 641 thee, *prosper* 642 avowe that, *admit to what* 644 to wys, *too smart* 645 That that, *that which,* preeve, *turn out* 647 lewed, *ignorant,* nyce, *foolish* 648 over-greet, *too great* 651 amende, *correct* 652 no fors, *no matter* 653 Syn, *since,* konnyng, *knowledge,* woost, *knows* 655 sly, *clever* 656 to telle be, *can be told* 658 hernes, *hidden places,* lanes blynde, *dead ends*

589 hostelrie, hostelry or inn; no location is specified or need be, but SK observed that five miles before Boughton (see lines 555–56) lies Ospringe, a customary lodging place for pilgrims on the way from London to Canterbury.

Where as thise robbours and thise theves by
    kynde°
Holden hir pryvee°, fereful residence,   660
As they that dar nat shewen hir presence;
So faren we, if I shal seye the sothe°."
    "Now," quod oure Hoost, "yit lat me talke to the.
Why artow° so discoloured of thy face?"
    "Peter°," quod he, "God yeve it harde
    grace°!   665
I am so used in the fyr to blowe
That it hath chaunged my colour, I trowe°.
I am nat wont° in no mirour to prie°,
But swynke soore° and lerne multiplie.
We blondren° evere and pouren° in the fir,   670
And for al that we faille of oure desir,
For evere we lakken oure conclusioun°.
To muchel° folk we doon illusioun,
And borwe gold, be it a pound or two,
Or ten, or twelve, or manye sommes mo°,   675
And make hem wenen° at the leeste weye
That of a pound we koude make tweye°.
Yet is it fals, but ay° we han good hope
It for to doon, and after it we grope.
But that science is so fer us biforn,   680
We mowen° nat, although we hadden sworn,
It overtake, it slit° awey so faste.
It wole us maken beggers atte laste."
    Whil this Yeman was thus in his talkyng,
This Chanoun drough hym° neer and herde al
    thyng   685
Which this Yeman spak, for suspecioun
Of mennes speche evere hadde this Chanoun.
For Catoun seith that he that gilty is

Demeth° alle thyng be spoke of hym, ywis°.
That was the cause he gan so ny° hym drawe   690
To his Yeman, to herknen° al his sawe°.
And thus he seyde unto his Yeman tho°,
"Hoold thou thy pees and spek no wordes mo,
For if thou do, thou shalt it deere abye°.
Thou sclaundrest° me heere in this
    compaignye,   695
And eek discoverest° that thou sholdest hyde."
    "Ye," quod oure Hoost, "telle on what so bityde°.
Of al his thretyng° rekke° nat a myte°."
    "In feith," quod he, "namoore I do but lyte°."
    And whan this Chanoun saugh it wolde nat
    bee,   700
But his Yeman wolde telle his pryvetee°,
He fledde awey for verray° sorwe and shame.
    "A," quod the Yeman, "heere shal arise game;
Al that I kan° anon now wol I telle.
Syn° he is goon, the foule feend hym quelle°!   705
For nevere heerafter wol I with hym meete
For peny ne for pound, I yow biheete°.
He that me broghte first unto that game,
Er that he dye, sorwe have he and shame.
For it is ernest to me, by my feith;   710
That feele I wel, what so° any man seith.
And yet for al my smert° and al my grief,
For al my sorwe, labour, and meschief°,
I koude nevere leve it in no wise°.
Now wolde God° my wit myghte suffise   715
To tellen al that longeth° to that art.
And nathelees yow wol I tellen part.
Syn that my lord is goon, I wol nat spare°;
Swich thyng as that I knowe, I wol declare."

Heere endeth the Prologe of the Chanouns Yemannes Tale.

Heere bigynneth the Chanouns Yeman his Tale.

    With this Chanoun I dwelt have seven yeer,   720
And of his science° am I never the neer°.

Al that I hadde I have lost therby,
And God woot° so hath many mo° than I.

---

659 by kynde, *naturally* **660 hir pryvee,** *their secret* **662 seye the sothe,** *tell you truth* **664 artow,** *are you* **665 Peter,** *by St. Peter,* **yeve it harde grace,** *give it bad luck* **667 trowe,** *believe* **668 wont,** *accustomed,* **prie,** *look* **669 swynke soore,** *work hard* **670 blondren,** *blunder,* **pouren,** *stare* **672 conclusioun,** *goal* **673 muchel,** *many* **675 sommes mo,** *more sums* **676 wenen,** *think* **677 tweye,** *two* **678 ay,** *always* **681 mowen,** *may* **682 slit,** *slides* **685 drough hym,** *drew himself* **689 Demeth,** *thinks,* **ywis,** *surely* **690 ny,** *near* **691 herknen,** *hear,* **sawe,** *saying* **692 tho,** *then*

694 deere abye, *pay for it dearly* **695 sclaundrest,** *slander* **696 eek discoverest,** *also reveal* **697 what so bityde,** *whatever happens* **698 thretyng,** *threatening,* **rekke,** *care,* **myte,** *tiny coin* **699 lyte,** *little* **701 pryvetee,** *secrets* **702 verray,** *genuine* **704 kan,** *know* **705 Syn,** *since,* **quelle,** *kill* **707 biheete,** *promise* **711 what so,** *whatever* **712 smert,** *pain* **713 meschief,** *misfortune* **714 wise,** *way* **715 wolde God,** *may God grant* **716 longeth,** *pertains* **718 spare,** *refrain* **721 science,** *knowledge,* **neer,** *nearer* **723 woot,** *knows,* **mo,** *more* (people)

669 multiplie, to transmute; i.e., the alchemical transformation of base to precious metals. **674 borwe gold,** earnest alchemists borrowed gold on the theory that it was necessary to initiate the process of transforming base metals; con artists capitalized on this belief. **688 Catoun,** Dionysius Cato, supposed author of *Disticha Catonis* (Cato's Couplets) 1.7.

Ther° I was wont° to be right fressh and gay
Of clothyng and of oother good array,   725
Now may I were an hose° upon myn heed;
And wher my colour was bothe fressh and reed,
Now is it wan° and of a leden hewe—
Whoso it useth°, soore shal he rewe°—
And of my swynk° yet blered is myn eye.   730
Lo, which° avantage is to multiplie°!
That slidyng° science hath me maad so bare
That I have no good° wher that evere I fare°;
And yet I am endetted° so therby
Of gold that I have borwed, trewely,   735
That whil I lyve I shal it quite° nevere.
Lat every man bewar by me forevere!
What maner° man that casteth hym° therto,
If he continue I holde his thrift ydo°.
For so helpe me God, therby shal he nat
          wynne,   740
But empte his purs and make his wittes
          thynne.
And whan he thurgh his madnesse and folye
Hath lost his owene good thurgh jupartye°,
Thanne he exciteth° oother folk therto
To lesen hir good°, as he hymself hath do.   745
For unto shrewes° joye it is and ese
To have hir felawes in peyne and disese°.
Thus was I ones lerned of° a clerk—
Of that no charge°, I wol speke of oure werk.
     Whan we been there as we shul exercise   750
Oure elvysshe° craft we semen wonder° wise,
Oure termes been so clergial° and so queynte°.
I blowe the fir til that myn herte feynte.
What° sholde I tellen ech proporcioun
Of thynges whiche that we werche° upon,   755
As on fyve or sixe ounces, may wel be,
Of silver, or som oother quantitee,

And bisye me to telle yow the names
Of orpyment°, brent° bones, iren squames°,
That into poudre grounden been ful smal;   760
And in an erthen pot how put is al,
And salt yput in, and also papeer,
Biforn thise poudres that I speke of heer;
And wel ycovered with a lampe° of glas;
And of muche oother thyng which that ther
          was;   765
And of the pot and glasses enlutyng°,
That of the eyr° myghte passe out nothyng;
And of the esy° fir, and smart° also,
Which that was maad; and of the care and wo
That we hadden in oure matires sublymyng°;   770
And in amalgamyng and calceniyng
Of quyksilver°, yclept° mercurie crude°?
For alle oure sleightes° we kan nat conclude°.
Oure orpyment° and sublymed° mercurie,
Oure grounden litarge° eek in the
          porfurie°,   775
Of ech of thise of ounces a certeyn°,
Noght helpeth us. Oure labour is in veyn.
Ne eek° oure spirites ascencioun°,
Ne oure matires° that lyen al fix adoun°,
Mowe° in oure werkyng nothyng us availle,   780
For lost is al oure labour and travaille°;
And al the cost, a twenty devel way,
Is lost also which we upon it lay°.
     Ther is also ful many another thyng
That is unto oure craft apertenyng°.   785
Though I by ordre hem nat reherce kan
By cause that I am a lewed° man,
Yet wol I telle hem as they come to mynde,
Thogh I ne kan nat sette hem in hir kynde°,
As boole armonyak°, vertgrees°, boras°,   790
And sondry° vessels maad of erthe and glas,

---

724 Ther, *where,* **wont,** *accustomed* **726 hose,** *stocking* **728 wan,** *pale* **729 it useth,** *practices it* (i.e., alchemy), **rewe,** *regret* **730 of my swynk,** *by my work* **731 which,** *what,* **to multiplie,** *to transmute* **732 slidyng,** *unreliable* **733 good,** *goods,* **fare,** *go* **734 endetted,** *in debt* **736 quite,** *repay* **738 What maner,** *whatever kind of,* **casteth hym,** *devotes himself* **739 thrift ydo,** *welfare destroyed* **743 jupartye,** *taking chances* **744 exciteth,** *incites* **745 lesen hir good,** *lose their goods* **746 shrewes,** *scoundrels* **747 disese,** *discomfort* **748 ones lerned of,** *once taught by* **749 no charge,** *no matter* **751 elvysshe,** *mysterious,* **semen wonder,** *seem wonderfully* **752 clergial,** *learned,* **queynte,** *intricate* **754 What,** *why* **755 werche,** *work* **759 orpyment,** *arsenic,* **brent,** *burned,* **squames,** *chips*

764 lampe, *lamp-shaped lid* **766 enlutyng,** *sealing* **767 eyr,** *air* **768 esy,** *moderate,* **smart,** *brisk* **770 matires sublymyng,** *refining materials* **772 quyksilver,** *mercury,* **yclept,** *called,* **crude,** *unrefined* **773 sleightes,** *tricks,* **conclude,** *succeed* **774 orpyment,** *arsenic,* **sublymed,** *purified* **775 litarge,** *lead monoxide,* **porfurie,** *marble mortar* (grinding bowl) **776 certeyn,** *certain* (amount) **778 Ne eek,** *nor also,* **spirites ascencioun,** *vapors rising* **779 matires,** *solids,* **al fix adoun,** *remaining in the bottom* **780 Mowe,** *might* **781 travaille,** *effort* **783 lay,** *took a chance* **785 is unto . . . apertenyng,** *pertains to* **787 lewed,** *unlearned* **789 in hir kynde,** *their natures* **790 boole armonyak,** *Armenian clay,* **vertgrees,** *copper acetate,* **boras,** *borax* **791 sondry,** *various*

---

730 blered is myn eye, my eye is blinded; i.e., I have been cheated. **762 salt . . . papeer,** salt and pepper; the bizarre concoction is typical of actual alchemical writing, but also parodic. **771 amalgamyng and calceniyng,** amalgamating and calcining; i.e., alloying with mercury and reducing to powder by heating. **782 a twenty devel way,** by twenty devils' paths; an exclamation of frustration or irritation. **786 by ordre hem nat reherce kan,** cannot relate them in an orderly way. The wrenched syntax contributes to the laboriousness of the Yeoman's disorderly and disconcerting tally of alchemical apparatus, terms, and processes.

Oure urynals° and oure descensories°,
Violes°, crosletz°, and sublymatories°,
Cucurbites° and alambikes° eek,
And othere swiche°, deere ynough a leek—   795
Nat nedeth it for to reherce hem alle—
Watres rubifiyng°, and boles galle°,
Arsenyk, sal armonyak°, and brymstoon°;
And herbes koude° I telle eek many oon,
As egremoyne°, valerian, and lunarie°,   800
And othere swiche, if that me liste tarie°;
Oure lampes brennyng bothe nyght and day,
To brynge aboute oure purpos, if we may;
Oure fourneys° eek of calcinacioun°,
And of watres albificacioun°;   805
Unslekked lym°, chalk, and gleyre of an ey°,
Poudres diverse, asshes, donge, pisse, and cley,
Cered° pottes, sal peter°, vitriole°,
And diverse fires maad of wode and cole;
Sal tartre°, alkaly°, and sal preparat°,   810
And combust matires° and coagulat°;
Cley maad with hors or mannes heer°, and oille
Of tartre°, alum glas°, berme°, wort°, and argoille°,
Resalgar°, and oure matires enbibyng°,
And eek of oure matires encorporyng°,   815
And of oure silver citrinacioun°,
Oure cementyng° and fermentacioun,
Oure yngottes°, testes°, and many mo.
  I wol yow telle, as was me taught also,
The foure spirites and the bodies sevene   820
By ordre, as ofte I herde my lord hem nevene°.
  The firste spirit quyksilver called is,
The seconde orpyment, the thridde, ywis,
Sal armonyak, and the ferthe brymstoon.

The bodyes sevene eek, lo, hem heere anoon: 825
Sol° gold is, and Luna° silver we threpe°,
Mars iren, Mercurie quyksilver we clepe°,
Saturnus leed, and Juppiter is tyn,
And Venus coper, by my fader kyn°.
  This cursed craft whoso wole exercise°,   830
He shal no good han° that hym may suffise,
For al the good he spendeth theraboute
He lese° shal, therof have I no doute.
Whoso that listeth outen° his folie,
Lat hym come forth and lerne multiplie.   835
And every man that oght° hath in his cofre°,
Lat hym appiere° and wexe° a philosophre.
Ascauns° that craft is so light° to leere°—
Nay, nay, God woot°, al be he° monk or frere,
Preest or chanoun, or any oother wyght°,   840
Though he sitte at his book bothe day and nyght
In lernyng of this elvysshe nyce loore°,
Al is veyn°, and parde°, muchel moore.
To lerne a lewed man this subtiltee—
Fy, spek nat therof, for it wol nat bee.   845
And konne he letterure° or konne he noon,
As in effect he shal fynde it al oon°.
For bothe two°, by my savacioun,
Concluden in multiplicacioun
Ylike° wel, whan they han al ydo°—   850
This is to seyn, they faillen bothe two.
  Yet forgat I to maken rehersaille
Of watres corosif°, and of lymaille°,
And of bodies mollificacioun°,
And also of hire induracioun°,   855
Oilles, ablucions°, and metal fusible°—
To tellen al wolde passen any bible°

---

792 urynals, *glass bottles,* **descensories,** *vessels for distilling* **793 Violes,** *small bottles,* **crosletz,** *crucibles,* **sublymatories,** *vessels for vaporizing solids* **794 Cucurbites,** *curved vessels,* **alambikes,** *vessels for distilling* **795 swiche,** *such* (things) **797 Watres rubifiyng,** *liquids that produce redness,* **boles gall,** *bull's bile* **798 sal armonyak,** *ammonium chloride,* **brymstoon,** *sulfur* **799 koude,** *could* **800 egremoyne,** *agrimony,* **lunarie,** *moonwort fern* **801 me liste tarie,** *I wished to delay* **804 fourneys,** *furnace,* **calcinacioun,** *reducing to powder* **805 watres albificacioun,** *whitening of liquids* **806 Unslekked lym,** *caustic lime,* **gleyre of an ey,** *egg white* **808 Cered,** *waxed,* **sal peter,** *saltpeter,* **vitriole,** *metal sulfate or sulfuric acid* **810 Sal tartre,** *potassium carbonate,* **alkaly,** *salt from boiled sea plants,* **sal preparat,** *purified salt* **811 combust matires,** *burned materials,* **coagulat,** *congealed* **812 heer,** *hair* **812–13 oille / Of tartre,** *cream of tartar,* **alum glas,** *rock alum,* **berme,** *yeast,* **wort,** *beer mash,* **argoille,** *wine-cast deposits* **814 Resalgar,** *red arsenic,* **matires**

enbibyng, *absorbent materials* **815 matires encorporyng,** *alloying materials* **816 silver citrinacioun,** *turning silver a yellowish color* **817 cementyng,** *fusing by heat* **818 yngottes,** *molds for casting metal,* **testes,** *testing vessels* **821 nevene,** *name* **826 Sol,** *the sun,* **Luna,** *the moon,* **threpe,** *assert* **827 clepe,** *call* **829 fader kyn,** *father's family* **830 exercise,** *practice* (it) **831 han,** *have* **833 lese,** *lose* **834 listeth outen,** *wishes to reveal* **836 oght,** *anything,* **cofre,** *treasure chest* **837 appiere,** *appear,* **wexe,** *become* **838 Ascauns,** *as if,* **light,** *easy,* **leere,** *learn* **839 woot,** *knows,* **al be he,** *even if he is* **840 wyght,** *person* **842 elvysshe nyce loore,** *otherworldly foolish learning* **843 veyn,** *empty,* **parde,** *by God* **846 konne he letterure,** (if) *he knows book learning* **847 al oon,** *all the same* **848 bothe two,** i.e., *the learned and the unlearned* **850 Ylike,** *alike,* **ydo,** *done* **853 watres corosif,** *acids,* **lymaille,** *metal filings* **854 mollificacioun,** *being softened,* **855 induracioun,** *being hardened* **856 ablucions,** *rinses,* **fusible,** *meltable* **857 bible,** *book*

---

795 deere ynough a leek, worth as much as a leek; i.e., worthless. **800 valerian,** like the others mentioned in this line, valerian is a plant. The husband of Cecilia in *SNT* is also named Valerian. **820 foure spirites . . . bodies sevene,** four substances that can be vaporized by heat: quicksilver (mercury), orpyment (arsenic), sal armonyak (ammonia), and brimstone (sulfur); seven metals that correspond to the seven planets. Variations on the classification are common in alchemy, and the lines describing the metals (826–29) have the appearance of a mnemonic jingle.

That owher is°. Wherfore, as for the beste,
Of alle thise names now wol I me reste.
For, as I trowe°, I have yow toold ynowe°   860
To reyse a feend°, al looke he° never so rowe°.
  A, nay, lat be! The philosophres stoon,
Elixer clept°, we sechen faste echoon°,
For hadde we hym°, thanne were we siker ynow°.
But unto God of hevene I make avow,   865
For al oure craft whan we han al ydo°,
With al oure sleighte° he° wol nat come us to.
He° hath ymaad us spenden muchel good
For sorwe of which almoost we wexen wood°,
But° that good hope crepeth in oure herte   870
Supposynge evere, though we sore smerte°,
To be releeved by hym afterward.
Swich supposyng and hope is sharp and hard.
I warne yow wel, it is to seken evere°,
That futur temps° hath maad men dissevere°   875
In trust therof from al that evere they hadde.
Yet of that art they kan nat wexen sadde°,
For unto hem it is a bitter sweete—
So semeth it—for nadde° they but a sheete
Which that they myghte wrappe hem inne
    a-nyght,   880
And a brat° to walken inne by daylyght,
They wolde hem selle and spenden on this craft.
They kan nat stynte° til nothyng be laft.
And everemoore where that evere they goon
Men may hem knowe by smel of brymstoon°.   885
For al the world they stynken as a goot;
Hir savour° is so rammyssh° and so hoot°
That though a man a mile from hem be,
The savour wole infecte hym, trusteth me.
And thus by smell and threedbare array°,   890
If that men liste° this folk they knowe may.
And if a man wole aske hem pryvely°
Why they been clothed so unthriftily°,
They right anon° wol rownen° in his ere

And seyn if that they espied° were   895
Men wolde hem slee by cause° of hir science°.
Lo, thus this folk bitrayen innocence!
  Passe over this; I go my tale unto.
Er that the pot be on the fir ydo°,
Of metals with a certeyn quantitee,   900
My lord hem trempeth°, and no man but he—
Now he is goon, I dar seyn° boldely—
For, as men seyn, he kan doon craftily.
Algate° I woot° wel he hath swich a name,
And yet ful ofte he renneth in a blame°.   905
And wite° ye how? Ful ofte it happeth so
The pot tobreketh°, and farewel, al is go°.
Thise metals been of so greet violence
Oure walles mowe° nat make hem resistence,
But if° they weren wroght of lym° and stoon;   910
They percen so, and thurgh the wal they goon.
And somme of hem synke into the ground—
Thus han we lost by tymes° many a pound—
And somme are scatered al the floor aboute;
Somme lepe into the roof. Withouten doute,   915
Though that the feend noght in oure sighte
    hym shewe°,
I trowe° he with us be, that ilke shrewe°!
In helle, where that he lord is and sire,
Nis ther° moore wo ne moore rancour ne ire.
Whan that oure pot is broke, as I have sayd,   920
Every man chit° and halt hym yvele apayd°.
  Somme seyde it was long on the fir makyng.
Somme seyde nay, it was on the blowyng—
Thanne was I fered°, for that was myn office°.
"Straw°," quod the thridde, "ye been lewed°
    and nyce°!   925
It was nat trempred° as it oghte be."
"Nay," quod the fourthe, "stynt° and herkne° me.
By cause oure fir ne was nat maad of beech,
That is the cause and oother noon, so theech°!"
I kan nat telle wheron it was along°,   930

---

858 **owher,** *anywhere* 860 **trowe,** *believe,* **ynowe,** *enough* 861 **reyse a feend,** *call up a demon,* **al looke he,** *although he looks,* **rowe,** *rough* 863 **clept,** *called,* **sechen faste echoon,** *each (of us) seek zealously* 864 **hym, it, siker ynow,** *certain enough* 866 **ydo,** *done* 867 **sleighte,** *cleverness,* **he,** *it* 868 **He,** *it,* **ymaad,** *made* 869 **wexen wood,** *go insane* 870 **But, except** 871 **sore smerte,** *hurt sorely* 874 **evere,** *forever* 875 **That futur temps,** *so that future times* (i.e., hopes for the future), **dissevere,** *separate* 877 **wexen sadde,** *become satisfied* 879 **nadde they,** *had they nothing* 881 **brat,** *rough coat* 883 **stynte,** *stop* 885 **brymstoon,** *sulfur* 887 **savour,** *smell,* **rammyssh,** *ramlike,* **hoot,** *intense* 890 **array,** *clothing* 891 **liste,** *wish* 892 **pryvely,** *secretly* 893 **unthriftily,** *poorly* 894 **right anon,**

immediately, **rownen,** *whisper* 895 **espied,** *discovered* 896 **by cause,** *because,* **science,** *knowledge* 899 **ydo,** *placed* 901 **trempreth,** *mixes* 902 **dar seyn,** *dare speak* 904 **Algate,** *even though,* **woot,** *know* 905 **renneth in a blame,** *is disgraced* 906 **wite,** *know* 907 **tobreketh,** *shatters,* **go,** *gone* 909 **mowe,** *might* 910 **But if,** *unless,* **lym,** *mortar* 913 **by tymes,** *in a moment* 916 **hym shewe,** *shows himself* 917 **trowe,** *believe,* **ilke shrewe,** *same wretch* 919 **Nis ther,** *there is no* 921 **chit,** *accuses* (others), **halt hym yvele apayd,** *considers himself badly treated* 924 **fered,** *afraid,* **office,** *responsibility* 925 **Straw,** *pshaw,* **lewed,** *ignorant,* **nyce,** *foolish* 926 **trempred,** *mixed* 927 **stynt,** *stop,* **herkne,** *hear* 929 **theech,** *may I prosper* 930 **wheron it was along,** *what it resulted from*

862–63 **philosophres stoon . . . / Elixer,** elixir (Arabic, "the philosopher's stone"), a mythic substance (solid, powder, or liquid) thought to transform base to precious metal, or even to extend human life. Compare *SNT* 8.487ff., where Almachius, who calls himself a philosopher (line 490), commands Cecilia to worship a stone idol, although Cecilia and the Christian God bring about conversion.

But wel I woot° greet strif us is among.
  "What," quod my lord, "ther is namoore to
    doone.
Of thise perils I wol be war eftsoone°.
I am right siker° that the pot was crased°.
Be as be may, be ye nothyng amased°;   935
As usage° is, lat swepe° the floor as swithe°.
Plukke up youre hertes and beeth glad and
    blithe."
  The mullok° on an heep ysweped was,
And on the floor ycast a canevas,
And al this mullok in a syve ythrowe°,   940
And sifted and ypiked many a throwe°.
  "Pardee°," quod oon, "somwhat of oure metal
Yet is ther heere, though that we han nat al.
And though this thyng myshapped have° as now,
Another tyme it may be wel ynow°.   945
Us moste putte oure good in aventure°.
A marchant, pardee, may nat ay° endure,
Trusteth me wel, in his prosperitee.
Somtyme his good is drenched° in the see,
And somtyme comth it sauf° unto the londe."   950
  "Pees," quod my lord, "the nexte tyme I wol
    fonde°
To bryngen oure craft al in another plite°,
And but° I do, sires, lat me han the wite°.
Ther was defaute in somwhat°, wel I woot°."
  Another seyde the fir was over-hoot.   955
But be it hoot or coold, I dar seye this,
That we concluden everemoore amys°.
We faille of that which that we wolden have,
And in oure madnesse everemoore we rave.
And whan we been togidres everichoon°,   960
Every man semeth a Salomon.
But al thyng which that shyneth as the gold
Nis nat gold, as that I have herd told;
Ne every appul that is fair to eye
Nis nat good, what so men clappe° or crye.   965

Right so, lo, fareth it° amonges us;
He that semeth the wiseste, by Jhesus,
Is moost fool whan it cometh to the preef°,
And he that semeth trewest is a theef.
That shul ye knowe er that I fro yow wende°   970
By that I of my tale have maad an ende.

Explicit prima pars. Et sequitur pars secunda.

  Ther is a chanoun of religioun
Amonges us wolde° infecte al a toun,
Thogh it as greet were as was Nynyvee,
Rome, Alisaundre, Troye, and othere three.   975
His sleightes° and his infinite falsenesse
Ther koude no man writen, as I gesse,
Though that he lyve myghte a thousand yeer.
In al this world of falshede nis° his peer,
For in his termes so he wole hym wynde°,   980
And speke his wordes in so sly a kynde°,
Whanne he commune° shal with any wight°,
That he wol make hym doten anon-right°,
But° it a feend be as hymselven is.
Ful many a man hath he bigiled er° this,   985
And wole° if that he lyve may a while.
And yet men ride and goon ful many a mile
Hym for to seke and have his aqueyntaunce,
Noght knowynge of his false governaunce°.
And if yow list to yeve me audience°,   990
I wol it tellen heere in youre presence.
  But worshipful chanons religious,
Ne demeth nat° that I sclaundre youre hous,
Although that my tale of a chanoun bee.
Of every ordre som shrewe° is, pardee°,   995
And God forbede that al a compaignye
Sholde rewe° o singuleer° mannes folye.
To sclaundre yow is nothyng myn entente,
But to correcten that is mys° I mente.
This tale was nat oonly told for yow,   1000
But eek for othere mo°. Ye woot° wel how

---

931 woot, *know* **933 war eftsoone,** *aware after this* **934 siker,** *certain,*
crased, *cracked* **935 amased,** *dismayed* **936 usage,** *habit,* **lat swepe,**
sweep, **as swithe,** *at once* **938 mullok,** *rubbish* **940 in a syve ythrowe,**
thrown in a sieve **941 ypiked many a throwe,** *picked through repeatedly*
942 Pardee, *by God* **944 myshapped have,** *has gone wrong* **945 ynow,**
enough **946 Us moste putte . . . in aventure,** *we must risk* **947 ay,** *al-*
ways **949 drenched,** *drowned* **950 sauf,** *safe* **951 wol fonde,** *will try*
952 plite, *condition* **953 but,** *unless,* **han the wite,** *have the blame* **954**
defaute in somwhat, *flaw in something,* **woot,** *know* **957 amys,**
wrongly **960 togidres everichoon,** *all together* **965 what so men clappe,**

whatever men jabber **966 fareth it,** *it goes* **968 preef,** *test* **970 wende,** *go*
973 wolde, *(who) would* **976 sleightes,** *tricks* **979 nis,** *none is* **980 wole**
hym wynde, *will wrap himself* **981 kynde,** *manner* **982 commune,** *con-*
verse, **wight,** *person* **983 doten anon-right,** *soon behave foolishly* **984**
But, *unless* **985 er,** *before* **986 wole,** *will* **989 governaunce,** *behavior* **990**
list to yeve me audience, *choose to listen to me* **993 Ne demeth nat,** *don't*
think **995 shrewe,** *wretch,* **pardee,** *by God* **997 rewe,** *regret,* **o singuleer,**
one individual **999 that is mys,** *what is amiss* **1001 othere mo,** *others*
more, **woot,** *know*

---

961 semeth a Salomon, seems a Solomon, who in scripture and legend was the ideal of a wise man. **971a** *Explicit prima pars. Et sequitur pars*
secunda. "Here ends part one. And here follows part two." **974 Nynyvee,** Nineveh, capital of the Assyrian Empire. **992 chanons religious,** canons regular; see 573n. This address may be simply rhetorical or may date from a time when Chaucer composed this section to be read before an audience such as the canons of King's Chapel at Windsor. If the latter, the address to the Host at line 1089 is evidence of revision.

That among Cristes aposteles twelve
Ther nas no traytour but Judas hymselve.
Thanne why sholde al the remenant have a blame
That giltlees were? By° yow I seye the same,   1005
Save oonly this, if ye wol herkne° me,
If any Judas in youre covent° be,
Remoeveth hym bitymes°, I yow rede°,
If shame or los° may causen any drede.
And beeth nothyng displesed, I yow preye,   1010
But in this cas° herkeneth what I shal seye.
　In Londoun was a preest, an annueleer,
That therinne had dwelled many a yeer,
Which° was so plesaunt and so servysable
Unto the wyf, where as he was at table,   1015
That she wolde suffre° hym no thyng for to paye
For bord ne clothyng, wente he never so gaye,
And spendyng silver hadde he right ynow°.
Therof no fors°, I wol procede as now,
And telle forth my tale of the chanoun   1020
That broghte this preest to confusioun.
　This false chanoun cam upon a day
Unto this preestes chambre, wher he lay,
Bisechynge° hym to lene° hym a certeyn°
Of gold, and he wolde quite° it hym ageyn.   1025
"Leene° me a marc°," quod he, "but dayes three,
And at my day I wol it quiten° thee.
And if so be that thow me fynde fals,
Another day do hange me by the hals°."
　This preest hym took° a marc, and that as
　　swithe°,   1030
And this chanoun hym thanked ofte sithe°,
And took his leve, and wente forth his weye,
And at the thridde day broghte his moneye,
And to the preest he took his gold agayn°
Wherof this preest was wonder glad and fayn°.   1035
　"Certes°," quod he, "nothyng anoyeth me°
To lene a man a noble°, or two, or thre,
Or what thyng were in my possessioun,
Whan he so trewe is of condicioun

That in no wise he breke wole his day°.   1040
To swich a man I kan never seye nay."
　"What," quod this chanoun, "sholde I be
　　untrewe?
Nay, that were thyng yfallen al of newe°.
Trouthe is a thyng that I wol evere kepe
Unto that day in which that I shal crepe   1045
Into my grave, and ellis God forbede.
Bileveth this as siker° as your Crede.
God thanke I, and in good tyme° be it sayd
That ther was nevere man yet yvele apayd°
For gold ne silver that he to me lente,   1050
Ne nevere falshede in myn herte I mente.
And sire," quod he, "now of my pryvetee°,
Syn° ye so goodlich han been unto me,
And kithed° to me so greet gentillesse,
Somwhat to quyte with° youre kyndenesse   1055
I wol yow shewe°, if that yow list to leere°,
I wol yow teche pleynly the manere
How I kan werken in philosophie°.
Taketh good heede, ye shul wel seen at eye°,
That I wol doon a maistrie° er I go."   1060
　"Ye," quod the preest, "ye, sire, and wol ye so?
Marie°, therof° I pray yow hertely."
　"At youre comandement, sire, trewely,"
Quod the chanoun, "and ellis God forbeede."
　Loo, how this theef koude his service
　　beede°!   1065
Ful sooth it is that swich° profred servyse
Stynketh, as witnessen thise olde wyse°,
And that ful soone° I wol it verifie
In this chanoun, roote of al trecherie,
That everemoore delit hath and gladnesse—   1070
Swiche feendly thoghtes in his herte impresse°—
How Cristes peple he may to meschief brynge.
God kepe us from his false dissymulynge°!
　Noght wiste° this preest with whom that he
　　delte,
Ne of his harm comynge he nothyng felte.   1075

1005 **By,** *concerning* 1006 **herkne,** *hear* 1007 **covent,** *religious house* 1008 **bitymes,** *at once,* **rede,** *advise* 1009 **los,** *reputation* 1011 **cas,** *instance* 1014 **Which,** *who* 1016 **suffre,** *allow* 1018 **ynow,** *enough* 1019 **no fors,** *no matter* 1024 **Bisechynge,** *asking,* **lene,** *loan,* **certeyn,** *amount* 1025 **quite,** *repay* 1026 **Leene,** *loan,* **marc,** *coin equal to two-thirds pound* 1027 **quiten,** *repay* 1029 **hals,** *neck* 1030 **took,** *gave,* **as swithe,** *quickly* 1031 **ofte sithe,** *many times* 1034 **took . . . agayn,** *returned* 1035 **fayn,** *pleased* 1036 **Certes,** *certainly,* **nothyng anoyeth me,** *it doesn't bother me* 1037 **noble,** *coin equal to about one-third pound* 1040 **breke wole his day,** *will fail to pay on the promised day* 1043 **were thyng**

yfallen al of newe, *i.e., would be the first time* 1047 **siker,** *certain* 1048 **in good tyme,** *fortunately* 1049 **yvele apayd,** *dissatisfied* 1052 **pryvetee,** *secrets* 1053 **Syn,** *since* 1054 **kithed,** *shown* 1055 **Somwhat to quyte with,** *something to repay* 1056 **shewe,** *show,* **list to leere,** *wish to learn* 1058 **philosophie,** *alchemy* 1059 **at eye,** *plainly* 1060 **doon a maistrie,** *demonstrate something special* 1062 **Marie,** *by Mary,* **therof,** *for that* 1065 **beede,** *offer* 1066 **swich,** *such* 1067 **witnessen thise olde wyse,** *old wise people make clear* 1068 **ful soone,** *very quickly* 1071 **impresse,** *make an impression* 1073 **dissymulynge,** *disguising* 1074 **Noght wiste,** *did not know*

1002–3 Matthew 26.47–49. **1012 annueleer,** a priest paid for a specified number of years to celebrate masses for the dead. **1047 Crede,** Creed (Lat. *credo,* "I believe"); a formal profession of faith. **1066–67 profred servyse / Stynketh,** proferred (unasked for) service stinks; proverbial.

O sely° preest, O sely innocent!
With coveitise anon thou shalt be blent°!
O gracelees, ful blynd is thy conceite°.
Nothyng ne artow war° of the deceite
Which that this fox yshapen° hath to thee.   1080
His wily wrenches° thou ne mayst nat flee.
Wherfore to go to the conclusioun
That refereth° to thy confusioun,
Unhappy man, anon I wol me hye°,
To tellen thyn unwit° and thy folye,   1085
And eek the falsnesse of that oother wrecche
As ferforth° as my konnyng° may strecche.

   This chanoun was my lord ye wolden weene°?
Sire hoost, in feith, and by the hevenes queene,
It was another chanoun and nat hee,   1090
That kan° an hundred foold moore subtiltee.
He hath bitrayed folkes many tyme.
Of his falsnesse it dulleth° me to ryme.
Evere whan that I speke of his falshede,
For shame of hym my chekes wexen rede°—   1095
Algates° they bigynnen for to glowe,
For reednesse have I noon right wel I knowe
In my visage; for fumes diverse
Of metals, which ye han herde me reherce,
Consumed and wasted han my reednesse.   1100
Now taak heed of this chanons cursednesse.

   "Sire," quod he to the preest, "lat youre man
     gon°
For quyksilver, that we hadde it anon;
And lat hym bryngen ounces two or three;
And whan he comth°, as faste shal ye see   1105
A wonder thyng, which ye saugh nevere er this."

   "Sire," quod the preest, "it shal be doon, ywis°."
He bad his servant fecchen hym this thyng;
And he al redy was at his biddyng
And wente hym forth and cam anon agayn   1110
With this quyksilver, shortly for to sayn,
And took thise ounces thre to the chanoun.
And he hem leyde faire and wel adoun,
And bad the servant coles° for to brynge
That he anon myghte go to his werkynge.   1115

   The coles right anon weren yfet°,
And this chanoun took out a crosselet°

Of his bosom and shewed it to the preest.
"This instrument," quod he, "which that thou
     seest,
Taak in thyn hand and put thyself therinne   1120
Of this quyksilver an ounce, and heer bigynne,
In name of Crist, to wexe a philosofre°.
Ther been ful fewe to whiche I wolde profre
To shewen hem thus muche of my science.
For ye shul seen heer, by experience,   1125
That this quyksilver I wol mortifye
Right in youre sighte anon, withouten lye,
And make it as good silver and as fyn
As ther is any in youre purs or myn,
Or elleswhere, and make it malliable,   1130
And elles holdeth me fals and unable°
Amonges folk forevere to appeere.
I have a poudre heer that coste me deere
Shal make al good, for it is cause of al
My konnyng°, which that I to yow shewen shal.   1135
Voyde° youre man and lat hym be theroute,
And shette the dore whils we been aboute
Oure pryvetee°, that no man us espie
Whils that we werke in this philosophie."

   Al as he bad fulfilled was in dede.   1140
This ilke° servant anonright out yede°,
And his maister shette the dore anon,
And to hire labour spedily they gon.

   This preest at this cursed chanons biddyng
Upon the fir anon sette this thyng,   1145
And blewe the fir, and bisyed hym ful faste°.
And this chanoun into the crosselet caste
A poudre, noot I° wherof that it was
Ymaad°, outher° of chalk, or of glas,
Or somwhat elles, was nat worth a flye,   1150
To blynde with this preest, and bad hym hye°
The coles for to couchen° al above
The crosselet. "For in tokenyng° I thee love,"
Quod this chanoun, "thyne owene handes two
Shul werche al thyng which shal heer be do."   1155
   "Graunt mercy°," quod the preest and was
     ful glad,
And couched coles as that the chanoun bad.
And while he bisy was, this feendly wrecche,

1076 sely, *foolish* **1077 blent,** *blinded* **1078 conceite,** *thought* **1079
Nothyng ne artow war,** *not at all are you aware* **1080 yshapen,** *planned*
1081 wrenches, *tricks* **1083 refereth,** *applies* **1084 hye,** *hurry* **1085 un-
wit,** *stupidity* **1087 forforth,** *far,* **konnyng,** *ability* **1088 weene,** *think*
1091 kan, *knows* **1093 dulleth,** *wearies* **1095 wexen rede,** *grow red*
1096 Algates, *at least* **1102 lat youre man gon,** *send your servant* **1105
comth,** *comes* **1107 ywis,** *certainly* **1114 coles,** *coals* **1116 yfet,** *brought*

1117 crosselet, *crucible* **1122 wexe a philosofre,** *become an alchemist*
1131 unable, *unfit* **1135 konnyng,** *skill* **1136 Voyde,** *send out* **1138
pryvetee,** *secrets* **1141 ilke,** *same,* **yede,** *went* **1146 ful faste,** *very intensely* **1148 noot I,** *I don't know* **1149 Ymaad,** *made,* **outher,** *either*
1151 hye, *pile* **1152 couchen,** *arrange* **1153 in tokenyng,** *as a sign that*
1156 Graunt mercy, *thank you*

1126 quyksilver . . . mortifye, to "mortify" or "kill" quicksilver—i.e., "live" silver—is the alchemical term for transforming it into solid silver.

This false chanoun—the foule feend hym
    fecche—
Out of his bosom took a bechen cole°   1160
In which ful subtilly was maad an hole,
And therinne put was of silver lemaille°
An ounce, and stopped was withouten faille,
This hole with wex, to kepe the lemaille in.
And understondeth that this false gyn°   1165
Was nat maad ther, but it was maad bifore;
And othere thynges I shal tellen moore
Herafterward, whiche that he with hym broghte.
Er he cam there, hym to bigile he thoghte.
And so he dide, er that they wente atwynne°;   1170
Til he had terved° hym, he koude nat blynne°.
It dulleth° me whan that I of hym speke.
On his falshede fayn° wolde I me wreke°
If I wiste° how, but he is heere and there;
He is so variaunt°, he abit° nowhere.   1175
    But taketh heede now, sires, for Goddes love.
He took this cole of which I spak above,
And in his hand he baar° it pryvely.
And whiles the preest couched° bisily
The coles, as I tolde yow er this,   1180
This chanoun seyde, "Freend, ye doon amys.
This is nat couched as it oghte be.
But soone I shal amenden it," quod he.
"Now lat me medle therwith but a while,
For of yow have I pitee, by Seint Gile.   1185
Ye been right hoot°; I se wel how ye swete.
Have heere a clooth, and wipe awey the wete."
And whiles that the preest wiped his face,
This chanoun took his cole—with sory grace°—
And leyde it above upon the myddeward°   1190
Of the crosselet, and blew wel afterward,
Til that the coles gonne faste brenne°.
    "Now yeve° us drynke," quod the chanoun
        thenne.
"As swithe° al shal be wel, I undertake°.
Sitte we doun and lat us myrie make."   1195

And whan that this chanounes bechen cole°
Was brent°, al the lemaille° out of the hole
Into the crosselet fil anon adoun—
And so it moste nedes°, by resoun,
Syn° it so evene° aboven it couched was.   1200
But therof wiste° the preest nothyng, alas.
He demed° alle the coles yliche° good,
For of that sleighte° he nothyng understood.
And whan this alkamystre° saugh° his tyme,
"Ris up," quod he, "sire preest, and stondeth
    by me;   1205
And for I woot° wel ingot° have ye noon,
Gooth, walketh forth, and bryng us a chalk stoon.
For I wol make it of the same shap
That is an ingot, if I may han hap°.
And bryngeth eek° with yow a bolle° or a
    panne   1210
Ful of water, and ye shul se wel thanne
How that oure bisynesse shal thryve and preeve°.
And yet, for ye shul han no mysbileeve
Ne wrong conceite° of me in youre absence,
I ne wol nat been out of youre presence,   1215
But go with yow and come with yow ageyn."
The chambre dore, shortly for to seyn,
They opened and shette and wente hir weye.
And forth with hem they carieden the keye
And coome agayn withouten any delay.   1220
What sholde I tarien° al the longe day?
He took the chalk and shoop° it in the wise°
Of an ingot as I shal yow devyse°.
    I seye, he took out of his owene sleeve
A teyne° of silver—yvele moot he cheeve°—   1225
Which that ne was nat but an ounce of weighte.
And taaketh heede now of his cursed sleighte.
    He shoop his ingot in lengthe and in breede°
Of this teyne, withouten any drede°,
So slyly that the preest it nat espide,   1230
And in his sleve agayn he gan it hide,
And fro the fir he took up his mateere,

1160 bechen cole, *beechwood charcoal* **1162 lemaille,** *filings* **1165 gyn,** *contrivance* **1170 wente atwynne,** *separated* **1171 terved,** *fleeced,* **blynne,** *stop* **1172 dulleth,** *numbs* **1173 fayn,** *happily,* **wreke,** *avenge* **1174 wiste,** *knew* **1175 variaunt,** *shifty,* **abit,** *stays* **1178 baar** *held* **1179 couched,** *arranged* **1186 right hoot,** *very hot* **1189 sory grace,** *bad luck* **1190 myddeward,** *middle* **1192 gonne faste brenne,** *burned intensely* **1193 yeve,** *give* **1194 As swithe,** *soon,* **undertake,** *declare* **1196 bechen cole,** *beechwood charcoal* **1197 brent,** *burned,* **lemaille,** *filings*

1199 moste nedes, *must necessarily* **1200 Syn,** *since,* **evene,** *squarely* **1201 wiste,** *knew* **1202 demed,** *thought,* **yliche,** *alike* **1203 sleighte,** *trick* **1204 alkamystre,** *alchemist,* **saugh,** *saw* **1206 woot,** *know,* **ingot,** *mold* **1209 han hap,** *have luck* **1210 eek,** *also,* **bolle,** *bowl* **1212 preeve,** *succeed* **1214 conceite,** *thought* **1221 tarien,** *delay* **1222 shoop,** *shaped,* **wise,** *manner* **1223 devyse,** *describe* **1225 teyne,** *small bar,* **yvele moot he cheeve,** *may he achieve evil* **1228 breede,** *breadth* **1229 drede,** *doubt*

1185 Seint Gile, St. Giles, patron saint of beggars and people who are crippled, but here possibly play on *guile.* **1231 in his sleve,** the small bar (only an ounce) hidden up his sleeve is in preparation for the third deception at lines 1317–18. In the first deception, the quicksilver evaporates and the silver filings melt from the hollow charcoal into the crucible, from which the canon fills the mold (ingot) he carved into the soft chalk. In the second deception, the silver filings melt from the hollow stick held by the canon. In all cases, the powder is a ruse.

And in th'yngot putte it with myrie cheere,
And in the water-vessel he it caste
Whan that hym luste°, and bad the preest as
　　faste,　　　　　　　　　　　　　　　1235
"Loke what ther is; put in thyn hand and grope.
Thow fynde shalt ther silver, as I hope."
What, devel of helle, sholde it elles be?
Shaving of silver silver is, pardee°!
He putte his hand in and took up a teyne　　1240
Of silver fyn°, and glad in every veyne
Was this preest whan he saugh that it was so.
"Goddes blessyng, and his moodres also,
And alle halwes°, have ye, sire chanoun,"
Seyde the preest, "and I hir malisoun°,　　1245
But°, and° ye vouchesauf° to techen me
This noble craft and this subtilitee,
I wol be youre in al that evere I may."
　　Quod the chanoun, "Yet wol I make assay°
The seconde tyme that ye may taken heede　　1250
And been expert of this, and in youre neede
Another day assaye in myn absence
This disciplyne and this crafty science.
Lat take° another ounce," quod he tho,
"Of quyksilver, withouten wordes mo,　　1255
And do therwith as ye han doon er this
With that oother, which that now silver is."
　　This preest hym bisieth° in al that he kan
To doon as this chanoun, this cursed man,
Comanded hym, and faste he blew the fir　　1260
For to come to th'effect° of his desir.
And this chanoun right in the meene while
Al redy was the preest eft° to bigile,
And for a contenaunce° in his hand he bar
An holwe° stikke—taak kepe° and bewar—　　1265
In the ende of which an ounce, and namoore,
Of silver lemaille° put was, as bifore
Was in his cole, and stopped with wex weel
For to kepe in his lemaille every deel°.
And whil this preest was in his bisynesse,　　1270
This chanoun with his stikke gan hym dresse°
To hym anon, and his poudre caste in
As he dide er—the devel out of his skyn
Hym terve°, I pray to God, for his falshede!
For he was evere fals in thoght and dede—　　1275

And with this stikke, above the crosselet,
That was ordeyned° with that false jet°,
He stired the coles til relente gan°
The wex agayn° the fir, as every man
But it a fool be woot° wel it moot nede°,　　1280
And al that in the stikke was out yede°,
And in the crosselet hastily it fel.
　　Now, goode sires, what wol ye bet than wel°?
Whan that this preest thus was bigiled ageyn,
Supposynge noght but treuthe, sooth to seyn,　　1285
He was so glad that I ne kan nat expresse
In no manere his myrthe and his gladnesse;
And to the chanoun he profred eftsoone°
Body and good. "Ye," quod the chanoun soone,
"Though poure I be, crafty thou shalt me
　　fynde.　　　　　　　　　　　　　　　1290
I warne° thee, yet is ther moore bihynde.
Is ther any coper herinne°?" seyde he.
　　"Ye," quod the preest, "sire, I trowe° wel
　　　ther be."
　　"Elles° go bye us som, and that as swithe°.
Now, good sire, go forth thy wey and hy the°."　　1295
　　He wente his wey, and with the coper cam,
And this chanon it in his handes nam°,
And of that coper weyed out but an ounce.
　　Al to symple is my tonge to pronounce
As ministre of my wit the doublenesse　　1300
Of this chanoun, roote of alle cursednesse.
He semed freendly to hem that knewe hym noght,
But he was feendly bothe in werk and thoght.
It weerieth me to telle of his falsnesse,
And nathelees yet wol I it expresse,　　1305
To th'entente that men may bewar therby,
And for noon oother cause, trewely.
　　He putte the ounce of coper in the crosselet,
And on the fir as swithe he hath it set,
And caste in poudre, and made the preest to
　　blowe,　　　　　　　　　　　　　　　1310
And in his werkyng for to stoupe lowe
As he dide er—and al nas° but a jape°.
Right as hym liste°, the preest he made his ape°.
And afterward in the ingot he it caste,
And in the panne putte it at the laste　　1315
Of water, and in he putte his owene hand,

1235 **luste,** *chose* 1239 **pardee,** *by God* 1241 **fyn,** *pure* 1244 **halwes,**
saints' 1245 **I hir malisoun,** (*may*) *I* (*have*) *their curse* 1246 **But,** *un-*
less, **and,** *if,* **vouchesauf,** *agree* 1249 **assay,** *attempt* 1254 **Lat take,** *take*
1258 **hym bisieth,** *busies himself* 1261 **th'effect,** *the outcome* 1263 **eft,**
again 1264 **a contenaunce,** *appearances* 1265 **holwe,** *hollow,* **taak**
kepe, *pay attention* 1267 **lemaille,** *filings* 1269 **deel,** *bit* 1271 **gan**
hym dresse, *approached* 1274 **terve,** *flay* 1277 **ordeyned,** *prepared,* **jet,**

device 1278 **relente gan,** *melted* 1279 **agayn,** *as a result of* 1280 **woot,**
knows, **moot nede,** *necessarily must* 1281 **yede,** *went* 1283 **wol ye bet**
than wel, *what more do you want* 1288 **profred eftsoone,** *offered at once*
1291 **warne,** *tell* 1292 **coper herinne,** *copper in here* 1293 **trowe,** *believe*
1294 **Elles,** *or else,* **as swithe,** *quickly* 1295 **hy the,** *hurry yourself* 1297
nam, *took* 1312 **nas,** *was nothing,* **jape,** *trick* 1313 **liste,** *wished,* **ape,**
i.e., he made a monkey of him

And in his sleve (as ye biforen-hand
Herde me telle) he hadde a silver teyne.
He slyly took it out, this cursed heyne°,
Unwityng° this preest of his false craft,   1320
And in the pannes botme° he hath it laft;
And in the water rombled to and fro,
And wonder pryvely° took up also
The coper teyne, noght knowynge° this preest,
And hidde it, and hym hente° by the breest,   1325
And to hym spak, and thus seyde in his game°:
"Stoupeth adoun, by God, ye be to blame°!
Helpeth me now, as I dide yow whileer°;
Putte in youre hand, and looketh what is theer."

    This preest took up this silver teyne anon,   1330
And thanne seyde the chanoun, "Lat us gon
With thise thre teynes whiche that we han wroght°
To som goldsmyth, and wite° if they been oght°.
For by my feith I nolde°, for myn hood,
But if that° they were silver fyn and good,   1335
And that as swithe preeved° it shal bee."

    Unto the goldsmyth with thise teynes three
They wente, and putte thise teynes in assay°
To fir and hamer. Myghte no man seye nay
But that they weren as hem oghte be.   1340

    This sotted° preest, who was gladder than he?
Was nevere brid° gladder agayn the day°,
Ne nyghtyngale in the sesoun of May.
Nas nevere° man that luste° bet° to synge,
Ne lady lustier in carolynge,   1345
Or for to speke of love and wommanhede,
Ne knyght in armes to doon an hardy dede,
To stonden in grace of his lady deere,
Than hadde this preest this soory craft to leere°,
And to the chanoun thus he spak and seyde,   1350
"For love of God, that for us alle deyde°,
And as I may deserve it unto° yow,
What shal this receite° coste? Telleth now!"

    "By oure Lady," quod this chanon, "it is deere°,
I warne yow wel; for save° I and a frere°,   1355
In Engelond ther kan no man it make."

    "No fors°," quod he, "now, sire, for Goddes sake,
What shal I paye? Telleth me, I preye."

    "Ywis°," quod he, "it is ful deere, I seye.
Sire, at o word, if that thee list° it have,   1360
Ye shul paye fourty pound, so God me save.
And nere° the freendshipe that ye dide er this
To me, ye sholde paye moore, ywis."

    This preest the somme of fourty pound anon
Of nobles fette°, and took hem everichon   1365
To this chanoun for this ilke receit°.
Al his werkyng nas° but fraude and deceit.

    "Sire preest," he seyde, "I kepe han no loos°
Of my craft, for I wolde it kept were cloos°;
And as ye love me kepeth it secree.   1370
For and° men knewen al my soutiltee°,
By God they wolden han so greet envye
To me by cause of my philosophye
I sholde be deed—ther were noon oother weye."

    "God it forbeede," quod the preest, "what
        sey ye?   1375
Yet hadde I levere° spenden al the good
Which that I have, or elles wexe I wood°,
Than that ye sholden falle in swich mescheef°."

    "For youre good wyl, sire, have ye right
        good preef°,"
Quod the chanoun, "and farwel, grant
        mercy°."   1380
He wente his wey, and never the preest hym sy°
After that day. And whan that this preest shoolde
Maken assay° at swich tyme as he wolde
Of this receit, farwel, it wolde nat be.
Lo, thus byjaped° and bigiled was he.   1385
Thus maketh he his introduccioun°
To brynge folk to hir destruccioun.

    Considereth, sires, how that in ech estaat°
Bitwixe men and gold ther is debaat°
So ferforth° that unnethe° is ther noon.   1390
This multiplying blent° so many oon
That in good feith I trowe° that it bee
The cause grettest of swich scarsetee.

1319 heyne, *wretch* **1320 Unwityng,** *unaware* **1321 botme,** *bottom* **1323 wonder pryvely,** *very secretly* **1324 noght knowynge,** *unknown to* **1325 hente,** *grabbed* **1326 in his game,** *as part of his scheme* **1327 to blame, at fault* **1328 whileer,** *just before* **1332 wroght,** *created* **1333 wite,** *learn,* **oght,** *(worth) anything* **1334 nolde,** *wish nothing* **1335 But if that,** *unless* **1336 as swithe preeved,** *quickly proved* **1338 assay,** *test of the purity of precious metals* **1341 sotted,** *besotted* **1342 brid,** *bird,* **agayn the day,** *as a result of dawn* **1344 Nas nevere,** *there was never,* **luste,** *yearned,* **bet,** *better* **1349 leere,** *learn* **1351 deyde,** *died* **1352 deserve it unto,** *earn it from* **1353 receite,** *formula* **1354 deere,** *costly* **1355 save,** *except for,*

frere, *friar* **1357 No fors,** *no matter* **1359 Ywis,** *certainly* **1360 list,** *wish (to)* **1362 nere,** *were it not for* **1365 nobles fette,** *gold coins fetched* **1366 ilke receit,** *same formula* **1367 nas,** *was nothing* **1368 kepe han no loos,** *care to have no fame,* **1369 cloos,** *secret* **1371 and,** *if,* **soutiltee,** *skill* **1376 levere,** *rather* **1377 wexe I wood,** *(may) I go insane* **1378 mescheef,** *misfortune* **1379 preef,** *proof* **1380 grant mercy,** *thank you* **1381 sy,** *saw* **1383 assay,** *a test* **1385 byjaped,** *tricked* **1386 introduccioun,** *beginning* **1388 estaat,** *social rank* **1389 debaat,** *conflict* **1390 ferforth,** *completely,* **unnethe,** *scarcely* **1391 blent,** *has blinded* **1392 trowe,** *believe*

1334 for myn hood, an idiom meaning "in exchange for my hood (or head)," i.e., "by all that's dear to me."

Philosophres speken so mystily°
In this craft that men kan nat come therby.   1395
For any wit that men han now-a-dayes
They mowe wel chiteren° as doon thise jayes°,
And in hir termes° sette° hir lust° and peyne,
But to hir purpos shul they nevere atteyne.
A man may lightly lerne°, if he have aught°,   1400
To multiplie and brynge his good to naught!
    Lo, swich° a lucre° is in this lusty° game.
A mannes myrthe it wol turne unto grame°,
And empten also grete and hevye purses,
And maken folk for to purchacen curses   1405
Of hem that han hir good therto ylent°.
O, fy, for shame, they that han been brent°,
Allas, kan they nat flee the fires heete?
Ye° that it use°, I rede° ye it leete°
Lest ye lese° al, for bet than nevere is late.   1410
Nevere to thryve were to long a date°.
Though ye prolle ay°, ye shul it nevere fynde.
Ye been as boold as is Bayard the blynde
That blondreth forth and peril casteth° noon.
He is as boold to renne agayn° a stoon   1415
As for to goon bisides in the weye°.
So faren° ye that multiplie, I seye.
If that youre eyen kan nat seen aright,
Looke that youre mynde lakke noght his° sight.
For though ye looken never so brode and
    stare,   1420
Ye shul nothyng wynne on that chaffare°,
But wasten al that ye may rape and renne.
Withdraweth the fir lest it to faste brenne;
Medleth° namoore with that art, I mene,

For if ye doon, youre thrift° is goon ful
    clene.   1425
And right as swithe° I wol yow tellen heere
What philosophres seyn in this mateere.
    Lo, thus seith Arnold of the Newe Toun,
As his *Rosarie* maketh mencioun;
He seith right thus, withouten any lye: 1430
"Ther may no man mercurie mortifie
But it be with his brother knowlechyng°."
How be that° he which that first seyde this thyng
Of philosophres fader was, Hermes.
He seith how that the dragon, doutelees,   1435
Ne dyeth nat but if that he be slayn
With his brother; and that is for to sayn,
By the dragon, Mercurie, and noon oother
He understood, and brymstoon by his brother,
That out of Sol and Luna were ydrawe°.   1440
"And therfore," seyde he—taak heede to my
    sawe°—
"Lat no man bisye hym this art for to seche°
But if that° he th'entencioun and speche
Of philosophres understonde kan.
And if he do, he is a lewed° man.   1445
For this science° and this konnyng°," quod he,
"Is of the secree of secretes°, pardee°."
    Also ther was a disciple of Plato
That on a tyme seyde his maister to,
As his book *Senior* wol bere witnesse,   1450
And this was his demande in soothfastnesse°,
"Telle me the name of the privee° stoon?"
    And Plato answerde unto hym anoon,
"Take the stoon that Titanos men name."

1394 **mystily,** *mysteriously* 1397 **mowe wel chiteren,** *might as well chatter,* **jayes,** *noisy birds* 1398 **termes,** *jargon,* **sette,** *place,* **lust,** *desire* 1400 **lightly lerne,** *learn easily,* **aught,** *anything* 1402 **swich,** *such,* **lucre,** *profit,* **lusty,** *greedy* 1403 **grame,** *grief* 1406 **that han hir good therto ylent,** *to whom they have lent their goods* 1407 **brent,** *burned* 1409 **Ye,** *you,* **use,** *practice,* **rede,** *advise,* **leete,** *abandon* 1410 **lese,** *lose* 1411 **date,** *time* 1412 **prolle ay,** *prowl forever* 1414 **casteth,** *considers* 1415 **renne agayn,** *run into* 1416 **goon bisides in the weye,** *go around on the* path 1417 **faren,** *do* 1419 **his,** *its (the mind's)* 1421 **chaffare,** *exchange* 1424 **Medleth,** *meddle* 1425 **thrift,** *prosperity* 1426 **right as swithe,** *as quickly as possible* 1432 **brother knowlechyng,** *brother's help* 1433 **How be that,** *however* 1440 **ydrawe,** *drawn* 1441 **sawe,** *saying* 1442 **seche,** *seek* 1443 **But if that,** *unless* 1445 **lewed,** *stupid* 1446 **science,** *knowledge,* **konnyng,** *skill* 1447 **secree of secretes,** *the secret of all secrets,* **pardee,** *by God* 1451 **in soothfastnesse,** *truly* 1452 **privee,** *secret*

1413 **Bayard,** a proverbial blind horse, brave because it could not see danger. 1422 **rape and renne,** seize and run, a proverbial idiom meaning "acquire by any means." 1428–32 **Arnold of the Newe Toun . . . ,** Arnaldus of Villanova, thirteenth-century French alchemist, wrote the *Rosarium Philosophorum* (The Philosopher's Rosary), but the quotations in lines 1431–47 echo his *De Lapide Philosophorum* (On the Philosopher's Stone), where the "mortification" or solidification of mercury (quicksilver) into silver is said to require sulfur, the "brother" of mercury. 1433 No MS includes "be," essential unless we construe "How that" as parallel to the same phrase in line 1435. 1434 **philosophres fader . . . Hermes,** Hermes Trismegistus was the legendary founding father of alchemy, the Greek equivalent of the Egyptian god of learning, Thoth. 1435–40 **dragon . . . ,** an alchemical metaphor for mercury, which was combined with its "brother," brimstone (sulfur), in efforts to transform the mercury into silver by "slaying" it. One or both derive in some mysterious way from gold and silver, the metals associated with the sun (**Sol,** line 1440) and moon (**Luna,** line 1440). Such occult combinations of metaphor, chemistry, and astrology are characteristic of alchemical treatises. 1448–71 **disciple of Plato . . . Senior . . . ,** Plato and his disciple have a similar discussion in a Latin version of an Arabic alchemical treatise, *Epistola Solis ad Lunam Crescentem* (The Sun's Letter to the Crescent Moon), published in the seventeenth century under the title *Senioris Zadith fil. Hamuelis Tabulis Chemica* (Chemical Table of Senior Zadith, son of Hamuel). 1454–55 **Titanos . . . Magnasia,** occult names for some mineral or substance.

"Which is that?" quod he. "Magnasia is the
    same," 1455
Seyde Plato. "Ye sire, and is it thus?
This is *ignotum per ignocius*°.
What is Magnasia, good sire, I yow preye?"
    "It is a water that is maad, I seye,
Of elementes foure," quod Plato. 1460
    "Telle me the roote°, good sire," quod he tho,
"Of that water, if it be youre wille."
    "Nay, nay," quod Plato, "certein, that I nylle°.
The philosophres sworn were everychoon
That they sholden discovere it unto noon, 1465
Ne in no book it write in no manere.
For unto Crist it is so lief° and deere
That he wol nat that it discovered bee

But where it liketh° to his deitee
Men for t'enspire, and eek for to deffende° 1470
Whom that hym liketh—lo, this is the ende."
    Thanne conclude I thus, sith° that God of
    hevene
Ne wil nat that the philosophres nevene°
How that a man shal come unto this stoon,
I rede°, as for the beste, lete it goon. 1475
For whoso maketh God his adversarie,
As for to werken anythyng in contrarie
Of his wil, certes° never shal he thryve,
Thogh that he multiplie terme° of his lyve.
And there a poynt°, for ended is my tale. 1480
God sende every trewe man boote of his bale°.
                        Amen.

Heere is ended the Chanouns Yemannes Tale.

1457 ignotum per ignocius, *explaining the unknown by the more unknown* **1461 roote,** *essential nature* **1463 nylle,** *will not* **1467 lief,** *beloved* **1469 it liketh,** *it is pleasing* **1470 deffende,** *forbid* **1472 sith,** *since* **1473 nevene,** *reveal* **1475 rede,** *advise* **1478 certes,** *surely* **1479 terme, the time* **1480 poynt,** *period* (full stop) **1481 boote of his bale,** *remedy for his suffering*

CANTERBURY TALES PART 9

INTRODUCTION

IT IS CONVENTIONAL TO LET THE *Manciple's Prologue* and *Tale* stand alone as part 9, but there is no good textual reason to do so. It regularly precedes part 10 in the reliable manuscripts, is explicitly referred to in the *Parson's Prologue* (10.1), and combines with parts 8 and 10 to create a geographical sequence as the pilgrims approach their destination. The Canon and his Yeoman meet the pilgrimage at Boughton in the Blean Forest (8.556), and the *Manciple's Prologue* opens in Harbledown (2, "Bobbe-up-and-doun") at the far edge of the Blean and only two miles from Canterbury. In the *Parson's Prologue,* the pilgrims enter a town, presumably Canterbury itself (10.12).

Yet a temporal discrepancy undercuts this geographical sequence. The Host says it is morning in the *Manciple's Prologue* (16), but following the Manciple's brief tale, it is already 4 p.m. in the *Parson's Prologue* (10.5). The discrepancy has encouraged a few critics to read the *Parson's Tale* as one of the tales intended for a return journey, but the signals to completion and closure in parts 8–10 suggest otherwise. The temporal leap is read allegorically by critics who consider the drunken Cook to be a figure of spiritual unpreparedness (8–17n); critics who argue that the *Manciple's Tale* sets up the Parson's rejection of fable for truth disregard the leap as an oversight left in need of revision.

Speech, language, and their consequences are dominant issues in the *Manciple's Prologue* and *Tale.* The altercation between the Manciple and the Cook in the prologue suggests professional competitiveness—a Londoner, the Cook prepares food, and the Manciple is responsible for supplying food to his employers, who live at the city's edge. Drunkenness and the Manciple's chiding render the Cook speechless and provide some of the most energetic drama in the entire Canterbury frame.

No one has explained satisfactorily why the Host calls for a tale from the Cook, who has already told a tale, albeit a fragmentary one, although the Host's reference to the Cook's "penaunce" (12), sleeplessness, and morning drunkenness are central to arguments that the Cook is spiritually unprepared. See Michael Kensak, "What Ails Chaucer's Cook? Spiritual Alchemy and the Ending of *The Canterbury Tales*" (2001, no. 1429).

In Ovid's *Metamorphoses* 2.531–632, the ultimate source of the plot of the *Manciple's Tale,* the central concern is Phoebus Apollo's punishing transformation of the tattletale crow from white to black. Chaucer maintains the concern with transformation but emphasizes speech and speechlessness by adding moralization and commentary on natural behavior and language use (163–234), much of it adapted from the *Roman de la Rose,* and most of it suggesting caution if not cynicism. The largest single addition, the concluding moralization (309–62), is a kind of self-cancellation—a loquacious recommendation not to speak or tell tales, whether false or true. Pervaded by a sense of expediency, the *Manciple's Prologue* and *Tale* suggest that we ought to distrust language, including our own speech, because it can get us into trouble.

The tale lacks the charm or pathos characteristic of Chaucer's other bird stories—the *Parliament of Fowls,* the *Nun's Priest's Tale,* and the falcon's lament in the *Squire's Tale.* Louise Fradenburg, "The Manciple's Servant Tongue" (1985, no. 1420), suggests that the tale be considered in light of the tradition in which poetry was offered as advice to princes, and she argues that it reflects Chaucer's anxious position as a poet and bureaucrat in the court of Richard II. A number of critics, including Britton J. Harwood, "Language and the Real: Chaucer's Manciple" (1972, no. 1425), suggest a more general examination of language whereby the Manciple's cynical distrust of language anticipates the proper use of language in the *Parson's Tale*. Donald C. Baker surveys critical approaches through 1980 in his Variorum edition of the tale (1984, no. 42). The survey is usefully updated in the notes and discussion of David Raybin, "The Death of a Silent Woman: Voice and Power in Chaucer's Manciple's Tale" (1996, no. 1435). See also the *Studies in the Age of Chaucer* colloquium on the tale (2003, no. 1423).

CANTERBURY TALES
PART 9

MANCIPLE'S TALE

PROLOGUE

Heere folweth the Prologe of the Maunciples Tale.

Woot° ye nat where ther stant a litel toun
Which that ycleped is° Bobbe-up-and-doun,
Under the Blee, in° Caunterbury weye?
Ther gan oure Hooste for to jape° and pleye,
And seyde, "Sires, what, Dun is in the myre!   5
Is ther no man for preyere ne for hyre°
That wole awake oure felawe al bihynde?
A theef myghte hym ful lightly° robbe and bynde.
See how he nappeth°! See how, for cokkes
      bones,
That he wol falle fro his hors atones°!   10
Is that a cook of Londoun, with meschaunce°?

Do hym° come forth—he knoweth his
      penaunce—
For he shal telle a tale, by my fey°,
Although it be nat worth a botel hey°.
   "Awake, thou Cook," quod he, "God yeve°
      thee sorwe!   15
What eyleth thee to slepe by the morwe°?
Hastow° had fleen° al nyght, or artow° dronke?
Or hastow with som quene° al nyght yswonke°,
So that thow mayst nat holden up thyn heed?"
   This Cook, that was ful pale and
      nothyng reed,   20

---

1 **Woot,** *know* 2 **Which that ycleped is,** *which is called* 3 **in,** *on* 4 **jape,** *joke* 6 **preyere ne for hyre,** *request nor for pay* 8 **lightly,** *easily* 9 **nappeth,** *sleeps* 10 **atones,** *soon* 11 **with meschaunce,** *bad luck to him*

12 **Do hym,** *have him* 13 **fey,** *faith* 14 **botel hey,** *bundle of hay* 15 **yeve,** *give* 16 **by the morwe,** *in the morning* 17 **Hastow,** *have you,* **fleen,** *fleas,* **artow,** *are you* 18 **quene,** *whore,* **yswonke,** *worked*

1–104 Lines lacking in several MSS, perhaps evidence of late composition; see MR 2.445. **2–3 Bobbe-up-and-doun . . . Blee,** Harbledown, on the edge of the Blean Forest and two miles from Canterbury. Compare 8.556n above. **5 Dun is in the myre,** Dun (a proverbial horse) is stuck in the mud; i.e., things have come to a halt. **8–17** Critics have read echoes of 1 Thessalonians 5.2–8, suggesting that Chaucer's imagery recalls St. Paul's comments on those who are spiritually unprepared. **9 cokkes bones,** cock's bones; euphemism for God's bones, a mild oath.

Seyde to oure Hoost, "So God my soule blesse,
As ther is falle on me swich hevynesse—
Noot I nat° why—that me were levere° slepe
Than the best galon wyn° in Chepe."
　　"Wel," quod the Maunciple, "if it may
　　　　doon ese　　　　　　　　　　　　　　　　　25
To thee, sire Cook, and to no wight° displese,
Which that heere rideth in this compaignye,
And that oure Hoost wole° of his curteisye,
I wol as now excuse thee of thy tale.
For in good feith thy visage is ful pale,　　　　30
Thyne eyen daswen eek°, as that me thynketh,
And wel I woot° thy breeth ful soure stynketh—
That sheweth wel thou art nat wel disposed.
Of me, certeyn, thou shalt nat been yglosed°.
See how he ganeth°, lo, this dronken wight,　　35
As though he wolde swolwe us anonright°.
Hoold cloos thy mouth, man, by thy fader kyn°!
The devel of helle sette his foot therin!
Thy cursed breeth infecte wole us alle.
Fy, stynkyng swyn°, fy, foule moote thee falle°!　40
A, taketh heede, sires, of this lusty man.
Now, sweete sire, wol ye justen atte fan?
Therto° me thynketh ye been wel yshape°!
I trowe° that ye dronken han wyn ape,
And that is whan men pleyen with a straw."　　45
And with this speche the Cook wax wrooth
　　and wraw°,
And on the Manciple he gan nodde faste
For lakke of speche, and doun the hors hym
　　caste,
Where as he lay til that men up hym took.
This was a fair chyvachee of° a cook!　　　　　50
Allas, he nadde holde° hym by his ladel°!
And er that he agayn were in his sadel,
Ther was greet showyng bothe to and fro
To lifte hym up, and muchel care and wo,

So unweeldy was this sory palled° goost.　　　55
And to the Manciple thanne spak oure Hoost:
　　"By cause drynke hath dominacioun
Upon this man, by my savacioun,
I trowe lewedly° he wolde telle his tale.
For were it wyn or oold or moysty° ale　　　　60
That he hath dronke, he speketh in his nose,
And fneseth° faste, and eek he hath the pose°.
He hath also to do moore than ynough
To kepen hym and his capul° out of the slough°.
And if he falle from his capul eftsoone°,　　　65
Thanne shal we alle have ynogh to doone°
In liftyng up his hevy dronken cors°.
Telle on thy tale; of hym make I no fors°.
　　"But yet, Manciple, in feith thou art to nyce°,
Thus openly repreve° hym of his vice.　　　　70
Another day he wole, peraventure°,
Reclayme thee and brynge thee to lure—
I meene, he speke wole of smale thynges,
As for to pynchen at thy rekenynges°
That were nat honeste, if it cam to preef°."　　75
　　"No," quod the Manciple, "that were a greet
　　　　mescheef!
So myghte he lightly° brynge me in the snare.
Yet hadde I levere° payen for the mare
Which he rit° on than he sholde with me stryve°.
I wol nat wratthen° hym, also moot I thryve°!　80
That that I spak, I seyde it in my bourde°.
And wite° ye what? I have heer in a gourde°
A draghte of wyn, ye, of a ripe grape,
And right anon° ye shul seen a good jape°.
This Cook shal drynke therof, if I that may.　85
Up° peyne of deeth, he wol nat seye me nay."
　　And certeynly, to tellen as it was,
Of this vessel the Cook drank faste, allas.
What neded hym? He drank ynough biforn.
And whan he hadde pouped in this horn　　　90

---

23 Noot I nat, *I don't know,* **me were levere,** *I would rather* **24 Than the best galon wyn,** *than* (have) *the best gallon of wine* **26 wight,** *person* **28 wole,** *will* **31 eyen daswen eek,** *eyes are dazed also* **32 woot,** *know* **34 yglosed,** *flattered* **35 ganeth,** *yawns* **36 anonright,** *soon* **37 fader kyn,** *father's relatives* **40 swyn,** *pig,* **foule moote thee falle,** *may evil happen to you* **43 Therto,** *for that,* **been wel yshape,** *are in good shape* **44 trowe,** *believe* **46 wax wrooth and wraw,** *grew angry and peevish* **50 chyvachee of,** *display of horsemanship by* **51 nadde holde,** *had not held,* **ladel,** *cooking ladle* **55 palled,** *pale* **59 trowe lewedly,** *think ignorantly* **60 oold or**

moysty, *old or fresh* **62 fneseth,** *sneezes,* **pose,** *head cold* **64 capul,** *horse,* **slough,** *mud* **65 eftsoone,** *again* **66 doone,** *do* **67 cors,** *body* **68 no fors,** *no matter* **69 to nyce,** *too foolish* **70 repreve,** (to) *accuse* **71 peraventure,** *perhaps* **74 pynchen at thy rekenynges,** *find errors in your accounts* **75 preef,** *proof* **77 lightly,** *easily* **78 hadde I levere,** *I would rather* **79 rit,** *rides,* **stryve,** *quarrel* **80 wratthen,** *anger,* **also may I thryve,** *as I may prosper* **81 bourde,** *joke* **82 wite,** *know,* **gourde,** *gourd-shaped bottle* **84 right anon,** *soon,* **jape,** *joke* **86 Up,** *upon*

---

24 Chepe, Cheapside, the market district of medieval London. **25 Maunciple,** as the purchaser of goods for a London law school, the Manciple was something of a professional rival of the Cook; see *GP* 1.567n. **42 justen atte fan,** joust at the quintain, a practice target that pivots and strikes the jousting knight (or the player of a derivative game) if he fails to avoid it. Apparently, the Cook is reeling in his saddle. **44 wyn ape,** the four traditional states of drunkenness are lamb-drunk (mild), lion-drunk (belligerent), ape-drunk (raucous), and pig-drunk (sloppy). **72 Reclayme thee . . . to lure,** i.e., "get you back"; derives from the language of falconry, where the "lure" is used to recall a bird from flight. **90 pouped in this horn,** blown in this horn, with double entendre: taken a drink and farted or vomited.

To the Manciple he took the gourde agayn°.
And of that drynke the Cook was wonder fayn°,
And thanked hym in swich wise as he koude.
  Thanne gan oure Hoost to laughen wonder loude,
And seyde, "I se wel it is necessarie,   95
Where that we goon, good drynke we with us carie.

For that wol turne rancour and disese°
T'acord and love, and many a wrong apese°.
  O Bacus, yblessed be thy name,
That so kanst turnen ernest into game!   100
Worship and thank be to thy deitee!
Of that mateere ye gete namoore of me.
Telle on thy tale, Manciple, I thee preye."
  "Wel, sire," quod he, "now herkneth what I seye."

Heere bigynneth the Maunciples Tale of the Crowe.

  Whan Phebus dwelled heere in this erthe adoun,   105
As olde bookes maken mencioun,
He was the mooste lusty bachiler°
In al this world, and eek the beste archer.
He slow Phitoun the serpent as he lay
Slepynge agayn° the sonne upon a day,   110
And many another noble worthy dede
He with his bowe wroghte°, as men may rede.
  Pleyen he koude° on every mynstralcie°,
And syngen that it was a melodie
To heeren of his cleere voys the soun.   115
Certes° the kyng of Thebes Amphioun,
That with his syngyng walled that citee,
Koude nevere syngen half so wel as hee.
Therto° he was the semelieste° man
That is or was sith° that the world bigan.   120
What nedeth it his fetures to discryve°?
For in this world was noon so fair on-lyve°.
He was therwith fulfild of gentillesse,
Of honour, and of parfit° worthynesse.
  This Phebus that was flour of bachilrie,   125
As wel in fredom° as in chivalrie,
For his desport° in signe eek of victorie
Of° Phitoun, so as telleth us the storie,
Was wont° to beren in his hand a bowe.
  Now hadde this Phebus in his hous a crowe   130
Which in a cage he fostred many a day,

And taughte it speke as men teche a jay.
Whit was this crowe as is a snowwhit swan,
And countrefete° the speche of every man
He koude whan he sholde telle a tale.   135
Therwith in al this world no nyghtyngale
Ne koude, by an hondred thousand deel°,
Syngen so wonder myrily and weel.
  Now hadde this Phebus in his hous a wyf
Which that he lovede moore than his lyf,   140
And nyght and day dide evere his diligence
Hir for to plese, and doon hire reverence—
Save oonly, if I the sothe° shal sayn,
Jalous he was and wolde have kept hire fayn°.
For hym were looth byjaped° for to be,   145
And so is every wight° in swich degree°.
But al in ydel, for it availleth noght°.
A good wyf that is clene° of werk and thoght
Sholde nat been kept in noon awayt°, certayn,
And trewely the labour is in vayn   150
To kepe a shrewe, for it wol nat bee.
This holde I for a verray nycetee°
To spille° labour for to kepe wyves;
Thus writen olde clerkes in hir lyves.
  But now to purpos as I first bigan: 155
This worthy Phebus dooth al that he kan
To plesen hire, wenynge° for swich plesaunce°,
And for his manhede and his governaunce°,
That no man sholde han put hym from hir grace°.

---

91 **took . . . agayn,** *returned* 92 **wonder fayn,** *wonderfully glad* 97 **disese,** *discomfort* 98 **apese,** *appease* 107 **lusty bachiler,** *vigorous knight* 110 **agayn,** *in* 112 **wroghte,** *accomplished* 113 **Pleyen he koude,** *he could play,* **mynstralcie,** *musical instrument* 116 **Certes,** *certainly* 119 **Therto,** *also,* **semelieste,** *most handsome* 120 **sith,** *since* 121 **discryve,** *describe* 122 **on-lyve,** *alive* 124 **parfit,** *perfect* 126 **fredom,** *generosity* 127 **desport,** *entertainment* 128 **Of,** *over* 129 **wont,** *accustomed* 134

countrefete, *imitate* 137 **deel,** *part* 143 **sothe,** *truth* 144 **wolde have kept hire fayn,** *would gladly have guarded her* 145 **byjaped,** *tricked* 146 **wight,** *man,* **swich degree,** *such social class* 147 **availleth noght,** *accomplishes nothing* 148 **clene,** *pure* 149 **awayt,** *surveillance* 152 **verray nycetee,** *true foolishness* 153 **spille,** *waste* 157 **wenynge,** *thinking,* **swich plesaunce,** *such pleasantness* 158 **governaunce,** *behavior* 159 **grace,** *favor*

99 **Bacus,** Bacchus, god of wine. 105 **Phebus,** Phoebus Apollo, god of music, poetry, and the sun. 109 **Phitoun,** the Python, killed by Apollo in Ovid's *Metamorphosis* 1.438–51. 116 **Amphioun,** played his lyre (not sang) so beautifully that walls built themselves around the city of Thebes. A familiar medieval figure; see *MerT* 4.1716. 143 Considerable variation in the MSS.

But God it woot°, ther may no man embrace°   160
As to destreyne° a thyng which that nature
Hath natureelly set in a creature.
    Taak any bryd° and put it in a cage,
And do al thyn entente and thy corage°
To fostre it tendrely with mete and drynke   165
Of alle deyntees that thou kanst bithynke°,
And keep it al so clenly as thou may,
Although his cage of gold be never so gay,
Yet hath this brid by twenty thousand foold
Levere° in a forest that is rude° and coold   170
Goon ete° wormes and swich wrecchednesse.
For evere this brid wol doon his bisynesse
To escape out of his cage, if he may.
His libertee this brid desireth ay°.
    Lat take° a cat and fostre hym wel with milk   175
And tendre flessh, and make his couche of silk,
And lat hym seen a mous go by the wal,
Anon he weyveth° milk and flessh and al,
And every deyntee that is in that hous,
Swich appetit hath he to ete a mous.   180
Lo, heere hath lust his dominacioun,
And appetit fleemeth° discrecioun.
    A she-wolf hath also a vileyns kynde°.
The lewedeste wolf that she may fynde,
Or leest of reputacioun, that wol she take   185
In tyme whan hir lust° to han a make°.
    Alle thise ensamples speke I by° thise men
That been untrewe and nothyng by° wommen.
For men han evere a likerous° appetit
On lower thyng to parfourne hire° delit   190
Than on hire wyves, be they never so faire,
Ne never so trewe, ne so debonaire°.
Flessh is so newefangel°, with meschaunce°,
That we ne konne° in nothyng han plesaunce°
That sowneth into° vertu any while.   195
    This Phebus, which that thoghte upon
      no gile,
Deceyved was for al his jolitee°.

For under hym another hadde shee,
A man of litel reputacioun,
Nat worth to Phebus in comparisoun.   200
The moore harm is, it happeth ofte so,
Of which ther cometh muchel harm and wo.
    And so bifel, whan Phebus was absent,
His wyf anon hath for hir lemman° sent.
Hir lemman? Certes, this is a knavyssh speche°!   205
Foryeveth it me, and that I yow biseche°.
    The wise Plato seith, as ye may rede,
The word moot nede° accorde with the dede.
If men shal telle proprely a thyng,
The word moost cosyn be to the werkyng.   210
I am a boystous° man, right thus seye I,
Ther nys no° difference, trewely,
Bitwixe a wyf that is of heigh degree,
If of hir body dishonest she bee,
And a poure wenche, oother than this—   215
If it so be they werke bothe amys°—
But that the gentile° in hire estaat above,
She shal be cleped° his lady, as in love;
And for that oother is a poure womman,
She shal be cleped his wenche or his lemman.   220
And, God it woot°, myn owene deere brother,
Men leyn that oon as lowe as lith° that oother.
    Right so bitwixe a titlelees tiraunt°
And an outlawe or a theef erraunt°
The same I seye—ther is no difference.   225
To Alisaundre was toold this sentence°,
That, for° the tirant is of gretter myght,
By force of meynee° for to sleen dounright°,
And brennen° hous and hoom, and make al
      playn°,
Lo, therfore is he cleped° a capitayn;   230
And for the outlawe hath but smal meynee,
And may nat doon so greet an harm as he,
Ne brynge a contree to so greet mescheef,
Men clepen hym an outlawe or a theef.
But for I am a man noght textueel°,   235

---

160 woot, *knows* **embrace,** *undertake* **161 destreyne,** *restrain* **163 bryd,** *bird* **164 corage,** *effort* **166 bithynke,** *think of* **170 Levere,** *rather,* **rude,** *rugged* **171 Goon ete,** *go eat* **174 ay,** *always* **175 Lat take,** *take for example* **178 weyveth,** *abandons* **182 fleemeth,** *drives out* **183 vileyns kynde,** *evil nature* **186 hir lust,** *it pleases her,* **make,** *mate* **187 by,** *about* **189 likerous,** *lecherous* **190 parfourne hire,** *perform their* **192 debonaire,** *meek* **193 newefangel,** *eager for newness,* **with meschaunce,** *bad luck to it* **194 konne,** *can,* **plesaunce,** *pleasure* **195 sowneth into,** *produces*

197 jolitee, *attractiveness* **204 lemman,** *lover* **205 knavyssh speche,** *low way to speak* **206 biseche,** *request* **208 moot nede,** *must necessarily* **211 boystous,** *rough* **212 nys no,** *is no* **216 amys,** *wrongly* **217 gentile,** *aristocrat* **218 cleped,** *called* **221 woot,** *knows* **222 lith,** *lies* **223 titlelees tiraunt,** *untitled usurper* **224 theef erraunt,** *roving robber* **226 sentence,** *meaningful saying* **227 for,** *because* **228 force of meynee,** *strength of his army,* **sleen dounright,** *slaughter* **229 brennen,** *burn,* **make al playn,** *flatten everything* **230 cleped,** *called* **235 noght textueel,** *not book learned*

160–62 This sentiment and the following examples of the natural inclinations of bird and cat are in *RR* 13941–14030 and elsewhere; the she-wolf (line 183), in *RR* 7763–66 and elsewhere. **207–10 Plato . . . werkyng,** see *GP* 1.741–42n. **222 leyn,** lay; double entendre: consider (lay a bet) and lay sexually. **226 Alisaundre,** Alexander the Great. The anecdote was familiar in political admonitions, going back to Cicero's *De Republica* 3.12.

I wol noght telle of textes never a deel°.
I wol go to my tale as I bigan.
Whan Phebus° wyf had sent for hir lemman
Anon° they wroghten al hire lust volage°.

 The white crowe that heeng ay° in the cage 240
Biheeld hire werk and seyde never a word.
And whan that hoom was come Phebus, the lord,
This crowe sang "Cokkow! Cokkow! Cokkow!"

 "What, bryd?" quod Phebus, "What song
  syngestow°?
Ne were thow wont° so myrily to synge 245
That to myn herte it was a rejoysynge
To heere thy voys? Allas, what song is this?"

 "By God," quod he, "I synge nat amys.
Phebus," quod he, "for al thy worthynesse,
For al thy beautee and thy gentilesse, 250
For al thy song and al thy mynstralcye,
For al thy waityng°, blered is thyn eye°
With oon of litel reputacioun,
Noght worth to thee as in comparisoun
The montance° of a gnat, so moote° I thryve°! 255
For on thy bed thy wyf I saugh° hym swyve°."

 What wol ye moore? The crowe anon hym tolde
By sadde tokenes° and by wordes bolde
How that his wyf had doon hire lecherye
Hym to° greet shame and to greet vileynye, 260
And tolde hym ofte he saugh it with his eyen.

 This Phebus gan aweyward for to wryen°.
Hym thoughte his sorweful herte brast atwo°.
His bowe he bente and sette therinne a flo°,
And in his ire his wyf thanne hath he slayn— 265
This is th'effect°, ther is namoore to sayn—
For sorwe of which he brak° his mynstralcie°,
Bothe harpe, and lute, and gyterne, and sautrie°,
And eek he brak his arwes and his bowe,
And after that thus spak he to the crowe: 270

 "Traitour," quod he, "with tonge of scorpioun,
Thou hast me broght to my confusioun°.
Allas, that I was wroght°! Why nere I° deed?

O deere wyf, O gemme° of lustiheed°,
That were to me so sad° and eek so trewe, 275
Now listow° deed with face pale of hewe
Ful giltelees, that dorste° I swere, ywys°!
O rakel° hand, to doon so foule amys!
O trouble° wit, O ire recchelees°,
That unavysed° smyteth° giltelees! 280
O wantrust°, ful of fals suspecioun,
Where was thy wit and thy discrecioun?
O every man, bewar of rakelnesse°!
Ne trowe° nothyng withouten strong witnesse.
Smyt° nat to soone er that ye witen° why, 285
And beeth avysed° wel and sobrely
Er ye doon any execucioun
Upon youre ire for suspecioun.
Allas, a thousand folk hath rakel ire
Fully fordoon° and broght hem in the mire°. 290
Allas, for sorwe I wol myselven slee°."

 And to the crowe, "O false theef," seyde he,
"I wol thee quite° anon thy false tale!
Thou songe whilom° lyk a nyghtyngale;
Now shaltow, false theef, thy song forgon°, 295
And eek thy white fetheres everichon°,
Ne nevere in al thy lif ne shaltou° speke.
Thus shal men on a traytour been awreke°;
Thou and thyn ofspryng evere shul be blake,
Ne nevere sweete noyse shul ye make, 300
But evere crie agayn° tempest and rayn,
In tokenynge° that thurgh thee my wyf is slayn."
And to the crowe he stirte° and that anon
And pulled his white fetheres everychon,
And made hym blak, and refte hym° al his
  song, 305
And eek his speche, and out at dore hym slong
Unto the devel, which° I hym bitake°—
And for this caas° been alle crowes blake.

 Lordynges, by this ensample I yow preye
Beth war and taketh kepe° what ye seye, 310
Ne telleth nevere no man in youre lyf

---

236 never a deel, *not a bit* **238 Phebus,** *Phebus's* **239 Anon,** *soon,* **hire lust volage,** *their passing pleasure* **240 heeng ay,** *hung always* **244 syngestow,** *do you sing* **245 Ne were thow wont,** *were you not accustomed* **252 waityng,** *watching,* **blered is thyn eye,** *you have been blinded* **255 montance,** *value,* **moote,** *might,* **thryve,** *prosper* **256 saugh,** *saw,* **swyve,** *screw* **258 sadde tokenes,** *strong evidence* **260 Hym to,** *to his* **262 wryen,** *turn* **263 brast atwo,** *burst apart* **264 flo,** *arrow* **266 th'effect,** *the outcome* **267 brak,** *broke,* **mynstralcie,** *musical instruments* **268 sautrie,** *dulcimer* **272 confusioun,** *ruin* **273 wroght,** *created,* **nere I,** *were I not* **274 gemme,** *jewel,* **lustiheed,** *delight* **275 sad,** *steadfast* **276**

listow, *you lie* **277 dorste,** *dare,* **ywys,** *for sure* **278 rakel,** *rash* **279 trouble,** *disturbed,* **ire recchelees,** *reckless anger* **280 unavysed,** *thoughtless,* **smyteth,** *strikes* **281 wantrust,** *distrust* **283 rakelnesse,** *rashness* **284 trowe,** *believe* **285 Smyt,** *strike,* **witen,** *know* **286 beeth avysed,** *consider* **290 fordoon,** *destroyed,* **mire,** *mud* **291 slee,** *slay* **293 quite,** *repay* **294 whilom,** *once* **295 forgon,** *lose* **296 everichon,** *everyone* **297 shaltou,** *shall you* **298 awreke,** *avenged* **301 agayn,** *at the approach of* **302 In tokenynge,** *as a sign* **303 stirte,** *went suddenly* **305 refte hym,** *deprived him of* **307 which,** *to whom,* **bitake,** *commit* **308 caas,** *reason* **310 kepe,** *care*

---

243 Cokkow, the crow speaks in bird talk and (in human speech) declares Phebus a cuckold at the same time. **271 scorpioun,** a common figure of treachery.

How that another man hath dight° his wyf.
He wol yow haten mortally, certeyn.
Daun Salomon, as wise clerkes seyn,
Techeth a man to kepen his tonge weel.   315
But, as I seyde, I am noght textueel°,
But nathelees thus taughte me my dame:
"My sone, thenk on the crowe, a Goddes name!
My sone, keep° wel thy tonge, and keep thy freend.
A wikked tonge is worse than a feend,   320
My sone; from a feend men may hem blesse°.
My sone, God of his endelees goodnesse
Walled a tonge with teeth and lippes eke,
For man sholde hym avyse° what he speeke.
My sone, ful ofte for to muche speche   325
Hath many a man been spilt°, as clerkes teche,
But for litel speche avysely°
Is no man shent°, to speke generally.
My sone, thy tonge sholdestow° restreyne
At alle tymes but° whan thou doost thy peyne°   330
To speke of God in honour and preyere.
The firste vertu, sone, if thou wolt leere°,
Is to restreyne and kepe wel thy tonge;
Thus lerne children whan that they been yonge.
My sone, of muchel spekyng yvele avysed°,   335
Ther lasse° spekyng hadde ynough suffised,
Comth muchel harm; thus was me toold and
    taught.

In muchel speche synne wanteth naught°.
Wostow° wherof a rakel° tonge serveth?
Right° as a swerd forkutteth and forkerveth°   340
An arm a-two, my deere sone, right so
A tonge kutteth freendshipe al a-two.
A janglere° is to God abhomynable.
Reed Salomon, so wys and honurable,
Reed David in his psalmes, reed Senekke.   345
My sone, spek nat, but with thyn heed thou
    bekke°.
Dissimule° as thou were deef if that thou heere
A janglere speke of perilous mateere.
The Flemyng seith, and lerne it if thee leste°,
That litel janglyng causeth muchel° reste.   350
My sone, if thou no wikked word hast seyd
Thee thar nat drede for to be biwreyd°
But he that hath mysseyd°, I dar wel sayn,
He may by no wey clepe° his word agayn.
Thyng that is seyd is seyd, and forth it gooth,   355
Though hym repente or be hym nevere so looth°.
He is his thral° to whom that he hath sayd
A tale of which he is now yvele apayd°.
My sone, bewar and be noon auctour° newe
Of tidynges, wheither they been false or
    trewe.   360
Wherso thou come, amonges hye or lowe°,
Kepe° wel thy tonge and thenk upon the crowe."

Heere is ended the Maunciples Tale of the Crowe.

---

312 **dight,** *had sex with* 316 **noght textueel,** *not book learned* 319 **keep,** *guard* 321 **blesse,** *protect by a blessing* 324 **hym avyse,** *consider* 326 **spilt,** *destroyed* 327 **avysely,** *thoughtfully* 328 **shent,** *hurt* 329 **sholdestow,** *you should* 330 **but,** *except,* **doost thy peyne,** *make the effort* 332 **leere,** *learn* 335 **yvele avysed,** *poorly considered* 336 **Ther lasse,** *where less* 338 **wanteth naught,** *lacks nothing* 339 **Wostow,** *do you know,* **rakel,** *rash*

340 **Right,** *just,* **forkutteth and forkerveth,** *cuts and carves completely* 343 **janglere,** *chatterer* 346 **bekke,** *nod* 347 **Dissimule,** *pretend* 349 **if thee leste,** *if you please* 350 **muchel,** *much* 352 **biwreyd,** *betrayed* 353 **mysseyd,** *misspoken* 354 **clepe,** *call back* 356 **looth,** *unwilling* 357 **thral,** *slave* 358 **yvele apayd,** *unhappy* 359 **auctour,** *author* 361 **hye or lowe,** *aristocracy or peasants* 362 **Kepe,** *guard*

314 **Daun Salomon,** "master" Solomon, thought to be the author of the book of Proverbs; see Proverbs 21.23. 321 **My sone,** the advisory "my son" formula recurs in Proverbs 23 and in other wisdom literature generally. The various proverbs and apothegms that follow recur in various sources, including Proverbs, Psalms, the *Distichs* of Cato, *RR,* and Albertanus de Brescia's *De arte loquendi et tacendi.* None of them counsels silence in such a long-winded way, but compare *RR* 7037–57. 344–45 Proverbs (attributed to Solomon) and David's Psalms are ultimate sources of several of the sentiments expressed in the Manciple's tally, but Seneca's works do not seem to be. 349–50 **Flemyng seith . . . reste,** a Flemish (Belgian) proverb.

CANTERBURY TALES PART 10

INTRODUCTION

IN THE *PARSON'S PROLOGUE*, the descending sun, lengthening shadows, and the astrological sign of Libra (signifying the scales or judgment) are clear signs of closure. As the pilgrims approach the outskirts of an unnamed village, the Host says that only one teller remains, signaling the end of the pilgrimage and the completion of the tale-telling contest. The Parson's rejection of fables for "Moralitee and vertuous mateere" (38) leads to his "meditacioun" (55) on the sacrament of confession or penance—the sacrament whereby sins are forgiven in medieval Christian tradition (and a number of Christian denominations today). When the Parson equates the pilgrimage to the spiritual journey to the heavenly Jerusalem (51), the entire Canterbury fiction becomes allegorical, for a moment at least, and the moral seriousness of the pilgrimage overtakes the lively give-and-take of the tale-telling contest. In a complex move, Chaucer indicates that his fiction is coming to an end, asks us once again to consider the relation of fiction to truth, and prompts us to consider his work as a story of human progress toward death and perhaps salvation—movement from the city of man to the City of God.

The sacrament of penance—the topic of the *Parson's Tale*—was thought to be a necessary step in the progress toward salvation. Baptism was the means to remove the effects of Adam's original sin that descended to all human beings, but penance was the means to eradicate the sins that the individual committed on the journey through life. Sinfulness was understood to be a state of being, not merely an accumulation of improper actions or misguided thoughts, and the effect of proper penance was to transform the individual from the state of being sinful to sinless. The sacrament required that the penitents be contrite—truly sorrowful—and that they confess all their sins to a priest, whose words of forgiveness were necessary to the action of the sacrament and the absolution of the sins. Intention and speech—the words of the penitent and of the priest—are equally important.

As a handbook or manual on penance, the *Parson's Tale* defines the sacrament and its functions and clarifies the variety of sins and their remedies under the conventional arrangement of the seven deadly sins (pride, envy, anger, sloth, avarice, gluttony, lechery). Such manuals were initially designed for confessors to help their penitents understand the sacrament, identify their sins systematically, and achieve contrition so that the sins could be purged. Over time, the Latin manuals were translated into the vernacular languages, becoming accessible to more people and, in the process, more meditational and affective, focused on personal examination of conscience. Reading a confessional manual was preparation for and part of the process of spiritual renewal—a medieval equivalent of self-help. It was a means to identify one's failings and inspire sincere sorrow, and the goal was the forgiveness of sins through the spoken sacrament, "shrift of mouthe" (87), as penance was known.

It is appropriate that such a treatise be assigned to the Parson because the pastoral duties of parish priests included instruction of their congregations about penance and administration of the sacrament to them. It has long been thought that by assigning this last tale to the Parson, Chaucer was submitting the rest of his tales to a higher, spiritual standard—perhaps a balance to the secular, philosophical standard of the *Knight's Tale*. Such readings can still stand, but they can be modified by the complex attitudes toward the priesthood (and knighthood) in Chaucer's age. Robert W. Swanson clarifies medieval pastoral responsibilities in "Chaucer's Parson and Other Priests" (1991, no. 1454). In "Chaucer's Parson and the Specter of Wycliffism" (2001, no. 1450), Katherine Little compares the *Parson's Tale* with its orthodox sources and contemporary vernacular material, showing how Chaucer's tale can be seen to emphasize reformed attitudes toward the priesthood, lay instruction, and the role of contrition in penance.

The most important sources of the *Parson's Tale* are two Latin treatises that Chaucer may have combined himself or were available to him in some version undiscovered by modern scholars. Raymund of Pennaforte's *Summa de paenitentia* (The Sum of Penance) underlies the discussion of penance at the opening and closing of the tale, and a version of William Peraldus's *Summa de vitiis et virtutibus* (The Sum of the Vices and Virtues) underlies the intervening descriptions of the vices and their remedies. For details, see Richard Newhauser's contribution to *Sources and Analogues* (2002, no. 187).

Reading through the *Parson's Tale* can encourage us to consider our own failings, but the process also prompts recollection of the pilgrims and tales that have come earlier in the Canterbury sequence. In general terms, "pride of dress" (415ff.) suggests the Monk, Squire, and others; "pride of table" (444ff.) suggests the Prioress and Franklin. The character name "Placebo" from the *Merchant's Tale* is mentioned in connection with flattery (617), and the "remedy" for lechery (930ff.) recalls issues in the marriage group. In "The *Parson's Tale* and the Quitting of the *Canterbury Tales*" (1978, no. 1451), Lee W. Patterson tallies some thirty-five instances where Chaucer's penitential treatise echoes preceding material. Many of them are conventional, found in Chaucer's sources, but several indicate that he may have been working on the *Parson's Tale* recurrently during the composition of the Canterbury fiction. Perhaps he adjusted the tale he had translated earlier to reflect the rest of the collection, or at times he may have composed later tales to anticipate this final one. Either way, the *Parson's Tale* invites readers to view the Canterbury pilgrims retrospectively from a penitential perspective, although this hindsight view does not obviate the vitality and variety of *The Canterbury Tales*. Our affective involvement in the penitential process helps us as readers identify the failings of the pilgrims with our own and it also helps to remind us that to be human is to sin.

When Chaucer asks forgiveness for his literary sins in his Retraction and then revokes a series of his works (1084–87), the penitential unity of pilgrims, audience, and author is complete. Retraction or apologies are conventional in medieval literature, but, typically, Chaucer puts his to great advantage, reminding us of his entire literary output at the same time that he retracts it and includes himself among those in need of penance. There is no Dantesque or Miltonic elevation of the poet here, but instead the acknowledgment that the lively variety of *The Canterbury Tales* cannot go on forever. Critics have read deathbed sincerity in the Retraction, and others have perceived wry ironies. Nothing is more Chaucerian than this combination of moral seriousness and artistic self-awareness.

For a series of essays that survey the scholarship and confront critical questions of part 10, see David Raybin and Linda Tarte Holley, eds., *Closure in The Canterbury Tales: The Role of the Parson's Tale* (2000, no. 1453). Thomas Bestul, "Chaucer's *Parson's Tale* and the Late-Medieval Tradition of Religious Meditation" (1989, no. 1443), addresses Chaucer's use of meditational materials. On the conventional nature of the Retraction, see Anita Obermeier, *The History and Anatomy of Auctorial Self-Criticism in the European Middle Ages* (1999, no. 1463).

CANTERBURY TALES PART 10

PARSON'S TALE

PROLOGUE

Heere folweth the Prologe of the Persouns Tale.

By that° the Maunciple hadde his tale al ended,
The sonne fro the south lyne° was descended
So lowe that he nas nat° to my sighte
Degrees nyne and twenty as in highte.
Foure of the clokke it was tho°, as I gesse,   5
For ellevene foot, or litel moore or lesse,
My shadwe was at thilke° tyme, as there
Of swiche feet° as my lengthe parted° were
In sixe feet equal of proporcioun.
Therwith° the moones exaltacioun—   10
I meene Libra—alwey gan ascende
As we were entryng at a thropes ende°.
For which oure Hoost, as he was wont to gye°
As in this caas° oure joly compaignye,

---

1 **By that,** *by* (the time) *that* 2 **south lyne,** *meridian* 3 **nas nat,** *was not* 5 **tho,** *then* 7 **thilke,** *that* 8 **swiche feet,** *such units,* **parted,** *divided* 10

Therwith, *also* 12 **thropes ende,** *edge of a village* 13 **wont to gye,** *accustomed to direct* 14 **caas,** *situation*

1 Hg writes "Maunciple" over an erasure; some late MSS have "Marchaunt" or "Yeman" depending on the order of the tales. **4–5 Degrees nyne and twenty . . . / Foure of the clokke,** these numbers vary in the MSS as a result of misreading the Roman numerals. But at 4 p.m. in mid-April, according to Nicholas of Lynn's *Kalendarium,* the sun is approximately 29 degrees below the meridian (the astronomical overhead circle that passes through the celestial poles). Chaucer's method of calculation here parallels his method in *MLT* 2.2–14, but the details are less precise than suggestive. Twenty-nine recalls *GP* 1.24, and 4 p.m. suggests the end of day and closure. **6 ellevene foot,** the angle of the sun at 4 p.m. casts horizontal shadows that are eleven units (feet) in length for every six units (feet) of the vertical, standing figure; see *MLT* 2.7–9. The narrator is not six feet tall, but the ratio of his height to his shadow is six to eleven. **10–11 moones exaltacioun . . . Libra,** an astronomical fiction or perhaps a reference to the impending rise of the moon. The exaltation (i.e., position of greatest influence) of the moon is in Taurus; the exaltation of Saturn is in Libra, the sign of the scales. Chaucer may have chosen Libra for the ways it suggests the Crucifixion (the shape of the scales), judgment (scales of justice), and/or freedom of choice (Lat. *liber*). Libra is the sign of the fall equinox, as Aries (*GP* 1.8) is the sign of the spring equinox.

Seyde in this wise, "Lordynges everichoon°, 15
Now lakketh us no tales mo than oon.
Fulfilled is my sentence and my decree.
I trowe° that we han herd of ech degree°.
Almoost fulfild is al myn ordinaunce°.
I pray to God, so yeve° hym right good
    chaunce 20
That telleth this tale to us lustily°.
    "Sire preest," quod he, "artow° a vicary,
Or arte a person? Sey sooth°, by thy fey°.
Be what thou be, ne breke thou nat oure
    pley°,
For every man save thou hath toold his tale. 25
Unbokele° and shewe us what is in thy male°,
For trewely me thynketh by thy cheere°
Thou sholdest knytte up° wel a greet mateere.
Telle us a fable anon, for cokkes bones!"
    This Persoun answerde al atones°, 30
"Thou getest fable° noon ytoold for° me,
For Paul, that writeth unto Thymothee,
Repreveth hem° that weyven° soothfastnesse,
And tellen fables and swich wrecchednesse.
Why sholde I sowen draf° out of my fest° 35
Whan I may sowen whete°, if that me lest°?
For which I seye, if that yow list° to heere
Moralitee and vertuous mateere,
And thanne that° ye wol yeve° me audience,
I wol ful fayn° at Cristes reverence 40
Do yow plesaunce leefful°, as I kan.
But trusteth wel, I am a southren man°.
I kan nat geeste 'rum, ram, ruf,' by lettre,
Ne, God woot°, rym° holde I but litel bettre.

And therfore, if yow list°—I wol nat glose°— 45
I wol yow telle a myrie° tale in prose
To knytte up al this feeste and make an ende.
And Jhesu for his grace wit° me sende
To shewe yow the wey in this viage°
Of thilke parfit° glorious pilgrymage 50
That highte° Jerusalem celestial.
And if ye vouchesauf°, anon I shal
Bigynne upon my tale, for which I preye
Telle youre avys°; I kan no bettre seye.
    "But nathelees, this meditacioun 55
I putte it ay° under correccioun
Of clerkes, for I am nat textueel°.
I take but the sentence°, trusteth weel.
Therfore I make protestacioun
That I wol stonde to correccioun." 60
    Upon this word we han assented soone,
For as us seemed° it was for to doone°
To enden in som vertuous sentence,
And for to yeve hym space° and audience,
And bede° oure Hoost he sholde to hym
    seye 65
That alle we to telle his tale hym preye.
    Oure Hoost hadde the wordes for us alle,
"Sire preest," quod he, "now faire yow
    bifalle°!
Telleth," quod he, "youre meditacioun.
But hasteth yow, the sonne wole adoun; 70
Beth fructuous° and that in litel space,
And to do wel God sende yow his grace.
Sey what yow list, and we wol gladly heere."
And with that word he seyde in this manere.

Explicit prohemium.

15 **everichoon,** *every one* 18 **trowe,** *think,* **degree,** *social rank* 19 **or-dinaunce,** *plan* 20 **yeve,** *give* 21 **lustily,** *pleasingly* 22 **artow,** *are you* 23 **sooth,** *truth,* **fey,** *faith* 24 **breke . . . oure pley,** *spoil our game* 26 **Un-bokele,** *unbuckle,* **male,** *purse* 27 **cheere,** *disposition* 28 **knytte up,** *con-clude* 30 **al atones,** *immediately* 31 **fable,** *fiction,* **for,** *by* 33 **Repreveth hem,** *blames them,* **weyven,** *turn from* 35 **draf,** *chaff,* **fest,** *fist* 36 **whete,** *wheat,* **me lest,** *it pleases me* 37 **list,** *wish* 39 **that,** *if,* **yeve,** *give* 40 **ful fayn,** *very happily* 41 **Do yow plesaunce leefful,** *give you legitimate* pleasure 42 **southren man,** *from the south* 44 **woot,** *knows,* **rym,** *rhyme* 45 **list,** *wish,* **glose,** *lie* 46 **myrie,** *merry* 48 **wit,** *intelligence* 49 **viage,** *journey* 50 **thilke parfit,** *that perfect* 51 **highte,** *is called* 52 **vouchesauf,** *agree* 54 **avys,** *opinion* 56 **ay,** *always* 57 **textueel,** *book learned* 58 **sen-tence,** *meaning* 62 **For as us seemed,** *because it seemed to us,* **for to doone,** *necessary* 64 **space,** *time* 65 **bede,** *asked* 68 **faire yow bifalle,** *may good things happen to you* 71 **fructuous,** *fruitful*

22–23 **vicary . . . person,** vicar or parson, i.e., a priest acting in the place of the holder of a benefice (church appointment) or the benefice holder himself. 25 **every man . . . hath toold his tale,** a sign of closure, although Chaucer evidently changed his mind about the number of tales each pilgrim would tell; see *GP* 1.792 and *SqT* 5.698. 29 **cokkes bones,** cock's bones; euphemism for God's bones, a mild oath. See *ManP* 9.9. 32 **Paul,** St. Paul rejects fiction and prefers truth in 1 Timothy 1.4, 4.7; 2 Timothy 4.4. 35–36 **draf . . . whete,** see *NPT* 7.3443n. 43 **geeste 'rum, ram, ruf' by lettre,** "tell a story in alliterative verse," often associated with the north and west of England. 51 **Jerusalem celestial,** heav-enly Jerusalem; repeated at line 80 below. This allusion to Revelation 21.2 lends a clear allegorical dimension to the journey to Canterbury. 73–74 These lines should follow 68, as they do in all MSS, so that *ParsP* ends with the word "grace" (line 71), but most recent editors have moved the lines on the assumption that it makes better sense. 74a **Explicit prohemium,** "Here ends the prologue."

Heere bigynneth the Persounes Tale.

Jer. 6. State super vias et videte et interrogate de viis antiquis, que sit via bona; et ambulate in ea, et invenietis refrigerium animabus vestris, &c.

Our sweete lord God of hevene, that wole° no man perisse° but wole that we comen alle to the knoweleche of hym and to the blissful lif that is perdurable°, / amonesteth° us by the pro- 75 phete Jeremie and seith in thys wyse, / "Stondeth upon the weyes and seeth and axeth of° olde pathes (that is to seyn, of olde sentences°) which is the goode wey; / and walketh in that wey, and ye shal fynde refresshynge for youre soules, &c." / Manye been the weyes espirituels° that leden folk to oure lord Jesu Crist and to the regne of glorie. / Of whiche weyes, ther is a ful noble wey and a ful covenable°, which may nat fayle to no man ne to womman, that thurgh synne hath mysgoon° fro the righte wey of Jerusalem celestial. / And 80 this wey is cleped° penitence, of which man sholde gladly herknen° and enquere with al his herte / to wyten° what is penitence, and whennes° it is cleped penitence, and in how manie maneres been the acciouns° or werkynges of penitence, / and how manie speces ther been of penitence, and whiche thynges apertenen° and bihouven° to penitence, and whiche thynges destourben° penitence. /

Seint Ambrose seith that penitence is the pleynynge° of man for the gilt that he hath doon, and namore to do anythyng for which hym oghte to pleyne. / And som doctour seith "Penitence is the waymentynge° of man that sorweth for his synne and pyneth hymself° for he hath mysdoon." / Penitence, with certeyne cir- 85 cumstances, is verray° repentance of a man that halt° hymself in sorwe and oother peyne for his giltes. / And for he shal be verray penitent, he shal first biwaylen the synnes that he hath doon and stidefastly purposen in his herte to have shrift° of mouthe and to doon satisfaccioun°, / and never to doon thyng for which hym oghte moore to biwayle or to compleyne, and continue in goode werkes, or elles his repentance may nat availle°. / For as seith Seint Ysidre, "He is a japer° and a gabbere° and no verray repentant that eftsoone° dooth thyng for which hym oghte repente." / Wepynge and nat for to stynte° to synne may nat avaylle°. / But 90 nathelees men shal hope that every tyme that man falleth, be it never so ofte, that he may arise thurgh penitence if he have grace—but certeinly it is greet doute. / For as seith Seint Gregorie, "Unnethe° ariseth he out of synne that is charged° with the charge of yvel usage°." / And therfore repentant folk that stynte° for to synne and forlete° synne er that synne forlete hem, Hooly Chirche holdeth hem siker° of hire savacioun. / And he that synneth and verraily repenteth hym in his laste, Hooly Chirche yet hopeth° his savacioun by the grete mercy of oure lord Jesu Crist, for his repentaunce—but taak the siker wey. /

And now sith° I have declared yow what thyng is penitence, now shul ye understonde that ther been three acciouns° of penitence. / The 95 firste accioun of penitence is that a man be baptized after that he hath synned. / Seint Augustyn seith, "But he be penytent for his olde synful lyf, he may nat bigynne the newe clene lif." / For certes if he be baptized withouten penitence of his olde gilt, he receyveth the mark of baptesme but nat the grace ne the remission of his synnes, til he have repentance verray°. / Another defaute° is this, that men doon deedly synne after that they

---

75 **wole,** *wishes,* **perisse,** *perish,* **perdurable,** *everlasting* 76 **amonesteth,** *advises* 77 **axeth of,** *ask about,* **sentences,** *meanings* 79 **weyes espirituels,** *spiritual ways* 80 **ful covenable,** *very appropriate,* **mysgoon,** *strayed* 81 **cleped,** *named,* **herknen,** *listen* 82 **wyten,** *know,* **whennes,** *why,* **acciouns,** *activities* 83 **apertenen,** *belong to,* **bihouven,** *are necessary,* **destourben,** *hinder* 84 **pleynynge,** *lamenting* 85 **waymentynge,** *lamenting,* **pyneth hymself,** *punishes himself* 86 **verray,**

genuine, **halt,** *holds* 87 **shrift,** *confession,* **satisfaccioun,** *acts of reparation* 88 **availle,** *be effective* 89 **japer,** *jokester,* **gabbere,** *chatterer,* **eftsoone,** *again* 90 **stynte,** *cease,* **avaylle,** *have effect* 92 **Unnethe,** *scarcely,* **charged,** *burdened,* **usage,** *habit* 93 **stynte,** *cease,* **forlete,** *abandon,* **siker,** *certain* 94 **hopeth,** *hopes for* 95 **sith,** *since,* **acciouns,** *activities* 98 **verray,** *true* 99 **defaute,** *fault*

74c–74e *Jer. 6* . . . , from Jeremiah 6.16, translated in lines 77–78. The line numbers for this prose tale are conventional for convenient reference. The numbers indicate the end of the respective lines. **84 Ambrose,** Pseudo-Ambrose, *Sermon* 25.1. **85 som doctour,** some doctor of the church, theologian; unidentified. **89 Ysidre,** Isidore of Seville, *Sententiae* 2.16.1. **92 Gregorie,** Gregory, *Morals* 4.27.51–52. **93** Compare the first half of this sentence with *PhyT* 6.286. **97 Augustyn,** Augustine, *Sermon* 351.2. **98 mark of baptesme,** the spiritual sign or character received by the soul in baptism that enables the soul to receive the other sacraments.

han receyved baptesme. / The thridde defaute is thatmen fallen in venial synnes after hir baptesme fro day to day. / Therof seith Seint 100 Augustyn that penitence of goode and humble folk is the penitence of every day. /

The speces° of penitence been three. That oon of hem is solempne°, another is commune°, and the thridde is privee°. / Thilke penance that is solempne is in two maneres, as to be put out of Hooly Chirche in Lente for slaughtre of children, and swich maner thyng. / Another thyng is whan a man hath synned openly, of which synne the fame° is openly spoken in the contree, and thanne Hooly Chirche by juggement destreyneth° hym for to do open° penaunce. / Commune penaunce is that preestes enjoynen° men comunly° in certeyn caas,° as for to goon, peraventure°, naked in pilgrimages, or barefoot. / Pryvee penaunce is thilke 105 that° men doon alday° for privee synnes, of whiche they shryve° hem prively and receyve privee penaunce. /

Now shaltow understande what is bihovely° and necessarie to verray perfit penitence. And this stant on° three thynges : / contricioun of herte, confessioun of mouth, and satisfaccioun. / For which seith Seint John Crisostom, "Penitence destreyneth a man to accepte benygnely every peyne that hym is enjoyned, with contricioun of herte, and shrift of mouth, with satisfaccioun, and in werkynge of alle maner humylitee." / And this is fruytful penitence agayn three thynges in whiche we wratthe° oure lord Jesu Crist, / this 110 is to seyn, by delit° in thynkynge, by recchelesnesse° in spekynge, and by wikked synful werkynge°. / And agayns thise wikkede giltes is penitence, that may be likned unto a tree. /

The roote of this tree is contricioun, that hideth hym° in the herte of hym that is verray repentaunt, right as the roote of a tree hydeth hym in the erthe. / Of the roote of contricion spryngeth a stalke that bereth braunches and leves of confessioun, and fruyt of satisfaccioun. / For which Crist seith in his gospel, "Dooth digne° fruyt of penitence." For by this fruyt may men knowe this tree, and nat by the roote that is hyd in the herte of man, ne by the braunches ne by the leves of confessioun. / And therfore oure lord Jesu 115 Crist seith thus, "By the fruyt of hem ye shul knowen hem." / Of this roote eek spryngeth° a seed of grace, the which seed is mooder° of sikernesse°, and this seed is egre° and hoot. / The grace of this seed spryngeth of God thurgh remembrance of the day of doome and on the peynes of helle. / Of this matere seith Salomon that in the drede of God man forleteth° his synne. / The heete of this seed is the love of God and the desiryng of the joye perdurable°. / This heete 120 draweth the herte of a man to God and dooth hym haten his synne. / For soothly, ther is nothing that savoureth° so wel to a child as the milk of his norice°, ne nothing is to him moore abhomynable than thilke milk whan it is medled° with oother mete°. / Right so the synful man that loveth his synne, hym semeth that it is to him moost sweete of anything. / But fro that tyme that he loveth sadly° oure lord Jesu Crist, and desireth the lif perdurable, ther nys to him nothing moore abhomynable. / For soothly, the lawe of God is the love of God; for which David the prophete seith, "I have loved thy lawe and hated wikkednesse and hate." He that loveth God kepeth his lawe and his word. / This tree saugh the prophete 125 Daniel in spirit upon the avysioun° of the king Nabugodonosor, whan he conseiled hym to do penitence. / Penaunce is the tree of lyf to hem that it receyven, and he that holdeth hym in

---

102 **speces,** *species,* **solempne,** *serious,* **commune,** *communal,* **privee,** *private* 104 **fame,** *reputation,* **destreyneth,** *compels,* **open,** *public* 105 **enjoynen,** *command,* **comunly,** *in groups,* **caas,** *situations,* **peraventure,** *perhaps* 106 **thilke that,** *that which,* **alday,** *regularly* **shryve,** *confess* 107 **bihovely,** *required of,* **stant on,** *depends upon* 110 **wratthe,** *make angry* 111 **delit,** *illicit pleasures,* **recchelesnesse,** *carelessness,* **werkynge,** *action* 113 **hym,** *itself* 115 **Dooth digne,** *produce worthy* 117 **spryngeth,** *grows,* **mooder,** *mother,* **sikernesse,** *certainty,* **egre,** *bitter* 119 **forleteth,** *abandons* 120 **perdurable,** *everlasting* 122 **savoureth,** *tastes,* **norice,** *nurse,* **medled,** *mixed,* **mete,** *food* 124 **sadly,** *firmly* 126 **upon the avysioun,** *after the dream*

99–100 Sorrow for one's sins is active in conjunction with baptism in removing "olde gilt" (line 98), and against sins, either "deedly" (i.e., mortal) or "venial," committed after baptism. Mortal sin deprives the soul of its inherent holiness through the severity of the sin and the complete intention of the sinner; venial sin is less serious or not fully intentional. See also lines 358ff. below. **101 Augustyn,** Epistles 265.8. **103 as to be put out of Hooly Chirche in Lente . . . ,** heinous sins required particularly strict penance; in this case, the denial of any participation in the church (excommunication) during the season leading up to Easter. **107 verray perfit penitence,** genuine perfect penitence, i.e., the state or condition of the penitent person who is completely realigned with God. **109 John Crisostom,** *Sermon on Penance,* attributed to Chrysostom in manuscripts and early editions. **115 Crist seith,** spoken by John the Baptist in Matthew 3.8. **116 Jesu Crist seith,** Matthew 7.20. **119 Salomon,** Proverbs 16.6. **125 David,** Psalms 119.123. **126 Daniel,** Daniel 4.1–24.

verray penitence is blessed, after the sentence of Salomon. /

In this penitence or contricioun man shal understonde foure thinges, that is to seyn: what is contricioun; and whiche been the causes that moeven a man to contricioun; and how he sholde be contrit; and what contricioun availleth to° the soule. / Thanne is it thus, that contricioun is the verray sorwe that a man receyveth° in his herte for his synnes, with sad° purpos to shryve hym°, and to do penaunce and nevermoore to do synne. / And this sorwe shal been in this manere, as seith Seint Bernard, "It shal been hevy and grevous, and ful sharpe and poynaunt in herte." / First, for man hath agilt° his lord and hys creatour; and moore sharpe and poynaunt for he hath agilt hys fader celestial; / and yet moore sharpe and poynaunt for he hath wrathed° and agilt hym that boghte° hym, which with his precious blood hath delivered us fro the bondes of synne and fro the crueltee of the devel and fro the peynes of helle. /

The causes that oghte moeve a man to contricioun been six. First, a man shal remembre hym of his synnes. / But looke he that thilke° remembraunce ne be to hym no delit by no wey, but greet shame and sorwe for his gilt. For Job seith, "Synful men doon werkes worthy of confusion." / And therfore seith Ezechie, "I wol remembre me° alle the yeres of my lyf in bitternesse of myn herte." / And God seith in the Apocalips, "Remembreth yow fro whennes° that ye been falle°." For biforn that tyme that ye synned ye were the children of God and lymes° of the regne° of God, / but for youre synne ye been woxen thral° and foul, and membres of the feend, hate of aungels, sclaundre° of Hooly Chirche, and foode of the false serpent, perpetueel matere° of the fir of helle. / And yet moore foul and abhomynable, for ye trespassen° so ofte tyme as dooth the hound that retourneth to eten his spewyng°. / And yet be ye fouler for youre longe continuyng in synne and youre synful usage°, for which ye be

roten in youre synne as a beest in his dong°. / Swiche manere of thoghtes maken a man to have shame of his synne and no delit, as God seith by the prophete Ezechiel, / "Ye shal remembre yow of youre weyes and they shuln° displese yow." Soothly, synnes been the weyes that leden folk to helle. /

The seconde cause that oghte make a man to have desdeyn of synne is this, that as seith Seint Peter, "Whoso that dooth synne is thral of synne," and synne put a man in greet thraldom°. / And therfore seith the prophete Ezechiel, "I wente sorweful in desdayn of myself." And certes, wel oghte a man have desdayn of synne, and withdrawe hym from that thraldom and vileynye. / And lo, what seith Seneca in this matere? He seith thus, "Though I wiste° that neither God ne man ne sholde nevere knowe it, yet wolde I have desdayn for to do synne." / And the same Seneca also seith, "I am born to gretter thynges than to be thral to my body, or than for to maken of my body a thral." / Ne a fouler thral may no man ne womman maken of his body than for to yeven° his body to synne. / Al° were it the fouleste cherl or the fouleste womman that lyveth, and leest of value, yet is he thanne moore foule and moore in servitute. / Evere fro the hyer degree that man falleth, the moore is he thral, and moore to God and to the world vile and abhomynable. / O goode God, wel oghte man have desdayn of synne sith° that thurgh synne ther° he was free, now is he maked bonde°. / And therfore seyth Seint Augustin, "If thou hast desdayn of thy servant, if he agilte° or synne, have thou thanne desdayn that thou thyself sholdest do synne." / Take reward° of thy value, that thou ne be to foul to thyself. / Allas, wel oghten they thanne have desdayn to been servauntz and thralles to synne, and soore been ashamed of hemself, / that God of his endelees goodnesse hath set hem in heigh estaat, or yeven hem wit, strengthe of body, heele°, beautee, prosperitee, / and boghte° hem fro the deeth with his herte blood, that they so

---

128 **availleth to,** *does for* 129 **receyveth,** *accepts,* **sad,** *firm,* **shryve hym,** *confess himself* 131 **agilt,** *sinned against* 132 **wrathed,** *angered,* **boghte,** *redeemed* 134 **looke he that thilke,** *he must beware that that* 135 **wol remembre me,** *will remind myself* 136 **whennes,** *where,* **been falle,** *are fallen,* **lymes,** *members,* **regne,** *kingdom* 137 **been woxen thral,** *have become enslaved,* **sclaundre,** *scandal,* **matere,** *fuel* 138 **trespassen,** *sin,* **spewyng,** *vomit* 139 **synful usage,** *habitual sin,* **dong,** *dung* 141 **shuln,** *shall* 142 **thraldom,** *servitude* 144 **wiste,** *know* 146 **yeven,** *give* 147 **Al,** *even though* 149 **sith,** *since,* **ther,** *when,* **bonde,** *slave* 150 **agilte,** *is guilty* 151 **reward,** *regard* 153 **heele,** *health* 154 **boghte,** *redeemed*

127 **Salomon,** Proverbs 28.13. 130 **Bernard,** Bernard of Clairvaux's associate, Nicholas of Clairvaux, *Sermon on the Feast of St. Andrew* 8. 134 **Job,** not in Job. 135 **Ezechie,** Hezekiah, in Isaiah 38.15. 136 **the Apocalips,** Revelation 2.5. 138 **hound,** Proverbs 26.11. 140–41 **Ezechiel,** Ezekiel 20.43. 142 **Peter,** John 8.34; compare 2 Peter 2.19. 143 **Ezechiel,** not in Ezekiel. 144–45 **Seneca,** the first reference is not in Seneca; the second is Seneca's *Moral Epistles* 65.21. 150 **Augustin,** *Sermons* 9.16.

unkyndely° agayns his gentilesse quiten° hym so vileynsly, to slaughtre of hir owene soules. / O goode God, ye wommen that been of so greet beautee, remembreth yow of the proverbe of Salomon, that seith, / "Likneth a fair womman that is a °155 fool of hire body lyk to a ryng of gold that were in the groyn° of a soughe°." / For right as a soughe wroteth° in everich ordure°, so wroteth she hire beautee in the stynkynge ordure of synne. /

The thridde cause that oghte moeve a man to contricioun is drede of the Day of Doome and of the horrible peynes of helle. / For as Seint Jerome seith, "At every tyme that me remembreth of the Day of Doome, I quake, / for whan I ete or drynke or whatso that I do, evere semeth me that the trompe° sowneth in myn ere: / 'Riseth up, ye °160 that been dede, and cometh to the juggement.'" / O goode God, muchel oghte a man to drede swich a juggement, "ther as we shullen been alle," as Seint Poul seith, "biforn the seete° of oure lord Jesu Crist," / where as he shal make a general congregacioun, where as no man may been absent. / For certes, there availleth noon essoyne° ne excusacioun. / And nat oonly that oure defautes shullen be jugged, but eek that alle oure werkes shullen openly be knowe. / And as °165 seith Seint Bernard, "Ther ne shal no pledynge availle, ne sleighte°. We shullen yeven° rekeninge of everich ydel word." / Ther shul we han a juge that may nat been deceyved ne corrupt. And why? For certes, alle oure thoghtes been discovered as to hym, ne for preyere ne for meede° he shal nat been corrupt. / And therfore seith Salomon, "The wratthe of God ne wol nat spare no wight for preyere ne for yifte°." And therfore at the Day of Doom ther nys noon hope to escape. / Wherfore, as seith Seint Anselm, "Ful greet angwyssh shul the synful folk have at that tyme. / Ther shal the stierne and wrothe° juge sitte above, and under hym the horrible put° of helle open to destroyen hym that noot biknowen° his synnes, whiche synnes openly been shewed biforn God and biforn every creature. / And in the °170 left syde, mo develes than herte may bithynke, for to harye° and drawe the synful soules to the peyne of helle. / And withinne the hertes of folk shal be the bitynge conscience, and withoute forth° shal be the world al brennynge°. / Whider shal thanne the wrecched synful man flee to hiden hym? Certes, he may nat hiden hym; he moste° come forth and shewen hym." / For certes, as seith Seint Jerome, "The erthe shal casten hym out of hym, and the see also, and the eyr also, that shal be ful of thonder clappes and lightnynges." / Now soothly, whoso wel remembreth hym of thise thynges, I gesse that his synne shal nat turne hym in delit, but to greet sorwe for drede of the peyne of helle. / And therfore seith Job to °175 God, "Suffre°, Lord, that I may a while biwaille and wepe er I go withoute returning to the derke lond covered with the derknesse of deeth, / to the lond of mysese° and of derknesse where as is the shadwe of deeth, where as ther is noon ordre or ordinaunce°, but grisly drede that evere shal laste." / Loo, heere may ye seen that Job preyde respit° a while, to biwepe and waille his trespas°, for soothly a day of respit is bettre than al the tresor of the world. / And forasmuche as a man may acquiten hymself biforn God by penitence in this world, and nat by tresor, therfore sholde he preye to God to yeve him respit a while, to biwepe and biwaillen his trespas. / For certes, al the sorwe that a man myghte make fro the bigynnyng of the world nys but a litel thyng at regard of° the sorwe of helle. / The cause why that Job clepeth° helle °180 "the lond of derknesse," / understondeth that he clepeth it "londe" or erthe for it is stable and nevere shal faille; "dirk," for he that is in helle hath defaute of light material°. / For certes, the derke light that shal come out of the fyr that evere shal brenne shal turne hym al to peyne that is in helle; for it sheweth hym to the horrible develes that hym tormenten. / "Covered with the derknesse of deeth"—that is to seyn that he that is in

---

unkyndely, *unnaturally,* quiten, *repaid* 156 groyn, *snout,* soughe, *sow* 157 wroteth, *roots,* everich ordure, *every kind of filth* 160 trompe, *trumpet* 162 seete, *throne* 164 essoyne, *excuse from appearing in court* 166 sleighte, *deception,* yeven, *give* 167 meede, *bribery* 168 yifte, *gift* 170 wrothe, *angry,* put, *pit,* noot biknowen, *will not acknowledge* 171

harye, *pull* 172 withoute forth, *outside,* brennynge, *burning* 173 moste, *must* 176 Suffre, *allow* 177 mysese, *suffering,* ordinaunce, *organization* 178 preyde respit, *requested relief,* trespas, *sin* 180 at regard of, *compared with* 181 clepeth, *calls* 182 hath defaute of light material, *lacks physical light*

155–56 **Salomon,** Proverbs 11.22; cf. *WBP* 3. 784–85. **159–61 Jerome,** *Letters* 66.10, and Pseudo-Jerome, *The Rule of Monarchy,* 30. **162 Poul,** Romans 14.10. **166 Bernard,** Pseudo-Bernard, *Sermon to the Prelates in Council* 5. **168 Salomon,** quotation not identified. **169–73 Anselm,** paraphrase of Anselm's *Meditation* 1: "On the Last Judgment" 78–79. **174 Jerome,** quotation not identified. **176–77 Job,** Job 10.20–22.

helle shal have defaute of the sighte of God, for certes the sighte of God is the lyf perdurable°. / "The derknesse of deeth" been the synnes that the wrecched man hath doon whiche that destourben° hym to see the face of God, right as dooth a derk clowde bitwixe us and the sonne. / 185 "Lond of misese°," by cause that ther been three maneres of defautes agayn° three thynges that folk of this world han in this present lyf, that is to seyn, honours, delices°, and richesses. / Agayns honour have they in helle shame and confusioun. / For wel ye woot° that men clepen° "honour" the reverence that man doth to man; but in helle is noon honour ne reverence. For certes, namoore reverence shal be doon there to a kyng than to a knave. / For which God seith by the prophete Jeremye, "Thilke folk that me despisen shul been in despit." / "Honour" is eek cleped° greet lordshipe; ther shal no man serven other but of° harm and torment. "Honour" is eek cleped greet dignitee and heighnesse, but in helle shul they been al fortroden of° develes. / And 190 God seith, "The horrible develes shulle goon and comen upon the hevedes° of the dampned folk." And this is forasmuche as° the hyer° that they were in this present lyf the more shulle they been abated° and defouled in helle. / Agayns the richesses of this world shul they han mysese of poverte. And this poverte shal been in foure thinges: / in defaute of tresor, of which that David seith, "The riche folk that embraceden and oneden° al hire herte to tresor of this world shul slepe in the slepynge of deeth; and nothyng ne shal they fynden in hir handes of al hir tresor." / And mooreover the myseyse of helle shal been in defaute° of mete° and drinke. / For God seith thus by Moyses, "They shul been wasted with hunger, and the briddes° of helle shul devouren hem with the bitter deeth, and the galle of the dragon shal been hire drynke, and the venym of the dragon hire morsels." / And fortherover, hire myseyse shal 195 been in defaute of clothyng, for they shulle be naked in body as of clothyng, save the fyr in which

they brenne° and othere filthes. / And naked shul they been of soule as of alle manere vertues, which that is the clothyng of the soule. Where been thanne the gaye robes and the softe shetes and the smale° shertes? / Loo, what seith God of hem by the prophete Ysaye, that under hem shul been strawed° motthes, and hire covertures° shulle been of wormes of helle. / And fortherover, hir myseyse shal been in defaute of freendes, for he nys nat poure that hath goode freendes. But there is no frend, / for neither God ne no creature shal been freend to hem, and everich° of hem shall haten oother with deedly hate. / "The sones and the 200 doghtren shullen rebellen agayns fader and mooder, and kynrede° agayns kynrede, and chiden° and despisen everich of hem oother," bothe day and nyght, as God seith by the prophete Michias. / And the lovynge children, that whilom° loveden so flesshly° everich oother, wolden everich of hem eten oother if they myghte. / For how sholden they love togidre in the peyne of helle, whan they hated ech of hem oother in the prosperitee of this lyf? / For truste wel, hir flesshly love was deedlyhate, as seith the prophete David, "Whoso that loveth wikkednesse, he hateth his soule." / And whoso hateth his owene soule, certes he may love noon oother wight° in no manere. / And 205 therfore in helle is no solas° ne no freendshipe, but evere the moore flesshly kynredes° that been in helle, the moore cursynges, the moore chidynges, and the moore deedly hate ther is among hem. / And fortherover, they shul have defaute of alle manere delices°. For certes, delices been after the appetites of the fyve wittes, as sighte, herynge, smellynge, savorynge, and touchynge. / But in helle hir sighte shal be ful of derknesse and of smoke, and therfore ful of teeres; and hir herynge ful of waymentynge and of gryntynge of teeth, as seith Jesu Crist; / hir nosethirles° shullen be ful of stynkynge stynk. And as seith Ysaye the prophete, "Hir savoryng shal be ful of bitter galle." / And touchynge of al hir body ycovered with "fir that nevere shal quenche and with wormes that nevere

---

184 **perdurable,** *everlasting* 185 **destourben,** *prevent* 186 **misese,** *suffering,* **defautes agayn,** *deprivations that parallel,* **delices,** *sensory pleasures* 188 **woot,** *know,* **clepen,** *call* 190 **cleped,** *called,* **other but of,** *another except in,* **fortroden of,** *trampled by* 191 **hevedes,** *heads,* **forasmuche as,** *because,* **hyer,** *higher,* **abated,** *degraded* 193 **oneden,** *united* 194 **defaute,** *lack,* **mete,** *food* 195 **briddes,** *birds* 196 **brenne,**

burn 197 **smale,** *fine* 198 **strawed,** *strewn,* **covertures,** *blankets* 200 **everich,** *each* 201 **kynrede,** *relative,* **chiden,** *accuse* 202 **whilom,** *once,* **flesshly** *passionately* 205 **wight,** *person* 206 **solas,** *comfort,* **flesshly kynredes,** *worldly relatives* 207 **delices,** *sensory pleasures* 209 **nosethirles,** *nostrils*

189 **Jeremye,** 1 Samuel 2.30. 191 **God seith,** Job 20.25. 193 **David,** Psalms 75.6 (Vulgate). 195 **Moyses,** Deuteronomy 32.24 and 33. 198 **Ysaye,** Isaiah 14.11. 201 **Michias,** Micah 7.6. 204 **David,** Psalms 11.5 (Vulgate 10.6). 208 **Jesu Crist,** Matthew 13.42, 25.30.

shul dyen," as God seith by the mouth of Ysaye. / And for as muche as they shul nat 210 wene° that they may dyen for peyne, and by hir deeth flee fro peyne, that may they understonden by the word of Job that seith, "Ther as is the shadwe of deeth." / Certes° a shadwe hath the liknesse of the thyng of which it is shadwe, but shadwe is nat the same thyng of which it is shadwe. / Right so fareth the peyne of helle. It is lyk deeth for the horrible anguissh, and why? For it peyneth hem evere as though they sholde dye anon; but certes they shal nat dye. / For as seith Seint Gregorie, "To wrecche caytyves° shal be deeth withoute deeth, and ende withouten ende, and defaute withoute failynge. / For hir deeth shal alwey lyven, and hir ende shal everemo bigynne, and hir defaute shal nat faille." / And therfore seith 215 Seint John the Evaungelist, "They shullen folwe deeth and they shul nat fynde hym, and they shul desiren to dye and deeth shal flee fro hem." / And eek Job seith that in helle is noon ordre of rule. / And al be it so that God hath creat alle thynges in right ordre, and nothing withouten ordre, but alle thynges been ordeyned and nombred, yet nathelees they that been dampned been nothyng in the ordre, ne holden noon ordre, / for the erthe ne shal bere hem no fruyt. / For as the prophete David seith, "God shal destroie the fruyt of the erthe as fro hem°," ne water ne shal yeve hem no moisture, ne the eyr no refresshyng, ne fyr no light. / For as seith Seint Basilie, "The 220 brennynge° of the fyr of this world shal God yeven in helle to hem that been dampned, / but the light and the cleernesse° shal be yeven in hevene to his children," right° as the goode man yeveth flessh° to his children and bones to his houndes. / And for they shullen have noon hope to escape, seith Seint Job atte laste that ther shal horrour and grisly drede dwellen withouten ende. / Horrour is alwey drede of harm that is to come, and this drede shal evere dwelle in the hertes

of hem that been dampned. And therfore han they lorn° al hire hope for sevene causes. / First, for God that is hir juge shal be withouten mercy to hem, and they may nat plese hym ne noon of his halwes°; ne they ne may yeve nothyng for hir raunsoun°; / ne they have no 225 voys to speke to hym; ne they may nat fle fro peyne; ne they have no goodnesse in hem that they mowe shewe° to delivere hem fro peyne. / And therfore seith Salomon, "The wikked man dyeth, and whan he is deed he shal have noon hope to escape fro peyne." / Whoso thanne wolde wel understande these peynes, and bithynke hym weel° that he hath deserved thilke° peynes for his synnes, certes, he sholde have moore talent° to siken° and to wepe than for to syngen and to pleye. / For as that seith Salomon, "Whoso that hadde the science° to knowe the peynes° that been establissed and ordeyned for synne, he wolde make sorwe." / "Thilke science," as seith Seint Augustyn, "maketh a man to waymenten° in his herte." / 230

The fourthe point that oghte maken a man to have contricioun is the sorweful remembraunce of the good that he hath left to doon° heere in erthe, and eek the good that he hath lorn°. / Soothly, the goode werkes that he hath lost, outher° they been the goode werkes that he hath wroght er he fel into deedly synne, or elles the goode werkes that he wroghte while he lay in synne. / Soothly, the goode werkes that he dide biforn that he fil in synne been al mortefied° and astoned° and dulled by the ofte synnyng. / The othere goode werkes that he wroghte whil he lay in deedly synne, thei been outrely dede° as to the lyf perdurable° in hevene. / Thanne thilke goode werkes that been mortefied by ofte synnyng, whiche goode werkes he dide whil he was in charitee°, ne mowe° nevere quyken° agayn withouten verray penitence. / And 235 therof seith God by the mouth of Ezechiel that if the rightful man returne agayn° from his rightwisnesse° and werke wikkednesse, shal he

---

211 **wene,** *think* 212 **Certes,** *certainly* 214 **wrecche caytyves,** *wretched captives* 220 **as fro hem,** *as far as they are concerned* 221 **brennynge,** *burning* 222 **cleernesse,** *brightness,* **right,** *just,* **flessh,** *meat* 224 **lorn,** *lost* 225 **halwes,** *saints,* **raunsoun,** *ransom* 226 **mowe shewe,** *may use* 228 **bithynke hym weel,** *consider well,* **thilke,** *those,* **talent,** *inclination,* **siken,** *sigh* 229 **science,** *knowledge,* **peynes,** *punishments* 230

waymenten, *lament* 231 **left to doon,** *left undone,* **lorn,** *lost* 232 **outher,** *either* 233 **mortefied,** *destroyed,* **astoned,** *stunned* 234 **outrely dede,** *utterly dead,* **perdurable,** *everlasting* 235 **charitee,** *spiritual love,* **mowe,** *may,* **quyken,** *come to life* 236 **returne agayn,** *turns away,* **rightwisnesse,** *goodness*

209–10 Ysaye, Isaiah 24.9 and 66.24. **211 Job,** 10.22. **214–15 Gregorie,** *Morals* 9.66.100. **216 John,** Revelation 9.6; the author of Revelation and the Gospel of John were thought to be the same. **217 Job,** see lines 176–77 above. **220 David,** Psalms 107.34–35 (Vulgate 106). **221 Basilie,** Basil, *Sermon on the Psalms* 28.7.6. **223 Job,** see lines 176–77 above. **227 Salomon,** Proverbs 11.7. **229 Salomon,** Ecclesiastes 1.17. **230 Augustyn,** quotation not identified. **236–37 Ezechiel,** Ezekiel 18.24.

live? / Nay, for alle the goode werkes that he hath wroght ne shul nevere been in remembraunce, for he shal dyen in his synne. / And upon thilke chapitre° seith Seint Gregorie thus, that we shulle understonde this principally, / that whan we doon deedly synne, it is for noght thanne to rehercen° or drawen into memorie the goode werkes that we han wroght biforn. / For certes, in the werkynge of the deedly synne, ther is no trust to no good werk that we han doon biforn, that is for to seyn as for to have therby the lyf perdurable in hevene. / But nathelees, the goode werkes 240 quyken° agayn, and comen agayn, and helpen, and availlen° to have the lyf perdurable in hevene whan we han contricioun. / But soothly, the goode werkes that men doon whil they been in deedly synne, for as muche as they were doon in deedly synne, they may nevere quyke agayn. / For certes, thyng that nevere hadde lyf may nevere quykene; and nathelees, al be it that they ne availle noght to han the lyf perdurable, yet availlen they to abregge° of the peyne of helle, or elles to geten temporal richesse, / or elles that God wole the rather° enlumyne and lightne the herte of the synful man to have repentance; / and eek they availlen for to usen° a man to doon goode werkes that the feend have the lasse power of his soule. / And thus the curteis lord Jesu Crist 245 wole that no good werk be lost, for in somwhat it shal availle. / But for as muche as the goode werkes that men doon whil they been in good lyf been al mortified by synne folwynge, and eek sith° that alle the goode werkes that men doon whil they been in deedly synne been outrely° dede as for to have the lyf perdurable, / wel may that man that no good werke ne dooth° synge thilke newe Frenshe song, *Jay tout perdu mon temps et mon labour.* / For certes, synne bireveth° a man bothe goodnesse of nature and eek the goodnesse of grace. / For soothly, the grace of the Holy Goost fareth° lyk fyr that may nat been ydel; for fyr fayleth anoon° as it forleteth his° wirkynge, and right so grace

fayleth anoon as it forleteth his werkynge. / 250 Then leseth° the synful man the goodnesse of glorie, that oonly is bihight° to goode men that labouren and werken. / Wel may he be sory thanne that oweth al his lif to God as longe as he hath lyved, and eek as longe as he shal lyve, that no goodnesse ne hath to paye with his dette to God, to whom he oweth al his lyf. / For trust wel, "He shal yeven° acountes," as seith Seint Bernard, "of alle the goodes that han be yeven hym° in this present lyf, and how he hath hem despended°, / noght so muche that ther shal nat perisse° an heer of his heed, ne a moment of an houre ne shal nat perisse of his tyme, that he ne shal yeve of it a rekening." /

The fifthe thyng that oghte moeve a man to contricioun is remembrance of the passioun° that oure lord Jesu Crist suffred for oure synnes. / 255 For as seith Seint Bernard, "Whil that I lyve I shal have remembrance of the travailles° that oure lord Crist suffred in prechyng, / his werynesse in travaillyng, his temptaciouns whan he fasted, his longe wakynges whan he preyde, his teeres whan that he weepe for pitee of good peple, / the wo and the shame and the filthe that men seyden to hym, of the foule spittyng that men spitte in his face, of the buffettes that men yaven° hym, of the foule mowes°, and of the repreves° that men to hym seyden, / of the nayles with whiche he was nayled to the croys, and of al the remenant of his passioun that he suffred for my synnes, and nothing for his gilt." / And ye shul understonde that in mannes synne is every manere of ordre or ordinaunce° turned upsodoun. / For it is sooth° that God 260 and resoun and sensualitee° and the body of man been ordeyned that everich of thise foure thynges sholde have lordshipe over that oother. / As thus: God sholde have lordshipe over resoun, and resoun over sensualitee, and sensualitee over the body of man. / But soothly whan man synneth, al this ordre or ordinaunce is turned upsodoun. / And therfore thanne, for as muche as the resoun of man ne wol nat be subget ne obeisant° to God, that

---

238 thilke chapitre, *that passage* **239 rehercen,** *recall* **241 quyken,** *come to life,* **availlen,** *are effective* **243 abregge,** *shorten* **244 rather,** *sooner* **245 usen,** *accustom* **247 sith,** *since,* **outrely,** *utterly* **248 no good werke ne dooth,** *does no good works* **249 bireveth,** *robs* **250 fareth,** *goes,* **fayleth anoon,** *disappears as soon,* **forleteth his,** *ceases its* **251 leseth,** *loses,* **bihight,** *promised* **253 yeven,** *give,* **han be yeven hym,** *have been given him,* **hem despended,** *spent them* **254 perisse,** *perish* **255 passioun,** *sufferings* **256 travailles,** *troubles* **258 yaven,** *gave,* **mowes,** *scowls,* **repreves,** *accusations* **260 ordinaunce,** *plan* **261 sooth,** *true,* **sensualitee,** *sensory responses* **264 obeisant,** *obedient*

---

238 Gregorie, Gregory's *Sermon on Ezekiel* 1.11.21. **248 *Jay tout perdu mon temps et mon labour,*** "I have completely lost my time and my work"; apparently the refrain from a popular French song, used also in Chaucer's short poem "Fortune" (line 7). **253–54 Bernard,** quotation not identified. **256–59 Bernard,** *Sermon on Wednesday of Holy Week* (Concerning the Lord's Passion) 11. **261–63** These notions of hierarchy and inversion are commonplace.

is his lord by right, therfore leseth it the lordshipe that it sholde have over sensualitee, and eek over the body of man. / And why? For sensualitee rebelleth thanne agayns resoun, and by that wey leseth resoun the lordshipe over sensualitee and over the body. / For right° as resoun is rebel to God,   265 right so is bothe sensualitee rebel to resoun and the body also. / And certes, this disordinaunce° and this rebellioun oure lord Jesu Crist aboghte° upon his precious body ful deere, and herkneth in which wise. / For as muche thanne as resoun is rebel to God, therfore is man worthy to have sorwe and to be deed. / This suffred oure lord Jesu Crist for man, after that he hadde be bitraysed° of his disciple, and distreyned° and bounde, so that his blood brast out at every nayle of his handes, as seith Seint Augustyn. / And forther over, for as muchel as resoun of man ne wol nat daunte° sensualitee whan it may, therfore is man worthy to have shame. And this suffred oure lord Jesu Crist for man when they spetten in his visage. / And forther   270 over, for as muchel thanne as the caytyf° body of man is rebel bothe to resoun and to sensualitee, therfore is it worthy the deeth. / And this suffred oure lord Jesu Crist for man upon the croys, where as ther was no part of his body free withouten greet peyne and bitter passioun. / And al this suffred Jesu Crist that nevere forfeted°. "To muchel am I peyned for the thynges that I nevere deserved, and to muche defouled for shendshipe° that man is worthy to have." / And therfore may the synful man wel seye, as seith Seint Bernard, "Acursed be the bitternesse of my synne, for which ther moste be suffred so muchel bitternesse." / For certes, after the diverse disordinaunces of oure wikkednesses was the passioun of Jesu Crist ordeyned in diverse thynges, / as thus. Certes, synful mannes soule   275 is bitraysed of° the devel by coveitise of temporeel prosperitee, and scorned by deceite whan he cheseth flesshly delices°; and yet is it tormented by inpacience of° adversitee, and bispet° by

servage° and subjeccioun of synne; and atte laste it is slayn fynally. / For this disordinaunce of synful man was Jesu Crist bitraysed, and after that was he bounde that cam for to unbynden us of synne and peyne. / Thanne was he byscorned, that oonly sholde han been honoured in alle thynges and of alle thynges. / Thanne was his visage, that oghte be desired to be seyn of al mankynde, in which visage aungels desiren to looke, vileynsly bispet. / Thanne was he scourged° that nothing hadde agilt°. And finally thanne was he crucified and slayn. / Thanne was acompliced° the word of   280 Ysaye that seith that he was wounded for oure mysdedes and defouled for oure felonies. / Now sith that° Jesu Crist took upon hymself the peyne of alle oure wikkednesses, muchel oghte synful man wepen and biwayle that for his synnes Goddes sone of hevene sholde al this peyne endure. /

The sixte thyng that oghte moeve a man to contricioun is the hope of three thynges: that is to seyn, foryifnesse of synne, and the yifte of grace wel for to do, and the glorie of hevene with which God shal guerdone° a man for his goode dedes. / And for as muche as Jesu Crist yeveth us thise yiftes of his largesse° and of his sovereyn bountee, therfore is he cleped° *Iesus Nazarenus rex Iudeorum.* / *Iesus* is to seyn "saveour" or "salvacioun," on whom men shul hope to have foryifnesse of synnes, which that is proprely salvacioun of synnes. /   285 And therfore seyde the aungel to Joseph, "Thou shalt clepen° his name Jesus, that shal saven his peple of hir synnes." / And heerof seith Seint Peter, "Ther is noon other name under hevene that is yeve° to any man by which a man may be saved, but only Jesus." / *Nazarenus* is as muche for to seye as "florisshynge," in which a man shal hope that he that yeveth hym remission of synnes shal yeve hym eek grace wel for to do. For in the flour is hope of fruit in tyme comynge, and in foryifnesse of synnes hope of grace wel for to do. / "I was atte dore of thyn herte," seith Jesus, "and

---

266 right, *just* **267 disordinaunce,** *disorder,* **aboghte,** *redeemed* **269 be bitraysed,** *been betrayed,* **distreyned,** *arrested* **270 daunte,** *subdue* **271 caytyf,** *wretched* **273 forfeted,** *sinned,* **shendshipe,** *disgrace* **276 bitraysed of,** *betrayed by,* **cheseth flesshly delices,** *chooses bodily*

pleasures, **inpacience of,** *impatience with,* **bispet,** *spit upon,* **servage,** *service* **280 scourged,** *whipped,* **nothing hadde agilt,** *sinned not at all* **281 acompliced,** *fulfilled* **282 sith that,** *since* **283 guerdone,** *reward* **284 largesse,** *generosity,* **cleped,** *called* **287 yeve,** *given*

---

269 be bitraysed of his disciple, been betrayed by his disciple, i.e., Judas; see, e.g., Matthew 26.47–50. **Augustyn,** not identified. **270 spetten in his visage,** spit in his face; see, e.g., Matthew 27.30. **273** Quotation not identified. **274 Bernard,** identified by Jill Mann as from Bernard's second sermon on Palm Sunday. **275 disordinaunces,** the MSS read "discordaunces" or some variant, but see lines 267 and 277. The sentence means that through divine order the passion or sufferings of Jesus paralleled (and compensated for) the process of human sin. **281 Ysaye,** Isaiah 53.5. **284 *Iesus Nazarenus rex Iudeorum,*** "Jesus of Nazareth, king of the Jews." **286 aungel,** Matthew 1.20–21.

cleped for to entre. He that openeth to me shal have foryifnesse of synne. / I wol entre into hym by my grace and soupe° with hym" by the goode werkes that he shal doon, whiche werkes been the foode of God, "and he shal soupe with me" by the grete joye that I shal yeven hym. / Thus shal man hope for° his werkes of penaunce that God shall yeven hym his regne°, as he bihooteth° hym in the gospel. /

Now shal a man understonde in which manere shal been his contricioun. I seye that it shal been universal and total, this is to seyn a man shal be ver-ray° repentant for alle his synnes that he hath doon in delit of his thoght, for delit is ful perilous. / For ther been two manere of consentynges. That oon of hem is cleped consentynge of affeccioun°, whan a man is moeved to do synne and deliteth hym longe for to thynke on that synne, / and his reson aperceyveth° it wel that it is synne agayns the lawe of God, and yet his resoun refreyneth° nat his foul delit or talent°, though he se wel apertly° that it is agayns the reverence of God. Although his re-soun ne consente noght to doon that synne in dede, / yet seyn somme doctours° that swich delit that dwelleth longe it is ful perilous al be it nevere so lite. / And also a man sholde sorwe, namely°, for al that evere he hath desired agayn the lawe of God with perfit consentynge of his re-soun, for therof is no doute that it is deedly synne in consentynge. / For certes, ther is no deedly synne that it nas first in mannes thought and after that in his delit, and so forth into consentynge and into dede. / Wherfore I seye that many men ne re-penten hem nevere of swiche thoghtes and delites, ne nevere shryven hem° of it, but oonly of the dede of grete synnes outward. / Wherfore I seye that swiche wikked delites and wikked thoghtes been subtile bigileres° of hem that shullen be damp-ned. / Mooreover man oghte to sorwe for his wikkede wordes as wel as for his wikkede dedes, for certes the repentaunce of a synguler synne and nat repente of alle his othere synnes, or elles repenten him of alle his othere synnes and nat of a

synguler synne, may nat availle°. / For certes, God Almighty is al good, and therfore he foryeveth al or elles right noght. / And heerof seith Seint Augustyn, "I woot° certeinly / that God is enemy to everich synnere." And how thanne, he that observeth o° synne, shal he have foryifnesse of the remenaunt of his othere synnes? Nay. / And fortherover, contricioun sholde be wonder sorwe-ful and angwissous°. And therfore yeveth hym God pleynly° his mercy. And therfore whan my soule was angwissous withinne me, I hadde remem-brance of God that my preyere myghte come to hym. / Fortherover, contricioun moste be con-tinueel, and that man have stedefast purpos to shriven hym, and for to amenden hym of his lyf. / For soothly, whil contricioun lasteth man may evere have hope of foryifnesse. And of this comth hate of synne that destroyeth synne bothe in himself and eek in oother folk, at his power. / For which seith David, "Ye that loven God hateth wikkednesse." For trusteth wel, to love God is for to love that he loveth and hate that he hateth. /

The laste thyng that man shal understonde in contricioun is this: wherof avayleth contricioun°? I seye that somtyme contricioun delivereth a man fro synne, / of which that David seith, "I seye," quod David, that is to seyn, "I purposed fermely° to shryve me and thow, Lord, relessedest my synne." / And right so° as contricion availleth noght withouten sad° purpos of shrifte°, if man have oportunitee, right so litel worth is shrifte° or satisfaccioun withouten contricioun. / And mooreover, contricion destroyeth the prisoun of helle; and maketh wayk° and fieble alle the strengthes of the develes; and restoreth the yiftes of the Hooly Goost and of alle goode vertues. / And it clenseth the soule of synne, and delivereth the soule fro the peyne of helle, and fro the com-paignye of the devel, and fro the servage of synne, and restoreth it to alle goodes espirituels°, and to the compaignye and communyoun of Hooly Chirche. / And fortherover, it maketh hym that whilom° was sone of ire to be sone of grace. And

---

290 **soupe,** *dine* 291 **for,** *because of,* **regne,** *kingdom,* **bihooteth,** *prom-ises* 292 **verray,** *truly* 293 **affeccioun,** *emotion* 294 **aperceyveth,** *per-ceives,* **refreyneth,** *restrains,* **talent,** *inclination,* **se wel apertly,** *sees clearly* 295 **doctours,** *theologians* 296 **namely,** *especially* 298 **shryven hem,** *confess themselves* 299 **bigileres,** *deceivers* 300 **may nat availle,** *is*

not effective 302 **woot,** *know* 303 **observeth o,** *acknowledges one* 304 **angwissous,** *anguished,* **pleynly,** *fully,* 308 **wherof avayleth contri-cioun,** *in what ways is contrition effective* 309 **purposed fermely,** *in-tended firmly* 310 **right so,** *just,* **sad,** *firm,* **shrifte,** *confession* 311 **wayk,** *weak* 312 **espirituels,** *spiritual* 313 **whilom,** *formerly*

289–90 **Jesus,** Revelation 3.20. 291 **in the gospel,** Luke 15.7. 302–3 **Augustyn,** Pseudo-Augustine, *De Vera et Falsa Poenitentia* (Concerning True and False Penance) 1.9.24. 304 **Jonah** 2.8. 307 **David,** Psalms 97.10 (Vulgate 96). 309 **David,** Psalms 32.5 (Vulgate 31). 313 **sone of ire,** son of anger; see Ephesians 2.3.

alle thise thynges been preved by hooly writ. / And therfore, he that wolde sette his entente to thise thynges, he were ful wys, for soothly he ne sholde nat thanne in al his lyf have corage° to synne, but yeven his body and al his herte to the service of Jesu Crist, and therof doon hym hommage°. / For soothly, oure sweete lord Jesu Crist hath spared us so debonairly° in our folies that if he ne hadde pitee of mannes soule, a sory song we mighten alle singe. /   315

Explicit prima pars Penitentie et sequitur secunda pars eiusdem.

The seconde partie° of penitence is confessioun, that is signe° of contricioun. / Now shul ye understonde what is confessioun, and wheither it oghte nedes be doon or noon°, and whiche thynges been covenable° to verray° confessioun. /

First shaltow° understonde that confessioun is verray shewinge° of synnes to the preest. / This is to seyn "verray" for he moste confessen hym of alle the condiciouns° that bilongen to his synne, as ferforth° as he kan. / Al moot° be seyd, and nothyng excused ne hyd ne forwrapped°; and noght avaunte° thee of thy goode werkes. / And 320 fortherover, it is necessarie to understonde whennes that° synnes spryngen°, and how they encreessen, and whiche they been. /

Of the spryngynge of synnes seith Seint Paul in this wise, that right° as by a man synne entred first into this world, and thurgh that synne deeth, right so thilke deeth entred into alle men that synneden. / And this man was Adam, by whom synne entred into this world whan he brak the comaundementz of God. / And therfore he that first was so mighty that he sholde nat have dyed bicam swich oon that he moste nedes dye, wheither he wolde or noon°, and all his progenye in this world that in thilke man synneden. / Looke that in th'estaat of innocence, whan Adam and Eve naked weren in paradys, and nothing ne hadden shame of hir nakednesse, / how that the ser- 325 pent that was moost wily of alle othere beestes that God hadde maked seyde to the womman, "Why comaunded God to yow, ye sholde nat eten of every tree in paradys?" / The womman answerde, "Of the fruyt," quod she, "of the trees in paradys we feden us, but soothly of the fruyt of the tree that is in the myddel of paradys God forbad us for to ete, and nat touchen it, lest peraventure° we should dyen." / The serpent seyde to the womman, "Nay, nay, ye shul nat dyen of deeth, for sothe! God woot° that what day that ye eten therof, youre eyen shul opene and ye shul been as goddes knowynge good and harm°." / The womman thanne saugh that the tree was good to feedyng, and fair to the eyen, and delitable to the sighte. She took of the fruyt of the tree and eet it, and yaf to hire housbonde and he eet, and anoon the eyen of hem bothe openeden. / And whan that they knewe that they were naked, they sowed of figeleves a maner° of breches° to hiden hire membres°. / There may ye seen that deedly 330 synne hath first suggestion of the feend, as sheweth heere by the naddre°; and afterward, the delit of the flessh, as sheweth heere by Eve; and after that, the consentynge of resoun, as sheweth heere by Adam. / For trust wel, though so were° that the feend tempted Eve, that is to seyn the flessh, and the flessh hadde delit in the beautee of the fruyt defended°, yet certes, til that resoun, that is to seyn Adam, consented to the etynge of the fruyt, yet stood he in th'estaat of innocence. / Of thilke° Adam tooke we° thilke synne original; for of hym flesshly° descended be we alle, and engendred° of vile and corrupt matiere. / And whan the soule is put in oure body, right anon is contract° original synne, and that that was erst° but oonly peyne° of concupiscence° is afterward bothe peyne

---

314 corage, *desire,* **doon hym hommage,** *acknowledge his lordship* **315 debonairly,** *graciously* **316 partie,** *part,* **signe,** *evidence* **317 noon,** *not,* **covenable,** *appropriate,* **verray,** *genuine* **318 shaltow,** *you shall,* **shewinge,** *revealing* **319 condiciouns,** *circumstances,* **ferforth,** *far* **320 moot,** *must,* **forwrapped,** *disguised,* **avaunte,** *boast* **321 whennes that,** *from what,* **spryngen,** *originate* **322 right,** *just* **324 wolde or noon,** *wished to or not* **327 lest peraventure,** *for fear perhaps* **328 woot,** *knows,*

harm, *evil* **330 maner,** *kind,* **breches,** *garment,* **membres,** *genitals* **331 naddre,** *serpent* **332 though so were,** *even though it was,* **fruyt defended,** *forbidden fruit* **333 thilke,** *that,* **tooke we,** *we received,* **flesshly,** *physically,* **engendred,** *born* **334 right anon is contract,** *immediately is incurred,* **that that was erst,** *that which was first,* **peyne,** *suffering,* **concupiscence,** *worldly desire*

315a Explicit prima pars Penitentie et sequitur secunda pars eiusdem, "Here ends the first part of Penance, and here follows the second part of the same." **322 Paul,** Romans 5.12. **325–30 Adam and Eve . . . ,** Genesis 3.1–7. **331–32** A common allegorization of the fall. **333 synne original,** in church doctrine, original sin is a state of sinfulness rather than an act of sinning (actual sin, line 357).

and synne. / And therfore be we alle born sones of wratthe and of dampnacioun perdurable°, if it nere° baptesme that we receyven which bynymeth° us the culpe°. But for sothe, the peyne dwelleth with us as to temptacioun, which peyne highte° concupiscence. / And this concupiscence 335 whan it is wrongfully disposed or ordeyned in man, it maketh hym coveite, by coveitise of flessh, flesshly synne by sighte of his eyen as to erthely thynges, and coveitise of hynesse by pride of herte. /

Now as for to speken of the firste coveitise°, that is concupiscence after the lawe of oure membres° that weren lawefulliche ymaked and by rightful juggement of God, / I seye for as muche as man is nat obeisaunt to God that is his lord, therfore is the flessh to hym disobeisaunt thurgh concupiscence, which yet is cleped norissynge° of synne and occasioun of synne. / Therfore, al the while that a man hath in hym the peyne of concupiscence, it is impossible but he be tempted somtime and moeved in his flessh to synne. / And this thyng may nat faille as longe as he lyveth. It may wel wexe fieble° and faille by vertu of baptesme and by the grace of God thurgh penitence, / but fully 340 ne shal it nevere quenche that he ne shal som-tyme be moeved in hymself, but if he were al re-freyded° by siknesse, or by malefice° of sorcerie, or colde drynkes. / For lo, what seith Seint Paul, "The flessh coveiteth agayn the spirit, and the spirit agayn° the flessh; they been so contrarie and so stryven that a man may nat alwey doon as he wolde." / The same Seint Paul, after his grete pe-naunce in water and in lond (in water by night and by day in greet peril and in greet peyne, in lond in famyne, in thurst, in coold and cloothlees, and ones stoned almoost to the deeth), / yet seyde he, "Allas, I, caytyf° man, who shal delivere me fro the prisoun of my caytyf body?" / And Seint Jerome, whan he longe tyme hadde woned° in desert where as he hadde no compaignye but of wilde beestes, where as he ne hadde no mete° but herbes and

water to his drynke, ne no bed but the naked erthe, for which his flessh was blak as an Ethiopeen for heete and ny° destroyed for coold, / yet 345 seyde he that the brennynge° of lecherie boyled in al his body. / Wherfore I woot wel sykerly° that they been deceyved that seyn that they ne be nat tempted in hir body. / Witnesse on Seint Jame the apostel that seith that every wight° is tempted in his owene concupiscence, that is to seyn that everich of us hath matere and occasioun to be tempted of the norissynge° of synne that is in his body. / And therfore seith Seint John the Evaun-gelist, "If that we seyn that we beth withoute synne, we deceyve us-selve and trouthe is nat in us." /

Now shal ye understonde in what manere that synne wexeth or encreesseth in man. The firste thyng is thilke norissynge of synne of which I spak biforn, thilke flesshly concupiscence. / 350 And after that comth the subjeccioun° of the devel, this is to seyn the develes bely°, with which he bloweth in man the fir of flesshly concupis-cence. / And after that, a man bithynketh hym° wheither he wol doon or no thilke thing to which he is tempted. / And thanne, if that a man with-stonde and weyve° the first entisynge of his flessh and of the feend, thanne is it no synne. And if it so be that he do nat so, thanne feeleth he anoon a flambe° of delit. / And thanne is it good to bewar and kepen hym° wel, or elles he wol falle anon into consentynge of synne; and thanne wol he do it if he may have tyme and place. / And of this matere seith Moyses by° the devel in this manere, "The feend seith. I wole chace and pursue the man by wikked suggestioun, and I wole hente° him by moevynge or stirynge of synne. I wol departe° my prise or my praye° by deliberacioun, and my lust° shal been ac-compliced in delit°. I wol drawe my swerd in consentynge." / For certes, right as a swerd de- 355 parteth° a thyng in two peces, right so consen-tynge departeth God fro man. "And thanne wol I sleen hym with myn hand in dede° of synne," thus seith the feend. / For certes, thanne is a man

---

certainly **348 wight,** *person,* **norissynge,** *nourishment* **351 subjec-cioun,** *suggestion,* **bely,** *bellows* **352 bithynketh hym,** *considers* **353 weyve,** *deflect,* **flambe,** *flame* **354 kepen hym,** *guard himself* **355 by,** *about,* **hente,** *seize,* **departe,** *single out,* **praye,** *prey,* **lust,** *desire,* **in delit,** *through pleasure* **356 departeth,** *divides,* **in dede,** *through the deed*

335 perdurable, *everlasting,* **if it nere,** *if it weren't for,* **bynymeth,** *removes from,* **culpe,** *guilt,* **highte,** *is called* **337 firste coveitise,** *the first kind of covetousness,* **after the lawe of oure membres,** *result-ing from sexual drive* **338 cleped norissynge,** *called nourishment* **340 wexe fieble,** *grow weak* **341 refreyded,** *cooled,* **malefice,** *evil work* **342 agayn,** *against* **344 caytyf,** *captive* **345 woned,** *lived,* **mete,** *food,* **ny,** *nearly* **346 brennynge,** *burning* **347 woot wel sikerly,** *know*

---

335 sones of wratthe, see 313n above. **concupiscence,** the love of or desire for any improper object; see lines 366–67. **336 coveitise of hy-nesse,** desire for worldly status; see 1 John 2.16. **342 Paul,** Galatians 5.17. **343–44 Paul,** 2 Corinthians 11.25–27; Romans 7.24. **345–46 Jerome,** *Letters,* To Eustochium 22.7. **348 Jame,** James 1.14. **349 John,** 1 John 1.8. **355–56 Moyses,** Exodus 15.9.

al deed° in soule. And thus is synne accompliced by temptacioun, by delit, and by consentynge; and thanne is the synne cleped° actueel. /

For sothe, synne is in two maneres: outher° it is venial or deedly sinne. Soothly, whan man loveth any creature moore than Jesu Crist oure creatour, thanne is it deedly sinne. And venial synne is it if man love Jesu Crist lasse than hym oghte. / For sothe, the dede of this venial synne is ful perilous, for it amenuseth° the love that men sholde han to God moore and moore. / And therfore, if a man charge° hymself with manye swiche venial synnes, certes, but if so be that he somtyme descharge hym of hem by shrifte°, they mowe° ful lightly° amenuse in hym al the love that he hath to Jesu Crist. / And in this wise skippeth° venial into 360 deedly synne. For certes, the moore that a man chargeth his soule with venial synnes, the moore is he enclyned to fallen into deedly synne. / And therfore, lat us nat be necligent to deschargen us of venial synnes. For the proverbe seith that manye smale maken a greet. / And herkne° this ensample. A greet wawe° of the see comth somtyme with so greet a violence that it drencheth° the shipe. And the same harm dooth somtyme the smale dropes of water that entren thurgh a litel crevace into the thurrok°, and into the botme of the shipe, if men be so necligent that they ne descharge hem nat bytyme°. / And therfore, althogh ther be a difference bitwixe thise two causes of drenchynge, algates° the shipe is dreynt°. / Right so fareth it somtyme of deedly synne, and of anoyouse° veniale synnes, whan they multiplie in a man so greetly that thilke worldly thynges that he loveth, thurgh whiche he synneth venyally, is as greet in his herte as the love of God, or moore. / And therfore, the love 365 of everything that is nat biset in God ne doon principally for Goddes sake, although that a man love it lasse than God, yet is it venial synne. / And deedly synne whan the love of anythyng weyeth° in the herte of man as muchel as the love of God, or moore. / "Deedly synne," as seith Seint Augustyn, "is whan a man turneth his herte fro God, which that is verray sovereyn bountee° that may nat chaunge, and yeveth° his herte to thyng that may chaunge and flitte°." / And certes, that is everything save God of hevene. For sooth is that if a man yeve his love the which that he oweth al to God with al his herte unto a creature, certes, as muche as he yeveth of his love to thilke creature, so muche he bireveth° fro God; / and therfore doth he synne. For he that is dettour to God ne yeldeth nat to God al his dette, that is to seyn al the love of his herte. / 370

Now sith man understondeth generally which is venial synne, thanne is it covenable° to tellen specially of synnes whiche that many a man peraventure° ne demeth hem° nat synnes, and ne shryveth hym nat of the same thynges, and yet nathelees they been synnes / soothly, as thise clerkes writen. This is to seyn that at every tyme that a man eteth or drynketh moore than suffyseth to the sustenaunce of his body, in certein he dooth synne. / And eek, whan he speketh moore than nedeth, it is synne. Eke whan he herkneth nat benignely° the compleint of the poure. / Eke whan he is in heele° of body and wol nat faste whan hym oghte faste, withouten cause resonable. Eke whan he slepeth moore than nedeth, or whan he comth by thilke enchesoun° to late to chirche, or to othere werkes of charite. / Eke whan he useth° his wyf withouten sovereyn° desir of engendrure° to the honour of God, or for the entente to yelde to his wyf the dette of his body. / Eke whan he 375 wol nat visite the sike and the prisoner, if he may. Eke if he love wyf or child or oother worldly thyng moore than resoun requireth. Eke if he flatere or blandishe° moore than hym oghte for any necessitee. / Eke if he amenuse° or withdrawe the almesse of° the poure. Eke if he apparailleth his mete° moore deliciously than nede is or ete to hastily by likerousnesse°. / Eke if he tale vanytees° at chirche or at Goddes service, or that he be a talkere of ydel wordes of folye or of vileynye, for he

---

357 al deed, *completely dead,* **cleped,** *called* **358 outher,** *either* **359 amenuseth,** *decreases* **360 charge,** *burdens,* **shrifte,** *confession,* **mowe,** *may,* **lightly,** *easily* **361 skippeth,** *passes quickly* **363 herkne,** *pay attention to,* **wawe,** *wave,* **drencheth,** *drowns,* **thurrok,** *hold,* **bytyme,** *in time* **364 algates,** *nevertheless,* **dreynt,** *drowned* **365 anoyouse,** *annoying* **367 weyeth,** *weighs* **368 sovereyn bountee,** *supreme goodness,* **yeveth,** *gives,* **flitte,** *pass quickly* **369 bireveth,** *steals* **371 covenable,** *appropriate,* **peraventure,** *perhaps,* **demeth hem,** *judges them* **373 benignely,** *kindly* **374 heele,** *health,* **thilke enchesoun,** *that reason* **375 useth,** *has sex with,* **sovereyn,** *ultimate,* **engendrure,** *begetting children* **376 blandishe,** *praise* **377 amenuse,** *reduce,* **almesse of,** *charity for,* **apparailleth his mete,** *prepare his food,* **likerousnesse,** *gluttony* **378 tale vanytees,** *speak foolishly*

---

358 venial . . . deedly, see 99–100n above. **362 the proverbe,** a common proverb. **368 Augustyn,** *De libero arbitrio* (On Free Will) 1.16, but widely quoted in various forms. **375 dette of his body,** marital obligation to sexual intercourse, 1 Corinthians 7.3; see *WBP* 3.130.

shal yelden acountes of it at the day of doome. / Eke whan he biheteth° or assureth to do thynges that he may nat perfourne. Eke whan that he by lightnesse° or folie mysseyeth° or scorneth his neighebore. / Eke whan he hath any wikked suspecioun of thyng ther he ne woot° of it no soothfastnesse°. / Thise thynges and mo withoute nombre been synnes, as seith Seint Augustyn. /

Now shal men understonde, that al be it so that noon erthely man may eschue° alle venial synnes, yet may he restreyne hym by the brennynge° love that he hath to oure lord Jesu Crist, and by preyeres and confessioun and othere goode werkes, so that it shal but litel greve°. / For as seith Seint Augustyn, "If a man love God in swich manere that al that evere he dooth is in the love of God, and for the love of God verraily°, for he brenneth in the love of God, / looke° how muche that a drope of water that falleth in a fourneys° ful of fyr anoyeth or greveth, so muche anoyeth a venial synne unto a man that is parfit in the love of Jesu Crist." / Men may also refreyne° venial synne by receyvynge worthily of the precious body of Jesu Crist, / by receyvyng eek of hooly water, by almesdede°, by general confessioun of *Confiteor* at masse and at complyn, and by blessynge of bisshopes and of preestes and oothere goode werkes. /

Sequitur de Septem Peccatis Mortalibus et eorum dependenciis circumstanciis et speciebus.

De Superbia.

Now is it bihovely° thyng to telle whiche been the Deedly Synnes, this is to seyn chieftaynes of synnes. Alle they renne in o lees, but in diverse maneres. Now been they cleped° chieftaynes for as muche as they been chief, and spryngers° of alle othere synnes. / Of the roote of thise sevene synnes thanne is pride the general roote of alle harmes, for of this roote spryngen certein braunches, as ire, envye, accidie or slewthe°, avarice or coveitise (to commune understondynge), glotonye, and lecherye. / And everich of thise chief synnes hath his braunches and his twigges, as shal be declared in hire chapitres° folwinge. /

And thogh so be that no man kan outrely telle° the nombre of the twigges and of the harmes that cometh of pride, yet wol I shewe a partie° of hem, as ye shul understonde. / Ther is

inobedience, avauntynge°, ypocrisie, despit°, arrogance, inpudence, swellynge of herte, insolence, elacioun°, inpacience, strif, contumacie°, presumpcioun, irreverence, pertinacie°, veyne glorie°, and many another twig that I kan nat declare. / Inobedient is he that disobeyeth for despit to the comandementz of God, and to his sovereyns, and to his goostly° fader. / Avauntour° is he that bosteth of the harm or of the bountee° that he hath doon. / Ypocrite is he that hideth to shewe° hym swich as he is and sheweth hym swiche as he noght is. / Despitous is he that hath desdeyn of his neighebore, that is to seyn of his evene-Cristene°, or hath despit to doon that hym oghte to do. / Arrogant is he that thynketh that he hath thilke bountees in hym that he hath noght, or weneth° that he sholde have hem by his desertes, or elles he demeth° that he be that he nys nat°. / Inpudent

---

379 biheteth, *promises,* **lightnesse,** *silliness,* **mysseyeth,** *speak wrongly of* **380 woot,** *knows,* **soothfastnesse,** *truth* **382 eschue,** *avoid,* **brennynge,** *burning,* **greve,** *damage* **383 verraily,** *truly* **384 looke,** *notice,* **fourneys,** *furnace* **385 refreyne,** *restrain* **386 almesdede,** *charitable giving* **387 bihovely,** *necessary,* **cleped,** *called,* **spryngers,** *originators* **388 accidie or slewthe,** *sloth* **389 hire chapitres,** *their sections* **390**

outrely telle, *completely count,* **partie,** *portion* **391 avauntynge,** *boasting,* **despit,** *disdain,* **elacioun,** *self-promotion,* **contumacie,** *insubordination,* **pertinacie,** *obstinacy,* **veyne glorie,** *pretentiousness* **392 goostly,** *spiritual* **393 Avauntour,** *braggart,* **bountee,** *good things* **394 hideth to shewe,** *disguises* **395 evene-Cristene,** *fellow Christian* **396 weneth,** *thinks,* **demeth,** *judges,* **that he nys nat,** *what he isn't*

---

381 Augustyn, a list similar to the preceding is in Pseudo-Augustine, *In Lectione Apostolica* 3. **383–84 Augustyn,** not identified in Augustine. **385 receyvynge . . . the precious body,** consuming the communion wafer, the Eucharist, which by the priest's words of consecration has become the body of Christ. **386 receyvynge . . . hooly water,** anointing with water blessed by a priest, a spiritual cleansing. *Confiteor,* "I confess," the opening words of a communal confession of sin that takes place at the beginning of the Mass and during compline (**complyn**), the last of the canonical hours, recited before going to bed. On the hours, see *MilT* 1.3655n. **386a Sequitur de Septem Peccatis Mortalibus et eorum dependenciis circumstanciis et speciebus,** "Here follow the Seven Deadly Sins and their subdivisions, and circumstances, and varieties." **386b De Superbia,** "Concerning Pride." **387 Alle they renne in o lees,** they all run on one leash; the seven deadly (or capital) sins are sometimes also called the "dogs of hell," with which the devil hunts his prey.

is he that for his pride hath no shame of his synnes. / Swellynge of herte is whan a man rejoyseth hym of harm that he hath doon. / Insolent is he that despiseth in his juggement alle othere folk as to regard of his value, and of his konning°, and of his spekyng, and of his beryng°. / Elacioun is whan he ne may neither suffre to have maister ne felawe. / Inpacient is he that wol nat been ytaught ne undernome° of his vice, and by strif werreieth° trouthe wityngly, and deffendeth his folye. / *Contumax*° is he that thurgh his indignacion is agayns everich auctoritee or power of hem that been his sovereyns. / Presumpcioun is whan a man undertaketh an emprise° that hym oghte nat do, or elles that he may nat do, and this is called surquidrie°. Irreverence is whan men do nat honour there as hem oghte to doon, and waiten to be reverenced. / Pertinacie is whan man deffendeth his folies, and trusteth to muchel in his owene wit. / Veyne glorie is for to have pompe and delit in his temporeel hynesse, and glorifie hym° in this worldly estaat. / Janglynge is whan men speken to muche biforn folk, and clappen as a mille°, and taken no kepe° what they seye. /

And yet is ther a privee spece° of pride that waiteth first for to be salewed° er he wole salewe, al be he lasse worth than that oother is peraventure°; and eek he waiteth or desireth to sitte, or elles to goon above hym° in the wey, or kisse pax, or been encensed, or goon to offryng biforn his neighebore, / and swiche semblable° thynges agayns his duetee°, peraventure, but that he hath his herte and his entente in swich a proud desir to be magnified and honoured biforn the peple. /

Now been ther two maneres of pride, that oon of hem is withinne the herte of man and that oother is withoute°. / Of whiche soothly thise forseyde thynges, and mo than I have seyd, apertenen°

to pride that is in the herte of man; and that othere speces of pride been withoute. / But natheles that oon of thise speces of pride is signe of that oother, right as the gaye leefsel° atte taverne is signe of the wyn that is in the celer°. / And this is in manye thynges, as in speche and contenaunce°, and in outrageous array of clothyng. / For certes, if ther ne hadde be no synne in clothyng, Crist wolde nat have noted and spoken of the clothyng of thilke riche man in the gospel. / And as seith Seint Gregorie that precious clothyng is cowpable° for the derthe° of it, and for his softenesse, and for his strangenesse° and degisynesse°, and for the superfluitee, and for the inordinat scantnesse of it. / Allas, may men nat seen, as in oure dayes, the synful costlewe° array of clothynge, and namely in to muche superfluitee°, or elles in to desordinat° scantnesse? /

As to the firste sinne, that is in superfluitee of clothynge which that maketh it so deere°, to harm° of the peple, / nat oonly the cost of embrowdynge°, the degise endentynge°, barrynge°, owndynge°, palynge°, wyndynge°, or bendynge°, and semblable° wast of clooth in vanitee, / but ther is also costlewe furrynge in hir gownes, so muche pownsonynge of chisels° to maken holes, so muche daggynge of sheres°, / forthwith° the superfluitee in lengthe of the forseide° gownes, trailynge in the dong and in the mire, on horse and eek on foote, as wel of men as of wommen, that al thilke trailyng is verraily as in effect wasted, consumed, thredbare, and roten with donge, rather than it is yeven to the poure, to greet damage of the forseyde poure folk. / And that in sondry wise°. This is to seyn that the moore that clooth is wasted, the moore it costeth to the peple for the scantnesse. / And fortherover, if so be that they wolde yeven° swich pownsoned and dagged clothyng to the

---

399 konning, *understanding,* **beryng,** *behavior* **401 undernome of,** *accused of,* **werreieth,** *battles against* **402 Contumax,** *(Lat.) obstinate* **403 emprise,** *enterprise,* **surquidrie,** *arrogance* **405 glorifie hym,** *take pride* **406 clappen as a mille,** *make noise constantly (like a mill wheel),* **kepe,** *care* **407 privee spece,** *secret species,* **salewed,** *greeted,* **peraventure,** *perhaps,* **sitte or . . . goon above hym,** *take precedence at table or in procession* **408 swiche semblable,** *other similar,* **agayns his duetee,** *beyond what is due him* **409 withoute,** *outside* **410 apertenen,** *pertain* **411 leefsel,** *bush used as a tavern sign,* **celer,** *storeroom* **412 contenaunce,** *behavior* **414 cowpable,** *blameworthy,* **derthe,** *high cost,* **strangenesse,**

unusualness, **degisynesse,** *trendiness* **415 costlewe,** *costly,* **superfluitee,** *excessiveness,* **desordinat,** *inappropriate* **416 deere,** *expensive,* **harm,** *detriment* **417 embrowdynge,** *embroidering,* **degise endentynge,** *fashionable notching,* **barrynge,** *striping,* **owndynge,** *wavy striping,* **palynge,** *vertical striping,* **wyndynge,** *wrapping,* **bendynge,** *bordering,* **semblable,** *similar* **418 pownsonynge of chisels,** *perforation with punches,* **daggynge of sheres,** *slashing with scissors* **419 forthwith,** *as well as,* **forseide,** *previously mentioned* **420 sondry wise,** *many ways* **421 yeven,** *give*

---

poure folk, it is nat convenient° to were for hire estaat°, ne suffisant to beete° hire necessitee, to kepe hem fro the distemperance° of the firmament°. / Upon that oother side, to speken of the horrible disordinat scantnesse of clothyng, as been thise kutted sloppes° or haynselyns°, that thurgh hire shortnesse ne covere nat the shameful membres° of man, to wikked entente. / Allas, somme of hem shewen the boce° of hir shape and the horrible swollen membres that semeth lik the maladie of hirnia, in the wrappynge of hir hoses°, / and eek the buttokes of hem faren° as it were the hyndre part of a she-ape in the fulle of the mone. / And mooreover the wrecched swollen membres that they shewe thurgh the degisynge°, in departynge° of hire hoses in whit and reed semeth that half hir shameful privee membres weren flayne°. / And if so be that they departen hire 425 hoses in othere colours, as is whit and blak, or whit and blew, or blak and reed, and so forth, / thanne semeth it as by variaunce of colour that half the partie° of hire privee membres were corrupt by the fir of Seint Antony, or by cancre, or by oother swich meschaunce°. / Of the hyndre part of hir buttokes, it is ful horrible for to see. For certes, in that partie of hir body ther as they purgen hir stynkynge ordure, / that foule partie shewe they to the peple prowdly in despit of honestitee, the which honestitee° that Jesu Crist and his freendes observede to shewen in hir lyve. / Now as of the outrageous array of wommen, God woot° that though the visages of somme of hem seme ful chaast and debonaire°, yet notifie° they in hire array of atyr° likerousnesse° and pride. / I sey 430 nat that honestitee in clothynge of man or womman is uncovenable°, but certes the super fluitee or disordinat scantitee of clothynge is reprevable°. /

Also the synne of aornement° or of apparaille is in thynges that apertenen° to rydynge, as in to manye delicat° horses that been hoolden for delit, that been so faire, fatte, and costlewe°; / and also to many a vicious knave that is sustened by cause of hem; in to curious° harneys, as in sadeles, in crouperes°, peytrels°, and bridles covered with precious clothyng and riche, barres and plates of gold and of silver. / For which God seith by Zakarie the prophete, "I wol confounde° the ryderes of swiche horses." / This folk taken litel reward° of the rydynge of Goddes sone of hevene, and of his harneys whan he rood upon the asse and ne hadde noon oother harneys but the poure clothes of his disciples; ne we ne rede nat that evere he rood on oother beest. / I speke this for the synne of 435 superfluitee, and nat for reasonable honestitee° whan reson it requireth. / And forther, certes, pride is greetly notified° in holdynge° of greet meynee° whan they be of litel profit or of right no profit. / And namely°, whan that meynee is felonous and damageous° to the peple, by hardynesse° of heigh lordshipe or by wey of offices°. / For certes, swiche lordes sellen thanne hir lordshipe to the devel of helle whanne they sustenen° the wikkednesse of hir meynee. / Or elles whan this folk of lowe degree, as thilke° that holden hostelries°, sustenen the thefte of hire hostilers°, and that is in many manere of deceites. / Thilke 440 manere° of folk been the flyes that folwen the hony, or elles the houndes that folwen the careyne°. Swiche forseyde folk stranglen spiritually hir lordshipes. / For which thus seith David the prophete, "Wikked deeth moote° come upon thilke lordshipes, and God yeve° that they moote descenden into helle al doun, for in hire houses been° iniquitees and shrewednesses°," and nat God of hevene. / And certes, but if° they doon amendement, right as God yaf his benisoun° to Laban by the service of Jacob, and to Pharao by the service of Joseph, right so God wol yeve his malisoun° to swiche lordshipes as sustenen the

convenient, *suitable*, estaat, *social class*, beete, *provide for*, distemperance, i.e., *bad weather*, firmament, *heavens* 422 kutted sloppes, *short-cut coats*, haynselyns, *jackets*, membres, *genitals* 423 boce, *bulge*, hoses, *leggings* 424 faren, *seem* 425 degisynge, *fashioning*, departynge, *separating*, flayne, *skinned* 427 partie, *portion*, meschaunce, *misfortune* 429 despit of honestitee, *scorn of decency* 430 woot, *knows*, debonaire, *meek*, notifie, *announce*, array of atyr, *display of dress*, likerousnesse, *lechery* 431 uncovenable, *unsuitable*, reprevable, *blameworthy* 432 aornement, *adornment*, apertenen, *pertain*, delicat, *elegant*, costlewe,

costly 433 to curious, *too ornate*, crouperes, *hindquarter straps*, peytrels, *chest straps* 434 confounde, *destroy* 435 reward, *regard* 436 honestitee, *honor* 437 notified, *made known*, holdynge, *keeping*, meynee, *entourage* 438 namely, *especially*, damageous, *harmful*, hardynesse, *insolence*, offices, *official appointments* 439 sustenen, *support* 440 thilke, *those*, holden hostelries, *own inns*, of hire hostilers, *by their innkeepers* 441 Thilke manere, *this kind*, careyne, *rotted flesh* 442 moote, *must*, yeve, *grant*, been, *are*, shrewednesses, *wickednesses* 443 but if, *unless*, yaf his benisoun, *gave his blessing*, malisoun, *curse*

427 fir of Seint Antony, erysipelas (St. Anthony's fire), which causes acute skin rash. 434 Zakarie, Zechariah 10.5. 435 rydynge of Goddes sone, Christ's entry into Jerusalem, e.g., Matthew 21.1–11. 442 David, Psalms 55.15 (Vulgate 54.16). 443 Laban . . . Joseph, Genesis 31 and 47.7.

wikkednesse of hir servauntz, but if they come to amendement. /

Pride of the table appeereth eek ful ofte, for certes riche men been cleped° to festes, and poure folk been put awey° and rebuked. / Also in excesse of diverse metes° and drynkes, and namely swiche manere bake metes° and dissh metes°, brennynge of° wilde fyr, and peynted and castelled with papir°, and semblable wast° so that it is abusioun° for to thynke. / And eek in to greet precious- 445 nesse of vessel and curiositee of mynstralcie°, by whiche a man is stired the moore to delices° of luxurie, / if so be that he sette his herte the lasse upon oure lord Jesu Crist, certeyn it is a synne. And certeinly the delices myghte been so grete in this caas that man myghte lightly falle by hem into deedly synne. / The especes° that sourden of° pride, soothly whan they sourden of malice ymagined°, avised°, and forncast°, or elles of usage°, been deedly synnes, it is no doute. / And whan they sourden by freletee unavysed° sodeynly, and sodeynly withdrawen ayeyn, al been they grevouse synnes, I gesse that they ne been nat deedly. /

Now myghte men axe° wherof that pride sourdeth and spryngeth and I seye somtyme it spryngeth of the goodes° of nature, and somtyme of the goodes of fortune, and somtyme of the goodes of grace. / Certes, the goodes of nature ston- 450 den outher° in goodes of body or in goodes of soule. / Certes, goodes of body been heele° of body, as strengthe, delivernesse°, beautee, gentries°, franchise°. / Goodes of nature of the soule been good wit, sharpe understondynge, subtil engyn°, vertu natureel, good memorie. / Goodes of fortune been richesses, highe degrees of lordshipes, preisinges of the peple. / Goodes of grace been science°, power to suffre spiritueel travaille, benignitee°, vertuous contemplacion, withstondynge of temptacion, and semblable° thynges. / Of whiche forseyde goodes, certes 455

it is a ful greet folye a man to priden hym in any of hem alle. / Now as for to speken of goodes of nature, God woot° that somtyme we han hem in nature as muche to oure damage as to oure profit. / As for to speken of heele of body, certes it passeth ful lightly°, and eek it is ful ofte enchesoun° of the siknesse of oure soule. For God woot, the flessh is a ful greet enemy to the soule, and therfore the moore that the body is hool, the moore be we in peril to falle. / Eke for to pride hym in his strengthe of body it is an heigh folye, for certes the flessh coveiteth agayn° the spirit, and ay the moore strong that the flessh is the sorier may the soule be. / And over al this, strengthe of body and worldly hardynesse° causeth° ful ofte many a man to peril and meschaunce°. / Eek for to 460 pride hym of his gentrie° is ful greet folie, for oftetyme the gentrie of the body binymeth° the gentrie of the soule. And eek we ben alle of o fader and of o mooder, and alle we been of o nature roten and corrupt, bothe riche and poure. / For sothe, o manere gentrie is for to preise, that apparailleth° mannes corage° with vertues and moralitees and maketh hym Cristes child. / For truste wel that over what man that synne hath maistrie, he is a verray cherl° to synne. /

Now been ther generale signes of gentillesse°, as eschewynge° of vice and ribaudye° and servage of° synne, in word, in werk, and contenaunce°, / and usynge vertu, curteisye, and clennesse, and to be liberal—that is to seyn, large by mesure°, for thilke that passeth° mesure is folie and synne. / 465 Another is to remembre hym of° bountee that he of oother folk hath receyved. / Another is to be benigne to his goode subgetis. Wherfore seith Senek, "Ther is nothing moore covenable° to a man of heigh estaat than debonairetee° and pitee. / And therfore thise flyes° that men clepeth° bees, whan they maken hire kyng, they chesen oon that hath no prikke° wherwith he may stynge." /

---

444 cleped, *called,* **put awey,** *turned away* **445 diverse metes,** *various foods,* **bake metes,** *meat pies,* **dissh metes,** *stews,* **brennynge of,** *flambéed with,* **castelled with papir,** *adorned with paper castles,* **semblable wast,** *similar waste,* **abusioun,** *outrage* **446 curiositee of mynstralcie,** *elaborateness of musical accompaniment,* **delices,** *the sensory delights* **448 especes,** *subcategories,* **sourden of,** *arise from,* **ymagined,** *devised,* **avised,** *considered,* **forncast,** *planned,* **usage,** *habit* **449 freletee unavysed,** *thoughtless weakness* **450 axe,** *ask,* **goodes,** *gifts* **451 outher,** *either* **452 heele,** *health,* **delivernesse,** *agility,* **gentries,** *aristocratic birth,* **franchise,** *freedom* **453 engyn,** *ingenuity* **455 science,** *knowledge,*

467 Senek, Seneca, *On Pity* 1.3.3, 1.19.2.

benignitee, *kindness,* **semblable,** *similar* **457 woot,** *knows* **458 lightly,** *quickly,* **enchesoun,** *cause* **459 coveiteth agayn,** *desires in conflict with* **460 hardynesse,** *boldness,* **causeth,** *provokes,* **meschaunce,** *misfortune* **461 gentrie,** *noble birth,* **binymeth,** *takes away* **462 apparailleth,** *adorns,* **corage,** *heart* **463 verray cherl,** *true servant* **464 gentillesse,** *nobility,* **eschewynge,** *avoiding,* **ribaudye,** *debauchery,* **servage of,** *bondage to,* **contenaunce,** *attitude* **465 large by mesure,** *generous with discretion,* **thilke that passeth,** *that which surpasses* **466 remembre hym of,** *recall* **467 covenable,** *appropriate,* **debonairetee,** *kindness* **468 flyes,** *insects,* **clepeth,** *call,* **prikke,** *stinger*

Another is, a man to have a noble herte and a diligent, to attayne to heighe vertuouse thynges. /
Now certes, a man to pride hym in the goodes of
grace is eek an outrageous folie, for thilke yiftes of
grace that sholde have turned hym to goodnesse
and to medicine turneth hym to venym and to
confusioun, as seith Seint Gregorie. / Certes 470
also, whoso prideth hym in the goodes of fortune, he is a ful greet fool. For somtyme is a man a
greet lord by the morwe that is a caytyf° and a
wrecche er it be nyght. / And somtyme the richesse
of a man is cause of his deth. Somtyme the delices°
of a man is cause of the grevous maladye thurgh
which he dyeth. / Certes, the commendacion of
the peple is somtyme ful fals and ful brotel° for to
triste°. This day they preyse, tomorwe they blame. /
God woot°, desir to have commendacioun eek of
the peple hath caused deeth to many a bisy man. /

Remedium contra peccatum Superbie.

Now sith° that so is, that ye han understonde
what is pride, and whiche been the speces of it,
and whennes pride sourdeth° and springeth, / 475
now shul ye understonde which is the remedie
agayns the synne of pride, and that is humylitee or
mekenesse. / That is a vertu thurgh which a man
hath verray° knoweleche of hymself, and holdeth
of hymself no pris° ne deyntee° as in regard of his
desertes, considerynge evere his freletee°. / Now
been ther three maneres° of humylitee, as humylitee in herte, and another humylitee in his mouth,
the thridde in his werkes. / The humilitee in herte
is in foure maneres: that oon is whan a man holdeth hymself as noght worth° biforn God of hevene.
Another is whan he ne despiseth noon oother
man. / The thridde is whan he rekketh° nat though
men holde him noght worth. The ferthe is
whan he nys nat sory of his humiliacioun. / 480
Also the humilitee of mouth is in foure thynges: in attempree° speche, and in humblesse of

speche, and whan he biknoweth° with his owene
mouth that he is swich as hym thynketh that he is in
his herte. Another is whan he preiseth the bountee°
of another man and nothyng therof amenuseth°. /
Humilitee eek in werkes is in foure maneres:
the firste is whan he putteth othere men biforn
hym. The seconde is to chese the loweste place
overal. The thridde is gladly to assente to good conseil. / The ferthe is to stonde gladly to the award°
of his sovereyns° or of hym that is in hyer degree.
Certein, this is a greet werk of humylitee. /

Sequitur de Invidia.

After pryde wol I speken of the foule synne of
envye, which is, as by the word of the philosophre,
sorwe of oother mennes prosperitee, and after
the word of Seint Augustyn it is sorwe of° oother
mennes wele°, and joye of othere mennes harm. /
This foule synne is platly° agayns the Hooly Goost.
Al be it so that every synne is agayns the Hooly
Goost, yet nathelees for as muche as bountee
aperteneth° proprely to the Hooly Goost, and envye comth proprely of malice, therfore it is proprely agayn the bountee of the Hooly Goost. / 485
Now hath malice two speces, that is to seyn,
hardnesse of herte in wikkednesse, or elles the
flessh of man is so blynd that he considereth nat
that he is in synne or rekketh° nat that he is in
synne, which is the hardnesse of the devel. / That
oother spece of malice is whan a man werreyeth°
trouthe whan he woot° that it is trouthe, and eek
whan he werreyeth the grace that God hath yeve°
to his neighebore, and al this is by envye. / Certes,
thanne is envye the worste synne that is. For
soothly, alle othere synnes been somtyme oonly
agayns o special vertu. / But certes, envye is agayns
alle vertues and agayns alle goodnesses. For it is
sory of° alle the bountees° of his neighebore, and in
this manere it is divers° from alle othere synnes. /
For wel unnethe° is ther any synne that it ne hath

---

471 caytyf, *captive* **472 delices,** *sensory delights* **473 brotel,** *brittle,*
triste, *trust* **474 woot,** *knows* **475 sith,** *since,* **sourdeth,** *arises* **477**
verray, *true,* **pris,** *value,* **deyntee,** *worth,* **freletee,** *weakness* **478**
maneres, *kinds* **479 noght worth,** *worth nothing* **480 rekketh,** *cares* **481**
attempree, *temperate,* **biknoweth,** *acknowledges,* **bountee,** *goodness,*

amenuseth, *detracts* **483 award,** *decision,* **sovereyns,** *rulers* **484 sorwe**
of, *sorrow at,* **wele,** *good fortune* **485 platly,** *directly,* **bountee**
aperteneth, *goodness belongs* **486 rekketh,** *cares* **487 werreyeth,** *battles,*
woot, *knows,* **yeve,** *given* **489 sory of,** *sorry about,* **bountees,** *advan-*
tages, **divers,** *different* **490 wel unnethe,** *scarcely*

---

470 Gregorie, *Morals* 33.12.25. **474a Remedium contra peccatum Superbie,** "Remedy for the Sin of Pride." Chaucer's source for the "cures"
or "corrections" of the sins is *Summa Virtutem de Remediis Anime* (Treatise on the Virtues That Cure the Soul), also known as *Postquam* (After),
which often follows treatises on the sins in manuscripts. Chaucer seems to have invented the idea of following each sin with its own remedy.
483a Sequitur de Invidia, "Here follows [the section] concerning Envy." **484 the philosophre,** i.e., Aristotle, but the reference is uncertain.
Augustyn, *Enarrationes in Psalmos* (Exposition of the Psalms) 104.17 (Vulgate 105.25).

som delit in itself, save only envye that evere hath in itself angwissh and sorwe. / The speces of envye been thise: there is first sorwe of other mannes goodnesse and of his prosperitee. And prosperitee is kyndely° matere of joye, thanne is envye a synne agayns kynde. / The secounde spece of envye is joye of oother mannes harm, and that is proprely lyk to the devel that evere rejoyseth hym of mannes harm. / Of thise two speces comth bakbityng°, and this synne of bakbityng or detraccion hath certeine speces, as thus. Som man preiseth his neighebore by a wikke entente, / for he maketh alwey a wikked knotte atte laste ende. Alwey he maketh a "but" atte laste ende, that is digne of° moore blame than worth is al the preisynge°. / The seconde spece is that if a man be good and dooth or seith a thing to good entente, the bakbiter wol turne all thilke goodnesse upsodoun° to his shrewed° entente. / The thridde is to amenuse° the bountee° of his neighebore. / The fourthe spece of bakbityng is this, that if men speke goodnesse of a man thanne wol the bakbitere seyn, "Pardee°, swich a man is yet bet than he," in dispreisynge of hym that men preise. / The fifte spece is this, for to consente gladly and herkne° gladly to the harm that men speke of oother folk. This synne is ful greet and ay° encreeseth after the wikked entente of the bakbiter. / After bakbityng cometh grucching° or murmuracion°; and somtyme it spryngeth of inpacience agayns God and somtyme agayns man. / Agayns God it is whan a man gruccheth agayn the peynes of helle, or agayns poverte, or los of catel°, or agayn reyn or tempest, or elles gruccheth that shrewes° han prosperitee, or elles for that goode men han adversitee. / And alle thise thynges sholde men suffre paciently, for they comen by the rightful juggement and ordinaunce° of God. / Somtyme comth grucching of avarice, as Judas grucched agayns the Magdaleyne whan she enoynte° the hevede° of oure lord Jesu Crist with hire precious oynement. / This maner

murmure is swich as whan man gruccheth of goodnesse that hymself dooth, or that oother folk doon of hir owene catel°. / Somtyme comth murmure of pride, as whan Simon the Pharisee grucched agayn the Magdaleyne whan she approched to Jesu Crist and weep at his feet for hire synnes. / And somtyme grucchyng sourdeth° of envye, whan men discovereth° a mannes harm that was pryvee°, or bereth hym on hond° thyng that is fals. / Murmure eek is ofte amonges servauntz, that grucchen whan hir sovereyns bidden hem doon leveful° thynges, / and for as muche as they dar nat openly withseye° the comaundementz of hir sovereyns yet wol they seyn harm and grucche and murmure prively for verray despit°, / whiche wordes men clepen° the develes Pater Noster, though so be that the devel ne hadde nevere Pater Noster, but that lewed° folk yeven° it swich a name. / Somtyme grucchyng comth of ire° or prive° hate that norisseth° rancour in herte, as afterward I shal declare. / Thanne cometh eek bitternesse of herte, thurgh which bitternesse every good dede of his neighebor semeth to hym bitter and unsavory. / Thanne cometh discord that unbyndeth alle manere of freendshipe. Thanne comth scornynge of his neighebore, al do he° never so weel. / Thanne comth accusynge, as whan man seketh occasioun to anoyen° his neighebor, which that is lyk to the craft of the devel that waiteth bothe night and day to accusen us alle. / Thanne comth malignitee, thurgh which a man anoyeth his neighebor prively if he may, / and if he noght may, algate° his wikked wil ne shal nat wante° as for to brennen° his hous pryvely, or empoysone or sleen° his bestes°, and semblable° thynges. /

Remedium contra peccatum Invidie.

Now wol I speken of the remedie agayns the foule synne of envye. First is the love of God principal,

---

491 **kyndely,** *naturally* 493 **bakbityng,** *secretive criticism of another* 494 **digne of,** *deserving of,* **preisynge,** *praising* 495 **upsodoun,** *upside down,* **shrewed,** *evil* 496 **amenuse,** *diminish,* **bountee,** *goodness* 497 **Pardee,** *by God* 498 **herkne,** *listen,* **ay,** *always* 499 **grucching,** *complaining,* **murmuracion,** *grumbling* 500 **catel,** *property,* **shrewes,** *bad people* 501 **ordinaunce,** *arrangement* 502 **enoynte,** *anointed,* **hevede,** *head* 503 **hir owene catel,** *their own property* 505 **sourdeth,** *arises,* **discovereth,**

reveals, **pryvee,** *secret,* **bereth hym on hond,** *accuses him of* 506 **leveful,** *legitimate* 507 **withseye,** *refuse,* **despit,** *spite* 508 **clepen,** *call,* **lewed,** *ignorant,* **yeven,** *give* 509 **ire,** *anger,* **prive,** *secret,* **norisseth,** *nourishes* 511 **al do he,** *although he may do* 512 **anoyen,** *harm* 514 **algate,** *nevertheless,* **wante,** *lack,* **brennen,** *burn,* **sleen,** *slay,* **bestes,** *beasts,* **semblable,** *similar*

---

502 **Judas . . . Magdaleyne,** see John 12.3–5, where the greedy Judas accuses Mary, sister of Martha (not Mary Magdalen), of being a spendthrift when she anoints the feet of Jesus. The other gospels do not name Judas or Mary here: Matthew 26.6–13, Mark 14.3–9, Luke 7.37–38. In Matthew and Mark, the woman anoints the head of Jesus. 504 **Simon,** Luke 7.37–40. 508 **develes Pater Noster,** devil's "Our Father," i.e., the devil's prayer. 512 Revelation 12.10. 514a **Remedium contra peccatum Invidie,** "Remedy for the sin of Envy."

and loving of his neighebor as hymself, for soothly that oon ne may nat been withoute that oother. / And truste wel that in the name 515 of thy neighebore thou shalt understonde the name of thy brother; for certes alle we have o fader flesshly° and o mooder, that is to seyn Adam and Eve; and eek o fader espiritueel°, and that is God of hevene. / Thy neighebore artow holden for° to love and wilne° hym alle goodnesse. And therfore seith God, "Love thy neighebore as thyselve," that is to seyn, to salvacioun bothe of lyf and of soule. / And mooreover thou shalt love hym in word and in benigne amonestynge° and chastisynge, and conforten hym in his anoyes°, and preye for hym with al thyn herte. / And in dede thou shalt love hym in swich wise that thou shalt doon to hym in charitee as thou woldest that it were doon to thyn owene persone. / And therfore thou ne shalt doon hym no damage in wikked word, ne harm in his body, ne in his catel°, ne in his soule, by entissyng° of wikked ensample°. / Thou shalt 520 nat desiren his wyf ne none of his thynges. Understoond eek that in the name of neighebor is comprehended his enemy. / Certes man shal loven his enemy by the comandement of God; and soothly thy freend shaltow° love in God. / I seye, thyn enemy shaltow love for Goddes sake, by his comandement. For if it were reson° that a man sholde haten his enemy, forsothe God nolde nat receyven us to his love that been his enemys. / Agayns three manere of wronges that his enemy dooth to hym, he shal doon three thynges, as thus. / Agayns hate and rancour of herte, he shal love hym in herte. Agayns chiding and wikkede wordes, he shal preye for his enemy. And agayn the wikked dede of his enemy, he shal doon hym bountee°. / For 525 Crist seith, "Loveth youre enemys, and preyeth for hem that speke yow harm, and eek for hem that yow chacen and pursewen°, and doth bountee to hem that yow haten." Loo, thus comaundeth us oure lord Jesu Crist to do to oure enemys. / For soothly, nature dryveth us to loven oure freendes, and parfey° oure enemys han moore nede to° love

than oure freendes. And they that moore nede have, certes to hem shal men doon goodnesse, / and certes in thilke dede have we remembraunce of the love of Jesu Crist that deyde° for his enemys. / And inasmuche as thilke love is the moore grevous° to parfourne°, insomuche is the moore gretter the merite, and therfore the lovynge of oure enemy hath confounded the venym of the devel. / For right as the devel is disconfited° by humylitee, right so is he wounded to the deeth by love of oure enemy. / Certes, thanne is love 530 the medicine that casteth out the venym of envye fro mannes herte. / The speces of this paas° shullen be moore largely in hir chapitres folwynge declared. /

Sequitur de Ira.

After envye wol I discryven° the synne of ire. For soothly, whoso hath envye upon his neighebor, anon he wole comunly fynde hym a matere of wratthe, in word or in dede, agayns hym to whom he hath envye. / And as wel comth ire of pryde as of envye; for soothly, he that is proude or envyous is lightly wrooth°. / This synne of ire, after the discryvyng of Seint Augustyn, is wikked wil to been avenged by word or by dede. / Ire, after the philosophre, 535 is the fervent blood of man yquiked° in his herte thurgh which he wole° harm to hym that he hateth. / For certes the herte of man by eschawfynge° and moevynge of his blood wexeth so trouble° that he is out of alle juggement of resoun. / But ye shal understonde that ire is in two maneres, that oon of hem is good, and that oother is wikked. / The goode ire is by jalousye of° goodnesse, thurgh which a man is wrooth with wikkednesse and agayns wikkednesse; and therfore seith a wys man that ire is bet than pley. / This ire is with debonairetee°, and it is wrooth withouten bitternesse; nat wrooth agayns the man, but wrooth with the mysdede of the man, as seith the prophete David, *Irascimini et nolite peccare.* / Now 540

---

516 **o fader flesshly,** *one physical father,* **espiritueel,** *spiritual* 517 **artow holden for,** *are you required,* **wilne,** *wish* 518 **benigne amonestynge,** *gentle admonishing,* **anoyes,** *troubles* 520 **catel,** *possessions,* **entissyng,** *enticing,* **ensample,** *example* 522 **shaltow,** *you shall* 523 **reson,** *reasonable* 525 **bountee,** *goodness* 526 **yow . . . pursewen,** *persecute . . . you* 527

parfey, *in faith,* **nede to,** *need of* 528 **deyde,** *died* 529 **grevous,** *difficult,* **parfourne,** *perform* 530 **disconfited,** *defeated* 532 **paas,** *step or section* 533 **discryven,** *describe* 534 **lightly wrooth,** *easily angered* 536 **yquiked,** *awakened,* **wole,** *wishes* 537 **eschawfynge,** *heating,* **wexeth so trouble,** *grows so disturbed* 539 **jalousye of,** *zeal for* 540 **debonairetee,** *humility*

---

515 **love of God . . . neighebor,** Matthew 22.37–39. 517 **seith God,** Matthew 22.39. 519 Matthew 7.12. 521 Exodus 20.17. 526 **Crist seith,** Matthew 5.44. 532a **Sequitur de Ira,** "Here follows [the section] concerning Anger." 535 **Augustyn,** *City of God* 14.15. 536 **after the philosophre,** according to Aristotle, *On the Soul* 1.1.24. 539 **bet than pley,** better than laughter; Ecclesiastes 7.4. 540 **David . . . ,** Psalms 4.5 (Vulgate): "Be angry and do not sin."

understondeth that wikked ire is in two maneres, that is to seyn, sodeyn ire or hastif ire, withouten avisement° and consentynge of resoun. / The menyng and the sens of this is that the resoun of man ne consente nat to thilke sodeyn ire and thanne it is venial. / Another ire is ful wikked that comth of felonie of herte avysed° and cast biforn°, with wikked wil to do vengeance; and therto his resoun consenteth, and soothly this is deedly synne. / This ire is so displesant to God that it troubleth his hous and chaceth the Hooly Goost out of mannes soule, and wasteth and destroyeth the liknesse of God—that is to seyn the vertu that is in mannes soule— / and put in hym the liknesse of the devel, and bynymeth° the man fro God that is his rightful lord. / This ire is a ful greet 545 plesaunce to the devel, for it is the develes fourneys° that is eschawfed° with the fir of helle. / For certes, right so as fir is moore mighty to destroyen erthely thynges than any oother element, right so ire is mighty to destroyen alle spiritueel thynges. / Looke how that fir of smale gleedes° that been almoost dede under asshen° wollen quike° agayn whan they been touched with brymstoon°. Right so ire wol everemo quyken agayn whan it is touched by the pride that is covered in mannes herte. / For certes fir ne may nat comen out of nothing, but if it were first in the same thyng natureelly, as fir is drawen out of flyntes with steel. / And right so as pride is ofte tyme matere of ire, right so is rancour norice° and keper of ire. / 550 Ther is a maner tree as seith Seint Ysidre that whan men maken fir of thilke tree, and covere the coles of it with asshen, soothly the fir of it wol lasten al a yeer° or moore. / And right so fareth it° of rancour. Whan it is ones° conceyved in the hertes of som men, certein it wol lasten peraventure° from oon Estre day unto another Estre day, and moore. / But certes thilke man is ful fer° fro the mercy of God al thilke while. /

In this forseyde develes fourneys ther forgen three shrewes°: pride that ay° bloweth and encreesseth the fir by chidynge and wikked wordes. / Thanne stant° envye and holdeth the hoote iren upon the herte of man with a peire of longe toonges of long rancour. / And 555 thanne stant the synne of contumelie°, or strif and cheeste°, and batereth and forgeth by vileyns reprevynges°. / Certes, this cursed synne anoyeth bothe to the man hymself and eek to his neighebor. For soothly, almoost al the harm that any man dooth to his neighebore comth of wratthe. / For certes, outrageous wratthe dooth al that evere the devel hym comaundeth, for he ne spareth neither Crist ne his sweete mooder. / And in his outrageous anger and ire, allas, allas, ful many oon at that tyme feeleth in his herte ful wikkedly bothe of Crist° and of alle his halwes°. / Is nat this a cursed vice? Yis, certes. Allas, it bynymeth° from man his wit and his resoun, and al his debonaire lif espiritueel° that sholde kepen° his soule. / 560 Certes, it bynymeth eek goddes° due lordshipe, and that is mannes soule and the love of his neighebores. It stryveth eek alday° agayn trouthe. It reveth hym° the quiete of his herte and subverteth his soule. /

Of ire comen thise stynkynge engendrures°: first hate that is oold wratthe; discord, thurgh which a man forsaketh his olde freend that he hath loved ful longe. / And thanne cometh werre°, and every manere of wrong that man dooth to his neighebore in body or in catel°. / Of this cursed synne of ire cometh eek manslaughtre. And understonde wel that homycide, that is manslaughtre, is in diverse wise°. Som manere of homycide is spiritueel, and som is bodily. / Spiritueel manslaughtre is in thre thynges. First, by hate, as Seint John seith, "He that hateth his brother is homycide." / 565 Homycide is eek by bakbitynge°. Of whiche bakbiteres seith Salomon that they han two swerdes with whiche they sleen hire neighebores. For soothly, as wikke is to bynyme° his good name as his lyf. / Homycide is eek in yevynge° of wikked conseil by fraude, as for to yeven conseil to areysen°

---

541 **avisement,** *consideration* 543 **avysed,** *considered,* **cast biforn,** *planned ahead* 545 **bynymeth,** *takes* 546 **fourneys,** *furnace,* **eschawfed,** *heated* 548 **gleedes,** *coals,* **asshen,** *ashes,* **wollen quike,** *will come to life,* **brymstoon,** *sulfur* 550 **norice,** *nurse* 551 **al a yeer,** *a whole year* 552 **fareth it,** *it happens,* **ones,** *once,* **peraventure,** *perhaps* 553 **ful fer,** *very far* 554 **forgen three shrewes,** *three villains work the forge,* **ay, always** 555 **stant,** *stands* 556 **contumelie,** *contentiousness,* **cheeste,** *quarreling,* **reprevynges,** *accusations* 559 **of Crist,** *toward Christ,* **halwes,** *saints* 560 **bynymeth,** *takes,* **debonaire lif espiritueel,** *gracious spiritual life,* **kepen,** *protect* 561 **goddes,** *God's,* **alday,** *always,* **reveth hym,** *steals from him* 562 **engendrures,** *offspring* 563 **werre,** *war,* **catel,** *property* 564 **in diverse wise,** *of many kinds* 566 **bakbitynge,** *secretive accusation,* **as wikke is to bynyme,** *it is as wicked to take* 567 **yevynge,** *giving,* **areysen,** *impose*

---

551 **maner tree . . . Ysidre,** kind of tree; "juniper" is derived from Greek for "fire" in Isidore of Seville, *Etymologies* 17.7.35. 552 **Estre,** Easter Sunday; on Easter eve, a fire representing Christ's resurrection is kindled. 565 **John,** 1 John 3.15. 566 **Salomon,** Proverbs 25.18.

wrongful custumes and taillages°. / Of whiche seith Salomon, "Leon rorynge and bere° hongry been like to the crueel lordshipes°," in withholdynge or abreggynge° of the shepe°, or the hyre°, or of the wages of servauntz, or elles in usures° or in withdrawynge of the almesse° of poure folk. / For which the wise man seith, "Fedeth hym that almoost dyeth for honger," for soothly but if thow feede hym, thou sleest hym. And alle thise been deedly synnes. / Bodily manslaughtre is whan thow sleest him with thy tonge in oother manere, as whan thou comandest to sleen a man, or elles yevest° hym conseil to sleen a man. / Manslaughtre in dede is in foure maneres. That oon is by lawe, right° as a justice dampneth° hym that is coupable° to the deeth. But lat the justice bewar that he do it rightfully, and that he do it nat for delit to spille blood, but for kepynge of rightwisenesse°. / Another homycide is that is doon for necessitee, as whan o man sleeth another in his defendaunt°, and that he ne may noon ootherwise escape from his owene deeth. / But certeinly, if he may escape withouten manslaughtre of his adversarie, and sleeth hym, he doth synne, and he shal bere penance as for deedly synne. / Eek if a man by caas° or aventure° shete° an arwe or caste a stoon with which he sleeth a man, he is homycide. / Eek if a womman by necligence overlyeth° hire child in hir slepyng, it is homycide and deedly synne. / Eek whan man destourbeth° concepcioun of a child, and maketh a womman outher bareyne° by drynkinge venemouse° herbes, thurgh which she may nat conceyve, or sleeth a child by drynkes wilfully, or elles putteth certeine material thynges in hire secree places to slee the child, / or elles doth unkyndely° synne by which man or womman shedeth hire nature° in manere or in place ther as a child may nat be conceived, or elles if a womman have conceyved and hurt hirself and sleeth the child, yet is it homycide. / What seye we eek of

wommen that mordren hir children for drede of worldly shame? Certes, an horrible homycide. / Homycide is eek if a man approcheth to a womman by desir of lecherye, thurgh which the child is perissed°, or elles smyteth° a womman wityngly°, thurgh which she leseth hir child. Alle thise been homycides and horrible deedly synnes. / Yet comen ther of ire manye mo synnes, as wel in word as in thoght and in dede; as he that arretteth upon° God, or blameth God of thyng of which he is hymself gilty; or despiseth God and alle his halwes°, as doon thise cursede hasardours° in diverse contrees. / This cursed synne doon they whan they feelen in hir hertes ful wikkedly of God° and of his halwes. / Also, whan they treten unreverently the sacrement of the auter, thilke sinne is so greet that unnethe° may it been releessed°, but that the mercy of God passeth° alle his werkes; it is so greet and he so benigne°. / Thanne comth of ire attry° angre. Whan a man is sharply amonested° in his shrifte° to forleten° his synne, / than wole he be angry and answeren hokerly° and angrily, and deffenden or excusen his synne by unstedefastnesse° of his flessh, or elles he dide it for to holde compaignye with his felawes, or elles, he seith, the feend enticed hym, / or elles he dide it for his youthe, or elles his complecccioun is so corageous° that he may nat forbere°, or elles it is his destinee, as he seith, unto a certein age, or elles, he seith, it cometh hym of gentillesse° of his auncestres, and semblable° thynges. / Alle this manere of folk so wrappen hem in hir synnes that they ne wol nat delivere° hemself. For soothly, no wight° that excuseth hym wilfully of his synne may nat been delivered of his synne til that he mekely biknoweth° his synne. / After this thanne cometh sweryng that is expres° agayn the comandement of God, and this bifalleth° ofte of anger and of ire. / God seith, "Thow shalt nat take the name of thy lord God in veyn or in ydel°." Also oure lord Jesu

---

custumes and taillages, *duties and taxes* **568 bere,** *bear,* **lordshipes,** *authorities,* **abreggynge,** *reducing,* **shepe,** *reward,* **hyre,** *payment,* **usures,** *usury,* **almesse,** *alms* **570 yevest,** *gives* **571 right,** *just,* **dampneth,** *condemns,* **coupable,** *guilty,* **rightwisenesse,** *righteousness* **572 defendaunt,** *defense* **574 caas,** *chance,* **aventure,** *accident,* **shete,** *shoots* **575 overlyeth,** *lies upon* **576 destourbeth,** *prevents,* **outher bareyne,** *either barren,* **venemouse,** *poisonous* **577 unkyndely,** *unnatural,* **shedeth hir nature,** *emit their procreative fluids* **579 perissed,** *destroyed,* **smyteth, strikes,** **wityngly,** *knowingly* **580 arretteth upon,** *finds fault with,* **halwes,**

saints, **hasardours,** *gamblers* **581 of God,** *against God* **582 unnethe,** *barely,* **releessed,** *forgiven,* **passeth,** *surpasses,* **benigne,** *gracious* **583 attry,** *poisonous,* **amonested,** *admonished,* **shrifte,** *confession,* **forleten,** *abandon* **584 hokerly,** *scornfully,* **unstedefastnesse,** *instability* **585 corageous,** *passionate,* **forbere,** *stop* (himself), **gentillesse,** *high birth,* **semblable,** *similar* **586 delivere,** *free,* **wight,** *person,* **biknoweth,** *acknowledges* **587 expres,** *specifically,* **bifalleth,** *happens* **588 in ydel,** *without purpose*

---

568 Salomon, Proverbs 28.15. **569** Proverbs 25.21. **582 sacrement of the auter,** the sacrament of the altar, the Eucharist. **585 complecccioun,** temperament. On medieval theory of the humors, see *GP* 1.333n. **588 God seith,** Exodus 20.7.

Crist seith by the word of Seint Mathew, / "Ne wol ye nat swere in alle° manere, neither by hevene for it is Goddes trone°, ne by erthe for it is the bench of his feet, ne by Jerusalem for it is the citee of a greet king, ne by thyn heed for thou mayst nat make an heer whit ne blak. / But seyeth by youre word, ye, ye, andnay, nay. And what that is moore, it is of yvel," seith Crist. / For Cristes sake, ne swereth nat so synfully in dismembrynge of Crist by soule, herte, bones, and body. For certes, it semeth that ye thynke that the cursede Jewes ne dismembred nat ynough the preciouse persone of Crist, but ye dismembre hym moore. / And if so be that the lawe compelle yow to swere, thanne rule yow after the lawe of God in youre sweryng, as seith Jeremye *4 capitulo,* "Thou shalt kepe three condicions: thou shalt swere in trouthe, in doom°, and in rightwisnesse°." / This is to seyn, thou shalt swere sooth°, for every lesynge° is agayns Crist, for Crist is verray° trouthe. And thynk wel this, that every greet swerere nat compelled lawefully to swere, the wounde shal nat departe from his hous whil he useth swich unleveful° sweryng. / Thou shalt sweren eek in doom whan thou art constreyned by thy domesman° to witnessen the trouthe. / Eek thow shalt nat swere for envye, ne for favour, ne for meede°, but for rightwisnesse and for declaracioun of it to the worship of God and helpyngof thyne evene-Cristene°. / And therfore, every man that taketh Goddes name in ydel°, or falsly swereth with his mouth, or elles taketh on hym the name of Crist, to be called a Cristene man, and lyveth agayns Cristes lyvynge and his techynge, alle they taken Goddes name in ydel. / Looke eek what Seint Peter seith, *Actuum 4 capitulo, Non est aliud nomen sub celo,* &c.: "Ther nys noon oother name," seith Seint Peter, "under hevene yeven° to men in which they mowe° be saved." That is to seyn, but the name of Jesu Crist. / Take kepe° eek how that the precious name of

590

595

Crist, as seith Seint Paul *ad Philipenses 2, In nomine Iesu,* &c.: that in the name of Jesu every knee of hevenely creatures, or erthely, or of helle sholden bowe, for it is so heigh° and so worshipful that the cursede feend in helle sholde tremblen to heeren it ynempned°. / Thanne semeth it that men that sweren so horribly by his blessed name, that they despise hym moore booldely than dide the cursede Jewes, or elles the devel that trembleth whan he heereth his name. /

Now certes, sith that° sweryng, but if° it be lawefully doon, is so heighly deffended°, muche worse is forsweryng° falsly and yet nedelees. / What seye we eek of hem that deliten hem in sweryng, and holden it a gentrie° or a manly dede to swere grete othes? And what of hem that of verray usage° ne cesse° nat to swere grete othes, al be the cause nat worth a straw°? Certes, it is horrible synne. / Swerynge sodeynly withoute avysement° is eek a synne. / But lat us go now to thilke horrible sweryng of adjuracioun° and conjuracioun°, as doon thise false enchauntours or nigromanciens° in bacyns° ful of water, or in a bright swerd, in a cercle, or in a fir, or in a shulder boon° of a sheep. / I kan nat seye but that they doon cursedly and dampnably, agayns Crist and al the feith of Hooly Chirche. /

What seye we of hem that bileeven in divynailes°, as by flight or by noyse of briddes°, or of beestes, or by sort°, by nygromancye, by dremes, by chirkynge° of dores, or crakynge of houses, by gnawynge of rattes, and swich manere wrecchednesse? / Certes, al this thyng is deffended° by God and by al Hooly Chirche. For which they been acursed til they come to amendement that on swich filthe setten hire bileeve°. / Charmes for woundes or maladie of men or of beestes, if they taken any effect it may be peraventure° that God suffreth° it, for folk° sholden yeve° the moore feith and reverence to his name. /

600

605

---

589 **alle,** *any,* **trone,** *throne* 592 **doom,** *court,* **rightwisnesse,** *righteousness* 593 **sooth,** *truth,* **lesynge,** *lie,* **verray,** *pure,* **unleveful,** *unlawful* 594 **domesman,** *judge* 595 **meede,** *payment,* **evene-Cristene,** *fellow Christian* 596 **in ydel,** *without purpose* 597 **yeven,** *given,* **mowe,** *might* 598 **kepe,** *care,* **heigh,** *high,* **ynempned,** *named* 600 **sith that,** *since,* **but if,** *unless,* **deffended,** *forbidden,* **forsweryng,** *perjuring* 601 **gentrie,** *fashionable thing,* **verray usage,** *simple habit,* **cesse,** *cease,* **nat worth a**

straw, i.e., *worth nothing* 602 **avysement,** *consideration* 603 **adjuracioun,** *exorcism,* **conjuracioun,** *calling spirits,* **nigromanciens,** *necromancers,* **bacyns,** *basins,* **boon,** *bone* 605 **divynailes,** *divination,* **briddes,** *birds,* **sort,** *drawing lots,* **chirkynge,** *creaking* 606 **deffenden,** *forbidden,* **bileeve,** *faith* 607 **peraventure,** *perhaps,* **suffreth,** *allows,* **for folk,** *so that people,* **yeve,** *give*

588–90 Crist seith, Matthew 5.34–37. **591 in dismembrynge,** swearing was thought to tear apart or dismember the body of Christ, since many oaths cite parts of Christ's body or aspects of his crucifixion. See *PardT* 6.474. **592 Jeremye *4 capitulo,*** Jeremiah, chapter 4 (4.2). **597 Peter . . . ,** Acts 4.12; the English translates and completes the Latin. **598 Paul . . . ,** Philippians 2.10; the English translates and completes the Latin. **603** Various kinds of divination and casting of spells were more often presented as sins of pride or avarice.

Now wol I speken of lesynges°, which generally is fals significacioun of word in entente to deceyven his evene-Cristene°. / Some lesynge is of which ther comth noon avantage to no wight°, and som lesynge turneth to the ese and profit of o man and to disese and damage of another man. / Another lesynge is for to saven his lyf or his catel°. Another lesynge comth of delit for to lye, in which delit they wol forge a long tale, and peynten it with alle circumstaunces, where al the ground° of the tale is fals. / Som lesynge comth for° he wole 610 sustene° his word; and som lesynge comth of reccheleesnesse°, withouten avisement°; and semblable° thynges. /

Lat us now touche the vice of flaterynge, which ne comth nat gladly but for drede or for coveitise. / Flaterye is generally wrongful preisynge°. Flatereres been the develes norices°, that norissen his children with milk of losengerie°. / For sothe, Salomon seith that flaterie is wors than detraccioun°. For somtyme detraccion maketh an hauteyn° man be the moore humble, for he dredeth detraccion. But certes flaterye, that maketh a man to enhauncen° his herte and his contenaunce°. / Flatereres been the develes enchauntours, for they make a man to wene of° hymself be lyk that he nys nat lyk. / They been lyk to Judas that bitraysen 615 a man to sellen hym to his enemy, that is to the devel. / Flatereres been the develes chapelleyns, that syngen evere *Placebo*. / I rekene flaterie in° the vices of ire for ofte tyme if o man be wrooth with another, thanne wol he flatere som wight° to sustene hym in his querele°. /

Speke we now of swich cursynge as comth of irous° herte. Malisoun° generally may be seyd every maner power or harm. Swich cursynge bireveth° man fro the regne° of God, as seith Seint Paul. / And ofte tyme swich cursynge wrongfully retorneth° agayn to hym that curseth, as a bryd that

retroneth agayn to his owene nest. / And over 620 alle thyngmen oghten eschewe° to cursen hire children and yeven° to the devel hire engendrure°, as ferforth° as in hem is. Certes, it is greet peril and greet synne. /

Lat us thanne speken of chidynge and reproche, whiche been ful grete woundes in mannes herte, for they unsowen° the semes° of freendshipe in mannes herte. / For certes, unnethes° may a man pleynly° been accorded with hym that hath hym openly revyled and repreved° in disclaundre°. This is a ful grisly° synne, as Crist seith in the gospel. / And taak kepe now that he that repreveth his neighebor outher° he repreveth hym by som harm of peyne that he hath on his body, as "mesel°," "croked harlot°," or by som synne that he dooth. / Now if he repreve hym by harm of peyne°, thanne turneth the repreve to Jesu Crist, for peyne is sent by the rightwys sonde° of God, and by his suffrance°, be it meselrie°, or maheym°, or maladie. / And if he repreve hym uncharitably of 625 synne, as "thou holour°," "thou dronkelewe harlot°," and so forth, thanne aperteneth° that to the rejoysynge of the devel that evere hath joye that men doon synne. / And certes, chidynge may nat come but out of a vileyns herte. For after the habundance of the herte speketh the mouth ful ofte. / And ye shul understonde that looke°, by any wey, whan any man shal chastise another, that he bewar from° chidynge and reprevynge. For trewely, but° he bewar he may ful lightly quyken° the fir of angre and of wratthe, which that he sholde quenche, and peraventure sleeth hym which that he myghte chastise with benignitee°. / For as seith Salomon, "The amyable° tonge is the tree of lyf," that is to seyn, of lyf espiritueel. And soothly, a deslavee° tonge sleeth the spirites of hym that repreveth and eek of hym that is repreved. / Loo, what seith Seint Augustyn, "Ther is nothyng so lyk

---

608 **lesynges,** *lies,* **evene-Cristene,** *fellow Christian* 609 **wight,** *person* 610 **catel,** *property,* **ground,** *basis* 611 **for,** *because,* **sustene,** *support,* **reccheleesnesse,** *thoughtlessness,* **avisement,** *consideration,* **semblable,** *similar* 613 **preisynge,** *praising,* **norices,** *nurses,* **losengerie,** *deceit* 614 **detraccioun,** *belittling,* **hauteyn,** *arrogant,* **enhauncen,** *puff up,* **contenaunce,** *behavior* 615 **wene of,** *believe* 618 **in,** *among,* **wight,** *person,* **querele,** *quarrel* 619 **irous,** *angry,* **Malisoun,** *cursing someone,* **bireveth,** *removes,* **regne,** *kingdom* 620 **retorneth,** *turns back* 621 **eschewe,** *avoid,* **yeven,** *give,* **engendrure,** *offspring,* **ferforth,** *far* 622

unsowen, *unstitch,* semes, *seams* 623 unnethes, *hardly,* pleynly, *fully,* repreved, *accused,* disclaundre, *slander,* grisly, *hideous* 624 outher, *either,* mesel, *leper,* croked harlot, *crippled scoundrel* 625 repreve hym by harm of peyne, *blames him for his suffering,* rightwys sonde, *righteous sending,* suffrance, *allowance,* meselrie, *leprosy,* maheym, *maiming* 626 holour, *lecher,* dronkelewe harlot, *drunken scoundrel,* aperteneth, *belongs* 628 ye . . . that looke, *you who see,* bewar from, *be cautious of,* but, *unless,* lightly quyken, *easily enliven,* benignitee, *goodness* 629 amyable, *friendly,* deslavee, *uncontrolled*

---

614 **Salomon seith,** unidentified. 616 **Judas,** see 269n above. 617 **syngen evere *Placebo*,** always sing "I will please," a metaphor for flattery. See *SumT* 3.2075 and *MerT* 4.1476. 619 **Paul,** 1 Corinthians 6.10. 623 **Crist seith,** Matthew 5.22. 627 **after the habundance,** from the abundance; Matthew 12.24. 629 **Salomon,** Proverbs 15.4.

the develes child as he thatofte chideth." Seint Paul seith eek, "The servant of God bihoveeth° nat to chide." / And how that° chidynge be a vi- 630 leyns thyng bitwixe alle manere folk, yet is it certes moost uncovenable° bitwixe a man and his wyf, for there is nevere reste. And therfore seith Salomon, "An hous that is uncovered° and droppynge°, and a chidynge wyf been lyke°." / A man that is in a droppynge hous in manye places, though he eschewe° the droppynge in o place, it droppeth on hym in another place; so fareth it by a chidynge wyf. But° she chide hym in o place, she wol chide hym in another. / And therfore, "Bettre is a morsel of breed with joye than an hous ful of delices with chidynge," seith Salomon. / Seint Paul seith, "O ye wommen, be ye subgetes° to youre housbondes as bihoveth° in God; and ye men, loveth youre wyves." *Ad Colossenses 3.* /

Afterward speke we of scornynge, which is a wikked synne, and namely whan he scorneth a man for his goode werkes. / For certes, swiche 635 scorneres faren° lyk the foule tode° that may nat endure to smelle the soote savour° of the vyne whanne it florissheth. / Thise scorneres been partyng felawes° with the devel, for they han joye whan the devel wynneth and sorwe whan he leseth°. / They been adversaries of Jesu Crist, for they haten that he loveth, that is to seyn salvacion of soule. /

Speke we now of wikked conseil, for he that wikked conseil yeveth° is a traytour. He deceyveth hym that trusteth in hym, *ut Achitofel ad Absolonem.* But natheless, yet is his wikked conseil first agayn hymself. / For as seith the wise man, every fals lyvynge° hath this propertee in hymself, that he that wole anoye° another man he anoyeth first hymself. / And men shul understonde that 640 man shal nat taken his conseil of fals folk, nor of angry folk, or grevous° folk, ne of folk that loven specially to muchel hir owene profit, ne to muche worldly folk, namely, in conseilynge of soules. /

Now comth the synne of hem that sowen and maken discord amonges folk, which is a synne that Crist hateth outrely°; and no wonder is. For he deyde° for to make concord. / And moore shame do they to Crist than dide they that hym crucifiede, for God loveth bettre that freendshipe be amonges folk than he dide his owene body, the which that he yaf° for unitee. Therfore been they likned to the devel, that evere been aboute° to maken discord. /

Now comth the synne of double tonge, swiche° as speken faire byforn folk and wikkedly bihynde, or elles they maken semblant° as though they speeke of good entencioun, or elles in game and pley, and yet they speke of wikked entente. /

Now comth biwreying° of conseil°, thurgh which a man is defamed. Certes, unnethe° may he restoore the damage. /   645

Now comth manace°, that is an open folye, for he that ofte manaceth, he threteth moore than he may parfourne° ful ofte tyme. /

Now cometh ydel wordes, that is withouten profit of° hym that speketh tho wordes and eek of hym that herkneth tho° wordes. Or elles ydel wordes been tho that been nedelees or withouten entente of natureel° profit. / And al be it that ydel wordes been somtyme venial synne, yet sholde men douten° hem, for we shul yeve rekenynge of hem bifore God. /

Now comth janglynge°, that may nat been withoute synne. And as seith Salomon, "It is a synne of apert folye°." / And therfore a philosophre seyde, whan men axed hym how that men sholde plese the peple, and he answerde, "Do manye goode werkes, and spek fewe jangles." /   650

After this comth the synne of japeres°, that been the develes apes, for they maken folk to laughe at hire japerie, as folk doon at the gawdes° of an ape. Swiche japeres deffendeth° Seint Paul. / Looke how that vertuouse wordes and hooly conforten hem that travaillen° in the service of

---

630 **bihoveeth,** *ought* 631 **how that,** *even though,* **uncovenable,** *unfitting,* **uncovered,** *roofless,* **droppynge,** *dripping,* **lyke,** *the same* 632 **eschewe,** *may avoid,* **But,** *unless* 634 **subgetes,** *subjects,* **bihoveth,** *is re-quired* 636 **faren,** *act,* **tode,** *toad,* **soote savour,** *sweet smell* 637 **partyng felawes,** *partners,* **leseth,** *loses* 639 **yeveth,** *gives* 640 **fals lyvynge,** *wicked action,* **anoye,** *damage* 641 **grevous,** *malicious* 642 **outrely,**

utterly, **deyde,** *died* 643 **yaf,** *gave,* **aboute,** *active* 644 **swiche,** *such,* **maken semblant,** *pretend* 645 **biwreying,** *betraying,* **conseil,** *confidences,* **unnethe,** *scarcely* 646 **manace,** *threats,* **parfourne,** *perform* 647 **profit of,** *benefit to,* **herkneth tho,** *listens to those,* **natureel,** *usual* 648 **douten,** *distrust* 649 **janglynge,** *chattering,* **apert folye,** *obvious folly* 651 **japeres,** *jokesters,* **gawdes,** *tricks,* **deffendeth,** *forbids* 652 **travaillen,** *labor*

630 **Augustyn,** identified by Jill Mann as from Augustine's *Confessions* 3.3.6. **Paul seith,** 2 Timothy 2.24. 631 **Salomon,** Proverbs 27.5; also in *WBP* 3.278–80 and *Mel* 7.1086. 633 **Salomon,** Proverbs 17.1 634 **Paul . . . Ad Colossenses,** Paul, [Epistle] to the Colossians 3.18–19. 639 *ut Achitofel ad Absolonem,* "as Achitophel (did) to Absolom"; 2 Samuel 17. 640 **wise man,** unidentified. 648 **yeve rekenynge of hem,** account for them; Matthew 12.36. 649 **Salomon,** Ecclesiastes 5.2. 650 **a philosophre,** Jill Mann explains that the anecdote is associated with Socrates in John of Salisbury's *Policraticus* 5.6 and mentioned elsewhere. 651 **Paul,** Ephesians 5.4.

Crist. Right so° conforten the vileyns wordes and knakkes° of japeris hem that travaillen in the service of the devel. / Thise been the synnes that comen of the tonge, that comen of ire, and of othere synnes mo°. /

Sequitur remedium contra peccatum Ire.

The remedie agayns ire is a vertu that men clepen mansuetude°, that is debonairetee°, and eek another vertu that men callen pacience or suffrance. /

Debonairetee withdraweth and refreyneth° the stirynges and the moevynges of mannes corage° in his herte in swich manere that they ne skippe nat out by angre ne by ire. / Suffrance suffreth 655 swetely alle the anoyaunces and the wronges that men doon to man outward. / Seint Jerome seith thus of debonairetee that it dooth noon harm to no wight°, ne seith°; ne for noon harm that men doon or seyn, he ne eschawfeth° nat agayns his resoun. / This vertu somtyme comth of nature, for as seith the philosophre, a man is a quyk° thyng, by nature debonaire and tretable° to goodnesse, but whan debonairetee is enformed of° grace, thanne is it the moore worth. /

Pacience that is another remedie agayns ire is a vertu that suffreth swetely every mannes goodnesse, and is nat wrooth for noon harm that is doon to hym. / The philosophre seith that pacience is thilke vertu that suffreth debonairely alle the outrages of adversitee and every wikked word. / This vertu maketh a man lyk to God, 660 and maketh hym Goddes owene deere child, as seith Crist. This vertu disconfiteth° thyn enemy. And therfore seith the wise man, if thow wolt venquysse° thyn enemy, lerne to suffre°. / And thou shalt understonde that man suffreth foure manere° of grevances in outward thynges, agayns the whiche foure he moot have foure manere of paciences. /

The firste grevance is of wikkede wordes. Thilke° suffrede Jesu Crist withouten grucchyng°, ful paciently, whan the Jewes despised and repreved° hym ful ofte. / Suffre thou therfore paciently, for the wise man seith if thou stryve with a fool, though the fool be wrooth° or though he laughe, algate° thou shalt have no reste. / That oother grevance outward is to have damage of thy catel°. Theragayns° suffred Crist ful paciently, whan he was despoyled° of al that he hadde in this lyf, and that nas° but his clothes. / The thridde grevance is 665 a man to have harm in his body. That suffred Crist ful paciently in al his passioun. / The fourthe grevance is in outrageous labour in werkes°. Wherfore I seye that folk that maken hir servantz to travaillen to grevously, or out of tyme as on haly° dayes, soothly they do greet synne. / Heer agayns° suffred Crist ful paciently, and taughte us pacience, whan he baar° upon his blissed shulder the croys upon which he sholde suffren despitous° deeth. / Heer may men lerne to be pacient, for certes noght only Cristen men been pacient for love of Jesu Crist, and for gerdoun° of the blisful lyf that is perdurable°, but certes the olde payens° that nevere were Cristene commendeden and useden the vertu of pacience. /

A philosophre upon a tyme, that wolde have beten his disciple for his grete trespas°, for which he was greetly amoeved° and broghte a yerde° to scoure with° the child, / and whan this child 670 saugh the yerde, he seyde to his maister, "What thenke ye to do?" "I wol bete thee," quod the maister, "for thy correccioun." / "For sothe," quod the child, "ye oghten first correcte youreself, that han lost al youre pacience for the gilt of a child." / "For sothe," quod the maister al wepynge, "thow seyst sooth. Have thow the yerde, my deere sone, and correcte me for myn inpacience." / Of pacience comth obedience, thurgh which a man is obedient to Crist and to alle hem to whiche he oghte to been obedient in Crist. / And understond wel that

---

Right so, *similarly,* knakkes, *jokes* 653 mo, *more* 654 clepen mansuetude, *call meekness,* debonairetee, *humility* 655 refreyneth, *restrains,* corage, *disposition* 657 wight, *person,* seith, *speaks,* eschawfeth, *heats up* 658 quyk, *living,* tretable, *inclined,* enformed of, *inspired by* 661 disconfiteth, *disturbs,* venquysse, *defeat,* suffre, *endure* 662 manere, *kinds* 663 Thilke, *this,* grucchyng, *complaining,* repreved, *accused* 664

wrooth, *angry,* algate, *nevertheless* 665 catel, *property,* Theragayns, *against this,* despoyled, *robbed,* nas, *was nothing* 667 outrageous labour in werkes, *excessive physical labor,* haly, *holy* 668 Heer agayns, *against this,* baar, *carried,* despitous, *scornful* 669 gerdoun, *reward,* perdurable, *everlasting,* payens, *pagans* 670 trespas, *offense,* amoeved, *provoked,* yerde, *stick,* scoure with, *beat*

653a Sequitur remedium contra peccatum Ire, "Here follows the remedy against the sin of Anger." 657 Jerome seith, not identified. 658 the philosophre, Aristotle, *On Interpretation* 11. 660 The philosophre, Aristotle, unidentified. 661 seith Crist, Matthew 5.9. wise man, Dionysius Cato, supposed author of *Disticha Catonis* (Cato's Couplets) 1.38. 664 wise man, Proverbs 29.9. 669–73 A philosophre . . . , the episode is unidentified.

obedience is perfit° whan that a man dooth gladly and hastily, with good herte entierly, al that he sholde do. / Obedience generally is to 675 parfourne° the doctrine of God and of his sovereyns°, to whiche hym° oghte to ben obeisaunt° in alle rightwisnesse°. /

Sequitur de Accidia.

After the synne of envye and of ire, now wol I speken of the synne of accidie°. For envye blyndeth the herte of a man, and ire troubleth a man, and accidie maketh hym hevy, thoghtful°, and wrawful°. / Envye and ire maken bitternesse in herte, which bitternesse is mooder° of accidie, and bynymeth hym° the love of alle goodnesse. Thanne is accidie the angwissh of troubled herte. And Seint Augustyn seith, "It is anoy° of goodnesse and joye of harm." / Certes, this is a dampnable synne, for it dooth wrong to Jesu Crist inasmuche as it bynymeth the service that men oghte doon to Crist with alle diligence, as seith Salomon. / But accidie dooth no swich diligence; he dooth alle thyng with anoy, and with wrawnesse°, slaknesse, and excusacioun, and with ydelnesse and unlust°. For which the book seith, acursed be he that dooth the service of God necligently. / Thanne is accidie enemy to 680 everich estaat° of man, for certes, the estaat of man is in three maneres. / Outher° it is th'estaat of innocence, as was th'estaat of Adam biforn that he fil into synne, in which estaat he was holden° to wirche°, as in heriynge° and adowrynge° of God. / Another estaat is the estaat of synful men, in which estaat men been holden to laboure in preiynge to God for amendement of hire synnes, and that he wole graunte hem to arysen out of hire synnes. / Another estaat is th'estaat of grace, in which estaat he is holden to werkes of penitence. And certes, to alle thise thynges is accidie enemy and contrarie. For he loveth no bisynesse at al. / Now certes, this

foule swyn° accidie is eek a ful greet enemy to the lyflode° of the body, for it ne hath no purveaunce° agayn temporeel necessitee, for it forsleuth° and forsluggeth°, and destroyeth alle goodes temporeles° by reccheleesnesse°. / 685

The fourthe thynge is that accidie is lyk to hem that been in the peyne of helle, by cause of hir slouthe and of hire hevynesse, for they that been dampned been so bounde that they ne may neither wel do ne wel thynke. / Of accidie comth first that a man is anoyed° and encombred for° to doon any goodnesse, and maketh that God hath abhomynacion of swich accidie, as seith Seint Johan. /

Now comth slouthe that wol nat suffre noon hardnesse° ne no penaunce. For soothly, slouthe is so tendre and so delicaat, as seith Salomon, that he wol nat suffre noon hardnesse ne penaunce, and therfore he shendeth° al that he dooth. / Agayns this roten-herted synne of accidie and slouthe sholde men exercise hemself to doon goode werkes, and manly° and vertuously cacchen corage° wel to doon, thynkynge that oure lord Jesu Crist quiteth° every good dede be it never so lite°. / Usage° of labour is a greet thyng, for it maketh, as seith Seint Bernard, the laborer to have stronge armes and harde synwes°, and slouthe maketh hem feble and tendre. / Thanne comth drede 690 to bigynne to werke anye goode werkes, for certes he that is enclyned to synne, hym thynketh it is so greet an emprise° for to undertake to doon werkes of goodnesse, / and casteth° in his herte that the circumstaunces of goodnesse been so grevouse and so chargeaunt° for to suffre that he dar nat undertake to do werkes of goodnesse, as seith Seint Gregorie. /

Now comth wanhope° that is despeir of the mercy of God, that comth somtyme of to muche outrageous sorwe, and somtyme of to muche drede, ymaginynge that he hath doon so muche synne that it wol nat availlen° hym, though

---

675 perfit, *perfect* **676 parfourne,** *perform,* **sovereyns,** *rulers,* **hym,** *i.e., the one who is ruled,* **obeisaunt,** *obedient,* **rightwisnesse,** *righteousness* **677 accidie,** *sloth,* **thoghtful,** *inactive,* **wrawful,** *peevish* **678 mooder,** *mother,* **bynymeth hym,** *deprives him of,* **anoy,** *annoyance* **680 wrawnesse,** *peevishness,* **unlust,** *lack of fervor* **681 everich estaat,** *every condition* **682 Outher,** *either,* **holden,** *obliged,* **wirche,** *work,* **heriynge,** *praising,* **adowrynge,** *adoring* **685 swyn,** *swine,* **lyflode,** *livelihood,* **purveaunce,** *provision,* **forsleuth,** *loses through delay,* **forsluggeth,**

neglects through sluggishness, **goodes temporeles,** *worldly goods,* **reccheleesnesse,** *lack of concern* **687 anoyed,** *wearied,* **encombred for,** *impeded* **688 hardnesse,** *hardship,* **shendeth,** *destroys* **689 manly,** *manfully,* **cacchen corage,** *take heart,* **quiteth,** *rewards,* **lite,** *little* **690 Usage,** *habit,* **synwes,** *sinews* **691 emprise,** *enterprise* **692 casteth,** *thinks,* **chargeaunt,** *burdensome* **693 wanhope,** *hopelessness,* **availlen,** *be of use to*

676a Sequitur de Accidia, "Here follows [the section] concerning Sloth." **678 Augustyn,** see line 484 and note. **679 Salomon,** perhaps Ecclesiastes 9.10. **680 the book,** Jeremiah 48.10, with "negligently" replacing "fraudulently." **687 Johan,** Revelation 3.16. **688 Salomon,** Proverbs 18.9. **690 Bernard,** not identified. **692 Gregorie,** not identified.

he wolde repenten hym and forsake synne, / thurgh which despeir or drede he abaundoneth al his herte to every maner synne, as seith Seint Augustyn. / Which dampnable synne, if that it continue unto his ende°, it is cleped° synnyng in° the Hooly Goost. / This horrible synne is so 695 perilous that he that is despeired, ther nys no felonye ne no synne that he douteth° for to do, as sheweth wel by Judas. / Certes, aboven alle synnes thanne is this synne moost displesant to Crist, and moost adversarie. / Soothly, he that despeireth hym is lyk the coward champioun recreant° that seith creant° withoute nede. Allas, allas, nedelees is he recreant and nedelees despeired. / Certes, the mercy of God is evere redy to every penitent and is aboven alle his werkes. / Allas, kan a man nat bithynke hym on the gospel of Seint Luc, 15, where as Crist seith that as wel shal ther be joye in hevene upon a synful man thatdooth penitence, as upon nynety and nyne rightful men that neden no penitence? / Looke forther° in the same 700 gospel, the joye and the feeste of the goode man that hadde lost his sone, whan his sone with repentaunce was retourned to his fader. / Kan they nat remembren hem eek that, as seith Seint Luc 23, how that the theef that was hanged bisyde Jesu Crist seyde "Lord, remembre of me whan thow comest into thy regne°"? / "For sothe," seyde Crist, "I seye to thee, today shaltow° been with me in Paradys." / Certes, ther is noon so horrible synne of man that it ne may, in his lyf, be destroyed by penitence, thurgh vertu° of the passion and of the deeth of Crist. / Allas, what nedeth man thanne to been despeired, sith that his mercy so redy is and large°? Axe° and have. / Thanne cometh sompnolence°, 705 that is sluggy° slombrynge, which maketh a man be hevy and dul in body and in soule, and this synne comth of slouthe. / And certes, the tyme that by wey of resoun men sholde nat slepe, that is by the morwe°, but if° ther were cause resonable. / For soothly, the morwetyde is moost covenable° a man to seye his preyeres, and for to thynken on God,

and for to honoure God, and to yeven almesse to the poure, that first cometh in the name of Crist. / Lo, what seith Salomon, "Whoso wolde by the morwe awaken and seke me, he shal fynde." / Thanne cometh necligence or recchelesnesse° that rekketh° of nothyng. And how that ignoraunce be mooder of alle harm, certes, necligence is the norice°. / Necligence ne dooth no fors°, whan 710 he shal doon a thyng, wheither he do it weel or baddely. /

Of the remedie of thise two synnes, as seith the wise man that he that dredeth God, he spareth nat to doon that hym oghte doon. / And he that loveth God, he wol doon diligence to plese God by his werkes and abaundone hymself with al his myght wel for to doon. / Thanne comth ydelnesse that is the yate° of alle harmes. An ydel man is lyk to a place that hath no walles; the develes may entre on every syde and sheten° at hym at discovert° by temptacion on every syde. / This ydelnesse is the thurrok° of alle wikked and vileyns thoghtes, and of alle jangles°, trufles°, and of alle ordure°. / Certes, the hevene is yeven to hem 715 that wol labouren, and nat to ydel folk. Eek David seith that they ne been nat in the labour of men, ne they shul nat been whipped with men, that is to seyn, in purgatorie. / Certes, thanne semeth it they shul be tormented with the devel in helle, but if they doon penitence. /

Thanne comth the synne that men clepen *tarditas*°, as whan a man is to laterede° or tariynge er he wole turne to God, and certes that is a greet folie. He is lyk to him that falleth in the dych and wol nat arise. / And this vice comth of a fals hope, that he thynketh that he shal lyve longe, but that hope faileth ful ofte. /

Thanne comth lachesse°, that is he that whan he biginneth any good werk anon he shal forleten° it and stynten°, as doon they that han any wight to governe° and ne taken of hym namore kepe anon as° they fynden any contrarie or any anoy°. / Thise been the newe sheepherdes that 720

---

695 ende, *death,* cleped, *called,* in, *against* 696 douteth, *fears* 698 recreant, *fearful,* seith creant, *says "I give up"* 701 Looke forther, *notice further* 702 regne, *kingdom* 703 shaltow, *you shall* 704 vertu, *the power* 705 large, *generous,* Axe, *ask* 706 sompnolence, *sleepiness,* sluggy, *sluggish* 707 by the morwe, *in the morning,* but if, *unless* 708 covenable, *appropriate* (for) 710 recchelesnesse, *lack of concern,*

rekketh, *cares,* norice, *nurse* 711 ne dooth no fors, *does not care* 714 yate, *gate,* sheten, *shoot,* at discovert, *in the open* 715 thurrok, *bilge,* jangles, *gossip,* trufles, *trifles,* ordure, *filth* 718 tarditas, (Lat.) *slowness,* to laterede, *too tardy* 720 lachesse, *laziness,* forleten, *abandon,* stynten, *stop,* wight to governe, *person to supervise,* kepe anon as, *care as soon as,* anoy, *trouble*

---

694 Augustyn, not identified in Augustine. 696 Judas, after betraying Jesus, Judas hanged himself, epitomizing despair; Matthew 27.5. 700–3 Luc, Luke 15.7, 11–24 and 23.42–43. 705 Axe and have, echoes Matthew 7.7. 709 Salomon, Proverbs 8.17. 712 Ecclesiastes 7.19. 714 yate, see *KnT* 1.1940 and *SNT* 8.2–3n. 716 David, Psalms 73.5 (Vulgate 72.5).

leten hir sheep wityngly° go renne to the wolf that is in the breres°, or do no fors° of hir owene governaunce. / Of this comth poverte and destruccioun, bothe of spiritueel and temporeel thynges. Thanne comth a manere cooldnesse that freseth° al the herte of a man. / Thanne comth undevocioun, thurgh which a man is so blent°, as seith Seint Bernard, and hath swiche langour in soule, that he may neither rede ne singe in hooly chirche, ne heere ne thynke of no devocioun, ne travaille° with his handes in no good werk, that it nys hym unsavoury° and al apalled°. / Thanne wexeth° he slough° and slombry, and soone wol be wrooth, and soone is enclyned to hate and to envye. / Thanne comth the synne of worldly sorwe which as is cleped *tristicia*° that sleeth man, as Seint Paul seith. / For certes, swich sorwe werketh to the 725 deeth of the soule and of the body also, for therof comth that a man is anoyed of his owene lif. / Wherfore swich sorwe shorteth ful ofte the lif of man, er that his tyme be come by wey of kynde°. /

Remedium contra peccatum Accidie.

Agayns this horrible synne of accidie, and the branches of the same, ther is a vertu that is called *fortitudo* or strengthe, that is an affeccioun° thurgh which a man despiseth anoyouse° thynges. / This vertu is so myghty and so vigorous that it dar withstonde myghtily, and wisely kepen hymself fro perils that been wikked, and wrastle agayn the assautes of the devel. / For it enhaunceth and enforceth° the soule, right as accidie abateth° it and maketh it fieble. For this *fortitudo* may endure by long sufraunce the travailles that been covenable°. / 730
This vertu hath manye speces, and the firste is cleped° magnanimitee, that is to seyn greet corage. For certes, ther bihoveth° greet corage agains accidie lest that it ne swolwe the soule by the synne of sorwe, or destroye it by wanhope°. / This vertu

maketh folk to undertake harde thynges and grevouse thynges, by hir owene wil, wysely and resonably. / And for as muchel as the devel fighteth agayns a man moore by queyntise° and by sleighte than by strengthe, therfore men shal withstonden hym by wit and by resoun and by discrecioun. / Thanne arn ther the vertues of feith and hope in God and in his seintes, to acheve and acomplice the goode werkes in the whiche he purposeth fermely to continue. / Thanne comth seuretee° or sikernesse°, and that is whan a man ne douteth° no travaille° in tyme comynge of the goode werkes that a man hath bigonne. / Thanne 735 comth magnificence, that is to seyn, whan a man dooth and parfourneth grete werkes of goodnesse, and that is the ende why that men sholde do goode werkes. For in the acomplissynge of grete goode werkes lith the grete gerdoun°. / Thanne is ther constaunce, that is stablenesse of corage, and this sholde been in herte by stedefast feith, and in mouth, and in berynge, and in chiere°, and in dede. / Eke ther been mo speciale remedies agains accidie in diverse werkes, and in consideracioun of the peynes of helle, and of the joyes of hevene, and in trust of the grace of the Hooly Goost, that wole yeve° hym myght to parfourne his goode entente. /

Sequitur de Avaricia.

After accidie wol I speke of avarice and of coveitise°, of which synne seith Seint Paule that the roote of alle harmes is coveitise, *ad Timotheum 6*. / For soothly, whan the herte of a man is confounded in itself and troubled, and that the soule hath lost the confort of God, thanne seketh he an ydel solas of worldly thynges. / 740
Avarice, after the descripcion of Seint Augustyn, is likerousnesse° in herte to have erthely thynges. / Som oother folk seyn that avarice is for to purchacen manye erthely thynges, and nothyng yeve to hem that han nede. / And understond that avarice ne stant nat oonly in lond ne catel°,

---

721 **wityngly,** *knowingly,* **breres,** *briars,* **do no fors,** *do not care* 722 **freseth,** *freezes* 723 **blent,** *blinded,* **travaille,** *labor,* **unsavoury,** *unpleasant,* **apalled,** *pale* 724 **wexeth,** *grows,* **slough,** *slow* 725 *tristicia,* (Lat.) *depression* 727 **kynde,** *nature* 728 **affeccioun,** *inclination,* **anoyouse,** *harmful* 730 **enforceth,** *strengthens,* **abateth,** *weakens,* **covenable,**

appropriate 731 **cleped,** *called,* **bihoveth,** *is needed,* **wanhope,** *despair* 733 **queyntise,** *cleverness* 735 **seuretee,** *security,* **sikernesse,** *certainly,* **douteth,** *fears,* **travaille,** *labor* 736 **gerdoun,** *reward* 737 **chiere,** *manner* 738 **yeve,** *give* 739 **coveitise,** *greed* 741 **likerousnesse,** *desire* 743 **catel,** *possessions*

---

721 **newe sheepherdes,** i.e., newfangled shepherds; the shepherd metaphor is recurrently applied to pastors, bad and good, but it is not in Chaucer's source. It underlies the idealization of the Parson in *GP* 1.496–514. 723 **Bernard,** *Sermons concerning the Song of Songs* 54. 725 **Paul,** 2 Corinthians 7.10. 727a **Remedium contra peccatum Accidie,** "Remedy against the sin of Sloth." 738a **Sequitur de Avaricia,** "Here follows [the section] concerning Avarice." 739 **Paule,** 1 Timothy 6.10. The phrase recurs at *PardP* 6.334 and 426. 741 **Augustyn,** *City of God* 14.15.

but somtyme in science° and in glorie, and in every manere of outrageous° thyng is avarice and coveitise. / And the difference bitwixe avarice and coveitise is this. Coveitise is for to coveite swiche thynges as thou hast nat, and avarice is for to withholde and kepe swiche thynges as thou hast withoute rightful nede. / Soothly, this avarice is a synne that is ful dampnable, for al hooly writ curseth it and speketh agayns that vice, for it dooth wrong to Jesu Crist. / For it bireveth° hym the love that men to hym owen, and turneth it bakward agayns alle resoun, / and maketh that the avaricious man hath moore hope in his catel° than in Jesu Crist, and dooth moore observance in° kepynge of his tresor than he dooth to service of Jesu Crist. / And therfore seith Seint Paul *ad Ephesios 5,* that an avaricious man is in the thraldom of ydolatrie. /

What difference is bitwixe an ydolastre° and an avaricious man, but that an ydolastre peraventure ne hath but o mawmet° or two and the avaricious man hath manye? For certes, every florin° in his cofre° is his mawmet. / And certes, the synne of mawmetrye is the firste thyng that God deffended° in the Ten Comaundmentz, as bereth witnesse *Exodi 20,* / "Thou shalt have no false goddes bifore me, ne thou shalt make to thee no grave° thyng." Thus is an avaricious man that loveth his tresor biforn God an ydolastre / thurgh this cursed synne of avarice. Of coveitise comen thise harde lordshipes°, thurgh whiche men been distreyned° by taylages°, custumes, and cariages°, moore than hire duetee° or resoun is. And eek they taken of hire bondemen° amercimentz°, whiche myghten moore resonably ben cleped° extorcions than amercimentz. / Of whiche amercimentz and raunsonynge of° bondemen, somme lordes stywardes seyn that it is rightful for as muche as a cherl hath no temporeel thyng that it ne is his lordes, as they seyn. / But certes, thise lordshipes doon wrong that bireven° hire bondefolk thynges that they nevere yave hem, *Augustinus de Civitate, libro 9.* / Sooth is

that the condicioun of thraldom° and the firste cause of thraldom is for synne, *Genesis, 9.* /   755

Thus may ye seen that the gilt disserveth thraldom, but nat nature. / Wherfore thise lordes ne sholde nat muche glorifien hem in hir lordshipes, sith that° by natureel condicion they been nat lordes of thralles, but for that thraldom comth first by the desert of synne. / And fortherover, ther as the lawe seith that temporeel goodes of boondefolk been the goodes of hir lordshipes, ye° that is for to understonde the goodes of the emperour, to deffenden hem° in hir right, but nat for to robben hem ne reven° hem. / And therfore seith Seneca, "Thy prudence sholde lyve benignely with thy thralles." / Thilke° that thou clepest thy thralles been Goddes peple, for humble folk been Cristes freendes; they been contubernyal° with the Lord. /   760

Thynk eek that of swich seed as cherles° spryngeth°, of swich seed spryngen lordes. As wel may the cherl be saved as the lord. / The same deeth that taketh the cherl, swich deeth taketh the lord. Wherfore I rede°, do right so with thy cherl as thou woldest that thy lord dide with thee, if thou were in his plit°. / Every synful man is a cherl to synne. I rede thee, certes, that thou, lord, werke in swiche wise with thy cherles that they rather love thee than drede. / I woot° wel ther is degree above degree, as reson is; and skile° it is that men do hir devoir ther as° it is due; but certes, extorcions and despit° of youre underlynges is dampnable. /

And fortherover, understoond wel that thise conquerours or tirauntz maken ful ofte thralles of hem that been born of as roial blood as been they that hem conqueren. / This name of   765 thraldom was nevere erst kowth° til that Noe seyde that his sone Canaan sholde be thral to his bretheren for his synne. / What seye we thanne of hem that pilen° and doon extorcions to Hooly Chirche? Certes, the swerd that men yeven first to a knyght whan he is newe dubbed signifieth that he sholde deffenden Hooly Chirche, and nat

---

science, *knowledge,* outrageous, *excessive* 746 bireveth, *robs* 747 catel, *possessions,* dooth moore observance in, *pays more attention to* 749 ydolastre, *idolator,* o mawmet, *one idol,* florin, *coin,* cofre, *money chest* 750 deffended, *forbade* 751 grave, *carved* 752 harde lordshipes, *harsh regimes,* distreyned, *overwhelmed,* taylages, *taxes,* cariages, *tolls,* duetee, *obligations,* bondemen, *serfs,* amercimentz, *fines,* cleped, *called*

753 raunsonynge of, *payments from* 754 bireven, *deprive* 755 thraldom, *slavery* 757 sith that, *since* 758 ye, *yes,* deffenden hem, *protect them,* reven, *steal* 760 Thilke, *those,* been contubernyal, *dwell* 761 cherles, *servants,* spryngeth, *grow from* 762 rede, *advise,* plit, *condition* 764 woot, *know,* skile, *reasonable,* hir devoir ther as, *their duty where,* despit, *scorn* 766 erst kowth, *before known* 767 pilen, *pillage*

748 **Seint Paul,** Ephesians 5.5. 750 *Exodi,* Exodus 20.3–4. 754 *Augustinus . . . ,* Augustine, *City of God* 19.15. 755 *Genesis,* 9.22–27. 759 **Seneca,** *Moral Epistles* 47.1. 766 **Noe . . . Canaan,** Genesis 9.25.

robben it ne pilen it. And whoso dooth is traitour to Crist. / And as seith Seint Augustyn, "They been the develes wolves that stranglen the sheepe of Jesu Crist"—and doon worse than wolves. / For soothly, whan the wolf hath ful his wombe°, he stynteth° to strangle sheepe. But soothly, the pilours° and destroyours of goodes of Hooly Chirche ne do nat so, for they ne stynte nevere to pile. / Now, as I have seyd, sith so is that synne was first cause of thraldom, thanne is it thus, that thilke tyme that al this world was in synne, thanne was al this world in thraldom and subjeccioun. / But certes, sith 770 the time of grace cam, God ordeyned that som folk sholde be moore heigh in estaat and in degree, and some folk moore lough°, and that everich sholde be served in his estaat and in his degree. / And therfore, in somme contrees ther° they byen° thralles, whan they han turned hem to the feith they maken hire thralles free out of thraldom. And therfore, certes, the lord oweth to his man that the man oweth to his lord. / The Pope calleth hymself servant of the servauntz of God; but for as muche as the estaat° of Hooly Chirche ne myghte nat han be°, ne the commune profit myghte nat han be kept, ne pees and reste in erthe, but if God hadde ordeyned that som men hadde hyer degree and som men lower, / therfore was sovereyntee ordeyned to kepe and mayntene and deffenden° hire underlynges or hire subgetz in resoun, as ferforth° as it lith° in hire power, and nat to destroyen hem ne confounde. / Wherfore I seye that thilke lordes that been lyk wolves, that devouren the possessiouns or the catel of poure folk wrongfully, withouten mercy or mesure°, / they shul receyven by the same 775 mesure that they han mesured to poure folk the mercy of Jesu Crist, but if it be amended. /

Now comth deceite bitwixe marchant and marchant. And thow shalt understonde that marchandise° is in manye maneres: that oon is bodily°, and that oother is goostly°. That oon is honeste and leveful°, and that oother is deshoneste and unleveful. / Of thilke bodily marchandise that is leveful and honeste is this, that there as God hath ordeyned that a regne or a contree is suffisaunt to hymself, thanne is it honeste and leveful that of habundaunce of this contree that men helpe another contree that is moore nedy. / And therfore, ther moote° been marchantz to bryngen fro that o contree to that oother hire marchandises. / That oother marchandise that men haunten° withfraude and trecherie and deceite, with lesynges° and false othes, is cursed and dampnable. / Espiritueel marchandise is proprely 780 symonye°, that is ententif° desir to byen thyng espiritueel, that is thyng that aperteneth° to the seintuarie° of God and to cure of the soule. / This desir, if so be that a man do his diligence° to parfournen it, al be it that his desir ne take noon effect, yet is it to hym a deedly synne; and if he be ordred°, he is irreguleer°. / Certes, symonye is cleped of° Symon Magus, that wolde han boght for temporeel catel° the yifte that God hadde yeven by the Hooly Goost to Seint Peter and to the apostles. / And therfore understoond that bothe he that selleth and he that beyeth thynges espiritueles been cleped symonials, be it by catel, be it by procurynge°, or by flesshly preyere° of his freendes, flesshly freendes or espiritueel freendes. / Flesshly in two maneres, as by kynrede or othere freendes. Soothly, if they praye° for hym that is nat worthy and able°, it is symonye if he take the benefice°, and if he be worthy and able, ther nys noon. / That 785 oother manere is whan a man or womman preyen for folk to avauncen hem oonly for wikked flesshly affeccioun that they han unto the persone, and that is foul symonye. / But certes, in service for which men yeven thynges espiritueels° unto hir servantz, it moot° been understonde that the service moot been honeste, and elles nat; and eek that it be withouten bargaynynge; and that the persone be able. / For as seith Seint Damasie, "Alle the synnes of the world at regard of this synne arn as thyng of noght," for it is the gretteste synne that may be, after the synne of Lucifer and Antecrist. / For by this

---

769 wombe, *stomach,* **stynteth,** *ceases,* **pilours,** *pillagers* **771 lough,** *low* **772 ther,** *where,* **byen,** *buy* **773 estaat,** *status,* **han be,** *have been* **774 deffenden,** *protect,* **ferforth,** *far,* **lith,** *lies* **775 mesure,** *measurement* **777 marchandise,** *trading,* **bodily,** *physical,* **goostly,** *spiritual,* **leveful,** *lawful* **779 moote,** *might* **780 haunten,** *practice,* **lesynges,** *lies* **781 proprely symonye,** *correctly* (called) *simony* (see 783n), **ententif,** *intentional,* **aperteneth,** *pertains,* **seintuarie,** *sacred things* **782 do his diligence,** *makes an effort,* **ordred,** *ordained,* **is irreguleer,** *may not perform or receive the sacraments* **783 cleped of,** *named after,* **for temporeel catel,** *with worldly goods* **784 procurynge,** *manipulating,* **flesshly preyere,** *worldly pleas* **785 praye,** *intercede,* **able,** *competent,* **benefice,** *clerical appointment* **787 thynges espiritueels,** *spiritual rewards,* **moot,** *must*

768 Augustyn, quotation not identified. **773 servant of the servauntz of God,** a signatory phrase used by popes since Gregory the Great in 591. **783 Symon Magus,** a magician who sought to buy power from the apostles; Acts 8.18–20. Simony is the buying and selling of church offices. **788 Seint Damasie,** Pope Damasus I; the quotation is found in Gratian, *Decretals* 2.1.7.27.

synne, God forleseth° the chirche and the soule that he boghte with his precious blood by hem that yeven chirches to hem that been nat digne°. / For they putten in theves that stelen the soules of Jesu Crist and destroyen his patrimoyne. / By 790 swiche undigne° preestes and curates han lewed° men the lasse° reverence of the sacramentz of Hooly Chirche. And swiche yeveres° of chirches putten out the children of Crist, and putten into the chirche the develes owene sone. / They sellen the soules that lambes sholde kepen to° the wolf that strangleth° hem. And therfore shul they nevere han part of the pasture of lambes, that is the blisse of hevene. /

Now comth hasardrie° with his apurtenaunces°, as tables° and rafles°, of which comth deceite, false othes, chidynges, and alle ravynes°, blasphemynge and reneiynge° of God, and hate of his neighebores, wast of goodes, mysspendynge of tyme, and somtyme manslaughtre. / Certes, hasardours ne mowe nat been° withouten greet synne whyles they haunte that craft. / Of avarice comen eek lesynges°, thefte, fals witnesse, and false othes. And ye shul understonde that thise been grete synnes, and expres° agayn the comaundementz of God, as I have seyd. / Fals witnesse is in word and eek 795 in dede. In word, as for to bireve° thy neighebores goode name by thy fals witnessyng, or bireven hym his catel or his heritage by thy fals witnessyng, whan thou for ire, or for meede°, or for envye berest fals witnesse, or accusest hym, or excusest hym by thy fals witnesse, or elles excusest thyself falsly. / Ware yow°, questemongeres° and notaries! Certes, for fals witnessyng was Susanna in ful gret sorwe and peyne, and many another mo. / The synne of thefte is eek expres agayns Goodes heeste°, and that in two maneres, corporeel or espiritueel. / Corporeel, as for to take thy neighebores catel° agayn his wyl, be it by force or by sleighte, be it by met or by mesure°. / By stelyng eek of false enditementz° upon hym, and in borwynge of thy neighebores catel, in entente nevere to payen it agayn, and semblable° thynges. / Es- 800 piritueel thefte is sacrilege, that is to seyn hurtynge of hooly thynges or of thynges sacred to Crist in two maneres: by reson of° the hooly place, as chirches or chirche hawes°, / for which every vileyns synne that men doon in swiche places may be cleped° sacrilege, or every violence in the semblable places. Also they that withdrawen falsly the rightes that longen° to Hooly Chirche. / And pleynly and generally, sacrilege is to reven° hooly thyng fro hooly place, or unhooly thyng out of hooly place, or hooly thyng out of unhooly place. /

Relevacio contra peccatum Avaricie.

Now shul ye understonde that the releevynge° of avarice is misericorde° and pitee largely taken°. And men myghten axe, why that misericorde and pitee is releevinge of avarice? / Certes, the avaricious man sheweth no pitee ne misericorde to the nedeful man, for he deliteth hym in the kepynge of his tresor, and nat in the rescowynge° ne releevynge of his evene-Cristene°. And therfore speke I first of misericorde. / Thanne is misericorde, 805 as seith the philosophre, a vertu by which the corage° of man is stired by the mysese° of hym that is mysesed°. / Upon which misericorde folweth pitee in parfournynge of charitable werkes of misericorde. / And certes, thise thynges moeven a man to misericorde of Jesu Crist: that he yaf hymself for oure gilt, and suffred deeth for misericorde, and forgaf us oure originale synnes, / and therby relessed us fro the peynes of helle, and amenused° the peynes of purgatorie by penitence, and yeveth grace wel to do, and atte laste the blisse of hevene. / The speces of misericorde been as for to lene°, and for to yeve, and to foryeven and relesse°, and for to han pitee in herte, and compassioun of the meschief of his evene Cristene, and eek to chastise there as nede is. / 810

---

789 **forleseth,** *completely loses,* **digne,** *worthy* 791 **By swiche undigne,** *because of such unworthy,* **lewed,** *unlearned,* **lasse,** *less,* **yeveres,** *givers* 792 **kepen to,** *protect from,* **strangleth,** *kills* 793 **hasardrie,** *gambling,* **apurtenaunces,** *accessories,* **tables,** *backgammon,* **rafles,** *dice,* **ravynes,** *robberies,* **reneiynge,** *denying* 794 **ne mowe nat been,** *cannot be* 795 **lesynges,** *lies,* **expres,** *explicitly* 796 **bireve,** *deprive,* **meede,** *payment* 797 **Ware,** *beware,* **questemongeres,** *lawsuit seekers* 798 **heeste,** *command* 799 **catel,** *possessions,* **by met or by mesure,** *in whatever quantity*

800 **eek of false enditementz,** *also (by means) of false documents,* **semblable,** *similar* 801 **by reson of,** *as the result of,* **chirche hawes,** *churchyards* 802 **cleped,** *called,* **longen,** *belong* 803 **reven,** *steal* 804 **releevynge,** *remedying,* **misericorde,** *compassion,* **largely taken,** *generously applied* 805 **rescowynge,** *rescuing,* **evene-Cristene,** *fellow Christian* 806 **corage,** *heart,* **mysese,** *distress,* **mysesed,** *distressed* 809 **amenused,** *reduced* 810 **lene,** *lend,* **relesse,** *release (from obligations)*

797 **Susanna,** a beautiful woman, victim of lust and false accusation; Daniel 13. **803a Relevacio contra peccatum Avaricie,** "Relief against the sin of Avarice." **806 the philosophre,** *Moralium Dogma Philosophorum,* attributed to William of Conches (ed. John Holmberg) 27.

Another manere of remedie agayns avarice is resonable largesse°. But soothly, heere bihoveth° the consideracioun of the grace of Jesu Crist and of his temporeel goodes, and eek of the goodes perdurables° that Crist yaf to us; / and to han remembrance of the deeth that he shal receyve, he noot° whanne, where, ne how; and eek that he shal forgon al that he hath save oonly that he hath despended° in goode werkes. /

But for as muche as som folk been unmesurable°, men oughten eschue fool largesse°, that men clepen wast°. / Certes, he that is fool large ne yeveth nat his catel°, but he leseth his catel. Soothly, what thyng that he yeveth for veyne glorie, as to mynstrals and to folk, for to beren his renoun in the world, he hath synne therof and noon almesse°. / Certes, he leseth foule° his good that ne seketh with the yifte of his good° nothing but synne. / He is lyk to an hors that seketh rather 815 to drynken drovy° or trouble water than for to drynken water of the clere welle. / And for as muchel as they yeven ther as they sholde nat yeven, to hem aperteneth thilke malisoun° that Crist shal yeven at the day of doome to hem that shullen been dampned. /

Sequitur de Gula.

After avarice comth glotonye, which is expres° eek agayn the comandement of God. Glotonye is unmesurable appetit to ete or to drynke, or elles to doon ynogh to° the unmesurable appetit and desordeynee° coveitise to eten or to drynke. / This synne corrumped° al this world as is wel shewed in the synne of Adam and of Eve. Looke eek what seith Seint Paul of glotonye. / "Manye," seith Seint Paul, "goon°, of whiche I have ofte seyd to yow and now I seye it wepynge that they been the enemys of the croys° of Crist, of whiche the ende is deeth, and of whiche hire wombe° is hire god, and hire glorie in confusioun° of hem that so devouren erthely

thynges." / He that is usaunt° to this synne of 820 glotonye, he ne may no synne withstonde. He moot been in servage° of alle vices, for it is the develes hoord ther° he hideth hym and resteth. / This synne hath manye speces. The firste is dronkenesse, that is the horrible sepulture° of mannes resoun. And therfore whan a man is dronken, he hath lost his resoun, and this is deedly synne. / But soothly, whan that a man is nat wont° to strong drynke, and peraventure° ne knoweth nat the strengthe of the drynke, or hath feblesse in his heed, or hath travailed°, thurgh which he drynketh the moore, al be he sodeynly caught with drynke, it is no deedly synne, but venyal. / The seconde spece of glotonye is that the spirit of a man wexeth al trouble°, for dronkenesse bireveth hym the discrecioun of his wit. / The thridde spece of glotonye is whan a man devoureth his mete° and hath no rightful manere of etynge. / The fourthe is 825 whan thurgh the grete habundaunce of his mete the humours in his body been destempred°. / The fifthe is foryetelnesse° by to muchel drynkynge, for which somtyme a man foryeteth er the morwe what he dide at even or on the nyght biforn. /

In oother manere been° distinct the speces of glotonye, after° Seint Gregorie. The firste is for to ete biforn tyme to ete. The seconde is whan a man get hym to delicaat° mete or drynke. / The thridde is whan men taken to muche over mesure°. The fourthe is curositee° with greet entente to maken and apparaillen° his mete. The fifthe is for to eten to gredily. / Thise been the fyve fyngres of the develes hand by whiche he draweth folk to synne. / 830

Remedium contra peccatum Gule.

Agayns glotonye is the remedie abstinence, as seith Galien, but that holde I nat meritorie° if he do it oonly for the heele° of his body. Seint

811 **resonable largesse**, *moderate generosity,* **bihoveth**, *is needed,* **perdurables**, *everlasting* 812 **noot**, *knows not,* **despended**, *spent* 813 **unmesurable**, *immoderate,* **eschue fool largesse**, *avoid foolish generosity,* **clepen wast**, *call waste* 814 **catel**, *possessions,* **almesse**, *charity* 815 **leseth foule**, *loses foully,* **good**, *possessions* 816 **drovy**, *dirty* 817 **aperteneth thilke malisoun**, *belongs that curse* 818 **expres**, *explicitly,* **doon ynogh to**, *satisfy,* **desordeynee**, *excessive* 819 **corrumped**, *corrupted* 820 **Manye . . . goon**, *(there are) many who walk about,* **croys**,

cross, **wombe**, *stomach,* **confusioun**, *damnation* 821 **usaunt**, *accustomed,* **servage**, *slavery,* **hoord ther**, *treasury where* 822 **sepulture**, *tomb* 823 **wont**, *accustomed,* **peraventure**, *perhaps,* **travailed**, *suffered* 824 **wexeth al trouble**, *grows all troubled* 825 **mete**, *food* 826 **destempred**, *out of balance* 827 **foryetelnesse**, *forgetfulness* 828 **oother manere been**, *another way are,* **after**, *according to,* **to delicaat**, *too fancy* 829 **over mesure**, *beyond moderation,* **curositee**, *intricacy,* **apparaillen**, *adorn* 831 **meritorie**, *meritorious,* **heele**, *health*

817a Sequitur de Gula, "Here follows [the section] concerning Gluttony." **820 Seint Paul**, Philippians 3.18–19; also in *PardT* 6.529–32. **826 humours**, see *GP* 1.333n. **828 Seint Gregorie**, *Morals* 30.18.60. **830 fyve fyngres**, the devil's five fingers is a commonplace in sermon literature. **830a Remedium contra peccatum Gule**, "Remedy against the sin of Gluttony." **831 Galien**, Galen, second-century Greek authority on medicine.

Augustyn wole that abstinence be doon for vertu and with pacience. / Abstinence, he seith, is litel worth but if a man have good wil therto, and but it be enforced by pacience and by charitee, and that men doon it for Godes sake, and in hope to have the blisse of hevene. /

The felawes of abstinence been attemperaunce that holdeth the meene° in alle thynges; eek shame that eschueth° alle deshonestee; suffisance° that seketh no riche metes ne drynkes, ne dooth no fors of° to outrageous apparailynge° of mete; / mesure° also that restreyneth by resoun the deslavee° appetit of etynge; sobrenesse also that restreyneth the outrage° of drynke; / sparynge° also that restreyneth the delicaat ese° to sitte longe at his mete and softely, wherfore som folk stonden of hir owene wyl to eten at the lasse leyser°. /   835

Sequitur de Luxuria.

After glotonye thanne comth lecherie, for thise two synnes been so ny cosyns° that ofte tyme they wol nat departe°. / God woot°, this synne is ful displesaunt thyng to God, for he seyde hymself, "Do no lecherie." And therfore he putte grete peynes° agayns this synne in the olde lawe. / If womman thral° were taken in this synne, she sholde be beten with staves to the deeth. And if she were a gentil womman, she sholde be slayn with stones. And if she were a bisshoppes doghter, she sholde been brent by Goddes comandement. / Fortherover, by° the synne of lecherie God dreynte° al the world at the diluge. And after that, he brente° fyve citees with thonder-leyt°, and sank hem into helle. /

Now lat us speke thanne of thilke stynkynge synne of lecherie that men clepe avowtrie° of wedded folk, that is to seyn if that oon of hem be wedded, or elles bothe. / Seint John seith that   840

avowtiers shullen been in helle in a stank° brennynge of fyr and of brymston—in fyr for the lecherie, in brymston for the stynk of hire ordure°. / Certes, the brekynge of this sacrement is an horrible thyng. It was maked of God hymself in paradys, and confermed by Jesu Crist, as witnesseth Seint Mathew in the gospel, "A man shal lete° fader and mooder, and taken hym to his wif, and they shullen be two in o flessh." / This sacrement bitokneth the knyttynge togidre of Crist and of Hooly Chirche. / And nat oonly that God forbad avowtrie in dede, but eek he comanded that thou sholdest nat coveite thy neighebores wyf. / In this heeste°, seith Seint Augustyn, is forboden alle manere coveitise to doon lecherie. Lo what seith Seint Mathew in the gospel, that whoso seeth° a womman to coveitise of his lust, he hath doon lecherie with hire in his herte. / Heere may ye   845 seen that nat oonly the dede of this synne is forboden, but eek the desir to doon that synne. / This cursed synne anoyeth° grevousliche hem that it haunten°. And first to hire soule, for he obligeth° it to synne and to peyne of deeth that is perdurable°. / Unto the body anoyeth it grevously also, for it dreyeth° hym, and wasteth, and shent° hym, and of his blood he maketh sacrifice to the feend of helle; it wasteth his catel° and his substaunce°. / And certes, if it be a foul thyng a man to waste his catel on wommen, yet is it a fouler thyng whan that for swich ordure° wommen dispenden upon men hir catel and substaunce. / This synne, as seith the prophete, bireveth° man and womman hir goode fame and al hire honour, and it is ful pleasaunt to the devel, for therby wynneth he the mooste partie° of this world. / And right° as a marchant   850 deliteth hym moost in chaffare° that he hath moost avantage of, right so deliteth the fend in this ordure. /

---

833 **meene,** *middle way,* **eschueth,** *avoids,* **suffisance,** *sufficiency,* **dooth no fors of,** *makes no effort,* **apparailynge,** *decoration* 834 **mesure,** *moderation,* **deslavee,** *uncontrolled,* **outrage,** *excess* 835 **sparynge,** *self-control,* **delicaat ese,** *extravagant ease,* **lasse leyser,** *less leisure* 836 **ny cosyns,** *close cousins,* **departe,** *separate* 837 **woot,** *knows,* **peynes,** *punishments* 838 **thral,** *servant* 839 **by,** *because of,* **dreynte,** *drowned,* **brente,** *burned,* **thonder-leyt,** *lightning* 840 **clepe avowtrie,**

call adultery 841 **stank,** *pond,* **ordure,** *filth* 842 **lete,** *leave* 845 **heeste,** *command,* **seeth,** *looks upon* 847 **anoyeth,** *damages,* **haunten,** *practices,* **obligeth,** *compels,* **perdurable,** *everlasting* 848 **dreyeth,** *dries,* **shent,** *ruins,* **catel,** *property,* **substaunce,** *wealth* 849 **ordure,** *filth* 850 **bireveth,** *deprives,* **mooste partie,** *greatest part* 851 **right,** *just,* **chaffare,** *trading*

Seint Augustyn, not identified. **835a Sequitur de Luxuria,** "Here follows [the section] concerning Lechery." **837 "Do no lecherie,"** Exodus 20.14? **838 beten . . . to the deeth,** beating a servant to death for lechery contradicts Leviticus 19.20; stoning and burning are punishments for lechery in Deuteronomy 22.21 and Leviticus 21.9. **839 diluge . . . fyve citees,** lechery is the reason for the deluge (flood) in Genesis 6.4–7. Five cities are grouped in Genesis 14.8: Sodom, Gomorrah, Admah, Zeboim, and Bela, although only the first two are specified in the account of their destruction in Genesis 19. **841 Seint John,** Revelation 21.8. **842 maked of God,** Genesis 2.18–25. **Seint Mathew,** Matthew 19.5. **843** The comparison between marriage and Christ's relation to his church is rooted in Ephesians 5.25. **844 coveite,** Exodus 20.17. **845 Seint Augustyn,** *Concerning the Sermon on the Mount* 1.36. **Seint Mathew,** Matthew 5.28. **850 the prophete,** reference unidentified.

This is that other hand of the devel, with fyve fyngres to cacche the peple to his vileynye. / The firste fynger is the fool° lookynge of the fool womman and of the fool man, that sleeth right as the basilicok sleeth folk by the venym of his sighte, for the coveitise of eyen folweth the coveitise of the herte. / The seconde fynger is the vileyns touchynge in wikkede manere, and therfore seith Salomon that whoso toucheth and handleth a womman, he fareth lyk hym that handleth the scorpioun that styngeth and sodeynly sleeth thurgh his envenymynge. As whoso toucheth warm pych° is shent° his fyngres. / The thridde is foule wordes that fareth° lyk fyr, that right anon brenneth° the herte. / The fourthe fynger is the kyssinge, 855 and trewely he werc a greet fool that wolde kisse the mouth of a brennynge ovene or of a fourneys. / And moore fooles been they that kissen in vileynye, for that mouth is the mouth of helle— and namely, thise olde dotardes holours°, yet wol they kisse though they may nat do, and smatre hem°. / Certes, they been lyk to houndes, for an hound whan he comth by the roser° or by othere beautees, though he may nat pisse yet wole he heve up his leg and make a contenaunce to pisse. / And for that many man weneth° that he may nat synne for no likerousnesse° that he dooth with his wyf, certes, that opinion is fals. God woot, a man may sleen hymself with his owene knyf, and make hymselven dronken of his owene tonne°. / Certes, be it wyf, be it child, or any worldlything that he loveth biforn God, it is his mawmet° and he is an ydolastre. / Man sholdeloven hys wyf by dis- 860 crecioun, paciently and atemprely°, and thanne is she as though it were his suster. / The fifthe fynger of the develes hand is the stynkinge dede of leccherie. / Certes, the fyve fyngres of glotonie the feend put in the wombe° of a man, and with his fyve fyngres of lecherie he gripeth hym by the reynes for to throwen hym into the fourneys of helle / ther as they shul han the fyr and the wormes that evere shul lasten, and wepynge and wailynge, sharpe hunger and thurst, and grymnesse of develes that shullen al to-trede° hem, withouten respit° and withouten ende. / Of leccherie, as I seyde, sourden° diverse speces, as fornicacioun that is bitwixe man and womman that been nat maried, and this is deedly synne and agayns nature. / Al that is enemy and destruccioun to na- 865 ture is agayns nature. / Parfay°, the resoun of a man telleth eek hym wel that it is deedly synne for as muche as God forbad leccherie. And Seint Paul yeveth hem the regne° that nys dewe° to no wight but to hem that doon deedly synne. / Another synne of leccherie is to bireve° a mayden of hir maydenhede°, for he that so dooth, certes he casteth a mayden out of the hyeste degree° that is in this present lif / and bireveth hire thilke precious fruyt that the book clepeth° "the hundred fruyt." I ne kan seye it noon oother weyes in Englissh, but in Latyn it highte *centesimus fructus.* / Certes, he that so dooth is cause of manye damages and vileynyes, mo than any man kan rekene°, right as he somtyme is cause of alle damages that beestes don in the feeld that breketh the hegge or the closure thurgh which he destroyeth that may nat been restoored. / For certes, namore may mayden- 870 hede be restoored than an arm that is smyten° fro the body may retourne agayn to wexe°. / She may have mercy, this woot° I wel, if she do penitence; but nevere shal it be that she nas corrupt. / And al be it so that I have spoken somwhat of avowtrie°, it is good to shewen mo perils that longen to avowtrie, for to eschue that foule synne. / Avowtrie in Latin is for to seyn approchynge of oother mannes bed, thurgh which tho° that whilom° weren o flessh abawndone° hir bodyes to othere persones. / Of this synne, as seith the wise man, folwen manye harmes. First, brekynge of feith; and certes, in feith is the keye of Cristendom. / And whan that feith is broken and 875 lorn°, soothly Cristendom stant veyn° and

---

853 fool, *foolish* **854 pych,** *pitch,* **is shent,** *are ruined* **855 fareth,** *act,* **brenneth,** *burns* **857 dotardes holours,** *doltish lechers,* **smatre hem,** *defile themselves* **858 roser,** *rosebush* **859 weneth,** *believes,* **likerousnesse,** *lechery,* **tonne,** *wine barrel* **860 mawmet,** *idol* **861 atemprely,** *temperately* **863 wombe,** *stomach* **864 to-trede,** *trample,* **respit,** *pause* **865 sourden,** *arise* **867 Parfay,** *by the faith,* **regne,** *kingdom* (reward),

nys dewe, *is not due* **868 bireve,** *deprive,* **maydenhede,** *virginity,* **hyeste degree,** *most perfect condition* **869 clepeth,** *calls* **870 rekene,** *count up* **871 smyten,** *struck,* **wexe,** *grow* **872 woot,** *know* **873 avowtrie,** *adultery* **874 tho,** *then,* **whilom,** *once,* **abawndone,** *abandon* **876 lorn,** *lost,* **veyn,** *empty*

---

852 fyve fyngres, see 830n. **853 basilicok,** basilisk, a mythical beast with the head of a cock and body of a serpent, supposed to kill with its glance or its breath. **854 Salomon,** Ecclesiasticus 26.10. **warm pych,** Ecclesiasticus 13.1. **859 with his owene knyf,** see *MerT* 5.1839–40. **867 Seint Paul,** Galatians 5.19–21. **869 highte** *centesimus fructus,* "is called the hundred fruit." The phrase is from Matthew 13.8, used as a metaphor for virginity by Jerome, *Against Jovinianus* 1.3, and others. **875 wise man . . . harmes,** Ecclesiasticus 23.33.

withouten fruyt. / This synne is eek a thefte, for thefte generally is for to reve° a wight his thyng agayns his wille. / Certes, this is the fouleste thefte that may be, whan a womman steleth hir body from hir housbonde and yeveth it to hire holour° to defoulen hire, and steleth hir soule fro Crist and yeveth it to the devel. / This is a fouler thefte than for to breke a chirche and stele the chalice, for thise avowtiers° breken the temple of God spiritually and stelen the vessel of grace, that is the body and the soule, for which Crist shal destroyen hem, as seith Seint Paul. / Soothly of this thefte douted° gretly Joseph, whan that his lordes wyf preyed hym of vileynye, whan he seyde, "Lo, my lady, how my lord hath take° to me under my warde° al that he hath in this world, ne nothyng of his thynges is out of my power but oonly ye that been his wyf. / And how sholde I thanne do 880 this wikkednesse and synne so horrible agayns God and agayns my lord? God it forbeede." Allas, al to litel is swich trouthe now yfounde! / The thridde harm is the filthe thurgh which they breken the comandement of God and defoulen the auctour° of matrimoyne, that is Crist. / For certes, insomuche as the sacrement of mariage is so noble and so digne°, so muche is it gretter synne for to breken it. For God made mariage in paradys, in the estaat of innocence, to multiplye mankynde to the service of God. / And therfore is the brekynge moore grevous. Of which brekynge comen false heires ofte tyme, that wrongfully occupien folkes heritages. And therfore wol Crist putte hem out of the regne of hevene, that is heritage to goode folk. / Of this brekynge comth eek ofte tyme that folk unwar° wedden or synnen with hire owene kynrede, and namely thilke harlotes° that haunten bordels° of thise fool wommen that mowe° be likned to a commune gonge° where as men purgen hire ordure°. / What seye we eek of putours° that 885 lyven by the horrible synne of putrie°, and constreyne wommen to yelden to hem a certeyn rente of hire bodily puterie, ye somtyme of his owene

wyf or his child, as doon this bawdes°? Certes, thise been cursede synnes. / Understoond eek that avowtrie is set gladly° in the Ten Comandementz bitwixe thefte and manslaughtre, for it is the gretteste thefte that may be, for it is thefte of body and of soule. / And it is lyk to homycide, for it kerveth a-two° and breketh a-two hem that first were maked o flessh, and therfore by the olde lawe of God they sholde be slayn. / But nathelees, by the lawe of Jesu Crist, that is lawe of pitee, whan he seyde to the womman that was founden in avowtrie and sholde han been slayn with stones after the wyl of the Jewes as was hir lawe, "Go," quod Jesu Crist, "and have namoore wyl to synne," or "wille namore to do synne." / Soothly, the vengeaunce of avowtrie is awarded to the peynes of helle, but if so be° that it be destourbed° by penitence. / Yet been 890 ther mo speces of this cursed synne, as whan that oon of hem is religious, or elles bothe; or of folk that been entred into ordre°, as subdekne, or dekne, or preest, or hospitaliers. And evere the hyer that he is in ordre, the gretter is the synne. / The thynges that gretly agreggen° hire synne is the brekynge of hire avow of chastitee, whan they receyved the ordre. / And fortherover, sooth is that hooly ordre is chief of al the tresorie of God, and his especial signe and mark of chastitee, to shewe that they been joyned to chastitee, which that is moost precious lyf that is. / And thise ordred folk been specially titled° to God, and of the special meignee° of God, for which whan they doon deedly synne, they been the special traytours of God and of his peple; for they lyven of° the peple to preye for the peple, and whyle they been suche traitours hire preyers availen nat° to the peple. / Preestes been aungeles, as by the dignitee of hir mysterye°, but for sothe, Seint Paul seith that Sathanas transformeth hym in° an aungel of light. / Soothly, 895 the preest that haunteth° deedly synne, he may be likned to the aungel of derknesse transformed in the aungel of light—he semeth aungel of light but for sothe he is aungel of derknesse. / Swiche

877 reve, *deprive* 878 holour, *lecher* 879 avowtiers, *adulterers* 880 douted, *feared*, take, *given*, warde, *control* 882 auctour, *author* 883 digne, *worthy* 885 unwar, *unaware*, thilke harlotes, *those lechers*, bordels, *brothels*, mowe, *may*, commune gonge, *public toilet*, ordure, *excrement* 886 putours, *pimps*, putrie, *prostitution*, bawdes, *pimps* 887

gladly, *appropriately* 888 a-two, *in half* 890 but if so be, *unless it happens*, destourbed, *prevented* 891 ordre, *organized religious life* 892 agreggen, *aggravate* 894 titled, *dedicated*, meignee, *household*, lyven of, *are supported by*, availen nat, *are of no use* 895 mysterye, *duties*, transformeth hym in, *transforms himself into* 896 haunteth, *practices*

879 Seint Paul, 1 Corinthians 3.17. 880–81 Joseph, Genesis 39.8–9; the story of Potiphar's wife. 889 quod Jesu Crist, John 8.11. 891 subdekne, or dekne . . . or hospitaliers, deacons and subdeacons are ordained church officers who help the priest with daily and liturgical duties; Knights Hospitallers were organized to build and maintain hospitals. 895 Seint Paul, 2 Corinthians 11.14.

preestes been the sones of Helie, as sheweth in the Book of Kynges that they weren the sones of Belial, that is the devel. / Belial is to seyn "withouten juge," and so faren they. Hem thynketh they been free and han no juge, namore than hath a free bole° that taketh which° cow that hym liketh in the town. / So faren they by wommen. For right as a free bole is ynough for al a town, right so is a wikked preest corrupcioun ynough for al a parisshe or for al a contree. / Thise preestes, as seith the book, ne konne° nat the mysterie° of preesthode to the peple, ne God ne knowe they nat. They ne holde hem nat apayd°, as seith the book, of soden flessh° that was to hem offred but they tooke by force the flessh that is rawe. / Certes, so thise shrewes°ne   900
holden hem nat apayed° of roosted flessh and sode flessh° with which the peple fedden hem in greet reverence, but they wole have raw flessh of folkes wyves and hir doghtres. / And certes, thise wommen that consenten to hire harlotrie doon greet wrong to Crist and to Hooly Chirche and alle halwes° and to alle soules, for they bireven alle thise hym° that sholde worshipe Crist and Hooly Chirche and preye for Cristene soules. / And therfore han° swiche preestes, and hire lemmanes° eek that consenten to hir leccherie, the malisoun° of al the court Cristiene°, til they come to amendement. / The thridde spece of avowtrie is somtyme bitwixe a man and his wyf; and that is whan they take no reward° in hire assemblynge°, but oonly to hire flesshly delit, as seith Seint Jerome, / and ne rekken° of nothyng but that they been assembled. By cause that they been maried al is good ynough, as thynketh to hem. / But in swich° folk hath the   905
devel power, as seyde the aungel Raphael to Thobie, for in hire assemblynge they putten Jesu Crist out of hire herte, and yeven hemself to alle ordure. / The fourthe spece is the assemblee of hem that been of hire kynrede°, or of hem that

been of oon affynytee°, or elles with hem with whiche hir fadres or hir kynrede han deled in the synne of leccherie. This synne maketh hem lyk to houndes that taken no kepe° to kynrede. / And certes, parentele° is in two maneres, outher goostly° or flesshly. Goostly as for to deelen with his godsibbes, / for right so as he that engendreth° a child is his flesshly fader, right so is his godfader his fader espiritueel. For which a womman may in no lasse synne assemblen with hire godsib than with hir owene flesshly brother. / The fifthe spece is thilke abhomynable synne of which that no man unnethe° oghte speke ne write, nathelees it is openly reherced° in hooly writ. / This cursed-   910
nesse doon men and wommen in diverse entente and in diverse manere. But though that hooly writ speke of horrible synne, certes, hooly writ may nat been defouled namore than the sonne that shyneth on the mixne°. / Another synne aperteneth to leccherie that comth in slepynge, and this synne cometh ofte to hem that been maydenes°, and eek to hem that been corrupt, and this synne men clepen polucioun°, that comth in foure maneres. / Somtyme of langwissynge° of body, for the humours been to ranke° and habundaunt in the body of man. Somtyme of infermetee, for the fieblesse of the vertu retentif° as phisik° maketh mencioun. Somtyme for surfeet° of mete and drynke. / And somtyme of vileyns thoghtes that been enclosed in mannes mynde whan he gooth to slepe, which may nat been withoute synne. For which men moste kepen° hem wisely, or elles may men synnen ful grevously. /

Remedium contra peccatum Luxurie.

Now comth the remedie agayns leccherie, and that is, generally, chastitee and continence that restreyneth alle the desordeynee moevinges°

898 bole, *bull*, **which,** *whichever* **900 konne,** *know*, **mysterie,** *duties*, **apayd,** *satisfied*, **soden flesh,** *boiled meat* **901 shrewes,** *wretches* **902 halwes,** *saints*, **bireven alle thise hym,** *rob all these of him* **903 han,** *have*, **lemmanes,** *lovers*, **malisoun,** *curse*, **court Cristiene,** *ecclesiastical court* **904 reward,** *regard*, **assemblynge,** *sexual intercourse* **905 rekken,** *care* **906 swich,** *such* **907 kynrede,** *relatives*, **oon affynytee,** *related by marriage*, **taken no kepe,** *pay no attention* **908 parentele,** *kinship*,

goostly, *spiritual* **909 engendreth,** *begets* **910 unnethe,** *hardly*, **reherced,** *discussed* **911 mixne,** *manure pile* **912 maydenes,** *virgins*, **clepen polucioun,** *call nocturnal emission* **913 langwissynge,** *weakness*, **to ranke,** *overripe*, **vertu retentif,** *power to retain fluids*, **phisik,** *medical science*, **surfeet,** *too much* **914 moste kepen,** *must guard* **915 desordeynee moevinges,** *inordinate impulses*

897 sones of Helie, sons of Eli; 1 Samuel 2.12 (1 Kings in the Vulgate). **898 withouten juge,** in Judges 19.22, "Belial" is interpreted as *absque iugo* (without a yoke); in French, *sans ioug* could easily be misread *sans iuge*. **900 the book,** 1 Samuel 2.13. **904 Jerome,** *Against Jovinianus* 1.49. **906 Raphael to Thobie,** Tobias 6.17. **908 godsibbes,** god-siblings, a special spiritual relationship; the children of one's godparents or godchildren of one's parents. Godparents accept spiritual responsibility for the children they sponsor at baptism. **910 hooly writ,** Romans 1.26–27 speaks vehemently against homosexuality. **914a Remedium contra peccatum Luxurie,** "Remedy against the sin of Lechery."

that comen of flesshly talentes°. / And evere 915
the gretter merite shal he han that moost restreyneth the wikkede eschawfynges° of the ardour
of this synne. And this is in two maneres, that is
to seyn chastitee in mariage and chastitee of
widwehode. / Now shaltow understonde that matrimoyne is leefful° assemblynge of man and of
womman that receyven by vertu of the sacrement
the boond thurgh which they may nat be departed
in al hir lyf, that is to seyn whil that they lyven bothe.
/ This, as seith the book, is a ful greet sacrement.
God maked it, as I have seyd, in paradys, and wolde
hymself be born in mariage. / And for to halwen
mariage°, he was at a weddynge, where as he turned
water into wyn, which was the firste miracle that he
wroghte in erthe biforn his disciples. / Trewe effect
of mariage clenseth fornicacioun and replenysseth
Hooly Chirche of good lynage, for that is the ende°
of mariage and it chaungeth deedly synne into
venial synne bitwixe hem that been ywedded, and
maketh the hertes al oon of hem that been
ywedded, as wel as the bodies. / This is verray° 920
mariage, that was establissed by God er that
synne bigan, whan natureel lawe was in his right
poynt° in paradys. And it was ordeyned that o man
sholde have but o womman, and o womman but o
man, as seith Seint Augustyn, by manye resouns. /
First, for° mariage is figured° bitwixe Crist and
Hooly Chirche. And that oother is for a man is
heved° of a womman, algate by ordinaunce° it
sholde be so. / For if a womman hadde mo men
than oon, thanne sholde she have moo hevedes
than oon, and that were an horrible thyng biforn
God, and eek a womman ne myghte nat plese to
many folk at oones. And also ther ne sholde nevere be pees ne reste amonges hem, for everich
wolde axen his owene thyng. / And fortherover,
no man ne sholde knowe his owene engendrure°,
ne who sholde have his heritage, and the womman

sholde been the lasse biloved fro the tyme that she
were conjoynt to many men. /
Now comth how that a man sholde bere hym
with his wif, and namely in two thynges, that is to
seyn in suffraunce° and reverence, as shewed
Crist whan he made first womman. / For he 925
ne made hire nat of the heved of Adam, for
she sholde nat clayme to greet lordshipe. / For ther
as the womman hath the maistrie, she maketh to
muche desray°. Ther neden none ensamples of
this; the experience of day by day oghte suffise. /
Also certes, God ne made nat womman of the foot
of Adam for she ne sholde nat been holden to lowe,
for she kan nat paciently suffre. But God made
womman of the ryb of Adam, for womman sholde
be felawe unto man. / Man sholde bere hym to° his
wyf in feith, in trouthe, and in love, as seith Seint
Paul, that a man sholde loven his wyf as Crist loved
Hooly Chirche, that loved it so wel that he deyde
for it. So sholde a man for his wyf if it were nede. /
Now how that a womman sholde be subget to
hire housbonde, that telleth Seint Peter. First,
in obedience. / And eek, as seith the decree, a 930
womman that is wyf, as longe as she is a wyf,
she hath noon auctoritee to swere ne bere witnesse withoute leve of hir housbonde that is hire
lord, algate° he sholde be so by resoun. / She
sholde eek serven hym in alle honestee and been
attempree° of hire array. I woot° wel that they
sholde setten hire entente to plesen hir housbondes, but nat by hire queyntise° of array. / Seint Jerome seith that wyves that been apparailled in silk
and in precious purpre° ne mowe° nat clothen hem
in Jesu Crist. What seith Seint John eek in thys matere? / Seint Gregorie eek seith that no wight seketh precious array but° oonly for veyne glorie° to
been honoured the moore biforn the peple. / It is
a greetfolye, a womman to have a fair array
outward and in hirself be foul inward. / A wyf 935

talentes, *capabilities* **916 eschawfynges,** *inflamings* **917 leefful,** *lawful*
919 halwen mariage, *make marriage holy* **920 ende,** *purpose* **921 ver-**
ray, *true,* **his right poynt,** *its proper state* **922 for,** *because,* **figured,** *sym-*
bolized, **heved,** *head,* **algate by ordinaunce,** *at any rate by decree* 924

engendrure, *offspring* **925 suffraunce,** *patience* **927 desray,** *disorder*
929 bere hym to, *behave toward* **931 algate,** *at least* **932 attempree,**
moderate, **woot,** *know,* **queyntise,** *cleverness* **933 purpre,** *purple,* **mowe,**
might **934 but,** *except,* **veyne glorie,** *empty pomp*

916 ardour, all manuscripts except one read "ordure," but the emendation has been accepted generally. **918 the book,** Ephesians 5.32.
God maked it, Genesis 2.24. **919 at a weddynge,** the wedding at Cana; John 2.1–11. See *WBP* 3.11. **921 Augustyn,** *On Good Marriage,*
20–21. **922 Crist and Hooly Chirche . . . heved,** Ephesians 5.23–24. **927 womman hath the maistrie,** female control, a concern in *WBPT*
3.818 and 1038–40. **928 ryb of Adam,** the account of Eve made from Adam's rib is Genesis 2.22, traditionally interpreted to indicate male-female fellowship. **929 Seint Paul,** Ephesians 5.25. **930 Seint Peter,** 1 Peter 3.1. **931 the decree,** Gratian's *Decretals* 2.33.5.17.
933 Seint Jerome, not found in Jerome; the claim is made of virgins rather than wives in St. Cyprian, *On the Clothing of Virgins,* 13.
Seint John, Revelations 17.4, where purple is associated with the Whore of Babylon. **934 Seint Gregorie,** *Sermons on the Gospels* 2.40.3; see
414n above.

sholde eek be mesurable° in lookinge and in berynge and in lawghynge, and discreet in alle hire wordes and hire dedes. / And aboven alle worldly thyng she sholde loven hire housbonde with al hire herte, and to hym be trewe of hir body. / So sholde an housbonde eek be to his wyf. For sith that° al the body is the housbondes, so sholde hire herte been, or elles ther is bitwixe hem two as in that no parfit mariage. / Thanne shal men understonde that for thre thynges a man and his wyf flesshly mowen assemble°. The firste is in entente of engendrure of children to the service of God, for certes that is the cause final of matrimoyne. / Another cause is to yelden everich° of hem to oother the dette of hire bodies, for neither of hem hath power over his owene body. The thridde is for to eschewe° leccherye and vileynye. The ferthe is for sothe° deedly synne. / As to the firste, it is meritorie°. The seconde also, for as seith the decree that she hath merite of chastitee that yeldeth to hire housbonde the dette of hir body, ye though it be agayn hir lykynge and the lust° of hire herte. / The thridde manere is venyal synne, and trewely scarsly may ther any of thise be withoute venial synne for the corrupcion and for the delit. / The fourthe manere is for to understonde, if they assemble oonly for amorous love and for noon of the forseyde causes, but for to accomplice thilke brennynge delit, they rekke° nevere how ofte, soothly it is deedly synne. And yet with sorwe° somme folk wol peynen hem° moore to doon than to hire appetit suffiseth. /

The seconde manere of chastitee is for to been a clene wydewe and eschue° the embracynges of man, and desiren the embracynge of Jesu Crist. / Thise been tho that han been wyves and han forgoon° hire housbondes, and eek wommen that han doon leccherie and been releeved by penitence. / And certes, if that a wyf koude kepen hire al chaast by licence° of hir housbonde so that she yeve° nevere noon occasion that

he agilte°, it were to hire a greet merite. / Thise manere° wommen that observen chastitee moste° be clene in herte as well as in body and in thoght, and mesurable° in clothynge and in contenaunce, and been abstinent in etynge and drynkynge, in spekynge, and in dede. They been the vessel or the boyste° of the blissed Magdelene, that fulfilleth Hooly Chirche of good odour. / The thridde manere of chastitee is virginitee, and it bihoveth° that she be hooly in herte and clene of body; thanne is she spouse to Jesu Crist, and she is the lyf of angeles. / She is the preisynge of this world, and she is as thise martirs in egalitee°; she hath in hire that° tonge may nat telle ne herte thynke. / Virginitee baar° oure lord Jesu Crist, and virgine was hymselve. /   950

Another remedie agayns leccherie is specially to withdrawen swiche thynges as yeve occasion to thilke vileynye, as ese°, etynge, and drynkynge, for certes whan the pot boyleth strongly, the beste remedie is to withdrawe the fyr. / Slepynge longe in greet quiete is eek a greet norice° to leccherie. /

Another remedie agayns leccherie is that a man or a womman eschue the compaignye of hem by whiche he douteth° to be tempted, for al be it so that the dede is withstonden, yet is ther greet temptacioun. / Soothly° a whit wal, although it ne brenne° noght fully by stikynge° of a candele, yet is the wal blak of the leyt°. / Ful ofte tyme I rede that no man truste in his owene perfeccioun but° he be stronger than Sampson, and hoolier than Danyel, and wiser than Salomon. /   955

Now after that I have declared yow as I kan the Sevene Deedly Synnes, and somme of hire braunches and hire remedies, soothly, if I koude, I wolde telle yow the Ten Comandementz. / But so heigh a doctrine I lete to divines°. Nathelees, I hope to God they been touched° in this tretice, everich of hem alle. /

---

936 **mesurable,** *modest* 938 **sith that,** *since* 939 **mowen assemble,** *might copulate* 940 **yelden everich,** *yield each,* **eschewe,** *avoid,* **for sothe,** *truly* 941 **meritorie,** *meritorious,* **lust,** *desire* 943 **rekke,** *care,* **with sorwe,** *alas,* **peynen hem,** *strive* 944 **eschue,** *avoid* 945 **forgoon,** *lost* 946 **licence,** *permission,* **yeve,** *give,* **agilte,** *sinned* 947 **manere,** *kind of,* **moste,** *must,* **mesurable,** *modest,* **boyste,** *container* 948 **bihoveth,**

is necessary 949 **as thise martirs in egalitee,** *equal to the martyrs, that,* *what* 950 **baar,** *bore* 951 **ese,** *ease* 952 **norice,** *nourishment* 953 **douteth,** *fears* 954 **Soothly,** *truly,* **brenne,** *burns,* **stikynge,** *attaching,* **leyt,** *flame* 955 **but,** *unless* 957 **divines,** *theologians,* **touched,** *touched upon*

---

940 **dette,** see 375n above. 941 **the decree,** unidentified, but see 931n. 947 **Magdelene . . . odour,** Matthew 26.7 and John 12.3.

Sequitur secunda pars Penitencie.

Now for as muche as the second partie of penitence stant in confessioun of mouth, as I bigan in the firste chapitre, I seye, Seint Augustyn seith, / "Synne is every word and every dede and al that men coveiten agayn the lawe of Jesu Crist." And this is for to synne in herte, in mouth, and in dede, by thy five wittes, that been sighte, herynge, smellynge, tastynge or savourynge, and feelynge. / Now is it good to understonde that that agreggeth muchel° every synne. / Thow shalt 960 considere what thow art that doost the synne, wheither thou be male or femele, yong or oold, gentil or thral°, frcc or scrvant, hool or syk, wedded or sengle, ordred or unordred°, wys or fool, clerk or seculeer°, / if she be of thy kynrede bodily or goostly° or noon, if any of thy kynrede have synned with hire or noon, and manye mo thynges. /

Another circumstaunce is this: wheither it be doon in fornicacioun or in avowtrie° or noon, incest or noon, mayden or noon, in manere of homicide or noon, horrible grete synnes or smale, and how longe thou hast continued in synne. / The thridde circumstaunce is the place ther thou hast do synne, wheither in oother mennes hous or in thyn owene, in feeld or in chirche or in chirche hawe°, in chirche dedicat° or noon. / For if the chirche be halwed° and man or womman spille his kynde° in with° that place by wey of synne, or by wikked temptacioun, the chirche is entredited° til it be reconciled° by the bishop; / and 965 the preest that dide swich a vileynye, to terme of al his lif he sholde namore synge masse, and if he dide he sholde doon deedly synne at every tyme that he so songe masse. / The fourthe circumstaunce is by whiche mediatours or by whiche messagers as for enticement or for consentement to bere compaignye with felaweshipe, for many a wrecche for to bere compaignye shal go to the devel of helle. / Wherfore° they that eggen° or consenten to the synne been parteners of the synne, and of the dampnacioun of the synnere. / The fifthe circumstaunce is how manye tymes that he hath synned, if it be in his mynde, and how ofte that he hath falle. / For he that ofte falleth in synne, he despiseth the mercy of God, and encreesseth hys synne, and is unkynde to Crist; and he wexeth° the moore fieble to withstonde synne, and synneth the moore lightly°, / and the latter ariseth°, 970 and is the moore eschew for to shryven hym°, namely, to hym that is his confessour. / For which that folk whan they falle agayn in hir olde folies, outher° they forleten° hir olde confessours al outrely°, or elles they departen hir shrift° in diverse places. But soothly, swich departed shrift deserveth no mercy of God of his synnes. / The sixte circumstaunce is why that a man synneth, as by whiche temptacioun, and if hymself procure thilke° temptacioun, or by the excitynge of oother folk; or if he synne with a womman by force, or by hire owene assent; / or if the womman, maugree hir heed°, hath been afforced, or noon. This shal she telle, for coveitise° or for poverte, and if it was hire procurynge or noon, and swiche manere harneys°. / The seventhe circumstaunce is in what manere he hath doon his synne, or how that she hath suffred that folk han doon to hire. / And the same shal 975 the man telle pleynly° with alle circumstaunces, and wheither he hath synned with comune bordel° wommen or noon, / or doon his synne in hooly tymes or noon, in fastyng tymes or noon, or biforn his shrifte, or after his latter shrifte, / and hath peraventure° broken therfore his penance enjoyned°, by whos help and whos conseil, by sorcerie or craft, al moste be toold. / Alle

---

960 that that agreggeth muchel, *what it is that intensifies greatly* **961 gentil or thral,** *aristocrat or slave,* **ordred or unordred,** *in religious orders or not,* **clerk or seculeer,** *clergy or lay person* **962 kynrede bodily or goostly,** *physical or spiritual family* **963 avowtrie,** *adultery* **964 chirche hawe,** *churchyard,* **dedicat,** *consecrated* **965 halwed,** *blessed,* **kynde,** *procreative fluid,* **in with,** *within,* **entredited,** *under interdiction* (prohibited), **reconciled,** *reconsecrated* **968 Wherfore,** *for what reason,* **eggen,** *urge* **970 wexeth,** *grows,* **lightly,** *easily* **971 latter** **ariseth,** (more) *slowly rises,* **eschew for to shryven hym,** *likely to avoid confessing himself* **972 outher,** *either,* **forleten,** *abandon,* **al outrely,** *utterly,* **departen hir shrift,** *divide their confession* **973 thilke,** *that* **974 maugree hir heed,** *despite her efforts,* **for coveitise,** *out of acquisitiveness,* **swiche manere harneys,** *such kind of conditions* **976 pleynly,** *openly,* **bordel,** *brothel* **978 peraventure,** *perhaps,* **enjoyned,** *assigned*

957a Sequitur secunda pars Penitencie, "Here follows the second part of Penance." **958–59 firste chapitre,** see lines 107–8. **Seint Augustyn,** *In Reply to Faustus* 22.27. **967** The syntax is elliptical, but the point is clear: the fourth circumstance of sin is what kind of go-between enticed or gained consent from the sinner to come together with others for the purpose or occasion of sinning.

thise thynges, after that° they been grete or smale, engreggen° the conscience of man, and eek the preest that is thy juge may the bettre been avysed of his juggement in yevynge° of thy penaunce, and that is after thy contricioun. / For understond wel that after tyme that a man hath defouled his baptesme by synne, if he wole come to salvacioun ther is noon other wey but by penitence and shrifte and satisfaccioun, / and namely by the two if ther be a confessour to which he may shriven hym, and the thridde if he have lyf to parfournen° it. /

Thanne shal man looke and considere that if he wole maken a trewe and a profitable confessioun ther moste° be foure condiciouns. / First, it moot° been in sorweful bitternesse of herte, as seyde the King Ezechye to God, "I wol remembre me alle the yeres of my lif in bitternesse of myn herte." / This condicioun of bitternesse hath fyve signes. The firste is that confessioun moste be shamefast°, nat for to covere ne hyden his synne, for he hath agilt° his God and defouled his soule. / And therof seith Seint Augustyn, "The herte travailleth° for shame of his synne." And for he hath greet shame fastnesse, he is digne° to have greet mercy of God. / Swich was the confessioun of the puplican° that wolde nat heven° up his eyen to hevene for he hadde offended God of hevene, for which shamefastnesse he hadde anon° the mercy of God. / And therof seith Seint Augustyn that swich shamefast folk been next° foryevenesse and remissioun. / Another signe is humylitee in confessioun. Of which seith Seint Peter, "Humbleth yow under the might of God." The hond of God is mighty in confessioun, for therby God foryeveth thee thy synnes, for he allone hath the power. / And this humylitee shal been in herte and in signe outward, for right° as he hath humylitee to God in his herte, right so sholde he humble his body outward to the preest that sit in Goddes place. / For which in no manere, sith° that Crist is sovereyn, and the preest meene° and mediatour bitwixe Crist and the

synnere, and the synnere is the laste by wey of resoun, / thanne sholde nat the synnere sitte as heighe as his confessour, but knele biforn hym or at his feet but if maladie destourbe° it. For he shal nat taken kepe° who sit there, but in whos place that he sitteth. / A man that hath trespased to a lord, and comth for to axe° mercy and maken his accord, and set him doun anon by the lord, men wolde holden hym outrageous and nat worthy so soone for to have remissioun ne mercy. / The thridde signe is how that thy shrift sholde be ful of teeres, if man may, and if man may nat wepe with his bodily eyen, lat hym wepe in herte. / Swich was the confession of Seint Peter, for after that he hadde forsake Jesu Crist, he wente out and weepe ful bitterly. / The fourthe signe is that he ne lette° nat for shame to shewen his confessioun. / Swich was the confessioun of the Magdelene that ne spared for no shame of hem that weren atte feeste for to go to oure lord Jesu Crist and biknowe° to hym hire synnes. / The fifthe signe is that a man or a womman be obeisant to receyven the penaunce that hym is enjoyned° for his synnes, for certes Jesu Crist, for the giltes of a man, was obedient to the deeth. /

The seconde condicion of verray° confession is that it be hastily doon°, for certes if a man hadde a deedly wounde, evere the lenger that he taried to warisshe° hymself, the moore wolde it corrupte and haste hym to his deeth, and eek the wounde wolde be the wors for to heele. / And right so fareth synne that longe tyme is in a man unshewed°. / Certes, a man oghte hastily shewen his synnes for manye causes, as for drede of deeth that cometh ofte sodenly and is in no certeyn what tyme it shal be, ne in what place. And eek the drecchynge° of o synne draweth in another, / and eek the lenger that he tarieth, the ferther he is fro Crist. And if he abide to his laste day, scarsly may he shryven hym or remembre hym of his synnes or repenten hym for° the grevous maladie of his deeth. / And for as muche as he ne hath nat in his

---

979 **after that,** *to the extent that,* **engreggen,** *burden,* **yevynge,** *giving* 981 **parfournen,** *perform* 982 **moste,** *must* 983 **moot,** *must* 984 **shamefast,** *humble,* **agilt,** *sinned against* 985 **travailleth,** *labors,* **digne,** *worthy* 986 **puplican,** *tax collector,* **heven,** *lift,* **anon,** *immediately* 987 **next,** *nearest to* 989 **right,** *just* 990 **sith,** *since,* **meene,** *the means* 991

destourbe, *prevent,* **taken kepe,** *consider* 992 **axe,** *ask* 995 **lette,** *refrain* 996 **biknowe,** *make known* 997 **enjoyned,** *assigned* 998 **verray,** *true,* **hastily doon,** *not delayed,* **warisshe,** *heal* 999 **unshewed,** *unrevealed* 1000 **drecchynge,** *continuing* 1001 **for,** *because of*

---

983 **Ezechye,** Hezekiah; Isaiah 38.15. 985 **Seint Augustyn,** *On True and False Confession* 1.10.25 (attributed to Augustine). 986 Luke 18.13. 987 **Seint Augustyn,** not identified. 988 **Seint Peter,** 1 Peter 5.6. 994 **Seint Peter,** Matthew 26.75. 996 **the Magdelene,** this name was mistakenly applied to the reformed sinner of Luke 7.37–38, 47 because she was often conflated with Mary Magdalen. In Luke, the public washing of Christ's feet is interpreted as an act of contrition.

lyf herkned° Jesu Crist whanne he hath spoken, he shal crie to Jesu Crist at his laste day and scarsly wol he herkne hym. / And understond that this condicioun moste han foure thynges. Thi shrift moste be purveyed° bifore and avysed°, for wikked haste dooth no profit. And that a man konne° shryve hym of his synnes, be it of pride, or of envye, and so forth of the speces and circumstances; / and that he have comprehended in hys mynde the nombre and the greetnesse of his synnes, and how longe that he hath leyn in synne; / and eek that he be contrit of his synnes and in stidefast purpos, by the grace of God, nevere eft° to falle in synne; and eek that he drede and countrewaite° hymself that he fle the occasiouns of synne to whiche he is enclyned. / Also thou shalt shryve thee of 1005 alle thy synnes to o man, and nat a parcel° to o man and a parcel to another, that is to understonde, in entente to departe° thy confessioun as for shame or drede, for it nys but stranglynge of thy soule. / For certes, Jesu Crist is entierly al good; in hym nys noon inperfeccioun; and therfore outher he foryeveth al parfitly or never a deel°. / I seye nat that if thow be assigned to the penitauncer for certein synne that thow art bounde to shewen hym al the remenaunt of thy synnes, of whiche thow hast be shryven to thy curaat°, but if it like to thee of thyn° humylitee. This is no departynge of shrifte. / Ne I seye nat, theras I speke of divisioun of confessioun, that if thou have licence° for to shryve thee to a discreet and an honeste preest, where thee liketh, and by licence of thy curat, that thow ne mayst wel shryve thee to him of alle thy synnes. / But lat no blotte be bihynde°; lat no synne been untoold, as fer as thow hast remembraunce. / And whan thou shalt be shriven 1010 to thy curaat, telle hym eek alle the synnes that thow hast doon syn thou were last yshryven. This is no wikked entente of divisioun of shrifte. /

Also the verray° shrifte axeth° certeine condiciouns. First, that thow shryve thee by thy free wil, noght constreyned, ne for shame of folk, ne for maladie, ne swiche thynges. For it is resoun° that he that trespasseth by his free wyl, that by his free wyl he confesse his trespas, / and that noon oother man telle his synne but he hymself. Ne he shal nat nayte° ne denye his synne, ne wratthe hym° agayn the preest for his amonestynge° to leve synne. / The seconde condicioun is that thy shrift be laweful, that is to seyn, that thow that shryvest thee, and eek the preest that hereth thy confessioun, been verraily° in the feith of Hooly Chirche, / and that a man ne be nat despeired of the mercy of Jesu Crist, as Caym or Judas. / And eek a man 1015 moot° accusen hymself of his owene trespas, and nat another; but he shal blame and wyten° hymself and his owene malice of his synne, and noon oother. / But nathelees, if that another man be occasioun or enticere of his synne, or the estaat of a persone be swich thurgh which his synne is agregged°, or elles that he may nat pleynly° shryven hym but he telle the persone with which he hath synned, thanne may he telle, / so that his entente ne be nat to bakbite the persone, but oonly to declaren his confessioun. /

Thou ne shalt nat eek make no lesynges° in thy confessioun, for humylitee peraventure° to seyn that thou hast doon synnes of whiche that thou were nevere gilty. / For Seint Augustyn seith if thou by cause of thyn humylitee makest lesynges on thyself, though thow ne were nat in synne biforn, yet artow° thanne in synne thurgh thy lesynges. / Thou most eek shewe thy synne 1020 by thyn owene propre mouth, but thow° be woxe dowmb°, and nat by no lettre°; for thow that hast doon the synne, thou shalt have the shame therfore. / Thow shalt nat eek peynte° thy confessioun by faire subtile wordes, to covere the moore° thy synne, for thanne bigylestow° thyself and nat the preest. Thow most tellen it pleynly, be it nevere so foul ne so horrible. / Thow shalt eek shryve thee to a preest that is discreet to conseille thee, and eek thou shalt nat shryve thee for veyne glorie°, ne for ypocrisye, ne for no cause, but oonly for the doute°

1002 **herkned,** *listened to* 1003 **purveyed,** *prepared for,* **avysed,** *considered,* **konne,** *knows how to* 1005 **eft,** *again,* **countrewaite,** *watch* 1006 **parcel,** *part,* **departe,** *portion out* 1007 **deel,** *bit* 1008 **curaat,** *local priest,* **but if it like to thee of thyn,** *unless it pleases you for your* 1009 **licence,** *permission* 1010 **bihynde,** *left behind* 1012 **verray,** *genuine,* **axeth,** *requires,* **resoun,** *reasonable* 1013 **nayte,** *disclaim,* **wratthe**

hym, *anger himself,* **amonestynge,** *admonishing* 1014 **verraily,** *truly* 1016 **moot,** *must,* **wyten,** *accuse* 1017 **agregged,** *increased,* **pleynly,** *fully* 1019 **lesynges,** *lies,* **peraventure,** *perhaps* 1020 **artow,** *are you* 1021 **but thow,** *unless you,* **woxe dowmb,** *grown dumb,* **nat by no lettre,** *not in writing* 1022 **peynte,** *disguise,* **moore,** *greater part of,* **bigylestow,** *you deceive* 1023 **veyne glorie,** *empty vanity,* **doute,** *fear*

1008 **penitauncer,** a priest appointed by the pope or a bishop to attend to special cases of penance. 1015 **Caym or Judas,** Cain and Judas are two standard figures of despair, based in Genesis 4.14 and Matthew 27.5. 1020 **Seint Augustyn,** Sermon 181.4.

of Jesu Crist and the heele° of thy soule. / Thow shalt nat eek renne° to the preest sodeynly to tellen hym lightly thy synne, as whoso° telleth a jape° or a tale, but avysely° and with greet devocioun. / And generally, shryve thee ofte. If thou ofte falle, ofte thou arise by confessioun. / And thogh 1025 thou shryve thee ofter than ones of synne of which thou hast be shryven, it is the moore merite. And, as seith Seint Augustyn, thow shalt have the moore lightly relessyng and grace of God, bothe of synne and of peyne°. / And certes, oones a yeere atte leeste wey it is laweful for to been housled°, for certes oones a yeere alle thynges renovellen°. /

Now have I toolde you of verray confessioun, that is the seconde partie of penitence. /

**Explicit secunda pars Penitencie et sequitur tercia
pars eiusdem de Satisfaccione.**

The thridde partie of penitence is satisfaccioun, and that stant moost generally in almesse° and in bodily peyne. / Now been ther three manere of almesses: contricion of herte, where a man offreth hymself to God; another is to han pitee of defaute° of his neighebores; and the thridde is in yevynge of good conseil and comfort goostly° and bodily, where men han nede, and namely in sustenaunce of mannes foode. / 1030 And tak kepe° that a man hath nede of thise thinges generally: he hath nede of foode, he hath nede of clothyng and herberwe°, he hath nede of charitable conseil and visitynge in prisone and in maladie, and sepulture° of his dede body. / And if thow mayst nat visite the nedeful with thy persone, visite him by thy message and by thy yiftes. / Thise been generally almesses or werkes of charitee of hem that han temporeel richesses or discrecioun in conseilynge. Of thise werkes shaltow heren° at the day of doome. /

Thise almesses shaltow doon° of thyne owene propre thynges°, and hastily and prively if thow mayst; / but nathelees if thow mayst nat doon it prively, thow shalt nat forbere to doon almesse though men seen it; so that it be nat doon for thank of the world, but oonly for thank of Jesu Crist. / For as witnesseth Seint Mathew, 1035 *capitulo* 5, "A citee may nat been hyd that is set on a montayne. Ne men lighte nat a lanterne and put it under a busshel, but men sette it on a candlestikke to yeve light to the men in the hous. / Right so shal youre light lighten bifore men, that they may seen youre goode werkes, and glorifie youre fader that is in hevene." /

Now as to speken of bodily peyne°, it stant in preyeres, in wakynges°, in fastynges, in vertuouse techynges of orisouns°. / And ye shul understonde that orisouns or preyeres is for to seyn a pitous wyl of herte that redresseth it in° God, and expresseth it by word outward to remoeven harmes and to han thynges° espiritueel and durable, and somtyme temporele thynges. Of whiche orisouns, certes, in the orisoun of the Pater Noster hath Jesu Crist enclosed° moost thynges. / Certes, it is privyleged of° thre thynges in his dignytee° for which it is moore digne than any oother preyere: for that Jesu Crist hymself maked it; / and it is short for it 1040 sholde be koud° the moore lightly°, and for to withholden it the moore esily in herte, and helpen hymself the ofter° with the orisoun, / and for a man sholde be the lasse wery to seyen it, and for a man may nat excusen hym to lerne it, it is so short and so esy; and for it comprehendeth in itself alle goode preyeres. / The exposicioun of this hooly preyere, that is so excellent and digne°, I bitake° to thise maistres of theologie, save thus muchel wol I

---

heele, *health* **1024 renne,** *run,* **whoso,** *someone who,* **jape,** *joke,* **avysely,** *thoughtfully* **1026 peyne,** *punishment* **1027 to been housled,** *to receive communion,* **renovellen,** *renewed* **1029 almesse,** *charity* **1030 defaute,** *the lack,* **goostly,** *spiritually* **1031 tak kepe,** *take note,* **herberwe,** *shelter,* **sepulture,** *burial* **1033 heren,** *hear* **1034 shaltow doon,** *you shall do,*

propre thynges, *personal property* **1038 bodily peyne,** *physical penance,* **wakynges,** *vigils,* **orisouns,** *prayers* **1039 redresseth it in,** *addresses itself to,* **han thynges,** *acquire things,* **enclosed,** *included* **1040 privyleged of,** *endowed with,* **his dignytee,** *its worthiness* **1041 koud,** *learned,* **lightly,** *easily,* **ofter,** *more often* **1043 digne,** *worthy,* **bitake,** *leave*

1026 Seint Augustyn, *On True and False Confession* 1.10.25 (attributed to Augustine). **1027 it is laweful,** it is required by law; the requirement to confess one's sins and receive communion annually was established at the Fourth Lateran Council of 1215–16, which inspired penitential treatises such as those of Raymund of Pennafort and Guilielmus Peraldus from which *ParsT* derives. **1028a Explicit secunda pars Penitencie et sequitur tercia pars eiusdem de Satisfaccione,** "Here ends the second part of Penance and follows the third part of the same concerning Satisfaction." **1036 Seint Mathew,** *capitulo* 5, chapter 5.14–16. **1039 Pater Noster,** Lord's Prayer; Matthew 6.9–13 and Luke 11.2–4.

seyn: that whan thou prayest that God sholde foryeve thee thy giltes as thow foryevest hem that agilten to thee, be ful wel war that thow ne be nat out of charitee. / This hooly orisoun amenuseth° eek venyal synne, and therfore it aperteneth° specially to penitence. /

This preyere moste be trewely° seyd and in verray° feith, and that men preye to God ordinatly° and discreetly and devoutly; and alwey a man shal putten his wyl to be subget to the wille of God. / This orisoun moste eek been seyd with 1045 greet humblesse and ful pure, honestly and nat to the anoyaunce of any man or womman. It moste eek been continued° with the werkes of charitee. / It avayleth eek agayn° the vices of the soule, for as seith Seint Jerome, "By fastynge been saved the vices of the flessh, and by preyere the vyces of the soule." /

After this thou shalt understonde that bodily peyne stant in wakynge°, for Jesu Crist seith, "Waketh and preyeth that ye ne entre in wikked temptacioun." / Ye shul understanden also that fastynge stant in thre thynges, in forberynge of° bodily mete and drynke, and in forberynge of worldly jolitee, and in forberynge of deedly synne. This is to seyn that a man shal kepen hym fro deedly synne with al his myght. /

And thou shalt understanden eek that God ordeyned fastynge. And to fastynge appertenen foure thinges: / largenesse° to poure folk, 1050 gladnesse of herte espiritueel, nat to been angry ne anoyed, ne grucche° for he fasteth, and also resonable houre for to ete by mesure°. That is for to seyn, a man shal nat ete in untyme° ne sitte the lenger at his table to ete for° he fasteth. /

Thanne shaltow understonde that bodily peyne stant in disciplyne or techynge by word, or by writynge, or in ensample. Also in werynge of heyres°, or of stamyn°, or of haubergeons° on hir naked flessh, for Cristes sake, and swiche manere penances. / But war thee wel that swiche manere penaunces on thy flessh ne make thee nat bitter or angry or anoyed of thyself. For bettre is to caste awey thyn heyre than for to caste away the sikernesse° of Jesu Crist. / And therfore seith Seint Paul, "Clothe yow, as they that been chosen of God, in herte of misericorde°, debonairetee°, suffraunce°, and swich manere of clothynge"; of whiche Jesu Crist is moore apayed° than of heyres, or haubergeouns, or hauberkes°. /

Thanne is disciplyne eek in knokkynge° of thy brest, in scourgynge with yerdes°, in knelynges, in tribulacions, / in suffrynge paciently 1055 wronges that been doon to thee, and eek in pacient suffraunce of maladies, or lesynge° of worldly catel°, or of wyf, or of child, or othere freendes. /

Thanne shaltow understonde whiche thynges destourben° penaunce, and this is in foure maneres, that is, drede, shame, hope, and wanhope°, that is, desperacion. / And for to speke first of drede, for which he weneth° that he may suffre no penaunce, / ther agayns is remedie for to thynke that bodily penaunce is but short and litel at regard of the peynes of helle, that is so crueel and so long that it lasteth withouten ende. /

Now again the shame that a man hath to shryven hym, and namely thise ypocrites that wolden been holden so parfite that they han no nede to shryven hem, / agayns that shame sholde a 1060 man thynke that by wey of resoun that he that hath nat been shamed to doon foule thynges, certes hym oghte nat been ashamed to do faire thynges, and that is confessiouns. / A man sholde eek thynke that God seeth and woot° alle his thoghtes and alle his werkes. To hym may nothyng been hyd ne covered. / Men sholden eek remembren hem of the shame that is to come at the day of doome to hem that been nat penitent and shryven in this present lyf. / For alle the creatures in hevene, in erthe, and in helle shullen seen apertly° al that they hyden in this world. /

Now for to speken of the hope of hem that been necligent and slowe to shryven hem, that stant in two maneres: / that oon is 1065 that he hopeth for to lyve longe and for to

---

1044 amenuseth, *reduces,* **aperteneth,** *pertains* **1045 trewely,** *sincerely,* **verray,** *genuine,* **ordinatly,** *in an orderly way* **1046 continued,** *extended* **1047 avayleth eek agayn,** *is effective also against* **1048 wakynge,** *keeping vigils* **1049 forberynge of,** *abstaining from* **1051 largenesse,** *generosity,* **grucche,** *complain,* **by mesure,** *appropriately,* **untyme,** *inappropriate times,* **for,** *because* **1052 heyres,** *hair shirts,* **stamyn,** *coarse cloth,*

haubergeons, *mail shirts* **1053 sikernesse,** *certainty* **1054 misericorde,** *mercy,* **debonairetee,** *graciousness,* **suffraunce,** *long-suffering,* **apayed,** *repaid,* **hauberkes,** *chain mail* **1055 knokkynge,** *beating,* **yerdes,** *yardsticks* **1056 lesynge,** *losing,* **catel,** *possessions* **1057 destourben,** *impede,* **wanhope,** *despair* **1058 weneth,** *thinks* **1062 woot,** *knows* **1064 apertly,** *openly*

1043 God sholde foryeve thee . . . to thee, from the Lord's Prayer; Matthew 6.12. **1047 Seint Jerome,** not found in Jerome, but attributed to him in Chaucer's source. **1048 Jesu Crist,** Matthew 26.41. **1054 Seint Paul,** Colossians 3.12.

purchacen° muche richesse for his delit, and thanne he wol shryven hym, and as he seith, hym semeth° thanne tymely ynough to come to shrifte. / Another is surquidrie° that he hath in Cristes mercy. / Agayns the firste vice, he shal thynke that oure lif is in no sikernesse°, and eek that alle the richesses in this world ben in aventure° and passen as a shadwe on the wal. / And as seith Seint Gregorie that it aperteneth° to the grete rightwisnesse° of God, that nevere shal the peyne stynte° of hem that nevere wolde withdrawen hem fro synne hir thankes°, but ay continue in synne. For thilke° perpetueel wil to do synne shul they han perpetueel peyne. /

Wanhope° is in two maneres: the firste wanhope is in the mercy of Crist, that oother is that they thynken that they ne myghte nat longe persevere in goodnesse. / The firste wanhope 1070 comth of that he demeth that he hath synned so greetly and so ofte, and so longe leyn in synne that he shal nat be saved. / Certes, agayns that cursed wanhope sholde he thynke that the passion° of Jesu Crist is moore strong for to unbynde than synne is strong for to bynde. / Agayns the seconde wanhope, he shal thynke that as ofte as he falleth he may arise agayn by penitence. And though he never so longe have leyn in synne, the mercy of Crist is alwey redy to receiven hym to mercy. / Agayns the wanhope that he demeth that he sholde nat longe persevere in goodnesse, he shal thynke that the feblesse of the devel may nothing doon but if men wol suffren° hym; / and eek he shal han strengthe of the helpe of God, and of al Hooly Chirche, and of the proteccioun of aungels, if hym list°. /   1075

Thanne shal men understonde what is the fruyt of penaunce, and after the word of Jesu Crist it is the endelees blisse of hevene, / ther° joye hath no contrarioustee of wo ne grevaunce, ther alle harmes been passed of this present lyf, ther as is the sikernesse° fro the peyne of helle, ther as is the blisful compaignye that rejoysen hem everemo everich of otheres joye, / ther as the body of man that whilom° was foul and derk is moore cleer than the sonne, ther as the body that whilom was syk, freele°, and fieble, and mortal, is inmortal, and so strong and so hool that ther may nothing apeyren° it, / ther as ne is neither hunger, thurst, ne coold, but every soule replenyssed with the sighte of the parfit knowynge of God. / This blisful regne may men purchace by poverte espiritueel, and the glorie by lowenesse, the plentee of joye by hunger and thurst, and the reste by travaille, and the lyf by deeth and mortificacion° of synne. /   1080

1066 **purchacen,** *acquire,* **hym semeth,** *it seems to him* **1067 surquidrie,** *overconfidence* **1068 sikernesse,** *certainty,* **in aventure,** *at risk* **1069 aperteneth,** *relates,* **rightwisnesse,** *righteousness,* **stynte,** *cease,* **hir thankes,** *voluntarily,* **thilke,** *this* **1070 Wanhope,** *despair*

1069 **Seint Gregorie,** *Morals* 34.19.36.

1072 **passion,** *suffering and death* **1074 suffren,** *allow* **1075 hym list,** *he chooses* **1077 ther,** *where,* **sikernesse,** *certainty* **1078 whilom,** *formerly,* **freele,** *frail,* **apeyren,** *harm* **1080 lowenesse,** *humility,* **mortificacion,** *destroying*

RETRACTION

Heere taketh the makere of this book his leve.

Now preye I to hem alle that herkne° this litel tretys or rede°, that if ther be anythyng in it that liketh° hem that therof they thanken oure lord Jhesu Crist, of whom procedeth al wit° and al goodnesse. / And if ther be anythyng that displese hem, I preye hem also that they arrette° it to the defaute° of myn unkonnynge°, and nat to my wyl that wolde ful fayn° have seyd bettre if I hadde had konnynge. / For oure book seith, "Al that is writen is writen for oure doctrine," and that is myn entente. / Wherfore I biseke yow mekely, for the mercy of God, that ye preye for me that Crist have mercy on me and foryeve me my giltes, / and namely° of my translacions and enditynges° of worldly vanitees, the whiche I revoke in my retracciouns: / ₁₀₈₅ as is the Book of Troilus; the Book also of Fame; the Book of the xxv Ladies; the Book of the

Duchesse; the Book of Seint Valentynes Day of the Parlement of Briddes; the Tales of Caunterbury, thilke that sownen into° synne; / the Book of the Leoun; and many another book, if they were in my remembrance, and many a song and many a leccherous lay°, that Crist for his grete mercy foryeve me the synne. / But of the translacioun of Boece de Consolacione and othere bookes of legendes° of seintes, and omelies°, and moralitee, and devocioun, / that thanke I oure lord Jhesu Crist and his blisful mooder, and alle the seintes of hevene, / bisekynge hem that they from hennes° forth unto my lyves ende sende me grace to biwayle my giltes and to studie to the salvacioun of my soule, and graunte me grace of verray° penitence, confessioun and satisfaccioun to doon in this present lyf, / thurgh the benigne° ₁₀₉₀

1081 herkne, *listen to,* **rede,** *read,* **liketh,** *pleases,* **wit,** *capability* **1082 arrette,** *attribute,* **defaute,** *fault,* **unkonnynge,** *lack of ability,* **fayn,** *gladly* **1085 namely,** *particularly,* **enditynges,** *writing* **1086 sownen**

into, *tend toward* **1087 lay,** *verse romance* **1088 legendes,** *lives,* **omelies,** *sermons* **1090 hennes,** *hence* **verray,** *genuine* **1091 benigne,** *goodly,* **boghte,** *redeemed*

1083 oure book, the Bible; Romans 15.4; also quoted in *NPT* 7.3441–42. **1085 revoke,** retract, but also rescue or restate; Chaucer's only other use of the verb is at *TC* 3.1118, where it means to call back to consciousness. **1086–88** This list of Chaucer's writings may be compared with the lists in *LGWP* F329–34 and 417–30. **Book of the xxv Ladies,** *Legend of Good Women,* where nineteen tales are told. The Roman numerals vary in the manuscripts. **1087 Book of the Leoun,** a lost, unidentified, or yet-to-be written book by Chaucer, perhaps a translation of Machaut's *Dit dou Lyon* or Deschamps's *Dict du Lyon.*

389

grace of hym that is kyng of kynges and preest over alle preestes, that boghte° us with the precious blood of his herte, / so that I may been oon of hem at the day of doome that shulle be saved. *Qui cum patre* &c.

Heere is ended the book of The Tales of Caunterbury compiled by Geffrey Chaucer of whos soule Jhesu Christ have mercy. Amen.

1092 *Qui cum patre,* the beginning of a Latin formulaic prayer: "He who with the Father and the Holy Spirit lives and reigns forever and ever. Amen."

CHAUCER IN HIS TIME

Not one of the 493 records printed and discussed in the *Chaucer Life-Records,* ed. M. M. Crow and C. Olson (1966), identifies Chaucer as an author. They chronicle the distinguished career of a courtier, diplomat, and civil servant. This must have been the character in which Chaucer viewed himself. His poetry he must have regarded as a fortunate talent by which he could advance his career in government. Only this can account for the fact that so many of his pieces were never finished and for the fact that, so far as we can tell, no manuscript of his works dates from before his death. Evidently, like Shakespeare, he gave no thought to the "publication" of his writings. The performance satisfied their intention. But this lack of interest in preserving an official canon contrasts with the hints we have of his desire to be remembered as a poet—in the *House of Fame,* at the conclusion of *Troylus and Criseyde,* in the lists of his titles in the *Legend of Good Women,* and the Retraction to *The Canterbury Tales.*

The life-records show Chaucer emerging from the class in society that has produced the most notable writers in England and elsewhere, the prosperous upper middle class that must continue to work for a living, but with cultivation, education, some leisure, and resources to collect and create in the intellectual and aesthetic sphere. Until F. J. Furnivall in 1876 discovered a deed of conveyance of a house on Thames Street in which Chaucer described himself as "me Galfridum Chaucer filium Johannis Chaucer vinetarii Londonie," his specific parentage was not known. But as early as 1598, Thomas Speght, in the biography attached to his edition, had surmised of his parents, "whether they were Merchants, (for in the places where they have dwelled, the Armes of the Merchants of the Staple have been seene in the glasse windowes), or whether they were of other calling, it is not necessary to search; but wealthy no doubt they were, and of good account in the commonwealth, who brought up their Sonne in such sort, that both he was thought fitte for the Court at home, and to be imployed for matters of State in forraine countreyes." This surmise has been largely confirmed by modern scholarship.

Chaucer's father and other relatives were wealthy vintners (wine importers and wholesale merchants), who served in the army, furnished provisions for the court, and occupied official positions both for the king and the City of London.

The nature of the first records reveals how fragmentary and fortuitous our knowledge of Chaucer is. These turned up in 1851 on some scraps used as stuffing in the covers of a manuscript recently bought by the British Library. They are a list of the expenses and gifts from 1356 to 1359 of the household of Elizabeth, Countess of Ulster and wife of Lionel, second son of Edward III. Her two attendants mentioned most frequently are Philippa Pan' and Galfrido Chaucer. Chaucer's function is not indicated; presumably he was a page. Philippa's identity has been much debated. The most attractive theory is that "Pan'" is a contraction of "Panneto," one form of the name of Sir Paon de Roet, father of Philippa Chaucer and Katherine Swynford, who was mistress and eventually (1396) wife of John of Gaunt, Duke of Lancaster, third son of Edward III. If this surmise is correct, Chaucer married the demoiselle with whom he had served as a young boy.

The date of Chaucer's birth is not known. In the Scrope-Grosvenor trial of 1386, he gave his age as "xl ans et plus armeez par xxvii ans"—forty years and more, having borne arms for twenty-seven years. Efforts have failed to make these terms precise, but the first part sets Chaucer's birth before 1346. The customary age for going to war was sixteen or seventeen, which would move the date back to 1342 or earlier. The twenty-seven years is quite accurate, because in 1359–1360 he served in the French war. In 1360 he was captured and ransomed for sixteen pounds—thirteen shillings fourpence less than for Sir Robert de Clinton's horse, as has been often remarked. Such military experience for Chaucer, as for his father before him, was clearly expected of one who hoped to be accepted by an aristocracy whose business was still war, even though his own ambitions might run in a totally different direction. Chaucer had no doubt been given a good elementary education before he joined the household of the countess.

Serving in a noble household and joining Prince Lionel on a military expedition must have been regarded as a continuation of his education.

But the period between the 1360 record of his military service and 1366, when he reappears traveling in Spain, is the longest gap in Chaucer's life-records after their commencement in 1357. Indeed, there are records every year from 1366 until the last one in 1400. The best supposition is that during these six years he was continuing his education in the Inns of Chancery and Inns of Court, which prepared him for an administrative career. In the Inns of Chancery, aspiring clerks were taught, first, the Chancery hand in which all official documents had to be written and, second, the forms and language (in Chaucer's time still Latin and French) in which they were enrolled. Without such training, Chaucer could not have been appointed controller of customs in 1374 with the provision that "rotulos suos dicta officia tangentes manu sua propria scribat"—that he write the rolls touching said office in his own hand. After two or three years in an Inn of Chancery, he could proceed to an Inn of Court, where he would hear lectures on law and government. The only evidence for such education comes much too late. Speght, in the 1598 life already referred to, said that "manye yeres since, master Buckley did see a recorde [of the Inner Temple], where Geffrye Chaucer was fined two shillinges for beatinge a Franciscane fryer in fletestreate." No records from the Inns of Court in Chaucer's day have survived, but Edith Rickert discovered that Master Buckley was keeper of the records of the Inner Temple in Speght's time, and so in a position to see such a record, and the offense and penalty are similar to others listed in the earliest records that do survive.

By 1366 this period was over and Chaucer reappears traveling in Spain, probably in connection with the Black Prince's campaign in support of Don Pedro of Castile, to whose fate Chaucer later alluded in the *Monk's Tale* (*CT* 7.2375ff.), but possibly simply on a pilgrimage to the shrine of St. James of Compostella (*CT* 1.466). In the same year the king granted Philippa Chaucer a life annuity of ten marks as a demoiselle in attendance upon Queen Philippa, and in 1367 the king granted Geoffrey his first annuity of twenty marks. Scholars have debated the timing and the wording of these grants. The facts that Philippa was referred to in her own person rather than as the wife of Geoffrey Chaucer and that she received her grant first make it appear that Chaucer had married above himself and that Philippa's connections in court would do his career no harm. Her father, Sir Paon de Roet, had come from Hainault in northern France in Queen Philippa's personal entourage, and he was Guienne King of Arms—that is, he was charged with recording the genealogies of the noble families in England's valuable territories in southern France.

From 1367 to 1374 Chaucer was "vallectus" (yeoman) in 1368 and was promoted to "armiger" (esquire) in the king's household, but without specific assignment. His status during this period is described in the *Liber Niger* of the household of Edward IV (the household ordinances of Edward III have not survived): "These Esquires of household of old be accustomed, winter and summer, in afternoones and eveninges to drawe to Lordes chambres within court, there to keep honest company after there Cunninge [i.e., skill, knowledge], in talking of Chronicles of Kinges, and of otheres pollicies, or in pipeing or harpeing, songinges, or other actes marcealles, to helpe to occupie the Court, and accompanie estraingers till the time require of departing." We can see how one with a gift for storytelling and poetry would be in demand. ("Chronicles of kings" are specifically referred to in the *Book of the Duchess,* ll. 57–58.) The contacts one made in such a situation would be the foundations for a career.

We see this career developing as Chaucer is assigned to carry messages abroad and serve on diplomatic missions, in 1368 and 1370 to France and in 1372–1373 on a six-month trip to Italy. On this trip he visited Genoa and Florence. Boccaccio was in Florence that winter, lecturing on Dante, and Petrarch was living in Padua, near Venice. There is no evidence that Chaucer met either, but it is hard to believe that one concerned with poetry would have missed the opportunity. Upon his return to England, he began immediately to show the influence of Dante and Boccaccio, and the Clerk (*CT* 4.27) says that he learned his tale from Petrarch in Padua. If Chaucer ever did meet either Boccaccio or Petrarch, it would have had to be at this time, because Petrarch died in 1374 and Boccaccio in 1375, before Chaucer's next trip to Italy in 1378.

Chaucer's extended absence in 1372–1373 involves a domestic situation that has troubled some scholars, notably Russell Krauss in *Three Chaucer Studies* (1932). One of the problems of Chaucer biography is his relation to Thomas Chaucer, one of the wealthiest men in England in the fifteenth century, whose daughter became Duchess of Suffolk, whose grandson married the sister of Edward IV, and whose great-grandson was declared heir apparent to Richard III, only to be killed in battle. Thomas Chaucer is referred to as the son of Geoffrey Chaucer in contemporary records, but his birth and early years are shrouded in mystery. After using the Chaucer coat of arms for a few years, he shifted to the de Roet arms of his mother. It has been suggested that the reason for his rapid advancement was that he was the illegitimate son of John of Gaunt by Philippa. From Gaunt's illegitimate children by Philippa's sister Katherine (legitimized by Gaunt's marriage to Katherine in 1396) were descended all of the English kings after Henry VI. If there is any truth in the conjecture that Philippa was also Gaunt's mistress—which is not unimportant in view of Chaucer's treatment of women in his writings and in view of the progress of his own career—it depends on the timing of events in 1373–1374.

When Chaucer departed for Italy in December 1372, Philippa was one of the demoiselles-in-waiting upon Gaunt's second wife, Constance of Castile, and Katherine (who that year bore Gaunt John Beaufort) was governess to his children by Blanche of Lancaster. Chaucer returned on May 23, 1373. On July 13 Gaunt went to lead a campaign in France. He returned to England in April 1374, and within two months Chaucer was made financially independent: on April 23 the king granted him a pitcher of wine daily (perhaps eighteen thousand dollars a year at present values); on May 10 he was given the house over Aldgate rent-free; on June 8 he was appointed controller of customs (another ten pounds—fifteen thousand dollars a year); and on June 13 he and Philippa together were granted another life annuity of ten pounds by John of Gaunt. All of this, together with previous grants and subsequent gifts and wardships, made Chaucer a prosperous man.

Philippa continued to receive gifts and payments from Gaunt, always in her own name, and the year before her death in 1387 she was admitted, again without her husband, to the fraternity of Lincoln Cathedral in a ceremony honoring the admission of Gaunt's oldest son, the future Henry

IV. Although her annuity was usually drawn at the hand of her husband, warrants transferring payments in 1378–1379 to receivers in Lincolnshire indicate that Philippa did not live with Chaucer over Aldgate the entire period after 1374, a circumstance that may throw light on the wry self-portrait in the *House of Fame* (ll.641–660). And while we are setting down these personal details, there is the curious business of the legal release granted in May 1380, by Cecily Champain to Geoffrey Chaucer for her "raptus." Despite arguments to the contrary, legal opinion holds that the word means what it says—that Chaucer had been sued for rape and had to seek legal quittance. Since the quittance came after the fact, this episode must have occurred around the time that Philippa was living in Lincolnshire. Skeat conjectured that "Litell Lowys," to whom the *Treatise on the Astrolabe* is addressed, might have been the consequence of this episode (*Astrolabe*, l. 27n).

Chaucer's earliest poetry is related to the household of John of Gaunt. Whether or not the *Prier a Nostre Dame* was written for Blanche of Lancaster, the *Book of the Duchess* was certainly composed as an elegy on her death in 1368. John Shirley asserted that the *Complaint of Mars* was likewise composed at the command of John of Gaunt. So both in documented fact and in undocumented tradition and surmise, Chaucer's literary and personal lives were entangled with the house of Lancaster.

But Chaucer's main career continued to be as esquire to the King. In 1376 and 1377, he was sent three times to France to negotiate for peace. This involved discussion of marriage between ten-year-old Richard (who succeeded his grandfather in 1377) and eleven-year-old Marie, daughter of the king of France, which appears to be satirized in the *Parliament of Fowls*. In 1378, he went again to Italy, leaving his power of attorney with his friends the poet John Gower and Richard Forester. This trip was to negotiate with Barnabo Visconti, ruler of Milan, whose fate is described in the *Monk's Tale* (*CT* 7.2399ff.). On these occasions, he was allowed to appoint a deputy in the office of controller.

In February 1385, Chaucer was given license to appoint a permanent deputy in his office. This represents another crux in his career. By October of that year he had been appointed a justice of the peace in Kent. In August 1386, he was elected a member of parliament from Kent. In October, the Aldgate residence was leased to Richard Forester.

That December, Adam Yardley replaced Chaucer as controller of customs. And in 1388, when the "Merciless Parliament" was investigating all of the grants made by Edward III and Richard II, he transferred his royal annuity to John Scalby. These events are all associated with the coup in the English government by which Thomas of Woodstock, youngest son of Edward III, replaced his brother John of Gaunt as the power behind the throne. All of the members of Richard's and Gaunt's households found themselves under suspicion. Richard's ineptitude, which was part of what led to this development, may be criticized in Alceste's speech to the god of love in the *Legend of Good Women* (ll.342ff.) and in *Lack of Steadfastnesse,* and Chaucer's own discouragement at the situation may be reflected in *Balade de Bon Conseil.* In any case, it may have been the prospect of freedom from administrative responsibility that led Chaucer to lay plans for an extensive work like *The Canterbury Tales.*

However, this period of comparative retirement did not last long. In 1389, Richard declared himself of age, dismissed Thomas of Woodstock from the Council, and took the rule into his own hands. Chaucer was immediately given the heaviest responsibilities of his career: clerkship of the king's works, overseeing the maintenance of Westminster Palace, the Tower of London, and many of the king's other castles, manors, and properties (such as the wool quay). In this capacity he supervised a large staff and handled great sums of money to pay for materials and labor. In connection with the large sums he had to carry about with him, Chaucer was robbed three times in four days in September 1390—at the "Fowle Ok" in Kent, at Hatcham in Surrey, and in Westminster. The beating and injuries mentioned in the inquest concerning these robberies may have been a factor in his giving up the clerkship the next June (1391). Meanwhile, he had been appointed subforester of Petherton Park, Somersetshire (1390). Probably this was a sinecure that allowed him to live near London, although he may have lived for a while in Somerset. Other than this, after his retirement from the clerkship of the king's works, Chaucer appears not to have held an official position.

In 1394, King Richard granted Chaucer a new annuity of twenty pounds, but he evidently had difficulty collecting the money due him. He was sued for debt; he transferred real estate; he borrowed money. Matters appeared to improve when the new king, Henry IV, doubled his annuity in an enrollment dated the day of his coronation, October 13, 1399. But this grant, too, had problems, since it was not actually made until February 1400, and backdated to October. In December 1399, Chaucer signed a fifty-three-year lease for a dwelling in Westminster Close. This may have been simply because he wanted to live in Westminster, but it has been pointed out that Westminster Abbey was a refuge for debtors, and his move there may have been connected with his financial exigency. (The question as to why he signed such a long lease in the last year of his life is explained by the conventions of English land tenure, where it is customary to buy the unexpired term of a long lease rather than to buy freehold.) A final record indicates that he received his last tun of wine on the royal grant before September 29, 1400. But he died before he could collect the money due him from Henry IV's annuity.

The date of Chaucer's death, inscribed on his sixteenth-century tomb in Westminster Abbey, is October 25, 1400. He was buried in the abbey because, as a resident of the close, he was a member of the parish. However, his burial there initiated the "Poets' Corner" in Westminster Abbey.

One gets the impression that Chaucer was most active as a writer when he was busiest as an administrator. Before 1374, he had translated all or part of the *Romaunt of the Rose* and written the *Book of the Duchess* and some other short poems. During his twelve years in the controller's office and in the midst of many trips abroad, he wrote *Parliament of Fowls, House of Fame, Boece, Troylus and Criseyde,* and *Palamon and Arcite* (the Knight's Tale). During his three years out of office he began *Legend of Good Women* and *The Canterbury Tales.* During the three years of the clerkship of the king's works, he no doubt continued work on *The Canterbury Tales* and began one, possibly two, astronomical treatises, *Astrolabe* and *Equatorie.* Except for the revision of the Prologue to *Legend of Good Women,* there is nothing except two "begging" balades that we can assign with assurance to the eight years of his retirement. His *Lenvoy a Scogan* implies that he may have felt his poetic gift was drying up. The *Complaint to His Purse* is a final plea to King Henry.

The "Chaucer Chronology" in the front endpapers of this edition summarize the important dates connected with Chaucer's life. Yet we go out pretty much as we came in. Little in the biographical records throws light on the personality of the poet or the meaning of the poems. Yet the charisma of the poems makes us endlessly curious about the nature of the man.

It is impossible to write a biography of Chaucer in the modern sense because the materials (manuscripts, letters, and observations by intimate contemporaries) are not available before the seventeenth century. Writing materials were too expensive; literacy was not sufficiently widespread. The best available biography is Derek Pearsall's *The Life of Geoffrey Chaucer* (1992, no. 182). Rich with beautiful illustrations of fourteenth-century life, Derek Brewer's *Chaucer and His World* (2d ed. 1992) has been reprinted as *The World of Chaucer* (2000, no. 167). Even more recent is the readable but extravagant set of surmises in *Who Murdered Chaucer? A Medieval Mystery,* by Terry Jones and others (2003, no. 178).

CHAUCER'S LANGUAGE AND VERSIFICATION

Chaucer's language is important, not only intrinsically as the language of a great poet, but also as an example of the language from which Modern Standard English developed. Chaucer did not create modern written English. That was evolved in the fifteenth century when the clerks in the English civil service—Chancery, as it was then called—switched government and parliamentary record keeping from French and Latin to English. Chaucer did his own writing as a civil servant in French and Latin. But the governing classes by his time were *speaking* English, even though they were still *writing* in French and Latin. So Chaucer took the brave step (which his friend John Gower did not, at first) of writing his poems for the entertainment of the court in the vernacular—the spoken language. Like Chancery Standard, when it developed in the next century, the language that Chaucer and his London companions developed for poetry used a vocabulary more than half French, with many French idioms and expressions (*man of law, playn eleccioun, parfay, entrechaunge*). The reason is that his literary models were French and he was writing for an audience still essentially bilingual.

The miracle is that the language of Chaucer's poetry is as close to the idiom of Modern English as it is. This is not true of his prose, or of fifteenth-century Chancery prose, even though the grammatical forms were quickly standardized. The greater facility of Chaucer's poetry illustrates what scholars have so often observed—that verse is the earliest mode of artistic expression in any language. It takes centuries to develop a lucid prose style, and this prose tradition must be passed from one generation to the next. When it ceases to be taught, it disappears, as Latin prose did after the fourth century and as Old English prose did after 1066.

Chaucer's spelling and pronunciation were more different from Modern English than his grammar and vocabulary because of two changes in pronunciation that affected the language between Chaucer's time and Shakespeare's: (1) long vowels all underwent what is called "the great vowel shift"; (2) inflectional endings weakened or disappeared. For convenience, the differences in pronunciation have been listed in the back endpapers of this edition. Here we discuss only the principles that underlie the changes.

1. In Chaucer's time, the difference between the vowels of *fat-fate, met-mete, bit-bite, god-good, but-about* was length, not quality. In the century following Chaucer, length ceased to have phonemic value in English, and the long vowels all shifted in quality, as indicated in the diagram on the following page. Spelling began to be standardized before this shift in sound was completed. This means that the spelling of the shifted vowels in Modern English is different from the spelling of equivalent sounds in other languages using the Latin alphabet: English *ice*—French *ici*, English *demon*—French *démon*. Hence, the generalization is that the long vowels of Middle English should be pronounced as the same spellings would be in Latin or any modern European language.

2. A second process that has gone on throughout the history of English is contraction of the sort that has led to the reduction of Old English *hlaford* to *lord* and is today leading to the reduction of *probably* to *probly*. Since spelling in the fourteenth century was still largely phonetic, the generalization is that there are no silent letters or syllables in Chaucer's English. The most widespread difference this makes in the pronunciation of Chaucer's English is that the inflectional endings *es* and *ed*, which have now been contracted, were then pronounced as separate syllables: *walkes, walked, stones.* Thus, there were many fewer monosyllabic words in Chaucer's English, which has important implications for rhythm and meter.

Consonants that have since become silent—*gnaw, folk*—were then pronounced. The spelling *gh* (then often spelled *h*) still had the palatal sound it has in Scots and German: *night* (*niht*), *bought* (*bohte*). When this sound occurred finally, it was already changing to *w,* as indicated by spellings like *bow* and *ynowe* (enough).

Also, most important, the many French words being introduced into English in Chaucer's time kept their French accent; *licóur, coráge.*

Pronunciation of all letters, Latinate vowels, al-

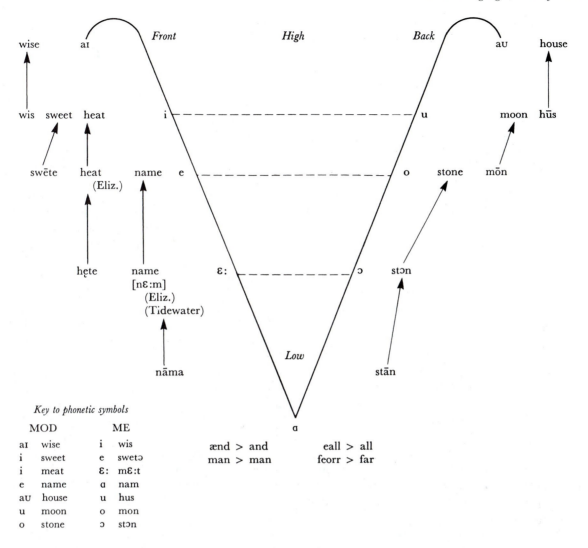

Key to phonetic symbols

MOD		ME	
aɪ	wise	i	wis
i	sweet	e	swetǝ
i	meat	ɛː	mɛːt
e	name	ɑ	nam
aʊ	house	u	hus
u	moon	o	mon
o	stone	ɔ	stɔn

ænd > and
man > man

eall > all
feorr > far

ternation of French and English accent, and pronunciation of palatals that have since become vocalized or become silent all mean that Chaucer's poetry has to be read more slowly than modern poetry. If it is hurried over, it loses its music. The fact that the differences in Chaucer's pronunciation were not understood in the seventeenth century resulted in his then being considered a rough and crude prosodist, although his "matter" was thought delightful. Most of the principles of his exquisite assonance and rhythm were rediscovered by Tyrwhitt and nineteenth-century philologists.

Chaucer's most important contribution to English poetry is the iambic pentameter line, for which he had no model in English. Most poetry after the Norman Conquest was either in relaxed alliterative verse or in tetrameter couplets mod-

eled on the French and Latin octosyllabics. The four-stress line in couplets or quatrains was the favorite form in English poetry from the *Owl and the Nightingale* to the *Pearl* and Gower's *Confessio Amantis.* Chaucer used it for three of his early poems, the *Romaunt of the Rose* (whatever part of it may be by him), *Book of the Duchess,* and *House of Fame.* Then he turned to the more sophisticated pentameter line. His models for this have frequently been debated. Since he evidently began to use it only after his trip to Italy, and since more than half his lines have feminine endings (thanks to the final *e*), there appears to have been an influence of the hendecasyllabic (eleven syllables), which Dante called the "most famous" line of the Italian poets. On the other hand, the decasyllabic was a line frequently employed in the

French poems that served Chaucer as his earliest models. Chaucer's task was to adapt this Continental syllable-counting meter to English stressed rhythm.

Both the French and Italian lines employed the movable caesura, and the movable caesura is a feature of Chaucer's line. However, in native English alliterative verse he found a fixed caesura with two strong stresses and a varying number of weak stresses in each half line. This has led to the assertion by some critics that Chaucer's rhythm—as distinguished from his meter—was really four-beat, two on each side of the caesura, superimposed on a more or less decasyllabic line (since a good many lines run to eleven syllables, and some have only nine). This scansion works well for the opening lines of the *Canterbury Tales: Whán thăt Ápríll / wĭth hĭs shóurĕs sóotĕ // Thĕ dróghtĕ˘ of Márch / haĭth pércĕd tŏ thĕ róotĕ*. Most authorities, however, hold that Chaucer regularly used five stresses in a line: *Whán thăt Ápríll / wĭth hĭs shóurĕs sóotĕ // Thĕ dróghtĕ˘ of Márch / haĭth pércĕd tó thĕ róotĕ*. The different levels of stress that were developing in Middle English made it possible for some stresses to be pronounced more heavily than others, so that while the line employed five stresses from a metrical point of view, the audience heard only the four maximal stresses. The chief mark of Chaucer's facility as a prosodist is the "naturalness" of his verse. The metrical stresses fall on the lexical stresses and reinforce the rhetorical emphasis without strain or distortion. When there are inversions either of stress or syntax, they are pleasurable instead of distracting. This is what is meant by "Chaucer's good ear." Keats said, "if poetry comes not as naturally as the leaves on a tree it had better not come at all." Even though Chaucer had no models for the English iambic pentameter, no subsequent poet has used it with more ease and expressiveness than he. For commentary and discussion, see nos. 145–63 in the Bibliography.

Chaucer's grammatical forms and syntax offer less trouble than his pronunciation and prosody. It is sufficient for us here to call attention to the *differences* between Chaucer's grammar and ours.

Nouns. In the case of the noun, Old English dative *e* was preserved in some prepositional phrases: *to groundĕ, in londĕ*. Some words have an uninflected genitive singular form from OE *e: sonne, fader, lady* (*his lady grace*). There are more plurals in *en* or *n* than in Modern English: *ashen, bosen, doghtren, foon*. Although plurals are usually syllabic *es*, in polysyllabic French words they are sometimes contracted to *s: barouns, conclusions;* when the word ends in *t*, this is sometimes represented by *z: advocatz, servantz*.

Nouns appear frequently in apposition to their governing words: *a barrel ale, a manner Latyn corrupt*. The partitive is expressed by *of: Of smale houndes hadde she, Of remedies of love she knew*. Nouns with the possessive ending *es* can be used as modifiers: *lyves creature* (living creature), *shames deth* (shameful death), *I shal nedes have* (I must needs have), *his / hir thankes* (thankfully, willingly). Double possessives continue to be divided as in Old English: *the Seintes Legende of Cupide* (the legend of the saints of Cupid), *the Kyng Priamus sone of Troye* (the son of King Priam of Troy).

Citations for and more examples of these and the following forms can be found by looking up the key words in Larry Benson, *Glossarial Concordance* (1993, no. 65).

Pronouns. The first-person pronoun is usually *I;* southern *ich* is used for emphasis and with contractions, *theech* (*thee ich*, may I prosper); northern *ik* is used in the Reeve's Tale. The second person singular is regularly *thou, thyn, thee*. Plural forms *ye, your, you* were already beginning to be used for the singular, generally reflecting formality or respect (e.g., in the *Clerk's Tale, CT* 4.306–50, Walter addresses Janicula with the singular; Janicula addresses Walter with the plural; and Walter addresses Griselda with the plural. Gentles usually address each other with the plural, like the lovers in *Franklin's Tale* and *Troylus,* but common folk use the singular, as in the *Miller's* and *Reeve's Tales;* Pandarus generally uses singular *thou* forms but addresses Criseyde with the plural *ye* forms as they approach Troylus's bedchamber, *TC* 2. 1716ff. Such distinctions provide nuances not available in Modern English.) Interrogative *thou* is often elided, *artow, thynkestow*.

The neuter singular was usually *it*, but the possessive continued to be Old English *his*, which should not be mistaken for personification (as in line 1 of *CT*). The feminine singular forms are *she* and *hir(e) / her(e)*, and the third-person plural forms, *they, hir(e) / her(e), hem*. There is confusion between feminine singular *her(e)* (her), plural *her(e)* (their), adverb *her* (here), and verb *her / heren* (to hear). In particular, plural *her* (their) should not be mistaken for singular *her* (her). With or without a final *e*, pronouns are always monosyllabic.

Plural of the demonstrative pronoun *that* is *tho*. *This*, often with a final *e*, *thise*, is either singular or plural. *Thilke* (*that ilke*, the same) is likewise either singular or plural. Both *that* and *the* are often elided, *th'estate*, *the tother*.

The relative pronoun may be omitted as a subject: *With hym ther was dwellynge a poure scoler, / **Had** lerned art*. Relative *that* is used as a collocation with pronouns and adverbs: *whom that* (but never *who that*), *if that*, *whan that*; it should not be mistaken for a demonstrative (as in line 1 of *CT*). Indefinite *man* is frequently used instead of the passive: *she wept if men smoot it*. The "ethical dative" or "dative of advantage" cannot be translated into Modern English: *To seken **hym** a chauntrie, And to the hors he goth **hym** faire*. The reflexive pronoun is usually the same as the personal: *To be my wyf and reule **hire** after me*; the *self* forms are usually intensive: *Ther walketh now the lymytour **hymself**.*

Adjectives. Adjectives that do not already end in *e* frequently take *e* when modifying plural nouns and in "weak" positions, i.e., following articles, demonstratives, or prepositions, or with vocatives: *a fair prelat / yven fair**e** wyves, a young Squier / the yong**e** sonne, an hard thyng / with hard**e** grace, ye be lief / soothly, lev**e** brother.*

Comparison of adjectives is generally the same as in Modern English except that the Old English mutated vowels of the comparative and superlative are sometimes preserved: *old / elder / eldest, long / lenger / lengest, strong / strenger / strengest*. The French-influenced *more-most* comparison was usually used with polysyllabic French words: *Moore delicaat, moore pompous / moost honourable.*

Adverbs. Adverbs are formed by adding *ly* or *liche*, but also by adding *e* unless the adjective already ends in *e*: *a clene sheepe / caste him clene out of his lady grace, a lyght gypoun / knokkeden ful light**e***. The *s* forms of the adverb occur more frequently than in Modern English: *whiles, eftson**es**, unneth**es**, as do the *en* forms, *about**en**, abov**en**, bifor**n***. *Very* is never used as an intensive adverb, but always as an adjective: *He was a verray, parfit, gentil knyght*. The intensive is expressed by special idioms like *for the maistrie, for the nones*. *Ther* and *ther-as* may be used as relatives: *for over al **ther** he com. As* is sometimes omitted from comparisons: *His nekke [as] whit was*

as; and omitted when correlative with *so*: *Ne was so worldly* [as] *for to have office.*

Prepositions. Prepositions may follow the words they govern: *seyde his maister to, rood hym agayns*, but seldom come at the end of the clause: *That men of yelpe, to shorte with oure weye*. An exception is the preposition *in*, which can occur at the end spelled *inne: Hire to delivere of wo that she was inne; Doun into helle, where he yet is inne.*

Verbs. The inflections of verbs are second-person (with *thou*) *est* (*st*), and third-person *eth* (*th*), usually spelled with thorn; *eth* is variously contracted, *rit* (*rideth*), *worth* (*wortheth*), *halt* (*holdeth*). Very occasionally (*BD* 73, 257, *HF* 426, as confirmed by the rhymes) we find northern third-person *es*, which also marks the dialect of the students in the Reeve's Tale.

The mark of the infinitive and the plural indicative and subjunctive is frequently, but not always, *en: they mak**en**, they slep**en**, He leet the feeste of his nativitee / Doon cry**en**.* A favorite contraction of *haven* is *han.*

The principle parts of the verbs were much as they are in Modern English, but in Chaucer's English there were more strong verbs (verbs that show tense by change of vowel): *delve / dolf / dolven, crepe / crop / cropen, shouve / shoof / shoven*. The past participles of strong verbs normally end in *en*, but the *n* is often dropped, *founden/ founde*. The preterite of *hoten, highte* has the passive sense "to be named / called." Past participles of both strong and weak verbs may take the prefix *y /i: ydon / I-yeven.*

The impersonal *it* of Modern English is often lacking: [it] *Bifil that in that seson*, and especially in idioms like *me thynketh* (it seems to me), *me liketh* (it pleases me), *hire lyste nat* (it did not please her).

One of the chief reasons for the different flavor of Chaucer's language is the scarcity of progressive forms, whose sense is expressed by simple verbs: *Ye goon* [are going] *to Canterbury, fowles maken* [were making] *melodye*. The auxiliary verb for the perfect tenses is usually a form of *be* rather than of *have: At nyght were* [had] *come into that hostelrye, That from the tyme of Kyng William were* [had] *yfalle*. Auxiliaries that have fallen out of use are *gan* (began), *what that the day gan sprynge, this noble duc gan ryde*, and *doon* (cause to be done), *he dide doon sleen hem* (he had them killed), *If that ye done us bothe dyen* (if you cause us both to die).

Infinitives frequently lack *to*. *Come soupen* and *if*

*yow liketh know**en*** are marked by *en,* but *hym liste ride* and *Bidde hym descende* are unmarked, like the infinitives in Modern English subjunctives (I shall go, I would go). The subjunctive is used more frequently than in Modern English: for condition, *if she telle it;* for wishes, *God yelde yow* (may God reward you); for hypotheses, *I trowe he were a geldyng;* for concessions, *Al were he short.*

Negation. The usual sign of negation is *ne* before the verb, *ne wolde,* frequently elided with the verb, *nolde, nas, nath.* This may be reinforced by a following *nat / nought, it ne seme naught,* which can be reduced by omitting *ne, it availeth noght.* But the more negatives loaded into a clause, the more

negative it is: *He nevere yet no vileyne ne sayde / In al his lyf unto no maner wight.*

Syntax. The conversational tone of Chaucer's writing is the result of less formal parallelism and subordination than we find in Modern written English. Among the syntax of oral language, we find Chaucer using **ellipsis:** *And* [we] *made forward erly for to ryse, And by his covenant* [he] *yaf rekenynge;* **parataxis:** *An horn he bar, the bawdryk was of grene; Bad nat every wight he sholde go selle;* **anacoluthon** (shift in grammar): *The reule of Seint Maure or Seint Beneit, / By cause that it was old and somdel streit, / This ilke Monk leet olde thynges pace.*

THE TEXT OF THIS EDITION

The text of *The Canterbury Tales* is a lightly corrected version of the one first published in *The Complete Poetry and Prose of Geoffrey Chaucer,* edited by John H. Fisher (1977).

Emendations to Fisher's text are limited to

1. corrections to accord with the base text, as follows:

   KnT 1.1323: "to" for "do"
   MLT 2.34: "Telle us a" for "Telle us as"
   SumT 3.1736: "wolde" for "wholde"
   Mel 7.1146: "therfore" for "therefore"
   ParsT 10.755: "Genesis, 9" for "Genesis, 5"
   ParsT 10.863: "fyngres" for "syngres"

2. adjustments in punctuation and rubrics for clarity, as follows:

   RvT 1.4129: dash added at end of line
   MLT 2.107: endline semicolon replaced comma
   MLT 2.471: midline question mark added, followed by capital letter
   MLT 2.706: colon added at end of line
   MLT 2.732: closing quotation marks added at end of line
   SumT 3.2217: endline comma changed to colon
   SumT 3.2218: quotation marks deleted
   SumT 3.2228: quotation marks added
   CIT 4.7: quotation marks deleted
   CIT 4.283: midline comma changed to semicolon
   Thop 7.833: rubric added: "[The Second Fit]"
   Thop 7.891: rubric changed: "[The Third Fit]" for "[The Second Fit]"
   Mel 7.1851: endline comma changed to semicolon
   CYT 8.1345: endline period changed to comma

No holograph of *The Canterbury Tales* survives. Our text is based upon the Ellesmere manuscript in the Huntington Library in San Marino, California (EL 26.C.9). The Ellesmere scribe has been identified by Linne Mooney as Adam Pinkhurst, who also produced during his long career the Hengwrt manuscript in the National Library of Wales (Peniarth 392D). Pinkhurst produced the Hengwrt before the Ellesmere, both before 1410, and it is possible that he completed the Hengwrt before Chaucer's death in 1400. The Ellesmere and Hengwrt are the earliest and two of the very best texts of *The Canterbury Tales.* Because the Ellesmere was produced as a single work, its text is more regular in dialect and spelling than that of Hengwrt, and it is more complete. The Ellesmere order of the tales is what most scholars today accept as the closest to Chaucer's intention.

Where the Ellesmere and the Hengwrt agree, the reading is usually taken as authoritative. Where they disagree, context and the evidence of other manuscripts help determine the reading. Because Fisher's textual notes are not exhaustive, I have further reduced them to examples that students may find instructive and instances where Fisher's emendations require explanation.

BIBLIOGRAPHY

Below is a selection of the works that pertain to Chaucer and *The Canterbury Tales*. It includes all works cited in this volume and works useful for exploring specific topics. It emphasizes studies written in English, materials that are generally available in university libraries, and discussions that reflect developments in Chaucer studies from 1900 forward, especially since 1975. Omitted are dissertations, collections of essays (except in several instances of particular focus and utility), and works of fewer than five pages. Selected essays in collections are listed individually, and the editors of the collections are not included in the Index of Authors. For a comprehensive bibliography, see nos. 1 and 51–57.

In the interest of saving space, individual entries are sometimes given in truncated form: subtitles of books are included when necessary for clarity or ease of location; multiple authors and editors are reduced to the lead name when other names are unnecessary to locate the work in libraries or online resources; titles of book series are generally not included. The cross listing at the end of the sections is intended to be helpful rather than exhaustive.

Electronic Resources

1. *Chaucer Bibliography Online.* <http://uchaucer.utsa.edu>. Annotated bibliography of Chaucer studies from 1975 to present.
2. *Chaucer Metapage.* <http://www.unc.edu/depts/chaucer/>. The monitored hub of Chaucer sites on the World Wide Web (WWW).
3. *The Canterbury Tales Project.* <http://www.cta.dmu.ac.uk/projects/ctp/>. Transcription and analysis of the manuscripts of *The Canterbury Tales*. See also *The* Canterbury Tales *Project Occasional Papers. Vols. I and II.* Ed. Norman Blake and Peter Robinson. Oxford: Office for Humanities Communication, 1993 and 1997.

Facsimiles — Complete Manuscripts, Including Diplomatic Transcriptions

4. *Cambridge Library, MS Gg.4.27: A Facsimile.* Introduction by Malcolm Parkes and Richard Beadle. 3 vols. Norman, OK: Pilgrim, 1980.
5. *The Canterbury Tales: A Facsimile and Transcription of the Hengwrt Manuscript, with Variants from the Ellesmere Manuscript.* Introduction by Donald C. Baker, A. I. Doyle, and M. B. Parkes. Norman: U of Oklahoma P, 1979.
6. *The Canterbury Tales by Geoffrey Chaucer: The New Ellesmere Chaucer Facsimile* (of Huntington Library MS EL 26 C 9). Ed. Daniel Woodward and Martin Stevens. San Marino, CA: Huntington Library; Tokyo: Yushodo, 1995. Monochromatic ed., 1997.
7. *Caxton's Canterbury Tales: The British Library Copies.* Ed. Barbara Bordalejo. Leicester: Scholarly Digital Editions, 2003.
8. *The Ellesmere Chaucer.* Reproduced in facsimile. 2 vols. Manchester: Manchester UP, 1911.
9. *The Ellesmere Manuscript of Chaucer's Canterbury Tales: A Working Facsimile.* Introduction by Ralph Hanna III. Rochester, NY: Boydell & Brewer, 1989.
10. *The Hengwrt Chaucer: Digital Facsimile.* Ed. Estelle Stubbs. Leicester: Scholarly Digital Editions, 2000.
11. *Magdalene College, Cambridge, MS Pepys 2006: A Facsimile.* Introduction by A. S. G. Edwards. Norman, OK: Pilgrim, 1986.
12. *A Six-Text Print of the Canterbury Tales.* Ellesmere, Hengwrt, Cambridge Gg.4.27, Petworth, Corpus, Lansdowne 851. London: Chaucer Society, first ser., nos. 1, 14–15, 25, 30–31, 37, 49, 1869–77.

Facsimiles — Individual Canterbury Tales

13. *The General Prologue on CD-ROM.* Ed. Elizabeth Solopova. Cambridge: Cambridge UP, 2000.
14. *The Miller's Tale on CD-ROM.* Ed. Peter Robinson. Cambridge: Cambridge UP, 2004.
15. *The Wife of Bath's Prologue on CD-ROM.* Ed. Peter Robinson. Cambridge: Cambridge UP, 1996.

Manuscripts and Textual Studies

16. Blake, N. F. "Geoffrey Chaucer and the Manuscripts of *The Canterbury Tales*." *JEBS* 1 (1997): 96–122.
17. Doyle, A. I., and M. B. Parkes. "The Production of Copies of the *Canterbury Tales* and the *Confessio Amantis* in the Early Fifteenth Century." In *Essays Presented to N. R. Ker,* edited by M. B. Parkes and A. G. Watson. London: Scolar, 1979.
18. Fredell, Joel. "The Lowly Paraf: Transmitting Manuscript Design in *The Canterbury Tales*." *SAC* 22 (2000): 213–80.
19. Hanna, Ralph. "The Hengwrt Manuscript and the Canon of *The Canterbury Tales*." *English Manuscript Studies, 1100–1700* 1 (1989): 64–84.
20. Horobin, S. C. P. "The 'Hooked G' Scribe and His Work on Three Manuscripts of the *Canterbury Tales*." *NM* 99 (1998): 411–17.

21. Horobin, Simon, and Linne R. Mooney. "A *Piers Plowman* Manuscript by the Hengwrt/Ellesmere Scribe and Its Implications for London Standard English." *SAC* 26 (2004): 65–112.

22. Lerer, Seth. "Medieval English Literature and the Idea of an Anthology." *PMLA* 118 (2003): 1251–67.

23. Mosser, Daniel W. "Reading and Editing the *Canterbury Tales:* Past, Present, and Future?" *Text* 7 (1994): 201–32.

24. Owen, Charles A., Jr. *The Statistical Determination of Affiliation in the Landmark Manuscripts of The Canterbury Tales.* Lewiston, NY: Mellen, 1993.

25. Partridge, Stephen. "Minding the Gaps: Interpreting the Manuscript Evidence of the Cook's Tale and the Squire's Tale." In *The English Medieval Book: Studies in Memory of Jeremy Griffiths,* edited by A. S. G. Edwards and others. London: British Library, 2000. 51–87.

26. Ramsey, Roy Vance. "The Hengwrt and Ellesmere Manuscripts of the *Canterbury Tales:* Different Scribes." *SB* 35 (1982): 133–54.

27. ———. "Paleography and Scribes of Shared Training." *SAC* 8 (1986): 107–44.

28. Samuels, M. L. "The Scribe of the Hengwrt and Ellesmere Manuscripts of the *Canterbury Tales.*" *SAC* 5 (1983): 49–55.

29. Seymour, M. C. *A Catalogue of Chaucer Manuscripts: Volume II, The Canterbury Tales.* Aldershot, UK: Scolar, 1997.

30. Stevens, Martin, and Daniel Woodward, eds. *The Ellesmere Chaucer: Essays in Interpretation.* San Marino, CA: Huntington Library; Tokyo: Yushodo, 1995.

See also nos. 157, 339, 848, 975–76, 998, 1314, 1440.

Editions — Complete

31. Benson, Larry D., gen. ed. *The Riverside Chaucer.* 3d ed. Boston: Houghton Mifflin, 1987.

32. Fisher, John H., ed. *The Complete Poetry and Prose of Geoffrey Chaucer.* 2d ed. Fort Worth, TX: Holt, Rinehart & Winston, 1989.

33. Ruggiers, Paul, ed. *Editing Chaucer: The Great Tradition.* Norman, OK: Pilgrim, 1984.

34. Skeat, Walter W., ed. *The Complete Works of Geoffrey Chaucer, Edited from Numerous Manuscripts.* 7 vols. Oxford: Clarendon, 1894–97.

Editions — *The Canterbury Tales* and Individual Tales

34a. Benson, Larry D. *The Canterbury Tales: Complete.* Boston: Houghton Mifflin, 2000.

35. Blake, N. F. *The Canterbury Tales by Geoffrey Chaucer, Edited from the Hengwrt Manuscript.* London: Arnold, 1980.

36. Donaldson, E. T., ed. *Chaucer's Poetry: An Anthology for the Modern Reader.* New York: Ronald, 1975.

37. Manly, John M., and Edith Rickert, eds. *The Text of the Canterbury Tales, Studied on the Basis of All Known Manuscripts.* 8 vols. Chicago: U of Chicago P, 1940.

38. *The General Prologue.* Ed. Malcolm Andrew, Daniel J. Ransom, Lynne Hunt Levy, and others. Variorum Chaucer, Vol. 2, Parts 1A and 1B. Norman: U of Oklahoma P, 1993.

39. *The Miller's Tale.* Ed. Thomas W. Ross. Variorum Chaucer, Vol. 2, Part 3. Norman: U of Oklahoma P, 1983.

40. *The Summoner's Tale.* Ed. John F. Plummer III. Variorum Chaucer, Vol. 2, Part 7. Norman: U of Oklahoma P, 1995.

41. *The Nun's Priest's Tale.* Ed. Derek Pearsall. Variorum Chaucer, Vol. 2, Part 9. Norman: U of Oklahoma P, 1984.

42. *The Manciple's Tale.* Ed. Donald C. Baker. Variorum Chaucer, Vol. 2, Part 10. Norman: U of Oklahoma P, 1984.

43. *The Squire's Tale.* Ed. Donald C. Baker. Variorum Chaucer, Vol. 2, Part 12. Norman: U of Oklahoma P, 1990.

44. *The Physician's Tale.* Ed. Helen Storm Corsa. Variorum Chaucer, Vol. 2, Part 17. Norman: U of Oklahoma P, 1987.

45. *The Prioress's Tale.* Ed. Beverly Boyd. Variorum Chaucer, Vol. 2, Part 20. Norman: U of Oklahoma P, 1987.

See also nos. 7, 13–15.

English Translations

46. Beidler, Peter G. "Chaucer and the Trots: What to Do about Those Modern English Translations." *ChauR* 19 (1985): 290–301.

47. Coghill, Nevill, trans. *The Canterbury Tales.* Harmondsworth, UK: Penguin, 1951. (verse)

48. Ecker, Ronald L., and Eugene J. Crook, trans. *The Canterbury Tales by Geoffrey Chaucer.* Palatka, FL: Hodges & Braddock, 1993. (verse)

49. Goldbeck, Janne. "The Absent Father: Translating Chaucer's *Canterbury Tales.*" *Rendezvous* 32.1 (1997): 87–93.

50. Wright, David, trans. *The Canterbury Tales.* New York: Random House, 1965. (prose)

Bibliographies — Comprehensive

51. *Studies in the Age of Chaucer.* Annual annotated bibliography, 1979—.

52. Bowers, Bege K., and Mark Allen, eds. *Annotated Chaucer Bibliography, 1986–1996.* Notre Dame, IN: U of Notre Dame P, 2002.

53. Baird-Lange, Lorrayne Y., and Hildegard Schnuttgen. *A Bibliography of Chaucer, 1974–1985.* Hamden, CT: Archon, 1988.

54. Baird, Lorrayne Y. *A Bibliography of Chaucer, 1964–1973.* Boston, MA: Hall, 1977.

55. Crawford, William R. *Bibliography of Chaucer, 1954–63.* Seattle: U of Washington P, 1967.

56. Griffith, Dudley David. *Bibliography of Chaucer, 1908–1953.* Seattle: U of Washington P, 1955.

57. Hammond, Eleanor Prescott. *Chaucer: A Bibliographical Manual*. 1908. Reprint, New York: Peter Smith, 1933.

See also no. 1.

Bibliographies — Selected

58. Allen, Mark, and John H. Fisher. *The Essential Chaucer: An Annotated Bibliography of Major Modern Studies*. Boston: Hall; London: Mansell, 1987. <http://colfa.utsa.edu/chaucer>.
59. Leyerle, John, and Anne Quick. *Chaucer: A Bibliographical Introduction*. Toronto: U of Toronto P, 1986.

Bibliographies — Individual Canterbury Tales

60. *Chaucer's "General Prologue" to the "Canterbury Tales." An Annotated Bibliography, 1900–1984*. Caroline D. Eckhardt. Toronto: U of Toronto P, 1990.
61. *Chaucer's "Knight's Tale." An Annotated Bibliography, 1900–1985*. Monica McAlpine. Toronto: U of Toronto P, 1991.
62. *Chaucer's Miller's, Reeve's, and Cook's Tales [An Annotated Bibliography: 1900–1992]*. Ed. T. L. Burton and Rosemary Greentree. Toronto: U of Toronto P, 1997.
63. *Chaucer's "Wife of Bath's Prologue" and "Tale." An Annotated Bibliography, 1900 to 1995*. Ed. Peter G. Beidler and Elizabeth M. Biebel. Toronto: U of Toronto P, 1998.
64. *Chaucer's "Pardoner's Prologue" and "Tale." An Annotated Bibliography, 1900–1995*. Marilyn Sutton. Toronto: U of Toronto P, 2000.

Dictionaries and Reference

65. Benson, Larry D. *A Glossarial Concordance to the Riverside Chaucer*. 2 vols. Hamden, CT: Garland, 1993.
66. Besserman, Lawrence. *Chaucer and the Bible: A Critical Review of Research, Indices, and Bibliography*. New York: Garland, 1988.
67. Davis, Norman, Douglas Gray, Patricia Ingham, and Anne Wallace-Hadrill. *A Chaucer Glossary*. Oxford: Clarendon, 1979.
68. De Weever, Jacqueline. *Chaucer Name Dictionary: A Guide to Astrological, Biblical, Historical, Literary, and Mythological Names in the Works of Geoffrey Chaucer*. New York: Garland, 1988.
69. Dillon, Bert. *A Chaucer Dictionary: Proper Names and Allusions, Excluding Place Names*. Boston: Hall, 1974.
70. Foster, Edward E., and David H. Carey. *Chaucer's Church: A Dictionary of Religious Terms in Chaucer*. Brookfield, VT: Ashgate, 2002.
71. Kurath, Hans, Sherman M. Kuhn, Robert E. Lewis, and others, eds. *The Middle English Dictionary*. Multiple vols. Ann Arbor: U of Michigan P, 1952–2001.
72. Magoun, Francis P., Jr. *A Chaucer Gazetteer*. Chicago: U of Chicago P; Stockholm: Almqvist & Wiksell, 1961.

73. Masui, Michio, ed. *A New Rime Index to The Canterbury Tales Based on Manly and Rickert's Text of the Canterbury Tales*. Tokyo: Shinozaki Shorin, 1988.
74. Oizumi, Akio. Programmed by Kunihiro Miki. *A Complete Concordance to the Works of Chaucer*. 12 vols. New York: Olms-Weidmann, 1991–94.
75. Rossignol, Rosalyn. *Chaucer: A to Z. The Essential Reference to His Life and Works*. New York: Facts on File, 1999.
76. Scott, Arthur F. *Who's Who in Chaucer*. London: Elm Tree, 1974.

Handbooks and Introductions

77. Ashton, Gail. *Chaucer: The Canterbury Tales*. New York: St. Martin's, 1998.
78. Boitani, Piero, and Jill Mann, eds. *The Cambridge Companion to Chaucer*. 2d ed. Cambridge: Cambridge UP, 2003.
79. Bourgne, Florence. *The Canterbury Tales. Geoffrey Chaucer*. Paris: Armand Colin/CNED, 2003.
80. Brown, Peter. *Chaucer at Work: The Making of the Canterbury Tales*. New York: Longman, 1994.
81. ———, ed. *A Companion to Chaucer*. Oxford: Blackwell, 2000.
82. Cooper, Helen. *The Canterbury Tales*. Oxford Guides to Chaucer. 2d ed. Oxford: Oxford UP, 1996.
83. Ellis, Steve, ed. *Chaucer: An Oxford Guide*. New York: Oxford UP, 2005.
84. Gray, Douglas, ed. *The Oxford Companion to Chaucer*. Oxford: Oxford UP, 2003.
85. Hallissy, Margaret. *A Companion to Chaucer's Canterbury Tales*. Westport, CT: Greenwood, 1995.
86. Hirsh, John C. *Chaucer and the Canterbury Tales: A Short Introduction*. Oxford: Blackwell, 2003.
87. Pearsall, Derek. *The Canterbury Tales*. Unwin Critical Library. London: Allen & Unwin, 1985.
88. Phillips, Helen. *An Introduction to the Canterbury Tales: Reading, Fiction, Context*. New York: St. Martin's, 2000.
89. Pope, Rob. *How to Study Chaucer*. 2d ed. New York: St. Martin's, 2001.
90. Rowland, Beryl, ed. *Companion to Chaucer Studies*. Rev. ed. New York: Oxford UP, 1979.
91. Wetherbee, Winthrop. *Geoffrey Chaucer: The Canterbury Tales*. 1989. Rev. Cambridge: Cambridge UP, 2004.

Language — General

92. Burnley, [John] David. "French and Frenches in Fourteenth-Century London." In *Language Contact in the History of English*, edited by Dieter Kastovsky and Arthur Mettinger. Frankfurt am Main: Lang, 2001. 17–34.
93. ———. *A Guide to Chaucer's Language*. Norman: U of Oklahoma P, 1983.
94. Davis, Norman. "Chaucer and Fifteenth-Century English." In *Geoffrey Chaucer*, edited by D. S. Brewer, Writers and Their Background. London: Bell, 1974. 58–84.

95. Eliason, Norman. *The Language of Chaucer's Poetry: An Appraisal of the Verse, Style, and Structure.* Anglistica 17. Copenhagen: Rosenkilde, 1972.

96. Elliott, R. W. V. *Chaucer's English.* London: Deutsch, 1974.

97. Furrow, Melissa. "Latin and Affect." In *The Endless Knot: Essays on Old and Middle English in Honor of Marie Borroff,* edited by M. Teresa Tavormina and R. F. Yeager. Cambridge, UK: Brewer, 1995. 29–41.

98. Greenwood, Maria. "What He Heard and What He Saw: Part Tenses and Characterization in Chaucer's 'General Prologue.'" In *L'Articulation langue-littérature dans les textes médiévaux anglais, II. Actes du colloque des 25 et 26 juin 1999 á l'Université de Nancy II,* edited by Colette Stévanovitch. Nancy: Publications de l'Association des Médiévistes Anglicistes de l'Enseignement Supérieur, 1999. 143–62.

99. Higuchi, Masayuki. *Studies in Chaucer's English.* Tokyo: Eichosha, 1996.

100. Horobin, Simon. *The Language of the Chaucer Tradition.* Cambridge, UK: Brewer, 2003.

101. Kerkhof, Jelle. *Studies in the Language of Geoffrey Chaucer.* 2d ed. Leiden: Leiden UP, 1982.

102. Kökeritz, Helge. *A Guide to Chaucer's Pronunciation.* 1954. Reprint, Toronto: U of Toronto P, 1978.

103. Potter, Russell A. "Chaucer and the Authority of Language: The Politics and Poetics of the Vernacular in Late Medieval England." *Assays* 6 (1991): 73–91.

104. Roscow, Gregory. *Syntax and Style in Chaucer's Poetry.* Cambridge, UK: Brewer, 1981.

105. Sandved, Arthur O. *Introduction to Chaucerian English.* Woodbridge, Suffolk, UK: Brewer, 1985.

106. Sauer, Walter. *Die Aussprache des Chaucer-Englischen: Ein Übungsbuch auf der Grundlage des Prologs der Canterbury Tales.* Heidelberg: Winter, 1998.

Language — Lexicon and Dialect

107. Baum, Paull F. "Chaucer's Puns." *PMLA* 71 (1956): 225–46. "Chaucer's Puns: A Supplementary List." *PMLA* 73 (1958): 167–70.

108. Benson, Larry D. "The 'Queynte' Punnings of Chaucer's Critics." *SAC Proceedings* 1 (1985): 3–50.

109. Blake, N. F. "Aspects of Syntax and Lexis in the *Canterbury Tales.*" *RCEI* 7 (1983): 1–20.

110. Brosnahan, Leger. "'And don thyn hood' and Other Hoods in Chaucer." *ChauR* 21 (1986): 45–52.

111. Burnley, J. D. *Chaucer's Language and the Philosopher's Tradition.* Cambridge, UK: Brewer, 1979.

112. Cannon, Christopher. *The Making of Chaucer's English: A Study of Words.* Cambridge: Cambridge UP, 1998.

113. DeWeever, Jacqueline. "Chaucerian Onomastics: The Formation of Personal Names in Chaucer's Works." *Names* 28 (1980): 1–31.

114. Dor, Juliette De Calewé. "Chaucer's Derivational Morphemes Revisited." In *Linguistic and Stylistic Studies in Medieval English,* edited by André Crépin. Paris: Publications de l'Association des Médiévistes Anglicistes de l'Enseignement Supérieur, 1984. 63–71.

115. Mazzon, Gabriella. "Social Relations and Form of Address in the Canterbury Tales." In *The History of English in a Social Context,* edited by Dieter Kastovsky and Arthur Mettinger. New York: Gruyter, 2000. 135–68.

116. Mersand, Joseph. *Chaucer's Romance Vocabulary.* 1937. Reprint, Port Washington, NY: Kennikat, 1968.

117. Pakkala-Wecktröm, Mari. "The Discourse of Seduction and Intrigue: Linguistic Strategies in Three Fabliaux in the *Canterbury Tales.*" *JHL* 3 (2002): 151–73.

118. Pearsall, Derek. "*The Franklin's Tale,* Line 1469: Forms of Address in Chaucer." *SAC* 17 (1995): 69–78.

119. Robertson, D. W., Jr. "Some Disputed Chaucerian Terminology." *Speculum* 52 (1977): 571–81.

120. Rogers, William E. "Individualization of Language in the Canterbury Frame Story." *AnM* 15 (1974): 74–108.

121. Ross, Thomas W. *Chaucer's Bawdy.* New York: Dutton, 1972.

122. Rothwell, W. "Chaucer and Stratford atte Bowe." *BJRL* 74 (1992): 3–28.

123. Scheps, Walter. "Chaucer's Use of Nonce Words, Primarily in the *Canterbury Tales.*" *NM* 80 (1979): 69–77.

124. Simes, G. R. "Chaucer and Bawdy." In *Words and Wordsmiths,* edited by Geraldine Barnes and others. Sydney: U of Sydney, 1989. 91–112.

125. Smith, Jeremy J. "Chaucer and the Invention of English." *SAC* 24 (2002): 335–46.

126. Yager, Susan. "Chaucer's *Peple* and *Folk.*" *JEGP* 100 (2001): 211–33.

See also nos. 859, 883, 890, 891, 1399.

Rhetoric and Style

127. Benson, Robert G. *Medieval Body Language: A Study of the Use of Gesture in Chaucer's Poetry.* Copenhagen: Rosenkilde, 1980.

128. Birney, Earle. *Essays on Chaucerian Irony.* Ed. Beryl Rowland. Toronto: U of Toronto P, 1985.

129. Diekstra, Fran. "The Language of Equivocation: Some Chaucerian Techniques." *DQR* 11 (1981): 215–36.

130. Elbow, Peter. *Oppositions in Chaucer.* Middletown, CT: Wesleyan UP, 1975.

131. Haas, Renate. "Chaucer's Use of the Lament for the Dead." In *Chaucer in the Eighties,* edited by Julian N. Wasserman and Robert J. Branch. Syracuse, NY: Syracuse UP, 1986. 23–37.

132. Hass, Robin R. "A Picture of Such Beauty in Their Minds: The Medieval Rhetoricians, Chaucer, and Evocative *Effictio.*" *Exemplaria* 14 (2002): 383–422.

133. Knox, Norman. "The Satiric Pattern of the *Canterbury Tales.*" In *Six Satirists,* edited by A. F. Sochatoff and others. Pittsburgh, PA: Carnegie Institute of Technology, 1965. 17–34.

134. MacDonald, Donald. "Proverbs, *Sententiae,* and *Exempla* in Chaucer's Comic Tales." *Speculum* 41 (1966): 453–65.

135. Manly, John M. "Chaucer and the Rhetoricians." (orig. pub. 1926). In *Chaucer Criticism,* Vol. 1. *The Canterbury Tales,* edited by Richard J. Schoeck and Jerome

Taylor. Notre Dame, IN: Notre Dame UP, 1960. 268–90.

136. Murphy, James J. "A New Look at Chaucer and the Rhetoricians." *RES* 15 (1964): 1–20.

137. Muscatine, Charles. *Chaucer and the French Tradition: A Study in Style and Meaning.* Berkeley: U of California P, 1957.

138. Payne, Robert O. "Chaucer and the Art of Rhetoric." In Rowland, no. 90, 42–64.

139. ———. "Rhetoric in Chaucer: Chaucer's Realization of Himself as a Rhetor." In *Medieval Eloquence,* edited by James J. Murphy. Berkeley: U of California P, 1978. 270–87.

140. Pazdziora, Marian. "The Sapiential Aspects of *The Canterbury Tales.*" *Kwartalnik Neofilologiczny* (Warsaw) 27 (1980): 413–26.

141. Presson, Robert K. "The Aesthetics of Chaucer's Art of Contrast." *English Miscellany* 15 (1964): 9–23.

142. Reiss, Edmund. "Chaucer and Medieval Irony." *SAC* 1 (1979): 67–82.

143. Taavitsainen, Irma. "Personality and Styles of Affect in the Canterbury Tales." In *Chaucer in Perspective,* edited by Geoffrey Lester. Sheffield: Sheffield Academic P, 1999. 18–34.

144. Winick, Stephen D. "Proverbial Strategy and Proverbial Wisdom in *The Canterbury Tales.*" *Proverbium* 11 (1994): 259–81.

See also nos. 455, 568a, 588, 755, 1121, 1124, 1353, 1372.

Prosody and Versification

145. Adams, Percy. "Chaucer's Assonance." *JEGP* 71 (1972): 527–39.

146. Baum, Paull F. *Chaucer's Verse.* Durham, NC: Duke UP, 1961.

147. Brody, Saul Nathaniel. "Chaucer's Rhyme Royal Tales and the Secularization of the Saint." *ChauR* 10 (1985): 113–31.

148. Cable, Thomas. "Issues for a New History of English Prosody." In *Studies in the History of the English Language: A Millennial Perspective,* edited by Donka Minkova and Robert Stockwell. Berlin: Mouton de Gruyter, 2002. 125–51.

149. Chickering, Howell. "Comic Meter and Rhyme in the 'Miller's Tale.'" *ChauY* 2 (1995): 17–47.

150. Dauby, Hélène. "Chaucer et l'Allitération." *L'Articulation langue-littérature dans les textes médiévaux anglais, II,* edited by Collette Stévanovitch. GRENDEL, no. 3. Nancy: Publications de l'Association des Médiévistes Anglicistes de l'Enseignement Supérieur, 1999. 133–42.

151. Duffell, Martin J. "'The craft so long to lerne': Chaucer's Invention of Iambic Pentameter." *ChauR* 34 (2000): 269–88.

152. Finnie, Bruce W. "On Chaucer's Stressed Vowel Phonemes." *ChauR* 3 (1975): 337–41.

153. Gaylord, Alan T. "Scanning the Prosodists: An Essay in Metacriticism." *ChauR* 11 (1976): 22–82.

154. ———, ed. *Essays on the Art of Chaucer's Verse.* New York: Routledge, 2001.

155. Knight, Stephen. *The Poetry of the Canterbury Tales.* Sydney: Angus, 1973.

156. ———. *Rymyng Craftily: Meaning in Chaucer's Poetry.* Sydney: Angus & Robertson, 1973.

157. Mann, Jill. "Chaucer's Meter and the Myth of the Ellesmere Editor of *The Canterbury Tales.*" *SAC* 23 (2001): 71–107.

158. Redford, Michael. "Middle English Stress Doubles: New Evidence from Chaucer's Meter." In *Development in Prosodic Systems,* edited by Paul Fikkert and Haike Jacobs. New York: Mouton de Gruyter, 2003. 159–95.

159. Robinson, Ian. *Chaucer's Prosody: A Study of the Middle English Verse Tradition.* London: Cambridge UP, 1971.

160. Solopova, Elizabeth. "Computer-Assisted Study of Chaucer's Meter." *Parergon* 18.1 (2000): 157–79.

161. Southworth, James G. *Verses of Cadence: An Introduction to the Prosody of Chaucer.* Oxford: Blackwell, 1954.

162. Stevens, Martin. "The Royal Stanza in Early English Literature." *PMLA* 94 (1979): 67–76.

163. Tarlinskaja, Marina G. *English Verse: Theory and History.* The Hague: Mouton, 1976.

See also nos. 73, 693, 777, 1015.

Prose

164. Bornstein, Diane. "Chaucer's *Tale of Melibee* as an Example of the *Style Clergial.*" *ChauR* 12 (1978): 236–54.

165. Chisnell, Robert E. "Chaucer's Neglected Prose." In *Literary and Historical Perspectives of the Middle Ages,* edited by Patricia W. Cummins, Patrick W. Conner, and Charles W. Connell. Morganton: West Virginia UP, 1982. 156–73.

Biography

166. Ackroyd, Peter. *Chaucer.* Chatto & Windus, 2004.

167. Brewer, Derek. *Chaucer and His World.* 2d ed. 1992. Reprinted as *The World of Chaucer.* Rochester, NY: Brewer, 2000.

168. Burrow, J. A. "The Poet as Petitioner." *SAC* 3 (1981): 61–75.

169. Cannon, Christopher. "*Raptus* in the Chaumpaigne Release and a Newly Discovered Document concerning the Life of Geoffrey Chaucer." *Speculum* 68 (1993): 74–94.

170. Carruthers, Leo. "Chaucer's In-Laws: Who Was Who in the War of the Roses." In *Mariages à la mode Anglo-Saxonne,* edited by Roger Lejosne and Dominique Sipière. Amiens: Sterne, 1995. 40–50.

171. Crow, Martin M., and Clair C. Olson, eds. *Chaucer Life Records. From Materials Compiled by John M. Manly and Edith Rickert, with the Assistance of Lillian Redstone and Others.* Oxford: Clarendon, 1966.

172. Delasanta, Rodney. "Chaucer and Strode." *ChauR* 26 (1991): 205–18.

173. Garbáty, Thomas J. "Chaucer, the Customs, and the Hainault Connection." *SAC Proceedings* 2 (1986): 95–102.

174. Gardner, John Champlin. *The Life and Times of Chaucer.* New York: Knopf, 1976.

175. Hornsby, Joseph A. "Was Chaucer Educated at the Inns of Court?" *ChauR* 22 (1988): 255–68.

176. Howard, Donald R. *Chaucer: His Life, His World, His Works.* New York: Dutton, 1987. Also pub. as *Chaucer and the Medieval World.* London: Weidenfeld & Nicolson, 1987.

177. Hulbert, James R. *Chaucer's Official Life.* 1912. Reprint, New York: Phaeton, 1970.

178. Jones, Terry, Robert F. Yeager, Terry Dolan, Alan Fletcher, and Juliette Dor. *Who Murdered Chaucer? A Medieval Mystery.* London: Methuen, 2003.

179. Kern, Alfred. *The Ancestry of Chaucer.* 1906. Reprint [New York: AMS], 1973.

180. Matheson, Lister M. "Chaucer's Ancestry: Historical and Philological Re-assessments." *ChauR* 5 (1991): 171–89.

181. Pearsall, Derek. "Chaucer's Tomb: The Politics of Reburial." *MAE* 64 (1995): 51–73.

182. ———. *The Life of Geoffrey Chaucer: A Critical Biography.* Oxford: Blackwell, 1992.

183. Rudd, Martin B. *Thomas Chaucer.* Research Publications of the U of Minnesota, 9. Minneapolis, 1926.

184. Sanderlin, S. "Chaucer and Ricardian Politics." *ChauR* 22 (1988): 171–84.

Sources and Analogues — General

185. Benson, Larry D., and Theodore Andersson, eds. *The Literary Context of Chaucer's Fabliaux.* Indianapolis, IN: Bobbs-Merrill, 1971.

186. Bryan, W. F., and Germaine Dempster, eds. *Sources and Analogues of Chaucer's "Canterbury Tales."* 1941. Reprint, London: Routledge & Kegan Paul; New York: Humanities, 1958.

187. Correale, Robert M., and Mary Hamel, eds. *Sources and Analogues of the Canterbury Tales, Volume I.* 2 vols. Rochester, NY: Brewer, 2002. (Vol. 2 forthcoming)

188. Diekstra, Fran. "Chaucer's Way with His Sources: Accident into Substance and Substance into Accident." *ES* 62 (1981): 215–36.

189. Miller, Robert P., ed. *Chaucer: Sources and Backgrounds.* New York: Oxford UP, 1977.

190. Morris, Lynn King. *Chaucer Source and Analogue Criticism: A Cross-Referenced Guide.* New York and London: Garland, 1985.

191. Pratt, Robert A. "Chaucer and the Hand That Fed Him." *Speculum* 41 (1966): 619–42.

See also nos. 397, 972.

Sources and Analogues — Editions

192. Albertano of Brescia. *Albertani Brixiensis Liber Consolationis et Consilii.* Ed. Thor Sundby. London: Chaucer Society, 2d ser., 8, 1873.

193. Boccaccio, Giovanni. *Tutte le Opere di Giovanni Boccaccio.* Gen. ed. Vittore Branca. Rev. ed. Milan: Mondadori, 1964.

194. ———. *De Casibus Vivorum Illustrium.* In no. 193, vol. 9. Trans. Louis B. Hall, *The Fates of Illustrious Men.* New York: Ungar, 1965.

195. ———. *De Claris Mulieribus.* In no. 193, vol. 10. Trans. Guido A. Guarino, *Concerning Famous Women.* New Brunswick, NY: Rutgers UP, 1963.

196. ———. *Il Decamerone.* In no. 193, vol. 4. Trans. G. H. McWilliam, *The Decameron.* Harmondsworth, UK: Penguin, 1972.

197. ———. *Il Filocolo.* In no. 193, vol. 1. Trans. Donald Cheney, with Thomas G. Bergin, *Filocolo.* New York: Garland, 1985, and in Havely, no. 207.

198. ———. *Il Filostrato.* In no. 193, vol. 2. Trans. Robert P. apRoberts and Anna Bruni Seldis, *Il Filostrato.* New York: Garland, 1986, and excerpts in Havely, no. 207.

199. ———. *Il Teseida.* In no. 193, vol. 2. Trans. Bernadette M. McCoy, *The Book of Theseus.* New York: Medieval Text Association, 1974, and in Havely, no. 207.

200. Boethius. *De Consolatione Philosophiae.* Ed. and trans. H. F. Stewart and E. K. Rand. Rev. ed. London: Loeb, 1968.

201. Caecilius Balbus [Pseudo]. *De Nugis Philosophorum, Quae Supersunt.* Ed. Edward Woefflin. Basil: Schweighauser, 1855.

202. Cato, "Dionysius." *Dicta Catonis [Disticha Catonis].* In *Minor Latin Poets,* 2 vols., rev. ed., translated by J. Wight Duff and Arnold M. Duff. Cambridge: Harvard UP; London: Heinemann, 1935. 1: 585–639.

203. Dante Alighieri. *Convivio.* Ed. Maria Simonelli. Bologna: Pátron, 1966. Trans. Richard H. Lansing, *Dante's Il Convivio (The Banquet).* New York: Garland, 1990.

204. Geoffrey of Monmouth. *The Historia Regum Britannie of Geoffrey of Monmouth.* Ed. and trans. Neil Wright. 5 vols. Cambridge: Brewer, 1985–95.

205. Gower, John. *Complete Works of John Gower.* Ed. G. C. Macauley. 4 vols. EETS. Oxford: Clarendon, 1899–1902.

206. Guillaume de Lorris and Jean de Meun. *Le Roman de la Rose.* Ed. Ernest Langlois. 5 vols. Paris: SATF, 1914–24; Ed. Felix Lecoy. 3 vols. Paris: Champion, 1965–70. Trans. Charles Dahlberg, *The Romance of the Rose.* Princeton: Princeton UP, 1983.

207. Havely, N. R. *Boccaccio — Sources of Troilus and the Knight's and Franklin's Tales.* Cambridge, UK: Brewer, 1980.

208. Innocent III, Pope (Lotario dei Segni). *De Miseria Condicionis Humane.* Ed. and trans. Robert E. Lewis. 1978. Reprint, London: Scolar, 1980.

209. Jerome, Saint. *Letter against Jovinian.* Trans. W. H. Fremantle, *The Principal Works of St. Jerome.* Vol. 6 of *A Select Library of Nicene and Post-Nicene Fathers of the Christian Church.* 2d ser. Reprint, Grand Rapids, MI: Eerdmans, 1989. And in Hanna and Lawler, no. 972.

210. Livy. *Livy, with an English Translation.* Ed. and trans. B. O. Foster and others. 14 vols. London: Loeb, 1919–59.

211. Martianus Dumiensis. *De Moribus.* In no. 217.

212. Nicholas of Lynn. *The Kalendarium of Nicholas of Lynn*. Ed. and trans. Sigmund Eisner and Gary Mac Eoin. Athens: U of Georgia P, 1980.

213. Ovid. *Ars Amatoria*. Ed. and trans. J. H. Mozley. Rev. ed. Ed. G. P. Goold. London: Loeb, 1979.

214. ———. *Metamorphoses*. Ed. and trans. F. J. Miller. 2 vols. Rev. ed. G. P. Goold. London: Loeb, 1976–77.

215. Petrarch. *Prose*. Ed. Guido Martellotti. Trans., in part, Aldo S. Bernardo and others, *Letters of Old Age*. Baltimore: Johns Hopkins UP, 1992. (tale of Griselda)

216. Petrus Alphonsus. *The Disciplina Clericalis of Petrus Alphonsi*. Trans. and ed. Eberhard Hermes. Eng. trans. P. R. Quarrie. Berkeley: U of California P, 1970.

217. Publilius Syrus. *Sententiae*. Includes *De Moribus* of Pseudo-Seneca, Martianus Dumiensis. Ed. Edward Woefflin. Leipzig: Tuebner, 1869.

217a. Sercambi, Giovanni. *Il Novelliere*. Ed. Luciano Rossi. Rome: Salerno, 1974.

Classical and Continental Relations

218. Boitani, Piero. *The Genius to Improve an Invention: Literary Transitions*. Notre Dame, IN: U of Notre Dame P, 2002.

219. ———, ed. *Chaucer and the Italian Trecento*. Cambridge: Cambridge UP, 1983.

220. Brewer, Derek. "The Relationship of Chaucer to English and European Traditions." In *Chaucer and Chaucerians: Critical Studies in Middle English Literature*. London: Nelson, 1966. 1–38.

221. Brown, Emerson, Jr. "Chaucer and the European Literary Tradition." In *Geoffrey Chaucer: A Collection of Original Articles*, edited by George D. Economou. New York: McGraw-Hill, 1976. 37–54.

222. Calabrese, Michael A. *Chaucer's Ovidian Arts of Love*. Gainesville: UP of Florida, 1994.

223. Crépin, André. "Chaucer and the French." In *Medieval and Pseudo-Medieval Literature*, edited by Piero Boitani and Anna Torti. Tübingen, Germany: Narr, 1984. 55–77.

224. Cummings, Hubertis. *The Indebtedness of Chaucer's Works to the Italian Works of Boccaccio*. 1916. Reprint, New York: Haskell, 1965.

225. Edwards, Robert R. *Chaucer and Boccaccio: Antiquity and Modernity*. New York: Palgrave, 2002.

226. Fyler, John M. *Chaucer and Ovid*. New Haven, CT: Yale UP, 1979.

227. Ginsberg, Warren. *Chaucer's Italian Tradition*. Ann Arbor: U of Michigan P, 2002.

228. Gutiérrez Arranz, José Maria. "The Classical and Modern Concept of *Auctoritas* in Geoffrey Chaucer's *The Canterbury Tales*." *SELIM* 6 (1996): 85–102.

229. Hagedorn, Suzanne C. *Abandoned Women: Rewriting the Classics in Dante, Boccaccio, & Chaucer*. Ann Arbor: U of Michigan P, 2004.

230. Harbert, Bruce. "Chaucer and the Latin Classics." In *Geoffrey Chaucer*, Writers and Their Background, edited by D. S. Brewer. London: Bell, 1974. 137–53.

231. Hardman, Phillipa. "Narrative Typology: Chaucer's Use of the Story of Orpheus." *MLR* 85 (1990): 445–54.

232. Hill, Ordelle. "Chaucer's 'Englished' Georgics." *MedPers* 4–5 (1989–90): 69–80.

233. Hoffman, Richard L. *Ovid and the Canterbury Tales*. Philadelphia: U of Pennsylvania P, 1966.

234. Jefferson, Bernard L. *Chaucer and the Consolation of Philosophy*. 1917. Reprint, New York: Haskell, 1965.

235. Koff, Leonard Michael, and Brenda Deen Schildgen, eds. *The Decameron and the Canterbury Tales: New Essays on an Old Question*. Madison, NJ: Fairleigh Dickinson UP, 2000.

236. McCall, John P. *Chaucer among the Gods: The Poetics of Classical Myth*. University Park: Pennsylvania State UP, 1979.

237. Minnis, A. J. *Chaucer and Pagan Antiquity*. Cambridge, UK: Brewer, 1982.

238. Neuse, Richard. *Chaucer's Dante: Allegory and Epic Theater in The Canterbury Tales*. Berkeley: U of California P, 1991.

239. Nolan, Barbara. *Chaucer and the Tradition of the Roman Antique*. Cambridge: Cambridge UP, 1992.

240. Nolan, Edward Peter. "Knocking the Mary out of the Bones: Chaucer's Ethical Mirrors of Dante." In *Through a Glass Darkly: Specular Images of Seeing and Knowing from Virgil to Chaucer*. Ann Arbor: U of Michigan P, 1990. 193–217.

241. Phillips, Helen. "Fortune and the Lady: Chaucer and the International 'Dit.'" *NMS* 38 (1999): 120–36.

242. Schless, Howard. *Chaucer and Dante: A Revaluation*. Norman, OK: Pilgrim, 1984.

243. Serrano Reyes, Jesús L. *Didactismo y moralismo en Geoffrey Chaucer y Don Juan Manuel: Un estudio comparativo textual*. Córdoba: Universidad de Córdoba, 1996.

244. Serrano Reyes, Jesús L., and others. *Seneca y Chaucer, I: Influencia Senequista en "The Canterbury Tales."* Córdoba: Universidad de Córdoba, 1996.

245. Shannon, Edgar F. *Chaucer and the Roman Poets*. Cambridge: Harvard UP, 1929.

246. Shoaf, Richard Allen. *Chaucer and the Currency of the Word: Money, Image, and Reference in Late Medieval Poetry*. Norman, OK: Pilgrim, 1983. [Relation to Dante]

247. Spearing, A. C. "Classical Antiquity in Chaucer's Chivalric Romances." In *Chivalry, Knighthood, and War in the Middle Ages*, edited by Susan J. Ridyard. Sewanee, TN: U of the South, 1999. 53–73.

248. Taylor, Karla. *Chaucer Reads "The Divine Comedy."* Stanford, CA: Stanford UP, 1989.

249. Thompson, N. S. *Chaucer, Boccaccio, and the Debate of Love: A Comparative Study of the Decameron and The Canterbury Tales*. Oxford: Clarendon, 1996.

250. Wallace, David. *Chaucer and the Early Writings of Boccaccio*. Cambridge, UK: Brewer, 1985.

251. ———. *Chaucerian Polity: Absolutist Lineages and Associational Forms in England and Italy*. Stanford, CA: Stanford UP, 1997.

252. Wilson, Grace G. "'Amonges Othere Wordes Wyse': The Medieval Seneca and the *Canterbury Tales*." *ChauR* 28 (1993): 135–45.

253. Wimsatt, James I. *Chaucer and His French Contemporaries: Natural Music in the Fourteenth Century*. Toronto: U of Toronto P, 1991.

See also nos. 375, 505–6, 781, 972.

English Relations, Contemporary and Later

254. Alderson, William L., and Arnold C. Henderson. *Chaucer and Augustan Scholarship.* Berkeley: U of California P, 1970.

255. Boitani, Piero. *English Medieval Narrative in the 13th and 14th Centuries.* Trans. Joan Krakover Hall. Cambridge: Cambridge UP, 1982.

256. Burrow, J. A. *Ricardian Poetry: Chaucer, Gower, Langland and the Pearl Poet.* New Haven, CT: Yale UP, 1971.

257. Crampton, Georgia R. *The Conditions of Creatures: Suffering and Action in Chaucer and Spenser.* New Haven, CT: Yale UP, 1974.

258. Davenport, W. A. *Chaucer and His English Contemporaries: Prologue and Tale in the Canterbury Tales.* New York: St. Martin's, 1998.

259. Donaldson, E. Talbot. *The Swan at the Well: Shakespeare Reading Chaucer.* New Haven, CT: Yale UP, 1985.

260. Fisher, John H. *The Importance of Chaucer.* Carbondale: Southern Illinois UP, 1992.

261. ———. *John Gower: Moral Philosopher and Friend of Chaucer.* New York: New York UP, 1964.

262. Hieatt, A. Kent. *Chaucer, Spenser, Milton: Mythopoetic Continuities and Transformations.* Montreal: McGill-Queen's UP, 1975.

263. Johnston, Alexandra F. "Chaucer's Records of Early English Drama." *Records of Early English Drama Newsletter* 13.2 (1988): 13–20.

264. Kirk, Elizabeth D. "Chaucer and His English Contemporaries." In *Geoffrey Chaucer: A Collection of Original Essays,* edited by George D. Economou. New York: McGraw-Hill, 1976. 111–27.

265. Krier, Theresa M., ed. *Refiguring Chaucer in the Renaissance.* Gainesville: UP of Florida, 1998.

266. Lerer, Seth. "The Chaucerian Critique of Medieval Theatricality." In *The Performance of Medieval Culture,* edited by James J. Paxson and others. Cambridge, UK: Brewer, 1998. 59–76.

267. Morse, Ruth, and Barry Windeatt, eds. *Chaucer Traditions: Studies in Honour of Derek Brewer.* Cambridge: Cambridge UP, 1990.

268. Miskimin, Alice S. *The Renaissance Chaucer.* New Haven, CT: Yale UP, 1975.

269. Pearsall, Derek. "The English Chaucerians." In *Chaucer and Chaucerians,* edited by D. S. Brewer. London: Nelson, 1966. 201–39.

270. Robinson, Ian. *Chaucer and the English Tradition.* Cambridge: Cambridge UP, 1972.

271. Thompson, Ann. *Shakespeare's Chaucer: A Study in Literary Origins.* New York: Barnes & Noble, 1978.

272. Weiss, Alexander. *Chaucer's Native Heritage.* Berne: Peter Lang, 1985.

273. Wright, Glenn. "Geoffrey the Unbarbarous: Chaucerian 'Genius' and Eighteenth-Century Antimedievalism." *ES* 82 (2001): 193–202.

See also nos. 289, 415, 559–60, 564, 784.

Audience

274. Bennett, Michael. "The Court of Richard II and the Promotion of Literature." In *Chaucer's English: Literature in Historical Context,* edited by Barbara Hanawalt. Minneapolis: U of Minnesota P, 1991. 3–20.

275. Boyd, Beverly. "Chaucer's Audience and the Henpecked Husband." *Florilegium* 12 (1993): 177–80.

276. Christianson, Paul. "Chaucer's Literacy." *ChauR* 11 (1976): 112–27.

277. Coleman, Janet. *Medieval Readers and Writers, 1350–1400.* New York: Columbia UP, 1981.

278. Eade, J. C. "'We ben to lewd or to slowe': Chaucer's Astronomy and Audience Participation." *SAC* 4 (1982): 53–85.

279. Fisher, John H. "Chaucer and the Written Language." In *The Popular Literature of Medieval England,* edited by Thomas J. Heffernan. Knoxville: U of Tennessee P, 1985. 237–51.

280. Green, Richard Firth. *Poets and Princepleasers: Literature and the English Court in the Late Middle Ages.* Toronto: U of Toronto P, 1980.

281. Mehl, Dieter. "Chaucer's Audience." *LeedsSE* 10 (1978): 58–74.

282. Middleton, Anne. "Chaucer's 'New Men' and the Good of Literature in the *Canterbury Tales.*" In *Literature and Society,* edited by Edward W. Said. Baltimore: Johns Hopkins UP, 1980. 15–56.

283. Reiss, Edmund. "Chaucer and His Audience." *ChauR* 14 (1980): 390–402.

284. Strohm, Paul. "Chaucer's Audience." *L&H* 5 (1977): 26–41.

285. ———. "Chaucer's Audience(s): Fictional, Implied, Intended, Actual." *ChauR* 18 (1983): 137–45.

286. ———. "Chaucer's Fifteenth-Century Audience and the Narrowing of the 'Chaucer Tradition.'" *SAC* 4 (1982): 3–32.

See also nos. 294, 310, 547, 1257.

Idea of the Author

287. De Looze, Lawrence. *Pseudo-Autobiography in the Fourteenth Century: Juan Ruiz, Guillaume de Machaut, Jean Froissart, and Geoffrey Chaucer.* Gainesville: UP of Florida, 1997.

288. Kimmelman, Burt. *The Poetics of Authorship in the Late Middle Ages.* New York: Lang, 1996.

289. Lerer, Seth. *Chaucer and His Readers: Imagining the Author in Late-Medieval England.* Princeton: Princeton UP, 1993.

290. Minnis, Alastair. "The Author's Two Bodies?: Authority and Fallibility in Late-Medieval Textual Theory." In *Of the Making of Books,* edited by P. R. Robinson and Rivkah Zim. Brookfield, VT: Ashgate, 1997. 259–79.

291. ———. *The Medieval Theory of Authorship.* Cambridge, UK: Brewer, 1982.

292. Olson, Glending. "Making and Poetry in the Age of Chaucer." *CL* 31 (1979): 272–90.

293. Walker, Denis. "The Structure of Literary Response in Chaucerian Texts." *Parergon* 3 (1985): 107–14.

See also nos. 1312, 1459, 1463–64, 1466.

Oral and Written Traditions

294. Amtower, Laurel. *Engaging Words: The Culture of Reading in the Later Middle Ages.* New York: Palgrave, 2000.

295. Axton, Richard. "Chaucer and the Idea of the Theatrical Performance." In *Divers Toyes Mengled: Essays on Medieval and Renaissance Culture in Honour of Andre Lascombes,* edited by Michel Bitot. Tours: Université François Ralelais, 1996. 83–100.

296. Blake, N. F. "Speech and Writing: An Historical Overview." *YES* 25 (1995): 6–21.

297. Coleman, Joyce. "On Beyond Ong: Taking the Paradox Out of 'Oral Literacy' (and 'Literate Orality')." In *Medieval Insular Literature between the Written and Oral II: Continuity of Transmission,* edited by Hildegard L. C. Tristram. Tübingen, Germany: Narr, 1997. 155–76.

298. Feinstein, Sandy. "Hypertextuality and Chaucer, or Re-ordering *The Canterbury Tales* and Other Readerly Prerogatives." *Readerly/Writerly Texts* 2 (1996): 135–48.

299. Ganim, John M. *Chaucerian Theatricality.* Princeton: Princeton UP, 1990.

300. ———. "Forms of Talk in *The Canterbury Tales.*" *PoeticaT* 34 (1991): 88–100.

301. Gellrich, Jesse. *Discourse and Dominion in the Fourteenth Century: Oral Contexts of Writing in Philosophy, Politics, and Poetry.* Princeton: Princeton UP, 1995.

302. ———. *The Idea of the Book in the Middle Ages: Language Theory, Mythology, and Fiction.* Ithaca, NY: Cornell UP, 1985.

303. Giaccherini, Enrico. "Theatrical Chaucer." *European Medieval Drama* 2 (1998): 85–98.

304. Grudin, Michaela Paasche. *Chaucer and the Politics of Discourse.* Columbia: U of South Carolina P, 1996.

305. Holsinger, Bruce W. "Langland's Musical Reader: Literature, Law, and the Constraints of Performance." *SAC* 21 (1999): 99–141.

306. Lindahl, Carl. "The Oral Undertones of Late Medieval Romance." In *Oral Tradition in the Middle Ages,* edited by W. F. H. Nicolaisen. Binghamton, NY: Medieval & Renaissance Texts & Studies, 1995. 59–75.

307. Neuss, Paula. "Images of Writing and the Book in Chaucer's Poetry." *RES* 32 (1981): 385–97.

308. Parks, Ward. "Oral Tradition and the 'Canterbury Tales.'" In *Oral Poetics in Middle English Poetry,* edited by Mark Amodio. New York: Garland, 1994. 149–79.

309. Rosenberg, Bruce. "The Oral Performance of Chaucer's Poetry." *Folklore Forum* 13 (1980): 224–37.

310. Rowland, Beryl. "Pronuntiatio and Its Effect on Chaucer's Audience." *SAC* 4 (1982): 33–51.

311. Sola Buil, Ricardo J. "*The Canterbury Tales* and Its Dramatic Background." *SELIM* 9 (1999): 111–27.

See also nos. 863, 1128, 1310.

Poetics and Narrative Technique

312. Ashley, Kathleen M. "Renaming the Sins: A Homiletic Topos of Linguistic Instability in the *Canterbury Tales.*" In *Sign, Sentence, Discourse: Language in Medieval Thought and Literature,* edited by Julian N. Wasserman and Lois Roney. Syracuse NY: Syracuse UP, 1989. 272–93.

313. Burlin, Robert B. *Chaucerian Fiction.* Princeton: Princeton UP, 1977.

314. Fichte, Joerg O. *Chaucer's "Art Poetical": A Study of Chaucerian Poetics.* Tübingen, Germany: Narr, 1980.

315. Hallissy, Margaret. "The End of English Literature: The Case of Geoffrey Chaucer." *Confrontation* 70–71 (2000): 13–19.

316. Hanning, Robert W. "'And countrefete the speche of every man/He coude, whan he sholde telle a tale': Towards a Lapsarian Poetics for *The Canterbury Tales.*" *SAC* 21 (1999): 29–58.

317. Jordan, Robert O. *Chaucer's Poetics and the Modern Reader.* Berkeley: U of California P, 1987.

318. Long, E. Hudson. "Chaucer as Master of the Short Story." *Delaware Notes,* 16 ser. (1943): 11–29.

319. McGerr, Rosemarie P. "Medieval Concepts of Literary Closure: Theory and Practice." *Exemplaria* 1 (1989): 149–79.

320. Payne, Robert O. *The Key of Remembrance: A Study of Chaucer's Poetic.* New Haven, CT: Yale UP, 1963.

321. Pearsall, Derek. "Towards a Poetics of Chaucerian Narrative." In *Drama, Narrative and Poetry in The Canterbury Tales,* edited by Wendy Harding. Toulouse: Presses Universitaires du Mirail, Collection Interlangues: Literatures, 2003. 99–112.

322. Ridley, Florence. "Chaucerian Strategies: Effects and Causes." In *Papers from the VIIth International Conference of SELIM,* edited by Bernardo Santano Moreno and others. Caceres: Universidad de Extremadura, 1995. 239–56.

323. Rowe, Donald W. "Metatextual Moments in Chaucer." *Graven Images* 1 (1994): 180–93.

324. Scala, Elizabeth. *Absent Narratives, Manuscript Textuality, and Literary Structure in Late Medieval England.* New York: Palgrave/Macmillan, 2002.

325. ———. "The Deconstucture of the Canterbury Tales." *Journal X* 4 (2000): 171–90.

326. Sklute, Larry. *Virtue of Necessity: Inconclusiveness and Narrative Form in Chaucer's Poetry.* Columbus: Ohio State UP, 1984.

327. Smallwood, T. M. "Chaucer's Distinctive Digressions." *SP* 82 (1985): 437–49.

328. Stevens, Martin. "Chaucer's 'Bad Art': The Interrupted Tales." In *The Rhetorical Poetics of the Middle Ages,* edited by John M. Hill and Deborah M. Sinnreich-Levy. Madison, NJ: Fairleigh Dickinson UP and Associated U Presses, 2000. 130–48.

329. Wood, Chauncey. "Affective Stylistics and the Study of Chaucer." *SAC* 6 (1984): 21–40.

See also no. 684.

Evolution and Order of *The Canterbury Tales*

330. Benson, Larry D. "The Order of *The Canterbury Tales.*" *SAC* 3 (1981): 77–120.

331. Blake, N. F. "Critics, Criticism, and the Order of the Canterbury Tales." *Archiv* 218 (1981): 47–58.

332. ———. *The Textual Tradition of the Canterbury Tales.* London: Arnold, 1985.

333. ———. "The Debate on the Order of the Canterbury Tales." *RCEI* 10 (1985): 31–42.

334. Dempster, Germaine. "The Fifteenth-Century Editions of the *Canterbury Tales* and the Problem of Tale Order." *PMLA* 64 (1949): 1123–42.

335. Fisher, John H. "Chaucer's Last Revision of the *Canterbury Tales.*" *MLR* 67 (1972): 241–51.

336. Forni, Kathleen. "'Queynte' Arguments: The Ellesmere Order May Be the Most 'Satisfactory' but Is It Chaucer's?" *ChauY* 5 (1998): 79–90.

337. Frese, Dolores Warwick. *An "Ars Legendi" for Chaucer's Canterbury Tales.* Gainesville: UP of Florida, 1991.

338. Furnivall, F. J. A. *A Temporary Preface to the Chaucer Society's Six-Text Edition of Chaucer's Canterbury Tales: Part I, Attempting to Show the Right Order of the Tales, and the Days and Stages of the Pilgrimage.* Chaucer Society, 2d ser., 3. London: Trübner, 1868.

339. Horobin, Simon. "Additional 35286 and the Order of the *Canterbury Tales.*" *ChauR* 31 (1997): 272–78.

340. Keiser, George. "In Defense of the Bradshaw Shift." *ChauR* 12 (1978): 191–201.

341. Lawton, David. "Chaucer's Two Ways: The Pilgrimage Frame of 'The Canterbury Tales.'" *SAC* 9 (1987): 3–40.

342. Olson, Glending. "The Terrain of Chaucer's Sittingbourne." *SAC* 6 (1984): 222–36.

343. Owen, Charles A., Jr. "The Alternative Reading of *The Canterbury Tales.*" *PMLA* 97 (1982): 237–50.

344. ———. "The Canterbury Tales: Beginnings (3) and Endings (2 + 1)." *ChauY* 1 (1992): 189–212.

345. ———. *Pilgrimage and Story-Telling in the Canterbury Tales: The Dialect of "Ernest" and "Game."* Norman: U of Oklahoma P, 1977.

346. Pearsall, Derek. "Pre-empting Closure in *The Canterbury Tales*: Old Endings, New Beginnings." In *Essays on Ricardian Literature,* edited by A. J. Minnis and others. Oxford: Clarendon, 1997. 23–38.

347. Pratt, Robert A. "The Order of the *Canterbury Tales.*" *PMLA* 66 (1951): 1141–67.

348. Spencer, Matthew, and others. "Analyzing the Order of Items in Manuscripts of *The Canterbury Tales.*" *ComH* 37 (2003): 97–109.

349. Tatlock, J. S. P. "*The Canterbury Tales* in 1400." *PMLA* 50 (1935): 100–139.

See also nos. 298, 426, 1343.

Voice, Narrative Persona, and the Narrator

350. Burrow, J. A. "Elvish Chaucer." In *The Endless Knot: Essays on Old and Middle English in Honor of Marie Borroff,* edited by M. Teresa Tavormina and R. F. Yeager. Cambridge, UK: Brewer, 1995. 105–11.

351. Donaldson, E. Talbot. "Chaucer the Pilgrim." *PMLA* 69 (1954): 928–36.

352. Fisher, John H. "Assertion of Self in the Works of Chaucer." *MedPers* 4–5 (1989–90): 1–24.

353. Harding, Wendy. "Gendering Discourse in the Canterbury Tales." *BAM* 64 (2003): 1–11.

354. Kane, George. *The Autobiographical Fallacy in Chaucer and Langland Studies.* London: Lewis, 1965.

355. Kuczynski, Michael. "Don't Blame Me: The Meta-ethics of a Chaucerian Apology." *ChauR* 37 (2003): 315–28.

356. Lawton, David. *Chaucer's Narrators.* Cambridge, UK: Brewer, 1985.

357. Leicester, H. Marshall. "The Art of Impersonation: A General Prologue to *The Canterbury Tales.*" *PMLA* 95 (1980): 8–22.

358. Mandel, Jerome. "Other Voices in the *Canterbury Tales.*" *Criticism* 19 (1977): 157–71.

359. Millns, Tony. "Chaucer's Suspended Judgments." *EIC* 27 (1977): 1–19.

360. Nolan, Barbara. "A Poet Ther Was: Chaucer's Voices in the *General Prologue.*" *PMLA* (1986): 154–69.

361. Riehle, Wolfgang. "Aspects of Chaucer's Narratorial Self-Representation in *The Canterbury Tales.*" In *Tales and "Their Telling Difference,"* edited by Herbert Foltinek and others. Heidelberg: Universitatsverlag, 1993. 133–47.

See also nos. 770, 813, 936.

Characterization

362. Braswell, Mary Flowers. "Poet and Sinner: Literary Characterization and the Mentality of the Late Middle Ages." *FCS* 10 (1984): 39–59.

363. Cigman, Gloria. "Chaucer and the Goats of Creation." *Literature and Theology* 5 (1991): 162–80.

364. Edwards, A. S. G. "Chaucer and the Poetics of Utterance." In *Poetics: Theory and Practice in Medieval English Literature,* edited by Piero Boitani and Anna Torti. Bury St. Edmunds, UK: Brewer, 1991. 57–67.

365. Engelhardt, George J. "The Ecclesiastical Pilgrims of the *Canterbury Tales*: A Study in Ethnography." *MS* 13 (1983): 41–51.

366. Friedman, John B. "Another Look at Chaucer and the Physiognomists." *SP* 78 (1981): 138–52.

367. Ginsberg, Warren. *The Cast of Character: The Representation of Personality in Ancient and Medieval Literature.* Toronto: U of Toronto P, 1983.

368. ———. "Chaucer's Disposition." In *The Endless Knot: Essays on Old and Middle English in Honor of Marie Borroff,* edited by M. Teresa Tavormina and R. F. Yeager. Cambridge, UK: Brewer, 1995. 129–40.

369. Manly, John M. *Some New Light on Chaucer.* 1926. Reprint, New York: Peter Smith, 1952.

370. Parr, Roger P. "Chaucer's Art of Portraiture." *SMC* 4 (1974): 428–36.

371. Specht, Henrik. "The Beautiful, the Handsome, and the Ugly: Some Aspects of the Art of Character Portrayal in Medieval Literature." *SN* 56 (1984): 129–46.

372. Wurtele, Douglas. "Some Uses of Physiognomical Lore in Chaucer's Canterbury Tales." *ChauR* 17 (1982): 130–41.

See also nos. 98, 420, 769, 769a, 850.

Philosophy

373. Baker, Denise N. "Chaucer and Moral Philosophy: The Virtuous Women of *The Canterbury Tales*." *MAE* 60 (1991): 241–56.

374. Dunleavy, Gareth W. "Natural Law as Chaucer's Ethical Absolute." *Transactions of the Wisconsin Academy of Sciences, Arts, and Letters* 52 (1963): 177–87.

375. Fisher, John H. "The New Humanism and Geoffrey Chaucer." *Soundings* 80 (1997): 23–39.

376. Foster, Edward E. *Understanding Chaucer's Intellectual and Interpretative World: Nominalist Fiction.* Lewistown, NY: Mellen, 1999.

377. Grudin, Michaela Paasche. "Credulity and the Rhetoric of Heterodoxy: From Averroes to Chaucer." *ChauR* 35 (2000): 204–22.

378. Kaske, R. E. "Causality and Miracle: Philosophical Perspectives in the 'Knight's Tale' and the 'Man of Law's Tale.'" In *Traditions and Innovations*, edited by David G. Allen and Robert A. White. Newark: U of Delaware P, 1990. 11–34.

379. Keiper, Hugo, Richard Utz, and Cristoph Bode, eds. *Nominalism and Literary Discourse: New Perspectives.* Atlanta, GA: Rodopi, 1997.

380. Mogan, Joseph J., Jr. *Chaucer and the Theme of Mutability.* The Hague: Mouton, 1969.

381. Myles, Robert. *Chaucerian Realism.* Cambridge, UK: Brewer, 1994.

382. Owen, Charles A., Jr. "The Problem of Free Will in Chaucer's Narratives." *PQ* 46 (1967): 433–56.

383. Patch, Howard. *The Goddess Fortuna in Medieval Literature.* Cambridge: Harvard UP, 1927.

384. ———. *The Tradition of Boethius: A Study of His Importance in Medieval Culture.* New York: Oxford UP, 1935.

385. Peck, Russell A. "Chaucer and the Nominalist Question." *Speculum* 53 (1978): 745–60.

386. Roney, Lois. "The Theme of Protagonist's Intention versus Actual Outcome." *ES* 64 (1983): 193–200.

387. Ruggiers, Paul G. "Platonic Forms in Chaucer." *ChauR* 17 (1983): 366–81.

388. Shepherd, Geoffrey. "Religion and Philosophy in Chaucer." In *Geoffrey Chaucer*, edited by D. S. Brewer. London: Bell, 1974. 262–89.

389. Taylor, Paul B. "Chaucer's Cosyn to the Dede." *Speculum* 57 (1982): 315–27.

390. Thundy, Zacharias. "Chaucer's Quest for Wisdom in *The Canterbury Tales*." *NM* 77 (1976): 582–98.

391. Utz, Richard, ed. *Literary Nominalism and the Theory of Rereading Late Medieval Texts.* Lewiston, NY: Edwin Mellen, 1995.

392. Yager, Susan. "Boethius, Philosophy, and Chaucer's 'Marriage Group.'" *CarmP* 4 (1995): 77–88.

See also nos. 600, 676, 793, 796–97, 805, 824, 826, 830, 948, 1061, 1267, 1318.

Religion and the Bible

393. Ames, Ruth. "Prototype and Parody in Chaucerian Exegesis." In *The Fourteenth Century*, edited by Paul Z. Szarmach and Bernard S. Levy. Binghamton: State U of New York at Binghamton, 1978. 87–105.

394. Astell, Anne. *Job, Boethius, and Epic Truth.* Ithaca, NY: Cornell UP, 1994.

395. Benson, C. David. "Varieties of Religious Poetry in 'The Canterbury Tales': 'The Man of Law's Tale' and 'The Clerk's Tale.'" *SAC Proceedings* 2 (1987): 159–67.

396. Benson, C. David, and Elizabeth Robertson, eds. *Chaucer's Religious Tales.* Cambridge, UK: Brewer, 1990.

397. Besserman, Lawrence. *Chaucer's Biblical Poetics.* Norman: U of Oklahoma P, 1998.

398. Biscoglio, Frances Minetti. *The Wife of "The Canterbury Tales" and the Tradition of the Valiant Women of Proverbs 31: 10–31.* San Francisco: Mellen Research UP, 1991.

399. Boenig, Robert. *Chaucer and the Mystics: The Canterbury Tales and the Genre of Devotional Prose.* Lewisburg, PA: Bucknell UP, 1995.

400. Borroff, Marie. "Dimensions of Judgment in the *Canterbury Tales*: Friar, Summoner, Pardoner, Wife of Bath." In *Traditions and Renewals: Chaucer, The Gawain-Poet, and Beyond.* New Haven, CT: Yale UP. 3–49.

401. Boyd, Beverly. *Chaucer and the Liturgy.* Philadelphia: Dorrance, 1967.

402. Gallick, Susan. "A Look at Chaucer and His Preachers." *Speculum* 50 (1975): 456–76.

403. Fleming, John V. "Chaucer's Ascetical Images." *C&L* 28 (1979): 19–26.

404. Fletcher, Alan J. "Chaucer the Heretic." *SAC* 25 (2003): 53–121.

405. Haskell, Ann. *Essays on Chaucer's Saints.* The Hague: Mouton, 1977.

406. Hill, John M. *Chaucerian Belief: The Poetics of Reverence and Delight.* New Haven, CT: Yale UP, 1991.

407. Jeffrey, David Lyle, ed. *Chaucer and Scriptural Tradition.* Ottawa: U of Ottawa P, 1984.

408. Kamowski, William. "Chaucer and Wyclif: God's Miracles against the Clergy's Magic." *ChauR* 37 (2002): 5–25.

409. Kelly, Henry Ansgar. "Sacraments, Sacramentals, and Lay Piety in Chaucer's England." *ChauR* 28 (1993): 5–22.

410. Leicester, H. Marshall, Jr. "Piety and Resistance: A Note on the Representation of Religious Feeling in the *Canterbury Tales*." In *The Endless Knot: Essays on Old and Middle English in Honor of Marie Borroff*, edited by M. Teresa Tavormina and R. F. Yeager. Cambridge, UK: Brewer, 1995. 151–60.

411. Madeleva, Sister Mary. *A Lost Language and Other Essays on Chaucer.* New York: Sheed, 1951.

412. Rhodes, Jim. *Poetry Does Theology: Chaucer, Grosseteste, and the Pearl-Poet.* Notre Dame, IN: U of Notre Dame P, 2001.

413. Schildgen, Brenda Deen. "Jerome's *Prefatory Epistles* to the Bible and *The Canterbury Tales*." *SAC* 15 (1993): 111–30.

414. Thomson, J. A. F. "Orthodox Religion and the Origins of Lollardy." *History* 74 (1989): 39–55.

415. Volk-Birke, Sabine. *Chaucer and Medieval Preaching: Rhetoric for Listeners in Sermons and Poetry.* Tübingen, Germany: Narr, 1991.

416. Wenzel, Siegfried. "Chaucer and the Language of Contemporary Preaching." *SP* 73 (1976): 138–61.

417. Woo, Constance. "The Spiritual Purpose of the Canterbury Tales." *Comitatus* 1 (1970): 85–109.

See also nos. 66, 70, 388, 525, 594–95, 611, 1076.

Astrology, Science

418. Brewer, Derek. "Chaucer and Arithmetic." In *Medieval Studies Conference, Aachen 1983,* edited by Wolf-Dietrich and Horst Weinstock. Frankfurt am Main: Peter Lang, 1984. 111–19.

419. Clark, George. "Chaucer's Third and Fourth of May." *RUO* 52 (1982): 257–65.

420. Curry, Walter C. *Chaucer and Medieval Sciences.* 1926. Enlarged ed., New York: Barnes & Noble, 1960.

421. Eisner, Sigmund. "The Ram Revisited: A Canterbury Conundrum." *ChauR* 28 (1994): 330–43.

422. Holley, Linda Tarte. *Chaucer's Measuring Eye.* Houston, TX: Rice UP, 1990.

423. Kummerer, K. R. "A Consistent Time Frame for Chaucer's Canterbury Pilgrimage." *Journal of the British Astronomical Society* 11.4 (2001): 203–13.

424. Mooney, Linne R. "Chaucer and Interest in Astronomy at the Court of Richard II." In *Chaucer in Perspective,* edited by Geoffrey Lester. Sheffield: Sheffield Academic P, 1999. 139–60.

425. North, J. D. *Chaucer's Universe.* Oxford: Clarendon, 1988.

426. Osborn, Marijane. *Time and the Astrolabe in The Canterbury Tales.* Norman: U of Oklahoma P, 2002.

427. Parker, R. H. "Accounting in Chaucer's *Canterbury Tales." Accounting, Auditing, Accountability* 12.1 (1999): 92–112.

428. Rutledge, Sheryl P. "Chaucer's Zodiac of Tales." *Costerus* 9 (1973): 117–43.

429. Smyser, Hamilton M. "A View of Chaucer's Astronomy." 45 (1970): 359–73.

430. Spencer, William. "Are Chaucer's Pilgrims Keyed to the Zodiac?" *ChauR* 4 (1970): 147–70.

431. Wood, Chauncey. *Chaucer and the Country of the Stars: Poetic Uses of Astrological Imagery.* Princeton: Princeton UP, 1979.

432. Wurtele, Douglas. "Another Look at an Old 'Science': Chaucer's Pilgrims and Physiognomy." In *From Arabye to Engelonde,* edited by A. E. Christa Canitz and Gernot R. Wieland. Ottawa: U of Ottawa P, 1999. 93–111.

See also nos. 366, 498, 665, 777, 1177.

Love, Marriage

433. Allman, W. W., and D. Thomas Hanks Jr. "Rough Love: Notes toward an Erotics of *The Canterbury Tales." ChauR* 38 (2003): 36–65.

434. Berggren, Ruth. "Who *Really* Is the Advocate of Equality in the Marriage Group?" *MSE* 6 (1977): 25–36.

435. Collins, Marie. "Love, Nature, and Law in the Poetry of Gower and Chaucer." In *Court and Poet,* edited by Glyn S. Burgess and others. Liverpool: Cairns, 1981. 113–28.

436. Denomy, Alexander J. *The Heresy of Courtly Love.* New York: Macmillan, 1947.

437. Edwards, Robert R. "Some Pious Talk about Marriage: Two Speeches from the *Canterbury Tales.*" In *Matrons and Marginal Women in Medieval Society,* edited by Robert R. Edwards and Vickie Ziegler. Woodbridge, Suffolk, UK: Boydell, 1995. 11–27.

438. Haahr, Joan G. "Chaucer's 'Marriage Group' Revisited: The Wife of Bath and the Merchant in Debate." In *Homo Carnalis: The Carnal Aspects of Medieval Human Life,* edited by Helen R. Lemay. [Binghamton]: Center for Medieval and Early Renaissance Studies, State University of New York at Binghamton, 1990. 105–20.

439. Hodge, James L. "The Marriage Group: Precarious Equilibrium." *ES* 46 (1965): 289–300.

440. Jacobs, Kathryn. *Marriage Contracts from Chaucer to the Renaissance Stage.* Gainesville: UP of Florida, 2001.

441. Kane, George. "Chaucer, Love Poetry, and Romantic Love." In *Acts of Interpretation,* edited by Mary Carruthers and Elizabeth D. Kirk. Norman, OK: Pilgrim, 1982. 237–55.

442. Kaske, R. E. "Chaucer's Marriage Group." In *Chaucer the Love Poet,* edited by Jerome Mitchell and William Provost. Athens: U of Georgia P, 1973. 45–66.

443. Kelly, H. A. *Love and Marriage in the Age of Chaucer.* Ithaca, NY: Cornell UP, 1975.

444. Kittredge, George Lyman. "Chaucer's Discussion of Marriage." *MP* 9 (1912): 435–67.

445. Lewis, C. S. *The Allegory of Love.* 1936. Reprint, Oxford: Oxford UP, 1958.

446. McCarthy, Conor. "Love, Marriage, and Law: Three Canterbury Tales." *ES* 83 (2002): 504–18.

447. Mandel, Jerome. "Courtly Love in the *Canterbury Tales.*" *ChauR* 19 (1985): 277–89.

448. Murtaugh, Daniel M. "Women and Geoffrey Chaucer." *ELH* 38 (1971): 473–92.

449. Nelson, Marie. "'Biheste is dette': Marriage Promises in Chaucer's *Canterbury Tales.*" *PLL* 38 (2002): 167–99.

450. O'Donoghue, Bernard. *The Courtly Love Tradition.* Manchester: Manchester UP, 1982.

451. Richmond, Velma Bourgeois. "'Pacience in Adversitee': Chaucer's Presentation of Marriage." *Viator* 10 (1979): 323–54.

452. Robertson, Elizabeth. "Marriage, Mutual Consent, and the Affirmation of the Female Subject in the *Knight's Tale,* the *Wife of Bath's Tale,* and the *Franklin's Tale.*" In *Drama, Narrative and Poetry in The Canterbury Tales,* edited by Wendy Harding. Toulouse: Presses Universitaires du Mirail, Collection Interlangues: Literatures, 2003. 175–93.

453. Slaughter, Eugene. *Virtue according to Love in Chaucer.* New York: Bookman, 1957.

454. Spearing, A. C. *The Medieval Poet as Voyeur: Looking and Listening in Medieval Love Narratives.* Cambridge: Cambridge UP, 1993.

455. Steadman, John M. "'Courtly Love' as a Problem of Style." In *Chaucer und seine Zeit: Symposium für Walter F.*

Schirmer, edited by Arno Esch. Tübingen, Germany: Narr, 1968. 1–33.

456. Taylor, Paul B. *Chaucer's Chain of Love.* Madison, NJ: Fairleigh Dickinson UP, 1996.

457. Wicher, Andrzej. "A Discussion of the Archetype of the Supernatural Husband and the Supernatural Wife As It Appears in Some of Geoffrey Chaucer's 'Canterbury Tales.'" *RealB* 7 (1990): 16–90.

458. Zong-qui, Cai. "Fragments I–II and III–V in the 'Canterbury Tales': A Re-examination of the Idea of the 'Marriage Group.'" *Comitatus* 19 (1988): 80–98.

See also nos. 392, 459, 470, 473–74, 1079, 1087, 1098.

Honor, Gentility, Pity

459. Baker, Donald C. "Chaucer's Clerk and the Wife of Bath on the Subject of Gentilesse." *SP* 59 (1962): 631–40.

460. Blamires, Alcuin. "Chaucer's Revaluation of Chivalric Honor." *Mediaevalia* 5 (1979): 245–69.

461. Brewer, Derek. "Honour in Chaucer." *E&S* 26 (1973): 1–19.

462. Burnley, David. *Courtliness and Literature in Medieval England.* New York: London, 1998.

463. Coghill, Nevill. *Chaucer's Idea of What Is Noble.* London: English Association, 1971.

464. Gray, Douglas. "'Pite for to Here — Pite for to Se': Some Scenes of Pathos in Late Medieval Literature." *PBA* 87 (1995): 67–99.

465. Guerin, Dorothy. "Chaucer's Pathos: Three Variations." *ChauR* 20 (1985): 90–112.

466. Harding, Wendy. "The Function of Pity in Three Canterbury Tales." *ChauR* 32 (1997): 162–74.

467. Justman, Stewart. "'The Reeve's Tale' and the Honor of Men." *SSF* 32 (1995): 21–27.

468. Kelso, Ruth. *The Doctrine of the English Gentleman in the Sixteenth Century.* Urbana: U of Illinois P, 1929.

469. Koretsky, Allen C. "The Heroes of Chaucer's Romances." *AnM* 17 (1976): 22–47.

470. Middleton, Anne. "War by Other Means: Marriage and Chivalry in Chaucer." *SAC Proceedings* 1 (1984): 119–33.

471. Monz, Dominic. *Gentelesse und Gentils: Der Weltliche Adel und Seine Werte in Geoffrey Chaucer's "Canterbury Tales."* Regensburg: Braun, 2002.

472. Penninger, Frieda Elaine. *Chaucer's 'Troilus and Criseyde' and 'The Knight's Tale': Fictions Used.* Lanham, MD: UP of America, 1993.

473. Saul, Nigel. "Chaucer and Gentility." In *Chaucer's England: Literature in Historical Context,* edited by Barbara A. Hanawalt. Minneapolis: U of Minnesota P, 1991. 41–55.

474. Silvia, D. S. "Geoffrey Chaucer on the Subject of Men, Women, and Gentillesse." *Revue des Langues Vivants* 33 (1967): 228–36.

475. Stugrin, Michael. "Ricardian Poetics and Late Medieval Cultural Pluriformity: The Significance of Pathos in the *Canterbury Tales.*" *ChauR* 15 (1981): 155–67.

476. Taylor, Paul Beekman. "The Uncourteous Knights of *The Canterbury Tales.*" *ES* 72 (1991): 209–18.

See also nos. 902, 1041, 1133, 1156.

Social Classes

477. Blamires, Alcuin. "Chaucer the Reactionary: Ideology and The General Prologue to The Canterbury Tales." *RES* 51 (2000): 523–39.

478. Brewer, Derek. "Class Distinction in Chaucer." *Speculum* 43 (1968): 290–305.

479. Knight, Stephen. "Politics and Chaucer's Poetry." In *The Radical Reader,* edited by Stephen Knight and Michael Wilding. Sydney: Wild and Woolley, 1977. 169–92.

480. Lindahl, Carl. "The Festive Form of the *Canterbury Tales.*" *ELH* 52 (1985): 531–74.

481. Patch, Howard. "Chaucer and the Common People." *JEGP* 29 (1930): 376–84.

482. Patterson, Lee. "'No Man His Reson Herde': Peasant Consciousness, Chaucer's Miller, and the Structure of the *Canterbury Tales.*" *SAQ* 86 (1987): 457–95.

See also nos. 517, 521, 772.

Imagery And Allegory

483. Boitani, Piero. "Chaucer and Lists of Trees." *RMS* 2 (1976): 28–44.

484. Brosamer, Matthew. "The Cook, the Miller, and Alimentary Hell." In *Chaucer and the Challenges of Medievalism,* edited by Donka Minkova and Theresa Tinkle. New York: Lang, 2003. 235–51.

485. David, Alfred. "An Iconography of Noses: Directions in the History of a Physical Stereotype." In *Mapping the Cosmos,* edited by Jane Chance and R. S. Wells Jr. Houston, TX: Rice UP, 1985. 76–97.

486. Doob, Penelope. *The Idea of the Labyrinth from Classical Antiquity through the Middle Ages.* Ithaca, NY: Cornell UP, 1990.

486a. Douglass, Rebecca M. "Ecocriticism in Middle English Literature." *SiM* 10 (1998): 136–63.

487. Economou, George D. "Chaucer's Use of the Bird in a Cage Image in *The Canterbury Tales.*" *PQ* 54 (1975): 679–84.

488. Emmerson, Richard K., and Ronald B. Herzman. *The Apocalyptic Imagination in Medieval Literature.* Philadelphia: U of Pennsylvania P, 1992.

489. Fisher, John H. "Chaucer's Horses." *SAQ* 60 (1961): 71–80.

490. Gillmeister, Heiner. *Chaucer's Conversion: Allegorical Thought in Medieval Literature.* New York: Lang, 1984.

491. Gross, Laila. "The Heart: Chaucer's Concretization of Emotions." *McNeece Review* 21 (1974–75): 89–102.

492. Haskell, Ann. "Chaucerian Women, Ideal Gardens, and the Wild Woods." In *A Wyf Ther Was: Essays in Honour of Paule Mertens-Fonck,* edited by Juliette Dor. Liége: U of Liége, 1992. 193–98.

493. Heffernan, Carol Falvo. "Wells and Streams in Three Chaucerian Gardens." *PLL* 15 (1979): 339–57.

494. Hermann, John P., and John J. Burke Jr., eds. *Signs and Symbols in Chaucer's Poetry*. University: U of Alabama P, 1981.

495. Howes, Laura L. *Chaucer's Gardens and the Language of Convention*. Gainesville: UP of Florida, 1997.

496. Huppé, Bernard F., and D. W. Robertson Jr. *Fruyt and Chaf: Studies in Chaucer's Allegories*. Princeton: Princeton UP, 1963.

497. Justman, Stewart. "Literal and Symbolic in the *Canterbury Tales*." *ChauR* 14 (1980): 199–214.

498. Lionarons, Joyce Tally. "Magic, Machines, and Deception: Technology in the *Canterbury Tales*." *ChauR* 27 (1993): 377–86.

499. Lynch, Kathryn. "Partitioned Fictions: The Meaning and Importance of Walls in Chaucer's Poetry." In *Art and Context in Late Medieval English Narrative*, edited by Robert R. Edwards. Cambridge, UK: Brewer, 1994. 107–25.

500. Richardson, Janette. *Blameth Nat Me: A Study of the Imagery in Chaucer's Fabliaux*. The Hague: Mouton, 1970.

501. Robertson, D. W., Jr. "The Doctrine of Charity in Medieval Literary Gardens." *Speculum* 26 (1951): 24–49.

502. ———. *A Preface to Chaucer: Studies in Medieval Perspective*. Princeton: Princeton UP, 1962.

503. Rowland, Beryl. *Blind Beasts: Chaucer's Animal World*. Kent, OH: Kent State UP, 1971.

504. ———. "The Horse and Rider Figure in Chaucer's Works." *UTQ* 35 (1966): 246–59.

505. Tinkle, Theresa. *Medieval Venuses and Cupids: Sexuality, Hermeneutics, and English Poetry*. Stanford, CA: Stanford UP, 1996.

506. Twycross, Meg. *The Medieval Anadyomene: A Study in Chaucer's Mythography*. Oxford: Blackwell, 1972.

507. Yamamoto, Dorothy. *The Boundaries of the Human in Medieval English Literature*. Oxford: Oxford UP, 2000.

See also nos. 337, 586, 596, 688, 791, 1098, 1330, 1422.

Various Themes

508. Aers, David. "Interpreting Dreams: Reflections on Freud, Milton, and Chaucer." In *Reading Dreams*, edited by Peter Brown. Oxford: Oxford UP, 1999. 84–98.

509. Biebel, Elizabeth M. "Pilgrims to Table: Food Consumption in Chaucer's *Canterbury Tales*." In *Food and Eating in Medieval Europe*, edited by Martha Carlin and Joel T. Rosenthal. Rio Grande, OH: Hambledon, 1998. 15–26.

510. Blodgett, E. D. "Chaucerian *Pryvetee* and the Opposition to Time." *Speculum* 51 (1976): 477–93.

511. Canfield, J. Douglas. *Word as Bond in English Literature from the Middle Ages to the Restoration*. Philadelphia: U of Pennsylvania P, 1989.

512. Cannon, Christopher. "Chaucer and Rape: Uncertainty's Certainties." *SAC* 22 (2000): 67–92.

513. Costigan, Edward. "'Privetee' in the *Canterbury Tales*." *SEL* 60 (1983): 217–30.

514. Dean, James. *The World Grown Old in Later Medieval Literature*. Cambridge, MA: Medieval Academy, 1997.

515. Delasanta, Rodney. "The Theme of Justice in *The Canterbury Tales*." *MLQ* 31 (1970): 298–307.

516. DeVries, David N. "Chaucer and the Idols of the Market." *ChauR* 32 (1999): 391–99.

517. Eaton, R. D. "Gender, Class, and Conscience in Chaucer." *ES* 84 (2003): 205–18.

518. Fichte, Jorge O. "Konkurrierende und Kontrastierende Zeitmuster in Chaucers *Canterbury Tales*." In *Zeitkonzeptionen Zeiterfahrung Zeitmessung: Stationen ihres Wandels vom Mittelalter bis zum Moderne*, edited by Trude Ehlert. Paderborn, Germany: Schöningh, 1997. 223–41.

519. Fields, Peter John. *Craft and Anti-craft in Chaucer's Canterbury Tales*. Lewistown, NY: Mellen, 2001.

520. Friman, Anne. "Of Bretherhede: The Friendship Motif in Chaucer." *Innisfree* 3 (1976): 24–36.

521. Ganim, John M. "Chaucer and the Noise of the People." *Exemplaria* 2 (1990): 71–88.

522. Hanning, Robert W. "'Parlous Play': Diabolic Comedy in Chaucer's *Canterbury Tales*." In *Chaucer's Humor: Critical Essays*, edited by Jean E. Jost. New York: Garland, 1994. 295–319.

523. ———. "Telling the Private Parts: 'Pryvetee' and Poetry in Chaucer's *Canterbury Tales*." In *The Idea of Medieval Literature*, edited by James M. Dean and Christian Zacher. Newark: U of Delaware P, 1992. 108–25.

524. Hieatt, Constance B. "'To boille the chiknes with the marybones': Hodge's Kitchen Revisited." In *Chaucerian Problems and Perspectives*, edited by Edward Vasta and Zacharias P. Thundy. Notre Dame, IN: U of Notre Dame P, 1979. 139–63.

525. Higgs, Elton D. "Temporal and Spiritual Indebtedness in the *Canterbury Tales*." In *New Perspectives on Middle English Texts*, edited by Susan Powell and Jeremy J. Smith. Cambridge, UK: Brewer, 2000. 151–67.

526. Joseph, Gerhard. "Chaucerian 'Game'—'Ernest' and the 'Argument of Herbergage' in the *Canterbury Tales*." *ChauR* 4 (1970): 83–96.

527. Justman, Stewart. "Medieval Monism and Abuse of Authority in Chaucer." *ChauR* 11 (1976): 95–111.

528. Kelly, Henry Ansger. "Meanings and Uses of *Raptus* in Chaucer's Time." *SAC* 20 (1998): 101–65.

529. Klene, Jean, C.S.C. "Chaucer's Contribution to the Popular Topos: The World Upside-Down." *Viator* 11 (1979): 321–34.

530. Lewis, Celia. "Framing Fiction with Death: Chaucer's *Canterbury Tales* and the Plague." In *New Readings of Chaucer's Poetry*, edited by Robert G. Benson and Susan Ridyard. Rochester, NY: Brewer, 2003. 139–64.

531. McIlhaney, Anne E. "Sentence and Judgment: The Role of the Fiend in Chaucer's *Canterbury Tales*." *ChauR* 31 (1996): 173–83.

532. Mann, Jill. "Anger and 'Glosynge' in the *Canterbury Tales*." *PBA* 76 (1990): 203–23.

533. ———. "Parents and Children in 'The Canterbury Tales.'" In *Literature in Fourteenth-Century England*, edited by Piero Boitani and Anna Torti. Cambridge, UK: Brewer, 1983. 165–83.

534. Olson, Glending. *Literature as Recreation in the Later Middle Ages.* Ithaca, NY: Cornell UP, 1982.

535. Orme, Nicholas. "Chaucer and Education." *ChauR* 16 (1981): 38–59.

536. Quinn, William A. "Chaucer's 'Janglerye.'" *Viator* 18 (1987): 309–20.

537. Roney, Lois. "Chaucer Subjectivizes the Oath: Depicting the Fall from Feudalism into Individualism in the 'Canterbury Tales.'" In *The Rusted Hauberk: Feudal Ideals of Order and Their Decline,* edited by Liam O. Purdon and Cindy L. Vitto. Gainesville: UP of Florida, 1994. 268–98.

538. Rose, Christine. "Reading Chaucer Reading Rape." In *Representing Rape in Medieval and Early Modern Literature,* edited by Elizabeth Robertson and Christine Rose. New York: Palgrave, 2001. 21–60.

539. Saunders, Corrine. *Rape and Ravishment in the Literature of Medieval England.* Cambridge, UK: Brewer, 2001.

540. Stanbury, Sarah. "EcoChaucer: Green Ethics and Medieval Nature." *ChauR* 39 (2004): 1–16.

541. Taylor, Paul B. "Time in the *Canterbury Tales.*" *Exemplaria* 7 (1995): 371–95.

542. Wilkins, Nigel. *Music in the Age of Chaucer.* Cambridge, UK: Brewer, 1980.

Visual Arts, Illustrations, and Portraits of Chaucer

543. Bowden, Betsy. "Visual Portraits of the Canterbury Pilgrims 1484 (?) to 1809." In no. 30, 171–204.

544. Davis, R. Evan. "The Pendant in the Chaucer Portraits." *ChauR* 17 (1982): 193–95.

545. Finley, William K., and Joseph Rosenblum, eds. *Chaucer Illustrated: Five Hundred Years of the Canterbury Tales in Pictures.* London: British Library, 2003.

546. Fleming, John V. "Chaucer and the Visual Arts of His Time." In *New Perspectives on Chaucer Criticism,* edited by Donald M. Rose. Norman, OK: Pilgrim, 1981. 121–36.

547. Hilmo, Maidie. "Framing the Canterbury Pilgrims for the Aristocratic Readers of the Ellesmere Manuscript." In *The Medieval Professional Reader at Work,* edited by Kathryn Kerby-Fulton and Maidie Hilmo. Victoria, BC: U of Victoria, 2001. 14–71.

548. Hussey, Maurice, comp. *Chaucer's World: A Pictorial Companion.* Cambridge: Cambridge UP, 1967.

549. Kendrick, Laura. "The Jesting Borders of Chaucer's *Canterbury Tales* and of Late Medieval Manuscript Art." In *Animating the Letter: The Figurative Embodiment of Writing from Late Antiquity to the Renaissance.* Columbus: Ohio State UP, 1999. 217–25.

550. Kolve, V. A. *Chaucer and the Imagery of Narrative: The First Five Canterbury Tales.* Stanford, CA: Stanford UP, 1984.

551. McGregor, James H. "The Iconography of Chaucer in Hoccleve's *De Regimine Principum* and the *Troilus* Frontispiece." *ChauR* 11 (1977): 338–50.

552. Miller, Miriam Youngerman. "Illustrations of the *Canterbury Tales* for Children: A Mirror of Chaucer's World?" *ChauR* 27 (1993): 293–304.

553. Mullaney, Samantha. "The Language of Costume in the Ellesmere Portraits." *Trivium* 31 (1999): 33–57.

554. Seymour, Michael. "Manuscript Portraits of Chaucer and Hoccleve." *Burlington Magazine* 124 (1982): 618–32.

555. Wentersdorf, Karl P. "The Symbolic Significance of *figurae scatologicae* in Gothic Manuscripts." In *Word, Picture, and Spectacle,* edited by Karl P. Wentersdorf and others. Kalamazoo: Western Michigan University, 1984. 1–19.

See also no. 182.

Reception and Guides to Criticism

556. Blamires, Alcuin. *"The Canterbury Tales": The Critics Debate.* London: Macmillan, 1987.

557. Boswell, Jackson Campbell, and Sylvia Wallace Holton. *Chaucer's Fame in England: STC Chauceriana 1475–1640.* New York: MLA, 2004.

558. Brewer, Derek, ed. *Geoffrey Chaucer: The Critical Heritage.* 2 vols. 1978. Reprint, London: Routledge, 1995.

559. Ellis, Steve. *Chaucer at Large: The Poet in the Modern Imagination.* Minneapolis: U of Minnesota P, 2000.

560. Leicester, H. Marshall. "Chaucer Criticism in 1996: Report to the Plenary Session of the New Chaucer Society, July 29, 1996." *Envoi* 6 (1997): 1–14.

561. Matthews, David. *The Making of Middle English, 1765–1910.* Minneapolis: U of Minnesota P, 1999.

562. Rooney, Anne. *Geoffrey Chaucer: A Guide through the Critical Maze.* Bristol: Bristol, 1989.

563. Rudd, Gillian. *The Complete Critical Guide to Geoffrey Chaucer.* New York: Routledge, 2001.

564. Saunders, Corrine. *Chaucer.* Blackwell Guides to Criticism. Oxford: Blackwell, 2001.

565. Spurgeon, Caroline F. E. *Five Hundred Years of Chaucer Criticism and Allusion 1357–1900.* 3 vols. 1908–17. Reprint, Cambridge: Cambridge UP, 1925; New York: Russell & Russell, 1960.

566. Trigg, Stephanie. *Congenial Souls: Reading Chaucer from Medieval to Postmodern.* Minneapolis: U of Minnesota P, 2002.

567. Utz, Richard. *Chaucer and the Discourse of German Philology: A History of Critical Reception and an Annotated Bibliography of Studies, 1793–1948.* Turnhout, Belgium: Brepols, 2002.

See also nos. 254, 265, 273, 286, 289.

General Studies and *The Canterbury Tales*

568. Aers, David. *Chaucer.* Atlantic Highlands, NJ: Humanities P International, 1986.

568a. Benson, C. David. *Chaucer's Drama of Style: Poetic Variety and Contrast in the Canterbury Tales.* Chapel Hill: U of North Carolina P, 1986.

569. Bishop, Ian. *The Narrative Art of "The Canterbury Tales": A Study of the Major Poems.* London: Everyman's University Library, 1987.

570. Brewer, Derek. *Chaucer the Poet as Storyteller.* London: Macmillan, 1984.

571. ———. *An Introduction to Chaucer.* London: Longman, 1984.

572. Coghill, Nevill. *The Poet Chaucer.* 2d ed. London: Oxford UP, 1967.

573. Corsa, Helen Storm. *Chaucer, Poet of Mirth and Morality.* Notre Dame, IN: U of Notre Dame P, 1964.

574. David, Alfred. *The Strumpet Muse: Art and Morals in Chaucer's Poetry.* Bloomington: Indiana UP, 1976.

575. Howard, Donald R. *The Idea of the Canterbury Tales.* Berkeley: U of California P, 1976.

576. Hussey, S. S. *Chaucer: An Introduction.* 2d ed. London: Methuen, 1981.

577. Kendrick, Laura. *Chaucerian Play: Comedy and Control in the "Canterbury Tales."* Berkeley: U of California P, 1988.

578. Kiser, Lisa. *Truth and Textuality in Chaucer's Poetry.* Hanover, NH: UP of New England, 1991.

579. Lawler, Traugott. *The One and the Many in The Canterbury Tales.* Hamden, CT: Archon, 1980.

580. Kean, P. M. *Chaucer and the Making of English Poetry.* 2 vols. London: Routledge, 1972.

581. Kittredge, George L. *Chaucer and His Poetry.* 1915. Reprint, Cambridge: Harvard UP, 1970.

582. McGavin, John J. *Chaucer and Dissimilarity: Comparisons in Chaucer and Other Late-Medieval Writing.* Madison, NJ: Fairleigh Dickinson UP, 2000.

583. Norton-Smith, John. *Geoffrey Chaucer.* London: Routledge, 1974.

584. Payne, Robert O. *Geoffrey Chaucer.* Boston: Twayne, 1986.

585. Richmond, Velma Bourgeois. *Geoffrey Chaucer.* New York: Continuum, 1992.

586. Rigby, S. H. *Chaucer in Context: Society, Allegory, and Gender.* Manchester: Manchester UP, 1996.

587. Ruggiers, Paul. *The Art of the Canterbury Tales.* Madison: U of Wisconsin P, 1965.

588. Russell, J. Stephen. *Chaucer and the Trivium: The Mindsong of the Canterbury Tales.* Gainesville: UP of Florida, 1998.

589. Shoaf, Allen. *Chaucer's Body: The Anxiety of Circulation in the Canterbury Tales.* Gainesville: UP of Florida, 2001.

590. Stone, Brian. *Chaucer.* Harmondsworth, UK: Penguin, 1989.

591. Traversi, Derek. *The "Canterbury Tales": A Reading.* Newark: U of Delaware P, 1983.

592. Whittock, Trevor. *A Reading of the Canterbury Tales.* Cambridge: Cambridge UP, 1968.

See also nos. 130, 345.

Social and Historical Criticism

593. Aers, David. *Chaucer, Langland, and the Creative Imagination.* London: Routledge, 1980.

594. ———. *Faith, Ethics, and the Church: Writing in England, 1360–1409.* Cambridge, UK: Brewer, 2000.

595. Aers, David, and Lynn Staley. *The Powers of the Holy: Religion, Politics, and Gender in Late Medieval English Culture.* University Park: Pennsylvania State UP, 1996.

596. Astell, Ann. *Political Allegory in Late-Medieval England.* Ithaca, NY: Cornell UP, 1999.

597. Barr, Helen. *Socioliterary Practice in Late Medieval England.* Oxford: Oxford UP, 2001.

598. Bennett, J. A. W. *Chaucer at Oxford and Cambridge.* Oxford: Cambridge, 1974.

599. Bisson, Lillian M. *Chaucer and the Late Medieval World.* New York: St. Martin's, 1999.

600. Bloomfield, Morton W. "Fourteenth-Century England: Realism and Rationalism in Wycliff and Chaucer." *ESA* 16 (1973): 59–70.

601. Bowers, John M. "Chaucer after Smithfield: From Postcolonial Writer to Imperialist Writer." In *The Postcolonial Middle Ages,* edited by Jeffrey Jerome Cohen. New York: St. Martin's, 2000. 53–66.

602. ———. "Chaucer's Canterbury Tales—Politically Corrected." In *Rewriting Chaucer: Culture, Authority, and the Idea of the Authentic Text,* edited by Thomas A. Prendergast and Barbara Kline. Columbus: Ohio State UP, 1999. 13–44.

603. Braswell, Mary Flowers. *Chaucer's "Legal Fiction": Reading the Records.* Teaneck, NJ: Fairleigh Dickinson UP, 2001.

604. Brewer, Derek. *Chaucer in His Time.* London: Nelson, 1963.

605. Brown, Peter, and Andrew Butcher. *The Age of Saturn: Literature and History in the Canterbury Tales.* Oxford: Blackwell, 1991.

606. Chute, Marchette. *Geoffrey Chaucer of England.* New York: Dutton, 1946.

607. Crane, Susan. *The Performance of Self: Ritual, Clothing, and Identity during the Hundred Years War.* Philadelphia: U of Pennsylvania P, 2002.

608. Dillon, Janette. *Geoffrey Chaucer.* New York: St. Martin's, 1993.

609. Green, Richard Firth. *A Crisis of Truth: Literature and Law in Ricardian England.* Philadelphia: U of Pennsylvania P, 1999.

610. Hornsby, Joseph Allen. *Chaucer and the Law.* Norman, OK: Pilgrim Books, 1988.

611. Hudson, Anne. *The Premature Reformation: Wycliffite Texts and Lollard History.* Oxford: Clarendon, 1988.

612. Johnston, Andrew James. *Clerks and Courtiers: Chaucer, Late Middle English Literature, and the State Formation Process.* Heidelberg: Winter, 2001.

613. Justice, Steven. *Writing and Rebellion: England in 1381.* Berkeley: U of California P, 1994.

614. Kaye, Joel. "Monetary and Market Consciousness in Thirteenth and Fourteenth Century Europe." In *Ancient and Medieval Economic Ideas and Concepts of Social Justice,* edited by S. Todd Lowry and Barry Gordon. New York: Brill, 1998. 371–403.

615. Knapp, Peggy. *Chaucer and the Social Contest.* New York: Routledge, 1991.

616. Knight, Stephen. "Chaucer and the Sociology of Literature." *SAC* 2 (1980): 15–51.

617. ———. *Geoffrey Chaucer.* Oxford: Blackwell, 1986.

618. Olson, Paul. *The Canterbury Tales and the Good Society.* Princeton: Princeton UP, 1986.

619. Patterson, Lee. *Chaucer and the Subject of History.* Madison: U of Wisconsin P, 1991.

620. ———, ed. *Literary Practice and Social Change in Britain, 1380–1530.* Berkeley: U of California P, 1990.

621. Peck, Russell A. "Social Conscience and the Poets." In *Social Unrest in the Middle Ages,* edited by Francis X. Newman. Binghamton, NY: Center for Medieval and Renaissance Studies, 1986. 113–48.

622. Strohm, Paul. *Social Chaucer.* Cambridge: Harvard UP, 1989.

623. ———. *Theory and the Premodern Text.* Minneapolis: U of Minnesota P, 2000.

624. Wallace, David. "In Flaundres." *SAC* 19 (1997): 63–91.

See also nos. 810, 812, 821–22.

Women and Feminist Criticism

625. Barnett, Pamela E. "'And Shortly for to Seyn They Were Aton': Chaucer's Deflections of Rape in the 'Reeve's' and the 'Franklin's Tales.'" *WS* 22 (1993): 145–62.

626. Blamires, Alcuin. *The Case for Women in Medieval Culture.* Oxford: Clarendon, 1997.

627. Cox, Catherine S. *Gender and Language in Chaucer.* Gainesville: UP of Florida, 1997.

628. Diamond, Arlyn. "Chaucer's Women and Women's Chaucer." In *The Authority of Experience: Essays in Feminist Criticism,* edited by Arlyn Diamond and Lee R. Edwards. Amherst: U of Massachusetts P, 1977. 60–83.

629. Dinshaw, Carolyn. *Chaucer's Sexual Poetics.* Madison: U of Wisconsin P, 1989.

630. Donnelly, Colleen. "Silence or Shame: How Women's Speech Contributes to Generic Conventionality and Generic Complexity in *The Canterbury Tales.*" *Lang&S* 24 (1991): 433–43.

631. Fyler, John M. "Man, Men and Woman in Chaucer's Poetry." In *The Olde Daunce: Love, Friendship, Sex, and Marriage in the Medieval World,* edited by Robert R. Edwards and Stephen Spector. Albany: State U of New York P, 1991. 154–76.

632. Hallissy, Margaret. *Clean Maids, True Wives, Steadfast Widows: Chaucer's Women and Medieval Codes of Conduct.* Westport, CT: Greenwood, 1993,

633. Hansen, Elaine Tuttle. *Chaucer and the Fictions of Gender.* Berkeley: U of California P, 1992.

634. Harley, Marta Powell. "Chaucer's Use of the Proserpina Myth in 'The Knight's Tale' and 'The Merchant's Tale.'" In *Images of Persephone: Feminist Readings in Western Literature,* edited by Elizabeth T. Hayes. Gainesville: UP of Florida, 1994. 20–32.

635. Haskell, Ann S. "The Portrayal of Women by Chaucer and His Age." In *What Manner of Woman?* edited by Marlene Springer. New York: New York UP, 1978. 1–14.

635a. Laskaya, Anne. *Chaucer's Approach to Gender in the Canterbury Tales.* Cambridge: Brewer, 1995.

636. Mann, Jill. "Chaucer and the 'Woman Question.'" In *This Noble Craft,* edited by Erik Kooper. Amsterdam: Rodopi, 1991. 173–88.

636a. ———. *Feminizing Chaucer.* Woodbridge, Suffolk, UK: Brewer, 2002.

637. Martin, Priscilla. *Chaucer's Women: Nuns, Wives, and Amazons.* Iowa City: U of Iowa P, 1990.

638. O'Brien, Timothy D. "Seductive Violence and Three Chaucerian Women." *CollL* 28.2 (2001): 178–96.

639. Salisbury, Eve. "Chaucer's 'Wife,' the Law, and Middle English Breton Lays." In *Domestic Violence in Medieval Texts,* edited by Eve Salisbury and others. Gainesville: UP of Florida, 2002. 73–93.

640. Stanbury, Sarah. "Women's Letters and Private Space." *Exemplaria* 6 (1994): 271–85.

641. Straus, Barrie Ruth. "Freedom through Renunciation: Women's Voices, Women's Bodies and the Phallic Order." In *Desire and Sexuality in the Premodern West,* edited by Jacqueline Murray and Konrad Eisenbichler. Toronto: U of Toronto P, 1996. 245–64.

642. ———. "Reframing the Violence of the Father: Reverse Oedipal Fantasies in Chaucer's Clerk's, Man of Law's, and Prioress's Tales." In *Domestic Violence in Medieval Texts,* edited by Eve Salisbury and others. Gainesville: UP of Florida, 2002. 122–38.

643. Sturges, Robert S. "*The Canterbury Tales*' Women Narrators: Three Traditions of Female Authority." *MLS* 13 (1983): 41–51.

644. Weisl, Angela Jane. "'Quiting Eve': Violence against Women in the *Canterbury Tales.*" In *Violence against Women in Medieval Texts,* edited by Anna Roberts. Gainesville: UP of Florida, 1998. 115–36.

645. Weismann, Hope Phyllis. "Antifeminism and Chaucer's Characterization of Women." In *Geoffrey Chaucer: A Collection of Original Essays,* edited by George D. Economou. New York: McGraw-Hill, 1976. 93–110.

646. Wynne-Davies, Marion. "'He Conquered Al the Regne of Femenye': Feminist Criticism of Chaucer." *Critical Survey* 4.2 (1992): 107–13.

See also nos. 398, 448, 709, 721, 963–64, 971, 975–76, 981, 1000, 1006, 1078, 1099, 1388–89.

Queer Studies

647. Bowers, John M. "Queering the Summoner: Same-Sex Union in Chaucer's *Canterbury Tales.*" In *Speaking Images: Essays in Honor of V. A. Kolve,* edited by R. F. Yeager and Charlotte C. Morse. Asheville, NC: Pegasus, 2001. 301–24.

648. Burger, Glenn. *Chaucer's Queer Nation.* Minneapolis: U of Minnesota P, 2003.

649. ———. "Shameful Pleasures: Up Close and Dirty with Chaucer, Flesh, and the Word." In *Queering the Middle Ages,* edited by Glenn Burger and Steven Kruger. Minneapolis: U of Minnesota P, 2001. 213–35.

650. Dinshaw, Carolyn. *Getting Medieval: Sexualities and Communities, Pre- and Postmodern.* Durham, NC: Duke UP, 1999.

651. Frantzen, Allen J. *Before the Closet: Same-Sex Love from Beowulf to Angels in America.* Chicago: U of Chicago P, 1998.

652. Lochrie, Karma. "Presumptive Sodomy and Its Exclusions." *Textual Practice* 13 (1999): 295–313.

653. Schibanoff, Susan. "Chaucer's Lesbians: Drawing Blanks?" *Medieval Feminist Newsletter* 13 (Spring 1992): 11–13.

See also nos. 657, 807, 809, 835, 839, 866, 990, 1198, 1206, 1209, 1219, 1238, 1242.

Race, the Other, and Postcolonial Studies

654. Collette, Carolyn P., and Vincent J. DiMarco. "The Matter of Armenia in the Age of Chaucer." *SAC* 23 (2001): 317–58.

655. Davis, Kathleen. "Time behind the Veil: The Media, the Middle Ages, and Orientalism Now." In *The Postcolonial Middle Ages,* edited by Jeffrey Jerome Cohen. New York: St Martin's, 2000. 105–22.

656. Delany, Sheila. *Chaucer and the Jews: Sources, Contexts, Meaning.* New York: Routledge, 2002.

657. Dinshaw, Carolyn. "Pale Faces: Race, Religion, and Affect in Chaucer's Texts and Their Readers." *SAC* 23 (2001): 19–41.

658. Fyler, John M. "Chaucerian Romance and the World beyond Europe." In *Literary Aspects of Courtly Culture,* edited by Donald Maddox and Sara Sturm-Maddox. Cambridge, UK: Brewer, 1994. 257–63.

659. Heffernan, Carol Falvo. *The Orient in Chaucer and Medieval Romance.* Rochester, NY: Boydell & Brewer, 2003.

659a. Heng, Geraldine. "Beauty and the East, a Modern Love Story: Women, Children, and Imagined Communities in *The Man of Law's Tale* and Its Others." In *Empire of Magic: Medieval Romance and the Politics of Cultural Fantasy.* New York: Columbia UP, 2003. 181–237.

660. Lynch, Kathryn L., ed. *Chaucer's Cultural Geography.* New York: Routledge, 2002.

661. Rose, Christine M. "The Jewish Mother-in-Law: Synagoga and the Man of Law's Tale." In *Hildegard of Bingen: Book of Essays,* edited by Maud Burnett McInerney. New York: Garland, 1998. 191–226.

661a. Said, Edward W. *Orientalism.* New York: Pantheon, 1978.

662. Sancéry, Arlette. "Représentations de l'Orient dans l'Angleterre médiévale." In *Angleterre et Orient au Moyen Âge,* edited by André Crépin. Paris: Association des Médiévistes Anglicistes de l'Enseignement Supérieur, 2002. 51–64.

663. Schildgen, Brenda Deen. *Pagans, Tartars, Moslems, and Jews in Chaucer's Canterbury Tales.* Gainesville: UP of Florida, 2001.

664. Tomasch, Sylvia. "Postcolonial Chaucer and the Virtual Jew." In *The Postcolonial Middle Ages,* edited by Jeffrey Jerome Cohen. New York: St. Martin's, 2000. 243–60.

See also nos. 601, 612, 909, 921, 924, 929, 932, 934, 974, 1112, 1275, 1284, 1292.

Psychology and Psychological Studies

665. Collette, Carolyn P. *Species, Phantasms, and Images: Vision and Medieval Psychology in The Canterbury Tales.* Ann Arbor: U of Michigan P, 2001.

666. Fradenburg, L. O. Aranye. *Sacrifice Your Love: Psychoanalysis, Historicism, Chaucer.* Minneapolis: U of Minnesota P, 2002.

667. Ginsberg, Warren. "The Lineaments of Desire: Wish-Fulfillment in Chaucer's Marriage Group." *Criticism* 25 (1983): 197–210.

668. Leicester, H. Marshall. *The Disenchanted Self: Representing the Subject in the Canterbury Tales.* Berkeley: U of California P, 1990.

669. Rudat, Wolfgang E. H. "The *Canterbury Tales*: Anxiety Release and Wish Fulfillment." *American Imago* 35 (1978): 407–18.

670. ———. *Earnest Exuberance in Chaucer's Poetics: Textual Games in the "Canterbury Tales."* Lewiston, NY: Mellen, 1994.

671. Scala, Elizabeth. "Historicists and Their Discontents: Reading Psychoanalytically in Medieval Studies." *TSLL* 44 (2002): 108–31.

672. Wolfe, Matthew C. "Jung and Chaucer: Synchronicity in *The Canterbury Tales.*" In *Archetypal Readings of Medieval Literature,* edited by Charlotte Spivack and Christine Herold. Lewiston, NY: Mellen, 202. 181–202.

673. Yiavis, Kostas. "Chaucer and the Death of the Father as a Figure of Authority." *Gramma Journal of Theory and Criticism* 9 (2001): 13–29.

See also nos. 854, 882, 866, 882, 973, 1070, 1086, 1228.

Structure and Frame

674. Allen, Judson Boyce, and Theresa Anne Mortiz. *A Distinction of Stories: The Medieval Unity of Chaucer's Fair Chain of Narratives for Canterbury.* Columbus: Ohio State UP, 1981.

675. Andreas, James R. "'Wordes Betwene': The Rhetoric of the Canterbury Links." *ChauR* 29 (1994): 45–64.

676. Astell, Ann. *Chaucer and the Universe of Learning.* Ithaca, NY: Cornell UP, 1996.

677. Baldwin, Ralph. *The Unity of the Canterbury Tales.* Copenhagen: Rosenkilde & Bagger, 1955.

678. Bloomfield, Morton. "*The Canterbury Tales* as Framed Narratives." *LeedsSE* 14 (1983): 44–56.

679. Condren, Edward I. *Chaucer and the Energy of Creation.* Gainesville: UP of Florida, 1999.

680. Cooper, Helen. *The Structure of the Canterbury Tales.* Athens: U of Georgia P, 1984.

681. Davidoff, Judith M. *Beginning Well: Framing Fictions in Late Middle English Poetry.* Rutherford, NJ: Fairleigh Dickinson UP, 1988.

682. Dean, James. "Dismantling the Canterbury Book." *PMLA* 100 (1984): 746–62.

683. Gittes, Katharine S. *Framing the Canterbury Tales: Chaucer and the Medieval Frame Tradition.* New York: Greenwood, 1991.

684. Jordan, Robert O. *Chaucer and the Shape of Creation: The Aesthetic Possibilities of Inorganic Structure.* Cambridge: Harvard UP, 1967.

685. Lumiansky, Robert M. *Of Sondry Folk: The Dramatic Principle of the Canterbury Tales.* Austin: U of Texas P, 1955.

686. Mandel, Jerome. *Geoffrey Chaucer: Building the Fragments of the Canterbury Tales.* Cranbury, NJ: Associated U Presses, 1992.

687. Olson, Glending. "Chaucer's Idea of a Canterbury Game." In *The Idea of Medieval Literature,* edited by James M. Dean and Christian Zacher. Newark: U of Delaware P, 1992. 72–90.

688. Rogers, William E. *Upon the Ways: The Structure of the Canterbury Tales.* Victoria, BC: U of Victoria, 1986.

689. Thompson, Charlotte. "Cosmic Allegory and Cosmic Error in the Frame of *The Canterbury Tales.*" *PCP* 18 (1983): 77–83.

See also nos. 341, 575, 720, 723.

Genre

690. Andreas, James R. "The Rhetoric of Chaucerian Comedy: The Aristotelian Legacy." *Comparatist* 8 (1984): 56–66.

691. Ashton, Gail. *The Generation of Identity in Late Medieval Hagiography: Speaking the Saint.* New York: Routledge, 2000.

692. Battles, Paul. "Chaucer and the Traditions of Dawn Song." *ChauR* 31 (1997): 317–38.

693. Benson, C. David. "The Aesthetic of Chaucer's Religious Tales in Rhyme Royale." In *Religion in the Poetry and Drama of the Late Middle Ages in England,* edited by Piero Boitani and Anna Torti. Cambridge, UK: Brewer, 1990. 101–17.

694. Cooke, Thomas D. *The Old French and Chaucerian Fabliaux: A Study of Their Comic Climax.* Columbia: U of Missouri P, 1978.

695. Crane, Susan. *Gender and Romance in Chaucer's Canterbury Tales.* Princeton: Princeton UP, 1994.

696. Finlayson, John. "Definitions of Middle English Romance." Parts I and II. *ChauR* 15 (1980): 44–62, 168–81.

697. Garbáty, Thomas J. "Chaucer and Comedy." In *Versions of Medieval Comedy,* edited by Paul G. Ruggiers. Norman: U of Oklahoma P, 1977. 173–90.

698. Herold, Christine. *Chaucer's Tragic Muse — the Paganization of Christian Tragedy.* Lewiston: NY: Mellen, 2003.

699. Hines, John. *The Fabliau in English.* New York: Longman, 1993.

700. Jordan, Robert. "Chaucerian Romance?" *Yale French Studies* 51 (1974): 223–34.

701. Kelly, Henry Ansgar. *Chaucerian Tragedy.* Cambridge, UK: Brewer, 1997.

702. Morse, Ruth. "Absolute Tragedy: Allusions and Avoidances." *PoeticaT* 38 (1993): 1–17.

703. Payne, F. Anne. *Chaucer and Menippean Satire.* Madison: U of Wisconsin P, 1981.

704. Rowland, Beryl. "What Chaucer Did to the Fabliaux." *SN* 51 (1979): 205–13.

705. Scanlon, Larry. *Narrative, Authority, and Power: The Medieval Exemplum and the Chaucerian Tradition.* Cambridge: Cambridge UP, 1994.

706. Smith, D. Vance. "Plague, Panic, and the Tragic Medieval Household." *SAQ* 98 (1999): 367–414.

707. Spencer, H. Leith *English Preaching in the Late Middle Ages.* Oxford: Clarendon, 1993.

708. Strohm, Paul. "Some Generic Distinctions in the *Canterbury Tales.*" *MP* 68 (1971): 321–28.

709. Weisl, Angela Jane. *Conquering the Reign of Femeny: Gender and Genre in Chaucer's Romance.* Cambridge, UK: Brewer, 1995.

710. Wetherbee, Winthrop. "Chaucer and the Tragic Vision of Life." *PoeticaT* 55 (2001): 39–53.

711. Wheatley, Edward. *Mastering Aesop: Medieval Education, Chaucer, and His Followers.* Gainesville: UP of Florida, 2000.

See also nos. 396, 469, 500, 630, 658–59, 832, 856, 887, 900, 905, 930, 1190, 1258, 1315, 1337, 1365, 1371, 1374, 1431.

The Pilgrimage Motif

712. Allen, Mark. "Moral and Aesthetic Falls on the Canterbury Way." *SCRev* 8 (1991): 36–49.

713. Dyas, Dee. *Pilgrimage in Medieval English Literature, 700–1500.* Cambridge, UK: Brewer, 2001.

714. Eisner, Sigmund. "Canterbury Day: A Fresh Start." *ChauR* 27 (1992): 31–44.

715. Georgianna, Linda. "Love So Dearly Bought: The Terms of Redemption in 'The Canterbury Tales.'" *SAC* 12 (1990): 85–116.

716. Howard, Donald R. *Writers and Pilgrims: Medieval Pilgrimage Narratives and Their Posterity.* Berkeley: U of California P, 1980.

717. Jonassen, Frederick B. "The Inn, the Cathedral, and the Pilgrimage of *The Canterbury Tales.*" In *Rebels and Rivals: The Contestive Spirit in The Canterbury Tales,* edited by Susanna Greer Fein and others. Kalamazoo, MI: Medieval Institute, 1991. 1–35.

718. Knapp, Daniel. "The Relyk of a Saint: A Gloss on Chaucer's Pilgrimage." *ELH* 39 (1972): 1–26.

719. Medcalf, Stephen. "Motives for Pilgrimage: *The Tale of Beryn.*" In *England in the Fourteenth Century,* edited by Nicholas Rogers. Stamford, CT: Watkins, 1993. 97–108.

720. Morgan, Gerald. "Moral and Social Identity and the Idea of Pilgrimage in the *General Prologue.*" *ChauR* 37.4 (2003): 285–314.

721. Morrison, Susan Signe. *Women Pilgrims in Late Medieval England: Private Piety as Public Performance.* New York: Routledge, 2000.

722. Pison, Thomas. "Liminality in *The Canterbury Tales.*" *Genre* 10 (1977): 157–71.

723. Reinheimer, David. "Chaucer's Mystery: Cycle Plays and Unity in the Canterbury Tales." *Publications of the Missouri Philological Association* 24 (1999): 1–10.

724. Reiss, Edmund. "The Pilgrimage Narrative and the *Canterbury Tales.*" *SP* 67 (1970): 295–305.

725. Stopford, J. *Pilgrimage Explored.* Rochester, NY: York Medieval, 1999.

726. Thundy, Zacharias P. "Significance of Pilgrimage in Chaucer's *Canterbury Tales.*" *Literary Half-Yearly* 20.2 (1979): 64–77.

727. Webb, Diana. *Pilgrimage in Medieval England.* New York: Hambledon, 2000.

728. Zacher, Christian. *Curiosity and Pilgrimage.* Baltimore: Johns Hopkins UP, 1976.

See also nos. 421, 426.

Names and Number of Pilgrims; Pilgrims without Tales

729. Bowers, John M. "Chaucer's Canterbury Tales—Politically Corrected." In *Rewriting Chaucer,* edited by Thomas A. Prendergast and Barbara Kline. Columbus: Ohio State UP, 1999. 13–44.

730. Brosnahan, Leger. "The Authenticity of 'And Preestes Thre.'" *ChauR* 16 (1982): 293–310.

731. Eckhardt, Caroline D. "The Number of Chaucer's Pilgrims: A Review and Reappraisal." *YES* 5 (1975): 1–18.

732. Eliason, Norman. "Personal Names in the *Canterbury Tales.*" *Names* 21 (1973): 137–52.

733. Garbáty, Thomas. "Chaucer's Guildsmen and Their Fraternity." *JEGP* 59 (1960): 691–709.

734. Gastle, Brian. "Chaucer's 'Shaply' Guildsmen and Mercantile Pretensions." *NM* 99 (1998): 211–16.

735. Goodall, Peter. "Chaucer's 'Burgesses' and the Aldermen of London." *MAE* 50 (1981): 284–91.

736. Hardwick, Paul. "Chaucer: The Poet as Ploughman." *ChauR* 33 (1998): 146–56.

737. Harwood, Britton J. "The 'Fraternitee' of Chaucer's Guildsmen." *RES* 39 (1988): 413–17.

738. Kirk, Elizabeth. "Langland's Plowman and the Recreation of Fourteenth-Century Religious Metaphor." *YLS* 2 (1988): 1–21. (the Plowman)

739. McColly, William B. "Chaucer's Yeoman and the Rank of His Knight." *ChauR* 20 (1985): 14–27.

740. Mertens-Fonck, Paule. "The Canterbury Tales: New Proposals of Interpretation." *Atti della Accademia Peloritana dei Pericolanti Classe di Lettere, Filosofia e Belle Arti* 69 (1995): 1–29.

741. Rogers, P. Burwell. "The Names of the Canterbury Pilgrims." *Names* 16 (1968): 339–46.

See also nos. 113, 849.

The Host

742. Allen, Mark. "Mirth and Bourgeois Masculinity in Chaucer's Host." In *Masculinities in Chaucer,* edited by Peter G. Beidler. Cambridge, UK: Brewer, 1998. 9–21.

742a. Carruthers, Leo. "Narrative Voice, Narrative Framework: The Host as 'Author' of *The Canterbury Tales.*" In *Drama, Narrative and Poetry in The Canterbury Tales,* edited by Wendy Harding. Toulouse: Presses Universitaires du Mirail, Collection Interlangues: Literatures, 2003. 51–67.

743. Cowgill, Bruce Kent. "'By *corpus dominus*': Harry Bailey as False Spiritual Guide." *JMRS* 15 (1985): 157–81.

744. Gaylord, Alan T. "*Sentence* and *Solaas* in Fragment VII of the *Canterbury Tales:* Harry Bailly as Horseback Editor." *PMLA* (1967): 226–35.

745. Hanawalt, Barbara A. "The Host, the Law, and the Ambiguous Space of Medieval London Taverns." In *Medieval Crime and Social Control,* edited by Barbara A. Hanawalt and David Wallace. Minneapolis: U of Minnesota P, 1999. 204–23.

746. Hussey, S. S. "Chaucer's Host." In *Medieval Studies Presented to George Kane,* edited by Edward Donald Kennedy and others. Woodbridge, Suffolk, UK: Brewer, 1988. 153–65.

747. Keen, William. "'To Doon Yow Ese': A Study of the Host in the General Prologue to the *Canterbury Tales.*" *Topic* 17 (1969): 5–18.

748. Leitch, L. M. "Sentence and Solaas: The Function of the Host in the *Canterbury Tales.*" *ChauR* 17 (1982): 5–20.

749. Page, Barbara. "Concerning the Host." *ChauR* 4 (1970): 1–13.

750. Pichaske, David R., and Laura Sweetland. "Chaucer on the Medieval Monarchy: Harry Bailey in the *Canterbury Tales.*" *ChauR* 11 (1977): 179–200.

751. Plummer, John F. "'Beth fructuous and that in litel space': The Engendering of Harry Bailly." In *New Readings of Chaucer's Poetry,* edited by Robert G. Benson and Susan J. Ridyard. Rochester, NY: Brewer, 2003. 107–18.

752. Richardson, Cynthia. "The Function of the Host in the *Canterbury Tales.*" *TSLL* 12 (1970): 325–44.

753. Scheps, Walter. "'Up roos oure Hoost, and was oure aller cok': Harry Bailly's Tale-Telling Competition." *ChauR* 10 (1975): 113–28.

See also nos. 1198, 1216, 1311–12.

Part 1

754. Brewer, Derek. "Knight and Miller: Similarity and Difference." In *Drama, Narrative and Poetry in The Canterbury Tales,* edited by Wendy Harding. Toulouse: Presses Universitaires du Mirail, Collection Interlangues: Literatures, 2003. 127–38.

755. Fisher, John H. "The Three Styles of Fragment I of the *Canterbury Tales.*" *ChauR* 8 (1973): 119–27.

756. Jenson, Emily. "Male Competition as a Unifying Motif in Fragment A of the *Canterbury Tales.*" *ChauR* 24 (1990): 320–28.

757. Siegel, Marsha. "What the Debate Is and Why It Founders in Fragment A of the *Canterbury Tales.*" *SP* 82 (1985): 1–24.

1 — The General Prologue

758. Andrew, Malcolm. "Context and Judgment in the 'General Prologue.'" *ChauR* 23 (1989): 316–37.

759. Badendyck, J. Lawrence. "Chaucer's Portrait Technique and the Dream Vision Tradition." *English Record* 21 (1970): 113–25.

760. Bowden, Muriel. *A Commentary on the General Prologue to the Canterbury Tales.* New York: Macmillan, 1948.

761. Cooney, Helen. "The Limits of Human Knowledge and the Structure of Chaucer's 'General Prologue.'" *SN* 63 (1991): 147–59.

762. Cooper, Helen. "Langland's and Chaucer's Prologues." *YLS* 1 (1987): 71–81.

763. Cunningham, J. V. "The Literary Form of the Prologue to the *Canterbury Tales.*" *MP* 49 (1952): 172–81.

764. Dauby, Hélène. "'In sangwyn and in pers': Les Couleurs dans le Prologue General des 'Canterbury Tales.'" In *Les Couleurs au Moyen Age.* Aix-en Provence: Université de Provence, 1988. 45–56.

765. Dobbs, Elizabeth. "Literary, Legal, and Last Judgments in *The Canterbury Tales.*" *SAC* 14 (1992): 31–52.

766. Eberle, Patricia J. "Commercial Language and the Commercial Outlook in the *General Prologue.*" *ChauR* 18 (1982): 161–74.

767. George, Jodi-Anne, ed. *Geoffrey Chaucer: The General Prologue to the Canterbury Tales.* New York: Columbia UP, 2000.

768. Higgs, Elton D. "The Old Order and the 'Newe World' in the General Prologue to the *Canterbury Tales.*" *HLQ* 45 (1982): 155–73.

769. Hodges, Laura. *Chaucer and Clothing: Clerical and Academic Costume in the General Prologue to The Canterbury Tales.* Rochester, NY: Brewer, 2005.

769a. ———. *Chaucer and Costume: The Secular Pilgrims in the General Prologue.* Cambridge, UK: Brewer, 2000.

770. Hoffman, Arthur. "Chaucer's Prologue: Two Voices." *ELH* 21 (1954): 1–16.

771. Lambdin, Laura C., and Robert T. Lambdin, eds. *Chaucer's Pilgrims: An Historical Guide to the Pilgrims in The Canterbury Tales.* Westport, CT: Greenwood, 1996.

772. Mann, Jill. *Chaucer and Medieval Estates Satire: The Literature of Social Classes and the General Prologue.* Cambridge: Cambridge UP, 1972.

773. Martin, Loy D. "History and Form in the General Prologue to the *Canterbury Tales.*" *ELH* 45 (1978): 1–17.

774. Mertens-Fonck, Paule. "Art and Symmetry in the 'General Prologue' to the 'Canterbury Tales.'" In *Actes du Congres d'Amiens 1982.* Société des Anglicistes de l'Enseignement Supérieur. Paris: Didier, 1987. 41–51.

775. Morgan, Gerald. "The Design of the General Prologue to the *Canterbury Tales.*" *ES* 58 (1977): 481–93.

776. ———. "Rhetorical Perspectives in the 'General Prologue' to the 'Canterbury Tales.'" *ES* 62 (1981): 411–22.

777. Owen, Charles A., Jr. "Chaucer's Witty Prosody in 'General Prologue,' Lines 1–42." In *Chaucer's Humor: Critical Essays,* edited by Jean Jost. New York: Garland, 1994. 261–70.

778. Sklute, Larry. "Catalogue Form and Catalogue Style in the General Prologue of the *Canterbury Tales.*" *SN* 52 (1980): 35–46.

779. Yusef, Abdul R. "The Spring Motif and the Subversion of Guaranteed Meaning in Chaucer's *The Canterbury Tales.*" *ESA* 38.2 (1995): 1–15.

See also nos. 38, 60, 106, 351, 357, 360.

1 — The Knight and His Tale

780. Amtower, Laurel. "Mimetic Desire and the Misappropriation of the Ideal in *The Knight's Tale.*" *Exemplaria* 8 (1996): 125–44.

781. Anderson, David. *Before the "Knight's Tale": Imitation of Classical Epic in Boccaccio's "Teseida."* Philadelphia: U of Pennsylvania P, 1988.

782. Bergen, Brooke. "Surface and Secret in the Knight's Tale." *ChauR* 26 (1991): 1–16.

783. Blake, Kathleen. "Order and the Noble Life in Chaucer's *Knight's Tale.*" *MLQ* 34 (1973): 3–19.

784. Bowers, John M. "Three Readings of *The Knight's Tale:* Sir John Clanvowe, Geoffrey Chaucer, and James I of Scotland." *JMEMSt* 34 (2004): 297–307.

785. Brewer, Derek. "Chaucer's Knight's Tale and the Problems of Cultural Translatability." In *Corresponding Powers,* edited by George Hughes. Rochester, NY: Brewer, 1997. 103–12.

786. Brooks, Douglas, and Alastair Fowler. "The Meaning of Chaucer's *Knight's Tale.*" *MAE* 39 (1970): 123–46.

787. Broughton, Laurel. "He Conquered Al the Regne of Femenye: What Chaucer's Knight Doesn't Tell about Theseus." In *Speaking in the Medieval World,* edited by Jean E. Godsall-Myers. Boston: Brill, 2003. 43–63.

788. Brown, Emerson, Jr. "Chaucer's Knight: What's Wrong with Being Worthy?" *Mediaevalia* 15 (1993): 183–205.

789. Carruthers, Mary. "Seeing Things: Locational Memory in Chaucer's *Knight's Tale.*" In *Art and Context in Late Medieval English Narrative,* edited by Robert R. Edwards. Cambridge, UK: Brewer, 1994. 93–106.

790. Chewning, Susannah Mary. "'Wommen . . . Folwen Alle the Favour of Fortune': A Semiotic Reading of Chaucer's *Knight's Tale.*" In *Semiotics 1993,* edited by Robert S. Corrington and John Deely. New York: Peter Lang, 1993. 373–79.

791. Clogan, Paul M. "The Imagery of the City of Thebes in 'The Knight's Tale.'" In *Typology and English Medieval Literature,* edited by Hugh T. Keenan. New York: AMS, 1968. 169–81.

792. Clopper, Lawrence. "The Engaged Spectator: Langland and Chaucer on Civic Spectacle and the *Theatrum.*" *SAC* 22 (2000): 115–39.

793. Cooney, Helen. "Wonder and Boethian Justice in the 'Knight's Tale.'" In *Noble and Joyous Histories: English Romances, 1375–1650,* edited by Eilean Ni Cuilleanain and J. D. Pheifer. Dublin: Irish Academic P, 1993. 27–58.

794. Cowgill, Bruce Kent. "*The Knight's Tale* and the Hundred Years' War." *PQ* 54 (1975): 670–79.

795. Diamond, Arlyn. "Unhappy Endings: Failed Love/ Failed Faith in Late Romances." In *Readings in Medieval English Romance,* edited by Carol M. Meale. Cambridge, UK: Brewer, 1994. 65–81.

796. Fichte, Joerg O. "Man's Free Will and the Poet's Choice: The Creation of Artistic Order in Chaucer's *Knight's Tale.*" *Anglia* 93 (1975): 335–60.

797. Finlayson, John. "*The Knight's Tale:* The Dialogue of Romance, Epic, and Philosophy." *ChauR* 27 (1992): 126–49.

798. Fowler, Elizabeth. "The Afterlife of the Civil Dead: Conquest in the *Knight's Tale.*" In *Critical Essays on Geoffrey Chaucer,* edited by Thomas Stillinger. New York: Hall, 1987. 59–81.

799. ———. "Chaucer's Hard Cases." In *Medieval Crime and Social Control,* edited by Barbara A. Hanawalt and David Wallace. Minneapolis: U of Minnesota P, 1999. 124–42.

800. Fradenburg, Louise O. "Sacrificial Desire in the *Knight's Tale.*" *JMEMSt* 27 (1997): 47–75.

801. Ganim, John. "Chaucerian Ritual and Patriarchal Discourse." *ChauY* 1 (1992): 65–86.

802. Hallissy, Margaret. "Writing a Building: Chaucer's Knowledge of the Construction Industry and the Language of the *Knight's Tale.*" *ChauR* 32 (1998): 239–59.

803. Hamaguchi, Keiko. "Domesticating Amazons in *The Knight's Tale.*" *SAC* 26 (2004): 331–54.

804. Hanning, Robert W. "'The Struggle between Noble Design and Chaos': The Literary Tradition of Chaucer's *Knight's Tale.*" *LittR* 23 (1980): 519–41.

805. Hazell, Dinah. "Empedocles, Boethius, and Chaucer: Love Binds All." *CarmP* 11 (2002): 43–74.

806. Helterman, Jeffrey. "The Dehumanizing Metamorphosis of *The Knight's Tale.*" *ELH* 38 (1971): 493–511.

807. Ingham, Patricia Clare. "Homosociality and Creative Masculinity in the Knight's Tale." In *Masculinities in Chaucer,* edited by Peter G. Biedler. Cambridge, UK: Brewer, 1998. 23–35.

808. Johnston, Andrew James. "The Keyhole Poetics of Chaucerian Theatricality: Voyeurism in the *Knight's Tale.*" *PoeticaT* 34 (2002): 73–97.

809. ———. "Wrestling with Ganymede: Chaucer's Knight's Tale and the Homoerotics of Epic History." *Germanische-Romanische Monatsschrift* 50 (2000): 21–43.

810. Jones, Terry. *Chaucer's Knight: The Portrait of a Medieval Mercenary.* Baton Rouge: Louisiana State UP, 1980.

811. ———. "The Image of Chaucer's Knight." In *Speaking Images: Essays in Honor of V. A. Kolve,* edited by Robert F. Yeager and Charlotte C. Morse. Asheville, NC: Pegasus, 2001. 205–36.

812. Keen, Maurice. "Chaucer's Knight, the English Aristocracy and the Crusade." In *English Court Culture,* edited by V. J. Scattergood and L. W. Sherborne. New York: St. Martin's, 1983. 45–61.

813. Klitgård, Ebbe. *Chaucer's Narrative Voice in "The Knight's Tale."* Copenhagen: Museum Tusculanum, 1995.

814. Lester, G. A. "Chaucer's Knight and the Medieval Tournament." *Neophil* 46 (1982): 460–68.

815. Luttrell, Anthony. "Chaucer's Knight and the Mediterranean." *Library of Mediterranean History* 1 (1994): 127–60.

816. Minnis, Alastair J. "'Goddes Speken in Amphibologies': The Ambiguous Future of Chaucer's *Knight's Tale.*" *PoeticaT* 55 (2001): 23–37.

817. Mroczkowski, Przemyslaw. "Chaucer's Knight and Some of His Fellow-Fighters." In *Genres, Themes, and Images in English Literature from the Fourteenth to the Fifteenth Century,* edited by Piero Boitani and Anna Torti. Tübingen, Germany: Narr, 1988. 40–58.

818. Murtaugh, Daniel M. "The Education of Theseus in *The Knight's Tale.*" *SELIM* 10 (2000): 141–65.

819. Muscatine, Charles. "Form, Texture, and Meaning in Chaucer's *Knight's Tale.*" *PMLA* 65 (1950): 911–29.

820. Noguchi, Shunichi. "Prayers in Chaucer's 'Knight's Tale.'" *PoeticT* 41 (1994): 45–50.

821. Olson, Paul. "Chaucer's Epic Statement and the Political Milieu of the Late Fourteenth Century." *Mediaevalia* 5 (1979): 61–87.

822. Pratt, John H. *Chaucer and War.* Lanham, MD: UP of America, 2000.

823. Robertson, D. W., Jr. "The Probable Date and Purpose of Chaucer's *Knight's Tale.*" *SP* 84 (1987): 418–39.

824. Roney, Lois. *Chaucer's "Knight's Tale" and Theories of Scholastic Psychology.* Tampa: U of South Florida P, 1990.

825. Scheps, Walter. "Chaucer's Duke Theseus and the *Knight's Tale.*" *LeedsSE* 9 (1976): 19–34.

826. Schweitzer, Edward C. "Fate and Freedom in *The Knight's Tale.*" *SAC* 3 (1981): 13–45.

827. Sherman, Mark A. "The Politics of Discourse in Chaucer's 'Knight's Tale.'" *Exemplaria* 6 (1994): 87–114.

828. Stein, Robert M. "The Conquest of Femenye: Desire, Power, and Narrative in Chaucer's *Knight's Tale.*" In *Desiring Discourse: The Literature of Love, Ovid through Chaucer,* edited by James J. Paxson and Cynthia A. Gravlee. Selinsgrove, PA: Susquehanna UP, 1998. 188–205.

829. Storm, Melvin. "From Knossos to Knight's Tale: The Changing Faces of Chaucer's Theseus." In *The Mythographic Art,* edited by Jane Chance. Gainesville: UP of Florida, 1990. 215–31.

830. Wasserman, Julian N. "Both Fixed and Free: Language and Destiny in Chaucer's *Knight's Tale* and *Troilus and Criseyde.*" In *Sign, Sentence, Discourse: Language in Medieval Thought and Literature,* edited by Julian N. Wasserman and Lois Roney. Syracuse NY: Syracuse UP, 1989. 194–222.

831. Wetherbee, Winthrop. "Chivalry under Siege in Ricardian Romance." In *The Medieval City under Siege,* edited by Ivy A. Corfis and Michael Wolf. Woodbridge, Suffolk, UK: Boydell, 1995. 207–23.

832. ———. "Romance and Epic in Chaucer's *Knight's Tale.*" *Exemplaria* 2 (1990): 303–28.

833. Woods, William. "Chivalry and Nature in *The Knight's Tale.*" *PQ* 66 (1987): 287–301.

See also nos. 61, 240, 378, 452, 472, 550, 634, 739.

1—*The Miller and His Tale*

834. Beidler, Peter G. "Art and Scatology in the *Miller's Tale*." *ChauR* 12 (1977): 90–102.

835. Blum, Martin. "Negotiating Masculinities: Erotic Triangles in the Miller's Tale." In *Masculinities in Chaucer,* edited by Peter G. Biedler. Rochester, NY: Brewer, 1998. 37–52.

836. Bowker, Alvin W. "Comic Illusion and Dark Reality in *The Miller's Tale*." *MLS* 4 (1977): 27–34.

837. Boyd, David Lorenzo. "Seeking 'Goddes Pryvete': Sodomy, Quitting, and Desire in 'The Miller's Tale.'" In *Word and Works,* edited by Peter S. Baker and Nicholas Howe. Toronto: U of Toronto P, 1998. 243–60.

838. Briggs, Frederick M. "Theophany in the 'Miller's Tale.'" *MAE* 65 (1996): 269–79.

839. Burger, Glenn. "Erotic Discipline . . . or 'Tee Hee, I Like My Boys to Be Girls': Inventing with the Body in Chaucer's 'Miller's Tale.'" In *Becoming Male in the Middle Ages,* edited by Jeffrey Cohen and Bonnie Wheeler. New York: Garland, 1997. 480–99.

840. Cooper, Geoffrey. "'Sely John' in the 'Legende' of the *Miller's Tale*." *JEGP* 79 (1980): 1–12.

841. Daniels, Richard. "Textual Pleasure in the Miller's Tale." In *The Performance of Middle English Culture,* edited by James J. Paxson and others. Cambridge, UK: Brewer, 1998. 111–23.

842. Donaldson, E. Talbot. "Idiom of Popular Poetry in the Miller's Tale." 1951. Reprinted in *Speaking of Chaucer.* New York: Norton, 1970. 13–29.

843. Donaldson, Kara Virginia. "Alisoun's Language: Body, Text, and Glossing in Chaucer's *The Miller's Tale*." *PQ* 71 (1992): 139–53.

844. Farrell, Thomas J. "Privacy and the Boundaries of Fabliau in the 'Miller's Tale.'" *ELH* 56 (1989): 773–95.

845. Fletcher, Alan J. "The Faith of a Simple Man: Carpenter John's Creed in the *Miller's Tale*." *MAE* 61 (1992): 96–105.

846. Friedman, John B. "Nicholas's 'Angelus ad Virginem' and the Mocking of Noah." *YES* 2 (1992): 162–80.

847. Gellrich, Jesse. "The Parody of Medieval Music in the *Miller's Tale*." *JEGP* 72 (1974): 176–88.

848. Hanna, Ralph, III. "'Pilate's Voice'/Shirley's Case." *SAQ* 91 (1992): 793–812.

849. Hough, Carole. "The Name of Chaucer's Miller." *N&Q* 244 (1999): 434–35.

850. Jambeck, Thomas J. "Characterization and Syntax in the *Miller's Tale*." *JNT* 5 (1975): 73–85.

851. Johnston, Andrew James. "The Exegetics of Laughter: Religious Parody in Chaucer's *Miller's Tale*." In *A History of English Laughter,* edited by Manfred Pfister. New York: Rodopi, 2002. 17–33.

852. Jones, George F. "Chaucer and the Medieval Miller." *MLQ* 16 (1955): 3–15.

853. Knapp, Peggy. "Robyn the Miller's Thrifty Work." In *Sign, Sentence, Discourse: Language in Medieval Thought and Literature,* edited by Julian N. Wasserman and Lois Roney. Syracuse NY: Syracuse UP, 1989. 294–303.

854. Leicester, H. Marshall. "Newer Currents in Psychoanalytic Criticism and the Difference 'It' Makes: Gender and Desire in the 'Miller's Tale.'" *ELH* 61 (1994): 473–99.

855. Lewis, Robert E. "The English Fabliau Tradition and Chaucer's *The Miller's Tale*." *MP* 79 (1982): 241–55.

856. Lochrie, Karma. "Women's 'Pryvetees' and the Fabliau Politics in the *Miller's Tale*." *Exemplaria* 6 (1994): 287–304.

857. Miller, Mark. "Naturalism and Its Discontents." *ELH* 67 (2000): 1–44.

858. Mosher, Harold F., Jr. "Greimas, Bremond, and the 'Miller's Tale.'" *Style* 31 (1997): 480–99.

859. Neuss, Paula. "Double Meanings: 1. Double Entendre in *The Miller's Tale*." *EIC* 24 (1974): 325–40.

860. Nolan, Barbara. "Playing Parts: Fragments, Figures, and the Mystery of Love in *The Miller's Tale*." In *Speaking Images: Essays in Honor of V. A. Kolve,* edited by R. F. Yeager and Charlotte Morse. Asheville, NC: Pegasus, 2001. 255–99.

861. Novelli, Cornelius. "Sin, Sight, and Sanctity in the *Miller's Tale*: Why Chaucer's Blacksmith Works at Night." *ChauR* 33 (1998): 168–75.

862. Parry, Joseph D. "Interpreting Female Agency and Responsibility in *The Miller's Tale* and *The Merchant's Tale*." *PQ* 80.2 (2001): 133–67.

863. Porter, Gerald. "The Miller in Oral and Written Narrative — an Aspect of Character or of Role? In *English Far and Wide,* edited by Risto Hiltunen and others. Turku, Finland: Turun Yliopisto, 1993. 59–74.

864. Prior, Sandra Pierson. "Parodying Typology and the Mystery Plays in the *Miller's Tale*." *JMRS* 16 (1986): 57–73.

865. Rowland, Beryl. "Chaucer's Blasphemous Churl: A New Interpretation of the *Miller's Tale*." In *Chaucer and Middle English Studies in Honour of Rossell Hope Robbins,* edited by Beryl Rowland. London: Unwin, 1974. 43–55.

866. Rudat, Wolfgang E. H. "Gender-Crossing in the 'Miller's Tale' — and a New Chaucerian Crux." *JEP* 16 (1995): 134–46.

867. Schweitzer, Edward C. "The Misdirected Kiss and the Lover's Malady in Chaucer's *Miller's Tale*." In *Chaucer in the Eighties,* edited by Julian N. Wasserman and Robert J. Blanch. Syracuse, NY: Syracuse UP, 1986. 223–33.

868. Silar, Theodore I. "Chaucer's Joly Absolon." *PQ* 69 (1990): 409–17.

869. Smith, Macklin. "Or I Wol Cast a Ston." *SAC* 8 (1986): 3–30.

870. Taylor, Paul Beekman. "Translating Spiritual to Corporeal in the Dusk of the Miller's Tale." In *Translating Chaucer.* Lanham, MD: UP of America, 1998. 39–50.

871. Vaughn, M. F. "Chaucer's Imaginative One-Day Flood." *PQ* 60 (1981): 117–23.

872. Walker, Greg. "Rough Girls and Squeamish Boys: The Trouble with Absolon in *The Miller's Tale*." *ES* 55 (2002): 61–91.

873. Woods, William F. "Private and Public Space in the *Miller's Tale*." *ChauR* 29 (1994): 166–78.

See also nos. 15, 39, 62, 149, 482, 484, 550, 876.

1 — The Reeve and His Tale

874. Arthur, Ross G. "'Why Artow Angry?': The Malice of Chaucer's Reeve." *ESC* 13 (1987): 1–11.

875. Brown, Peter G. "The Confinement of Symkyn: The Function of Space in the *Reeve's Tale*." *ChauR* 14 (1980): 225–36.

876. Carroll, Virginia Schaefer. "Women and Money in *The Miller's Tale* and *The Reeve's Tale*." *MedPers* 3 (1988): 76–88.

877. Ellis, Deborah. "Chaucer's Devilish Reeve." *ChauR* 27 (1992): 150–61.

878. Everest, Carol. "Sex and Old Age in the *Reeve's Prologue*." *ChauR* 31 (1996): 99–114.

879. Fein, Susanna Greer. "'Lat the Children Pleye': The Game betwixt the Ages in *The Reeve's Tale*." In *Rebels and Rivals: The Contestive Spirit in the Canterbury Tales*," edited by Susanna Greer Fein and others. Kalamazoo, MI: Medieval Institute, 1991. 73–104.

880. Friedman, John B. "A Reading of Chaucer's *Reeve's Tale*." *ChauR* 2 (1967): 8–19.

881. Grennan, Joseph E. "The Calculating Reeve and His Camera Obscura." *JMRS* 14 (1984): 245–59.

882. Harwood, Britton J. "Psychoanalytic Politics: Chaucer and Two Peasants." *ELH* 68 (2001): 1–27.

883. Horobin, S. C. P. "J. R. R. Tolkien as a Philologist: A Reconsideration of the Northernisms in Chaucer's *Reeve's Tale*." *ES* 82 (2001): 97–105.

884. Kohanski, Tamarah. "In Search of Malyne." *ChauR* 27 (1993): 228–38.

885. Lancashire, Ian. "Sexual Innuendo in the *Reeve's Tale*." *ChauR* 6 (1972): 159–70.

886. Moore, Bruce. "The Reeve's Rusty Blade." *MAE* 58 (1989): 304–12.

887. Olson, Glending. "The Reeve's Tale as Fabliau." *MLQ* 35 (1974): 219–30.

888. Plummer, John F. "'Hooly Chirches Blood': Simony and Patrimony in Chaucer's *Reeve's Tale*." *ChauR* 18 (1983): 49–60.

889. Scase, Wendy. "Tolkien, Philology, and *The Reeve's Tale*: Toward the Cultural Move in Middle English Studies." *SAC* 24 (2002): 325–34.

890. Tolkien, J. R. R. "Chaucer as Philologist: *The Reeve's Tale*." In *Transactions of the Philological Society*. London: Nutt, 1934. 1–70.

891. Williams, Jeni. "Competing Spaces: Dialectology and the Place of Dialect in Chaucer's Reeve's Tale." In *Debating Dialect*, edited by Robert Penhallurick. Cardiff: U of Wales P, 2000. 46–65.

892. Woods, William F. "Symkyn's Place in the *Reeve's Tale*." *ChauR* 39 (2004): 17–40.

893. Yager, Susan. "'A Whit Thyng in Her Ye': Perception and Error in the *Reeve's Tale*." *ChauR* 28 (1994): 393–404.

See also nos. 62, 467, 625.

1 — The Cook and His Tale

894. Bertolet, Craig E. "'Wel Bet Is Token Appul Out of Hoord': Chaucer's Cook, Commerce, and Civic Order." *SP* 99 (2002): 229–46.

895. Kang, Ji-Soo. "The (In)completeness of the *Cook's Tale*." *Medieval English Studies* (Seoul) 5 (1997): 145–70.

896. Scattergood, V. J. "Perkyn Revelour and the *Cook's Tale*." *ChauR* 19 (1984): 14–23.

897. Strohm, Paul. "'Lad with Revel to Newegate': Chaucerian Narrative and Historical Meta-Narrative." In *Art and Context in Late Medieval English Narrative*, edited by Robert R. Edwards. Cambridge, UK: Brewer, 1994. 163–76.

898. Wallace, David. "Chaucer and the Absent City." In *Chaucer's England: Literature in Historical Context*, edited by Barbara A. Hanawalt. Minneapolis: U of Minnesota P, 1991. 59–90.

899. Woods, William. "Society and Nature in the 'Cook's Tale.'" *PLL* 32 (1996): 189–205.

See also nos. 25, 62, 484, 524, 1429.

Part 2

2 — The Man of Law and His Tale

900. Archibald, Elizabeth. "Contextualizing Chaucer's Constance: Romance Modes and Family Values." In *The Endless Knot: Essays on Old and Middle English in Honor of Marie Borroff*, edited by M. Teresa Tavormina and R. F. Yeager. Cambridge, UK: Brewer, 1995. 161–75.

901. Astell, Anne W. "Apostrophe, Prayer, and the Structure of Satire in the Man of Law's Tale." *SAC* 13 (1991): 81–97.

901a. Barefield, Laura D. "Women's Patronage and the Writing of History: Nicholas Trevet's *Les Cronicles* and Geoffrey Chaucer's *Man of Law's Tale*." In *Gender and History in Medieval English Romance and Chronicle*. New York: Lang, 2003. 37–72.

902. Bestul, Thomas H. "The *Man of Law's Tale* and the Rhetorical Foundations of Chaucerian Pathos." *ChauR* 9 (1975): 216–26.

903. Black, Nancy B. *Medieval Narratives of Accused Queens*. Gainesville: UP of Florida, 2003.

904. Block, Edward A. "Originality, Controlling Purpose, and Craftsmanship in Chaucer's *Man of Law's Tale*." *PMLA* 68 (1953): 572–616.

905. Bloomfield, Morton W. "The *Man of Law's Tale*: A Tragedy of Victimization and Christian Comedy." *PMLA* 87 (1972): 384–90.

906. Bolton, W. F. "Pinchbeck and the Chaucer Circle in Law Reports and Records of 11–13 Richard II." *MP* 84 (1987): 401–6.

907. Bullón-Fernández, María. "Engendering Authority: Father and Daughter, State and Church in Gower's 'Tale of Constance' and Chaucer's 'Man of Law's Tale.'" In *Re-visioning Gower*, edited by R. F. Yeager. Asheville, NC: Pegasus, 1998. 129–46.

908. Caie, Graham. "'This Was a Thrifty Tale for the Nones': Chaucer's Man of Law." In *Chaucer in Perspective*, edited by Geoffrey Lester. Sheffield: Sheffield Academic P, 1999. 47–60.

909. Cigman, Gloria. "The Evil Outsider in Chaucer's *Man of Law's Tale*." *BAM* 62 (2003): 1–9.

910. Clark, Susan L., and Julian N. Wasserman. "Constance as Romance and Folk Heroine in Chaucer's *Man of Law's Tale.*" *RUS* 64 (1978): 13–24.

911. Clogan, Paul M. "The Narrative Style of the *Man of Law's Tale.*" *M&H* 8 (1977): 217–33.

912. Culver, T. D. "The Imposition of Order: A Measure of Art in the *Man of Law's Tale.*" *YES* 2 (1972): 13–20.

913. Delany, Sheila. "Womanliness in the *Man of Law's Tale.*" *ChauR* 9 (1974): 63–72.

914. Dinshaw, Carolyn. "The Law of Man and Its 'Abhomynacions.'" *Exemplaria* 1 (1989): 117–48.

915. ———. "New Approaches to Chaucer." In no. 78, 270–89.

916. Dugas, Don-John. "The Legitimization of Royal Power in Chaucer's *Man of Law's Tale.*" *MP* 95 (1997): 27–43.

917. Edwards, A. S. G. "Critical Approaches to the *Man of Law's Tale.*" In no. 396, 85–94.

918. Fowler, Elizabeth. "The Empire and the Waif: Consent and Conflict of Laws in the *Man of Law's Tale.*" In *Medieval Literature and Historical Inquiry,* edited by David Aers. Cambridge, UK: Brewer, 2000. 55–67.

918a. Hanning, Robert W. "Custance and Ciapelletto in the Middle of It All." In no. 235, 177–211.

919. Kikuchi, Akio. "The Legend of the 'Martyr King': Political Representation in *The Man of Law's Tale.*" *Shiron* 39 (2000): 1–19.

920. Landman, James. "Proving Constant: Torture and *The Man of Law's Tale.*" *SAC* 20 (1998): 1–39.

921. Lavezzo, Kathy. "Beyond Rome: Mapping Gender and Justice in *The Man of Law's Tale.*" *SAC* 24 (2002): 149–80.

922. Lee, Brian S. "Christian Adornment in *The Man of Law's Tale.*" *PMAM* 10 (2003): 31–48.

923. Lewis, Robert E. "Chaucer's Artistic Use of Pope Innocent III's *De Miseria Conditionis* in the *Man of Law's Tale.*" *PMLA* 81 (1966): 485–92.

924. Lynch, Kathryn. "Storytelling, Exchange, and Constancy: East and West in Chaucer's *Man of Law's Tale.*" *ChauR* 33 (1999): 409–22.

925. McCarthy, Conor. "Injustice and Chaucer's Man of Law." *Parergon* 20 (2003): 1–18.

926. McKenna, Isobel. "The Making of a Fourteenth-Century Sergeant of the Law." *RUO* 45 (1975): 244–62.

927. Manning, Stephen. "Chaucer's Constance: Pale and Passive." In *Chaucerian Problems and Perspectives,* edited by Edward Vasta and Zacharias P. Thundy. Notre Dame, IN: U of Notre Dame P, 1979. 13–23.

928. Nicholson, Peter. "The *Man of Law's Tale*: What Chaucer Really Owed to Gower." *ChauR* 26 (1991): 153–74.

929. Niebrzydowski, Sue. "Monstrous (M)othering: The Representation of the Sowdanesse in Chaucer's *Man of Law's Tale.*" In *Consuming Narratives,* edited by Herbert McAvoy and Teresa Walters. Cardiff: U of Wales P, 2002. 196–207.

930. Paull, Michael R. "The Influence of the Saint's Legend Genre in the *Man of Law's Tale.*" *ChauR* 5 (1971): 179–84.

931. Raybin, David. "Custance and History: Woman as Outsider in Chaucer's *Man of Law's Tale.*" *SAC* 12 (1990): 65–84.

932. Robertson, Elizabeth. "The 'Elvyssh' Power of Constance: Christian Feminism in Geoffrey Chaucer's *The Man of Law's Tale.*" *SAC* 23 (2001): 143–80.

933. Scheps, Walter. "Chaucer's Man of Law and the Tale of Constance." *PMLA* 89 (1974): 285–95.

934. Schibanoff, Susan. "Worlds Apart: Orientalism, Antifeminism, and Heresy in Chaucer's *Man of Law's Tale.*" *Exemplaria* 8 (1996): 59–96.

935. Schlauch, Margaret. *Constance and the Accused Queens.* New York: New York UP, 1927.

936. Spearing, A. C. "Narrative Voice: The Case of Chaucer's *Man of Law's Tale.*" *NLH* 32 (2001): 715–46.

937. Weissman, Hope Phyllis. "Late Gothic Pathos in the *Man of Law's Tale.*" *JMRS* 9 (1979): 133–53.

938. Wetherbee, Winthrop. "Constance and the World in Chaucer and Gower." In *John Gower: Recent Readings,* edited by R. F. Yeager. Kalamazoo: Medieval Institute, Western Michigan U, 1989. 65–93.

939. Wood, Chauncey. "Chaucer's Man of Law as Interpreter." *Traditio* 23 (1967): 149–90.

940. Wurtele, Douglas. "'Proprietas' in Chaucer's Man of Law's Tale." *Neophil* 60 (1976): 577–93.

See also nos. 378, 396, 550, 642, 655, 657–62.

Part 3

941. Carruthers, Mary. "Letter and Gloss in the Friar's and Summoner's Tales." *JNT* 2 (1972): 208–14.

942. East, W. G. "By Preeve Which That Is Demonstratif." *ChauR* 12 (1977): 78–82.

943. Hanning, Robert W. "Roasting a Friar, Mis-Taking a Wife, and Other Acts of Textual Harassment in Chaucer's *Canterbury Tales.*" *SAC* 7 (1985): 3–21.

944. Kamowski, William. "The Sinner against the Scoundrels: The Ills of Doctrine and 'Shrift' in the Wife of Bath's, Friar's, and Summoner's Narratives." *Religion and Literature* 25 (1993): 1–18.

945. Owens, Charles A., Jr. "Fictions Living Fictions: The Poetics of Voice and Genre in Fragment D [3] of the *Canterbury Tales.*" In *Poetics: Theory and Practice in Medieval English Literature,* edited by Piero Boitani and Anna Torti. Bury St. Edmunds, UK: Brewer, 1991. 37–55.

946. Szittya, Penn R. "The Green Man as Loathly Lady: The Friar's Parody of the Wife of Bath's Tale." *PMLA* 90 (1975): 386–94.

947. Wallace, David. "Chaucer's Body Politic: Social and Narrative Self-Regulation." *Exemplaria* 2 (1990): 221–40.

948. Wasserman, J. N. "The Ideal and the Actual: The Philosophical Unity of *Canterbury Tales* MS. Group III." *Allegorica* 7 (1982): 65–99.

3 — The Wife of Bath and Her Tale

949. Aguirre Daban, Manuel. "The Riddle of Sovereignty." *MLR* 88 (1992): 273–82.

950. Beidler, Peter G., ed. *Geoffrey Chaucer: "The Wife of Bath": Complete Authoritative Text with Biographical and Historical Contexts, Critical History and Essays from Five Contemporary Critical Perspectives*. New York: Bedford-St. Martin's, 1996.

951. Biebel, Elizabeth. "A Wife, a Batterer, a Rapist: Representations of 'Masculinity' in the Wife of Bath's Prologue and Tale." In *Masculinities in Chaucer*, edited by Peter G. Beidler. Rochester, NY: Brewer, 1998. 63–75.

952. Blamires, Alcuin. "Refiguring the 'Scandalous Excess' of Medieval Women: The Wife of Bath and Liberality." In *Gender in Debate,* edited by Thelma S. Fenster and Clare A. Lees. New York: Palgrave, 2002. 57–78.

953. ———. "Wife of Bath and Lollardy." *MAE* 58 (1989): 224–42.

954. Carruthers, Mary. "The Wife of Bath and the Painting of Lions." *PMLA* 94 (1979): 209–22. Reprinted with an "Afterword" in *Feminist Readings in Middle English Literature,* edited by Ruth Evans and Lesley Johnson. New York: Routledge, 1994. 22–53.

955. Carter, Susan. "Coupling the Beastly Bride and the Hunter Hunted: What Lies behind Chaucer's *Wife of Bath's Tale?*" *ChauR* 37 (2003): 329–45.

956. Cary, Meredith. "Sovereignty and the Old Wife." *PLL* 5 (1969): 375–88.

957. Charles, Casey. "Adversus Jerome: Liberation Theology in the *Wife of Bath's Prologue.*" *Assays* 6 (1991): 55–71.

958. Colmer, Dorothy. "Character and Class in the *Wife of Bath's Tale.*" *JEGP* 72 (1974): 329–39.

959. Cooper, Helen. "The Shape-Shiftings of the Wife of Bath, 1395–1670." In no. 267, 168–84.

960. Delany, Sheila. "Sexual Economics, Chaucer's Wife of Bath and the Book of Margery Kempe." 1975. Reprinted in *Feminist Readings in Middle English Literature,* edited by Ruth Evans and Lesley Johnson. New York: Routledge, 1994. 72–87.

961. ———. "Strategies of Silence: In the Wife of Bath's Recital." *Exemplaria* 2 (1990): 49–69.

962. Delasanta, Rodney. "Alisoun and the Saved Harlots: A Cozening of Our Expectations." *ChauR* 12 (1978): 218–35.

963. Dickson, Lynne. "Deflection in the Mirror: Feminine Discourse in the *Wife of Bath's Prologue* and *Tale.*" *SAC* 15 (1993): 61–90.

964. Dor, Juliette. "The Wife of Bath's 'Wandrynge by the Weye' and Conduct Literature for Women." In *Drama, Narrative and Poetry in The Canterbury Tales,* edited by Wendy Harding. Toulouse: Presses Universitaires du Mirail, Collection Interlangues: Literatures, 2003. 139–55.

965. Fischer, Olga C. M. "Gower's *Tale of Florent* and Chaucer's *Wife of Bath's Tale.*" *ES* 66 (1985): 205–25.

966. Fleming, John V. "Sacred and Secular Exegesis in the *Wyf of Bath's Tale.*" In *Retelling Tales,* edited by Thomas Hahn and Alan Lupack. Rochester, NY: Brewer, 1997. 73–90.

967. Friedman, John Block. "Alice of Bath's Astral Destiny: A Re-appraisal." *ChauR* 25 (2000): 66–81.

968. Galloway, Andrew. "Marriage Sermons, Polemical Sermons, and *The Wife of Bath's Prologue.*" *SAC* 14 (1992): 3–30.

969. Gottfried, Barbara. "Conflict and Relationship, Sovereignty and Survival: Parables of Power in the *Wife of Bath's Prologue.*" *ChauR* 19 (1985): 202–24.

970. Hagen, Susan K. "The Wife of Bath: Chaucer's Inchoate Experiment." In *Rebels and Rivals: The Contestive Spirit in The Canterbury Tales,"* edited by Susanna Freer Fein and others. Kalamazoo, MI: Medieval Institute, 1991. 105–24.

971. Hahn, Thomas. "Old Wives' Tales and Masculine Intuition." In *Retelling Tales,* edited by Thomas Hahn and Alan Lupack. Rochester, NY: Brewer, 1997. 91–108.

972. Hanna, Ralph, III, and Traugott Lawler, eds. *Jankyn's Book of Wikked Wyves.* Athens: U of Georgia P, 1997.

973. Herold, Christine. "Archetypal Chaucer: The Case of the Disappearing Hag in *The Wife of Bath's Tale.*" In *Archetypal Readings of Medieval Literature,* edited by Charlotte Spivack and Christine Herold. Lewiston, NY: Mellen, 2002. 47–65.

974. Ingham, Patricia Clare. "Pastoral Histories: Utopia, Conquest, and the *Wife of Bath's Tale.*" *TSLL* 44 (2002): 34–46.

975. Kennedy, Beverly. "Cambridge MS. Dd.4.24: A Misogynous Scribal Revision of the *Wife of Bath's Prologue.*" *ChauR* 30 (1996): 343–58.

976. ———. "The Rewriting of the Wife of Bath's Prologue in Cambridge Dd.4.24." In *Rewriting Chaucer,* edited by Thomas A. Prendergast and Barbara Kline. Columbus: Ohio State UP, 1999. 203–33.

977. Knapp, Peggy. "Alisoun Weaves a Text." *PQ* 65 (1986): 387–401.

978. Lawton, Lesley. "'Glose Whoso Wole': Voice, Text and Authority in *The Wife of Bath's Prologue.*" In *Drama, Narrative and Poetry in The Canterbury Tales,* edited by Wendy Harding. Toulouse: Presses Universitaires du Mirail, Collection Interlangues: Literatures, 2003. 157–74.

979. Lindley, Arthur. "'Vanysshed Was This Daunce, He Nyste Where': Alisoun's Absence in *The Wife of Bath's Prologue and Tale.*" *ELH* 59 (1992): 1–21.

980. Longsworth, Robert. "The Wife of Bath and the Samaritan Woman." *ChauR* 34 (2000): 372–87.

981. McCarthy, Conor. "The Position of Widows in the Later Fourteenth-Century English Community and the *Wife of Bath's Prologue.*" In *Authority & Community in the Middle Ages,* edited by Donald Mowbray and others. Phoenix Mill, Gloucestershire, UK: Sutton, 1999. 101–15.

982. McKinley, Kathryn. "The Silenced Knight: Questions on Power and Reciprocity in the *Wife of Bath's Tale.*" *ChauR* 30 (1996): 359–78.

983. Malvern, Marjorie. "'Who Peyntede the Leon, Tel Me Who?'" Rhetorical and Didactic Roles Played by an Aesopic Fable in the *Wife of Bath's Prologue.*" *SP* 80 (1983): 238–52.

984. Matthews, William. "The Wife of Bath and All Her Sect." *Viator* 7 (1974): 413–43.

985. Minnis, Alastair. "Anthropologizing Alisoun: The Case of Chaucer's Wife of Bath." *RealB* 12 (1996): 203–21.

986. Morrison, Susan Signe. "Don't Ask; Don't Tell: The Wife of Bath and Vernacular Translations." *Exemplaria* 8 (1996): 97–123.

987. Oberembt, Kenneth J. "Chaucer's Anti-misogynist Wife of Bath." *ChauR* 10 (1976): 287–302.

988. Patterson, Lee. "'For the Wyves Love of Bathe': Feminine Rhetoric and Poetic Resolution in the *Roman de la Rose* and the *Canterbury Tales*." *Speculum* 58 (1983): 656–95.

989. ———. *Putting the Wife in Her Place.* [London]: [Birbeck College], 1995.

990. Pugh, Tison. "Queering Genres, Battering Males: The Wife of Bath's Narrative Violence." *JNT* 33 (2003): 115–42.

991. Puhvel, Martin. "The Death of Alys of Bath's 'Revelour' Husband." *NM* 103 (2002): 328–40.

992. Robertson, D. W., Jr. "The Wife of Bath and Midas." *SAC* 6 (1984): 1–20.

993. Root, Jerry. "'Space to Speke': The Wife of Bath and the Discourse of Confession." *ChauR* 28 (1994): 252–74.

994. Saunders, Corinne. "Women Displaced: Rape and Romance in Chaucer's *Wife of Bath's Tale*." *Arthurian Literature* 13 (1995): 115–31.

995. Schibanoff, Susan. "The New Reader and Female Textuality in Two Early Commentaries on Chaucer." *SAC* 10 (1988): 71–108.

996. Shapiro, Gloria. "The Wife of Bath as Deceptive Narrator." *ChauR* 6 (1971): 130–41.

997. Smith, Warren S. "The Wife of Bath Debates Jerome." *ChauR* 32 (1997): 129–45.

998. Solopova, Elizabeth. "The Problem of Authorial Variants in the Wife of Bath's Prologue." In *The Canterbury Tales Project Occasional Papers Volume II*, edited by Norman Blake and Peter Robinson. Oxford: Office for Humanities Communications, 1997. 133–42.

999. Speed, Diane. "Quest and Question in *The Wife of Bath's Tale*." *Sydney Studies in English* 22 (1996): 3–14.

1000. Straus, Barrie Ruth. "The Subversive Discourse of the Wife of Bath: Phallocentric Discourse and the Imprisonment of Language." *ELH* 55 (1988): 527–54.

1001. Strohm, Paul. "Treason in the Household." In *Hochon's Arrow: The Social Imagination of Fourteenth-Century Texts*. Princeton: Princeton UP, 1992. 121–44.

1002. Thundy, Zacharias P. "Matheolus, Chaucer, and the Wife of Bath." In *Chaucerian Problems and Perspectives*, edited by Edward Vasta and Zacharias P. Thundy. Notre Dame, IN: U of Notre Dame P, 1979. 24–58.

1003. Van, Thomas A. "False Texts and Disappearing Women in the *Wife of Bath's Prologue and Tale*." *ChauR* 29 (1994): 179–93.

1004. Weissman, Hope Phyllis. "Why Chaucer's Wife Is from Bath." *ChauR* 15 (1980): 11–36.

1005. Wimsatt, James I. "The Wife of Bath, the Franklin, and the Rhetoric of St. Jerome." In *A Wyf Ther Was*, edited by Juliette Dor. Liége: University of Liége, 1992. 275–81.

1006. Wynne-Davies, Marion. "'The Elf-Queen with Hir Joly Compaignye': Chaucer's Wife of Bath's Tale." In *Women and Arthurian Literature: Seizing the Sword*. New York: St. Martin's, 1996. 14–35.

See also nos. 14, 63, 400, 438, 444, 452, 459, 638–39, 643, 721.

3 — The Friar and His Tale

1007. Geltner, G. "Faux Semblants: Antifraternalism Reconsidered in Jean de Meun and Chaucer." *SP* 101 (2004): 357–80.

1008. Hahn, Thomas, and Kaeuper, Richard W. "Text and Context: Chaucer's *Friar's Tale*." *SAC* 5 (1983): 67–101.

1009. Havely, N. R. "Chaucer's Friar and Merchant." *ChauR* 13 (1979): 337–45.

1010. Jost, Jean. "Ambiguous Brotherhood in the *Friar's Tale* and the *Summoner's Tale*." In *Masculinities in Chaucer*, edited by Peter G. Beidler. Rochester, NY: Brewer, 1998. 77–90.

1011. Kline, Daniel T. "'Myne by Right': Oath Making and Intent in *The Friar's Tale*." *PQ* 77 (1998): 271–93.

1012. Kolve, V. A. "'Man in the Middle': Art and Religion in Chaucer's *Friar's Tale*." *SAC* 12 (1990): 5–46.

1013. Leicester, H. Marshall, Jr. "'No Vileyns Word': Social Context and Performance in Chaucer's *Friar's Tale*." *ChauR* 17 (1982): 21–39.

1014. Lenaghan, R. T. "The Irony of the *Friar's Tale*." *ChauR* 7 (1973): 281–94.

1015. Murtaugh, Daniel M. "Riming Justice in the *Friar's Tale*." *NM* 74 (1973): 107–12.

1016. Richardson, Janette. "Friar and Summoner, the Art of Balance." *ChauR* 9 (1975): 227–36.

1017. Ridley, Florence. "The Friar and the Critics." In *The Idea of Medieval Literature*, edited by James M. Dean and Christian Zacher. Newark: U of Delaware P, 1992. 160–72.

1018. Williams, Arnold. "Chaucer and the Friars." *Speculum* 28 (1953): 499–513.

1019. Williams, David. "'From Chaucer's Pan to Logic's Fire': Intentionality in Chaucer's *Friar's Tale*." In *Literature and Ethics: Essays Presented to A. E. Malloch*, edited by Gary Wihl and David Williams. Montreal: McGill-Queen's UP, 1988. 77–95.

See also nos. 381, 400.

3 — The Summoner and His Tale

1020. Adams, John F. "The Structure of Irony in the *Summoner's Tale*." *EIC* 12 (1962): 126–32.

1021. Andreas, James R. "'Newe Science' from 'Olde Bokes': A Bakhtinian Approach to the *Summoner's Tale*." *ChauR* 25 (1990): 138–51.

1022. Berlin, Gail Ivy. "Speaking to the Devil: A New Context for *The Friar's Tale*." *PQ* 69 (1990): 1–12.

1023. Clark, Roy Peter. "Doubting Thomas in Chaucer's *Summoner's Tale*." *ChauR* 11 (1976): 164–78.

1024. Cox, Catherine S. "'Grope Wel Bihynde': The Subversive Erotics of Chaucer's Summoner." *Exemplaria* 7 (1995): 145–77.

1025. Fleming, John V. "Anticlerical Satire as Theological Essay: Chaucer's *Summoner's Tale.*" *Thalia* 6 (1983): 5–22.

1026. Fletcher, Alan J. "The Summoner and the Abominable Anatomy of Antichrist." *SAC* 18 (1996): 91–117.

1027. Hanks, D. Thomas, Jr. "Chaucer's *Summoner's Tale* and 'the first smel of fartes thre.'" *ChauY* 4 (1997): 33–43.

1028. Haselmayer, L. A. "The Apparitor and Chaucer's Summoner." *Speculum* 12 (1973): 43–57.

1029. Hasenfrantz, Robert. "The Science of Flatulence: Possible Source for the *Summoner's Tale.*" *ChauR* 30 (1996): 241–61.

1030. Kabir, Ananya Jahanara. "From Twelve Devouring Dragons to the *Develes Ers:* The Medieval History of an Apocryphal Punitive Motif." *Archiv* 238 (2001): 280–98.

1031. Lancashire, Ian. "Moses, Elijah and the Back Parts of God: Satiric Scatology in Chaucer's *Summoner's Tale.*" *Mosaic* 14 (1981): 17–30.

1032. Matsuda, Takami. "The *Summoner's Prologue* and the Tradition of the Vision of the Afterlife." *PoeticaT* 55 (2001): 75–82.

1033. O'Brien, Timothy D. "'Ars-metrik': Science, Satire, and Chaucer's Summoner." *Mosaic* 23.4 (1990): 1–22.

1034. Olson, Glending. "The End of *The Summoner's Tale* and the Uses of Pentecost." *SAC* 21 (1999): 209–45.

1035. Shippey, Tom. "Bilingualism and Betrayal in Chaucer's 'Summoner's Tale.'" In *Speaking in the Medieval World,* edited by Jean E. Godsall-Myers. Boston: Brill, 2003. 125–44.

1036. Somerset, Fiona. "'As just as is a squyre': The Politics of 'Lewed Translacion' in Chaucer's *Summoner's Tale.*" *SAC* 21 (1999): 187–207.

1037. Szittya, Penn R. "The Friar as False Apostle: Antifraternal Exegesis and the *Summoner's Tale.*" *SP* 71 (1974): 19–46.

1038. Zietlow, Paul N. "In Defense of the Summoner." *ChauR* 1 (1966): 4–19.

See also nos. 40, 400, 477, 647, 1010, 1016.

Part 4

1039. Cherniss, Michael D. "The *Clerk's Tale* and *Envoy,* the Wife of Bath's Purgatory, and the *Merchant's Tale.*" *ChauR* 6 (1972): 235–54.

1040. Hardman, Phillipa. "Chaucer's Tyrants of Lombardy." *RES* 31 (1980): 172–78.

1041. Levy, Bernard S. "*Gentilesse* in Chaucer's *Clerk's* and *Merchant's* Tales." *ChauR* 11 (1977): 306–18.

4—The Clerk and His Tale

1042. Ashton, Gail. "Patient Mimesis: Griselda and the *Clerk's Tale.*" *ChauR* 32 (1998): 232–38.

1043. Bronfman, Judith. *Chaucer's Clerk's Tale: The Griselda Story Received, Rewritten, Illustrated.* New York: Garland, 1994.

1044. Campbell, Emma. "Sexual Poetics and the Politics of Translation in the Tale of Griselda." *CL* 55 (2003): 191–216.

1045. Carruthers, Mary J. "The Lady, the Swineherd, and Chaucer's Clerk." *ChauR* 17 (1983): 221–34.

1046. Chickering, Howell. "Form and Interpretation in the *Envoy* to the *Clerk's Tale.*" *ChauR* 29 (1995): 352–72.

1047. Delasanta, Rodney. "Nominalism and the *Clerk's Tale* Revisited." *ChauR* 31 (1997): 209–31.

1048. Edden, Valerie. "Sacred and Secular in the *Clerk's Tale.*" *ChauR* 26 (1992): 369–76.

1049. Farrell, Thomas J. "The Chronotopes of Monology in Chaucer's *Clerk's Tale.*" In *Bakhtin and Medieval Voices,* edited by Thomas J. Farrell. Gainesville: UP of Florida, 1995. 141–57.

1050. ———. "The *Envoy de Chaucer* and the *Clerk's Tale.*" *ChauR* 24 (1990): 329–36.

1051. Finlayson, John. "Petrarch, Boccaccio, and Chaucer's *Clerk's Tale.*" *SP* 97 (2000): 255–75.

1052. Finnegan, Robert Emmett. "'She Should Have Said No to Walter': Griselda's Promise in *The Clerk's Tale.*" *ES* 75 (1994): 302–21.

1053. Georgianna, Linda. "*The Clerk's Tale* and the Grammar of Assent." *Speculum* 70 (1995): 793–821.

1054. Gilmartin, Kristine. "Array in the *Clerk's Tale.*" *ChauR* 13 (1979): 234–46.

1055. Grudin, Michaela Paasche. "Chaucer's *Clerk's Tale* as Political Paradox." *SAC* 11 (1989): 63–92.

1056. Harding, Wendy. "The Dynamics of Law in the *Clerk's Tale.*" *ChauY* 4 (1997): 49–59.

1057. ———. "Griselda's 'Translation' in the *Clerk's Tale.*" In *Medieval Translator, 6,* edited by Roger Ellis and others. [Turnhout, Belgium]: Brepols, 1998. 194–210.

1058. Heninger, S. K. "The Concept of Order in Chaucer's *Clerk's Tale.*" *JEGP* 56 (1957): 282–95.

1059. Kellogg, Alfred L. "The Evolution of the *Clerk's Tale:* A Study in Connotation." In *Chaucer, Langland, Arthur: Essays in Middle English Literature.* New Brunswick, NY: Rutgers UP, 1972. 276–329.

1060. Lavezzo, Kathy. "Chaucer and Everyday Death: *The Clerk's Tale,* Burial, and the Subject of Poverty." *SAC* 23 (2001): 255–87.

1061. Lynch, Kathryn L. "Despoiling Griselda: Chaucer's Walter and the Problem of Knowledge in *The Clerk's Tale.*" *SAC* 10 (1988): 41–70.

1062. McClellan, William. "A Postmodern Performance: Counter-Reading Chaucer's *Clerk's Tale* and Maxine Hong Kingston's 'No Name Woman.'" In *The Performance of Medieval Culture,* edited by James J. Paxson and others. Cambridge, UK: Brewer, 1998. 18–96.

1063. McKinley, Kathryn L. "*The Clerk's Tale:* Hagiography and the Problematics of Lay Sanctity." *ChauR* 33 (1998): 99–111.

1064. Mann, Jill. "Satisfaction and Payment in Middle English Literature." *SAC* 5 (1983): 17–48.

1065. Middleton, Anne. "The Clerk and His Tale: Some Literary Contexts." *SAC* 2 (1980): 121–50.

1066. Morse, Charlotte C. "Critical Approaches to the *Clerk's Tale.*" In no. 396, 71–83.

1067. ———. "The Exemplary Griselda." *SAC* 7 (1985): 51–86.

1068. Myles, Robert. "Confusing Signs: The Semiotic Point of View in the *Clerk's Tale.*" In *Chaucer and Language: Essays in Honour of Douglas Wurtele,* edited by Robert Myles and David Williams. Montreal: McGill-Queens UP, 2001. 107–27.

1069. Newton, Allyson. "The Occlusion of Mothering in Chaucer's *Clerk's Tale.*" In *Medieval Mothering,* edited by John Carmi Parsons and Bonnie Wheeler. New York: Garland, 1996. 63–77.

1070. Pearlman, E. "The Psychological Basis of the *Clerk's Tale.*" *ChauR* 11 (1977): 248–57.

1071. Ramsey, Roger. "Clothing Makes a Queen in *The Clerk's Tale.*" *JNT* 7 (1977): 104–15.

1072. Rothman, Irving N. "Humility and Obedience in the *Clerk's Tale,* with the Envoy Considered as an Ironic Affirmation." *PLL* 9 (1973): 115–27.

1073. Severs, J. Burke. *The Literary Relationships of Chaucer's Clerkes Tale.* 1942. Reprint, Hamden, CT: Archon, 1972.

1074. Sledd, James. "The *Clerk's Tale:* The Monsters and the Critics." *MP* 51 (1953): 73–82.

1075. Stanbury, Sarah. "Regimes of the Visual in Premodern England: Gaze, Body, and Chaucer's *Clerk's Tale.*" *NLH* 28 (1997): 261–89.

1076. Stepsis, Robert. "*Potentia Absoluta* and the Clerk's Tale." *ChauR* 10 (1975): 129–46.

1077. Van Dyke, Carolynn. "The Clerk's and the Franklin's Subjected Subject." *SAC* 17 (1995): 45–66.

1078. Waugh, Robin. "A Woman in the Mind's Eye (and Not): Narrators and Gazes in Chaucer's *Clerk's Tale* and Two Analogues." *PQ* 79 (2000): 1–18.

See also nos. 444, 446, 459, 607, 642.

4—The Merchant and His Tale

1079. Benson, Donald R. "The Marriage 'Encomium' in the *Merchant's Tale:* A Chaucerian Crux." *ChauR* 14 (1979): 48–60.

1080. Brown, Emerson, Jr. "Chaucer, the Merchant, and Their Tale: Getting beyond Old Controversies: Part I." *ChauR* 13 (1978–79): 141–56; "Part II," 247–62.

1081. Bugge, John. "Damyan's Wanton *Clyket* and an Ironic New *Twiste* to the Merchant's Tale." *AnM* 14 (1973): 53–62.

1082. Burger, Glenn. "Present Panic in *The Merchant's Tale.*" *SAC* 24 (2002): 49–73.

1083. Burnley, J. D. "The Morality of *The Merchant's Tale.*" *YES* 6 (1976): 16–25.

1084. Cahn, Kenneth S. "Chaucer's Merchants and the Foreign Exchange: An Introduction to Medieval Finance." *SAC* 2 (1980): 81–119.

1085. Cooke, Jessica. "Januarie and May in Chaucer's *Merchant's Tale.*" *ES* 78 (1997): 407–16.

1086. Crocker, Holly A. "Performative Passivity and Fantasies of Masculinity in the *Merchant's Tale.*" *ChauR* 38 (2003): 178–98.

1087. Dove, Mary. "'Swiche Olde Lewed Wordes': Books about Medieval Love, Medieval Books about Love and the Medieval Book of Love." In *Venus and Mars,* edited by Andrew Lynch and Philippa Maddern. Nedlands: U of Western Australia P, 1995. 11–33.

1088. Edwards, A. S. G. "The Merchant's Tale and Moral Chaucer." *MLQ* 51 (1990): 409–26.

1089. Edwards, Robert R. "Narration and Doctrine in the *Merchant's Tale.*" *Speculum* 66 (1991): 342–67.

1090. Field, Rosalind. "January's 'Honeste Thynges': Knighthood and Narrative in the *Merchant's Tale.*" *RMS* 20 (1994): 37–49.

1091. ———. "'Superfluous Ribaldry': Spurious Lines in the *Merchant's Tale.*" *ChauR* 28 (1994): 353–67.

1092. Heffernan, Carol Falvo. "Contraception and the Pear Tree Episode of Chaucer's *Merchant's Tale.*" *JEGP* 94 (1995): 31–41.

1093. Jager, Erik. "The Carnal Letters in Chaucer's Earthly Paradise." In *The Tempter's Voice: Language and the Fall in Medieval Literature.* Ithaca, NY: Cornell UP, 1993. 241–98.

1094. Jonassen, Frederick B. "Rough Music in Chaucer's *Merchant's Tale.*" In *Chaucer's Humor: Critical Essays,* edited by Jean E. Jost. New York: Garland, 1994. 229–58.

1095. Jost, Jean. "May's Mismarriage of Youth and Elde: The Poetics of Sexual Desire in Chaucer's *Merchant's Tale.*" In *Feminea Medievalia I,* edited by Bonnie Wheeler. Dallas, TX: Academia, 1993. 117–38.

1096. Kohler, Michelle. "Vision, Logic, and the Comic Production of Reality in the *Merchant's Tale* and Two French Fabliaux." *ChauR* 39 (2004): 137–50.

1097. Lucas, Angela M. "The Mirror in the Marketplace: Januarie through the Looking Glass." *ChauR* 33 (1998): 123–45.

1098. Neuse, Richard. "Marriage and the Question of Allegory in the *Merchant's Tale.*" *ChauR* 24 (1989): 115–31.

1099. Rose, Christine. "Women's 'Pryvete,' May, and the Privy: Fissures in the Narrative Voice in the *Merchant's Tale,* 1944–86." *ChauY* 4 (1997): 61–77.

1100. Shores, David L. "The *Merchant's Tale:* Some Lay Observations." *NM* 71 (1970): 119–33.

1101. Simmons-O'Neill, Elizabeth. "Love in Hell: The Role of Pluto and Proserpine in Chaucer's *Merchant's Tale.*" *MLQ* 51 (1990): 389–407.

1102. Smarr, Janet Levarie. "Mercury in the Garden: Mythographical Methods in the *Merchant's Tale* and *Decameron* 7.9." In *The Mythographic Art,* edited by Jane Chance. Gainesville: UP of Florida, 1990. 199–214.

1103. Stock, Lorraine Kochanske. "Making It in the *Merchant's Tale:* Chaucer's Signs of January's Fall." *Semiotica* 63 (1987): 171–83.

1104. Tatlock, J. S. P. "Chaucer's *Merchant's Tale.*" *MP* 33 (1935): 367–81.

1105. Tucker, Edward F. J. "'Parfite Blisses Two': January's Dilemma and the Themes of Temptation and Doublemindedness in the Merchant's Tale." *ABR* 33 (1982): 172–81.

1106. Wentersdorf, Karl P. "Theme and Structure in *The Merchant's Tale:* The Function of the Pluto Episode." *PMLA* 80 (1965): 522–27.

1107. Wurtele, Douglas. "The Blasphemy of Chaucer's Merchant." *AnM* 21 (1981): 91–110.

See also nos. 136, 438, 444, 446, 634, 636, 862, 1009.

Part 5

1108. Goodman, Jennifer. "Dorigen and the Falcon: The Element of Despair in Chaucer's *Squire's* and *Franklin's Tales.*" In *Feminea Medievalia I,* edited by Bonnie Wheeler. Dallas, TX: Academia, 1993. 69–90.

1109. Lee, Brian S. "The Question of Closure in Fragment V of *The Canterbury Tales.*" *YES* 22 (1992): 190–200.

1110. Lynch, Kathryn. "East Meets West in Chaucer's Squire's and Franklin's Tales." *Speculum* 70 (1995): 530–51.

1111. Peterson, Joyce E. "The Finished Fragment: A Reassessment of the *Squire's Tale.*" *ChauR* 5 (1970): 62–74.

5 — The Squire and His Tale

1112. Ambrisco, Alan S. "'It Lyth Nat in My Tonge': Occupatio and Otherness in the *Squire's Tale.*" *ChauR* 38 (2004): 205–28.

1113. Berry, Craig A. "Flying Sources: Classical Authority in Chaucer's *Squire's Tale.*" *ELH* 68 (2001): 287–313.

1114. Braddy, Haldeen. "The Genre of Chaucer's *Squire's Tale.*" *JEGP* 41 (1942): 279–90.

1115. Dane, Joseph A. "'Tyl Mercurius House He Flye': Early Printed Editions and Critical Reading of the *Squire's Tale.*" *ChauR* 34 (2000): 309–16.

1116. DiMarco, Vincent. "The Dialogue of Science and Magic in Chaucer's *Squire's Tale.*" In *Dialogische Strukturen/Dialogic Structures,* edited by Thomas Kuhn and Ursula Schaefer. Tübingen, Germany: Narr, 1996. 50–68.

1117. ———. "The Historical Basis of Chaucer's *Squire's Tale.*" *Edebiyat,* n.s., 1.2 (1989): 1–22.

1118. Edwards, Robert R. "The Failure of Invention: Chaucer's *Squire's Tale.*" In *Ratio and Invention.* Nashville, TN: Vanderbilt UP, 1989. 131–45.

1119. Fyler, John M. "Domesticating the Exotic in the *Squire's Tale.*" *ELH* 55 (1988): 1–26.

1120. Goodman, Jennifer R. "Chaucer's *Squire's Tale* and the Rise of Chivalry." *SAC* 5 (1983): 127–36.

1121. Haller, Robert S. "Chaucer's Squire's Tale and the Uses of Rhetoric." *MP* 62 (1965): 285–95.

1122. Heffernan, Carol F. "Chaucer's *Squire's Tale:* The Poetics of Interlace or the 'Well of English Undefiled.'" *ChauR* 32 (1997): 32–45.

1123. Jordan, Carmel. "Soviet Archeology and the Setting of the *Squire's Tale.*" *ChauR* 22 (1987): 128–40.

1124. Kamowski, William. "Trading the 'Knotte' for Loose Ends: The *Squire's Tale* and the Poetics of Chaucerian Fragments." *Style* 31 (1997): 391–412.

1125. Lightsey, Scott. "Chaucer's Secular Marvels and the Medieval Economy of Wonder." *SAC* 23 (2001): 289–316.

1126. Neville, Marie. "The Function of the *Squire's Tale* in the Canterbury Scheme." *JEGP* 50 (1951): 167–79.

1127. Sharon-Zisser, Shirley. "The *Squire's Tale* and the Limits of Non-mimetic Fiction." *ChauR* 26 (1992): 377–94.

See also nos. 25, 43, 660, 663, 1427.

5 — The Franklin and His Tale

1128. Arnovick, Leslie K. "Dorigen's Promise and Scholars' Premises: The Orality of the Speech Act in the *Franklin's Tale.*" In *Oral Poetics in Middle English Poetry,* edited by Mark C. Amodio. New York: Garland, 1994. 125–47.

1129. Battles, Dominique. "Chaucer's *Franklin's Tale* and Boccaccio's *Filocolo* Reconsidered." *ChauR* 34 (1999): 38–59.

1130. Bleeth, Kenneth. "The Rock and the Garden: The Limits of Illusion in Chaucer's *Franklin's Tale.*" *ES* 74 (1993): 113–23.

1131. Braswell, Mary Flowers. "The Magic of Machinery: A Context for Chaucer's *Franklin's Tale.*" *Mosaic* 18 (1985): 101–10.

1132. Brown, Carole Koepke. "'It Is True to Conceal Art': The Episodic Structure of Chaucer's *Franklin's Tale.*" *ChauR* 27 (1992): 162–85.

1133. Carruthers, Mary J. "The Gentilesse of Chaucer's Franklin." *Criticism* 23 (1981): 283–300.

1134. David, Alfred. "Sentimental Comedy in the *Franklin's Tale.*" *AnM* 6 (1965): 19–27.

1135. Eaton, R. D. "Narrative Closure in Chaucer's *Franklin's Tale.*" *Neophil* 84 (2000): 309–21.

1136. Fein, Susanna. "Boethian Boundaries: Compassion and Constraint in the *Franklin's Tale.*" In *Drama, Narrative and Poetry in The Canterbury Tales,* edited by Wendy Harding. Toulouse: Presses Universitaires du Mirail, Collection Interlangues: Literatures, 2003. 195–212.

1137. Flake, Timothy H. "Love, *Trouthe,* and the Happy Ending of the *Franklin's Tale.*" *ES* 77 (1996): 209–26.

1138. Gravlee, Cynthia A. "Presence, Absence, and Difference: Reception and Deception in *The Franklin's Tale.*" In *Desiring Discourse: The Literature of Love, Ovid through Chaucer,* edited by James J. Paxson and Cynthia A. Gravlee. Selinsgrove, PA: Susquehanna UP, 1998. 177–87.

1139. Greenberg, Nina Manasan. "Dorigen as Enigma: The Production of Meaning in the *Franklin's Tale.*" *ChauR* 33 (1999): 329–49.

1140. Hamaguchi, Keiko. "In Defense of Dorigen: Dorigen's Complaint in the Franklin's Tale." In *Fiction and Truth: Essays on Fourteenth Century Literature,* edited by Hisao Tsuru. Tokyo: Kirihara Shoten, 2000. 195–211.

1141. Jonassen, Frederick B. "Carnival Food Imagery in Chaucer's Description of the Franklin." *SAC* 16 (1994): 99–117.

1142. Knight, Stephen. "Ideology in *The Franklin's Tale*." *Parergon* 28 (1980): 3–31.

1143. Knopp, Sherron. "Poetry as Conjuring Act: The *Franklin's Tale* and *The Tempest*." *ChauR* 38 (2004): 337–54.

1144. Lucas, Angela. "Keeping Up Appearances: Chaucer's Franklin and the Magic of the Breton Lay." In *Literature and the Supernatural,* edited by Brian Cosgrove. Blackrock, Ireland: Columba, 1996. 11–32.

1145. Luengo, Anthony E. "Magic and Illusion in *The Franklin's Tale*." *JEGP* 77 (1978): 1–16.

1146. McEntire, Sandra J. "Illusions and Interpretations in the *Franklin's Tale*." *ChauR* 31 (1996): 145–63.

1147. McGregor, Francine. "What of Dorigen? Agency and Ambivalence in the *Franklin's Tale*." *ChauR* 31 (1997): 365–78.

1148. Mann, Jill. "Wife-Swapping in Medieval Literature." *Viator* 32 (2001): 92–119.

1149. Miller, Robert P. "The Epicurean Homily on Marriage by Chaucer's Franklin." *Mediaevalia* 6 (1980): 151–86.

1150. Morgan, Gerald. "A Defence of Dorigen's Complaint." *MAE* 46 (1977): 77–97.

1151. ———. "Experience and the Judgment of Poetry: A Reconsideration of *The Franklin's Tale*." *MAE* 70 (2001): 204–25.

1152. Pakkala-Weckström, Mari. "'Have Her My Trouthe — Til That Myn Herte Breste': Dorigen and the Difficulty of Keeping Promises in the *Franklin's Tale*." In *Variation Past and Present,* edited by Helena Raumolin-Brunberg and others. Helsinki: Société Néophilologique, 2002. 287–300.

1153. Pearcy, Roy J. "Chaucer's Franklin and the Literary Vavasour." *ChauR* 8 (1973): 33–59.

1154. Pitcher, John A. "'Word and Werk' in Chaucer's *Franklin's Tale*." *L&P* 49 (2003): 77–109.

1155. Pulham, Carol A. "Promises, Promises: Dorigen's Dilemma Revisited." *ChauR* 31 (1996): 76–86.

1156. Riddy, Felicity. "Engendering Pity in the *Franklin's Tale*." In *Feminist Readings in Middle English Literature,* edited by Ruth Evans and Lesley Johnson. London: Routledge, 1994. 54–71.

1157. Robertson, D. W., Jr. "Chaucer's Franklin and His Tale." *Costerus,* n.s., 1 (1974): 1–26.

1158. Ronquist, E. C. "The Franklin, Epicurus, and the Play of Values." In *Chaucer and Language: Essays in Honour of Douglas Wurtele,* edited by Robert Myles and David Williams. Montreal: McGill-Queen's UP, 2001. 44–60.

1159. Saul, Nigel. "The Social Status of Chaucer's Franklin: A Reconsideration." *MAE* 52 (1983): 10–26.

1160. Schutz, Andrea. "Negotiating the Present: Language and Trouthe in the *Franklin's Tale*." In *Speaking in the Medieval World,* edited by Jean E. Godsall-Myers. Boston: Brill, 2003. 105–24.

1161. Scott, Anne. "'Considerynge the Beste on Every Side': Ethics, Empathy, and Epistemology in the *Franklin's Tale*." *ChauR* 29 (1995): 390–415.

1162. Seaman, David M. "'As Thynketh Yow': Conflicting Evidence and the Interpretation of *The Franklin's Tale*." *M&H* 17 (1991): 41–58.

1163. Smith, Warren S. "Dorigen's Lament and the Resolution of the *Franklin's Tale*." *ChauR* 36 (2002): 374–90.

1164. Specht, Henrik. *Chaucer's Franklin in the Canterbury Tales: The Social and Literary Background of a Chaucerian Character.* Copenhagen: Akademisk Forlag, 1981.

1165. Straus, Barrie Ruth. "'Truth' and 'Woman' in Chaucer's *Franklin's Tale*." *Exemplaria* 4, Special Issue (1992): 135–68.

1166. Sweeney, Michelle. *Magic in Medieval Romance from Chrétien de Troyes to Geoffrey Chaucer.* Dublin: Four Courts, 2000.

1167. Traversi, Derek. "The Franklin's Tale." In *The Literary Imagination: Studies in Dante, Chaucer, and Shakespeare.* Newark: U of Delaware P, 1982. 87–119.

1168. Wheeler, Bonnie. "*Trouthe* without Consequences: Rhetoric and Gender in the *Franklin's Tale*." In *Feminea Medievalia I,* edited by Bonnie Wheeler. Dallas, TX: Academia, 1993. 91–116.

See also nos. 118, 444, 446, 452, 537, 625, 639, 1005, 1077.

Part 6

1169. Amoils, E. R. "Fruitfulness and Sterility in the Physician's and Pardoner's Tales." *ESA* 17 (1974): 17–37.

1170. Haines, R. Michael. "Fortune, Nature, and Grace in Fragment C [6]." *ChauR* 10 (1976): 220–35.

1171. Joseph, Gerhard. "The Gifts of Nature, Fortune, and Grace in the *Physician's, Pardoner's,* and *Parson's Tales*." *ChauR* 9 (1975): 237–45.

1172. Lee, Brian S. "Justice in the *Physician's Tale* and the *Pardoner's Tale*: A Dialogic Contrast." *ChauY* 4 (1997): 21–32.

1173. Pelen, Marc M. "Murder and Immorality in Fragment VI (C) of the *Canterbury Tales*: Chaucer's Transformation of Theme and Image from the *Roman de la Rose*." *ChauR* 29 (1994): 1–25.

1174. Trower, Katherine B. "Spiritual Sickness in the Physician's and Pardoner's Tales: Thematic Unity in Fragment VI of the *Canterbury Tales*." *ABR* 29 (1978): 67–86.

6—*The Physician and His Tale*

1175. Bloch, R. Howard. "Chaucer's Maiden's Head: *The Physician's Tale* and the Poetics of Virginity." *Representations* 28 (1989): 113–34.

1176. Bott, Robin. "'O, Keep Me from Their Lust Worse Than Killing': Ideologies of Rape and Mutilation in Chaucer's *Physician's Tale* and Shakespeare's *Titus Andronicus*." In *Representing Rape in Medieval and Early Modern Literature,* edited by Elizabeth Robertson and Christine M. Rose. New York: Palgrave, 2001. 189–211.

1177. Braswell, Laurel. "The Moon and Medicine in Chaucer's Time." *SAC* 8 (1986): 145–56.

1178. Brown, Emerson. "What Is Chaucer Doing with the Physician and His Tale?" *PQ* 60 (1981): 129–49.

1179. Brown, William H. "Chaucer, Livy, and Bersuire: The Roman Materials in *The Physician's Tale*." In *On Language: Rhetorica, Phonologica, Syntactica,* edited by Caroline Duncan-Rose and Theo Venneman. New York: Routledge, 1988. 39–51.

1180. Delany, Sheila. "Slaying Python: Marriage and Misogyny in a Chaucerian Text." In *Writing Women: Women Writers and Women in Literature Medieval to Modern.* New York: Schocken, 1983. 47–75.

1181. Farber, Lianna. "The Creation of Consent in the *Physician's Tale*." *ChauR* 39 (2004): 151–64.

1182. Fletcher, Angus. "The Sentencing of Virginia in the *Physician's Tale*." *ChauR* 34 (2000): 300–308.

1183. Harley, Marta Powell. "Last Things First in Chaucer's *Physician's Tale:* Final Judgment and the Worm of Conscience." *JEGP* 91 (1992): 1–16.

1184. Hirsh, John C. "Chaucer's Roman Tales." *ChauR* 31 (1996): 45–57.

1185. ———. "Modern Times: The Discourse of the *Physician's Tale*." *ChauR* 27 (1993): 387–95.

1186. Mandel, Jerome H. "Governance in the *Physician's Tale*." *ChauR* 10 (1978): 76–84.

1187. Middleton, Anne. "*The Physician's Tale* and Love's Martyrs: 'Ensamples Mo Than Ten' as a Method in the *Canterbury Tales*." *ChauR* 8 (1973): 9–32.

1188. Pitcher, John A. "Chaucer's Wolf: Exemplary Violence in *The Physician's Tale*." *Genre* 36 (2003): 1–27.

1189. Prior, Sandra Pierson. "Virginity and Sacrifice in Chaucer's *Physician's Tale*." In *Constructions of Widowhood and Virginity in the Middle Ages,* edited by Cindy L. Carlson and Angela Jane Weisl. New York: St. Martin's, 1999. 165–80.

1190. Sanok, Catherine. "The Geography of Genre in the *Physician's Tale* and *Pearl*." *NML* 5 (2002): 177–201.

1191. Skerpan, Elizabeth. "Chaucer's Physicians: Their Texts, Contexts, and the *Canterbury Tales*." *JRMMRA* 5 (1984): 4–56.

1192. Uebel, Michael. "Public Fantasy and Logic of Sacrifice in *The Physician's Tale*." *ANQ* 15.3 (2002): 30–33.

1193. Ussery, Huling E. *Chaucer's Physician: Medicine and Literature in Fourteenth-Century England.* New Orleans: Tulane U Dept. of English, 1971.

See also no. 44.

6—The Pardoner and His Tale

1194. Beidler, Peter G. "The Plague and Chaucer's Pardoner." *ChauR* 16 (1982): 257–69.

1195. Bishop, Ian. "The Narrative Art of the *Pardoner's Tale*." *MAE* 36 (1967): 15–24.

1196. Braswell, Mary Flowers. "Chaucer's Palimpsest: Judas Iscariot and *The Pardoner's Tale*." *ChauR* 29 (1995): 303–10.

1197. Bullough, Vern. "Medieval Masculinities and Modern Interpretations: The Problem of the Pardoner." In *Conflicted Identities and Multiple Masculinities,* edited by Jacqueline Murray. New York: Garland, 1999. 93–110.

1198. Burger, Glenn. "Kissing the Pardoner." *PMLA* 107 (1992): 1143–56.

1199. Calabrese, Michael A. "'Make a Mark That Shows': Orphean Song, Orphean Sexuality, and the Exile of Chaucer's Pardoner." *Viator* 24 (1993): 269–86.

1200. Chance, Jane. "'Disfigured is thy face': Chaucer's Pardoner and the Protean Shape-Shifter Fals-Semblant (A Response to Britton J. Harwood)." *PQ* 67 (1988): 423–37.

1201. Condren, Edward I. "The Pardoner's Bid for Existence." *Viator* 4 (1973): 177–205.

1202. Copeland, Rita. "The Pardoner's Body and the Discipline of Rhetoric." In *Framing Medieval Bodies,* edited by Sarah Kay and Miri Rubin. New York: Manchester UP, 1994. 138–59.

1203. Cox, Catherine S. "Water of Bitterness: The Pardoner and/as the Sotah." *Exemplaria* 16 (2004): 131–64.

1204. Delasanta, Rodney. "Sacrament and Sacrifice in the Pardoner's Tale." *AnM* 14 (1973): 43–52.

1205. Dillon, Janette. "Chaucer's Game in the Pardoner's Tale." *EIC* 41 (1991): 208–21.

1206. Dinshaw, Carolyn. "Chaucer's Queer Touches/A Queer Touches Chaucer." *Exemplaria* 7 (1995): 75–92.

1207. ———. "Eunuch Hermeneutics." *ELH* 55 (1988): 27–51.

1208. Fletcher, Alan J. "The Topical Hypocrisy of Chaucer's Pardoner." *ChauR* 25 (1990): 110–26.

1209. Fowler, Elizabeth. "Character and Habituation of the Reader: The Pardoner's Thought Experiment." In *Literary Character: The Human Figure in Early English Writing*. Ithaca, NY: Cornell UP, 2003. 32–94.

1210. Frantzen, Allen J. "*The Pardoner's Tale,* the Pervert, and the Price of Order in Chaucer's World." In *Class and Gender in Early English Literature,* edited by Britton J. Harwood and Gillian R. Overing. Bloomington: Indiana UP, 1994. 131–48.

1211. Green, Richard Firth. "The Pardoner's Pants (and Why They Matter)." *SAC* 15 (1993): 131–45.

1212. Gross, Gregory W. "Trade Secrets: Chaucer, the Pardoner, the Critics." *MLS* 25.4 (1995): 1–36.

1213. Halverson, John. "Chaucer's Pardoner and the Progress of Criticism." *ChauR* 4 (1970): 184–202.

1214. Harwood, Britton J. "Chaucer's Pardoner: The Dialectics of Inside and Outside." *PQ* 67 (1988): 409–22.

1215. Hoerner, Fred. "Church Office, Routine, and Self-Exile in Chaucer's Pardoner." *SAC* 16 (1994): 69–98.

1216. Jungman, Robert E. "The Pardoner's Quarrel with the Host." *PQ* 55 (1976): 279–81.

1217. Kellogg, A. L., and L. A. Haselmayer. "Chaucer's Satire on the Pardoner." *PMLA* 66 (1951): 251–77.

1218. Kelly, Henry Ansgar. "The Pardoner's Voice, Disjunctive Narrative, and Modes of Effemination." In *Speaking Images: Essays in Honor of V. A. Kolve,* edited by R. F. Yeager and Charlotte C. Morse. Asheville, NC: Pegasus, 2001. 411–44.

1219. Kruger, Steven F. "Claiming the Pardoner: Toward a Gay Reading of Chaucer's *Pardoner's Tale*." *Exemplaria* 6 (1994): 115–39.

1220. McAlpine, Monica E. "The Pardoner's Homosexuality and How It Matters." *PMLA* 95 (1980): 8–22.

1221. Matsuda, Takami. "Death, Prudence, and Chaucer's *Pardoner's Tale*." *JEGP* 91 (1992): 313–24.

1222. Maxfield, David K. "St. Mary Rouncivale, Charing Cross: The Hospital of Chaucer's Pardoner." *ChauR* 28 (1993): 148–63.

1223. Merrix, Robert P. "Sermon Structure in the *Pardoner's Tale*." *ChauR* 17 (1983): 235–49.

1224. Minnis, Alastair. "Reclaiming the Pardoner." *JMEMSt* 33 (2003): 311–34.

1225. Nitecki. Alicia K. "The Convention of the Old Man's Lament in the *Pardoner's Tale*." *ChauR* 16 (1981): 76–84.

1226. Osborn, Marijane. "Transgressive Word and Image in Chaucer's Enshrined *Coillions* Passage." *ChauR* 37 (2003): 365–84.

1227. Patterson, Lee. "Chaucerian Confession: Penitential Literature and the Pardoner." *M&H* 7 (1976): 153–73.

1228. ———. "Chaucer's Pardoner on the Couch: Psyche and Clio in Medieval Literary Studies." *Speculum* 76 (2001): 638–80.

1229. Pittock, Malcolm. "The Pardoner's Tale and the Quest of Death." *EIC* 24 (1974): 107–23.

1230. Purdon, Liam. "The Pardoner's Old Man and the Second Death." *SP* 89 (1992): 334–49.

1231. Reed, Shannon. "Who Is Afraid of the Pardoner?" *Journal X* 5 (2000–2001): 109–16.

1232. Richardson, Gudrun. "The Old Man in Chaucer's *Pardoner's Tale:* An Interpretative Study of His Identity and Meaning." *Neophil* 87 (2003): 323–37.

1233. Sedgewick, G. G. "The Progress of Chaucer's Pardoner, 1880–1940." *MLQ* 1 (1940): 431–58.

1234. Snell, William. "Chaucer's *Pardoner's Tale* and Pestilence in Late-Medieval Literature." *SIMELL* 10 (1995): 1–16.

1235. Steimatsky, Noa. "The Name of the Corpse: A Reading of the *Pardoner's Tale*." *HUSL* 15 (1987): 36–43.

1236. Storm, Melvin. "The Pardoner's Invitation: Quaestor's Bag or Becket's Shrine?" *PMLA* 97 (1982): 810–18.

1237. Strohm, Paul. "Chaucer's Lollard Joke: History and Textual Unconscious." *SAC* 17 (1995): 23–42.

1238. Sturges, Robert S. *Chaucer's Pardoner and Gender Theory: Bodies of Discourse.* New York: St. Martin's, 2000.

1239. Thomas, Susanne Sara. "Textual Exhibitionism: The Pardoner's Affirmation of Text over Context." *Mediaevalia* 22 (1998): 13–47.

1240. Vance, Eugene. "Chaucer's Pardoner: Relics, Discourse, and Frames of Propriety." *NLH* 20 (1989): 723–45.

1241. Williams, David. "'Lo, How I Vanysshe': The Pardoner's War against Signs." In *Chaucer and Language: Essays in Honour of Douglas Wurtele,* edited by Robert Myles and David Williams. Montreal: McGill-Queen's UP, 2001. 143–73.

1242. Zeikowitz, Richard E. "Silenced but Not Stifled: The Disruptive Queer Power of Chaucer's Pardoner." *DR* 82.1 (2002): 55–73.

See also nos. 64, 290, 400, 648–50, 652, 1007, 1442, 1456, 1477.

Part 7

1243. Astell, Ann. "Chaucer's 'Literature Group' and the Medieval Causes of Books." *ELH* 59 (1992): 269–87.

1244. Brown, Emerson, Jr. "Fragment VII of Chaucer's 'Canterbury Tales' and the 'Mental Climate' of the Fourteenth Century." In *Traditions and Innovations,* edited by David G. Allen and Robert A. White. Newark: U of Delaware P, 1990. 50–58.

1245. Gruenler, Curtis. "Desire, Violence and the Passion of Fragment VII of *The Canterbury Tales*: A Girardian Reading." *Renascence* 52 (1999): 35–56.

See also no. 744.

7—The Shipman and His Tale

1246. Abraham, David H. "*Cosyn* and *Cosynage*: Pun and Structure in the *Shipman's Tale*." *ChauR* 11 (1977): 319–27.

1247. Adams, Robert. "The Concept of Debt in *The Shipman's Tale*." *SAC* 6 (1984): 85–102.

1248. Beidler, Peter G. "Contrasting Masculinities in the *Shipman's Tale:* Monk, Merchant, and Wife." In *Masculinities in Chaucer,* edited by Peter G. Beidler. Rochester, NY: Brewer, 1998. 131–42.

1249. Buckmaster, Dale, and Elizabeth Buckmaster. "Studies of Accounting and Commerce in Chaucer's *Shipman's Tale*." *Accounting, Auditing, & Accountability* 12.1 (1999): 113–28.

1250. Finlayson, John. "Chaucer's *Shipman's Tale,* Boccaccio, and the 'Civilizing' of Fabliau." *ChauR* 36 (2002): 336–51.

1251. Fulton, Helen. "Mercantile Ideology in Chaucer's *Shipman's Tale*." *ChauR* 36 (2002): 311–28.

1252. Ganim, John M. "Double Entry in Chaucer's *Shipman's Tale:* Chaucer and Bookkeeping before Pacioli." *ChauR* 30 (1996): 294–305.

1253. Hahn, Thomas. "Money, Sexuality, and Context in the *Shipman's Tale*." In *Chaucer in the Eighties,* edited by Julian N. Wasserman and Robert J. Blanch. Syracuse, NY: Syracuse UP, 1986. 235–49.

1254. Hamaguchi, Keiko. "*Debt* and the Wife as Verbal Exchange in *The Shipman's Tale*." In *A Pilgrimage through English Literature,* edited by Hiroe Futamura and others. Tokyo: Nan' Un-Do, 1993. 123–44.

1255. Jager, Eric. "*The Shipman's Tale:* Merchant's Time and Church's Time, Secular and Sacred Space." In *Chaucer and the Challenges of Medievalism,* edited by Donka Minkova and Theresa Tinkle. Frankfurt: Lang, 2003. 253–60.

1256. Joseph, Gerhard. "Chaucer's Coinage: Foreign Exchange and the Puns of the *Shipman's Tale*." *ChauR* 17 (1983): 341–47. ·

1257. Keen, William P. "Chaucer's Imaginable Audience and the Oaths of *The Shipman's Tale*." *Topic* 50 (2000): 91–103.

1258. Nicholson, Peter. "The Shipman's Tale and the *Fabliaux*." *ELH* 45 (1978): 583–96.

1259. Rogers, William E., and Paul Dower. "Thinking about Money in Chaucer's *Shipman's Tale*." In *New Readings of Chaucer's Poetry,* edited by Robert G. Benson and Susan J. Ridyard. Rochester, NY: Brewer, 2003. 119–38.

1260. Sayers, William. "Chaucer's Shipman and the Law Marine." *ChauR* 37 (2002): 145–58.

1261. Scattergood, V. J. "The Originality of the *Shipman's Tale*." *ChauR* 11 (1977): 210–31.

1262. Silverman, Albert H. "Sex and Money in Chaucer's *Shipman's Tale*" *PQ* 32 (1953): 329–36.

1263. Thormann, Janet. "The Circulation of Desire in *The Shipman's Tale*." *L&P* 39.3 (1993): 1–15.

1264. Woods, William F. "Metaphoric Comedy in the *Shipman's Tale*." In *Chaucer's Humor: Critical Essays,* edited by Jean E. Jost. New York: Garland, 1994. 207–28.

See also nos. 427, 638, 1340–41.

7—The Prioress and Her Tale

1265. Adams, Robert. "Chaucer's 'Newe Rachel' and the Theological Roots of Medieval Anti-Semitism." *BJRL* 77 (1995): 9–18.

1266. Alexander, Philip S. "Madame Eglentyne, Geoffrey Chaucer and the Problem of Medieval Anti-Semitism." *BJRL* 74 (1992): 109–20.

1267. Bauer, Kate. "'We Thrughoutly Hauen Cnawyng': Ideas of Learning and Knowing in Some Works of Chaucer, Gower, and the Pearl-Poet." In *Satura: Studies in Medieval Literature in Honour of Robert R. Raymo,* edited by Nancy R. Reale and Ruth E. Sternglantz. Donington: Shaun Tyas, 2001. 205–26.

1268. Besserman, Lawrence L. "Ideology, Antisemitism, and Chaucer's *Prioress's Tale*." *ChauR* 36 (2001): 48–72.

1269. Boenig, Robert. "Alma Redemptoris Mater, Gaude Maria, and the Prioress's Tale." *N&Q* 244 (1999): 321–26.

1270. Calabrese, Michael. "Performing the Prioress: 'Conscience' and Responsibility in Studies of Chaucer's *Prioress's Tale*." *TSLL* 44 (2002): 66–91.

1271. Collette, Carolyn P. "Chaucer's Discourse of Mariology: Gaining the Right to Speak." In *Art and Context in Late Medieval English Narrative,* edited by Robert R. Edwards. Cambridge, UK: Brewer, 1994. 127–47.

1272. ———. "Critical Approaches to the 'Prioress's Tale' and the 'Second Nun's Tale.'" In no. 396, 95–107.

1273. ———. "Sense and Sensibility in the *Prioress's Tale*." *ChauR* 15 (1981): 138–50.

1274. D'Arcy, Anne Marie. "'Cursed Folk of Herodes Al New': Suppressionist Typology and Chaucer's Prioress." *E&S* 55 (2002): 117–56.

1275. Delany, Sheila. "Chaucer's Prioress, the Jews, and the Muslims." *Medieval Encounters* 5 (1999): 198–213.

1276. Despres, Denise. "Cultic Anti-Judaism and Chaucer's 'Litel Clergeon.'" *MP* 91 (1994): 413–27.

1277. Dutton, Marsha L. "Chaucer's Two Nuns." In *Monasteries and Society in Medieval Britain. Proceedings of the 1994 Harlaxton Symposium,* edited by Benjamin Thorpe. Stamford: Watkins, 1999. 296–311.

1278. Ferris, Sumner. "The Mariology of the *Prioress's Tale*." *ABR* 32 (1981): 232–54.

1279. Ferster, Judith. "'Your Praise Is Performed by Men and Children': Language and Gender in the *Prioress's Prologue* and *Tale*." *Exemplaria* 2 (1990): 149–68.

1280. Fradenburg, Louise O. "Criticism, Anti-Semitism, and the *Prioress's Tale*." *Exemplaria* 1 (1989): 69–115.

1281. Frank, Hardy Long. "Seeing the Prioress Whole." *ChauR* 25 (1991): 229–37.

1282. Frank, Robert Worth, Jr. "Miracles of the Virgin, Medieval Anti-Semitism, and the *Prioress's Tale*." In *The Wisdom of Poetry,* edited by Larry D. Benson and Siegfried Wenzel. Kalamazoo: Western Michigan P, 1982. 177–88.

1283. Friedman, Albert B. "The Prioress's Tale and Chaucer's Anti-Semitism." *ChauR* 9 (1974): 118–29.

1284. Gaynor, Stephanie. "He Says, She Says: Subjectivity and the Discourse of the Other in the Prioress's Portrait and Tale." *Medieval Encounters* 5 (1999): 375–90.

1285. Hahn, Thomas. "The Performance of Gender in the Prioress." *ChauY* 1 (1992): 11–34.

1286. Holsinger, Bruce W. "Pedagogy, Violence, and the Subject of Music: Chaucer's *Prioress's Tale* and the Ideologies of *Song*." *NML* 1 (1997): 157–92.

1287. Koretsky, Allen C. "Dangerous Innocence: Chaucer's Prioress and Her Tale." In *Jewish Presences in English Literature,* edited by Derek Cohen and Deborah Haller. Montreal: McGill-Queen's UP, 1990. 10–24.

1288. Maleski, Mary. "The Culpability of Chaucer's Prioress." *ChauY* 5 (1998): 41–60.

1289. Meale, Carol M. "Women's Pity and Women's Power: Chaucer's Prioress Reconsidered." In *Essays on Ricardian Literature,* edited by A. J. Minnis and others. Oxford: Clarendon, 1997. 39–60.

1290. Oliver, Kathleen M. "Singing Bread, Manna, and the Clergeon's *Greyn*." *ChauR* 31 (1997): 357–64.

1291. Osberg, Richard H. "A Voice for the Prioress: The Context of English Devotional Prose." *SAC* 18 (1996): 25–54.

1292. Paley, Karen Surman. "The Assassination of the 'Litel Clergeon': A Post-colonial Reading of the Prioress's Tale." *Diversity* 3 (Summer 1995): 39–65.

1293. Patterson, Lee. "'The Living Witnesses of Our Redemption': Martyrdom and Imitation in Chaucer's *Prioress's Tale*." *JMEMSt* 31 (2001): 507–60.

1294. Power, Eileen. "Madam Eglentyne: Chaucer's Prioress in Real Life." In *Medieval People*. 10th ed. London: Methuen, 1963.

1296. Rambuss, Richard. "Devotion and Defilement: The Blessed Virgin Mary and the Corporeal Hagiographics of Chaucer's *Prioress's Tale*." In *Textual Bodies*, edited by Lori Hope Lefkovitz. Albany: State U of New York P, 1997. 75–99.

1297. Rex, Richard. *"The Sins of Madame Eglentyne" and Other Essays on Chaucer*. Newark: U of Delaware P, 1995.

1298. Ridley, Florence. *The Prioress and the Critics*. U of California English Studies 30. Berkeley: U of California P, 1965.

1299. Saito, Isumu. "'Greyn' of Martyrdom in Chaucer's *Prioress's Tale*." In *Arthurian and Other Studies Presented to Sunichi Noguchi*, edited by Takashi Suzuki and Tsuyoshi Mukai. Cambridge, UK: Brewer, 1993. 31–38.

1300. Spector, Stephen. "Empathy and Enmity in the Prioress's Tale." In *The Olde Daunce*, edited by Robert R. Edwards and Stephen Spector. Albany: State U of New York P, 1991. 211–28.

1301. Wood, Chauncey. "Chaucer's Use of Signs in His Portrait of the Prioress." In no. 494, 81–101.

See also nos. 45, 122, 638, 642–43, 656, 663–64, 1307.

7 — The Tale of Sir Thopas

1302. Burrow, J. A. "Chaucer's *Sir Thopas* and *La Prise de Neuvile*." In *English Satire and Satiric Tradition*, edited by Claude Rawson. Oxford: Blackwell, 1984. 44–55.

1303. Cohen, Jeffrey Jerome. "Diminishing Masculinity in Chaucer's *Tale of Sir Thopas*." In *Masculinities in Chaucer*, edited by Peter G. Beidler. Rochester, NY: Brewer, 1998. 143–55.

1304. Conley, John. "The Peculiar Name *Thopas*." *SP* 73 (1976): 42–61.

1305. Gaylord, Alan T. "Chaucer's Dainty 'Dogerel': The 'Elvyssh' Prosody of *Sir Thopas*." *SAC* 1 (1979): 83–104.

1306. ———. "The 'Miracle' of *Sir Thopas*." *SAC* 6 (1984): 65–84.

1307. Hamel, Mary. "And Now for Something Different: The Relationship between the *Prioress's Tale* and the *Rime of Sir Thopas*." *ChauR* 14 (1980): 251–59.

1308. Jones, E. A. "'Loo, Lordes Myne, Heere Is a Fit!': The Structure of Chaucer's *Sir Thopas*." *RES* 51 (2000): 248–52.

1309. Kooper, E. S. "Inverted Images in Chaucer's *Tale of Sir Thopas*." *SN* 56 (1984): 147–54.

1310. Lerer, Seth. "'Now Holde Youre Mouth': The Romance of Orality in the *Thopas-Melibee* Section of the *Canterbury Tales*." In *Oral Poetics in Middle English Poetry*, edited by Mark C. Amodio. New York: Garland, 1994. 181–205.

1311. Olson, Glending. "A Reading of the Thopas-Melibee Link." *ChauR* 10 (1975): 147–53.

1312. Patterson, Lee W. "'What Man Artow?': Authorial Self-Definition in *The Tale of Sir Thopas* and *The Tale of Melibee*." *SAC* 11 (1989): 117–75.

1313. Scattergood, V. J. "Chaucer and the French War: *Sir Thopas* and *Melibee*." In *Court and Poet*, edited by Glyn S. Burgess and others. Liverpool: Cairns, 1981. 287–96.

1314. Tschann, Judith. "The Layout of *Sir Thopas* in the Ellesmere, Hengwrt, Cambridge Dd.4.24 and Cambridge Gg.4.27 Manuscripts." *ChauR* 20 (1985): 1–13.

1315. Wright, Glenn. "Modern Inconveniences: Rethinking the Parody in *The Tale of Sir Thopas*." *Genre* 30 (1997): 167–94.

See also nos. 327, 361, 744.

7 — The Tale of Melibee

1316. Aers, David. "Chaucer's *Tale of Melibee*: Whose Virtues?" In *Medieval Literature and Historical Inquiry*, edited by David Aers. Cambridge, UK: Brewer, 2000. 68–81.

1317. Burger, Glenn. "Making a History of Sexuality in Melibee." In *Chaucer and Language: Essays in Honour of Douglas Wurtele*, edited by Robert Myles and David Williams. Montreal: McGill-Queen's UP, 2001. 61–70.

1318. Dobyns, Ann. "Chaucer and the Rhetoric of Justice." *Disputatio* 4 (1999): 75–89.

1319. Ferster, Judith. "Chaucer's *Tale of Melibee*: Advice to the King and Advice to the King's Advisers." In *Fictions of Advice: The Literature and Politics of Counsel in Late Medieval England*. Philadelphia: U of Pennsylvania P, 1996. 89–107.

1320. ———. "Chaucer's *Tale of Melibee*: Contradictions and Context." In *Inscribing the Hundred Years' War in French and English Cultures*, edited by Denise N. Baker. Albany: State U of New York P, 2000. 79–89.

1321. Hoffman, Richard L. "Chaucer's Melibee and Tales of Sondry Folk." *Classica et Medievalia* 30 (1969): 552–77.

1322. Johnson, Lynn Staley. "Inverse Counsel: Contexts for the *Melibee*." *SP* 87 (1990): 137–55.

1323. Jones, Christine. "Chaucer after the Linguistic Turn: Memory, History, and Fiction in the Link to Melibee." In *Chaucer and Language: Essays in Honour of Douglas Wurtele*, edited by Robert Myles and David Williams. Montreal: McGill-Queen's UP, 2001. 71–82.

1324. Kennedy, Kathleen E. "Maintaining Love through Accord in the *Tale of Melibee*." *ChauR* 39 (2004): 165–76.

1325. Mann, Jill. "Newly Identified Quotations in Chaucer's *Tale of Melibee* and the *Parson's Tale*." In *The Medieval Book and a Modern Collector*, edited by Takami Matsuda and others. Cambridge, UK: Brewer, 2004. 61–71.

1326. Moore, Stephen G. "Apply Yourself: Learning While Reading the *Tale of Melibee*." *ChauR* 38 (2003): 83–97.

1327. Owen, Charles A., Jr. "The *Tale of Melibee*." *ChauR* 7 (1973): 267–80.

1328. Pakkala-Weckström, Mari. "Prudence and the Power of Persuasion — Language and *Maistrie* in the *Tale of Melibee*." *ChauR* 35 (2001): 399–411.

1329. Stillwell, Gardner. "The Political Meaning of Chaucer's *Tale of Melibee.*" *Speculum* 19 (1944): 433–44.

1330. Strohm, Paul. "The Allegory of the *Tale of Melibee.*" *ChauR* 2 (1967): 32–42.

1331. Waterhouse, Ruth, and Gwen Griffiths. "*Sweete Wordes* of Nonsense: Deconstruction of the Moral *Melibee.*" *ChauR* 23 (1989): 53–63.

See also nos. 164, 744, 1310–13.

7 — The Monk and His Tale

1332. Beichner, Paul E. "Daun Piers, Monk and Business Administrator." *Speculum* 34 (1959): 611–19.

1333. Berndt, David E. "Monastic *Acedia* and Chaucer's Characterization of Daun Piers." *SP* 68 (1971): 435–50.

1334. Delasanta, Rodney. "'Namoore of This': Chaucer's Priest and Monk." *TSL* 13 (1968): 117–32.

1335. Fry, Donald K. "The Ending of the *Monk's Tale.*" *JEGP* 71 (1972): 355–68.

1336. Jensen, Emily. "'Winkers' and 'Janglers': Teller/Listener/Reader Response in the *Monk's Tale,* the Link, and the *Nun's Priest Tale.*" *ChauR* 32 (1997): 183–95.

1337. Kang, Du-Hyoung. "The Problem of Tragedy in *The Canterbury Tales.*" *Journal of English Language and Literature* (Korea) 37 (1991): 825–41.

1338. Norsworthy, Scott. "Hard Lords and Bad Food Service in the *Monk's Tale.*" *JEGP* 100 (2001): 313–32.

1339. Olsson, Kurt. "Grammar, Manhood, and Tears: The Curiosity of Chaucer's Monk." *MP* 76 (1978): 1–17.

1340. Pardee, Sheila. "Sympathy for the Monastery: Monks and Their Stereotypes in *The Canterbury Tales.*" *JRMMRA* 14 (1993): 65–79.

1341. Pearsall, Derek. "'If heaven be on this earth, it is in cloister or in school': The Monastic Ideal in Later Medieval English Literature." In *Pragmatic Utopias: Ideals and Communities, 1200–1630,* edited by Rosemary Horrox and Sarah Rees Jones. Cambridge: Cambridge UP, 2001. 11–25.

1342. [Scanlon, Larry, ed.]. "Colloquium on *The Monk's Tale.*" *SAC* 22 (2000): 381–440.

1343. Seymour, M. C. "Chaucer's Early Poem *De casibus virorum illustrum.*" *ChauR* 24 (1989): 163–65.

1344. Wenzel, Siegfried. "Why the Monk?" In *Words and Works,* edited by Peter S. Baker and Nicholas Howe. Toronto: U of Toronto P, 1998. 261–69.

1345. Wetherbee, Winthrop. "The Context of the *Monk's Tale.*" In *Language and Style in English Literature,* edited by Michio Kawai. Tokyo: Eihosha, 1991. 159–77.

1346. White, Robert B., Jr. "Chaucer's Daun Piers and the Rule of St. Benedict: The Failure of an Ideal." *JEGP* 70 (1971): 13–30.

1347. Zatta, Jane. "Chaucer's Monk: 'A Mighty Hunter before the Lord.'" *ChauR* 29 (1994): 111–33.

See also nos. 327, 698, 701–2, 710.

7 — The Nun's Priest and His Tale

1348. Baswell, Christopher. "Aenas in 1381." *NML* 5 (2002): 8–58.

1349. Bloomfield, Morton W. "The Wisdom of the Nun's Priest's Tale." In *Chaucerian Problems and Perspectives,* edited by Edward Vasta and Zacharias P. Thundy. Notre Dame, IN: U of Notre Dame P, 1979. 70–82.

1350. Boitani, Piero. "'My Tale Is of a Cock' or, The Problems of Literal Interpretation." In *Literature and Religion in the Later Middle Ages,* edited by Richard G. Newhauser and John A. Alford. Binghamton, NY: Medieval & Renaissance Texts & Studies, 1995. 25–42.

1351. Brody, Saul Nathaniel. "Truth and Fiction in the *Nun's Priest's Tale.*" *ChauR* 14 (1979): 33–47.

1352. Broes, Arthur T. "Chaucer's Disgruntled Cleric: The Nun's Priest's Tale." *PMLA* 78 (1963): 156–62.

1353. Camargo, Martin. "Rhetorical Ethos and the *Nun's Priest's Tale.*" *Comparative Literature Studies* 33 (1996): 173–86.

1354. Chapin, Arthur. "Morality Ovidized: Sententiousness and the Aphoristic Moment in the *Nun's Priest's Tale.*" *Yale Journal of Criticism* 8.1 (1995): 7–33.

1355. Crépin, André. "The Cock, the Priest, and the Poet." In *Drama, Narrative and Poetry in The Canterbury Tales,* edited by Wendy Harding. Toulouse: Presses Universitaires du Mirail, Collection Interlangues: Literatures, 2003. 227–36.

1356. Fehrenbacher, Richard W. "'A Yeerd Enclosed Al About': Literature and History in the *Nun's Priest's Tale.*" *ChauR* 29 (1994): 134–48.

1357. Gallacher, Patrick. "Food, Laxatives, and the Catharsis in Chaucer's Nun's Priest's Tale." *Speculum* 51 (1976): 49–68.

1358. Goldstein, R. James. "Chaucer, Freud, and the Economy of Wit: Tendentious Jokes in the *Nun's Priest's Tale.*" In *Chaucer's Humor: Critical Essays,* edited by Jean E. Jost. New York: Garland, 1994. 145–62.

1359. Hoy, Michael. "The Nun's Priest's Tale." In *Chaucer's Major Tales,* edited by Michael Hoy and Michael Stevens. London: Bailey, 1969. 135–62.

1360. Kaylor, Noel Harold. "*The Nun's Priest's Tale* as Chaucer's *Anti-tragedy.*" In *The Living Middle Ages: Studies in Mediaeval English Literature and Its Tradition,* edited by Uwe Boker and others. Stuttgart: Belser, 1989. 87–102.

1361. Kempton, Daniel. "The Nun's Priest's Festive Doctrine: 'Al That Written Is.'" *Assays* 8 (1995): 101–18.

1362. Knight, Stephen. "Form, Content and Context in *The Nun's Priest's Tale.*" In *Studies in Chaucer,* edited by G. A. Wilkes and A. P. Reimer. Sydney: U of Sydney, 1981. 64–85.

1363. McAlpine, Monica E. "The Triumph of Fiction in the Nun's Priest's Tale." In *Art and Context in Late Medieval English Narrative,* edited by Robert R. Edwards. Cambridge, UK: Brewer, 1994. 79–92.

1364. Mann, Jill. "The *Speculum Stultorum* and the *Nun's Priest's Tale.*" *ChauR* 9 (1975): 262–82.

1365. Manning, Stephen. "The Nun's Priest's Morality and the Medieval Attitude toward Fables." *JEGP* 59 (1960): 403–16.

1366. Oerlemans, Onno. "The Seriousness of the *Nun's Priest's Tale*." *ChauR* 26 (1992): 317–28.

1367. Pelen, Marc M. "The Escape of Chaucer's Chauntecleer: A Brief Revaluation." *ChauR* 36 (2002): 329–35.

1368. Pizzorno, Patrizia Grimaldi. "Chauntecleer's Bad Latin." *Exemplaria* 4 (1992): 387–409.

1369. Pratt, Robert A. "Some Latin Sources of the Nonnes Preest on Dreams." *Speculum* 52 (1977): 538–70.

1370. ———. "Three Old French Sources of the Nonnes Preestes Tale." *Speculum* 47 (1972): 422–44, 646–68.

1371. Scanlon, Larry. "The Authority of Fable: Allegory and Irony in the *Nun's Priest's Tale*." *Exemplaria* 1 (1989): 43–68.

1372. Schauber, Ellen, and Ellen Spolsky. "Stalking a Generative Poetics." *NLH* 12 (1981): 397–413.

1373. Scheps, Walter. "Chaucer's Anti-fable: *Reduction ad Absurdum* in the *Nun's Priest's Tale*." *LeedsSE* 4 (1970): 1–10.

1374. Shallers, A. Paul. "The 'Nun's Priest's Tale': An Ironic Exemplum." *ELH* 42 (1975): 319–37.

1375. Thomas, Paul R. "'Have Ye No Mannes Herte?' Chauntecleer as Cock-Man in the *Nun's Priest's Tale*." In *Masculinities in Chaucer*, edited by Peter G. Beidler. Rochester, NY: Brewer, 1998. 187–202.

1376. Travis, Peter W. "Chaucer's Heliotropes and the Poetics of Metaphor." *Speculum* 72 (1997): 399–427.

1377. ———. "Reading Chaucer *Ob Ovo*: Mock-*Exemplum* in the *Nun's Priest's Tale*." In *The Performance of Medieval Culture*, edited by James J. Paxson and others. Cambridge, UK: Brewer, 1998. 161–81.

See also nos. 41, 597, 613, 711, 1334, 1336, 1454.

Part 8

1378. Cowgill, Bruce Kent. "Sweetness and Sweat: The Extraordinary Emanations in Fragment Eight of the *Canterbury Tales*." *PQ* 74 (1995): 343–57.

1379. Grennen, Joseph E. "Saint Cecilia's 'Chemical Wedding': The Unity of *Canterbury Tales*, Fragment VIII." *JEGP* 65 (1966): 466–81.

1380. Kealy, J. Kiernan. "Voices of the Tabard: The Last Tales of the Canterbury Tales." In *From Arabye to Engelond*, edited by A. E. Christa Canitz and Gernot R. Wieland. Ottawa: U of Ottawa P, 1999. 113–29.

1381. Longsworth, Robert M. "Privileged Knowledge: St. Cecilia and the Alchemist in the *Canterbury Tales*." *ChauR* 27 (1992): 87–96.

1382. Olson, Glending. "Chaucer, Dante, and the Structure of Fragment VIII (G) of the *Canterbury Tales*." *ChauR* 16 (1982): 222–36.

1383. Rosenberg, Bruce A. "The Contrary Tales of the Second Nun and the Canon's Yeoman." *ChauR* 2 (1968): 278–91.

1384. Scattergood, John. "Chaucer in the Suburbs." In *Medieval Literature and Antiquities*, edited by Myra Stokes and T. L. Burton. Cambridge, UK: Brewer, 1987. 145–62.

8—The Second Nun and Her Tale

1385. Arthur, Karen. "Equivocal Subjectivity in Chaucer's *Second Nun's Prologue* and *Tale*." *ChauR* 32 (1998): 217–31.

1386. Børch, Marianne. "Chaucer's *Second Nun's Tale*: Record of a Dying World." *ChauY* 5 (1998): 19–40.

1387. Connolly, Thomas. *Mourning into Joy: Music, Raphael, and Saint Cecilia*. New Haven, CT: Yale UP, 1994.

1388. Damon, John. "Seinte Cecile and Cristes Owene Knyghtes: Violence, Resignation, and Resistance in the Second Nun's Tale." In *Crossing Boundaries: Issues of Cultural and Individual Identity in the Middle Ages and the Renaissance*, edited by Sally McKee. Turnhout, Belgium: Brepols, 1999. 41–56.

1389. Filax, Elaine. "A Female I-deal: Chaucer's Second Nun." In *Sovereign Lady: Essays on Women in Middle English Literature*, edited by Muriel Whitaker. New York: Garland, 1995. 133–56.

1390. Hirsh, John C. "The Politics of Spirituality: The Second Nun and the Manciple." *ChauR* 12 (1977): 129–46.

1391. Jankowski, Eileen S. "Chaucer's *Second Nun's Tale* and the Apocalyptic Imagination." *ChauR* 36 (2001): 128–48.

1392. Johnson, Lynn Staley. "Chaucer's Tale of the Second Nun and the Strategies of Dissent." *SP* 89 (1992): 314–33.

1393. Johnston, Mark E. "The Resonance of the *Second Nun's Tale*." *MHLS* 3 (1980): 25–38.

1394. Kennedy, Thomas C. "The Translator's Voice in the Second Nun's *Invocacio*: Gender, Influence, and Textuality." *M&H* 22 (1995): 95–110.

1395. Luecke, Janemarie. "Three Faces of Cecilia: Chaucer's Second Nun's Tale." *ABR* 33 (1982): 35–48.

1396. Peck, Russell A. "The Ideas of *Entente* and Translation in Chaucer's *Second Nun's Tale*." *AnM* 8 (1967): 17–37.

1397. Raybin, David. "Chaucer's Creation and Recreation of the *Lyf of Seynt Cecile*." *ChauR* 32 (1997): 196–212.

1398. Sanok, Catherine. "Performing Feminine Sanctity in Late Medieval England: Parish Guilds, Saints' Plays, and the *Second Nun's Tale*." *JMEMSt* 32 (2002): 269–303.

1399. Weise, Judith. "Chaucer's Tell-Tale Lexicon: Romancing Seinte Cecyle." *Style* 31 (1997): 440–79.

See also nos. 512, 643, 1134, 1184, 1272, 1277.

8—The Canon's Yeoman and His Tale

1400. Bruhn, Mark J. "Art, Anxiety, and Alchemy in the *Canon's Yeoman's Tale*." *ChauR* 33 (1999): 288–315.

1401. Campbell, Jackson J. "The Canon's Yeoman as Imperfect Paradigm." *ChauR* 17 (1982): 171–81.

1402. Duncan, Edgar H. "The Literature of Alchemy and Chaucer's Canon's Yeoman's Tale: Framework, Theme and Characters." *Speculum* 43 (1968): 633–56.

1403. Hartung, Albert E. "'Pars Seconda' and the Development of the *Canon's Yeoman's Tale.*" *ChauR* 12 (1977): 111–28.

1404. Harwood, Britton J. "Chaucer and the Silence of History: Situating the Canon's Yeoman's Tale." *PMLA* 102 (1987): 338–50.

1405. Kanno, Masahiko. "Lexis and Structure in *The Canon's Yeoman's Tale.*" *InG* 10 (1989): 45–58.

1406. Keiser, George R. "The Conclusion of the Canon's Yeoman's Tale: Readings and (Mis)readings." *ChauR* 35 (2000): 1–21.

1406a. Knapp, Peggy. "The Work of Alchemy." *JMEMSt* 30 (2000): 575–99.

1407. Landman, Mark H. "The Laws of Community, Margery Kempe, and the *Canon's Yeoman's Tale.*" *JMEMSt* 28 (1998): 389–425.

1408. Linden, Stanton J. *Darke Hierogliphicks: Alchemy in English Literature from Chaucer to the Restoration.* Lexington: U of Kentucky P, 1996.

1409. McCracken, Samuel. "Confessional Prologue and the Topography of the Canon's Yeoman." *MP* 68 (1971): 289–91.

1410. Patterson, Lee. "Perpetual Motion: Alchemy and the Technology of the Self." *SAC* 15 (1993): 25–57.

1411. Raybin, David. "'And Pave It Al of Silver and Gold': The Humane Artistry of *The Canon's Yeoman's Tale.*" In *Rebels and Rivals: The Contestive Spirit of The Canterbury Tales,* edited by Susanna Freer Fein and others. Kalamazoo, MI: Medieval Institute, 1991. 189–212.

1412. Staley, Lynn. "The Man in Foul Clothes and a Late Fourteenth-Century Conversation about Sin." *SAC* 24 (2002): 1–47.

1413. Thomas, Susanne Sara. "Representing (Re)production: The Canon's Yeoman's Revelations of Textual Impotence." *Crossings* 1 (1997): 159–73.

See also nos. 19, 1414.

Part 9

1414. Weil, Eric. "An Alchemical Freedom Flight: Linking the Manciple's Tale to the Second Nun's and Canon's Yeoman's Tales." *MedPers* 6 (1991): 162–70.

Part 9—The Manciple and His Tale

1415. Allen, Mark. "Penitential Sermons, the Manciple, and the End of the *Canterbury Tales.*" *SAC* 9 (1987): 77–96.

1416. Burrow, J. A. "Chaucer's Canterbury Pilgrimage." *EIC* 36 (1986): 97–119.

1417. Craun, Edwin D. *Lies, Slander, and Obscenity in Medieval English Literature: Pastoral Rhetoric and the Deviant Speaker.* Cambridge: Cambridge UP, 1997.

1418. Davidson, Arnold B. "The Logic of Confusion in the *Manciple's Tale.*" *AnM* 19 (1979): 5–13.

1419. Dean, James. "The Ending of the *Canterbury Tales,* 1952–1976." *TSLL* 21 (1979): 17–33.

1420. Fradenburg, Louise. "The Manciple's Servant Tongue." *ELH* 52 (1985): 85–118.

1421. Fumo, Jamie C. "Thinking upon the Crow: The *Manciple's Tale* and Ovidian Mythology." *ChauR* 38 (2004): 355–75.

1422. Ginsberg, Warren. "Chaucer's Canterbury Poetics: Irony, Allegory, and the *Prologue* to *The Manciple's Tale.*" *SAC* 18 (1996): 55–89.

1423. [Grady, Frank]. "Colloquium: *The Manciple's Tale.*" *SAC* 25 (2003): 285–337.

1424. Grudin, Michaela Paasche. "Chaucer's *Manciple's Tale* and the Poetics of Guile." *ChauR* 25 (1991): 329–42.

1425. Harwood, Britton J. "Language and the Real: Chaucer's Manciple." *ChauR* 6 (1972): 268–79.

1426. Hazelton, Richard. "The *Manciple's Tale*: Parody and Critique." *JEGP* 60 (1963): 1–31.

1427. Houwen, L. A. J. R. "Natural Law in the Manciple's Tale and the Squire's Tale." In *Chaucer in Perspective,* edited by Geoffrey Lester. Sheffield: Sheffield Academic, 1999. 100–117.

1428. Kensak, Michael. "Apollo *Exterminans:* The God of Poetry in Chaucer's *Manciple's Tale.*" *SP* 98 (2001): 143–57.

1429. ———. "What Ails Chaucer's Cook? Spiritual Alchemy and the Ending of *The Canterbury Tales.*" *PQ* 80.3 (2001): 213–31.

1430. McGavin, John J. "How Nasty Is Phoebus's Crow?" *ChauR* 21 (1987): 444–58.

1431. Owen, Charles A., Jr. "Chaucer's Manciple: Voice and Genre." In *Retelling Tales: Essays in Honor of Russell Peck,* edited by Thomas Hahn and Alan Lupack. Rochester, NY: Brewer, 1997. 259–74.

1432. Patton, Celeste A. "False 'Rekenynges': Sharp Practice and the Politics of Language in Chaucer's *Manciple's Tale.*" *PQ* 71 (1992): 399–417.

1433. Pelen, Marc M. "The Manciple's 'Cosyn' to the Dede." *ChauR* 25 (1991): 343–51.

1434. Powell, Stephen D. "Game Over: Defragmenting the End of the *Canterbury Tales.*" *ChauR* 37 (2002): 40–58.

1435. Raybin, David. "The Death of a Silent Woman: Voice and Power in Chaucer's Manciple's Tale." *JEGP* 95 (1996): 19–37.

1436. Scattergood, V. J. "The Manciple's Manner of Speaking." *EIC* 24 (1974): 124–46.

1437. Striar, Brian. "The *Manciple's Tale* and Chaucer's Apolline Poetics." *Criticism* 33 (1991): 173–204.

1438. Wood, Chauncey. "Speech, the Principle of Contraries, and Chaucer's Tales of the Manciple and the Parson." *Mediaevalia* 6 (1980): 209–29.

See also nos. 42, 1180.

Part 10

1439. Dean, James. "Chaucer's Repentance: A Likely Story." *ChauR* 24 (1989): 64–76.

1440. Vaughan, Míceál F. "Creating Comfortable Boundaries: Scribes, Editors, and the Invention of the Parson's Tale." In *Rewriting Chaucer,* edited by Thomas A. Prendergast and Barbara Kline. Columbus: Ohio State UP, 1999. 45–90.

1441. Wurtele, Douglas. "The Penitence of Geoffrey Chaucer." *Viator* 11 (1980): 355–61.

See also nos. 484, 682.

10 — The Parson and His Tale

1442. Baumlin, Tita French. "Theology and Discourse in the *Pardoner's Tale,* the *Parson's Tale,* and the *Retraction.*" *Renascence* 14 (1989): 127–49.

1443. Bestul, Thomas. "Chaucer's *Parson's Tale* and the Late-Medieval Tradition of Religious Meditation." *Speculum* 64 (1989): 600–619.

1444. Brown, Emerson, Jr. "The Poet's Last Words: Text and Meaning at the End of the *Parson's Prologue.*" *ChauR* 10 (1976): 236–42.

1445. Delasanta, Rodney. "Penance and Poetry in the *Canterbury Tales.*" *PMLA* 93 (1978): 240–47.

1446. Finke, Laurie A. "'To Knytte up al this Feeste': The Parson's Rhetoric and the Ending of the *Canterbury Tales.*" *LeedsSE* 15 (1984): 95–107.

1447. Finlayson, John. "The Satiric Mode and the *Parson's Tale.*" *ChauR* 6 (1971): 94–116.

1448. Hartung, Albert E. "*The Parson's Tale* and Chaucer's Penance." In *Literature and Religion in the Later Middle Ages,* edited by Richard G. Newhauser and John A. Alford. Binghamton, NY: Medieval & Renaissance Texts & Studies, 1995. 61–80.

1449. Jost, Jean E. "The *Parson's Tale:* Ending 'Thilke Parfit Glorious Pilgrymage That Highte Jerusalem Celestial.'" *PMAM* 3 (1995): 94–109.

1450. Little, Katherine. "Chaucer's Parson and the Specter of Wycliffism." *SAC* 23 (2001): 225–53.

1451. Patterson, Lee W. "The *Parson's Tale* and the Quitting of the *Canterbury Tales.*" *Traditio* 34 (1978): 331–80.

1452. Pitard, Derrick G. "Sowing Difficulty: *The Parson's Tale,* Vernacular Commentary, and the Nature of Chaucerian Dissent." *SAC* 26 (2004): 299–330.

1453. Raybin, David, and Linda Tarte Holley, eds. *Closure in The Canterbury Tales: The Role of the Parson's Tale.* Kalamazoo, MI: Medieval Institute, 2000.

1454. Swanson, Robert W. "Chaucer's Parson and Other Priests." *SAC* 13 (1991): 41–80.

1455. Travis, Peter W. "Deconstructing Chaucer's Retraction." *Exemplaria* 3, Special Issue (1991): 135–58.

1456. Waters, Claire M. "Holy Duplicity: The Preacher's Two Faces." *SAC* 24 (2002): 75–113.

1457. Wenzel, Siegfried. "Chaucer's Parson's Tale: 'Every Tales Strengthe.'" In *Europäische Lehrdictung. Festschrift für Walter Naumann zum 70 Geburtstag,* edited by Hans Gerd Rötzer and Herbert Walz. Darmstadt, Germany: Wissenschaftliche Buchgesell, 1981. 86–98.

1458. Wurtele, Douglas J. "The Anti-Lollardry of Chaucer's Parson." *Mediaevalia* (1989): 151–68.

See also nos. 341, 345, 611, 1171, 1325, 1414–15, 1419, 1429, 1434, 1438.

10 — Chaucer's Retraction

1459. Furrow, Melissa. "The Author and Damnation: Chaucer, Writing, and Penitence." *FMLS* 33 (1997): 244–57.

1460. Haines, Victor Yelverton. "Where Are Chaucer's 'Retracciouns'?" *Florilegium* 10 (1988–91): 127–49.

1461. Knapp, Robert. "Penance, Irony, and Chaucer's Retraction." *Assays* 2 (1983): 45–67.

1462. McGerr, Rosemarie Potz. "Retraction and Memory: Retrospective Structure in the *Canterbury Tales.*" *CL* 37 (1985): 97–113.

1463. Obermeier, Anita. *The History and Anatomy of Auctorial Self-Criticism in the European Middle Ages.* Atlanta: Rodopi, 1999.

1464. Pigg, Daniel F. "Figuring Subjectivity in 'Piers Plowman C,' the Parson's 'Tale,' and 'Retraction': Authorial Insertion and Identity Politics." *Style* 31 (1997): 428–39.

1465. Reiss, Edmund. "Chaucer and Medieval Irony." *SAC* 1 (1979): 97–113.

1466. Renoir, Alain. "Tradition and Moral Realism: Chaucer's Conception of the Poet." *SN* 35 (1963): 199–210.

1467. Sayce, Olive. "Chaucer's Retractions: The Conclusion of the *Canterbury Tales* and Its Place in Literary Tradition." *MAE* 40 (1971): 230–48.

1468. Schricker, Gale C. "On the Relation of Fact and Fiction in Chaucer's Poetic Endings." *PQ* 60 (1981): 13–27.

See also nos. 1439, 1441–42, 1448, 1455.

Chaucer's Canon and Apocryphal Tales

1469. Adams, Jenny. "Exchequers and Balances: Anxieties of Exchange in *The Tale of Beryn.*" *SAC* 26 (2004): 267–97.

1470. Bonner, Frances W. "The Genesis of the Chaucer Apocrypha." *SP* 48 (1951): 461–81.

1471. Bowers, John M. "*The Tale of Beryn* and *The Siege of Thebes:* Alternative Ideas of *The Canterbury Tales.*" *SAC* 7 (1985): 23–50.

1472. Brown, Peter. "Journey's End: The Prologue to the *Tale of Beryn.*" In *Chaucer and Fifteenth-Century Poetry,* edited by Julia Boffey and Janet Cowman. London: King's College Centre for Late Antique and Medieval Studies, 1991. 143–74.

1473. Brusendorff, Aage. *The Chaucer Tradition.* London: Oxford UP, 1925.

1474. Costomiris, Robert. "The Yoke of Canon: Chaucerian Aspects of *The Plowman's Tale.*" *PQ* 71 (1992): 185–98.

1475. Forni, Kathleen. *The Chaucerian Apocrypha: A Counterfeit Canon.* Gainesville: UP of Florida, 2001.

1476. Heffernan, Thomas J. "Aspects of the Chaucerian Apocrypha: Animadversions on William Thynne's Edition of the *Plowman's Tale.*" In no. 267, 155–67.

1477. Jonassen, Frederick B. "Cathedral, Inn, and Pardoner in the Prologue of the *Tale of Beryn.*" *FCS* 18 (1991): 109–32.

1478. Jost, Jean E. "From Southwark's Tabard Inn to Chaucer's Cheker-of-the-Hope: The Un-Chaucerian *Tale of Beryn.*" *FCS* 21 (1994): 133–48.

1479. Kohl, Stephan. "Chaucer's Pilgrims in Fifteenth-Century Literature." *FCS* 7 (1982): 221–36.

1480. McCarl, Mary Rhinelander, ed. *The Plowman's Tale: The c. 1532 and 1606 Editions of a Spurious Canterbury Tale.* New York: Garland, 1997.

1481. Shippey, T. A. "The Tale of Gamelyn: Class Warfare and the Embarrassments of Genre." In *The Spirit of Medieval Popular Romance,* edited by Ad Putter and Jane Gilbert. New York: Longman, 2000. 78–96.

1482. Skeat, Walter W. *The Chaucerian Canon with a Discussion of the Works Associated with the Name of Geoffrey Chaucer.* Oxford: Oxford UP, 1900.

1483. Spearing, A. C. "Lydgate's Canterbury Tale: *The Siege of Thebes* and Fifteenth-Century Chaucerianism." In *Fifteenth-Century Studies,* edited by Robert F. Yeager. Hamden: CT: Archon, 1984. 333–64.

1484. Taylor, Andrew. "The Curious Eye and the Alternative Endings of *The Canterbury Tales.*" In *Part Two: Reflections on the Sequel,* edited by Paul Budra and Betty A. Schellenberg. Toronto: U of Toronto P, 1998. 34–52.

1485. Winstead, Karen. "The *Beryn* Writer as a Reader of Chaucer." *ChauR* 22 (1988): 225–33.

See also nos. 34 (vol. 7), 621, 719.

CLASSIFICATIONS

ABBREVIATIONS

Chaucer's Works

ABC	An ABC
Adam	Adam Scriveyn
Anel	Anelida and Arcite
Astr	Treatise on the Astrolabe
Bal Compl	A Balade of Complaint
BD	Book of the Duchess
Bo	Boece
Buk	The Envoy to Bukton
CkT, CkP	The Cook's Tale, The Cook's Prologue
ClT, ClP	The Clerk's Tale, The Clerk's Prologue
Compl d'Am	Complaynt d'Amours
CT	The Canterbury Tales
CYT, CYP	The Canon's Yeoman's Tale, The Canon's Yeoman's Prologue
Equat	The Equatorie of the Planetis
For	Fortune
Form Age	The Former Age
FranT, FranP	The Franklin's Tale, The Franklin's Prologue
FrT, FrP	The Friar's Tale, The Friar's Prologue
Gent	Gentilesse
GP	The General Prologue to The Canterbury Tales
HF	The House of Fame
KnT, KnP	The Knight's Tale, The Knight's Prologue
Lady	A Complaint to His Lady
LGW, LGWP	The Legend of Good Women, The Prologue to the Legend of Good Women
ManT, ManP	The Manciple's Tale, The Manciple's Prologue
Mars	The Complaint of Mars
Mel, MelP	The Tale of Melibee, The Prologue to the Tale of Melibee
MercB	Merciles Beaute
MerT, MerP	The Merchant's Tale, The Merchant's Prologue
MilT, MilP	The Miller's Tale, The Miller's Prologue
MkT, MkP	The Monk's Tale, The Monk's Prologue
MLT, MLP	The Man of Law's Tale, The Man of Law's Prologue

NPT, NPP	The Nun's Priest's Tale, The Nun's Priest's Prologue
PardT, PardP	The Pardoner's Tale, The Pardoner's Prologue
ParsT, ParsP	The Parson's Tale, The Parson's Prologue
PF	The Parliament of Fowls
PhyT	The Physician's Tale
Pity	The Complaint unto Pity
Prov	Proverbs
PrT, PrP	The Prioress's Tale, The Prioress's Prologue
Purse	The Complaint of Chaucer to His Purse
Ret	Chaucer's Retraction
Rom	The Romaunt of the Rose
Ros	To Rosemounde
RvT, RvP	The Reeve's Tale, The Reeve's Prologue
Scog	The Envoy to Scogan
ShT	The Shipman's Tale
SNT, SNP	The Second Nun's Tale, The Second Nun's Prologue
SqT, SqP	The Squire's Tale, The Squire's Prologue
Sted	Lak of Stedfastnesse
SumT, SumP	The Summoner's Tale, The Summoner's Prologue
TC	Troilus and Criseyde
Th, ThP	The Tale of Sir Thopas, The Prologue to the Tale of Sir Thopas
Truth	Truth
Ven	The Complaint of Venus
WBT, WBP	The Wife of Bath's Tale, The Wife of Bath's Prologue
Wom Nob	Womanly Noblesse
Wom Unc	Against Women Unconstant

Miscellaneous

Dd	University Library, Cambridge Manuscript Dd.4.24
EETS	Early English Text Society
El	The Ellesmere Manuscript. San Marino, CA. Huntington Library Manuscript EL 26.C.9.

Hg	The Hengwrt Manuscript. Aberystwyth. National Library of Wales. MS Peniarth 392.D.
MED	*Middle English Dictionary.* Ed. Hans Kurath and others. Ann Arbor: U of Michigan P, 1952–2001.
MR	Manly, John M., and Edith Rickert, eds. *The Text of the Canterbury Tales, Studied on the Basis of All Known Manuscripts.* 8 vols. Chicago: U of Chicago P, 1940.
OED	*Oxford English Dictionary.* Ed. J. A. Simpson and E. S. C. Weiner. 2d ed. Oxford: Clarendon, 1989.
PL	Patrologia Latina. *Patrologiae cursus completus, sive biblioteca universalis, integra, uniformis, commoda, oeconomica, omnium SS. Patrum, doctorum scripto-rumque ecclesiasticorum . . .* [Series Latina . . .]. Ed. J-P Migne. 221 vols. Paris: Migne, 1844–91.
PP	Langland, William. *Piers Plowman: A Parallel-Text Edition of the A, B, C and Z Versions.* Vol. I: Text. Ed. A. V. C. Schmidt. London: Longman, 1995.
RI	*The Riverside Chaucer.* 3d ed. Gen ed. Larry D. Benson. Boston: Houghton Mifflin, 1987.
RR	*Roman de la Rose* (see citation no. 206)
SATF	Société des Anciens Textes Française
SK	Skeat, Walter W., ed. *The Complete Works of Geoffrey Chaucer.* 7 vols. Oxford: Clarendon, 1894–97.

Journals

ABR	*American Benedictine Review*
AnM	*Annuale Medievale*
ANQ	*American Notes and Queries*
BAM	*Bulletin des Anglicistes Médiévistes*
BJRL	*Bulletin of the John Rylands University Library of Manchester*
CarmP	*Carmina Philosophiae*
ChauR	*Chaucer Review*
ChauY	*Chaucer Yearbook*
C&L	*Christianity and Literature*
CL	*Comparative Literature*
CollL	*College Literature*
ComH	*Computers and the Humanities*

DQR	*Dutch Quarterly Review*
DR	*Dalhousie Review*
E&S	*Essays and Studies*
EIC	*Essays in Criticism*
ELH	*ELH: English Literary History*
ES	*English Studies*
ESA	*English Studies in Africa*
ESC	*English Studies in Canada*
FCS	*Fifteenth-Century Studies*
FMLS	*Forum for Modern Language Study*
HLQ	*Huntington Library Quarterly*
HUSL	*Hebrew University Studies in Language and the Arts*
InG	*In Geardagum*
JEBS	*Journal of the Early Book Society*
JEGP	*Journal of English and Germanic Philology*
JEP	*Journal of Evolutionary Psychology*
JHL	*Journal of Historical Linguistics*
JMEMSt	*Journal of Medieval and Early Modern Studies*
JNT	*Journal of Narrative Technique*
JRMMRA	*Journal of the Rocky Mountain Medieval and Renaissance Association*
JMRS	*Journal of Medieval and Renaissance Studies*
L&H	*Literature and History*
L&P	*Literature and Psychology*
Lang&S	*Language & Style*
LeedsSE	*Leeds Studies in English*
LittR	*Literary Review* (Madison, NJ)
M&H	*Medievalia et Humanistica*
MAE	*Medium Aevum*
MedPers	*Medieval Perspectives*
MHLS	*Mid-Hudson Language Studies*
MLQ	*Modern Language Quarterly*
MLR	*Modern Language Review*
MLS	*Modern Language Studies*
MP	*Modern Philology*
MS	*Mediaeval Studies*
MSE	*Massachusetts Studies in English*
N&Q	*Notes and Queries*
Neophil	*Neophilologica*
NLH	*New Literary History*
NM	*Neuphilologische Mitteilungen*
NML	*New Medieval Literatures*
PBA	*Proceedings of the British Academy*
PCP	*Pacific Coast Philology*

PLL	*Papers on Language and Literature*	*SEL*	*Studies in English Literature, 1500–1900*
PMAM	*Publications of the Medieval Association of the Midwest*	*SELIM*	*SELIM: Journal of the Spanish Society for Mediaeval English Language and Literature*
PMLA	*Publications of the Modern Language Association*	*SiM*	*Studies in Medievalism*
PoeticaT	*Poetica: An International Journal of Linguistic Literary Study* (Tokyo)	*SIMELL*	*Studies in Medieval English Language and Literature*
PQ	*Philological Quarterly*	*SMC*	*Studies in Medieval Culture*
		SN	*Studia Neophilologica*
RCEI	*Revista Canaria de Estudios Ingleses*	*SP*	*Studies in Philology*
RealB	*RealB: The Yearbook of Research in English and American Literature*	*SSF*	*Studies in Short Fiction*
RES	*Review of English Studies*	*TSL*	*Tennessee Studies in Literature*
RMS	*Reading Medieval Studies*	*TSLL*	*Texas Studies in Language and Literature*
RUO	*Revue de l'Université d'Ottawa*		
RUS	*Rice University Studies*	*UTQ*	*University of Toronto Quarterly*
SAC	*Studies in the Age of Chaucer*	*YES*	*Yearbook of English Studies*
SAQ	*South Atlantic Quarterly*	*YLS*	*Yearbook of Langland Studies*
SB	*Studies in Bibliography*		
SCRev	*South Central Review*	*WS*	*Women's Studies*

INDEX OF AUTHORS

The Pronunciation of Chaucer's English

See "Chaucer's Language and Versification," pp. 961–965
Transcriptions in brackets are in the International Phonetic Alphabet (IPA).

Accent

1. Native words on their root syllables (as in Modern English): *sóndry, Eńgelond, tóward, yrónne, anón*

2. French loan words often retain their final French accent: *coráge, pilgrymáges, resoún, compaigńye, vertú*

3. Classical loan words (usually names) frequently anglicized: *Dárdanus (TC* II.618), *Dámyssene (CT* VII.2007), *Sáturnus (CT* I.2443); but sometimes still on the penult: *Zephírus* or antepenult: *Tarquínius (LGW* 16882)

Consonants

As in Modern English except:
1. There are no "silent" letters: *knyght, gnawe, sing, wreke, Southwerk, domb*

2. There is no syncope of inflectional endings: *walked, banes*

3. *c* is pronounced [k] before consonants and back vowels and when doubled (as in Modern English): *croppes, corages, apothecaries, recche*

   c is pronounced [s] before and after front vowels (as in French): *centre, circuit, specially*

4. *g* is pronounced [g] initially before consonants and back vowels (as in Modern English): *ground, goon*

   g is pronounced [g] medially before consonants, when doubled, and with umlaut vowels (again, Modern English is a clue to the pronunciation): *pilgrimes, dogge, bigynne*

   g is pronounced [ǰ] in French loan words: *gentil, engendered, straunge*

   gh (sometimes spelled merely *h*) is pronounced [χ] or [ç] medially and finally after back or front vowels: *droghte (drohte), though (thoh), nyght (nyht), right (riht)*

5. *h* is pronounced initially in native words: *hous*

   h is silent in French loan words: *hostel, habounde, heroun*

   h is weakened or silent in unstressed particles: *him, his, hit, hem, hir*

6. *f, s, th* largely unvoiced except intervocalically: *as, of, that,* but *ryse, halfe, bathed*

7. *r* is fully pronounced, probably trilled

Vowels

Middle English vowels are pronounced as they are in Latin and the Continental languages (e.g., German, French, Spanish):

1. The short vowels

   e [ɛ]: *sette, perced*

   i, y [ɪ]: *sitte, thynk*

   o [ɔ]: *long, anon; o* from Old English *u* today pronounced [ə] should be pronounced [ʊ]: *come, som, yonge, sonne*

   u [ʊ]: *but, putten, dulle*